THE WORLD
OF POMPEII

———— .◆. ————

The World of Pompeii draws together the vast amount of data available on Pompeii and allows readers, for the first time, to see the buried cities of Campania in the round. Although there is increasing specialization in the subject area, leading scholars are brought together to provide a comprehensive overview that has not been available since Mau and Kelsey's *Pompeii: its life and art*, published over one hundred years ago.

The picture of the settlements under Vesuvius is being revised by the on-going archaeological work and this volume details life as lived by the elite to the lower classes, using the results of the latest discoveries. The volume is also accompanied by a CD that includes detailed maps of Pompeii. Highly illustrated and including a large number of site maps this volume provides a wide-ranging survey of the site and Pompeian studies. There is also a web-companion with *marginalia*, at http://homepage.mac.com/pfoss/Pompeii/WorldofPompeii/.

John J. Dobbins is Professor of Classical Art and Archaeology at the University of Virginia, USA.

Pedar W. Foss is Associate Professor of Classical Studies at DePauw University, USA.

THE ROUTLEDGE WORLDS

THE GREEK WORLD
Edited by Anton Powell

THE ROMAN WORLD
Edited by John Wacher

THE BIBLICAL WORLD
Edited by John Barton

THE EARLY CHRISTIAN WORLD
Edited by Philip F. Esler

THE CELTIC WORLD
Edited by Miranda Green

THE MEDIEVAL WORLD
Edited by Peter Linehan and Janet L. Nelson

THE REFORMATION WORLD
Edited by Andrew Pettegree

THE ENLIGHTENMENT WORLD
Edited by Martin Fitzpatrick, Peter Jones,
Christa Knellwolf and Iain McCalman

THE HINDU WORLD
Edited by Sushil Mittal and Gene Thursby

Forthcoming:

THE EGYPTIAN WORLD
Edited by Toby Wilkinson

THE BABYLONIAN WORLD
Edited by Gwendolyn Leick

THE VIKING WORLD
Edited by Stefan Brink and Neil Price

THE RENAISSANCE WORLD
Edited by John Jeffries Martin

THE ELIZABETHAN WORLD
Edited by Susan Doran and Norman Jones

THE OTTOMAN WORLD
Edited by Christine Woodhead

THE BYZANTINE WORLD
Edited by Paul Stephenson

THE WORLD OF POMPEII

Edited by

John J. Dobbins
and
Pedar W. Foss

Routledge
Taylor & Francis Group
LONDON AND NEW YORK

First published 2007
First published in paperback 2008
by Routledge
270 Madison Ave, New York, NY 10016

Simultaneously published in the UK
by Routledge
2 Park Square, Milton Park, Abingdon, Oxon OX14 4RN

Routledge is an imprint of the Taylor & Francis Group, an informa business

Typeset in Garamond by
Florence Production Ltd, Stoodleigh, Devon
Printed and bound in Great Britain by
CPI Antony Rowe, Chippenham, Wiltshire

British Library Cataloguing in Publication Data
A catalogue record for this book is available from the British Library

Library of Congress Cataloging in Publication Data
A catalog record for this book has been requested

ISBN10: 0–415–17324–8 (hbk)
ISBN10: 0–415–47577–5 (pbk)

ISBN13: 978–0–415–17324–7 (hbk)
ISBN13: 978–0–415–47577–8 (pbk)

In honor of August Mau and Francis W. Kelsey
and
John H. D'Arms

CONTENTS

—·◆·—

vii

PART II: THE COMMUNITY

PART III: HOUSING

PART IV: SOCIETY AND ECONOMY

ILLUSTRATIONS

———•◆•———

MAPS

FIGURES

TABLES

CONTRIBUTORS

———— •◆• ————

Jean-Pierre Adam is an Architect-Archaeologist and presently teaches at the École du Louvre, the École de Chaillot (préparation Monuments Historiques), the Université de Roma III, and the École polytechnique de Lausanne. He directed the Paris bureau of the Institut de Recherche sur l'Architecture Antique (IRAA) of CNRS, from 1972 to 2003. He taught at the Université de PARIS IV until 2002 and at the Université du Liban until 2004. His research activities include archaeological projects and publications on Roman Italy, the Greek world, Pharaonic Egypt and the history of construction techniques. He also works in collaboration with the Musée du Louvre and the Musée du Moyen Age.

Penelope M. Allison has taught ancient history and archaeology at the University of Sydney, Australian National University and University of Sheffield. She has held research fellowships at the University of Sydney and in the Faculty of Classics, Cambridge. At present she is a Lecturer in the School of Archaeology and Ancient History at the University of Leicester. Her current research interests concern gender and space in the Roman world and household archaeology in western New South Wales, Australia. Her major publications include: *The Archaeology of Household Activities* (1999), *Casa della Caccia Antica*, Häuser in Pompeji, vol. 11 (2002) and *Pompeian Households: an analysis of the material culture* (2004).

Frances Bernstein is an independent consultant living in the Washington, DC area. Her Ph.D. in Greek and Roman History is from the University of Maryland. Dr Bernstein's dissertation focused on the role of women at Pompeii. She served for four years as Principal Investigator for the Earthwatch Project at Pompeii, a house-by-house study of *lararia* and the role of women in domestic religion. She currently directs the Cumae-Isis project, an excavation of the so-called "Temple of Isis" at Cuma, Italy. She has taught at the Catholic University of America, American University, the University of Maryland and Mary Washington University.

Joanne Berry is an Associate Lecturer in the Department of Classics and Ancient History, University of Wales, Swansea, UK. She also works for the Classical Press of Wales. She gained her Ph.D. from the University of Reading in 1997. Her dissertation was a study of the social and economic organization of the Roman house, based on the evidence of domestic artifacts found in the houses of Pompeii.

Paolo Carafa is Associate Professor and has been teaching the Archaeology of Magna Grecia at the University of Calabria since 1999 and Classical Archaeology at the University of Rome, *La Sapienza*, since 2001. Carafa has been involved in coordinating scientific research teams with the aim of reconstructing the topography and landscapes of the centers and territories being investigated through different phases of antiquity. Carafa's interests also include artistic production in the Hellenistic period, Latin epigraphy, archaic architecture in mid-Thyrrenian Italy, and romanization of Campania, mainly in the city of Pompeii, and in Magna Grecia.

Christina Chiaramonte is Associate Professor of pre-Roman Italian Civilization at the Università degli Studi di Milano. She excavated at Pompeii in the 1980s and published her studies on the Etruscan and Samnite phases of the Vesuvian city. For many years she has taken part in excavations of the Etruscan city of Tarquinia and she has published the relevant results. Presently she is studying the necropoleis of Campalanno.

John R. Clarke is Annie Laurie Howard Regents Professor of Art History at the University of Texas, Austin. He is author of five books on the art and culture of ancient Rome: *Roman Black-and-White Figural Mosaics* (1979), *The Houses of Roman Italy: ritual, space, and decoration, 100 BC–AD 250* (1991), *Looking at Lovemaking: constructions of sexuality in Roman art 100 BC–AD 250* (1998), *Art in the Lives of Ordinary Romans: visual representation and viewers in Italy, 100 BC–AD 315* (2003); *Roman Sex, 100 BC–AD 250* (2003). Among his seventy articles and chapters are studies of style and chronology of Roman wall paintings and mosaics; explorations of iconography; work on gender and sexuality in the ancient world; and analyses of visual art 1960 to the present. He is currently completing a book entitled *Looking at Laughter: humor, power, and transgression in Roman visual culture, 100 BC–AD 315*.

Sarah Cormack received her Ph.D. from Yale University, and has taught at the University of Michigan and Duke University. She is currently an Adjunct Faculty Member in the Art Department at Webster University, Vienna. Her study of monumental tombs of the Roman period in Turkey has recently been published, *The Space of Death in Roman Asia Minor* (2004).

Stefano De Caro teaches Ancient Topography at the Università Federico II di Napoli. He is also Regional Director for Cultural Property and Natural Resources in Campania. He has conducted excavations and studies in Molise and Campania, in particular at Pompeii, being interested in topography, urbanism, rustic and luxury villas, and ancient painting. De Caro has published over a hundred articles, monographs and exhibition catalogues.

John DeFelice is Assistant Professor of History at the University of Maine at Presque Isle. He completed his doctoral research at Miami University in Oxford, Ohio after completing his undergraduate studies at Gordon College in Wenham, Massachusetts. His dissertation was titled "The women of Pompeian inns: a study of law, occupation and status" (published as *Roman Hospitality*, 2001). The book is presently in revision for a second edition.

Jean-Paul Descœudres received his Ph.D. at the University of Basel. He is currently Ordinary Professor for Classical Archaeology at the University of Geneva and Honorary Professor in the School of Philosophical and Historical Inquiry at the University of Sydney, and Editor-in-chief of *Mediterranean Archaeology*. He was Director of the Australian Expedition to Pompeii from 1978 till 1986 and Director of the Genevan "Pompei extra muros" excavations since 1998.

Jens-Arne Dickmann is a Senior Lecturer at the Institut für Altertumswissenschaften at Ruprecht-Karls-Universität Heidelberg (Germany). He earned his Ph.D. at the Ludwig-Maximilians-Universität in Munich. In his dissertation, *"Domus frequentata. Anspruchsvolles Wohnen im pompejanischen Stadthaus,"* he explored the spatial organization of townhouses at Pompeii and their changes and re-buildings from the second century BC onwards until AD 79. Since then he has worked on the antiquities collection of the Earls of Pembroke at Wilton House (UK) and on the history of childhood in ancient Greece. On behalf of the Deutsches Archäologisches Institut (DAI) at Rome starting in 1997 he directed, together with Felix Pirson, the international excavation, documentation and conservation project in the Casa dei Postumii at Pompeii.

John J. Dobbins is Professor of Classical Art and Archaeology at the University of Virginia. He has excavated in Spain, Greece, Syria, and Italy where his current research focuses on the Hellenistic theater at Morgantina, Sicily, and on Pompeii where, for over ten years, he has been the Director of the Pompeii Forum Project (http://pompeii. virginia.edu). He is a Fellow of the Institute for Advanced Technology in the Humanities at the University of Virginia and has published on Pompeii, Roman sculpture, lamps, a Roman villa in Tuscany, the Athenian Acropolis, and houses and mosaics at Antioch. He also lectures widely for the Archaeological Institute of America and has been the Charlottesville President of the AIA for more than twenty years.

J. Clayton Fant is Professor of Classical Studies and Professor of History at the University of Akron. He has also taught at the University of Michigan and Wellesley College. After Williams College he earned his Ph.D. at the University of Michigan; he is a Fellow of the American Academy in Rome. In the 1980s he studied the imperially owned marble quarry at Dokimeion in central Turkey, leading to a number of publications. More recently he has studied the marble yards of Rome and continues to explore the use of marble at Pompeii with traditional methods as well as in collaboration with experts in provenience. He is working on a book with the provisional title "Marble and the Caesars."

Pedar W. Foss is Associate Professor of Classical Studies at DePauw University in Greencastle, Indiana. He has carried out fieldwork in Greece, Italy, Tunisia and Turkey. His publications concern domestic life at Pompeii, archaeological survey and

Geographic Information Systems (http://cgma.depauw.edu). He has also edited for the *Journal of Roman Archaeology* and, as of 2008, the *American Journal of Archaeology*.

James Franklin is Professor of Classical Studies at Indiana University. While completing his Ph.D. at Duke University, he was named a Fellow of the American Academy in Rome, and his dissertation eventually became a volume in its Papers and Monographs series. His research interests, largely in the political life of ancient Pompeii, have been supported by awards from the American Council of Learned Societies and the National Endowment for the Arts, as well as The University of Michigan and Indiana University. He has several times directed Summer Sessions of the Vergilian Society of America at Cuma, and he has twice served as the Professor-In-Charge of the Intercollegiate Center for Classical Studies, Rome. He is the author of three books and numerous articles on various aspects of ancient Pompeii.

Herman Geertman is the Director Emeritus of the Royal Dutch Institute at Rome and Emeritus Chair of Classical Archaeology at the University of Leiden. He received his MA and Ph.D. in Classical Archaeology at the University of Utrecht. His fields of interest and publications include Late Roman and Early Medieval Rome, especially the Christianization of the City; theory and practice of Classical architecture, especially Vitruvius; Hellenistic and Roman town planning, especially the development of Pompeii; and Theoretical Archaeology.

Michele George is Associate Professor of Classics at McMaster University in Hamilton, Canada. She is a graduate of the University of Toronto and McMaster University. She has published on various aspects of Roman domestic architecture at Pompeii, in Italy, and other parts of the Roman empire, including as editor of *The Roman Family in the Empire* (2005). She is currently working on an analysis of Roman slavery and material culture.

Pietro Giovanni Guzzo has been the Director of the Archaeological Superintendency at Pompeii since 1995 and since 1998 the President of the Board of Directors in the same Superintendency. Prior to this, he served several Superintendencies in Italy in various capacities. As Archaeological Inspector at the Superintendency of Calabria he conducted excavations at Sibaris and directed the recovery of the Riace bronzes. He is a member of numerous learned societies and has been elected to various positions within the Ministry of Culture. He has taught at several institutions for higher learning in Italy, and has published widely on Italic archaeology, Magna Grecia and Pompeii.

Gemma Jansen has been researching the water systems and sanitation within the Roman towns of Pompeii, Herculaneum and Ostia. In addition, she has recently finished research on the most beautiful and spectacular toilets of the Roman empire: those of the emperor Hadrian at his villa near Tivoli, Italy. Currently she is participating in a large-scale project of the Austrian Archaeological Institute at Vienna concerning the water supply lines of Ephesos, Turkey.

Wilhelmina Jashemski is Professor Emerita in History at the University of Maryland, where she taught for almost thirty-five years. She is the pioneer of the field of garden archaeology, and began the first systematic and scientific studies of the flora, fauna and environment of the Vesuvian area, where she began working in 1961. Her work on gardens has now spanned the entire Roman world. Her achievements were marked by the Archaeological Institute of America's Gold Medal for Distinguished Archaeological Achievement in 1996.

Rick Jones is a Reader in Roman Archaeology at the University of Bradford, where he was previously a Senior Lecturer and Lecturer, following studies at the Universities of Manchester and London. He has co-directed excavations at Pompeii with Damian Robinson since 1994. He co-edited *Sequence and space in Pompeii* (1997) with Sara Bon. Previously he led fieldwork in Britain, Spain and France. His research focuses are ancient urbanism and social interactions on the Roman frontier.

Willem M. Jongman teaches ancient history at the University of Groningen. His *The Economy and Society of Pompeii* (1988) was a noted attempt to reintegrate Pompeii into contemporary debate on ancient economy and society. It was awarded several important prizes, and was recently named as one of the most notable books on the ancient economy of the last two centuries. His most recent research has involved the Roman standard of living. He is currently writing a book on the growth and decline of Italian urban culture and society.

Ann Olga Koloski-Ostrow is Associate Professor and Chair of the Department of Classical Studies at Brandeis University. She holds an MA in Latin and Greek and a Ph.D. in Classical Art and Archaeology from the University of Michigan. She is the author of *The Sarno Bath Complex: Architecture in Pompeii's Last Years* (1990), and editor and contributor to *Naked Truths: Women, Sexuality, and Gender in Classical Art and Archaeology* (1997 and 2000), and *Water Use and Hydraulics in the Roman Empire* (2001).

Anne Laidlaw is Professor Emerita of Classics at Hollins College. She received her MA and Ph.D. in Classical Archaeology at Yale University. She excavated in the House of Sallust in Pompeii to clarify the patterns of Roman First-Style wall paintings analogous to those found at Cosa, a study that resulted in *The First Style in Pompeii, Painting and Architecture* (1985). In 2005 she resumed her study of the House of Sallust as a member of the University of Perugia team led by Professor Filippo Coarelli. She has published a number of articles on Roman painting, co-authored *Karthago II* (1997) and has lectured widely.

Estelle Lazer is a freelance archaeologist. Her Ph.D., from the Department of Anatomy and Histology at the University of Sydney, was based on an analysis of the human skeletal remains from Pompeii. She is an Honorary Research Associate in Archaeology, Anatomy and Architecture at the University of Sydney. She has studied human remains from a number of sites in various countries, including Italy and Cyprus. She teaches undergraduate courses in archaeology and anatomy at the Universities of Sydney and New South Wales. Her other major research area is Sub-Antarctic and Antarctic historic sites. She is currently involved in the development of a GIS-linked database of sites and artifacts for the Australian Antarctic Division.

Roger Ling is Professor of Classical Art and Archaeology in the University of Manchester. His specialist interest is Roman archaeology. In addition to excavations in Britain and survey work in Turkey, he has directed a project in the Insula of the Menander at Pompeii, in course of publication as a five-volume monograph. He is also the author of general books on Pompeii, on ancient mosaics, and on Roman painting.

Eric M. Moormann holds the Chair of Classical Archaeology at Radboud University, Nijmegen (The Netherlands) and also reads at Amsterdam University. His Ph.D., published in 1988, discussed the representation of sculpture in wall paintings. He has published extensively on mural painting from the Vesuvian area, Rome and Ostia. A catalogue of the classical sculptures in the Allard Pierson Museum at Amsterdam came out in 2000. A monograph on Nero's Golden House at Rome, written in collaboration with P. G. P. Meyboom, is due shortly. He currently co-directs a restoration and research project in the *hierothesion* of Kommagene at Nemrud Dagi (Eastern Turkey). Another topic of interest is the reception history of antiquity in Western culture, especially that of Pompeii.

Salvatore Ciro Nappo is a classical archaeologist and a graduate of the Università Federico II di Napoli under Prof. A. De Franciscis in 1981. He subsequently attended the Scuola di Specializzazione in Archeologia Classica, and in 1986 completed an advanced degree in the integrated conservation of cultural patrimony. His scientific interests lie primarily in the areas of Roman architecture and painting. He has directed excavations at Napoli (Palazzo Corigliano), Irpinia (Aequum Tuticum), Stabiae (Villa Ariadne) and Pompei (*insulae* I.14, I.16, I.21, I.22, Murecine). He has also been responsible for the restoration of houses and wall decoration in Regions I and II at Pompeii. Among his publications are: *Pompei—Guida alla città sepolta* (1998), . . . *Mitis Sarni Opes: gli scavi di Murecine* (2000) and "La decorazione parietale dell' Hospitium dei Sulpici in località Murecine a Pompei" (MEFRA 113, 2001).

Christopher Parslow is Professor of Classical Studies and Archaeology at Wesleyan University. He is interested in all aspects of the sites buried by the eruption of Vesuvius. His first book, *Rediscovering Antiquity: Karl Weber and the Excavations of Pompeii, Herculaneum and Stabiae* (Cambridge 1995) explored the life of Karl Weber, the Swiss military engineer who supervised the Bourbon-era excavations at those sites, and his contributions to the history of archaeology. He is currently completing a monographic study of the Praedia Iuliae Felicis (Regio II.4.1–12) in Pompeii.

Kees Peterse is the Head of PANSA BV, a scientifically based company dedicated to the reconstruction of Roman architecture. His graduation from the Polytechnic at 's-Hertogenbosch was followed by Ph.D. research in Classical Archaeology at the Radboud University of Nijmegen, focussing on early masonry techniques and early domestic architecture in Pompeii. Anticipating his current position, he was director of Peterse Architectuur BV, founded by his father. During 1997–98 he was a visiting lecturer at the University of Texas at Austin. He currently works on the virtual reconstruction of Roman Nijmegen, both the buildings and their settings. The fruits of his efforts are on display in various museums.

Felix Pirson is currently Head of the Istanbul Department of the Deutsches Archäologisches Institut, after a term as a "Wissenschaftlicher Assistent" at the Institute of Classical Archaeology at Leipzig University. After degrees from Munich University and the Faculty of Classics at Cambridge (UK), he obtained his Ph.D. for a dissertation on rented apartments at Pompeii and Herculaneum. He has worked with Jens-Arne Dickmann on the publication of a jointly directed research project at Pompeii, which was conducted by the Deutsches Archäologisches Institut (DAI) and an international team of archaeologists, scientists and conservators between 1997–2002. His other fields of research include images of war in antiquity and the archaeology of Pergamum.

Damian Robinson is the Director of the Oxford Centre for Maritime Archaeology and a William Golding Fellow at Brasenose College Oxford. Prior to this he was a Lecturer in Classical Archaeology at the University of Oxford and a British Academy Postdoctoral Fellow in Roman Archaeology at the University of Bradford, where he carried out research into the social and economic development of Pompeii. His Ph.D. was also from the University of Bradford and involved a spatial analysis of the urban fabric of Pompeii. With Rick Jones, he directs the Anglo American Project in Pompeii.

Haraldur Sigurdsson is a volcanologist of Icelandic origin, and Professor of Oceanography at the University of Rhode Island. He has conducted research on most of the major volcanic eruptions in historic time, with a particular emphasis on the impact of large explosive eruptions on human cultures, such as the eruptions of Tambora in 1815 and Krakatau in 1883. His current research focuses on the great Bronze Age eruption of Santorini in the Aegean Sea, and its impact on the Minoan culture. He began studies on the Vesuvius eruption of AD 79 in 1976.

Alastair M. Small is an Honorary Fellow in Classics at the University of Edinburgh and Professor Emeritus of the University of Alberta. He has been working for more than forty years on the archaeology and history of South Italy in the Iron Age and Roman periods, on which he has numerous publications. He is currently directing a project of excavation, geophysics and field survey in a Roman imperial estate at Vagnari in Puglia. He has taught the archaeology of Pompeii for many years, and published a study of the imperial cult in the Macellum.

Volker Michael Strocka is Ordinary Professor of Classical Archaeology at the Archäologisches Institut of the Albert-Ludwigs-Universität of Freiburg, Germany. He studied at Munich, Basel, Freiburg and Paris, and received his doctorate at Freiburg in 1965. From 1975 to 1981 he was First Director of the headquarters of the Deutsches Archäologisches Institut at Berlin. He has directed long-term documentation and excavation projects at Ephesos (wall paintings and the re-erection of the Library of Celsus) and Pompeii (the "Häuser in Pompeji" series), and shorter ones in Thugga (Tunisia) and Nysa (Turkey). His interests and publications are manifold: ancient sculpture, Roman architecture and wall paintings, ancient libraries, and Greek and Roman art history.

Rolf A. Tybout is the author of a monograph on first-century BC Roman architectural wall painting ("Second Style") based on his 1989 Leiden dissertation. His subsequent publications include studies on Vitruvius, the social significance of Roman wall painting and Greek funerary inscriptions. He is also active in the field of musicology, publishing articles on the German composer Hans Pfitzner. He is currently working in the field of Greek epigraphy and is one of the editors of the *Supplementum Epigraphicum Graecum.*

Andrew Wallace-Hadrill is the Director of the British School at Rome and Professor of Classics at the University of Reading. Among his numerous publications on the Roman world, his 1994 book *Houses and Society in Pompeii and Herculaneum* won the James R. Wiseman award. He co-directs with Prof. Michael Fulford a project on Pompeii Regio I Insula 9. He is also director of the Herculaneum Conservation Project.

Katherine E. Welch is Associate Professor of Fine Arts at the Institute of Fine Arts at New York University, with her Ph.D. from the same institution. A specialist in Roman architecture, sculpture and painting, she is the winner of a Rome Prize and has been a Fellow of the American School of Classical Studies at Athens. Her publications range from studies of the Roman amphitheater to those of the art and architecture of Italy (particularly Rome), Greece and Asia Minor.

Carroll William Westfall came to Notre Dame in 1998 as Frank Montana Professor and Chairman of the School of Architecture, serving as chairman until 2002. Earlier he taught at Amherst College, the University of Illinois in Chicago, and, after 1982, at the University of Virginia. He received his Ph.D. from Columbia University. His initial work led to numerous articles and a book, *In This Most Perfect Paradise* (1974), a study of Early Renaissance Rome. His more recent studies of the relationship between the history, theory and practice of architecture are found in his contribution to the 1991 book *Architectural Principles in the Age of Historicism* written with Robert Jan van Pelt. His current focus is on tradition and classicism in architecture and the American city and the architect's capacity to nourish the Christian faith.

PREFACE

———— •◆• ————

John J. Dobbins and Pedar W. Foss

For whom is this book intended? Our audience is the same as that of Mau and Kelsey, or at least the same as the Mau–Kelsey audience that we have observed during the last thirty years: scholars (especially Pompeii scholars); college and university teachers; students of archaeology; students in general enrolled in the ubiquitous courses on Pompeii taught at colleges and universities around the world; and the general public interested in learning more about Pompeii. This does not mean, however, that we present this book as "the new Mau:" far from it. August Mau's *Pompeji in Leben und Kunst* (*Pompeii: its life and art*, as translated by Francis W. Kelsey) was a unique creation of a single pioneer scholar, and a product of the late nineteenth century, just as our *The World of Pompeii* is a unique assemblage of essays by numerous scholars working at Pompeii in the late twentieth and early twenty-first centuries. In many ways, this volume is as much an introduction to Pompeian studies as a study of Pompeii.

It was very difficult to produce this book, and far more time-consuming than we had imagined during the planning stages. Many delays were due to the nature of the publication, but many were due to the editors. We regret the former, and apologize for the latter. In the end, we hope that authors and readers alike will appreciate the good qualities of this very special book, and not dwell on the delays. This project began in the late 1990s because a suitably comprehensive, topically oriented, historically organized, and up-to-date treatment of Pompeii, Herculaneum and the other sites buried by Vesuvius did not exist in English. At the time, a number of useful studies had just been published.[1] However, the second edition of Mau and Kelsey, published in 1902, was still being used in classrooms, which spoke to the quality of its panoptic vision.

August Mau was born in Kiel in 1840; he died in Rome in 1909. Working out of the Deutsches Archäologisches Institut in Rome, Mau was introduced to Pompeii at a time when research at the site was becoming internationalized. His first publication, concerned with wall painting, appeared in 1873, and his record began to flourish in 1874, breaking through with his work on Overbeck's fourth edition of *Pompeji* (1884).[2] That encyclopedic treatment inspired his own effort fifteen years later. It was commissioned, as his own preface states, first in English. The English translation was accomplished by Francis W. Kelsey, who was born in Ogden, New York, in 1858 and died in Ann Arbor, Michigan, in 1927. Kelsey had been Professor of Latin Language and Literature at the University of Michigan for ten years before *Pompeii: its life and art* came out. He went on to enjoy one of the most distinguished careers in classical archaeology. Kelsey was working on his own grand treatment of Pompeii at the time of his death; it may be apt in some small way that both editors began their careers as graduate students in the building that bears his name, the Kelsey Museum of Art and Archaeology at Michigan.[3]

Mau's ability to synthesize the information available to him in a detailed and compelling manner has proved hard to match. In addition, given the advances made in the century since Mau's publication, it seems well-nigh impossible for one or even two individuals to comparably distill over 250 years of work in multiple languages, at the oldest continually excavated set of sites in the world, using about the same number of pages that Mau and Kelsey had. Our approach had to be different. We decided to invite scholars from around the world (Australia, Canada, England, France, Germany, Italy, the Netherlands and the United States) to contribute chapters which, when compiled, might form the book we wished to have on our shelves as the "first to consult."

Multiple voices speak about these sites (sometimes in concert, at other times in contradiction), and we have attempted as best we can to knit them together coherently yet distinctively. Any disagreement that can be detected across chapters is not altogether undesirable; these sites are too large, too old and too complex for a simple and convenient picture to be drawn from them of life in ancient Italy. The reader is encouraged to consider the strengths and weaknesses of all the arguments in relation to each other. Meanwhile, we have tried to ensure that references are sufficiently detailed to allow readers to pick their way through that long tradition of scholarship and reach the sources of the evidence if they so choose. The labyrinthine problems of Pompeian scholarship are, in fact, addressed in the final chapter.

The book is divided into four sections. John Dobbins edited "Beginnings" (Chapters 1–8) and "The Community" (Chapters 9–16), as well as Chapter 39. The sections on "Housing" (Chapters 17–28) and "Society and Economy" (Chapters 29–38) were overseen by Pedar Foss. While these chapters may be read in order, and are arranged thematically for easy consultation, there are plenty of issues and key pieces of evidence that appear in several different chapters across the sections we have created. In order to facilitate reading the relationships between chapters, we have inserted many cross-references, which appear in this fashion: (cf. Jashemski, Ch. 31). Each chapter has its own set of bibliographical references in the endnotes, so that the sources most important to individual topics remain self-contained. As editors, we encouraged, but did not require, authors to provide bibliographies; many did provide them. As a result, each chapter is a self-contained unit, and we felt that a final comprehensive bibliography was unnecessary.

Citations use the "short title" format, meaning that once a source has been cited in full within a chapter, its next mention is made in the form of an author and/or abbreviated title. In almost all cases we have followed the system of abbreviations for periodicals, series and books set by the *American Journal of Archaeology*.[4] We have abbreviated references to the Museo Archeologico Nazionale di Napoli collection as "MNN," and abbreviations for ancient authors come from the *Oxford Classical Dictionary*, 3rd edn. "Public" inscriptions are capitalized; "private" *graffiti/dipinti* are italicized, although such distinctions can be difficult and seem arbitrary.

Major sites, buildings (in English), streets (in Italian) and city gates (in Italian) are labeled in Figures 12.1 and 28.1, and on the four maps following the Preface and on the CD. Because the sites are not oriented to cardinal points, directions can be confusing. For Pompeii, "Map North" is at the top. For Herculaneum (Map 4), it is at the left, although publications often use the top for "Map North." This explains why the so-called *cardines* seem to run east–west, and the *insulae orientales* are at the south. *Caveat lector.* See Laidlaw, Ch. 39, Appendix 2, for map orientations in the early published sources.

For all buildings cited in the chapters, a street address is given which correlates to the large city plans of Pompeii and Herculaneum (Maps 3 and 4). In the former case, addresses are tripartite, consisting of the Region (I–IX), *insula* (city-block), and entrance number(s) (commas indicate multiple entrances) for the building on the street (except when a structure takes up an entire *insula*, in which case the address is bipartite). Several names for the same structures have often appeared in the literature; for a concordance to Pompeii, one can refer to H. B. Van der Poel (ed.), *Corpus Topographicum Pompeianum, Pars II, Toponymy*, Rome, 1983. The numbering scheme for spaces within buildings at Pompeii follows Carratelli and Baldassarre, *Pitture e mosaici*, unless otherwise noted. In the case of Herculaneum, there are no "Regions," and so addresses have only an *insula* and address number.

The editors wish to acknowledge first and foremost the excellent work of the authors and their patience over the long course of this volume's gestation. While it is a desideratum in such a book to summarize satisfactorily the state of knowledge in a particular area, there is much in these chapters that is new, and we thank the authors for working to find a balance between outline and originality. We are also grateful to the translators of the non-English contributions; they made possible our ability to edit those chapters confidently while preserving the style and approach of each author.[5] We are indebted to Pietro Giovanni Guzzo and the Soprintendenza Archeologica di Pompei for providing plans of Pompeii and Herculaneum and for permission to publish Soprintendenza photographs and photographs taken by the authors. Appreciation is also well deserved by Richard Stoneman and Routledge, for their willingness to see the project through. And finally, we gratefully acknowledge the dedication of Sue Leaper and Florence Production in producing this book.

John Dobbins wishes to acknowledge the support given to the Pompeii Forum Project which, in turn, led to his collaboration with Pedar Foss on the present book: the Institute for Advanced Technology in the Humanities (IATH) at the University of Virginia; the National Endowment for the Humanities; the Ceres Foundation; and Gilbert and Judy Shelton. Scott Craver and Eric Field provided invaluable help with the maps. I am grateful to my wife, Kathy Dobbins, for her encouragement.

Pedar Foss wishes to mention his appreciation for a Semple Fellowship Grant from the University of Cincinnati in 1997, which helped get the project started, as well as a John and Janice Fisher Time-Out from DePauw University in 2004, which helped to push the project to completion.[6] Finishing would not have been possible without the patient support of my wife, Rebecca Schindler, and the sublime distractions of my sons Simon and Jakob.

Finally, we would like to include in the dedication, John H. D'Arms, who we had hoped could contribute a chapter on "The public life of Pompeii," and whose untimely passing during the creation of this volume left us all to mourn a great scholar, mentor and friend. *Benemerenti*. From the beginning we had intended to dedicate this book to the memories of August Mau and Francis W. Kelsey. The inclusion of John D'Arms renders the dedication especially personal and poignant.[7] We remember, too, Jos A. K. E. DeWaele, Professor of Classical Archaeology at the University of Nijmegen, who was killed in a minibus accident while en route to Pompeii in 2001.[8] References to his work on the Doric temple in the Triangular Forum appear in several chapters.

NOTES

1 L. Eschebach, *Gebäudeverzeichnis und Stadtplan de antiken Stadt Pompeji*, Köln, 1993; W. F. Jashemski, *The Gardens of Pompeii, Herculaneum and the Villas Destroyed by Vesuvius: Appendices*, New Rochelle, NY, 1993, vol. 2; A. Wallace-Hadrill, *Houses and Society in Pompeii and Herculaneum*, Princeton, NJ, 1994; R. Laurence, *Roman Pompeii. Space and Society*, London, 1994; P. Zanker, *Pompeji. Stadtbild und Wohngeschmack*, Mainz am Rhein, 1995; C. Parslow, *Rediscovering Antiquity. Karl Weber and the Excavation of Herculaneum, Pompeii and Stabiae*, Cambridge, 1995; R. Laurence and A. Wallace-Hadrill (eds), "Domestic space in the Roman world: Pompeii and beyond," *Journal of Roman Archaeology*, Suppl. Ser. no. 22, 1997; S. E. Bon and R. Jones (eds), *Sequence and Space in Pompeii*, Oxbow Monograph no. 77, Oxford, 1997; G. P. Carratelli and I. Baldassarre (eds), *Pompei, pitture e mosaici*, 11 vols, Rome, 1990–2003.

2 A. Mau, "Osservazioni intorno alle decorazioni murali di Pompei," *Giornale degli scavi di Pompei*, Nuova serie, 1870 (1873), vol. 2, no. 19, coll. 386–95. See H. B. Van der Poel (ed.), *Corpus Topographicum Pompeianum, Pars IV, Bibliography*, Rome, 1977, for listings of his publications.

3 M. D. Bridges, "Francis Willey Kelsey (1858–1927)," *Contexts for Classics*, http://www.umich.edu/~cfc/kelsey.htm (September 19, 2004).

4 The current list of *AJA* abbreviations is available online at: www.ajaonline.org/index.php?ptype=page&pid=8 (May 1, 2007).

5 The editors gratefully acknowledge the joint financial support of the Carl H. and Martha S. Lindner Center for Art History at the University of Virginia and the Faculty Development Program at DePauw University for providing a subvention to cover translation costs for the book.

6 At DePauw, Sara Robertson did much of the work on the glossary, Jinyu Liu made several essential suggestions, I consulted Julia Bruggemann, Emmanuel Harris and Bob Hershberger on translations, and Mary Giles, Carl Huffman and Brooke Cox helped with illustrations. Neal Abraham arranged for additional time to work on the project. Sean Lockwood of the University of Cincinnati and Elise Friedland of Rollins College provided valuable assistance as well. I thank them all.

7 Pedar and I (along with authors Clayton Fant and Ann Koloski-Ostrow, and translator Maureen B. Fant) were graduate students of John D'Arms at the University of Michigan. In his final years John was President of the American Council of Learned Societies (ACLS) and his limited and precious research time was spent at the American Academy in Rome. On our last encounter I was examining the ambiguities and potential implications of Cicero's brief comment on Pompeii in *Pro Sulla* 60–62. Knowing that John was working at a nearby desk, and realizing that for their whole lives professors are connected to their former students, I invaded his research time with questions about *Pro Sulla*. At the time I appreciated our brief exchanges on a Pompeii topic in the stacks of the American Academy, and now I cherish them all the more. Thank you for much, John D'Arms (John Dobbins, ed.).

8 Jos DeWaele visited the University of Virginia once to deliver a lecture and he and I overlapped once in our research in Pompeii. His personal charisma and professional generosity revealed themselves on both occasions. I regret that my encounters with him were so few (John Dobbins, ed.).

MAPS

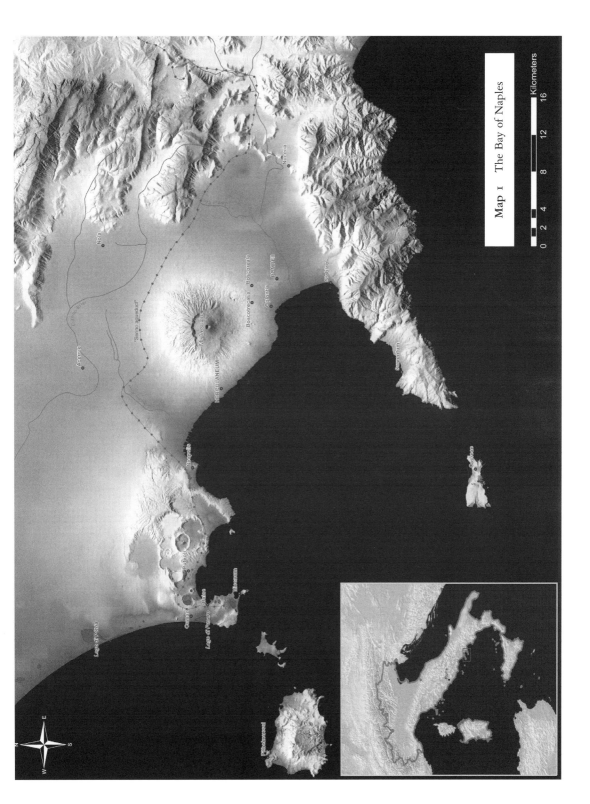

Map 1   The Bay of Naples

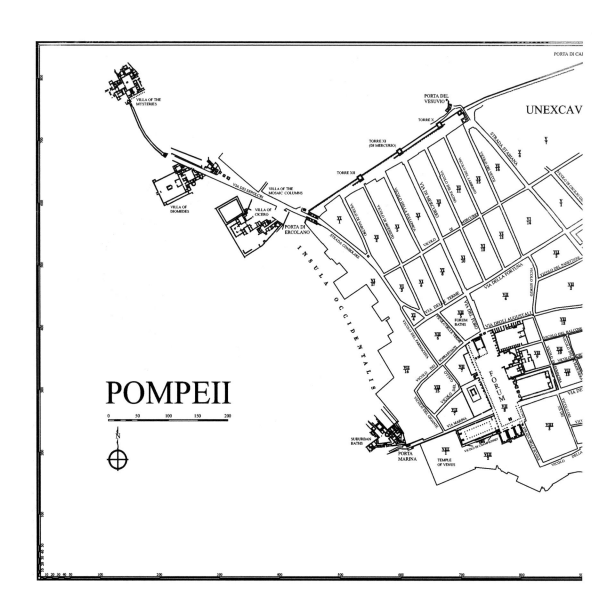

POMPEII

Map 2   Plan of Pompeii. Streets, gates, towers and principal monuments

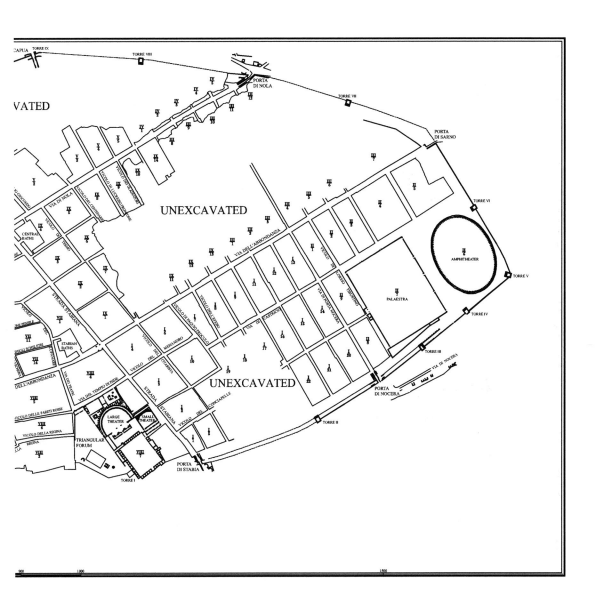

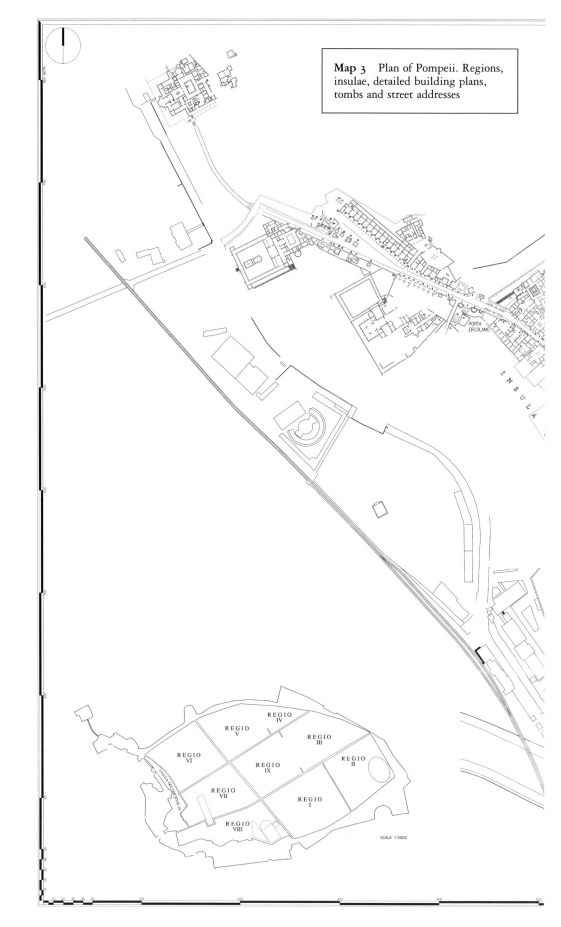

Map 3 Plan of Pompeii. Regions, insulae, detailed building plans, tombs and street addresses

PORTA
ERCOLANO

INSULA

REGIO
IV

REGIO
V

REGIO
III

REGIO
VI

REGIO
IX

REGIO
II

INSULA OCCIDENTALIS

REGIO
VII

REGIO
I

REGIO
VIII

SCALA 1:5000

PORTA CAPUA

PORTA
VESUVIO

ULA OCCIDENTALIS

PORTA
MARINA

Map 3 *Continued*

PORTA NOLA

PORTA DI STABIA

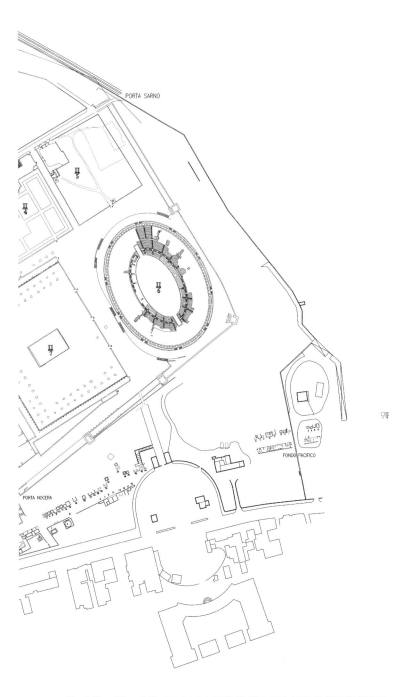

PORTA SARNO

II
5

II
4

II
6

II
7

PORTA NOCERA

FONDO PACIFICO

Map 3. Plan of Pompeii. Regions, insulae, detailed building plans, tombs and street addresses
(after a map provided by the Soprintendenza Archeologica di Pompeii).
Il progetto è finanziato dall'American Express attraverso il World Monuments Watch, un programma del World Monuments
Fund Base cartografica: The Rica Maps of Pompeii, 1984. Digitalizzazione a cura dello STUDIO DI ARCHITETTURA
SCALA: 1:1000

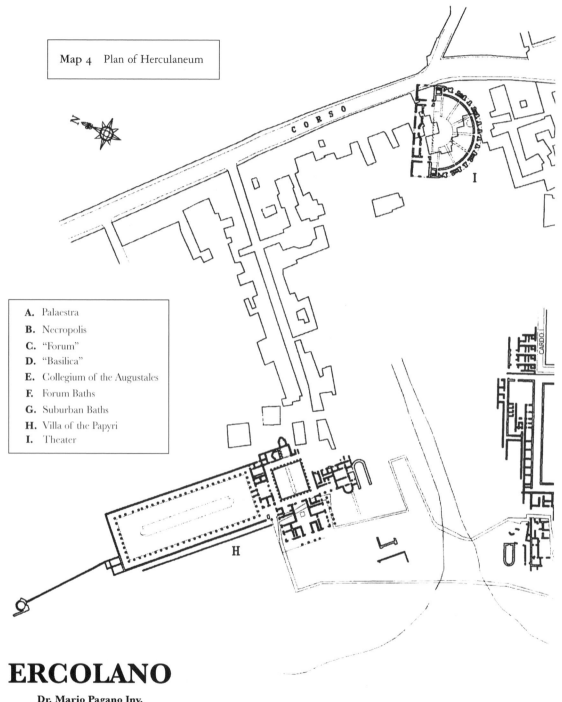

Map 4   Plan of Herculaneum

A. Palaestra
B. Necropolis
C. "Forum"
D. "Basilica"
E. Collegium of the Augustales
F. Forum Baths
G. Suburban Baths
H. Villa of the Papyri
I. Theater

CORSO

CARDO I.

I

H

ERCOLANO

Dr. Mario Pagano Inv.
Arch. Ubaldo Pastore Dis.

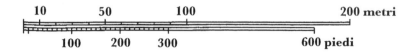

RESINA

B

C

DECUMANUS MAXIMUS

D

E

F

VI

V

VII

A

Ins. Or. II

DECUMANUS INFERIOR

II

III

IV

Ins. Or. I

G

Excavated Structures
Area documented by 18th-c. drawings
Limit of the Excavations
Coastline in A.D. 79
Modern town

PART I

BEGINNINGS

———·◆·———

CITY AND COUNTRY
An introduction

——·◆·——

Pietro Giovanni Guzzo

In 310 BC, during the second Samnite war, the Romans and their naval allies carried out a raid against Nuceria. Livy (9.38.2–3) describes the territorial context as dominated by the fortified city of Pompeii, in which the families that cultivated the surrounding countryside took refuge.

But Strabo (5.4.8) tells us that both Pompeii and Herculaneum had a more ancient history: thanks also to archaeological finds, modern historical criticism considers Pompeii to have already been fortified by the end of the sixth century BC. Parallel evidence is lacking for Herculaneum; it will be better to suspend judgment, but to keep in mind that Strabo records a closely parallel development for the two cities.

For Pompeii's archaic period, except for the walls and the votive offerings at the Temple of Apollo, the evidence is scarce and uncertain; and in the surrounding countryside only unrecorded finds at Boscoreale can be mentioned. Near Castellammare di Stabia, at Santa Maria delle Grazie, however, a necropolis with trench tombs is known. Its grave goods consist of local and Etruscan products (some inscribed) in use from the end of the seventh until the fifth century BC. To complete our picture of the archaic Stabian settlement we have a small rural nucleus at Gesini di Casola, consisting of burials from the middle of the sixth to the first half of the fifth century BC, and the toponym Petra Herculis (Pliny the Elder, *HN* 32.17) for the islet of Rovigliano, located probably at the landing place.

It is possible that Pompeii had gradually downgraded the archaic Stabian settlement's role as a port. Pompeii's predominance was facilitated by the control it could exercise on the mouth of the Sarno, located just south of the fortified hill of the city. On the right bank of the mouth of the Sarno is attested, at least from the fifth century BC, the Sanctuary of Poseidon at Bottaro (Figure 28.1, A).

The approximate chronological coincidence between the end of the Stabian necropolis and the establishment of the cult at Bottaro seems significant.

The trade on the Nola plateau used the river Sarno. The Samnites were establishing themselves in this area during the fifth century BC, replacing the Aurunci, who occupied it earlier. The Italic toponyms of both Nuceria and Nola contain the root Nou-, which indicates a "new" settlement.

By the end of the fourth century BC, the city of Pompeii had elaborated a new urban layout that gradually filled up with buildings over its entire fortified area (*c.* 66 ha, or 165 acres). If we look at the main urban road axes (Maps 1–2), we can extend our examination to the surrounding countryside as well. The principal axis is the north–south road that links Porta Vesuvio and Porta di Stabia; east of it two streets head toward the towns of Nola and Sarno. The southern necropolis outside Porta Nocera follows the orientation of the road to Nuceria, which, on the way, crossed the ancient course of the river Sarno at Scafati. From Porta Ercolano, another very important road, to judge from the antiquity of its route, entered the city. It is, in fact, the only road that interrupted the regularity of the urban design by *insulae*, dividing *insula* 3 of Regio VI in two.

From this layout we can infer that Pompeii was linked, from Porta Ercolano, to a coast road that passed the area later known as Oplontis (present-day Torre Annunziata), on its way to the coast, where it turned toward Neapolis and Cumae, via Herculaneum.

From the archaic period, inside the fortified city, this coast road intersected with the north–south road that linked the southern slopes of Vesuvius with Stabiae. Furthermore, it was possible to travel up the valley of the Sarno from Pompeii along a number of river and land corridors. These routes intersected at the port at the mouth of the Sarno: it is therefore possible to infer that Pompeii developed profitably.

It is, in fact, Pompeii's role as distribution point of the agricultural products of the district, whence they were sent on to external markets, that suggests that the countryside was farmed intensively—just as Livy describes it. But the archaeological evidence is practically nonexistent. To this phase can be ascribed a few tombs at Pozzano di Castellammare and a sanctuary in the same township, at Privati, with architectural terracottas made from moulds used in the decoration of the "Doric temple" of the Triangular Forum in Pompeii (Figure 6.2).

It has been observed that the northern suburban villas of Pompeii show the same orientation as the roads that articulate Regio VI, one of the earliest of post-archaic Pompeii (Figure 28.2).[1] It has therefore been proposed that the countryside north of the city had been "centuriated" in continuation of the axes of the city streets, since there was originally a gate, later closed, also at the northern extremity of the Via di Mercurio (Figure 11.3). The farms and the suburban villas would have been built on this grid; some of these constituted the nucleus of the villas, oriented differently, whose Second-Style decoration tells us they were enlarged after the establishment of the Sullan colony (80 BC).

Between the third and second centuries BC, the Samnite magistrates administered the roads that ran south from Pompeii. There is epigraphic evidence for a "Stabian bridge," which facilitated transit perhaps not only into town but also between the suburban sanctuaries of *fondo* Iozzino and S. Abbondio (dedicated to Bacchus), on opposite banks of the river Sarno (Figure 28.1, B–C). The location of the saltpans, documented by Oscan and Latin inscriptions, is uncertain.

The replacement of the previous owners by the Roman colonists brought a period of internal turbulence, but the volcanic deposits from the eruption of AD 79 make it impossible to identify fully the successive centuriations of the *ager*. The toponym *pagus (Augustus) Felix suburbanus* (*CIL* X, 814, 853–7, 924, 1027, 1028, 1030, 1042, 1074c), of uncertain location, suggests that the corresponding nucleus served as a

Figure 1.1 View of the *dolia* in courtyard (I) of the Villa Regina at Boscoreale (cf. Figure 28.4). Photo: Soprintendenza Archeologica di Pompei.

base for the Sullan colonists. The electoral *programmata* and other inscriptions mention other *pagi* in the territory, which have not yet been identified. It is certain that the agricultural exploitation of the Pompeian, Nucerian and Stabian countryside continued over time until the fatal interruption.

The number of the agricultural settlements is gradually increasing thanks to continuing excavations (Figure 28.1). As D'Arms[2] has already pointed out, we do not in any case know the respective size or the relationship between buildings and fields; for Villa Regina, an area between three and eight *iugera* of vineyards has been calculated on the basis of the capacity of the *dolia* (Figures 1.1, 28.4, 28.5). Most of the buildings have rustic rooms, few with frescoed decorations, a sign that the presence of the owner was probably occasional. Sometimes the decoration is quite costly, as in the "*tablinum*" of the farm at Carmiano 1963, with a Third-Style Bacchic scene; or at Terzigno (Boccia al Mauro), with Second-Style megalographic paintings (1997 excavations). There are plenty of simple decorations that allude to the tutelary gods of the harvest, as in the farm of Villa Regina at Boscoreale; and signs of Egyptian cults, as in the Villa of Agrippa Postumus at Boscotrecase (Figure 28.1, no. 31).

The principal crop was the vine; wine was traded in the western Mediterranean. Manpower was provided by slaves, as iron shackles attest, but it is possible that free peasants still survived.

In addition to the farms, the territory was occupied by luxurious villas of *otium*: this typology expands from Cumae and Baiae southward along the coast of the Bay from some time in the first century BC, after the establishment of the Sullan colony.

Figure 1.2 Detail of a Second-Style wall painting from the west wall of *atrium* (5) in the villa at Oplontis (modern Torre Annunziata). Photo: Soprintendenza Archeologica di Pompei.

Villas of the kind can be suburban, as that attributed, without foundation, to the Pisones at Herculaneum, with its bronze and marble sculptures, in addition to some 1,800 papyrus scrolls mostly written upon in Greek. Farther from the city are the so-called villa of the Poppaei, at Oplontis (Figures 1.2, 31.5), and that of San Marco at Stabiae, more recent than the destruction of that city by Sulla. Less well preserved, but of equal importance, is the villa at contrada Sora, Torre del Greco, from which come the relief with Orpheus and Eurydice, a replica of Praxiteles' Satyr Pouring, and a bronze of Hercules and the stag (the latter two in the Palermo museum).

The villas situated inland, from that "of the Mysteries" to those attributed to P. Fannius Synistor, N. Popidius Florus (at Boscoreale), to Agrippa Postumus (at Boscotrecase), also include a *rustica* part, showing that they have combined two functions. The prevalent Second-Style decorations place the enlargement in the post-colonial phase.

Both the precision and the size of the frescoed decorations and, when preserved, the artistic furnishings (from the villa "of the Pisones" to that of Oplontis) indicate the owners' high position. It should be recalled how landholdings were always being bought and sold for speculation, and for this reason it is difficult and probably useless to assign, as owners, names known from the sources (such as the *matrona* Rectina) to properties brought to light by archaeology. To make matters worse, the damage inflicted by the series of earthquakes preceding the eruption (of which at least that of AD 62 is known) will have brought about even more buying and selling.

The fertility of the soils and the favorable opportunities for trade caused the Pompeian countryside to be densely populated: Pliny records how enormous crowds from the farms took refuge at Stabiae, seeking to escape in boats.

After AD 79 came a period of total abandonment, not least because the volcanic debris impeded people's movement near the coast. Nocera equipped itself with an outlet at Vietri sul Mare, picking up again the archaic axis of communication on which Marcina was located. There is evidence of subsequent life in the territory of Pompeii, even in the immediate vicinity of the Porta Vesuvio. The roads from Nocera to the embarkation at Stabiae were reopened, and Stabiae continued to be occupied until late antiquity, as numerous burials and a Hadrianic mile post attest.

NOTES

1 Maureen B. Fant translated the Italian text. F. Zevi, "Urbanistica di Pompei," in F. Zevi (ed.), *La Regione sotterrata dal Vesuvio. Studi e prospettive. Atti del Convegno Internazionale*, Naples, 1979, pp. 353–65; A. Oettel, *Fundkontexte roemischer Vesuvvillen im Gebiet um Pompeji. Die Grabungen von 1894 bis 1908*, Mainz, 1996.
2 J. H. D'Arms, "Ville rustiche e ville di otium," in F. Zevi (ed.), *Pompei 79. Raccolta di studi per il decimono centenario dell'eruzione vesuviana*, Naples, 1979, pp. 25–39.

BIBLIOGRAPHY

Adamo Muscettola, S., "La trasformazione della città tra Silla e Augusto," in F. Zevi (ed.), *Pompei 1*, Naples, 1991, pp. 77–114.

Amodio, D., "Sui vici e le circoscrizioni elettorali di Pompei," *Athenaeum* n.s. 84, 1996, pp. 457–8.

Camardo, D. and A. Ferrara, "Petra Herculis: un luogo di culto alla foce del Sarno," *AION* 12, 1990, pp. 169–80.

Casale, A. and A. Bianco, "Primo contributo alla topografia del suburbio pompeiano," *Antiqua*, suppl. 15, 1979, pp. 27–56.

Cicirelli, C., "Le ville rustiche," in M. Borriello, A. D'Ambrosio, S. De Caro and P. G. Guzzo (eds), *Pompei. Abitare sotto il Vesuvio*, Ferrara, 1996, pp. 29–33.

—— *Le ville romane di Terzigno*, Terzigno, 1989.

Conticello De' Spagnolis, M., *Il pons Sarni di Scafati e la via Nuceria–Pompeios*, Rome, 1994.

Cristofani, M., "Presenze etrusche tra Stabia e Pontecagnano," *Atti e memorie della Società Magna Grecia* s. 3a, 1, 1992, pp. 61–6.

D'Arms, J. H., "Ville rustiche e ville di 'otium'," in F. Zevi (ed.), *Pompei 79*, Naples, 1979, pp. 65–86.

De Caro, S., "Lo sviluppo urbanistico di Pompei," *Atti e memorie della Società Magna Grecia*, s. 3a, 1, 1992, pp. 67–90.

—— "La città sannitica. Urbanistica e architettura," in F. Zevi (ed.), *Pompei 1*, Naples, 1991, pp. 23–46.

—— "Villa rustica in località Petraro (Stabiae)," *Rivista Istituto Italiano di Archeologia e Storia*, s. 2a, 10, 1987, 1988, pp. 5–89.

—— *La villa rustica in località Villa Regina di Boscoreale*, Rome, 1994.

—— "Le ville residenziali," in M. Borriello, A. D'Ambrosio, S. De Caro and P. G. Guzzo (eds), *Pompei. Abitare sotto il Vesuvio*, Ferrara, 1996, pp. 21–7.

Esposito, E., "L'ager Nucerinus: note storiche e topografiche," *Rendiconti Accademia Archeologia*, 1984, vol. 58, pp. 221–40.

Frederiksen, M., *Campania*, ed. with additions, N. Purcell, Rome, 1984.

Lo Cascio, E., "La società pompeiana dalla città sannitica alla colonia romana," in F. Zevi (ed.), *Pompei 1*, Naples, 1991, pp. 111–30.

Marzocchella, A., *et al.*, *Guida al territorio del Sarno. Tracce storiche, archeologiche e mitiche*, Ercolano, 1994.

Miniero, P., "Ricerche sull'Ager Stabianus," in R. I. Curtis, (ed.), *Studia Pompeiana et Classica in Honor of W. F. Jashemski*, New Rochelle, NY, 1988, pp. 231–92.

Murolo, N., "Le saline Herculeae di Pompei. Produzione del sale e culto di Ercole nella Campania antica," in *Studi sulla Campania preromana*, Rome, 1995, pp. 105–23.

Oettel, A., *Fundkontexte römischer Vesuvvillen im Gebiet um Pompeji. Die Grabungen von 1894 bis 1908*, Mainz, 1996.

Pagano, M., *Portici archeologica*, Rome, 1997.

—— "Torre del Greco. Scavo di una villa rustica," *RivStPom*, 2, 1988, vol. 2, pp. 240–3.

—— "La villa romana di contrada Sora a Torre del Greco," in *Cronache Ercolanesi*, 1991, vol. 21, pp. 149–86.

—— *Picta Fragmenta. Decorazioni parietali dalle città sepolte*, Yokohama, 1997, pp. 57–9.

Scatozza Höricht, L. A., "Ville nel territorio ercolanese," *Cronache Ercolanesi*, 1985, vol. 15, pp. 131–65.

Stefani, G., *Pompei. Vecchi scavi sconosciuti*, Rome, 1994.

Tchernia, A., "Il vino: produzione e commercio," in F. Zevi (ed.), *Pompei 79*, Naples, 1979, pp. 87–96.

Ward-Perkins, J. B., "Note di topografia e urbanistica," in F. Zevi (ed.), *Pompei 79*, Naples, 1979, pp. 25–39.

Zevi, F., "Urbanistica di Pompei," in F. Zevi (ed.), *La Regione sotterrata dal Vesuvio, Studi e prospettive: Atti del Convegno Internazionale*, Naples, 1982, pp. 353–65.

CHAPTER TWO

HISTORY AND
HISTORICAL SOURCES

———•◆•———

Jean-Paul Descœudres

The sources of information at our disposal to reconstruct the history of Pompeii can be subdivided into two main categories: the written and the unwritten. The first includes some fifty passages in ancient (Greek and Latin) literature and over 11,000 inscriptions found in the city itself.[1] The second category is much more diverse and comprises geographical, geomorphological, and topographical data and, most importantly, the archaeological evidence which means all material remains left behind by the Pompeians. The first part of this chapter aims at a brief examination and assessment of these various sources, illustrating each kind with specific examples. In the second part an attempt is made to sketch a historical survey of the town by combining the information gained from the sources presented in the first part.

THE SOURCES

Written evidence

Ancient literature

There exists no historical account of Pompeii by an ancient writer, and the roughly fifty passages in the extant Greek and Roman literature that mention the town[2] do so almost without exception incidentally and in passing.[3] Three times it is mentioned as having been destroyed by the earthquake that ravaged large parts of Campania on February 5, AD 62,[4] eleven times in the context of the gigantic eruption of Mt Vesuvius that buried it together with Herculaneum and Stabiae on August 24–25, AD 79.[5] Six times it figures in general descriptions of Campania, and on some of these occasions its name is said to derive from *pompe*, the "procession" that Hercules led on his way back to Greece, returning from Spain.[6] Two of these passages give an extremely condensed summary of its pre-Roman existence. According to Strabo, Pompeii "belonged first to the Oscans, then to the Tyrrhenians and to the Pelasgians, and finally to the Samnites until they, too, were expelled,"[7] whereas Pliny says that "its inhabitants were Oscan, Greek, Umbrian, Etruscan, and Campanian."[8] Most interesting from a historical point of view are the five passages dealing with political events. Thus, we gather from Livy that in 310 BC a Roman fleet under the command of Publius Cornelius landed in Pompeii to raid the territory of Nuceria,[9] and three authors inform us about Pompeii's participation in the Social Wars between 91 and 89 BC.[10] Thanks to Tacitus we also know about a bloody brawl that took place in Pompeii's amphitheater in AD 59 between Nucerians and Pompeians.[11]

Epigraphic sources[12]

OFFICIAL INSCRIPTIONS

Generally, these were meant to last and are therefore carved in stone, form part of a mosaic or *signinum* floor, are incised on bronze plaques, or composed of letters made of metal. Such inscriptions are found on statues and, above all, on public buildings where they commemorate the magistrates under whose administration they were erected, enlarged, embellished or repaired. For instance, an Oscan inscription in the Temple of Apollo announces that: "the quaestor O[ppius] Campanus, with the consent of the Council and using Apollo's money had it built."[13] Similarly, an inscription made of white marble chips placed in the *signinum* floor of the ramp that leads to the entrance porch, provides the visitor of the Temple of Dionysus near S. Abbondio south of the city with the names of the two aediles responsible for its building:

O. EPIDIUS O. FILIUS TREBIUS MEZIUS TREBII FILIUS AEDILES[14]

while another inscription, placed on a travertine slab above the amphitheater's main entrance, announces that (cf. Table 33.1 for municipal offices):

> Gaius Quinctius Valgus, son of Gaius, and Marcus Porcius, son of Marcus, the *duumviri* for five years, for the sake of the colony's honor had this amphitheater built at their own expense and dedicated it to the colonists to use forever.[15]

Exceptionally, official writings may also be of temporary character, such as the so-called *eituns* inscriptions[16] or other municipal announcements (including the list of candidates for the annual elections of the magistrates) set up in the forum (Figure 23.12).[17]

PRIVATE MESSAGES

Unofficial messages are, as a rule, of temporary nature and not meant for posteriority. They comprise some 2,600 election posters, such as: "the garlic sellers ask you to vote for Gnaeus Helvius Sabinus,"[18] or, more ambiguously, "the petty thieves ask you to vote for Vatia as aedile,"[19] and other advertisements painted on house walls,[20] as well as thousands of messages scratched in the plaster of both private and public walls.[21] The vast majority of these messages are rather trivial,[22] but as a whole they form an invaluable source for the social history of the town and also help us gain an idea of its political organization.[23] A few of them can be dated, either by virtue of their content,[24] or because they include the date when they were written,[25] and so can provide most useful chronological fixed points. Thus, we know thanks to a Gaius Pumidius Dipilus that the Basilica was completed before 78 BC. He scratched, like many others, his name into the plaster on the interior of the building (on the north wall, to be precise), and added the date of his visit: October 3 of the year when Marcus Lepidus and Quintus Catulus were consuls in Rome.[26]

Of quite exceptional historical value are two *graffiti* in the House of C. Iulius Polybius (IX.13.1–3),[27] placed one above the other on the same wall.[28] The meaning of the one below, which reads:

Caesar ut ad Venerem venet sanctissimam ut tui te uexere pedes caelestes Auguste millia milliorum ponderis auri fuit[29]

becomes clearer thanks to the one above:

Munera Poppaea misit Veneri sanctissimae brullum helencumque unio mixtus erat.[30]

Since the marriage between Nero and Sabina Poppaea only lasted from AD 63 to AD 65, their visit to Pompeii and their generous offerings to the Temple of Venus must have occurred some time after the earthquake, perhaps on the occasion of Nero's performance in the theater of Naples in 64.[31]

Among the unofficial inscriptions are also those by which private people publicly announce a dedication to a divinity, or a gift to the community. A famous example of the first category is Sextius Ruma's votive offering to Neptune, thanks to which we know of the existence of a sanctuary consecrated to this god, most probably situated in the vicinity of the harbor:

SEX POMPEIVS SEX L RVMA NEPTVNO V S L (*CIL* X 2).[32]

An Oscan dedication in the Sanctuary of Apollo provides an intriguing example of the second category:

L MUMMIS L KUSUL.

It is written on the pedestal for a now lost offering, undoubtedly of Greek origin, placed against one of the columns in the southern *porticus* of the sanctuary, facing the temple.[33] Several ancient authors mention that after sacking Corinth in 146 BC, Lucius Mummius distributed some of his booty among various municipalities.[34] The inscription in the Sanctuary of Apollo shows that Pompeii was one of the municipalities that benefited from these gifts. On the other hand, it adds nothing to our knowledge of the history of the Temple of Apollo,[35] since it is quite obvious that the pedestal, and thus the inscription, was not originally designed to be placed in its present location. To fit the available space on the narrow plinth in front of the *porticus* columns, the base had to be reduced in size, which explains why its rear has been cut off. A second base, with an almost identical profile, was placed in the same *porticus* further east and has been adjusted even more roughly to fit its secondary position.[36]

More exceptional are inscriptions the content of which seems rather casual but which have nevertheless been made to last, such as the well-known type of floor mosaic representing a guard dog with the warning *cave canem*, known from several houses. Unique is the inscription, also laid down in stone as part of a mosaic pavement, in front of the House of the Faun (VI.12): it greets the visitor with the Latin *HAVE*, and was placed there long before Pompeii became a Roman colony and Latin its official language.

Finally, there are the famous receipts of the accountant L. Caecilius Iucundus[37] and the more recently discovered commercial transactions of the bankers Sulpicii from Puteoli,[38] each set including over a hundred wax-covered wooden sheets. Both date from before AD 62, which suggests that even if the bankers Sulpicii and the accountant Caecilius survived the earthquake, their businesses did not.

Non-literary sources

Environmental evidence

The close connection that exists between a settlement's history and its natural environment is particularly clear in Pompeii's case, due to the fact that both the lava spur on which it is built and the ash under which it was buried until its rediscovery in 1748 are the results of the activity of the volcano that rises some 20 km to the northwest.[39] Geomorphological studies have revealed that the ancient coast line was much closer to the town than it is today, thus confirming the statements made by ancient writers that Pompeii was a harbor city, situated on the mouth of the river Sarno (Figure 28.1, dashed line).[40] Moreover, Pompeii's geology and topography show that its plateau, with its steep rise above the Sarno valley, offers the advantage of a natural defense, but as it is formed of volcanic deposits, a certain level of technological know-how is required to reach drinking water which only occurs at a depth of over 20 m, as Maiuri's excavation of a well near the Porta Vesuvio revealed in 1928.[41]

Archaeological evidence

TOWN PLAN[42]

The history of every settlement is, to a larger or lesser extent, reflected in its plan. In Pompeii's case, the town's five main historical phases can be recognized without difficulty (cf. Figures 7.5 and 7.6). The first settlement is likely to have been situated in the southwestern part of the town, often referred to as *"Altstadt,"*[43] as its narrow and curving lanes suggest. A first extension to the north, for which the Via di Mercurio forms the main axis and which corresponds roughly to Regio VI, is likely to go back to the sixth century BC.[44] The tripartite arrangement of the eastern part, with the Via Stabiana as *cardo* and the Via di Nola and the Via dell'Abbondanza as *decumani*, is clearly linked to the town wall and is unlikely to predate the fourth century BC.[45] A further subdivision can be observed in Regions I, II and III, where the house blocks along the Via di Nocera are of distinctly different shape and smaller size than those elsewhere; it has been suggested that this phase belongs to the late third century, and that the urban space may have been reorganized in order to accommodate an influx of new inhabitants, possibly as a result of Nuceria's destruction in 216 at the hands of Hannibal.[46] To the fifth phase, finally, Pompeii's Roman period, belong the large area dedicated to public use in the northeastern corner as well as the private dwellings built on top of the city wall along the town's western and southwestern edges (Figures 26.1 and 26.4).[47]

BUILDING MATERIALS AND CONSTRUCTION TECHNIQUES

According to a view commonly accepted until recently, Pompeii's historical development is also reflected in its building materials (cf. Adam, Ch. 8; Wallace-Hadrill, Ch. 18; Peterse, Ch. 24).[48] In particular, a first urban phase has often been named the "Limestone period," in the belief that this stone, in reality travertine, was the prevailing, if not only, building material during the period *c.*425–200 BC. Similarly, the following phase, from *c.*200 to 80 BC, is frequently referred to as the "Tufa period."[49] As has been rightly pointed out, the basis for this chronology is most unreliable, and the exceptions to the rule too numerous for the system to be of much help.[50] More useful information could undoubtedly be gained from a systematic analysis of the construction techniques,[51] as Maiuri's study of the post-62 techniques shows, thanks to which the extent of the earthquake damage can be gauged.[52]

ARCHITECTURE[53]

Buildings, single or in groups, provide important insights into the history of the whole town (cf. Ling, Ch. 9). Thus, the erection along the forum's southwestern edge of a basilica, a characteristically Roman building type, at the end of the second century is not only a most noteworthy change in Pompeii's cityscape, it also reflects a change in the town's socio-political outlook. The same can be said about the transformation of the Temple of Jupiter into a Capitolium shortly after 80 BC, when the city became a Roman colony,[54] or the transformation of many peristyle gardens into industrially used areas after the earthquake of AD 62.[55]

SCULPTURE, WALL PAINTINGS AND MOSAICS[56]

The preference for a particular subject-matter, or the combination of a number of pictorial themes in the decoration of private and public buildings, give us insights into the changing ethic and religious attitudes of Pompeians through time.[57]

POTTERY, METAL VESSELS, COINS AND OTHER SMALL OBJECTS (*INSTRUMENTUM DOMESTICUM*)[58]

To illustrate the usefulness of this source of information with regard to Pompeii's economic history it may suffice to mention the example of the fish-sauce (*garum*) containers made in Pompeii and exported as far as southern France.[59] The archaeological evidence nicely confirms the literary sources according to which Pompeii was one of the most famous *garum* producers, alongside Carthage, Clazomenae, and Leptis Magna (cf. Jones and Robinson, Ch. 25).[60]

STRATIGRAPHICAL DATA

Mainly interested in the recovery of artistically valuable objects, the early excavators limited themselves to removing the volcanic deposits under which these treasures laid buried, and when Giuseppe Fiorelli introduced a more scientific and systematic approach when he became director in 1860, he decided to excavate the town to its AD 79 level, so as to bring it back to the appearance it had just prior to its death. Most of his successors adhered to this decision, and it was only under Amedeo Maiuri's directorship that a first important series of soundings and trial trenches was carried out all over the city in order to investigate its pre-79 past.[61] Although soundings below the 79 level have since been dug in ever increasing numbers, only a few have so far been fully reported and published.[62] It is likely that new projects, several of which have just started at the time of writing (summer 1998), will make substantial contributions to our still very fragmentary knowledge of pre-Roman Pompeii.[63]

FLORAL, FAUNAL AND ANTHROPOLOGICAL REMAINS

The study of plant remains (either in the form of roots, carbonized fruit and wood, or of pollen) by archaeobotanists, and of animal and human bones by archaeozoologists and anthropologists, respectively, is an even more recent addition to the range of tools with which the city's history can be reconstructed.[64] While a few hints in the ancient literature[65] and the mention in several election posters of the *aliarii*, *pomarii* and *lupinarii*, the garlic sellers, market gardeners and greengrocers, suggest that the growing of fruit, vegetables and flowers was a significant part of Pompeii's economy, it is mainly thanks to recent archaeobotanical studies that its importance can be assessed more accurately.[66] The same is true with regard to the wine industry (Figure 31.6)[67]—about which Pliny is rather critical, observing that Pompeian wines "do not improve with age" and that: "it has been observed that they are rather dangerous as they may cause a headache which lasts till noon on the following day."[68]

A BRIEF OUTLINE OF POMPEII'S HISTORY

Origins

The first permanent settlement on the plateau which was later to be occupied by the town of Pompeii does not appear to go back beyond the sixth century BC.[69] As the plan of the city suggests, the first Pompeians probably settled on the southwestern corner of the plateau, and as archaeological evidence shows, the town soon expanded northwards, possibly before the middle of the sixth century BC.[70] At the same time, the whole area that was later to be covered by the Roman town, covering a surface of some 66 ha (165 acres), seems to have been enclosed by a simple wall, built of large tufa blocks (cf. Chiaramonte, Ch. 11).[71]

This wall doesn't appear to have had a proper military function and served, rather, as an enclosure for fields, pastures and vineyards—some of which still existed until the town's final destruction in AD 79. That some dwellings or small country sanctuaries existed here as early as the sixth century cannot be excluded.[72] This would explain the sporadic discovery of Archaic material, mainly pottery fragments, over much of the area, except for the most eastern parts.[73] Among them a substantial number of fragments stem from Etruscan *bucchero* vessels.[74] Several bear inscriptions in Greek letters, but all of them are in Etruscan. They suggest that the earliest Pompeii was an Etruscan town—at least in terms of its cultural habits.[75] This tallies with the character of its first monumental temples, that of Apollo on the western side of the later forum[76] and the distinctly Italic features of the so-called Doric Temple in the "Triangular Forum" (cf. De Caro, Ch. 6).[77]

This first period comes to an apparently abrupt end around 470 BC, possibly in the wake of the Etruscans' defeat at the hands of Hieron of Syracuse in 474. The first town wall appears to have been destroyed around this period, and its successor, built along the same line and, in places, directly on top of it, appears to have been short-lived.[78] From about 460 BC on, Pompeii shrouds itself in total silence for over a century,[79] and it looks as if the town was reduced to an insignificant hamlet, if it continued at all to exist.

The Samnite period

Since the middle of the fifth century the Samnite people were pushing from their original homeland in the Apennines towards the coast; in 424 BC they occupied Capua, which had been the most important Etruscan center in Campania, a few years later Cumae, a Greek foundation. It is likely that Pompeii, too, was occupied, or resettled, by Samnites. They spoke Oscan, one of the three main dialects that form the Italic branch of the Indo-European family of languages (the other two being Umbrian and Latin).[80]

Samnite Pompeii must have started as a very modest settlement some time around the middle of the fourth century BC or a little later. In 310 BC it appears to be still too small to prevent a minor expedition of Roman marines from landing in the mouth of the Sarno directly at its feet.[81] However, it regains its urban character a few decades later when it is surrounded again by a town wall, this time built of Sarno "limestone."[82] It is at this time that Pompeii acquires the town plan which it is to retain, except for minor alterations, until its final destruction. The layout is as regular as topographical features and pre-existing traffic lines permit.

From the late third century BC[83] the town starts to flourish and grows at an ever increasing pace which reaches almost boom proportions in the second half of the second century. In a short period of time, Pompeii transforms itself from a small provincial place to a Hellenized urban center with all the necessary amenities such as a theater (Figure 14.3), a large sports complex (*palaestra*), and a public bath with a second *palaestra* (Figure 15.2). Its civic center, hitherto little more than a large open space, begins to undergo a process of monumentalization that transforms it into a large, paved square, a proper forum, surrounded by porticoes. The Temple of Apollo is rebuilt from scratch, and just opposite rises now a large basilica which, just as its models in Rome, forms the city's commercial and judiciary center. Even more impressive is the wealth in the private sphere, with many of Pompeii's leading families living in huge, palace-like mansions, luxuriously decorated with floor mosaics, stuccoed wall decorations, and marble and bronze sculptures.[84]

Yet, despite its wealth and its loyalty to Rome (of which it is an ally (*socius*) since the end of the fourth century), Pompeii has only very limited political rights. It is hardly surprising, therefore, that it participates in the revolt of Rome's Italian allies in 91 BC, the so-called Social Wars. After some initial difficulties, Rome rapidly reasserts itself, and in 89 an army under Sulla's command brings Campania back under Roman control. Herculaneum falls after a short siege,[85] Stabiae is totally destroyed.[86] Pompeii, too, is besieged, but seems to have held out (Figures 25.7 and 25.8).[87] It certainly suffered no substantial damage.[88]

Yet, although the revolt failed in military terms, it achieved its main aim. In 89 BC, Rome granted all Italic communities south of the Po full citizenship. Nevertheless, a few years later, in 80 BC, Pompeii was made a Roman colony, quite obviously as a punishment for its participation in the rebellion and its resistance against Sulla's army. One of the three men in charge of establishing the colony, the *tresviri coloniae deducendae*, was the dictator's nephew, Publius Cornelius Sulla.[89]

Roman Pompeii

The town's new official name, *Colonia Cornelia Veneria Pompeianorum*, alludes twice to the victor of the Social Wars, Sulla, since it includes both the name of his family, the ancient and powerful gens of the Cornelians, and that of his divine protectress, Venus. It is likely that at least some of the leading indigenous families that were known to have taken an anti-Roman position during the war, were dispossessed and their properties distributed among the Roman colonists. The number of colonists is not known, but it could have tallied with the size of a legion and been as high as 4,000–5,000.[90]

Epigraphic evidence suggests that the transformation of the Samnite town into a Roman colony had only a very limited effect on Pompeii's social and economic structure and that many Samnite families succeeded in keeping their leading positions.[91] This is not to say that the town did not undergo considerable changes in the process. To start with, the Temple of Jupiter at the north end of the forum, on which work had started shortly before the outbreak of the war (and which probably had not been completed) was transformed into a Capitolium, dedicated to Rome's Capitoline triad of Jupiter Maximus, Iuno and Minerva (Figure 12.5).[92] To the south of the forum, a new temple was erected, consecrated to Venus. Built on a large terrace overlooking the mouth of the Sarno and the Gulf of Naples, it was the first building to be seen when approaching the town from the sea.[93]

No less significant is the fact that a number of private dwellings were built on top of the city wall, offering their owners magnificent views to the Gulf of Naples, and at the same time demonstrating that a city wall was no longer necessary, now that Pompeii was a Roman colony.[94]

Yet, perhaps the most significant change in the townscape occurred in its south-eastern corner, where a number of private dwellings—possibly of dispossessed Samnites —were removed[95] to make space for a large amphitheater (Figure 14.2). As an inscription announces,[96] the building, called *spectacula* since the term amphitheater did not yet exist, was paid for by two leading colonists, Marcus Porcius and Quinctius Valgus (see above). Both are also known from other inscriptions, and the latter could well be identical with a Valgus mentioned by Cicero for the lack of scruples with which he enriched himself under Sulla's dictatorship.[97]

Little more than half a century later the town experiences another series of substantial changes, and again the impulse comes from Rome where Augustus begins his principate in 27 BC. In an attempt to emulate Augustus' transformation of Rome from a city built of bricks to one made of marble, Pompeii's upper class embarks on a huge building and renovation program. Erected by the priestess Mamia,[98] a temple dedicated to the Genius Augusti replaces a series of shops on the forum's east side, and there is hardly a public building which does not undergo some kind of enlargement and/or embellishment. In general, such works are carried out at the expense of magistrates who, in this way, demonstrate their *pietas* and *mores maiorum* (respect for the gods and the ancestral customs), and above all their *publica magnificentia* (social responsibility and care for the community). Thus, M. Tullius—among the most powerful men of the Augustan period—is recorded for his donation that enabled the building of the temple dedicated to Fortuna Augusta immediately to the north of the forum,[99] while a member of another old and influential Pompeian family, Holconius Rufus, had the old theater completely rebuilt in marble.[100]

Some years later another important building was erected thanks to the *publica magnificentia* of a wealthy Pompeian, this time a woman. The huge complex is generally known as Eumachia Building (Figure 12.13), after the woman who had it built, as the inscription on the front porch states:

> Eumachia, Lucius' daughter, public priestess, built at her own expenses in her name and in the name of her son Marcus Numistrius Fronto the entrance hall, the galleries and the courtyard surrounded by colonnades, and she dedicated them to Concordia and Pietas Augusta.[101]

Unfortunately, the inscription doesn't mention the building's function, but because Eumachia's portrait statue, placed at the rear of the building, had been donated by the fullers (as its dedicatory inscription informs us; Figure 34.2[102]) it was for a long time believed to be the city's wool-market. Today, most scholars believe that it served more than one purpose,[103] and one might compare it to a modern shopping center.

By dedicating her building to the imperial Concordia and Pietas, Eumachia was obviously referring to the central power in Rome and to events involving the imperial family. It was first thought Eumachia was alluding to the concord between Nero and Agrippina,[104] but as Mau observed, the wall paintings of the building, which belong to the so-called Third Style, are incompatible with a Neronian date. It is, therefore, more likely that Eumachia alludes to Livia,[105] and this is confirmed by the building itself which in its layout and through its sculptural decoration clearly refers to the *porticus* which Livia dedicated to Concordia in 7 BC. It is most likely that the second reference to the imperial family also alludes to a particular event and building in Rome, namely to the altar erected to Pietas Augusta by the senate in AD 22. This means that the building was dedicated after 22, which tallies neatly with the epigraphic evidence. For, contrary to what has often been claimed,[106] the Marcus Numistrius Fronto mentioned in the inscription as Eumachia's son cannot be identical with the Marcus Numistrius Fronto who was *duumvir* in AD 3 according to *CIL* X, 892.[107] There can be only one reason for the son to be mentioned by his mother, and his name to appear after hers (rather than vice versa): Eumachia was a widow and her son Marcus not yet of adult age. We may then reconstruct the sequence of events as follows. Marcus Numistrius Fronto sr., *duumvir* in AD 3, died some ten to fifteen years later, leaving behind a considerable fortune and an adolescent son (born in the first decade of the century). When the latter is about to come of age, around AD 25, Eumachia decides to make an important donation to enhance his success and display the good relations that exist between mother and son (but cf. Small, Ch. 13).

Among the most impressive new buildings is the huge sport center (Figure 14.4) next to the amphitheater, in which the youth associations created under Augustus, the *collegia iuvenum*, may have exhibited their *virtus* (physical fitness).[108]

No less striking than these changes in the appearance of the town are those that are taking place at the social level. The *patres familias* are still ruling over their families, but now they themselves are part of a larger family, the state, to whose head, Augustus, they are accountable. Their power has been eclipsed by his—the *pater patriae*. The shift is clearly reflected in domestic architecture, where many houses are now transformed so as to give the peristyle garden a greater importance, at the cost of the old *atrium/tablinum* complex (cf. Wallace-Hadrill, Ch. 18).[109]

Of far-reaching consequences was the provision of piped water, as a result of the aqueduct built on Augustus' initiative for the naval base at Misenum (Map 1). It brought about a considerable improvement in the quality of life of the Pompeians who, until that time, had relied on wells and cisterns.[110]

As for *l'histoire événementielle*, there is nothing to report until AD 59, when a bloody riot between Pompeians and Nucerians broke out in the amphitheater,[111] which led the Roman senate to ban public meets between the *collegia iuvenum*, the youth associations of Pompeii, for a period of ten years.[112]

Long before this period came to an end, the town was struck by a much more important event.

The last seventeen years

On February 5, AD 62, Pompeii was devastated by an earthquake which, as Seneca reports, caused the town to collapse.[113] Archaeological evidence fully confirms his statement: earthquake damage has been observed throughout the town, and it seems clear that numerous, if not most, houses had become uninhabitable. Hardly any building in Pompeii appears to have escaped completely unscathed.

In 79, when the city was buried by Mt Vesuvius, many houses were unoccupied or under reconstruction and not all public buildings had been fully restored. This is commonly interpreted as a consequence of the severity of the catastrophe of 62. Seventeen years later, it has been argued traditionally, the whole city was still a huge builders' yard (cf. Dobbins, Ch. 12).[114]

While comparisons with similar catastrophes in modern times (such as the destruction of Lisbon in 1755, or of Messina in 1908) show that 17 years would not be an inconceivably long reconstruction period, it is nonetheless worth pointing out that the link between archaeologically observable earthquake damage in Pompeii and the historically recorded event of AD 62 is not as firm and secure as many scholars would like to believe. The 62 earthquake signaled the beginning of an increased volcanic activity that culminated in Mt Vesuvius' explosion on August 24, 79. It is highly unlikely that there were no further quakes between 62 and 79, and although no other earthquake concerning Pompeii itself is recorded in the ancient sources, we know that in 64 an earthquake caused the theater in nearby Naples to collapse.[115] The possibility must therefore always be borne in mind that any earthquake damage observed on buildings in Pompeii may have been caused not by "the" earthquake (i.e., of 62), but by "an" earthquake (i.e., any time between 62 and 79).[116] Indeed, it appears that some buildings that apparently had been repaired look as if they had been damaged again shortly before 79.

The Pompeians set out to rebuild their town by and large as it had been prior to the disaster. The major exceptions appear to have been the transformation of the east side of the forum and the construction of a large bath complex in IX.4, a block previously occupied by private dwellings.[117]

Also, the water supply system appears to have been completely revised and may not have been fully operational by the time of the fatal eruption in 79.[118] On the other hand, many an old mansion was subdivided and modified to allow parts of it to be let as separate apartments and other areas to be used for various commercial activities.[119] These encroachments of commercial and industrial activities upon space previously used for residential or representative purposes have often been interpreted as reflections of profound changes in Pompeii's socio-economic fabric. According to this view, the town's economy was shifting from a predominantly rural system to one in which commerce and industrial production were playing major roles, and a class of merchants and tradesmen, often of servile origin, was replacing the landed aristocracy. While some scholars see the change as a direct result of the earthquake, others have argued that the disaster might have done no more than accelerated an already ongoing process.[120]

As for single events of socio-historical importance we know of two. The first is the visit by Nero and his wife Poppaea in AD 64,[121] the second, which no doubt had a greater, but as yet little explored, impact on the town and some of its inhabitants, is Vespasian's decision that all public land which had been unlawfully privatized (especially within the city's *pomerium*) was to be returned to the municipality. The text of the decree was inscribed on stone and was probably placed in front of all city gates. Several of them have been found: one, in front of the Porta Ercolano, as early as 1763 (Figure 37.1, b).[122] It provided the first firm proof that the site being excavated was not, as had been believed since 1748, Stabiae, but Pompeii:

EX AUCTORITATE
IMP CAESARIS
VESPASIANI AUG
LOCA PUBLICA A PRIVATIS
POSSESSA T SUEDIUS CLEMENS
TRIBUNUS CAUSIS COGNITIS ET
MENSURIS FACTIS REI PUBLICAE
POMPEIANORUM RESTITUIT.

The date of the decree is still debated, but according to J. L. Franklin Jr, the tribunus Titus Suedius Clemens participated in an election campaign in AD 77,[123] which suggests a date in the very last years of the town.[124]

THE FINAL DESTRUCTION: AUGUST 24–25, AD 79

Until the 1950s it was generally believed, not least on the basis of Pliny's letters,[125] that the end of Pompeii had been caused by a heavy and rapid fall of pumice stones and ash. This volcanic rain, sometimes quite explicitly compared to heavy snow fall, had buried the town so gently as to leave it practically intact under its cover. Thanks to recent volcanological research based on the study of the volcanic deposits in the

Vesuvian region, and on the observations of eruptions in various parts of the world in modern times, it has been possible to gain a better understanding of the sequence of events that took place on August 24–25, 79 and their devastating effect on Pompeii and its inhabitants.[126] It is clear that by the end of August 25, the landscape around Mt Vesuvius had changed so dramatically, and Pompeii and Herculaneum been buried so completely, that it would have been impossible to even approximately locate the place where the two cities once stood. As remarks Plutarch: "those who went there by daylight felt ignorance and uncertainty as to where these [cities; sc. Pompeii and Herculaneum] had been situated."[127]

NOTES

1 H. Mouritsen, *Election, Magistrates and Municipal Elite. Studies in Pompeian Epigraphy*, Rome, 1988, p. 9.

2 Conveniently listed in *RE*, 1952, vol. XXI, 2, 2001–2 s.v. Pompeii (Van Buren).

3 For instance, Cicero, *Fam.* 7.1.3 and *Att.* 10.16.4 where Cicero mentions his villa in Pompeii.

4 Seneca, *QNat.* 6.1.1–3 and 6.26.3–4; Tacitus, *Ann.* 15.22. The correct date, AD 62, is that mentioned by Tacitus: see R. Lecocq, *AntCl*, 1949, vol. 18, pp. 85–91. and G. O. Onorato, *RendAccLinc*, 1949, vol. VIII/4, fasc. 11–12, pp. 644–61.

5 The most famous and detailed account is that given by Pliny the Younger in two letters addressed to Tacitus: *Ep.* 6.16 and 20. They are an invaluable source of information about the catastrophe, but tell us hardly anything about the effect it had on the towns and their inhabitants and the many villas and farms in the countryside. Cassius Dio's description of the event in his *Roman History* (66.21.1; 66.22.1–66.24.1) is much less useful from a modern, volcanological point of view, and tells us no more than Pliny about its effects. For a commented English translation of both sources, see, e.g., E. A. Fisher and R. A. Hadley in *Pompeii and the Vesuvian Landscape*, Washington, 1979, pp. 9–15.

6 Solinus, *Collectanea rerum memorabilium* 2.5; Martianus Capella 6.642; Isidorus, *Etymologiarum* 15.51. A rather more plausible etymology was proposed by August Mau who, considering that *pompe* is the Oscan equivalent of Latin *quinque*, thought that the name might derive from a family name, the Oscan counterpart of the Roman Quintii. "Pompeii was thus the city of the clan of the Pompeys, as Tarquinii was the city of the Tarquins, and Veii the city of the Veian clan." According to Amedeo Maiuri (in *EAA*, 1960, vol. 6, p. 309, s.v. Pompei), the name of Pompeii is likely to allude to a subdivision of the town's population into five groups which, as has recently been pointed out by S. De Caro (in *AttiMemSMGr*, 1992, ser. 3/1, p. 79, n. 61) seems to be reflected in Pompeii's layout into five regions.

7 Strabo, *Geographia* 5.4.8.

8 Pliny the Elder, *HN* 3.60–2.

9 Livy, *Ab urbe condita* 9.38.2–3.

10 Velleius Paterculus (*Historia Romana* 2.16.2); Appianus (*BCiv.* 1.39 and 50), and Orosius (*Historia adversus paganos* 5.22).

11 Tacitus, *Ann.* 14.17.

12 For a general introduction to Pompeian epigraphy, see Mouritsen, *Pompeian Epigraphy*, pp. 9–11; also J. L. Franklin, Jr, "Literacy and the parietal inscriptions of Pompeii," in M. Beard *et al.*, *Literacy in the Roman World*, JRA Suppl. Ser no. 3, Ann Arbor, MI, 1991, pp. 77–98. Most inscriptions are in Latin, some in Greek, a few in Oscan. The Latin and Greek ones are published in the *Corpus Inscriptionum Latinarum* (*CIL*): volume IV contains the *inscriptiones parietariae*, inscriptions (painted or scratched) on walls, as well as inscriptions on *amphorae*. The main volume appeared in 1871, first (for wax tablets) and second supplements in 1898 and 1909, while the first four fascicles of the third supplement came out in 1952, 1955, 1963 and 1970; a fifth is in preparation (see H. Solin in F. Zevi (ed.), *Pompei 79*, Naples, 1979, p. 287, n. 8 and A. Varone, *Erotica Pompeiana. Iscrizioni d'amore sui muri di Pompei*, Rome, 1994, p. 189 s.v. Della Corte, ms.; 190 s.v. Solin, ms.). The official inscriptions cut in stone, the *tituli*, are to be found in volume 1, fasc. 2 (1918) 642–6 if they are of Republican

date, in vol. 10 (1883) and in *Ephemeris Epigraphica*, 1899, vol. 8, pp. 86–90 if they belong to the Imperial period. Vol. 10 also includes the *signacula*, the seal stamps, and stamp marks. Inscriptions of all kinds found subsequently have mostly been published in *Notizie degli Scavi* and are reported in *L'Année Epigraphique*. Cf. Laidlaw, Ch. 39.

For the Oscan inscriptions, see E. Vetter, *Handbuch der italischen Dialekte*, Heidelberg, 1953, pp. 46–67 and, for an update, R. Antonini, *Studi Etruschi*, 1977, vol. 45, pp. 317–40.

For selected inscriptions of all kinds, see, e.g., G. O. Onorato, *Iscrizioni Pompeiane*, Florence, 1957–58, vol. 1–2 and P. Moreau, *Sur les murs de Pompéi*, Paris, 1993.

13 The letters were outlined by bronze pins inlaid in the slate margin of the *opus sectile* floor of the *cella*, and although the metal has long been removed, the holes have survived. See August Mau, *Pompeii: Its Life and Art*, 1902, p. 81, n. 1: *O. KAMP{ANIIS . . . KVA}ISSTUR KOMBENN{IEIS TANGINUD} APPELLUNEIS EITIU{VAD . . . OPS}ANNU AAMAN-{AFF}ED*. Unfortunately, it remains unclear whether the inscription refers to the floor only or to the entire building. For a brief discussion of the Oscan language and script, see E. T. Salmon, *Samnium and the Samnites*, Cambridge, 1967, pp. 112–26 (with further literature). For a fuller account, A. Prosdocimi in: *Popoli e civiltà dell'Italia Antica*, Rome, 1978, vol. 6, pp. 825–912 (with addenda in vol. 6bis [1984] 39–41).

14 See M. Wolf, "Der Tempel von S. Abbondio in Pompeji," in *Koldewey Gesellschaft, Bericht 41. Tagung f. Ausgrabungswissenschaft und Bauforschung*, May–June 2000 (2002), p. 61.

15 *CIL* X, 852.

16 The term designates six Oscan inscriptions which clearly belong together (Vetter, *Handbuch*, pp. 54–7 nos. 23–8). Painted in red on tufa façades of Samnite residences in the Regions III, VI and VII they all follow the same formula, instructing someone to go through a particular lane to a particular spot of the city wall. The inscription on the so-called House of Pansa (VI.6), for instance, reads:

> EKSUK AMVIANUD EIT(UNS)
> ANTER TIURRI XII INI
> VERU SARINA PUF
> FAAMAT MR AALIRIIS V

which may be translated as follows:

> through this lane they ought to go
> between tower XII and
> the Sarina gate, where
> Maras Adirius, the son of Vibius, commands.

It is generally agreed that the inscriptions represent military instructions for the defense of the city, almost certainly issued on the occasion of Sulla's siege in 89 BC (see Mau, *Pompeii: Its Life and Art*, p. 240, and, for a more detailed discussion, A. Sogliano, *Pompei nel suo sviluppo storico: Pompei preromana*, Rome, 1937, pp. 284–91).

17 As represented on the famous painting from the estate of Julia Felix, now in the National Mus. in Naples, inv. 9068 (for a good color reproduction, see *RivStPomp*, 1989, vol. 3, p. 87, fig. 10).

18 *Cnaeum Heluium Sabinum aliarii rogant* (*CIL* IV, 3485).

19 *Vatiam aedilem furunculi rogant* (*CIL* IV, 576).

20 For a good selection of such advertisements, see A. Staccioli, *Manifesti elettorali nell'antica Pompei*, Milan, 1992.

21 For selections of such inscriptions, see, e.g., E. Diehl, *Pompejanische Wandinschriften und Verwandtes*, 2nd edn, Bonn, 1930; J. Lindsay, *The Writing on the Wall*, London, 1960; W. Krenkel, *Pompejanische Wandinschriften*, Leipzig, 1963.

22 Of the type "Lucius painted this" (*CIL* IV, 7535), or "I got laid here" (*CIL* IV, 2217), "I'm yours for one *as*" (*CIL* IV, 5372), "Perarius, you're a thief" (*CIL* IV, 4764), or "profit is joy" (*CIL* X, 875).

23 See P. Castrén, *Ordo Populusque Pompeianus. Polity and Society in Roman Pompeii*, Rome, 1975; J. L. Franklin, Jr, *Pompeii: the Electoral Programmata, Campaigns and Politics*, AD 71–79,

Papers and Monographs of the American Academy at Rome 28, Rome, 1980; Mouritsen, *Pompeian Epigraphy*. Cf. Franklin, Ch. 33.

24 E.g., *CIL* IV, 4814: *Neroni feliciter* (long live Nero!); *CIL* X, 623: AUGUSTO CAESARI PARENTI PATRIAE (to Augustus, the father of the fatherland).

25 E.g., *CIL* IV, 5214, written on November 6, 15 (see Mau, *Pompeii: Its Life and Art*, p. 226). Cf. also the imprint of a Vespasianic coin on a wall in the House of the Ancient Hunt (VII. 4.48) decorated in Fourth Style: J.-P. Descœudres *et al.*, Australian Museum, *Pompeii Revisited*, Sydney, 1994, p. 167 with figs, 106–7.

26 *CIL* IV, 1842: *C(aius) Pumidius Dipilus heic fuit a(nte) d(iem) V nonas octobreis M(arco) Lepid(o) Q(uinto) Catul(o) co(nsulibus)*.

27 A. de Franciscis, "La casa di C. Iulius Polybius," *RivStPomp*, 1988, vol. 2, pp. 15–36.

28 First published by C. Giordano, *RendNap*, 1974, n.s., vol. 49, p. 22, fig. 2 and reported in *L'Année Epigraphique*, 1977 (1981), pp. 60–1, nos. 217–18.

29 "As Caesar came to the most sacred [Temple of] Venus, as your divine feet, Augustus, brought you to it, there was an unbelievable quantity of gold."

30 "As gifts to the most sacred Venus, Poppaea offered a beryl, an *elenchus* [a pear-shaped pearl], to which was added a *unio* [a particularly large pearl]."

31 Tacitus, *Ann.* 15.34 and Suetonius, *Nero* 20.

32 See G. Fiorelli, *NSc* 1881, p. 121; S. De Caro, *PompHercStab*, 1983, vol. 1, pp. 210–11; A. D'Ambrosio, *La stipe votiva in località Bottaro (Pompei)*, Rome, 1984.

33 See A. Martelli, "Per una nuova lettura dell'iscrizione Vetter 61," *Eutopia*, 2002, vol. II 2, p. 73 fig. 1. The object placed on the base might have been a tripod, as E. Lippolis, "*Triumphata Corintho*: La preda bellica e I doni di Lucio Mummio Achaico," *ACl*, 2004, vol. 55, pp. 35–6, suggests.

34 See, in particular, Livy, *Epit.* Oxyr. 53 and, for further refs, Lippolis, "*Triumphata Corintho*," pp. 33–4.

35 *Pace* Martelli, "Per una nuova lettura dell'iscrizione Vetter 61," pp. 78–81.

36 See Martelli, "Per una nuova lettura dell'iscrizione Vetter 61," p. 79 figs 5–6.

37 The tablets, first published in *CIL* IV, 3340 nos. 1–153, have been exhaustively studied by J. Andreau, *Les affaires de Monsieur Jucundus*, Rome, 1974.

38 See L. Bove, *Documenti di operazioni finanziarie dall'archivio di Sulpici*, Rome, 1984; G. Camodeca, *L'archivio puteolano dei Sulpicii*, 1992; id., *Tabulae Pompeianae Sulpiciorum*, I–II, 1999.

39 See E. and L. Eschebach, *Pompeji*, Cologne, 1995, pp. 1–13 with refs to earlier literature.

40 Most recently: G. Stefani and G. Di Maio, "Considerazioni sulla linea di costa del 79 d.C. e sul porto dell'antica pompei", *RivStPomp*, 2003, vol. 14, pp. 141–95 (with refs to earlier literature). Strabo, *Geographia* V 4:8: "Pompaia is the port-town of Nola, Nuceria, and Acherrae, as it lies on the Sarno river which takes the cargoes inland and sends them out to sea."

41 *NSc*, 1931, pp. 548ff.

42 Other than Map 3 in this volume, the most easily accessible plan is that by H. Eschebach, first published in: *Die städtebauliche Entwicklung des antiken Pompeji*, RM-EH 17, Berlin, 1970, and since reproduced in countless publications at various scales. An updated version has been published by J. Müller-Trollius in: L. Eschebach, *Gebäudeverzeichnis und Stadtplan der antiken Stadt Pompeji*, Cologne, 1993. The RICA maps of Pompeii (*Corpus Topographicum Pompeianum*, Rome, 1984, vol. 3) are based on aerial photogrammetry but include a great deal of data gathered in the field and in the archives (see H. B. Van der Poel (ed.), *Corpus Topographicum Pompeianum*, Rome, 1986, vol. 3A, pp. xi–xix). On the whole, the two plans match as closely as one might expect, but there are some striking discrepancies (note, e.g., the area of the Suburban Baths below the Porta Marina, or the distance between the Porta Ercolano and Tower XII which measures 95 m on Eschebach's plan, 96 m on the RICA map). Also based on an aerial survey is the new, computer-generated plan produced by the so-called NEAPOLIS project: *NEAPOLIS. Planimetria della città antica di Pompei*, Rome, 1994; see also B. Conticello in: *Pompeii Rediscovered*, Exhibition Catalogue New York, Rome, 1990, pp. 8–9.

43 The term, coined by F. Haverfield, *Ancient Town-planning*, Oxford, 1913, pp. 63–5, has been kept by successive scholars such as A. von Gerkan, *Der Stadtplan von Pompeji*, Berlin, 1940, and F. Castagnoli, *Ippodamo di Mileto e l'urbanistica a pianta ortogonale*, Rome, 1957, pp. 26–32, and further elaborated by H. Eschebach in his monumental study, *Die städtebauliche Entwicklung*

des antiken Pompeji, posthumously followed by his *Pompeji*, Cologne, 1995 (edited by his wife, Liselotte). For further literature, see L. Richardson, jr, *Pompeii. An Architectural History*, Baltimore, MD, 1988, p. 36, n. 1, to which may be added S. Sakai, "Some considerations of the urbanism in the so-called Neustadt of Pompeii," *OpuscPomp*, 1991, vol. 1, pp. 35–57.

44 S. De Caro, "Lo sviluppo urbanistico di Pompei," *AttiMemSocMGr* ser. iii, 1, 1992, pp. 67–90; for a brief report on recent discoveries of sixth-century BC architectural remains in this region (VI 9.3–5), see F. Coarelli, F. Pesando and A. Zaccaria Ruggiu, *RivStPomp*, 2003, vol. 14, p. 290 (also in *Archeo*, 2004, vol. 20/1, pp. 42–9).

45 For the chronology of the town wall, see M. Miller, *Befestigungsanlagen in Italien vom 8. bis 3. Jahrhundert vor Christus*, Hamburg, 1995, pp. 462–3 (with refs to the earlier literature); H. Etani, S. Sakai and H. Kiriyama, "Archaeological investigation at Porta Capua, Pompeii," *OpPomp*, 1997, vol. 7, pp. 145–58; S. Sakai, "Gli scopi e gli obiettivi della missione archeologica giapponese a Pompei," in F. Senatore (dir.), *Pompei, il Vesuvio e la Penisola Sorrentina*, 1999, Naples, pp. 45–54; id., "La storia sotto il suolo del 79 d.C. Considerazioni sui dati provenienti dalle attività archeologiche svolte sulle fortificazioni di Pompei," *OpPomp*, 2000/1, vol. 10, pp. 87–100.

The early-third-century wall (C) was repaired and reinforced on several occasions, but remained basically unchanged until Roman times. Its building can be dated with certainty and accuracy to *c.*280 BC, on the basis of the stratigraphic excavations carried out in the early 1980s by S. De Caro ("Nuove indagini sulle fortificazioni di Pompei", *AION* 1985, vol. 7, pp. 75–114) and C. Chiaramonte (*Nuovi contributi sulle fortificazioni pompeiane*, Milan, 1986).Very little is known about its two possible predecessors. For wall A, commonly known as the Pappamonte wall, there is some evidence suggesting it might date back to the middle of the sixth century (De Caro, "Nuove indagini," p. 90), but its military character remains most doubtful (see Sakai, "La missione archeologica giapponese a Pompei," pp. 52–4; *contra*: F. Coarelli, *Pompeii*, New York, 2002, pp. 27–45). Wall B is later than wall A but precedes C. Only a few stretches of it have been identified and it appears to have been rather short-lived. It served most certainly as a defensive wall, but its absolute chronology is uncertain. Cf. Chiaramonte, Ch. 11.

46 De Caro, "Lo sviluppo urbanistico," p. 88 (see now also H. Geertman, "Lo studio della città antica," in P. G. Guzzo (ed.), *Pompei. Scienza e società. Conv. Int. Napoli 1998*, Naples, 2001, pp. 131–5; cf. Geertman, Ch. 7).

47 F. Noack and K. Lehmann-Hartleben, *Baugeschichtliche Untersuchungen am Stadtrand von Pompeji*, Berlin, 1936; V. Kockel, *AA*, 1986, pp. 506–14; P. Zanker, *Pompeji. Stadtbilder als Spiegel von Gesellschaft und Herrschaftsform*, *TrWPr*, 1987, vol. 9, p. 21, fig. 9; 23–4; id., *Pompeii: Public and Private Life*, Cambridge, MA and London, 1998, pp. 61–77.

48 Most succinctly, A. Hoffmann in F. Zevi (ed.), *Pompei AD 79*, Naples, 1979, p. 107.

49 For instance, F. Coarelli (ed.), *Guida archeologica di Pompei*, Milan, 1976, pp. 31–4.

50 For instance, M. Bonghi Jovino, *Ricerche a Pompei. L'insula 5 della Regio VI dalle origini al 79 d.C.*, Rome, 1984, and, for a much harsher assessment, Richardson, *Pompeii*, p. 370.

51 For a preliminary sketch of such a study, see Richardson, *Pompeii*, pp. 376–81.

52 A. Maiuri, *L'ultima fase edilizia di Pompei*, Rome, 1942.

53 Richardson, *Pompeii*, the first and so far only general survey of Pompeii's architecture, has to be used with great caution, as it ignores much of the research published in languages other than English.

54 A. Maiuri, *Alla ricerca di Pompei preromana*, Naples, 1973, pp. 101–24; Zanker, *Pompeji. Stadtbilder*, pp. 14, 18 with n. 31.

55 Maiuri, *L'ultima fase*, pp. 216–17; and, for a particular example of such a transformation, A. Meneghini, "Trasformazione di una residenza domestica in impianto commerciale a Pompei," *RivStPomp*, 1999, vol. 10, pp. 11–22.

56 A complete corpus of all sculptural finds from Pompeii is still wanting; H. Döhl and P. Zanker in Zevi (ed.), *Pompei*, pp. 177–210, give a general idea of the range of this material. For more detailed studies of particular aspects, see H. von Rohden, *Die Terrakotten von Pompeji*, Berlin, 1880; E. J. Dwyer, *Pompeian Domestic Sculpture. A Study of Five Pompeian Houses and their Contents*, Rome, 1982; W. Wohlmayr, *Studien zur Idealplastik der Vesuvstädte*, Buchloe, 1989; A. D'Ambrosio and M. Borriello, *Le terrecotte figurate di Pompei*, Rome, 1990;

R. Bonifacio, *Ritratti Romani da Pompei*, Rome, 1997. For the wall paintings and mosaics, see now the magnificent repertory published by the Istituto della Enciclopedia Italiana: *Pompei, pitture e mosaici*, Rome, 1990ff., vols. I–XI.

57 K. Schefold's work remains fundamental in this area, see esp. his *Pompejanische Malerei, Sinn und Ideengeschichte*, Zurich, 1952; transl. into French by J.-M. Croisille: *La peinture pompéienne. Essai sur l'évolution de sa signification*, Brussels, 1972.

58 As is well known, numerous small objects found during the early excavations are no longer identifiable, either because they were given as souvenirs to prominent visitors, or because their descriptions in the excavation diaries are too summary for them to be identified among the finds stored in the National Museum in Naples. For a preliminary account of this material, see A. Carandini (ed.), *L'instrumentum domesticum di Ercolano e Pompei*, Rome, 1977; for the bronze vessels and implements, E. Pernice, *Die hellenistische Kunst in Pompeji, IV: Gefässe und Geräte aus Bronze*, Berlin, 1925; more recently, S. Tassinari, *Il vasellame bronzeo di Pompei*, Rome, 1993.

59 R. I. Curtis, "A personalized floor-mosaic from Pompeii," *AJA*, 1984, vol. 88, p. 561.

60 Pliny, *HN* 31.94. Cf. also Clarke, Ch. 21, p. 330.

61 See Maiuri, *Pompeii preromana*. Among the most important of these deep soundings are those in the forum area, including the Temple of Jupiter and the Temple of Apollo. The results of the latter have been published by S. De Caro, *Saggi nell'area del tempio di Apollo a Pompei*, Naples, 1986.

62 No more than brief preliminary reports without adequate documentation exist, for instance, for the excavations carried out in the 1960s both in the House of the Faun (A. Bruckner in B. Andreae and H. Kyrieleis (eds), *Neue Forschungen in Pompeji*, Recklinghausen, 1973, pp. 205–9) and the House of Sallust (A. Laidlaw in *Eius virtutis studiosi: Classical and Post-Classical Studies in Memory of Frank Edward Brown*, Washington, DC, 1993, pp. 217–31), in the 1970s in the House of Lucretius Fronto (H. Brunsting and S. L.Wynia in W. J. Th. Peters (ed.), *La Casa di Marcus Lucretius Fronto a Pompei*, Amsterdam, 1993, pp. 3–37), and in the early 1980s in the forum area and in the House of Bacchus (P. Arthur, *AntJ*, 1986, vol. 66, pp. 29–44). Among the rare and most commendable exceptions is the exemplary publication of the excavations carried out by a team from the University of Milan under the direction of Maria Bonghi Jovino between 1976 and 1979 in the so-called House of the Etruscan Column: Bonghi Jovino, *Ricerche a Pompei*.

63 [*Postscriptum* October 2004: This forecast has proven accurate: see now, for summaries of the main projects presently being carried out, P. G. Guzzo and M. P. Guidobaldi (eds), *Nuove ricerche archeologiche a Pompei ed Ercolano*, Naples, 2005.]

64 There exists no full study of the skeletal remains from Pompeii, however incredible this may sound (for a brief assessment of the potential of such a study, see E. Lazer in Descœudres *et al.*, *Pompeii Revisited*, pp. 147–9); ead. in S. E. Bon and R. Jones (eds), *Sequence and Space in Pompeii*, Oxford, 1997, pp. 107–17; cf. Lazer, Ch. 38. (For Herculaneum see S. C. Bisel and J. F. Bisel, "Health and nutrition at Herculaneum: an examination of human skeletal remains," in W. F. Jashemski and F. G. Meyer (eds), *The Natural History of Pompeii*, Cambridge and New York, 2002, pp. 251–75.) The same is true for the faunal remains, which until very recently were usually not even mentioned in excavation reports. See, however, W. F. Jashemski, *The Gardens of Pompeii, Herculaneum, and the Villas destroyed by Vesuvius*, New Rochelle, 1979, pp. 216–18, 242, 247, 255; J. Richardson, G. Thompson and A. Genovese, "New directions in economic and environmental research at Pompeii," in Bon and Jones (eds), pp. 88–101; Jashemski and Meyer (eds), *The Natural History of Pompeii*.

65 Columella, *Rust.* 10.127–36 (on cabbage); 12.10.1 (on onions).

66 See Jashemski, *Gardens*, vol. I, pp. 233–88; cf. Jashemski, Ch. 31.

67 Jashemski, *Gardens*, vol. I, pp. 200–32.

68 Pliny the Elder, *HN* 14.70. Another industry which appears to have been of considerable importance is the wool and textile industry: see W. Moeller, *The Wool Trade of Ancient Pompeii*, *Studies of the Dutch Archaeological and Historical Soc.*, Leiden, 1976, vol. 3.

69 Sporadic occupation may have occurred as early as the Late Bronze Age, which would explain the occasional find of pottery fragments datable to this period. In the city's main and doubtless oldest sanctuary, dedicated to Apollo, the earliest offerings belong to the late seventh and

early sixth centuries BC, except for a handful of possibly earlier objects (among them a bronze fibula of the eighth century) which might have been heirlooms and which at any rate are not numerous enough to suggest the presence of a cult place, let alone a settlement, before c.600 BC. Reports by P. Carafa in S. Bon and R. Jones (eds), *Sequence and Space*, Oxford, 1997, pp. 13–31, and in C. Stein and J. H. Humphrey (eds), *Pompeian Brothels, Pompeii's Ancient History, Mirrors and Mysteries, Art and Nature at Oplontis, & The Herculaneum "Basilica,"* JRA Suppl. Ser. no. 47, 2002, 47–61 mention traces of early occupation, said to go back possibly to the seventh century or even earlier ("between the Iron Age and the mid 7th c. BC" [*sic*]), from the area just west of the so-called Doric Temple. Unfortunately, none of the alleged evidence is illustrated or described in such detail as to allow it to be assessed. Also, cf. Carafa, Ch. 5. As for O. Elia's claim that remains of huts and even of a fortification wall discovered under the Temple of Isis belonged to the Early Iron Age (*Studi della città antica*, 1970), it has long been put to rest by A. Varone who re-opened Elia's trenches in the 1980s. His report, published in *RivStPomp*, 1989, vol. 3, pp. 226–31, seems to have escaped the attention of M. Fulford and A. Wallace-Hadrill, "Excavations beneath the House of Amarantus (I 9, 11–12)," *PBSR* 1999, vol. 67, p. 106.

70 The only architectural remains going back to the Archaic period known so far, in the form of extant structures or of architectural terracottas, are limited to the area of the *Altstadt* (Temple of Apollo: see De Caro, *Tempio di Apollo*; so-called Doric Temple: J. A. K. E. De Waele (ed.), *Il tempio dorico del Foro Triangolare di Pompei*, Rome, 2001) and to that of regio VI (*insula* 5: M. Bonghi Jovino, *Ricerche a Pompei. L'insula 5 della Regio VI dalle origini al 79 d.C.*, 1984; *insula* 9: F. Coarelli and F. Pesando, "Il 'Progetto' Regio VI: campagna di scavo 2002," *RivStPomp*, 2003, vol. 14, p. 290). Everywhere else, pre-fourth-century finds, in most cases pottery fragments, have been discovered without architectural context and almost without exception in association with later material; this is also true for the following, which have sometimes been cited as proofs that the so-called *Neustadt*, too, was occupied as early as the sixth century BC: I.9.11–12 (where a few pottery fragments of the late sixth century BC provide no more than a *terminus post quem* for the wall foundations in which they were embedded, *pace* Fulford *et al.*, "Excavations beneath the House of Amarantus"); VII.3 (where the interpretation of a hypogeum within the complex of the Stabian Baths as an Etruscan chamber tomb of the Archaic period, originally put forth by Maiuri, *Alla ricerca di Pompei preromana*, pp. 43–51, has long been laid to rest: see, e.g., H. Riemann, "Das vorsamnitische Pompeji," in B. Andreae and H. Kyrieleis (eds), *Neue Forschungen in Pompeji*, Recklinghausen, 1975, pp. 225–33); VII.4.62 (where the only sixth-century sherd was found in a Hellenistic context: A. D'Ambrosio and S. De Caro, "Un contributo all'architettura e all'urbanistica di Pompei in età ellenistica. I saggi nella casa VII, 4, 62," *AION*, 1989, vol. 11, pp. 173–215); and VII.9.47 (where according to the excavators no datable finds were found to allow the remains of a wall built of so-called Pappamonte tufa to be attributed to the Archaic period: P. Carafa, "The investigations of the University of Rome 'La Sapienza' in Regions VII and VIII: the ancient history of Pompeii," in Stein and Humphrey (eds), JRA Suppl. Ser. no. 47, 2002, 54–6).

71 See above, n. 45.

72 The Archaic beech grove observed in VI.5 by Bonghi Jovino, *Ricerche a Pompei* might have had a sacred function, as Coarelli, *Pompeii*, pp. 27–45 has recently suggested.

73 Several find-spots could now be added to the distribution map published in: F. Zevi (ed.), *Pompei*, Naples, 1992, vol. I, p. 11 (reproduced in Descœudres *et al.*, *Pompeii Revisited*, p. 4 fig. 4), but they hardly alter the general picture that clearly emerges from it. The "revised" version published by J.-A. Dickmann and F. Pirson, "L'indagine nella Casa dei Postumii," in F. Senatore (ed.), *Pompei tra Sorrento e Sarno*, Rome, 2001, pp. 63–85, has to be used with caution, as it contains several errors.

74 See the statistics for the offerings in the Temple of Apollo published by De Caro, *Tempio di Apollo*.

75 As for the ethnic origin of its inhabitants, for which archaeology is unable to provide any clues, the literary sources suggest that they were natives: see above, with nn. 7–8.

76 De Caro, *Tempio di Apollo*.

77 De Waele (ed.), *Il Tempio dorico*.

78 See above, n. 45.

79 No finds published so far can be assigned to this period. Particularly noteworthy is their complete absence among the offerings at the Temple of Apollo and at the so-called Doric temple, as the sequence in both sanctuaries is otherwise unbroken, ranging from the early sixth century BC to the Roman period.

80 It is known to us from numerous inscriptions (most of them of the third and second centuries BC), written either in the Latin, Greek or Oscan alphabet—the latter a derivative from Etruscan. In Pompeii, Oscan was replaced as the official language by Latin in 80 BC when the town was transformed into a Roman colony, but a number of inscriptions show that it continued to be spoken, at least occasionally, until the very end of the town's existence.

81 See n. 9.

82 See n. 45.

83 See above for a possible link with the destruction of Nocera in 216 BC.

84 The largest and undoubtedly best known of these second-century dwellings, covering a floor surface of some 3,000 m², is the so-called House of the Faun (VI.12; on which most recently F. Zevi, "Die Casa del Fauno in Pompeji und das Alexandermosaik," *RM*, 1998, vol. 105, pp. 21–65; id., "Pompei: Casa del Fauno," in R. Cappelli (ed.), *Studi sull'Italia dei Sanniti*, 2000, pp. 118–37). Yet, members of the middle and lower classes, too, "lived in surprising comfort" (the remark made by E. Packer in Andreae and Kyrieleis (eds), *Neue Forschungen*, p. 142, although aimed at the Imperial period, is just as valid for the second century).

85 As reports Velleius Paterculus (*Hist. Rom.* II 16.2).

86 Pliny, *HN* 3.70.

87 The city, obviously in expectation of such an attack, had shortly before restored and strengthened its fortifications by adding a series of towers to the city wall. It had also carefully prepared a detailed defense plan, as the so-called *eituns* inscriptions suggest (see n. 16).

88 It is widely believed that some circular holes on the surface of the town wall in some areas may have been caused by Sulla's artillery, following a proposal first made by A. W. van Buren, "Further Studies in Pompeian Archaeology," *MAAR*, 1925, vol. 5, pp. 110–11; it is also possible that houses close to the wall may have suffered some damage, as has recently been proposed for the House of the Labyrinth (V. M. Strocka, *Casa del Labirinto (Häuser in Pompeji, 4)*, Munich, 1991, p. 61. Cf. Jones and Robinson, Ch. 25.

89 Cicero, *Pro Sulla* 60–2. The other two may have been Quinctius Valgus and Marcus Porcius, on whom see below.

90 The settlement of such a large number of newcomers (plus their dependants) in a town with an estimated population of between 10,000 and 15,000, would no doubt have created a considerably more traumatic upheaval than what appears to have happened—which leads almost unavoidably to the conclusion that a significant number of Sulla's veterans were not settled in the town itself, but were given plots of land in its immediate surroundings.

91 The administrative structure of the colony was described in the *lex*, the "constitution," with which it was provided at its foundation. As this document has not been recovered, the reconstruction of Pompeii's political structure has to be based on indirect, mainly epigraphical, evidence and on comparisons with other, similar colonies: see H.-J. Gehrke, "Zur Gemeindeverfassung von Pompeji," *Hermes*, 1983, vol. 111, pp. 471–90 and Mouritsen, *Pompeian Epigraphy*, esp. pp. 28–30 (with refs to earlier lit.).

92 See n. 54.

93 L. Jacobelli and P. Pensabene, "La decorazione architettonica del tempio di Venere a Pompei," *RivStPomp*, 1995/6, vol. 7, pp. 45–75 (with the earlier lit.).

94 Zanker, *Pompeji. Stadtbilder*; id. *Pompeii: Public and Private Life*.

95 A. de Franciscis, "Attività archeologica," *CronPomp*, 1975, vol. 1, p. 245.

96 *CIL* X, 852.

97 Cicero, *Leg. Agr.* 3.8.

98 *CIL* X, 816.

99 *CIL* X, 820.

100 *CIL* X, 833–4.

101 *CIL* X, 810-11. Cf. Dobbins, Ch. 12; Welch, Ch. 36.

102 *CIL* X, 813.

103 E.g., Richardson, *Pompeii*, p. 198; J. J. Dobbins, "Problems of chronology, decoration, and urban design in the forum at Pompeii," *AJA*, 1994, vol. 98, pp. 647, 653.

104 H. Nissen, *Pompejanische Studien*, 1877, pp. 301–2.

105 G. Spano, "L'edificio di Eumachia in Pompei," *RendNap*, 1961, vol. 36, pp. 14ff.

106 For instance, by Spano, "L'edificio di Eumachia," 15; W. O. Moeller, "The date of dedication of the Building of Eumachia," *CronPomp*, 1975, vol. 1, pp. 234–5; V. Kockel, "Archäologische Funde und Forschungen in den Vesuvstädten, II," *AA*, 1986, p. 457; K. Wallat, *Die Ostseite des Forums von Pompeji*, 1997, Frankfurt am Main, p. 272.

107 P. Castrén, *Ordo populusque Pompeianus*, pp. 165–6 no. 160, 1; p. 198 no. 280, 1.

108 See Zanker, *Pompeji. Stadtbilder*, pp. 36–8 (the link with the youth associations remains hypothetical, as Richardson, *Pompeii*, p. 214 emphasizes).

109 A good example for this is the famous House of the Vettii (VI.15.1–2): for its plan see, e.g., Coarelli (ed.), *Guida*, p. 269.

110 For the impact the introduction of piped water had on domestic architecture and especially on gardens, see Jashemski, *Gardens*, vol. I, pp. 32–3; for a particular example, F. Sear in Descœudres *et al.*, *Pompeii Revisited*, pp. 100–2.

111 Tacitus, *Ann.* 14.17.

112 See W. O. Moeller, "The Riot of AD 59 at Pompeii," *Historia*, 1970, vol. 19, pp. 84–95 and A. Los, "Quand et pourquoi a-t-on envoyé les prétoriens à Pompéi?," in: *Nunc de suebis dicendum est. Studia archaeologica et historica Georgio Kolendo ab amicis et discipulis dicata*, Warsaw, 1995, pp. 165–70.

113 Seneca, *QNat.* 6.1.1–3 and 6.26.3–4; see Sigurdsson, Ch. 4.

114 See, e.g., Dobbins, "Problems of chronology," pp. 629–94, on the work being carried out on the east side of the forum in order to give it a monumental appearance.

115 No doubt this event, reported by Tacitus (*Ann.* 15.34.1) and Suetonius (*Nero* 20), made it into the history books only thanks to Nero who had been performing in the theater just before.

116 The occurrence of at least one further earthquake between 62 and 79 was first postulated by K. Schefold, *RM*, 1953/4, vol. 60/1, p. 114, n. 32; the body of evidence confirming his hypothesis has since been steadily growing. See J.-P. Descœudres, *RivStPomp*, 1987, vol. 1, p. 34 with n. 63; *Archäologie und Seismologie*, Colloquium Boscoreale 1993, Munich, 1995, passim.

117 P. Bargellini in *Les thermes Romains*, Collection Ecole Française de Rome, Rome, 1991, vol. 142, pp. 115–28. Cf. Dobbins, Ch. 12; Koloski-Ostrow, Ch. 15.

118 T. L. Heres, "The structures related to the water supply of Pompeii: materials and chronology," *Meded*, 1991–2, vol. 51–2, pp. 42–61. Cf. Jansen, Ch. 16.

119 See n. 55.

120 For this debate, see J. Andreau, *Histoire des séismes et histoire économique. Le tremblement de terre de Pompéi (62 ap. J.-C.)*, in *Annales, Économies, Sociétés, Civilisations*, 1973, vol. 28, pp. 369–95; Andreau in Zevi (ed.), *Pompeii 79*, pp. 40–4; A. Wallace-Hadrill, *Houses and Society in Pompeii and Herculaneum*, Princeton, NJ, 1994, pp. 122–3.

121 See nn. 29–31; also M. Mastroroberto, "Una visita di Nerone a Pompei: le *deversoriae tabernae* di Moregine," in A. D'Ambrosio, P. G. Guzzo and M. Mastroroberto (eds), *Storie da un'eruzione*. Exhib. Catalogue Naples–Bruxelles 2003–2004, 2003, pp. 479–523, who convincingly argues that the splendidly decorated *hospitium* south of Pompeii was built for this occasion.

122 *CIL* X, 1018. For the one at the Porta Vesuvio, see G. Spano, *NSc* 1910, p. 399, for the third, at the Porta Nocera, Castrén, *Ordo Populusque*, p. 117.

123 *Pompeii: The Electoral Programmata, Campaigns and Politics AD 71–79*, Rome, 1980, p. 96.

124 L. Jacobelli, "Pompei fuori le mura: lo spazio pubblico e privato," in: F. Senatore (dir.), *Pompei tra Sorrento e Sarno. Atti 3° e 4° ciclo conferenze Pompei 1999–2000*, Rome 2001, pp. 29–61.

125 See n. 5.

126 Cf. Sigurdsson, Ch. 4; H. Sigurdsson, S. Cashdollar and S. R. J. Sparks, *AJA*, 1982, vol. 86, pp. 315ff.; F. Lin Sutherland in Descœudres *et al.*, *Pompeii Revisited*, pp. 72–5; R. Scandone in *Archäologie und Seismologie*, pp. 137–42.

127 Plutarch, *Moralia* (398 E).

CHAPTER THREE

REDISCOVERY
AND RESURRECTION

———•◆•———

Pedar W. Foss

INTRODUCTION

The rediscovery of the settlements overwhelmed by Vesuvius possesses a history as interesting, and nearly half as long, as their occupation in antiquity. Their recovery ushered in archaeology and art history as primary methods, alongside philology and ancient history, for approaching and reconstructing the past. Their contents provided creative inspiration for architects, painters, wallpaper manufacturers, poets, novelists, filmmakers and forgers. It is not an exaggeration to say that Pompeii and Herculaneum have influenced the last several centuries of our age more profoundly and extensively than those cities ever impacted the Roman world of their own day.

The narrative of discovery—the dramas of dilettantes, kings, engineers, institutions and academics who scrabbled to unearth a captured glimpse of an ancient Roman landscape—began to be woven into the history of the emerging cities when the first published reports appeared in 1748, only a decade after excavations began at Herculaneum.[1] By this time there was already fierce competition among authorities to claim credit for the discovery, even as the court of Charles VII of Bourbon, King of the Two Sicilies, tried to keep news about the discoveries under strict control.

The newly found ancient cities were both *treasures* and *stages*: full of objets d'art which adorned royal palaces and eventually public museums, reproduced in fine engravings—crowded artifactual compilations leavened by vignettes and landscapes in grand oversize volumes given as royal presents (*Le Antichità di Ercolano*) or sold to erudite subscribers (e.g., Gell, Mazois, the Niccolini).[2] These richly illustrated and imagined folios were soon translated, copied, plagiarized and distilled into site-guides to meet growing demand, and they served as backdrops and prop-encyclopedias for literary characters that began to populate a parallel, almost mythic, Pompeian past. Actors and actresses dramatized the romantic pathos of a civilization at its apex but in the throes of moral decline, soon to be obliterated by the violent caprice of nature or by some sort of supernatural justice.[3]

Rediscovery has been a continuous process. The sites have become a de facto laboratory for excavation and recording methods, publication standards, the conservation and analysis of the entire range of artifacts and ecofacts, the study of human–environment relations, and cultural resource management. Together, the buried cities of Vesuvius form the longest continuously excavated archaeological zone in the world—an honor they can never lose, and a burden they can never shift.

Every year, several million tourists, thousands of artifact reproductions, hundreds of state employees, scores of tourist guides, dozens of different languages and a steady flow of television documentaries are engaged. For some, it is simply their job; Pompeii and Herculaneum have created their own economy. For others, it is a cultural obligation, a pale echo of Goethe's "see Naples and die!" Still others envision the romantic possibility of existing in the everyday of an ordinary Roman town, and finding themselves suddenly under the pressure of the extraordinary forces that struck old, young, rich and poor alike on an August day in AD 79. Finally, there are the scholars and the artists dedicated to interrogating and interpreting these unique sites. This is, in short, *their* story.

THE DISCOVERERS

A loose annotated chronology follows of the principal persons responsible for excavating in the Vesuvian area and disseminating its discoveries, and of others who creatively converted these discoveries into elements of contemporary culture and art. The list of course cannot be complete, and it is biased towards the early periods because the purpose of this volume otherwise is to summarize recent developments. The story begins at the end of the sixteenth century, but it should be noted that encounters with the ruined settlements began soon after the eruption itself, as rescuers, salvagers, looters and eventually new settlers returned to the area, braving the constant threats of eruption or earthquake.[4] Refer to the map of excavation progress (Figure 3.1; cf. also Laidlaw, Ch. 39 for details about early documentation).

1594–1600   Domenico Fontana helps to lay out a canal from the Sarno river to Torre Annunziata to provide water to gunpowder factories there. The tunnel cuts underground through a part of Pompeii (known then only as *cività*, "ancient town"), and reveals buildings, wall paintings, and two inscriptions, but this discovery neither encourages further investigation nor immediately reveals the identity of the place.[5]

1710–16   An Austrian general in the service of Charles VI, Emmanuel Maurice de Guise-Lorraine (Duc d'Elbeuf), acting on the tip of a local marble worker, pursues excavations in a well-shaft at Resina, southeast of Naples, in order to acquire sculpture for decorating his villa. He discovers numerous portrait busts and statues which later prove to have belonged to the *scaenae frons* of the theater of Herculaneum.[6]

1738   Charles VII of Bourbon decides to build a summer palace at Portici, neighboring Resina on the northwest. He enlists Rocque Joaquin de Alcubierre, a Spanish-born military engineer, to survey the site and meanwhile investigate the area to see what antiquities might be found to adorn the new property, since it is well known locally (especially after d'Elbeuf) that ancient remains are below the surface.[7] After initial diggings, regular work begins on October 22 through tunnels dug around 20 m below the surface, threatened constantly by lethal vapors and the danger of collapse.[8]

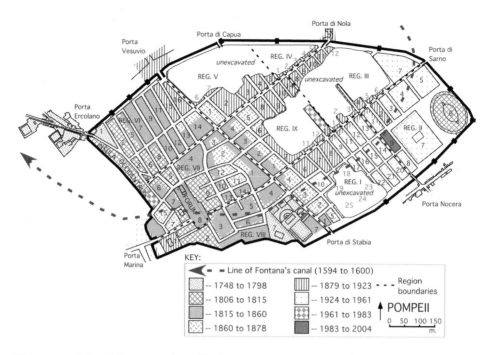

Figure 3.1 Map of the progression of fresh excavations at Pompeii (after Nappo, *Pompeii*, p. 17; Eschebach, *Die städtebaulichte Entwicklung*, and B. Marzolla's 1845 plan (Ciarallo and De Carolis, *Around the Walls*, fig. 10)).

Subsequent discoveries include the first large-scale mythological panel-paintings, from the Basilica (1741–45), two marble equestrian statues of local nobility, the Nonii Balbi (1746), and the Villa of the Papyri with its library of carbonized scrolls (1750); cf. Dickmann, Ch. 27. Just two months after the Villa is first located (but well before its size or importance are known), de Alcubierre hands over command of daily field operations to a Swiss officer named Karl Jakob Weber (Figure 28.3). Weber's background in languages, architecture, engineering and the military gives him the essential qualifications of the first archaeologists: the abilities to supervise many men moving large quantities of earth, to make careful reports of notable finds and safely convey them to the palace, and to make accurate plans of the ancient architecture.[9] Weber proves adept, and makes the important advance of linking finds to their architectural contexts, essential to interpreting their meaning.[10] King Charles establishes a Royal Academy in 1755 to oversee publication of the excavations,[11] and work continues intermittently at Herculaneum until 1780 (Map 4).[12]

1748 Excavations commence at the site of Pompeii, about 11 km further southeast, under the mistaken impression that it is ancient Stabiae, and because the cover of *lapilli* and ash makes much easier digging than the solidified mud-flow that binds Herculaneum.[13] On April 19, 1748, de Alcubierre makes this brief note in his journals: "This morning [the workmen] have come across a dead man amongst the ash and the earth, discovered with 18 bronze coins and one silver coin." This nameless skeleton becomes the first intact human victim of Vesuvius discovered by the excavations; many more are to follow.[14]

Under the direction of de Alcubierre, work remains sporadic and scattered until 1755. Workmen, chained convicts and forced laborers captured from Barbary ships unearth paintings, statues, coins and other small finds within the buildings, while a diarist records items of interest or value, sometimes noting their approximate depth below ground level.[15] Camillo Paderni, curator of what has become the royal museum at the Portici palace, selects paintings for removal to the museum and, for a time at least, destroys the remainder (so that those selected paintings will retain their unique value). The buildings are refilled when they have been stripped.[16] Proof of the town's name finally comes on August 20, 1763, when an inscription including the words REI PUBLICAE POMPEIANORUM is retrieved from outside the Porta Ercolano (Figure 37.1, b).[17] Within a month, the practice of re-filling previous excavation areas ceases, and the town begins to be exposed to the air, which delights visitors but greatly hastens the decay of the monuments and any remaining decoration.[18]

1758 Johann Joachim Winckelmann makes the first of four visits over ten years to the Bay of Naples in his capacity as a correspondent for the court of Augustus III at Dresden. Winckelmann is an ambitious onetime schoolteacher from Prussia who has so applied himself to learning, networking and writing that he earns an official post in Rome and makes his fame as the foremost antiquarian of his day (he is still often called the "Father of Classical Archaeology"). Despite (or because of) his reputation, he finds himself hindered from seeing, inspecting and drawing everything he would like by bureaucrats already upset about previous unauthorized reports that are pre-empting the official publication series. In two detailed letters that complain (not always accurately) about mismanagement and secrecy of the excavations even as he publicizes the tantalizing scholarly returns of the sites, Winckelmann makes Pompeii and Herculaneum topics of conversation across Europe.[19]

1765 Francesco la Vega takes over on-site direction (and overall direction in 1780, after de Alcubierre's death) until 1804, when his brother Pietro succeeds him. Francesco leaves the excavated buildings uncovered and takes measures to preserve *in situ* everything which is not so valuable that it must be removed to the museum. He also pursues Weber's concern for context, documentation and preservation, although exposure to the elements and to increasing numbers of memento-hungry visitors takes a serious toll.[20] In the 1780s the royal collection of antiquities is moved from the shadow of the mountain at Portici to a renovated Naples Museum.[21] This has the dual result of protecting already-extracted treasures from the possibility of another eruption (of which there are at least seven instances during this period alone[22]), and of making the objects more accessible to the public. Back at the site, excavation alternates between the area of the Triangular Forum, Theater district and Temple of Isis on the south edge, and the northwest corner of the city near the Porta Ercolano and along the via dei Sepolcri. The two areas are connected by a carriage-path to facilitate tourists, and become completely joined by excavations along connecting streets subsequent to the French seizure of power in 1799.[23]

During la Vega's tenure and until the arrival of Napoleon's armies, the Englishman Sir William Hamilton requests the post of envoy to the court of King Ferdinand IV in Naples, where he pursues his interests in art, antiquities and volcanology. Encyclopedic in his curiosity (like his model, the Roman senator and naturalist Pliny the Elder, who perished in the AD 79 eruption) he produces the lavishly illustrated *Campi Phlegraei* in 1776.[24] His scientific and artistic observations of past and present Vesuvian eruptions create a natural historical framework for the archaeological remains. Furthermore, the art and artifacts that Hamilton collects and sells to the British Museum, his letters to the Society of Antiquaries in London and his publications have profound repercussions for the promotion of classical culture and images in Britain.[25]

As a patron of ancient art for contemporary tastes, Hamilton is hardly alone. Estates of English, French, Italian (and eventually Russian and German) nobility begin to show an appetite for Pompeian style in their furniture and in their wall and ceiling decoration during the 1760s. These are specially commissioned, time-consuming and expensive decorative undertakings. About a decade later, however, Jean-Baptiste Réveillon develops a wallpaper factory in Paris that conveniently reproduces Pompeian fresco designs on a large scale for a wider but still upscale market.[26] By the early nineteenth century, designers have compiled motif- and style-books for an expanding audience, and it is about a hundred years after the movement starts before Pompeian style begins dying out.[27]

1808   Michele Arditi and Antonio Bonucci begin a renewed program of excavations, aided by funding for a work-force of more than 1,500 persons provided by Caroline, sister of Napoleon Bonaparte and Queen of Naples (as the wife of King Joachim Murat). Under the French, the entire circuit of the town walls begins to be revealed. Workmen also clear portions of the forum area and the amphitheater, and join the principal areas of excavation for visitors. Procedurally, workers first uncover a portion of an ancient street, and then dig sideways into the buildings through their entrances, prohibiting any consistent stratigraphic observations. Clearance is rapid until the Bourbon kings regain control soon after Waterloo in 1815, and work slows because of scarce funding. (Impatience with the pace of excavations is always proved foolish in hindsight, because it inevitably indicates carelessness in recording and preserving crucial interpretive data.)

Despite reduced resources, Francesco Avellino (1839–50) and S. Spinelli (1850–63) continue to oversee a steady effort to reveal more than a third of the total urban area, largely in the western portion of the city.[28] A major problem is simply that the crown does not own most of the land under which the ancient city lies, and despite ambitious expropriation plans (first mapped out in Scognamiglio's famous plan of 1807, which also marks Fontana's sixteenth-century canal), the state does not come entirely into control of the walled portion of the city until 1909.[29] After the government acquires property over one of the original Bourbon shafts, work recommences at Herculaneum in 1828. Open-air excavation is undertaken for the first time, uncovering streets, houses, shops and the baths intermittently until 1875.[30]

Pompeii becomes more popular than ever during the Romantic period as a regular tourist stop on the Grand Tour, as a source of ideas, motives and patterns for European decorative arts, and as inspiration for artistic attempts to "revive" the past.[31] This is due in large part to well-illustrated publications that begin to bring Pompeii to a larger and broader European audience. First comes the *Pompeiana* of Sir William

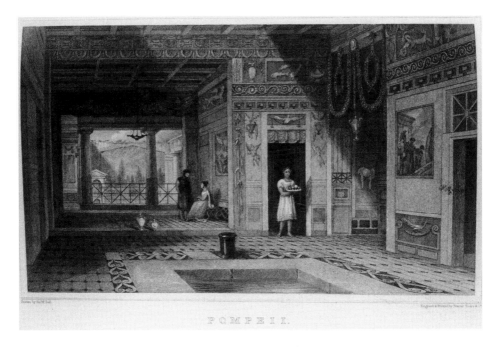

Figure 3.2   Reconstruction of the House of the Tragic Poet (VI.8.5),
from Gell, *Pompeiana*.

Gell in 1817–19, expanded to two volumes by 1832, and with several subsequent
printings (Figures 3.2 and 15.5). The four-volume opus of Charles François Mazois,
Les ruines de Pompéi, appears between 1824 and 1838 (although it covers the French
excavations of 1809–13; Figure 15.4). The Niccolini family (father Antonio, and
sons Fausto and Felice) publishes even more expansive and expensive works: a finds
catalog in sixteen volumes (the *Real Museo Borbonico*, 1824–57), and a four-volume
site catalog (*Le case ed i monumenti di Pompei*, 1854–96).[32] Included are: plans, elevations,
decorative details and commentary. They also present illustrations of a site becoming
re-populated—some show well-dressed visitors lending scale to the buildings, and
others show resurrected Pompeians conducting their lives in tidy reconstructions as
prosperous city-dwellers unaware of imminent doom.[33] The charmingly decorated
(but not overwhelmingly large) House of the Tragic Poet (VI.8.5), excavated between
1824 and 1826, becomes a favorite setting (Figure 3.2).[34]

Settings give birth to script in 1825, when Giovanni Pacini's opera *"L'ultimo giorno
di Pompei"* ("Pompeii's last day") opens successfully in Naples, its scenery designed
by the elder Niccolini.[35] Other media for melodrama soon follow: painting (the
Russian Karl Bryullov's *Last Days of Pompeii*, 1828), poetry (the American Sumner
Lincoln Fairfax's *The Last Night of Pompeii*, 1832) and the novel (the Englishman
Edward Bulwer-Lytton's *The Last Days of Pompeii*, 1834, which is dedicated to Gell).[36]
The story of Vesuvius' wrath upon ordinary people is now truly an international
phenomenon, building upon the increasing intersection and mutual reinforcement
of elite patronage, academic interest, artistic expression, and the popular romanticizing
of a tragedy that befell an entire population.

Two other novels of the age, while not reaching the popularity of Bulwer-Lytton's work, are notable: Théophile Gautier's *Arria Marcella*, 1852, and Wilhelm Jensen's *Gradiva—ein pompejanisches Phantasiestück*, 1904. In both, the protagonist crosses a temporal boundary to encounter the Pompeian past directly.[37] Visitors, readers and viewers, faced with the ashy aftermath, are understandably attracted to such ways of replacing the ghosts of the place with more lively and lifelike images. Accordingly, perhaps, novels about Pompeii are largely superseded in the twentieth century by cinematic adaptations of *The Last Days of Pompeii* (filmed at least a dozen times), all promising the visceral excitement of cataclysm (and sometimes of Roman amphitheaters and orgies as well) while seeing the characters through a cathartic morality play.[38]

1863   During a twelve-year tenure as *Soprintendente* of the Pompeian excavations (though he is active with Campanian material both before and after), Giuseppe Fiorelli shepherds a revolution in archaeological method and procedure at Pompeii. First, he excavates from the top down in an effort to recover and reconstruct as much of the architecture as possible. Second, he invents a procedure for pouring plaster into cavities left by organic substances (e.g., wood, animals, humans) that have rotted away. The resulting casts for the first time give form to furniture, doors, and many victims of the eruption, revealed in the agonized poses they took when the fourth pyroclastic surge swept over the town (cf. Sigurdsson, Ch. 4; Lazer, Ch. 38; Figure 38.1). Administratively, Fiorelli reorganizes the site, dividing it into its present nine *Regiones* (cf. Figure 7.2) and systematically naming individual buildings by region, *insula* (city-block), and entrance number, instead of the confusing "Spinelli" numbers previously in use. He also redacts and publishes the excavation notes for Pompeii, back to the start of operations, in the *Pompeianarum Antiquitatum Historia*. He keeps and publishes regular reports of his own excavations in the *Giornale degli Scavi* and other journals, recording artifactual context (cf. Laidlaw, Ch. 39). Finally, he introduces an entrance-fee to the excavations. Access is no longer dependent on permissions from select authorities; more democratic visitation is possible. Likewise, researchers from all countries are now invited to work at Pompeii, and a burst of new scholarship results.[39] The site becomes a world-famous model for archaeological enterprise.

Fiorelli's general procedures hold force for nearly fifty years. Michele Ruggiero (1875–93), Giulio De Petra (1893–1900), Ettore Pais (1901–4), and Antonio Sogliano (1905–10) continue to excavate eastward, more methodically than their early eighteenth-century predecessors, and interested in preserving and often reconstructing the remains *in situ*.[40] Ruggiero's prize find is probably the collection of writing tablets belonging to the banker L. Caecilius Iucundus, which gives unprecedented information about quotidian economic transactions and social life (cf. Jongman, Ch. 32).[41] The show-house for De Petra's excavations is the House of the Vettii (VI.15.1) (1894–5), a singularly conserved and reconstructed *exemplum* of Roman domesticity, the redecoration of which, perhaps ironically, was put in place by owners who were freed slaves.[42]

Assisting in the excavation of the House of the Vettii is a scholar named August Mau. Mau is one of several Germans who, around the time of both Italy's (1870) and Germany's (1871) political unifications, not only undertake programs of specialized research, but also another kind of unification: comprehensive, synthetic treatments of the buried cities.[43] The great historian Theodor Mommsen begins to edit the *Corpus Inscriptionum Latinarum* (*CIL*), including inscriptions from the Vesuvian cities in volume X, in 1853; Helbig publishes his analysis of Pompeian wall painting in 1868; Nissen follows with a study of ancient urbanism based on Pompeii in 1877; and Overbeck presents a synthesis of Pompeian art and architecture in 1856, revised in 1884 by Mau, who offers his own version in 1899 (first in English; one year later in German). Mau's work, partly because of its thoroughness, coherence and organizational clarity, and partly because of its translation into numerous languages, earns the status of the principal handbook to Pompeii.[44] In addition, Mau's stylistic categorization and chronological sequence for wall painting styles helps to stretch Pompeii's history from the span of its last days to several centuries of complex life (cf. Strocka, Ch. 20).

The interest of institutions in the United States only appears near the end of the nineteenth century, as the Metropolitan Museum of Art in New York and the Museum of Fine Arts in Boston acquire paintings and fine objects auctioned off from unofficial excavations of rural villas in the Vesuvian countryside (cf. Moormann, Ch. 28).[45] Much later, the J. Paul Getty Museum compiles a third major Pompeian collection. In the early 1970s, the Getty rebuilds the Villa of the Papyri on Weber's plan in Malibu, California. The ostentatious vision of a wealthy patron, and a favorite image for college art classes, the "Getty Villa" like its predecessor suffers from earthquakes, and has now been redesigned away from its roots as a classical reproduction towards being classical "in inspiration."[46]

After 150 years of disarticulation, a growing concern with integration and detailed reconstruction culminates in the work of Vittorio Spinazzola (1911–23), who carefully uncovers and painstakingly restores (particularly the upper floors, hitherto ignored) the remainder of the street frontage of the via dell'Abbondanza, as well as several houses and shops along that route. In so doing, he creates a fuller architectural impression of a living town along this thoroughfare than anywhere else in Pompeii. Spinazzola is not a true innovator in these methods or techniques (which began with Fiorelli), but he is exceptionally diligent in their application.[47]

The directorships of these men happen to correspond with great waves of new excavations and discoveries in the eastern Mediterranean. Heinrich Schliemann (who visited Pompeii in 1864 and 1868 as part of his several Grand Tours),[48] Wilhelm Dörpfeld (who worked with Mau on the theater at Pompeii from 1902–6) and Sir Arthur Evans, reveal the cultures of the Bronze-Age Aegean; archaeological excavations (e.g., at Nineveh and Babylon) commence in the Near East; Flinders Petrie introduces rigorous excavations to Egypt; Howard Carter discovers Tutankhamun's tomb.[49] Pompeii is eclipsed as a source of intense archaeological interest for the public; it is no longer fresh. In addition, the sciences and scientific thinking are beginning to modify the perspectives and procedures of excavators; archaeology is increasingly becoming a quest for information above objects. At Pompeii, however, little advancement or innovation is occurring; methodologically, the site is being left behind.

1924   For thirty-seven years during the middle of the twentieth century, Amedeo Maiuri dominates the scene. One of his first major initiatives is to engage in large-scale, open-air excavations at Herculaneum in 1927. (An attempt by the American Charles Waldstein between 1903–7 had failed to open the site, but Mussolini's new Fascist government makes it easier for Maiuri to expropriate the land above the site, relocate the residents and employ hundreds of workers.) Continuing the procedures perfected under Spinazzola for stabilizing upper stories, Maiuri uncovers about five city-blocks of a town where wood and other organic remains are particularly well preserved.[50]

Back at Pompeii, after first continuing his predecessor's work along the via dell' Abbondanza, Maiuri clears much of the southeastern portion of the city (Figure 23.1), the entire circuit wall (one of the original goals of the French period), the extensive area of tombs outside the Porta Nocera, and the Villa of the Mysteries northwest of town. That villa and the House of the Menander (I.10.4) earn special publications (1931, 1933) because of their rich finds of painting and silver.[51] Then, in August and September 1943, Allied planes, as part of the landing at Salerno to the south, drop numerous bombs on Pompeii, in the belief that German ammunition is being stored there, causing heavy damage to the site, but also "excavating" new sites, such as the Temple of Dionysus at S. Abbondio (cf. Small, Ch. 13).[52] Maiuri afterwards supervises repairs, and employs hundreds of unskilled laborers (as part of the post-war economic revitalization program, the "Cassa per il Mezzogiorno") to unearth ten additional city-blocks with minimal documentation. The newly exposed buildings are not always properly consolidated and they deteriorate significantly.[53] Maiuri does, however, dig below the ground level (beginning in 1930 and following Sogliano's early efforts) to gather evidence about the pre-AD 79 phases of the city, a task that continues over much of the latter half of the twentieth century and into the twenty-first.[54]

1961   Alfonso de Franciscis institutes a program of restoration work and slows down new digging, opening only two major locations (the House of C. Julius Polybius [IX.13.1] and the Villa at Oplontis (Figure 31.5)), using modern techniques of recording and excavation.[55] During this time major progress is made, however, in mapping Pompeii's urban development[56] and in the scientific study of the plants and gardens that once adorned the town (cf. Jashemski, Ch. 31).[57] International colloquia and museum exhibitions also appear with increasing frequency around the 1900th anniversary of the eruption.[58]

After the serious earthquake of 1980, repairs take up much of the energies of Fausto Zevi and Giuseppina Cerulli Irelli (1977–82, 1982–84). Baldassare Conticello (1984–94) continues the restoration of Maiuri's excavations in Regiones I–II, and finishes old excavations there. The Suburban Baths are also completely cleared (cf. Koloski-Ostrow, Ch. 15).[59] Major initiatives are undertaken to publish certain individual houses in great detail, to redact pictorial evidence of the excavations, and to use computers to document, analyze and reconstruct the site.[60]

1994   Under the current director, Pietro Giovanni Guzzo, the Archaeological Super-intendency of Pompeii is made financially autonomous, having become administratively and scientifically autonomous under Giuseppina Cerulli Irelli, allowing the considerable gate receipts to fund local needs rather than be spread throughout Italy.[61] Extensive cleaning and consolidation efforts are proceeding to protect the site and make it more welcoming to visitors (since 1996, Pompeii has been on the World Monuments Fund's list of 100 most endangered sites: http://www.world monumentswatchorg/; Pompeii was on the list in 1996, 1998, and 2000).[62] Additional signage, audio tours and excellent bookstores help to make visits more informative; an itinerary around the city walls offers a park-like ambience, and new entrances are complete.[63] Sondages are under way at various points throughout the city (the results

Figure 3.3   Recently unearthed portion (the seafront) of the Villa of the Papyri
at Herculaneum (March 1, 2003). View north.

of several are presented in this volume) to continue clarifying the long history of the
town's development. In place, however, is a moratorium on virgin excavation, leaving
approximately one-third of the ancient town preserved for future digging and future
improvements in methodology, preservation and reconstruction. Coming full circle
at Herculaneum, the Villa of the Papyri, site of the first discoveries to make an international impact, is partially (and controversially) disinterred 250 years later, and opened
to the general public for the first time on March 1, 2003 (Figure 3.3; Map 4, H).

CONCLUSION

In the effort to rediscover the discoverers, Herculaneum has been relatively well
served by a recent retrospective, the publications of day-notes, and a bibliographic
summary.[64] Historiographic sources and studies (including excavation diaries, travellers'
writings, re-assessments of early large-format publications and collections of artists'
views), as well as new museum exhibitions and continuing scientific colloquia, are
also positive steps.[65] However, a comprehensive synthesis of the entire history of
excavations, as Parslow has done for the first twenty-five years, remains a desideratum.[66]

After being so long in the forefront of archaeological advances and cultural impact,
and after suffering a prolonged period of methodological stagnation and relative
cultural disinterest, Pompeii and Herculaneum seem to be enjoying a second wind

in both the academic and popular venues.[67] No other sites in the Mediterranean remain so new and so old, in so many ways, at the same time. Their continual reinvention, in the true sense of the word, exemplifies the deep and abiding human desire to forge connections between the past and the present. After all, as the residents of those towns discovered, the future is ultimately unpredictable.

NOTES

1 In order of appearance: Anton Francesco Gori, *Notizie del memorabile scoprimento dell'antica città di Ercolano*, Florence, 1748 and Marcello Venuti, *Descrizione delle prime scoperte dell'antica città di Ercolano ritrovata vicino a Portici*, Rome, 1748 (C. C. Parslow, *Rediscovering Antiquity. Karl Weber and the excavation of Herculaneum, Pompeii and Stabiae*, Cambridge, 1995, pp. 30–1; R. Brilliant, *Pompeii AD 79. The treasure of rediscovery*, New York, 1979, pp. 38–40).

2 Regale Accademia Ercolanese di Archeologia, *Le Antichità di Ercolano esposte*, 9 vols, Naples, 1754–92. Subsequent volumes bring the total to eleven, the last of which is published in 1855. The first volumes are distributed only as gifts of the court; none are available for sale until 1770 (A. E. Cooley, *Pompeii*, London, 2003, pp. 71–2). Grand volumes that are for sale include: W. Gell (engravings by J. P. Gandy), *Pompeiana: the topography, edifices, and ornaments of Pompeii*, London, 1817/19; C. F. Mazois, *Les ruines de Pompéi dessinées et mesurées pendant les années 1809–1810–1811*, 4 vols, Paris, 1824–38; A. Niccolini (ed.), *Real Museo Borbonico*, 16 vols, Naples, 1824–57; A. Niccolini, F. Niccolini and F. Niccolini, *Le case ed i monumenti di Pompei designati e descritti*, 4 vols, Naples, 1854–96. Cf. Laidlaw, Ch. 39.

3 The Biblical "parallel" of Sodom and Gomorrah was first used to explain why the disaster occurred probably during the eruption itself: a large charcoal *graffito* was found scrawled 1.8 m above the floor on a wall in House IX.1.26. It reads *sodoma gomora* (*CIL* IV, 4976). The early Christian writer Tertullian also makes the association (in *De pallio* 2, but see also *Ad nat.* 1.9). See C. Giordano and I. Kahn, *The Jews in Pompeii, Herculaneum, Stabiae and in the Cities of Campania Felix*, W. F. Jaskemski, trans., 3rd edn, Rome, 2001, pp. 75–6; M. Wyke, *Projecting the Past: ancient Rome, cinema and history*, London and New York, 1997, pp. 149–50.

4 Cooley, *Pompeii*, pp. 50–64; R. Ling, *The Insula of the Menander at Pompeii*, Oxford, 1997, vol. I, pp. 10–11; C. Amery and B. Curran, Jr, *The Lost World of Pompeii*, Los Angeles, CA, 2002, p. 30.

5 The discovery in 1689 of an inscription with the words "decurio Pompeiis" did spark sondages by Giuseppe Macrini, who argued that *cività* was Pompeii, but other scholars mistakenly insisted that it referred to a villa of the late republican general and politician Pompey the Great. See G. E. Macrini, *De Vesuvio*, Naples, 1699; Amery and Curran, *Lost World*, pp. 30–2; G. W. Bowersock, "The rediscovery of Herculaneum and Pompeii," *The American Scholar*, 1978, vol. 47, p. 464. For Fontana, see also Parslow, *Rediscovering Antiquity*, p. 44; Cooley, *Pompeii*, pp. 62–3 and n. 30; Gell, *Pompeiana*, pp. 18–19.

6 The site of Herculaneum had been postulated near Resina already by the topographer Ambrogio Leone on a map of 1503 (M. Brion, *Pompeii and Herculaneum: the glory and the grief*, J. Rosenberg, trans., London, 1960, p. 41) and by the sixteenth-century Neapolitan scholar Fabio Giordano (M. Pagano, "Storia degli scavi," in M. Pagano (ed.), *Gli antichi Ercolanesi. Antropologia, società, economia*, Naples, 2000, p. 24). Fragments of an inscription that began to appear on January 10–13, 1739 (*CIL* X, 1443), announcing the construction of the theater by one Lucius Annius Mammianus Rufus, led to the secure identification of the site as Herculaneum (see Parslow, *Rediscovering Antiquity*, pp. 22–31, 234–5 for d'Elbeuf's work and the intrigues regarding the struggle to identify the town first and thereby claim credit for its discovery).

7 For background, see R. B. Litchfield, "Naples under the Bourbons: an historical overview," in *The Golden Age of Naples: art and civilization under the Bourbons (1734-1805)*, Detroit, MI, 1981, vol. 1, pp. 1–14.

8 Parslow, *Rediscovering Antiquity*, pp. 19–22, 27–9.

9 Parslow, *Rediscovering Antiquity*, pp. 38–46.

10 For Weber's contribution to the development of archaeological method, see Parslow, *Rediscovering Antiquity*, passim, esp. pp. 277–81.

11 For the publication, see above, n. 2. Charles ascends to the throne of Spain as Charles III in 1759, leaving Naples to his young son Ferdinand under the direction of Bernardo Tanucci, the Prime Minister. As the original sponsor and enlightened patron of the excavations, however, Charles remains informed about progress at the sites (Parslow, *Rediscovering Antiquity*, p. 153).

12 R. E. L. B. De Kind, *Houses in Herculaneum*, Amsterdam, 1998, p. 42.

13 *23 Marzo {1748}—Con el motivo de haver estado en los dias pasados al reconocimiento del rio que conduze el agua à la Polvarera en la Torre de la Anunciada, y noticias que tenia precedentemente en particular del Intendente D. Juan Bernardo Boschi, de haver alli un paraje llamado la civita, como 2 millas distante de la dicha Torre, donde se han hallado de particular algunas estatuas y otros residuos de la antigua ciudad Estabia: me pareciò reconocer el paraje y tomar algunos informes, y he venido à creer que puedan alli encontrarse algunos monumentos y alajas antiguas con menos travajo, que se consigne en este paraje*

[With the purpose of determining the state of affairs during the past few days while inspecting the canal that brings water to the gunpowder works at Torre Annunziata, and based on previous reports, particularly those made by the quartermaster general D. Juan Bernardo Boschi, according to whom there is a place there called "ancient town", about two miles from the said Torre, where there have been found some notable statues and other remnants of the ancient city of Stabia: I decided to explore the place and take some notes, and I have come to believe that it is possible to come across some monuments and ancient jewelry with as little effort as can be allocated to the site]

(Giuseppe Fiorelli (ed.), *Pompeianarum Antiquitatum Historia*, Naples, 1860, vol. I, p. 1)

Official inventories are originally made in Spanish, so that the court can follow the progress and keep track of the finds (all of which technically belong to the monarch, who guards that right jealously). Stabiae itself begins to be exposed on June 7, 1749 (Parslow, *Rediscovering Antiquity*, p. 46). Cf. Laidlaw, Ch. 39, Appendix 1 for lists of supervising officials.

14 Fiorelli, *Pompeianarum Antiquitatum Historia*, vol. I, p. 2. To date, *c.* 1,150 bodies have been recovered from the excavations at Pompeii alone (Cooley, *Pompeii*, pp. 44–9); 229 were found during 1982–3 at the waterfront in Herculaneum (J. Judge, "Buried Roman town gives up its dead," *National Geographic*, 1982, vol. 162:6, pp. 687–93; R. Gore, "The dead do tell tales at Vesuvius," *National Geographic*, 1984, vol. 165:5, pp. 557–65; Luigi Capasso, *I fuggiaschi di Ercolano. Paleobiologia delle vittime dell'eruzione vesuviana del 79 d.C.*, Rome, 2001, pp. 27–9; S. C. Bisel and J. F. Bisel, "Health and nutrition at Herculaneum: an examination of human skeletal remains," in W. F. Jashemski and F. G. Meyer (eds), *The Natural History of Pompeii*, Cambridge, 2002, pp. 251–75; cf. Lazer, Ch. 38.

15 Parslow, *Rediscovering Antiquity*, pp. 36–7, 45, 47–8. "Barbary" refers to the North African coast, from which privateers were encouraged by the Turkish authorities to attack Christian ships and settlements to bring back loot and slaves, of whom many ended up rowing for their new masters on subsequent raids. European powers acted in kind, capturing Muslim slaves for labor, sale, ransom or exchange. See S. Bono, *Schiavi Musulmani nell'Italia Moderna*, Naples, 1999.

16 Paderni has the sanction of his superiors, including Tanucci, for this practice. See S. C. Nappo, *Pompeii: guide to the lost city*, London, 1998, p. 16; Parslow, *Rediscovering Antiquity*, pp. 206–8.

17 *CIL* X, 1018; cf. Descœudres, Ch. 2. The inscription of T. Suedius Clemens marks the sacred boundary (*pomerium*) of the city of Pompeii at its northwest corner. Burial and building were not permitted within a *pomerium*, so this marker also began the so-called "Via dei Sepolcri" that led to Herculaneum (Roman cemeteries cluster alongside roads); cf. Cormack, Ch. 37.

18 C. Parslow, "The open-air excavations at Pompeii in the eighteenth-century: new methods, new problems," in P. G. Guzzo (ed.), *Pompei. Scienza e società*. Convegno Internazionale, Naples, November 25–27, 1998, Milan 2001, pp. 20–1. Parslow, *Rediscovering Antiquity*, p. 228 stresses that the find of the inscription was probably not the cause of the change in policy.

19 J. J. Winckelmann, *Sendschreiben von den Herculanischen Entdeckungen*, Dresden, 1762; J. J. Winckelmann, *Nachrichten von den neuesten Herculanischen Entdeckungen*, Dresden, 1764. It was

when the latter was published in *lingua franca* that Winckelmann's views affected European opinion and earned him a temporary ban from visiting the sites of Campania. See W. Leppman, *Winckelmann*, New York, 1970; Parslow, *Rediscovering Antiquity*, pp. 215–32.

20 Tourists acquired artifacts as souvenirs, and personalized excavations (often seeded with already-discovered artifacts) were staged for important visitors; see Cooley, *Pompeii*, pp. 76–7. See also A. Wilton and I. Bignamini (eds), *Grand Tour. The lure of Italy in the eighteenth century*, London, 1996.

21 Brilliant, *Pompeii AD 79*, pp. 84–5.

22 J. Thackray, "'The modern Pliny'. Hamilton and Vesuvius," in I. Jenkins and K. Sloan, *Vases & Volcanoes. Sir William Hamilton and his collection*, London, 1996, pp. 65–74.

23 Parslow, "Open-air excavations," pp. 21–4; Nappo, *Pompeii*, p. 16.

24 W. Hamilton, *Campi Phlegraei, Observations on the volcanos of the Two Sicilies, as they have been communicated to the Royal Society of London*, Naples, 1776; Amery and Curran, *Lost World*, pp. 160–7.

25 Hamilton's collection provides designs for Josiah Wedgwood and Thomas Bentley, whose reproductions of ancient vases helped make them rich. See I. Jenkins, "Contemporary minds. Sir William Hamilton's affair with antiquity," in Jenkins and Sloan, *Vases & Volcanoes*, pp. 40–64.

26 P. Ackerman, *Wallpaper. Its history, design and use*, New York, 1923, pp. 43–4.

27 Amery and Curran, *Lost World*, pp. 170–83; E. Colle, "L'evoluzione del gusto pompeiano in Europa," in S. De Caro (ed.), *Le Case e i monumenti di Pompei nell'opera di Fausto e Felice Niccolini*, Novara, 1997, pp. 26–39; F. Bologna, "The rediscovery of Herculaneum and Pompeii in the artistic culture of Europe in the eighteenth century," in *Rediscovering Pompeii*, Rome, 1990, pp. 79–91; R. Winkes, "The influence of Herculaneum and Pompeii on American art of the 18th and 19th centuries," in L. Franchi dell'Orto (ed.), *Ercolano 1738-1988: 250 anni di ricerca archeologica*, Rome, 1993, pp. 127–32.

28 A. Ambrosio (ed.), *Discovering Pompeii*, Milan, 1998, pp. 8–9; Nappo, *Pompeii*, p. 17. This period is perhaps the least-studied era in the history of Pompeian excavations.

29 S. A. Muscettola, "Problemi di tutela a Pompei nell'Ottocento: il fallimento del progetto di esproprio murattiano," in Guzzo, *Scienza e Società*, pp. 29–49. Attempts to purchase adjacent suburban properties continue today.

30 De Kind, *Houses in Herculaneum*, pp. 42–4.

31 The Grand Tour was an extended exploration of the principal cities, museums and sites of Europe (and sometimes the Levant) for generally young and aristocratic northern Europeans (and a few Americans) seeking to add personal experience of the arts to their classical educations and to meet other social and cultural pilgrims like themselves. Italy was central to the Tour, which had no fixed itinerary, but had essential stops such as Venice and Rome. Naples and Pompeii were frequently included; notable visitors were (to mention a very few): Horace Walpole (1740), Goethe (1787), Stendhal (1817), Percy Bysshe Shelley (1819), Sir Walter Scott (1832), Charles Dickens (1844) and Mark Twain (1867). See Amery and Curran, *Lost World*, pp. 148–67; Cooley, *Pompeii*, pp. 74–8; W. Leppmann, *Pompeii in Fact and Fiction*, London, 1968, pp. 92–128, 154–63; R. Trevelyan, *The Shadow of Vesuvius*, London, 1976, pp. 74–84.

32 See above, n. 2, for full citations of these books. Also notable are: E. Breton, *Pompeia décrite et dessinée*, Paris, 1855; T. H. Dyer, *Pompeii: its history, buildings and antiquities*, London, 1867.

33 See R. Cassanelli, "Pompei nella pittura dell'Ottocento," in De Caro, *Le Case e i monumenti*, pp. 40–7. See also Brilliant, *Pompeii AD 79*, esp. pp. 140–85.

34 Other monuments such as the Villa of Diomedes, the via delle Tombe/dei Sepolcri, the forum, the Temple of Isis, and the amphitheater are also popular locations.

35 P. L. Ciapparelli, "L'avventura editoriale dei Niccolini," in De Caro, *Le Case e i monumenti*, p. 10.

36 Brilliant, *Pompeii AD 79*, p. 173. Even prior to these works, Madame de Staël's *Corinne* (1807) put Romanticism and Pompeii squarely together (Leppmann, *Pompeii in Fact and Fiction*, pp. 92–109). See also L. Fino, *Ercolano e Pompei: vedute neoclassiche e romantiche*, Naples, 1988.

37 Jensen's novel, which relies heavily on dream sequences, catches the notice of Carl Jung and Sigmund Freud, and the latter uses the book to pen the first psychoanalytical study of a literary work: *Der Wahn und die Träume in W. Jensens "Gradiva,"* Vienna, 1907 (Leppmann, *Pompeii in Fact and Fiction*, pp. 149–54). The device of time-travel has since reappeared in R. East's *AD 62: Pompeii* (2003).

38 The films were anticipated by theatrical "pyrodramas" (with music and fireworks) produced regularly in the 1880s and 1890s (Wyke, *Projecting the Past*, pp. 147–82; Brilliant, *Pompeii AD 79*, pp. 183–5; for an even earlier example in Vienna, see Cooley, *Pompeii*, p. 76).

39 M. David, "Fiorelli e i modi della documentazione in archeologia," in De Caro, *Le case e i monumenti*, pp. 52–7; Cooley, *Pompeii*, pp. 83–96; Brilliant, *Pompeii AD 79*, pp. 123–9; Nappo, *Pompeii*, pp. 17–18.

40 Cf. J. Sogliano, *Pompei e la regione sotterrata dal Vesuvio nell'anno LXXIX*, Naples, 1879; J. Sogliano, *Gli scavi di Pompei dal 1873 al 1900*, Rome, 1904. Excavation reports also regularly appear in the *Notizie degli Scavi di Antichità*.

41 J. Andreau, *Les affaires de Monsieur Jucundus*, Rome, 1974.

42 See J. R. Clarke, *The Houses of Roman Italy, 100 BC–AD 250. Ritual, space, and decoration*, Berkeley, CA, 1991, pp. 208–35.

43 The Deutsches Archäologisches Institut in Rome, founded in 1829, and gaining official status and additional support after German unification, facilitates their work. The establishment of foreign schools in addition to national archaeological services helps foster internationalization, institutionalization and regulation of archaeology as an academic discipline.

44 Th. Mommsen (ed.), *CIL X, Inscriptiones Bruttiorum, Lucaniae, Campaniae, Siciliae, Sardiniae Latinae*, Berlin, 1883 (parietal inscriptions such as *graffiti* and *dipinti* are covered by K. Zangemeister in vol. IV, 1871); W. Helbig, *Wandgemälde der vom Vesuv verschütteten Städte Campaniens*, Leipzig, 1868; H. Nissen, *Pompejanische Studien zur Städtekunde des Altertums*, Leipzig, 1877; J. Overbeck, *Pompeji in seinen Gebäuden, Alterhümern und Kunstwerken*, Leipzig, 1884; A. Mau, *Pompeii: its life and art*, F. W. Kelsey, trans., London, 1899 (cf. Laidlaw, Ch. 39).

45 M. L. Anderson, "Pompeii and America," in *Rediscovering Pompeii*, pp. 93–103; Brilliant, *Pompeii AD 79*, p. 213.

46 http://www.getty.edu/.

47 F. Delpino, "Vittorio Spinazzola. Tra Napoli e Pompei, fra scandali e scavi," in Guzzo, *Scienza e Società*, pp. 50–61; V. Spinazzola, *Pompei alla luce degli scavi nuovi di via dell'Abbondanza (anni 1910-1923)*, 3 vols, Rome, 1953; Brilliant, *Pompeii AD 79*, pp. 220–9.

48 D. A. Traill, *Schliemann of Troy. Treasure and deceit*, New York, 1995, pp. 28–9, 38–9.

49 Brilliant, *Pompeii AD 79*, pp. 197–204.

50 A. Maiuri, *Ercolano: i nuovi scavi (1927-1958)*, Rome, 1958 (includes only the architecture; the paintings, inscriptions and finds meant for a second volume were never published); De Kind, *Houses in Herculaneum*, pp. 44–7; Franchi dell'Orto, *Ercolano 1738-1988*.

51 A. Maiuri, *La Villa dei Misteri*, 2 vols, Rome, 1931; A. Maiuri, *La casa del Menandro e il suo tesoro di argentaria*, 2 vols, Rome, 1933. See also A. Maiuri: "Gli scavi di Pompei dal 1879 al 1948," in *Pompeiana. Raccolta di studi per il secondo centenario degli scavi di Pompei*, Naples, 1950, pp. 9–40.

52 http://www.classics.cam.ac.uk/Pompeii/pompeii.html cites 162 bombs; S. Ellis, in an online Archaeology Magazine feature (http://www.archaeology.org/interactive/pompeii/field/10.html), counts 163. A soprintendenza sketch plan notes 160 bombs (cf. Laidlaw, Ch. 39 Appendix 2). An unexploded shell was recently found in the House of the Surgeon (VI.1.10): *The Independent* (July 15, 2006).

53 The city-blocks are in regions I and II. See Brilliant, *Pompeii AD 79*, pp. 232–67; J.-P. Descœudres, *Pompeii Revisited. The life and death of a Roman town*, Sydney, 1994, pp. 47–50; F. Zevi, "Aspetti dell'archeologia pompeiana nel Novecento: gli scavi del Maiuri a Pompei," in Guzzo, *Scienza e Società*, pp. 72–9 (with a chronology of Maiuri's activities); Nappo, *Pompeii*, pp. 18–19.

54 A. Maiuri, *Alla ricerca di Pompei preromana*, Naples, 1973; A. Maiuri, *L'ultima faze edilizie di Pompei*, Rome, 1942; A. Sogliano, *Pompei nel suo sviluppo storico. Pompei preromana (dalle origine all'anno 80 a.C.)*, Rome, 1937. For recent excavations below the 79 level, cf. Carafa, Ch. 5; Chiaramonte, Ch. 11; Dobbins, Ch. 12; Wallace-Hadrill, Ch. 18 (re: House of Amarantus); Jones and Robinson, Ch. 25.

55 A. de Franciscis, *The Pompeian Wall Paintings in the Roman Villa of Oplontis*, Recklinghausen, 1975; A. de Franciscis, "La Casa di C. Iulius Polybius," *RStPomp*, 1988, vol. 2, pp. 14–34; A. Ciarallo and E. De Carolis (eds), "La Casa di Giulio Polibio: studi interdisciplinari," Tokyo-Pompeii, 2001.

56 H. Eschebach, *Die städtebaulichte Entwicklung des antiken Pompeji*, *RM* Suppl. 17, Rome, 1970; H. B. Van der Poel (ed.), *Corpus Topographicum Pompeianum*, 5 vols, Rome, 1977–86 (which also includes extensive bibliographies and indices, though its photogrammatic mapping remains only partially complete).

57 W. F. Jashemksi, *The Gardens of Pompeii, Herculaneum and the Villas Destroyed by Vesuvius*, 2 vols, New Rochelle, NY, 1979–93.

58 Volumes with multilingual contributions become common. B. Andreae and H. Kyrieleis (eds), *Neue Forschungen in Pompeji*, Recklinghausen, 1975; J. B. Ward-Perkins and A. Claridge, *Pompeii AD 79*, London, 1976; *Pompei 1748-1980. I tempi della documentazione*, Rome, 1981; F. Zevi (ed.), *Pompeii 79: Raccolta di studi per il decimonono centenario dell'eruzione vesuviana*, Naples, 1984.

59 Nappo, *Pompeii*, p. 19.

60 *Häuser in Pompeji* is a monograph series sponsored by the Deutsches Archäologisches Institut (now at twelve volumes) that compiles photographs, drawings, descriptions and finds for notably elaborate houses from Pompeii. For the quintessential photographic catalog of the site, see: G. P. Carratelli and I. Baldassarre (eds), *Pompei, pitture e mosaici*, 10 vols, Rome, 1990–95 and its accompanying volume of drawings and paintings: *Pompei: pitture e mosaici: la documentazione nell'opera di disegnatori e pittori dei secoli XVIII e XIX*, Rome, 1995. For electronic initiatives, see: *Rediscovering Pompeii*, pp. 42–77, 105–27; *Neapolis: progetto-sistema per la valorizzazione integrale delle risorse ambientali e artistiche dell'area vesuviana*, 3 vols, Rome, 1988–94 (a failed attempt at computerization). See also P. M. Allison, *Pompeian households: an on-line companion*, in R. Scaife (ed.), *The Stoa: a consortium for electronic publication in the humanities*, 2001, http://www.stoa.org/projects/ph/home.

61 Bylaw 352/97; see P. G. Guzzo, "Autonomia della Soprintendenza Archeologia di Pompei. Impostazione e strumenti," in Guzzo, *Scienza e Società*, pp. 119–25.

62 The World Monuments Fund, the Soprintendenza Archeologica di Pompei, and the Samuel H. Kress Foundation sponsored a symposium in Pompeii, November 20–22, 2003, entitled "Symposium on Conservation at Pompeii and Other Sites in the Shadow of Vesuvius: A Review of Best Practices." The symposium brought together conservators and archaeologists who are actively working on the preservation and presentation of Pompeii and nearby sites.

63 A. Ciarallo and E. De Carolis (eds), *Around the Walls of Pompeii*, Milan, 1998.

64 Franchi dell'Orto, *Ercolano 1738–1988*; A. Maiuri (M. Capasso, ed.), *Dallo scavo di Ercolano allo svolgimento dei papiri: scritti e documenti inediti*, Naples, 1991; U. Pannuti, *Il "Giornale degli scavi" di Ercolano, 1738-1756*, Rome, 1983; I. C. McIlwaine, *Herculaneum: a guide to printed sources*, Naples, 1988.

65 M. Pagano, *I diari di scavo di Pompei, Ercolano e Stabia di Francesco e Pietro La Vega (1764–1810)*, Rome, 1997; C. Grell, *Herculanum et Pompei dans les récits des voyageurs français du XVIIIe siècle*, Rome, 1982; C. Robotti, *Immagini di Ercolano e Pompei*, Naples, 1987; *Italiensiche Reise: immagini pompeiane nelle raccolte archeologiche germaniche*, Naples, 1989; *Rediscovering Pompeii*; Guzzo, *Scienza e Società*.

66 Parslow, *Rediscovering Antiquity*. A forthcoming book by the same author (*Pompeii: history, archaeology, reception* [Cambridge]) may address this need. Cooley, *Pompeii* is a good introduction and is topically strong, rather than comprehensive. It relies primarily on secondary studies rather than the archival sources employed by Parslow. However, A. E. Cooley and M. G. L. Cooley, *Pompeii. A Sourcebook*, London, 2004, is a highly useful resource; see P. W. Foss, "Summarising Pompeii and its sources," *JRA*, 2005, vol. 18, pp. 583–6. The oversized, lavishly illustrated nature and limited print-run of Brilliant, *Pompeii AD 79* emulates the grand publications of the nineteenth century. Its awkward citation of sources makes it difficult to use; though insightful, it is more helpful as a narrative than as a reference.

67 R. Harris' *Pompeii: a novel* (2003) carefully incorporates much recent scholarship without deadening the drama or emotion of its narrative. A major motion picture is apparently in the works (Associated Press, "Report: Roman Polanski and Robert Harris team up to make Pompeii epic," *International Herald Tribune*, February 4, 2007).

CHAPTER FOUR

THE ENVIRONMENTAL AND GEOMORPHOLOGICAL CONTEXT OF THE VOLCANO

———— •✦• ————

Haraldur Sigurdsson

INTRODUCTION

The region surrounding an active volcano is subject to very rapid changes in geomorphology and environmental conditions. A new cone can be built up in a matter of months or a few years during periods of frequent lava flow eruptions, only to be destroyed by a violent Plinian explosive eruption and caldera collapse after centuries of dormancy. This intermittent pattern of activity is characteristic of the evolution of Vesuvius volcano, which suddenly terminated a long dormant period with catastrophic consequences in AD 79. This chapter reviews the volcanic history of Vesuvius, and presents a reconstruction of the AD 79 eruption, based on modern volcanological studies of the deposits in Pompeii, Herculaneum and numerous other sites in Campania, where the so-called "Pompeii pumice" is exposed at the surface. The effects of the eruption were truly prodigious. In addition to the death of thousands of inhabitants and total loss of two important Roman cities, the landscape of Campania was totally transformed. A deposit ranging in thickness from a meter to tens of meters was laid over all the farms and agricultural lands surrounding Vesuvius, and the advance of pyroclastic flows into the Bay of Naples pushed out the coastline several hundred meters and obliterated all ports south of Naples.

EARLY VESUVIUS ACTIVITY

For the last two million years, the region of central and southern Italy has been the scene of active volcanism and associated crustal movements. This region is known among geologists as the Roman Comagmatic Province and extends along the Tyrrhenian coast, from the Vulsini area in northern Latium, to Vesuvius in the south. In north Latium the volcanic activity became largely extinct about 100,000 years ago, but farther south, however, in the Campanian volcanic region, activity has continued up to the present day.

Vesuvius has a prominent volcanic history in the past thousands of years, and its violent explosive eruptions have repeatedly laid waste to large areas of Campania. Most of the early activity in Vesuvius consisted of numerous small eruptions of lava, accompanied by minor explosive eruptions. This activity built up the ancestral Monte

Somma strato-volcano that was up to 300,000 years old.[1] The Somma foundation of Vesuvius includes the prominent arcuate ridge to the north and east of the active volcanic cone.

The earliest known major explosive eruption of Vesuvius occurred about 25,000 years ago, forming the so-called Codola pumice-fall deposit.[2] Recently another important early event has also been recognized: the Sarno eruption, which occurred about 22,000 years ago. About 17,000 years ago the third major Plinian explosive eruption occurred which deposited a widespread layer known as the Basal pumice. These events may be regarded as marking the termination of Somma's activity and the birth of Vesuvius. During the early huge explosive eruptions the summit of Monte Somma may have collapsed, thus forming the caldera-like structure in which the modern cone of Vesuvius is nestled. The Monte Somma caldera wall has restricted the spread of lava flows from Vesuvius; consequently, lava flows younger than 17,000 years are not found on the north flank of Monte Somma. Similarly, the caldera rim influenced and restricted the northward distribution of pyroclastic flows and surges in AD 79.

The Codola eruption was the first of eight major explosive eruptions of Vesuvius in the past 25,000 years. These highly explosive eruptions produced Plinian pumice-fall deposits, often associated with pyroclastic flows and surges. Typically, a 1,400 to 4,000-year period of quiescence has preceded each Plinian explosive event, as marked by well-developed paleosoils under the Plinian deposits. Each Plinian eruption is regarded as the beginning of a new eruptive cycle. The major volcanic cycle that preceded the AD 79 eruption was the fifth cycle of Vesuvius' activity and began with the Plinian eruption of the Avellino pumice, which was deposited on a thick paleosoil, radiocarbon dated as 3,360 ± 40 years before present, or about 1600 to 1700 BC. The ash and pumice-fall deposit from the Bronze-Age Avellino eruption occurred primarily to the east and east-northeast of the volcano. This eruption was very similar in magnitude, composition and extent to that of AD 79, and also produced pyroclastic flows and surges in the final stages of the event. The event also had a severe environmental impact on the Campanian region, and Bronze-Age ceramics buried by the Avellino pumice attest that the Vesuvius region was inhabited at that time.[3]

The soils immediately underlying the AD 79 pumice deposit reveal volcanic ash layers, which show that a number of small eruptions occurred in Vesuvius after the Avellino explosion, but prior to the great event that devastated Pompeii and Herculaneum. It is of great importance to establish in detail the evolution of the volcano just before the great explosive event, as such knowledge will aid in predicting or forecasting future lethal eruptions. We would like to know, for example, what was the period of dormancy or quiescence before the AD 79 eruption, and what was the style of activity during the last minor eruption preceding the great disaster?

Near the volcano, at Terzigno, about 6 km southeast of the crater, the interval between the Bronze-Age Avellino eruption and the AD 79 eruption is marked by the deposition of over 10 m of relatively thin volcanic ashes and sands (Figure 4.1). This deposit contains a valuable record of the low-level activity of the volcano between the great eruptions, spaced some 1,700 years apart. The Avellino pumice-fall deposit is overlain by a paleosoil, which has been dated by the radiocarbon method at 3,000 years before present, indicating a 300–400-year break in activity after the Avellino eruption.[4]

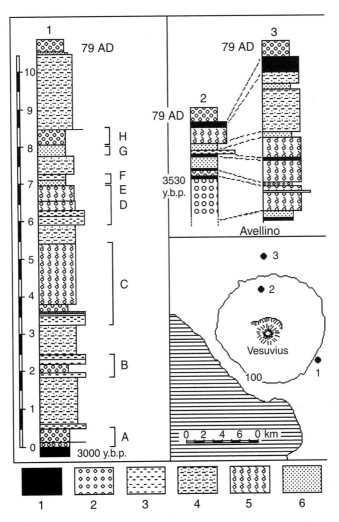

Figure 4.1 The volcanic activity of Vesuvius, prior to the great AD 79 explosive eruption, can be studied in soil profiles and sand quarries around the volcano. The diagram (modified from Arno *et al.* 1987) shows three sections through the pre-AD 79 deposits. The insert map shows the location of these sections (1, 2 and 3) around the volcano. Section 1 is at Terzigno, southeast of the crater. Section 2 is east of S. Anastasia, and section 3 is northwest of Somma Vesuviana. Legend to deposit symbols: (1) paleosoil, with C-14 age dates indicated; (2) pumice-fall deposit; (3) sandy surge deposit; (4) fluviatile sands and other reworked deposits; (5) ash-flow deposit; (6) ash-fall deposit. The letters A to H indicate the deposits from eight relatively minor eruptions, which Arno *et al.* (1987) have identified in the interval between the Avellino eruption and AD 79. It is estimated that the time interval between the last of these events (eruption H) and the AD 79 eruption is about 700 years.

During a period of about 1,700 years, following the Bronze-Age Avellino eruption, at least eight minor explosive eruptions occurred in Vesuvius. The first of these events (eruption "A" of Rosi and Santacroce 1986) spread a white pumice-fall layer over the soil on top of the Avellino deposit. The A eruption deposit is covered by a thick layer of sands and gravels, representing a long period of erosion of loose volcanic ashes from the flanks of the volcano above. The next eruption (B) was also explosive, depositing a greenish-gray pumice layer, and fine ash beds (Figure 4.1). Again, a sand and gravel deposit was laid down, during a long period of erosion of the volcano's flanks. The third explosive eruption in this sequence, probably around 1,000 BC, is eruption C of Rosi and Santacroce. It deposited three ash and *lapilli*-fall layers, followed by a pumice-rich and hot mudflow deposit in the Terzigno area. After yet another period of volcanic quiescence, erosion and deposition of fluviatile sands, the fourth eruption took place (D), depositing ash falls, a surge bed and mudflow.

The four final volcanic events, prior to the great eruption of AD 79, were small explosive eruptions, that deposited thin and dark layers of ash, *lapilli* and fine scoriae around the volcano (eruptions E, F, G and H). This episode was followed by a long period of volcanic quiescence and erosion of the loose deposits from the flanks of Vesuvius, during which a 2 m-thick layer of fluviatile sands and gravels was deposited over the Terzigno area (Figure 4.1). The duration of this break in activity before the AD 79 eruption can be crudely inferred from the thickness of the reworked sand layer. The total thickness of reworked sands deposited at Terzigno in the 1,700-year interval between the Avellino and AD 79 eruptions is about 5.4 m (excluding the primary volcanic layers). Of this, the final period of quiescence just prior to AD 79 represents 2.2 m thickness, or equivalent to a period of dormancy of the volcano of about 700 years. It is no wonder that the Romans did not consider the mountain a threat, or were not even aware of its volcanic character until that fateful day in AD 79.

It is commonly regarded that the magnitude of an explosive eruption increases with the length of the repose period preceding that eruption. This would also seem to be the case of the AD 79 event, and its exceptional violence and intensity may thus be directly related to the very long quiescence of Vesuvius of 700 years. During such a long period of repose, magma may be accumulating at a steady rate in the subterranean reservoir of the volcano, leading to a build-up of magma volume, causing the melting and assimilation of rocks surrounding the reservoir, and an increase in the volatile content of the magma. The longest known dormancy period known for the volcano in historical times was about 300 years preceding the 1631 eruption, which also was a violent explosive event, although much smaller than the AD 79 eruption. By comparison the current dormant period since the 1944 eruption is only fifty-six years.

The German archaeologist Hans Eschebach has studied the stratigraphy of the earlier deposits which underlie the AD 79 volcanic layer and the Roman soil in Pompeii. Among his important findings is the discovery that the city of Pompeii is situated on an ancient lava flow from Vesuvius, which is at a depth of about 1.5 to 3 m below the Roman surface. He also proposed, on basis of myths and interpretation of decorations on ancient Roman coins, that Vesuvius erupted in the fourth century BC. On the basis of ten test pits, Eschebach has described a yellowish-brown volcanic ash deposit, 1 to 3 m thick, overlying the ancient lava flow. This deposit has not been studied by volcanologists, and it is not clear what volcanic processes were responsible, but from Eschebach's descriptions it is most likely that it is a surge deposit or pyroclastic flow. The age is also unknown, but the deposit is likely to represent a major eruption of Vesuvius, such as the Bronze-Age Avellino eruption. Dating of the deposit by the radiocarbon method would resolve this question, and establish the age of the last major event to impact the site of Pompeii before AD 79.

THE VOLCANO BEFORE AD 79

The earliest historical information about Vesuvius dates from the first century BC. In 73 BC a revolt of gladiator slaves led by Spartacus posed a serious threat to the cities around Vesuvius, and this episode gives a glimpse of the volcano before the eruption. Spartacus was sold into slavery in Capua near Vesuvius, where he organized a break-out with seventy other gladiators and sought shelter in the crater of Vesuvius. The band was besieged in the crater by an army led by Claudius Glaber, who was sent from Rome to mop up this trouble. According to Plutarch:

> There was only one way up this hill and that was narrow and difficult and closely guarded by Glaber; in every other direction there was nothing but sheer cliffs. The top of the hill was covered with wild vines which the gladiators twisted into strong rope-ladders long enough to reach down the cliff-face. They all got out of the crater and down safely by means of these ladders except one man who stayed at the top to deal with the arms, and he, once the rest had got down, dropped the arms down to them and then descended last and reached the plain safely. The Romans knew nothing of this and thus the gladiators were able to get around behind them and throw them into confusion by an unexpected attack, first routing them and then capturing their camp. And now they were joined by numbers of herdsmen and shepherds of these parts, all sturdy men and fast on their feet.
>
> (Plutarch, *Life of Crassus* 9.1–3)

Soon Spartacus' army numbered 70,000 men and the Romans were to experience other humiliating defeats by the slave army near Vesuvius and again near Herculaneum. Spartacus was finally conquered and crucified outside Rome after having defeated nine Roman armies.

The tale of Spartacus contains meager but very important information about the topography of Vesuvius some 150 years before the great eruption of AD 79. The chroniclers of the rebellion of Spartacus note that in earlier days the volcano was covered by a dense forest, famous for its wild boars. By the first century BC the primeval forest had given way to the axe and the plough. Writing at the time of Augustus in the first century AD, the Greek geographer Strabo identified Vesuvius as an extinct volcano, with a barren and ash colored summit.

> Above these places lies Mt. Vesuvius, which, save for its summit, has dwellings all around, on farm-lands that are absolutely beautiful. As for the summit, a considerable part of it is flat, but all of it is unfruitful, and looks ash-coloured, and it shows pore-like cavities in masses of rock that are soot-coloured on the

surface, these masses of rock looking as though they had been eaten out by fire; and hence one might infer that in earlier times this district was on fire and had craters of fire, and then, because the fuel gave out, was quenched.

(Strabo, *Geographia* 5.4.8)

There has been much speculation about the shape of Vesuvius before the AD 79 eruption, but it is generally believed to have been a single truncated cone. The idea that Vesuvius had a single peak before AD 79 stems mainly from Strabo's description. Similarly, Dio Cassius, writing in the third century AD, states that "once Vesuvius was equally high at all points" (*Roman History* 66.21.1). A wall painting dating to *c.* AD 50 has survived in the *lararium* of court (49) in the House of the Centenary in Pompeii, and it has been taken as evidence of the appearance of Vesuvius prior to the AD 79 eruption (Figure 4.2). Here, the volcano is shown as a single, steep peak, with the lower slopes covered by vineyards, and with trees and bushes growing near the summit, where the slopes were too steep for cultivation, but supplied firewood and land for grazing. This was the pastoral aspect of the slumbering giant up to AD 79. The figure draped in bunches of grapes is the god Dionysus (Bacchus), and the

Figure 4.2 Wall painting from kitchen *lararium* of the House of the Centenary (IX.8.3, 6) at Pompeii depicting Mt Vesuvius and Dionysus, *c.* AD 50. Museo Nazionale, Naples, inv. no. 112286. Drawn by Christie Padget.

snake represents the household gods. We may infer that the volcano was cone-shaped and with a single major peak prior to the AD 79 event, but other contemporary paintings from Herculaneum show a twin-peaked mountain—possibly Vesuvius—and thus the question of the pre-eruption topography remains open.[5] These observations are not necessarily contradictory, however, as today the volcano has the aspect of single peak from some directions, while it is twin-peaked when seen from other viewpoints. It is clear, nevertheless, that the Monte Somma ridge affected the distribution of the pyroclastic flow and surges from the AD 79 eruption to the north and east. Thus Vesuvius most likely already had a caldera rim at this time.

Pliny the Elder was familiar with the Campanian region and it is evident from his writings that he had visited its cities on many occasions. In Book thirty-five of his *Natural History* descriptions can be found of some of the painted scenes actually discovered in the ruins of Herculaneum and Pompeii. Campania was in his day a blessed and fruitful country, clad with vines that supplied wines famous throughout the Roman World. He mentions Herculaneum and Pompeii, "not far from Vesuvius" (*HN* 3.62). Nowhere in his writings, however, is there an indication that he was aware of the volcanic nature of this mountain that eventually took his life. Strabo (63 BC–AD 30) recognized the volcanic nature of Vesuvius, although the volcano had not erupted in his lifetime. Seneca (2 BC–AD 65) refers to various volcanoes in his works (Etna, Thera, Vulcano), but notably not Vesuvius. Many other historians writing in the Augustan age (31 BC–AD 14), including Diodorus Siculus (*The Library of History* 4.21.5) and Vitruvius (*De arch.* 2.6.1–2), recognized Vesuvius' volcanic character.

THE EARTHQUAKE OF AD 62 AND OTHER PRECURSORS

Large volcanic eruptions are typically preceded by a variety of signals that can be felt or observed at the surface, months or years before eruption begins, and the AD 79 eruption was no exception. These symptoms may include inflation of the volcano and surrounding land, earthquakes, increased thermal activity, change in ground water table and increased volcanic gas emission. Minor phreatic or steam explosions also typically occur shortly before the main eruption, and evidence has been presented showing that a phreatic eruption preceded the main AD 79 event. All of these phenomena are linked to the upward flow of magma within the Earth's crust, either from a deep source to a reservoir at 5 to 10 km below the volcano, or out of this magma reservoir towards the surface via a narrow conduit.

On February 5, AD 62 the volcano gave the first signs of returning to activity, when a large earthquake rocked the area, centered near Pompeii. Seneca wrote a contemporary account of the earthquake and other pre-eruption phenomena under the heading *De Terrae Motu* (Earthquakes) in Book VI of his *Natural Questions*:

> I have just heard that Pompeii, the famous city in Campania, has been laid low by an earthquake which also disturbed all the adjacent districts . . . In fact, it occurred in days of winter, a season which our ancestors used to claim was free from such disaster. This earthquake was on the Nones of February, in the

consulship of Regulus and Verginius. It caused great destruction in Campania, which had never been safe from this danger but had never been damaged and time and again had got off with a fright. Also, part of the town of Herculaneum is in ruins and even the structures which are left standing are shaky . . . To these calamities others were added: they say that a flock of hundreds of sheep was killed, statues were cracked, and some people were deranged and afterwards wandered about unable to help themselves . . . Yet certain things are said to have happened peculiar to this Campanian earthquake, and they need to be explained. I have said that a flock of hundreds of sheep was killed in the Pompeian district. There is no reason you should think this happened to those sheep because of fear. For they say that a plague usually occurs after a great earthquake, and this is not surprising. For many death-carrying elements lie hidden in the depths. The very atmosphere there, which is stagnant either from some flaw in the earth or from inactivity and the eternal darkness, is harmful to those breathing it. Or, when it has been tainted by the poison of the internal fires and is sent out from its long stay it stains and pollutes this pure, clear atmosphere and offers new types of disease to those who breathe the unfamiliar air . . . I am not surprised that sheep have been infected, sheep which have a delicate constitution, the closer they carried their heads to the ground, since they received the afflatus of the tainted air near the ground itself. If the air had come out in greater quantity it would have harmed people too; but the abundance of pure air extinguished it before it rose high enough to be breathed by people.

(Seneca, *QNat.* 6.1.1; 6.1.1–2; 6.1.3.; 6.27.1–2; 6.27.4)

The death of hundreds of sheep by mysterious poisoning on the slopes of Vesuvius, as reported by Seneca, is perhaps the best evidence that the volcano was returning back to life in AD 62 and that the earthquake was also related to the volcano. Increased emission of volcanic gases commonly occurs before eruptions, including large quantities of carbon dioxide.

From Seneca and other sources it is evident that the earthquake was strongest in Pompeii and Herculaneum. In Pompeii, the Porta Vesuvio and Porta Ercolano, aqueducts and waterworks were broken, including lead-pipes which served as plumbing to residential houses. The Roman Senate sent aid for restoration, which was still in progress seventeen years later when the volcano dealt the final blow. At Herculaneum, the richer city, restoration proceeded much faster and was mostly complete by the time of the eruption, but an inscription records that restoration of the Temple of Mater Deum was not completed until AD 76 (*CIL* X, 1406). Earthquakes are common in Campania and the people probably took this one in their stride. One prominent banker in Pompeii, Lucius Caecilius Iucundus, commemorated the earthquake with two amusing marble reliefs in his house, where the crashing of arches and columns and the heaving of the ground are shown, with the two equestrian statues suddenly coming to life as the riders struggle to regain their balance.

THE AD 79 ERUPTION

In Campania most of the year AD 79 was uneventful until June 24, when news came of the death of Emperor Vespasian and the rise of his son Titus. Emperor Vespasian fell ill with fever in Campania and died on June 23, 79, exactly two months before the eruption of Vesuvius. Titus, who was already co-ruler in the last years of his father's reign, assumed the title Imperator Titus Flavius Vespasianus. In mid-August, about six weeks after Titus became emperor, earthquake activity was renewed, as documented by Pliny the Younger. The shocks were small but frequent and caused only minor damage. By August 20, the earthquake tremors increased in strength and noises were heard like distant thunder. At the same time the springs ceased to flow and wells dried up. Unknown to the Pompeians, the volcano was waking from a slumber which had lasted for 700 years.

The destruction of Pompeii and Herculaneum during the AD 79 eruption has been the subject of many studies, beginning with the visit of the French scholar Dolomieu to Herculaneum in the eighteenth century. One of the earliest observations of the nature of the volcanic deposits was made by Gell and Gandy who observed that Pompeii had been buried by a shower of ash, pumice and stones that created stratigraphic layers. This view was echoed in most later studies where the fate of the cities was attributed to very heavy and rapid fall of pumice and ash in the case of Pompeii and inundation by mudflows in the case of Herculaneum.[6] This hypothesis failed, however, to account for evidence of very high temperatures in the "mudflow" deposits, such as melted glass and carbonized wood and bones.

In 1902 the devastatingly explosive eruption of Mont Pelée on the Caribbean island of Martinique dramatically illustrated another volcanic process that had an important bearing on the AD 79 event. A deadly cloud of hot volcanic gas and particles traveled down the slopes of the volcano at hurricane speed, killing 25,000 people. These deadly clouds were described as glowing avalanches or *nuées ardentes* by Lacroix because of the transport of incandescent fragments.[7] Following the recognition of *nuées ardentes* in 1902, Merrill saw the Vesuvius eruption in a new light, and proposed that the fatal blows had been dealt by *nuées ardentes*. Merrill's work went unnoticed, however, and the idea of mudflows continued to prevail. In the last two decades tremendous progress has been made towards an understanding of *nuées ardentes*. These clouds evolve into two parts as they travel down the slope of a volcano, with a high-concentration mixture of gas and particles at the base, called a pyroclastic flow. The upper part of the *nuée ardente* is a low-concentration, highly turbulent mixture of gas and particles, called a pyroclastic surge. Surges commonly extend over a much larger area than their associated pyroclastic flows, but often leave very thin deposits. As deposits of the AD 79 eruption were examined in the light of a new appreciation for these processes, it became clear that both pyroclastic surges and flows were an important part of this event.[8] We have presented a new reconstruction of the eruption on the basis of a combination of the stratigraphic evidence from the volcanic deposits and the letters of Pliny the Younger, where we contrasted the different effects of the pumice-fall, pyroclastic surges, and pyroclastic flows on communities around the volcano, and established a chronology for the main events during the eruption.[9]

A detailed account of the AD 79 eruption can be pieced together from two lines of evidence: two letters of Pliny the Younger (*Ep.* 6.16 and 6.20), and numerous features in the volcanic deposits documented in 1985 by Sigurdsson *et al.*[10] We have a vivid contemporary account of the disaster because of the death of the famous Roman scholar Pliny the Elder during the eruption. Pliny the Elder was in command of the naval port of Misenum, 32 km across the bay from Vesuvius (Map 1), where he was accompanied by his sister and her seventeen-year-old son, Pliny the Younger. During the two days of the eruption, the family was to experience grave danger, which led to Pliny the Elder's death, whereas Pliny the Younger and his mother narrowly escaped. At the request of the historian Cornelius Tacitus, Pliny the Younger recorded the circumstances of his uncle's death and his eyewitness account of the eruption.

Our reading of the volcanic deposits relies on a number of measurable variables, such as thickness, grain size, sorting, the type of rock components (pumice, stones, ash etc.). In addition, there are numerous factors that provide evidence of heat (melting of glass, charcoal), and high lateral velocity (e.g., roof tiles and other building materials in the deposit). Well-recognized volcanological principles allow us to differentiate between fallout deposits (ash and pumice-fall) and pyroclastic flow and surge deposits. One of the most important parameters in the study of an eruption is the mass eruption rate of magma, which is typically of the order of millions of kilograms per second. This parameter is measured from grain size features of the deposit (which are dependent on the eruption column height), and in the case of the AD 79 event, we have determined the variation in mass eruption rate at several stages of the eruption.

In Pliny the Younger's letter we read that it was near the seventh hour after sunrise (*hora fere septima*) on August 24, when they noted the eruption cloud over Vesuvius, i.e. about noon (*Ep.* 6.16.4). Thus began the Plinian phase of the eruption, with a 14 km-high eruption cloud of pumice and ash. The top of the column was sheared by the stratospheric wind, carrying a plume of ash and pumice to the southeast, over Pompeii. The pumice-fall in Pompeii continued virtually without break, accumulating at a rate of 10 to 15 cm per hour to form a 280 centimeter-thick layer, consisting of white pumice in the lower part and grey pumice in the upper part of the layer (Figure 4.3). During the next twelve hours, the eruption column increased steadily from a height of 14 to 33 km over the volcano. On land, the pumice deposit can now be traced as far as Agropoli, 74 km southeast of Vesuvius. Much of the distal ashfall has been eroded, however, and accounts written shortly after the eruption tell of much more extensive ashfall. Dio Cassius notes that ashfall occurred in North Africa, Egypt, Palestine, and elsewhere in the Levant following the eruption (*Roman History* 66.23.4).

People in Pompeii, Oplontis, and elsewhere in the zone of heavy pumice-fall were faced with two problems during the afternoon and evening of August 24. First, the pumice-fall was accompanied by fall of dense lithic fragments, some fist-sized. These lithics, falling at terminal velocities of over 50 m per second, were dangerous projectiles, and surely injured or killed some people outdoors. Fortunately, pyroclastics of this type were only 10 percent of the total fall. Second, the weight of accumulating pumice would have collapsed roofs in Pompeii during the afternoon, probably after two or three hours of pumice-fall. This must have led to widespread evacuation of buildings and exodus from the city. Pompeii and other areas southeast of Vesuvius were in darkness at this time, caused by the dense eruption plume overhead (Figure 4.4).

During the first twelve hours of activity the heavy pumice-fall mainly affected an area southeast of Vesuvius, bounded by Terzigno to the east and Oplontis to the west. Just after midnight on August 24, the style of activity changed as Vesuvius

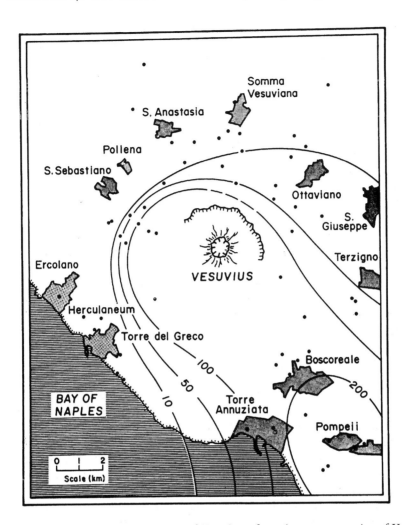

Figure 4.3   The distribution of the pumice fallout layer from the AD 79 eruption of Vesuvius. Isopachs (lines of equal thickness) show the total thickness of the pumice deposit today, in centimeters. Solid dots indicate the locations where measurements were made. Note that the thickest deposit is over Pompeii. The distribution of the pumice-fall deposit is largely controlled by the prevailing high-level winds, which were blowing from the northwest at the time of the eruption (adapted from Carey and Sigurdsson, 1987).

produced the first of six pyroclastic surges and flows, which were to interrupt the pumice-fall during the next seven hours, killing people within a 10 km radius from the crater. The first surge (labeled S-1 in the stratigraphy of Sigurdsson *et al.* 1985) spread over the south and west flank of Vesuvius, overwhelming Villa Regina at Boscoreale, Oplontis, and all the west coast to Herculaneum. Small tongues of this surge extended down the valleys above Somma Vesuviana and Ottaviano on the north and northeast flank. This first and smallest of the surges did not, however, reach the *villae rusticae* at Terzigno or the city of Pompeii. The effects of this surge were remarkably similar to the effects of the surges of the 1982 eruption of

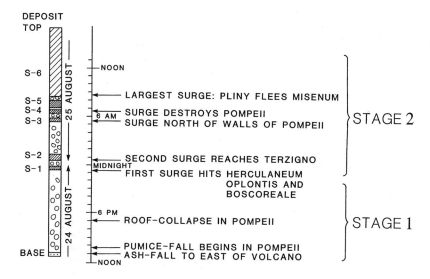

Figure 4.4 The chronology of the AD 79 eruption, based on the study of the volcanic deposits and interpretation of the letters of Pliny the Younger. The deposit shown (far left) is that of Oplontis, where most or all of the layers are preserved. S-1 to S-6 indicate pyroclastic surge and pyroclastic flow events. The intervening layers decorated with open circles represent the pumice-fall deposits. Total thickness of the deposit shown here is approximately 4 m. The eruption is divided into two stages. During Stage 1, the eruption produced a high Plinian column, resulting solely in pumice and ash fallout. During Stage 2 the eruption column collapsed repeatedly (at least six times), producing deadly, hot and destructive pyroclastic surges (S-1 to S-6) that were progressively larger and more destructive.

El Chichon in Mexico, which devastated nine towns and villages. The effects of the S-1 surge are best studied and most dramatic in Herculaneum. During the preceding twelve-hour period of activity, the city had only received a light sprinkling of ashfall, less than 1 cm. With the erupting volcano in full view, and being only 7 km from the crater, the population must have been uneasy. Many Herculaneans must have left their city during this period, and fled toward safety in Naples to the north where these lucky refugees became permanent residents of the Herculaneum Quarter.

People remaining in Herculaneum may have seen the precursor of the surge as a *nuée ardente* sweeping down the cone of the volcano. During the 1980 Mt St Helens eruption, the main surge moved at 60 to 250 m per second. The S-1 surge, however, is much finer grained and of smaller extent, and probably more similar to the southern Mt St Helens surge, which traveled at only 30 m per second. Even at this lower velocity, the surge would have taken no more than four minutes to reach Herculaneum. People in the city were without doubt on the alert that night, and probably in the streets watching the spectacle of the ominous eruption column, with its lower trunk glowing from incandescent tephra, and its upper part illuminated by flashes of lightning. The cascade of the *nuée ardente* down the flank would have been immediately noticed and recognized as a threat. Flight from the eruption to the waterfront and along the coast toward Naples was the most obvious solution.

Just after midnight when the eruption column had grown to its peak height, the first surge cloud swept into Herculaneum at sufficient velocity to topple the colonnade and portico around the *palaestra* and to transport building rubble 2 to 4 m. It probably left most walls intact, but stripped the roof tiles off some buildings. Temperatures in the surge were high enough to carbonize dry wood but not green wood. When the surge poured over the waterfront in the lee of the great city wall, its velocity decreased locally, so that deposition increased on the beach and the adjacent chambers. As the hot surge entered the ocean it caused the water to boil and give off small steam explosions. People on the beach and in the chambers were engulfed in a swirling ash-cloud that carried flying roof tiles and other debris. Thus, one of the victims may have been struck down by the red tile found resting against her forehead. Breathing in the surge cloud was impossible and, like the victims of Mt St Helens, the Herculaneans were asphyxiated.

The northward spread of the first *nuée ardente* was apparently restricted by the 300-meter-high arcuate Monte Somma rim. Only two minor lobes of the S-1 surge surmounted this barrier and flowed down the valleys above Somma Vesuviana and Ottaviano (Figure 4.5). This indicates that the body of the *nuée ardente* in the Valle del Gigante exceeded 300 m in thickness. A large part of the surge was funneled down the Valle del Gigante and onto the lowlands to the west, over the Cava Montone area and toward Herculaneum. The *nuée ardente* segregated early into a fast-moving surge and a more slowly moving pyroclastic flow. The flow reached Herculaneum shortly after the surge, and came into the city from the east, flowing into the *palaestra* where it filled a large cross-shaped swimming pool. The flow did not advance through the city, but rather down a valley along its southern edge and onto the beach in front of the Suburban Thermae. Here the pyroclastic flow (F-1) engulfed and carbonized a large boat on the beach and advanced into the ocean before coming to rest. Where exposed on the waterfront, the F-1 flow rests directly on top of the S-1 surge. Here the flow contains gas pipes, produced by the escape of steam expelled from the underlying surge, which by now had become soaked by seawater.

Fall of gray pumice continued as before, following the emplacement of the first surge and flow, and led to accumulation of pumice-fall layer A-4, during one hour, south of the volcano. The height of the eruption column had, however, decreased to 22 km in response to the collapse that generated the first pyroclastic surge and flow. Elsewhere, the new desert-like surface created by the first surge remained bare, with protruding, smoking carbonized tree trunks and steam rising from rivers and the coast. One hour later, near 1 a.m., the second *nuée ardente* was generated from the crater, and formed a surge with a volume about three times that of the first event. The S-2 surge cloud spilled out the Valle del Gigante and over the Somma rim to the north, devastating all the north flank of Vesuvius within 7 km of the crater. It destroyed the *villae rusticae* at Terzigno beyond the reach of the first surge, but ran its course south of Boscoreale before reaching Pompeii.

On the west flank the surge left a deposit similar to that of the May 18, 1980 Mt St Helens blast, and was probably moving at 100 to 200 m per second. In Herculaneum, where its effects were particularly severe, it struck with sufficient force to break down the masonry walls and roofs unaffected by the first surge. The surge was closely followed by the pyroclastic flow F-2, which flowed north of Herculaneum and onto the beach. Flows also advanced down valleys on the north flank leading to

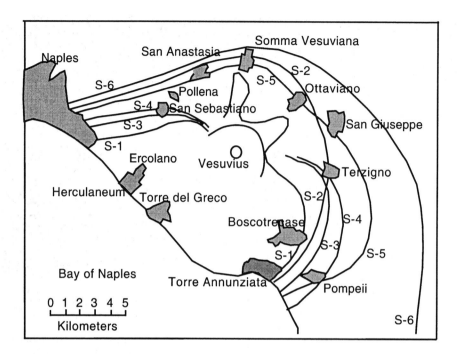

Figure 4.5   The distribution of pyroclastic surges around Vesuvius during the AD 79 eruption.

Pollena, Santa Anastasia, and Somma Vesuviana, but no pyroclastic flows are known to have affected the south flank at this time. In many southern outcrops, the S-2 surge is split by a thin pumice-fall layer, from which the surge can be inferred to have come in two rapid pulses to the south.

Pumice-fall continued after passage of the great S-2 surge, and the A-5 gray pumice layer accumulated during about four hours, until about 5 a.m. During this Plinian phase a larger proportion of lithics was erupted than before, probably indicating increased erosion of the vent. These included both lavas and fragments from the carbonate basement. Around 5:30 a.m. the third surge was generated. It extended even farther south, running up against the northern city wall of Pompeii but not entering the city. The surge was followed by a pyroclastic flow in the northwest, which flowed directly over the remains of Herculaneum and completely buried the city so that only the theater protruded. This and subsequent flows extended the new coastline an additional 400 m to the west of the Herculaneum waterfront.

The pumice-fall was now darker and more lithic-rich. It continued for about an hour, until 6:30 a.m., forming layer A-6. Subsequently a fourth surge was generated (S-4), which followed the previous pattern and spread even farther south, this time overwhelming Pompeii and Bottaro (Figure 4.6). As the surge cloud came over the northern city wall of Pompeii, it rolled over an area already blanketed by 2.4 m of pumice-fall. Most roofs had collapsed, and only the walls of two- and three-story buildings stood above the bleak wasteland. Most of the inhabitants had abandoned the city to escape the collapsing roofs, but a surprising number of people were

Figure 4.6 Photograph of the AD 79 volcanic deposits in the Porta Nocera necropolis, south of Pompeii. On the right is one of the buried tombs. The deposit consists of pumice fallout in the lower part (*c.* 2 m thick), grading from nearly white pumice at the base, to dark grey top. A sharp boundary marks the abrupt change to pyroclastic surge deposition (S-4 here, about 10 cm thick). This is overlain by about 80 cm-thick pyroclastic surge and flow (S-5) and then massive pyroclastic flow from S-6.

moving about on top of the pumice-fall when the lethal fourth surge struck at about 6:30 a.m. Their deaths are tragically recaptured in the plaster casts of hollows in the deposits. They were asphyxiated in the surge cloud, which tore through the city, removing roofs and collapsing many walls.

The fourth surge was followed by the fifth surge a few minutes later. Even larger, it was accompanied by a pyroclastic flow in many areas to the south, such as Oplontis. The large surge cloud that passed over Pompeii (S-6) continued to the south and overwhelmed the city of Stabiae, where Pliny the Elder had sought refuge in the villa of his friend Pomponianus, 14 km south of the crater. The previous afternoon Pliny had abandoned his plans of making landfall on the southwest coast under the volcano, because of very heavy fall of hot pumice and lithics on his ships and because sailing near the coast was made impossible by thick floating rafts of pumice. He therefore gave up his rescue mission and headed for the comparative safety of Stabiae to the south. Judging from the stratigraphic section at the Villa Ariadne, nearly 2 m of pumice-fall accumulated at Stabiae during the eruption. It is not surprising, as

Pliny the Younger states, that his uncle had difficulty opening his door the next morning, because of the thick pumice layer in the courtyard:

> They debated whether to stay indoors or take their chance in the open, for the buildings were now shaking with violent shocks, and seemed to be swaying to and fro, as if they were torn from their foundations. Outside, on the other hand, there was the danger of falling pumice-stones, even though they were light and porous; however, after comparing the risks they chose the latter.
>
> (*Ep.* 6.16.15–16)

The black eruption plume overhead caused darkness at Stabiae "blacker and denser than any ordinary night" (*Ep.* 6.16.17), but they could see daylight underneath the cloud, probably to the northeast and west.

"Then the flames and smell of sulfur which gave warning of the approaching fire drove the others to take flight" (*Ep.* 6.16.18). This event must represent the advance of the sixth and largest surge over the south flank toward Stabiae at about 7 a.m. on August 25. At Villa Ariadne the surge deposited a 5 cm layer on top of the pumice-fall and thus clearly affected Stabiae. By his nephew's admission, Pliny the Elder was an overweight man with a weak constitution and he did not take flight with the others, but collapsed in the arms of his two slaves as he choked in the dusty surge cloud. Near the volcano the sixth surge left a major deposit, which is often 0.5 to 1 m thick in outcrops. It grades upward into a pyroclastic flow, e.g. at Oplontis and Boscoreale; thicker parts of this deposit at Pompeii also resemble pyroclastic flow.

Severe earth tremors also threatened Pliny the Younger and his mother that morning at Misenum and they decided to abandon the tottering buildings and leave town. En route they witnessed a tidal wave and over the volcano "a fearful black cloud was rent by forked and quivering bursts of flame, and parted to reveal great tongues of fire, like flashes of lightning magnified in size" (*Ep.* 6.20.9). They were witnessing the great *nuée ardente* that generated the sixth surge about 7 a.m., and took the life of Pliny the Elder. "Soon afterwards the cloud sank down to earth and covered the sea; it had already blotted out Capri and hidden the promontory of Misenum from sight" (*Ep.* 6.20.11). Both are about 30 km from Vesuvius. Pliny the Younger then describes their experience as they fled the surge cloud rolling across the Bay of Naples:

> Ashes were already falling, not as yet very thickly. I looked around: A dense black cloud was coming up behind us, spreading over the earth like a flood. . . . Darkness fell and ashes began to fall again, this time in heavy showers. We rose from time to time and shook them off. . . . At last the darkness thinned and dispersed into smoke or cloud; then there was genuine daylight, and the sun actually shone out.
>
> (*Ep.* 6.20.13–18)

The surge traveled across the Bay of Naples and reached Misenum, where fine ash from the turbulent surge cloud settled. It must have cooled on its long path, because Pliny mentions no heat. The deposit left by the surge at Misenum was probably only a few centimeters and soon eroded away, because no deposit remains today. The passage of a surge cloud over a long distance across water was also documented in the 1883 Krakatau eruption in Indonesia, where surge clouds from the volcano engulfed islands and settlements on the south coast of Sumatra.[11]

WANING ERUPTION AND AFTERMATH

The activity of Vesuvius following the sixth and largest surge is not chronicled in Pliny, but the deposits bear evidence of continued eruption. Within 10 km of the volcano this later activity laid down surges and accretionary *lapilli* beds consisting of at least twenty units. Many of these beds are pumice-free and mostly composed of lithics, thus indicating the small role of juvenile magma at this stage. These deposits were probably formed by a large number of small phreatic or phreatomagmatic explosions, resulting from interaction of groundwater and magma remaining in the volcano's conduit. This activity may have persisted for days or weeks.

When the eruption came to an end, pyroclastic surges that left a deposit with a volume equivalent to 0.23 km^3 of dense rock had totally devastated 300 km^2 around Vesuvius. By comparison, the volcano produced about 0.14 km^3 of pyroclastic flows during the eruption and 0.16 km^3 of accretionary *lapilli* beds during the final phreatomagmatic phase. These figures do not take into account the unknown volumes of tephra that entered the Bay of Naples. Including 2.6 km^3 of gray pumice and 1 km^3 (dense-rock equivalent) of white pumice, the total deposit produced by the eruption is thus equivalent to about 4 km^3 of dense rock; about 90 percent was magmatic material, and the remainder rock fragments torn from the walls of the Vesuvius conduit.

Titus hastened to Campania on receiving news of the eruption and its widespread destruction and returned there again the following year. He appointed two *curatores restituendae Campaniae* (Suetonius, *Titus* 8.4) to organize aid and reconstruction in the region and these appointments were drawn by lot from those of consular rank. Titus provided the necessary funds from his own resources and from the property of the many people who had died in the eruption without heirs. Contemporary accounts indicate that refugees from the devastated areas around Vesuvius fled to the neighboring towns of Capua, Nola, Neapolis and Surrentum and the shrewd Titus gave special privileges to the towns which had offered assistance to these refugees.

Except for brief remarks by the Latin poets Martial and Statius, the first mention of the AD 79 Vesuvius eruption after Pliny the Younger's letters is the *Epitome* of Dio Cassius. Writing about one and a half centuries after the eruption, Dio gives a garbled account of the event, influenced by superstition and mythology. From Dio's account we learn that Vesuvius was still active in his time, with minor explosions usually occurring "every year" (*Roman History* 66.22.1) and that the volcanic ash from the 79 eruption that reached Rome was blamed for the terrible pestilence that visited the city (*Roman History* 66.24.5). The AD 79 eruption may also be described in a Coptic Gnostic text discovered at Nag' Hammadi entitled "The Apocalypse of Adam":

> Fire, pumice and asphalt will be thrown upon these people. And fire and dazzling will come over those aeons and the eyes of the manifestations of the luminaries

will become dark. And the aeons will not see by them in those days. And great clouds of light come down upon them and also other clouds of light come down upon them from the great aeons.[12]

Goedicke has suggested that the author of the "Apocalypse" had used Pliny's account of the eruption, in describing a cosmic warning of the impending coming of the Savior of the World.[13]

NOTES

1 C. Principe, M. Rosi, R. Santacroce and A. Sbrana, *Workshop on Explosive Volcanism: Guidebook on the Field Excursion to Phlegrean Fields and Vesuvius,* Rome, 1982.

2 V. Arno, C. Principe, M. Rosi, R. Santacroce, A. Sbrana and M. F. Sheridan, "Eruptive history," in R. Santacroce (ed.), *Somma-Vesuvius,* CNR *Quaderni de "La ricerca scientifica",* 114, vol. 8, Rome, 1987, pp. 53–103.

3 C. Albore Livadie, "Palma Campania (Napoli). Resti di abitato dell'età del bronzo o antico," *NSc,* 1980, ser. 8, vol. 34, pp. 59–101. G. Mastrolorenzo *et al.,* "The Avellino 3780-yr-B.P. catastrophe as a worst-case scenario for a future eruption at Vesuvius," *Proceedings of the National Academy of Sciences,* 2006, vol. 103.12, pp. 4366–70.

4 Rosi and Santacroce, "L'attività del Somma-Vesuvio precedente l'eruzione del 1631;" Arno *et al.,* "Eruptive history."

5 G. B. Alfano and I. Friedlander, *Die Geschichte des Vesuv,* Berlin, 1929; P. Preusse, "Ein Wort zur Vesuvgestaltung und Vesuvtatigkeit im Altertum," *Klio,* 1934, vol. 27, pp. 295–310; R. B. Stothers and M. R. Rampino, "Volcanic eruptions in the Mediterranean before AD 630 from written and archaeological sources," *Journal of Geophysical Research,* 1983, vol. 88, pp. 6357–71; E. Renna, *Vesuvius Mons,* Naples, 1992.

6 F. Ippolito, "Sul meccanismo del seppellimento di Pompei e di Ercolano," *Pompeiana,* 1950, pp. 387–95; A. Rittmann, "L'eruzione Vesuviana del 79, studio magmalogico e volcanologico," *Pompeiana,* 1950, pp. 456–74.

7 A. Lacroix, "Les derniers jours d'Herculaneum et de Pompéi interprétés à l'aide de quelques phénomènes récents du volcanisme," *La Géographie Bulletin de la Société de Géographie,* 1908, vol. 18: n. 5, pp. 281–96.

8 L. Lirer, T. Pescatore, B. Booth and G. P. L. Walker, "Two Plinian pumice-fall deposits from Somma Vesuvius, Italy," *Geological Society of America, Bulletin,* 1973, vol. 84, pp. 759–72; R. S. J. Sparks and G. P. L. Walker, "The ground surge deposit: a third type of pyroclastic rock," *Nature,* 1973, vol. 241, pp. 62–4.

9 H. Sigurdsson, S. Cashdollar and R. S. J. Sparks, "The eruption of Vesuvius in AD 79: reconstruction from historical and volcanological evidence," *AJA,* 1982, vol. 86, pp. 39–51; H. Sigurdsson, S. Carey and J. M. Espindola, "The 1982 eruptions of El Chichon volcano, Mexico: stratigraphy of pyroclastic deposits," *Journal of Volcanology and Geothermal Research,* 1984, vol. 23, pp. 11–37; Sigurdsson *et al.* "The eruption of Vesuvius in AD 79," pp. 332–87; H. Sigurdsson, W. Cornell and S. Carey, "Influence of magma withdrawal on compositional gradients during the AD 79 Vesuvius eruption," *Nature,* 1990, vol. 345, pp. 519–21; H. Sigurdsson, S. Carey and C. Mandeville, "Krakatau: submarine pyroclastic flows of the 1883 eruption of Krakatau volcano," *National Geographic Research,* 1991, vol. 7, pp. 310–27; H. Sigurdsson, T. Pescatore, A. Varone and A. M. Ciarallo, "The eruption of Vesuvius AD 79. Volcanology, sedimentology and archeology," in *Excursion Guide A4,* 15th International Association of Sedimentologists, April 1994, pp. 83–104; S. Carey and H. Sigurdsson, "Temporal variations in column height and magma discharge rate during the AD 79 eruption of Vesuvius," *Geological Society of America, Bulletin,* 1987, vol. 99, pp. 303–14. [See also now: G. Luongo *et al.,* "Impact of AD 79 explosive eruption on Pompeii, I. Relations amongst the depositional mechanisms of the pyroclastic products, the framework of the buildings and the associated destructive events," *Journal of Volcanology and Geothermal Research,* 2003, vol. 126, pp. 201–23; G. Luongo *et al.,* "Impact of the AD 79 explosive eruption on Pompeii,

II. Causes of death of the inhabitants inferred by stratigraphic analysis and areal distribution of the human casualties," *Journal of Volcanology and Geothermal Research*, 2003, vol. 126, pp. 169–200.—Eds]

10 Sigurdsson *et al.*, "The eruption of Vesuvius in AD 79," pp. 332–87.

11 Sigurdsson *et al.*, "Krakatau."

12 A. Bohlig and P. Labib, "Koiptisch-Gnostische Apokalypsen aus Codex V von Nag Hammadi," *Wissenschaftliche Zeitschrift der Martin-Luther-Universität*, Sonderband 107, Halle-Wittenberg, 1963.

13 H. Goedicke, "An unexpected allusion to the Vesuvius eruption in AD 79," *Classical Journal*, 1968, vol. 25, pp. 340–1.

BIBLIOGRAPHY

Albore Livadie, C., "Palma Campania (Napoli). Resti di abitato dell'età del bronzo o antico," *NSc*, 1980, ser. 8, vol. 34, pp. 59–101.

Alfano, G. B. and Friedlander, I., *Die Geschichte des Vesuv*, Berlin, 1929.

Arno, V., Principe, C., Rosi, M., Santacroce, R., Sbrana, A. and Sheridan, M. F., "Eruptive history," in R. Santacroce (ed.), *Somma-Vesuvius*, CNR *Quaderni de "La ricerca scientifica"*, 114, vol. 8, Rome, 1987, pp. 53–103.

Bohlig, A. and Labib, P., "Koiptisch-Gnostische Apokalypsen aus Codex V von Nag Hammadi," *Wissehschaftliche Zeitschrift der Martin-Luther-Universitaat*, Halle-Wittenberg, 1963, Sonderband, 107.

Carey, S. and Sigurdsson, H., "Temporal variations in column height and magma discharge rate during the AD 79 eruption of Vesuvius," *Geological Society of America, Bulletin*, 1987, vol. 99, pp. 303–14.

Delibrias, G., DiPaola, G. M., Rosi, M. and Santocroce, R., "La storia eruttiva del complesso vulcanico Somma Vesuvio ricostruita dalle successioni piorclastiche del Monte Somma," *Rend. Società Italiana di Mineralogie e Petrologia*, 1979, vol. 35, pp. 411–38.

Eschebach, H., "Ein nicht uberlieferter, auch Pompeji betreffender Vesuvausbruch?," *RM*, 1976, vol. 83, pp. 71–111.

Goedicke, H., "An unexpected allusion to the Vesuvius eruption in AD 79," *Classical Journal*, 1968, vol. 25, pp. 340–1.

Ippolito, F., "Sul meccanismo del seppellimento di Pompei e di Ercolano," *Pompeiana*, 1950, pp. 387–95.

Lacroix, A., "Les derniers jours d'Herculaneum et de Pompéi interprétés à l'aide de quelques phénomènes récents du volcanisme," *La Géographie Bulletin de la Société de Géographie*, 1908, vol. 18: n. 5, pp. 281–96.

Lirer, L., Pescatore, T., Booth, B. and Walker, G. P. L., "Two Plinian pumice-fall deposits from Somma Vesuvius, Italy," *Geological Society of America, Bulletin*, 1973, vol. 84, pp. 759–72.

Maiuri, A., *Herculaneum*, Rome, 1977.

Merrill, E. T., "Notes on the eruption of Vesuvius in AD 79," *AJA*, 1918, vol. 22, pp. 304–9.

——, "Further note on the eruption of Vesuvius in AD 79," *AJA*, 1920, vol. 24, pp. 262–8.

Moore, J. G. and Rice, C. J., "Chronology and character of May 18, 1980, explosive eruptions of Mount St. Helens," *Explosive Volcanism, Inception, Evolution and Hazards*, Washington, DC, 1984, pp. 133–42.

Preusse, P., "Ein Wort zur Vesuvgestaltung und Vesuvtatigkeit im Altertum," *Klio*, 1934, vol. 27, pp. 295–310.

Principe, C., Rosi, M., Santacroce, R. and Sbrana, A., *Workshop on Explosive Volcanism: Guidebook on the Field Excursion to Phlegrean Fields and Vesuvius*, Rome, 1982.

Renna, E., *Vesuvius Mons*, Naples, 1992.

Rittmann, A., "L'eruzione Vesuviana del 79, studio magmalogico e volcanologico," *Pompeiana*, 1950, pp. 456–74.

Rosi, M. and Santacroce, R., "L'attivita del Somma-Vesuvio precedente l'eruzione del 1631: dati stratigrafici e vulcanologici," in C. A. Livadie (ed.), *Tremblements de terre, éruptions volcaniques et vie des hommes dans la Campanie antique*, Naples, 1986, pp. 15–33.

Sheridan, M. F., Barberi, F., Rosi, M. and Santacroce, R., "A model for Plinian eruptions of Vesuvius," *Nature*, 1981, vol. 289, pp. 282–5.

Sigurdsson, H., Carey, S. and Espindola, J. M., "The 1982 eruptions of El Chichon volcano, Mexico: stratigraphy of pyroclastic deposits," *Journal of Volcanology and Geothermal Research*, 1984, vol. 23, pp. 11–37.

——, —— and Mandeville, C., "Krakatau: submarine pyroclastic flows of the 1883 eruption of Krakatau volcano," *National Geographic Research*, 1991, vol. 7, pp. 310–27.

——, Cashdollar, S. and Sparks, R. S. J., "The eruption of Vesuvius in AD 79: reconstruction from historical and volcanological evidence," *AJA*, 1982, vol. 86, pp. 39–51.

——, Cornell, W. and Carey, S., "Influence of magma withdrawal on compositional gradients during the AD 79 Vesuvius eruption," *Nature*, 1990, vol. 345, pp. 519–21.

——, Carey, S., Cornell, W. and Pescatore, T., "The eruption of Vesuvius in AD 79," *National Geographic Research*, 1985, vol. 1, pp. 332–87.

——, Pescatore, T., Varone, A. and Ciarallo, A. M., "The eruption of Vesuvius AD 79. Volcanology, sedimentology and archeology," in *Excursion Guide A4*, 15th International Association of Sedimentologists, April 1994, pp. 83–104.

Sparks, R. S. J. and Walker, G. P. L., "The ground surge deposit: a third type of pyroclastic rock," *Nature*, 1973, vol. 241, pp. 62–4.

Stothers, R. B. and Rampino, M. R., "Volcanic eruptions in the Mediterranean before AD 630 from written and archaeological sources," *Journal of Geophysical Research*, 1983, vol. 88, pp. 6357–71.

Vogel, J. S., Cornell, W., Nelson, D. E. and Southon, J. R., "Vesuvius/Avellino, one possible source of seventeenth century BC climatic disturbances," *Nature*, 1990, vol. 344, pp. 534–7.

CHAPTER FIVE

RECENT WORK ON EARLY POMPEII

———•◆•———

Paolo Carafa

The earliest phases of the settlements in the centuries prior to the Roman conquest of Campania have not generally received a great deal of attention from scholars.[1] But for some years now, thanks especially to the Soprintendenza Archeologica, numerous research projects have been contributing new material or new proposals and have reopened the debate on the history and, consequently, on the urban structure of the small Vesuvian center.[2] The chronologies of the various phases of the urban fortifications and of the earliest and most important sanctuaries by now rest on solid foundations (cf. De Caro, Ch. 6);[3] we have sufficient evidence to reconstruct the evolution of the building techniques used at Pompeii between the sixth and second centuries BC, which have never been so well documented. Although much of this research is still in progress and the picture we see today could change quickly, we have sought to reconsider, in the light of the new data, the entire archaeological documentation relative to the phases of the built-up area prior to the end of the second century BC.

Most scholars deny that a stable settlement might have existed at Pompeii before the beginning of the sixth century BC.[4] The conviction is based essentially on the fact that no archaic necropoleis or structures securely datable before the sixth century BC have yet been identified,[5] as well as on the dating of some public monuments, whose existence presupposes the completed birth of a city, specifically:

- The Temple of Apollo (*c.*600–575 BC). Chronology based on the earliest architectural terracottas attributable to the decoration of a temple and on the material collected in the sanctuary's votive deposits.[6]
- The first fortification, built of so-called *pappamonte* tufa (600–550 BC), possibly *c.*550 BC. Chronology established on the basis of stratigraphy.[7]
- The so-called Doric Temple (600–550 BC), possibly *c.*550 BC. Chronology based on the form of the Doric capitals preserved and on the earliest architectural terracottas attributable to the decoration of the temple.[8]

The ancients, however, had a completely different notion of the history of this small town on the slopes of Vesuvius. Mythological and historical tradition associated the birth of Pompeii with the Labors of Hercules in Italy.[9] In terms of "absolute chronology" that means an era before the Trojan War (1193–1183 BC, according to Eratosthenes of Cyrene). This complex tradition has, of course, been revised several times and variously interpreted,[10] and we do not intend to seek exact confirmation of the myth in the scant archaeological data available. Still, the finding of pottery and bronze datable to the protohistoric and archaic periods in a number of different excavations (Figure 5.1) may merit closer attention.

Fortunately we possess an up-to-date list of a series of objects from Pompeii datable before *c.*600 BC.[11] The material is very scanty, a few dozen pieces, some intact, some fragments, but it sheds a little light on a long span of time that would otherwise remain absolutely unattainable for us. The earliest object so far known from Pompeii is a stone axe, found outside the Porta Nocera and believed to be Eneolithic.[12] With the first phases of the Bronze Age (first half of the second millennium BC) the evidence becomes a little more solid, as the pottery fragments collected in the excavation of the House of Lucretius Fronto[13] and of a stretch of fortification east of tower III show.[14] For the ninth and eighth centuries BC the evidence is not more plentiful, but is more widely scattered over the plateau (impasto fragments from the Isaeum;[15] impasto fragments from the House of Lucretius Fronto;[16] pottery and bronze from the House of Ganymede;[17] bronze fibula and impasto cup from the Sanctuary of Apollo;[18] bronze fibula from the area of the Doric Temple;[19] bronze pendants without precise provenience[20]).

Can we begin to consider the presence of such early material as evidence of the first stable occupation of the area? I believe we can. The very recent discovery at Bottaro of a necropolis with some thirty burials datable starting from the centuries just before the middle of the second millennium BC clearly confirms the existence of a settlement of considerable antiquity in the surrounding area.[21] It may be worth

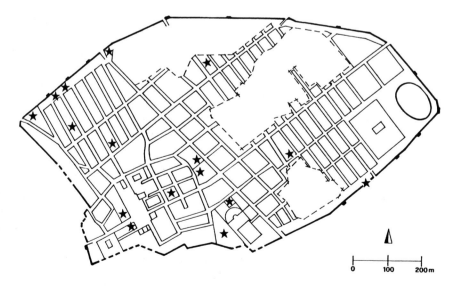

Figure 5.1 Pompeii: distribution of protohistoric and Archaic finds
(after Carafa 1997).

pointing out that, as the most recent attempts at reconstruction of the territory surrounding the mouth of the Sarno (ancient Sarnus) have proved, the lava plateau (Figure 11.1) on which Pompeii stands represents the only site easily defendable and suitable for settling in an almost flat and marshy area, periodically subject to flooding of the river.[22] Although we lack the support of funerary evidence for the subsequent centuries, it is important to note that some objects datable to the eighth century BC have been collected in the two earliest sanctuaries of what was to become the city. This might be evidence that both cults were present far earlier than the period in which the two sanctuaries were built up and, thus, may attest that an organized community had settled on the plateau at least from the end of the Iron Age.[23] If we also accepted the proposal that a sacred beech wood stood in the northwest part of the area later enclosed by the fortification,[24] this picture could be articulated further.

Placing the birth of the settlement so early would lead us to the possibility that the protohistoric villages of the interior—whose existence is known thanks to the famous necropoleis of S. Marzano sul Sarno, Sarno, S. Valentino Torio and Striano[25]— had a corresponding coastal center, more ancient than the "city" that would have been founded at the beginning of the sixth century BC spurred by the Etruscan component, culturally dominant and well attested at the borders of the Sarno plain.[26] It has already been proposed that Pompeii was a "port of trade"[27] or at least that the *area sacra* of Apollo was associated with an emporium,[28] but not before the end of the seventh century BC. There remains only to await what emerges from continuing excavations of the stratigraphy beneath the pavements of the Roman city, to verify the existence of further elements that might give greater substance to the few facts we possess so far.

At the present state of the research, whether we accept the existence of a protohistoric settlement or not, it is an established fact that the earliest structures identified at Pompeii cannot be dated before the beginning of the sixth century BC.[29] These are the *pappamonte* walls found mainly in the southwest area of the plateau (Figure 5.2). It is not possible to reconstruct, even partially, the plan of even one of these buildings. We can, however, observe that their orientation is always consistent with that of the later *insulae* and, more important, that they too lie outside the area considered to be the Pompeian *Altstadt*. We should also point out that where levels attributable to the Archaic period, or even virgin earth, are reached, structures of this type have not always been encountered.[30] This would seem to show that, despite the established existence of at least two large cult buildings and a fortification that by now enclosed the entire plateau, the density of the buildings in the infant city was still rather low.

If we consider the context in which these buildings were constructed, we should point out the importance of a fact that we consider essential to understanding the urban phenomenon at Pompeii. Albeit in a general context characterized by heavy political tensions and profound territorial changes,[31] the necropoleis of the Sarno valley (mentioned above) are not abandoned, as is generally held, but continue to be used at least until the next century.[32] From this it follows that the foundation of Pompeii cannot possibly be the direct result of the concentration on the lava plateau that dominated the mouth of the Sarno of a population previously distributed in settlements along the course of the river. If we also duly consider that a settlement probably already existed in the area of Pompeii for at least two centuries, it would

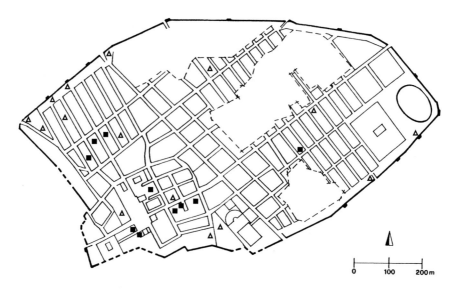

Figure 5.2 Pompeii: distribution of remains of *pappamonte* buildings (squares)
and Archaic finds (triangles).

seem unlikely that this building activity represented the foundation of a new city,
including the construction of the first fortification.

Some two generations after construction of the walls, the great sanctuaries and
some small *pappamonte* structures, the archaeological record of Pompeii drops off un-
expectedly. The fortification was restored in the course of the fifth century BC,[33]
but the votive deposits of the Sanctuary of Apollo receive no more gifts[34] and, more
in general, traces of material datable to the years between the end of the sixth and
approximately the end of the fourth century BC are quite scarce throughout the
city. Various explanations for this phenomenon have been put forth,[35] and without
facts it is difficult to prefer one interpretation over another. Nevertheless, it is certain
that after this temporary stasis, building activity resumed with vigor. In addition to
a new rebuilding of the walls (Figure 11.2) and the construction of a small bath
in the area of the Stabian Baths, which have long been recognized,[36] a good number
of structures datable to the early Hellenistic period and distributed throughout the
area enclosed by the fortification have now been identified (Figure 5.3). These are not,
however, great *domus* with *atrium* (no standing Pompeian house is datable with certainty before the second century BC[37]), but rather buildings of limited area, again
poorly constructed, with walls in *pozzolana* and foundations made of limestone and
lava chips (cf. Jones and Robinson, Ch. 25). Thanks to the recent resumption of
extensive stratigraphic excavations, we know this new type of construction better than
has been possible for the earliest *pappamonte* structures. In at least three cases, we can
reconstruct the general plan of the buildings.

Under the *atrium* of the House of the Forms of Crete (VII.4.62), has been identified
part of a small complex with two banquet rooms probably opening onto a colonnade.[38] This may be a public building, built between the end of the fourth and the
beginning of the third century BC, which makes it extremely interesting for the

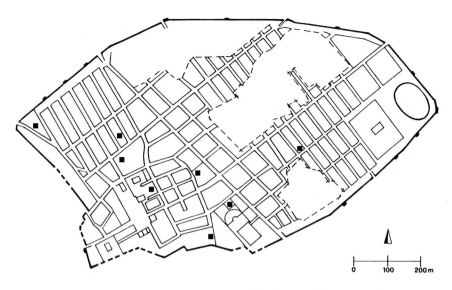

Figure 5.3 Pompeii: distribution of buildings of limestone and
lava fragments.

reconstruction of the urban plan of Pompeii before the creation of the large *insulae*.
A small square structure (*c*.20 m²) identified under the *atrium* of the House of Joseph
II (VIII.2.38–39)[39] is datable to the same period. The available evidence (only a few
stretches of the foundations are preserved) is too scanty for us to determine its function.
Its small size, however, would rule out that it was a dwelling. However, the structure
identified under the House of the Wedding of Hercules (VII.9.47)[40] can almost
certainly be interpreted as a habitation. The remains preserved (Figure 5.4) permit
reconstruction of a rectangular building (*c*.90 m²) open towards the south and preceded
by a small wooden portico on the north side. It consists of two small adjacent rooms
that face out on a third, larger, space that may have been a small unroofed courtyard.
Both the rooms and the hypothetical courtyard are floored in tamped earth. The
presumed courtyard contains two circular pits, one for garbage and the other used
as a latrine. The walls must have been faced or decorated, as the numerous white
and colored fragments of plaster recovered during the excavation indicate. A rather
limited number of bricks of the building have been collected in the layers of the
house's collapse, but it would seem beyond doubt that the roof was tiled. The associated
stratigraphy indicates a life for the structure between the end of the fourth/beginning
of the third century BC and the middle of the second century BC.

The density of the structures is rather low in the Hellenistic phase as well. In all
cases examined the buildings are surrounded by large empty areas and, at least in
the case of the excavation in the House of the Wedding of Hercules, these areas are
characterized by dark soils that have nothing to do with streets, squares or any other
type of urban elements. The landscape within the walls of Pompeii must have looked
very different from the dense streets and buildings of the now numerous cities that
occupied the territories between Rome and the *ager Picentinus*. The great walls, the
two ancient sanctuaries, the small buildings separated by empty lots resembled—

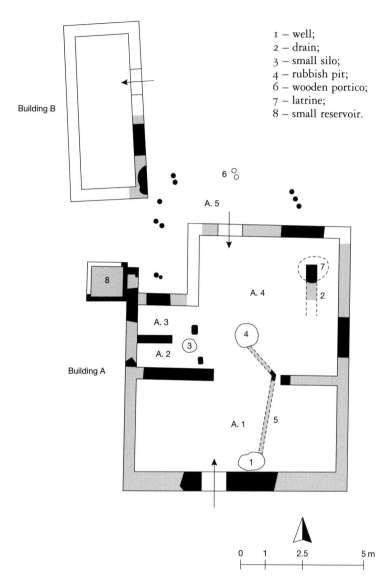

1 – well;
2 – drain;
3 – small silo;
4 – rubbish pit;
6 – wooden portico;
7 – latrine;
8 – small reservoir.

Figure 5.4 Pompeii: reconstructed plan of Samnite house under the House of the Wedding of Hercules (VII.9.47) (after Carandini *et al.* 2001). Surviving remains in black; reconstructed structures in grey and white.

perhaps much more than modern scholars would expect—Italic *oppida* of the central-southern regions.[41]

To reconstruct the history and appearance of a settlement we can no longer see may be one of the main duties of archaeological research. All the information we need is waiting to be recovered. At Pompeii, the work has just begun, but we may be able to propose a key to understanding what we have looked at so far. The city destroyed by Vesuvius was preceded by a settlement that, at the present state of the research, we are beginning to recognize as a dispersed settlement where structures of different sizes and degrees of monumentality coexisted among spaces not yet well defined, but definitely not occupied by structures (cf. Jones and Robinson, Ch. 25). We do not yet have a secure terminus for dating its birth but, if the indications from the protohistoric finds were to be confirmed, we could trace it back as far as the second millennium BC. Gradually this settlement began to evolve until it became like one of the cities or small towns desired by Rome in the course of her progressive expansion in central Italy. The different aspects of this change cannot yet be said to be fully understood, and only continued research can help us reconstruct the stages of so long a process.

NOTES

1 Maureen B. Fant translated the Italian text. H. Eschebach, "Ausgrabungen und Baugeschichte," *RM*, 1982, vol. 89, pp. 219–313; C. Reusser, "Archaische Funde," *RM*, 1982, vol. 89, pp. 353–72; M. Bonghi Jovino (ed.), *Ricerche a Pompei. L'insula 5 della Regio VI dalle origini al 79 d.C.*, Rome, 1984; S. De Caro, "Nuove indagini sulle fortificazioni di Pompei," *AION*, 1985, vol. 7, pp. 75–114; P. Arthur, "Problems of the urbanization of Pompeii: excavations 1980–1981," *The Antiquaries Journal*, 1986, vol. 61.1, pp. 29–44; S. De Caro, *Saggi nell'area del tempio di Apollo a Pompei. Scavi stratigrafici di A. Maiuri nel 1931-32 e 1942-43*, Naples, 1986; A. D'Ambrosio and S. De Caro, "Un contributo all'urbanistica e all'architettura di Pompei in età ellenistica. I saggi nella casa VII, 4, 62," *AION*, 1989, vol. VII, pp. 173–215.

2 S. De Caro, "Lo sviluppo urbanistico di Pompei," *Atti e memorie della Società Magna Grecia*, 1992, ser. 3, 1, pp. 67–90; *Neapolis Project, Progetto-sistema per la valorizzazione integrale delle risorse ambientali e artistiche dell'area vesuviana*, Rome, 1994; J. J. Dobbins, "Problems of chronology, decoration, and urban design in the forum at Pompeii," *AJA*, 1994, vol. 98, pp. 629–94; J. J. Dobbins, L. F. Ball, J. G. Cooper, S. L. Gavel and S. Hay, "Excavations in the Sanctuary of Apollo at Pompeii, 1997," *AJA*, 1998, vol. 102, pp. 739–56; S. E. Bon, R. Jones, B. Kurchin and D. J. Robinson, "The context of the House of the Surgeon: investigations in Insula VI,1 at Pompeii," in S. E. Bon and R. Jones (eds), *Sequence and Space in Pompeii*, Exeter, 1997, pp. 7–12; P. Carafa, "What was Pompeii before 200 BC? Excavations in the House of Joseph II, in the Triangular Forum and in the House of the Wedding of Hercules," in Bon and Jones (eds), *Sequence and Space*, pp. 13–31; P. Carafa and M. T. D'Alessio, "Lo scavo nella Casa di Giuseppe II (VIII, 2, 38–39) e nel portico occidentale del Foro Triangolare a Pompei. Rapporto preliminare," *RivStPom*, 1997, vol. 7, pp. 137–45; H. W. Horsnaes, "From Iron Age to Pompeii. Urbanization in Southern Campania—a case study," *Acta Hyperborea*, 1997, vol. 7, pp. 195–227; A. Wallace-Hadrill and M. Fulford, "Unpeeling Pompeii," *Antiquity*, 1998, vol. 72, 128–45; H. Geertman, "The layout of the city and its history: the Dutch project," in J. Berry (ed.), *Unpeeling Pompeii: Studies in Region I of Pompeii*, Milan, 1998, pp. 17–25; M. Fulford and A. Wallace-Hadrill, "Towards a history of pre-Roman Pompeii: excavations beneath the House of Amarantus (I.9.11–12), 1995–8," *PBSR*, 1999, vol. 67, pp. 37–144; A. Carandini, P. Carafa and M. T. D'Alessio, "Nuovi progetti, nuove domande, nuovi metodi," in S. De Caro and P. G. Guzzo (eds), *Pompei*, Milan, 2001, pp. 127–9.

3 F. Pesando, "La porta presso la Torre di Mercurio e le fasi della fortificazione di Pompei," in F. Carocci, E. De Albentiis, M. Gargiulo and F. Pesando (eds), *Le insulae 3 e 4 della Regio VI di Pompei. Una storia urbanistica*, Rome, 1990, pp. 217–26; De Caro, *Tempio di Apollo*; J. A. K. E. De Waele, B. D'Agostino and P. S. Lulof (eds), *Tempio dorico del Foro Triangulare di Pompei*, Rome, 2001.

4 M. Cristofani, "La fase 'etrusca' di Pompei," in *Pompei*, ed. F. Zevi, Naples, 1991, pp. 13ff.; De Caro, "Lo sviluppo urbanistico;" N. Murolo, "Le saline herculeae di Pompei. Produzione del sale e culto di Ercole nella Campania antica," in *Studi sulla Campania preromana*, Rome, 1995, pp. 105–24; L. Cerchiai, *I Campani*, Milan, 1995.

5 Cristofani, "La fase 'etrusca' di Pompei;" De Caro, "Lo sviluppo urbanistico," pp. 107ff.

6 De Caro, *Tempio di Apollo*.

7 De Caro, "Nuove indagini."

8 J. A. K. E. De Waele, B. D'Agostino and P. S. Lulof (eds), *Tempio dorico del Foro Triangulare di Pompei*, Rome, 2001. J. A. K. E. De Waele, "The 'Doric' Temple on the Forum Triangulare in Pompeii," *Opuscola Pompeiana*, 1993, vol. 3, pp. 105–18; Horsnaes, "From Iron Age to Pompeii," p. 202.

9 J. Berard, *La Magna Grecia*, Turin, 1963, p. 397; M. De Vos, "Ercole e Priamo," in A. Mastrocinque (ed.), *Ercole in Occidente*, Trento, 1993, pp. 88ff.

10 M. Torelli, "Gli aromi e il sale. Afrodite ed Ercole nell'*emporia* arcaica dell'Italia," in A. Mastrocinque (ed.), *Ercole in Occidente*, pp. 91–117; Cerchiai, *I Campani*, pp. 153ff.

11 Reusser "Archaische Funde," pp. 353–72; B. Limata, "Su alcuni pendagli bronzei da Pompei," in *Studi sulla Campania preromana*, Rome, 1995, pp. 99–103; Carafa and D'Alessio, "Lo scavo nella Casa di Giuseppe II," p. 145; Horsnaes, "From Iron Age to Pompeii," pp. 197–99.

12 De Caro, "Nuove indagini," p. 107.

13 S. L. Wynia, "The excavations in and around the House of Marcus Lucretius Fronto," in *La regione sotterrata dal Vesuvio*, Naples, 1982, pp. 329–31.

14 De Caro, "Nuove indagini," pp. 101–3.

15 A. Varone, "Attività dell'Ufficio Scavi: 1989," *RivStPom*, 1989, vol. 3, p. 231.

16 H. Brusting and S. L. Wynia, "I mobilia," in J. Jh. W. Peters (ed.), *La casa di Marcus Lucretius Fronto a Pompei e le sue pitture*, Amsterdam, 1993, p. 15.

17 Reusser, "Archaische Funde," pp. 355ff., Abb. 1 and 2, Taf. 134.1–2.

18 De Caro, *Tempio di Apollo*, p. 112 n. 909, tav. L, and p. 110, n. 909 tav. L.

19 Reusser, "Archaische Funde," p. 369.

20 Limata, "Su alcuni pendagli bronzei."

21 V. Mastroroberto, "La necropoli di S. Abbondio: una comunità dell'età del Bronzo a Pompei," in P. G. Guzzo and R. Peroni (eds), *Archeologia e Vulcanologia in Campania*, Naples, 1998, pp. 135–50.

22 *Neapolis*, pp. 245–52.

23 Carafa, "What was Pompeii before 200 BC?," p. 26.

24 Bonghi Jovino, *Ricerche a Pompei*, pp. 364–5; De Caro, "Lo sviluppo urbanistico," p. 72.

25 Cerchiai, *I Campani*, pp. 30–6.

26 Most recently, V. Bellelli, "Anomalie pompeiane," *Prospettiva*, 1995, vol. 77, pp. 9–10.

27 Arthur, "Urbanization of Pompeii," p. 39.

28 Most recently, G. Tagliamonte, *I figli di Marte*, Rome, 1994, p. 70.

29 Horsnaes, "From Iron Age to Pompeii."

30 House VI.5.4: Bonghi Jovino, *Ricerche a Pompei*; House of the Forms of Crete: A. D'Ambrosio and S. De Caro, "Un contributo all'urbanistica e all'architettura di Pompei in età ellenistica. I saggi nella casa VII, 4, 62," *AION*, 1989, vol. 11, pp. 173–215; Chalcidicum of the Basilica: A. Maiuri, *Alla ricerca di Pompei preromana*, Naples, 1975, pp. 209 and 211; so-called Temple of the Lares Publici: H. Eschebach and L. Eschebach, *Pompej*, Cologne, 1995; House of Joseph II and Triangular Forum: Carafa and D'Alessio, "Lo scavo nella Casa di Giuseppe II;" House of Ganymede: Eschebach, "Ausgrabungen und Baugeschichte;" see also Bon *et al.*, in Bon and Jones (eds), *Sequence and Space*.

31 See, for example, L. Cerchiai, "Il processo di strutturazione del politico: i Campani," *AION*, 1987, vol. 9, p. 46.

32 Arthur, "Urbanization of Pompeii," p. 40.

33 De Caro, "Lo sviluppo urbanistico," p. 75.

34 De Caro, *Tempio di Apollo*, p. 23.

35 De Caro, "Lo sviluppo urbanistico," p. 76; Horsnaes, "From Iron Age to Pompeii," p. 218.

36 De Caro, "Lo sviluppo urbanistico," p. 78; H. F. Eschebach, *Die Stabianer Thermen in Pompeji*, Berlin, 1979.

37 M. T. D'Alessio, "La nascita della casa ad atrio in un centro italico medio-tirrenico: il caso di Pompei," in M. Tosi and M. Pearce (eds), *Papers from the EAA Third Annual Meeting at Ravenna 1997*, vol. II, *Classical and Medieval*, BAR i.s. 718, 1998, pp. 81–5.

38 D'Ambrosio and De Caro, "Pompei in età ellenistica."

39 Carafa and D'Alessio, "Lo scavo nella Casa di Giuseppe II," p. 140.

40 Carafa, "What was Pompeii before 200 BC?," pp. 21–3.

41 Carafa, "What was Pompeii before 200 BC?," p. 28; see also S. L. Dyson, "Some random thoughts on a collection of papers in Roman Archaeology," in Bon and Jones (eds), *Sequence and Space*, p. 156.

BIBLIOGRAPHY

Arthur, P., "Problems of the urbanization of Pompeii: excavations 1980–1981," *The Antiquaries Journal*, 1986, vol. 61.1, pp. 29–44.

Bellelli, V., "Anomalie pompeiane," *Prospettiva*, 1995, vol. 77, pp. 2–15.

Berard, J., *La Magna Grecia*, Turin, 1963.

Bon, S. E., R. Jones, B. Kurchin and D. J. Robinson, "The context of the House of the Surgeon: investigations in Insula VI,1 at Pompeii," in S. E. Bon and R. Jones (eds), *Sequence and Space in Pompeii*, Exeter, 1997, pp. 7–12.

Bonghi Jovino, M. (ed.), *Ricerche a Pompei. L'insula 5 della Regio VI dalle origini al 79 d.C.*, Rome, 1984.

Brusting, H. and S. L. Wynia, "I mobilia," in J. Jh. W. Peters (ed.), *La casa di Marcus Lucretius Fronto a Pompei e le sue pitture*, Amsterdam, 1993, pp. 15–37.

Carafa, P., "What was Pompeii before 200 BC? Excavations in the House of Joseph II, in the Triangular Forum and in the House of the Wedding of Hercules," in S. E. Bon and R. Jones (eds), *Sequence and Space in Pompeii*, Exeter, 1997, pp. 13–31.

—— and M. T. D'Alessio, "Lo scavo nella Casa di Giuseppe II (VIII, 2, 38–39) e nel portico occidentale del Foro Triangolare a Pompei. Rapporto preliminare," *RivStPom*, 1997, vol. 7, pp. 137–45.

Carandini, A., P. Carafa and M. T. D'Alessio, "Nuovi progetti, nuove domande, nuovi metodi," in S. De Caro and P. G. Guzzo (eds), *Pompei*, Milan, 2001, pp. 127–9.

Cerchiai, L., "Il processo di strutturazione del politico: i Campani," *AION*, 1987, vol. 9, pp. 41–54.

——, *I Campani*, Milan, 1995.

Cristofani, M., "La fase 'etrusca' di Pompei," in F. Zevi (ed.), *Pompei*, Naples, 1991, pp. 9–22.

D'Alessio, M. T., "La nascita della casa ad atrio in un centro italico medio-tirrenico. Il caso di Pompei," in M. Tosi and M. Pearce (eds), *Papers from the EAA Third Annual Meeting at Ravenna 1997*, vol. II, *Classical and Medieval*, British Archaeological Reports, i.s. 718, 1998, pp. 81–5.

D'Ambrosio, A. and S. De Caro, "Un contributo all'urbanistica e all'architettura di Pompei in età ellenistica. I saggi nella casa VII, 4, 62," *AION*, 1989, vol. 11, pp. 173–215.

De Caro, S., "Nuove indagini sulle fortificazioni di Pompei," *AION*, 1985, vol. 7, pp. 75–114.

——, *Saggi nell'area del tempio di Apollo a Pompei. Scavi stratigrafici di A. Maiuri nel 1931–32 e 1942–43*, Naples, 1986.

——, "Lo sviluppo urbanistico di Pompei," *Atti e memorie della Società Magna Grecia*, 1992, ser. 3, vol. 1, pp. 67–90.

——, "Intervento," in P. G. Guzzo and R. Peroni (eds), *Archeologia e vulcanologia in Campania*, Naples, 1998, pp. 217–18.

De Vos, M., "Ercole e Priamo," in A. Mastrocinque (ed.), *Ercole in Occidente*, Trento, 1993, pp. 81–9.

De Waele, J. A. K. E., B. D'Agostino and P. S. Lulof (eds), *Tempio dorico del Foro Triangulare di Pompei*, Rome, 2001.

——, "The 'Doric' Temple on the Forum Triangulare in Pompeii," *Opuscola Pompeiana*, 1993, vol. 3, pp. 105–18.

Dobbins, J. J., "Problems of chronology, decoration, and urban design in the forum at Pompeii," *AJA*, 1994, vol. 98, pp. 629–94.

——, L. F. Ball, J. G. Cooper, S. L. Gavel and S. Hay, "Excavations in the Sanctuary of Apollo at Pompeii, 1997," *AJA*, 1998, vol. 102, pp. 739–56.

Dyson, S. L., "Some random thoughts on a collection of papers in Roman archaeology," in S. E. Bon and R. Jones (eds), *Sequence and Space in Pompeii*, Exeter, 1997, pp. 150–7.

Eschebach, H., "Ausgrabungen und Baugeschichte," *RM*, 1982, vol. 89, pp. 219–313.

—— and L. Eschebach, *Pompeji*, Cologne, 1995.

Fulford, M. and A. Wallace-Hadrill, "Towards a history of pre-Roman Pompeii: excavations beneath the House of Amarantus (I.9.11–12), 1995–8," *PBSR*, 1999, vol. 67, pp. 37–144.

Geertman, H., "The layout of the city and its history: the Dutch project," in J. Berry (ed.), *Unpeeling Pompeii: Studies in Region I of Pompeii*, Milan, 1998, pp. 17–25.

Horsnaes, H. W., "From Iron Age to Pompeii. Urbanization in Southern Campania—a case study," *Acta Hyperborea*, 1997, vol. 7, pp. 195–227.

Limata, B., "Su alcuni pendagli bronzei da Pompei," in *Studi sulla Campania preromana*, Rome, 1995, pp. 99–103.

Maiuri, A., *Alla ricerca di Pompei preromana*, Naples, 1975.

Mastroroberto, V., "La necropoli di S. Abbondio: una comunità dell'età del Bronzo a Pompei," in P. G. Guzzo and R. Peroni (eds), *Archeologia e Vulcanologia in Campania*, Naples, 1998, pp. 135–50.

Murolo, N., "Le saline herculeae di Pompei. Produzione del sale e culto di Ercole nella Campania antica," in *Studi sulla Campania preromana*, Rome, 1995, pp. 105–24.

Neapolis Project, "Progetto-sistema per la valorizzazione integrale delle risorse ambientali e artistiche dell'area vesuviana," project documents, Rome, 1994.

Pesando, F., "La porta presso la Torre di Mercurio e le fasi della fortificazione di Pompei," in F. Carocci, E. De Albentiis, M. Gargiulo and F. Pesando (eds), *Le insulae 3 e 4 della Regio VI di Pompei. Una storia urbanistica*, Rome, 1990, pp. 217–26.

Reusser, C., "Archaische Funde," *RM*, 1982, vol. 89, pp. 353–72.

Tagliamonte, G., *I figli di Marte*, Rome, 1994.

Torelli, M., "Gli aromi e il sale. Afrodite ed Ercole nell'*emporia* arcaica dell'Italia," in A. Mastrocinque (ed.), *Ercole in Occidente*, Trento, 1993, pp. 91–117.

Varone, A., "Attività dell'Ufficio Scavi: 1989," *RivStPom*, 1989, vol. 3, pp. 225–38.

Wallace-Hadrill, A. and M. Fulford, "Unpeeling Pompeii," *Antiquity*, 1998, vol. 72, pp. 128–45.

Wynia, S. L., "The excavations in and around the House of Marcus Lucretius Fronto," in F. Zevi (ed.), *La regione sotterrata dal Vesuvio, Studi e prospettive: Atti del Convegno Internazionale*, Naples, 1982, pp. 225–38.

CHAPTER SIX

THE FIRST
SANCTUARIES

———— •◆• ————

Stefano De Caro

What we know of Pompeii's earliest sanctuaries comes essentially from research conducted in the nineteenth century, leading to the first stratigraphic investigations of the city's earliest phases.[1]

Although our picture of these phases is still full of gaps, it is nevertheless clear that the central place in the archaic city belonged to the Sanctuary of Apollo, located at the intersection of the two perpendicular streets that divide the *Altstadt*, whatever this represents within the great first circuit of walls built of *pappamonte*, the gray local tufa. *Pappamonte* was also used for the earliest structure in this sanctuary, an *opus quadratum* wall that probably marks the boundary of the temenos on the side on which the House of Triptolemus would later be built. Votive offerings, sometimes consisting of valuable Middle Corinthian craters, provide evidence of the cult in that sacred space since the beginning of the sixth century BC. Such finds attest both the intensity of the nascent city's relationships with Greek trading circuits, and the consistency of the aristocratic ideal that the dedicands felt with the imagery of the banquets and of the departures of warriors represented. In this first phase the sanctuary probably consisted of a votive column and an altar, as in the *area sacra* of the Lapis Niger in Rome. Nor does the allusion seem far-fetched, because the evidence of the inscriptions scratched on the *bucchero* vases found in the sanctuary show that the city was decidedly Etruscan in this period, even if the god worshiped, Apollo, is the one who most represents the link of these southern Etruscans with the world of the Greek colonies, Cumae in particular, where the cult of the god was certainly very important.

In the last quarter of the sixth century BC a temple of Etruscan type was erected and decorated with architectural terracottas (Figure 6.1) that have been reconstructed with sufficient precision and that belong to that late archaic southern Latian and Campanian *koiné* that included both Etruscan or Etruscanizing areas (Segni, Satricum, Anagni, Capua, Fratta, Nola) and Greek areas (Pithekoussai, Cumae, Poseidonia, Velia, Surrentum). For all the sixth and part of the fifth century BC, the ceramics offered in the sanctuary, especially Attic red- and black-figure pottery, attest that both it and the city were flourishing.

The other great sanctuary of the archaic city was located on a sort of spur of the lava flow on which the built-up area was planted. At the end of the sixth century

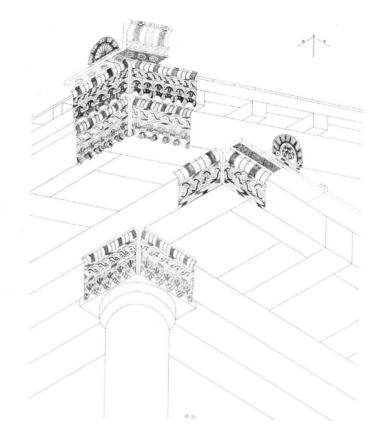

Figure 6.1 The Sanctuary of Apollo in the archaic period, reconstruction (VII.7).

BC a temple was erected here that dominated the plain beneath it where the Sarno emptied into the sea. The temple, in turn, was highly visible to the ships that hugged the coastline of the gulf of Cumae. The divinity worshiped in it was Athena, a cult that recalls the much more famous one of the nearby cape Athenaion. Fragments of a terracotta acroterial statue pertain to both Athena and her favorite, Hercules, engaged in the Labor of the Cerynthian Hind.

The temple structure has more than a few architectural affinities with Greek temples, in particular its beautiful Doric capitals, which are very similar to those of the Temple of Apollo Lycaeus (the so-called *Tavole Palatine*) at Metapontum, but the plan has noteworthy similarities to temple B of Pyrgi. This mixed Greek-Etruscan language, together with the position of the temple, within the urban circuit but at the edge of the *Altstadt*, almost a beacon for ships, lends itself well to a cult associated with a commercial center.

Still within the perimeter of the archaic city, but this time on the opposite side of the *Altstadt*, in the heart of Regio VI, *insula* 5, was located another sanctuary, probably a *lucus*, a sacred beech grove (likely to have been specially planted, since they usually grow at higher altitude) in which a votive column and an altar were installed in the sixth century BC. It became suffocated by the urbanization of the Hellenistic city, but the venerable column was respected, embedded in a wall (The House of the Etruscan Column, VI.5.17–18, between rooms [2] and [4]) but still quite visible, proudly displayed by generations of the owners of the house as a sign of ancient times.

Evidence of the break that must have occurred with the Samnite conquest of the city can be glimpsed in the sanctuaries as elsewhere. The sudden diminution of the ceramics dedicated in the Sanctuary of Apollo seems to indicate a sharp drop in the offerings, probably a reflection of the inevitable loss of status of the Etruscan aristocracies whose cult center it was, as well as perhaps of the slow integration of the new Samnite dominant class.

The first signs of the incipient Hellenism of the new social structure are evident around the middle of the fourth century BC in the series of architectural terracottas, antefixes with Athena and Hercules protomes, and *antepagmenta* (door jambs) in relief, which decorated the renovated Temple of Athena in the Triangular Forum (Figure 6.2). The pronounced presence of Hercules elements in the figural decoration of the temple, as for that matter, in the archaic phase, and the recent discovery of a bronze statuette of the hero, who was very popular among the Samnites, seem to confirm that the sanctuary also contained his cult. Certainly the local mythology, perhaps in part already from the Hellenistic period, abounds in his presence, from the Petra Herculis, the rocky islet opposite the present-day mouth of the Sarno, to the triumphal procession (*pompe*) that was conducted here by the hero returning from the Labor of Geryon and that, according to a typical Hellenistic popular etymology, gave the name to the city. The presence of the same antefixes and statuettes of Athena with Phrygian helmet—perhaps reproductions of the cult statue—in the sanctuaries of the Sorrento peninsula, at Privati di Castellammare di Stabia and in the Athenaion at Punta Campanella, indicates that by now a common religious culture was taking hold in the area of the *touta nucerina* (the Samnite administrative district).

Figure 6.2   Antefixes with the heads of Athena and Hercules from the temple in the Triangular Forum, Pompeii (VIII.7).

The last significant phase in the history of the pre-Roman sanctuaries of Pompeii occurs during the second century BC. A systematic modernization and beautification was carried out according to the aesthetic canon of Hellenistic cities when the flourishing of commerce due to the proximity of the new (194 BC) large Roman harbor of Puteoli made Pompeii suddenly rich. First, the old Temple of Apollo in the piazza of the forum, still covered in its wooden structure by polychrome Etruscan terracottas, was replaced around the middle of the century by a new stone building of Hellenistic style, a Corinthian hexastyle temple on a high podium with an *omphalos* of tufa and a beautiful pavement of inlaid green and white stone arranged to form cubes in perspective (cf. Small, Ch. 13 and Figure 13.1). On the border of the band of slate, an inscription in the Oscan language, unfortunately with lacunae, records the name of the KVAISSTUR, U. KAMP[ANIS] (Ovius Campanus), who had the building built with the money offered to Apollo, by decree of the assembly.

A lucky find in a garden of the so-called House of the Golden Bracelet (or of the Wedding of Alexander and Roxane, VI.17 [*Ins. Occ.*].42) has recently given us, with every likelihood, conspicuous remains of the terracotta decoration of the pediment and frieze. The first, consisting of a series of figures in high relief on rectangular slabs, and recognizable as a pediment from the typical triangular pieces for the outer corners with the still more characteristic reclining figures, depicts the myth of Apollo and Marsyas, the Silenus who, defeated in a music contest, was flayed alive as punishment for his arrogance. In front of the enthroned god kneels as supplicant Olympos, the Phrygian shepherd and pupil of Marsyas, who seeks mercy from the god for his master. In their midst may be a Scythian, in the gesture of transmitting to his companion the god's order to proceed with the punishment of the Silenus (Figure 6.3). On other slabs appear figures of Muses, a Nike, symbolizing the victory of the god, the goddess Artemis, and, reclining, the river Meander. The quality of the terracottas, modeled by hand and conserving significant traces of the rich original polychrome, is very high; theme and style seem to reveal the influence of Asian Hellenism. The continuous frieze, certainly from the same workshop, to judge from the technique and the taste for fleshy plasticism, presents the theme, already well attested in the tradition of Magna Graecia especially at Tarentum, of the frieze with scrollwork with Erotes. The date of the pedimental terracottas, well into the second century BC, their size, and, especially, the highly specific subject, certainly all point to the Temple of Apollo as it was reconstructed in this period. In any case this revival of the cult of Apollo should perhaps be connected—more than to the recovery of archaic traditions or to the importance sometimes attributed to the god by the Oscan communities, such as that of the Mamertines at Messana—to its centrality in the community of the Italic *negotiatores* of Delos (which we know consisted largely of Campanians) in the second century BC.

This rebuilding of the temple, which involved the total destruction of the earlier sanctuary, whose elements were religiously buried within the *area sacra*, was accompanied by a reorganization of the space surrounding and overlooking the piazza and the street that rose from Porta Marina with the construction of a platform containing a cistern and delimited by a tufa staircase. But soon this project was abandoned for the new, more ambitious project of organizing the contiguous piazza of the forum. The forum was now redesigned on the Hellenistic model of the "piazza with temple," porticoed, paved in tufa slabs and with the longitudinal axis centered

Figure 6.3   Terracotta slab with Apollo and Olympos, from the
House of the Golden Bracelet (VI.17 [*Ins. Occ.*].42), probably from the pediment
of the Hellenistic Temple of Apollo.

on the façade of the main temple of the city (Figures 10.8, 12.1, 12.2 and 12.3; cf. Ling, Ch. 9 and Dobbins, Ch. 12). The new temple was sacred to Jupiter, to whom an *area sacra* may have been dedicated earlier nearby. We may have the foundations of an open-air altar under which was found a votive deposit dating to the end of the third century BC and containing terracotta votive objects, architectural terracottas, coins and arms. The temple was built like that of Apollo, with a high podium and a hexastyle façade with Corinthian columns of Nucera tufa (Figure 12.5). The walls, of *opus incertum*, were decorated, in the so-called First Pompeian Style, with faux marble encrustation. In front of the temple stood a large altar, aligned lengthwise with the principal axis of the temple, probably faced with tufa slabs. A row of pillars, becoming gradually thicker from south to north, was constructed on the eastern border of the Sanctuary of Apollo to link the slightly divergent orientations of the new piazza and the sanctuary (Figure 12.16).

   Even the internal space of the Sanctuary of Apollo was also now closed off by a tufa portico and offered an ideal setting for the location of votive monuments (Figure 13.1). Only a few bases of Samnite honorific statues remain, certainly eliminated by the Romans after the Social War, and the bronzes of Apollo and Diana as archers. The former is of better quality than the latter; if our interpretation of an Oscan *graffito* containing the name of a Mummius on the base is correct (cf. Descœudres, Ch. 2), it may come from the plunder of Corinth, sacked and destroyed by the Romans in 146 BC. Recent excavations have brought to light, in the fill of the sanctuary's cisterns and in some votive deposits in the western portico of the forum, some of the objects, notably terracotta statuettes and miniature vases, offered by the faithful to the god. The types are those common in all Hellenistic sanctuaries, generic female figurines of Tanagra type or small animals. They were certainly largely of local production, as the remains of moulds found in the same votive deposits attest. Also from these dumps come interesting remains of the First-Style decoration of the sanctuary, with stucco shields decorated with Apollonian *episemata*, or shield devices, in relief, a crow and the Delphic tripod.

Contemporary with the sanctuaries in the forum area, the sanctuaries of the so-called Triangular Forum, beginning with the Athenaion, also received the attention of the architects charged by the citizen magistrates with the beautification of Pompeii. After restoration in the fourth century BC, the Athenaion evidently had new problems. The roofs were once again dismantled and the old architectural terracottas eliminated; some of the Hercules and Athena antefixes even wound up in the area of the forum, in the terrace fill under the Eumachia Building, together with a great deal of votive material from the same place. The *cella* and the colonnade were probably radically restructured too, to judge from the tufa blocks and column drums that remain. It is also possible that the only surviving metope of the temple, a slab with depiction of the punishment of Ixion, in which the theme and the Greek iconography are rendered in a dissonant Italic stylistic idiom, also dates to this phase rather than to the fourth century BC.

As in the Sanctuary of Apollo, the area around this temple, too, received a Doric colonnade of tufa with architrave of smooth metopes and triglyphs that defined a roughly triangular piazza (whence the modern name). On the side facing the city, the entrance onto the via del tempio di Iside was monumentalized with the construction of an Ionic propylaeum (in part reworked in a later period), a columned entrance with six columns and two engaged columns of slender and elegant proportions arranged scenographically to attract the attention of visitors from the via dell'Abbondanza. In the space in front of the temple an ancient well cut into the lava was now made monumental with a very elegant circular *aedicula* whose eight Doric columns probably supported a conical roof. The architrave bore an Oscan inscription: NI(UMSIS) TREBIIS TR(EBIEIS), MED(DISS) TUV(TIKS) AAMANAFFED, recalls the magistrate of the *touta*, Numerius Trebius, son of Trebius, who promoted the construction.

In the context of Pompeian urban development of this phase, all carefully planned, it is certainly highly significant that right next to the older *palaestra* (VIII.7.29) of the *vereia* (an association of elite Samnites) the Samnite city had admitted a sanctuary consecrated to a foreign goddess such as Isis. The presence of the Egyptian gods so early is not very odd, considering the nature and characteristics of the economic development of Pompeii, founded, as we have said, on the close commercial relationships with the Hellenistic East, established through the emporium of Puteoli. The dominant presence of the Alexandrian element in this current is demonstrated at Puteoli by the construction, before 105 BC, of a Temple of Serapis. The evidence of the Isaeum of Pompeii is, therefore, perfectly parallel. It was used both by the Egyptian colony of artisans and merchants certainly established at Pompeii (numerous typical names are preserved in inscriptions) and by local devotees, who multiplied rapidly, attracted, as people were by the thousands throughout the Mediterranean basin, by this religion's message of salvation. The presence of this first Pompeian Isaeum in the quarter of the gymnasium and its *paideia* provides a key to understanding the notable degree of acceptance of a foreign religion by the Samnite culture of Pompeii and, more in general, of the class of the Italic *negotiatores*. Not much remains of this first Isaeum—some tufa elements reused in the reconstruction of the building undertaken after the earthquake of AD 62. But we can assume that the general appearance of the building, with its peculiar plan probably due to cult reasons, was substantially repeated in the later one. It is possible that some of the sculptures found in the sanctuary adorned the earliest sanctuary buildings. Among the recent finds relative to this cult, a fragment of a small black-glaze bowl, perhaps dating to the first century BC, from a dump outside the Porta di Nola, deserves mention. On it a devotee of Isis, with the typically Alexandrian name of Philadelphos, records in Greek his vow to the "benign gods," a characteristic ritual formula used to designate the triad Horos–Apollo–Harpocrates (. . . *kai theon eueilaton Philadelphos euchen*).

Another sanctuary erected in this quarter in the same period is that which faces the via di Stabia and is attributed to Jupiter Meilichios. Thus identified on the basis of an Oscan inscription found outside the Porta di Stabia, the sanctuary consists of the temple, a small tetrastyle prostyle building, possibly Corinthian, with a monumental staircase on the front and decorated with First-Style paintings and figured capitals—one now lost had the bearded head of a god—and by a small open area preceded by a short two-columned portico added after 62. In the center of the courtyard, aligned lengthwise with the temple, was an elegant altar of Hellenistic style in blocks of tufa decorated with a frieze of triglyphs and metopes and a pulvinus with Ionic volutes. Inside the *cella* were found the late Hellenistic terracotta cult statues, two standing figures, identified as Jupiter and Juno, and a bust of Athena perhaps introduced later; their presence together has suggested that after the earthquake of 62, the Capitoline triad was moved here.

The ancient funerary cult of Zeus Meilichios originated on the Peloponnesus and spread to Sicily and Magna Graecia, whence it probably reached Pompeii. The attribution of the sanctuary to this god is, however, problematic. For one thing, it requires that a cult, which is chthonic by definition, and therefore elsewhere strictly extra-urban, had been moved into the city. For another, its date, which is only the end of the second century BC (or, more probably, considering the use of *opus quasi reticulatum*, the late first century BC), would lead to an anachronistic, late Hellenistic, importation of a Greek cult otherwise typically archaic. Nor are there traces of an earlier cult structure on the same site, as proved by unproductive stratigraphic excavations in the area. I believe that the temple is therefore to be attributed to Asklepios, and have proposed returning to the identification (Winckelmann's) of the male statue as that god, and of the female statue as a Hygieia. An Asklepieion appears, moreover, well established in the quarter of the Theaters, alongside another exotic and salvific sanctuary as an Isaeum (the same is true, for example, at Ampurias in Spain), and more appropriate to the spirit of the times than to the topographical position, intra-urban and marginal at the same time. As for the bust of Athena found here, it is quite possible that after the earthquake of 62, what remained of the cult of the ancient Athenaion, now in ruins in the Triangular Forum, was brought here.

I have proposed, rather, to identify the Sanctuary of Zeus Meilichios as the sacral complex on the same ancient road to Stabiae, but outside the city, which was partially explored in the 1950s, on the *fondo* Iozzino (Figure 28.1, B). Here, a large retaining wall of *opus quadratum* in Sarno limestone encloses some *sacella*. Fragments of *bucchero*, Campanian red-figure pottery and some terracotta statues attest the long life of the sanctuary and the importance of its cults, some certainly chthonic (a clay statue has been identified as a Hekate). We do not know whether this extra-urban sanctuary on the *fondo* Iozzino housed the public cult of Ceres, which the Roman colony seems to have inherited together with that of a Venus Physica from the Samnite city. These temples have definitely not been identified in the city, and it is not impossible that the Samnite Kerres/Ceres here had the features of the Greek Malophoros.

Another sanctuary going back to the pre-Roman period was located in *contrada* Bottaro (Figure 28.1, A), in this same area between the city and the sea. In fact, this sanctuary must have been located, as the sand dunes observed during the excavation indicate, directly on the bank of the lagoon delta where the port of Pompeii was located. The sanctuary was probably dedicated to Poseidon, if an inscription with dedication to Neptune by a freedman of Sextus Pompeius found in the same area can be attributed to its Roman phase; remains of the archaic and Hellenistic deposits, and fragments of the temple building, already destroyed in antiquity, with part of the Oscan inscription dedicating the pavement, have also been found.

We conclude this survey with the small Sanctuary of Dionysus-Liber on the hill of S. Abbondio (Figure 28.1, C). The cult must date back to the archaic period, but the best-documented phase is the Hellenistic, with a small Doric tetrastyle prostyle temple, adorned with a beautiful little tufa pediment in which the god celebrates his sacred marriage with Ariadne. The cult, prohibited in exactly this period in Rome by the *senatus consultus de Bacchanalibus*, shows that it was alive and beloved in this Campanian city, certainly in connection with the flourishing viticulture of the area, not by chance attested already from this period by a local production of Greek-Italic amphorae.

NOTE

1   Maureen B. Fant translated the Italian text.

BIBLIOGRAPHY

Bonghi Jovino, M. (ed.), *Ricerche a Pompei. L'insula 5 della Regio VI dalle origini al 79 d.C.*, Rome, 1984.

Cristofani, M., "La fase 'etrusca' di Pompei," in F. Zevi (ed.), *Pompei*, Naples, 1991, pp. 9–22.

D'Ambrosio, A., *La stipe votiva in località Bottaro*, Naples, 1984.

—— and M. R. Borriello, *Le terrecotte figurate di Pompei*, Rome, 1990.

D'Agostino, B., "Il processo di strutturazione del politico nel mondo osco-lucano. La protostoria," AION 1987, vol. 9, pp. 32ff.

De Caro, S. (ed.), *Alla ricerca di Iside*, Naples, 1993.

——, *Saggi nell'area del tempio di Apollo a Pompei. Scavi stratigrafici di A. Maiuri nel 1931–32 e 1942–43*, Naples, 1986.

——, "La città sannitica, urbanistica e architettura," in F. Zevi (ed.), *Pompei 1*, Naples, 1991, pp. 23–46.

De Waele, J., "De Dorische Tempel op het Forum Triangulare te Pompei," *Hermeneus*, 1982, vol. 54, pp. 27–35.

——, B. D'Agostino, P. S. Lulof (eds), *Tempio dorico del Foro Triangulare di Pompei*, Rome, 2001.

Elia, O. and G. Pugliese Carratelli, "Il santuario dionisiaco di S. Abbondio," in G. Pugliese Carratelli (ed.), *Pompei 79: Studi su Pompei ed Ercolano*, Naples, 1979, pp. 442ff.

Maiuri, A., "Greci ed Etruschi a Pompei," *Atti della Reale Accademia d'Italia. Memorie*, ser. 7, 1943, vol. 4, pp. 121–49 (reprinted in *Alla ricerca di Pompei preromana*, pp. 135–59).

——, *Notizie degli Scavi*, 1942, pp. 253ff.

——, *Alla ricerca di Pompei preromana*, Naples, 1973.

Richardson, L., jr, "The Archaic Doric Temple of Pompeii," *PP*, 1974, vol. 29, pp. 281ff.

Russo, D., *Il tempio di Giove Meilichio a Pompei*, Naples, 1991.

Varone, A., "Saggi stratigrafici nel tempio di Iside," *RivStPom*, 1989, vol. 3, pp. 229ff.

CHAPTER SEVEN

THE URBAN
DEVELOPMENT OF THE
PRE-ROMAN CITY

———— ·◆· ————

Herman Geertman

The origins of the town of Pompeii date back to the archaic period when, sometime between the eighth and sixth centuries BC, an urban nucleus grew up in connection with two sanctuaries, one to Apollo and the other to Minerva or Hercules (cf. De Caro, Ch. 6). The settlement was located on the promontory of a high lava plateau near the mouth of the river Sarno. Only certain elements of this original nucleus were conserved in the later Roman town buried by Vesuvius in AD 79; today these can be seen in the irregular plan of the southwest zone of the town which clearly contrasts with the regular appearance of the northern and eastern zones.

The urban history of Pompeii, or, in other words, the answer to the question of how this city originated and how it developed into its present shape and appearance, is one of the most complicated and difficult aspects with which Pompeian research confronts us.[1] All of us have in mind the layout of the city that was destroyed in AD 79: a city with a more or less oval shape, situated on a lava promontory, with its civic center in the southwestern zone, urban areas with a regular appearance in the north and east, apparently planned and intersected by large arteries, and all surrounded by the city walls.

At the beginning of the twentieth century, only part of all this was known, namely the structures within the western zone, the outline of the principal roads in the eastern zone, the gates and the city walls. Two things lie at the base of the discussions that have been going on since that time on the city's development. On the one hand, the recognition of the so-called *Altstadt* by Haverfield in 1913, and on the other hand the excavations that since 1910 have uncovered a large part of the eastern zone of the city—the work of Spinazzola and later of Maiuri. It was these excavations that allowed for an analysis of the city as a whole and made it possible to try to reconstruct the origins and the history of its urban structure. This was done in 1940 by Armin von Gerkan, in a brief and fundamental study of a strictly archaeological character dealing with the material evidence in situ. Following Haverfield, Gerkan also recognizes an *Altstadt* and a *Neustadt*. The suburban roads around the *Altstadt*, the pre-Samnite city, would have offered, in a later period under Samnite rule, a starting point for the expansion of the urban area and the construction of new walls and gates (Figure 7.1; Map 2).[2]

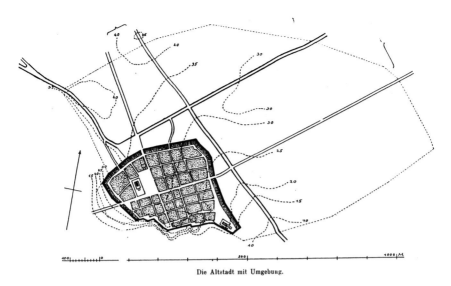

Die Altstadt mit Umgebung.

Figure 7.1   Pompeii: reconstruction of the first town and of the main roads
in the surrounding area by A. von Gerkan, *Stadtplan*, Pl. 2. The *Altstadt* is the shaded area.

Gerkan convincingly demonstrates the ungrounded nature of Fiorelli's 1858 thesis
that the entire urban plan was the product of a ritual Roman *limitatio* for which the
via Stabiana and the via di Nola were the *cardo* and *decumanus*. Fiorelli's thesis, which
was the basis for his division of the site into nine *regiones* (Figure 7.2),[3] was later
developed further by Nissen and Mau, and was still defended as late as 1937 by
Antonio Sogliano.[4] It is only in the case of the *Altstadt* that Gerkan admits with
some particular reservations, the possibility of a *limitatio*.

Gerkan considers the *Neustadt* to be the product of one single project. He explains
the differences in the forms, dimensions and orientations of the *insulae* by the relief
of the site and the presence of suburban roads. The form of the extended city is
rectangular—Figure 7.3 shows my interpretation of this concept. According to Gerkan,
the *insulae* are also rectangular, a solution imitating the well-known city of Naples
and applied in Pompeii to the extent that was permitted by the circumstances.
However, in the new situation, the original old city maintained its central function.
So much for Gerkan's research. After his publication, the thesis of the original presence
of an *Altstadt* and of suburban roads has not been seriously contested even though
several scholars, such as Hans Eschebach and John Ward Perkins, have proposed
alternatives to single concrete solutions.[5] The unitary nature of the so-called *Neustadt*
is also generally accepted. The expansion of the city would have been the product
of one single action. The chronology of the observed phenomena and, related to these,
the Greek nature of the new layout, have remained more problematic and discussed.

In 1956, this last aspect was taken up again by Ferdinando Castagnoli.[6] He assigns
the expansion of the city to the period after the Battle of Cumae (474 BC), when the
Greek presence was dominant in the coastal zone of Campania. The regular layout
of the new city of Pompeii, based essentially, according to Castagnoli, on a system

83

Pompeii

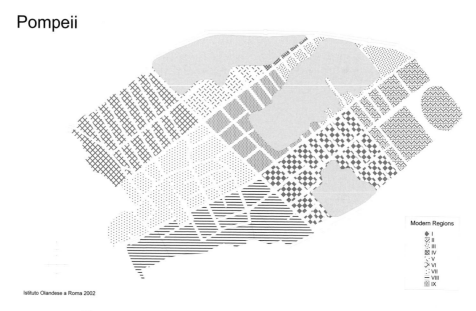

Istituto Olandese a Roma 2002

Figure 7.2   Pompeii: division of the urban area into nine regions
by G. Fiorelli (1858).

of principal orthogonal streets and rectangular *insulae*, fits into the Greek Hippodamian urbanization of the fifth and fourth centuries BC.

A fundamental critique to this appreciation of the phenomena was presented in 1989 by Paolo Sommella.[7] The proportions of the shapes of the *insulae* form his starting point. He points out that these proportions do not comply with those associated with Greek urbanization from the sixth to the fourth centuries, but are similar to the much less extreme proportions of the Hellenistic period, and show a likeness to the adaptations that this new urbanization was undergoing in the Italian, and especially Roman environment. In other words, he brings forward the date of the expansion of Pompeii to the late fourth and third centuries BC, when Rome stabilized its power in south Italy.[8]

The walls are a separate subject of discussion. While Gerkan and Castagnoli considered the first phase of the walls to belong to the project of the *Neustadt*, Sommella accepts the results of the excavations by Stefano De Caro. These have surprisingly revealed the existence of a first course of the city walls, executed in *pappamonte* tuff, which dates back to the first half of the sixth century BC, when there was still no trace of a *Neustadt*. De Caro concluded that, at one time, the *Altstadt* comprised within its new defensive system a first zone of the surrounding agricultural territory where agricultural activity and herds would be protected.[9] The motive for this may have been to provide protection from Greek or Etruscan expansion, or it may have been due to internal tensions between the indigenous populations of the region. Moreover, his investigations made evident that this wall followed the same line as the still standing later walls that we know.[10] According to De Caro, the new area within the walls remained agricultural for a long time and was not systematically built over.

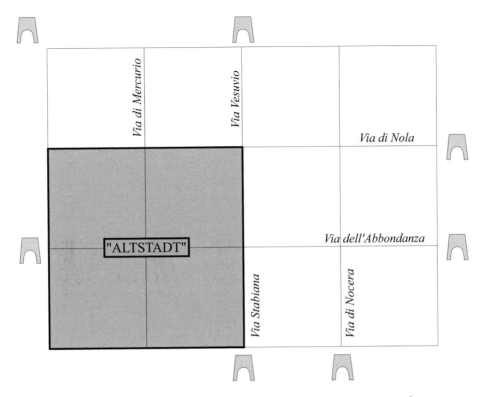

Figure 7.3 Plan of Pompeii interpreted according to the concept of rectangular and orthogonal design.

If the situation was, indeed, like that reconstructed by De Caro, this implies that we should distinguish between two separate phenomena that evolve from different moments in history: (1) an expansion of the city that consisted of the enclosure of an open area for agricultural purposes, and (2) the gradual building of new quarters in the agricultural area to produce what is frequently called the *Neustadt*. This new knowledge inevitably leads to another question: If the building up of the agricultural area is not linked to the original expansion of the *Altstadt*, at what point is it necessary and justified to link it to one of the later phases, such as the Samnite phase, of the walls?

This question is closely related to research on the urbanistic development of the city that I have conducted, together with others, in Pompeii.[11] The questions that lie at the base of this research are: What is the nature of the extension of the town outside the ancient core of Pompeii? Is it the result of one unitary plan that led to the creation of city walls, gates and a regulated network of new streets and quarters, as Gerkan and Castagnoli, among others, thought? Or is the extension of the *Altstadt* the effect of a spontaneous development that was not dictated by a regulated plan? Or, as a third possibility, can one recognize a stratification in the phenomena that unites the two previous options?

The subject of our research is the extension of the town outside the ancient core of Pompeii. Such an extension meant the creation both of a new network of streets and of new quarters. Investigation started from the following working hypotheses: the urban expansion had a systematic character that was decided by public authorities; given the several notable differences between the new quarters, the latter developed sequentially rather than at one single moment (in other words, the urban context that we see today is considered to be the result of one or more regulated plans); such plans are identifiable through the analysis of metrological phenomena and through observations concerning topography and construction.

To test these hypotheses, three levels of data have been gathered. The first level concerns the layout of the principal streets, the position of the gates of the city and their relation to the surrounding territory; the second level concerns the individual quarters and their articulation; the third level contains the original partition of each *insula* and its first (that is, the oldest recognizable) construction. Summarizing the still provisional results of the research one may present the following picture.

GATES AND STREET NETWORKS

The network of streets that structured the new urban area was formed from five axes, two going from east to west, and three from north to south (Figure 7.4). The position and orientation of the principal north–south axis and of the northern east–west axis are dictated by the altimetric condition of the terrain. Starting from the crossroads of these two axes, the principal north–south axis, the via Stabiana and its continuation on the via Vesuvio, was measured out into three equal parts which fixed the exact position of the southern transversal axis, the continuation of the via dell'Abbondanza. The northern transversal axis, from the crossroads with the via Consolare to the Porta di Nola, has the same length as the via Stabiana between the two gates, while half of this length is found in the tract of the south axis which connects the via Stabiana with the via di Nocera. One third of this length is found not only in the three tracts of the via Stabiana but also in the via di Mercurio, principal axis of region VI. The regular position and calculation of the principal roads make it clear that this grid was the result of an act of planning.

If the dimensions are, indeed, as they have been described above, this implies that the course of the walls, at the principal points of the gates, is part of the supposed regulated plan; it also implies that the described network of main roads is part of the original expansion of the urban area, then still in its agricultural phase. At this point one can usefully introduce the observations made by Fausto Zevi, who has brought to our attention that the orientation of the via di Mercurio and of the entire region VI are related to the orientation discovered in the area outside the walls to the north of the city (Figure 28.2). In the near future, therefore, attention will need to focus not only on the development of the city, but also on its ties with the organization of the surrounding territory.[12]

THE EXPANSION OF THE *ALTSTADT*

The building up of the new area within the walls appears to have taken place considerably later than the enclosure of the space itself. A first phenomenon that should be discussed in this context is the relation between the gates and the principal streets of the expanded area (i.e., what would become the *Neustadt*). The position of

Pompeii

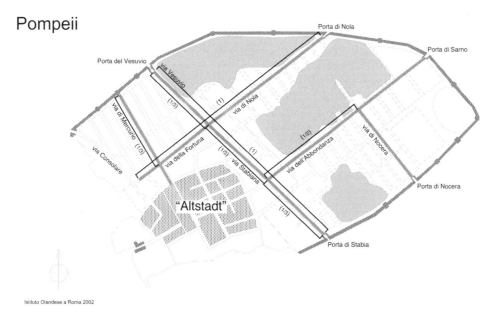

Istituto Olandese a Roma 2002

Figure 7.4 Pompeii: first town, wall and gates; main roads of the agricultural area, later transformed into streets of the built-up town.

the five gates in the city wall corresponds to the network of streets, but it is surprising that none of these gates is really on axis with the street that passes through it. It seems likely that the first plan saw the construction of a fortification wall and a regular division of the area inside the walls, comprising the positioning of the main routes and the gates. When, at a later date, the agricultural area within the walls was converted into a built-up area and proper streets were laid down, the existing situation was taken as a point of departure but the precise course of the main streets along straight lines was defined by the rules governing good building.

Due to the absence of sufficiently extensive excavations, the exact chronology of this second phase is still uncertain. Somewhere in the Samnite period, between the fourth and the second centuries BC when Campania was increasingly influenced by the newly emerging power of Rome, the existing built-up area of the town was expanded by the addition of new quarters.[13] This aspect will be further discussed below. A second question is whether the seemingly systematic character was the result of one unitary plan or of more regulated plans undertaken in phases. Generally, one is inclined to put most emphasis on the similarities of the rectangular shapes of the *insulae* in the different quarters, while the deviant shape, more or less square, which is found on the east side of the via Stabiana, can be explained by assuming pre-existing structures of some kind at this point near the Porta di Stabia. Our research, however, has led us to different conclusions. Three separate systems of division and orientation can be distinguished: the northwest zone which has the via di Mercurio as its axis, the orientation of which is determined by the forum; the zone of the squared *insulae*, the orientation of which has been determined by the north–south axis of the via Stabiana; and finally the east zone which has the via di Nocera as its

Pompeii

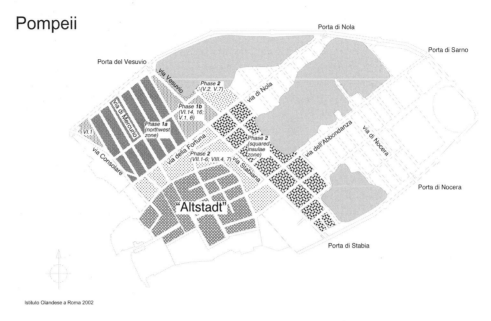

Figure 7.5 First town; northern and central extensions of the built-up area.

axis and perpendicularly the via di Nola and the via dell'Abbondanza. To find an answer to the subsequent question of whether or not they were created contemporaneously, particular attention was paid to the presence of two clusters of *insulae* of irregular shape to the north and east side of the squared *insulae* along the via Stabiana (Figure 7.5). Close examination of how these clusters connect the three main zones to each other has offered the possibility of establishing a relative chronology for their layout and excludes the possibility that they were contemporary, even though they may all have been laid out over a short time-span. The sequence starts with the quarter north of the forum (region VI), where twelve *insulae* in the form of parallelograms were planned on the two sides of the via di Mercurio. Subsequently, to the east of these, four *insulae* of a different shape were added along the via Vesuvio (VI.14 and 16; V.1 and 6).

In a second phase, a double series of *insulae* was planned to the east of the old city, whose square form was determined by the strong north–south slope of the ground. The zone became fully connected with the northwest quarter by the addition of two other *insulae* (V.2 and 7) of exceptionally large width to fill up the open space at the other side of the via di Nola. More or less contemporary to the described process of expansion must have been the building up of the area between the old city and the two new quarters (VII.1–6; VIII.4 and 7). The fact that some of the streets here are not straight demonstrates that older streets already existed and that the building was conducted only to a certain extent as part of a regular plan.

The two new quarters formed a belt around the old city. This situation, of a built-up area to the west and an open area to the east, was intended to exist for a certain period as seems to be suggested by a curious and possibly significant feature. The façades of the last two houses of the last two blocks along the via di Nola (V.2.18

88

and IX.5.11) do not respect the regular frontline of the preceding houses and blocks but protrude forward, narrowing the street from thirty feet to twenty-three feet so as to form a sort of closure of the street and the built-up area. Immediately beyond this point the frontline of the block on the south side of the street recedes significantly, about ten feet, creating a sort of *largo* between the first two blocks of the eastern expansion. Only further down does the street return to its normal width. A reasonable explanation might be that at this point of the via di Nola, immediately outside the last houses of the built-up area, market activities had developed and that this situation still lives on in the deviating façades.

It is not known when the large eastern quarter was added. The new quarter has *insulae* of a regular rectangular form and streets that intersect them at right angles (Figure 7.6). Presumably this whole area to the east was destined to be covered by *insulae*, but later, in the first century BC, parts gave way to the amphitheater and other particular buildings.[14] The new quarter was connected to the already existing zones of the town by the insertion of a series of *insulae* of irregular form. It might be argued that the creation of the eastern quarter was previous to, or contemporaneous with, the creation of the zone of squared blocks along the via Stabiana and that the connecting irregular blocks offered the necessary deviant orientation for the squared blocks. This hypothetical sequence of events, however, is not acceptable because it does not explain the curious configuration of the *insulae* V.1–2–3 and is even contradicted by it. The same difficulty is encountered when supposing a sequence in which the creation of the squared blocks is considered previous to, or contemporaneous with, the creation of the northern quarter.

The final conclusion is that the regulated unitary masterplan that was behind the building-up of the *Neustadt*, where there was previously nothing, never existed and

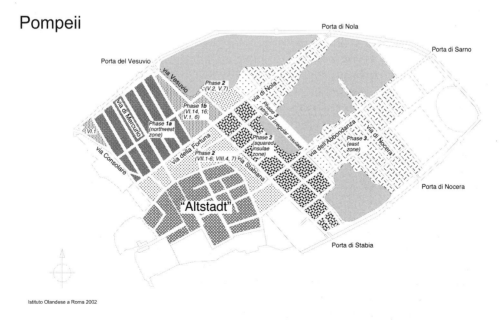

Figure 7.6   First town; northern, central and eastern extensions of the built-up area.

that, rather, we are dealing with a series of regulated measures, separated in time and programmed and decided upon by the community of the city of Pompeii.[15] The earliest phase leads back, as we have seen, to the sixth century when a large area of *c.*66 ha was enclosed and a wall, gates and a network of main roads were constructed. The fact that this network was regular and that it later became the starting point for the systematic building up of the area, are indications that the control over this area had always been, without interruption, communal. We can also assume that the exploitation of the soil was mainly concerned with the production of cereals and that a rotation system was applied that also included the grazing of cattle. It appears that this area outside the *Altstadt* also knew the development of sparse habitation. Traces of structures previous to the construction of the *insulae* have been found in several places; the orientation of these structures generally follows the main division of this area.[16] The chronology of the construction of the *insulae* is a hard question to answer. The sequence of three phases presented above excluded the possibility of them being contemporaneous, but gives no information on the time difference between the construction phases, which may have been very short, and even less on the reasons for the expansion. Are we dealing with the immigration of new groups of people, and can this process be reasonably connected to specific historical events?[17] Or are we dealing with internal social-economic developments and the birth of new civic groups?[18] Or was the expansion the effect of a social and political articulation of the community and not of a demographic and urbanistic evolution?[19] None of these questions can be answered without a program of deliberate excavations (cf. Jones and Robinson, Ch. 25).[20] Some considerations of a more general nature can, however, be formulated. Before the third century BC, only sparse habitation is found in the whole of the agricultural area. Towards the end of the fourth century BC, or perhaps shortly after that, the city wall is reconstructed extensively, during which process the city gate at the end of the via di Mercurio was dismantled (Figures 11.2 and 11.3). If we connect these facts to the building up of the northern zone of the city, it means that this area was designed shortly after 300 BC.[21] In a next phase, probably not long afterwards as was indicated above, the area east of the via Stabiana was added. Both cases concerned an area where the new arrangement partly needed to be adjusted to the already existing situation of gates, main roads and commercial and agricultural structures. A proposition has been made to connect the building-up of the eastern area with the destruction of Nocera by Hannibal and the settling of the inhabitants of Nocera in Pompeii. One could doubt the likelihood of giving up the protected agricultural area in times when the besieging of the city was feared. However, the expansion in the eastern direction cannot have taken place long after the beginning of the second century BC. The most recent studies in Region I show that the construction of this area with *insulae* was, in that period, a fact.[22]

THE DIVISION OF THE INDIVIDUAL *INSULAE*

The 120 or more *insulae* of Pompeii are not individual blocks separated by a network of streets. Rather, one must think of urban zones, surrounded by a network of principal streets, which functioned as quarters. One of the methods to study them as contextual units is to attempt to identify the original partition of each *insula* in order to define both the technical criteria that were adopted by the surveyors of the land, and the social and economic criteria that guided the municipal authority in the partition of lots, and the buyers in their choice of future property. At first sight, identifying the original partition of *insulae* seems a hard task. Buildings have often been restructured, divided into different properties, or joined with other properties to form a single large complex. Fortunately, reality is less dramatic. The studies of Salvatore Ciro Nappo in Region I and the result of our own studies have confirmed that this type of research is useful (cf. Nappo, Ch. 23).[23] The methods of research come from different angles: in the first place by an attentive observation of the wall structures, which often preserve, however many later alterations have taken place, signs of the original situation; second, by an accurate metrological analysis of the façades of the *insulae*; third by the signs of property to which the sidewalks in front of the houses also belong. In many cases these appear to respect the divisions of ownership. Among other things it may be the case that the surface of the sidewalk or the fabric of the borders change exactly in line with a partition wall between two properties, or a block may have been placed at that point, perpendicular to the façade. Evidently, the arrangement and the maintenance of the space in front of the façade were the task of the private individual, and, furthermore, not only the task but also the right, even though these spaces were obviously not part of the private property.[24] What has been mentioned above reminds us once again that the ambivalent space of the surrounding street plays a role in the definition of the *insula* as a contextual unity.

Once an *insula* has been studied by these methods, one tries to reconstruct its original organization, or at least the oldest recognizable division. Some observations concerning the *insulae* VI.1 and VI.14, situated on the crossroads of the via Vesuvio and the via di Nola, will be illustrative (Figure 7.7). The situation of *insula* V.1 in AD 79 is characterized by a rather regular division into three zones, all of which comprised a large house with a transversal part at the back and a smaller house, whether or not temporarily connected to the large house, which may be considered as dependent on the first and even originally built as a property for rent (Figures 7.7 and 7.8).[25] It is tempting to interpret a situation this regular as systematic and intended, as it is also tempting to regard it as original. However, the study of the wall structures and the sidewalks and the analysis of the metric data bring us to a different conclusion. The original partition (Figure 7.9) presents a regular parallelogram of 142 × 330 Oscan feet, divided into three zones.[26] The central zone from the beginning offers space to three plots of 55, 47.5 and 47.5 ft (150 ft in total), with large houses situated on the via Vesuviana that had a deep garden with a rear exit onto the small street to the east. Along the via di Nola, perpendicular to the others, another plot is located, with the same depth of 140 ft, but wider still, 60 ft, also covered by a house with a deep garden and a rear exit onto the alley on the east side. On average each of these four houses covers an area of about 16 percent of the total surface. The six houses that take up the remaining space are much smaller, and none covers more than 6 percent of the total surface. As far as can be deduced from the oldest wall structures, the six houses were habitations and their construction was independent, unrelated to the neighboring large houses. The situation that presents itself for a study of the original policies of division and assignment (Figure 7.9) turns out to be essentially different from the situation of building and ownership that was present in the first century of our era (Figure 7.8). The reconstructed scheme

Figure 7.7   Plan of *insulae* VI.13, VI.14 and V.1 (excerpted from Map 3).

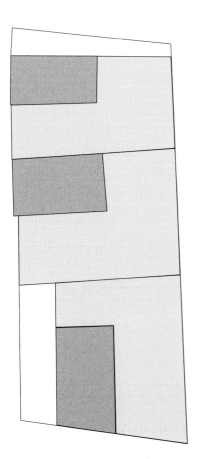

Figure 7.8   *Ins.* V.1: configuration of the main property limits in AD 79.

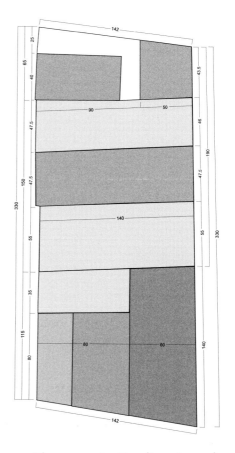

Figure 7.9   *Ins.* V.1: dimensions and articulation of the area; reconstruction of the original plots and property limits.

of land division shows in the first place that a rigidly unitary assignment of plots is clearly absent and that, to a certain extent, the division follows the needs and economic possibilities of the first owners and builders of the plots. Second, it shows that the division conformed to social and commercial factors. The concentration at the crossroads on the southwest corner of three smaller houses suggests commercial activities and the location of the other smaller houses on the least important north side of the *insula* may imply the presence of workshops. *Insula* VI.14, located on the opposite side of the via di Vesuvio offers another example of the same phenomena. As discussed above the irregular trapezoidal shape of the *insula* is caused by the fact that the *insula* was created to fill in the space that was left open between the regular blocks of region VI and the continuation of the via Stabiana. Metrological analysis of its dimensions and articulation suggests a close relationship with *insula* V.1 (Figures 7.10 and 7.11). The south façade reveals that the large surface that had to be organized and divided, was conceived ideally as a double *insula* to which was given twice the width of 140 feet. This dimension does not occur elsewhere and distinguishes the two *insulae* from their more narrow western neighbors in Region VI. The greater houses of VI.14 are

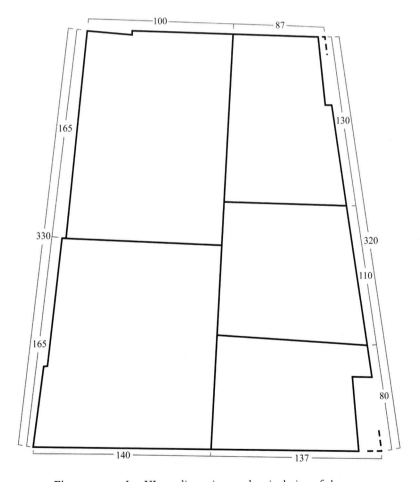

Figure 7.10 *Ins.* VI.14: dimensions and articulation of the area.

Figure 7.11 *Ins.* VI.14 and *ins.* V.1: reconstruction of the original partition into plots.

located in the central and southern part of the *insula*, four of them in front of similar houses in V.1. Here, too, the southeast corner at the crossroads and the northern side of the *insula* offer a different picture, similar to what is seen in V.1. It is a phenomenon that recurs in many varieties all over the city. Its consistent occurrence may help to define the nature and function of the *insulae* placed within the context of streets and neighborhoods. The subject will be presented and discussed extensively in the final publication of the project.

NOTES

1 Translation from Italian by Noor Winckel and Joanne Berry. Illustrations: Figures 7.2, 7.4–7.6, H. Knikman; Figures 7.3, 7.8–7.11, P. Deunhouwer. The text presented here is a re-elaboration of two previous contributions and takes into account the discussion that followed the presentation of the latter at the Naples conference, November 1998: Herman Geertman, "The layout of the city and its history. The Dutch project," in J. Berry (ed.), *Unpeeling Pompeii. Studies in Region I of Pompeii*, Milan, 1998, pp. 17–25; Herman Geertman, "Lo studio della città antica. Vecchi e nuovi approcci," in P. G. Guzzo (ed.), *Pompei. Scienza e Società. 250° Anniversario degli Scavi di Pompei.* Convegno Internazionale, Naples, November 25–27, 1998, Milan, 2001, pp. 131–5.

2 F. J. Haverfield, *Ancient Town-Planning*, Oxford, 1913, pp. 63–6; A. von Gerkan, *Der Stadtplan von Pompeji*, Berlin, 1940.

3 Fiorelli's division of the town into IX *regiones*, although no longer accepted as an explanation of the ancient urban structure, is still in use for practical and administrative reasons: I.1.1 indicates Region I, block (*insula*) 1, entrance from the street 1.

4 A. Sogliano, *Pompei nel suo sviluppo storico. Pompei preromana (dalle origini all'anno 80 av.C.)*, Rome, 1937, pp. 38ff. For the propositions and analyses by Giuseppe Fiorelli, Heinrich Nissen and August Mau, see L. García y García, "Divisione Fiorelliana e piano regolatore di Pompei," *Opuscula Pompeiana*, 1993, vol. 3, pp. 55–70.

5 H. Eschebach, *Die städtebauliche Entwicklung des antiken Pompeji*, Heidelberg, 1970, pp. 17ff., Abb.14; J. B. Ward Perkins, *Cities of Ancient Greece and Italy: Planning in Classical Antiquity*, New York, 1974, pp. 24ff. and 118ff., fig. 41; idem, "Note di topografia e urbanistica," in F. Zevi (ed.), *Pompei 79*, Naples, 1979, pp. 25–39, fig. 9.

6 F. Castagnoli, *Ippodamo di Mileto e l'urbanistica a pianta ortogonale*, Rome, 1956, pp. 26–34.

7 P. Sommella, *Urbanistica Pompeiana. Nuovi momenti di studio*, Rome, 1989, pp. 17–26, reprinted in: *Neapolis, II. Temi progettuali*, Rome, 1994 (Soprintendenza Archeologica di Pompei, Monografie 7), pp. 179–88.

8 Cf. on this subject also S. De Caro, "Lo sviluppo urbanistico di Pompei," *Atti e Memorie della Società Magna Grecia*, 1992, vol. n.s. 3, 1, pp. 67–90, tavv. iii–viii.

9 S. De Caro, "Nuove indagini sulle fortificazioni di Pompei," *AIONArchStAnt*, 1985, vol. 7, pp. 75–114, spec. 109.

10 De Caro "Nuove indagine"; P. G. Guzzo, "Alla ricerca della Pompei sannitica," in *Studi sull'Italia dei Sanniti*, Milan, 2000, pp. 107–17. See also the discussion in Guzzo (ed.), *Pompei. Scienza e Società*, p. 159 (F. Coarelli) and p. 161 (H. Geertman).

11 The project runs under the care of the University of Leiden, The Dutch Institute at Rome and the Netherlands Organization for Scientific Research. Members of the team: Herman Geertman (director), Hans Knikman, Natasja Rabouw, Catherine Saliou, Astrid Schoonhoven, Noor Winckel.

12 F. Zevi, "Urbanistica di Pompei," in *La regione sotterrata dal Vesuvio. Studi e prospettive* (Atti del convegno internazionale nov. 1979), Naples, 1982, pp. 353–65. See also De Caro, "Lo sviluppo urbanistico," p. 89.

13 Guzzo, "Alla ricerca della Pompei sannitica," pp. 107–17. See also the discussion in Guzzo (ed.), *Pompei. Scienza e Società*, p. 159 (F. Coarelli).

14 The eastern part, near the via di Nocera, has been altered profoundly. The image of a city not completely filled in and still green in the southeastern part is the situation of the final period, but there was a previous time when this situation was definitely different, see for instance A. De Simone, "Le insulae su via di Nocera, regiones I e II," in *Restaurare Pompei*, Milan, 1990, pp. 111–20; S. Nappo, "Alcuni esempi di tipologie di case popolari della fine III, inizio II secolo a.C. a Pompei," *Rivista di Studi Pompeiani*, 1993–94, vol. 6, pp. 77–104; House I.16.7 may serve as another example. The façade has been constructed in *opus quadratum* of large blocks of limestone, perfectly regular. Some of the blocks have been placed in such a way that they form three splayed windows. This in itself is not peculiar, as such windows are familiar features of *opus quadratum* façades, however, these windows are positioned about 1.50 m above the present threshold, while their normal position is at a height of 2.70–3.30 m. The façade continues beneath the street level, still covered by its plaster, which means that at this point the original level of the house presumably lies two rows of limestone blocks, about 1.30–1.40 m, underneath the present threshold. Little has remained of this level of construction in this zone.

15 Or maybe by the Nucerian League to which Pompeii belonged; cf. Guzzo, "Alla ricerca della Pompei sannitica," pp. 107–17.

16 E.g., a rectangular structure, slightly out of axis, in the southeast corner of *insula* I.9.

17 S. C. Nappo, "Urban transformation at Pompeii in the late 3rd and early 2nd c. BC," in R. Laurence and A. Wallace-Hadrill (eds), *Domestic Space in the Roman World: Pompeii and beyond*, 1997 (JRA Suppl. Ser. no. 22), pp. 91–120, proposes to connect the eastern expansion to the displacements of people during the Hannibalic wars at the end of the third century BC.

18 M. Torelli, "Conclusioni," in Guzzo (ed.), *Pompei. Scienza e Società*, p. 150.

19 A. Carandini, "Nuovi progetti, nuove domande, nuovi metodi," in Guzzo (ed.), *Pompei, Scienza e Società*, pp. 127–9. Carandini considers the possibility that the whole of the walled area knew sparse habitation in the earliest period and that the so-called *Altstadt* should also be considered as part of the series of new living-areas, reflecting a new political arrangement within the

community. This thesis is attractive for its simplicity but the contrast between the so-called *Altstadt* and the so-called *Neustadt* is too great not to derive from significant physical circumstances.

20 As hoped for by H. Geertman in Guzzo (ed.), *Pompei. Scienza e Società*, p. 135, and by F. Coarelli, ibid., p. 159.

21 A. V. Schoonhoven, *Metrology and Meaning in Pompeii. The Urban Arrangement of Regio VI*, Ph.D. diss., University of Leiden 2003, published as Studi della Soprintendenza Archeologica di Pompei, vol. 20 (Rome, 2006), chapter 2.2.

22 Berry (ed.), *Unpeeling Pompeii*. Cf. P. G. Guzzo, "Alla ricerca della Pompei sannitica," pp. 107–17, esp. p. 112.

23 Nappo, "Urban transformation at Pompeii in the late 3rd and early 2nd c. BC," pp. 91–120; H. Geertman, "The layout of the city and its history. The Dutch project," pp. 17–25; C. Saliou, "Les trottoirs de Pompéi: une première approche," *BABesch* 74, 1999, pp. 161–218; Schoonhoven, *Metrology and Meaning in Pompeii*, chapter 2.2.

24 Saliou, "Les trottoirs de Pompéi," pp. 161–218.

25 The present names of the three large houses are the House of the Little Bull (V.1.7), House of L. Caecilius Iucundus (V.1.26) and the House of the Greek Epigrams (V.1.18).

26 As far as the conversion of the metric data is concerned, it has to be noted that the measurements of the *insula* as a whole, as well as the values of the division seem to be very precise. The Oscan foot normally varies between 27.40 and 27.70 cm. The average value that came out of the analysis of the partition of *Insula* V.1 is 27.534 cm. The western façade of the *insula*, ideally measuring 330 ft, measures 329.37 ft (90.69 m), while the central zone, ideally 150 ft, measures 149.92 ft (41.28 m, outer walls included). Also in the case of the façades of the three houses that occupy this central zone, one finds values close to round numbers: 46.92 + 47.50 + 55.50 (obviously ideally 47.5 + 47.5 + 55). Generally we notice that the values of the broad divisions tend to be more precise than those of the single façades, where variations may occur such as 39 + 41 + 42 + 38, together 160 ft. This does not automatically mean that the land surveyors were more precise than the builders. Where the situation is clear and not disturbed by later interventions, it often seems that the variations in width have mostly to do with the measurement of the surface of the single plots or with the property of the dividing walls.

BIBLIOGRAPHY

Carandini, A., "Nuovi progetti, nuove domande, nuovi metodi," in P. G. Guzzo (ed.), *Pompei. Scienza e Società. 250° Anniversario degli Scavi di Pompei*, Convegno Internazionale, Naples, November 25–27, 1998, Milan, 2001, pp. 127–9.

Castagnoli, F., *Ippodamo di Mileto e l'urbanistica a pianta ortogonale*, Rome, 1956, pp. 26–34.

De Caro, S., "Lo sviluppo urbanistico di Pompei," *Atti e Memorie della Società Magna Grecia*, 1992, vol. n.s. 3, 1, pp. 67–90.

——, "Nuove indagini sulle fortificazioni di Pompei," *AIONArchStAnt*, 1985, vol. 7, pp. 75–114.

De Simone, A., "Le insulae su via di Nocera, regiones I e II," in *Restaurare Pompei*, Milan, 1990, pp. 111–20.

Eschebach, H., *Die städtebauliche Entwicklung des antiken Pompeji*, Heidelberg, 1970.

García y García, L., "Divisione Fiorelliana e piano regolatore di Pompei," *Opuscula Pompeiana*, 1993, vol. 3, pp. 55–70.

Geertman, H., "Lo studio della città antica. Vecchi e nuovi approcci," in P. G. Guzzo (ed.), *Pompei. Scienza e Società. 250° Anniversario degli Scavi di Pompei*. Convegno Internazionale, Naples, November 25–27, 1998, Milan, 2001, pp. 131–5.

——, "The layout of the city and its history. The Dutch project," in J. Berry (ed.), *Unpeeling Pompeii. Studies in Region I of Pompeii*, Milan, 1998, pp. 17–25.

Guzzo, P. G., "Alla ricerca della Pompei sannitica," in *Studi sull'Italia dei Sanniti*, Milan, 2000, pp. 107–17.

Haverfield, F. J., *Ancient Town-Planning*, Oxford, 1913, pp. 63–6.

Laurence, R. and A. Wallace-Hadrill (eds), *Domestic Space in the Roman World: Pompeii and beyond* (JRA Suppl. Ser. no. 22), Portsmouth, 1997 .

Nappo, S. C., "Alcuni esempi di tipologie di case popolari della fine III, inizio II secolo a.C. a Pompei," *Rivista di Studi Pompeiani*, 1993–94, vol. 6, pp. 77–104.

——, "Urban transformation at Pompeii in the late 3rd and early 2nd c. BC," in R. Laurence and A. Wallace-Hadrill (eds), *Domestic Space in the Roman World: Pompeii and beyond* (JRA Suppl. Ser. no. 22), Portsmouth, 1997, pp. 91–120.

Saliou, C., "Les trottoirs de Pompéi: une première approche," *BABesch* 74, 1999, pp. 161–218.

Schoonhoven, A. V., *Metrology and Meaning in Pompeii. The Urban Arrangement of Regio VI*, Ph.D. diss., University of Leiden 2003, published as Studi della Soprintendenza Archeologica di Pompei, vol. 20 (Rome, 2006).

Sogliano, A., *Pompei nel suo sviluppo storico. Pompei preromana (dalle origini all'anno 80 av.C.)*, Rome, 1937.

Sommella, P., *Urbanistica Pompeiana. Nuovi momenti di studio*, Rome, 1989, pp. 17–26, reprinted in: *Neapolis, II. Temi progettuali*, Rome, 1994 (Soprintendenza Archeologica di Pompei. Monografie 7), pp. 179–88.

Torelli, M., "Conclusioni," in P. G. Guzzo (ed.), *Pompei. Scienza e Società*, p. 150.

von Gerkan, A., *Der Stadtplan von Pompeji*, Berlin, 1940.

Ward Perkins, J. B., *Cities of Ancient Greece and Italy: Planning in Classical Antiquity*, New York, 1974, pp. 24ff. and 118ff., Figure 41.

——, "Note di topografia e urbanistica," in F. Zevi (ed.), *Pompei 79*, Naples, 1979, pp. 25–39.

Zevi, F., "Urbanistica di Pompei," in F. Zevi (ed.), *La regione sotterrata dal Vesuvio. Studi e prospettive* (Atti del convegno internazionale nov. 1979), Naples, 1982, pp. 353–65.

CHAPTER EIGHT

BUILDING MATERIALS, CONSTRUCTION TECHNIQUES AND CHRONOLOGIES

—— ·◆· ——

Jean-Pierre Adam

Because of its prosperity and its privileged status as a meeting place for Greek, Etruscan and Roman cultures, Pompeii is an indispensable reference point for the study of Roman architecture, as much in the area of building methods as in programmatic urban planning.[1]

Even so, the architectural richness of this small provincial city, disclosed to us by the tragic but providential accident of Vesuvius's eruption, must be qualified: except for its amphitheater, Pompeii did not have significantly large monuments on the scale of other examples of Roman architecture. The smallish size of the town's architecture, which is an advantage in interpreting and understanding its buildings, is due to the minor importance of the town itself, and also to the fact that it was bypassed in the big building schemes of the Empire, which often razed the edifices of the Republic. This adds to its interest: Pompeii retains an urban architecture that spans the period between the fourth century BC to AD 79, and yet there is still about one-third of the city to be revealed.

The building materials used at Pompeii are astonishing in their variety and provide visitors with a wide range of textures and colors, even though the picturesque ruins are for the most part made of wall-surfaces that were intended to be plastered.

ASHLAR CONSTRUCTION

The region around Pompeii has two kinds of stone: limestone and volcanic rock. The local limestone is the sedimentary deposit of the Sarno valley (*calcare di Sarno*), which has botanical fossils and alveoles giving it a rough texture when cut. This limestone was mainly used for ashlar masonry in large blocks and in *opus incertum*, and was the material used in the earliest Pompeian construction method; this chronological period, from 425 to 200 BC, has been called the "limestone era" or the "first Samnite Period." The sequence from the "limestone period" to the "tufa period" which followed it is based almost entirely on the building sequences of the city walls. In fact, because the original rampart enclosing the western sector of the town has disappeared, the greater enclosure—still in place in AD 79—went through several phases: Sarno limestone in a dressed ashlar masonry, then a second phase with tufa blocks (called

Figure 8.1 House of the Surgeon (VI.1.10), one of the earliest houses in the town, built of large blocks of Sarno limestone.

Nocera tufa) in the second half of the third century BC (cf. Chiaramonte, Ch. 11). Sarno limestone was certainly used in the construction of houses as well, even though only a few survive: for example, the House of the Surgeon (VI.1.10) with its austere façade, unmodified since its building (Figure 8.1; cf. Jones and Robinson, Ch. 25). However, it is not possible to lump all the construction phases of the town together on the basis of the materials used, because the pace of quarrying stone and the schedule of urban building campaigns can be quite different. Still, it is interesting to note that the ashlar blocks of Sarno limestone in *opus quadratum* exhibit oblique, sometimes even curved, edges. This shaping is due to the fact that the quarrymen sawed the blocks by juxtaposing them, so as to get a perfect fit.

Sarno limestone, because of its rough texture, does not take a smooth finish and cannot be cut into fine mouldings. That is why the finest architecture in Pompeii is made of the warmly colored, fine-grained volcanic tufa, the famous tufa of Nocera. In this so-called "tufa period" (also called the "second Samnite Period") beginning *c.*200 BC and lasting until the Roman conquest, the masons perfected their craft and used all the techniques of Hellenistic architecture, giving the town monuments which, though of small size, were its finest architectural manifestations. Apart from the enlargement of the defensive wall with the doubling of its thickness, Pompeian masons exerted their skills on both public monuments such as the temples of the forum, the Basilica, and the Stabian Baths and on a large number of private houses with grandly designed masonry façades, such as the House of the Large Fountain (VI.8.22; Figure 8.2), the House of the Faun (VI.12.2) and the House of Pansa

Figure 8.2 A wall of *opus quadratum* in Nocera tufa; House of the Large Fountain
(VI.8.22); second century BC.

(VI.6.1). While simple block-capitals finished off the pilasters framing the entrance doors in the early phases, these sober designs were quickly superseded with finely sculpted Doric or Corinthian capitals upholding canonically proportioned entablatures. The classical orders of the façades were also used indoors, to decorate *atria* when these had monumental columns, as in the House of the Ceii (I.6.15), the House of the Labyrinth (VI.11.10), or the House of Obellius Firmus (IX.14.4). The peristyles of internal gardens were specially embellished with tufa columns to create lovely, permanent microcosms—privileged, private spaces—evoking a pervasive Greek artistic and cultural ambience (cf. Wallace-Hadrill, Ch. 18).

Even though Nocera tufa can be carved to a sharp, smooth surface, walls and columns made of it bear traces of white stucco. This indicates that, as in Greece itself and in areas which sought to imitate the Greeks, the Pompeians were seeking to imitate the immaculate look and feel of marble. Marble was not available locally, so plaster was applied to simulate its effect, as the builders of the Temple of Zeus at Olympia and the masons of Agrigento had done, to hide what they evidently considered to be the coarseness of the stone they were using.

It is important to note that, after Sarno limestone went out of use for cut-stone walls, tufa persisted in use for ashlar masonry until AD 79.

Marble, except for its use as flooring-material or in counter-tops for taverns, is rare at Pompeii (cf. Fant, Ch. 22). Still, architectural elements in marble are of good quality, as can be seen in the handsome colonnade in front of the Macellum on the northeast side of the forum or, more significantly, in the astonishing door frame of the Eumachia Building (the wool market), decorated with leaf scrolls and peopled with various animals. There may, indeed, be an artificial paucity of architectural marble if we recall that, after the earthquake of AD 62, carved decorations of damaged buildings in the forum were stockpiled for restoration. Immediately after the disaster of AD 79, Titus designated two magistrates as *consulares Campaniae resituendae* to organize the retrieval of the public and private goods from the site of the buried city (Suetonius, *Titus* 8.4). Excavations were organized to recuperate, insofar as was possible, the more valuable building materials and other objects, especially those of the public monuments and the buildings of the forum. This activity, which was undertaken by digging deep holes through the *lapilli* and the ashes, stripped Pompeii of a large amount of its public adornment of both marble and bronze. Marble revetment was salvaged, as were carved architectural marble and statues. Among the rare surviving instances of what must have been a widespread use of marble, the construction site of the Temple of Venus near the Porta Marina had a large number of marble blocks undergoing work for use in the never-to-be-finished temple.

In place of marble, Pompeian builders had recourse to a fine white limestone brought to the town during the Augustan period; the most important instance of its use was in the porticoes of the forum (Figures 10.6, 12.4 and 12.14).

Finally, because it was hard and thus difficult to cut, lava rock was generally used only in big blocks for road surfaces, as slabs for the sides of fountains, and as rough stone of small grade for rubble walls (Figure 10.3).

HAULAGE AND LIFTING

Transport and lifting of stone and other building materials is recorded in stockpiles of building materials on construction sites of the town. For haulage, the most significant evidence comes from the building site of the Temple of Venus on the via Marina, where there were large blocks of marble. The biggest is 3.07 m wide, a meter high, and 0.73 m deep; it weighs 5.8 tons (Figure 8.3). These were brought from a far off quarry, and the site masons roughed out what they needed on the blocks themselves. Two at least bear saw marks to make sheets of marble revetment (Figure 8.4). The haulage of such blocks must have been on single-axle high-wheeled wagons pulled by two oxen. Just such a wagon loaded with building materials in a construction site is depicted in a large wall painting discovered in the Villa San Marco at Stabiae and now in the museum at Castellamare (Figure 8.5). The same type of wagon appears in a more legible relief sculpture in the Museo Nazionale in Rome (Figure 8.6). In addition, the remains of two heavy transport vehicles were found in 1981, also at Stabiae in the nearby Villa of Ariadne: these were two-axle, four-wheeled wagons with pivoting forward shafts. Until this discovery, it was not known if the Romans were familiar with such a mechanism, even though such vehicles were often depicted (e.g., on mosaic floors from the Baths of the Cisiarii at Ostia). We do not, in fact, know if building-materials were hauled with two-axle vehicles (the wagons from Stabiae were used to haul people).

Figure 8.3 Marble block roughed out in the quarry and probably intended for the building site of the Temple of Venus (VIII.1.3–5). 3.07 m wide, 1.00 m high and 0.73 m deep, weighing 5.8 tons.

Figure 8.4 Marble block bearing saw-marks, from the building site of the Temple of Venus.

Figure 8.5 Fresco from the *caldarium* in the bath at the Villa San Marco at Stabiae showing a building site. On the left, a *carrus* (single-axle, high-wheeled wagon) unloads building materials. In the middle, workmen use a pyramidal lifting device called a "goat."

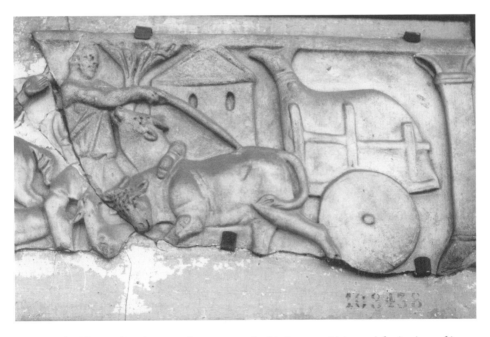

Figure 8.6 The single-axle type of wagon was the kind most widely used for haulage of heavy materials; this relief in the Museo Nazionale in Rome clarifies the structure of the wagon in the Stabiae painting (Figure 8.5).

Figure 8.8 Foundation blocks intended to support the orthostates of the Temple of Venus. The horizontal clamps have been set in place and the square dowel-holes for vertical dowels have been cut, as well as the channel to introduce the molten lead seal; the holes of the tips of lifting-grips can also be seen on the sides of the blocks.

Figure 8.7 Lifting-bosses not yet chiseled off, from the stylobate slabs of the portico of the Central Baths (IX.4), under construction in AD 79.

The methods of lifting stones are recorded on the blocks left at construction sites; the dressing of the surfaces often is supplemented by marks which show us how the blocks were manipulated and lifted.

The main lifting methods of Greek, and then Roman, masons were in use at Pompeii. Good evidence of these methods is available to us, in part because reconstruction and restoration work from the earthquake of AD 62 was still going on in AD 79.

Bosses or tenons to hold lifting ropes were used: they are still apparent, for example, on blocks intended as the floor of the peristyle in the Central Baths (Figure 8.7). Such bosses would, of course, have been chiseled off once the building was finished.

Another method for lifting was to cut small holes into the face surfaces of blocks to accommodate the tips of lifting grips. These marks, which would have been filled in when the building was finished, can be seen on the marble blocks of a funerary monument on the via dei Sepolcri outside the Porta Ercolano (*PErc* 35).

Finally, the most common method for lifting was by the lewis, a multi-component reusable hook of standardized parts which slipped into dovetailed or wedge-shaped slots cut into the blocks as needed.

Following methods inherited from Greek architects, blocks were firmly fixed to one another by means of iron clamps sealed with lead. The clamps could be in the shape of a double-dovetail or a double-T or, most frequent, a *pi* (Figure 8.8). This horizontal clamping was generally complemented with vertical dowels, which were also indispensable to set column drums.

Figure 8.9   An example of *opus africanum* or *opera a telaio* with limestone pillars and
infill of *opus incertum* made of lava rock stone (I.12.1); third century BC.

OPUS AFRICANUM

Together with ashlar masonry in limestone, another type of construction appears in
the early years of Pompeian building, namely a composite structure characteristically
found in North Africa and so-called, for that reason, *opus africanum* [the technique
is also known as "limestone framework," as in Ch. 24—Eds] (Figure 8.9). If this
building technique is indeed of Punic origin, it is possible that it appeared in Campania
by way of Sicily, since early examples of it are found in Mozia (Motiae) and Selinus.
Whatever the case might have been, the Italian term for it is *opera a telaio*, the
"woven" or "square" system.

The technique consists of vertical piers with crossing courses, both of large blocks.
This framework provides a skeleton of support which was in-filled with *opus incertum*.
In the oldest examples, this masonry is set in clay, but later the rubble infill was set
in lime mortar (cf. Peterse, Ch. 24 for analysis of the mortar).

105

MASONRY CONSTRUCTION

Walls in *opus quadratum* must, of course, be painstakingly constructed of blocks of standard size. By contrast, masonry built of smaller components set in mortar can be made with a much wider range of materials, both natural and man-made. Pompeian masonry can incorporate hard black lava rock, red porous lava rock, volcanic scoriae, three types of volcanic tufa, a calcareous tufa, as well as bricks and re-used roof-tiles.

In the earliest masonry techniques at Pompeii, the emplecton structure as defined by Vitruvius (*De arch.* 2.8) was used: this was a core of rubble or *opus caementicium* faced with stone on the external surfaces. Figure 8.10 illustrates the construction of such a wall whose core is Roman concrete and whose facings are *opus incertum* or *opus reticulatum* (cf. Figure A8.1 in the appendix to this chapter). During the third century BC, clay mortars were slowly replaced with lime-based mortars, loosely mixed in the cores but of high quality on the outside.

Typologically and in terms of date, the earliest type of stone facing was a rather rustic one called *opus incertum*, in which the stones, roughly cut and approximately graded as to size, were randomly set without much pattern or organization.

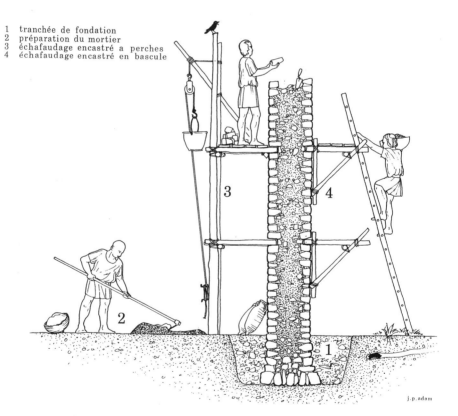

1 tranchée de fondation
2 préparation du mortier
3 échafaudage encastré a perches
4 échafaudage encastré en bascule

Figure 8.10 Section of a masonry wall during its construction,
showing (1) foundation trench, (2) preparation of mortar, (3) socketed scaffolding with
standards, and (4) cantilever scaffolding.

Figure 8.11 Wall of the Odeion (VIII.7.16–20), *c.*80 BC., one of the earliest examples of *opus reticulatum* at Pompeii. The quoining assumes a serrated pattern in order to correspond to the setting of the facing stones at a 45° degree angle.

After the implantation of a colony of veterans by Sulla in 80 BC, Pompeii received new buildings, notably the amphitheater and the Odeion (or *theatrum tectum*), in which a new type of stone facing, *opus reticulatum*, came to be used. This is a more systematic technique, in which the square ends of pyramid-shaped stones form the exterior wall facing. The square ends of the facing stones are set at a 45° angle to form a netlike, or reticulate, pattern (Figure 8.11). This technique, which appeared in Rome toward the end of the second century BC, is standardized and thus more rapidly assembled as well as stronger than *opus incertum*. With *opus reticulatum* come polychrome effects in masonry, made from combining different kinds of materials, such as tufas, lava rock and bricks. Many walls even have a mixture of materials in a deliberately designed color pattern; such walls are mainly found in structures rebuilt after the earthquake of AD 62, but almost all were intended to be stuccoed. What is clear, however, is that *opus reticulatum* did not go out of use in the imperial period but persisted as a widespread and elegant masonry technique, both at Pompeii and in the rest of central and southern Italy. Many of the walls of Hadrian's Villa at Tivoli attest to this.

Masonry with facing stones cut into rectangles, called *opus vittatum*, is rare at Pompeii. The technique was first used as quoining for structures in *opus reticulatum*

Figure 8.12 A mixed construction incorporating *opus reticulatum* in various natural stones, with quoins in *opus mixtum* of rubble and brick.

and in small buildings such as secondary water towers in the water supply system (Figure 16.4). Increased use of *opus vittatum* came in reconstruction work after the earthquake of AD 62: the facing stones are of a friable yellow tufa from the region of Pozzuoli.

Brick appears precociously early in Campania, as the columns of the Basilica, (*c.*110 BC) indicate, and brick was used relatively early on in walls as well. Thus, the Odeion incorporated quoins of brick set in a serrated pattern (Figure 8.11). The combination of brick and rubble is called *opus mixtum*, a general term covering many different techniques: the bricks can be used as quoining, or set in horizontal courses variously spaced and of varying thickness (Figure 8.12). One of the most significant examples of *opus mixtum* is the Porta Ercolano (shortly after 80 BC), which incorporated panels of lava facing stones framed with quoins of tufa and brick. In spite of their elegance, the walls of this monument were covered with a white stucco intended to imitate marble revetment. By contrast, shops newly built around the Central Baths after the earthquake of AD 62 had façades that combined various tufa facings with brick, in calculated geometric designs that may well have been built to be seen without any stucco covering.

Brick as a uniform facing-material for rubble walls came to be used only after the earthquake of AD 62. The technique was used for reconstruction work, as for example in the Eumachia Building in the forum (Figures 12.13 and 12.14), as well as quite commonly for public monuments such as the three buildings of the Curia, also facing the forum at the south end.

Finally, mixed construction of rubble and wood, what was called *opus craticium* and which we know as a form of half-timbering, was mainly used for internal partitions

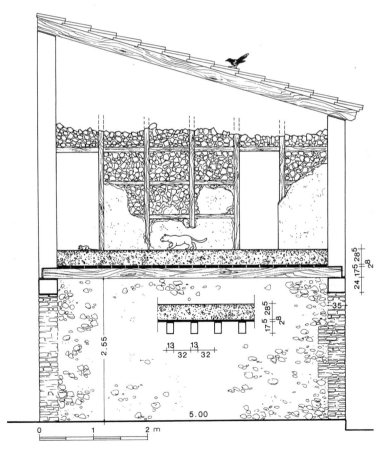

Figure 8.13 Section through a two-story building showing several materials and techniques, including a wall of *opus craticium* on the second story.

Figure 8.14 Detail of the ladder stair of shop
(*Ins. Or.* II.9), Herculaneum.

Figure 8.15 Staircase with treads and risers
at (IV.20), Herculaneum.

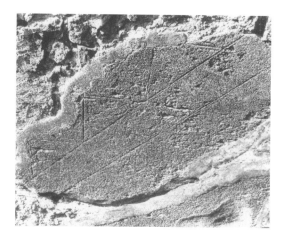

Figure 8.16 Traces of marks to set a
wooden staircase in the corridor of the House
of the Faun (VI.12), Pompeii.

and, because of its lightness, for the external walls of upper floors projected or
cantilevered over the street (Figure 8.13). At Pompeii, the relatively shallow burying
of the structures did not allow for the preservation of much structural wood, whereas
at Herculaneum, because of the thick cover of *lapilli* and ash, structural wood as well
as floors, door frames and furniture were found in situ (Figure 27.6).

Arches and vaults in Pompeian architecture were mainly built of rubble masonry;
only the great gangways (*vomitoria*) of the amphitheater incorporated arches made of
tufa voussoirs, perfectly cut and assembled. In general, and because there were no
large-scale monuments, vaults at Pompeii were of modest size: the largest were the
rubble masonry vaults of the large rooms in the Stabian Baths, about 8 m in span.

Figure 8.17 The wall slots for the ends of floor joists for the upper floor of the House of the Silverware (VI.7.22). The marks of the floorboards of the upper room can be seen in a narrow line above the slots, and below them the groove marks for the ceiling laths. The holes on the wall below are put-log supports for scaffolding as seen in Figure 8.10.

Figure 8.18 Traces of a shed roof for the peristyle of the House of Oppius Gratus (IX.6.5). The first row of roof tiles were built into the masonry. The supports for the joists are separated from the tiles by laths.

Figure 8.19   Reconstruction of the carpentry of the *atrium* roof of the House of the Wooden Partition (III.11), Herculaneum.

With respect to vaults, many of the rooms of Pomepeian houses were decorated with false vaults. These were, in fact, carpentered structures, as outlined by Vitruvius (7.3). Supports were fixed in a semicircle to the walls below the room's ceiling, then a lattice of lathes was applied which was, in turn, covered with painted plaster.

CARPENTRY

Besides its use in partitions and half-timbered structures, carpentered wood was used in the floors, ceilings and staircases of houses of two or more stories.

The traces of wooden stairs are easy to discern from the traces of supports on wall surfaces. At Herculaneum, two types of stairs survive: a ladder stair with steps or treads, but no risers, as in the shop at no. 9 in the East *Insula*, IIA (Figure 8.14), and a real staircase with both treads and risers, as in no. 20 in *Insula* IV (Figure 8.15). A preparatory sketch for a wooden staircase is incised in the plaster of a corridor of the House of the Faun (Figure 8.16). Marks of floor joists (Figure 8.17) and roof joists can also be seen on wall surfaces, rarely surviving at Pompeii but found partially preserved at Herculaneum. Floor joists were closely spaced because a mortar bed was laid on the wooden floor boards to take a smooth walkable surface.

The meticulous excavations of V. Spinazzola have allowed us to reconstruct the techniques of structural wood used by the Pompeian builders. Whenever possible, they avoided using complex angular trussing: instead, they covered spans horizontally by running median bearing walls through the middle of buildings. Against these walls, simple shed roofs could be built, and such roofs were the structure of choice to cover the porticoes of private peristyles (Figure 8.18). Roofing *atria* took more care and know-how on the carpenter's part, especially in the case of Tuscan *atria* which did not have columns around the *impluvium* to give support to the heavy beams (Figure 8.19). The spans could be considerable (8 m in the House of the Vettii, 10 m in the House of Sallust). The structure of Tuscan *atria* consisted of two parallel bearing beams pinioned to the walls of the room which supported two cross beams at right angles. The center was open to form the *compluvium*, and at the intersections of the sides, purlins were set to take the rafters and lathes onto which the roof tiles were affixed.

NOTE

1   Guy P. R. Métreau translated the French text.

BIBLIOGRAPHY

Adam, J.-P., *Dégradation et restauration de l'architecture pompéienne*, Paris, 1983.
——, *Observations techniques sur les suites du séisme de 62 à Pompéi*, Naples, 1983.
——, *Roman Building: materials and techniques*, London, 1994.
Carrington, R., "Notes on the building materials of Pompeii," *Journal of Roman Studies*, 1933, vol. 23, pp. 125ff.
De Vos, A. and De Vos, M., *Pompei, Ercolano, Stabia, Guide Laterza*, Rome, 1982.
Etienne, R., *La vie quotidienne à Pompéi*, Paris, 1966.
Eschebach, H., *Die Stabianer Thermen in Pompeji*, Berlin, 1979.
Fiorelli, G., *Gli scavi di Pompei dal 1861 al 1872*, Naples, 1873.
——, *Pompeianorum antiquitatum historia*, Naples, 1860–64.
Giovannonni, G., *La tecnica della costruzione presso i Romani*, Rome, 1925.
Jashemski, W. F., *The Gardens of Pompeii, Herculaneum, and the Villas Destroyed by Vesuvius*, New Rochelle, NY, 1979.
Maiuri, A., *Pompei ed Ercolano fra case ed abitanti*, Milan, 1959.
——, *Introduzione allo studio di Pompei, la città ed i monumenti pubblici*, Naples, 1949.
Mau, A., *Pompeji in Leben und Kunst*, Leipzig, 1882.
Thedenat, H., *Pompéi*, numerous editions from 1906–27.

APPENDIX TO CHAPTER EIGHT

A note on Roman concrete (*opus caementicium*) and other wall construction

——•◆•——

John J. Dobbins

This brief discussion of Roman concrete with its various facings (*opus incertum, opus quasi reticulatum, opus reticulatum* and *opus testaceum*; Figure A8.1) and other wall construction is for readers who are new to the field and who will need this information as they read the chapters that follow.

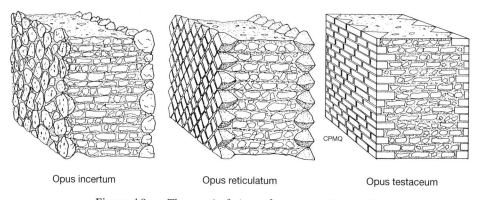

Opus incertum   Opus reticulatum   Opus testaceum

Figure A8.1 Three main facings of *opus caementicium* walls.
Drawing by L. F. Ball.

The masonry (i.e., the wall construction) found at Pompeii is quite diverse and poses a challenge to those who want to understand it in detail. The goal here is merely to introduce some standard descriptive terms. Technical terms are found in the glossary, and several chapters, such as those by Adam (Ch. 8) and Peterse (Ch. 24), discuss and illustrate various types of wall construction. Here are presented the different types of facing that are associated with walls constructed in Roman concrete followed by brief comments on other constructions.

During the second century BC the Romans developed a building material that made wall construction for major buildings easier, and that ultimately revolutionized Roman architectural design. This material is known as Roman concrete (*opus caementicium*), and is discussed by Adam under Masonry Construction (Ch. 8, p. 106). Instead of cutting individual stone blocks for constructing a wall (called ashlar masonry, or *opus quadratum*; Figures 8.1 and 8.2) as had been done in earlier construction, the Romans developed an alternative to this labor-intensive process in which the wall core was a mix of various materials covered by a facing on both sides. The wall core consists of rock, broken terracotta roof tiles, broken brick (the *caementa*), a volcanic ash from the Bay of Naples that the Romans called *pulvis puteolanis*, lime and water. In addition to being much easier to produce than ashlar masonry, *opus caementicium* had the additional advantage of curing, or setting up, rock hard, even under water. This method of construction was used in straight walls, in curved walls, in vaults and in harbor facilities.

The four major facings used for Roman concrete walls are *opus incertum* (irregular, or uncertain, work—"*opus*" means "work"), *opus reticulatum* (a network, or reticulate pattern), *opus quasi reticulatum* (more regular than *opus incertum*, but not quite *opus reticulatum*) and *opus testaceum* (brickwork) (Figure A8.1).

Roman concrete walls could be constructed within wooden formwork, or between string lines that would guide the builders. Whatever the manner of construction, the facing was built up vertically along with the core; it was not inserted later. It should be emphasized that the wall core was not as viscous, or liquid-like, as modern cement. Rather, it was much chunkier and was delivered by workers basket after basket as the masons constructed the wall and made sure that the facing pieces (stone or brick) were in place. Figure 8.10 depicts the construction of an *opus caementicium* wall.

The stones used in *opus incertum* facing were approximately the size of cobbles, and were typically limestone or lava. The stone for *opus quasi reticulatum* and *opus reticulatum* was volcanic tufa (or more correctly "tuff," although many archaeologists, including this author, use the term "tufa"). These tufa stones were cut in the shape of elongated pyramids (some of the facing stones in Figure 8.10 appear to be of this sort). The square ends form the face of the wall while the pointed ends of the elongated pyramids penetrate into the wall core. The Roman bricks used in *opus testaceum* are thinner than modern bricks and are frequently triangular-shaped so that one pointed edge can project into the wall core.

Figure 8.11 (at the *theatrum tectum*, or covered theater; cf. Parslow, Ch. 14) presents several interesting construction details. The wall is constructed in the *opus quasi reticulatum* technique, but the door jambs, where the wall must be straight and sharp-edged, are in *opus testaceum*, or brick-faced Roman concrete.[1] The interface between the two materials and techniques is achieved by means of toothlike projections called quoins, which usually are rectangular, but here are serrated. Above the doorway is a "relieving arch" that deflects the downward pressure from the lintel to the jambs. The lintel itself is wooden and is therefore a modern restoration, and the stones immediately above a wooden lintel are always modern replacements. When standing in front of an actual wall it is usually possible to distinguish between the ancient and the modern construction.

Figure 8.12 demonstrates not only *opus reticulatum* in the center of the wall, but also the *opus vittatum mixtum* technique of alternating one course of small blocks (limestone or tufa) with two courses of brick to form the facing of the wall.

Once the construction was finished, no one saw the wall core because it was covered by the wall facings just described. In most cases, no one saw the facings either because they were covered by a variety of additional decorative treatments, such as stucco, fresco or marble veneer (cf. Strocka, Ch. 20; Clarke, Ch. 21; Fant, Ch. 22). In some cases, such as the south wall of the Macellum, it is likely that the facing (there *opus reticulatum*) was not covered with any decorative treatment.

Some early walls display a combination of cut blocks and mortared rubble resembling *opus caementicium* (Figure 8.9). This technique of making masonry, or cut block, chains is described in Chapters 8 and 24 and is called variously "limestone framework," *opus africanum*, and *opera a telaio* (woven work, in Italian).

Here are a few additional technical and archaeological observations. Given that Pompeii lived for centuries and that individual walls, and even whole buildings, were knocked down and replaced, it is obvious that a lot of building debris would have been available for reuse in new construction. A close look at Pompeian walls reveals chunks of *opus incertum* facing that still retain their original plaster built into later walls. Or one might see a patch of floor mosaic reused in a later wall. Another issue is modern restoration. Pompeii has been under excavation for more than 250 years and many walls have been restored. Sometimes a horizontal row of differently colored bricks is inserted to mark the line between ancient and modern construction. More often this is not done and one must be very wary in evaluating an individual wall.

NOTE

1   The differentiation between *opus quasi reticulatum* and *opus reticulatum* is a matter of judgment. This wall is considered to be *opus reticulatum* by Adam in Chapter 8.

PART II
THE COMMUNITY

———•◆•———

CHAPTER NINE

DEVELOPMENT OF POMPEII'S PUBLIC LANDSCAPE IN THE ROMAN PERIOD

—·◆·—

Roger Ling

The detailed evolution of Pompeii's public landscape in the Roman period is full of uncertainties. There are question-marks over the dates of several buildings; it is difficult to decide, indeed, whether some of them date to the period after the foundation of the colony or go back to Samnite times. Where the dates of buildings are known, it is often unclear what preceded them: the dearth of excavations beneath the levels of 79 prevents us, in most cases, from judging whether they were constructed on "virgin" sites, whether they replaced domestic or commercial buildings, or whether they were substitutes for previous public edifices. The following account will, therefore, be hedged with many "ifs", "buts" and "maybes".[1]

By the time of the Social War the development of the street-system was complete apart from minor adjustments, and most of the city-blocks were built up. The forum, towards the southwest corner of the city, was the hub of civic and commercial activity, and, though much of its east side seems still to have been occupied by shops and workshops rather than the public buildings which existed later, there were certainly public buildings to the south and west (Figure 12.15). At the southwest corner the Basilica, perhaps a law-court and stock-market combined, can be dated on the basis of its architectural detail and First-Style plasterwork, in which are cut *graffiti* in the Oscan alphabet, to the second half of the second century (Figure 12.8). To the north of this the Temple of Apollo, with a dedicatory inscription in Oscan set in its pavement, already existed on the forum's western flank. At the south end may have stood administrative buildings, precursors of the trio in existence in 79. It is even possible that the Temple of Jupiter, whether dedicated to the Capitoline deity of the Romans or to some other, already overlooked the *piazza* from the north (Figures 10.8 and 12.5).

On the southern edge of the city was an enclave of buildings of Greek character. The so-called Triangular Forum with its Doric temple of the sixth century BC already formed a religious precinct. Adjacent to it was the large theatre, built during the second century BC (Figure 14.3). Immediately to the south of this was a large open space surrounded by a colonnade, perhaps to be interpreted as a gymnasium,[2] and to the northwest was a small *palaestra* (exercise area) (VIII.7.29).

Two blocks to the north, the Stabian Baths occupied a strategic position next to the intersection of two of the major arterial routes, the strada Stabiana and the via dell'Abbondanza (Figures 15.1, 15.2, 15.3 and 15.4). Public baths were an amenity increasingly essential to the life-style of Campanian and other south-Italian communities, and a central location was advantageous at a time when very few private householders had adequate bathing facilities on their own premises.

Apart from these buildings we can say little about the public landscape of the city before 80 BC. The arrival of the Roman colonists, however, led to a number of clear-cut developments: an influx of veteran soldiers with different social and cultural priorities demanded the provision of a number of buildings that were not previously available.

As in all Greek and Roman cities, the public building works of Pompeii were supervised, and in many cases funded, by wealthy individuals who advertised their generosity in dedicatory inscriptions. The survival of such inscriptions in at least two cases links new buildings with the colonists. The first was the "covered theatre" (*theatrum tectum*), the dedication of which names two leading colonists, C. Quinctius Valgus and M. Porcius, as its founders (*CIL* X, 844–5) (Figure 14.1). Built immediately to the east of the pre-existing large theatre, this is often called an "odeion" and interpreted, like the Greek buildings of that name, as a concert-hall for musical performances and recitations; but it is highly unlikely that Roman ex-soldiers would have been much interested in promoting Greek culture in this way. More plausible is Paul Zanker's suggestion that the building, whose auditorium would have held between 1,500 and 2,000 people, may have served as an assembly chamber for meetings of the colonists.[3] Its architectural form tallies well enough with that of assembly-halls or council-chambers in certain Hellenistic cities in the Aegean area, notably Priene and Miletus in Asia Minor. The fact that it was situated next to the large theatre does not imply that it, too, was intended for public entertainments. The position of both buildings was dictated by the convenience of a hill-slope in which the auditoria could be hollowed.

The second new building was the amphitheatre, financed by the same two colonists, Quinctius Valgus and Porcius, but at a slightly later date (*CIL* X, 852) (Figure 14.2). The official title was actually not *amphitheatron*, a Greek term used of such buildings only at a later date, but the Latin SPECTACULA. This reflects the fact that the entertainments staged in the arena were of purely Roman type, the gladiatorial combats and wild-beast hunts which had evolved in central Italy, perhaps from games conducted at funerals, and whose brutality and bloodshed set them apart from the popular entertainments of the Greeks. As such, the amphitheatre may have been designed, initially at least, to respond more to the demands of the Roman colonists than to those of the indigenous Pompeians: it may be significant that the founders here felt it necessary to state that they were acting "for the honour of the colony" (COLONIAE HONORIS CAUSA) and did so "at their own expense" (DE SUA PECUNIA). The building was sited away from other public buildings, in the eastern angle of the city. It is not certain whether, as often claimed, this was because the site in question was open land and thus available for development: recent excavations have indicated that the blocks in the eastern quarter were much more fully built up in their early stages (second century BC) than was later the case.[4] Marginalizing the amphitheatre had the advantage of keeping potentially rowdy crowds away from the city-centre; at the same time, spectators from communities further up the Sarno valley, such as Nuceria, could be channelled in and out through the nearest city-gates. The chosen site also had more immediate advantages. The oval auditorium, which was not supported on a network of concrete vaults like later amphitheatres, exploited the slope of the defensive ramparts on the south and east (Figure 23.1). Only the north and west sides needed to be constructed upon new earthen banks, formed from the upcast obtained by digging the arena.

Other buildings of the colonial phase can be identified on historical or archaeological grounds. Pre-eminent was the Temple of Venus (VIII.1.3–5), the patron goddess of the colony. This was constructed on a lofty platform at the southwest corner of the city, adjacent to the Porta Marina, where the goddess would be able to control and protect the route by which visitors arrived from the commercial port. It may well have been visible from the sea and thus have formed a conspicuous landmark, a kind of symbol of the city. The emphasis on the approach from the sea was further reinforced by the rebuilding of the Porta Marina. While the defensive walls, now redundant, were generally neglected or swallowed up by private development, the arched gateways seem to have been maintained as a means of monumentalizing access and thus asserting civic pride.

Of the buildings in the forum area, it is inconceivable that the colonists did not make changes to the dominant temple at the northern end (Figures 10.8 and 12.5). Even if this was already dedicated to Jupiter, there was probably now a rebuilding that laid emphasis on the Capitoline version of that god's cult, in which Jupiter shared honours with Juno and Minerva. It may have been at this stage that the base for the cult-statue within the temple was transformed into a three-chambered podium, while the whole building was radically re-designed and monumentalized.[5] At the south end of the forum the *Comitium*, or voting enclosure, though perhaps begun in the pre-colonial period, was brought to completion in the first years of the colony.

Much of the building work of the colonists was carried out in a distinctive technique of *quasi reticulatum* in black lava with cornering in brickwork (often arranged to form a series of superposed wedges; Figure 8.11). The use of this technique characterizes another major new building, the Forum Baths (Figure 15.4). Situated in the block immediately to the north of the Capitoline temple, these represented a state-of-the-art project incorporating not just bathing facilities but also shops and upstairs apartments, and were clearly intended as an amenity for the general population, among whom the bathing habit had taken a firm hold, rather than for the colonists alone. Significantly, a pair of inscriptions which have been ascribed to the Forum Baths records the magistrates who supervised the work as operating at public expense (EX PEQUNIA PUBLICA) rather than paying from their own pockets. Evidently the Stabian Baths were now inadequate to the requirements of the city, and a new establishment was needed to relieve pressure on them. At the same time the Stabian Baths themselves were modernized, as an inscription reveals, by the addition of a *laconicum* (dry-heat room) and *destrictarium* (room for rubbing down after exercise) and by the reconstruction of the Baths' *palaestra* and its porticoes. The position of the new baths, like the old, was strategically chosen to benefit as large a slice of the urban population as possible. They served the northern and western quarters, leaving the Stabian Baths to cater to dwellers in the centre and east. It is interesting that both sets of baths were fitted in irregular *insulae*, which straddled the transition between the old quarter of the city and the more regular developments to the north and east. If, as Eschebach argues, there was formerly some kind of physical boundary or *pomerium* round the old quarter,[6] these blocks may have been relatively sparsely built up, thus providing the only feasible sites which were both centrally positioned and large enough to accommodate the baths.

The buildings of the colonists made an important mark on Pompeii's public landscape; they set the stamp on its transformation from the Hellenized Samnite city of the second century BC to the Roman city of the early Imperial period. The process was continued, after an apparent hiatus during the civil wars of the last decades of the Republic, under the emperor Augustus.

The Augustan period gave the Roman world a new stability and security buttressed by an ideological programme which emphasized concepts such as the revival of traditional religious and moral values. In Pompeii, as in hundreds of other communities, prominent local citizens sought to express their gratitude to the new regime, and in some cases to secure their personal advancement, by sponsoring building projects which honoured the emperor or promoted his ideals. A good example was the erection by M. Tullius, a leading magistrate of the last decades of the first century BC, of a temple dedicated to Fortuna Augusta, one of various cults which grew up around the emperor and his tutelary spirits. Tullius had received honours from the emperor, and the building of the temple was a statement of his loyalty. Moreover, its location at a busy crossroads two streets north of the forum was well suited to advertise the cult and, with it, the munificence and political correctness of the donor (Figure 10.7). The land on which the temple was built formed part of Tullius's private property, and he was fortunate to be able to turn this circumstance to advantage.

Another prominent citizen of the Augustan period was M. Holconius Rufus, who held all the chief posts in the local administration, acted as a priest of the imperial cult, and like Tullius was rewarded by the emperor with a grant of the military tribunate (Figure 36.3). He, too, was active in public building. During his third tenure of the *duovirate*, i.e., not long before 2 BC, the year of his fourth tenure, he and his fellow *duovir*, C. Egnatius Postumus, built a wall which obstructed the lights of houses adjacent to the Sanctuary of Apollo (Figure 12.1). An inscription found in the sanctuary records the compensation paid to the householders who were affected (*CIL* X, 787). It is normally believed that the layout of the precinct, with its rigid axial planning and colonnaded courtyard, goes back to the second century BC, but recent trial excavations have yielded dating evidence that points to building activity in the late first century BC (Figure 13.1).[7] Since the wall that impinged upon neighbouring properties was clearly the west precinct boundary, and since this is an integral part of the overall plan, it seems that Holconius and his colleague were responsible for a radical rebuilding and enlargement which resulted in the suppression of an early street along the west side. In either case their concern for the cult of Apollo acquires added significance when one remembers that Apollo was Augustus's patron deity. It was natural to demonstrate allegiance to the new regime by promoting the interests of its leader's favourite god.

Another prominent benefactor of the Augustan period was the public priestess Mamia, who put up a Sanctuary of the Genius of Augustus (Figure 12.12; cf. Dobbins, Ch. 12; Small, Ch. 13).[8] The provenance of the inscription that records this dedication is uncertain, but it has been plausibly linked with one of the buildings on the east side of the forum, the so-called Temple of Vespasian.[9] If this is correct, Mamia owned (or bought) the plot in question, because she, like M. Tullius, records that the temple was built not just at her own expense but on her own land. An Augustan date for the building is supported by the imagery of the reliefs on the altar which stood in front of the temple.[10] We may, therefore, suspect that the monumentalization of the forum's east front, with the old shops and workshops giving way to large public complexes, began in Augustan times.

Elsewhere in the city M. Holconius Rufus appears again, this time with his brother (or son) Holconius Celer, another leading figure in the imperial cult and the local administration, carrying out major alterations to the large theatre: they built a *crypta* (probably an annular corridor which supported an extra tier of seating at the back of the auditorium), *tribunalia* (the boxes constructed over the side-passages, or *parodoi*, which led to the area in front of the stage), and the *theatrum* (presumably the seating in general) (Figure 14.3). Apparently the Holconii not only enlarged and refurbished the auditorium but also, by adding *tribunalia*, completed the conversion of the theatre from its old Hellenistic form, in which the auditorium was separate from the stage-building, to something approaching the standard Roman type in which the two elements were unified in a single structure. Investing in civic theatres was a widespread cultural phenomenon of the reign of Augustus, for which the emperor himself set a precedent by his dedication of the monumental Theatre of Marcellus in Rome.[11]

A further major building of the Augustan period cannot, for lack of evidence, be connected with any individual benefactors but fits the same pattern of conformance to government ideology: the so-called Large Palaestra (II.7), situated next to the amphitheatre (cf. Parslow, Ch. 14). This was a *campus* (training-ground) for the military corps of upper-class youths, which Augustus promoted as part of a policy of producing model citizens and supporters of his regime. When not in use for drills and other displays, it would have been open to the general public as a pleasant intramural open space, analogous to the monumental *porticus*, such as the Porticus of Octavia and the Porticus of Livia, which the emperor created (in continuance of a Republican tradition) in the capital. It was provided with a central swimming pool and planted with plane trees whose estimated age at the time of the eruption is the chief argument for an Augustan date (Figure 14.4). The importance of the *campus* is attested by the fact that the space was obtained by suppressing six blocks of the pre-existing street-grid. Recent excavations have yielded traces of early properties which must have been bought or expropriated. One reason for placing the *campus* in the eastern part of the city may have been that this quarter was less densely populated than others, so that the cost of the development and the degree of disruption that it caused were less than they would have been elsewhere.

While the buildings so far mentioned were the result of local initiative, a final contribution of the Augustan age to Pompeii's public landscape was apparently due to government investment. The city's supply of running water was probably furnished by a branch of the aqueduct constructed by Augustus's minister Agrippa to supply the fleet at Misenum (Map 1). In improving the quality of life in the city the provision of fresh water was of immeasurable importance. Its chief visual impact was in the creation of two new street-side features: the regular series of towers that maintained the pressure of flow from the distributing tank at the Porta Vesuvio, and the public fountains that were located at street corners to service the needs of those residents of neighbouring blocks who did not have water piped into their own homes (Figure 16.3). The arrival of running water will also have led to improvements in the functioning of the public baths. The dedication of a new *labrum* in the Forum Baths, dated to AD 3/4, may have been one consequence of it (Figure 15.4). The building of the Suburban Baths outside the Porta Marina may have been another.

The reign of Augustus was a seminal phase in the history of Pompeii's public landscape, but it merely marked the beginning of a development that continued under Augustus's successors. Sometimes it is difficult to know whether buildings should be dated to the Augustan or Julio-Claudian periods. On the east side of the forum, for instance, the Building of Eumachia, whose precise function is uncertain but was certainly in some sense commercial, contained references to Augustan propaganda, including replicas of the statues of Aeneas and Romulus from the Forum Augustum in Rome, but its dedicatory inscriptions, which record that Eumachia constructed the building in her own name and that of her son, M. Numistrius Fronto, and dedicated it to Concordia Augusta and Pietas, fit a period early in the reign of Tiberius, and especially the years AD 22–24, when there was emphasis on the close relations between the emperor and his mother Livia, and concepts such as concord and filial devotion (*pietas*) would have been in fashion (Figures 12.13 and 12.14). A post-Augustan date is supported by details of the building's Third-Style wall paintings, known from nineteenth-century drawings (cf. Descœudres, Ch. 2; Dobbins, Ch. 12; Small, Ch. 13).[12] The Macellum, the principal food-market, at the northeast corner of the forum, is not securely dated and it too could belong to the Julio-Claudian phase (Figure 12.9). Its southern neighbour, usually called the Sanctuary of the Lares Publici but identified by Zanker, plausibly, as a sanctuary for the imperial cult,[13] may have been added even later, perhaps not until after the earthquake of AD 62 (Figures 12.10 and 12.11).

The monumental development of the forum may, therefore, have continued through the early imperial period. Other buildings around it, such as the vegetable market to the north of the Sanctuary of Apollo, and the three administrative buildings on the south side, could also have taken their final form at this time. What is striking is the piecemeal nature of the development, which produced façades on different alignments and plans with shifts of orientation. The whole picture is one of individual initiative, in which leading magistrates vied with each other to make an impact upon the urban landscape in this most prestigious area of the city.

But, as time went on, there was an effort to unify this heterogeneous architecture. Although there had been an early attempt to build a colonnade round the *piazza*, dated, on the basis of an inscription, to the 80s BC,[14] this may never have got much further than the southern end. Work was carried forward and largely completed during the imperial period, substituting a superior material, limestone, for the volcanic tuff of the original project (Figures 12.3 and 12.4). Similar improvements were made in the paving. At the same time, the honorary statues which had proliferated and been distributed in a somewhat haphazard fashion were apparently tidied up, the equestrian figures being lined up in front of the western colonnade (Figure 23.12), the standing figures perhaps set inside the eastern, while at the southern end was installed a symmetrical grouping of monumental bases which must have carried statues of particularly important personages, perhaps Augustus and members of the ruling house. A centrally located base towards the northern end is thought by Zanker to have carried an altar of the imperial cult,[15] but a statue of one of the emperors is again a possibility. To left and right of the Temple of Jupiter the forum space was defined by a pair of monumental arches (Figure 10.8), though at a later stage, probably between AD 23 and 29, the one at the right was replaced by another set further back to allow a clear view of the colonnade (here marble rather than limestone) in front of the Macellum (Figure 12.5). Further north a smaller arch, dating perhaps to the reign of Caligula (AD 37–41), was built across the entrance to the via di Mercurio, providing a visual focus to the colonnaded street behind the Tiberian arch (Figure 10.7).

The monumentalization of the forum and main streets fits with a trend which was common to cities of the early imperial period. Formal axial planning, spaces defined by colonnades, the use of superior building materials—all were fundamental to the new urban landscape (cf. Westfall, Ch. 10). From the Fora of Caesar and Augustus in Rome, they were disseminated to the new colonies of northern Italy and the provinces and served as models to be emulated by old cities too.

At Pompeii the process was continued after the disastrous earthquake of AD 62. It has traditionally been argued that the city was crippled by the earthquake and that many public buildings were still in a state of ruin at the time of the final eruption seventeen years later; only in houses and other projects involving private finance was the work of reconstruction well advanced.[16] But research by John Dobbins has shown, for the buildings on the east side of the forum at least, that this view is misguided.[17] The appearance of devastation and incompleteness created, for example, by the disappearance of statues and the absence of marble wall-veneers should be credited to the activities of salvagers and plunderers after the city's burial: the tops of buildings would have been poking out of the ash, and it would have been easy to locate potential sources of valuable or reusable material. Rather than being incomplete, the buildings to the east of the forum seem to have been largely restored; moreover, their appearance was enhanced by the liberal use of marble veneers, and there was a deliberate effort to unify the façades by linking them and blocking the last vestiges of two east–west streets which formerly debouched in the forum. One edifice, the Imperial Cult Building, may have been constructed *ex novo*: the way in which it uses a play of curved and rectangular recesses to model interior space recalls certain elements in Nero's Golden House in Rome and, from our knowledge of Roman architecture, would have been unusually avant garde before this time.

A difference of the post-earthquake period lay in the source of funding. To restore their major public buildings after the earthquake the Pompeians must have had financial support from the central government. The traditional pattern of reliance upon private munificence was clearly impracticable: the extent of the work required would have placed an unreasonable burden on the magistrates. Presumably money was provided by the emperor, as it had been in the case of other natural disasters, such as the earthquake which had struck various cities of Asia Minor in AD 17.

In addition to the buildings of the forum, a priority in the programme of reconstruction would have been the Sanctuary of Venus. This is usually said still to have resembled a builder's yard in AD 79; but again the state of incompleteness could be partially due to post-eruption stone-robbing. Here, however, a further factor may have been the radical nature of the rebuilding: the old sanctuary was being replaced by a new and grander project. That the temple precinct was enlarged after the middle of the first century AD is shown by the fact that new foundations were cut through rooms of the so-called Villa Imperiale which were painted in the Fourth Style.[18] The most likely date for this development, since it presupposes the abandonment of the

Villa Imperiale, would be after the earthquake. If so, the Temple of Venus would offer another illustration of the vigour with which the programme of recovery was pursued.

One last modification to the public landscape of Pompeii is securely placed after the earthquake: the building of the Central Baths (Figure 15.6). Situated like the other intramural baths at a major crossroads, the intersection of the strada Stabiana and the via di Nola, these were evidently necessitated by increasing pressure upon the Forum and Stabian Baths. At the same time, they introduced modern developments in the architecture of thermal establishments such as had become established in the great imperial baths of the capital. Aided by technical improvements in wall-heating and in the production of window glass, the designers of the new baths were able to dispense with the old dark, inward-looking architecture and replace it with spacious rooms lit by large south-west-facing windows. The site for the new baths was obtained by taking over a whole block and demolishing the pre-existing houses, presumably after expropriation. Such a drastic redevelopment may have been more easily undertaken in the aftermath of the earthquake, which had left properties damaged or deserted; nonetheless it shows that Pompeii was no moribund city simply struggling to recover from the disaster of 62. It was alive and receptive to new urban forms. Had it survived, the public landscape would have continued to evolve in sympathy with the changing requirements of new generations just as it had done in the past.

NOTES

1 For an earlier account of the development of Pompeii's public landscape (divergent in some respects from the present one) see P. Zanker, *Pompeji: Stadtbilder als Spiegel von Gesellschaft und Herrschaftsform (Trierer Winckelmannsprogramme IX)*, Mainz, 1988; cf. P. Zanker, *Pompeji. Stadt und Wohngeschmack*, Mainz, 1995, pp. 33–140; P. Zanker, *Pompeii. Public and Private Life*, Cambridge, MA, 1998, pp. 27–133. [The author's most recent thinking on issues in this chapter are expressed in his *Pompeii: History, Life and Afterlife*, Stroud, 2005.—Eds]

2 Zanker, *Pompeji. Stadtbilder*, pp. 12–13; Zanker, *Pompeji. Stadt und Wohngeschmack*, pp. 52–6; Zanker, *Pompeii*, pp. 46–9.

3 Zanker, *Pompeji. Stadtbilder*, p. 19; Zanker, *Pompeji. Stadt und Wohngeschmack*, pp. 73–4; Zanker, *Pompeii*, pp. 65–8.

4 S. C. Nappo, "Pompei: la casa *Regio* I, *ins.* 20, n. 4 nelle sue fasi. Considerazioni e problemi", in L. Franchi dell'Orto (ed.), *Ercolano 1738-1988: 250 anni di ricerca archeologica. Atti del Convegno Internazionale Ravello–Ercolano–Napoli–Pompei 30 ottobre–5 novembre 1988*, Rome, 1993, pp. 667–76.

5 For a different view, which ascribes the conversion of the Capitolium to a phase of voluntary Romanization before the Social War, see H. Lauter, "Bemerkungen zur späthellenistischen Baukunst in Mittelitalien", *JdI*, 1979, vol. 94, pp. 430–4; cf. V. M. Strocka, *Casa del Labirinto (VI 11, 8-10) (Häuser in Pompeji 4)*, Munich, 1991, pp. 108–9.

6 H. Eschebach, "Die städtebauliche Entwicklung des antiken Pompeji", RM-EH 17, Heidelberg, 1970, pp. 24–40.

7 A. L. Slayman, "The new Pompeii. Excavations beneath the AD 79 level illuminate the history of the famous Roman resort", *Archaeology*, Nov./Dec. 1997, p. 34; J. J. Dobbins, L. F. Ball, J. G. Cooper, S. L. Gavel and S. Hay, "Excavations in the Sanctuary of Apollo at Pompeii, 1997", *AJA*, 1998, vol. 102, pp. 739–56.

8 For a proposal that the dedication read "GENIO COLONIAE" rather than "GENIO AVG(VSTI)" see I. Gradel, "Mamia's dedication: emperor and genius. The imperial cult in Italy and the Genius Coloniae in Pompeii", *AnalRom*, 1992, vol. 20, pp. 43–58; cf. J. J. Dobbins, "Problems of chronology, decoration, and urban design in the forum at Pompeii", *AJA*, 1994, vol. 98, pp. 662–3, 694 note 153.

9 See Zanker, *Pompeji. Stadtbilder*, pp. 28–30; Zanker, *Pompeii*, pp. 87–93; Dobbins, "Problems of chronology", pp. 661–3.

10 J. J. Dobbins, "The altar in the sanctuary of the Genius of Augustus in the forum at Pompeii", *RM*, 1992, vol. 99, pp. 251–63.

11 Generally on M. Holconius and the theatre see J. H. D'Arms, "Pompeii and Rome in the Augustan age and beyond: the eminence of the Gens Holconia", in R. I. Curtis (ed.), *Studia pompeiana et classica in honor of Wilhelmina F. Jashemski 1: Pompeiana*, New Rochelle, NY, 1988, pp. 53–8.

12 The Tiberian date: A. Mau and F. W. Kelsey, *Pompeii: Its Life and Art*, London and New York, 1902, pp. 111–12. A. Mau, *Pompeji in Leben und Kunst*, Leipzig, 1908, pp. 106–8. On the basis of the wall-paintings W. Ehrhardt (*Stilgeschichtliche Untersuchungen an römischen Wandmalereien von der späten Republik bis zur Zeit Neros*, Mainz, 1987, pp. 5–7) would go even later, to the reign of Nero. Others prefer an Augustan date: e.g. L. Richardson, jr, "Concordia and Concordia Augusta: Rome and Pompeii", *PP*, 1978, vol. 33, pp. 267–9; V. Kockel, "Funde und Forschungen in den Vesuvstädten II", *AA*, 1986, pp. 457–8; D'Arms, "Pompeii and Rome", p. 53; Zanker, *Pompeji. Stadtbilder*, pp. 30–1; Zanker, *Pompeii*, pp. 93–101; Dobbins, "Problems of chronology", p. 647.

13 Zanker, *Pompeji. Stadtbilder*, p. 28; Zanker, *Pompeji. Stadt und Wohngeschmack*, p. 94; Zanker, *Pompeii*, pp. 85–7; cf. Dobbins, "Problems of chronology", pp. 685–8.

14 Lauter ("Bemerkungen zur späthellenistischen Baukunst in Mittelitalien", pp. 422–3) suggests a slightly earlier date, around 95 BC.

15 Zanker, *Pompeji. Stadtbilder*, p. 33; Zanker, *Pompeji. Stadt und Wohngeschmack*, p. 115; Zanker, *Pompeii*, pp. 105–7.

16 The idea is explored most fully in J. Andreau, "Histoires des séismes et histoire économique: le tremblement de terre de Pompéi (62 ap. J.-C.)," *AnnEconSocCiv*, 1973, vol. 28, pp. 369–95.

17 Dobbins, "Problems of chronology"; cf. also K. Wallat, *Die Ostseite des Forums von Pompeji*, Frankfurt am Main, 1997, and idem, "Der Zustand des Forums von Pompeji am Vorabend des Vesuvausbruchs 79 n.Chr", in T. Fröhlich and L. Jacobelli (eds), *Archäologie und Seismologie. La regione vesuviana dal 62 at 79 d.C. Problemi archeologici e sismologici* (Colloquium Boscoreale, 26–27 November 1993), Munich, 1995, pp. 75–92.

18 This is overlooked by Zanker, who ascribes the enlargement of the sanctuary to the Augustan period (*Pompeji. Stadtbilder*, p. 26; *Pompeji. Stadt und Wohngeschmack*, pp. 86–7; *Pompeii*, pp. 78–9).

BIBLIOGRAPHY

Andreau, J., "Histoires des séismes et histoire économique: le tremblement de terre de Pompéi (62 ap. J.-C.)", *AnnEconSocCiv*, 1973, vol. 28, pp. 369–95.

D'Arms, J. H., "Pompeii and Rome in the Augustan age and beyond: the eminence of the Gens Holconia", in R. I. Curtis (ed.), *Studia pompeiana et classica in honor of Wilhelmina F. Jashemski I: Pompeiana*, New Rochelle, NY, 1988, pp. 51–73.

Dobbins, J. J., "The altar in the sanctuary of the Genius of Augustus in the forum at Pompeii", *RM*, 1992, vol. 99, pp. 251–63.

——, "Problems of chronology, decoration, and urban design in the forum at Pompeii", *AJA*, 1994, vol. 98, pp. 629–94.

——, Ball, L. F., Cooper, J. G., Gavel, S. L. and Hay, S., "Excavations in the sanctuary of Apollo at Pompeii, 1997", *AJA*, 1998, vol. 102, pp. 739–56.

Ehrhardt, W., *Stilgeschichtliche Untersuchungen an römischen Wandmalereien von der späten Republik bis zur Zeit Neros*, Mainz, 1987.

Eschebach, H., *Die städtebauliche Entwicklung des antiken Pompeji*, RM-EH 17, Heidelberg, 1970.

Gradel, I., "Mamia's dedication: emperor and genius. The imperial cult in Italy and the Genius Coloniae in Pompeii", *AnalRom*, 1992, vol. 20, pp. 43–58.

Kockel, V., "Funde und Forschungen in den Vesuvstädten II", *AA*, 1986, pp. 443–569.

Lauter, H., "Bemerkungen zur späthellenistischen Baukunst in Mittelitalien", *JdI*, 1979, vol. 94, pp. 390–459.

Ling, R. *Pompeii: History, Life and Afterlife*, Stroud, 2005.

Mau, A. and Kelsey, F. W. *Pompeii: Its Life and Art* (2nd edn), London and New York, 1902.

——, *Pompeji in Leben und Kunst* (2nd edn), Leipzig, 1908.

Nappo, S. C. "Pompei: la casa *Regio* I, *ins*. 20, n. 4 nelle sue fasi. Considerazioni e problemi", in L. Franchi dell'Orto (ed.), *Ercolano 1738–1988: 250 anni di ricerca archeologica. Atti del Convegno Internazionale Ravello–Ercolano–Napoli–Pompei 30 ottobre–5 novembre 1988* (Ministero per i Beni Culturali ed Ambientali, Soprintendenza Archeologica di Pompei, Monografie, 6), Rome, 1993, pp. 667–76.

Richardson, L., jr, "Concordia and Concordia Augusta: Rome and Pompeii", *PP*, 1978, vol. 33, pp. 260–72.

Slayman, A. L., "The new Pompeii. Excavations beneath the AD 79 level illuminate the history of the famous Roman resort", *Archaeology*, November/December 1997, pp. 26–34.

Strocka, V. M., *Casa del Labirinto (VI 11, 8–10)* (Häuser in Pompeji 4), Munich, 1991.

Wallat, K., "Der Zustand des Forums von Pompeji am Vorabend des Vesuvausbruchs 79 n.Chr", in T. Fröhlich and L. Jacobelli (eds), *Archäologie und Seismologie. La regione vesuviana dal 62 al 79 d.C. Problemi archeologici e sismologici* (Colloquium Boscoreale, 26–27 November 1993), Munich, 1995, pp. 75–92.

——, *Die Ostseite des Forums von Pompeji*, Frankfurt am Main, 1997.

Zanker, P., *Pompeji: Stadtbilder als Spiegel von Gesellschaft und Herrschaftsform* (Trierer Winckelmannsprogramme IX), Mainz, 1988.

——, *Pompeji. Stadt und Wohngeschmack*, Mainz, 1995.

——, *Pompeii. Public and Private Life*, Cambridge, MA, 1998.

CHAPTER TEN

URBAN PLANNING, ROADS, STREETS AND NEIGHBORHOODS

———•◆•———

Carroll William Westfall

Pompeii reveals to us how the Romans used their acute skills as architects and urban designers to serve their distinctive and clearly defined civic needs. In 89 BC the Romans took over an already flourishing Pompeii and spent 150 years rebuilding, refitting and reconstructing it. In AD 79 they were still not finished reshaping Pompeii, as any Roman city was always a work in progress. Described here is Pompeii's urban character based on what is visible today.[1]

The city the Romans conquered was principally a commercial center, rich in great private luxury, but rather poor in public buildings, shrines and places of resort. Like their predecessors, the Romans spent lavishly on private pleasures, but their sense of civic duty also led them to spend liberally on religious and civic buildings and on public recreational facilities. The city they built within the Pompeii they inherited presents an impressive urban order in the service of the civil order.[2]

Pompeii exemplifies the urban legacy of Rome and presents an instructive example of a traditional town built to sustain and foster a life of civility. Population density was high by modern standards with the 167-acre city holding perhaps 10,000 to 12,000 residents,[3] a number that swelled each day as people came from the countryside to enjoy the city's markets and diversions. The same general urban character pervaded the city's background buildings: atrium houses, row houses and other common types of residential party-wall construction, often with shops fronting the streets. The typical street cross-section had building walls rising directly from a sidewalk with curbs defining footpaths, although some streets lacked sidewalks on one or both sides, and some were narrower than others. The solidly built-up blocks were arrayed in an irregular grid pattern in which most streets change their alignment every few blocks, a condition the Romans exploited to great advantage as they imposed their urban order on the city.

The Romans defined four districts within the city (Figure 10.1): (1) a district for outdoor amusements centered at the amphitheater, (2) a genteel residential district in the area of the Central Baths, (3) a cultural district for theatrical entertainment, and (4) the district the forum dominates. Each district can be traversed in a walk of fifteen or so minutes; each possesses a distinctive character; all are connected one with another, and all form their most impressive linkages with the forum, the city's urban and civil center.

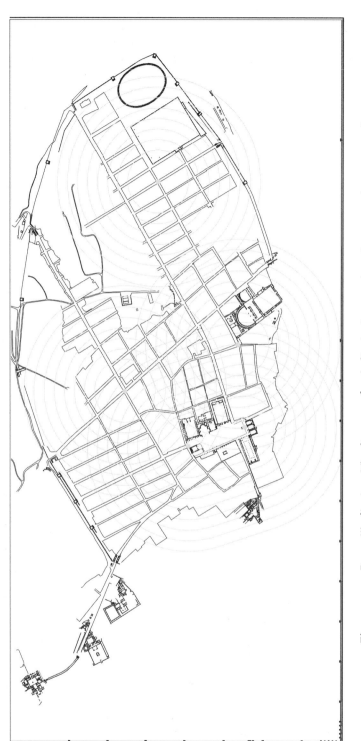

Figure 10.1 Pompeii's districts. The diameter of each district is approximately 500 m; the structures in black postdate the Roman takeover. Map compliments of H. Knickman; districts overlain by K. M. Hanna.

The district notable for offering outdoor amusements lay far to the east of the forum.[4] Most prominent here is the amphitheater, one of the first structures the Romans built. The neighboring *palaestra* provides the city's largest outdoor open area. The amphitheater and *palaestra* lie just beyond the urban villas strung along via dell'Abbondanza where many of the buildings have rooms opening onto colonnades fronting graceful gardens, water features and orchards (Figure 23.1). In this district many of the *insulae* host agriculture including, most invitingly, viticulture (Figure 31.6). Here were pleasant places to take the air and a cup of wine in simple shelters nestled within spacious high-walled enclosures.

A great variety of large and small houses largely defines the district to the north located around the Central Baths, which were being built in AD 79 (Figure 15.6). These baths were so important that they occupied an entire *insula*, obliterating all traces of the *insula*'s previous use, and even intruded into the back street, rendering that street impassable to cart traffic.[5]

The baths stand at this district's center, at the intersection of the two major streets, strada Stabiana and via della Fortuna. Strada Stabiana probably began as a north–south country road passing outside Pompeii's putative original nucleus. The via di Nola–via della Fortuna route may also have lain outside that nucleus since it, like strada Stabiana, fails to run directly into the forum. Shops provide most of the frontage of both streets, as one would expect on well-traveled thoroughfares, and the new baths would have added more than a dozen shops. Both streets provide an entrance to the baths, but neither entrance would have rivaled the shops. When designing

Figure 10.2 Via Stabiana at its intersection with via della Fortuna–via di Nola, from southeast. Visible are a water tower, a small shrine, remains of a portico, a fountain and stepping stones. Photo: J. J. Dobbins.

Figure 10.3 Via Stabiana at its intersection with via degli Augustali, from south. Visible are a water tower, a fountain, an arcade and stepping stones. Photo: J. J. Dobbins.

this inward-looking building, it was more important to have shops along the streets than imposing façades for the baths.

Opposite the baths, and uniquely in Pompeii, one corner of the strada Stabiana–via della Fortuna intersection is notched out to form a small plaza (the southeast corner of VI.14).[6] Here the Romans placed a portico fronting the shops (only traces remain), a water standpipe, a shrine, a fountain and the usual curb stones and related stepping stones across the roadway (Figure 10.2). Their placement seems consciously calculated to inflect the pedestrian toward the forum.

Similar inflections occur at the via degli Augustali and the via dell'Abbondanza intersections along strada Stabiana. The Romans enlivened the via degli Augustali intersection with a standpipe, a fountain and a feature encountered nowhere else in Pompeii, namely, an arched portico straddling the sidewalk and protecting a shop (Figure 10.3). These features invest the intersecting and unremarkable via degli Augustali with an importance worthy of its destination, the forum.

Farther south, strada Stabiana meets via dell'Abbondanza, the street connecting the amphitheater district to the forum. As via dell'Abbondanza approaches this intersection from the west it bends and widens to form the broad largo Stabiana stretching from the entrance to the Stabian Baths to the intersection itself (Figure 10.4). To the east the street narrows and jogs to the north thereby creating the impression for one approaching from the west that via dell'Abbondanza ends at strada Stabiana. The Romans exploited these conditions brilliantly. They placed a fountain and standpipe on the east side of the intersection (Figure 16.4). In the opposite direction, they raised the pavement to make a forecourt for the expanded and rebuilt Stabian Baths and built a tetrapylon honoring the Holconius family (Figures 10.4 and 15.3). The visibility of the tetrapylon's southwest pier from the edge of the forum lying at some distance up the rising slope of via dell'Abbondanza connects this intersection with the city's center (Figure 10.5).

This intersection, appealing and richly equipped as it is, is less the center of a district than a linkage between the other four. It is, itself, linked most closely to the city's cultural district. In pre-Roman times this district centered around the Triangular Forum whose nucleus was a ruined temple, a theater and a small *palaestra* (VIII.7.29). The Romans reconditioned the temple ruin, edged much of the area it occupied with a Doric colonnade, expanded the theater (Figure 14.3), added a roofed theater, or odeion (Figure 14.1), outfitted a large peristyle that ultimately became a gladiators' barracks, and built (though cf. De Caro, Ch. 6) a temple to Jupiter Meilichios, and a sanctuary to Isis (Figure 13.3). A new entrance to the Triangular Forum, the Ionic Propylon, integrated this newly important area into the civil and architectural order of Pompeii.[7] The propylon is visible frontally from via dell'Abbondanza at the western end of the largo Stabiana. This zone has been interpreted as an especially honorific and ceremonial passageway within the city.[8] The Ionic Propylon is also visible obliquely from strada Stabiana (at its intersection with via del Tempio di Iside) where it constitutes the only conspicuous, beckoning urban element between the largo Stabiana and the Porta di Stabia at the city walls.

The forum, the focus of the Romans' most intense energies and grandest ambitions, is the center of the fourth and most important district. In pre-Roman Pompeii, the

Figure 10.4 Strada Stabiana (foreground) with largo Stabiana and via dell'Abbondanza ascending toward the forum, from east. Visible are the tetrapylon, the step to the level of the largo, and at the right, the corner of a fountain and a water tower. Photo: J. J. Dobbins.

Figure 10.5 View toward largo Stabiana from the upper end of via dell'Abbondanza near its intersection with the forum, from west. The southwest pier of the tetrapylon is visible in the distance. Photo: J. J. Dobbins.

forum was simply an open market area with porous edges that a person could enter from a number of streets (Figure 12.15). The Romans converted it into an urban center and focused attention on it from throughout the city (cf. Dobbins, Ch. 12). They collected the shops scattered around its edges into a *macellum* at the northeast corner, lined the forum's open area with colonnades, rebuilt the eastern side with four impressive new imperial buildings, modified the opposite side, apparently added public buildings at the south end, and at the north end probably rebuilt the Temple of Jupiter. The Romans also transformed the forum's physical relationship to the rest of the city. They eliminated some entrances thereby making the forum's presence within the city dependent on a few entrances, each of which connected the forum to the city's larger urban order.[9]

The least important entrance served the area south of the forum. The Romans blocked via delle Scuole with a fountain, curbstones and a Doric tufa column aligned with similar columns in the forum colonnade. Much more important is the pair of streets, via dell'Abbondanza and, almost in a direct line with it, via Marina to the west that together form the only route across the city passing through the forum (Figures 12.1 and 12.2).[10] In both streets, preparation for entering the forum begins at some distance away where the usual façades one encounters on Pompeii's major streets give way to monumental walls. In via dell'Abbondanza these are the walls of the Eumachia Building on the north, and on the south, the enclosure traditionally identified as the *Comitium* (VIII. 3) with its entrance from this street set on a platform reached by three steps along the line of the sidewalk. At the forum's edge a person encounters bollards and a curb like those at the other forum entrances, excluding cart traffic from the forum. Because the colonnade here was still under construction in AD 79, the intended form of this entrance remains obscure, but clearly the Romans had made the street's breaching of the colonnade conspicuous by orienting an obviously wider intercolumniation on the street's center.

The approach to the forum from the west is more monumental. In moving from the sea front, just beyond the Porta Marina, up the steep incline toward the forum, one encounters on the right the massive Roman precinct wall of the Sanctuary of Venus, which intrudes into the street and narrows it considerably. Above and to the left, at the higher sidewalk level onto which the neighboring houses front, one sees several columns (these are some of the twelve columns that form a colonnade in front of these houses, visible in Figure 10.6). Given that streetside colonnades are indicators of urban significance, the visitor is at once informed of the importance of this entrance to the city. Next, and also on the left, is the intersecting, narrow vicolo del Gigante. At this point one may continue to walk in the street or ascend three steps to a broad sidewalk that fronts several houses in *insula* VII.7. Immediately after this point the street widens as one passes the corner of the Sanctuary of Venus. On the right the high north wall of the Basilica stretches to the end of the street and is relieved only by a doorway located midway along its length. Midway along *insula* VII.7, opposite the north entrance to the Basilica just mentioned, begins the plain, stark wall enclosing the Temple of Apollo whose entrance lies half way between this point and the forum. At the street's head stood the two-story unfluted, limestone, Tuscan and Ionic colonnade, still under construction along the west side of the forum in AD 79. Its intercolumniation for the street is more generous here just as it is across the forum, suggesting that the two sides were understood to be parts of a pair (Figure 10.6).

Figure 10.6 Via Marina from within the forum, from east. Visible are the forum's Tuscan colonnade, the Basilica (left), the Sanctuary of Apollo (right), the entrance to the Sanctuary of Venus (marked by modern white signs) and part of the colonnade flanking via Marina. Photo: J. J. Dobbins.

The Romans exploited the lack of parallelism between the exterior walls of the Basilica and Sanctuary of Apollo to produce complementary forced perspectives. When one looks toward the forum, the street's diverging sides defeat perspective's tendency to narrow vistas and make objects seem farther away. The forum therefore appears large in the immediate distance. When one looks away from the forum and toward the Porta Marina (Figure 10.6), the convergence of the curbs and walls accentuates the perspective and appears to push everything farther away. In the distance two features catch one's eye. On the left, beyond the Basilica, the entrance to the precinct of the Temple of Venus is inviting and totally open. On the right and a little farther away is the first column of the via Marina colonnade. This prominent column announces the Porta Marina which the steep decline renders invisible from near the forum. A final touch invests this area with importance: from the forum to the precinct of the Temple of Venus the pavement is enriched with small white limestone pieces inserted in the corners of the dark lava pavers.[11]

These entrances pale in comparison with the forum's northeast entrance. The connection between the forum and the rest of the city begins in the constricted area between the Macellum and the flank of the Temple of Jupiter (Figure 12.5). The Romans made this an important largo. They built a large arch (so-called "of Tiberius") at the back of the temple (visible in Figure 10.8); it either replaced or duplicated the one they had built and then destroyed near the front of the temple. They introduced an elegant Corinthian colonnade, and made the façade of the Macellum equally grand. Furthermore, they defined this area with a subtle telling detail. Around the entire forum ran a pair of steps. The lower tread formed an apron approximately 1.80 m deep; the upper tread was the stylobate for the forum colonnade. Within the Macellum largo the apron reduces its depth to that of a normal step, a detail that stressed the linkage between the forum and the area just beyond it while also making it distinct.

Beyond the Macellum largo and through the great arch is via degli Augustali, the street whose intersection with strada Stabiana we examined earlier. The extension of the Macellum largo northward is via del Foro, a street with an urban character unique in Pompeii.

Via del Foro's west side is faced with shops and the unpretentious men's entrance to the Forum Baths, one of the first Roman additions to the city. Shop fronts interspersed with house entrances originally lined the street's east side, but at an early date the Romans added a portico of thirteen brick and stucco Tuscan columns, beginning at via della Fortuna and running for most of the block's length (Figure 10.7). Later modifications at the portico's southern end produced an emphatic entrance (VII.4.10) to some rooms behind the shops. That entrance preserves two original columns, but all the other columns in the portico were transformed at some unknown date into compound piers except for the three columns nearest via della Fortuna which, either then or at some other time, were removed. The Temple of Fortuna Augusta occupies the space from which the three columns had been removed. Dedicated in AD 3/4 (the only dateable work here), the temple was paid for by M. Tullius whose name is traditionally given to the portico.

The temple's design and siting wring the greatest possible urbanistic advantage from the corner site. The temple's steps project into via del Foro, and its lower podium is deep enough to hold an altar visible from within the forum (Figures 10.7 and 10.8). A northward tilt of the building's principal axis brings the temple's front

Figure 10.7 Via del Foro. Overview from south, showing the Porticus Tulliana, the Temple of Fortuna Augusta with its altar on the lower terrace of the temple podium, the so-called Arch of Caligula with via del Mercurio beyond, and the sidewalk and facades of the street's western side. Photo: J. J. Dobbins.

out into the intersection making it magnetic to those approaching from via delle Terme. Travelers on this street, which continues a route beginning at the important Porta Ercolano, were drawn here for their entrance to the forum rather than to the shorter back-alley route through the narrow vicolo delle Terme (Map 2).

The temple's design and siting make it visually important from the east as well. From the distant notched intersection at strada Stabiana, the bright marble temple flank beckoned people to take the brief ascent up via della Fortuna, a high-class street linked with big houses and subsidiary shops.

Also visible while making that ascent is the flank of the other important element at via del Foro, the so-called Arch of Caligula (seen in Figure 10.7). Serving as the entrance to via di Mercurio, its flank is conspicuous because the façade line in the last block on the north side of via della Fortuna before the arch (VI.10) was set back, possibly in conjunction with the temple's construction.[12]

The wide via di Mercurio lying beyond the arch is devoted to large houses with almost no shops. The other blocks north of via della Fortuna–via delle Terme are similarly luxurious, although some lesser dwellings and shops are intermixed. This distinctly patrician district stands in contrast to the humble, utilitarian, character of the blocks with narrow, irregular streets which the new Roman buildings on the forum's east side cut off from the forum.

The intersection with its arch, temple, baths and portico collects the routes attracted here and then funnels them along via del Foro into the forum. Drawing people down the street's slight descent is the "Arch of Tiberius" opening into the largo in front of the Macellum; next is the high flank of the Temple of Jupiter, and beyond that lies the vast open area of the forum with its brilliant limestone pavement and bright limestone colonnades. Here a person has obviously reached Pompeii's center.

Figure 10.8 Forum. Overview from south. Towards the Temple of Jupiter, flanked by two arches and with Vesuvius behind. The photograph is taken near the intersection of major north–south and east–west urban axes. Visible through the arch at the right is the altar of the Temple of Fortuna Augusta (cf. Fig. 10.7 for a closer view of the altar). Photo: J. J. Dobbins.

From the forum a person can also be directed to all the districts in the city. In front of a large statue base centered near the forum's south end is a small area (perhaps 3 m^2) that serves as the city's specially charged center of gravity (Figure 12.2).[13] This area is both the focus of the elements of the urban ensemble and the area from which the linkages between the forum and the city's districts are especially clear.

Four axes intersect here to define that focus. One is the forum's long axis culminating in the Temple of Jupiter with Vesuvius looming behind it (Figure 10.8). The second is the prolongation of via Marina leading to the precinct of Venus and the sea just beyond the Porta Marina; the entrance to that precinct and the easternmost column of the colonnade draw a person's attention to what remains hidden farther along (Figure 10.6). The third is the prolongation of via dell'Abbondanza. It is connected indirectly through the Ionic Propylon to the Triangular Forum, while from the head of via dell'Abbondanza the visibility of the southwest pylon of the tetrapylon connects it directly to strada Stabiana (Figure 10.5). From that elaborate intersection people can be carried on into the farther arena district or up and down strada Stabiana. The final axis is northward, along a line of sight running through the Macellum largo and the so-called Arch of Tiberius along via del Foro to reach the quite distinctively visible altar on the podium of the Temple of Fortuna Augusta (Figure 10.8). From here one can easily continue up via di Mercurio, follow the bustling route toward the Porta Ercolano, or descend along the attractive via della Fortuna to reach the broad expanses of Pompeii's northeastern areas. The Romans made the forum both goal and beginning of all the important routes of sight and travel within the city. None could doubt that here was the center of their distinctive and impressive conjunction of civil and urban order.

NOTES

1 Most of what follows is based on observations made during two-week periods in June of 1995, 1996 and 1997 as a member of the Pompeii Forum Project directed by John J. Dobbins. Fundamental to this work was the on-site collaboration with team member Mark Schimmenti, Associate Professor of Architecture at the University of Tennessee.

2 Using the term urban order here is meant to provide a parallel to the Roman civil term, *ordo* (the body of magistrates that within a municipal constitution form the city council), thereby suggesting the reciprocity between the urban and the architectural on the one hand and the political and civil on the other.

3 W. Jongman, *The Economy and Society of Pompeii*, Amsterdam, 1988, pp. 108–12.

4 Its center might be said to be at the intersection of via di Castricio and via di porta Nocera, although nothing distinctive marks that intersection. All street names are modern.

5 The bath's walls extend beyond the original curb line into vicolo di Tesmo (between *insulae* V.4 and V.5). A new, narrow sidewalk of large lava blocks set beyond the bath's walls intrudes far enough into the original, heavily rutted street to make it probably the narrowest street in Pompeii and quite impassable for carts. None of this is shown on the Eschebach plan; but see Map 3.

6 The notch in the building allotments seems to be as old as this area's platting according to the work of the University of Leiden group headed by Herman Geertman and communicated to me orally.

7 The Propylon and associated Doric colonnade, both built of tufa, have generally been thought to be Samnite structures with Augustan repairs and minor modifications; see for example L. Richardson, jr, *Pompeii: An Architectural History*, Baltimore, MD and London, 1988, pp. 67–73. However, excavations conducted in the summer of 1996 by the University of Rome "La Sapienza" point to a date between the earthquake of AD 62 and the eruption of 79, although the evidence is not without its ambiguities: A. Carandini, "Nuovi progetti, nuove domande, nuovi metodi," in P. G. Guzzo (ed.), *Pompei. Scienza e Società. 250° Anniversario degli Scavi di Pompei*. Convegno Internazionale, Naples, November 25–27, 1998, Milan, 2001, pp. 127–9. For a commentary on the previous article, see P. G. Guzzo and F. Pesando, "Sul colonnato nel foro triangulare di Pompei: indizi in un delitto perfetto," *Eutopia* II n.s., 2002, pp. 111–21.

8 A. Wallace-Hadrill, "Public honour and private shame: the urban texture of Pompeii," in T. J. Cornell and K. Lomas (eds), *Urban Society in Roman Italy*, London, 1995, pp. 39–62 (especially 47–50).

9 Three additional, older, inconspicuous surviving entrances remained unblocked or unimproved: vicolo di Championnet south of the Basilica, another between the western and central municipal buildings at the forum's south end, and the third through the pair of openings to the west of the Temple of Jupiter, an area apparently being altered in AD 79.

10 Via delle Scuole and via del Foro have a similar slight misalignment with one another, but the great distance between them and the intruding forum colonnades have not allowed them to be perceived as parts of a pair.

11 Richardson, *Pompeii*, p. 278, n. 14, postulates that this pavement treatment marks this section as a processional way associated with the Temple of Venus. This would correspond with a similar putative use for the unflecked via dell'Abbondanza postulated by Wallace-Hadrill, "Public honour and private shame: the urban texture of Pompeii," pp. 39–62. Similar flecking occurs in front of the Temple of Fortuna Augusta in via del Foro, discussed below.

12 In *insula* VI.10 the building alignment is parallel to the temple's flank and is skewed relative to the line formed by the north street face of *insulae* VI.12, 13 and 14. [The "Arch of Caligula" was also topped by a bronze equestrian statue, making it even more visible (cf. Welch, Ch. 36; Figure 36.2.—Eds]

13 Recall that Roman perspective schemes vanished to an area and not a point as occurs in the perspective system invented in the early fifteenth century. For useful comments see L. Bek, *Towards Paradise on Earth* (*Analecta Romana*, IX), Odense, 1980, esp. part III, 1. That an imperial equestrian statue sat atop the base is, sadly, mere conjecture.

CHAPTER ELEVEN

THE WALLS AND GATES

——·◆·——

Cristina Chiaramonte

The history of the research on, and studies of, the fortifications of Pompeii[1] is long and complex for two main reasons. On the strictly archaeological level, the surviving remains should be attributed to a number of defensive circuits whose placement in time and space has posed a number of problems. On the more broadly historical level, the phases of the walls reflects, as is natural, the process of the birth and urban development of a city that in the pre-Roman period was a crossroads of relationships, exchanges and conflicts between the native Oscan world and the Etruscan, Greek and Campano-Samnite worlds. Although it may not be legitimate to apply mechanically the dates of the great events in history to restorations and rebuildings of the fortifications, it is inevitable for us to connect interventions representing an enormous commitment for the community to political emergencies requiring improvement or adaptation of the defenses to new techniques of warfare.

Taking into account a long history of research and studies, and the relative bibliography, which is the product of at least two periods of fervid debate on the subject—the 1930s and 1940s and the 1970s and 1980s—what we know today about the walls can be summed up briefly as follows. The ridge of the terrace on which Pompeii stood was first surrounded by walls in the first half of the sixth century BC. Remains of the walls have been identified at Porta Nocera[2] and between Porta Nocera and Tower III, beneath the Tower of Mercury and at Porta Vesuvio; traces of it have come to light at Porta Ercolano (see Map 2). The circuit of this fortification, roughly coinciding with that of the subsequent ones in the northwest and southeast sectors, seems to have defined for the first time the area of more than 65 ha (160 acres) that the city was to keep up to the end. From that time on a wall surrounded the entire plateau along the so-called "tactical ridge," defined by the conformation of the margins of the lava front which in protohistoric times had formed the hill on which the city stood (Figure 11.1).

The excavation data relating to the wall indicated not a double curtain but a single curtain of five or six courses, not very high (2 to 3 m), in *opus quadratum* with rectangular blocks in horizontal courses, 40 to 50 cm high, 75 to 100 cm long, and about 55 cm thick. Recent observations, however, have proposed a double wall, 100 cm high (though this requires verification by excavation).[3] The material used

Figure 11.1   Houses of Region VIII on the lava spur at Pompeii.
Photo: J. J. Dobbins.

was a local sandstone known as *pappamonte* and the soft lava called *cruma di lava*, both occurring in the more archaic building phases of the city, but only the second was also utilized in later periods. The wall had a foundation trench only a few centimeters deep and no *agger* (earth mound) backing. The two gates that anchor part of the archaic road network to the building of the wall (*intra* and *extra moenia*) can be placed at Porta Vesuvio and the Tower of Mercury.[4] The pottery found in sondages indicates that the wall was built in the first half of the sixth century BC and was destroyed at the beginning of the next century.

Sometime between the first half of the fifth and the fourth century BC a new fortification was built. The date comes from stratified material, but cannot be pin-pointed more closely.[5] This new wall was completely independent of the first wall, though it approximately followed its course along the edge of the plateau. The new wall was a double curtain of Sarno limestone. Its overall thickness was 4.30 m, in *opus quadratum* with a flat layer of slabs projecting into the intramural fill, which in turn contained compacted limestone chips and crumbs. The foundations are shallow, limited substantially to just the base slab, but in such a way as not to allow great upward development. Remains of this fortification—called *ad ortostati* for the appearance of its lowest course of large rectangular slabs, or orthostats, set vertically—came to light during Maiuri's sondages at Porta Ercolano, Porta Vesuvio, Porta di Stabia and at the Tower of Mercury, and in those of 1982 between the amphitheater and Tower III.[6]

The walls had stairs for access to the bastions and may have been reinforced by towers. In order to circumscribe the period of these new defenses to the first half of the fifth century BC, we note the presence of a small intrapomerial street (i.e., one inside the city limits) related to it. This street is dated to the first decades of the century, and in the same period the curtain of *pappamonte* and soft lava had been obliterated.[7]

The third fortification of the city was first built at the end of the fourth century BC and is still in good part visible along the perimeter of the city (Figure 11.2). It encloses an oval area, with a northeast–southwest axis of 1,200 m and a northwest–southeast axis of 720 m. The double curtain of orthostats was demolished and a curtain rebuilt with Sarno limestone with internal pillars and an *agger* backing. Later in the third century, an inner curtain of Nocera tufa was added, set back about 5 m from the outer face. This was higher than the outer one, and it, too, had solid closely spaced buttresses projecting inward, and with an *agger* that sloped toward the city

Figure 11.2 Samnite city wall in Sarno limestone near the Porta Nocera. First half of the third century BC. Photo: J. J. Dobbins.

as far as a low retaining wall. On the same occasion the outer curtain was rebuilt and raised with courses of tufa. Before the Social War broke out, various points of the outer curtain were rebuilt in *opus incertum*; the towers visible today were built, and for access to them the *agger* had to be lowered. Thus came into being the last double-curtain fortification with an *agger* on the city side, eight gates and at least thirteen towers.

We do not know exactly the original height of the outer curtain, but the foundations, far sturdier than those of the earlier walls,[8] suggest that it was considerable. We know that the sloping *agger*, interrupted to build the inner curtain of Nocera tufa, had a low wall of clustered limestone fragments serving as weight-bearing spine; we presume, given the height of the curtain, that it was quite wide, wide enough to permit a useable slope.[9] Recent sondages at the walls confirm substantially the two different moments of construction of the curtains, as Maiuri had maintained in his day and contrary to what some scholars still believe today.[10]

The city gates were probably renovated when the curtain was doubled, with arches of Nocera tufa and the typical decoration of protomes of divinities in relief on the keystones. They must have been partially rebuilt in great haste on the eve of the Social War and for this reason display a mixed construction technique with limestone and tufa blocks and lava insertions in *opus incertum*. Four gates (Stabia, Nocera, Nola and Sarno) were of simple type, with barrel-vaulted space containing the actual gate, preceded by a long, narrow passage between the gate itself and two outside bastions where attackers would have been exposed from above on both sides. Porta Vesuvio was destroyed by the earthquake of 62 and never rebuilt. Porta Marina is a deep passage covered by a barrel vault that leads up the plateau. A pedestrian corridor, a guard post and a passageway wide enough to bring up war machines—the whole structural conception of this gate makes it a case unto itself. It belongs to the first years of the Roman colony and was probably rebuilt at the same time as the adjacent Temple of Venus.

Porta Ercolano with its three arches, including the symmetrical pedestrian passages, was the monumental entrance to the city in its final period. The construction with façade in *opus mixtum vittatum* (block-and-brick) and the traces of what must have been First-Style decoration are evidence of this.

Recent excavations by a Japanese team at the walls in the vicinity of the so-called Porta di Capua, between Porta Vesuvio and Porta di Nola, have not identified traces of the gate.[11] Before the Social War the towers were inserted into the double curtain and projected from the outer curtain by 2–2.50 m on average. They had walls of *opus incertum* of limestone and lava and were faced with thick white plaster forming ashlar-type blocks in relief to simulate *opus quadratum* (Figure 11.3). A Doric entablature, with triglyphs and metopes, adorned the top. The remains of the collapse of Tower VIII indicate that from the beginning the towers bore inscribed numbers, starting from Porta di Stabia and continuing counterclockwise around the walls.[12] The interior, with barrel vault and internal stairs, had three stories. The uppermost story had wide windows for artillery; the middle story, at the height of the wall-walk, to which it was connected by gates on both flanks, had narrow slits for the archers. From a lower mezzanine a gate toward the city permitted walking down the escarpment or along its top inside the wall. The exit from the ground-floor guardroom, lighted by narrow slits, was through a postern on the flank.

Figure 11.3   Tower XI, or the Tower of Mercury, on the north side of the fortifications.
Photo: J. J. Dobbins.

The different interpretations, both archaeological and historical, of these facts, which have been amassed over time through mostly focused investigations, have sought to answer the basic questions of who gave Pompeii its walls, when and why, and the urban layout anchored to them (cf. also Carafa, Ch. 5).

A fundamental point of departure for anyone wishing to trace the history of the studies remains the works of Amedeo Maiuri,[13] whose conclusions, after systematic research and sporadic minor interventions, can be briefly summarized as follows. Though he recognized the *pappamonte* wall as archaic, he suspended judgment, awaiting new evidence, on its chronology and course. He identified Greek methods in the construction, between 474 and 430 BC, of the double limestone curtain. He attributed to a first intervention of the Samnites, between 400 and 300 BC, its demolition and the construction, along the same course, of the limestone wall with *agger* to which the inner tufa curtain would be added (300–180 BC). Among the various rebuildings that preceded the outbreak of the Social War were the construction of the towers and the consequent lowering of the *agger*.

Maiuri's proposal of phases, which was related to the debate over the Greek and Etruscan hegemony of Pompeii, was surrounded by heated arguments from those who did not believe in so large a city from the beginning of the fifth century BC and those who, while accepting the proposed chronologies, did not see a Greek model in the earliest fortification but, rather, an "Etruscan-Italic" one. Von Gerkan in 1940, going back to an intuition of Haverfield, who already in 1913 had identified the original nucleus of Pompeii in the area around the forum,[14] proposed a chronology for the extension of the original nucleus and the construction of the first fortification along the edge of the hill, at the end of the fifth century BC by the Samnites. Decades later, Eschebach[15] substantially restated von Gerkan's positions. Only after the resumption of the stratigraphic excavations both in the city[16] and at the walls, did debate reopen on the development of Pompeii in the light, especially, of the new elements that emerged on the earliest *pappamonte* wall and of the research conducted between the area of the *Altstadt* and the Temple of Apollo.[17]

The recent studies of the structures and of pottery and architectural material from stratigraphy, as well as those of the epigraphic evidence, have also freed the problem of the urban formation of Pompeii from the old Etruscans–Greeks dichotomy. Once the inevitable connection of political and cultural elements of Etruscan, Greek and Italic stamp in the archaic Tyrrhenian was acknowledged, the following conclusions, today shared by most, were reached.[18] A first set of walls in *pappamonte* and soft lava went up along the "tactical ridge" of the hill in the first half of the sixth century BC, spurred by the Etruscan component which amply permeated the native population of the earliest village. To the Etruscan element, then, should be attributed the urban rationalization of a center in typical position of high ground dominating the coast at the mouth of a river. The function of the masonry would have been, among other things, to incorporate and control a stretch of the piedmont road, i.e., the gully corresponding to the future via di Stabia, which, following the lava spur from Vesuvius, reached the sea and the Sorrentine peninsula from the hinterland.[19] The Sanctuary of Athena, on the edge of the city, would have dominated this road from the end of the sixth century BC.

Inside a much larger circuit wall we thus find the first residential nucleus, the so-called old city, the *Altstadt*, for which the choice between two hypotheses remains uncertain: that it is contemporary with the walls or that it pre-existed them. The latter hypothesis is supported by the inexact topographic coordination between the already substantially regular plan of the small built-up area and the course of the walls.

It seems clear, rather, that in the same period as that of the walls, at the intersection of the north–south and east–west axes of the original built-up area, the strikingly Etruscanizing Sanctuary of Apollo was erected in the context of a single settlement plan. There followed the definition of a road network based on the intersection of the roads corresponding to the future east side of the forum with via delle Scuole, and via Marina with the first stretch of via dell'Abbondanza.

Most of the fortified area remained available for farming and grazing and only the area corresponding to the future Regiones VI, VII and VIII was partially occupied by masonry houses, whence we infer planned growth and a political orientation to the whole project.

Few architectural remains can be assigned to the Pompeii of the fifth and fourth centuries BC, when the Greek and Etruscan structures collapsed and the Samnites came to dominate the entire Campanian region. The most important of these is certainly the double curtain of orthostats; we have sufficient evidence on its course and construction technique, and have elements for its relative chronology, but little data for an absolute chronology. These include the early fifth-century BC fragments that date the narrow street that defined the city limits, which was laid over the collapse of the *pappamonte* walls and probably associated with the later limestone curtain.[20]

Pompeii's Temple of Athena, in the Triangular Forum, is also dated about 500 BC and the duo of walls and great temple could be said to echo, with the same ideological weight, that of the archaic *pappamonte* walls and the Temple of Apollo.

The new fortification—probably to be attributed again to the Etruscan city, placed on guard by the great tumult that within a few decades would lead to the Samnite conquest of the region—had a corresponding road system. This extended the corridors that existed in the original nucleus, as proved by traces of pre-existing gates identified at Porta di Stabia, Porta Vesuvio and Porta Ercolano. We do not know, however, how much of the intramural area was built up in this period, especially now that a rereading of the results of Maiuri's excavations and comparison with situations recorded in recent investigations suggest that the date should be lowered to the third century BC also for houses, notably the House of the Surgeon, traditionally dated to the fourth century and considered among the earliest (cf. Jones and Robinson, Ch. 25).[21]

The installation of the fortification with limestone curtain and *agger* is to be considered part of the planned building development of Pompeii in the third century, when the city had effectively entered the orbit of Rome with the entire federation of Nuceria. The model applied, which we soon find again in the Latin colony of Paestum, was a rectangular plan with a north–south axis. Once again the natural slope of the strada Stabiana was used, and two east–west axes, via di Nola and via dell'Abbondanza which divided the city in three bands, dictated the position of the Porta di Nola and Porta di Sarno. The secondary partitions of the three stretches of the via di Stabia thus defined the positions of towers or posterns that must have preceded those still visible and that were distributed along the eastern walls at the exact center of the distance between two gates or between a gate and a corner of the curtain (Figure 11.4; cf. also Geertman, Ch. 7).

It would seem that the radical restructuring of the walls from a conceptually simple curtain with *agger* to double curtain with *agger* should be seen in relation to the imminent danger of incursions by Hannibal. The final intervention, on the eve of the Social War, was the construction, or more probably the reconstruction, of the towers in *opus incertum* (cf. Jones and Robinson, Ch. 25 for damage to those walls in the siege).

Pompeii and its urban territory, for centuries fortified and constructed upon, received its definitive urban fabric, still today largely recognizable, between the third and second centuries. This must have followed a radical operation of leveling and burying which preserved or incorporated only what coincided with the established grid. This is probably the cause of the diversity of the stratigraphy beneath Pompeii,

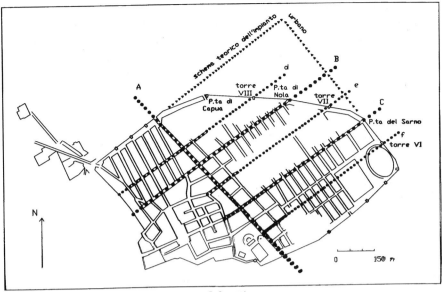

SCHEMA DELL'IMPIANTO URBANISTICO DI III SECOLO A.C. NEL SUO MODELLO TEORICO (DE CARO. 1991).

Figure 11.4 Schematic plan of Pompeii in the third century BC
(after De Caro, "La città sannitica").

and of diversity within the same Region or even the same house.[22] The sondages that shed light on pre-Roman Pompeii are still too few and too irregularly located, but the evidence they have provided has sufficed for us to understand how long and articulated the history of the city was already when, with the Sullan conquest, it entered to all effects into the orbit of Rome. The main stages of this history are defined in the constant attention that the citizenry gave to their system of defenses, which survived in its last version to our own day, a mighty bulwark into which flowed centuries of experiences of different peoples.

NOTES

1 Maureen B. Fant translated the Italian text. A. Maiuri, "Studi e ricerche sulla fortificazione di Pompei," *MonAnt*, 1930, vol. 33, coll. 113–286; idem, "Greci ed Etruschi a Pompei," *Atti della Reale Accademia d'Italia. Memorie*, ser. 7, 1943, vol. 4, pp. 121–49 (reprinted in *Alla ricerca di Pompei preromana*, pp. 135–59); and bibliographical references in the following notes.

2 In particular a trial trench supervised by me for the Pompeii Soprintendenza Archeologica, at the Porta di Nocera, has yielded precise data on the technique, the relative chronology and the absolute chronology of the *pappamonte* wall. See S. De Caro, "Nuove indagini sulle fortificazioni di Pompei," *AION*, 1985, vol. 7, pp. 75–114, especially pp. 79–80.

3 S. Lorenzoni, E. Zanettin and A. Casella, "La più antica cinta muraria di Pompei. Studio petro-archeometrico," *Rassegna di Archeologia*, 2001, vol. 18B, pp. 35–49.

4 For the gate at the Tower of Mercury, see F. Pesando, "La porta presso la Torre di Mercurio e le fasi della fortificazione di Pompei," in F. Pesando *et al.*, *Le insulae 3 e 4 della Regio VI di Pompei. Un'analisi dell'urbanistica*, Rome, 1990, pp. 217–26.

5 De Caro, "Nuove indagini," pp. 91–6.

147

6 De Caro, "Nuove indagini," pp. 99–104.

7 De Caro, "Nuove indagini," pp. 81–4, fig. 17.1.

8 At Porta di Nola the presence of foundations with four layers of blocks placed sloping inward has been recorded: C. Chiaramonte Treré (ed.), *Nuovi contributi sulle fortificazioni di Pompeii, Quaderni di ACME*, 1986, vol. 6.

9 De Caro, "Nuove indagini."

10 Maiuri, "Greci ed Etruschi a Pompei." L. Richardson, jr, *Pompeii. an architectural history*, Baltimore, MD, 1988, p. 49 maintains that the entire fortification, including the two curtains and the *agger*, should be associated typologically with the Athenian walls of the fourth century BC, whose model appears for the first time in Italy in Greek Sicily of the first half of the third century BC.

11 H. Etani, S. Sakai and Y. Hori, "Preliminary reports: archaeological investigation at Porta Capua, Pompeii," *Opuscula Pompeiana*, 1997, vol. 7, pp. 145–58, with earlier bibliography.

12 Chiaramonte Treré, *Nuovi contributi sulle fortificazioni di Pompei.*

13 Maiuri, "Greci ed Etruschi a Pompei;" idem, "Studi e ricerche sulla fortificazione di Pompei."

14 F. Haverfield, *Ancient Town-Planning*, Oxford, 1913; A. von Gerkan, *Der Stadtplan von Pompeij*, Berlin, 1940.

15 H. Eschebach, *Die städtebauliche Entwicklung des antiken Pompeji*, RM-EH 17, Heidelberg, 1970.

16 M. Bonghi Jovino (ed.), *Ricerche a Pompei. L'insula 5 della Regio VI dalle origini al 79 d.C.*, Rome, 1984.

17 De Caro, "Nuove indagini;" idem, *Saggi nell'area del tempio di Apollo,* Naples, 1986; Chiaramonte Treré, *Nuovi contributi sulle fortificazioni di Pompei.*

18 A. D'Ambrosio and S. De Caro, "Un contributo all'urbanistica e all'architettura di Pompei in età ellenistica. I saggi nella casa VII, 4, 62," *AION*, 1989, vol. 11, pp. 173–215; C. Chiaramonte Treré, "Sull'origine e lo sviluppo del'architettura residenziale di Pompei sannitica," *ACME— Annali della Facoltà di Lettere e Filosofia dell'Università degli Studi di Milano*, 1990, vol. 43.3, pp. 5–34; M. Cristofani, "La fase "etrusca' di Pompei," in F. Zevi (ed.), *Pompei*, Naples, 1991, pp. 9–22; S. De Caro, "La città sannitica: urbanistica e architettura," in F. Zevi (ed.), *Pompei* I, Naples, 1991, pp. 23–46; S. De Caro, "Lo sviluppo urbanistico di Pompei," *Atti e memorie della Società Magna Grecia*, 1992, vol. s. 3a, 1, pp. 67–90; P. Sommella, "Città e territorio nella Campania antica," in G. Pugliese Carratelli (ed.), *L'Evo Antico*, Naples, 1991, pp. 178–9; C. Chiaramonte Treré, "Note in margine all'assetto edilizio e produttivo di Pompei in età ellenistica," in *Splendida Civitas nostra, Studi archeologici in onore do Antonio Frova*, Rome, 1995, pp. 9–21; Lorenzoni *et al.*," La più antica cinta muraria di Pompei. Studio petro-archeometrico."

19 De Caro, "Lo sviluppo urbanistico."

20 De Caro, "Nuove indagini."

21 C. Chiaramonte Treré, "Sull'origine e lo sviluppo del'architettura residenziale di Pompei sannitica," pp. 5–34.

22 Chiaramonte Treré, "Note in margine all'assetto edilizio e produttivo di Pompei in età ellenistica," p. 12. Much evidence attests how abrupt differences in the level of bedrock beneath Pompeii can be found within a short distance. Maiuri noted how in the sondages in the House of the Large Fountain, in Regio VI, the foundations of the façade were set into bedrock 1.20 m deep; about five m away were the remains of an archaic *pappamonte* structure at 0.50 m (A. Maiuri, "Saggi nella Casa della Fontana Grande," *NSc* 1944–55, pp. 130–5).

BIBLIOGRAPHY

Bonghi Jovino, M. (ed.), *Ricerche a Pompei. L'insula 5 della Regio VI dalle origini al 79 d.C.*, Rome, 1984.

Chiaramonte Treré, C. (ed.), "Nuovi contributi sulle fortificazioni di Pompei," *Quaderni di ACME*, 1986, vol. 6.

——, "Sull'origine e lo sviluppo del'architettura residenziale di Pompei sannitica," *ACME*, 1990, vol. 43.3, pp. 5–34.

———, "Note in margine all'assetto edilizio e produttivo di Pompei in età ellenistica," in *Splendida Civitas nostra, Studi archeologici in onore do Antonio Frova*, Rome, 1995, pp. 9–21.

Cristofani, M., "La fase 'etrusca' di Pompei," in F. Zevi (ed.), *Pompei*, Naples, 1991, pp. 9–22.

D'Ambrosio, A. and S. De Caro, "Un contributo all'urbanistica e all'architettura di Pompei in età ellenistica. I saggi nella casa VII, 4, 62," *AION*, 1989, vol. 11, pp. 173–215.

De Caro, S., "Nuove indagini sulle fortificazioni di Pompei," *AION*, 1985, vol. 7, pp. 75–114.

———, *Saggi nell'area del tempio di Apollo a Pompei. Scavi stratigrafici di A. Maiuri nel 1931–32 e 1942–43*, Naples, 1986.

———, "La città sannitica: urbanistica e architettura," in F. Zevi, (ed.), *Pompei*, Naples, 1991, pp. 23–46.

———, "Lo sviluppo urbanistico di Pompei," *Atti e memorie della Società Magna Grecia*, 1992, vol. s. 3a, 1, pp. 67–90.

Eschebach, H., *Die städtebauliche Entwicklung des antiken Pompeji*, RM-EH 17, Heidelberg, 1970.

Haverfield, F. *Ancient Town-Planning*, Oxford, 1913.

Lorenzoni, S., E. Zanettin and A. Casella, "La più antica cinta muraria di Pompei. Studio petro-archeometrico," *Rassegna di Archeologia*, 2001, vol. 18B, pp. 35–49.

Maiuri, A. "Studi e ricerche sulla fortificazione di Pompei," *MonAnt*, 1930, vol. 33, coll. 113–286.

———, "Greci ed Etruschi a Pompei," *Atti della Reale Accademia d'Italia*. Memorie, ser. 7, 1943, vol. 4, pp. 121–49 (reprinted in *Alla ricerca di Pompei preromana*, pp. 135–59).

Richardson, L., jr, *Pompeii. An Architectural History*, Baltimore, MD, 1988, pp. 44–50.

Sommella, P., "Città e territorio nella Campania antica," in G. Pugliese Carratelli (ed.), *L'Evo Antico*, Naples, 1991, pp. 178ff.

Von Gerkan, A., *Der Stadtplan von Pompeji*, Berlin, 1940.

CHAPTER TWELVE

THE FORUM AND
ITS DEPENDENCIES

——— •♦• ———

John J. Dobbins

INTRODUCTION*

Today's visitors spend little time in the city center, moving on instead to the "must see" houses with frescoes, the baths and the brothel. This is understandable because the forum is quite ruined and appears as if it will not reward attention, but such visitors are deceived because the forum, which was Pompeii's urban space *par excellence*, is interesting in its own right and important for what it tells us about Roman urbanism. Archaeologists know that the forum is rich in information—the chapters by Descœudres, Ling and Small attest to that. However, in spite of the considerable data that we have, archaeologists cannot agree on certain basic information, such as the dates and functions of some buildings, or more seriously, on the overall evolution of the most important public zone of the city.

The forum was the focal point of Pompeii's life, housing its institutions of government, its main market, and major cult buildings (Figures 12.1, 12.2 and Table 33.1).[1] It drew citizens and visitors alike to its colonnades, buildings and open space as people pursued their daily lives of marketing, attending meetings, dealing with officials and participating in religious festivals. In many ways the forum at Pompeii emulated the Forum Romanum in Rome, just as every town throughout the empire looked to Rome for inspiration. As in Rome, the history of the forum in Pompeii is that of the systematic building up and aggrandizing of the most important part of the city.[2] The eruption of AD 79 halted the process of urban development and preserved much of the evidence that inevitably would have been destroyed or obscured if Pompeii had endured throughout antiquity. In its final phase, the Pompeian forum provides a window onto civic aspirations, building techniques and urban design schemes of the third quarter of the first century AD. This is especially true because the earthquake of 62 thrust the Pompeians into a period of building activity that may never have occurred if disaster had not struck. By identifying what the Pompeians rebuilt or built anew and how they changed the forum, we gain an insight into what was important to them urbanistically during the 60s and 70s. The period bracketed by the earthquake and the eruption thus provides us with an unparalleled opportunity to study urban change and development within a very narrowly circumscribed period.

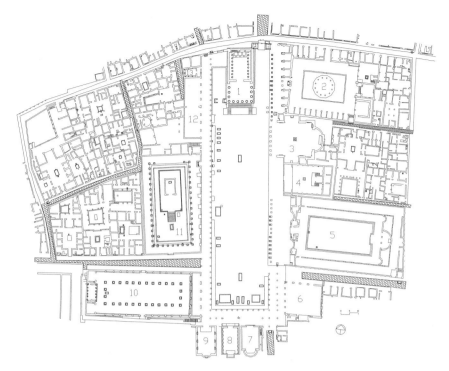

Figure 12.1   Pompeii forum. Plan.
Plan with current streets highlighted and buildings numbered.

1 Temple of Jupiter; 2 Macellum; 3 Imperial Cult Building (also called Sanctuary of the Public Lares); 4 Sanctuary of Augustus (also called Temple of Vespasian); 5 Eumachia Building; 6 *Comitium*; 7–9 Civic buildings; 10 Basilica; 11 Sanctuary of Apollo; 12 Northwest Building; 13 Public latrine.

On the other hand, peeling away the layers of urban development and getting back to the early forum is an especially difficult challenge. The pages that follow tell the story in a new way that, at this writing, is controversial.

This chapter builds on the pioneering efforts of August Mau to interpret the architectural remains of the forum. The forum was excavated during the 1810s and 1820s, but the first systematic attempt to come to grips with the newly discovered buildings was made by Mau in specialized articles and in the comprehensive treatment of the whole city that this present volume seeks to honor. My colleagues and I in the Pompeii Forum Project disagree with many of Mau's assessments, most fundamentally the validity of his "tufa period," but that does not diminish the esteem in which we hold him for his critical eye, astute observations and prompt publications (cf. Laidlaw, Ch. 39, n. 3 for an acknowledgment of Mau's accuracy).[3] Many others since Mau have studied the forum, but this essay cannot review all contributions.

The Pompeii Forum Project (http://pompeii.virginia.edu), which is currently investigating the forum, is an interdisciplinary, collaborative effort to understand the evolution of the forum, including the chronologies of individual buildings, the relationships among the buildings that formed the urban ensemble, and the dynamics of urban change that produced the forum that we see today. The most important factors that

Figure 12.2 Pompeii forum. Balloon view.
Compliments of Aristide Caratzas.

shaped the city center were influences from Rome, local patronage and the response to the earthquake of AD 62.

THE FORUM TODAY

Entrances

Today's forum is approached by three primary and three secondary entrances (Figures 12.1 and 12.2). The primary approaches are the two east–west streets near the southern end (via Marina and via dell'Abbondanza) and via del Foro that enters the forum through the arch at the northeast corner. The secondary entrances are at the northwest from vicolo dei Soprastanti, at the southwest along vicolo di Championnet, and at the southeast along via delle Scuole. An alley between buildings 8 and 9 (Figure 12.1) may have served the houses to the south. The major entrances provide far more than simple utilitarian access to the forum. Using urban devices, such as arches, wide column spacing, street widening, framed vistas, and the sculpture galleries associated with the Macellum and the Eumachia Building, the entrances call attention to the importance of the forum to those approaching, and for those within the forum they link its space to the city beyond its limits (cf. Westfall, Ch. 10).

Colonnade, forum pavement and monument bases

The forum's vast open area is defined by the remains of the once continuous colonnade that wrapped its east, south and west sides and established the forum as a monumental urban space.[4] The colonnade was a unifying screen for the diverse buildings behind it, although it employed different materials and orders: Luna marble in front of the Macellum (Corinthian order); limestone in front of the Eumachia Building (Tuscan) and along the west side of the forum (Tuscan lower and Ionic upper); and tufa along the south and the southeastern section as far as via dell'Abbondanza (the Doric colonnade of Popidius). In front of the Imperial Cult Building are the foundations for seven of eight large columns. No trace of a colonnade remains in front of the Temple of Augustus where the stylobate is a modern reconstruction, but it is reasonable to restore a colonnade at that location. The reconstructed stylobate continues in front of the Eumachia Building as far as via dell'Abbondanza.[5] Associated with the colonnades in front of the Macellum and the Eumachia Building are statue bases placed against the east sides of the columns. By means of these sculpture galleries, the forum colonnade in front of the two buildings was given special emphasis.[6]

Universally recognized as the colonnade that gave the forum space its first organized and monumental character is the tufa Doric colonnade of Popidius.[7] Beam pockets preserved on the back of the entablature are evidence that the colonnade once carried a second story (Figure 12.3). Compare the similar treatment of the limestone colonnade in front of the Basilica where the second story, but not its flooring, has been re-erected (Figure 12.4). Stairways at the northeast corner of the east South Building and at southeast corner of the Basilica gave access to the second story of the colonnade.[8] The full extent of the colonnade of Popidius is not known as it was being replaced with a limestone and marble colonnade when Vesuvius erupted, as the unfinished nature of the western branch of the limestone colonnade makes clear.[9] A more fundamental question is the date, because the colonnade played a major role in the first

Figure 12.3   Forum. Overview from south.

Figure 12.4   Forum. Overview from southwest.

systematic shaping of the forum. Does the tufa colonnade belong to the pre-Roman Samnite period of the second century BC, as is generally believed, or to the period after the Romans conquered Pompeii in 89 BC? This issue is treated below.

Early imperial paving slabs of Caserta limestone are preserved in a continuous section in the south and southeast regions, on both sides of the Temple of Jupiter, and randomly throughout the rest of the forum (a stretch of modern cement paving in front of the Temple of Jupiter dates from 2002).[10] Between the forum pavement and the stylobate on which the columns stand is a partially preserved broad apron, or step, also of Caserta limestone (as are the stylobates), that sets the forum's inner surface apart from the surrounding higher level of the enveloping porticoes. For much of its modern history most of the forum surface was dirt because most paving slabs had been salvaged after the eruption, but in 1995 a lawn was introduced over much of the area to reduce persistently blowing dust and to retard erosion. An unfortunate consequence of the lawn is that visitors can no longer traverse the previously open public space.[11]

Numerous statue bases occupy the central area.[12] Most prominent are the large axially-aligned bases, probably for equestrian statues, and the group of large bases at the forum's south end. Along the west side is a large speaker's platform, or *suggestum*, several equestrian bases, and bases for individual standing statues, these latter identified by inscriptions. None of the statues survives (but cf. Figure 23.12).

Temple of Jupiter (the Capitolium)

At its north end the forum is dominated by the Temple of Jupiter set against the dramatic backdrop of Mt Vesuvius, the flanking arches enhancing the scenographic effect of the temple's setting (Figures 10.8, 12.5).[13] Even though the arches are not of the same scale or symmetrically arranged, to the eye of a person at the southern end of the forum they register as nearly equal pendants framing the temple (Figure 10.8). In typical Etrusco-Italic fashion, the Temple of Jupiter is raised on a high podium from which it dominated the forum as its sacred precinct. Three substantial north–south segmental vaults of concrete construction constitute the structure of the podium and receive some illumination from small light shafts in the floor of the temple above.[14] This accommodation for light suggests that the podium served some function, perhaps as the *aerarium*, or city treasury, but it may have served other purposes as well.[15] The present door to the podium near its exterior southeast corner (opposite the façade of the Macellum) is a secondary entrance roughly cut through the wall of the podium. An earlier entrance, belonging to an earlier phase of the temple, descended from the temple's stairway into the central vault of the podium as steps preserved inside the podium attest.[16]

The present temple is hexastyle Corinthian with a deep *pronaos*, or porch, of tufa columns.[17] The interior Ionic colonnade is set close to the *cella* walls allowing a broad nave to approach the rear of the *cella* where a platform contains three vaulted chambers that must have served the Capitoline cult in some way. Maiuri's investigations revealed that the vaulted structures were added around an earlier columnar arrangement whose columns are now visible through openings left by Maiuri in the later fabric.[18]

From the forum the *pronaos* is approached by two narrow staircases that flank a *rostrum*, or podium, that accommodated an altar and that may also have served as a

Figure 12.5　Temple of Jupiter, from southeast.

speaker's platform.[19] Above the *rostrum* is a broad staircase that ascends to the *pronaos*. The temple suffered damage in the earthquake of 62 as depicted in the famous relief of the quake in progress, and as attested in the out-of-plane damage to the east and west *cella* walls.[20] Damage to the podium's crown molding may have been caused by elements of the superstructure falling upon it. The repair of the walls appears to be ancient, but the temple seems not to have been fully repaired, its statue of Jupiter stored elsewhere and the head discovered in the *cella*. Major problems attending the Temple of Jupiter remain its construction history and the role it played in the early development of the forum.[21]

The south end: South Buildings, *"Comitium"* and Basilica

At the southern end of the forum, and deriving importance from the north–south axis shared with the Temple of Jupiter, are three civic buildings here designated the South Buildings.[22] It is impossible to assign specific functions to the three civic buildings, but it is possible that they served as the city council chamber (analogous to the *Curia*, or Senate House, in Rome), an archive for city documents (analogous to the *Tabularium* in Rome), and possibly an office for the two chief magistrates, the *duumviri*.[23] The east South Building reveals two phases of construction. Its façade and apsidal end are replacements contemporary with the completely new construction in brick-faced concrete of the west and central South Buildings, developments apparently dating to the post-62 period. The inner forum colonnade in front of the civic buildings also displays modifications to its original tufa form.

Figure 12.6 Plan of *insula* VIII.3 (outline emphasized) with *Comitium* at northwest corner.

Figure 12.7 *Comitium* and southeast corner of the colonnade of Popidius, from southwest.

Figure 12.8 Basilica, from east.

Also belonging to the suite of civic buildings at the forum's southern end are a squarish building traditionally called the *Comitium*,[24] but probably a voting place, and the Basilica[25] that served as a court, and possibly a bourse and meeting place for magistrates.

The *Comitium*, along with part of the colonnade of Popidius, was carved out of the northwest corner of residential block VIII.3 (Figures 12.6 and 12.7). The intimate structural relationship between the *Comitium* and the colonnade indicates that they were constructed at the same time, although the precise date remains debatable (the Pompeii Forum Project argues for a date between 89 and 80 BC). Most of the broad openings that once characterized the *Comitium*'s north and west walls were blocked at a subsequent point in the building's history. The flexibility provided by the original multiple doorways and the two elevated tribunals (exterior southwest corner and interior south side) made the building a suitable location for conducting elections.[26]

The Basilica is generally considered to be one of the most magnificent buildings at Pompeii and is frequently cited in discussions of Roman architecture to illustrate "basilica" as a Roman building form (Figure 12.8).[27] This is somewhat ironic as virtually all commentators date the Basilica to the *pre-Roman* Samnite period of the late second century BC following Mau in his assignment of the building to his "tufa period." The Pompeii Forum Project departs from this dating and argues below that the Basilica belongs to the early Roman period, immediately after the Sullan conquest.

The interior of the Basilica consists of an ample nave surrounded by an ambulatory and at the western end a raised tribunal.[28] From the interior, steps lead down to a *chalcidicum*, or porch, at the level of the forum colonnade (Figure 12.4). While the Basilica is generally characterized as being of tufa construction, its tufa is limited to the piers and north and south walls of the *chalcidicum*, the engaged columns of the interior walls, and the columns of the tribunal. The walls are constructed of lava *opus incertum*; the columns of the nave are assembled from bricks specifically designed for the purpose. Remains of First-Style wall painting cover the interior walls.

West side, northeast corner and arches

Flanking the forum's west side, but not actually within the forum is the Sanctuary of Apollo, one of the oldest cult places in Pompeii, dating from the sixth century BC, but experiencing many changes throughout its long history (Figure 13.1).[29] Immediately north of the sanctuary is the *mensa ponderaria* where Roman standards of measure were displayed and where purchasers could verify the volume of goods purchased.[30] A room to its north may have been an office for an official overseeing the standards of measure. Next is the Northwest Building, a simple long structure of *opus testaceum* that was constructed after 62 and appears not to have been finished. It is divided into several units serving four different purposes. The first is a large rectangular space with brick piers defining its forum façade.[31] It is sometimes identified as a granary, but it would have been ineffective in that capacity as its broad openings would have provided no protection against dampness, rodents and insects. Today, the building houses a variety of objects recovered in the excavations (amphorae, sculpture, furniture, etc.) as well as some plaster casts of victims of the Vesuvian eruption. Simplicity of design and proximity to the *mensa ponderaria* and to the

Macellum on the opposite side of the forum support the argument that it was a market building.[32] The next spaces are a public latrine, and two large shoplike rooms that open to the street to the north. As the shop entrances are raised high above the sidewalks, it is more likely that they were offices rather than typical shops. Under the shops and accessible by a door opening onto the forum is a pair of vaulted, subterranean chambers that may have served as the city *aerarium*, or as a repository for products that required cool storage, such as wine or olive oil. Immediately to the east, at the northwest corner of the forum, are two small stairways that provide communication between the forum and vicolo dei Soprastanti. Opposite the long rectangular market building is a small arch that provided a link between the forum colonnade and the Temple of Jupiter. A similar arch once stood on the east side of the temple, but it was removed in antiquity and the places where its piers were located were filled in with limestone paving slabs in a pattern that identifies the location of the arch. Further back, at the northeast corner of the Temple of Jupiter, is a larger arch that communicates with via del Foro. While the arches are early imperial, their precise dates, the date of the removal of the one, and the individuals to whom they were dedicated are unknown.[33]

East side[34]

Macellum

At the northeast corner of the forum is the Macellum, the main food market (Figure 12.9).[35] A monumental marbled entrance that includes statue bases and an *aedicula*, or templelike statue niche, is flanked by shops and/or offices and leads to a once-

Figure 12.9   Macellum. Overview of interior, from northwest.
Photo: L. F. Ball.

colonnaded interior with shops on the south, a shrine and two large flanking spaces at the far east end, and a pavilion (no longer extant) supported on twelve bases in the center.[36] Fish scales found in the drain below the pavilion suggests that fish were sold there. Balancing the interior southern shops are exterior northern shops. The shrine contains a base for the main statue and two niches in each side wall. The two statues (Figures 36.5 and 36.6) in the southern wall were discovered by the excavators, but their identities remain in doubt (the current statues are plaster casts; the originals are in the Museo Nazionale in Naples). Alastair Small makes a case that the figures are members of the imperial family.[37] The specific functions of the two large rooms flanking the shrine are impossible to determine. The northern space appears to be religious in nature due to its elevated templelike structure and low altar, while the southern space with its benchlike structure eludes definitive identification.[38] Also debatable are the precise foundation date for the Macellum (although a date in the 30s or 40s seems reasonable), the nature of the predecessor buildings on the site, and the condition after the earthquake.

Imperial Cult Building

To the south of the Macellum is a large open-fronted structure, whose design is the most advanced among the buildings on the forum in its curvilinear plan and articulation of interior wall surfaces, traditionally designated the Sanctuary of the Public Lares (Figure 12.10).[39] While the building cannot be identified with certainty, it appears to be a sanctuary for the imperial cult, built after 62, and designated here the Imperial Cult Building. The building emphasizes interior space in the manner of Roman architectural design beginning with Nero's Domus Aurea in the 60s,

Figure 12.10   Imperial Cult Building from southwest.

Figure 12.11 Imperial Cult Building. Reconstruction by J. G. Cooper.

continuing with the Palace of Domitian in the 90s, and culminating in the Pantheon in the 120s. Its interior is dominated by a large apse, and two large lateral *exedrae*. Each *exedra* contains a statue base and each preserves the footings for a pair of columns that screened its entrance. In addition, numerous niches for over-lifesize statues are evident throughout while the apse with its raised ledges for sculpture could have accommodated at least nine statues probably set between columns. The building is very prescient in dematerializing wall surfaces in the manner of the later Aula Regia in the Palace of Domitian in Rome.[40] The interior was richly clad in marble revetment, all salvaged after the eruption save three pieces pinned behind the base in the south *exedra*. Preparations in the form of the standard tangs and wedges, and impressions of revetment slabs in the mortar of the setting bed confirm the existence of the marble veneer.[41]

An integral part of the building were eight large columns that did double duty in serving as both forum colonnade columns and façade columns for the Imperial Cult Building. They stood on ample footings of which seven are still in situ.[42] By comparing the dimensions of these footings to the smaller footings and surviving columns of the colonnade in front of the Macellum we calculate a column height of *c*.10.33 m, or 35 Roman feet. These columns stood slightly in advance of the Macellum columns and presumably of the columns in front of the Sanctuary of Augustus. In this way the façade of the building was marked by its taller columns and its slight projection from the flanking colonnades. For reasons argued in detail elsewhere, at the ends of the façade we restore arches that span the forum colonnade and echo the blind arches of the zone immediately in front of the interior apse.[43] The façade, set off by arches as a discrete urban zone, coopted the forum colonnade and perforce drew into the interior of the building anyone walking along the east portico of the forum (Figure 12.11).

There is no scholarly consensus on the date of this precocious building, but its design and physical relationships to adjacent buildings lead to the conclusion that is belongs to the post-62 rebuilding of the east side of the forum.[44]

Sanctuary of Augustus

The small Sanctuary of Augustus nicely illustrates the essential components of a Roman sanctuary, and also demonstrates the fundamental problems of identification and date that face anyone studying the Pompeian forum (Figure 12.12).[45] The sacred space is defined by a precinct wall that provides an ample entrance from the forum. A vestibule immediately inside was probably covered. The main space is an open court with a temple built up against the rear wall and an altar in front of the temple. Three service or sacristy rooms lie to the east of the court. The walls of the court form a series of shallow bays that are capped alternately by triangular and lunette-shaped pediments (i.e., the same treatment as the exterior south and east walls of the Eumachia Building). The temple is approached by stairways on the sides of the podium.[46] Within the small temple are the remains of a base for the cult statue. The marble altar in the courtyard is original.[47] It bears evidence of having been repaired, probably following damage in the earthquake. Its four sculptural panels present Augustan themes and support the notion that the temple was dedicated to the first emperor.

The temple itself was decorated inside and out with marble veneer that was salvaged after the eruption. The walls of the courtyard retain their rough coat of plaster, but they never received their final coat. The vestibule had not yet been decorated. The

Figure 12.12   Sanctuary of Augustus, from west.

163

façade on the forum, however, was decorated with marble veneer whose impressions still can be seen in the mortar. In the angle at the juncture with the Imperial Cult Building can be seen traces of an earlier decoration in painted plaster.[48]

In 1875 Giuseppe Fiorelli identified the sanctuary as that dedicated by the priestess Mamia to the Genius of Augustus (*CIL* X, 816).[49] However, throughout most of the twentieth century scholars identified it as the Temple of Vespasian. Mau's arguments in favor of a Flavian date and Maiuri's excavations that found no earlier temple proved persuasive and convinced most that the temple, allegedly unfinished at the time of the eruption, was to have been dedicated to Vespasian, the most recently deified emperor.[50] Some recent opinion has returned to Fiorelli's identification of the sanctuary as that dedicated by the priestess Mamia to the Genius of Augustus.[51] It is not disputed that Mamia was an Augustan-period priestess; indeed, Kockel has established that Mamia's tomb outside the Porta Ercolano dates to the late Augustan or Tiberian period.[52]

More recently, however, Ittai Gradel has challenged both the traditional reading of the inscription and the consensus that the present building is Mamia's dedication.[53] Gradel's new restoration of a critical lacuna in the inscription replaces the traditional

M[a]MIA P(ublii) F(ilia) SACERDOS PVBLIC(a)
GENI[o Aug(usti) s]OLO ET PEC[unia sua]

with

M[a]MIA P(ublii) F(ilia) SACERDOS PVBLIC(a)
GENI[o coloniae s]OLO ET PEC[unia sua].[54]

Thus, Mamia's dedication is not seen as a reference to the emperor, but rather to the *genius* of the colony. In addition, Gradel disassociates the inscription from the present sanctuary and argues instead that the Genius of Pompeii was worshiped in the so-called Sanctuary of the Public Lares, a structure that he dates to the pre-earthquake period. While his bold new reading invites a rethinking of the notion of a sanctuary to the Genius of Augustus, it is not possible to assign the much later Imperial Cult Building to Mamia, and the remains beneath it are such that they provide no evidence for assigning the preceding structures to her either.[55]

It is a commonplace that Augustus did not allow himself to be worshiped directly in Italy, but did permit his *genius* to receive cult; however, Duncan Fishwick's assessment that the municipalities in Italy did *not* worship the *genius* of Augustus supports Gradel's reading of the Mamia inscription and also requires that we rethink the identification of the temple.[56] Following Fishwick and Gradel, it seems prudent to rule out a Mamian dedication of any cult place to the *genius* of Augustus. Nonetheless, the altar in the present sanctuary is so replete with Augustan imagery, and the sanctuary has such a long history, including severe earthquake damage and repair, that it seems reasonable to recognize Augustus as the object of the cult, hence the designation here as the Sanctuary of Augustus. This leaves open the question of whether or not this sanctuary was dedicated by Mamia, and, if not, where her dedication was located.

Figure 12.13   Eumachia Building, interior, from southwest. Photo: L. F. Ball.

The Eumachia Building

Although a detailed understanding of the undoubtedly multiple uses of the Eumachia Building (Figure 12.13) may always elude us, the building offers a wealth of architectural, sculptural and epigraphic evidence.[57] Although this writer prefers a date in the first decade of the first century AD, it must be admitted that the evidence for dating is ambiguous.[58] Mau's Tiberian date was followed by many throughout the twentieth century.[59] Descœudres supports it in this volume and sees the dedicatory inscription as added confirmation.[60] Richardson identifies the Eumachia Building typologically as a *porticus* that is related historically, architecturally and ideologically to the building program of Augustus at Rome. Kockel, too, prefers an Augustan date for the building.[61]

Scale and siting lend special prominence to the Eumachia Building. Its size is considerable (approximately 67 m × 40 m), and it was the first building one saw upon entering the forum from via Marina. For the person approaching the forum along the upward grade of via dell'Abbondanza, the Eumachia Building's articulated southern façade marked the final stretch of road. Inscriptions on the frieze of the forum colonnade (fragmentary) and over the southeast entrance (complete) called attention to the donor and pointed to the building's wider civic meaning. They record that Eumachia, public priestess and daughter of Lucius Eumachius, in her own name and in that of her son, Marcus Numistrius Fronto, constructed the building with her own funds and dedicated it to Concordia Augusta and Pietas (*CIL* X, 810, 811).[62] The three parts of the building named in the inscription (*chalcidicum*, *porticus* and *crypta*) are identified, respectively, as the space between the forum colonnade and the main façade, the interior colonnade, and the corridor behind the interior colonnade. Through

Figure 12.14 Eumachia Building, *chalcidicum*, from south.

her dedication of a *porticus* at Pompeii, Eumachia emulated the dedication in Rome in 7 BC of the *Porticus Liviae*, a dedication to Concordia that Livia shared with her son, Tiberius. Building type, joint benefaction with her son (surely in the hope of advancing his career), and dedication to Concordia Augusta indicate that the most prominent woman in Pompeii was consciously expressing her civic responsibilities and aspirations in the same architectural, familial and religious language employed by the most prominent woman in Rome.[63]

The *chalcidicum* presents an articulated façade to the forum (Figure 12.14). Curved and square *exedrae*, as well as sculpture niches, flank the main portal. Fragmentary inscriptions for statues of Aeneas and Romulus connect the sculptural program of the *chalcidicum* with the Forum of Augustus in Rome (*CIL* X, 808, 809). It is not known if the statue bases against the forum colonnade continued the Augustan program or served as a Pompeian analogy, perhaps honoring local *summi viri*.[64] The ample portal is framed with an inhabited scroll carved in marble that evokes the acanthus scroll of the Ara Pacis Augustae in Rome.[65] To the right of the portal is a small room that appears to have been a porter's lodge. To the left, in the space between the façade wall and the interior wall, a service passage leads to an alley between the Eumachia Building and the Sanctuary of Augustus.

The *porticus* surrounded the open-air central court, its east end terminating in a large apse flanked by two smaller apses communicating with two light wells by windows (Figure 12.13). Excavations by Maiuri demonstrated that the apse with its central statue base and flanking statue niches replaced a rectilinear pre-earthquake recess.[66] The templelike projection at the center of the eastern branch of the *porticus* emphasized the apsidal sculpture gallery and invested it with an aura of religious sanctity. The apse may have contained the statue(s) whose fragments where found in

1820. Richardson is likely correct in reconstructing a sculptural program consisting of a statue of Livia on the central base flanked by statues of Concordia and Pietas in the niches.[67]

There are three entrances to the *crypta*. Two are located at the western ends of the interior portico; a third is a stepped ramp leading from the southeast entrance. A porter's lodge, still containing Third-Style wall painting, flanks this entrance. At the center of the eastern branch of the *crypta*, a sculpture niche contained a marble statue of Eumachia and an inscription recording that the fullers dedicated it (Figures 34.2 and 36.4).[68] Ample windows with low marble sills connected the *crypta* to the *porticus*. Thus the *crypta* was adequately lighted and was capable of being secured by shutters and doors, while access to the building as a whole could easily be monitored by porters at the two entrances. Both entrances to the southeast porter's lodge, the southeast entrance proper, the top of the entrance ramp, and the main entrance from the forum all preserve thresholds with cuttings for doors. This indicates that the whole building could be completely secured.

A convincing explanation of the function of the building has long eluded scholars. On the basis of the fullers' inscription and the vats allegedly found next to the south *porticus*, early commentators identified the building as a fullery. Mau correctly rejected the theory and suggested instead that the building served as a market for wool, or clothing in general. In associating the Eumachia Building with *porticus* in Rome, Richardson argues for a multipurpose use, possibly including the sale of luxury goods, and not excluding the woollen trade.[69] Most recently, a case has been made that the building was a slave market.[70] To date, Richardson's interpretation seems to be the most convincing.

It is not surprising that such an important building would have been repaired after the earthquake; indeed, repairs abound.[71] The newly restored building with its marble façade and lavish marble interior joined the others on the forum's east side in celebrating a new period of urban splendor at Pompeii in the years after AD 62.

THE HISTORY OF THE FORUM

Overview

It is impossible to write an uncontroversial history of the forum at Pompeii because the evidence is incomplete and scholarly opinion is so divergent that there is no agreement even on fundamental issues (cf. De Caro, Ch. 6 and Ling, Ch. 9). The following is a condensed account based on the current research of the Pompeii Forum Project.

At this point in Pompeian archaeology it is also impossible to provide a detailed account of the very early history of the forum area. Given the area's proximity to the coast to the west and to the Sarno river to the south, it is likely that the forum area addressed commercial needs from an early date, especially in conjunction with the Sanctuary of Apollo that appears to have been thriving in the sixth and later centuries BC.

The forum of the second century BC probably consisted of a large open space, functioning mainly as a market, and including public buildings at the south and southwest, shops on the east, and the Sanctuary of Apollo on the west, whose early

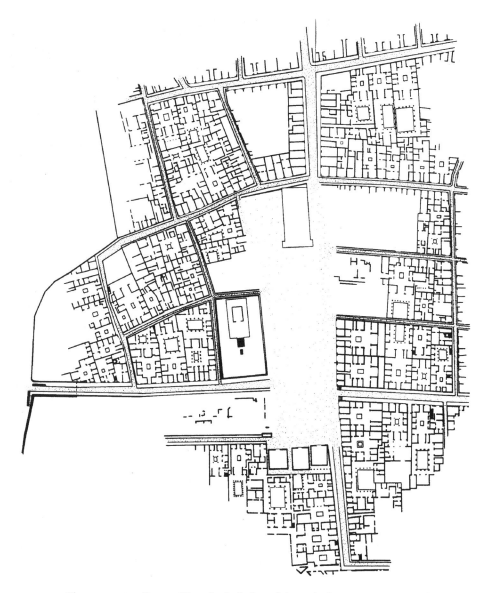

Figure 12.15 Forum. Hypothetical plan of the early forum. L. F. Ball.

form eludes us (Figure 12.15). Following the Roman conquest in 89 BC, the forum experienced three particularly vigorous building periods: (1) the early Roman period beginning in 89 BC; (2) the principate of Augustus, 27 BC to AD 14, and the early imperial period up to 62; and (3) the years after the earthquake, between 62 and 79. To the early Roman period can be attributed the tufa colonnade of Popidius, the *Comitium*, the Basilica, the east pier-wall of the Sanctuary of Apollo, the *mensa ponderaria*, probably the Temple of Jupiter, and the earlier forum pavement. It is likely that the east South Building, and possibly predecessors of the central and west South Buildings belong to this period as well. To the Augustan period belong the Eumachia Building, the Sanctuary of Augustus (the so-called Temple of Vespasian), probably the forum's limestone pavement, and the Sanctuary of Apollo in its present form. Located one block north of the forum and linked to it by via del Foro is the Augustan-period Temple of Fortuna Augusta (Figure 10.7).[72] The Macellum, which is not closely dated, is generally considered to be post-Augustan and clearly pre-earthquake. To the years after 62 belong the Imperial Cult Building (traditionally called the Sanctuary of the Public Lares), the west and central South Buildings, the Northwest Building, considerable repair work throughout the forum, and the installation of the still unfinished limestone colonnade.

The early forum

The decade from 89 to 80 BC was a watershed in Pompeian history because in that decade Pompeii became Roman: the Latin language; a Roman constitution; Roman standards of measure; the construction of the Forum Baths, the amphitheater, the *theatrum tectum*; and an influx of Roman settlers and the attendant social changes that they inevitably introduced. Strangely, no scholar discusses developments in the forum during this decade. The reason lies at least partly in the traditional opinion from the time of Mau that the forum's monumentalization belongs to the second century BC, to the "tufa period," that included the tufa colonnade of Popidius, Temple of Jupiter, Basilica, and Sanctuary of Apollo in its current form.[73] This opinion sees no architectural or urbanistic activity in the forum between the second century BC and Augustus or later. At the same time, the whole notion of the tufa period has, itself, come under considerable criticism as Pompeianists find ever more evidence contrary to it.[74] Moreover, the idea that the very center of Pompeii was architecturally sterile during the most crucial century of its history is highly improbable. Recent study by the Pompeii Forum Project seeks to clarify this situation.

We can reconstruct the pre-regularized forum in a general way (Figure 12.15). As the *Comitium* and part of the *porticus* of Popidius were carved out of the northwest corner of residential block VIII.3 (Figure 12.6), we reconstruct pre-*Comitium* houses there. Maiuri's excavations revealed shops in front of the Eumachia Building and the Sanctuary of Augustus, behind which we posit houses; at the south he found three non-aligned façade walls belonging to three non-domestic buildings that preceded the present civic buildings; and beneath the Basilica, walls that suggest a non-domestic building.[75] At that earlier time the forum was an irregular space. Its present north–south axis was not precisely defined, whether or not the Temple of Jupiter existed at the time. No side was straight, and each building presented its own façade and individual orientation to the forum. The elements did not relate to each other in a design sense or to any grander overriding principle.

The structures in the southern part of the forum are important in reconstructing the early regularized forum: the colonnade of Popidius; the east precinct wall of the Sanctuary of Apollo; the Basilica, especially its *chalcidicum*, that faces the forum colonnade; and the *Comitium*. Of primary importance is the *relationship* that exists among these urban components. Our first task is to recognize that these components form one contemporaneous ensemble. Then we will address the date.

The role of the colonnade of Popidius in shaping the forum is crucial. Its southern wing defines the south end as a straight line, while its northern returns both define the east and west edges of the forum and establish the central axis. So strong was the organizing impact of the colonnade that all subsequent buildings conform to it. While the earlier street grid and property lots did not allow whole buildings to assume orthogonal relationships to the forum axis, their façades invariably responded to the axis defined by the colonnade. The façades therefore tend to be wedge-shaped in order to conform to incompatible axes (Figure 12.16). More important, whenever such a wedge-shaped element is an integral part of a given building in the forum, the Popidian colonnade is a *terminus post quem* for that building.

As described above, the eastern branch of the tufa colonnade of Popidius is doubled in front of the *Comitium*, as was its southern branch, although there its inner file was altered over time. Understanding the relationship between the *Comitium* and the Popidian colonnade is crucial because it illustrates that the two are parts of a contemporaneous ensemble. In front of the *Comitium* the two eastern files of the colonnade are irregular in informative ways. Most obviously, they have different numbers of columns, which therefore don't align with each other: nine columns in the outer (forum side) file; eight in the inner (*Comitium* side) (Figure 12.6). The irregular spacing of the inner colonnade is chronologically crucial because that colonnade clearly responds to the pier spacing of the *Comitium*. One column is associated

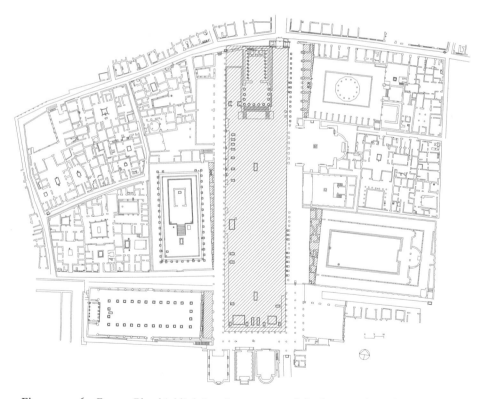

Figure 12.16 Forum. Plan highlighting the open area of the forum and the façade-wedges.

with the *Comitium*'s northwest corner while the intercolumniations of other columns relate, albeit imperfectly, to the openings in the *Comitium*. If the *Comitium*'s west wall had not existed when the colonnade was built, the colonnade would certainly not have been arranged in this awkward manner. We would expect the east file columns to be regularly spaced, to register on those in the west file and we would expect the same number of columns in each. Instead, the east colonnade responds to the design of the *Comitium* piers, so the colonnade is therefore contemporary with or later than the *Comitium*.

At the same time, the location and orientation of the *Comitium*'s west wall were determined not by the *Comitium* itself, but by the tufa colonnade. This is obvious from the fact that the tufa colonnade defines the location and orientation of the *Comitium*'s west wall. In the absence of the colonnade, the *Comitium* could have occupied the full corner of the block (VIII.3) in which it is located (Figure 12.6). It is clear that the presence of the colonnade constrained the builders of the *Comitium*. Moreover, the colonnade defines the southeast corner of the forum, with no regard for the design needs of the *Comitium*. The southeast corner of the colonnade determined both the location and orientation of the east side of the forum. Then the *Comitium* wall was set according to the colonnade. This means that the *Comitium* presupposes the colonnade, but we have just seen that the colonnade presupposes the *Comitium*. Definitively, therefore, the two are contemporary parts of one project.

We can recognize a similarly intimate relationship between the Basilica and the colonnade. The façade-wedge is again instructive for it implies that the Basilica responded to the tufa colonnade which either pre-dated the Basilica or was contemporary with it (Figure 12.16). If the Basilica had been the earlier of the two structures there would have been no need for the accommodation achieved by the façade-wedge. We would expect an orthogonal *chalcidicum*, not a wedge.

The piers of the *chalcidicum* confirm that the Basilica was responding to the colonnade in front of it because the Doric pilaster strips on the outer sides of the piers conform to the colonnade of Popidius. That conformity is not only in motif, but also in height (widths vary). The Basilica, then, also appears to be part of the Popidian ensemble.

The Basilica is also linked to the Sanctuary of Apollo by the triforal gateway where via Marina enters the forum. The south side of the gateway is formed by the north façade of the Basilica where a pilaster, like those on the *chalcidicum* façade, responds to the two tufa columns in via Marina. Similarly, the north side of the gateway is formed by the southeast corner of the sanctuary where two pilasters and capitals identical in design and height to those of the Basilica's *chalcidicum* decorate the corner. The pilaster facing south responds to the Basilica and to the tufa columns in via Marina; that facing east responds to the forum colonnade. Since the pilasters are integral to the building fabric in both the Sanctuary of Apollo and the Basilica, they, and the Popidian colonnade that defines their form, all appear to be part of one coherent design. The use of the same profile on the sanctuary and Basilica capitals supports the link. Furthermore, the east wall of the Sanctuary of Apollo aligns with the façade of the Basilica and continues the ensemble.

In sum, it appears that there was a tufa ensemble in the forum, the Popidian ensemble. Its closely linked and contemporaneous components include the colonnade of Popidius, the east wall of the Sanctuary of Apollo, the gateway to the forum at via Marina, the Basilica and the *Comitium*.

We turn now to the date of the ensemble and start with the colonnade of Popidius whose Latin dedicatory inscription names Vibius Popidius, *quaestor*, as the one who had the colonnade constructed.[76] The inscription includes no date, but the analysis of Giovanni Onorato, whose 1951 study dates the inscription to a period after 89 BC because it is in Latin, and before 80 BC because the Roman colony at Pompeii did not include the office of *quaestor*, is convincing.[77] Popidius was a member of a distinguished Samnite family, the same family whose stamp appears on roof tiles from the Basilica.[78] Popidius appears to have cooperated with the new Roman regime, including a major urban benefaction after the traditional Roman fashion, taking full credit in the new official language of Pompeii—Latin.

The *Comitium* dates to the Roman period because of its association with the colonnade and inscription of Popidius, but there is other evidence as well. In carving the *Comitium* out of the northwest corner of the residential *insula* VIII.3, the house at VIII.3.31 was truncated, losing part of its northern side to the *Comitium*; the filled doors that once led to *cubicula* and an *ala* are still visible. Another complete house was apparently lost where the *Comitium* now stands. While the act of suppressing private property to construct a civic building is not datable in itself, the arrival of the Romans constitutes an historical moment when such a transfer of property might be expected to occur, an argument that supports a Roman date without actually proving it.[79]

Most definitive, the *Comitium* was constructed using the Roman foot of 0.295 m and not the Oscan foot of 0.275 m. Pier dimensions, individual ashlar blocks, and openings between the piers are in Roman feet of 0.295 m.

The Basilica, too, (Figures 12.4 and 12.8) displays a similarly intimate relationship with the colonnade. The façade-wedge is again instructive for it implies that the Basilica responded to the tufa colonnade, which either pre-existed the Basilica or was contemporary with it (Figure 12.16). If the Basilica had been the earlier of the two structures there would have been no need for the wedge-shaped *chalcidicum*. Similarly, as discussed above, the tufa piers of the *chalcidicum* confirm that the Basilica was responding to the original tufa colonnade in front of it. Equally important, the Basilica's façade piers are an integral structural part of the Popidian colonnade, supporting the inner ends of its joists and rafters. Additionally, the Roman foot is also employed throughout the Basilica.[80] And, finally, Pompeii Forum Project excavations have discovered pottery of the first century BC in association with the construction of the Basilica (forthcoming). The Basilica, then, is part of the Popidian ensemble too.

The above evidence and analysis point to the conclusion that there was one grandiose project to create a regularized forum. No single piece of evidence dates the whole, but the weight of all the evidence leads to the conclusion that the Popidian ensemble was the first major urbanistic project of Roman Pompeii, an emphatic and unambiguous assertion of the Roman presence.

The Augustan and early imperial period

The Popidian ensemble appears to have done little to develop the east side of the forum, save to provide a columnar screen for the early shops and whatever other structures existed on that side.[81] During the Augustan period—a time of major urban development in Rome—and later, the Pompeians focused on the apparently shabby east side of their forum and transformed it into a much grander civic space. New buildings were the Eumachia Building, the Sanctuary of Augustus (the so-called Temple of Vespasian), possibly the predecessor to the Imperial Cult Building,[82] and the Macellum. Changes to the Temple of Jupiter, discussed above, and the present limestone forum pavement may date to the Augustan period as well. To this period also belong the three arches (one demolished in antiquity) associated with the Temple of Jupiter.[83] Especially controversial are the Augustan-period modifications made to the Sanctuary of Apollo that were identified by the Pompeii Forum Project during its 1997 excavations.[84]

From 62–79

Like the great fire in Rome in 64, or in London in 1666, the earthquake at Pompeii presented its inhabitants with a need to rebuild, as well as an opportunity to rebuild in a manner and on a scale that they might never have undertaken if disaster had not struck. The conventional view holds that the forum was still in shambles when Vesuvius erupted. The designation "builders' yard" is frequently applied to the post-62 forum. Mau laid the foundation for this widely held opinion, and the archaeological investigations and building analyses of Maiuri ostensibly confirmed the opinion. While most commentators on Pompeii follow Mau and Maiuri to a considerable degree, the present author challenged the conventional view in 1994.[85] Apart from abundant evidence provided by the forum buildings themselves, a strong argument against the conventional view is human nature. The extensive repair and redecoration of houses in post-62 Pompeii confirm that the residents possessed the will and the means to recover from the disaster. It is inexplicable that such a vigorous domestic recovery was not accompanied by a comparable rebuilding in the public realm.

Not slapdash or casual, the recovery was conducted according to a grand and coherent plan whose hallmarks were the monumentalizing and the unifying of the urban center. These processes were achieved by: (1) linking façades; (2) blocking the two central streets that had fragmented the eastern side of the forum; (3) upgrading building material; and (4) emphasizing the now more prominent northeastern and southeastern entrances to the forum. While all the four buildings on the east side are distinct, their façades are connected, forming one continuous urban façade that at the same time blocks the streets that had once divided the forum's east side into three blocks (Figure 12.2). All façades on the east side were revetted with marble, and the Imperial Cult Building, which has no traditional façade, bore marble revetment throughout.

The elimination of the two central streets had the practical effect of rerouting traffic from the east to the northeastern and southeastern corners of the forum. The now more heavily used entrances acquired a grander design compatible with their enhanced role in the new scheme. The north entrance on the east side is the more elaborate of the two. Two arches signaled the presence and the importance of the forum to those approaching from the north and east. The so-called Arch of Tiberius framed a view into a small separate piazza, or largo, almost a vestibule to the larger forum, defined by the flank of the Temple of Jupiter, the new Corinthian colonnade in front of the Macellum, and the arch itself. In contrast, a smaller and now largely broken arch, located at the north end of the Macellum colonnade invited one into the sculpture gallery that was at once a grand forecourt to the Macellum and a sculptural announcement of the public nature of the forum.

At the south end of the forum, the western and central civic buildings were rebuilt along with the front of the eastern building, thereby creating one single façade. An apse was also added to the eastern building. The sturdily built Basilica, whose engaged columns functioned as buttresses during the earthquake, may not have sustained great damage. The reworking of the Ionic capitals in the Sanctuary of Apollo bespeaks an attempt to salvage capitals damaged in a fall. The adding of additional stucco to the columns appears to be part of the recovery effort as well.

These four interrelated processes took place in the context of damage, repair, and new building. The product was a new creation, different from the old and much more than simply a repair of damaged buildings. This is not to suggest that the entire forum had been repaired by 79; it had not. The western branch of the forum colonnade had not been completed, and it appears that the Temple of Jupiter had not been repaired either. Nonetheless, judging from what had been accomplished and what was in progress it is possible to conclude that the recovery was vigorous.

While the evidence above does not prove that the rebuilding plan was inspired by Rome or that the planner was Roman, such a case can be made, but other evidence must be adduced. From the foundation of the Roman colony architectural design at Pompeii had been inspired by Rome. There is no reason to suspect that Roman influence diminished during the 60s. The design of the Imperial Cult Building is without parallel at Pompeii, but fits comfortably within developments at Rome. And finally, if the following suggestion that Rome provided post-earthquake assistance is correct, the presence of Roman plans and possibly Roman planners at Pompeii are the more easily explained.

Who paid for the recovery at Pompeii? There are three possibilities: private benefactions, the Pompeian treasury and the imperial treasury. No written documentation from Pompeii survives on this issue. Private monies may have been available, but it is clear that much effort was committed to restoring private dwellings. It is impossible to assess the ability of the Pompeian treasury to support the extensive repairs that have been documented throughout the forum, but in view of the enormity of the project local civic funds must have been inadequate. The only remaining source was the imperial treasury. While no direct proof of such assistance survives, there are ample records of imperial assistance to towns, many further from Rome than Pompeii, that suffered natural disasters, especially earthquakes. Direct imperial interventions at Pompeii and neighboring towns are known on other occasions.[86] Given these imperial actions and the other considerations already mentioned, it is likely that Rome provided both the inspiration and the revenue for the recovery at Pompeii.

Urban, social and economic implications

By observing what the Pompeians rebuilt we can determine what was important to them. The implications of this simple truth are profound. In the absence of written accounts of the post-earthquake period, the patterns and extent of recovery in the forum provide the only access we have to the thinking of the Pompeians on the nature of the city and its proper physical embodiment. The present reading of the monuments documents the lavish attention that the Pompeians showered on the forum as they seized the opportunity to lend a new grandeur to their corporate, civic existence. In terms of scale, materials, and sheer magnificence, the forum was primary in the post-62 architectural hierarchy, a position consistent with the equal pre-eminence of the city in the hierarchy of abstract values. If the usual interpretation that the public buildings languished during the recovery can no longer be supported, then we must reassess as well the values that have been imputed to the Pompeians on that basis.

A vigorous public building program meant that craftsmen from all aspects of the building trade descended upon Pompeii; the city itself could not have supplied all necessary workers. The craftsmen, in turn, were customers for greengrocers, bakers, farmers, fullers, leasers of rooms, owners of *thermopolia*, prostitutes, sellers of lamps and oil, etc. Public building must have been, at least to some extent, a force in the post-62 economy, and yet this aspect of Pompeii's economic life (and its related social implications) are systematically discounted because it has been believed that the public buildings had been abandoned. Whether in compressed form as part of an overview of Pompeii or in an extended discussion, as that of Andreau,[87] an assessment of Pompeii's economic recovery always includes the observation that the public buildings were left unrepaired, or, at best, still under construction. The data of the Pompeii Forum Project invite a new approach to studies of the social and economic history of Pompeii: rather than being viewed as a symbol of depressed economic conditions at Pompeii after AD 62 and an indication that the elite had fled the city, the forum with its vigorous and ambitious post-earthquake building program can play its appropriate role in any future study.

NOTES

*My colleagues and I in the Pompeii Forum Project are grateful to Pietro Giovanni Guzzo, Soprintendente alle Antichità di Pompei, to Antonio D'Ambrosio, Direttore degli Scavi, and to the staff at the Soprintendenza Archeologica and the Direzione degli Scavi for facilitating our work in the forum at Pompeii. Invaluable support has been provided by the National Endowment for the Humanities, the Institute for Advanced Technology in the Humanities (IATH) at the University of Virginia, Gilbert and Judy Shelton, and the Ceres Foundation.

A note on the figures. This chapter provides several views that are not usually seen. Figure 12.4 is from the top of the staircase at the southeast corner of the Basilica; Figures 12.3 and 12.7 are from the top of the staircase at the northeast corner of the east South Building; Figures 12.5, 12.10 and 12.12 are from atop scaffolding set in front of the Sanctuary of Augustus in 1996; Figure 12.9 is from atop a ladder set against the north wall of the Macellum. Figures 12.3 and 12.7 overlap. In addition, Figure 13.1 was taken atop a tall ladder set in the inner southeast corner of the Sanctuary of Apollo. Illustrations are by the author unless otherwise noted.

1 A. Mau, *Pompeii: its life and art*, trans. Francis W. Kelsey, New York, 1902, pp. 45–60 provides a still-valuable overview of the forum. For an overview of the civic institutions and the role of the forum in the life of the city, see J. B. Ward-Perkins and A. Claridge, *Pompeii AD 79*, Boston, 1978, pp. 39–51; and Table 33.1.

2 The Roman influence emphasized here pertains to the period after Pompeii became officially Roman, i.e., 89 BC. The degree of Roman influence at Pompeii before the arrival of Sulla's army (89 BC) and the establishment of an official Roman colony (80 BC) is a subject of debate.

3 The author is the director of the Pompeii Forum Project. This chapter, which disagrees at many points with traditional views of the forum, including some expressed in this book, is based on the current research of the Pompeii Forum Project. As the product of a collaborative research endeavor, this essay owes a debt to other project members, especially Larry F. Ball,

James G. Cooper, Harrison Eiteljorg III, Stephen L. Gavel, Karim M. Hanna, Kirk Martini, Mark Schimmenti and Carroll William Westfall.

4   For the forum colonnade, see Mau, *Pompeii*, pp. 40–54; L. Richardson, jr, *Pompeii: an architectural history*, Baltimore, MD and London, 1988, pp. 145–7 and 261–7. The width of the open space from stylobate to stylobate is 32.65 m. Its length from the rear of the Temple of Jupiter to the south stylobate is 147.45 m. Using a Roman foot of 0.295 m, these dimensions equal 110.6 by 499.8 Roman feet, i.e., an ideal of 110 by 500 Roman feet (Figure 12.16).

5   J. J. Dobbins, "The Pompeii Forum Project 1994–95," in S .A. Bon and R. Jones (eds), *Sequence and Space in Pompeii*, Oxford, 1997, pp. 73–87; see esp. pp. 75–80.

6   Knowing the identities of those statues would add immeasurably to our understanding of Pompeii's public presentation of itself. Although that information is forever lost, it is quite possible that the statues represented important figures in the city's history, but one cannot rule out the possibility that distinguished Romans were among those depicted.

7   Also known as "the *porticus* of Popidius," parts of this tufa colonnade are preserved along the south side of the forum, on the east side in front of the *Comitium*, and at the points of entry of via dell'Abbondanza and via Marina. This is the same colonnade called by Richardson, *Pompeii*, p. 145, the Porticus of Vibius, and dated by him to the 80s BC.

8   Figures 12.3 and 12.4, respectively, are taken from the tops of these two stairways.

9   Two tufa columns at the junction between via Marina and the forum, a tufa column in an analogous position in via dell'Abbondanza, and another tufa column at the south end of the Eumachia Building's *chalcidicum* indicate the continuation of the tufa colonnade to at least those points, but it is reasonable to consider that it originally continued as far to the north as did its later replacement.

10 Richardson, *Pompeii*, pp. 209–10, 372; excavations by Amedeo Maiuri revealed an earlier pavement of cement edged by tufa, dated by him to the tufa period: "Saggi nel area del Foro," *Alla ricerca di Pompei preromana*, Naples, 1973, pp. 63–70 (= *NSc*, 1941, pp. 386–98). Precise dates for the pavements are difficult to ascertain, Maiuri's certainty notwithstanding; one could reasonably date the tufa pavement to the Roman colony and the limestone to the imperial period.

11 The forum slopes downwards almost imperceptibly from north to south. At its south end are drain holes that allow water to escape in order to avoid flooding.

12 Mau, *Pompeii*, pp. 46–8; idem, "Die Statuen des Forums von Pompeji," *RM*, 1896, vol. 11, pp. 160–6; Richardson, *Pompeii*, pp. 268–9. Cf. Welch, Ch. 36.

13 Mau, *Pompeii*, pp. 61–9 remains an excellent introduction to the temple. The most thorough archaeological study to date is A. Maiuri, "Saggi negli edifici del Foro: V.—Tempio di Giove," *Pompei preromana*, pp. 101–24 (= *NSc*, 1942, pp. 285–320). See also A. Sogliano, "Il foro di Pompei," *Memoria Reale Accademia Nazionale dei Lincei*, 1925, Ser. 6, vol. 1, fasc. 3, pp. 14ff. A more recent study within the context of Hellenistic architecture is H. Lauter, "Zur späthellenistischen Baukunst in Mittelitalien," *JdI*, 1979, vol. 94, pp. 430–6. Richardson, *Pompeii*, pp. 138–45, provides an excellent summary of the temple's history that includes Maiuri's work, and offers an initial construction date in the Sullan period. Cf. Small, Ch. 13.

14 The vaults are located under the *pronaos* and *cella*; they do not extend under the steps. Arnold and Mariette De Vos, *Pompei, Ercolano, Stabia* (*Guida archeologica Laterza*), Bari, 1982, p. 46 call these barrel vaults but, in fact, they are segmental. One wonders how much light penetrated to the interior of the podium from the enclosed *cella*. The segmental vaults are divided into sections by concrete cross walls; doors through the vault walls and through the cross walls permit access to all interior spaces. On the exterior, the later pavement has covered part of the podium base; this is especially clear on the east side (note, too, that there is an obvious north-to-south slope to the pavement). At the presently visible podium base on the east side of the temple are two steps and a large cavetto molding with a roundel above, the latter visible only at the temple's southeast corner (all lava). Also on the podium's east side, the corresponding cavetto crown molding employs Sarno limestone in the area of the *pronaos* and tufa next to the *cella* wall; the division of materials is less precise on the west side, where fewer blocks of Sarno limestone are used in the *pronaos* area. The steps and base molding are applied to the surface of the podium and are not load bearing. See Maiuri, *Pompei preromana*, figs. 56, 65 for profile drawings that do not correspond precisely to the description provided here.

15 The vast interior offered far more space than the city treasure would have required, but the dim light and the cool, damp interior may have been useful for commodities, such as wine or olive oil, that would have benefited from secure storage in such conditions.

16 Maiuri, *Pompeii preromana*, p. 106 and fig. 58. These steps remain visible.

17 The *pronaos* and temple walls rest on a platform that forms a step above the podium's crown molding. The platform is travertine (with considerable restoration) in the *pronaos* and tufa behind. From below, the travertine registers as a white band emphasizing the *pronaos* of the temple.

18 While the present chambers are too restricted for the display of cult statues, the earlier arrangement, employing columns to create three spaces at the end of the *cella*, could have accommodated three over-lifesize statues. See Maiuri, *Pompei preromana*, fig. 63, for a detailed plan of the vaulted chambers.

19 R. B. Ulrich, *The Roman Orator and the Sacred Stage: The Roman Templum Rostratum*, Collection Latomus 22, Brussels, 1994, pp. 224–48 presents the Capitolium and several other buildings in and near the forum as derived from the *"templum rostratum"* at Rome. His work is important not only for recognizing specific Roman sources in Pompeian architecture, but also for highlighting the general, pervasive influence of Rome at Pompeii.

20 The relief from the House of Lucius Caecilius Iucundus is frequently illustrated, e.g., T. Kraus, *Pompeii and Herculaneum: the living cities of the dead*, New York, 1975, fig. 9; S. C. Nappo, *Pompei: guida alla città sepolta*, Vercelli, 1998, p. 12; cf. Small, Ch. 13, n. 26.

21 Mau, *Pompeii*, pp. 66–7, believed that the temple was not especially old, probably dating to the period just before the planting of the Roman colony. Maiuri, *Pompei preromana*, pp. 101–24, dates the temple to 150–120 BC with major revisions after the arrival of the Romans. H. Lauter, "Zur späthellenistischen Baukunst," pp. 430–6 dates the conversion of a Samnite-period temple to the Capitoline cult to the late second century BC. Zanker, *Pompeii*, pp. 63–4 adheres to Maiuri's date for this development at the time of the foundation of the Sullan colony. Richardson, *Pompeii*, pp. 138–45 rejects the idea of a pre-Sullan temple altogether, and argues that the temple was a Capitolium from the start. Cf. Small, Ch. 13. The Pompeii Forum Project is currently working on the temple and at this writing is inclined to date the initial construction to the Sullan colony based on the extensive use of the Roman foot as a module in the initial design and construction of the vaulted podium. If this is right, the temple would have been a Capitolium from the start. The later change that suppressed the central stairway that descended to the vaults, and redesigned the stairs (and at least the *pronaos*), would belong to a later, perhaps late Republican or Augustan revision. If the Sullan date is correct, the temple would assume an important role in the Popidian ensemble, discussed below.

22 Mau, *Pompeii*, pp. 121–3; Richardson, *Pompeii*, pp. 269–73.

23 Richardson, *Pompeii*, pp. 269–73, makes a good case for the east South Building being the *curia*, the center South Building being the *tabularium*, and the west South Building being an Augusteum, or center of emperor worship. While Richardson says that the entrance to the latter is undramatic, the approach, whether viewing the "Augusteum" from the via Marina entrance, or from further north, reveals that the forum's west colonnade serves as a tunnel of space that frames the west South Building's façade, directs one's view into the building, and emphasizes that this is an important space. Ulrich, *Templum Rostratum*, pp. 228–30 argues that the central building is the *curia*.

24 Mau, *Pompeii*, pp. 119–20; Richardson, *Pompeii*, 145–7; Ulrich, *Templum Rostratum*, pp. 230–1. The most thorough study to date is G. Fuchs, "Fragmenta Saeptorum: Untersuchungen am sogenannten Comitium in Pompei," *RM*, 1957, vol. 64, pp. 154–97.

25 Mau, *Pompeii*, pp. 70–9; Richardson, *Pompeii*, pp. 95–9; Ulrich, *Templum Rostratum*, pp. 225–8. The most thorough study of the Basilica is K. Ohr, *Die Basilika in Pompeji*, Berlin, 1991.

26 Richardson, *Pompeii*, pp. 145–7, who also dates the building to the early years of the Roman colony, argues that this is a law court, which is entirely possible, but its design is also well suited for voting activities. In Rome and other Roman cities the *Comitium* was an assembly place. Whether the building served such a function in Pompeii is impossible to determine. Critics observe that Roman *comitia* are circular in form, but the present building was carved out of the northwest corner of a rectilinear city block (Figure 12.6), as mentioned immediately

above, and that fact influenced its form far more than did its function. (Here, form does not necessarily follow function.) It is possible that assemblies took place in the covered theater, but the form of the *Comitium* does not preclude such assemblies there. Instead of inventing a new name for what might have been a multipurpose building, the traditional designation is retained. In J. J. Dobbins, "Problems of chronology, decoration, and urban design in the forum at Pompeii," *AJA*, 1994, vol. 98, pp. 691–2, I asserted that the *Comitium*'s north façade echoes the Eumachia Building's south façade. Our subsequent close analysis suggests that the reverse is true, namely that the Eumachia Building's south façade echoes the *Comitium*'s north façade.

27 That the Basilica is a magnificent structure is not challenged here. It is cited as exemplary of the Roman basilica in such works as A. Boëthius, *Etruscan and Early Roman Architecture*, Harmondsworth, 1978, p. 152; M. Trachtenberg and I. Hyman, *Architecture, from Prehistory to Post-Modernism*, New York, 2002, p. 142; F. S. Kleiner and C. J. Mamiya (eds), *Gardner's Art through the Ages*, 12th edn, Belmont, CA, 2005, p. 255; and it is used to illustrate a widely circulated translation of Vitruvius: *Vitruvius, The Ten Books on Architecture*, trans. M. H. Morgan, New York, 1960, pp. 133–4.

28 Nineteenth-century images confirm that the excavated tribunal was poorly preserved and that what one now sees is largely a reconstruction. See C. F. Mazois, *Les ruines de Pompéi*, Paris, 1812–38, vol. 3, pls 16 and 29; *Pompéi: travaux et envois des architectes Français au XIXe siècle*, Rome, 1981, p. 40, fig. 32; p. 154, cat. no. 25; Giorgio Sommer, photograph no. 1225; Zanker, *Pompeii*, fig. 20.

29 S. De Caro, *Saggi nell'area del tempio di Apollo a Pompei. Scavi stratigrafici di A. Maiuri nel 1931–32 e 1942–43 (AnnArchStorAnt)*, vol. 3, Naples, 1986; Mau, *Pompeii*, pp. 80–90; Richardson, *Pompeii*, pp. 89–95; cf. De Caro, Ch. 6, and Small, Ch. 13. There is no definitive study of this important sanctuary.

30 Mau, *Pompeii*, pp. 92–3; Richardson, *Pompeii*, pp. 89, 372; De Vos and De Vos, *Guida Laterza*, p. 48. Constructed of Caserta limestone, the *mensa*, or table, dates to the Samnite period; its cavities were enlarged to conform to Roman measures and a Latin inscription was added (*CIL* X, 793) in the Augustan period. P. Castrén, *Odro Populusque Pompeianus*, Rome, 1975, pp. 94, 101 and 155 discusses the magistrates whose names appear in the inscription.

31 Mau, *Pompeii*, pp. 91–3, including the *mensa ponderaria*; Richardson, *Pompeii*, pp. 275–6.

32 The *mensa ponderaria*, the room to its north, and the south end of the Northwest Building are modern, the original structures having been destroyed during World War II (confirmed by excavations and investigations of the Pompeii Forum Project in 2001 and by a contemporary documentary photograph). The table of measures itself is a plaster cast of the original, now off display. For a plan of World War II Allied bomb strikes in the forum, see K. Wallat, *Die Ostseite des Forums von Pompeji*, Frankfurt am Main, 1997, pl. 5.

33 Richardson, *Pompeii*, pp. 206–9.

34 Two studies treat the buildings of the forum's east side, exclusive of the *Comitium*: Dobbins, "Problems of chronology;" K. Wallat, *Die Ostseite des Forums von Pompeji*.

35 Mau, *Pompeii*, pp. 94–101; A. Maiuri, *L'ultima fase edilizia di Pompei*, Rome, 1942, pp. 54–61; Richardson, *Pompeii*, pp. 198–202; Dobbins, "Problems of chronology," pp. 645–7, 668–85; Wallat, *Die Ostseite des Forums*, pp. 153–200.

36 A modern roofed portico has been built in the northwestern corner of the interior to protect still-surviving Fourth-Style wall paintings. The subjects of the paintings include foodstuffs of the sort that may have been sold in the market and mythological themes. Early publications and nineteenth-century photographs indicate that more paintings were visible at the Macellum's east end. Outlines of those paintings are barely visible today. In the late 1990s the modern portico was rebuilt and some of the southern shops were roofed and gated to provide secure storage for objects found in recent excavations.

37 A. Small, "The shrine of the imperial family in the Macellum at Pompeii," in A. Small (ed.), *Subject and Ruler: the cult of the ruling power in classical antiquity*, JRA Suppl. Ser. no. 17, 1996, pp. 115–36. Cf. Small, Ch. 13 and Welch, Ch. 36.

38 Small, "The shrine of the imperial family in the Macellum at Pompeii," pp. 131–5, considers both spaces to be open-air cult areas, the southern one serving as a *triclinium* for cult-related banquets or for the display of imperial images.

39 Mau, *Pompeii*, pp. 102–5; idem, "Der staedtische Larentempel in Pompeji," *RM*, 1896, vol. 11, pp. 285–301; Richardson, *Pompeii*, pp. 273–5; Dobbins, "Problems of chronology," pp. 640–6, 685–8; idem, "The Pompeii Forum Project 1994–95," in Bon and Jones (eds), *Sequence and Space*, pp. 73–87; see esp. pp. 78–85; idem, "The Imperial Cult Building in the forum at Pompeii," in Small (ed.), *Subject and Ruler*, pp. 99–114; Wallat, *Die Ostseite des Forums*, pp. 129–52; Zanker, *Pompeii*, pp. 85–7; cf. Small, Ch. 13.

40 For a detailed plan of the Aula Regia see H. Finsen, *Domus Flavia sur le Palatin; Aula Regia— Basilica*, *AnalRom*, Supplement II, Rome, 1962. For a general discussion of the Palace of Domitian, including the Aula Regia, see William L. MacDonald, *The Architecture of the Roman Empire: an introductory study*, New Haven, CT, 1982, pp. 47–74.

41 For the technique of marble revetment, see Larry F. Ball, "How did the Romans install revetment?," *AJA*, 2002, vol. 106, pp. 551–73. Cf. Fant, Ch. 22.

42 The eighth is located in the south *exedra*.

43 Dobbins, "The Pompeii Forum Project 1994–95," pp. 83–7 and fig. 7.13.

44 Dobbins, "Problems of chronology," pp. 640–46, 686–7; Richardson, *Pompeii*, p. 273. For a pre-62 date, see Mau, Wallat and Zanker in n. 39.

45 Mau, *Pompeii*, pp. 106–9; Richardson, *Pompeii*, pp. 191–4; Dobbins, "Problems of chronology," pp. 639–45, 661–8; Wallat, *Die Ostseite des Forums*, pp. 107–27; Zanker, *Pompeii*, pp. 87–93. K. Wallat has proposed that the frieze surrounding the main portal to the Eumachia Building belongs to the Sanctuary of Augustus: "Der Marmorfries am Eingangsportal des Gabäudes der Eumachia (VII 9.1) in Pompeji und sein ursprünglicher Anbringungsort," *AA*, 1995, pp. 345–73.

46 Ulrich, *Templum Rostratum*, pp. 231–4.

47 J. J. Dobbins, "The altar in the Sanctuary of the Genius of Augustus in the forum at Pompeii," *RM*, 1992, vol. 99, pp. 251–63.

48 Dobbins, "Problems of chronology," p. 641; idem, "The Imperial Cult Building in the forum at Pompeii," in Small (ed.), *Subject and Ruler*, pp. 107–9; A. Mau, *Pompejanische Beiträge*, Berlin, 1879; idem, "Osservazioni sul creduto tempio del Genio di Augusto," *Atti della Reale Accademia di Archeologia, Lettere e Belle Arti*, Naples, 1893 [published in 1894], pp. 181–8; K. Wallat, "Der Zustand des Forums von Pompeji am Vorabend des Vesuvausbruchs 79 n. Chr.," in T. Frölich and L. Jacobelli (eds), *Archäologie und Seismologie. La regione vesuviana dal 62 al 79 d.C. Problemi archeologici e sismologici* (Colloquium Boscorele, November 26–27, 1993), Munich, 1995, pp. 75–92, esp. pp. 85–6; idem, "Opus Testaceum in Pompeji," *RM*, 1993, vol. 100, pp. 353–82, esp. p. 359; idem, *Die Ostseite des Forums*, p. 131 and fig. 158.

49 G. Fiorelli, *Descrizione di Pompei*, Naples, 1875, pp. 261–2.

50 Overbeck and Mau, 1884, 183 and Maiuri, *Pompeii preromana*, pp. 88–91.

51 For the Augustan dating of the sanctuary see V. Kockel, "Funde und Forschungen in den Vesuvstädten," *AA*, 1986, pp. 457–8, esp. p. 457, n. 52; P. Zanker, *Pompeji: Stadtbilder als Spiegel von Gesellschaft und Herrschftsform*, Mainz, 1987, pp. 28–30; idem, *Pompei: Società, immagini urbane e forme dell'abitare*, Turin, 1993, pp. 103–5; idem, *Pompeii*, pp. 87–93; Richardson, pp. 192–4; Dobbins, "The altar in the Sanctuary of the Genius of Augustus," pp. 251–63; idem, "Problems of chronology," pp. 639–45, 661–8.

52 V. Kockel, *Die Grabbauten vor dem Herkulaner Tor in Pompeji*, Mainz, 1983, pp. 57–9. Kockel, however, adhering to Maiuri's conclusions, chooses not to associate the inscription with the so-called Temple of Vespasian (n. 95). Cf. Bernstein, Ch. 34, for her tomb.

53 I. Gradel, "Mamia's Dedication: Emperor and Genius. The Imperial Cult in Italy and the Genius Coloniae in Pompeii," *AnalRom*, 1992, vol. 20, pp. 43–58; idem, *Emperor Worship and Roman Religion*, Oxford and New York, 2002.

54 The traditional reading of the inscription: Mamia, daughter of Publius and public priestess, (dedicated the temple) to the genius of Augustus on her own and with her own money. Instead of "genius of Augustus," Gradel reads the missing section as "genius of the colony."

55 H. Eschebach and L. Eschebach, *Pompeji vom 7. Jahrhundert v. Chr. Bis 79 n. Chr.*, Cologne, 1995, figs 15.1 and 15.2.

56 D. Fishwick, "The inscription of Mamia again: The cult of the *Genius Augusti* and the temple of the imperial cult on the *Forum* of Pompeii," *Epigraphica*, 1995, vol. 57, pp. 17–38.

57 Mau, *Pompeii*, pp. 110–18; Richardson, *Pompeii*, pp. 194–8; Wallat, *Die Ostseite des Forums*, pp. 31–105.

58 Dobbins, "Problems of chronology," pp. 639–40, 647–61, 688–9; cf. Small, Ch. 13 and Descœudres, Ch. 2.

59 Mau, *Pompeii*, pp. 110–18.

60 Cf. Descœudres, Ch. 2. While it is agreed that the son mentioned in the inscription was not the *duumvir* of AD 3, it is not necessary to reconstruct the historical events as does Descœudres. We do not know the birth date of the young Marcus. It is quite possible that Eumachia's dedication followed closely on Livia's and that the age of the son was less important than the fact that, like Tiberius, he be included in the dedication of the mother. Furthermore, the dedication to Pietas does not in itself relate the building to the Ara Pietatis in Rome. Barring clearer evidence to the contrary, a building date in the first decade AD remains reasonable. The architectural, sculptural and epigraphic references to the *Porticus Liviae*, the Ara Pacis, and the Forum Augustum not only strengthen the argument that Eumachia's *publica magnificentia* derives from the Augustan building program, but also provide a *terminus post quem* of 2 BC (the dedication of the Forum Augustum) for the construction of the Eumachia Building. The building materials and techniques are consistent with those of dated Augustan buildings at Pompeii, thus permitting Eumachia's dedication to be recognized as a major component of an Augustan-period development on the forum at Pompeii.

61 L. Richardson, jr, "Concordia and Concordia Augusta: Rome and Pompeii," *PP*, 1978, vol. 33, pp. 260–72. V. Kockel, "Funde und Forschungen in den Vesuvstädten," *AA*, 1986, pp. 457–8.

62 In the late 1990s the inscription over the southeast door fell from the building and as of this writing neither the original nor a copy has been restored to the building.

63 The dedication to Concordia Augusta affords us a specific example of an abstraction being explicitly associated with Augustus and the Augustan regime. For discussions of Concordia and of the Augustan transformation in form and meaning of the Temple of Concord in the Forum Romanum, see Richardson, "Concordia and Concordia Augusta," and B. A. Kellum, "The city adorned: programmatic display at the *Aedes Concordiae Augustae*," in K. A. Raaflaub and M. Toher (eds), *Between Republic and Empire: interpretations of Augustus and his Principate*, Berkeley and Los Angeles, CA, 1990, pp. 276–307.

64 It is possible that the sculpture gallery was a feature only of the post-62 rebuilding rather than part of the original design.

65 See above, n. 44, for Wallat's study assigning the frieze to the portal of the Sanctuary of Augustus.

66 Maiuri, *Pompeii preromana*, pp. 92–3.

67 Richardson, "Concordia and Concordia Augusta," p. 269.

68 The marble statue is in Naples at the Museo Nazionale; on site is a plaster cast. The original inscription remains in situ: EVMACHIAE.L.F/SACERD.PVBL/FVLLONES (*CIL* X, 813).

69 Richardson, *Pompeii*, p. 198. De Vos and De Vos, *Guida Laterza*, p. 41 also express the current trend toward rejecting both the fullery and wool market hypotheses.

70 Elizabeth Fentress, "On the block: *catastae, chalcidica* and *cryptae* in Early Imperial Italy," *JRA*, 2005, vol. 18, pp. 220–34.

71 Dobbins, "Problems of chronology," pp. 655–61; cf. Fant, Ch. 22 and Figure 22.3.

72 *CIL* X, 820, 824, 825; A. Mau, "Der Temple der Fortuna Augusta in Pompeji," *RM*, 1896, vol. 11, pp. 269–84; Mau, *Pompeii*, pp. 130–2; Maiuri, *L'ultima fase*, pp. 67–8; Richardson, *Pompeii*, pp. 202–6.

73 Mau, *Pompeii*, p. 40. Lauter, "Zur späthellenistischen Baukunst," is the most recent extensive presentation of the traditional second-century date and is followed by many general studies on Pompeii. Two more recent articles, partly in response to the Pompeii Forum Project's dating, reassert the second-century date for the tufa colonnade in the Sanctuary of Apollo: P. G. Guzzo and F. Pesando, "Sul colonnato nel foro triangulare di Pompei: indizi in un delitto perfetto," *Eutopia*, 2002, vol. II n.s., Issue 1, pp. 111–21; A. Martelli, "Per una nuova lettura dell'iscrizione Vetter 61 nel contesto del santuario di Apollo a Pompei," *Eutopia*, 2002, vol. II n.s., Issue 2, pp. 71–81.

74 A. Carandini, P. Carafa and T. D'Alessio, "Nuove progetti, nuove domande, nuove metodi," in P. G. Guzzo (ed.), *Pompei: Scienza e Società. 250° Anniversario degli Scavi di Pompei. Convegno Internazionale. Napoli, 25–27 novembre 1998*, Milan, 2001, pp. 127–9; M. G. Fulford and A. Wallace-Hadrill, "Towards a history of pre-Roman Pompeii: excavations beneath the House of Amarantus (I.9.11–12), 1995–8," *PBSR*, 1999, vol. 67, pp. 37–144, esp. 37–40; idem, "Unpeeling Pompeii," *Antiquity*, 1998, vol. 72, pp. 128–45, esp. 128–29 and passim; idem, "The house of Amarantus at Pompeii (I.9.11–12): an interim report on survey and excavations in 1995–96," *RStPomp*, 1995–96 (publ. 1998), vol. 5, pp. 77–113; P. Carafa, "What was Pompeii before 200 BC? Excavations in the House of Joseph II, in the Triangular Forum and in the House of the Wedding of Hercules," in S. E. Bon and R. Jones (eds), *Sequence and Space in Pompeii*, Oxford, 1997, pp. 13–31, esp. 20–21 for a late date for the tufa portico in the Triangular Forum; idem, "The investigations of the University of Rome 'La Sapienza' in Regions VII and VIII: the ancient history of Pompeii," in C. Stein and J. H. Humphrey (eds), *Pompeian Brothels, Pompeii's Ancient History, Mirrors and Mysteries, Art and Nature at Oplontis, & the Herculaneum "Basilica"*, JRA, Suppl. Ser. no. 47, 2002, pp. 47–61, esp. 51–2 (tufa portico); S. C. Nappo, "Urban transformation at Pompeii in the late 3rd and early 2nd c. BC," in R. Laurence and A. Wallace-Hadrill (eds) *Domestic Space in the Roman World: Pompeii and Beyond*, JRA, Suppl. Ser. no. 22, 1997, pp. 91–120, esp. 91 concerning Sarno limestone. Our own investigations in the Augustan-period Eumachia Building argue that the original colonnade was tufa and that the post-62 colonnade was marble: Dobbins, "Problems of chronology," pp. 659–60.

75 Maiuri, *Pompei preromana*: Eumachia Building, pp. 53–63 and figs 19–25 (= *NSc*, 1941, pp. 371–86); Sanctuary of Augustus, i.e., Maiuri's Temple of Vespasian, pp. 88–91 and fig. 44 (=*NSc*, 1942, pp. 267–70); South Buildings, pp. 99–101 and figs 54–5, Tav. I (= *NSc*, 1942, pp. 281–5; Basilica, pp. 191–223 and fig. 109 especially (=*NSc*, 1951, pp. 225–60).

76 The inscription (*CIL* X, 794) reads V.POPIDIVS / EP.F.Q. / PORTICVS / FACIENDAS / COERAVIT; "Vibius Popidius, son of Epidius, Quaestor, had the colonnades made."

77 G. Onorato, "Pompei municipium e colonia romana," *RendNap*, 1951, vol. 26 n.s., pp. 115–56.

78 Maiuri, *Pompei preromana*, p. 197; Castrén, pp. 207–9.

79 Cicero, *Pro Sulla*, 60–62, documents the long-standing dissension between the Pompeians and the Roman colonists, but he provides no details.

80 K. Ohr, *Die Basilika in Pompeji*, Berlin, 1991, p. 1, embraces the traditional date between 150 and 100 BC. Ohr posits a foot of 0.2935 m, a Roman foot although he does not say so specifically, and argues against Maiuri's assumption of an Oscan foot module (p. 34, n. 142). Ohr's measured plans present the evidence; the Roman foot is found repeatedly throughout the Basilica.

81 Remains of a small rectangular building beneath the Sanctuary of Augustus align with the colonnade and therefore can be dated between the construction of the colonnade and that of the sanctuary. Little is known about this early building, which Maiuri dates to the republican period, but it cannot have lent any grandeur to the forum. See Mauiri, *Pompei preromana*, pp. 88–9 and fig. 44. Two observations are of urban interest. The first is that the outer wall (Maiuri's wall A-A') is on the same alignment as the inner file of the columns in front of the *Comitium*. This reveals a design decision to relate the building to a prominent component of the Popidian ensemble and it also links the building to the latter chronologically. The second is that this building blocked the access of vicolo degli Scheletri to the forum. Such a blocking was the first step in the process that ultimately led to the post-62 unified façade that linked all forum buildings north of via dell'Abbondanza.

82 H. Eschebach and L. Eschebach, *Pompeji vom 7. Jahrhundert v. Chr. Bis 79 n. Chr.*, Cologne, 1995, figs 15.1 and 15.2.

83 See above: West side, northeast corner and arches.

84 John J. Dobbins, Larry F. Ball, James G. Cooper, Stephen L. Gavel and Sophie Hay, "Excavations in the Sanctuary of Apollo at Pompeii, 1997," *AJA*, 1998, vol. 102, pp. 739–56. Two already-cited articles challenge our conclusions: Guzzo and Pesando, "Sul colonnato nel foro triangulare di Pompei: indizi in un delitto perfetto," esp. 118–19 which deal with the Sanctuary of Apollo, and Martelli, "Per una nuova lettura dell'iscrizione Vetter 61 nel contesto del santuario do

Apollo a Pompei." A detailed response will appear elsewhere. Martelli argues that a dedicatory inscription to Lucius Mummius, in Oscan, on a statue base set against one of the columns of the sanctuary's portico dates the portico to the second century BC. While the inscription surely relates to the distribution of booty to Italian cities after the conquest of Corinth by Mummius in 146 BC, the base has been modified and is in a secondary setting. It cannot be used to date the colonnade (cf. Descœudres, Ch. 2). Guzzo and Pesando perpetuate some mistakes of Maiuri, dismiss the excavations of 1997 without discussing them, and fail to develop arguments to support their case that the colonnade of Popidius and the colonnade of the Sanctuary of Apollo date to the second century BC. Cf. De Caro, Ch. 6 and Small, Ch. 13.

85 J. J. Dobbins, "Problems of chronology," pp. 629–94.

86 Tacitus (*Ann.* 14.17) records a riot in the amphitheater that drew a punitive response from Rome. In the period after the earthquake, Vespasian sent to Pompeii T. Suedius Clemens who restored to the city of Pompeii plots of land which were in the possession of private individuals (Mau, *Pompeii*, pp. 407–8; *CIL* X, 1018). After 79 Titus sent to Campania a commission to oversee the work of salvage (Suetonius, *Titus* 8.3–4).

87 J. Andreau, "Histoire des séismes et histoire économique, le tremblement de terre de Pompéi (62 ap. J.-C.)," *AnnEconSocCiv*, 1973, vol. 28, pp. 369–95.

SELECT BIBLIOGRAPHY

De Caro, S., *Saggi nell'area del tempio di Apollo a Pompei. Scavi stratigrafici di A. Maiuri nel 1931–32 e 1942–43* (AnnArchStorAnt), vol. 3, Naples, 1986.

Dobbins, J. J., "The altar in the sanctuary of the Genius of Augustus in the forum of Pompeii," *RM*, 1992, vol. 99, pp. 251–61.

——, "Problems of chronology, decoration, and urban design in the forum at Pompeii," *AJA*, 1994, vol. 98, pp. 629–94.

——, "The imperial cult building in the forum of Pompeii," in A. Small, (ed.), *Subject and Ruler: the cult of the ruling power in classical antiquity. Papers in honour of the 65th birthday of Duncan Fishwick*, JRA Suppl. Ser. no. 17, 1996, pp. 99–114.

——, "The Pompeii Forum Project 1994–95," in S. A. Bon and R. Jones (eds), *Sequence and Space in Pompeii*, Oxford, 1997, pp. 73–87.

——, Ball, L. F., Cooper, J. G., Gavel, S. L. and Hay, S., "Excavations in the Sanctuary of Apollo at Pompeii, 1997," *AJA*, 1998, vol. 102, pp. 739–56.

Fishwick, D., "The inscription of Mamia again: The Cult of the *Genius Augusti* and the Temple of the Imperial cult on the *Forum* of Pompeii," *Epigraphica*, 1995, vol. 57, pp. 17–38.

Fuchs, G., "Fragmenta Saeptorum: Untersuchungen am sogenannten Comitium in Pompei," *RM*, 1957, vol. 64, pp. 154–97.

Gradel, I, "Mamia's Dedication: Emperor and Genius. The Imperial Cult in Italy and the Genius Coloniae in Pompeii," *AnalRom*, 1992, vol. 20, pp. 43–58.

Guzzo, P. G. and F. Pesando, "Sul colonnato nel foro triangulare di Pompei: indizi in un delitto perfetto," *Eutopia*, 2002, vol. II n.s., Issue 1, pp. 111–21.

Kockel, V., "Funde und Forschungen in den Vesuvstädten II," *AA*, 1986, pp. 443–569 (for the forum see esp. pp. 454ff.).

Lauter, H., "Zur spälthellenistischen Baukunst in Mittelitalien," *JdI*, 1979, vol. 94, pp. 390–457 (pp. 416–36 for the forum buildings).

Maiuri, A., *L'ultima fase edilizia di Pompei*, Rome, 1942.

——, *Alla ricerca di Pompei preromana*, Naples, 1973.

Martelli, A., "Per una nuova lettura dell'iscrizione Vetter 61 nel contesto del santuario di Apollo a Pompei," *Eutopia*, 2002, vol. II n.s., Issue 2, pp. 71–81.

Mau, A., *Pompejanische Beiträge*, Berlin, 1879.

——, "Il portico del foro di Pompei," *RM*, 1891, vol. 6, pp. 168–76.

——, "Osservazioni sull'Edificio di Eumachia in Pompei," *RM*, 1892, vol. 7, pp. 113–43.

——, "Osservazioni sul creduto tempio del Genio di Augusto," *Atti della Reale Accademia di Archeologia, Lettere e Belle Arti*, 1891–1893 [published in 1894] vol. 16, pp. 181–8.

——, "Der staedtische Larentempel in Pompeji," *RM*, 1896, vol. 11, pp. 285–301.

——, "Die Statuen des Forums von Pompeji," *RM*, 1896, vol. 11, pp. 160–6.

——, "Der Tempel des Vespasian in Pompeji," *RM*, 1900, vol. 15, pp. 133–8.

——, *Pompeii: its life and art*, trans. Francis W. Kelsey, New York, 1902.

Ohr, K., *Die Basilika in Pompeji*, Berlin, 1991.

Overbeck, J. and A. Mau, *Pompeji in seinen Gebäuden, Alterthümern und Kunstwerken*, 4th edn, Leipzig, 1884.

Richardson, L., jr, "Concordia and Concordia Augusta: Rome and Pompeii," *PP*, 1978, vol. 33, pp. 260–72.

——, *Pompeii: an architectural history*, Baltimore, MD and London, 1988.

Small, A., "The shrine of the imperial family in the Macellum at Pompeii," in A. Small (ed.), *Subject and Ruler: the cult of the ruling power in classical antiquity*, JRA Suppl. Ser. no. 17, 1996, pp. 115–36.

Sogliano, A., "Il foro di Pompei," *Memoria Reale Accademia Nazionale dei Lincei*, 1925, Ser. 6, vol. 1, fasc. 3, pp. 14ff.

Ulrich, R., *The Roman Orator and the Sacred Stage: The Roman Templum Rostratum*, Latomus Collection 22, Brussels, 1994.

Wallat, K., "Opus Testaceum in Pompeji," *RM*, 1993, vol. 100, pp. 353–82.

——, "Der Marmorfries am Eingangsportal des Gabäudes der Eumachia (VII 9,1) in Pompeji und sein ursprünglicher Anbringungsort," *AA*, 1995, 345–73.

——, "Der Zustand des Forums von Pompeji am Vorabend des Vesuvausbruchs 79 n. Chr.," in T. Frölich and L. Jacobelli (eds), *Archäologie und Seismologie. La regione vesuviana dal 62 al 79 d.C. Problemi archeologici e sismologici* (Colloquium Boscorele, November 26–27, 1993), Munich, 1995, pp. 75–92.

——, *Die Ostseite des Forums von Pompeji*, Frankfurt am Main, 1997.

CHAPTER THIRTEEN

URBAN, SUBURBAN AND RURAL RELIGION IN THE ROMAN PERIOD

———— ·◆· ————

Alastair M. Small

The Vesuvian sites offer us a wonderfully vivid picture of Roman religion in the Late Republic and Early Empire.[1] It is, however, an incomplete, and perhaps even a distorted picture, for much of the evidence has been irretrievably lost. Most of the marble fittings, statues and inscriptions were stripped from the temples of Pompeii after the eruption, and many of the minor artifacts and almost all the biological remains which might have yielded evidence for cult practices vanished without trace when the ruins of the most important sanctuaries were excavated in the late eighteenth and early nineteenth centuries. Although two-thirds of the urban area have been excavated, it is certain that many cult buildings, including some of the most important, remain to be discovered.[2] In Herculaneum, where less than half the city has been excavated, no public temple has yet been uncovered except for two small shrines in the Area Sacra Suburbana overlooking the sea.

In spite of the gaps in the evidence, the spatial distribution of the public temples in Pompeii says much about the role of official religion in the civic life of the city. In the excavated areas there are large expanses with no temples at all. The known temples all cluster in Region VII in the vicinity of the Great Theatre, and in Region VIII around the forum and basilica—that is to say, in the two main areas developed for public buildings. The reason is clear: temples within the city walls were the responsibility of the *decurions* and city magistrates; they were as much part of the official fabric of the city as the markets or public meeting places; and they formed an integral part of the urban landscape of the city centres. The local subdivisions of the city (*vici*) had their own cult places, but these were small crossroads shrines.

In pre-Roman Pompeii the most important temple was dedicated to Apollo (Figure 13.1; De Caro, Ch. 6), whose cult went back to the origins of the city in the early sixth century BC.[3] The temple was rebuilt in the second century BC in the Corinthian order in a precinct planted with trees and shrubs, larger than the peristyle now visible.[4] It formed part of the western edge of the main public open space, which was to become the forum of the Roman city. At the north end of this space there was another cult centre where Maiuri excavated a votive deposit of the fourth and third centuries BC.[5] A temple seems to have been built for this cult around the end of the second century BC on a podium which was re-used in the Roman Capitolium.[6]

Figure 13.1 Temple and precinct of Apollo, Pompeii (VII.7.31–32). Photo: J. J. Dobbins.

If there was any continuity of cult from the one phase to the other, then the earlier building was probably dedicated to Jupiter.

There was also a temple in the Triangular Forum, built in the archaic period, and renovated in the fourth century BC[7] which was dedicated, almost certainly, to Minerva.[8] Two temples were built in the second century BC in the vicinity of the Great Theatre— a shrine of uncertain dedication, once thought to be the temple of Jupiter Meilichios referred to in an Oscan inscription at the Porta di Stabia, and a temple of Isis, the earliest in Italy known to have been dedicated to this Egyptian goddess.

Several extra-mural sanctuaries have been identified, all of which go back to the pre-Roman period (Figure 28.1 A–C). The best known is a small temple of Dionysus situated on the top of a low hill at S. Abbondio near what was then the mouth of the Sarno river.[9] There was also a sanctuary at Bottaro in the so-called Borgo Marinaro, probably dedicated to Neptune,[10] and another in the Contrada Iozzino to the south of the city, beside the road that leads from the Porta di Stabia, which is perhaps to be identified with the Temple of Jupiter Meilichios referred to in the Oscan inscription. Its situation, surrounded by graves, would be appropriate for the cult of this chthonic god.[11]

These remains point to the importance of religion in the public life of Pompeii in the immediately pre-Roman period, and the ease with which cults of alien origin could win official approval and be absorbed into the city's culture. In that respect Pompeii was probably typical of Campanian cities in the late Hellenistic period, but it differed from Rome where the magistrates did not tolerate non-traditional cults thought likely to endanger the well-being of the state.[12] In 186 BC the Roman senate took alarm at rumours of a new form of the cult of Dionysus which had recently reached Italy (Livy 39.8–19) and instructed the magistrates to suppress it ruthlessly, even in non-Roman communities such as Pompeii.[13] Their decree allowed exemptions under special circumstances for small groups of bacchants who worshipped at long established sanctuaries, and the cult at S. Abbondio must have been registered as one of these, for the sanctuary remained in use, though it ceased to be supported by the city government.[14]

The imposition of the Roman colony on the Samnite community in 80 BC led to significant changes. The priesthoods were reformed according to Roman practice (cf. *CIL* X, 93). In the new colony there were *pontifices* who administered Roman religious law, and *augures* who interpreted the omens sent by the gods (especially in the flight of birds). There was also a public priestess, drawn from one or other of the leading families of the city,[15] who must have performed sacrifices at the Temple of Venus, and may have had a role in other cults as well. We also know of a public priestess of Ceres, and a priest of Mars.

Most of the pre-Roman sanctuaries continued,[16] but they must have been brought within the religious laws that governed the cults of the new colony. In the Sanctuary of Apollo (Figure 13.1) the magistrates replaced the old altar with a new one, in accordance with a decree of the *decurions*, as they recorded in an inscription (*CIL* X, 800). That must imply some reorganisation of the cult. Probably at the same time the precinct was separated from the forum by piers of increasing thickness which masked the difference in alignment between forum and temple. In spite of these changes the forum remained the scene of the great festival of Apollo, the *ludi apollinares*, held each year on 6–13 July on the model of a similar festival in Rome, with bull-fights, pantomimes and other entertainments (*CIL* X, 1074d).

In the shrine of uncertain dedication near the Greek Theatre the *cella* was rebuilt, and several changes were made in the precinct.[17] The altar was retained, but was probably turned around to fit the reduced space.[18]

The most drastic modification of an existing cult was the conversion of the temple at the north end of the forum into a Capitolium to house the three-fold cult of Jupiter, Juno and Minerva, imported from the Capitoline hill in Rome.[19] The new temple demonstrated the supremacy of Rome's most prestigious cult, and emphasised the *romanitas* of the new colony. The head and bust of the statue of Jupiter survive, a colossal piece based on a late-classical Greek original.[20] Unlike other Pompeian temples, the Capitolium had no precinct of its own. Its courtyard was the whole forum which provided a conspicuous setting for its ceremonies.

Equally important in the cult life of the Roman colony was the new Temple of Venus. Venus had been the patron goddess of Sulla whose veterans formed the first colonists, and the official name of the colony, *Colonia Veneria Cornelia* (*CIL* I, 1252; X, 787; 10 BC), connects it both with Venus and with Sulla who belonged to the *gens* Cornelia. But the cult title *Victrix*—the Victorious—with which Sulla worshipped the goddess was not used at Pompeii, presumably because it evoked Sulla's bloody victory over the Samnites in the wars of the late 80s. Instead she was worshipped as Venus Pompeiana—or as Venus Fisica, the goddess of Nature. The two were sometimes combined as Venus Fisica Pompeiana.[21] The cult became very popular, to judge by the number of *graffiti* that allude to it (*CIL* IV, 26, 538, 1520, 2457, 4007, 6865), and Pompeii became well known as the city of Venus.[22]

Her temple was situated just inside the Porta Marina.[23] It was built on a vast artificial platform and must have been intended to be conspicuous from the sea like several other famous temples of Aphrodite/Venus who was born from the sea, and whose cult was popular with sailors.[24]

The three main temples—the Capitolium, the Temple of Apollo and the Temple of Venus, were all embellished in the Augustan period or shortly afterwards. The entrance steps of the Capitolium were rebuilt with flanking bastions which may have supported statues of the Dioscuri, sons of Jupiter,[25] and the altar was reset on a raised platform in the centre of the temple steps, where it is shown blazing at the time of the earthquake in a relief on the *lararium* of L. Caecilius Iucundus.[26] In the precinct of Apollo the gaps between the piers that connected the sanctuary with the forum were filled in and the area was reshaped as the colonnaded courtyard visible today.[27] A new portico was also built around the Temple of Venus. It was destroyed together with the temple in the earthquake of AD 62, and rebuilding had not progressed far by the time of the eruption.

The porticoes surrounding these temples were large enough to accommodate many participants in the cult festivals. A painting of the marriage of Hercules and Hebe found in the *oecus* of the House of the Wedding of Hercules (VII.9.47) gives a vivid impression of a festival at the Temple of Venus (Figure 13.2): the doors of the temple have been opened to reveal the cult statue standing inside, bedecked with jewellery, flanked by smaller statues of Priapus and Cupid.[28] On either side of the temple a procession makes its way. Several groups carry cult objects on *fercula*, and others bring a white heifer for sacrifice.

The great temples were designed for large numbers of people to participate in the cult. By contrast, the Temple of Isis had a much smaller precinct intended to serve a more intimate community of initiates, and it was hidden from public view by a high wall flanking the south side of the via del Tempio di Iside. Nevertheless, the cult continued to benefit from the official status it had been given before the foundation of the Sullan colony,[29] and became even modish under Vespasian.[30] The sanctuary was largely reconstructed after the earthquake of AD 62 and was fully functional at

Figure 13.2 Painting from the House of the Wedding of Hercules/
House of Mars and Venus (VII.9.47) showing a procession to the Temple of Venus,
Pompeii. From M. Della Corte, *Iuventus*, pl. I.

Figure 13.3   Temple of Isis, Pompeii (VIII.7.28).

the time of the eruption: the excavators of 1764 recorded finding ashes and fragments of burned bones lying on the altar.

The temple (Figure 13.3) differs markedly from Graeco-Roman norms, and was clearly designed to suit the theatrical requirements of the cult.[31] It stands on a high podium near the centre of the porticoed courtyard. Sockets in the stylobate show that there were doors or screens between the columns by which the view from the portico to the central court could be controlled. Both the *pronaos* and the *cella* are unusually wide in proportion to their depth, and a staircase running up against the south wall gave direct access to the *cella* from outside, for use by the priests who could enter or leave the *cella* without being seen by the spectators in the eastern portico. The plinth was extended on either side of the *pronaos* to support two small *aediculae* which must have held other cult statues. Each has an altar in front of it. The main altar was set off-centre, southeast of the temple steps so as not to obstruct the view into the temple from the portico.

In the extreme southeast corner of the court there was a walled enclosure, open to the sky, with a flight of steps which led to an underground vaulted chamber where there was a large bowl set on a pedestal. It probably contained Nile water for use in purification ceremonies.

Several statues or parts of statues were found inside the temple precinct.[32] Some were of Isis and other Egyptian divinities, but there were also statuettes of Dionysus and Venus Anadyomene which point to syncretism of the Isis cult with Graeco-Roman cults connected with fertility and regeneration.

The theatrical nature of the cult is vividly illustrated by two paintings from Herculaneum (where there must also have been a temple of Isis), which show Isiac ceremonies.[33] In one a priest stands at the top of a flight of steps in front of a temple holding a pot of Nile water, while attendant priests and devotees raise their hands in prayer, and shake their sacred rattles (*sistra*). In the other a masked man dances in the shrine to the sound of flutes, tambourines and *sistra*.

The Mysteries of the Great Mother, Cybele, and her castrated lover Attis were also popular in the Vesuvian cities and countryside.[34] In its extreme form the cult involved orgiastic rituals culminating in the self-castration of its devotees, but it was subjected to strict controls when it was introduced to Rome during the Hannibalic War. There is no epigraphic or structural evidence for a temple of Cybele in Pompeii, but a lively fresco on the wall of the shop at IX.7.1 on the via dell'Abbondanza shows a procession in honour of the goddess.[35] Her cult statue is seated on a wooden litter beside which stand four bearers with garlands in their hair. Behind her are two rows of worshippers led by a priest and priestess, some of them playing the pan pipes or double flute, others beating tambourines or clashing cymbals.

At Herculaneum, too, there was a temple of Cybele, in her role as Mother of the Gods. The building has not yet been located, but we know of its existence from an inscription (*CIL* X, 1406) which records that it was rebuilt by Vespasian in AD 76 after it had been destroyed in the earthquake. This act of personal patronage by the emperor to a relatively small city, fourteen years after the disaster in which the temple had collapsed, is a remarkable sign of the importance the new Flavian dynasty attached to ecstatic cults of eastern origin.[36]

The early excavators, digging their tunnels through the remains of Herculaneum, reported finding traces of several temples, but the evidence for them is difficult to assess.[37] The only sanctuaries visible today are two small temples of the Augustan period located on an artificial platform known as the Area Sacra Suburbana overlooking the sea to the right of the modern entrance to the site (Figure 13.4; Map 4).[38] Each has an altar in front. The smaller shrine nearest the entrance was dedicated to Venus (appropriately, since it overlooked the sea); the larger one to Minerva, Vulcan, Mercury and Neptune. An inscription found in the precinct shows that a *collegium* of *Venerei* had their seat there, probably in the adjacent series of small chambers to the east. They must have maintained the cult of Venus in the nearby shrine.

The evidence from Pompeii shows how a Roman city developed and controlled religious cult at the level of the city's subdivisions, with a series of shrines set up at crossroads (*compita*). There was a board of *magistri* for each ward (*vicus*) of the city, and for each district (*pagus*) in the countryside. They carried out sacrifices at *compita*, especially on the three-day festival of the *Compitalia* held at the turn of each year. We know the names of several who held office at Pompeii in 47 and 46 BC (*CIL* IV, 60): some were free-born; others were freedmen. There are remains of one painted altar of this period, on the via dell'Abbondanza at IX.11.1. It was decorated *c*.20 BC with a frieze of the Twelve Gods (only nine are now visible). Below them the four *magistri* are shown at an altar, together with two *lares*, and a snake representing the *genius* of the place.[39]

In 7 BC the Roman senate ordered a reform of the system of local wards,[40] which required, among other things, that the image of the *genius* of Augustus should be displayed on the compital shrines together with those of the *lares compitales*. The new

Figure 13.4 View east and down at the two small temples in the Area Sacra Suburbana in Herculaneum, dedicated to Venus (right) and Minerva, Vulcan, Mercury and Neptune (left). Photo: A.M. Small.

combined cult was administered in the city by *ministri augusti*, most of whom were slaves. The reform gave a socially important role to the lowest members of Roman society, and fostered their loyalty to the emperor; but it involved them in some expense, because they were expected to make dedications on important occasions connected with the dynasty.[41]

Three compital shrines at Pompeii,[42] and one at Herculaneum (at the junction of *cardo* III and the *decumanus maximus*) show the effects of this reform. They are simple altars of masonry or cut stone, set in front of house walls which were painted with scenes of the cult. On one such shrine set against the wall of IX.12.7, the *genius Augusti* is shown sacrificing at an altar attended by a flute player wearing a toga, and by two small tunic-clad figures representing the *ministri*. One holds a *patera* of offerings in his left hand and a garland in his right while the other drags a pig to the altar. In a lower register two snakes, manifestations of the *genius* of the place, sup from eggs on another altar.[43]

There were many other images of popular piety in the streets of Pompeii, for inn-keepers, shopkeepers and artisans regularly painted the façades of their houses with pictures of their favourite divinities. There is a particularly good group in Reg. IX.7 on the north side of the via dell'Abbondanza.[44] At IX.7.1 there is the procession scene of Cybele, already mentioned. A little further down the road, Venus Pompeiana is depicted on the outside wall of a felt-maker's workshop at IX.7.7, riding a triumphal chariot drawn by elephants, and holding the branch of Minerva in her right hand,

and a sceptre in her left, which she supports on the upturned rudder of Fortuna;[45] to the left, Mercury is shown alighting, purse in hand, at a temple, while below him is a picture of a stall where a woman salesperson deals with a young customer. At Herculaneum there is an unusual image of the Sabine god Semo Sancus painted on the wall of a wine-shop at VI.14. Below him is an array of wine jugs each marked with a different price.[46] Fortuna, sometimes conflated with Isis, protected the Pompeian latrines and those who used them.[47]

Some owners of private houses also displayed images of their patron deities on their house fronts, or in the *fauces* between the front door and the atrium, as in the House of the Vettii (VI.15.1) where Priapus greeted the visitor with grossly extended phallus balanced against a money purse in a pair of weigh-scales. He was a talisman against the evil eye, protecting the riches of the house.[48] But the real family cults took place further inside houses, at the shrines (*lararia*) where the images of the household gods were displayed. A pious household would decorate the images with garlands on the kalends, ides and nones of each month; and would offer simple sacrifices of wine, spelt and honey cakes to them. On days which were especially significant for the family, such as the birthday or marriage day of the *paterfamilias*, or the day when his son put on his *toga virilis*, a pig would be sacrificed to his *genius*. The cult was male-oriented, though women might make offerings to their *juno*, the female equivalent of the *genius*.

In 30 BC, at the very beginning of the principate, the senate passed a decree which required offerings of undiluted wine to be made to Octavian (soon to become Augustus) at both public and private banquets.[49] With this, the image of the emperor, or more probably of the emperor's *genius*, became a necessary part of family cult. In both Pompeii and Herculaneum the *genius Augusti* is represented in private *lararia*, wearing the *toga praetexta* and patrician shoes of the emperor, and pouring sacrificial offerings from a *patera* onto an altar.[50] He is usually flanked by two *lares*, shown as young and jovial male figures wearing a short tunic, and pouring a libation of wine from a ritual vessel (*rhyton*). Two snakes representing the *genius* of the place (or perhaps the *genius* and *juno* of the family) are often depicted in a lower register, feeding at an altar (Figure 13.5).

More than 300 *lararia* have been recorded from Pompeii (Figures 23.4 and 35.1), and there were many also in Herculaneum.[51] Their quality varies according to their location and the social standing of the people who created them. In the houses of the poor, and in areas of grand houses used especially by slaves, they usually consist of cult images painted on a wall or in a niche, with an altar or shelf below on which offerings would be placed. The *lararia* of the rich were generally grander structures, with a pediment and sometimes columns in stucco or wood, which housed small figurines in bronze or terracotta.[52] They were intended for display, and were often set in the *atrium* where visitors would be expected to venerate the images on entering and leaving the house.[53] A common alternative setting was in a peristyle where a *lararium* might close an axial view.

Domestic cult was not confined to *lararia*. There are enough figurines found in bedchambers (*cubicula*) to show that pious Pompeians wanted to sleep in the company of bedroom gods,[54] even without a proper *lararium* in the room: a group of figurines was found in a cupboard in the *cubiculum* of an upstairs apartment in the Casa a Gratticio at Herculaneum (Figure 27.6).[55] Small portable altars of terracotta, bronze

Figure 13.5 *Lararium* in the House of the Vettii (VI.15.1), Pompeii. Istituto Centrale per il Catalogo e la Documentazione (ICCD), N G15740.

or stone are frequent finds at Vesuvian sites, and may sometimes have been set up for temporary use without the need for a *lararium*.[56]

The cults represented in domestic *lararia* conform, by and large, to the established cults of the community, and are likely to have involved the household as a whole— the nuclear family and its dependents, including its slaves. In a number of houses, however, in both Pompeii and Herculaneum, there are small shrines (*sacraria*), usually situated in the interior of the house, though sometimes in the garden (Figure 31.1, niche on right), which must have been designed for more private cults.[57] Some were purpose built, with vaulted ceilings, and niches for the cult statues; others were converted from *cubicula*. Their religious character is indicated by paintings on the walls and in the niches, by cult statuettes, and by small portable altars for burning incense, or in some cases by more solid altars of masonry. Some, such as an underground chamber in the House of Popidius Priscus at Pompeii (VII.2.20) which measured only 1.12 × 1.24 m, are so small that they can hardly have had room for more than a single individual. They suggest that the *paterfamilias* or the matron of the house felt the need for much more private devotion. Others could have accommodated small numbers of participants in a cult, away from public view. One such is a narrow room which opened onto the garden peristyle of the House of the Lararium (I.6.4). The vault and lunettes were decorated with stuccoes alluding to the union of mortals and immortals (Diana and Endymion in the lunettes, the rape of Ganymede, probably, in a medallion in the centre of the vault). The sacred nature of the room is confirmed by a group of alabaster doves, symbols of Venus, found inside it.[58]

Sacraria such as these provided a suitable setting for the secret rites of the Bona Dea which were strictly confined to female participants. One has recently been identified in the Villa of Risi di Prisco at Boscoreale. Inside the room there was a *lararium* containing a small marble statuette of the goddess, reclining on a *kline*, and pouring an offering from a *patera* for a snake coiled around her right arm.[59] The goddess is also represented on a silver appliqué for a box kept in the *lararium*, and on a terracotta basin below it. The same image is found in a *sacrarium* at the bottom of the garden of house IX.9.6 at Pompeii, and in several other Pompeian *sacraria* which must also have been used for the cult of the goddess.[60]

Several houses have vaulted rooms painted with emblems of mystery cults set in a paradise of flowering and fruiting plants inhabited by birds. It is often supposed that these were intended merely to diffuse a vaguely religious aura; but in some cases the allusions to cult strongly suggest that the rooms were the *sacraria* of private mysteries which could combine elements from several cults. An outstanding example is a room found in 1978 in the House of the Golden Bracelet (VI.17.42). It opened directly onto the garden, and was painted in the second quarter of the first century AD with garden scenes of astonishing beauty,[61] inset with symbols of Dionysus. Similar garden paintings have been found in vaulted rooms in several other Pompeian houses. In some cases the dionysiac motifs are linked with others drawn from the cult of Isis, as in the House of the Floral Cubiculum (I.9.6),[62] or the House of the Fruit Orchard (I.11.5).[63] The rooms are all small, and if they were used for mystery cults, as the motifs and vaulted construction suggest, they can have served only a few devotees. Most are situated near to a garden or peristyle, appropriate to the theme of the painting. They convey the message that the god is the source of life and regeneration, in which the initiate may hope to share through participation in the cult.

In the house at II.1.12 there was a *sacrarium* of the Phrygian god Sabazius, who was worshipped with orgiastic ceremonies and initiation rites that had absorbed many elements from the cult of Dionysus.[64] The cult was suppressed by the praetor in Rome in 139 BC, and it remained outside the law. There was nothing on the exterior the house to identify the Sabazian sanctuary inside: in fact, paintings of Venus and Cupid, Dionysus, Mercury and Priapus in the doorway suggested an attachment to more conventional gods. But the worshipper who entered the doorway looked across a peristyle planted with poplars to an altar, and an open-fronted room beyond it. The word *antrum* roughly cut on the pier to the left of the room identifies it as a cave, and so probably the birthplace of the god, for in the principal version of the cultic myth Persephone was impregnated by Zeus in the form of a snake, and gave birth to Sabazius in a cave. On the opposite pier, an ithyphallic dancer brandishing a tambourine hints at the orgiastic character of the cult. At the back of the room there was a podium on which the birth scene may have been represented. Two other rooms, suitably proportioned for *triclinia* may have been used for cult banquets. Two ritual vessels, decorated in relief with snakes, lizards, tortoises and bunches of grapes were found in the vicinity of the altar in the peristyle, together with two hands entwined with similar cult emblems. The sanctuary can be dated by masonry features after the earthquake of AD 62.

The cult of Dionysus had no official temple or priest, but in private circles it was immensely popular, as the innumerable representations of the god and his entourage found in the Vesuvian sites shows. He is depicted as the god of wine in an unusual painting found in a *lararium* in the House of the Centenary (IX.8.3.6), now in Naples Museum, which shows him draped in clusters of grapes and pouring wine from a *kantharos* to be lapped up by his companion panther. Behind him is Mt Vesuvius (Figure 4.2).[65] The villas on the slopes of the mountain produced excellent wine, and not surprisingly a small shrine for the cult of the god is incorporated into the pressing room (IX–IX*bis*) of the rural villa in the area of Villa Regina at Boscoreale (Figure 28.4), and in several other wine-producing villas in the neighbourhood.[66] A much more complex aspect of Dionysiac cult is vividly represented in the famous chamber of the Villa of the Mysteries at Pompeii, decorated *c.*50 BC with a continuous grand frieze depicting women taking part in a series of rituals presided over by Dionysus and (probably) his mother Semele. The great painting and its sources have been endlessly discussed, without any definitive interpretation emerging; but its prevailing message is the liberating power that Dionysus exercises over his initiates.[67]

The earliest Christian meeting-places in the Vesuvian cities are also likely to have been *sacraria*, hidden from public view in the inner recesses of private houses. The evidence for Christianity in Pompeii and Herculaneum is of uneven value, and has been much debated, but when the more dubious arguments are discounted there remains a residue of archaeological documentation which should leave little doubt that there were Christians in Pompeii before the eruption. The clearest indication is a *graffito* scratched in charcoal on a wall of an inn situated on the via del Balcone Pensile (VII.11.11–14), which was recorded by several authorities at the time of the excavation in 1862 but had vanished within two years. The beginning and end are uncertain, but the word *christianos* clearly occurred on the fourth line.[68] There has been much debate about the well-known magic square

ROTAS
OPERA
TENET
AREPO
SATOR

found scratched on a column of the Great Palaestra (II.7), and on the south wall of the peristyle of the House of Paquius Proculus at (Reg. I.7.1). It was certainly a Christian cryptogram,[69] and may have been inscribed by Jewish Christians at the time of the eruption, though some suppose that the liturgical formula "pater noster" encoded in the cryptogram could not have been in use at this date, and that the graffiti must have been inscribed at some later time by looters digging through the ruins of the city.[70] The *graffito Sodoma Gomora* alluding to the destruction of the cursed cities in *Genesis* 19, presents the same problems. It was written in charcoal on the wall of a house at IX.1.26, evidently by a Jew or Christian, alluding to the destruction of the cursed cities in *Genesis* 19.[71] Much more dubious is a cross-shaped groove found on a wall of the House of the Bicentenary at Herculaneum (V.15), which Maiuri held to be the placement for a Christian cross, but which is open to other interpretations.[72]

Jews are well attested at Pompeii and there is some evidence for them at Herculaneum,[73] but no synagogue has yet been found in either city, and there is little evidence of Jewish religious practices or beliefs. A few items, however, allude to themes in the Bible. The most interesting (apart from the *graffito* of Sodom and Gomorrah) is a painting in the burlesque style from Pompeii found on a wall of the peristyle in the House of the Doctor at VIII.5.24, which shows pygmies enacting a scene resembling the judgment of Solomon in I *Kings* 3.16ff.[74] It is likely to be based on an Alexandrian original, but it would have had little point if the owner of the house had not been familiar with the Jewish story.

In spite of the popularity of mystery cults offering hope of a more blissful after-life, the Pompeians continued to practise the traditional cult of the dead (cf. Cormack, Ch. 37). Only very small children whose first teeth had not yet erupted were buried; older children and adults were regularly cremated and their ashes placed in terracotta urns or glass vases, usually with a few grave goods and a bronze coin—"Charon's fee"—to pay for their journey to the underworld. The urns might be buried directly in the ground or set in niches in tombs such as those that line the road outside the Porta Ercolano (Figure 37.1), depending on the wealth and social pretensions of the family. The relatives of the dead might gather at their family tombs several times each year to eat a ceremonial meal and offer gifts of incense and flowers and libations of wine and oil to the dead. The occasion might be a family event such as the birthday of the dead person, or the communal festival of the dead, the *Parentalia*, held annually between 13 and 21 February, which culminated on the last day with a general procession through the city to the graves outside the walls.[75] Many tombs were equipped for these ceremonies. Some had walled enclosures, probably planted as gardens, where the family group could hold the funerary feast in pleasant surroundings. The best attested example is a tomb at Scafati which had a walled precinct planted with trees.[76] The tomb of Gnaeus Vibius Saturninus on the via dei Sepolcri at Pompeii had an elaborate open-air *triclinium*.[77] Many of the tombs were equipped with funnels through which libations could be poured directly onto the funerary urns to feed the shades of the dead.[78]

Much less is known of burials at Herculaneum since the open excavations have not extended to the city gates and the graves beyond them on the landward side. Some tombs were encountered in the early excavations lining the road to Pompeii to the southeast of the city (Map 4, B), but little is known of these. The only funerary monument currently visible is the remarkable tomb of Marcus Nonius Balbus (Figures 15.13, B and 27.3, lower right). It shares the same terrace as the two small sanctuaries of the Area Sacra Suburbana, and adjoins the Suburban Baths which were built with funds left by Balbus in his will. Since the terrace lay just outside the city gate leading to the sea, the burial did not infringe the ancient prohibition on burying or cremating a corpse within the city;[79] but it was nevertheless the only tomb permitted by the city authorities in this position. Balbus was the patron of the city at the beginning of the principate, a supporter of Octavian/Augustus who had been proconsul of Crete and Cyrene. The tomb is in the form of an altar, and an inscription on the front of it states that the *decurions* had decreed that the marble altar should be made, constituted (by religious ceremony) and inscribed at public expense in the place where his ashes were collected; also that the public procession held each year on the festival of the *Parentalia* should start from that place.[80] Recent excavations inside the tomb have revealed Balbus's funerary urn. It contained the ashes of his pyre, and the uncremated bone of one of his fingers. It illustrates the ritual of *os resectum*,—the removal of a finger from a corpse before cremation—which was prompted by the belief that at least a token part of the body must be returned uncremated to the earth if a burial was to be valid by religious custom and the family was to be purified from the taint of death.[81] On the west side of the altar there were three steps which gave access to it for sacrifice. Beside it there was a statue of Balbus (b), the recipient of the sacrifice, in cuirass and military cloak. The monument in effect elevates the status of the dead Nonius to that of a heroic being.

In Pompeii, as elsewhere in the Roman world, there was a substratum of popular religion for which there was no dogma or myth, but which aimed to control supernatural forces by magic.[82] Various symbols were used to invoke fertility or good luck, or ward off the evil eye. The most common was the erect phallus (*fascinus*)[83] which is found in a wide variety of contexts in Pompeii and Herculaneum.[84] Many amulets were imported from Egypt, or made in imitation of Egyptian types, for Egyptian magical practices associated with the cult of Hermes Trismegistos were becoming influential in the Greco-Roman world in this period. Still more exotic is an ivory figurine of the Indian goddess Laksmi, found in the House of the Indian Statuette (I.8.5), which was perhaps brought to Pompeii by a merchant as a talisman.[85] Some magical amulets had a more sinister purpose, like two lead curse tablets (*defixiones*) which were found buried in the Tomb of the Epidii, pierced with two nails and bound around with a lead strip. The inscriptions inside are barely legible, but one seems to devote various body parts of an enemy to the gods of the underworld (*CIL* IV, 9251–2).

Prodigies—unusual events which violated the natural order—needed to be expiated by special rites prescribed by religious law. They included objects struck by lightning (*fulgur*), which were ceremonially buried. There is a good example in the small courtyard at the back of the House of the Four Styles (I.8.17) where Maiuri excavated a pit filled with broken tiles and other building rubble. It was covered by a low mound of soil, marked with a flat tile roughly inscribed FVLGVR.[86]

The fatalistic belief that the stars ruled human destiny through a chain of cause and effect spread to Italy from Alexandria. It, too, was derived from the cult of Hermes Trismegistos who was believed to be the source of astrology as well as of magic,[87] but it was given added credibility by stoic philosophers[88] who held that the stars were emanations of the divine providence that determined human behaviour. The seven planets (including the sun and the moon) were especially important: each was identified with a particular god, and gradually (during the first three centuries AD) the idea took hold that each planetary deity presided in turn over human destiny. The logical consequence was the development of the seven-day planetary week. The earliest evidence we have for this comes from the Vesuvian cities. A *graffito* on the wall of a *triclinium* in the small house at V.4.b in Pompeii gave the names of the planetary deities in the order in which we know them in the calendar, beginning with Saturn,[89] and a painting in the Fourth Style discovered at Pompeii somewhere in *Ins. Occ.* VI in 1760 and now in the Naples Museum shows the busts of Saturn, Sol, Luna, Mars, Mercury, Jupiter and Venus.[90]

In the Roman world there was no clear boundary between philosophy and religion, for most philosophers believed that the universe was ruled by divine intelligence, and even the Epicureans, who argued that the world was essentially irrational, admitted that there were gods, though they thought they were irrelevant to human affairs. Philosophy, however, was the religion of the leisured and educated rich, and so was more relevant to life in the suburban villa than in the town. Villa owners often expressed their philosophical inclinations in visual form, as we can see, for instance, in an inset panel from a mosaic found in the suburban villa of T. Siminius Stephanus outside the Porta Vesuvio at Pompeii (Figure 28.2, top right), which shows a group of philosophers gathered around a semicircular bench in the open air. It probably represents Plato and others in the Academy.[91] The prevailing philosophy was epicureanism which inculcated the avoidance of stress, and suited the life-style of many Pompeian villa owners. In the luxurious Villa of the Papyri near Herculaneum the owner had a library of (predominantly) epicurean works, and surrounded himself with images of Epicurus and other philosophers.[92] By contrast, the owner of the modest productive villa at Pisanella (Figure 28.1, no. 13) spent little on architectural embellishment, but he concealed a remarkable hoard of gold and silver in the cistern of his pressing room, including two silver beakers decorated with revelling skeletons of philosophers and poets, like a parody of the sculptures in the Villa of the Papyri. Inscriptions convey the epicurean message that the end of life is pleasure: tomorrow is uncertain, so one should enjoy oneself while one can.[93]

The beginning of the principate brought a number of innovations to the religious life of the Vesuvian cities, as it did throughout the empire. Not only was the emperor the *pontifex maximus* (after 12 BC), and so vested with special authority to regulate the official cults of the Roman state; he was also a distant, all-powerful figure and the subject of spontaneous worship. The cult of the living emperor was not institutionalised in the city of Rome where such a violation of the traditions of the ancestors might arouse the indignation of the senatorial class; but beyond the city boundaries there was no need for restraint.[94] Before the end of the first century BC the Pompeians erected a temple to Augustus[95] in the centre of the east side of the forum. It stands within its own precinct, in the middle of which is the altar,[96] which survived the despoliation of the marble fittings after the eruption. Each side is decorated with symbols of the cult carved in low relief. The main scene, on the front, shows a mythical sacrifice carried out by Augustus at the dedication of his temple: a group of people stands in front of the temple which has four Corinthian columns partially concealed by a curtain: Augustus with veiled head pours incense from a *patera* onto a tripod altar, while a *victimarius* prepares to despatch the bull. The first recorded priest to serve the cult was M. Holconius Rufus, the most important member of the aristocracy of Pompeii at the time, who held the duovirate (the chief annual magistracy in the city) for the fourth time in 2/1 BC.[97] He was succeeded by his brother, M. Holconius Celer.

In AD 3 (*CIL* X, 824) the magistrates of Pompeii authorised the building of a temple to Fortuna Augusta, in which Augustus was associated with the fickle goddess of chance. It stands a little to the north of the forum area at the crossing of two main streets—the via del Foro and the via di Nola (Figure 12.2, top left). Inscriptions show that the building was paid for by M. Tullius, one of the leading members of the Pompeian aristocracy (*CIL* X, 820), and that a new college of *ministri* was appointed to attend to the details of the cult. Like the *ministri Augusti* who served the cult of the Lares Compitales, they were initially drawn from slaves.[98] The date of the temple (AD 3) is significant, for one of Augustus' grandsons (and adopted sons), Lucius Caesar, had died in the previous year, and his oldest grandson and principal heir, Gaius Caesar, had been badly wounded in Armenia (in AD 2 or perhaps 3) and was to die in AD 4. Augustus himself ascribed their deaths to cruel fortune.[99]

Another aspect of the imperial cult was the deification of virtues appropriate to the imperial family. In Pompeii this is exemplified by the so-called Eumachia Building, immediately adjacent to the Temple of Augustus.[100] It consists of a colonnaded area (*chalcidicum*) outside the entrance, and an internal courtyard surrounded by another colonnade (*porticus*), with a subterranean passageway (*crypta*) below it. An inscription placed over the entrances tells us that Eumachia, the public priestess, dedicated all three parts of the building to *Concordia Augusta* and *Pietas* in the names of her son M. Numistrius Fronto and herself. It was inspired by the Porticus that Livia dedicated to Concord at Rome in 7 BC, and celebrated both the concord of the imperial family, and Eumachia's personal piety. It was probably built late in the reign of Augustus after the death of her husband and son.[101] It may have contained a shrine of the Julian family.[102] Since the building probably served various civic purposes, the cult of the imperial family and its virtues was integrated into the routine life of the city.

Another building where civic functions may have taken place in the ambience of the emperor cult was the Macellum, built late in the reign of Claudius, and repaired after the earthquake of AD 62.[103] The courtyard may have been a butchers' market (*macellum*); but it was dominated by a small temple at the eastern end with a cult statue of the emperor holding a globe, and other sculptures of the imperial family, or perhaps of local notables who had paid for the building or were connected with the cult (Figures 36.5 and 36.6).[104] To the north and south there were open spaces behind a screen set aside for cult purposes.

Between the Macellum and the Temple of Augustus was another building opening onto the forum which may have been designed for the imperial cult (Figure 12.10).[105] It was the latest and most innovative structure to be erected in the forum area. On architectural grounds it should be dated late in the reign of Nero or to the reign of Vespasian. It was perhaps dedicated to the *domus divina* of the Flavians, for the plan provided a conspicuous setting for three statues—one in the central apse (for Vespasian?) and two in the side wings (for Titus and Domitian?): an architectural counterpart of bronze coins of the beginning of Vespasian's reign, which show Vespasian on the obverse, and Titus and Domitian facing each other on the reverse.[106] There was an altar in the centre of the building, equidistant from the three statues.

By the time of the eruption, the east side of the forum had been redeveloped as a showplace for various aspects of imperial cult. This was the official centre of the city which the new temples for cults associated with the emperor shared with the Samnite Temple of Apollo and the Capitolium of the Roman colony, marking a new epoch in the religious life of the community. The forum provided ample space for processions in which the images of the emperor and his family would be displayed on official festivals.

In Pompeii, Augustus, Claudius and Nero all had priests, and Agrippina (or perhaps Livia) a priestess, in their own lifetime.[107] They were drawn from the highest ranking members of the Pompeian aristocracy who no doubt paid for some of the expenses of these cults. In this they were assisted by the *augustales*, a group of rich freedmen who formed a college for honouring the emperor with banquets and other festivities.[108]

At Herculaneum, too, there were sanctuaries for the cult of the emperor though they are less well recorded, and some no doubt remain to be discovered when the forum is excavated. Several buildings which contained statues of the imperial family were erected facing each other on either side of the *decumanus maximus*.[109] Only one is currently visible at VI.21 (Map 4, E).[110] It is a large covered room with raised central roof, and a shrine in the centre of the west end. An inscription states that it was sacred to Augustus, and that two brothers, Aulus Lucius Proculus and Aulus Lucius Iulianus, gave a banquet for the local senate and *augustales* on the occasion of its dedication. It may have served both as a temple of Augustus and as a seat for the *augustales*.[111] The side walls of the shrine were painted in the Fourth Style with large panels showing scenes of the last episodes in the Hercules legend: his struggle with Achelous and his apotheosis. The hero had a double relevance as the mythical founder of the city, and as the ideal prototype of the emperors whose statues once occupied the shrine.[112]

On the other side of the *decumanus maximus*, the tunnel-diggers of the late 1730s and early 1740s came upon large parts of a colonnaded building which they thought must be a basilica, but which is much more likely to have been a *porticus*, with central courtyard open to the sky, comparable in many respects to the Eumachia Building or the Macellum at Pompeii. It is now inaccessible, but from the early records we can infer that it was most probably built during the reign of Claudius for the cult of the emperor and his family.[113] It contained numerous statues of the Julio-Claudian and Flavian dynasties. An inscription found with a bronze statue of Claudius reveals that it was put up in AD 48/49 and paid for by a legacy left by a soldier named Seneca of the 13th urban cohort.[114] The urban cohorts were mostly used for policing Rome, but were deployed when necessary in the Italian cities. Six other inscriptions record statues of members of the family of Claudius which were paid for and dedicated by Lucius Mammius Maximus, an *augustalis*.[115] He and Seneca of the urban cohort are typical of men whose origins were outside the governing circle of their municipality, but who aimed to achieve public recognition, living or dead, through devotion to the imperial family. Another, more humble, inscription shows that the cult of the emperor and his family could evoke genuine piety: it records a statuette set up in response to a dream or vision by an unknown individual in honour of Julia the daughter of Titus. It assimilates the princess to Hygia, the goddess of health.[116]

In the 150 years that followed the foundation of the Roman colony great changes took place in religious thought and behaviour in the Vesuvian cities, as elsewhere in Italy. The votive offerings of terracotta statuettes, typical of the pre-Roman Iron Age, gradually ceased to be made in the sanctuaries, and are rare after the end of the first century BC.[117] For private individuals, the routine making and fulfilling of vows through votive offerings was no longer the principal way of regulating relations with the gods. A large proportion of the population consisted of displaced persons, moved around by the institution of slavery, military action or long-distance trade, for whom local cults had no special meaning. To a large extent they must have found comfort in the closed communities of the mystery cults that offered salvation through initiation rites and secret knowledge. The torch-lit rituals, the drums and rattles and the ecstatic dancing of these cults were emotionally exciting. Mystery cults demanded a degree of commitment unknown in traditional religion, but in return they offered the joy of religious ecstasy; and many ordinary people, especially slaves and freedmen who had lost contact with their origins, must have found comfort and a new sense of identity in their ready-made societies.[118]

The rituals of the traditional cults continued, though probably with diminished vigour. Throughout the period there was a process of transformation, prompted by the idea, widespread in Greek philosophy in the Hellenistic period, that the universe was ruled by a single divine force of which the various gods were manifestations. Such gods would be more relevant to the enlarged and cosmopolitan world of the Roman Empire. One aspect of this was syncretism: the blending of characteristics of different gods, such as Isis and Fortuna; another was the combination of cults in the same sacred space. In Pompeii new cults were introduced into old temples: the cults of Venus and Diana, and probably of Hermes and Hermaphrodite, were instituted in the portico of the temple of Apollo early in the first century AD; and, as we have seen, statues of Dionysus and Venus were set up in the precinct of Isis.

The cult of the emperor and his family fitted easily into this elastic framework. It could not offer the personal satisfaction of the mystery cults, but it provided an outlet for both the rich and the ordinary people of Pompeii and Herculaneum to express their civic loyalty and their social ambitions through religious formulae. It was probably the most effective force for social cohesion in the community.

Perhaps the best gauge of religious thought at Pompeii is the state of the temples and shrines at the time of the eruption. The evidence is to some extent confused by the subsequent plundering of the site, but there can be little doubt that whereas the shrines of the imperial cult and the temples of Dionysus and Isis were fully restored after the earthquake of AD 62, and the Sanctuary of Sabazius was newly developed, the temples of Apollo and Venus and the Capitolium were still not usable in AD 79. The gods of the mystery cults and the new imperial divinities were given priority over the more traditional deities. Even more impressive is the fact that so many household *lararia* were reconstructed and repainted after the earthquake. The household cults lay at the core of Roman religion, and the Pompeians, like Aeneas at Troy, rescued their household gods as they could when disaster struck them.[119]

NOTES

1   There is no single substantial monograph covering all aspects of religion in the Vesuvian sites. The following, however, are useful, in addition to the more specific studies cited below: R. M. Peterson, *The Cults of Campania*, Papers and Monographs of the American Academy in Rome, Rome, 1919; R. Étienne, *La vie quotidienne à Pompéi*, Paris, 1966; C. Cicirelli, *Vita religiosa nell'antica Pompei* (Exhibition catalogue), Pompeii, Soprintendenza Archeologica di Pompei, 1995; A. Varone, *Pompei, i misteri di una città sepolta. Storia e segreti di un luogo in cui la vita si è fermata duemila anni fa*, 2nd edn, Rome, 2000, pp. 106–27, "La vita religiosa"; V. Catalano, *Case abitanti e culti di Ercolano, nuova edizione con gli indices a cura di L García y García e G. Panzera*, Rome, 2002. R. Ling, *Pompeii. History, Life and Afterlife*, Stroud, 2005, pp. 107–14, "Religion".

2   The cults of Mars (*CIL* IV, 879) and Ceres (*CIL* X, 812, 1074a) are attested by inscriptions though their sanctuaries have not yet been located. Ceres must have been especially important since she had a public priestess (cf. Bernstein, Ch. 34; Cormack, Ch. 37). In Herculaneum there is epigraphic evidence for cults of Jupiter, Hercules, Nemesis and Cybele (V. Tran-Tam-Tinh, *Le culte des divinités orientales à Herculanum*, Leiden, 1971, p. 2, and refs to *CIL*). There are also numerous indications of the cult of Isis.

3   S. De Caro, *Saggi nell'area del tempio di Apollo a Pompei. Scavi stratigrafici di A. Maiuri nel 1931–32 e 1942–43*, Naples, 1986.

4   P. Arthur, "Problems of the urbanization of Pompeii. Excavations of 1980–1981", *AntJ*, 1986, vol. 66, pp. 34–5.

5   A. Maiuri, *Alla ricerca di Pompei preromana*, Naples, 1973, pp. 116–19.

6   Maiuri, *Pompei preromana*, pp. 101–25; P. Zanker, *Pompeii. Public and Private Life*, Cambridge, MA and London, 1998, pp. 53–4.

7   L. Richardson, jr, "The archaic doric temple of Pompeii", *PP*, 1974, vol. 29, pp. 281–90; J. A. K. E. De Waele (ed.), *Il tempio dorico del foro triangolare di Pompei*, Rome, 2001; idem, "Excavations in the Doric Temple in the Triangular Forum at Pompeii", *Opuscula Pompeiana*, 1997, vol. 7, pp. 51–73; T. D'Alessio, *Materiali votivi dal Foro Triangolare di Pompei*, Rome, 2001, esp. p. 173.

8   J. A. K. E. De Waele, "The Doric Temple on the Forum Triangulare in Pompeii", *Opuscula Pompeiana*, 1993, vol. 3, p. 117. Cf. De Caro, Ch. 6.

9   O. Elia and G. Pugliese Caratelli, "Il santuario dionisiaco di Pompei", *PP*, 1979, vol. 34, pp. 442–81.

10 A. D'Ambrosio, *La stipe votiva in località Bottaro (Pompei)*, Naples, 1984; F. Zevi, "I greci, gli etruschi, il Sele (Note sui culti arcaici di Pompei)", in S. A. Muscettola, Giovanna Greco and Luigi Cicala (eds), *I culti della Campania antica: Atti del convegno internazionale di studi in ricordo di Nazarena Valenza Mele, Napoli, 15–17 maggio 1995*, Rome, 1998, pp. 21–2.

11 A. D'Ambrosio and M. Borriello, *Le terrecotte figurate di Pompei*, Rome, 1990; S. De Caro, "Novità isiache in Campania", *PP*, 1994, vol. 49, pp. 9–11.

12 M. Beard, J. North and S. Pryce, *Religions of Rome. Volume I–A History; Volume II–A Sourcebook*, 1998, vol. I, pp. 87–98.

13 J.-M. Paillier, *Bacchanalia: la repression de 186 av. J.-C. à Rome et en Italie: vestiges, images, tradition*, Paris and Rome, 1988.

14 Inscriptions on the ramp and altar show that the sanctuary was maintained by the aediles, chief magistrates of the city in the Samnite period (Elia and Pugliese Caratelli, "Il santuario dionisiaco di Pompei"). There is no subsequent evidence for official patronage, and the senatorial decree prohibited the use of civic funds to support the cult.

15 P. Castrén, *Ordo Populusque Pompeianus. Polity and Society in Roman Pompeii*, Acta Instituti Romani Finlandiae 8, Rome, Bardi, 1975, p. 71.

16 The Temple of Minerva Athena in the Foro Triangolare had probably already fallen into disuse after the end of the third century BC: D'Alessio, *Materiali votivi dal Foro Triangolare di Pompei*, p. 174.

17 D. Russo, *Il tempio di Giove Meilichio a Pompei*, Naples, 1991, p. 128.

18 P. Zanker, *Pompeii. Public and private life*, Cambridge, MA and London, 1998, pp. 52–53 and 214 n. 32.

19 The date of this development is controversial. The structural sequence was established by Maiuri, *Pompei preromana*, pp. 101–24. H. Lauter, "Zur späthellenistischen Baukunst in Mittelitalien", *JdI*, 1979, vol. 94, pp. 430–6 dates the conversion of the temple for the Capitoline cult to the late second century BC, and sees it as an act of "self-Romanization" by the Samnite community. Zanker, *Pompeii*, pp. 63–4 returns to Maiuri's date for this development at the time of the foundation of the Sullan colony (the position followed here). L. Richardson, jr, *Pompeii, An Architectural History*, Baltimore, MD and London, 1988, pp. 138–45 rejects the idea of a pre-Sullan temple altogether, and argues that the temple was a Capitolium from the start. Cf. Dobbins, Ch. 12.

20 *Museo di Napoli* I.2, pp. 96–7 no. 1; H. Döhl and P. Zanker, "La scultura", in F. Zevi (ed.), *Pompei 79. Raccolta di studi per il decimonono centenario dell'eruzione vesuviana*, Naples, 1979, p. 182, fig. 20.

21 For Venus Fisica, see R. Schilling, *La religion romaine de Vénus depuis les origines jusqu'au temps d'Auguste*, Paris, 1954; for the identification, cf. *CIL* IV, 1520: *Candida me docuit nigras odisse puellas./Odero s(i) potero, sed non invitus amabo./Scripsit Venus Fisica Pompeiana* (derived from Propertius 1.1.5; cf. De Felice, Ch. 30, n. 26).

22 Martial, IV.44.5; Statius, *Silvae* V.3.164.

23 A. Mau, "Der Tempel der Venus Pompeiana", *RM*, 1900, vol. 15, pp. 270–308; Richardson, *Pompeii*, pp. 277–301.

24 E.g., the temples on the Acrocorinth, at Knidos, and on Mt Eryx in Sicily.

25 Shown on the relief from the *lararium* of L. Caecilius Juncundus: F. Chapouthier, *Les Dioscures au service d'une déesse*, Paris, 1935, p. 303. Cf. Welch, Ch. 36.

26 J. Andreau, *Les affaires de Monsieur Jucundus*, Collection de l'École Française de Rome 19, Paris and Rome, École Française de Rome, 1974, fig. 4.

27 J. J. Dobbins *et al.*, "Excavations in the Sanctuary of Apollo at Pompeii, 1997", *AJA*, 1998, vol. 102, pp. 739–56.

28 M. Della Corte, *Iuventus*, Arpino, 1924, pl. I.; P.G. Guzzo, *Pompei. Storia e paesaggi della città antica*, Milano, 2007, 169, 171 (fig.). Guzzo, following Marcattili, interprets the temple shown on the painting as the temple of Asclepius, accepting De Caro's argument (above, Chapter 6) that this was the real dedication of the "Temple of Jupiter Meilichius": F. Marcattili, "Il cosidetto tempio di Giove Meilichio nel fregio della casa delle Nozze di Ercole (VII,9,47): immagini di culto e topografia sacra," in I. Colpo, I. Favaretto and F. Ghedini (eds.), *Iconografia 2001. Studi sull'immagine*, Atti del Convegno (Padova, 2001), Rome, 2002, 319–30. The cult statue, however, indicates that the building should be the temple of Venus, shown schematically in the painting.

29 This is implied by the fact that a portrait herm of C. Norbanus Sorex (Figure 36.7) and a statue of Isis erected by L. Caecilius Phoebus required the permission of the *decurions*: *CIL* X, 814, 849. For the numerous Isiac remains at Pompeii, see V. Tran-Tam-Tinh, *Essai sur le culte d'Isis à Pompéi*, 1964.

30 Cf. J. H. W. G. Liebeschuetz, *Continuity and Change in Roman Religion*, Oxford, 1996, pp. 180–2.

31 Museo Archeologico Nazionale di Napoli, *Alla ricerca di Iside. Analisi, studi e restauri dell'Iseo pompeiano nel Museo di Napoli*, Rome, 1992; F. Zevi, "Sul tempio di Iside a Pompei", *PP*, 1994, vol. 49, pp. 37–56.

32 S. Adamo Muscettola, "La decorazione architettonica e l'arredo", in *Alla ricerca di Iside*, pp. 67–71.

33 V. Tran-Tam-Tinh, *Le culte des divinités orientales à Herculanum*, pp. 29–48, 83–6. There is no record of the building in which the paintings were found.

34 M. Vermaseren, *Cybele and Attis. The Myth and the Cult*, London, 1977, pp. 12–28; S. De Caro, "Un graffito ed altre testimonianze del culto della Magna Mater nella villa romana di Oplontis", in R. I. Curtis (ed.), *Studia Pompeiana & Classica in Honor of Wilhelmina F. Jashemski*, New Rochelle, NY, 1989, vol. 1, pp. 89–96.

35 T. Fröhlich, *Lararien und Fassadenbilder in der Vesuvstädten. Untersuchungen zur "volkstümlichen" pompejanischen Malerei*, RM-EH 32, 1991, pl. 59.2.

36 Cf. S. Adamo Musecettola, "I flavi tra Iside e Cibele", *PP*, 1994, vol. 49, 83–118.

37 Catalano, *Case abitanti e culti*, pp. 137–92.

38 A. Maiuri, *Ercolano, i nuovi scavi*, 2 vols, Rome, 1958, pp. 175–85; Pagano, *Ercolano*, p. 24.

39 V. Spinazzola, *Pompei alla luce degli scavi nuovi di Via dell'Abbondanza (Anni 1910–1923)*, 2 vols, Rome, 1953, pl. XVIII; Fröhlich, *Lararien*, pp. 34–5 and pl. 60.1–2, 61.2.

40 G. Niebling, "Laribus augustis magistri primi. Der Beginn des Compitalkultes der Lares und des Genius Augusti", *Historia*, 1956, vol. 5, pp. 303–478.

41 P. Castrén, *Ordo Populusque Pompeianus*, pp. 75, 105.

42 Fröhlich, *Lararien*, pp. 335 (IX.11.1 = F66), 338 (IX.12.6 = F70) and 339 (IX.12.7 = F71).

43 H. Hänlein Schäfer, "Die Ikonographie des Genius Augusti in Kompital- und Hauskult der frühen Kaiserzeit", in A. M. Small (ed.), *Subject and Ruler: The Cult of the Ruling Power in Classical Antiquity. Papers in honour of the 65th birthday of Duncan Fishwick*, JRA Suppl. Ser. no. 17, 1996, pp. 82–3 and fig. 4.

44 Spinazzola, *Pompei alla luce degli scavi nuovi*, pl. I.

45 To the right of the depiction of Mercury. Spinazzola, *Pompei alla luce degli scavi nuovi*, pls II, XI; Schilling, *La religion romaine de Vénus*, pl. XVI.

46 M. Pagano, "Semo Sancus in una insegna di bottega a Ercolano", *Cronache Ercolanesi*, 1988, vol. 18, pp. 209–14.

47 Fröhlich, *Lararien*, pp. 40, 59, 296–7, Taf. 10.1; G. C. M. Jansen, "Paintings in Roman toilets", in E. M. Moorman (ed.), *Functional and Spatial Analysis of Wall Painting* (Proceedings of the Fifth International Congress on Ancient Wall Painting), Leiden, 1993, p. 33 note 5; P. G. Guzzo, "Ritrovamenti in contesti non cultuali: Pompei", in E. A. Arslan (ed.), *Iside: il mito, il mistero, la magia* (Exhibition catalogue), Milan, 1997, pp. 344–5.

48 J. Clarke, *The Houses of Roman Italy, 100 BC–AD 250. Ritual, space, and decoration*, Berkeley, Los Angeles, CA, 1991, pp. 211–14; K. W. Slane and M. Dickie, "A Knidian phallic vase from Corinth", *Hesperia*, 1993, vol. 62, pp. 486–94.

49 Dio 15.19.7; D. Fishwick, *The Imperial Cult in the Latin West: Studies in the Ruler Cult of the Western Provinces of the Roman Empire*, vol. I.1, Leiden, New York, Copenhagen, Cologne, 1987, pp. 84–5.

50 Hänlein Schäfer, "Die Ikonographie des Genius Augusti". This interpretation contradicts the view that the political themes of the imperial myth did not normally occur in private houses (Zanker, *Pompeii*, p. 24).

51 G. K. Boyce, *Pompeian Lararia*, Memoirs of the American Academy in Rome 14, 1937; D. G. Orr, "Roman domestic religion. The evidence of the household shrines", *ANRW*, II.16.2., 1978, pp. 1557–91; Fröhlich, *Lararien*. For *lararia* in Herculaneum: Catalano, *Case abitanti e culti*, 175–8.

52 S. Adamo Muscettola, "Osservazioni sulla composizione dei larari con statuette in bronzo di Pompei ed Ercolano", in *Toreutik und figürliche Bronzen römischer Zeit*, Berlin, 1984, pp. 9–32; "I culti domestici", in *Abitare sotto il Vesuvio* (Exhibition catalogue), Ferrara, 1997, pp. 175–9.

53 Fröhlich, *Lararien*, p. 24.

54 *Lares cubiculi*: Suet. *Aug.* 7; *Domit.* 17; Dio 67.16; Adamo Muscettola, "Osservazioni sulla composizione dei larari", p. 12.

55 Adamo Muscettola, "Osservazioni sulla composizione dei larari", p. 25; A. Maiuri, *Ercolano, i nuovi scavi*, 2 vols, Rome, 1958, p. 414.

56 E.g., R. Duthoy, "Culti familiari e privati della Campania. Arulae fittili pompeiane", in *Hommages à Albert Grenier*, Collection Latomus 58, Brussels, 1962, pp. 559–66 in terracotta; J. B. Ward-Perkins and A. Claridge, *Pompeii AD 79*, London, 1976, cat. 212–13, in bronze.

57 F. Di Capua, "Sacrari pompeiani", in *Pompeiana. Raccolta di studi per il secondo centenario degli scavi di Pompei*, Naples, 1950, pp. 60–85.

58 F. Pesando, *"Domus". Edilizia privata e società pompeiana fra III e I secolo a.C.*, Rome, 1997, p. 39; Spinazzola, *Pompei alla luce degli scavi nuovi*, pp. 446, 871.

59 G. Stefani (ed.), *Uomo e ambiente nel territorio vesuviano. Guida all'Antiquarium di Boscoreale*, Pompei, 2003, 112–14.

60 Di Capua, "Sacrari pompeiani", pp. 64–6, 78.

61 (Various authors) *Il giardino dipinto nella casa del bracciale d'oro a Pompei e il suo restauro* (Exhibition catalogue), Florence, 1991; W. F. Jashemski, *The Gardens of Pompeii, Herculaneum and the Villas Destroyed by Vesuvius*, vol. 2, New Rochelle, NY, 1993, pp. 166–7.

62 F. Le Corsu, "Un oratoire pompéien consacré á Dionysos–Osiris", *Revue Archéologique*, 1967, pp. 239–54.

63 Jashemski, *The Gardens of Pompeii*, vol. 1, pp. 77–9; vol. 2, pp. 17–22.

64 R. Turcan, "Sabazios à Pompéi", in *Ercolano 1738–1988. 25 Anni di ricerca archeologica*, Rome, 1993, pp. 499–512; R. Pace, "Il Complesso dei riti magici a Pompei II.1.11–12", *RStPomp*, 1997, vol. 8, pp. 73–97. For Sabazian hands from other contexts in Herculaneum and Pompeii, see M. Vermaseren, *Corpus Cultus Iovis Sabazii (CCIS) I. The hands*, Leiden, 1983, pp. 5–10, nos. 12–19.

65 Located in court (49)—frequently illustrated, e.g., in T. Kraus and L. von Matt, *Pompeii and Herculaneum. The Living Cities of the Dead*, New York, 1975, p. 21, fig. 11.

66 S. De Caro, *La villa rustica in località Villa Regina a Boscoreale*, Rome, 1994, pp. 41–2.

67 R. Turcan, "Pour en finir avec la femme fouettée", *Revue Archéologique*, 1982, pp. 291–302; R. Ling, *Roman Painting*, Cambridge and New York, 1991, pp. 101–4; G. Sauron, *La grande fresque de la Villa des Mystères à Pompéi*, Paris, 1998.

68 M. Guarducci, "La più antica iscrizione col nome dei Cristiani", *Römische Quartalschrift*, 1962, vol. 57, pp. 116–25. She transcribes the line as Bovios audi(t) christianos: Bovius listens to Christians, and interprets it as a malignant comment, suitable for the wall of a drinking house.

69 The literal meaning is "the sower Arepo holds the wheels with care", or perhaps "The sower holds the wheels of the plough with care", but the point of the cryptogram is the complex symbolism. TENET forms a Greek cross; the words are an anagram of PATERNOSTER, written twice in the form of a Greek cross with the two bars intersecting at the letter N, combined with A O (for alpha and omega, the beginning and the end) written twice (between the arms of the cross or at their extremities); the letters at the edge of the square form the word ROTAS (wheels) or its palindrome SATOR (sower) twice, recalling the four wheels in the vision of *Ezekiel* (chapters 10 and 11) that surrounded the cherubim, sent by Jahweh to punish Jerusalem for abominations by slaying all except for the righteous who were protected by the sign of the *tau*. The cryptogram remained in use for a long time as a Christian talisman. The subject is contentious and the bibliography is immense. For a convenient summary, see C. Giordano and I. Kahn, *The Jews in Pompeii, Herculaneum and Stabiae, and in the Cities of Campania Felix*, Rome, 2001, pp. 76–82, and at greater length, A. Baldi, *La Pompei giudaico-cristiana*, Cava dei Tirreni, Di Mauro, 1964, pp. 41–62.

70 J. Carcopino, "Le Christianisme secret du 'carré magique'", *Museum Helveticum* 5, 1948, 16–59. The argument is risky, however. The adoption of the seven-day planetary week before AD 79 (discussed below) might be questioned on similar grounds if it were not certainly attested at Pompeii and Herculaneum in contexts which pre-date the eruption.

71 *CIL* VI, 4976.

72 The excavator, Maiuri, argued that it was the seating for a wooden cross set there as an object of devotion by a Christian worshipper who tore it away at the time of the eruption: A. Maiuri, "La croce di Ercolano", *Rend Pont Acc* (1939), ser. 3, vol. 15, Rome 1940, pp. 193–218; but the groove could equally have held a shelf, or the support for a wooden *lararium*. For the contrasting arguments, see R. Olivieri Farioli, "La 'Croce' di Ercolano, Rassegna di studi", *RendNap*, 1970, vol. 45, pp. 57–71; and for bibliography with recent update, Catalano, *Case, abitanti e culti*, p. 184.

73 A. Varano, *Presenze giudaiche e cristiane a Pompei*, Naples, M. D'Auria, 1979; Giordano and Kahn, *The Jews in Pompeii*. Much of the evidence consists of names of Jewish origin rendered into Latin.

74 MNN inv. 113197. Giordano and Kahn, *The Jews in Pompeii*, p. 58, fig. 14. Some scholars suppose that it must represent a similar but unauthenticated story told of an Egyptian pharaoh.

75 For festivals of the dead, see J. M. C. Toynbee, *Death and Burial in the Roman World*, London, 1971, pp. 61–4.

76 Jashemski, *Gardens of Pompeii*, pp. 145–51.

77 *PErc* 523; V. Kockel, *Die Grabbauten vor dem herkulaner Tor in Pompeji,* Mainz am Rhein, von Zabern, 1983, pp. 109–11.

78 Kockel, *Grabbauten*, pp. 39–41.

79 In Table X of the law of the XII Tables: *hominem mortuum in urbe ne sepelito neve urito*: Cicero, *de legibus* 2.23.58.

80 A. Maiuri, "Un decreto onorario di M. Nonio scoperto recentemente ad Ercolano", *RendLinc*, 1942, ser. 7.8, pp. 1–26; U. Pappalardo, "Nuove testimonianze su Marco Nonio Balbo ad Ercolano", *RM*, 1997, vol. 194, p. 423.

81 G. Grévin, "La crémation à l'époque romaine: un os resectum dans le monument funéraire de Marcus Nonius Balbus à Herculanum", *RM*, 1997, vol. 194, pp. 429–32 (appendix to Pappalardo, "Nuove testimonianze"); G. Rohde, *RE* XVIII.2 cols 1534–6 s.v. *os resectum*.

82 A. Varone, "Religion and superstition", in L. Franchi dell'Orto and A. Varone (eds), *Rediscovering Pompeii* (Exhibition catalogue), Rome, 1992, pp. 135–6.

83 For the use of the *fascinus* to avert the evil eye, see Pliny, *HN* 28.39.

84 Cf. e.g., R. Ling, "Street plaques at Pompeii", in M. Henig (ed.), *Architecture and Architectural Sculpture in the Roman Empire*, Oxford, 1990, pp. 51–66; Catalano, *Case abitanti e culti*, pp. 84–5.

85 *Museo di Napoli* I.1, p. 230 no. 1 and colour plate on p. 113. A. Butterworth and R. Laurence, *Pompeii: the living city*, New York, pp. 54–5, suggest it was a tripod table leg. A graffito of a merchant ship, and several showing parts of a ship, found in the same building suggest that the owner was involved in overseas trade: F. P. Maulucci Vivolo, *Pompei: I graffiti figurati*, Foggia, 1993, p. 198.

86 A. Maiuri, "'Fulgur conditum' o della scoperta di un bidental a Pompei", *RendNap*, 1941, vol. 21, pp. 55–72.

87 Cf. G. Fowden, *The Egyptian Hermes: a historical approach to the late pagan mind*, Cambridge and New York, 1986, p. 162.

88 Liebeschuetz, *Continuity and Change in Roman Religion*, pp. 119–26.

89 *CIL* IV, 6779. Mercury was already illegible when the house was excavated in 1901.

90 *Museo di Napoli* I.1, p. 161 no. 262. See C. R. Long, "The Pompeii Calendar Medallions," *AJA*, 1992, vol. 96.3, pp. 477–501.

91 *Museo di Napoli* I.1, p. 117 no. 11. According to Kraus, the scene could equally well be a gathering of scholars active at one of the Diadochian courts: Kraus and von Matt, *Pompeii and Herculaneum*, p. 166 and fig. 215.

92 M. R. Wojcik, *La villa dei Papiri ad Ercolano. Contributo alla ricostruzione dell'ideologia della nobilitas tardo-repubblicana*, Rome, 1986; the library was particularly well supplied with the works of Philodemus, who interpreted Epicurean philosophy to the Roman elite in the first century BC: M. Gigante, *Philodemus in Italy: the books from Herculaneum*, translated by Dirk Obbink, Ann Arbor, MI, 1995.

93 K. M. D. Dunbabin, "Sic erimus cuncti . . . The skeleton in Graeco-Roman art", *JdI*, 1986, vol. 101, pp. 185–255, esp. pp. 224–31. AA.vv., *Il tesoro di Boscoreale*, Milan, 1988.

94 E. Magaldi, "Il culto degli imperatori a Pompei ed edifici che hanno rapporto con esso", *Rivista di Studi Pompeiani*, 1937, vol. 2, pp. 159–90, though out of date in some respects, is still useful for the imperial cults in Pompeii.

95 The dedication is controversial, and depends in part on whether a fragmentary inscription of the Public Priestess Mamia belongs to this building, for which there is no firm evidence (See I. Gradel, "Mamia's dedication: Emperor and Genius. The imperial cult in Italy and the Genius Coloniae in Pompeii", *AnalRom*, 1992, vol. 20, pp. 42–58). It records a dedication made by her at her own expense and on her own ground to a Genius, perhaps but not certainly of Augustus. I follow Fishwick in holding that the inscription does not belong to this building and that the temple was dedicated to Augustus himself in his own lifetime: D. Fishwick, "The inscription of Mamia again: the cult of the Genius Augusti and the

Temple of the Imperial Cult on the Forum of Pompeii", *Epigraphica*, 1995, vol. 57, pp. 17–38. In a recent article, however, Torelli upholds the view that the dedication was to the Genius of Augustus: M. Torelli, "Il culto imperiale a Pompei", in S. Adamo Muscettola, Giovanna Greco and Luigi Cicala (eds), *I culti della Campania antica*, pp. 245–70. The traditional view that the temple was dedicated to Vespasian is to be rejected on grounds of chronology and style: see n. 96 and cf. Dobbins, Ch. 12.

96 J. J. Dobbins, "The altar in the sanctuary of the Genius of Augustus in the Forum of Pompeii", *RM*, 1992, vol. 99, pp. 251–61.

97 Castrén, *Ordo Populusque Pompeianus*, p. 176. Cf. Figure 36.3.

98 Castrén, *Ordo Populusque Pompeianus*, pp. 76–7, 276. Cf. Jongman, Ch. 32.

99 Suet. Tib. 23: *atrox fortuna*.

100 For the sequence of buildings on this side of the forum, see J. J. Dobbins, "Problems of chronology, decoration, and urban design in the forum at Pompeii", *AJA*, 1994, vol. 98, pp. 629–94; cf. Dobbins, Ch. 12.

101 L. Richardson, jr, "Concordia and Concordia Augusta; Rome and Pompeii", *PP*, 1978, vol. 33, pp. 267–9. For the date see J. J. Dobbins, "Problems of chronology", pp. 647–61, 688–9. Her husband, also called M. Numistrius Fronto, died in AD 3 (*CIL* X, 892). Torelli, "Culto imperiale", pp. 251–62. As Torelli points out, the dedication to *Pietas* without the epithet *Augusta* alludes to the personal piety of Eumachia rather than to the piety of the imperial family, and probably implies that she dedicated the building jointly in her son's name and her own after her son's death. But cf. Descœudres, Ch. 2.

102 J. R. Fears, "The cult of virtues and Roman imperial ideology", *ANRW*, II.17.2, 1981, p. 892.

103 A. M. Small, "The shrine of the imperial family in the Macellum at Pompeii", in A. M. Small (ed.), *Subject and Ruler*, pp. 115–36.

104 Two statues survive, one of a priestess, the other of a young man, identified as Gnaeus Alleius Nigidius Maius and his daughter Alleia (priestess of Venus and Ceres) by S. Adamo Muscettola, "I Nigidi Mai di Pompei: far politica tra l'età neroniana e l'età flavia", *RIA*, 1991–2, s. III, vol. 14–15, pp. 193ff; and as Spurius Turranius Proculus Gellianus and Holconia (public priestess, and daughter, perhaps, of M. Holconius Celer, the second priest of Augustus) by Torelli, "Culto imperiale", p. 265. I have argued (in "The shrine of the imperial family ..." pp. 126–30) that they are probably Agrippina and Britannicus. Certainty is impossible.

105 J. J. Dobbins, "The imperial cult building in the forum of Pompeii", in A. M. Small, (ed.), *Subject and Ruler*, pp. 99–114.

106 H. Mattingly, *Coins of the Roman Empire in the British Museum II: Vespasian to Domitian*, London, 1930, pp. 1–2 nos. 1–6, AD 69–70.

107 M. Holconius Celer began serving as priest of Augustus, and continued after the emperor's death as priest of divus Augustus. For these priests, see Castrén, *Ordo Populusque Pompeianus*, pp. 68–72.

108 R. Duthoy, *Culti familiari e privati della Campania. Arulae fittili pompeiane*; S. E. Ostrow, "Augustales along the Bay of Naples: a case for their early growth", *Historia*, 1985, vol. 34, pp. 64–101. Cf. Jongman, Ch. 32; Franklin, Ch. 33.

109 A. Allroggen-Bedel, "Das sogennante Forum von Herculaneum und die borbonischen Grabungen von 1739", *CronErcol*, 1974, vol. 4, pp. 97–109. For a reconstruction, see M. Pagano, *Ercolano, itinerario archeologico raggionato*, Naples, 1997, p. 46.

110 Pagano, *Ercolano*, pp. 44–9. Cf. Dickmann, Ch. 27.

111 R. Étienne, "A propos du cosidette édifice des augustales d'Herculanum", in *Ercolano 1738–1988: 250 anni di ricerca archeologica*, Atti del Convegno Internazionale Ravello-Ercolano-Napoli-Pompei 30 ottobre–5 novembre 1988, Rome, 1993, pp. 345–50.

112 U. Pappalardo, "Spazio sacro e spazio profano: il Collegio degli Augustali ad Ercolano", in E. M. Moorman (ed.), *Functional and Spatial Analysis of Wall Painting* (Proceedings of the Fifth International Congress on Ancient Wall Painting), Leiden, 1993, pp. 90–5.

113 Allroggen-Bedel, "Das sogennante Forum von Herculaneum und die borbonischen Grabungen von 1739."

114 *CIL* X, 1416, with MNN inv. 5593. Other statues from the building, now in Naples Museum, include a bronze statue of Augustus (inv. 5595), two colossal statues of emperors restored by Tagliolini as Augustus and Claudius (inv. 6040, 6056), and a marble statue of Titus (inv. 6059): Allroggen-Bedel 1983, p. 148; *Museo di Napoli* I.2 p. 79 nos. 72, 74–6.

115 Allroggen-Bedel has shown that the inscriptions to Livia as *Diva Augusta*, Antonia and probably Germanicus, all of which were dedicated by Mammius Maximus (*CIL* X, 1413, 1417, 1415) were found in this building, as were the later dedications to Domitilla, wife of Vespasian, and Domitia, wife of Domitian (*CIL* X, 1419, 1422): (*CronErco* 1974, p. 107; 1983, pp. 148–50). It seems likely that Mammius' other dedications to Agrippina (*CIL* X, 1418) and to Divus Iulius, Divus Augustus and Britannicus (Catalano, *Case abitanti e culti*, p. 174) belong to the same Claudian group and were also found in the building.

116 IVLIA HYGIA/EX VISU: Catalano, *Case abitanti e culti*, pp. 162–5.

117 Cf. A. D'Ambrosio, and M. Borriello, *Le terrecotte figurate di Pompei*, Rome, 1990, p. 15.

118 R. Turcan, *The Cults of the Roman Empire*, Oxford, 1996, pp. 15–18.

119 Figurines of household gods are missing from many *lararia*, and some wooden *lararia* seem to have been ripped from the walls complete with their contents at the time of the eruption: Catalano, *Case abitanti e culti*, pp. 177, 183. Some of the dead have been found holding statuettes of divinities: cf. e.g., S. De Caro, "Novità isiache in Campania", *PP*, 1994, vol. 49, p. 8.

BIBLIOGRAPHY

AA.vv., *Il tesoro di Boscoreale*, Milan, 1988.

Adamo Muscettola, S., "Osservazioni sulla composizione dei larari con statuette in bronzo di Pompei ed Ercolano", in *Toreutik und figürliche Bronzen römischer Zeit*, Berlin, 1984, pp. 9–32.

——, "I Nigidi Mai di Pompei: far politica tra l'età neroniana e l'età flavia", *RIA*, 1991–2, s. III, vol. 14–15, 193 ff.

——, "La decorazione architettonica e l'arredo", in *Alla ricerca di Iside*, Rome, 1992, pp. 63–75.

——, "I culti domestici", in *Abitare sotto il Vesuvio* (Exhibition catalogue), Ferrara, 1997, pp. 175–9.

Allroggen-Bedel, A., "Das sogennante Forum von Herculaneum und die borbonischen Grabungen von 1739", *CronErcol*, 1974, vol. 4, pp. 97–109.

——, "Dokumente des 18 Jahrhunderts zur Topographie von Herculaneum", *CronErcol*, 1983, vol. 13, pp. 139–58.

Andreau, J., *Les affaires de Monsieur Jucundus*, Collection de l'École Française de Rome 19, Paris and Rome, 1974.

Arthur, P., "Problems of the urbanization of Pompeii. Excavations of 1980–1981", *AntJ*, 1986, vol. 66, pp. 29–44.

Baldi, A., *La Pompei giudaico-cristiana*, Cava dei Tirreni, 1964.

Beard, M., North, J. and Pryce, S., *Religions of Rome. Volume I—A History; Volume II–A Sourcebook*, Cambridge, 1998.

Boyce, G. K., *Pompeian Lararia*, Memoirs of the American Academy in Rome 14, 1937.

Castrén, P., *Ordo Populusque Pompeianus. Polity and Society in Roman Pompeii*, Acta Instituti Romani Finlandiae 8, Rome, 1975.

Catalano, V. *Case abitanti e culti di Ercolano, nuova edizione con gli indices a cura di L García y García e G. Panzera*, Rome, 2002.

Chapouthier, F., *Les Dioscures au service d'une déesse*, Paris, 1935.

Cicirelli, C., *Vita religiosa nell'antica Pompei* (Exhibition catalogue), Pompeii, Soprintendenza Archeologica di Pompei, 1995.

Clarke, J., *The Houses of Roman Italy, 100 BC–AD 250. Ritual, space, and decoration*, Berkeley, Los Angeles, CA and Oxford, 1991.

D'Alessio, T. *Materiali votivi dal Foro Triangolare di Pompei* (Corpus delle stipi votive in Italia; v. 12), Rome, 2001.

D'Ambrosio, A., *La stipe votiva in località Bottaro (Pompei)*, Naples, 1984.

——, and Borriello, M., *Le terrecotte figurate di Pompei*, Rome, 1990.

Della Corte, M., *Iuventus*, Arpino, 1924.

De Caro, S., *Saggi nell'area del tempio di Apollo a Pompei. Scavi stratigrafici di A. Maiuri nel 1931–32 e 1942–43*, Naples, 1986.

——, "Un graffito ed altre testimonianze del culto della Magna Mater nella villa romana di Oplontis", in R. I. Curtis (ed.), *Studia Pompeiana & Classica in Honor of Wilhelmina F. Jashemski*, New Rochelle, NY, 1989, vol. 1, pp. 89–96.

——, "Novità isiache in Campania", *PP*, 1994, vol. 49, pp. 7–21.

——, *La villa rustica in località Villa Regina a Boscoreale*, Rome, 1994.

De' Spagnolis Conticello, M., "Sul rinvenimento della villa e del monumento funerario dei Lucretii Valentes", *RStPomp*, 1993–4, vol. 6, pp. 147–66.

De Vos, A. and De Vos, M., *Pompei, Ercolano, Stabia. Guide Archeologiche Laterza*, Rome and Bari, 1982.

De Vos, M., "Aegyptiaca romana", *PP*, 1994, vol. 49, pp. 130–59.

De Waele, J. A. K. E. (ed.), *Il tempio dorico del foro triangolare di Pompei*, Rome, 2001.

——, "Excavations in the Doric Temple in the Triangular Forum at Pompeii", *Opuscula Pompeiana*, 1997, vol. 7, pp. 51–73.

——, "The Doric Temple on the Forum Triangulare in Pompeii", *Opuscula Pompeiana*, 1993, vol. 3, pp. 105–18.

Di Capua, F., "Sacrari pompeiani", in *Pompeiana. Raccolta di studi per il secondo centenario degli scavi di Pompei*, Naples, 1950, pp. 60–85.

Dobbins, J. J., "The altar in the sanctuary of the Genius of Augustus in the Forum of Pompeii", *RM*, 1992, vol. 99, pp. 251–61.

——, "Problems of chronology, decoration, and urban design in the forum at Pompeii", *AJA*, 1994, vol. 98, pp. 629–94.

——, "The imperial cult building in the forum of Pompeii", in A. Small, (ed.), *Subject and Ruler: The Cult of the Ruling Power in Classical Antiquity. Papers in honour of the 65th birthday of Duncan Fishwick*, JRA Suppl. Ser. no. 17, 1996, pp. 99–114.

——, Ball, L. F., Cooper, J. G., Gavel, S. L. and Hay, S., "Excavations in the Sanctuary of Apollo at Pompeii, 1997", *AJA*, 1998, vol. 102, pp. 739–56.

Döhl, H. and Zanker, P., "La scultura", in F. Zevi (ed.), *Pompei 79. Raccolta di studi per il decimonono centenario dell'eruzione vesuviana*, Naples, 1979, pp. 172–210.

Dunbabin, K. M. D., "Sic erimus cuncti . . . The skeleton in Graeco-Roman art", *JdI*, 1986, vol. 101, pp. 185–255.

Duthoy, R., "Culti familiari e privati della Campania. Arulae fittili pompeiane", in *Hommages à Albert Grenier, Collection Latomus* 58, Brussels, 1962, pp. 559–66.

——, "Les augustales", *ANRW* II.16.2, 1978, pp. 1254–309.

Elia, O. and Pugliese Caratelli, G., "Il santuario dionisiaco di Pompei", *PP*, 1979, vol. 34, pp. 442–81.

Étienne, R., *La vie quotidienne à Pompéi*, Paris, 1966.

——, "A propos du cosidette édifice des augustales d'Herculanum", in *Ercolano 1738–1988: 250 anni di ricerca archeologica*, Atti del Convegno Internazionale Ravello-Ercolano-Napoli-Pompei 30 ottobre–5 novembre 1988, Rome, 1993, pp. 345–50.

Fears, J. R., "The cult of virtues and Roman imperial ideology", *ANRW* II.17.2, 1981, pp. 736–826.

Fishwick, D., *The Imperial Cult in the Latin West: Studies in the Ruler Cult of the Western Provinces of the Roman Empire*, vol. I.1, Leiden, New York, Copenhagen, Cologne, 1987.

——, "The inscription of Mamia again: the cult of the Genius Augusti and the Temple of the Imperial Cult on the Forum of Pompeii", *Epigraphica*, 1995, vol. 57, pp. 17–38.

Fowden, G., *The Egyptian Hermes: a historical approach to the late pagan mind*, Cambridge and New York, 1986.

Fröhlich, T., *Lararien und Fassadenbilder in der Vesuvstädten. Untersuchungen zur "volkstümlichen" pompejanischen Malerei*, RM-EH 32, 1991.

Gigante, M., *Philodemus in Italy: the books from Herculaneum*, translated by Dirk Obbink, Ann Arbor, MI, 1995.

Giordano, C. and Kahn, I., *The Jews in Pompeii, Herculaneum, Stabiae and in the Cities of Campania Felix*, 3rd edn revised and enlarged by L. García y García (English translation by Wilhelmina F. Jashemski), Rome, 2001.

Gradel, I., "Mamia's dedication: Emperor and Genius. The imperial cult in Italy and the Genius Coloniae in Pompeii", *AnalRom*, 1992, vol. 20, pp. 42–58.

Grévin, G., "La crémation à l'époque romaine: un os resectum dans le monument funéraire de Marcus Nonius Balbus à Herculanum", *RM*, 1997, vol. 194, pp. 429–32 (appendix to Pappalardo, "Nuove testimonianze").

Guzzo, P. G., "Ritrovamenti in contesti non cultuali: Ercolano", in E. A. Arslan (ed.), *Iside: il mito, il mistero, la magia* (Exhibition Catalogue), Milan, 1997, pp. 346–7.

———, "Ritrovamenti in contesti non cultuali: Pompei", in E. A. Arslan (ed.) *Iside: il mito, il mistero, la magia* (Exhibition Catalogue), Milan, 1997, pp. 344–5.

Hänlein Schäfer, H., "Die Ikonographie des Genius Augusti in Kompital- und Hauskult der frühen Kaiserzeit", in A. Small (ed.), *Subject and Ruler: The Cult of the Ruling Power in Classical Antiquity. Papers in honour of the 65th birthday of Duncan Fishwick*, JRA Suppl. Ser. no. 17, 1996, pp. 73–98.

Jansen, G. C. M., "Paintings in Roman toilets", in E. M. Moorman (ed.), *Functional and Spatial Analysis of Wall Painting* (Proceedings of the Fifth International Congress on Ancient Wall Painting), Leiden, 1993, pp. 29–33.

Jashemski, W. F., *The Gardens of Pompeii, Herculaneum and the Villas Destroyed by Vesuvius*, 2 vols, New Rochelle, NY, 1979–93.

Kockel, V., *Die Grabbauten vor dem herkulaner Tor in Pompeji*, Mainz am Rhein, 1983.

Kraus, T. and von Matt, L., *Pompeii and Herculaneum. The Living Cities of the Dead*, trans. R. E. Wolf, New York, 1975.

Lauter, H., "Zur späthellenistischen Baukunst in Mittelitalien", *JdI*, 1979, vol. 94, pp. 390–459.

Le Corsu, F., "Un oratoire pompéien consacré à Dionysos–Osiris", *RA*, 1967, pp. 239–54.

Liebeschuetz, J. H. W. G., *Continuity and Change in Roman Religion*, Oxford, 1996.

Ling, R., "Street plaques at Pompeii", in Henig, M. (ed.), *Architecture and Architectural Sculpture in the Roman Empire*, Oxford, 1990, pp. 51–66.

———, *Roman Painting*, Cambridge and New York, 1991.

Magaldi, E., "Il culto degli imperatori a Pompei ed edifici che hanno rapporto con esso", *Rivista di Studi Pompeiani*, 1937, vol. 2, pp. 159–90.

Maiuri, A., "'Fulgur conditum' o della scoperta di un bidental a Pompei", *RendNap*, 1941, vol. 21, pp. 55–72.

———, "Un decreto onorario di M. Nonio scoperto recentemente ad Ercolano", *RendLinc*, 1942, ser. 7.8, pp. 1–26.

———, *Ercolano, i nuovi scavi*, 2 vols, Rome, 1958.

———, *Alla ricerca di Pompei preromana*, Naples, 1973.

Mau, A., "Der Tempel der Venus Pompeiana", *RM*, 1900, vol. 15, pp. 270–308.

Maulucci Vivolo, F. P., *Pompei: i graffiti figurati*, Foggia, Bastogi, 1993.

Museo di Napoli I.1 = Le collezioni del Museo Nazionale di Napoli, vol. I.1: I mosaici, le pitture, gli oggetti di uso quotidiano, gli argenti, le terrecotte invetriate, i vetri, i cristalli, gli avori, Rome and Milan, 1986.

Museo di Napoli I.2 = La scultura greco-romana, le sculture antiche della collezione Farnese, le collezioni monetali, le oreficerie, la collezione glittica, Rome and Milan, 1989.

Niebling, G., "Laribus augustis magistri primi. Der Beginn des Compitalkultes der Lares und des Genius Augusti", *Historia*, 1956, vol. 5, pp. 303–478.

Olivieri Farioli, R., "La 'Croce' di Ercolano: Rassegna di studi", *RendNap*, 1970, vol. 45, pp. 57–71.

Orr, D. G., "Roman domestic religion. The evidence of the household shrines", *ANRW* II.16.2., 1978, pp. 1557–91.

Ostrow, S. E., "Augustales along the Bay of Naples: a case for their early growth", *Historia*, 1985, vol. 34, pp. 64–101.

Pace, R., "Il 'Complesso dei riti magici' a Pompei II.1.11–12", *RStPomp*, 1997, vol. 8, pp. 73–97.

Pagano, M., "Semo Sancus in una insegna di bottega a Ercolano", *CronErcol*, 1988, vol. 18, pp. 209–14.

——, *Ercolano, itinerario archeologico raggionato*, Naples, 1997.

Paillier, J.-M., *Bacchanalia: la repression de 186 av. J.-C. à Rome et en Italie: vestiges, images, tradition*, Paris and Rome, 1988.

Pappalardo, U., "Spazio sacro e spazio profano: il Collegio degli Augustali ad Ercolano", in E. M. Moorman (ed.), *Functional and Spatial Analysis of Wall Painting* (Proceedings of the Fifth International Congress on Ancient Wall Painting), Leiden, 1993, pp. 90–5.

——, "Nuove testimonianze su Marco Nonio Balbo ad Ercolano", *RM*, 1997, vol. 194, pp. 417–28.

Pesando, F., *"Domus". Edilizia privata e società pompeiana fra III e I secolo a.C.*, Rome, 1997.

Peterson, R. M., *The Cults of Campania*, Papers and Monographs of the American Academy in Rome, 1919, p. 1.

Richardson, L., jr, "The archaic doric temple of Pompeii", *PP*, 1974, vol. 29, pp. 281–90.

——, "Concordia and Concordia Augusta: Rome and Pompeii", *PP*, 1978, vol. 33, pp. 260–72.

——, *Pompeii, an Architectural History*, Baltimore, MD and London, 1988.

Rohde, G., "*os resectum*", RE XVIII.2 cols 1534–6.

Russo, D., *Il tempio di Giove Meilichio a Pompei*, Naples, 1991.

Sauron, G., *La grande fresque de la Villa des Mystères à Pompéi*, Paris, 1998.

Schilling, Robert, *La religion romaine de Vénus depuis les origines jusqu'au temps d'Auguste*, Paris, 1954.

Slane, K. W. and Dickie, M., "A Knidian phallic vase from Corinth", *Hesperia*, 1993, vol. 62, pp. 483–505.

Small, A. M., "The shrine of the imperial family in the Macellum at Pompeii", in Small (ed.), *Subject and Ruler: The Cult of the Ruling Power in Classical Antiquity. Papers in honour of the 65th birthday of Duncan Fishwick*, JRA Suppl. Ser. no. 17, 1996, pp. 115–36.

—— (ed.), *Subject and Ruler: The Cult of the Ruling Power in Classical Antiquity. Papers in honour of the 65th birthday of Duncan Fishwick*, JRA Suppl. Ser. no. 17, 1996.

Spinazzola, V., *Pompei alla luce degli scavi nuovi di Via dell'Abbondanza (Anni 1910–1923)*, 2 vols, Rome, 1953.

Stefani, G. (ed.), *Uomo e ambiente nel territorio vesuviano. Guida all'Antiquarium di Boscoreale*, Pompeii, 2003.

Torelli, M., "Il culto imperiale a Pompei", in S. Adamo Muscettola, G. Greco and L. Cicala (eds), *I culti della Campania antica: Atti del convegno internazionale di studi in ricordo di Nazarena Valenza Mele, Napoli, 15–17 maggio 1995*, Rome, 1998, pp. 245–70.

Toynbee, J. M. C., *Death and Burial in the Roman World*, London, 1971.

Tran-Tam-Tinh, V., *Essai sur le culte d'Isis à Pompéi*, Paris, 1964.

——, *Le culte des divinités orientales à Herculanum*, Leiden, 1971.

——, "La vita religiosa", in F. Zevi (ed.), *Pompei 79. Raccolta di studi per il decimonono centenario dell'eruzione vesuviana*, Naples, 1984, pp. 56–64.

Turcan, R., "Pour en finir avec la femme fouettée", *RA*, 1982, pp. 291–302.

——, "Sabazios à Pompéi", in *Ercolano 1738–1988. 25 Anni di ricerca archeologica*, Rome, 1993, pp. 499–512.

——, *The Cults of the Roman Empire*, Oxford, 1996.

Varone, A., "Religion and Superstition", in L. Franchi dell'Orto and A. Varone (eds), *Rediscovering Pompeii* (Exhibition catalogue), Rome, 1992, pp. 135–6.

———, *Presenze giudaiche e cristiane a Pompei*, Quaderni della Società per lo Studio e la Divulgazione dell'Archeologia Biblica 1, Naples, 1979.

———, *Pompei, i misteri di una città sepolta. Storia e segreti di un luogo in cui la vita si è fermata duemila anni fa*, 2nd edn, Rome, 2000.

Vermaseren, M., *Corpus Cultus Iovis Sabazii (CCIS) I. The hands.* (Études Préliminaires aux Religions Orientales dans l'Empire Romain publiées par M.J. Vermaseren; v. 100). Leiden, 1983, pp. 5–10, nos. 12–19.

———, *Cybele and Attis. The Myth and the Cult*, London, 1977.

Ward-Perkins, J. B. and Claridge, A., *Pompeii AD 79*, London, 1976.

Wojcik, M. R., *La villa dei Papiri ad Ercolano. Contributo alla ricostruzione dell'ideologia della nobilitas tardo-repubblicana*, Rome, 1986.

Zanker, P., *Pompeii. Public and private life*, Cambridge, MA and London, 1998.

Zevi, F., "Sul tempio di Iside a Pompei", *PP*, 1994, vol. 49, pp. 37–56.

———, "I greci, gli etruschi, il Sele (Note sui culti arcaici di Pompei)", in *I culti della Campania antica*, Rome, 1998, pp. 21–2.

CHAPTER FOURTEEN

ENTERTAINMENT
AT POMPEII

———•••———

Christopher Parslow

Mau–Kelsey remains a fundamental resource on the buildings in Pompeii dedicated to public entertainment since no complete archaeological investigations of these buildings were undertaken in the twentieth century. All, however, have been the subject of individual studies devoted to the epigraphical evidence and analysis of the standing structures. In 1906, Mau published a detailed study of the theater, while Girosi treated the architecture of the amphitheater in 1932.[1] In the late 1940s and the 1950s, Spano wrote essays on the amphitheater as well as the *theatrum tectum*, whose roof Murolo sought to reconstruct.[2] Only a handful of soundings have been made into pre-AD 79 levels. Mau's excavations in the orchestra of the theater revealed a series of basins evidently used for aquatic displays (*sparsiones*) in Imperial times while Maiuri exposed the remains of an earlier *cavea*.[3] In the 1970s, De Franciscis laid trenches in and around the amphitheater, the results of which remain largely unpublished.[4] The most significant discovery occurred in the mid-1930s when Maiuri cleared the "Palestra Grande," a building whose existence already had been indicated by its depiction in the famous painting commemorating the riot of AD 59 in the amphitheater.[5] The trend in more recent studies has been to place these monuments within their social and historical context, especially for the pivotal periods of the Sullan colony and the Augustan era, but while these may enhance and clarify the work of Mau–Kelsey, none have superseded it.[6]

As the first permanent auditorium, the theater fulfilled a variety of functions in the life of the Samnite city, from serving as the site for dramatic presentations and games to holding assemblies of the people.[7] The theater was first laid out in the early second century BC on a natural declivity along the southern edge of the city.[8] In its original plan it was little more than a semicircular *cavea* with wooden seating, a horseshoe-shaped orchestra, and a simple detached stage, though subsequent modifications and restorations have obscured most traces of this earliest phase. Its setting meant that the upper tiers of seats stood level with the adjacent Triangular Forum, whose porticoed entrance and colonnade were designed to function as a kind of monumental foyer to the theater, especially during the ceremonial processions (*pompae*) associated with festivals. While spectators defiled from the colonnade of the Triangular Forum toward their seats, magistrates and officiants could continue down a large stairway to a point behind the stage, and then parade through the *paradoi* into the orchestra and to their seats.

Changes in the social and political makeup of the city caused by the arrival of the Sullan colonists in the 80s BC were reflected as well in the transformation of its public spaces. While much has been made of Cicero's notice (*Pro Sulla* 60–62) about tensions between the native population and the colonists who took control of the city, the architectural evidence suggests an atmosphere of mutual tolerance in which the new leaders practiced a diplomatic blend of a victor's right of imposition with a realist's sense of compromise in the interest of coexistence. If the amphitheater served the more militaristic interests of the veterans who made up the colonists, the small roofed theater was a response to the natives' fascination with Hellenistic culture. Both buildings elevated Pompeii's image as a cultural mecca in this region as it outstripped its neighbors in the sheer number of its facilities for entertainment, and, as a consequence, both also enhanced the social and economic development of the entire city in significant ways.

The building identified as a *theatrum tectum* in its dedicatory inscription (*CIL* X, 844) was an architectural innovation, its design modeled after the *bouleuteria* of Hellenistic cities but its construction essentially Roman with Samnite flourishes.[9] Though built adjacent to the old theater and reaching roughly the same height, its thick outer walls retain a masonry core for the *cavea*, making it an early example of what would become the canonical free-standing Roman theater (Figure 14.1).

The *theatrum tectum*'s design, together with the inscription, help date construction securely to the early years of the colony. Its rectilinear plan was laid out in Roman

Figure 14.1 View of the orchestra and *cavea* of the *theatrum tectum* in Pompeii (VIII.7.16–20). The west tribunal is at the left; note the Telamones figures at the ends of the *analemmata* at the left and in the foreground, right. View from just inside the east *parados*. Photo: J. J. Dobbins.

feet, and *opus quasi reticulatum* and brickwork quoining were used in the construction (Figure 8.11). Of the two *duoviri*, the Roman magistrates responsible for letting the building contract and approving the work, one was C. Quinctius Valgus, a wealthy Sullan partisan known to have endowed at least two other cities, while the other was M. Porcius who appears on several monuments datable to this same period. Yet the kneeling *telamones* adorning the ends of the *analemmata* first appeared in the earlier Samnite theater at Pietrabbondante, as did the winged lions' paws carved at the ends of the balustrade of upright tufa slabs that divides the four rows of the *ima cavea* from the seventeen rows of the *media cavea*. The seats, where these survive, are also of carved tufa. Two stairs, reached from a corridor behind the building, deposited the bulk of the spectators at the top of *cavea*. Special box seats (*tribunalia*) for organizers of the events and their guests were arranged above the *paradoi* which were vaulted over, as was done in the theater as well. The building's thicker east and west walls supported trusses that carried a pitched roof and were pierced with windows along the top to help light the interior.[10]

Such an elegant structure could not have been intended to serve the interests of the veterans alone by functioning solely as a kind of reunion hall where they could assemble independently from the natives; the spacious stage and the use of the term *theatrum* in the inscriptions both argue against such a limited function.[11] Its fusion of cultural traits suggests instead that it sought to acknowledge, as well as to serve, the interests of the entire community. It could be used on any occasion that required a setting that was both free from exposure to the elements and more intimate than that offered by the open-air theater.

In contrast, the amphitheater served a specific function which required a building of relatively simple, but purely Roman, design (Figure 14.2).[12] It dates to the quinquennial duovirate of the same two individuals who oversaw construction of the *theatrum tectum*, though Valgus and Porcius claim in the building inscriptions (*CIL* X, 852) that they built what they termed a SPECTACULA with their own funds and gave the site in perpetuity to the colonists, by which they meant all Pompeians. The year of their office is generally fixed as 70 BC, to coincide with the censorial year in Rome, making this the oldest standing amphitheater in the Roman world.

The site chosen for its construction, in the southeast corner of the city inside the walls, featured relatively flat land that was encumbered by few existing structures (Figure 23.1).[13] Though stratigraphical studies have yet to determine the exact appearance of the amphitheater in its earliest phase, it is likely to have been simply a great oval bowl of earth, created by excavating out the area for the arena and supporting the sloped fill in part with the existing city walls and elsewhere by a retaining wall reinforced by buttresses connected by arches. The arena stands some 6 m below the level of the ground outside and has none of the substructures seen in amphitheaters of later date. The built structures within the earthen *cavea* probably were limited to vaulted corridors cut through the fill that provided access to the arena, perhaps only the two main corridors on the north and southwest façades above whose entrances stood the dedicatory inscriptions. Since the slope of the *cavea* was too steep for spectators to sit comfortably on the earth itself, the seating would have consisted entirely of wooden bleachers accessed from the top by means of six stone stairways built onto the building's façade, a design recalling that of the *theatrum tectum*.

Figure 14.2 The amphitheater of Pompeii (II.6). The arena is in the center. Portions of the original tufa seating in the *cavea* are visible on the right. View from the south.

No other city in the Vesuvian landscape, with the possible exception of Naples, could boast of having two theaters and an amphitheater already in the early first century BC. Nuceria, Pompeii's closest neighbor and biggest rival, had only a single theater, while its amphitheater may only be Neronian in date. Sarno had only a theater, and Puteoli only an amphitheater, while Surrentum and Capua had both. Even Rome's first permanent theater, the free-standing Theater of Pompey, dates only to 55 BC, while Statilius Taurus built Rome's first stone amphitheater only in 29 BC. Residents from the numerous small towns and villas throughout the Sarno valley flocked to Pompeii on festival days to enjoy a variety of entertainment that ranged from the local *fabulae Atellanae* and mime performed in the theaters, to gladiatorial shows and animal hunts (*venationes*) in the *spectacula*. These three basic structures would serve Pompeii until its destruction, though over time each underwent modifications and restorations.

The Augustan era, with its emphasis on urbanization and civic benefaction, brought the most significant changes to the physical appearance of these buildings. The theater acquired a considerably more monumental appearance, due in large part to M. Holconius Rufus, the most distinguished Pompeian of this period (cf. Ling, Ch. 9). Together with his brother, and with their own money, they revetted the *ima cavea* in marble to provide a more suitable setting for the *bisellia* of the *decuriones*. Above the vaulted *paradoi* they added *tribunalia* similar to those in the *theatrum tectum*, while behind the existing *cavea* they constructed a *crypta*, evidently the vaulted, annular corridor that supported a *summa cavea* of wooden bleachers and presented a new two-storied, arcaded

Figure 14.3 The theater of Pompeii (VIII.7.20–21). Part of the stage (without flooring) at left; at the left, above the vaulted west *parados*, is a tribunal; note the four marble steps for the seats of the *ima cavea*. Above the *media cavea* are the remains of the *crypta*, which supported the *summa cavea*; several of the tufa sockets to support the *vela* are visible along the top of the theater's outer wall. View from just inside the east *parados*. Photo: J. J. Dobbins.

façade toward the Triangular Forum. Tufa sockets cantilevered along the top of this held the masts of the *vela*, a canopy to shade spectators (Figure 14.3). The Holconii recorded their accomplishments in at least three identical inscriptions (*CIL* X, 833–5) and even their architect, the freedman M. Artorius Primus, inscribed his name on the theater (*CIL* X, 841).[14] In thanks for Holconius Rufus' generous contributions, the *decuriones* decreed him a monument, perhaps a *bisellium*, centered in the first row of the *media cavea*, along with an inscription recording his public offices (*CIL* X, 838). The stage building also received its final form in this period and featured a brick *scaenae frons* with a main door (*porta regia*) in its central apsed niche flanked by two doors recessed in rectangular niches. At about the same time, the *duovir* M. Oculatius Verus paved the orchestra of the *theatrum tectum* in polychrome marble and inscribed it with his name in bronze letters (*CIL* X, 845).

Oculatius had contributed this pavement in lieu of offering public games (PRO LUDIS), as required by the laws governing Pompeian magistrates.[15] In much the same way, the amphitheater gradually assumed a more monumental form. Eight inscriptions (*CIL* X, 853–7) carved into its travertine podium record that individual *duoviri* chose to contribute specific *cunei* of tufa seats rather than sponsor games or provide torches for processions (PRO LUDIS ET LUMIN[IBUS]). The fact that one inscription names the *magistri* of the *Pagus Augustus Felix Suburbanus*, a group organized only in 7 BC, suggests that the process of adding permanent seating began in the Augustan period. Since no precise chronology for the architectural development of the amphitheater has been established, however, it is unclear to what extent the network of underground access tunnels, corridors and stairs pre-dated, or is contemporary with, the start of this process. The installation of seating helped clearly differentiate the spectators according to class and rank, as the laws dictated. This was especially evident in the *ima cavea*, which was physically separated from the rest of the *cavea* and where the *bisellia* of magistrates and the games' sponsors occupied the prime rows in the center of the long sides. Subsequent benefactors must have added the remaining *cunei* over time, but there is no physical or epigraphical evidence to confirm this.

The importance of gladiatorial spectacles in the social and economic life of the city in the early Empire also is illustrated by the construction of the single largest public building in Pompeii adjacent to the amphitheater. It is essentially an enormous rectangular open space enclosed by porticoes on three sides and, on the fourth, by a single wall with five doors toward the amphitheater.[16] In the center of the west portico an *exedra* with two columns marking its entrance and a large pedestal against its west wall is likely a shrine, though the dedication is unknown, while two small rooms adjacent to this may be for the *ostiarius* who monitored the foot traffic entering from the blind alley from the Via di Porta Nocera. A double row of plane trees once stood before the porticoes (Map 3, II.7), the size of their root cavities indicating they were roughly a century old, though a late Augustan or early Tiberian date for the building seems more likely.[17] In the center of the green space stands an immense pool, which marks the terminus of the city's aqueduct. Its runoff flushed a public latrine, built sometime later in the south portico, which is the largest in Pompeii but hardly seems adequate for the needs of crowds in the amphitheater (Figure 14.4).

Construction of this building almost certainly was not undertaken by private individuals as was Valgus' and Porcius' *spectacula*. The need to raze the equivalent of six entire city blocks, even if these were characterized primarily by small vineyards and market gardens, underscores that this was an important public project decreed by the *decuriones* and paid for with public funds. The building's function is often linked to Augustus' reorganization of the *collegium iuvenum*, a paramilitary youth organization with an emphasis on competitive athletic and equestrian activities, and Maiuri consequently designated it the "Palestra Grande."[18] Its proximity to the amphitheater, however, suggests its actual uses were far more broad-ranging and it is more likely a *campus*, a building type attested elsewhere.[19] As the numerous *graffiti* etched into its 120 columns vividly illustrate (*CIL* IV, 8515–814), its covered halls, shaded *allées*, and open spaces made it not only an ideal meeting place and urban park but also a marketplace for both local and itinerant merchants and tradesmen, who probably affixed temporary awnings or displays to the columns. But its heaviest use came during festivals, when it provided water, shelter, sanitary facilities and concession stands for Pompeians and for visitors from neighboring towns who might camp here for the duration of the *munus*.

Literary and archaeological sources provide a rare glimpse into many aspects of *munera* at Pompeii.[20] Painted announcements found throughout the city and on tombs lining the roads outside the walls advertise such details as the names of sponsors, the number of pairs of gladiators, the duration of the games, and whether or not *venationes* would be offered or the *vela* unfurled to shade spectators in the stands.[21] Others for games in Nuceria, Nola, Puteoli and Cumae illustrate how far enthusiastic fans might travel to attend these spectacles. Tacitus (*Ann.* 14.17) documented the grim consequences of the resulting intense inter-city rivalries in his account of the riot of AD 59 at Pompeii. Little is known for certain about this fatal brawl between triumphant Pompeians and disgruntled Nucerians but the episode was captured by a local painter in a bird's eye perspective showing the fighting as it spills out into the areas around the amphitheater and the *campus*.[22] In particular, it is unclear precisely what kind of events were outlawed and whether the city really endured the full ten-year ban on "spectacles of this kind" that Rome imposed. The repercussions on the city's economy, likewise, are impossible to assess because of the upheavals caused by the earthquake four years later, an event whose effects are far more tangible.

The importance of entertainment in the life of the city was reaffirmed by the speed with which the Pompeians restored these structures in the years after the earthquake, while several religious sanctuaries and even public baths lay in ruins. It is clear, however, that gladiatorial spectacles took precedence over theatrical displays.[23] The *theatrum tectum* may have been knocked out of service entirely while the *scaenae frons* of the theater had to be heavily restored and the *summa cavea* sustained serious damage and had not yet been repaired by AD 79.[24] The *quadriporticus* behind the theater, originally constructed around the time of the *theatrum tectum*, was converted into a gladiatorial *ludus*, a training ground and dormitory for gladiators.[25] Columns in the *campus* had to be re-anchored to the stylobate with lead clamps and many were receiving a new coat of stucco. The amphitheater was extensively restored, including a new *summa cavea* and brick buttresses to support the vaulted ceilings of the main access tunnels. The arena's podium was brightly painted with a frieze of panels depicting gladiatorial contests, *venationes*, winged Victories and faux-marbre motives.[26] Two inscribed statue niches (*CIL* X, 858–9) flanking the northern entrance to the arena indicate that this work was carried out by C. Cuspius Pansa and his son, whose duovirate has been dated to AD 79.

The area surrounding the amphitheater and *campus* was similarly revitalized to capitalize on the crowds returning to this quarter of the city. While the aediles allocated spaces to concession stands in the arcaded façade of the amphitheater (*CIL* IV, 1096–7) and the tree-lined area between it and the *campus*, property owners in the adjacent area converted their homes and vineyards into taverns and restaurants (e.g., perhaps, Figures 31.6 and 31.7).[27] One notable example of such an enterprise is the *Praedia*, or "Properties," of Julia Felix (II.4.1–12), a unique complex of shops, baths and garden reception rooms north of the amphitheater on the Via dell' Abbondanza (cf. Nappo, Ch. 23; Figures 23.11–13). The elegant baths, the only ones identified so far in this part of Pompeii, featured the entire spectrum of facilities found in the larger public baths but included a *laconicum* (29) and an open-air *natatio* (34) (cf. Koloski-Ostrow, Ch. 15). They were flanked by a *popina* and a sprawling *caupona* (at no. 7) which offered patrons the choice of dining while reclining or sitting upright. Their proximity allowed these establishments to draw their business from one another. The main reception rooms stood on the west side of the *Praedia* behind a gracious colonnade of white marble pillars with Corinthian capitals (Figure 23.13). Chief among these rooms was a barrel-vaulted *nymphaeum* (83) with a waterstair

Figure 14.4 The northern half of the *campus* or "Great Palaestra" (II.7) of Pompeii. On the right, in front of the north colonnade, are the two rows of plaster casts of the root cavities of the plane trees. The *natatio* is visible on the left while the *exedra* with its shrine is in the distance. View from the east (from the top of the amphitheater).

Figure 14.5 View of the *euripus* in the *viridarium* of the *Praedia* of Julia Felix (II.4) in Pompeii.

fountain in the rear wall and a blue painted frieze showing flora and fauna of the Nile delta. Patrons reclining on its masonry *triclinium* looked out onto a *viridarium* adorned with a *euripus* and an eclectic assortment of garden statuary (Figure 14.5).[28] Other reception rooms had been fashioned out of an old *domus* that stood south of the colonnade (at nos. 10–11). Those facing onto a large *hortus* to the east were decorated with particularly fine paintings, including one with a set of Apollo and the Muses and another (92) with a frieze of still-life panels. The sumptuousness of the architecture and the quality of the decoration indicate that the *Praedia* were intended to cater to a clientele limited to the upper echelons of Pompeian society. As in the grand *thermae* in Rome, patrons could linger here for hours, enjoying a bath or a meal, relaxing in the shade of a vine arbor, and perhaps even hearing a poetry recital, before heading off to their beloved games.[29]

NOTES

1 A. Mau, "Das grosse Theater in Pompeji," *RM*, 1906, vol. 21, pp. 1–56; M. Girosi, "L'Anfiteatro di Pompei," *MemNap*, 1936, vol. 5, pp. 29–55. For the theater, see also A. W. Byvanck, "Das grosse Theater in Pompeji," *RM*, 1940, vol. 25, pp. 107–24.

2 G. Spano, "Osservazioni intorno al 'Theatrum Tectum' di Pompei," *Annali dell'Istituto Superiore di Scienze e Lettere di Santa Chiara*, 1949, vol. 1, pp. 111–39, and idem, "Alcune osservazioni nascenti da una descrizione dell'anfiteatro di Pompei," *Annali dell'Istituto dell'Università di Magistero di Salerno*, 1952, vol. 1, pp. 357–419; M. Murolo, "Il cosidetto 'Odeo' di Pompei ed il problema della sua copertura," *RendNap*, 1959, n.s. 34, pp. 89–101.

3 Mau's work was initially reported by his excavators, R. Paribeni, "Relazioni degli scavi esequiti nel mese di settembre 1902," *NSc*, 1902, pp. 512–15, and A. Sogliano, "Esplorazioni nel teatro scoperto," *NSc*, 1906, pp. 100–7; see also A. Maiuri, "Saggi nella cavea del 'Teatro grande'," *NSc*, 1951, pp. 126–34.

4 A. De Franciscis, *Fasti Archaeologici*, 1971–72, vol. 26–7, n. 8186, and idem, "Attività archeologica," *CronPomp*, 1975, vol. 1, pp. 245–6.

5 A. Maiuri, "Scavo della 'Grande Palestra' nel quartiere dell'Anfiteatro," *NSc*, 1939, pp. 165–238.

6 See especially P. Zanker, *Pompeii: public and private life*, Cambridge, MA, 1998, esp. pp. 65–72, 107–14; S. De Caro, "La città in età imperiale," in F. Zevi (ed.), *Pompei*, Naples, 1992, vol. 2, pp. 11–38, esp. pp. 26–9; S. Adamo Muscettola, "La trasformazione della città tra Silla e Augusto," in F. Zevi (ed.), *Pompei*, Naples, 1992, vol. 1, pp. 73–112; F. Zevi, "Pompei dalla città sannitica alla colonia sillana: Per un'interpretazione dei dati archeologici," in *Les élites municipales de l'Italie péninsulaire des Gracques à Néron*, Rome, 1996, pp. 125–38.

7 L. Richardson, jr, *Pompeii: an architectural history*, Baltimore, MD, 1988, pp. 75–80.

8 For similarities in the plans of the theaters at Pompeii, Pietrabbondante and Sarno, see H. Lauter, "Die hellenistischen Theater der Samniten und Latiner in ihrer Bezeihung zur Theaterarchitektur der Greichen," in P. Zanker (ed.), *Hellenismus in Mittelitalien*, Göttingen, 1976, pp. 413–30.

9 Richardson, *Pompeii*, pp. 131–4; Zanker, *Pompeii*, pp. 65–8; W. Johannowsky, "La situazione in Campania," in P. Zanker (ed.), *Hellenismus in Mittelitalien*, 1976, p. 272.

10 Murolo, "Il cosidetto 'Odeo' di Pompei ed il problema della sua copertura," pp. 91–101; G. Izenour, *Roofed Theaters in Classical Antiquity*, New Haven, CT, 1992, pp. 66–72; R. Meinel, *Das Odeion: Untersuchungen an überdachten antiken Theatergebäuden*, Frankfurt, 1979, pp. 36–44, 155.

11 Zanker, *Pompeii*, p. 66, proposed it was an assembly hall for the veterans, a notion refuted in part by Zevi, "Pompei dalla città sannitica alla colonia sillana: Per un'interpretazione dei dati archeologici," p. 131.

12 Girosi, "L'Anfiteatro di Pompei," pp. 29–57; Spano, "Alcune osservazioni nascenti da una descrizione dell'anfiteatro di Pompei," pp. 357–419; Richardson, *Pompeii*, pp. 134–8; J. C.

Golvin, *L'amphithéâtre romain*, Paris, 1988, pp. 33–7; K. Welch, "The arena in late-Republican Italy: a new interpretation," *JRA*, 1994, vol. 7, pp. 59–80.

13 De Franciscis's excavations (see n. 4) revealed what he believed were the remains of private houses under the amphitheater.

14 M. Fuchs, *Untersuchungen zur Ausstattung römischer Theater in Italien und den Westprovinzen des Imperium Romanum*, Mainz am Rhein, 1987, pp. 44–6.

15 See especially, from Pompeii, *CIL* X, 829: EX EA PECUNIA QUOD EOS E LEGE IN LUDOS AUT IN MONUMENTO CONSUMERE OPORTUIT ("from the money which the law required them to spend on games or a monument"), and the Lex Coloniae Genetivae Juliae ("Charter of Urso"), #70–71 (E. G. Hardy, *Three Spanish Charters and Other Documents*, Oxford, 1912, pp. 31–2). The inscription is no longer in situ.

16 Maiuri, "Scavo della 'Grande Palestra' nel quartiere dell'Anfiteatro," pp. 165–231.

17 W. Jashemski, *The Gardens of Pompeii, Herculaneum and the Villas Destroyed by Vesuvius*, vol. 1, New Rochelle, NY, 1979, pp. 160–1, fig. 246.

18 M. Della Corte, *Iuventus*, Arpino, 1924; De Caro, "La città in età imperiale," pp. 27–8.

19 M. Della Corte, "Il campus di Pompei," *RendLinc* Ser. 8.2, 1947, pp. 555–68; H. Devijver and F. van Wonterghem, "Il campus nell'impianto delle città romane: Testimonianze epigrafiche e resti archeologici," *Acta Archaeologica Lovaniensia*, 1981, vol. 20, pp. 33–68, and idem, "Ancora sul campus delle città romane," *Acta Archaeologica Lovaniensia*, 1982, vol. 21, pp. 93–8.

20 P. Sabbatini-Tumolesi, *Gladiatorium paria: Annunci di spettacoli gladiatorii a Pompei*, Rome, 1980. See also George, Ch. 35, n. 18 for additional bibliography.

21 R. Graefe, *Vela erunt: Die Zeltdächer der römischer Theater und ähnlicher Anlager*, Mainz, 1979, pp. 36–40, pl. 28–35 (theater), 67–70, pl. 77–82 (amphitheater).

22 MNN inv. no. 112222 (1.70 × 1.85 m), from the west wall of courtyatd (n) in I.3.23 ("House of the Riot in the Amphitheater"); G. De Petra, *Giornale degli Scavi*, n.s. 1, 1868–9, pp. 185–7; *Pompei: Pitture e Mosaici*, Rome, 1990, vol. 1, pp. 80–1; T. Fröhlich, *Lararien- und Fassadenbilder in den Vesuvstädten*, RM-EH 32, Mainz, 1991, pp. 241–7, pl. 23.2.

23 A. Maiuri, *L'ultima fase edilizia di Pompei*, Rome, 1942, pp. 83–9.

24 The state of the *theatrum tectum* in the last period is difficult to access given its extensive restorations. Francesco La Vega, who first excavated and restored it in 1793, believed it had been damaged in the earthquake and never restored, but offered no evidence to support this conclusion; see M. Pagano, *I diari di scavo di Pompei, Ercolano e Stabiae di Francesco e Pietro La Vega (1764–1810): Raccolta e studio di documenti inediti*, Rome, 1997, pp. 124–5.

25 At VIII.7.16; Richardson, *Pompeii*, pp. 83–7.

26 *Pompei: Pitture e Mosaici, La documentazione nell'opera di disegnatori e pittori dei secoli XVIII e XIX*, Rome, 1995, pp. 105–11.

27 Examples from the *insulae* immediately adjacent to these buildings include Regio II.1.8, II.2.2 ("House of D. Octavius Quartio"), II.3.9, II.5.5 (Figure 31.6), II.8.2, II.8.5, II.8.6 and II.9.6.

28 Though excavated first in 1755–57, the *Praedia* had been reburied and were not visible in Mau–Kelsey's day; they were only re-excavated and restored in the early 1950s. For a summary of the excavation history and the finds, along with pertinent bibliography, see C. Parslow, "Documents illustrating the excavations of the Praedia of Julia Felix in Pompeii," *RStPomp*, 1989, vol. 2, pp. 37–48. See also C. Parslow, *The Praedia of Iuliae Felicis in Pompeii (Regio II.4.1–12)*, forthcoming.

29 The so-called Portico dei Triclini in the Pagus Maritimus of Pompeii (Murecine) consisted of a small bath complex attached to a porticoed *viridarium* which was surrounded by at least five rooms, each with a *triclinium* equipped with elaborate water features and decorated with fine wall paintings. It has been identified as the seat of a commercial enterprise or the Collegium of maritime merchants, though it is likely a bathing and dining establishment on the model of the *Praedia*. See, M. Pagano, "L'edificio dell'agro Murecine a Pompei," *RendNap* n.s. 58, 1983, pp. 325–62. The site has recently been re-excavated and buried yet again; see S. C. Nappo, "Nuova indagine archeologica in località Morecine a Pompei," *RStPomp*, 1999, vol. 10, pp. 185–90. The present contribution was completed in 1999.

BIBLIOGRAPHY

Adamo Muscettola, S., "La transformazione della città tra Silla e Augusto," in F. Zevi (ed.), *Pompei*, Naples, 1992, vol. 1, pp. 73–112.

Byvanck, A. W., "Das grosse Theater in Pompeji," *RM*, 1940, vol. 25, pp. 107–24.

De Caro, S., "La città in età imperiale," in F. Zevi (ed.), *Pompei*, Naples, 1992, vol. 2, pp. 11–38.

De Franciscis, A., "Attività archeologica," *CronPomp*, 1975, vol. 1, pp. 245–6.

——, *Fasti Archaeologici*, 1971–72, pp. 26–7, n. 8186.

Della Corte, M., "Il campus di Pompei," *RendLinc Ser.*, 1947, vol. 8.2, pp. 555–68.

——, *Iuventus*, Arpino, 1924.

De Petra, G., *Giornale degli Scavi*, 1868–69, n.s. 1, pp. 185–7.

Devijver, H. and F. van Wonterghem, "Ancora sul campus delle città romane," *Acta Archaeologica Lovaniensia*, 1982, vol. 21, pp. 93–8.

——, "Il campus nell'impianto delle città romane: Testimonianze epigrafiche e resti archeologici," *Acta Archaeologica Lovaniensia*, 1981, vol. 20, pp. 33–68.

Fröhlich, T., *Lararien- und Fassadenbilder in den Vesuvstädten*, RM-EH 32, Mainz, 1991.

Fuchs, M., *Untersuchungen zur Ausstattung römischer Theater in Italien und den Westprovinzen des Imperium Romanum*, Mainz am Rhein, 1987.

Girosi, M., "L'Anfiteatro di Pompei," *MemNap*, 1936, vol. 5, pp. 29–55.

Golvin, J. C., *L'amphithéâtre romain*, Paris, 1988.

Graefe, R., *Vela erunt: Die Zeltdächer der römischer Theater und ähnlicher Anlager*, Mainz, 1979.

Hardy, E. G., *Three Spanish Charters and Other Documents*, Oxford, 1912.

Izenour, G., *Roofed Theaters in Classical Antiquity*, New Haven, CT, 1992.

Jashemski, W., *The Gardens of Pompeii, Herculaneum and the Villas Destroyed by Vesuvius*, 2 vols, New Rochelle, NY, 1979–93.

Johannowsky, W., "La situazione in Campania," in P. Zanker (ed.), *Hellenismus in Mittelitalien*, Göttingen, 1976, pp. 267–99.

Lauter, H., "Die hellenistichen Theater der Samniten und Latiner in ihrer Bezeihung zur Theaterarchitektur der Greichen," in P. Zanker (ed.), *Hellenismus in Mittelitalien*, Göttingen, 1976, pp. 413–30.

Maiuri, A., "Saggi nella cavea del 'Teatro grande'," *NSc*, 1951, pp. 126–34.

——, "Scavo della 'Grande Palestra' nel quartiere dell'Anfiteatro," *NSc*, 1939, pp. 165–238.

——, *L'ultima fase edilizia di Pompei*, Rome, 1942.

Mau, A., "Das grosse Theater in Pompeji," *RömMitt*, 1906, vol. 21, pp. 1–56.

Meinel, R., *Das Odeion: Untersuchungen an überdachten antiken Theatergebäuden*, Frankfurt, 1979.

Murolo, M., "Il cosidetto 'Odeo' di Pompei ed il problema della sua copertura," *RendNap*, 1959, n.s. 34, pp. 89–101.

Nappo, S. C., "Nuova indagine archeologica in località Moregine a Pompei," *RStPomp*, 1999, vol. 10, pp. 185–90.

Pagano, M., *I diari di scavo di Pompei, Ercolano e Stabiae di Francesco e Pietro La Vega*, 1764–1810: *Raccolta e studio di documenti inediti*, Rome, 1997.

——, "L'edificio dell'agro Murecine a Pompei," *RendNap*, 1983, n.s. 58, pp. 325–62.

Paribeni, R., "Relazioni degli scavi esequiti nel mese di settembre 1902," *NSc*, 1902, pp. 512–15.

Parslow, C., "Documents illustrating the excavations of the Praedia of Julia Felix in Pompeii," *RStPomp*, 1989, vol. 2, pp. 37–48.

Pompei: Pitture e Mosaici, vol. 1, Rome, 1990.

Pompei: Pitture e Mosaici, vol. 2, *La documentazione nell'opera di disegnatori e pittori dei secoli XVIII e XIX*, Rome, 1995.

Richardson, L., jr, *Pompeii: an architectural history*, Baltimore, MD, 1988, pp. 75–80.

Sabbatini-Tumolesi, P., *Gladiatorium paria: Annunci di spettacoli gladiatorii a Pompei*, Rome, 1980.

Sogliano, A., "Esplorazioni nel teatro scoperto," *NSc*, 1906, pp. 100–7.

Spano, G., "Alcune osservazioni nascenti da una descrizione dell'anfiteatro di Pompei," *Annali dell'Instituto dell'Università di Magistero di Salerno*, 1953, vol. 1, pp. 357–419.

——, "Osservazioni intorno al 'Theatrum Tectum' di Pompei," *Annali dell'Instituto Superiore di Scienze e Lettere di Santa Chiara*, 1949, vol. 1, pp. 111–39.

Welch, K., "The arena in late-Republican Italy: a new interpretation," *JRA*, 1994, vol. 7, pp. 59–80.

Zanker, P., *Pompeii: public and private life*, trans. D. Schneider, Cambridge, MA, 1998.

——, *Pompeji: Stadtbilder als Spiegel von Gesellschaft und Herrschaftsform*, Mainz am Rhein, 1987.

Zevi, F., "Pompei dalla città sannitica alla colonia sillana: Per un'interpretazione dei dati archeologici," in *Les élites municipales de l'Italie péninsulaire des Gracques à Néron*, Rome, 1996, pp. 125–38.

CHAPTER FIFTEEN

THE CITY BATHS OF POMPEII AND HERCULANEUM[1]

—— •◆• ——

Ann Olga Koloski-Ostrow

INTRODUCTION TO CITY BATHS AND MAU'S CONTRIBUTION

Pompeii gives us no fewer than four sets of public baths, financed and built by the town officials. These baths have the following modern names: the Stabian Baths, of the second century BC (Figures 15.1, 15.2 and 15.3); the Forum Baths, c.80–55 BC (Figures 15.4 and 15.5); the Central Baths, still unfinished at the time of the eruption of Mt Vesuvius in AD 79 (Figure 15.6)[2]; and the Suburban Baths outside the Porta Marina, of early imperial date (Tiberian?), which seem to have been publicly owned even if reserved for a private clientele.[3]

City authorities, however, were not the only ones building baths at Pompeii. Private entrepreneurs, especially in the last years of the city, added to the bathing landscape of new buildings and new amenities as well. Three other complexes of a semi-private nature were fully excavated after Mau was first published. These baths were privately built[4]: the *Palaestra*/Sarno Baths in Region VIII.2.17–23, c.AD 50–79 (Figures 15.9, 15.10 and 15.11); the *Praedia* of Julia Felix in Region II, c.AD 62–79 (Figure 15.8); and the Republican Baths of Region VIII, early first century BC (Figure 15.7). At least one or two additional public or semi-private baths, those of M. Crassus Frugi and of Agrippa, both perhaps Tiberian, are known only from inscriptions.[5] Two or three more bathing establishments very likely lie unexcavated beneath the eruption debris of AD 79. By the end of Pompeii's history, there were at least nine bathing establishments available to the public in this relatively small commercial center.

Mau was one of the first scholars to appreciate the potential of the Pompeian baths known to him—Stabian, Forum, and Central in particular—to serve as models for understanding the Roman bath in general.[6] He observed how knowledge of ancient bathing arrangements at Pompeii could be applied, as he put it, "to the imposing but barren remains of Rome itself." He likewise realized how the Pompeian remains could help trace the development of the public bath in a single city over almost 200 years. Mau also understood the architectural, social and historical complexity of baths. Baths were ubiquitous because they were essential to the Roman experience of civilized life. They were a clear and definite symbol of Romanization as Rome encroached ever more on the "barbarian" world.[7]

It is not our purpose here to trace the history of public bathing in Roman life, the architectural history of the bath, or the complex organization of materials and labor necessary to build a Roman bath.[8] The custom of public bathing, however, had made its mark on the architecture of Pompeii by the first century AD, and we consider that mark in some detail. Fagan suggests that earthquakes, especially that of AD 62, may have allowed for greater real-estate speculation in the heart of the city in the first century AD, and that the arrival of the aqueduct no doubt further stimulated improvements to the baths from the time of Augustus onwards. Although these two suggestions in themselves are not new,[9] Fagan breaks new ground for bath studies by pointing out that Pompeii was vigorously responding to Roman desires for the latest in public bathing facilities, and that these desires were prompted by inherent needs in the bathing habit itself.[10]

Roman tastes were rather complex, and inspired multi-faceted bath buildings. Inside the single enclosure of a public bath were opportunities for a wide variety of activities spanning private, commercial and public needs. Private uses of the bath involved attending to personal hygiene (cleansing, bathing, sweating, making use of available latrines) or enjoying some (more-or-less) quiet leisure. The physical evidence makes it clear that the *thermae* were equipped with all sorts of amenities extraneous to the main function of bathing—libraries, theaters, shaded walkways and restaurants.[11]

Our sources[12] mention that buying and eating a variety of foods, purchasing bathing supplies, procuring sexual favors and settling business were some of the viable commercial activities within the walls of the bath. The baths serviced other needs as well, such as providing a warm place for socially interacting with friends and for enjoying light entertainment. Public baths built by imperial officials were important benefactions in a city. The number of inscriptions that attest to the offer of free bathing as a benefaction suggests that entrance fees (*balneatica*) were not uncommon in city baths.[13] While some scholars have argued that publicly owned baths had no entrance fees, the evidence is too inconclusive for proclaiming an empire-wide norm. Privately owned facilities, which were open to the public, clearly could charge fees, at least judging from literary evidence by the time of Augustus.[14] Baths, therefore, contributed to the economic well-being of the cities in which they were built.

Mau's treatment of the city baths of Pompeii and bathing customs as an integral part of Roman daily life, especially during the empire,[15] began one of the most important discussions in bath scholarship, which is still going on today.[16] As Fagan shows, the archaeological remains confirm the written record and demonstrate that the number of baths at Pompeii grows steadily in the first century BC and still more dramatically in the first century AD. This growth in bath architecture in the city is definitely in step with the heightened profile of public bathing in Roman life in general. Let us now consider some specific observations about the architectural structure of Pompeian baths.

GENERAL CHARACTERISTICS OF THE CITY BATHS

Single-axis row type with *palaestra*

Pompeii's four largest baths, Stabian, Republican, Forum and Central, are early examples of a bath type that is combined with a *palaestra*, the "single-axis row type" in the current language of bath architecture.[17] The essential parts of each of the Pompeian bath-houses are the same.[18] An open courtyard, or *palaestra*, surrounded by a colonnade, served as the space for gymnastic exercises and sometimes is connected with an open-air swimming tank, as in the Stabian Baths (Figures 15.1, 15.2 and 15.3).

From the street, one passed through a passageway or anteroom to enter the *apodyterium*, or changing room. Cold bathing generally took place in a separate room called the *frigidarium*.[19] Perhaps to avoid too sudden a change of temperature for the bathers,[20] a room moderately heated, the *tepidarium*, was placed between the dressing room and the *caldarium*, where hot baths were taken. At one end of the *caldarium* was a bath basin of masonry, often faced with marble, called the *alveus*. Ordinarily, on the opposite side of the room was a semicircular niche, *schola*, in which stood the *labrum*, a large, shallow, circular basin resting upon an original concrete support. Cold or lukewarm water fed into this basin from pipes connected to a tank near the furnace room, the *praefurnium*. In one of the city baths of Pompeii, the Central, we also find a *sudatorium*,[21] or sweat room with extremely hot and dry air (Figure 15.6, r). In all four of these main city baths, there is at least one public latrine.[22]

Sergius Orata and the hypocaust system

While baths were originally heated only by means of braziers (see, for example, the male *tepidarium* of the Forum Baths below and Figure 15.5), at the beginning of the first century BC the technology of *balneae pensiles*, "hanging baths," was invented.[23] Mau completely accepted that Sergius Orata, a rather mysterious entrepreneur on the Bay of Naples, was the inventor and that the invention was the equivalent of the hypocaust heating system for baths in particular. The exact meaning of the Latin is somewhat troubling, and the Orata connection has not been proven beyond a doubt.[24]

A bath equipped with a hypocaust system was constructed with its functional floors raised on small brick pillars, *suspensurae*. These pillars supported the four corners of floor tiles, which were approximately 2 ft square. The elevation of the floor thus created hollow spaces underneath for the circulation of hot air, which was introduced from the furnace, *hypocausis*. As the floor became warm, the temperature of the room above was evenly modified. At first confined only to floors, the hollow space was eventually, perhaps as early as the Republican period,[25] extended to the walls by means of small quadrangular flues and by the use of "nipple tiles," *tegulae mammatae*, large rectangular tiles with conical projections, about 2 in. high, at each corner. These were laid on their edges, with the projections pressed against the wall, thus leaving an air space on the inside.[26] We turn now from aspects of the specific technology of Pompeian baths to their overall planning and design.

Zones of the bathing block

Two of the city baths at Pompeii, Forum and Central, occupy complete city blocks and are bordered by rows of shops on one or more sides. Their plans show a clear separation of functions into two distinct zones: a *palaestra* with associated rooms, and a bath block of vaulted rooms and service spaces.[27] The bath block, consisting of the main rooms named above, is composed of a row of independently vaulted, parallel, rectangular rooms (Figures 15.1, 15.2, 15.4, 15.6 and 15.7). In all but the Republican and Central Baths, the bath block is separated into two duplicate sections with shared heating facilities. The Central Baths are designed with an additional service corridor laid out along the back of the entire bath block, isolating it from the street.[28]

The surviving decoration and appointments of the Stabian, Forum and Central baths were well described by Mau. The Republican, *Palaestra*/Sarno Baths, and Suburban Baths receive careful treatment in more recent studies.[29] Below are general descriptions to accompany each plan (Figures 15.1, 15.2, 15.4, 15.6, 15.7 and 15.11), and at the end of each description is a discussion of their particular features. The selected features are worth highlighting because of their contributions to a methodology for studying baths, terminology, origins and development, chronology, architectural design, technology, and/or the social function of baths.

STABIAN BATHS (TERME STABIANE, VII.1.8)

Description

Because it is the oldest, most irregular, and largest of the bathing establishments at Pompeii, more has been written about the Stabian Baths than any other in the city. Mau placed the original construction in the second century BC, and this dating has generally been accepted with certain refinements to various phases of its architectural history.[30]

The Stabian Baths occupy most of its city block. Streets lie on three sides (Figures 15.1, 15.2 and 15.3), while the north side is bounded by the House of P. Vedius Siricus (VII.1.25, 47). A row of shops (all labeled L, Figure 15.1) along the south and west sides of the baths open onto two of the bordering streets, via dell'Abbondanza and vicolo del Lupanare. The third street on the east side, the Strada Stabiana, gives its name to the baths.

The main entrance (A) on the south side (Figure 15.1)[31] opens directly into *palaestra* (C) which has a colonnade on three sides. A strip of relatively smooth pavement with a raised margin replaces the colonnade on the west side. Mau[32] tells us that two heavy stone balls were found here, which, according to him, were used in a game resembling some form of bowling. He rather vaguely identified the room R (Figure 15.1; in Mau and Kelsey Figure 86, room K) as a space for the players of this game. At the middle of the west side of the *palaestra* was a swimming pool (D) with two rooms, both labeled F, to the north and south of it (Figure 15.1; in Mau and Kelsey Figure 86, rooms E and G).

In the northwest corner of the building is a side entrance to the baths (H). Mau interpreted room T (Figure 15.1; in Mau and Kelsey Figure 86, room J) as the office of the superintendent in charge of the building as a whole. Mau suggested that room E (Figure 15.1; D in his plan, Figure 86), located in the southwest corner of the *palaestra*, was a *destrictarium*, a room for removal of dirt and oil with a strigil after outdoor exercises. The identification seems to have been based on a polychrome stucco depiction on the outside walls of rooms E and F facing the *palaestra*,[33] specifically a boxer and an athlete cleaning himself with a strigil. An inscription (*CIL* X, 829), tossed aside in antiquity and found in one of the smaller rooms[34] indicates that a *laconicum* and a *destrictarium* were built in these baths soon after 80 BC. Other

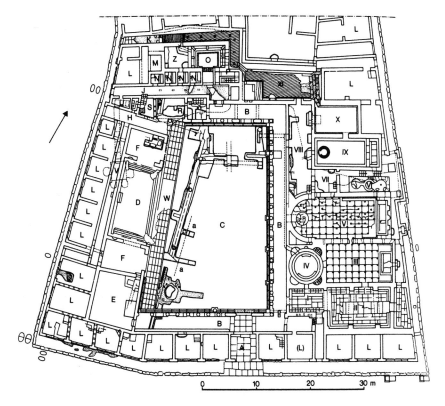

Figure 15.1 Stabian Baths, Pompeii (VII.1.8), plan from A. and M. De Vos,
Laterza Pompei, 1982, p. 198, after Eschebach.

extensive changes were made at the same time, including a rebuilding of the colonnade and repairs to the *palaestra*.

On the southeast side of the open courtyard are the men's baths, rooms I–V (Figure 15.1; in Mau and Kelsey Figure 86, rooms I–VIII)—the sequence includes a vestibule, *frigidarium* (the round room IV, originally a *laconicum*), *apodyterium*, *tepidarium* and *caldarium*. The women's baths, rooms VIII–XI (Figure 15.1; in Mau and Kelsey Figure 86, rooms 1–6), are to the north of these with the furnace room (VI) between them (Figure 15.1; in Mau and Kelsey Figure 86, room IX). The sequence repeats the pattern of the men's baths: *apodyterium*, *tepidarium* and *caldarium*. The only differences between the male and female sections of these baths are: (1) that the *frigidarium* in the women's section is represented by a large concrete tank for cold bathing, apparently a later addition in the northeast corner of the *apodyterium*, instead of a separate round room with a tub, and (2) the dimensions of the rooms in the women's section are slightly smaller.

The small series of four rooms labeled N (cf. Figure 15.1; in Mau and Kelsey Figure 86, rooms *e-e*) appear to be for individual, private bathing, perhaps also for sexual encounters. These rooms seem not to have been heated and were not in service at the time of the eruption of AD 79.[35]

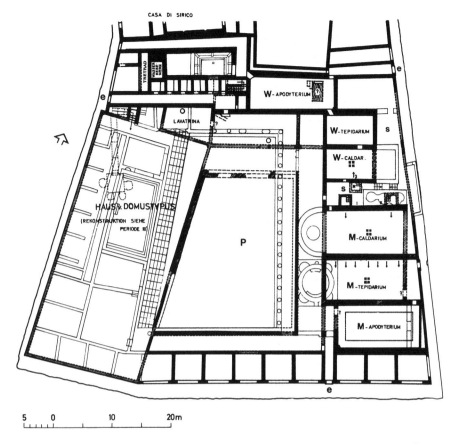

Figure 15.2   Stabian Baths, Pompeii (VII.1.8), plan from Yegül, *Baths and Bathing*, 1992, fig. 58, after Eschebach, Phases III–IV.

Special features or problems

First, the phasing of the building has been hotly disputed since Mau's first description. In the first full publications of the Stabian Baths,[36] six building periods were distinguished, the first consisting only of the "Greek" bath, of the fifth century BC, with individual cubicles at the northwest corner of the later complex (Figure 15.1, rooms labeled N), the fifth the post-80 BC rebuilding by Vulius and Aninius, and the sixth coming from restorations after the earthquake of AD 62. This phasing, particularly in the intervening stages from one to five (Figure 15.2), has been challenged by Richardson.[37] Eschebach's unusually early date for the Stabian Baths was based on the assumption that the oblique west edge of the *palaestra* was determined by the line of the Old City wall of Pompeii and was contemporaneous with it, which, in fact, can not be established unequivocally.[38] In any case, we can say that in the early phases of the Stabian Baths, the water supply came from a deep well located near the vicolo del Lupanare.[39] This fact is significant because it counters the standard interpretation of baths, which makes them entirely dependent on the aqueducts.[40]

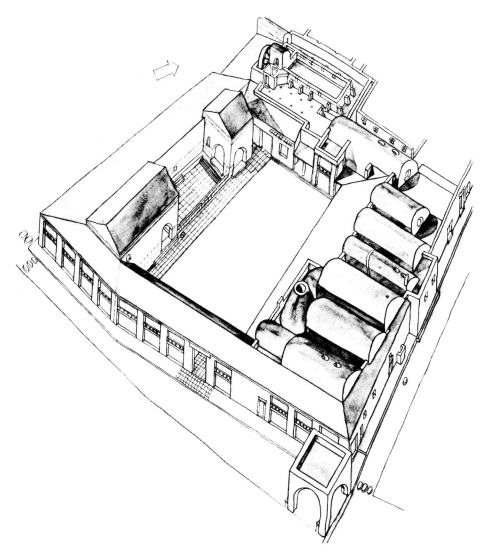

Figure 15.3 Stabian Baths, Pompeii (VII.1.8), perspective drawing from Yegül, *Baths and Bathing*, 1992, fig. 60, restored perspective after Eschebach.

Second, the design of the Stabian Baths' east wing marks a significant point of departure in bath planning[41] which must be hailed as remarkable for its functionality and resourcefulness. The disposition of interrelated rooms in a straight sequence suggests the order of usage: a direct progression from unheated areas to heated ones and back again. This "single-axis row type" was also efficient in the arrangement of its heating apparatus. The construction of parallel, barrel-vaulted halls provided a sturdy structural advantage. The short sides of these rooms could easily be articulated with apses or large windows, as we see demonstrated fully below by the Central Baths. This bath type, manifested in the early Stabian Baths, was widely diffused in both public and domestic spheres.[42]

How can we be sure that the duplication of rooms found in these baths and others was really meant for a division of the sexes? In answer, an inscription, written in black paint over the northwest entrance (Figure 15.1, corridor labeled K) from the vicolo del Lupanare reads *Mulier*, "Woman."[43] This entrance wound around by way of a vaulted corridor to the sequence of bathing rooms (Figure 15.1, rooms VIII–XI) which we now call the women's section. As far as I know, this is the only painted sign we have that may label gender division within a bath. Mau combined the evidence of the sign with three other important characteristics of these rooms—their slightly smaller dimensions, their lack of access to the *palaestra*, and their lack of a separate circular room for a *frigidarium*—to create a model for identifying the "female" section in many other city baths at Pompeii and elsewhere. Literary evidence in Varro and Aulus Gellius, for example, supports such a gender division as well.[44]

FORUM BATHS (TERME DEL FORO, VII.5)

Description

The Forum Baths, excavated and published by 1824, were the first public bath complex discovered in Pompeii,[45] and Mazois' nineteenth-century plan remains valid for understanding their layout and design (Figure 15.4). The Pompeians rebuilt an entire city block north of the forum in the second quarter of the first century BC, just after Pompeii had become an official Roman colony. As in the Stabian, the center of the bathing block was situated behind lines of shops, some of the largest in Pompeii, on three sides—south, east and north. The bath design is the "single-axis row type" with a duplication of rooms meant for men and women.[46] The Forum Baths are the only one of the four main public baths in the city that was completely restored after the earthquake of AD 62 and that was largely operational in AD 79.[47]

The larger, presumably male section, has three entrances (Figure 15.4, a', a'', a'''): the first, on the west side, by way of a short flight of steps, which passed by a small latrine (d), leads directly into the *palaestra* (A); the second, east entrance (probably the main one because of a small cubicle off it for the bathman, or custodian) leads by way of a fairly long vaulted passageway into either the *palaestra* (A) or the *apodyterium* (B); and the third, north entrance, leads by way of a rather shorter barrel-vaulted passageway directly into the *apodyterium*. The *apodyterium* is a rectangular, barrel-vaulted chamber with a plaster-faced bench around three sides on which one could sit while dressing, and where servants could wait for their masters.[48] There are no niches around the walls, as in the dressing rooms of the Stabian Baths, and presumably wooden shelves or cabinets, now vanished, once lined the walls instead. Holes for the shelves are still visible in the walls of both male and female sections. Light enters the room through a window in the lunette at the south end, originally closed, according to Mau,[49] by a pane of glass half an inch thick, which was set in a bronze frame that turned on two pivots. On either side of the window are huge Tritons with vases on their shoulders in stucco relief. They are surrounded by dolphins with a mask of Oceanus underneath. Much of this decoration is almost impossible to see today. The same wall contains a small niche for a lamp, and is still blackened by soot. From this room one had access to either the *frigidarium* (C), the *palaestra* (A), or the *tepidarium* (D).

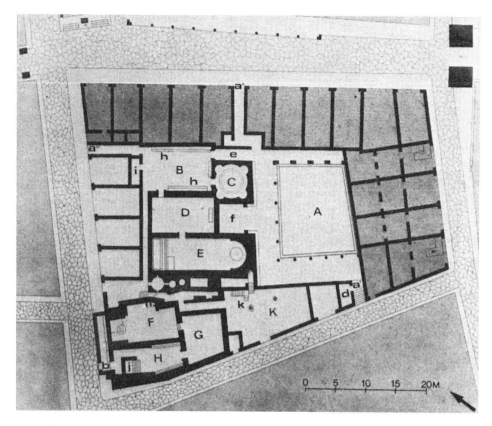

Figure 15.4   Forum Baths, Pompeii (VII.5), plan from A. and M. De Vos,
Laterza Pompei, 1982, p. 50, plan of Mazois.

The *frigidarium* (C) is a circular room with four small, half-domed niches to fill out the corners of an inscribing square;[50] it is very similar in size and decoration, heavy with painted vegetation, to the *frigidarium* of the Stabian Baths (Figure 15.1, room IV). A circular pool takes up most of the room.

The *tepidarium* (Figure 15.4, room D), west of the *apodyterium* and of about the same dimensions, has the best preserved decoration of the whole complex. Niches, possibly for additional locker space, surround the walls. Broad-shouldered Atlantes made of molded terracotta stand out as bold projections separating the niches. Each figure sustains a cornice with uplifted hands and straining musculature.

According to Mau,[51] the south-facing window was once closed by a pane of glass, again in a bronze frame. The decoration on the ceiling, which includes Cupid leaning on his bow, Apollo riding on a griffin, Ganymede with the eagle, Cupids on sea horses, to name the best preserved, utilizes white stucco and painted panels of white, blue, or violet ground. Unlike the two *tepidaria* of the Stabian Baths (Figure 15.1, rooms III and X), this one is not raised on *suspensurae*, but was heated by braziers, one of which still sits in its south end (Figure 15.5). Inscriptions tell us that various bronze furnishings were donated to these baths by P. Nigidius Vaccula.[52]

Figure 15.5 Forum Baths, Pompeii (VII.5), the *tepidarium*. Sir William Gell, *Pompeiana. The Topography, Edifices and Ornaments of Pompeii, the Results of Excavations since 1819*, London, 1832.

Only part of the vaulted ceiling of the *caldarium* (Figure 15.4, room E) was destroyed in the eruption of AD 79. Most of the room is well preserved, including the marble-lined bath basin, alabaster *labrum*,[53] yellow walls, windows in the *schola* to the south, and a lamp niche.

Special features and problems

More than 500 lamps were found in the north–south corridor (Figure 15.4, e) which connected the *palaestra* to the *apodyterium*.[54] We learn from Vitruvius (V.10.1) that late afternoon and early evening were the times to visit the baths, and light would have been waning.

The women's section (rooms F, G, H and K) is rather awkwardly placed in the remaining corner of the block. Since it contains a system of heating which is more sophisticated than the men's baths, the women's baths are thought to be later, perhaps an extension built in the Augustan period.[55] Both the *tepidarium* and the *caldarium* (G and F, respectively) were provided with hollow floors and hot air spaces in the walls. The *caldarium* has lost much of its decoration, its bath basin, its heating apparatus, and all but the base of its *labrum*. Mau speculated that the sorry state of these rooms may have been caused by the earthquake of AD 62.[56] The impressions of the cylindrical tanks for hot, lukewarm and cold water can still be seen in the *praefurnium* (Figure 15.4). Interestingly, just beyond the area for the tanks is a cistern which was supplied in part by rain water from the roof, and in part by a feed pipe connected with the water system of the city.[57]

CENTRAL BATHS
(TERME CENTRALI, IX.4.5, 10, 18)

Description

Begun after the earthquake of AD 62, the Central Baths were still under construction at the time of the eruption. They occupy an entire city block at the southeast corner of the Strada Stabiana and the via di Nola. The north and west sides of the complex are given over to fairly uniform one-room shops. The most significant difference in the design of the Central Baths is that it had only a single series of bathing rooms (Figure 15.6). Mau[58] speculated that these baths were built for men, but that women might possibly have used them at certain hours, in the event that the women's sections

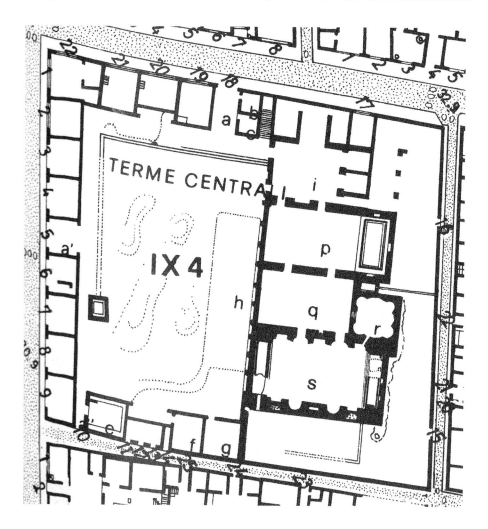

Figure 15.6 Central Baths, Pompeii (IX.4), plan from A. and M. De Vos, *Laterza Pompei*, 1982, p. 207, map of Region IX after Eschebach.

of the Forum and Stabian Baths were overcrowded. In contrast, Richardson[59] has posited that the strong architectural emphasis on the *palaestra* and on large bath rooms with a lack of amenities and annexes suggest that the overall design of the Central Baths catered to "the young and vigorous." It is also possible that mixed bathing was practiced here.

Entrances from three streets lead to the ample *palaestra* at nos. 5, 10 and 18. Two service entrances (on the east side at nos. 15 and 16, Figure 15.6) lead directly into the large corridor on the east side of the building. The main entrance may have been from the north (no. 18) through a vestibule (a) into first the *palaestra* and then into room (i), the likely *apodyterium*, though the room was never finished. On the other hand, the entrance through room (a') at no. 5 into the *palaestra* from the west opens from a larger street. Archaeologists in Mau's day found that the remains of the demolished residential block, which had been leveled to make room for the grand space of the *palaestra*, had not yet been entirely cleared by the architects who were building the bath (Figure 22.4). The east side of the *palaestra* contains the depression where a large outdoor swimming pool was to be laid, as well as the water channel leading to the latrine. Waste water from the pool would have flushed the latrine (e).[60]

The *frigidarium* (p) is somewhat unusual in the Central Baths. Rather than a round room with a tub, as in the Stabian and Forum Baths, here the *frigidarium* is a rather large, rectangular room with a basin, nearly five feet deep, for cold baths along the east wall, opposite the three windows. This is an innovation that also occurs in the Sarno Baths (see below, Sarno Baths, level 4). The *tepidarium* and *caldarium* (q and s, respectively) also each had three large windows opening onto the *palaestra*. In accordance with the recommendation of Vitruvius, the *caldarium* was so placed as to receive the greatest possible amount of sunlight, particularly in the afternoon hours when the baths were to be in use. While none of the rooms were finished and only bits of decoration, mostly stucco fragments, have been found,[61] hollow floors and walls had been built in the *tepidarium*, *caldarium* and *sudatorium* (r), of which the latter may be an important innovation for the Central Baths. No marble had yet been laid in the bath basins, and the two furnaces (to be located in the L-shaped corridor opposite entrance no. 15, Figure 15.6) had not been built.

Special features and problems

The five smaller windows on the south side of the *caldarium* (s) looked out on a narrow garden.[62] Mau noted that the workmen had begun to construct a wall along the south edge of the garden, visible just south of room (s), to cut off the sight of the slaves passing between the two furnaces that were to be located along the service corridor. Another garden was likely destined for the oblong court between the bathing rooms and the street at the northeast corner.[63]

The round sweating room, the *sudatorium* (r) was made more ample by means of four semicircular niches, and was lit by three small round windows just above the cornice of the domed ceiling. Mau thought that another round opening at the apex was probably designed for a bronze shutter, which could have been opened or closed with a chain in order to regulate the temperature in the room.[64] One could enter either the *tepidarium* or the *caldarium* from the *sudatorium*.

Mau surmised that room (i) along with the small rooms on its north and east sides was a kind of general store for the sale of edibles and bather's conveniences, rather than an *apodyterium*.[65] Given the size of the baths, however, it seems that an ample *apodyterium* would have been in order, so Mau's hypothesis is difficult to accept.

The rantings of Seneca (especially *Ep.* 86.8–9) against the rapid growth of luxury baths and bathing habits in the first century find a vivid reflection in the Central Baths.[66] The Pompeians would have been able to boast the most modern facility in their city's history, if it had not been destroyed before its completion.

OTHER IMPORTANT BATHS AT POMPEII

Aside from the briefest of references to the *Praedia* of Julia Felix and to the *Palaestra/Sarno Bath* complex, Mau was not aware of the evidence presented in this section. If Mau's thoughtful observations on the three main public baths, Stabian, Forum and Central Baths, are taken together with this additional evidence, however, we have in Pompeii one of the most informative sites anywhere with regard to the history of baths and bathing.[67] The growth of the bathing industry, easily discerned in the written testimony, can now be tested in the physical evidence, since Pompeii has bath-houses datable to the Republican and early Imperial periods side-by-side.

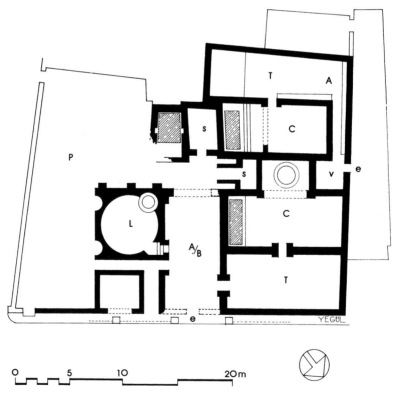

Figure 15.7 Republican Baths, Pompeii (VIII.5.36), plan from Yegül, *Baths and Bathing*, 1992, fig. 57.

Republican Baths, VIII.5.36

The Republican Baths of Region VIII have been dated to the early first century BC, the years just before Pompeii became a Roman colony, and close in date to the construction of the Forum Baths.[68] The overall plan (Figure 15.7) is similar to the two other early establishments at Pompeii, the Stabian and the Forum Baths. The Republican Baths also belong to the single-axis row type with a *palaestra*. These baths, however, were built on a much smaller scale, occupy only a modest part of *insula* 5, and were rather primitive in terms of the hypocaust and other appointments. Since Maiuri's publication in 1950, almost nothing more has been said about these baths.[69] On the strength of their small scale, abandonment, presumably in the Augustan period when better quality baths were finding a warm reception in the city, and lack of surviving inscriptions naming public officials, Maiuri suggested that these baths might have been privately owned. This would put them in a special category of baths, privately owned public facilities which catered to their own (higher paying?) clientele. Fagan[70] supports Maiuri's proposition since, as he points out, written testimony does verify that wealthy Romans were not averse to investing in baths. Fagan also uses this modest, handsome building complex, which operated for no less than fifty years, as further valuable archaeological evidence to demonstrate the increasing popularity of public bathing from the Republic into the Empire. Perhaps by the time of Augustus, all the new innovations in bathing elsewhere in the city were drawing away patronage from the more modestly appointed Republican Baths. These baths may have fallen into disuse simply because it was harder and harder for the proprietor to pay his bills. In any case, the Republican Baths provide a fascinating glimpse into the rise and fall of a privately owned public bath.

Praedia of Julia Felix, II.4

The *Praedia* of Julia Felix (II.4) is certainly one of the best preserved establishments designed and run by a private entrepreneur at Pompeii and in the entire archaeological record (Figure 15.8). Inside we find taverns, dining areas, rooms for relaxation or napping, gardens, a *nymphaeum*, a well-appointed though small latrine (37, cf. also Figure 23.11), and a swimming pool along with the principal bathing suite. The complex belongs largely to the period after the earthquake of AD 62, which is why it includes some of the more modern technical features found in the Central Baths and in the Suburban Baths in Herculaneum (see below).[71] From the *frigidarium* (32) with its rectangular basin (39) for bathing, one passed into the *tepidarium* (41), and from there either into the *laconicum/sudatorium* (29), a room with a circular cupola, or out to a room on the west, the *caldarium* (42). Both *tepidarium* and *caldarium* were fitted with *suspensurae* and the decoration in all rooms is lavish. Ample windows in the *caldarium* look onto the garden (Figure 14.5). The design of the *caldarium* with respect to the garden is reminiscent of the similar arrangement in the Central Baths, only more intimate and of a more human scale.

Partially uncovered and reburied in the years 1755–57, the *Praedia* of Julia Felix was fully excavated only between 1936 and 1953.[72] Mau knew of the *Praedia*, therefore, only from an inscription (*CIL* IV, 1136)[73] which identified the baths in the complex as *balneum Venerium et Nongentum* (cf. Bernstein,. Ch. 34, for the full text).[74] The use of *nongentum* in this context, which is still not clearly understood, apparently derives

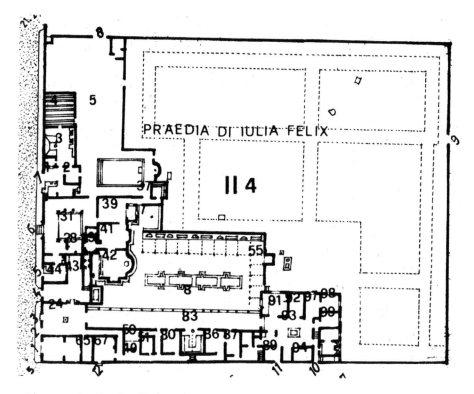

Figure 15.8 *Praedia* of Julia Felix, Pompeii (II.4), plan from A. and M. De Vos, *Laterza Pompei*, 1982, p. 143, after Eschebach.

from a passage in Pliny (*HN* 33.31) from which we understand that in colloquial language the *equites* were known as "the nine hundred." A bath suitable for "the nine hundred" would then be one designed to attract the patronage of "the best people."[75] *Venerium* most likely refers to the "elegant" services at these baths. Fagan[76] suggests that the whole unit (Figure 15.8) may have been an attempt to reproduce, albeit on a smaller scale, the luxuries now available in Rome, most notably in the *Thermae* of Nero, excluding the dining rooms. The location of the complex near the amphitheater must have been good for business.

Palaestra/Sarno Baths, VIII 2.17–23

Other enterprising private citizens who wanted to take advantage of the bathing passion erected two other baths, *Palaestra* and Sarno, on the opposite side of the city. These baths cascaded down the steep southern slopes of Region VIII on at least two, possibly three, levels.[77] The *Palaestra* Baths (VIII.2.21–23, partially visible in Figure 15.9), accessible from the via delle Scuole at the intersection of the vicolo della Regina, contained the usual bathing suite, a latrine, a small *palaestra* with *exedras*, and a balcony with an exceptional view towards the southern valley and sea beyond. Unlike the nearby Sarno Baths, the *Palaestra* seems to have been in service at the time of the eruption.

The Sarno Baths (VIII.2.17–20), situated just north of the *Palaestra* Baths, is an enormous building occupying one-third of *insula* 2. Unquestionably for Pompeii, it is not a structure of a common design (Figure 15.10, exterior view from the via delle Ginestre), comprising five existing stories and a sixth, presumably wooden, story above level 1, which has not survived. Luxury apartments occupied level 1 (Figure 15.9, and the lost level above it) and level 3, which had their own access to the main bath at level 4 (Figure 15.11) and the associated bath rooms of level 5. Level 2 was a service area. The many irregular spaces clinging to the slopes of this remarkable

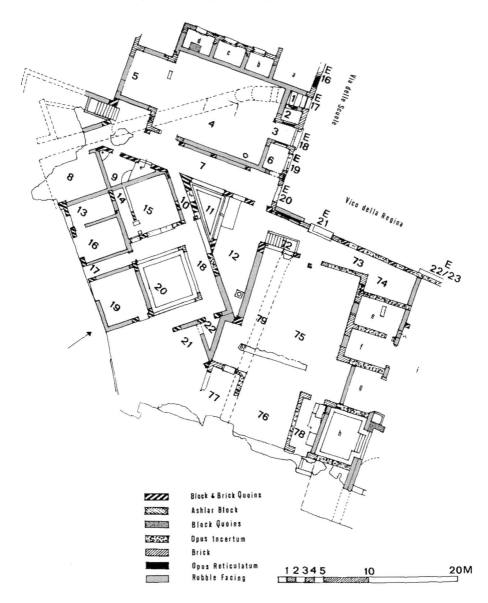

Figure 15.9 *Palaestra*/Sarno Complex, Pompeii (VIII.2.17–23), plan of level 1.

239

Figure 15.10   Sarno Baths, Pompeii (VIII.2.17–23), view of lower exterior of complex.

hillside must have served functions similar to those served by the halls and alcoves discovered in the *praedia*: rooms for dining, reception, drinking, resting, sleeping and enjoying sexual favors.

Level 4 was undergoing renovations at the time of the eruption, suggesting that these baths were not in service, perhaps since the earthquake of AD 62. A new hypocaust heating system was being laid in rooms (51–52), the *tepidarium* and *caldarium*, respectively (Figure 15.11). Both rooms have large windows with southern exposure to capture the warmth of the afternoon sun. The apparatus in the *praefurnium* (room 49, Figure 15.11) was not yet fully installed.

All of the surviving decoration[78] can be dated to the period after *c.*AD 50. There is no *palaestra*, which, if we follow Mau, might suggest that the baths were reserved for women. More likely, however, the disposition of this bath, constructed on a narrow, concrete platform hugging the hillside, did not make inclusion of a *palaestra* feasible. The row of seven cubicles running off to the southeast of the main bathing block along corridor 55 (Figure 15.11, rooms 56–62) may have been additional rooms to rent, rooms for prostitution, or even possibly private changing areas.[79] At least they hold no archaeological evidence, neither individual immersion tubs nor depressions for such, suggesting that bathing took place therein (cf. the four rooms labeled N, Figure 15.1, in the Stabian Baths). The importance of the entire labyrinthine complex (VIII.2.17–23, *Palaestra*/Sarno Baths combined) for bath studies is that it gives us a generally well-preserved example of a "semi-public" facility, serving the apartments above it and, at the same time, allowing access to the general public directly from the street (cf. especially entrance 17, Figure 15.9).

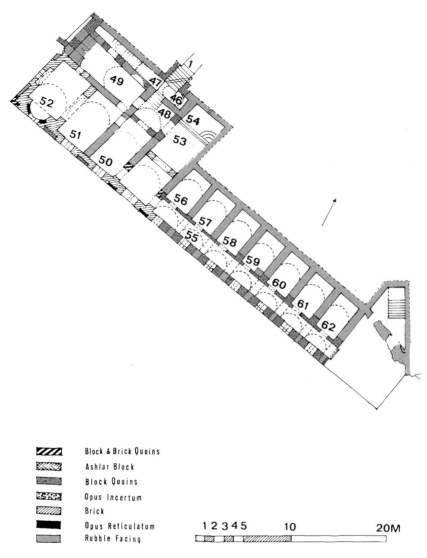

Block & Brick Quoins
Ashlar Block
Block Quoins
Opus Incertum
Brick
Opus Reticulatum
Rubble Facing

1 2 3 4 5   10   20M

Figure 15.11   Sarno Baths, Pompeii (VIII.2.17–23), plan of level 4.

Suburban baths, M. Crassus Frugi; *balneus Agrippae*; Suburban Baths, Porta Marina

After the construction of the Republican and Forum Baths and renovations to the Stabian Baths in the Augustan period, no new baths were built in the early imperial period, until near the end of the Julio-Claudian reign, during the last years of Pompeii. Mau, however, was not unfamiliar with the "suburban" bath when he recorded an inscription, found in 1749 near the Porta Ercolano, which advertised a set of baths as follows: THERMAE M CRASSI FRVGI AQVA MARINA ET BALN AQVA DVLCI IANVARIVS L—"the bathing establishment of Marcus Crassus Frugi. Warm sea

241

baths and freshwater baths. (Superintendent) the freedman Januarius."[80] Mau identified the owner of these baths as M. Crassus Frugi (consul, AD 64) who, according to Pliny the Elder, owned a hot spring which gushed up out of the sea.[81] Although the owner's exact identification cannot be established with certainty, the inscription does attest to the fact that senatorial families could own baths. Some of the entrepreneurs dabbling in baths, therefore, were Romans of rank and power. The institution of the bath had clearly gained the attention of serious money-makers already in the late Republic and early Empire.

From recent excavations we know that more than one set of baths, datable to the early Empire, was constructed outside the city. *CIL* IV, 3878, found outside the Porta Nocera may refer to a "suburban" bath building. The text is only a *graffito*, but it records *balneus Agrippae*.[82] More compelling extra-mural evidence in this early period, however, are the so-called Suburban Baths, discovered in 1986. They were constructed just outside the Porta Marina, probably under the Emperor Tiberius.[83] These baths have many hallmarks of the "new" bath architecture: single-axis row type, large windows facing southwest, and an outdoor pool with a fountain. The bath-house was a two-story structure built to a higher standard of luxury and efficiency than the earlier baths in the town. The upper story, as in the *Palaestra*/Sarno complex, was let out and subdivided into three apartments, with views towards the port and the Bay of Naples.

On the ground floor, inside the *apodyterium*, the discoveries were no less than sensational. The upper part of one wall was decorated with a series of eight numbered erotic scenes, I–VIII, under each of which the decorator had painted empty boxes on a long, narrow yellow table.[84] These erotic scenes are unparalleled in their completeness, for their variety of positions and combinations of sexual couplings, and in the knowledge which they provide of their original context. From traces of iron work on the floor, the archaeologists concluded[85] that below the painted wall, the *apodyterium* was actually fitted with a table and boxes, into which bath customers could put their clothes. Customers then were faced with a choice about how to remember which box was theirs: by sexual position in the painting, I–VIII, or by number. Roman humor seems to be at play here with the juxtaposition of boxes and a table painted on the wall above the real boxes and the real table in the room.[86] As these "revealing" paintings in the Suburban Baths show,[87] Roman baths left everyone exposed in every possible way. It seems very unlikely that these paintings were serious "manuals" for sexual behavior. Rather, they seem amusing flights of fancy to remind bathers of all the sexual possibilities which might develop from the bathing experience and which could as well be pursued afterwards.

Baths in private houses: new research

New research within the last ten years, considerably altering the picture of life at Pompeii depicted by Mau, has shown that there were at least thirty examples of private baths in the town.[88] There is, in fact, no reason to assume that having a private suite would keep one away from public facilities, but the assumption is tempting. While Mau was certainly aware of houses[89] which included private baths, he was not aware of the extent to which private bath construction was fostered throughout the city.

De Haan[90] has divided the private baths of Pompeii into three main groups based on measurements and the complexity of their arrangements. Twenty-two of her examples consist of only two rooms, the heated *apodyterium*, which was therefore also the *tepidarium*, and *caldarium* with tub and *labrum*. Six of the larger complexes had additional rooms, including an outdoor *piscina*.[91] Her studies have examined many other important aspects as well, including water disposal, supply, and heating. Most private baths were remarkably pragmatic in nature and her calculations have shown that these baths had relatively modest requirements for water. The evidence is inconclusive regarding how often private baths were put in use. Given the amount of work required to heat them, however, we can safely assume that they were probably fired up only infrequently.

BATHS OF HERCULANEUM

While life in Herculaneum is treated elsewhere in this volume, the two main bath buildings in that town deserve attention in the context of Pompeii's baths. Mau reviewed the early excavation history of Herculaneum,[92] but he did not compare Pompeii and Herculaneum in terms of individual buildings and building types, institutions, or daily life. The baths of Herculaneum contribute to our understanding of the bathing custom in Campania.

Baths of the Forum, Herculaneum
(Terme del Foro, VI.1–10)

First excavated in 1860–75, these baths represent the first public building in Herculaneum to come to light. Although smaller than the baths of Pompeii with a less perfected heating apparatus, the Baths of the Forum show the same distribution of rooms within each of the two gendered divisions (Figure 15.12).

The entrance to the men's *thermae* (*cardo* III at no. 1) leads through a corridor passing a latrine (Figure 15.12, a and a') on the left in one direction to the portico of the *palaestra*, and in the other, by way of a small doorway, to the changing room, *apodyterium* (A). This latter, the best preserved room in the men's bath, is decorated with a simple red dado on white walls, a strigilated stucco vault, and a pavement in black, white and gray marble chips. A *cippolino* marble washing basin, the *labrum*, rests in the apse at the west end of the room. A plain stucco bench of concrete runs around three side of the room with niches above for clothes and sandals. Light enters through a large window in the south wall. A small, undecorated, square room off the north side of the *apodyterium* serves as the anti-chamber to the *frigidarium* (B). The *frigidarium* pool is painted blue and the red walls above it are broken by four deep niches. The ceiling of the *frigidarium* is domed with a skylight. In the poorly preserved vault of the ceiling Maiuri[93] observed a painted scene of a fishpond in blue ground teeming with fat eels, mullet, and an enormous polyp grasping a *murena*, a fish favored by the Romans. The shimmering reflections from the real waters below onto the watery painting above must have created the illusion of an aquarium for the bathers.

The great *tepidarium* (C) is also surrounded by a bench with shelves above to accommodate additional bathers. A coarse black and white mosaic pavement includes

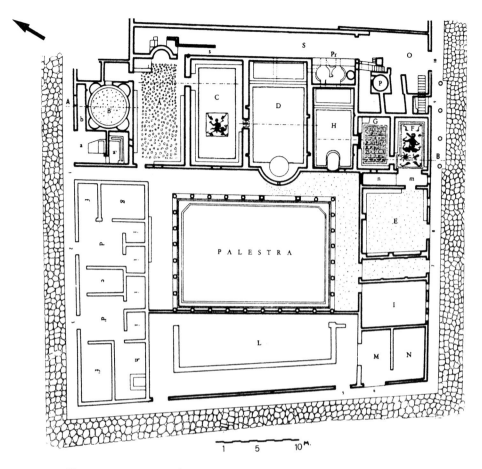

Figure 15.12   Baths of the Forum, Herculaneum (VI.1–10), plan from
A. and M. De Vos, *Laterza Pompei*, 1982, p. 296.

a galloping Triton, a basket of fruit, and four dolphins.[94] Unfortunately, much of
the floor has now caved into the space of the hypocaust below. The *caldarium* (D) is
arranged with an immersion bath at the northeast end, and a cold water *labrum* at
the southwest end.

The *palaestra*, accessible only from the men's section, is flanked by a portico along
three sides, with brick columns and pilasters which have been faced with stucco. The
arrangement is very similar both to the Stabian and the Forum Baths in Pompeii.

The area of the baths reserved for women (Figure 15.12, E–H) is smaller, less well
decorated, and does not include a *frigidarium*. The entrance (off *cardo* IV at no. 8)
leads to a large, square room (E), where, according to Maiuri, the clients waited their
turn.[95] The small room (n) was probably for the supply of bath linens, which could
be collected before entering the *apodyterium* (F). The Triton mosaic on the floor of
the *apodyterium*, similar to the one in the men's *caldarium*, is coarsely executed. Shelves
with recesses and a bench below run around three sides of the room. The *tepidarium*
(G), fitted with *suspensurae* and paved with a geometrical meander motif, is smaller

than the *apodyterium* and also has extra niches and benches for bathing clients. The *caldarium*, also with *suspensurae*, is equipped with a large marble bath in the east end, a podium for the *labrum* in the west end, and two elegant colored marble benches along the north and south walls.

The furnace (*praefurnium*) that services both the men's (D) and women's (H) *caldaria* is located off a corridor(s) just behind this block of rooms to the east. This bath complex presents a very important picture of typical bathing arrangements in the first century AD. The well-preserved furnace area (Pr and room P) includes a circular well, reservoirs, staircases possibly used in the inspection of the boilers, the *praefurnium* itself with its massive iron door for each of the two boilers, and an iron poker,[96] all important components for operating the heating system.

Suburban Baths of Herculaneum (Terme Suburbane)

Below *cardo* V in the southwest corner of Herculaneum and to the south of a large open square (Figure 27.3, right edge)[97] stands the imposing Suburban Baths (Figure 15.13). Excavations, which began only in the late 1960s, have been very difficult due to the proximity of the water table.

The entrance to the building is a large stuccoed and painted portal which leads immediately down a wooden staircase to a vestibule. This room (A) is illuminated by a skylight high above and constructed as a tetrastyle atrium with a series of arches and over-arches above the *impluvium*, or floor basin to receive water from the roof. A herm, possibly Apollo, disguises the pipes that originally discharged water into a marble basin before it. The two symmetrical rooms to the southwest (Figure 15.13, d and e) may have been for the distribution of bath supplies, given their wooden counters. The *praefurnium* (P) opens off the vestibule to the south. A rather large day room (D) probably served as a waiting room, which was well lighted by three large windows which would have looked upon the sea.[98] A long service corridor (N) leads to a room (S) where sexual favors may have been granted, judging from the *graffiti* found there,[99] and to the back side of the *sudatorium* (L). The *frigidarium* (F), *apodyterium*

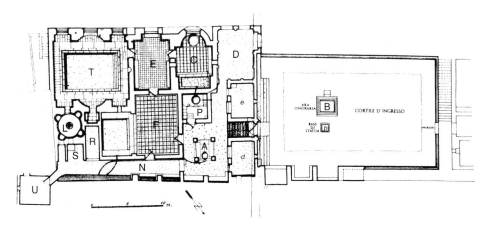

Figure 15.13 Suburban Baths, Herculaneum (VI.1–10), plan from A. and M. De Vos, *Laterza Pompei*, 1982, p. 279, after Maiuri. B and b: tomb and statue base of M. Nonius Balbus.

(E), *tepidarium* (T) and *caldarium* (C) are elegantly decorated, with floors paved in black and white marble tiles, Fourth-Style paintings, and stuccoed reliefs on the walls. The *tepidarium* (T) is mostly taken up with a large swimming pool, which could have been heated.[100]

Conforming to the prescription of Vitruvius (V.10), the *sudatorium* (L) was at the back of the *tepidarium*, communicating with it, and constructed as a circular room with four apses projecting from its rim. The room is on a raised platform, created with *suspensurae*, and was originally heated from fires in a second *praefurnium* (R).

The Suburban Baths date to the beginning of the Flavian period, AD 70s. Given their luxury appointments, it is generally agreed that they were probably reserved for a select (higher paying) clientele or that they were a private club. Although only about one fourth of the city of Herculaneum is excavated, we already have two impressive bathing establishments to demonstrate the claim that the bathing habit was maintained in this city of Vesuvius as well.

NEW RESEARCH RELATED TO BATH STUDIES

Water: supply (aqueducts), distribution (*castellum aquae*) and disposal (city sanitation)

Discussion of the city baths inevitably leads us to larger questions of urban infrastructure. We now return to Pompeii for a brief consideration of its water supply, distribution and disposal (cf. Jansen, Ch. 16). Many places in a Roman town needed water—public fountains, baths, *nymphaea*, public latrines, markets (for washing fruits and vegetables and for clearing away blood from cut meats and fish), the amphitheater (where blood was a major problem), grand *palaestra*, the theater (for cooling the audience on hot days), temples (for various rituals) and so on.[101] Public areas, including various monuments and buildings alike, often depended on water and gained beauty and functionality from good access to water. A good source of water had the power to shape urban topography—and even change local history. The supply and drainage of Pompeii's water system is treated in the next chapter, but some general comments must be made here on the impact of various new studies with regard specifically to the city baths.

The water-supply system in the final years of Pompeii was quite sophisticated. It consisted of an aqueduct,[102] three large pressure mains, fourteen water-towers,[103] and secondary and tertiary water mains. The *castellum aquae*, or the "water castle," had the function of dividing the incoming water into the three water mains (Figure 16.3).[104] Wiggers and his team have shown that the introduction of so many towers at Pompeii made it possible to supply water under relatively low pressure to owners of houses as well as to public buildings, such as baths.

Much new water research involves large-scale projects, which are giving us an important framework for future explorations in ancient water technology. The German hydraulic engineer, Garbrecht, has published many important studies on water power, the oldest dam constructions, water-supply in Jericho, water reservoirs in the Fayum, and on the water-supply and hydraulics of the Roman *thermae*, which are especially useful for understanding the city baths of Pompeii.[105] Fahlbusch, another hydraulic engineer who worked closely with Garbrecht for many years, has compared Greek and Roman water-supply systems. He has convincingly shown that a well-functioning water-system was often a decisive factor in urban development.[106] Much of this new work has serious implications for the thorough study of Pompeii's water system which is still to be accomplished.

Latrines and the sewers throughout the Roman world have not received the attention they deserve, except for several recent important studies.[107] At Pompeii, more often than not, latrines are built inside a city bath (cf. Stabian, Republican, Forum, Central, and *Palaestra* Baths, and also in the *Praedia* of Julia Felix), and they mostly date after 80 BC. It may be that they were constructed more as Romanizing elements built for political advantage in Pompeii, since public latrines mainly appear after the city became a colony, than as improvements to desperate sanitary conditions.[108] What were their features of technology and design? Given their physical layout, is there more to say about them in the context of Roman social customs? What are the reasons Romans built them? These are only a few of the questions which need to be addressed more fully.

Medicine and health

Certainly by the reign of Augustus, citizens at Pompeii frequented the city baths as much for their general cleansing and tonic effects as for their specific healing benefits. Pliny, after all, tells us in his *Natural History*, "Everywhere in many lands gush forth beneficent waters, here cold, there hot, there both ... in some places tepid and lukewarm, promising relief to the sick" (Pliny *HN* 31, 1–2). Public baths, and their attached latrines and sewer systems, therefore lead us to some discussion of health and sanitation. Much new research has confirmed that water was frequently, widely, and enduringly used in classical medicine. There was a keen appreciation of the specific and general properties of different types of water—that from mineral and thermal springs was particularly valued. Water was applied locally to afflicted parts of the body; swimming and static immersion were common medical treatments, above all for rheumatic and urinary diseases; and draughts were freely administered for a host of internal ailments.[109] Water was, of course, also a source of enjoyment and delectation. We are now closer to an honest appraisal of the inherent pleasures and dangers of the public baths than ever before.[110]

POMPEII AND NEW DIRECTIONS FOR BATH RESEARCH

DeLaine has correctly pointed out the "subtle discrimination"[111] that public baths have suffered from scholars during the last century. Because they are rather common structures, that is, more examples of baths exist than of any other kind of Roman public building, we too often assume that nothing new can be said about them. We think we understand them fully from the already published sources, as a class, their form, their systems of operations, their social and medical roles. Baths seem just too familiar to pursue further as topics of scholarly debate. DeLaine revealed an even more elusive discrimination inflicted upon them. By any standard, baths and their attached toilets, "sweaty bodies and sewers"[112] belong to "low" rather than "high" Roman cultural life. They are not the stuff of religion, philosophy, literature and politics, and so for much of the last century had not made a serious claim on scholarship. DeLaine's new analysis of the Baths of Caracalla[113] is a groundbreaking attempt to unravel the preparatory stages involved in the creation of a specific building. She concerns herself with what she calls the "generating processes" of a building project: design, construction and the supply of building materials, which leads her to a quantitative as well as a qualitative analysis of the bath complex. Her results are illuminating for the history of one bath building, for techniques in ancient architecture, and for our appreciation of the building industry and economics of ancient Rome.

The studies of just the last ten years—on baths large and small, on baths as cultural process, on baths within the contexts of Romanization and urbanization, on baths catalogued and drawn, on baths in the history of Roman technology and engineering— are finally beginning to address baths as the truly multi-faceted operations that Mau originally claimed for the city baths at Pompeii.

NOTES

1 I thank the editors, John J. Dobbins and Pedar W. Foss, for their invitation to be a part of this project, for their encouragement, and for their many helpful suggestions. Crispin Corrado Goulet, Garrett G. Fagan, Nathalie de Haan and Andrew Wilson were most generous as readers with their time and expertise, which greatly improved the manuscript. They have my sincere gratitude. I am fully responsible for not always accepting their good advice. Many other friends and colleagues have shared their ideas with me over the years about Pompeii and its baths. I apologize to anyone I have inadvertently omitted, but offer my thanks to: Giuseppina Cerulli Irelli, Dora Crouch, Antonio D'Ambrosio, the late John D'Arms, Stephano De Caro, Janet DeLaine, Simon Ellis, Liselotte (and the late Hans) Eschebach, James L. Franklin, Anne Haeckl, William Harris, John H. Humphrey, Gemma C. M. Jansen, Eleanor W. Leach, Anne Laidlaw, Roger Ling, Mario Pagano and Lawrence Richardson, jr. Special thanks go to Steven Ostrow for unending support and important criticisms, and to my two intrepid explorer-sons, Aaron and Benjamin, for whom the baths were rest and shade from the unrelenting Campanian sun.

The following abbreviations are frequently used in the notes:

A. and M. De Vos, *Laterza Pompei*, 1982: A. and M. De Vos, *Guide archeologiche Laterza: Pompei, Ercolano, Stabia*, Bari, Italy, Gius. Laterza & Figli, 1982.

Fagan, *Bathing in Public*: G. G. Fagan, *Bathing in Public in the Roman World*, Ann Arbor, MI, University of Michigan Press, 1999.

Maiuri, *Pompeii*, 1965: A. Maiuri, *Pompeii*, Rome, Istituto Poligrafico dello Stato, 1965.

Maiuri, *Herculaneum*, 1970: A. Maiuri, *Herculaneum*, Rome, Istituto Poligrafico dello Stato, 1970.

Mau and Kelsey, 1907: A. Mau and F. Kelsey, *Pompeii: its life and art*, New York, Macmillan Co., 1907.

Richardson, *Pompeii*, 1988: L. Richardson, jr, *Pompeii: an architectural history*, Baltimore, MD, Johns Hopkins University Press, 1988.

Yegül, *Baths and Bathing*, 1992: F. Yegül, *Baths and Bathing in Classical Antiquity*, Cambridge, MA, Massachusetts Institute of Technology Press, 1992.

2 A. Mau and F. Kelsey, *Pompeii: its life and art*, New York, 1907, pp. 186–211; F. Yegül, *Baths and Bathing in Classical Antiquity*, Cambridge, MA, 1992, pp. 57–66; L. Richardson, jr, *Pompeii: an architectural history*, Baltimore, MD, 1988, pp. 100–5, pp. 147–53, pp. 286–9, pp. 303–7; A. and M. De Vos, *Guida archeologica di Pompei*, Bari, 1982, pp. 49–52, pp. 194–202, pp. 206–9; H. Manderscheid, *Ancient Baths and Bathing: A Bibliography for the Years 1988–2001*, JRA Suppl. Ser. no. 55, 2004.

3 H. Jacobelli, "Die Suburbanen Thermen in Pompei: Architektur, Raumfunktion und Ausstattung," *Archaeologisches Korrespondenzblatt*, 1993, vol. 23, pp. 327–35; J. DeLaine and D. E. Johnston (eds), *Roman Baths and Bathing. Part 2. Design and Context*, JRA Suppl. Ser. no. 37.2, 2000.

4 On the Sarno Baths see A. O. Koloski-Ostrow, *The Sarno Bath Complex*, Rome, "L'Erma" di Bretschneider, 1990, p. 1, which lists all notices of the Terme del Sarno chronologically; on the *praedia* see C. Parslow, *The Praedia Iuliae Felicis in Pompeii*, Ph.D. Dissertation, Duke Univeristy, 1989; and on the Republican Baths of Region VIII see A. Maiuri, "Pompei. Scoperta di un edificio termale nella Regio VIII, *Insula* 5, no. 36," *NSc*, 1950, vol. 66, pp. 116–36. I. Nielsen, *Thermae et balnea*, Aarhus, 1993, proposes 90–80 BC for the date of Republican Baths. J. DeLaine, "Some observations on the transition from Greek to Roman Baths in Hellenistic Italy," *MeditArch*, 1989, vol. 2, p. 120, argues that, in terms of construction and decoration, the Republican Baths may "just as easily belong to the middle of the second century BC."

5 Mau, *Pompeii: its life and art*, p. 189 on a bath perhaps owned by one, *M. Crassus Frugi*, located somewhere outside the Porta Ercolano; and on the *balneus Agrippae*, CIL IV, 3878.

6 Mau, *Pompeii: its life and art*, pp. 186ff.

7 Cf., e.g., Tacitus, *Agricola* 21.

8 On the history of public bathing in Roman life see G. G. Fagan, *Bathing in Public in the Roman World*, Ann Arbor, MI, 1999, pp. 40–84. Cf. Yegül, *Baths and Bathing*, pp. 6–91 on the Greek bath, on bathing and baths in the Roman world, and on the origins and early development of Roman baths. (See also review of Yegül, *Baths and Bathing* by A. O. Koloski-Ostrow in *AJA*, April 1994, vol. 98, pp. 380–1.) On the "generating processes" of bath construction, see J. DeLaine, *The Baths of Caracalla: a study in the design, construction and economics of large-scale public buildings in Imperial Rome*, Portsmouth, RI, JRA Suppl. Ser. no. 25, 1997 (reviewed by A. O. Koloski-Ostrow on the web page of the *Bryn Mawr Classical Review*, Dec. 1998, 1–6. The reference number is 1998.11.41. html), and R. Taylor, *Roman Builders: a study in architectural process*, Cambridge, 2003, pp. 70–129.

9 Mau, *Pompeii: its life and art*; Maiuri, *Pompeii*, Rome, 1965, *passim*.

10 On which see Fagan, *Bathing in Public*, pp. 56–68.

11 J. P. V. D. Balsdon, *Life and Leisure in Ancient Rome*, London, Bodley Head, 1974; M. Borrielli and A. Ambrosio, *Forma Italiae. Regio I*, Vol. XIV: *Baiae-Misenum*, Firenze, L. S. Olschki, 1979; J. Carcopino, *Daily Life in Ancient Rome*, New Haven, CT, Yale University Press, 1960; A. Carandini, *et al.*, *Ostia, StMisc*, 1968, vol. I; 1970, vol. II; 1973, vol. III; 1977, vol. IV; F. Coarelli, *Guide archeologiche Laterza: Roma*, Rome, Gius. Laterza & Figli, 1981; B. Crova, "Le terme romane nella Campania," *VIII Convegno di Storia dell'Architettura*, 1953, pp. 271–88; J. DeLaine, "Recent research on Roman baths," *JRA*, 1988, vol. 1, pp. 11–32; *ead.*, "Some observations on the transition from Greek to Roman Baths in Hellenistic Italy," 111–25; *ead.*, "Roman baths and bathing," *JRA*, 1993, vol. 6, pp. 348–58; K. A. Dunbabin, "*Baiarum Grata Voluptas*: pleasures and dangers of the baths," *PBSR*, 1989, vol. 57, pp. 6–49; Fagan, *Bathing in Public*, pp. 76–7, 88, 176–8; R. Ginouvès, *Balaneutikè: recherches sur le bain dans l'antiquité grecque*, Paris, 1962; W. Heinz, *Römische Thermen. Badewesen und Badeluxus im römischen Reich*, Munich, 1983; C. F. Kaufmann, *The Baths of Pozzuoli*, Oxford, 1959; D. Krencker, *et al.*, *Die Trierer Kaiserthermen*, Augsburg, 1929; W. L. MacDonald and B. Boyle, "The small baths at Hadrian's Villa," *JSAH*, 1980, vol. 39, 5–27; H. Manderscheid, "Römische Thermen. Aspekte von Architektur, Techniek und Ausstattung," *Geschichte der Wasserversorgung*, 1988, vol. III, Mainz am Rhein; *id.*, "Bemerkung zur Wasserbewirtschaftung der suburbanen Thermen in Pompeji," *Archäologisches Korrespondenzblatt*, 1993, vol. 23, pp. 337–46; *id.*, "Standard und Luxus in römishchen Bädern. Überlegungen aus der Sicht der Hydrotechnik," in N. de Haan and G. C. M. Jansen (eds), *Cura Aquarum in Campania: Proceedings of the 9th International Congress on the History of Water Management and Hydraulic Engineering in the Mediterranean Region* (Pompeii, 1–8 October 1994), *Bulletin antieke beschaving. Annual Papers on Classical Archaeology*, 1996, supplement 4, pp. 109–15; I. Nielsen, *Thermae et balnea*, Aarhus, 1990; M. Pasquinucci (ed.), *Terme romane e vita quotidiana*, Mostra, Modena, 1987; Yegül, *Baths and Bathing*. Specifically on libraries in baths, see T. K. Dix and G. W. Houston, "Libraries in Roman Baths?" *Balnearia*, 1995, vol. 4, 2–4.

12 Seneca *Ep.* 56, for example, see Mau, *Pompeii: its life and art*, p. 200; Richardson, *Pompeii*, p. 152, where notice is taken of the largest cookshops and wineshops located opposite both the Forum Baths and the Stabian Baths.

13 On the matter of free bathing benefactions, see Fagan, *Bathing in Public*, p. 127 with n. 77, and pp. 160–1 with n. 65. Pliny, *HN* 36.121, indicates that 170 *gratuita balinea* were offered in Rome in his day. Cf. F. Cenerini, "Evergetismo ed epigrafia: *Lavationem in perpetuum*," *RivStorAnt* 17–18 (1987–88), pp. 199–220, which thoroughly treats the issue of free bathing.

14 For a survey of bathing references in Augustan poets, see J. Griffin, *Latin Poets and Roman Life*, London, 1985, pp. 88–111. Fagan, *Bathing in Public*, p. 51, focuses on Horace and Ovid, their regular encounters with baths, and the useful information on entrance fees in these authors. Cf., for example, Horace *Sat.* 1.3.137–9.

15 Mau, *Pompeii: its life and art*, pp. 186–211.

16 Cf. DeLaine, "Recent Research on Roman Baths;" *ead.*, "Roman Baths and Bathing;" K. A. Dunbabin, "*Baiarum Grata Voluptas*," pp. 6–49; Yegül, *Baths and Bathing*; Fagan, *Bathing in Public*; Taylor, *Roman Builders*.

17 Developed by D. Krencker, *et al.*, *Die Trierer Kaiserthermen*, Augsburg, 1929.; See also Yegül, *Baths and Bathing*, p. 57; Mau, *Pompeii: its life and art*, p. 186.

18 Mau, *Pompeii: its life and art*, pp. 186ff.; Richardson, *Pompeii*, pp. 148ff.; Yegül, *Baths and Bathing*, pp. 61–4, e.g.

19 *Frigidaria* are round only in the Forum and Stabian Baths at Pompeii because they are ex-*laconica*.

20 Mau, *Pompeii: its life and art*, pp. 188ff.

21 H. Eschebach has argued that the *frigidaria* of both the Forum and Stabian Baths were once *laconica*. Cf. H. Eschebach, "Untersuchengen in den Stabianer Thermen zu Pompeji," *RM*, 1973, vol. 80, pp. 235–42. See also W. Heinz, *Romische Thermen*, pp. 33–4. Neilsen, *Thermae et balnea*, proposed the now widely accepted terminology of *sudatorium* instead of *laconicum* in the Central Baths.

22 Cf. G. C. M. Jansen, "Sewers and tapwater as urban innovations at Herculaneum," in *XIV Congreso Internacional de Arqueología Clásica Tarragona*, Taragona, 1993, pp. 218–20; *ead.*, *Water in de Romeinse stad. Pompeji, Herculaneum, Ostia*, Leuven, 2002; R. Neudecker, *Die Pracht der Latrine*, Munich, Dr Friedrich Pfiel, 1994; A. O. Koloski-Ostrow, "Finding social meaning in the public latrines of Pompeii," in de Haan and Jansen (eds), *Cura Aquarum*, pp. 79–86.

23 Mau, *Pompeii: its life and art*, p. 187. Cf. N. de Haan, "The significance of Roman private baths for the development of public baths," *Proceedings of the Second International Conference on Ancient Baths*, Varna, 22–27 April, 1996, forthcoming. I am grateful to Dr de Haan for allowing me to see her paper before publication. She discusses Orata, private baths and the invention of the hypocaust.

24 G. G. Fagan, "Sergius Orata: inventor of the hypocaust?" *Phoenix*, 1996, vol. 50, pp. 56–66.

25 Cf. Mau, *Pompeii: its life and art*, p. 187.

26 For various discussions of the hypocaust technique, cf. Mau and Kelsey 1907, p. 187; J. Benedum, "Die *Balnea Pensilia* des Asklepiades von Prusa," *Gesnerus*, 1967, vol. 24, pp. 93–107; J. Hilton Turner, "Sergius Orata, pioneer of radiant heating," *CJ*, 1947/48, vol. 43, pp. 486–7; A. Iorio, "Sistema di riscaldamento nelle antiche terme pompeiane," *Bullettino della Commissione archeologica comunale di Roma*, 1978–79, vol. 86, pp. 167–89; F. Kretzschmer, "Hypocausten," *Saalburg-Jahrbuch. Bericht des Saalburg-Museums*, 1953, pp. 7–41; E. Künzl, "Operationsräume im römischen Thermen," *Bonner Jahrbücher des Rheinischen Landesmuseums in Bonn und des Vereins von Altertumsfreunden im Rheinlande*, 1986, vol. 186, pp. 491–509; Maiuri, *Pompeii*; J. P. Oleson and J. W. Humphrey, *Greek and Roman Technology: a sourcebook*, London, Routledge, 1997; T. Rook, "The development and operation of Roman hypocausted baths," *JAS*, 1978, vol. 5, pp. 269–82.

27 Yegül, *Baths and Bathing*, pp. 57–91.

28 Yegül *Baths and Bathing*, p. 57. There is no clear evidence of two sets of rooms in the Republican Baths according to A. Maiuri, "Pompeii. Scoperta di un edificio termale nella Regio VIII, Insula 5, no. 36," *NSc*, 1950, vol. 66, pp. 116–36.

29 See notes 3 and 4.

30 Cf. Mau, *Pompeii: its life and art*, p. 189. H. Eschebach's effort to date the earliest phase of the baths to the fifth century BC has not been widely accepted. Cf. H. Eschebach, "Untersuchungen in den Stabianer Thermen," pp. 235–42; *id.*, *Die Stabianer Thermen in Pompeji*, Berlin, 1979. For arguments against Eschebach's dating see I. Nielsen, "Considerazioni

sulle primi fasi dell'evoluzione dell'edificio termale romano," *AnalRom*, 1985, vol. 14, pp. 81–112; *ead.*, *Thermae et balnea*; Richardson, *Pompeii*, pp. 100–5; Yegül, *Baths and Bathing*, p. 57, p. 434, n. 19; J. DeLaine, "Some observations on the transition from Greek to Roman baths in Hellenistic Italy."

31 Cf. Mau, *Pompeii: its life and art*, plan, fig. 86.

32 Mau, *Pompeii: its life and art*, p. 189.

33 A. and M. De Vos, *Laterza Pompei*, p. 199.

34 Cf. Mau, *Pompeii: its life and art*, p.195; Richardson, *Pompeii*, p. 102. On *CIL* X, 829 see J. Delorme, *Gymnasion: Etude sur les monuments consacres a l'education en Grece*, Paris, 1960, pp. 224–6. *Duumvirs* C. Vulius and P. Aninius are named.

35 Mau, *Pompeii: its life and art*, p. 190; A. and M. De Vos, *Laterza Pompei*, p. 202. Possibly there was a *praefurnium* for heating these rooms. Cf. Richardson, *Pompeii*, p. 102. It was located off to the west in conjunction with the deep well, adjacent to the vicolo del Lupanare. Archaeological proof, however, is lacking. Cf. J. Oleson, "Water-lifting devices at Herculaneum and Pompeii in the context of Roman technology," in de Haan and Jansen (eds), *Cura Aquarum*, pp. 67–77.

36 H. Eschebach, "Untersuchungen in den Stabianer Thermen;" *id.*, *Die Stabianer Thermen in Pompeji*.

37 Richardson, *Pompeii*, pp. 103–5.

38 See especially, Yegül, *Baths and Bathing*, pp. 434–5, n. 19.

39 See n. 35.

40 See DeLaine, "Recent research on Roman Baths," p. 24. Cf. E. Brödner, *Die römischen Thermen und das antike Badewesen*, Darmstadt, Wissenschaftliche Buchgesellschaft, 1983; Heinz, *Römische Thermen*.

41 Yegül, *Baths and Bathing*, p. 61.

42 Yegül, *Baths and Bathing*, pp. 63–4. Cf. Nielsen, *Thermae et balnea*; and G. G. Fagan, "Bathing in the backwaters," review of A. Farrington, *The Roman Baths of Lycia. An architectural study*, Oxford, 1995, in *JRA*, 1997, vol. 10, pp. 520–3.

43 A. and M. De Vos, *Laterza Pompei*, p. 201—no longer visible, unfortunately. G. G. Fagan has suggested to me that *mulier* might be shorthand for *mulieribus*, "for women."

44 Varro *Ling.* 9.68 and *Aul. Gell.* 10.3.3. I am grateful to G. G. Fagan for these citations.

45 Richardson, *Pompeii*, pp. 147ff. with n. 11. Also see, L. Eschebach, "Die Forumstermen in Pompeji, Regio VII, Insula 5," *AntW*, 1991, vol. 22, pp. 257–87. She proposes a rather far-fetched building history.

46 The female section seems to be a later addition. See below.

47 Here, too, the female section seems to be the exception.

48 The same arrangement can be found in *apodyteria* of the male and female sections of the Stabian Baths—rooms II and XI in Figure 15.1.

49 Mau, *Pompeii: its life and art*, p. 204.

50 Richardson, *Pompeii*, p. 148.

51 Mau, *Pompeii: its life and art*, p. 205.

52 *CIL* X, 818; Richardson, *Pompeii*, p. 148.

53 The *labrum* was inscribed by Gnaeus Melissaeus Aper and Marcus Staius Rufus, *duumvirs* in AD 3–4. Cf. Mau, *Pompeii: its life and art*, p. 206; A. and M. De Vos, *Laterza Pompei*, p. 52 for the full inscription.

54 A. and M. De Vos, *Laterza Pompei*, p. 51.

55 Mau, *Pompeii: its life and art*, pp. 206–7; Fagan, *Bathing in Public*, p. 59.

56 Mau, *Pompeii: its life and art*, p. 207.

57 Mau, *Pompeii: its life and art*, p. 207; Richardson, *Pompeii*, pp. 151–2; A. T. Hodge, "*In Vitruvianum Pompeianum*: urban water distribution reappraised," *AJA*, 1996, vol. 100, pp. 261–76; H. Mygind, "Hygienische Verhältnisse im alten Pompeji," *Janus*, 1921, vol. 25, pp. 324–85; Oleson, "Water-lifting devices."

58 Mau, *Pompeii: its life and art*, p. 208.

59 Richardson, *Pompeii*, p. 289.

60 Koloski-Ostrow, "Finding social meaning in the public latrines of Pompeii."

61 Mau, *Pompeii: its life and art*, pp. 209ff.; Richardson, *Pompeii*, pp. 286–9.

62 Mau, *Pompeii: its life and art*, p. 210; W. F. Jashemski, *The Gardens of Pompeii, Herculaneum, and the Villas Destroyed by Vesuvius*, New Rochelle, NY, 1979, p. 164, accepts this interpretation.

63 Mau, *Pompeii: its life and art*, p. 211; and Jashemski, *Gardens*, p. 164.

64 Mau, *Pompeii: its life and art*, p. 211.

65 Cf. Yegül, *Baths and Bathing*, p. 63.

66 Cf. Fagan, *Bathing in Public*, p. 65.

67 Fagan, *Bathing in Public*, pp. 65–7, makes a strong case for this point.

68 A. Maiuri, "Pompeii. Scoperta di un edificio termale nella Regio VIII, *Insula* 5, no. 36," postulated a construction date of *c*.90–80 BC.

69 Cf. Yegül, *Baths and Bathing*, fig. 57, but no word of them in his text.

70 Fagan, *Bathing in Public*, pp. 233–316, includes lists of inscriptions of constructional and nonconstructional benefactions.

71 A. and M. De Vos, *Laterza Pompei*, p. 145; U. Pappalardo, "The Suburban Baths of Herculaneum," in J. DeLaine and D. E. Johnston (eds), *Roman Baths and Bathing. Part 2. Design and Context*, JRA Suppl. Ser. no. 37.2, 2000, pp. 229–38.

72 C. Parslow, *The Praedia Iuliae Felicis in Pompeii*; id., *Rediscovering Antiquity. Karl Weber and the excavation of Herculaneum, Pompeii, and Stabiae*, Cambridge, 1995.

73 Mau, *Pompeii: its life and art*, pp. 489–90; A. and M. De Vos, *Laterza Pompei*, pp. 141–2.

74 Cf. Koloski-Ostrow, *The Sarno Bath Complex*, p. 58, and notes 92–3.

75 Cf. M. Delle Corte, *Case ed abitanti di Pompei*, Naples, 1965, pp. 390–1, no. 821 with his note 2 concerning "i nongenti," custodians of electoral urns.

76 Cf. Fagan, *Bathing in Public*, pp. 65–6.

77 Cf. Koloski-Ostrow, *The Sarno Bath Complex*, *passim*, for the Sarno Baths.

78 Cf. Koloski-Ostrow, *The Sarno Bath Complex*, pp. 61–79.

79 Cf. Koloski-Ostrow, *The Sarno Bath Complex*, p. 41; Cf. Fagan, *Bathing in Public*, p. 67, for other suggestions.

80 Cf. Mau, *Pompeii: its life and art*, p. 408.

81 Pliny *HN* 31.5, discussed in Mau, *Pompeii: its life and art*, p. 408. Cf. Fagan, *Bathing in Public*, pp. 62–3, with n. 74, for closer discussion of the modes of bathing implied in this inscription, and for dating problems connected with Pliny's Crassus.

82 Fagan, *Bathing in Public*, p. 63, suggests a possible connection with Agrippa Postumus, who may have owned a villa at Boscotrecase in the outskirts of Pompeii.

83 L. Jacobelli, "Lo scavo delle Therme Suburbane. Notizie preliminari," *Rivista di studi pompeiani*, 1987, vol. 1, pp. 151–4; *ead.*, "Terme Suburbane: stato attuale delle conoscenze," *Rivista di studi pompeiani*, 1988, vol. 2, pp. 202–8; *ead.*, "Le Terme Suburbane di Pompei: architettura e distribuzione degli ambienti," in DeLaine and Johnston (eds), *Roman Baths and Bathing. Part 2. Design and Context*, pp. 221–8; *ead.*, *Le pitture erotiche delle therme suburbane di Pompei*, Rome, 1995, pp. 20–3. For a compelling discussion of sex and laughter in the Suburban Baths, see J. R. Clarke, *Looking at Lovemaking: constructions of sexuality in Roman art 100 BC–AD 250*, Berkeley, Los Angeles, CA, and London, 1998, pp. 212–40. His text includes a clear plan (fig. 89, p. 213) as well as an interior of the *apodyterium* 7.

84 There are actually sixteen painted boxes, but boxes numbered IX–XVI are not under erotic scenes.

85 Cf. Jacobelli, *Le pitture erotiche*.

86 We might compare paintings of birds, flowers, and greenery in rooms enclosing real plantings or lining actual garden walls, such as at the Villa at Oplontis.

87 For example, one woman on top with a man below, another man is on top while a woman has her leg over his shoulder, a woman fellates a man who has interrupted his reading, a foursome of man/man/woman/woman are in a sexual chain, and so on.

88 N. de Haan, "Privatbäder in Pompeji und Herkulaneum und die städtische Wasserversorgung," *Mitteilungen des Leichtweiß—Instituts für Wasserbau der Technischen Universität Braunschweig*, 1992, vol. 117, pp. 423–45; *ead.*, "Die Wasserversorgung der Privatbäder in Pompeji," in de Haan and Jansen (eds), *Cura Aquarum*, pp. 59–65; *ead.*, *Römische Privatbäder, Entwicklung, Verbreitung und sozialerStatus*, diss. Katholieke Universiteit, Nijmegen, 2003.

89 Mau, *Pompeii: its life and art*, pp. 267, 297, 306–7, 346, 357, 362–3—most notably the Casa del Fauno and Nozze d'argento.

90 N. de Haan, "Privatbäder in Pompeji und Herkulaneum;" *ead.*, "Dekoration und Funktion in den Privatbäderen von Pompeji und Herculaneum," in E. Moorman (ed.), *Functional and Spatial Analysis of Wall Painting*, Proceedings of the Fifth International Congress on Ancient Wall Painting, 1993, Supplement 3, *Bulletin antieke beschaving. Annual Papers of Classical Archaeology*, Leiden, pp. 34–7; *ead.* and Jansen (eds) 1996, pp. 59–65; *ead.*, *Römische Privatbäder.*

91 Cf. Casa delle Nozze d'argento, V.2.1; A. and M. De Vos, *Laterza Pompei*, pp. 211–12.

92 Mau, *Pompeii: its life and art*, pp. 21 and 26.

93 Maiuri, *Herculaneum*, Rome, 1970, p. 37; and A. and M. De Vos, *Laterza Pompeii*, pp. 296ff.

94 The same subject with slight variation is in the women's *apodyterium* of these baths.

95 Maiuri, *Herculaneum*, p. 39.

96 Maiuri, *Herculaneum*, p. 40.

97 The square contains the honorary statue bases dedicated to M. Nonius Balbus (cf. Small, Ch. 13). Cf. A. and M. De Vos, *Laterza Pompeii*, pp. 278–82. For the baths see U. Pappalardo, "The Suburban Baths of Heculaneum," in DeLaine and Johnston (eds), *Roman Baths and Bathing. Part 2. Design and Context*, pp. 229–38.

98 Maiuri, *Herculaneum*, p. 70.

99 A. and M. De Vos, *Laterza Pompeii*, p. 280, where all the best examples are listed. For example: *Apelles cubicularius cum Dextro Caesar(is) pranderunt hic iucundissime et futuere simul.*

100 A. and M. De Vos, *Laterza Pompeii*, p. 281.

101 Cf. A. O. Koloski-Ostrow *et al.*, "Water in the Roman town: new research from *Cura Aquarum* and the *Frontinus* Society," *JRA*, 1997, vol. 10, pp. 181–91.

102 In general see: R. J. A. Wilson, "*Tot aquarum tam multis necessariis molibus . . .* recent studies on aqueducts and water supply," *JRA*, 1996, vol. 9, pp. 5–29; G. Fabre, J.-L. Fiches and J.-L. Paillet (eds), *L'aqueduc di Nîmes et le Pont du Gard: archéologie, géosystème, historie*, Paris, Conseil général du Gard, 1991; *id.* and Ph. Leveau, *Le Pont du Gard. L'eau dans la ville antique*, Paris, Caisse nationale des monuments historiques et des sites: CNRS éditions, 1992; A. T. Hodge (ed.), *Future Currents in Aqueduct Studies*, Leeds, F. Cairns, 1991; and *id.*, *Roman Aqueducts and Water Supply*, London, 1992.

103 J. B. M. Wiggers, "The urban water supply of Pompeii," in de Haan and Jansen (eds), *Cura Aquarum*, pp. 29–32.

104 A. T. Hodge, "Anomalies in the flow at Pompeii Castellum," in de Haan and Jansen (eds), *Cura Aquarum in Campania*, pp. 13–18; *id.*, "*In Vitruvianum Pompeianum.*"

105 G. Garbrecht and E. Netzer, "Die Wasserversorgung des geschichtlichen Jericho und seiner königlichen Anlagen (Gut, Winterpaläste)," *Mitteilungen des Leichtweiß—Instituts für Wasserbau der Technischen Universität Braunschweig*, 1991, vol. 115, on Jericho; *id.* and H. Jaritz, "Untersuchung antiker Anlagen zur Wasserspeicherung in Fayum/Ägypten," *Mitteilungen aus dem Leichtweiß—Instituts für Wasserbau der Technischen Universität Braunschweig*, 1990, vol. 107; *id.* and H. Manderscheid, "'Etiam fonte novo antoniniano.' L'acquedotto antoniniano delle terme di Caracalla," *ArchCl*, 1992, vol. 44, pp. 93–234; *id.* and H. Manderscheid, 1994 "Die Wasserbewirtschaftung römischer Thermen," *Mitteilungen des Leichtweiß—Instituts für Wasserbau der Technischen Universität Braunschweig*, 1994, vols 118 A–C; *id.* and H. Manderscheid, 1995 "Die Wasserversorgung der Caracallathermen durch die Aqua Antoniniana," *AntW*, 1995, vol. 26, pp. 193–202 on water-supply in *thermae*.

106 H. Fahlbusch, "Elemente griechischer und römischer Wasserversorgungsanlagen," 1987, *Wasserversorgung* II, pp. 133–63.

107 R. Neudecker, *Die Pracht der Latrine*, Munich, 1994; P. Reimers, "'*Opus Omnium Dictu Maximum*' literary sources for the knowledge of Roman city drainage," *OpRom* XVII, 1989, vol. 10, pp. 137–41; *id.*, "Roman sewers and sewerage networks—neglected areas of study," *Munuscula Romana*, 1991, pp. 111–16; A. Scobie, "Slums, sanitation and mortality in the Roman world," *Klio*, 1986, vol. 68:2, pp. 399–433; Jansen, *Water in de Romeinse Stad.*

108 Koloski-Ostrow, "Finding social meaning in the public latrines of Pompeii;" Scobie, "Slums, sanitation, and mortality;" and A. O. Koloski-Ostrow, *The Archaeology of Sanitation in Roman Italy: water, sewers, and toilets*, Chapel Hill, NC, forthcoming.

109 Cf. R. Jackson, "Waters and spas in the classical world," in R. Porter, *The Medical History of Waters and Spas*, London, 1990, 1–13.

110 Dunbabin, "Baiarum Grata Voluptas."

111 DeLaine, "Recent research on Roman baths," pp. 11–32.
112 DeLaine, "Recent research on Roman baths," p. 11.
113 DeLaine, *The Baths of Caracalla*; Taylor, *Roman Builders*.

BIBLIOGRAPHY

Borrielli, M. and A. Ambrosio, *Forma Italiae. Regio I, Vol. XIV: Baiae-Misenum*, Florence, 1979.

Brödner, E., *Die römischen Thermen und das antike Badewesen*, Darmstadt, 1983.

Crova, B., "Le terme romane nella Campania," *VIII Convegno di Storia dell'Architettura*, 1953, pp. 271–88.

DeLaine, J., "Recent research on Roman baths," *JRA*, 1988, vol. 1, pp. 11–32.

——, "Some observations on the transition from Greek to Roman baths in Hellenistic Italy," *Mediterranean Archaeology*, 1989, vol. 2, pp. 111–25.

——, "Roman baths and bathing," *JRA*, 1993, vol. 6, pp. 348–58.

——, *The Baths of Caracalla: A Study in the Design, Construction and Economics of Large-Scale Public Buildings in Imperial Rome*, JRA Suppl. Ser. no. 25, 1997.

DeLaine, J. and Johnston, D. E. (eds), *Roman Baths and Bathing*, Proceedings of the first International Conference on Roman Baths held at Bath, England, 30 March–4 April, 1992, Pt. 1: *Bathing and Society*, Pt. 2: *Design and Context*, JRA Suppl. Ser. no. 37.1, 37.2, 1999 and 2000.

Delorme, J., *Gymnasion: Étude sur les monuments consacres a l'education en Grèce*, Paris, 1960.

De Vos, A. and M. De Vos, *Guide archeologiche Laterza: Pompei, Ercolano, Stabia*, Rome, 1982.

Dunbabin, K. A., "Baiarum Grata Voluptas: pleasures and dangers of the baths," *Papers of the British School in Rome*, 1989, vol. 57, pp. 6–49.

Eschebach, H., "Untersuchungen in den Stabianer Thermen zu Pompeji," *RM*, 1973, vol. 80, pp. 235–42.

——, *Die Stabianer Thermen in Pompeji*, Berlin, 1979.

Fagan, G. G., "Sergius Orata: inventor of the hypocaust?" *Phoenix*, 1996, vol. 50, pp. 56–66.

——, *Bathing in Public in the Roman World*, Ann Arbor, MI, 1999.

——, "The genesis of the Roman public bath: recent approaches and future directions," *AJA*, 2001, vol. 105, pp. 403–26.

Fahlbusch, H., "Elemente griechischer und römischer Wasserversorgungsanlagen," *Wasserversorgung*, 1987, vol. II, pp. 133–63.

Garbrecht, G. and H. Manderscheid, "Die Wasserbewirtschaftung römischer Thermen," *Mitteilungen des Leichtweiß-Instituts für Wasserbau der Technischen Universität Braunschweig*, 1994, vols 118 A–C.

Ginouvès, R., *Balaneutikè: recherches sur le bain dans l'antiquité grecque*, Paris, 1962.

Haan, N. de, "Privatbäder in Pompeji und Herkulaneum und die städtische Wasserversorgung," *Mitteilungen des Leichtweiß-Instituts für Wasserbau der Technischen Universität Braunschweig*, 1992, vol. 117, pp. 423–45.

——, "Die Wasserversorgung der Privatbäder in Pompeji," in de Haan and Jansen (eds), *Cura Aquarum*, pp. 59–65.

——, *Römische Privatbäder, Entwicklung, Verbreitung und sozialerStatus*, Ph.D. dissertation, Nijmegen, Katholieke Universiteit, forthcoming.

Haan, N. de and G. C. M. Jansen (eds), *Cura Aquarum in Campania: Proceedings of the 9th International Congress on the History of Water Management and Hydraulic Engineering in the Mediterranean Region* (Pompeii, 1–8 October 1994), *Bulletin Antieke Beschaving—Annual Papers on Classical Archaeology*, Supplement 4, Leiden, 1996.

Heinz, W., *Römische Thermen. Badewesen und Badeluxus im römischen Reich*, Munich, 1983.

Hodge, A. Trevor (ed.), *Future Currents in Aqueduct Studies*, Leeds, 1991.

——, *Roman Aqueducts and Water Supply*, London, 1992.

——, "Anomalies in the flow at the Pompeii *Castellum*," in de Haan and Jansen (eds), 1996, pp. 13–18.

——, "*In Vitruvianum Pompeianum*: urban water distribution reappraised," *AJA*, 1996, vol. 100, pp. 261–76.

Iorio, A., "Sistema di riscaldamento nelle antiche terme pompeiane," *Bullettino della Commissione archeologica comunale di Roma*, 1978–79, vol. 86, pp. 167–89.

Jacobelli, L., "Terme Suburbane: stato attuale delle conoscenze," *Rivista di studi pompeiani*, 1988, vol. 2, pp. 202–8.

——, *Le pitture erotiche delle terme suburbane di Pompei*, Rome, 1995.

Jansen, G. C. M., "Sewers and tapwater as urban innovations at Herculaneum," in *XIV Congreso Internacional de Arqueología Clásica Tarragona*, 1993, vol. 2, pp. 18–20.

——, *Water in de Romeinse stad. Pompeii, Herculaneum, Ostia*, Leuven, 2002.

Jashemski, W. F., *The Gardens of Pompeii, Herculaneum, and the Villas Destroyed by Vesuvius*, New Rochelle, NY, 1979.

Kaufmann, C. M., *The Baths of Pozzuoli, A Study of the Medieval Illuminations of Peter of Eboli's Poem*, Oxford, 1959.

Koloski-Ostrow, A. O., *The Sarno Bath Complex*, Rome, 1990.

——, "Finding social meaning in the public latrines of Pompeii," in de Haan and Jansen (eds), *Cura Aquarum*, pp. 79–86.

——, *The Archaeology of Sanitation in Roman Italy: Water, Sewers, and Toilets*, Chapel Hill, NC, forthcoming.

Koloski-Ostrow, A. O., N. de Haan, G. de Kleijn and S. Piras, "Water in the Roman town: new research from *Cura Aquarum* and the *Frontinus* Society," *JRA*, 1997, vol. 10, pp. 181–91.

Kretzschmer, F., "Hypocausten," *Saalburg-Jahrbuch*, 1953, vol. 12, pp. 7–41.

Künzl, E., "Operationsräume im römischen Thermen," *Bonner Jahrbücher des Rheinischen Landesmuseums in Bonn und des Vereins von Altertumsfreunden im Rheinlande*, 1986, vol. 186, pp. 491–509.

Maiuri, A., "Pompeii. Scoperta di un edificio termale nella Regio VIII, Insula 5, no. 36," *Notizie degli Scavi*, 1950, vol. 66, pp. 116–36.

——, *Pompeii*, Rome, 1965.

——, *Herculaneum*, Rome, 1970.

Manderscheid, H., "Römische Thermen. Aspekte von Architektur, Techniek und Ausstattung," *Wasserversorgung*, 1988, vol. III, pp. 99–125.

——, "Bemerkungen zur Wasserbewirtschaftung der suburbanen Thermen in Pompeji," *Archaeologisches Korrespondenzblatt*, 1993, vol. 23, pp. 337–46.

——, "Standard und Luxus in römischen Bädern. Überlegungen aus der Sicht der Hydrotechnik," in de Haan and Jansen (eds), *Cura Aquarum*, 1994, pp. 109–15.

——, *Ancient Baths and Bathing: A Bibliography for the Years 1988–2001*, JRA Suppl. Ser. no. 55, 2004.

Mau, A. and Kelsey, F., *Pompeii: its life and art*, New York, 1907.

Mygind, H., "Hygienische Verhältnisse im alten Pompeji," *Janus*, 1921, vol. 25, pp. 251–81, 324–85.

Nielsen, I., "Considerazioni sulle primi fasi dell'evoluzione dell'edificio termale romano," *AnalRom*, 1985, vol. 14, pp. 81–112.

——, *Thermae et balnea*, Aarhus, 1993.

Oleson, J. P., "Water-lifting devices at Herculaneum and Pompeii in the context of Roman technology," in de Haan and Jansen (eds), 1996, pp. 67–77.

——, and Humphrey, J. W., *Greek and Roman Technology: a sourcebook*, London, 1997.

Parslow, C., *The Praedia Iuliae Felicis in Pompeii*, Ph.D. Dissertation, Durham, NC, Duke University, 1989.

——, *Rediscovering Antiquity. Karl Weber and the excavation of Herculaneum, Pompeii, and Stabiae*, Cambridge, 1995.

Pasquinucci, M. (ed.), *Terme romane e vita quotidiana*, Mostra, Modena, 1987.

Reimers, P., "'*Opus Omnium Dictu Maximum*' literary sources for the knowledge of Roman city drainage," *Opuscula Romana*, 1989, vol. XVII: 10, pp. 137–41.

——, "Roman sewers and sewerage networks—neglected areas of study," *Munuscula Romana*, 1991, pp. 111–16.

Richardson, L., jr, *Pompeii: an architectural history*, Baltimore, MD, 1988.

Scobie, A., "Slums, sanitation, and mortality in the Roman world," *Klio*, 1986, vol. 68: 2, pp. 399–433.

Taylor, R., *Roman Builders: a study in architectural process*, Cambridge, 2003.

Turner, J. Hilton, "Sergius Orata, pioneer of radiant heating," *Classical Journal*, 1947/48, vol. 43, pp. 486–7.

Wiggers, J. B. M., "The urban water supply of Pompeii," in de Haan and Jansen (eds), 1996, pp. 29–32.

Wilson, R. J. A., *"Tot aquarum tam multis necessariis molibus . . .* Recent studies on aqueducts and water supply," *JRA*, 1996, vol. 9, pp. 5–29.

Yegül, F. K. *Baths and Bathing in Classical Antiquity*, Cambridge, MA, 1992.

CHAPTER SIXTEEN

THE WATER SYSTEM
Supply and drainage

——— •◆• ———

Gemma Jansen

At Pompeii and Herculaneum great care was given to the water supply, sanitation and drainage.[1] Various methods accomplished the task—some simple, others more sophisticated. Different methods of providing water existed side by side: groundwater was hauled up from wells, and in houses rainwater was collected and stored. In addition, a network of lead pipes brought water to the baths, street fountains and private consumers. Sanitary provisions were abundant; in addition to the several public toilets, many toilets were built in private homes and shops. And finally, drainage accommodated the different kinds of material that had to be removed: urine and feces disappeared into cesspits; rainwater was led out of town along the sloping streets; and waste water from the baths was carried away in sewers.

This kaleidoscope of large and small, public and private, provisions functioned well and resulted in a good working system of water supply and disposal. This chapter presents the three types of water supply, sanitation, and different methods of disposal.

WELLS

From an early period the inhabitants of Pompeii used wells. The geological substrata of the town consisted of alternating layers of porous volcanic material and hard lava banks. At a depth of 20 to 30 m was a 5 m-thick aquifer. Skill and perseverance were needed to reach this water as the porous walls of the well shaft collapsed easily. Furthermore, there was always the danger of deadly gas which even now can occur below a depth of 10 m. Due to these difficulties Pompeii had only a few wells. Some were in private houses; others were dug along the streets and served the general public.

In Herculaneum the groundwater could be found at a depth of only 8 to 10 m. Despite the fact that the substrata were formed out of hard tuff lava banks, many houses had their own private wells. Several windlasses with which water could be hauled up have been found in the houses.

In both towns a special kind of well was dug in establishments that needed a lot of water, such as the baths and *fullonicae*. Water was raised from the aquifer to a roof tank by a large water-lifting mechanism: a bucket-chain hung in the broad well shaft operated by a man walking a tread-wheel.[2] In the roof tank the water was stored and later distributed over the building by lead pipes. With help of these devices one could be ensured of an abundant supply of daily water.

RAINWATER CATCHMENT AND STORAGE

Besides drawing groundwater from wells, the inhabitants of Pompeii and Herculaneum collected rainwater on the roofs of their homes and led it into subterranean cisterns. Every house, or more accurately, every court was equipped with provisions for rainwater catchment. These were simple in design, but appropriate for collecting and storing rainwater and keeping it cool, clear and fresh.

In the *atrium*, rainwater was collected on the inward-sloping roof (Figures 8.19, 16.1) whose square opening, the *compluvium*, was decorated with waterspouts in form of dogs, bears or lions. These waterspouts directed the rainwater into a basin situated

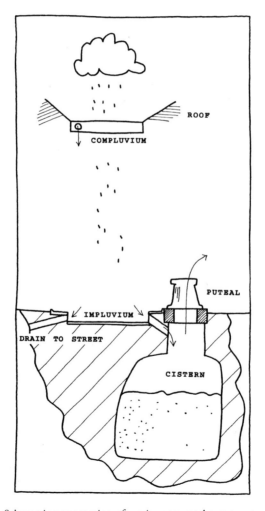

Figure 16.1   Schematic presentation of a rainwater catchment system in an *atrium*.

Figure 16.2 Settling box in peristyle gutter and perforated lead sheet in front of cistern entrance, both to prevent dirt from entering the cistern (Pompeii, I.9.11–12).

underneath, the *impluvium* (Figures 16.1, 21.4), which guaranteed that only clear water entered the cistern. As the *impluvium* had two drains, one to the street and one to the cistern, the water could be regulated by closing one of these drains. After long periods of drought the rainwater which fell into the *impluvium* was polluted with dust and dirt from the roofs. This rainwater was led directly to the streets by closing the drain to the cistern. When the water became clear, the drain to the street was closed and the water was allowed to enter the cistern.

Water from the cistern could be obtained from the cistern mouth, a stone slab with a hole in the middle for lowering buckets. The rims show signs of wear caused by ropes with which the buckets of water were hauled up. The cistern mouth was closed with a stone cover or decorative "well"-head, a so-called *puteal* (Figure 18.2). These protected the cistern water against sunlight and dirt. Moreover, in this way the cistern presented no danger to playing children or inattentive grown-ups.

In peristyles rainwater was collected on the portico roof. The water fell from these roofs in a stone gutter lying on the floor and it was from here conducted into the cistern. Because the water could not be manipulated here as in the *impluvium* one built in small settling boxes (Figure 16.2). A perforated lead sheet fixed in front of the cistern entrance prevented debris, such as twigs and leaves, from entering the cistern.

WATER PIPE SYSTEM

At a still unknown time in the history of Pompeii and Herculaneum, a long-distance pipeline and an intra-urban pressure system was introduced.[3] This provision went beyond the capabilities of the individual citizen. For carrying out such a large-scale project it was imperative that there should be an adequate organizational structure, not only with regard to planning and construction but also regarding maintenance, supervision and repairs. These tasks were taken on by the municipal government

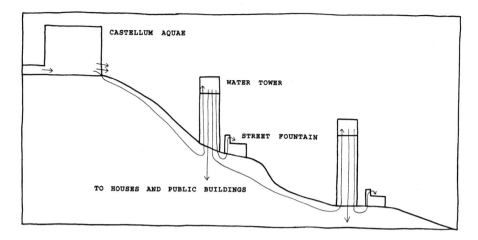

Figure 16.3 Schematic presentation of the elements of the municipal water pipe system of Pompeii.

(Table 33.1). The introduction of this system was revolutionary for the water supply, as water was delivered to people's homes at a certain pressure. Of this advantage the inhabitants of both towns made grateful use by installing many fountains in their houses (Figures 14.5, 23.16 and 31.4).

In Augustan times a large aqueduct ran through Campania (Map 1). One of the assumptions is that Pompeii and Herculaneum were fed by branches of this aqueduct. However, the connection has not yet been found and the only thing known is the 90 m-long pipeline which has been excavated just north of Pompeii.[4] This is a typical Roman long-distance supply channel: U-shaped with a vaulted ceiling and large enough for a (small) man to walk through. In the excavated section two inspection shafts are still intact.

The urban system started at the main distribution center where the water, brought to the city by this aqueduct, was discharged. This water distribution center, called a *castellum aquae*, was a small building in which the water flow was divided and distributed among three large lead pipes.[5] As the building was situated at the highest point of the town, water was easily conducted to the several districts through pressurized pipelines. Because of the steep slope of the hill on which the city was built and, consequently, the difference in elevation between different parts of the town, the pressure in the main pipes varied considerably. Especially in lower parts of the town, the pressure must have been unacceptably high, necessitating the construction of towers up to 6 m high as minor distribution centers at street crossings (Figures 16.3 and 16.4). To release pressure, the main pipe was led in a groove up the side of the tower to a small and open basin at the top. That the water sometimes overflowed this basin can be deduced from the heavy calcium incrustations on some of the towers. In this way the water was depressurized and the downstream head of pressure was reduced to the height of the tower above the final destination. From the top of the tower small consumer pipes descended. These were smaller than the mains and attached to the tower with lead strips and iron nails.

Through the pipes, which ran down from the towers and under the sidewalks, water was led to its destinations: the baths, some urban reservoirs, street fountains and private consumers. People with no adequate water supply of their own could turn to the street fountains, a common feature in Pompeii and according to Eschebach's map not further away from one's house than 50 m (Figure 16.4).[6] Most of the street fountains were equipped with a basin, so it was possible for more than one person at a time to draw water and at the same time to create a reserve.

A private water pipe entered the house near the front or side door and headed immediately for the *impluvium* in the *atrium*.[7] Here the pipe was connected to a lead box to which several other pipes were fitted (Figure 16.5). These pipes were connected to fountains in and around the *impluvium* and could be closed by stopcocks, set between the lead box and each of the pipes. The most striking feature is the fact that it was not possible to close off the entire system within the house with one master valve. It was only possible to close each fountain independently.

In domestic settings water was mainly used for fountains whose overflow was drained into cisterns. Pipes leading to private baths and toilets were more rare.

The advent of piped water from the aqueduct introduced certain changes. Wells and rainwater catchment became supplementary. Public wells were replaced by street fountains and baths were no longer supplied with groundwater, but were converted to the pipe system. Some wells in private houses remained functional and rainwater catchment systems remained in use with the small change that the surplus from the fountains was now also stored in the cisterns.

Figure 16.4   Water tower and street fountain at the intersection of the via Stabiana and the via dell'Abbondanza at Pompeii; view from the south.

Figure 16.5   Lead distribution box with four pipes and four stopcocks,
House of the Hanging Balcony, Pompeii (VII.12.28).

SANITATION

On several walls in Pompeii inscriptions, such as *cacator cave malu(m) aut contempseris habeas Iove iratum* and *cacator sic valeas ut tu hoc locum trasea(s)* can be read.[8] From these it can be concluded that some relieved themselves in the street, and also that others took offence at this habit. This did not mean that there were not enough toilets in the town. On the contrary, both towns had several large and small public toilets and nearly every household had its own private one (cf. Jones and Robinson, Ch. 25).[9] In all these toilets water was needed, both to rinse the sponges, the Roman equivalent of our toilet paper, and to flush the toilet. Households that were not connected to the water pipe system or apartments on upper floors had toilets built in niches in the wall (Figure 16.6). In this way one could sit right above the drainpipe which was let into the wall and not much water was required for flushing. More water was needed in flush toilets, which mostly occur in kitchen areas. To flush the toilet with a bucket of water a small plateau of tiles was built in front of the toilet seat which slanted slightly towards the drain underneath the seat (Figure 16.7).

The porous and permeable subsoil of Pompeii made it possible to connect toilets to well-functioning cesspits. A cesspit was a kind of leach field: liquid material seeped into the ground and solid material remained in the pit. This result was achieved by constructing the pit's walls in such a way that liquids could get out through the seams between the bricks. The cesspits were round or square and the upper part was built of bricks. They could be up to 11 m deep. The opening through which a cesspit had to be emptied was often situated in the sidewalk of a nearby street or in an adjoining garden. In this way the pit could be emptied without causing a mess in the house. It is possible that the contents of the pits were used as a fertilizer on the fields outside the city or gardens within.

Figure 16.6   Niche toilet on an upper floor with drainpipe in the wall, Pompeii (V.1.30).

Figure 16.7   Flush toilet with raised tile floor in kitchen, House of Apollo (VI.7.23), Pompeii.

DISPOSAL OF RAIN AND WASTE WATER

Rainwater, the overflow from the fountains, and waste water had to be removed. Because of the sloping streets of both Pompeii and Herculaneum the rainwater automatically flowed downwards and left through the city gates. Even now, after a shower of rain the streets of Pompeii change into fast-flowing brooklets. At such times the high sidewalks and stepping stones prove to be no superfluous luxury. The Pompeians did not just sit back and watch the water leave their city; they tried to manipulate it to prevent the flooding of some streets and to reduce the flow in others.[10] One method of manipulating the water was to construct a small elevation at the entrance to a side street, to prevent the rainwater from flowing into it. Another method was to raise the pavement slightly and thus force the water to change direction. In this way the water was manipulated without obstructing the traffic. Special measures were taken at the city gates. Since the gates were closed at night, the rainwater was led into a large drain beside the gate. This drain passed through the city's walls. Although it cannot be seen where the water went after it left the gates, it seems safe to assume that it was directed to the river Sarno or to the sea.

Because excreta were disposed of in cesspits and rainwater was carried away by the streets it seems that Pompeii did not need a sewer. But Pompeii had a sewer anyway. It was not a complete network but it consisted of different and separate branches, built to solve specific problems. One branch was specially designed to drain the forum. Other branches were connected to buildings where large amounts of water had to be disposed of, such as the baths and the Great Palaestra. The toilets of the baths and the *palaestra* were connected to the sewer as well.

As soon as branches of a sewer were laid out, they started to be used to get rid of other waste as well. In places where there was a lot of rainwater in the streets, a connection was made to the sewer to remove the excess. Toilets could then be connected to the sewer as well.

In contrast to Pompeii, Herculaneum had a rather systematic sewer system. Underneath all of the streets a sewer was installed. Inhabitants of Herculaneum were forced to do so, as cesspits did not work very well in the compact tuff substrata. Most of the toilets were, therefore, connected to this extensive sewer network.

NOTES

1 For a general introduction into the water supply systems of Pompeii see H. Eschebach, "Die Gebrauchswasserversorgung des antiken Pompeji," *Antike Welt*, 1979, vol. 10, pp. 3–24; and N. de Haan and G. C. M. Jansen (eds), *Cura Aquarum in Campania: proceedings of the Ninth International Congress on the History of Water Management and Hydraulic Engineering in the Mediterranean Region* (Pompeii, 1–8 October 1994), *Bulletin Antieke Beschaving–Annual Papers on Classical Archaeology*, 1996, Supplement 4. For an introduction into the systems of water supply, sanitation and wastewater disposal of Herculaneum see A. Maiuri, *Ercolano, I Nuovi Scavi 1927–1958*, Rome, 1958, pp. 51–3, 49–51, 467–9 and G. Jansen, "Water systems and sanitation in the houses of Herculaneum," *Mededelingen van het Nederlands Instituut te Rome*, 1991, vol. 50, pp. 145–66. See also Koloski-Ostrow, Ch. 15.

2 J. P. Oleson, *Greek and Roman Mechanical Waterlifting Technology*, Toronto, 1984, pp. 213–15, 241–8 and J. P. Oleson, "Waterlifting devices at Herculaneum and Pompeii in the context of Roman technology," in N. de Haan and G. Jansen (eds), *Cura Aquarum*, pp. 67–77.

3 For this discussion see Eschebach, "Die Gebrauchswasserversorgung des antiken Pompeji," p. 7; Chr. Ohlig, "DE AQUIS POMPEIANORUM, Das Castellum Aquae in Pompeji: Herkunft, Zuleitung und Verteilung des Wassers," diss. Nijmegen, 2001, pp. 49–83.

4 As the eastern and highest part of Herculaneum is not excavated yet, a substantial part of the water pipe system is still missing: the aqueduct remains hidden underneath modern Herculaneum together with the main distribution center.

5 For recent research into this main distribution center see Chr. Ohlig, "Vitruvs 'castellum aquae' und die Wasserverteilung in antiken Pompeji," *Sftenreihe der Fronchritinusgesellschaft*, 1995, vol. 19, pp. 124–47 and idem, "Anmerkungen zum Funktionsmodell des Castellum Aquae im antiken Pompeji," in N. de Haan and G. Jansen (eds), *Cura Aquarum*, pp. 19–27; idem, "DE AQUIS POMPEIANORUM." [For concerns about lead piping affecting the health of the population, cf. Lazer, Ch. 38. Calcium deposits from the hard water (see below) would have helped insulate the water from lead contamination.—Eds]

6 Eschebach, "Die Gebrauchswasserversorgung des antiken Pompeji," fig. 11.

7 G. Jansen, "Water pipe systems in the houses of Pompeii: distribution and use," in A. O. Koloski-Ostrow (ed.), *Water Use and Hydraulics in the Roman City*, AIA Colloquia and Conference *Papers*, no. 3, Boston, 2001, pp. 27–40.

8 Found on the outside of the house walls: (*CIL IV*, 7716) "Shitter beware: if you ignore (this warning), may you endure the wrath of Jove" in II.5 and (*CIL IV*, 6641) "Shitter: you can hold it long enough to pass this place" in V.6. Trans. P. Foss.

9 A. O. Koloski-Ostrow, "Finding social meaning in the public latrines of Pompeii," in N. de Haan and G. Jansen (eds), *Cura Aquarum*, pp. 79–86 for public toilets, and G. Jansen, "Private toilets at Pompeii: appearance and operation," in S. E. Bon and R. Jones (eds), *Sequence and Space in Pompeii*, Oxford, 1997, pp. 121–34 for private ones.

10 M. Koga, "The surface drainage system of Pompeii," in *Opuscula Pompeiana*, 1992, vol. II, pp. 57–72; G. Jansen, "Systems for the disposal of waste and excreta in Roman cities. The situation at Pompeii, Herculaneum and Ostia," in X. Dupré Raventos and J.-A. Remolà (eds), *Sordes Urbis, La eliminación de residuos en la ciudad romana*, Rome, 2000, pp. 37–49.

BIBLIOGRAPHY

Eschebach, H., "Die Gebrauchswasserversorgung des antiken Pompeji," *Antike Welt*, 1979, vol. 10, pp. 3–24.

Haan, N. de and G. Jansen (eds), *Cura Aquarum in Campania, Proceedings of the Ninth International Congress on the History of Water Management and Hydraulic Engineering in the Mediterranean Region* (Pompeii, 1–8 October 1994). *Bulletin Antieke Beschaving—Annual Papers on Classical Archaeology* 1996, Supplement 4.

Jansen, G., "Water systems and sanitation in the houses of Herculaneum," *Mededelingen van het Nederlands Instituut te Rome*, 1991, vol. 50, pp. 145–66.

——, "Private toilets at Pompeii: appearance and operation," in S. E. Bon and R. Jones (eds), *Sequence and Space in Pompeii*, Oxford, 1997, pp. 121–34.

——, "Water pipe systems in the houses of Pompeii: distribution and use," in A. O. Koloski-Ostrow (ed.), *Water Use and Hydraulics in the Roman City*, AIA Colloquia and Conference Papers, no. 3, Boston, MA, 2001, pp. 27–40.

——, "Systems for the disposal of waste and excreta in Roman cities. The situation at Pompeii, Herculaneum and Ostia," in X. Dupré Raventos and J.-A. Remolà (eds), *Sordes Urbis, La eliminación de residuos en la ciudad romana*, Rome, 2000, pp. 37–49.

Koga, M., "The surface drainage system of Pompeii," in *Opuscula Pompeiana*, 1992, vol. II, pp. 57–72.

Koloski-Ostrow, A. O., "Finding social meaning in the public latrines of Pompeii," in de Haan and Jansen (eds), *Cura Aquarum*, pp. 79–86.

Maiuri, A., *Ercolano, I Nuovi Scavi 1927–1958*, Rome, 1958.

Ohlig, Chr., "Vitruvs 'castellum aquae' und die Wasserverteilung in antiken Pompeji," *Sftenreihe der Fronchritinusgesellschaft*, 1995, vol. 19, pp. 124–47.

——, "Anmerkungen zum Funktionsmodell des Castellum Aquae im antiken Pompeji," in de Haan and Jansen (eds), *Cura Aquarum*, pp. 19–27.

——, "DE AQUIS POMPEIANORUM, Das Castellum Aquae in Pompeji: Herkunft, Zuleitung und Verteilung des Wassers," diss. Nijmegen, 2001.

Oleson, J. P., *Greek and Roman Mechanical Waterlifting Technology*, Toronto, 1984.

——, "Waterlifting devices at Herculaneum and Pompeii in the context of Roman technology," in de Haan and Jansen (eds), *Cura Aquarum*, pp. 67–77.

PART III

HOUSING

—◆—

CHAPTER SEVENTEEN

DOMESTIC SPACES AND ACTIVITIES

———— •◆• ————

Penelope M. Allison

THE "*ATRIUM*-HOUSE" TYPE

The vast majority of houses in Pompeii and Herculaneum take the form of rooms around inner courtyards, many, especially in Pompeii, conforming in plan to what has become known as the "*atrium* house." Nineteenth- and early twentieth-century excavators of these towns concentrated their interest on such houses, because they saw in them the materialization of textual references to Roman houses, particularly those in the architectural manuals of Vitruvius on how to build an ideal town house.[1] On the basis of Vitruvius' recommendations these scholars also labeled the constituent parts of this "*atrium* house" according to his specifications for the locations, proportions and aspects of particular room types (Figure 17.1). Other texts, such as Varro's study of the origins of Latin words, have likewise been "ransacked for labels" (cf. Wallace-Hadrill, Ch. 18).[2]

The so-called "*atrium* houses" in Pompeii and Herculaneum generally comprise a core group of rooms around the nucleus of a front hall, often with an opening in the center of the roof through which rainwater collected in a catchment pool beneath (Figures 18.1, 18.2, 27.1 and 27.2). Vitruvius refers to front halls in Roman town houses as *cava aedium* and *atria*. Varro describes how the inner courtyard of a house came to be called a *cavum aedium* and how the word *atrium* had been taken from the Etruscans. Modern scholars have generally adopted the latter term for the extant front halls of Roman town houses.

Small closed rooms and some open-fronted rooms are located on one or both sides of these front halls in Campanian houses. Vitruvius' stipulation that proportions for the *alae* should be related to the *atrium* has been used to provide this label for the open rooms. Varro describes how the rooms around the *cava aedium* had acquired their names from their original purposes: *cellae* for concealing; *penariae* where food is kept; *cubicula* for lying or resting; *cenacula* for dining. He also indicated that these terms had not remained static.

The front hall of an "*atrium* house" was usually entered from the street through a narrow corridor at the center of one end. Opposite this entrance a relatively large open-fronted room was frequently located, open on its opposite side onto a colonnaded

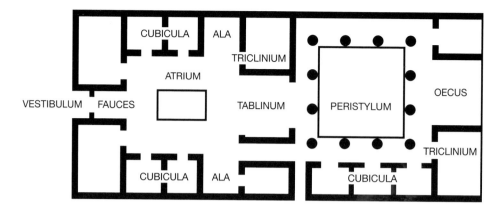

Figure 17.1 Hypothetical house plan labeled with Vitruvian terminology (modeled after Mau, *Pompeii*, figure 115).

garden. Following Vitruvius' specifications that the width of the *fauces* be proportional to the *tablinum*, scholars apply the former label to the entranceway, and the latter to the room opening towards the garden. Rooms at the corners of the front hall were often relatively large and oblong in shape. In houses that had gardens, these corner rooms might also open, with a wider opening, onto the garden. Scholars label them *triclinia*, following Vitruvius' recommendation that the length of a *triclinium* must be twice its width. The application of this label to these rooms in Pompeian houses has been used to identify them as dining rooms.[3]

The term "peristyle" has been used to label the colonnaded gardens of Pompeian houses although these invariably followed the same axis as the front hall and so-called *tablinum*, whereas Vitruvius prescribed that the *peristylum* should lie crossways to the *tablinum*. Around these colonnaded gardens are located rooms of varied sizes, shapes and degrees of openness, depending on the size of the house. Smaller closed rooms have been labelled *cubicula*. Some larger oblong rooms have been called *triclinia*, while more open large rooms have been labeled *exedrae* or *oeci*, because Vitruvius indicates that these were often squarer and more spacious than *triclinia*. Smaller open rooms are also often referred to as *exedrae*. Further rooms are sometimes found down internal corridors leading either from the front hall or colonnaded garden.

There is little doubt that there was some correspondence between the spatial arrangements of many Campanian houses and literary sources such as Vitruvius' architectural manual, written probably during the reign of Augustus; Varro's dictionary, written in the first century BC; and Pliny the Younger's post-AD 79 letters describing his country villas.[4] It is, indeed, possible that terms used by such authors were those used by Pompeians to label various parts of their houses. However, it is by no means certain what they would have called each actual room. Eleanor Leach has investigated the use in ancient written sources of many labels currently applied to Pompeian houses and found a lack of correspondence.[5] More importantly, it is by no means certain that, even if Pompeians used such labels, we can identify activities that took place in so-labeled rooms at Pompeii through activities associated with labels in textual sources.[6] It is probable that labels and their uses changed over time, as Varro states. While the basic structure of spaces in Campanian houses may have remained relatively unchanged for several centuries, their labels and, more probably their functions, might not have (cf. Wallace-Hadrill, Ch. 18).

The application of textual nomenclature to spaces in excavated houses is more a convenient categorization system for modern scholars than a reliable guide to the activities that took place therein.[7] In order to identify activities, our best surviving evidence is for those that took place in AD 79. The combination of structural remains, decorative remains, fixtures and finds' assemblages provide the most reliable evidence for how these houses and their various spaces would have been used immediately prior to the eruption.

However, contrary to popular belief, the archaeological record at Pompeii does not represent a town "frozen in time," with assemblages documenting habitual domestic life.[8] Not only would much household material have been moved during the final eruption, but excavated remains have indicated that some houses were undergoing change, possibly due to seismic activity in the years before the final eruption (cf. Sigurdsson, Ch. 4).[9] Therefore, an analysis of the finds' assemblages in an individual house is not necessarily an appropriate method for establishing patterns of room use under normal conditions. However, investigation of the most prolific patterns of artefact distribution across a large sample, particularly of less mobile contents such as furniture, in relation to each room type and its decoration, can provide an understanding of how the various parts of Pompeian houses might have functioned (Table 17.1).[10]

The front hall area

Through my investigation of thirty Pompeian "*atrium* houses," it has become evident that front halls sometimes had display furniture, such as statuary, marble tables, basins and religious shrines, which suggests that they were reception areas for guests, furnished to impress visitors. However, these halls were frequently furnished with cupboards and chests (Figure 17.2), containing a full range of domestic utensils, and storage vessels such as *amphorae*. The front hall must have served both as a reception area and as the main circulation area for all members of the households—men, women, children and slaves—where daily necessities were stored and where domestic industries (e.g., spinning and weaving) and the procurement of household commodities took place.

The use of the front part of the house for a wide range of household activities is borne out in many of the small undecorated rooms around the front hall that often had shelving and evidence of domestic, utilitarian and bulk storage, and must have served as storerooms. Varro's terms for storerooms, *cellae* or *penariae*, might seem more appropriate for these spaces, rather than the commonly used term *cubicula*.[11] It is also often assumed that rooms labeled *cubicula* were bedrooms.[12] Small decorated rooms, also labeled *cubicula* tended to have different assemblages from the undecorated ones. A limited number had evidence of bedding but more often they contained small quantities of personal material (e.g., caskets, small vessels, items related to dress, toilet and lighting). Low recesses in the walls (of both decorated and undecorated rooms) have previously been interpreted as recesses for the ends of beds. However, the spatial distribution of these recesses throughout Pompeian houses, and the assemblages with which they were often associated, indicate that they probably had

Table 17.1 Summary of activities represented in distribution patterns of household assemblages across room types. Conventional Latin terms shown in brackets to assist in identification of these types

Room types	Display	Religious	Domestic storage	Food preparation	Food serving/consumption	Lighting	Sleeping	Personal	Water access	Household industries	Bulk storage
Front hall area											
Front Halls (*atria*)	•	•	•						•	•	•
Small closed side rooms (undec) (*cubicula*)		•	•							•	•
Small closed side rooms (dec) (*cubicula*)			•						•	•	
Small open side rooms (*alae*)			•				•?	•			
Long corner rooms (*triclinia*)			•			•					
Open space at end of front hall (*tablina*)			•		•	•	•?				
Main garden area											
Garden and ambulatories (*peristyla*)	•	•	•	•	•				•	•	•
Small closed rooms (undec) (*cubicula*)		•	•	•						•	•
Small closed rooms (dec) (*cubicula*)			•	•					•	•	
Small open side rooms (*exedrae*)			•					•			
Long corner rooms (*triclinia*)			•	•	•		•?	•			
Large open rooms (*oeci/exedrae*)			•	•	•	•					
Other areas on ground floor											
Kitchen (*culina*)		•		•	•				•	•	
Other room types away from main axis			•	•				•	•	•	•
Upper storeys	•		•		•					•	•

Figure 17.2 Cupboard in front hall of the House of the Ceii (I.6.15).

a variety of functions.[13] Such rooms were unlikely to have been individual sleeping rooms. In fact, the concept of numerous individual spaces set aside for sleeping is a relatively recent phenomenon and belongs with "Separate Spheres" ideologies of the nineteenth century.[14] We might, rather, consider that Pompeians slept wherever convenient, according to status, interpersonal relationships and the season. Overbeck suggested, more than 150 years ago, that these small closed rooms in Pompeian houses were unlikely to all have had the same uses and names.[15] Evidence of private activities suggests that analogy with a "boudoir" rather than with a bedroom (in the modern sense) might be appropriate.[16]

The assemblage patterns in so-called *alae* suggest that activities of the front hall continued into these open spaces. The open spaces between the front hall and the garden areas, the so-called *tablina*, also appear to have the kind of domestic storage (in wooden cupboards) witnessed in front halls. Contents of so-called *triclinia* suggest that they had no specific function at the time of the eruption, although the argument (based on literary sources) that these rooms were winter dining rooms might be used to explain the lack of definitive evidence for their function in August, the time of the eruption.[17]

In summary, there is ample evidence that both household members and outsiders—those who needed to be impressed, and those more involved in domestic, industrial or commercial activities—used the front areas of Pompeian "*atrium* houses." Notably lacking is evidence for food preparation and eating in this part of the house.

The main garden area

The colonnaded garden areas of Pompeian "*atrium* houses," often called *peristyla* (Figures 23.18 and 23.20), had formal entertainment fixtures (e.g., pools and fountains, statue bases, wooden or masonry dining couches), as well as other luxury furniture and statuary, all suggesting that this area was meant to be entered by, and to impress, visitors. However, many of the assemblages, particularly in the ambulatories, also bore witness to more utilitarian activities, including bulk and domestic storage. The location of braziers in the ambulatories, even in some of the larger houses, indicates that cooking was likely to have been carried out in these colonnaded garden areas and, indeed, that cooking on braziers was not confined to poorer households.[18] The frequent occurrence of cistern mouths and puteals (covers over cistern mouths or well-heads) in open gardens and ambulatories demonstrates that residents accessed domestic water storage here for various household activities, probably on a daily basis. Jashemski has also shown that these colonnaded gardens were not merely formal entertainment areas but were often planted with large fruit-bearing trees, providing produce for the household and possibly external distribution (cf. Jashemski, Ch. 31).[19]

The number and uses of small closed rooms around the garden (also labeled *cubicula*) undoubtedly varied according to house size and status. However, the predominant pattern is that undecorated rooms were storage areas for a variety of material, including utilitarian and bulk storage. Decorated rooms were similarly used, although they had less evidence for permanent shelving and less utilitarian material. Their contents included items for toilet, particularly personal ablution, with a marked lack of evidence for sleeping. The contents in both decorated and undecorated rooms also included material for less specialized and more communal activities (e.g., for dining and food preparation), than that in comparable small rooms around the front hall. The small open rooms around colonnaded gardens generally lacked contents, implying that they were probably relatively empty. When contents were recorded, they appeared to mimic those found in the garden ambulatories (e.g., braziers and chests) or in the surrounding small closed rooms (e.g., personal care items).

The long, narrow, closed rooms off the garden, so-called *triclinia*, were generally empty, but sometimes food-preparation fixtures and chests and cupboards with domestic utensils (frequently related to food preparation) were found there. A greater amount of contents was reported in the large open rooms, the so-called *oeci* or *exedrae*. Domestic storage was likewise common here, as were beds, couches and tables (Figure 20.8 for couch recess). While food-preparation equipment was frequently recorded in the narrower rooms, serving equipment or tableware was not. The pattern was the reverse in more open rooms, suggesting they were more likely to be used for dining and entertainment than the closed ones.

Colonnaded gardens seem to have been the most ostentatious spaces, particularly in larger homes. They were undoubtedly places for display and entertainment,[20] particularly dining.[21] But even in houses with a wealth of display items in the garden and spacious, richly decorated banqueting rooms, utilitarian domestic activities were not excluded. There were latrines in the area, and domestic storage, weaving and other household activities took place here, either in the ambulatories of the gardens or even the dining rooms themselves. Bulk storage was found side-by-side with banqueting halls. Food preparation and cooking were possibly carried out in front of diners. Colonnaded gardens of Pompeian houses cannot be considered sparsely furnished, formal courts. Such perspectives stem from the study of the architectural remains of Roman houses stripped of their contents, and from analogies with eighteenth-century French and Italian villas and English country houses. Rather,

Figure 17.3 Kitchen in the House of the Vettii (VI.15.1); after Sogliano, *Monumenti antichi*, 1898, vol. 8, fig. 13. The pot on the tripod on the bench was not found in this location.

these garden areas were probably buzzing with daily household activities, and during the evening meal diners must have looked out on cupboards and *amphorae* as well as statuary and pergolas.

Other areas

Almost all *"atrium* houses" possessed a room with a fixed hearth. Such rooms have been identified as kitchens; they often contained cooking and food-preparation utensils (Figure 17.3). They could be located anywhere in the plan of the house but were mainly near the garden or off the front hall/garden axis. Their frequent location near rooms identified for dining suggests that little need was seen to separate cooking from dining. The presence of braziers in garden areas supports this impression and also indicates that not all cooking was carried out in so-designated kitchens.

In the larger houses, many other rooms were located away from the front hall/garden axis, but the combination of their locations and fixtures indicate that they were not a coherent group. Some were located off the front hall, some off the garden area or secondary entranceways, and others in lower ground-floor areas. With the exception of some larger rooms on lower ground floors (e.g., in *insula* VIII.2) that seem to have been used for entertainment, most contents indicate that such rooms were used for utilitarian activities (e.g., heating water, baking bread, storage and animal quarters). It is traditionally assumed that they were service areas or servants' quarters.[22] There is certainly less evidence of decorated rooms in these areas than in the front hall/garden axis. However, evidence of shelving and utilitarian contents indicates that storage and service activities took place in the main part of the house. There seems little reason to assume that slaves had their own quarters (cf. George, Ch. 35).[23] These observations, and the frequent reports of luxury and personal items in these areas, away from the main axes of the house, should make us question assumptions about Pompeian houses being strictly divided into service and non-service areas. It is important to remember that spatial separation of domestic, industrial and commercial activities is largely a modern concept.

Upper storeys

While poor recording, post-eruption disturbance, and lack of structural remains render it more difficult to identify the activities in upper-storey rooms than in ground-floor rooms, the general pattern suggests that upper-floor rooms had a similar range of contents as those on the ground floor, with perhaps less evidence for industrial activities and (at the other end of the scale) less entertainment or display. They indicate that the occupants used these spaces for basic domestic activities such as sleeping, eating and possibly small unpretentious gatherings. This suggests that living quarters separate from the main household might have been prominent on the upper floor, even if a separate entranceway was not evident.[24] Occupants of such accommodation may have carried out industrial or commercial activities elsewhere and have had little need of ostentatious furnishings. Other upper-floor areas showed little evidence of habitation and seem to have been used for bulk storage.

The foregoing discussion has concentrated on the assemblages in "*atrium*," or more specifically "*atrium*-peristyle houses" in Pompeii for the patterns they produce of normal domestic life in the latter half of the first century AD. Given these patterns' lack of precise concordance with the separation of household activities which have been hypothesized through combining architectural evidence with textual analogy, we should be wary of trying to interpret the use of space in Herculanean or Pompeian houses at earlier periods, with less legible assemblages, without a rigorous examination of relationships between Roman texts and these material remains, of changing attitudes to domestic space as witnessed in the ancient authors, and of patterns of change in the development of Campanian houses (cf. Wallace-Hadrill, Ch. 18).[25]

OTHER HOUSE TYPES

"*Atrium* houses" included the largest houses in Pompeii, although some houses of this type were quite small. But not all houses in Pompeii and Herculaneum conformed to this plan. There were many variations: small front halls or courtyards with few or no side rooms (e.g., Figures 23.3 and 24.2); small courtyards, roofed or unroofed, with a limited number of surrounding rooms and large non-colonnaded rear gardens, seemingly used for agricultural purposes.[26] Nomenclature applied to the spaces of so-called *atrium* houses (e.g., *fauces, cubicula, alae, triclinia, tablina, oeci, viridaria*) has also been applied to spaces in these types of houses. While these might provide convenient labels for modern scholars discussing architectural components, not only are they often far removed from Vitruvius' architectural specifications, but such labels should not be used as indications of the activities carried out in the rooms of such houses. Without detailed analyses of contents across a sample of houses, as outlined above, it is difficult to ascribe specific activities to spaces in these types of houses. It is more likely that spaces in such smaller houses had more limited spatial separation of activities.

Not all dwellings in Pompeii can be considered "houses." There is ample evidence that parts of many larger establishments were separated off, particularly rooms above or behind street frontages. These probably constituted shops and workshops with attached accommodation, perhaps rented out by the owners of the larger establishments (cf. Pirson, Ch. 29; Nappo, Ch. 23).[27] Such apartments usually consisted of only one or two living spaces. While the upper rooms often indicate a range of domestic activities, the fixtures and contents of lower rooms on the street indicate that commercial or industrial, as well as domestic, activities were carried out in these areas (e.g., I.10.5–6).[28]

Once we are better informed about the total archaeological record at Pompeii for all types of houses, we might better be able to discuss its relationships with textual sources on the spatial distribution of activities in Roman houses, and relationships between domestic life at Pompeii and other parts of the Roman world (and in other periods).

NOTES

1 Vitr., *De arch.* 6, esp. 6.3.

2 Varro, *Ling.* 5.161–2; A. Wallace-Hadrill, *Houses and Society in Pompeii and Herculaneum*, Princeton, NJ, 1994, p. 6.

3 E.g., L. Richardson, jr, "A contribution to the study of Pompeian dining-rooms," *Pompeii Herculaneum Stabiae*, 1983, vol. 1, pp. 63–4.

4 Pliny, *Ep.* 2.17, 5.6.

5 E. W. Leach, "Oecus on Ibycus: investigating the vocabulary of the Roman house," in S. E. Bon and R. Jones (eds), *Sequence and Space in Pompeii*, Oxbow monograph 77, Oxford, 1997, pp. 50–72. See now E. W. Leach, *The Social Life of Painting in Ancient Rome and the Bay of Naples*, Cambridge, 2004.

6 See L. Nevett, "Perceptions of domestic space in Roman Italy," in B. Rawson and P. Weaver (eds), *The Roman Family in Italy*, Oxford, 1997, pp. 290–1.

7 P. M. Allison, "How do we identify the use of space in Roman housing?" in E. M. Moormann (ed.), *Functional and Spatial Analysis of Wall Painting. Proceedings of the Fifth International Congress on Ancient Wall Painting*, BABesch Suppl. no. 3, Leiden, 1993, pp. 1–8; P. M. Allison, "Room use in Pompeian houses," in J.-P. Descœudres *et al.*, *Pompeii Revisited: the life and death of a Roman town*, Sydney, 1994, p. 89; P. M. Allison, "Using the material and the written sources: turn of the millennium approaches to Roman domestic space," *AJA*, 2001, vol. 105: pp. 181–208; P. M. Allison, *Pompeian Households: an analysis of the material culture*, Los Angeles, CA, 2004, pp. 43–177; Nevett, "Perceptions," p. 283.

8 P. M. Allison, "Artefact assemblages: not the Pompeii premise," in E. Herring, R. Whitehouse and J. Wilkins (eds), *Papers of the Fourth Conference of Italian Archaeology, London 1990*, London 1992, vol. 3 pt. I, pp. 49–56.

9 See Pliny, *Ep.* 6.20; T. Fröhlich and L. Jacobelli (eds), *Archäologie und Seismologie: la regione vesuviana dal 62 al 79 d.C. Problemi archeologici e sismologici*, Munich, 1995.

10 P. M. Allison, *The Distribution of Pompeian House Contents and its Significance*, Ph.D. thesis, University of Sydney 1992, Ann Arbor, MI, 1994; P. M. Allison, "Artefact distribution and spatial function in Pompeian houses," in Rawson and Weaver. *Roman Family*, pp. 321–54;

Allison, *Pompeian Households*; for the data behind that publication, see: P. M. Allison, "Pompeian households: an on-line companion," in R. Scaife (ed.), *The Stoa: a consortium for on-line publication in the humanities*, http://www.stoa.org/projects/ph/home/.

11 A. Mau, *Pompeii: its life and art* (transl. and ed. by F. W. Kelsey), London, 1899, fig. 110; J.-P. Descœudres, "Rome and Roman art," in A. Cremin (ed.), *The Enduring Past: archaeology of the ancient world for Australians*, Sydney, 1987, figs. 10.12–13.

12 E.g., M. Grant, *Cities of Vesuvius: Pompeii and Herculaneum*, London, 1971, figs. 6–11; A. G. McKay, *Houses, Villas and Palaces in the Roman World*, Southampton, 1977, figs 8, 9 and 11; Wallace-Hadrill, *Houses and Society*, p. 57. Cf. A. M. Riggsby, "'Public' and 'private' in Roman culture: the case of the *cubiculum*," *JRA*, 1997, vol. 10, pp. 36–56.

13 P. M. Allison, "House contents in Pompeii: data collection and interpretative procedures for a reappraisal of Roman domestic life and site formation processes," *Journal of European Archaeology*, 1995, vol. 3.1, pp. 163–7; Allison, *Pompeian Households*, pp. 43–8.

14 See A. Vickery, "Golden Age to Separate Spheres? A review of the categories and chronology of English women's history," *Historical Journal*, 1993, vol. 36, pp. 383–414.

15 J. Overbeck, *Pompeji in Seinen Gebäuden, Alterthümern und Kunstwerken für Kunst- und Alterthumsfreunde*, Leipzig, 1856, p. 192.

16 For example, the assemblages in these types of rooms included bronze vessels, needlework items and lamps, which imply that these were private spaces where one might meet with intimates.

17 Richardson, "Dining-rooms," pp. 63–4.

18 Cf. E. Salza Prina Ricotti, "Cucine e quartieri servili in epoca romana," *RendPontAcc*, 1978–80, vol. 51–2: pp. 240, 278.

19 W. F. Jashemski, *The Gardens of Pompeii, Herculaneum and the Villas Destroyed by Vesuvius*, New Rochelle, NY, 1979, vol. 1, p. 604.

20 E. Dwyer, *Pompeian Domestic Sculpture: a study of five Pompeian houses and their contents*, Rome, 1982, pp. 116–19, 123–8; S. De Caro, "The sculptures of the Villa of Poppaea at Oplontis: a preliminary report," in E. B. MacDougall (ed.), *Ancient Roman Villa Gardens*, Washington, DC, 1987, pp. 77–133; R. Neudecker, *Die Skulpturen-Austattung römischer Villen in Italien*, Mainz, 1988.

21 P. Soprano, "I triclini all'aperto di Pompei," *Pompeiana. Raccolta di studi per il secondo centenario degli scavi di Pompei*, Naples, 1950, pp. 288–310; L. Richardson, jr, "Water triclinia and biclinia in Pompeii," in R. Curtis (ed.), *Studia pompeiana & classica in honour of Wilhelmina F. Jashemski*, New York, 1988, pp. 305–12; K. Dunbabin, "Triclinium and stibadium," in W. J. Slater (ed.), *Dining in a Classical Context*, Ann Arbor, MI, 1991, pp. 121–48.

22 E.g., A. Maiuri, *La Casa del Menandro e il suo tesoro di argenteria*, Rome, 1933, pp. 186–224.

23 See M. George, "*Servus* and *domus*: the slave in the Roman house," in R. Laurence and A. Wallace-Hadrill (eds), *Domestic Space in the Roman world: Pompeii and beyond*, JRA Suppl. Ser. no. 22, 1997, pp. 15–24.

24 Cf. F. Pirson, "Rented accommodation at Pompeii: the *Insula Arriana Polliana*," in Laurence and Wallace-Hadrill, *Domestic Space*, pp. 175–8.

25 E.g., A. Wallace-Hadrill, "Rethinking the Roman atrium house," in Laurence and Wallace-Hadrill, *Domestic Space*, pp. 219–40.

26 See esp. J. E. Packer, "Middle and lower class housing in Pompeii and Herculaneum: a preliminary report," in B. Andreae and H. Kyrieleis (eds), *Neue Forschungen in Pompeji*, Recklinghausen, 1977, pp. 133–42; S. Nappo, "The urban transformation at Pompeii in the late third and early second centuries BC," in Laurence and Wallace-Hadrill, *Domestic Space*, pp. 91–120.

27 See esp. Pirson, "Rented accommodation," pp. 165–81.

28 R. Ling, *The Insula of the Menander at Pompeii 1: the structures*, Oxford, 1997, pp. 145–8; P. M. Allison, *The Insula of the Menander at Pompeii 3: the finds, a contextual study*, Oxford, 2006, pp. 154–7, 335–6.

CHAPTER EIGHTEEN

THE DEVELOPMENT OF THE CAMPANIAN HOUSE

———.◆.———

Andrew Wallace-Hadrill

THE HISTORY OF THE QUESTION

When, a century ago, Mau wrote about the Pompeian house, he could state with confidence that "the development of the Italic house can be traced at Pompeii over a period of almost four hundred years".[1] That confidence, characteristic of the advances of systematic nineteenth-century science, would have been impossible a hundred years previously; and new advances today make it inappropriate to continue repeating the time-honoured schema of the evolution of "the Italic house". At the start of the twenty-first century, we must register that we know rather less about such an evolution than was supposed, though the evidence is gradually accumulating that will help us pose the questions better.

Until the early part of the nineteenth century, descriptions of "the Roman house" rested on collections by antiquarians and philologists of passages from literary sources, with pride of place given to Vitruvius' detailed account in book 6 of the *De architectura*. It is revealing that Wilhelm Becker, the father of *Handbücher* on Roman antiquities, in the first (1838) edition of his *Gallus*, which attached systematic documentation on Roman domestic life to a fictional narrative, explicitly denied any link between the Pompeian house and that described by Vitruvius, and persisted in ignoring the archaeological evidence.[2] Yet, the opposite viewpoint had been argued by François Mazois in his own account of a fictional visit to a typical Roman aristocratic house, *Le palais de Scaurus* (1819), and then in his monumental publication of *Les ruines de Pompéi, deuxieme partie, les abitations* (1824).[3] Mazois sought to show not only that there was close fit between the Pompeian evidence and Vitruvius (and other literary descriptions of elite Roman houses), but also that the fragments of the marble plan of Severan Rome confirmed the same typology in the metropolis.

Mazois' point of view prevailed, and in later editions of Becker, in the handbook by Marquardt that replaced him, and in later handbooks of which Mau himself was the author, the convergence between the parts of the house described by Vitruvius and the analysis of the "typical" Pompeian house became canonical.[4] Nor is there anything inherently unreasonable in the assumption that what Vitruvius described might be found not just at Rome, but even in provincial Pompeii. Vitruvius, though making explicit reference to Roman magistrates and linking architectural forms to the exigencies of Roman public life (6.5.2), nowhere suggests he is describing a limited metropolitan phenomenon. On the contrary, he writes of "our" usage in contrast to that of the Greeks (6.6.7), and when he labels it, he does so as *italico more* ("Italic custom") not as "Roman" (6.7.7). In the *tota Italia* of Augustus, a "national" cultural common tongue was ideologically desirable. Moreover, a substantial presence of the Roman ruling class on the Bay of Naples since the beginning of the second century BC was likely to have led to close contact between Roman and local Campanian practices, and it would be strange indeed if there were not multiple points of contact between literary texts of the late republic and early empire, and Campanian architecture of precisely the same period.

But if it is possible to speak in a general way of the "Italic" house by Vitruvius' day, we are on dangerous ground in projecting such a unity into a remote past. The evolution allegedly visible at Pompeii helped build a history of domestic form in Italy, but the evidential basis for this supposed evolution can no longer be regarded as sound. The method of analysis developed in the 1870s by Giuseppe Fiorelli depended on observable contrasts in construction techniques and materials of houses still standing in AD 79 (cf. Adam, Ch. 8). Among the houses excavated to that date, i.e., those in the western part of the city, he distinguished two characteristic groups that he took to be chronologically prior. The first were those with *atria* constructed of local calcareous stone from the bed of the Sarno, customarily referred to as "limestone" (*calcare, Kalkstein*), though it is more strictly a travertine, complete with fossilised leaves and reeds. This stone was occasionally put together in large ashlar fitted blocks (*opus quadratum*, in Vitruvius' terminology); it appeared in façades, and more commonly in walls of *opus Africanum* (Figure 8.9).[5] The House of the Surgeon (VI.1.10) was taken as the type-house of this group, and frequently identified as the oldest house in the city, articulated completely around the *atrium*, without a rear garden (Figure 8.1). Fiorelli dated this group as early as the fifth century BC, though Mau more cautiously allowed any time before 200 BC.[6]

Fiorelli's second distinctive group were the *tufo* houses, those employing the grey, fine-grained volcanic tuff of neighbouring Nuceria, especially for ashlar façades and architectural details, notably column capitals and *impluvium* basins (cf. Adam, Ch.8; Figure 8.2). While the Sarno stone houses are generally of modest dimensions, Nuceria tuff appears on some of the great show-houses, notably the House of the Faun (VI.12; see Map 3). Its frequent association with "Hellenistic" architectural details (e.g. Corinthian capitals, mosaic pavements and false marbling or First-Style mural plasterwork) pointed to a second-century BC date, a phase often referred to as Hellenistic Pompeii (cf. Strocka, Ch. 20; Clarke, Ch. 21; Fant, Ch. 22).

Other types of domestic construction were less distinctive than Sarno limestone and tuff: the vast majority of Pompeian walls are constructed of rubblework constructions based on lumps of Sarno stone and/or dark-grey lava joined by a lime and sand mortar (the Vitruvian term *opus incertum* is no more than a catch-all; cf. Dobbins, Appendix to Ch. 8; Figures 8.17 and A8.1). However, Fiorelli and Mau dated a number of techniques after the foundation of the Sullan colony of 80 BC; specifically, mortared stones laid in a more or less precise net-pattern (*opus quasi-reticulatum* and *reticulatum*), and the construction of load-bearing elements, especially piers, pillars and quoins in fired brick or tile (*opus latericium* or *testaceum*), or in alternating rows of brick and rectangular stone blocks (*opus vittatum mixtum*) (Figures 8.11, 8.12 and A8.1).[7]

While subsequent work has tended to confirm the first-century BC dating of these latter techniques, the key element for the evolutionary thesis is the early dating of Sarno stone (cf. Peterse, Ch. 24). It fits so neatly with a cherished Roman myth of Italian cultural development: from an "ancestral" simplicity suitable for sturdy rustics such as the Samnites (culturally unsophisticated, but still holding laudable peasant values), to the transformation brought by the wealth of eastern conquest and cultural "Hellenisation" in all its moral ambivalence. The move from the House of the Surgeon, modest in dimensions, bereft of ornament or decoration, but sturdy and four-square in construction, to the breathtaking palatial sophistication of the House of the Faun, seems to summarise such a transformation.

But this chronology can draw little comfort from a series of stratigraphic tests conducted during the past century. The matter was first put to the test in 1926 by Amedeo Maiuri in what was to prove a pioneering excavation.[8] He chose the House of the Surgeon itself to test the controversy between Fiorelli, who asserted the priority of Sarno stone construction, and Heinrich Nissen, who pointed out that different building materials served different functions, and architectural details such as capitals and *impluvium* basins could be cut easily in soft Nuceria tuff, but with great difficulty in the coarse-textured Sarno stone. His excavation found in favour of Fiorelli, in that the tuff *impluvium*, indeed, belonged to a second phase of the house; but it simultaneously upset his chronology, since the presence of abundant Campanian black-ware pointed to a third-century BC date.

It is likely that even a third-century date is too high for the House of the Surgeon (Figure 25.4). Maiuri neither published his ceramics nor preserved them for future study; but a series of similar subsoil excavations in the last twenty years seems to show consistently that no domestic structure standing in AD 79 can be confidently dated before 200 BC (cf. Carafa, Ch. 5).[9] Similar results emerge from houses in widely scattered locations in the city: from the House of the Etruscan Column (VI.5.17–18) in the north,[10] to the House of The Emperor Joseph II (VIII.2.39) at the western edge of the "Triangular Forum" (cf. Tybout, Ch. 26); from the House of the Wedding of Hercules (VII.9.47, 65) east of the forum,[11] to the House of Amarantus (I.9.12) in the rectangular grid of the southeastern quarter.[12] The House of Amarantus is a particularly close typological parallel for the House of the Surgeon, with its ashlar façade in Sarno stone, and *opus Africanum* construction of the *atrium* courtyard. Yet the evidence indicates a date between the second and mid-first century BC for the walls that stand.

A second clear result that emerges from excavation of Sarno stone *atria* is that again and again they are preceded by earlier structures, following the same alignments, but built of flimsier materials, whether un-mortared Sarno stone, or the crumbly local tuff called *pappamonte*, or simply of postholes for wooden structures (see Jones and Robinson, Ch. 25). The alternative picture now emerging is of a Pompeii with a long history before the second century, but one we can scarcely see. It seems to have been laid out, so far as the interior alignments of houses indicate, on the same street grid. It also seems to have been constructed less solidly, doubtless of mud-brick or pisé walls on stone foundations.[13] Because the alignments remain the same for centuries, and because the later foundations for heavier walls may cut deeper than the earlier ones, the evidence is largely disturbed, and we are unlikely to gain more than a fragmentary picture of such early houses.

However, it does not follow that no sequential development is visible in the domestic structures still standing in AD 79. Excavation confirms the picture already visible—in the almost universal spread of blocked windows and doors, and the patchwork of constantly changing construction techniques and materials—that Pompeian houses were subject to repeated and intensive modification, often ebbing and flowing beyond the property boundaries in place during the final phase.[14] But the intense history of construction and modification belongs to a much shorter period than Mau could have guessed—at most the last three centuries of the city's history, when Pompeii was already touched by the enormous wealth flowing into Italy from Rome's eastern conquests.

THE *ATRIUM* NUCLEUS

Even if the surviving evidence will not permit us to observe the evolution of the Italic house from its "origins", the traceable transformations of the last two centuries BC and the first century AD are substantial: the pace of change is frenetic, whether one looks at construction techniques, decoration, or simply the traces of constant rebuilding (cf. Nappo, Ch. 23; Peterse, Ch. 24; Tybout, Ch. 26). The nucleus of the Roman house is the *atrium*. Whether one considers this (in evolutionist terms) an "original core" from which a more complex house develops, or regards it as a basic element of the syntax of the house—the variations upon which generate the extant house forms—it is hard to describe or analyse the Pompeian house except from this point of view (cf. Allison, Ch. 17).

The Vitruvian prescription for an *atrium* (with which his account of the Roman house opens) focuses foremost on the varying types of roof-construction (Figure 8.19): the five variants of Tuscanic, Corinthian, tetrastyle, displuviate and testudinate (6.3.1) give the appearance of a canon almost like that of the orders. For that reason, it has been widely assumed that a space must be roofed to qualify as an "*atrium*", and in particular that the rainwater basin of the central *impluvium* is a necessary marker of a true *atrium*. But this assumption hampers discussion in two ways. The first is that, even when the evidence is preserved so clearly and to such a height as is the case at Pompeii, it is frequently impossible to determine what the roofline of the building was. Even the tell-tale *impluvium* basin is not so certain a signal of an inwardly sloping "compluviate" roof of the classic Tuscanic *atrium*, since there are cases where the basin acted as a sump for the run-off to collect water from a wholly open area, and did not correspond to a limited opening in the roof. As most Pompeian houses are known primarily from their ground plans, this is a significant disadvantage. The second is that in emphasising the *atrium* as a sheltered internal space, we miss its functional connection to the central open court of the standard Mediterranean house, whether in Greece, or elsewhere in Italy and the Roman world. Of course it does matter if the central court is roofed over, and what effect that has on the status and functionality of the house. But in any case, the *atrium* is simply a central space, whether open to the sky or partly enclosed, around which individual rooms are ordered.[15]

Looking at the ground-plans, and setting aside for a moment the roofs, the regularity of the syntax that determines how rooms are organized around the central space is striking. One feature above all emerges as characteristic of the Romano-Pompeian house, and that is the presence of rooms opening directly onto the central area without substantial walls and narrow doors to limit movement from one area to another. The classic example is the *tablinum*, conventionally situated on axis with the entrance passage, and forming the central focus of the vista from the entrance door, though in a number of houses the *tablinum* may also be found off-centre, or even to one side. So familiar is this conventional image that it is easy to forget how unusual it is in domestic architecture for rooms not to be entirely isolable from each other. Indeed, as in the House of the Wooden Partition (III.11) in Herculaneum, temporary wooden structures or even curtains could partially isolate the *tablinum* (cf. Figure 27.2). Nevertheless, the distinctive design feature is the absence of such a structural partition (cf. Allison, Ch. 17).

The same form is replicated in the *alae* of the classic Vitruvian type, much smaller rooms than the *tablinum*, and normally, as their name ("wings") implies, flanking it on either side. Their characteristic, too, is the absence of a separating wall, so that one can move unimpeded between the central space of the *atrium*, to the *alae* at the sides, and to the *tablinum* at the end. The phenomenon of the "open" room is not limited to the *atrium*. Around the peristyle walkway may also be found open rooms, though these more usually show in their thresholds and jambs signs of widely opening shutters: according to their size these are generally termed (following Vitruvius) *exedrae* and *oeci*. The vital implication of all these open rooms for human encounters is that they offer positive encouragement for people to move freely in and out, whereas a room only accessible through a narrow doorway seems more "private", not to be entered without explicit permission. Since, according to Vitruvius (6.5.1), one of the basic social requirements of Roman domestic architecture is that it distinguish "common" space accessible without invitation from "private" space of limited access, the structural distinction of "open" and "closed" rooms is likely to be socially significant.

The *atrium* nucleus, based on a rhythm of "open" and "closed" rooms, implies equally ritualised patterns of social encounter. The circumstances of imperial Rome and Ostia, where such *domus* were the exception, and multiple-occupancy properties or *insulae* the norm, have given rise to the impression that *atrium* houses were limited to the rich. Though this was true of high-density population centres, even in AD 79 houses built round an *atrium* nucleus were more like the norm. The enormous flexibility of the *atrium* scheme made this possible. The classic arrangement with central *tablinum* opposite the door, flanked by two *alae*, and with a "Tuscanic" *impluvium* at the centre, on the scale, e.g., of the House of Pansa (VI.6.1, 12), requires a broad plot of ground (Figure 18.1). But many more modest houses, such as the House of the Fruit Orchard (I.9.5) or the House of the Lararium (I.6.4), dispense with one side (Figure 18.2), settling for a *tablinum* with only one *ala* and corresponding side-rooms. Others dispense with side-rooms entirely, so that the atrium area occupies the whole width of the plot (cf. Peterse, Ch. 24). Curiously enough, this is the case with some houses of considerable magnificence, such as the House of Paquius Proculus (I.7.1, 20), which by dint of painted doors on the side walls gives the *impression* of a far more ample space than it has at its disposal (Figure 21.4). Similarly, the Samnite House at Herculaneum (V.1), which has no side-rooms except a staircase to rooms above (Figure 27.1), gives the impression of being a traditional *atrium* house (whence its name).

The fact that reasonably grand houses could permit variations on the *tablinum/alae* formula should encourage us to recognise similar principles at work in the much

Figure 18.1 View north from the *atrium* to the peristyle in the House of Pansa (VI.6.1).
Photo: P. W. Foss.

Figure 18.2 The *atrium* of the House of the Lararium (I.6.4).
Photo: P. W. Foss.

more modest "terraced" houses of Pompeii. Recent work in the southeast quarter has suggested that many of the rectangular blocks were laid out around 200 BC, with modest houses on a standard set of patterns in narrow strips 25 to 30 ft wide (Nappo, Ch. 23; Figure 23.2). Front rooms were grouped around a court that appears to have been originally open, on principles clearly linked to those of the *atrium*. Usually there are no side-rooms, and the court occupies the full width of the plot. The *tablinum* may be set off-centre on the opposite side of the court from the entrance (Figure 23.3); more rarely, as in the House of the Ship Europa (I.15.1), it may be set on the central axis (cf. Map 3). An interesting variation is found in House (I.20.4), where the entrance is at the edge of the plot, instead of the centre, and the *tablinum* and its flanking rooms rest on an axis at a right-angle to that of the entrance. These variations demonstrate that even in modest houses, datable as early as any of the grander ones, the "open" areas of court and *tablinum* serve a social function, and the appeal of axiality is not forgotten.

At the other end of the spectrum, the *atrium* nucleus allowed multiplication. The House of the Faun (VI.12) is the classic example of a well-attested phenomenon of houses with twin *atria* (cf. Map 3). Here, it is evidently part of the architectural design, not the result of amalgamating two previously independent units. There has been much speculation over the function of the doubled *atrium*, and it has been argued that a secondary *atrium* serves as a "private" side for the use of the family, while the main *atrium* is the show-piece for visitors.[16] Certainly, doubling up the *atrium* nucleus would provide the owner with greater flexibility. But this doubling, like the removal of side-rooms, again signals how flexible the idea of the *atrium* was, a basic building block from which the grandest and the more modest houses alike could be adapted.

The *atrium* nucleus was deeply embedded in how the Pompeian house was conceived. As the Romans imagined, it was rooted in tradition. The term "Tuscanic" for the typical arrangement of the *atrium* roof implies an Etruscan origin, which antiquarians such as Varro were happy to assert.[17] The *atrium* form is notable in a number of fourth-century BC Etruscan tombs, and excavations are now indicating the antiquity of the arrangement (and cf. Figure 24.5).[18] The houses of fifth-century Marzabotto provide clear evidence for houses with the "cruciform" pattern of *atrium* and *tablinum* flanked by *alae*.[19] Something similar is distinguishable at sixth-century Regisvillae, and (rather less clearly) in the "House of the Impluvium" at Roselle.[20] The great *atrium* houses at the foot of the Palatine have sixth-century origins, and though traces of the earliest phases are frustratingly fragmentary, the suggestion is attractive that some type of *atrium* organisation goes back to the beginning.[21] The great villa on the outskirts of Rome on the Via Flaminia (Auditorium site) has an equally long history, and at least by the third century BC the canonical *atrium* arrangement is certain.[22]

How similar patterns reached Pompeii cannot yet be told for certain. Either what is attested in Etruria is part of a more widespread Italic phenomenon; or if we are dealing with a specifically Etruscan tradition that was taken up by the Romans, it is possible that it reached Pompeii through imitation of third-century Roman settlements. Certainly, the *atrium* house emerges as standard at the Latin colony of Fregellae from the earliest visible phases in the third century.[23] Similarly, in Cosa we find large *atrium* houses around the forum with the classic cruciform *atrium* pattern dating back to the early second century; more modest terraced houses of the same date are based on open courts reminiscent of those at Pompeii.[24] One way or another, the language of domestic architecture as we meet it in Pompeii during the last two centuries BC belongs to a common language widely diffused through the rapidly Romanising cities of Italy.

HELLENISATION AND ROMANISATION

Pompeian house form was subject to evolution, and the period where our evidence survives is one of rapid change in all fields of Italian material culture. It is traditional and convenient to refer to this transformation, especially in the last two centuries BC, by the term "Hellenisation". But the term conceals a range of assumptions that should be treated with caution. The extensive imitation, or appropriation, of a wide range of eastern Mediterranean cultural goods is beyond doubt. But the picture of an authentic native culture becoming absorbed into a Greek cultural ambit is misleading. It underestimates the continuous and profound impact of Greek models in preceding centuries, especially in an area that lay on the borders of Greek south Italy, and it conceals the fact that the cultural change goes hand-in-hand with the political absorption of Italian cities into the Roman sphere. "Hellenisation" is shorthand for the cultural process by which Italy became Roman. This is the period during which Pompeii is transformed from an Oscan-speaking independent "ally" into a Latin-speaking colony operating under Roman law. The idea that the Pompeian house is transformed from an "Italic" model to a compromise between Greek and Italic makes little sense.

"Hellenistic" influence on the Pompeian house is clear at many levels, from the articulation of the house as a whole, to the shaping and disposition of individual rooms, to their furnishing and decoration. The House of the Faun (VI.12) may be the classic example of second-century Hellenisation. The house has frequently been compared to the royal palaces of Hellenistic cities such as Pergamum or Alexandria, not only because of its exceptional size (nearly 3,000 m^2), but because of its articulation around two magnificent colonnaded gardens or "peristyles". The rooms around these peristyles, though we can only guess how the inhabitants used them, let alone named them, fit the typology of the Greek room names transmitted by Vitruvius, *oeci* or *exedrae*, rather than that of the traditional Roman reception room, *triclinium* (cf. Allison, Ch. 17). The culmination of the decorative system of the house, the Alexander mosaic, is placed on the central visual axis between the first and second peristyles, in a room referred to as an *exedra* (37), echoing the vocabulary form of the Hellenistic public gymnasium, with large sitting-out spaces (especially on the central axes) used for philosophical discussion, etc. (cf. Clarke, Ch. 21).[25]

The decoration of the house consciously transports the viewer into the Hellenistic world, with its image of Alexander in battle against the Persian king, with mosaics evoking the flora and fauna of the Nile, and mythological and religious icons of Greek culture such as the panther-borne Dionysus, or the erotic embrace of a satyr. The eponymous bronze statuette of a Faun points to the same Greek world of satyrs, though by an attractive conjecture, it may also be word-play on the name of the owners, the distinguished Oscan family of the Satrii or Sadirii.[26] The wall-decoration above these pavements is the most extensive surviving example of the false marble panelling characteristic of the First Style, well attested on contemporary second-century Delos (cf. Strocka, Ch. 20; Fant, Ch. 22).

The standard account of Pompeian house development sees the addition of the peristyle to the *atrium* nucleus as the hallmark of the Hellenisation of the Italic house. But the House of the Faun shows how complex the transformation actually is. The peristyles do not follow a model based on domestic architecture. The ordinary Greek house was frequently organised around a courtyard, which in second-century Delos, for example, may be enhanced by a colonnade. The palaces of Pergamum are also organised around colonnaded peristyles, off which rows of banqueting rooms open. But the peristyles of the House of the Faun do not exist to articulate the rooms, which are few in number. The model is that of the public gymnasium, with an occasional *exedra*, and a set of baths to one side. In this sense, far from showing the influence of Hellenistic domestic architecture, the peristyles are an attempt to lift the house beyond the merely domestic, and to add the magnificence of a public building, rich with evocations of the opulent East.[27]

The peristyle only gradually transforms the underlying articulation of the house. If the traditional pattern was a group of rooms around an *atrium* court, with a garden plot (*hortus*) behind, the colonnades of the peristyle initially serve to give luxury and magnificence to the garden plot (cf. Jashemski, Ch. 31). The terraced houses of the early second century, which are too modest to have peristyles, may still have a few rooms looking out on the backyard and the *hortus*. Only as the image of the colonnade becomes embedded does the focus shift from the *atrium* to the peristyle as the place to locate major reception rooms. Rooms originally constructed to open on the *atrium* are re-orientated to face the peristyle. If the *tablinum*, for instance, starts as a room with a wide opening on the *atrium*, and at most a view through a back window towards the garden, by the first century AD it becomes normal to remove the back wall entirely, so that the *tablinum* becomes a transitional area that pulls the visitor through to the peristyle behind. In the House of Paquius Proculus (I.7.1, 20), the enormous *atrium* with its eye-catching mosaic floor ceases to be the focus for habitable rooms, which are set around the peristyle (Figure 21.4). The *tablinum* is deep and high, and its lack of a back wall pulls the eye through to the peristyle beyond with a fountain at its centre.

In view of the enthusiasm with which houses draw on the architecture and decoration of the Hellenistic world, it is remarkable how tenaciously the *atrium* survives at Pompeii. Indeed, we are not dealing with a mere "survival", but with a key part of the self-image of the inhabitants, comparable to the toga-clad statues on tombs outside the city gates. It is the very awareness that peristyles and mosaics and mythological paintings and statues in the garden point to a non-Italian world that enables the *atrium* to act as a guarantee of Italian identity. Vitruvius explicitly associates the architectural form with Roman social rituals of *clientela* (6.5.2). That does not mean that every Pompeian house with an *atrium* and *tablinum* received clients, but the symbolic associations of the form gave it widespread appeal and potency.

We can trace, then, a shift of emphasis over the course of two centuries, as entertainment comes to centre on the peristyle rather than the *atrium*. But while countless features are imitated from the Greek world, the Pompeian house does not thereby become assimilated to the Greek house. On the contrary, the cultural distinctiveness of the face it presents to the visitor is underlined, making what was probably a common Italic house-form in the third century BC a marker of "Roman" identity in an Italy increasingly culturally homogeneous under the forcible impact of Roman control.

PAST THE *ATRIUM* HOUSE

The classic domestic image of the high empire is the multiple-occupancy *insula* on many floors of robust brick-clad concrete. Was Pompeii heading in the same direction when its evolution was interrupted, and were the days of the *atrium* house already numbered? Perhaps so, but the thesis of an such an "evolution" starting at Pompeii and ending at Ostia attributes too much importance to the casual survival of evidence from two sites, each unique in its own way. Pompeii betrays no sign of developing brick and concrete multi-floor *insulae*—although the single example in Herculaneum in the Palaestra complex (*Insula Orientalis* II) shows that the model was already known beyond Rome, where it had probably developed by the late first century BC. The key factor behind such construction is population pressure, expressed in rising rents that permit capital outlay.

By the early first century AD, there was some growth of population associated with commercial prosperity, and a fairly active rental market developed at Pompeii. While the Ostian-type *insula* is not favoured, the *atrium* house could be adapted to multiple occupancy—again, the "*atrium* house" is not a single model of construction, but a set of paradigms that allowed many different expressions. A model of multiple occupancy is the Insula Arriana Polliana (VI.6), thanks to the *dipinto* that in AD 79 was advertising the availability for rent of shops with upper rooms (*tabernae cum pergulis*), up-market apartments (*cenacula equestria*), and houses (*domus*) (cf. Pirson, Ch. 29).[28] The plan of the *insula* (Map 3) shows how the construction of a particularly magnificent *atrium*-peristyle house, the House of Pansa (Figure 18.1), did not exclude rental activity, but positively encouraged it. The house occupies the core of the plot, leaving room around the edges for a penumbra of lesser properties, shops in the main façade, and to the side, small residences built around a courtyard nucleus, while staircases direct to upper apartments appear occasionally between the other units. The size (and implicit wealth) of the House of Pansa left little room for rival owners in the block, and enabled it to exploit the rental potential of the land spared by its own architecture.

All three types of rented unit, *tabernae*, *cenacula* and *domus*, seem to be widespread in Pompeii and Herculaneum. Shops incorporated in the façades of larger houses are likely to have belonged to them more often than not. Three possibilities are common: the shop independent of the main house with stairs up to a room above (Figure 8.14), the shop linked directly to the *atrium* behind, and the independent shop beneath upper rooms accessible from within the *atrium*. The last two of these types normally imply letting; the first type also may have been let, though we cannot prove it.

Rented *cenacula* are most easily recognised from separate staircases accessible directly from the street. It is reasonable to infer that inhabitants of such apartments had a strictly commercial relationship with the owners of the whole property. But we cannot exclude the possibility that the upper rooms accessible from staircases internal to the *atrium* could also be let.[29] Just as it would be difficult to trace archaeologically the presence of lodgers in a modern family house, we should not assume that the *atrium* house was always the sole preserve of a family group.

CONCLUSION

The history of domestic form at Pompeii and Herculaneum is one of constant change and adaptation. We should beware the picture of a steady, unilinear evolution. One house that can be traced through in-depth excavation is the House of Amarantus (I.9.12; Figure 19.1).[30] At first sight it seems an early example of a "limestone period" *atrium* house, constructed with Sarno stone in *opus quadratum* and *opus Africanum*. Yet excavation suggests it was built no earlier than the second century BC, and possibly later. It further reveals that the *impluvium* set axially between *fauces* and *tablinum* was no more than a flowerbed with a raised border, placed to mimic a rainwater basin. A compluviate roof can be excluded; instead, like other row houses in the area, it was constructed around an open court. At some point, the *tablinum* was raised by half a metre, and its back wall demolished, to open directly on a newly organised peristyle. Simultaneously, the side bedroom, previously accessible to the *atrium*, was turned round to face the peristyle. These changes may seem typical of second-century BC Hellenisation, but they are archaeologically datable to the mid-first century AD, when Fourth-Style decoration was applied.

In the adjoining house at no. 11, we have a clear example of an upper floor installed for *cenacula*: the brick columns of the colonnade are blocked in to sustain the weight of an upper storey, and new latrines are installed at both levels. Simultaneously, a narrow opening on the street is created for a stairway that leads directly to these rooms. But while such upper rooms were attributed by Maiuri to the "commercialisation" of the city in the aftermath of the earthquake of AD 62/63, in this case it is clear that they were installed some decades earlier. By the last years of the city, the upper floor collapsed, probably from seismic activity, and the door to the external stair was blocked in. In the same period, the *atrium* of the linked house 12 was reduced to a storage area for the bar at no. 11, and its front room changed to a donkey stable.

The persistence of the *atrium* form may be attributed above all to its adaptability. The same basic pattern serves the magnificent public reception area of the House of the Faun or the basic front courtyard of the House of Amarantus, with its *amphorae* and its donkey. Certainly by the early imperial period when Vitruvius is writing, the *atrium* house may be seen as the symbol of an authentic Roman style. Yet the use and ideology of domestic space changed constantly through time, and it is dangerous to project the same ideology back onto a remote past, even if it remains plausible that predecessors of the same form had a long history. The fact that the empire brought new social and economic pressures does not mean that the *atrium* house became irrelevant, giving way to a new architecture shaped around the needs of landlords maximising rental income. The Pompeii of AD 79 shows that the old forms were entirely capable of adapting to these needs.

NOTES

1 A. Mau, *Pompeii: its life and art*, (transl. and ed. by F. W. Kelsey), rev. edn, London, 1902, p. 245. The present text was last revised in 2002. Much has been published subsequently that bears on the questions discussed, notably the excavation of F. Coarelli's group. See F. Coarelli and F. Pesando (eds), *Rileggere Pompei. I. L'insula 10 della Regio VI*, Studi della Soprintendenza Archeologica di Pompei no. 12, Rome, 2006.

2 W. Becker, *Gallus, oder Römische Scenen aus der Zeit Augusts*, Leipzig, 1838. An English translation was printed by J. W. Parker of London in 1844.

3 C. F. Mazois, *Le palais de Scaurus*, Paris, 1819; C. F. Mazois, *Les ruines de Pompéi dessinées et mesurées pendant les années 1809–1810–1811*, 4 vols, Paris, 1824–38.

4 *Gallus* had gone through nine editions by 1888. J. Marquardt, *Das Privatleben der Römer*, in *Handbuch der römischen Alterthümer*, Band 7 (2 vols), Leipzig, 1879–82; A. Mau, *Führer durch Pompeji*, Naples, 1893; Mau, *Pompeii*.

5 The (modern) term refers to its frequency in North Africa, where it dates back to the Punic period. It originated as a drystone construction with a framework of chains of large blocks laid in alternate vertical and horizontal layers, holding together a rubble infill of smaller blocks of the same stone.

6 Mau, *Pompeii*, p. 280.

7 Mau, *Pompeii*, pp. 41–3.

8 A. Maiuri, "Saggi nella 'Casa del Chirurgo' (Reg.VI, Ins.I, n.10)", *NSc*, 1930, pp. 381–95, reprinted in: A. Maiuri, *Alla ricerca di Pompei preromana*, Naples, 1973, pp. 1–13.

9 The more extensive investigations of the Anglo-American project of R. Jones and D. Robinson *et al.* have recently confirmed the down-dating of this house (cf. Ch. 25). For the general picture, see C. Chiaramonte Treré, "Sull'origine e lo sviluppo dell'architettura residenziale di Pompei sannitica", *Acme*, 1990, vol. 43, pp. 5–34; A. D'Ambrosio, and S. De Caro, "Un contributo all'architettura e all'urbanistica di Pompei in età ellenistica. I saggi nella casa VII, 4, 62", *AION*, 1989, vol. 11, pp. 173–215.

10 M. Bonghi Jovino *et al.*, *Ricerche a Pompei. L'insula 5 della Regio VI dalle origini al 79 d.C. I (campagne di scavo 1976–1979)*, 2 vols, Rome, 1984; those results have now been modified by the excavations of F. Coarelli, F. Pesando *et al.* in the same house.

11 P. Carafa and M. T. d'Alessio, "Lo sviluppo urbanistico di Pompei alla luce delle recenti scoperte. Considerazioni preliminari in margine alle nuove ricerche nelle Regiones VIII e VII", *RStPomp*, forthcoming; A. Carandini, "Nuovi progetti, nuove domande, nuovi metodi", in P. G. Guzzo (ed.), *Pompei. Scienza e società*. Convegno Internazionale, Napoli 25–27 novembre 1998, Milan, 2001, pp. 127–9.

12 See below, and n. 30.

13 On the importance of mud walls and the links with Fregellae, see F. Pesando, "Forme abitative e controllo sociale: la documentazione archeologica delle colonie latine in età repubblicana", in *Habitat et société*, Actes des Rencontres 22–23–24 octobre 1998, Antibes, 1999, p. 247; P. G. Guzzo, "Alla ricerca della Pompei sannitica", in *Studi sull'Italia dei Sanniti*, Milan, 2000, p. 109.

14 Magisterially documented by R. Ling, *The Insula of the Menander at Pompeii*, vol. 1, Oxford, 1997. See also now Coarelli and Pesando, *Rileggere Pompei*.

15 See my discussion in "Rethinking the atrium house", in R. Laurence and A. Wallace-Hadrill (eds), *Domestic Space in the Roman World: Pompeii and beyond*, JRA Suppl. Ser. no. 22, 1997, pp. 219–40.

16 This is rightly questioned by J.-A. Dickmann, *Domus frequentata: Anspruchsvolles Wohnen im pompejanischen Stadthaus*, Munich, 1999, pp. 53ff. For a recent study of the design of the House of the Faun, see E. Dwyer, "The unified Plan of the House of the Faun", *JSAH*, 2001, vol. 60.3, pp. 328–43.

17 Varro, Ling. 5.161, *Tuscanicum dictum a Tuscis, posteaquam illorum cavum aedium simulare coeperant. atrium appellatum ab Atriatibus Tuscis: illinc enim exemplum sumptum.*

18 On the excavations of archaic houses on the Palatine, see A. Carandini and P. Carafa (eds), *Palatium e Sacra Via* I, Bollettino di Archeologia, 1995 [2000], vols 31–34.

19 G. Colonna, "Urbanistica e architettura", in M. Pallottino *et al.*, *Rasenna. Storia e civiltà degli Etruschi*, Milan, 1986, pp. 371–530; G. Sassatelli, *La città etrusca di Marzabotto*, Bologna, 1989.

20 L. Donati, *La Casa dell'Impluvium: architettura etrusca a Roselle*, Rome, 1994.

21 See Carandini and Carafa, *Palatium e Sacra Via* I.

22 N. Terrenato, "The Auditorium site and the origins of the Roman villa", *JRA*, 2001, vol. 14, pp. 5–32.

23 F. Coarelli and P. G. Monti (eds), *Fregellae 1. Le fonti, la storia, il territorio*, Rome, 1998.

24 E. Fentress, *Cosa V. An intermittent town, excavations 1991–1997*, MAAR suppl., Ann Arbor, MI, 2003.

25 Vitr., *De arch.* 5.11.2; cf. Varro, *Rust.* 2 praef. for the borrowing of names linked to the gymnasium. For the Alexander mosaic, see also: B. Cohen, *The Alexander Mosaic: stories of victory and defeat*, New York, 1997.

26 F. Pesando, "Autocelebrazione aristocratica e propaganda politica in ambiente privato: la casa del Fauno a Pompei", *Cahiers du Centre Gustave-Glotz*, 1996, vol. 7, pp. 189–228, at 221ff.; cf. F. Meyboom, *The Nile Mosaic of Palestrina. Early evidence of Egyptian religion in Italy*, Leiden/New York/Köln, 1995, 167–72.

27 See Dickmann, *Domus frequentata*; F. Pesando, *Domus. Edilizia privata e società pompeiana fra III e I secolo a.C.*, Rome, 1997, pp. 80–120.

28 See F. Pirson, "Rented accommodation at Pompeii: the *Insula Arriana Polliana*", in Laurence and Wallace-Hadrill, *Domestic Space*, pp. 165–81; in detail: F. Pirson, *Mietwohnungen in Pompeji und Herkulaneum. Untersuchungen zur Architektur, zum Wohnen und zur Sozial- und Wirtschaftsgeschichte der Vesuvstädte*, Studien zur Antiken Stadt no. 5, Munich, 2000, pp. 23ff.

29 Pirson, *Mietwohnungen*, p. 141.

30 See an interim report on survey and excavations in 1995–6: M. Fulford and A. Wallace-Hadrill, "The House of Amarantus at Pompeii (I.9.11–12)", *RStPomp*, 1995–96 [1998], vol. 7, pp. 77–113; M. Fulford and A. Wallace-Hadrill, "Towards a history of pre-Roman Pompeii: excavations beneath the House of Amarantus (I.9.11–12), 1995–8", *PBSR*, 1999, vol. 67, pp. 37–144; A. Wallace-Hadrill, "Excavation and standing structures in Pompeii Insula I.9", in P. G. Guzzo and M. P. Guidobaldi (eds), *Nuove ricerche archeologiche a Pompei ed Ercolano*, Studi della Soprintendenza Archeologica di Pompei no. 10, Naples, 2005, pp. 101–8.

CHAPTER NINETEEN

INSTRUMENTUM DOMESTICUM— A CASE STUDY[1]

——.•.——

Joanne Berry

THE PROBLEM OF STUDYING ARTEFACTS

The *instrumentum domesticum* of Pompeii is unique: the destruction and preservation of the town has preserved a full range of everyday household objects, representing many of the different activities that took place within the domestic environment. The value of this evidence is underlined by the sheer quantity and diversity of these objects: there are over 50,000 artefacts stored on-site alone,[2] consisting of jewellery, statuary and furniture, tables, kitchen and storage vessels, lamps, tools and toilet objects in a variety of different materials such as gold, silver, bronze, iron, terracotta, glass, bone and organic materials. Pompeii thus offers the archaeologist and historian a unique opportunity to study ancient domestic life, and to understand better the issues of household organisation, domestic consumption and production, social status and aspirations.

It is only recently that archaeologists and historians have begun to exploit this potential.[3] Roman artefacts have traditionally been studied from the point of view of their production and distribution throughout the Mediterranean world, with the result that the focus has been centred on the question of when and where they were made, and whither they were exported. This is partly to do with the nature of the available evidence, which often consists of scattered finds, artefacts from abandoned sites, or grave goods. Yet the fact that artefacts such as *amphorae*, lamps and finewares are studied in isolation without reference to each other and absent their original context, has had the result that interest in the assemblage of artefacts found in the uniquely well-preserved towns of Pompeii and Herculaneum has been limited. Instead, the traditional focus of Pompeian scholars has been the architecture and decoration of these towns.

To be fair, it is actually very difficult to study the artefacts of Pompeii because the excavations have never been published systematically. Some of the archival documentation is available in the *Pompeianarum Antiquitatum Historia*, the *Giornali degli Scavi di Pompei*, and the *Notizie degli Scavi di Antichità*, but these publications cover only particular periods of the excavations and the attention given to artefactual evidence varies (cf. Laidlaw, Ch. 39). Many exhibition catalogues feature ornate, expensive or unusual items, and recently a series of typological studies of different classes of material has appeared, but attempts to study and publish the artefacts of Pompeii in their original context have been rare.[4] This means that a student wishing to undertake this task in a particular house or group of houses generally needs to consult the original excavation daybooks and inventories which are to be found in Pompeii, Naples and Rome.[5] Interest in this type of study has recently risen, as it has become clear that artefactual material can bring a whole new dimension to the interpretation of houses.[6] This chapter elaborates on the nature of the *instrumentum domesticum* of Pompeii, and, through a detailed case study of the House of the Beautiful Impluvium (I.9.1-2), illustrates some of the ways in which this evidence can shed light on the realities and complexities of domestic life in AD 79.

Unfortunately, the remarkable range and diversity of artefacts from Pompeii does not represent all objects in use in AD 79. The first phase (pumice-fall) of the eruption probably lasted about eighteen hours, which means that most inhabitants had time to escape from Pompeii before the devastating pyroclastic flows of the second phase (cf. Sigurdsson, Ch. 4, Figure 4.4).[7] The fact that only approximately 1,150 bodies[8] have been found on site seems to confirm this theory (cf. Lazer, Ch. 38). Most escapees probably managed to salvage some of their most valuable belongings; many skeletons were found with jewellery, coins and silverwares.

Second, organic artefacts have perished, either having burned and been destroyed during the eruption, or having slowly decomposed in the centuries after the eruption. Evidence for wooden furniture, basketry, foodstuffs, curtains, clothes, etc. consists of mere carbonised scraps of material or fragments of wood (and, in the case of wooden furniture, nails and ornamental studs). In some cases, excavators have been able to make plaster-cast reproductions from the void left by the decomposition of organic substances, but this is only possible if the object (generally bodies or wooden furniture; Figures 38.1 and 17.2) was buried in the last stages of the eruption when flows of ash and other detritus ejected from Vesuvius settled compactly over the town.[9] It is impossible to reconstruct the form of organic objects buried by *lapilli* in the earlier stages of the eruption, since loose *lapilli* filled in any void created by organic decomposition.

Third, there is wide evidence of post-eruption disturbance. It is likely that many surviving inhabitants returned to the town after the eruption in order to salvage as much as possible (cf. Foss, Ch. 3). In the excavation reports, larger houses are more often noted to contain disturbed volcanic fill than smaller houses, and it seems likely that after the eruption roof-tops were still visible in certain parts of the town, and this enabled people to navigate their way to the largest, wealthiest houses. In addition, clandestine excavations have occurred since the rediscovery of Pompeii in 1748 and down to the present day.

The tradition of excavation and documentation (or non-documentation) at Pompeii complicates this picture. The first excavations were little more than treasure-hunting, and the quality of documentation often reflects this attitude. Artefactual studies have highlighted the shabby methods of excavation and recording. Tradition-bound attitudes to the storage and display of both units and artefacts have plagued the history of Pompeian scholarship, hindering the collection and interpretation of artefacts.[10] The excavation reports are a notoriously difficult source, hand-written and full of discrepancies and inconsistencies; the quality and level of detail improves during the 250-year history of the excavations, but at no time can the *Giornali degli Scavi* be compared to modern archaeological standards.

Finally, the interpretation of this material is complex. Most scholars now accept that the final years of Pompeii saw frequent seismic disturbances, although not all agree on the effects this disturbance had on urban life. Did it stimulate reconstruction or did it cause economic decline and abandonment (cf. Jongman, Ch. 32; Franklin, Ch. 33)?[11] Certainly, the widespread evidence of both finished and on-going repairs/reconstruction points to a notable degree of disturbance in the everyday organisation of households, although houses would have been damaged to differing degrees by the earth tremors. Our problem is to assess the changes brought about by the seismic activity, since we have no understanding of how domestic activities were organised before tremors began in AD 62. The artefactual evidence is synchronic; it does not permit us to draw easy comparisons to earlier periods or to understand clearly the effects of earthquake damage on everyday domestic activities unless we also undertake a detailed architectural and archaeological study of each house.[12] Evidence of building work seems to suggest that most inhabitants were attempting to get on with their lives as best as possible, undertaking gradual repairs to their homes, and continuing with their normal daily activities. Building work might temporarily have affected the distribution of artefacts in houses, and may have involved lifestyle changes, but these changes need not have been negative or permanent. With this in mind, it is likely that even if the distribution of artefacts was temporarily disturbed, the complete domestic assemblage of each house as a whole was unaltered to a large degree, and many normal household activities still took place. In addition, even under normal circumstances, the distribution of artefacts in a house is more likely to represent storage than use, and the different areas of each house must have been used in many more ways than the literary sources suggest (cf. Allison, Ch. 17).[13]

Despite these problems, no other Roman site can match the sheer number and range of artefacts excavated at Pompeii. This evidence has not been perfectly conserved during excavation, nor was it ever a 'time-capsule' perfectly preserved by the volcanic material,[14] but it does offer an unparalleled opportunity to investigate the functioning of houses in one part of the Roman empire. What, therefore, can the *instrumentum domesticum* reveal about inhabitants and their activities?

A CASE STUDY

The House of the Beautiful Impluvium (I.9.1–2) consists of a *fauces*, *atrium*, peristyle, kitchen and latrine, attached shop, and eight other rooms (Figures 19.1 and 19.2).[15] Most rooms are decorated in Third-Style wall painting. An upper floor was reached by means of stairways from room (3) and room (4), and there is a cellar under the kitchen (6) and latrine (5). The house appears to have been undergoing renovation in AD 79; the *atrium* was still undecorated.

Excavations took place in two distinct periods. Matteo Della Corte excavated the shop at no. 2 in 1913–14 and published the results in the *Notizie degli Scavi di Antichità*. Unfortunately, the quality of reporting is poor, giving little attention to a detailed examination of either the structural condition of the shop or its contents. In fact, the recorded artefacts probably do not comprise the sum actually uncovered. The main discovery was the remains of a wooden cupboard containing a mixture of artefacts (Figure 19.3). These included a bronze bracelet, a necklace consisting of nineteen blue glass-paste beads, and the rim of a small bronze box or pyxis often associated with

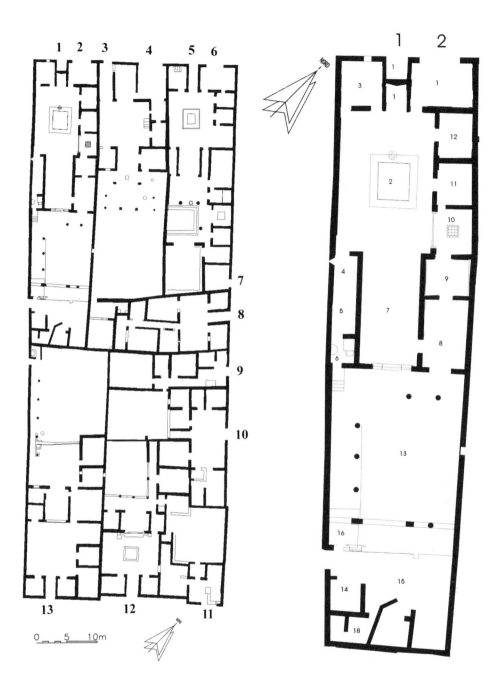

Figure 19.1 Plan of *insula* I.9. Drawn by Raphael Helman and Marie-Noelle Janssens; The British School at Rome.

Figure 19.2 Plan of the House of the Beautiful Impluvium (I.9.1–2). Drawn by Raphael Helman and Marie-Noelle Janssens; The British School at Rome.

Figure 19.3   Artefacts from shop (I.9.2). Photo: Sophie Hay and Anthony Sibthorpe.

female toilet activities. There was also a simple terracotta lamp and a collection of thirty-four glass 'pawns'—probably gaming-counters—eighteen of which were black and sixteen white. In the same cupboard a collection of different knives was discovered: seven of which had a single straight edge and six of which had wide triangular blades. Only two of these blades (the triangular ones) had handles.

Other recorded artefacts from shop no. 2 were either assigned no provenance, or were found in the higher levels of eruptive ash. The unprovenanced artefacts consisted of three decorated bronze 'saucepans' (*casseruole*) with slightly different shapes; these are generally interpreted as table vessels, but their precise function is unknown.[16] Also found in the shop without a firm provenance were two small bronze feet from a chair or stool. Artefacts in the higher levels of ash consisted of a *terra sigillata* bowl, a large bronze bell, a buckle and a couple of small iron objects claimed to belong to a bridle. The bowl is interesting since it is elaborately decorated with scenes from a hunt. The figures are somewhat blurred, however, suggesting that the original mould was worn or of poor quality. Given the lack of a staircase from the shop to the room above, these artefacts presumably belonged to the upper rooms of the House of the Beautiful Impluvium, although it is strange to think of horse-harness equipment kept on an upper floor. Another possibility is that these objects were, indeed, part of the shop's contents and were stored on a shelf high up on the wall, though there is no reported evidence (the shop has since been heavily restored, obscuring much of the original condition of the walls). As with many shops along the via dell'Abbondanza, the mixture of reported artefacts makes it difficult to interpret what was actually going on in the shop in AD 79. However, the collection of knives is unusual. The blades are all similar in shape and in good condition, and one would expect knives in a domestic or craft context to be different—because they would perform different tasks—and to show signs of use. This may indicate that this was

Figure 19.4   Artefacts from the House of the Beautiful Impluvium (I.9.1).
Photo: Sophie Hay and Anthony Sibthorpe.

a cutler's shop—a place where knives were finished and sold,[17] although the other objects found here are not what one might expect to find in such a shop.

The rest of the house and its two neighbours to the east (I.9.3, I.9.5) were excavated October–December 1951, January–February 1952 and April 1952, but remain unpublished. These excavations were part of a campaign of public works to promote employment in the Naples area, and progressed extremely quickly (cf. Foss, Ch. 3). Excavation notebooks report extensive post-eruption disturbance in all three houses, and many household objects were likely salvaged after the eruption. Only the lowest levels of eruptive fill in the House of the Beautiful Impluvium were composed of undisturbed *lapilli*. In addition, some of the 1952 excavation reports seem to be missing, so our picture is even more limited and difficult to interpret. This is a shame, since the extant records reveal a remarkable set of artefacts that suggest prosperous inhabitants (Figure 19.4).

The main evidence for prosperity comes from the remains of a wooden chest and attached wooden cupboard found along the west wall of the *atrium* (2) along with all their bronze, iron and bone fittings, and a bronze key. Inside the chest and cupboard was a wide mixture of different artefacts, ranging from jewellery and personal items to tablewares and lamps. These included a silver mirror, a silver jug, a silver crochet-hook, a gold ring, two gold bracelets, two silver-plated bronze bowls, three bronze *casseruole*, a bronze plate, two *terra sigillata* plates and a bowl, two glass beakers, a glass jug, a glass bottle, a bronze bucket, two pairs of tweezers and four glass perfume-bottles. It is fairly common to find such a mixture stored within containers in Pompeian houses,[18] but the fact that many objects were made from precious metals is unusual. More importantly, the cupboard also contained a hoard of 298 silver coins and three gold coins; most were Vespasianic and Domitianic, apart from a few Republican issues. It is possible that the prosperity of this household came from activities in the attached shop. A wall painting of the god of trade, Mercury, carrying a bag of money towards the door was uncovered in the entranceway (1) of the house.

In direct contrast to this vivid collection, we have only a partial idea of contents in other areas of the house. By the front door a terracotta jug, a *terra sigillata* plate and a commonware terracotta plate were found, which may have fallen from the floor above during the eruption. Various artefacts were reported from the *atrium* and attached rooms (many without exact find-spots), including bronze vessels (jugs, a *casseruola* fused to an iron tripod, and a bucket), a few lamps, a small *terra sigillata* plate, and a series of plaques, studs and rings that the excavators interpreted as equestrian equipment. There was a bronze candelabrum in the *ala* (10), and rare ivory ornaments from a bed in room (11). A small bronze *amphora* was found in room (3), along with a bronze perfume-bottle, a large bronze basin, a small terracotta jar, a terracotta bowl, a bone spindle, and a *terra sigillata* bowl and plate. A stone base and another bronze bucket and a bronze cooking-pot were found in the *tablinum* (7), and another bronze basin in the area of the kitchen and latrine (5 and 6). Due to the missing notes, the area around the peristyle was less well-recorded, and artefacts consist of the remains of another wooden cupboard (including seven bone hinges) which contained a bronze lamp, a bell, an iron razor, and two bronze objects described as *zoccoli di piede di cavallo* (literally, "horse-hooves"). Another terracotta lamp was also found in the peristyle (13). Other artefacts were given no find-spot at all in the excavation reports, including a gold earring and a small violet gem for a ring, another two bronze *casseruole* and a bronze jug, a bronze ink-pot (*calamaria*), and a gaming die. There were also many unprovenanced hinges, nails, studs, fragments of locks, an ivory ornament, and another two bronze feet from a stool similar to those found in shop no. 2.

This distribution of artefacts is somewhat confusing, and in most cases probably related to storage rather than use: it is more illuminating to consider the activities that these artefacts probably represented. There are both male and female toilet-objects, including a razor, perfume-bottles, parts of two different necklaces, the stone from a ring, a mirror and two pairs of tweezers. There were also several shells, which may have been used to mix make-up. These imply that at least some of the inhabitants had the time and inclination to care for and adorn their bodies. A die suggests leisure activity. Only limited evidence for cooking (one bronze pot) is recorded—suggesting, misleadingly, that the house was not properly inhabited in AD 79. Terracotta vessels were used predominantly in cooking, and, given the nature and speed of excavation, it would not be surprising if the excavators had simply omitted to record these 'worthless' pots. This explanation makes sense when we examine the evidence for dining. There is wide evidence for tablewares of all sorts—in silver, bronze, glass and *terra sigillata*. Large bronze bowls and jugs would have been used for ablutions before and after meals, and smaller glass and *terra sigillata* bowls and plates, glass beakers, and bronze jugs and *casseruole* would have been used to serve and consume food and drink.[19] Interestingly, these vessels were found distributed *throughout* the house, and they indicate that the inhabitants had the ability to hold formal dinners and entertain guests. The most difficult artefacts to explain are those related to equestrian equipment—parts of bridles and the strange bronze hooves. This suggests that the inhabitants of the house kept a donkey or mule, perhaps connected to the unknown commercial activity out of the attached shop.

In the case of the House of the Beautiful Impluvium, some excavation reports are missing and there is evidence of wide post-eruption disturbance. In addition, building work seems to have been taking place, and parts of the house were in need of redecoration. Based on this evidence for building work and the lack of recorded cooking equipment, we might conclude that the House of the Beautiful Impluvium was uninhabited at the time of the eruption. But when we examine the other categories of artefact, we see that this could not be the case. The uncovered artefacts represent a range of domestic activities, including dining and dicing, toilet activities and personal adornment. The range of tablewares and personal objects indicate that the house was still occupied in AD 79; the sheer quantity of coins and other valuable objects suggest that the inhabitants were prospering. The fact that few terracotta pots, *amphorae* or tools of any kind (that would represent cooking, storage and specific work activities) are documented, probably means that they were overlooked in the reporting of the rapid 1950s' excavations.

The analysis of *instrumentum domesticum* adds a new dimension to the study of Pompeian houses. It both allows a more accurate interpretation of the nature and organisation of domestic life in each household in AD 79, and illustrates the complexity of each house and shop and the range of activities carried out which are not normally visible in the architectural and decorative record. Architecture and decoration alone do not give an accurate picture of the activities that took place in a house or shop. Yet the artefacts found within these spaces often complicate rather than clarify the picture. The artefactual record is by no means complete and is often difficult to interpret. This makes it important to look at the ensemble of artefacts within a house, to identify the range of activities that are taking place rather than to focus on the issue of room-use. Many activities, such as dining, are to be expected; but the artefacts help to reveal how such activities might take place alongside, for example, commercial activities as part of normal everyday activity. The artefactual evidence brings to life our understanding of each individual house and adds to our understanding of the nature of domestic life.

NOTES

1 I would like to thank Pietro Giovanni Guzzo and Antonio d'Ambrosio for permission to carry out the primary research upon which this chapter is based. I am also grateful for the guidance of Franco Striano, Ciro Sicignano and Luigi Matrone in the *Casa di Bacco*.

2 These figures exclude the massive quantity of artefacts to be found in the National Museum at Naples, and in museums around the world.

3 P. M. Allison, *Pompeian Households: an analysis of the material culture*, Los Angeles, 2004; J. Berry, 'Household artefacts: towards a reinterpretation of Roman domestic space', in R. Laurence and A. Wallace-Hadrill (eds), *Domestic Space in the Roman World: Pompeii and beyond*, JRA Suppl. Ser. no. 22, 1997, pp. 183–95; J. Berry, 'The conditions of domestic life in Pompeii AD 79: a case-study of houses 11 and 12, Insula 9, Region I', *PBSR*, 1997, vol. 65, pp. 103–25. There has been recent success in tracking down some of the contents of a few of the earliest excavated houses, such as the House of the Faun (VI.12); cf. M. Borriello, A. d'Ambrosio, S. De Caro and P. G. Guzzo, *Pompei. Abitare sotto il Vesuvio*, Ferrara, 1996.

4 Catalogues include Borriello *et al.*, *Abitare*; B. Conticello, *Rediscovering Pompeii*, Rome, 1990; M. R. Borriello (ed.), *Le collezioni del Museo Nazionale di Napoli*, Rome/Milan, 1989; T. Budetta and M. Pagano, *Ercolano: legni e piccoli bronzi. Testimonianze dell'arredo e delle suppellettini della casa romana*, Mostra, Soprintendenza Archeologica di Pompei, 1988; J. P. Ward-Perkins and A. Claridge, *Pompeii AD 79*, London, 1976. Studies of individual types of artefacts include (on pottery): V. Di Giovanni, 'Produzione e consumo di ceramica da cucina nella Campania romana (II a.C.–II d.C.)', in *Les céramiques communes de Campanie et de Narbonnaise (Ier s.av.J-C.–IIe s.ap. J-C.). La vaisselle de cuisine et de table*, Naples, 1996, pp. 65–103; G. Gasperetti, 'Produzione e consumo della ceramica da mensa e dispensa nella Campania romana', in *Céramiques communes*, pp. 19–63; V. Castiglione Morelli del Franco, 'La ceramica nell'instrumentum domesticum della casa di C. Polibio a Pompei', in *Céramiques communes*, pp. 105–12; V. Di Giovanni and G. Gasperetti, 'Materiali per l'elaborazione di una tipologia della ceramica comune di Pompei', *Société française de la céramique antique en Gaule*, Suppl. Actes du Congres de Versailles, Paris, 1993, pp. 267–79; C. Panella, 'Per uno studio delle anfore di Pompei', *StMisc*, 1974, vol. 22, pp. 151–62; (on bronze vessels): S. Tassinari, *Il vassellame bronzeo di Pompei*, Rome, 1993; (on terracotta figurines): M. R. Borriello and A. d'Ambrosio, *Le terrecotte figurate di Pompei*, Rome, 1990; (on bronze lamps): M. Conticello de Spagnolis and E. De Carolis, *Le lucerne di bronzo di Ercolano e Pompei*, The Vatican, 1988; N. Valenza Mele, *Catalogo delle lucerne in bronzo. Museo Nazionale di Napoli*, Rome, 1983; (on jewellery): V. Castiglione Morelli del Franco, 'Le oreficerie della casa di C. Giulio Polibio', in *La regione sotterrata dal Vesuvio. Studi e prospettivi*. Atti del convegno internazionale 11–15 novembre 1979, Naples, 1982, pp. 789–808; (on medical instruments): R. Jackson, 'A set of Roman medical instruments from Italy', *Britannia* 1986, vol. 17, pp. 119–67; (on glass vessels from Herculaneum): L. A. Scatozza Höricht, *I vetri romani di Ercolano*, Rome, 1986.

5 Cf. V. Castiglione Morelli del Franco, 'Il giornale dei soprastanti di Pompei e le Notizie degli Scavi', in L. Franchi dell'Orto (ed.), *Ercolano 1738–1988. 250 anni di ricerca archeologica*. Atti del Convegno Internazionale Ravello-Ercolano-Napoli-Pompei 30 ottobre–5 novembre 1988, Rome, 1993, pp. 659–66, on the archives. At Naples there is the *Archivio Storico della Soprintendenza Archeologica di Napoli e Caserta*, the *Archivio di Stato*, the *Biblioteca Nazionale Vittorio Emanuele*, the *Biblioteca di Storia Patria*; at Pompeii the archives of the *Soprintendenza* are held in the *Casa di Bacco*; at Rome documentation can also be found in the *Archivio dell'Istituto Archeologico Germanico*.

6 J. Berry (ed.), *Unpeeling Pompeii*, Catalogue of the exhibition held at the Auditorium of Pompeii 1 October–15 December 1998, Milan, 1998; Berry, 'Household artefacts'; Berry, 'Conditions of domestic life'; Borriello *et al.*, *Abitare sotto il Vesuvio*; S. T. A. M. Mols, 'Osservazioni sulla forma e tecnica del mobilio ligneo di Ercolano', in Franchi dell'Orto, *Ercolano 1738–1988*, pp. 489–98; Allison, *Pompeian Households*; E. J. Dwyer, *Pompeian Domestic Sculpture: a study of five Pompeian houses and their contents*, Rome 1982; E. J. Dwyer, 'Sculpture and its display in private houses of Pompeii', in *Pompeii and the Vesuvian Landscape*, Washington, DC, 1979, pp. 59–77.

7 H. Sigurdsson, S. Cashdollar and S. R. J. Sparks, 'The eruption of Vesuvius in AD 79: reconstruction from historical and volcanological evidence', *AJA*, 1982, vol. 86, pp. 39–51.

8 See E. De Carolis, G. Patricelli and A. Ciarallo, 'Rinvenimenti di corpi umani nell'area urbana di Pompei', *RStPomp*, 1998, vol. 9, pp. 75–123.

9 G. Fiorelli discovered this technique in 1863. By 1874 this technique was used commonly in the excavations. Initially used to make casts of bodies, the technique was later applied to make casts of voids left by wooden furniture. Unfortunately it has not been used consistently, and much depends on the ability of the excavators to recognise the presence of a void before it is completely unearthed and destroyed, and to have the necessary materials and time to make the plaster-cast.

10 Tassinari, *Vassellame bronzeo*; C. F. Moss, *Roman Marble Tables*, Ph.D. thesis, Princeton University, 1988, p. 6; M. Annecchino, 'Suppellettile fittile per uso agricolo in Pompei e nell'agro vesuviano', in *Regione sotterata dal Vesuvio*, p. 755; M. Annecchino, 'Suppellittile fittile da cucina di Pompei', in M. Annecchino (ed.), *L'Instrumentum Domesticum di Ercolano e Pompeii nella prima età imperiale*, Rome, 1977, p. 105; M. Annecchino, 'Fritillus. Un piccolo vaso di terracotta', *CronPomp*, 1977, vol. 3, p. 198; J.-P. Morel, 'La ceramica e il vetro', in F. Zevi

(ed.), *Pompei 79. Raccolta di studi per il decimonono centenario dell'eruzione Vesuviana*, Naples, 1979, p. 243; A. Rocco, 'Pompeiana Supplex', in A. Maiuri (ed.), *Pompeiana. Raccolta di studi per il secondo centenario degli scavi di Pompei*, Naples, 1950, p. 279.

11 For different points of view, see J. J. Dobbins, 'Problems of chronology, decoration, and urban design in the forum at Pompeii', *AJA*, 1994, vol. 98, pp. 629–94; J. Andreau, 'Histoire des séismes et histoire economique: le tremblement de terre di Pompeii (62 ap. J.-C.)', *AnnÉconSocCiv*, 1973, vol. 28, pp. 369–95; P. Allison, 'On-going seismic activity and its effects on the living conditions in Pompeii in the last decades', in *Archäologie und Seismologie. La regione Vesuviana dal 62 al 79 D.C. Problemi archeologici e sismologici*, Colloquim Boscoreale 26–27 Novembre 1993, Munich, 1995, pp. 183–9; and other papers in *Archäologie und Seismologie*.

12 For an example of this approach, see Berry, 'Conditions of domestic life'.

13 Cf. P. Allison, 'Artefact distribution and spatial function in Pompeian houses', in B. Rawson and P. Weaver (eds), *The Roman Family in Italy. Status, sentiment, space*, Oxford, 1997, pp. 321–54 on the unreliability of the literary sources for determining room function.

14 L. Binford, 'Behaviour archaeology and the "Pompeii premise"', *Journal of Anthropological Research*, 1981, vol. 37, pp. 195–208; against this view, P. Allison, 'Artefact assemblages: not "the Pompeii premise"', in E. Herring, R. Whitehouse and J. Wilkins (eds), *Papers of the Fourth Conference of Italian Archaeology*, London, 1992, vol. 3, pt. I, pp. 49–56.

15 *Insula* I.9 is currently the focus of a British School at Rome project. For a more detailed description of the architecture and decoration of this house, see A. Wallace-Hadrill, 'Region I Insula 9. The British Project', in Berry, *Unpeeling Pompeii*, pp. 49–55.

16 Tassinari, *Vassellame bronzeo*, pp. 230ff. discusses the function of bronze vessels.

17 Cf. W. H. Manning, *Catalogue of the Romano-British Iron Tools, Fittings and Weapons in the British Museum*, London, 1985, pl. XVI. A reconstruction of a cutler's shop can be found in the Museum of London; cf. J. Hall and R. Merrifield, *Roman London*, London, 1986, p. 37 for an illustration.

18 E.g., A. Pasqui, 'La villa Pompeiana della Pisanella presso Boscoreale', *Monumenti Antichi dell'Accademia dei Lincei*, 1897, vol. 7, pp. 411–15, 477; Allison, 'Artefact distribution', pp. 333ff.

19 Tassinari, *Vassellame bronzeo*, pp. 230ff.

CHAPTER TWENTY

DOMESTIC DECORATION
Painting and the "Four Styles"

———•◆•———

Volker Michael Strocka

INTRODUCTION

We can hardly imagine how colorful were the houses of Pompeii or any other Roman city during the early imperial period. Today the walls are largely bare, revealing mostly structural and chronological details. Originally they were all plastered, and many were brightly painted. Exterior walls were usually simply whitewashed above a red or black socle, but façades and especially entryways of houses or shops received additional ornamentation in the form of colorful faux masonry, figural shop signs, representations of gods, or apotropaic symbols. On the interior, hardly a room aside from cellars, storage rooms and narrow corridors contained walls without ornamental and/or figural paintings (Figure 20.1). Even ceilings were brightly painted; these echoed floors in colorful terrazzo or black-and-white mosaics, sometimes with colorful *emblemata* (cf. Clarke, Ch. 21).[1]

There was nothing random about the elements of the decoration; their selection was governed by firm conventions, less according to room function than the laws of commensurability. The relative quantity of decorative extravagance corresponded to a hierarchy of room purposes and an ongoing, deliberate escalation in the representation of private luxury. Naturally the amount and quality of painted decoration was always determined by a homeowner's financial means, resulting in interiors of vastly different degrees of opulence but dating to the same period.

Each wall was divided up according to a pre-selected decorative scheme, usually without taking into consideration doors, windows or niches. Following ancient traditions, each wall had a dado course and main zone, and often an additional upper zone. The decoration of each horizontal zone was usually governed by particular rules. What all three normally had in common was a symmetrical division into three, five, or occasionally two vertical sections. In Roman wall decoration, there was no such thing as a neutral space for hanging up pictures. Instead, pictures were painted on the wall and incorporated into the decorative scheme described above. The viewer was usually confronted with an unobstructed view of the entire wall-space, because there were seldom items of furniture in the way (but cf. Allison, Ch. 17; Berry, Ch. 19). Closets were often built-in, and banqueting couches (*klinai*) and tables rarely

Figure 20.1   House of Julia Felix (II.4.2), "zebra-pattern" decoration on west wall of passage (90b) near *atrium* (93) (Fourth Style). Photo: Arch. Inst. Bochum 73/8/7 (G. Fittschen-Badura).

extended past the dado, which tended to be simply decorated where it was anticipated such furniture would stand.

DECORATIVE SCHEMES

The following, basic decorative strategies usually pertained to the design of the main zone, though sometimes they occurred only in the dado or upper zone:[2]

1   Imitation of marble revetment in fields, and/or with architectural elements. This may be limited to the dado or extend into the main zone (cf. Fant, Ch. 22; Figure 20.2).

2   Colonnaded architectural schemes that articulate the wall-surface while at the same time creating the illusion of space. These often have a central *aedicula* and illusionistic vistas, or a framed central painting (usually containing a mythological theme; Figures 1.2, 20.4 and 26.2).

3 Large single figures or figural scenes (megalography). These are rare; they may be arranged paratactically in friezes or be divided by monumental architectural elements (Figure 20.11).

4 The main zone is divided into fields that either stand side by side, or are separated from one another using ornamental pilaster strips or architectural vistas. Fields may contain central framed paintings flanked by *emblemata* in axial symmetry, or paratactically arranged vignettes. In extravagant cases, the central field of the wall is highlighted by an *aedicula*. This is, by far, the most common scheme (Figures 20.5–10).

5 Extensive garden or landscape paintings. These are generally reserved for great peristyles, but can sometimes be found in *cubicula* (cf. Jashemski, Ch. 31). These scenes are often populated by wild animals, and occasionally Pygmies or Egyptian motifs. Such vistas may fill the entire wall above the dado, be divided into fields or be separated by architectural elements (Figures 23.21, 31.1).

6 Endlessly repeating patterns that resemble carpets. These do not appear until the final (Fourth) style. They entirely cover either the main or the upper zone.

The first scheme came into use with the First Style. The other types were used from the Second Style until late antiquity in stylistically variable forms. Ceiling paintings were based on coffering in the first two styles; in later periods they were divided into complicated patterns of fields in an undefined space that emphasized axes or diagonals (cf. Clarke, Ch. 21; Figure 21.5).

TECHNIQUE[3]

All Campanian wall paintings were painted in *buon fresco*. Pigments were applied to fine calcite plaster while it was still moist, in one-day sections, following preliminary sketches (*sinopie*). When the paint was almost dry, it was burnished with small marble rollers to increase its luminous quality. Additional decorative elements, such as vignettes or fine details in the figural paintings, were added onto the dry walls in tempera technique with the addition of special binding media. The top layer of fine plaster, approximately 1–5 mm thick, covered one or more layers of coarser plaster, together several centimeters thick. The thickness, quality and composition of plaster layers changed over time.

CHRONOLOGY

The wall paintings of Herculaneum, Pompeii and Stabiae were admired for nearly a century and a half without accounting for stylistic differences. Eventually, in the latter nineteenth century, the German archaeologist August Mau demonstrated that it was possible to distinguish between four stylistic periods, based on numerous observations of relative chronology and precise typological gradations in the wall paintings of Pompeii. In 1882 he presented his revolutionary conclusions in an exhaustive study, at least with respect to the first three styles. In all essential points, his observations have remained valid. Some fine-tuning in chronology has occurred, however. The dates of the transitions from the First to Second Style and from the Third to Fourth Style are now thought to be approximately two decades earlier than Mau's dates (Table 20.1).

Figure 20.2 House of the Faun (VI.12), northwest corner of the second peristyle (39) (First Style, *c*.100 BC).

The First Style (third–second centuries BC)[4]

The earliest kind of identifiable Campanian wall decoration imitates the elements of Greek masonry in colored plaster (Figures 20.2, 27.1). Strict tectonic rules of monumental stone construction are followed rather freely, but the ancient division of the wall into zones is preserved. The smooth dado or socle is often topped by a molded string course, while the main zone, at eye level, is richly structured in orthostates and courses of ashlar masonry blocks; it is usually crowned by a molded cornice, rarely by a complete entablature. The upper zone is often smooth and monochromatic; in later examples, this is motivated by the creation of vistas through rows of half-columns and pilasters.

Different combinations of these few elements and changes in their proportions multiplied into an astonishing number of variations which were further differentiated by the use of different color schemes, polychrome marbling, painted moldings and other ornamentation. The imitation of expensive types of marble suggests that real revetments (in use as early as the fourth century BC) were copied (cf. Fant, Ch. 22). While possible, a more important consideration may have been to effect an artificial reality, created by the illusion of fabulous wealth and the playful distribution of structural elements that far surpassed physical reality. The First Style is related and equal in this intent to the following three styles.

305

Table 20.1 A chronological survey of painting styles

FIRST STYLE	
Pompeii (VI.2.4), House of Sallust	175–150 BC
Pompeii (VIII.1), Basilica	130/120
Pompeii (VI.12), House of the Faun	120/100
Pompeii (VI.11.8–10), House of the Labyrinth	100
SECOND STYLE	
Phase Ia	100–80 BC
Rome, Palatine Hill, House of the Griffons	100–90
Phase Ib	80–50
Brescia, republican temples	after 89
Pompeii, Villa of the Mysteries	after 80
Phase Ic	70–50
Pompeii (VI.11.8–10), House of the Labyrinth	70–60
Boscoreale, Villa of P. Fannius Synistor	60
Oplontis, Villa of Poppaea	60–50
Phase IIa	50–30
Pompeii (VI.17 [*Ins. Occ.*]. 41), House with private library	50–40
Pompeii (V.2.i), House of the Silver Wedding	40
Pompeii (V.1.18), House of the Greek epigrams	40–30
Rome, Palatine Hill, House of "Augustus"	30
Pompeii (I.6.2), House of the Cryptoporticus	30
Pompeii (IX.14.2, 4), House of M. Obellius Firmus	30
Phase IIb	30–20
Rome, Palatine Hill, House of "Livia"	30–20
Rome, Palatine Hill, Aula Isiaca	30–20
Masada (Israel)	after 36
Herodion (Israel)	after 24
Pompeii (V.5.3), Gladiatorial Barracks	30–20
THIRD STYLE	
Early Phase	
Rome, Pyramid of Cestius	before 12, *c.*20 BC
Pompeii, Villa Imperiale	20–10
Oplontis, Villa of Poppaea	20–1
Pompeii (IX.8.3, 6), House of the Centenary, room (41)	10–1

The palette is warm and bright. Ocher, red shading to violet, and dark green predominate; black, white and, rarely, blue also appear. Faux marbling incorporates the same colors. Where monochromatic ashlar blocks or orthostates are painted, the colors are mixed in bright profusion, whereas in the Greek East the colors changed by registers. Figural representations are entirely subordinate to the architectonic structural system. On the Greek island of Delos, a frieze placed at eye level may include miniature depictions of *erotes* at play or scenes from comedy. At Pompeii, however, figural scenes are rendered upon the masonry surfaces themselves: mythological scenes, figures developed out of the marbling, or illusionistic objects such as a towel suspended in front of an orthostate. The dominance of the modeled architectural system on the walls displaces larger figural representations—always signs of particular ostentation—to the floor mosaics, as in the House of the Faun (VI.12).

The chronology of the First Style in Pompeii remains uncertain. Architectural wall

Table 20.1 *(continued)*

Middle Phase	
Boscotrecase, Villa of Agrippa Postumus	AD 1–10
Rome, Esquiline Hill, Auditorium of Maecenas	1–10
Pompeii, Villa of the Mysteries, *tablinum* (2)	10–20
Pompeii (VII.3.29), House of M. Spurius Mesor	10–20
Pompeii (VII.9.1, 43), Eumachia building	10–20
Rome, Tomb of Pomponius Hylas	19–37
Pompeii (VII.4.59), House of the Bronzes	20–30
Pompeii (VI.11.8–10), House of the Labyrinth, baths	20–30
Late Phase	
Pompeii (IX.9.b, c), House of C. Sulpicius Rufus	35–40
Pompeii (II.7), Palaestra, north wing	before 42, *c.*35–40
Pompeii (VI.14.20), House of Orpheus, *triclinium* (l)	35–40
Pompeii (IX.1.22), House of M. Epidius Sabinus, *triclinium* (t')	*c.*40
Pompeii (VII.4.56), House of the Grand Duke, *tablinum* (11)	*c.*40
Pompeii (I.6.15), House of the Ceii	35–45
Pompeii (V.4.a), House of M. Lucretius Fronto	40–45
Pompeii (V.1.26), House of L. Caecilius Iucundus, *tablinum* (i)	40–45
FOURTH STYLE	
Rome, "Domus Transitoria"	after AD 41
Stabiae, Villa of Ariadne, *atrium*	45–50
Stabiae, Villa of San Marco, upper peristyle	45–50
Pompeii (VI.15.1), House of the Vetti, *alae* (h) and (i)	*c.*50
Pompeii (I.10.4), House of the Menander	50–55
Pompeii (VI.15.7, 8), House of the Prince of Naples	50–60
Pompeii (V.2.i), House of the Silver Wedding	shortly before 60
Pompeii (VII.9.7–8), Macellum	shortly before 62
Pompeii (I.6.4), House of the Lararium	61/62
Pompeii (VI.15.1), House of the Vetti, remainder of decoration	soon after 62
Pompeii (VI.16.7), House of the Gilded Cupids	soon after 62
Rome, Domus Aurea	64–68
Jerusalem, Mirgov Ladakh Street	before 70
Pompeii (VII.4.48), House of the Hunt	after 71
Pompeii (VII.12.18), Big Lupanar	after 72

designs were modeled in plaster in Greece as early as the fourth century BC (Athens, Kolophon, Olynthos, Samothrace).[5] As at Morgantina on Sicily, such decorative schemes were certainly also used in Pompeii by the third century BC. The oldest preserved examples are the *atrium, ala* and *tablinum* of the House of Sallust (VI.2.3–5); judging by the style of the pilaster capital in the *ala*, it can be dated no later than the second quarter of the second century BC. The basilica at Pompeii was probably built and decorated around 130–120 BC; the House of the Faun was thoroughly rebuilt toward the end of the second century and was extensively decorated with opulent stucco work that approaches the proportions and sequences of slabs of the Second Style. The First Style in the House of the Labyrinth (VI.11.9–10) is part of the second phase of the house, which is dated by architectural details and mosaics to *c.*100 BC.[6] There is no example of the First Style in Pompeii that must necessarily date to after the founding of the Roman colony in 80 BC (but cf. Dobbins, Ch. 12).

The Second Style (*c.*100–20 BC)[7]

The revolutionary transformation of the solid First-Style system into an illusionistic play of infinite possibilities can only have taken place around 100 BC in Rome, the new center of the Mediterranean world, a city extremely unstable both politically and socially. The new style was a qualitative innovation; instead of representing the architectural structure of the wall in modeled plaster relief, the entire wall was rendered *trompe l'oeil*. The Second Style used plaster moldings only at the edges of walls or as framing around lunettes. In the very earliest example, the House of the Griffons on the Palatine in Rome, it was not enough simply to paint in the orthostates, masonry courses and cornices in shadows and highlights. Instead, the painterly possibilities were immediately exploited for more complex representations (e.g. at Pompeii, Figures 20.4, 21.1): offset podia seen from above, columns and pilasters placed in front of screen walls, foreshortened coffered ceilings seen from below, and perspectivally rendered pediments. It was not possible to depict such depth and complexity in modeled plaster (cf. Clarke, Ch. 21).

The perspectival effect of superimposed planes of space soon led to the next step: open vistas appearing to look beyond the wall onto colonnades, peristyle courts, gardens, the sea or the distant blue sky. This illusionistic space was not staged as a consistent expansion of the real space of the room, but conceived as a separate pictorial space for each wall. A dado or podium always blocks direct access, and even in those places where the podium recedes, a base molding or step prevents the fictive extension of the floor. Each wall is framed by pilasters or posts that do not stand proud of the wall, but are, instead, bisected by the corner and continue at right angles on the next wall in the same role as framing elements (Figure 21.1). The painters certainly mastered the use of perspective, but only rarely used a single central vanishing point. Especially long walls exhibit parallel lines of recession; several vanishing points can be present in a single wall. These are rarely the results of mistakes; instead, the overall effect of the decorative scheme from different viewpoints is emphasized.

The open vistas so characteristic of the Second Style are reserved for the most prominent rooms of a house or villa. The vast majority of Second-Style walls in Pompeii are decorated with closed architectures that deviate increasingly from First-Style formulas and develop a considerable range of permutations (Figures 20.3, 27.4).

There have been attempts to show that the fictive architectural murals of the Second Style derived from theatrical set painting—indeed, some have interpreted them as depictions of entire stage façades (*scaenae frontes*) (Figure 26.2).[8] This theory is correct insofar as the new wall-painting style could not have evolved so quickly, had it not been for theater painting, which had used foreshortening, shading and architectural perspective with ever increasing sophistication starting in the fifth century BC. However, Second-Style fictive architectures developed out of First-Style wall designs and were not meant to be representational. Instead, from the beginning they depicted fanciful, disorienting compositions that offered viewers a multitude of associations, including an element of irony toward the end of the style. Far exceeding the First Style in this regard, the display of opulence, the perspectival visions and the "props" increasingly and lavishly strewn throughout, all conspired to evoke the seductive magic of a hyperreality—a fanciful fictive world (Figures 1.2, 20.4).

Figure 20.3 House of Ceres (I.9.13), *cubiculum* (c) (Second Style, *c*.50–40 BC).
Photo: ICCD N 38760.

In addition to architectural designs, the Second Style includes the category of the landscape frieze with loosely varying topographical or figural motifs, apparently inspired by Alexandrian Nilotic landscapes. Monumental figural scenes (megalography) are rare; where they do appear, they are always integrated into the overall spatial illusion of the architectonic wall design. By pulling individual figures or groups from Hellenistic wall painting or panel painting, painters let them "step out" from the framework and suggest their actual presence in the architecture (e.g., Dionysiac scenes in the Great Frieze of *oecus* [5] in the Villa of the Mysteries or the controversially interpreted mythological figures of hall (H) in the Villa of P. Fannius Synistor at Boscoreale). Only in the second phase of the Second Style (*c*.50–20 BC) does an autonomous, framed picture in the center of the wall become generally accepted.

H. G. Beyen has done commendable work on the chronology of the Second Style. His classification of phases Ia-b-c and IIa-b, as well as his analysis of the datable characteristics in each, has justly stood the test of time. However, his absolute chronology is set a bit too low. In his day the House of Augustus was not yet known. Closely correlated with the Temple of Apollo on the Palatine, the House of Augustus

Figure 20.4 Pompeii (VI.17 [*Ins. Occ.*].41), *exedra* (Second Style, *c.*50–40 BC).

must have been vowed in 36 BC and completed in 28 BC at the latest. Its paintings, which belong to the transition from IIa to IIb, must date to around 30 BC. On the other hand, we can now be certain that the frescoes of the House of the Griffons in Rome were painted around 100 BC (90 at the latest).

Extravagant open architectures with receding vistas most easily allow us to trace relative stylistic development. The complexity and scale of the central vista increase until the end of Phase Ic. Then a counter-movement takes place—the central motif is transformed into an increasingly independent picture, and new vistas may be opened up to the sides as wall surfaces are re-emphasized. Architectural features become increasingly delicate, mannered and elongated, until they are partly replaced by fantastic vegetal creations (in IIb). More and more plant-derived patterns and motifs infiltrate the architectural order as early as Phase Ic. Increasingly frequent in Phases IIa (and particularly IIb) are ironic deviations from the norm, and fantastic hybrid creatures that enliven the wall structures. In the end, these hybrids take on tectonic functions in entirely unrealistic ways.

Colors also indicate stylistic sub-phases. At the beginning, they hardly differ from color schemes favored in the First Style. The range of colors expands from Ic on (and especially in Ic); mixed shades and expensive colors such as blue and cinnabar red are applied more frequently. In general, warm and glowing colors are used, and the realism of highlights and deeper shading in Phase Ic also make them more "painterly" than before. In Phase II the colors become increasingly light. At the end, cool, broken colors are preferred. Highlights and shadows continue to be painted, but they serve less to evoke the three-dimensionality of objects than to emphasize painterly, unreal qualities and to increase a general sense of unease.

The Third Style (*c.*20 BC–AD 40/50)[9]

The late Second Style uses increasingly delicate architectural elements to configure the surface decorations; the Third Style takes this trend further, towards a radically new way of structuring them. The podium no longer projects, and we no longer see architectonic vistas in the main zones; instead, these are banished to the upper zone where they only appear in miniaturized and entirely unrealistic form (Figure 20.5).

Figure 20.5   Pompeii, Villa Imperiale, *cubiculum* (B), north wall (Third Style, *c.*20 BC).
Photo: DAI Berlin 83.3.580 (P. Grunwald).

Figure 20.6 Pompeii, Villa Imperiale, *oecus* (A), south wall with death of Icarus (Third Style, *c.*20 BC). Photo: DAI Berlin 84.2.559 (P. Grunwald).

The main zone consists either of simple blocks of color (plain or bearing vignettes), arranged paratactically and divided by spindly elements such as columns or candelabra, or else the middle of the wall contains a non-perspectival *aedicula* that frames and highlights a separate figural painting (Figures 20.6 and 23.7).

Mau christened the most delicate form of this scheme the "candelabrum style," after its most characteristic element. However, we should not consider it a separate "style," but rather a restrained decorative strategy consisting of a closed wall with fields articulated by extremely thin elements, usually placed paratactically, during the late Second and early Third Styles. The architectural elements are entirely free of any traditional proportions or realism, unless we envision ephemeral festival ornaments of wood or metal (Figure 20.7). The serene and precisely framed blocks of color contrast with finely detailed ornaments of crystalline patterns or stylized plants and blossoms in a manner that recalls Classical, or even Archaic Greek, ornament. The basic impression of stillness and simplicity created by the above-named elements

Figure 20.7   House of the Priest Amandus (I.7.7), *triclinium* (b), north wall
(Third Style, *c.*AD 30–40). Photo: GFN N 35349.

is, however, extremely complex. Strict symmetry, linear precision in the depiction of all elements, and the highlighting of miniature motifs and ornaments produce an air of mannered elegance.

Figural representations and the compositions of paintings in the central fields also take part in the new style. Outlines of figures are emphasized, and they are often placed on a pale background devoid of spatial depth. Three-dimensionality is represented using tiny, linear brush strokes with little shading or projection. Compositions, resembling reliefs, tend to avoid energetic motion. Cool and broken colors are used in the paintings as well as the wall schemes (which does not exclude saturated red, yellow or black for large fields). As imaginative as the many variations are, no wall of the Third Style lacks articulation by means of relatively abstract dividing elements, entablatures and lines of architectural derivation.

Landscape painting is limited to vignettes, pinakes or central panels. A special type of landscape develops, consisting of many parts wherein mythological scenes are miniaturized and strewn throughout, sometimes continuously. Garden painting, which becomes more common during this period, is also never found without a strong division into fields using non-perspectival architectures. Tendril scrolls and scattered

Figure 20.8 *Thermopolium* (I.8.8), *triclinium* (10), east wall, with a niche for a dining couch (Third Style, *c*.AD 20–30). Photo: GFN N 38290.

blossoms, appearing first on ceilings, introduce new, free possibilities of wall decoration. Central pictures, originating in the late Second Style, gain increased prominence, although formats vary greatly (Figure 20.8). Compositions derive from the repertoire of Hellenistic panel paintings, but those prototypes are modified in the classicizing taste described above. A systematic effort is now made at formal and thematic integration of the central pictures within a room into a single program (*Bildprogramm*). Also characteristic are miniaturistic figural vignettes in the side panels, and scenes made up of small figures on the predellas that become common under the main fields and in the friezes above them.

There are extraordinarily few fixed chronological dates. Around 20 BC, the burial chamber of the Pyramid of Cestius in Rome was probably painted; the mention of M. Vipsanius Agrippa as heir suggests that the monument was completed before 12 BC. Several rooms of the House of the Centenary (IX.8.3, 6), especially *triclinium* (41), are decorated in a consistent manner and dated by a *graffito* to before AD 15.[10] Frescoes in the Third Style, now lost, in the *atrium* and *tablinum* of House VI.14.5 included several *graffiti* with consular dates between AD 17 and 29.[11] According to its earliest inscription, the preserved paintings in the tomb of Pomponius Hylas in Rome date to the period AD 19–37.[12] A *graffito* was scratched before AD 42 into a column in the north hall of the *palaestra* in Pompeii; thus, its paintings must be older. No other absolute dates have yet been found.

A relative chronology of Third-Style walls cannot rest on as firm a foundation as the consistent and logical development of the Second Style. The earliest examples (Villa Imperiale, outside the Porta Marina) simplify and disembody the forms of the late Second Style. The latest walls (*tablina* in the Houses of M. Lucretius Fronto [V.4.a, 11], and of L. Caecilius Iucundus [V.1.26]) create hybrid forms transitional to the Fourth Style, to which they contribute isolated floral elements and painterly effects. The Third Style appears to be sober and restrained, but also particularly detailed and miniaturistic, during the middle and late Augustan era. Developments during the reigns of Tiberius and Caligula (Figures 20.8, 20.13) are characterized by the enlargement of ornaments, the increased enlivening of the compositions by the use of rigidly stylized floral elements (plants in the socle, undulating branches), the increased use and layering of non-perspectival architectural schemes, and the use of warmer colors. There is no evidence to indicate that the Third Style was in use after the 40s of the first century AD.

The Third Style developed during the second decade of the principate in conscious reaction to the mannerism of the late Second Style. The classicizing, eclectic nature of the Third Style, its avoidance of passionate or painterly elements, and its refined simplicity and precision all fit perfectly with the character of the Augustan state, just as it was expressed in other genres of Augustan art. The regnal years of the emperor Tiberius (AD 14–37) first saw unbroken continuity, then gradually stagnation, in a coarsening and multiplication of the unchanged repertoire of forms. The short reign of Caligula (AD 37–41) may have initiated an about-face. It was not until Claudius that a new style, the Fourth Style, was conceived.

The Fourth Style (*c.*AD 40/50–79/100)[13]

If the Third Style is classicizing, then the Fourth Style is consciously the opposite. Once again, warm colors, dark shadows and highlights are used, as well as more relaxed brushstrokes—in short, it is a painterly style that avoids the linearity and simplicity of its predecessor. There is a love of contrasts, such as those between flat undifferentiated surfaces and perspectival vistas, or between realistic details in an irrational context. Dynamic forms are preferred, especially undulating plants (volutes, tendrils, blossoms and garlands [Figure 21.4]), and animals (swans, dolphins, griffins, etc.). A typical element rarely left out of even the most humble decorative schemes is the filigree "embroidery" border in all its endless variations (Figures 20.9 and 23.15).

None of these innovations can be explained as developments out of the Third Style, since their effect is to negate all of the latter's principles, but seem, rather, a conscious revival of the Second Style (IIb), without copying its works precisely. Since the typological innovations of the Third Style are largely retained, although dominated by an overall organic, ornamental and irrational character, the Fourth Style is an entirely new kind of decorative scheme with a nearly infinite repertoire. However, the compositional types of the Third Style do continue, with variations. These include the three-part or five-part wall scheme with central *aedicula*, the bisected narrow wall, the restrained division into fields, and, especially, the field-and-divider-strip pattern in the main zone, where dividers are either filled (as before) with candelabra, arabesques and other ornaments, or contain vistas onto fantastical architectures (Figure 20.10).

Figure 20.9   House of the Moralist (III.4.2–3), *triclinium* (g), south wall
(Fourth Style, *c.*AD 50). Photo: Arch. Inst. Freiburg 81/9/8 (W. Gut).

The flat dado divided into fields often decorated with bundles of plants, the interior frames and vignettes of the fields flanking the main zone, the more or less prominent central scenes, and the architectural fantasies in the upper zone are also all retained. New elements include rare architectural vistas serving as a stage for mythological scenes in the main zone, which may even extend into the dado; large garden paintings and landscapes set within window-like frames but not subdivided in themselves (Figures 20.11, 31.1); and the still rare wallpaper patterns or ornamental friezes in the main zone. Circular and diagonal schemes become favored in ceiling paintings (Figure 21.5). Once again, the painting style and the dynamic, three-dimensional compositions of figural scenes recall late Classical and Hellenistic prototypes, although they can hardly be considered exact copies.

Scholars have diligently tried to distinguish workshops and oeuvres of individual painters who almost never signed their work.[14] Persuasive solutions are scarce. Even if it is possible, through careful analysis, to identify the personal style of a painter of figural scenes in several different paintings, we still cannot know the full range of any one workshop's repertoire of motifs, with its fluctuating personnel. Pattern books presumably contained figural types and compositions, as well as architectural and ornamental variations. It is hard to imagine that such a treasury of forms was restricted to a single workshop for any period of time. Undoubtedly there were local differences within the Fourth Style (e.g., between Pompeii and Herculaneum), as

Figure 20.10 House of Queen Margherita (V.2.1), room (o) (Fourth Style, *c.*AD 50–60).
Photo: DAI Rom 56.1260.

well as regional variations (e.g., the Rhine provinces as compared to Campania), but these have not yet been systematically documented.

There is also still no consensus on the chronology of the Fourth Style. According to Beyen, it began as early as the final years of Tiberius, while Schefold dates the beginning to the independent rule of Nero after AD 59. Meanwhile, it is widely agreed that the new style was already burgeoning in the cities of Campania before the disastrous earthquake of AD 62, but in individual cases it remains uncertain whether that earthquake or some theoretical later quake should be considered the *terminus ante sive post quem* for any damaged or repaired decoration. At certain sites it is hardly possible to imagine any other context for damage and repairs than the earthquake of AD 62 (Figure 20.12).[15] Fortunately, there are several find contexts independent of the earthquake that can be dated quite precisely. Based on coins, construction details and inscriptions, the ceiling paintings of the so-called Domus Transitoria under the Flavian Palace on the Palatine must be considered Claudian. Motifs of the Fourth Style can already be seen in Room K of the Magdalensberg, the predecessor of Virunum founded by Claudius in the eastern Alps. A *graffito* of February, AD 60, on one of the columns of the peristyle of the House of the Silver Wedding (V.2.i), unequivocally dates its decoration and all of the stylistically connected rooms slightly earlier. In Rome, the Domus Aurea of the emperor Nero, built AD 64–68, is filled with decoration executed in the advanced Fourth Style. All of the

Figure 20.11   House of the Ceii (I.6.15) garden (h), north wall (Fourth Style, *c.*AD 70–79).
Photo: DAI Berlin 83.2.135 (P. Grunwald).

Figure 20.12   House of the Lararium (I.6.4), room (h), south wall (Fourth Style,
painting interrupted by the earthquake of AD 62). Photo: P. Grunwald.

Figure 20.13 House of the Ceii (I.6.15), *cubiculum* (f), east wall (late Third Style).
Photo: DAI Berlin 80.2.260 (P. Grunwald).

Figure 20.14 House of the Menander (I.10.4), room (19), south wall (early Fourth Style).
Photo: GFN N 35759.

frescoes in the House of the Hunt (VII.4.48) were painted after AD 71, judging from the impressions of coins left in the wet plaster of the socle.

Scholars have yet to agree on a generally accepted view of the development of the Fourth Style, since apparently anything goes, stylistically, from the 40s to AD 79. However, we can observe a change in the arrangement and rendering of a repertoire of forms that stays nearly constant. The Fourth Style under Claudius gives the impression of a fresh new kind of invention, superabundant but delicate in ornamental details (Figure 21.4). It features stark contrasts between sections opened up with illusionistic depth and others that emphasize the flatness of the wall. The Neronian Fourth Style heightens illusionism, elegance and refinement in that it reduces the contrasts, and the repertoire of variations on the standardized system of forms becomes richest. The Fourth Style under Vespasian apparently likes to pile on all the effects. Forms grow heavier, and details are rendered more coarsely (Figure 20.11).

The Fourth Style apparently develops during the first years of emperor Claudius' reign (AD 41–54) as a deliberate retort to a Third Style that had stagnated under Tiberius (compare Figures 20.13 and 20.14). The revival of the forms and aesthetics of the late Second Style (IIb) can best be understood in the context of the systematic efforts of the emperor Claudius to associate himself with the young Augustus. A new beginning is made, in heightened form, in order to overcome paralysis and improprieties under Tiberius and Caligula. Of course, so general a phenomenon as a *"Zeitstil"* (period-style) is not only the product of political ideas, but also of accompanying changing mentalities. The Fourth Style was a psychologically necessary answer to the antiquated Third Style, just as the Second Style was to the First, and the Third to the Second.

NOTES

1 Constanze Witt translated the German text. For general surveys of wall painting at Pompeii, see: A. Mau, *Geschichte der decorativen Wandmalerei in Pompeji*, Berlin, 1882; H. G. Beyen, "Das stilistische und chronologische Verhältnis der letzten drei pompejanischen Stile," *Antiquity and survival*, 1958, vol. 2, pp. 349–64; K. Schefold, *Vergessenes Pompeji*, Bern, 1962; A. Barbet, *La peinture murale romaine: les styles décoratifs pompéiens*, Paris, 1985; G. Cerulli Irelli, *et al.* (eds), *Pompejanische Wandmalerei*, Stuttgart 1990, with extensive bibliography (also published in Japanese, English, French and Italian); R. Ling, *Roman Painting*, Cambridge, 1991; V. M. Strocka, "Pompeiani, stili," *Enciclopedia dell'Arte Antica*, Supplemento IV, Rome, 1996, pp. 414–25. L. Laken, 'Zebra patterns in Campanian wall-painting: a matter of function," *BABesch*, 2003, vol. 78, pp. 167–89; E. W. Leach, *The Social Life of Painting in Ancient Rome and the Bay of Naples*, Cambridge, 2004.

For catalogues and documentation of wall painting at Pompeii, see: I. Bragantini, M. De Vos and F. Parise Badoni (eds), *Pitture e pavimenti di Pompei. Repertorio delle fotografie del Gabinetto Fotografico Nazionale*, Rome, 1981–86, vols I–III; V. M. Strocka (ed.), *Häuser in Pompeji*, Tübingen/Munich, 1984–2004, vols I–XII (continuing series); G. Pugliese Carratelli and I. Baldassarre (eds), *Pompei. Pitture e mosaici*, 11 vols, Rome, 1990–2003.

2 For studies of various painting genres, see: C. M. Dawson, *Romano-Campanian Mythological Landscape Painting*, New Haven, CT, 1944; W. J. Th. Peters, *Landscape in Romano-Campanian mural painting*, Assen, 1963; J.-M. Croisille, *Les natures mortes campaniennes*, Brussels, 1965; R. Ling, "Studius and the beginning of Roman landscape painting," *JRS*, 1977, vol. 67, pp. 1–16; D. Michel, "Pompejanische Gartenmalereien," in *Tainia. Festschrift für Roland Hampe*, Mainz, 1980, pp. 373–404; E. W. Leach, *The Rhetoric of Space. Literary and artistic representations of landscape in Republican and Augustan Rome*, Princeton, NJ, 1988; Th. Fröhlich, *Lararien- und Fassadenbilder in den Vesuvstädten*, RM-EH, 32, Mainz, 1991.

3 For sources on techniques, painters and workshops, see: S. Augusti, *I colori pompeiani*, Rome, 1967; P. Mora, "Proposta sulla tecnica della pittura murale romana," *Bollettino dell'Istituto Centrale del Restauro*, 1967, pp. 63–84; A. Barbet and C. Allag, "Techniques de préparations des parois dans la peinture murale romaine," *MÉFR*, 1972, vol. 84, pp. 935–1069; M. De Vos, "La bottega di pittori di via di Castricio," in *Pompei 1748–1980. I tempi della documentazione*, Rome, 1981, pp. 119–30; H. Eristov, "Peinture romaine et textes antiques: information et ambiguités. A propos du 'Recueil Milliet'," *RA*, 1987, pp. 109–23; P. M. Allison, "'Workshops' and 'Patternbooks'," *KölnJb*, 1991, vol. 24, pp. 79–84; J. de Mol, "Some remarks on proportions in Fourth Style wall-paintings in Pompeii," *KölnJb*, 1991, vol. 24, pp. 159–63; E. M. Moormann (ed.), *Meded*, 1995, vol. 54: many of the articles in this volume are concerned with workshop questions.

4 Bibliography for the First Style: I. Baldassarre, "Pitture parietali e mosaico pavimentale dal IV al II sec. a. C.," *DialArch*, 1984, vol. 2, pp. 65–76; A. Laidlaw, *The First Style in Pompeii. Painting and architecture*, Rome, 1985; A. Laidlaw, "Der Erste Stil," in Cerulli Irelli, *Pompejanische Wandmalerei*, pp. 205 ff.; A. Rouveret, *Histoire et imaginaire de la peinture ancienne (Ve siècle av. J.-C.–Ie siècle ap. J.-C.)*, BÉFAR, vol. 274, Rome, 1989, pp. 166–212.

5 See, e.g., V. J. Bruno, "Antecedents of the Pompeian First Style," *AJA*, 1969, vol. 73, pp. 305–17; V. J. Bruno, *Hellenistic Painting Techniques: the evidence of the Delos fragments*, Leiden, 1985; R. Ginouvès (ed.), *Macedonia from Philip II to the Roman Conquest*, Princeton, NJ, 1994, pp. 136–8; N. Cahill, *Household and City Organization at Olynthus*, New Haven, CT, 2002, esp. p. 85; P. W. Lehmann, *Samothrace, vol. III: the Hieron*, Princeton, NJ, 1969, pp. 207–8, 216.

6 V. M. Strocka, *Casa del Labirinto (VI 11, 8–10)*, Häuser in Pompeji, Bd. 4, Munich, 1991, esp. pp. 66–7.

7 Bibliography for the Second Style: H. G. Beyen, *Die pompejanische Wanddekoration vom zweiten bis zum vierten Stil*, The Hague, 1938–60, vols I–II; G. Carettoni, "La casa di Augusto sul Palatino," *RM*, 1983, vol. 90, pp. 373–419; B. Wesenberg, "Römische Wandmalerei am Ausgang der Republik. Der Zweite Pompejanische Stil," *Gymnasium*, 1985, vol. 92, pp. 470–88; R. A. Tybout, *Aedificiorum figurae. Untersuchungen zu den Architekturdarstellungen des frühen zweiten Stils*, Amsterdam, 1989; V. M. Strocka, "Der Zweite Stil," in Cerulli Irelli, *Pompejanische Wandmalerei*, pp. 213–22; E. Heinrich, *Der Zweite Stil in pompejanischen Wohnhäusern*, Munich, 2002.

8 E.g.: Beyen, *Pompejanische Wanddekoration*, n. 5.

9 Bibliography for the Third Style: F. L. Bastet and M. De Vos, *Proposta per una classificazione del terzo stile pompeiano*, The Hague, 1979; W. Ehrhardt, *Stilgeschichtliche Untersuchungen an römischen Wandmalereien von der späten Republik bis zur Zeit Neros*, Mainz, 1987; V. M. Strocka, "Die römische Wandmalerei von Tiberius bis Nero," in *Pictores per provincias, Cahiers d'archéologie romaine*, Lausanne, 1987, vol. 43, pp. 29–44; U. Pappalardo, "Der Dritte Stil," in Cerulli Irelli, *Pompejanische Wandmalerei*, pp. 223–32; P. H. von Blanckenhagen and C. Alexander, *The Paintings from Boscotrecase*, RM-EH, 6, Heidelberg, 1962.

10 Mau, *Geschichte der decorativen Wandmalerei*, pp. 383–5; A. Mau, *BdI*, 1882, pp. 23f.; Ehrhardt, *Stilgeschichtliche*, pp. 4, 42f.

11 *CIL* IV, 1552–6.

12 *CIL* VI², 5540.

13 Bibliography for the Fourth Style: V. M. Strocka, "Ein mißverstandener Terminus des Vierten Stils: Die Casa del Sacello Iliaco in Pompeji (I 6, 4)," *RM* 1984, vol. 91, pp. 125–40; W. C. Archer, "The paintings in the alae of the Casa dei Vetti and a definition of the Fourth Pompeian Style," *AJA*, 1990, vol. 94, pp. 95–123; G. Cerulli Irelli, "Der letzte pompejanische Stil," in Cerulli Irelli, *Pompejanische Wandmalerei*, pp. 233–8; H. Eristov, *Les éléments architecturaux dans la peinture campanienne du quatrième style*, Paris, 1994; V. M. Strocka, "Neubeginn und Steigerung des Principats. Zu den Ursachen des claudischen Stilwandels," in V. M. Strocka (ed.), *Die Regierungszeit des Kaisers Claudius (41–54 n. Chr.)—Umbruch oder Episode?* Mainz, 1994, pp. 191–220; V. M. Strocka, "Die Chronologie des Vierten Stils, von keinem Erdbeben erschüttert," in Th. Fröhlich (ed.), *La regione vesuviana dal 62 al 79 d. C.: problemi archeologici e sismologici*, Munich, 1995, pp. 175–82; P. M. Allison and F. B. Sear, *Casa della Caccia antica (VII 4, 48)*, Häuser in Pompeji XI, Munich, 2002, esp. pp. 66–86.

14 See, e.g., L. Richardson, jr, *A Catalogue of Identifiable Figure Painters of Ancient Pompeii, Herculaneum and Stabiae*, Baltimore, MD, 1999.

15 E.g., The House of the Vettii (VI.15.1), *alae* (h) and (i); The House of the Prince of Naples (VI.15.7–8); and the House of the Lararium (I.6.4), a house damaged by the earthquake of 62 while in the process of being repainted, which afterward continued to be inhabited having been only crudely repaired.

CHAPTER TWENTY-ONE

DOMESTIC DECORATION
Mosaics and stucco

————•◆•————

John R. Clarke

Throughout the documented history of domestic decoration at Pompeii,[1] two themes remain constant: the coordination of floor, wall and ceiling decoration, and the relation of these ensembles of mosaic, painting and stucco to the function of the spaces they adorned (cf. Strocka, Ch. 20).[2] The coordination of systems for decorating the interior surfaces of the Roman house developed logically from domestic construction techniques. Houses were built on a "slab" made of pounded earth and cement, and all walls and ceilings of a house received a coating of plaster. The articulation of that coating helped determine the character of each space. Two basic approaches characterized the decoration of walls—either emphasizing solid surfaces by sheathing them with real or painted imitations of precious colored marbles (the First Style), or opening them up with perspective schemes seeming to recede behind the physical boundary of the wall (Second Style). Likewise, owners decorated floors either as flat surfaces, or set elaborately framed illusionistic mosaic pictures into them. Because Roman interior decoration used permanent materials (fresco on plaster walls and ceilings, stucco moldings, and mosaic or cement floors), and because owners often took special pains to preserve rooms decorated in earlier styles as "period rooms,"[3] scholars have been able to chart with great accuracy the fashions in Roman interior design from 200 BC through AD 79.

The patterns that governed how decorative systems signaled the functions of the spaces they adorned arose from the ways that Pompeians used their houses for business, domestic ritual, entertainment and repose. Dynamic spaces, including the *atrium*, passageways, and the peristyle, received all-over patterns on their floors and simple systems on their walls and ceilings. With the exception of the floor of the *fauces* or vestibule, decorators avoided placing complex figural imagery on floors or walls, since it would encourage the viewer to tarry. In static spaces—the *tablinum, triclinium, oecus, cubiculum* and *exedra*—the case was exactly the opposite: here, artists incorporated elaborate illusionistic images into floor, wall and ceiling schemes to tempt the visitor to stop and contemplate their meaning.[4]

323

FIRST-STYLE STUCCO AND MOSAIC

The First Style covers the period *c*.200–80 BC. One result of Pompeii's great prosperity during the second century BC was that wealthy citizens built elaborate houses— several much larger than palaces excavated in the Greek East. The artists commissioned to decorate these houses borrowed their vocabulary from palaces, temples and stoas to create grandiose interiors. Using inexpensive plaster and paint, they imitated costly marble masonry, thereby introducing into the private house the wealth and status associated with Hellenistic rulers (cf. Wallace-Hadrill, Ch. 18; Strocka, Ch. 20; Fant, Ch.22). The "illusion" in the First Style is a rather literal one: like faux-marble techniques used to this day, it succeeds if the viewer is fooled into believing that painted plaster walls are really constructed in, or sheathed with, precious marbles. Rather than being work for painters, the First Style was carried out by stuccoists, skilled in applying and carving plaster to make the fluted pilasters, moldings and capitals that substituted for their marble counterparts. These architectural elements form the credible basis of First-Style schemes: successive rows of marble blocks and moldings of the wall's socle, middle zone and upper zone were framed by stucco pilasters and capitals placed at doorways and room openings. All received the colors of bright and expensive marbles, and employed the same moldings found in masonry. The First Style is much like a plaster cast of architectural forms.

Most First-Style houses received simple pavements made of either red or black cement. Crushed red pottery or roof tiles colored the red pavements, called both *opus signinum* and *cocciopesto*. The term *lavapesta* designates cement floors black in color because of the crushed black volcanic rock that forms its aggregate. Although usually plain, sometimes mosaicists would decorate cement floors with geometric designs outlined in rows of cubic stones, called *tesserae*. Mosaicists made *tesserae* by cutting white limestone or marble into uniform shapes.[5]

At both Delos and Pompeii appears another type of pavement, made of chips of travertine, lava, limestone, or even colored glass; sometimes the mosaicist arranged the chips in a geometric design.[6] Mosaicists also used rectangular tesserae to create polychrome basket-weave patterns. More rare and costly were so-called *opus sectile* pavements, consisting in this period of colored limestone cut into geometric shapes to create brilliant accents on the floors of important spaces in the house.[7]

All of these pavements with their abstract, decorative patterns imitated carpets in both their compositions and placement within rooms. However, in the latest phase of the First Style, around 100 BC, designers began to insert illusionistic mosaic pictures into floors. These pictures were prefabricated in a workshop using extremely small colored *tesserae* (1–5 mm), specially shaped and arranged to imitate the individual brushstrokes of a painting. Because the *tesserae*-"brushstrokes" often created snaky forms, the technique is called *opus vermiculatum* or "worm style." Executed by specialists on marble or terracotta trays, these paintings in stone were portable. The patron would choose these insets or *emblemata* from the workshop and they would be carried to the site for installation into the usual mosaic floor worked in much larger, uniform cubic *tesserae* (5–10 mm); sometimes they were inserted into cement or chip pavements.

Since figural elements were extremely rare on First-Style walls, use of illusionistic *emblemata* on the floor must have stemmed from a desire to make decoration showier. But whereas geometric pavements in red or black cement made few demands on the viewer, illusionistic *emblemata* created curious problems, since they required a certain suspension of disbelief—particularly because they could be walked on. The spectator's viewing position assumes paramount importance when one part of the floor is singled out as a field for illusionism, because the *emblema*, unlike a painting on a wall, is visible right side up from less than half of the room and makes sense from an even more limited area. It constitutes a kind of illusionistic hole in the flat surface underfoot, forcing the viewer to circle it to understand its imagery.[8]

In Pompeii excavators have found thirty-four *emblemata* in twenty-one houses to date. There are twenty-three subjects, of which seven recur. The fact that there is a degree of repetition in subjects suggests the circulation of copy-books or even cartoons throughout Italy. One scholar has posited that the workshop responsible for the several versions of an underwater still-life found at Pompeii was the same one that created the great mosaics of the Sanctuary of Fortuna Primigenia at Praeneste.[9] Various *emblemata* of doves drinking seem to be copies of a lost original by Sosos of Pergamon. In the House of the Faun (VI.12) an *emblema* of a Satyr and Maenad coupling has a close double in a mosaic from Thmuis in Egypt.[10] The most famous mosaic in the *opus vermiculatum* technique, however, is the Alexander Mosaic, not an *emblema* since its large size (5.82 m × 3.13 m with its perspectival geometric border; 5.12 m × 2.71 m without it) required manufacture *in situ*. Composed of millions of *tesserae* and placed in large *exedra* (37), on axis with the *fauces* and *tablinum*, most scholars consider it a mosaic copy of the famous painting of the Battle of Issos, commissioned by Cassander (d. 298 BC) from Philoxenos of Eretria (cf. Wallace-Hadrill, Ch. 18).[11] The mosaic uses the same four base colors—white, black, red and yellow—associated with classical Greek painting.

Although a commission such as the Alexander Mosaic is a refined work of mosaic art that must have represented a large investment for the owner of the house, the *emblemata* in the rest of the house vary in quality and represent not so much a unified program as a compendium of the models in circulation around 100 BC among late Hellenistic workshops. In addition to the Alexander Mosaic and the *emblemata*, mosaicists created chip pavements, cement floors and polychrome *opus sectile* pavements with lively geometric designs in the House of the Faun. These last adorned important spaces, including the sloping floor of the *fauces*, the pool of the *impluvium* and the *tablinum*.

If the pavements within the House of the Faun record the Pompeian fascination with things Greek, the mosaic inscription in the sidewalk in front of the house incorporates a Latin greeting for both passersby and visitors: *have* "Hail!"[12] Mosaic greetings at the entryways of houses, executed in a variety of techniques that use bits of colored marble set in *opus signinum* (House of the Faun) or *tesserae* to spell out words, reveal something of the owner's values. At Pompeii we read: *salve lucru(m)* "Hail to money" (VII.1.47); *lucrum gaudium* "Money is a joy!" (VI.14.39); *lucru(m) ac(c)ipe* "Take the money" (VII.3.?);[13] and *cras credo* "I believe in tomorrow" (II.8.6).

SECOND-STYLE MOSAIC AND STUCCO

Unlike the First Style's structural decoration, where imitation marble blocks in relief articulate all wall surfaces, with special framing elements at openings, the Second Style (*c.*80–20 BC) employs columns painted in perspective. Regularly spaced, they form a fictive colonnade that appears to hold up the ceiling. Central to the success

Figure 21.1 Villa of the Mysteries, *cubiculum* (16), east and south alcoves.
Photo: Michael Larvey.

of the Second-Style room is the coordination of this *trompe l'oeil* painting with stucco and mosaic. A bedroom in the Villa of the Mysteries provides a clear picture of how wall painter, stuccoist, and mosaicist coordinated their skills to differentiate areas with separate functions within the same space (Figure 21.1). A mosaic carpet with a pattern of red and black crosses defines the dynamic, circulation space of the anteroom. Two contrasting bedside carpet mosaics meet at right angles by the closet, separating the two alcoves that housed beds. They coordinate closely with the scheme of the wall painting, where a red and green pilaster folded around the outside corner of the closet meets them. The pilasters end in elaborate stucco capitals. Each alcove also has a different stucco pattern in its vaulted ceiling.

Figure 21.2   House of the Cryptoporticus (I.6.2), room (i), view of threshold
band from south. Photo: Michael Larvey.

Such functional division employing wall, floor and ceiling decoration also occurs
in dining rooms, where decoration differentiates the static space for the dining couches
from the dynamic area for the servers.[14] An excellent example is room (i) of the
House of the Cryptoporticus (I.6.2) where changes in the mosaic pavement, the wall
painting and stucco differentiate a dynamic passageway between two doorways from
the east part of the room, where dining couches would have been set up. An *emblema*
at the center of the back of the room creates a focus of interest for the diners reclining
on couches arranged around it. In Figure 21.2 we see the end of the threshold band
that marks the transition between the two functions of the space. A pattern of colored
marble rectangles and white *tesserae* set into a black tessellated pavement decorates
the passageway space to the left, whereas a polychrome threshold band made of squares
and rectangles marks the place where the dining area of the room begins. Patterns
typical of Second-Style mosaics, including the shaded meander, fish scales, and roundels
framed with two-stranded braids, fill the squares and rectangles. The wall-painter
marked this same point with the image of a female herm that supports a rectangular
section of architrave in perspective. This architrave "carries" a frieze of deeply projecting

stucco consoles surmounted by a band that articulates a barrel vault directly over the position of the mosaic threshold band.

Figural stuccoes develop markedly during the Second-Style period. Whereas First-Style stuccoes included few figural elements, with the Second Style stucco frees itself from its task of creating architectural framing and begins to incorporate motifs from painting. Stucco establishes its own decorative repertoire in this period. On the northeast vaulted ceiling of the cryptoporticus in the House of the Cryptoporticus (*c.*40–20 BC) stuccoists created a series of lacunars framed by the Ionic *kymation*, and filled with motifs that included crossed shields and weapons. The vaults of the north *ala* and of the *tepidarium* of the bath complex on the eastern side of the cryptoporticus preserve elaborate decoration. In the *tepidarium* is a lunette showing amorini playing with Hercules' quiver; trees occupy the background. All of these stucco decorations are white, contrasting with the rich colors of the Second-Style walls and the polychromy of the mosaic floors.

Stuccoes in the House of the Cryptoporticus, like those in the Villa of the Mysteries, take their inspiration from wood lacunar ceilings and favor the heavy framing of architectural elements. With the last phase of the Second Style (*c.*40–20 BC), however, stucco ceiling decoration reduces the framing elements to emphasize figural landscapes of the "sacro-idyllic" type. Although none are preserved at Pompeii, the vaulted ceilings of the *cubicula* of the House under the Farnesina in Rome (*c.*20 BC) underscore the stuccoists' close observation of painted landscapes of this type and their translation of polychrome paintings into white reliefs.[15]

Mosaics become "bilingual" during the period of the Second Style, with old-style, shaded three-dimensional color mosaic carpets appearing at the same time as new, two-dimensional black-and-white mosaics. In some houses, like that of the Crypto-porticus, one can find polychrome three-dimensional designs (e.g., room (i)) in one room, and the flat black-and-white design in an adjoining room (the entrance to (e)). Large expanses of black-and-white mosaics appear at the Villa of Fannius Synistor at Boscoreale and at the Villa of Ariadne at Stabiae, where excavators found a *sinopia* (preliminary sketch) scratched into the wet cement and a meander pattern painted with a brush in lampblack.[16] Similar *sinopie* guided the mosaicists who laid the Second-Style floors of the Villa of Settefinestre near Cosa.[17]

With the disappearance of *emblemata* the floors of static spaces receive flat patterns, and illusionistic pictures begin to migrate to the walls—a trend that fully estab-lishes itself in the late Second Style (*c.*40–20 BC). In the dynamic spaces of *atria* and peristyles it is the all-over patterns, without figural imagery, that dominate both mosaic and cement floors.

Figural decoration on Pompeian floors takes a new direction at this time. Mosaicists begin to translate the imagery of the precious *emblemata* into whole-floor figural designs made of the same cubic *tesserae* as the decorative parts of the floors. The floor of *caldarium* (48) in the bath of the House of the Menander (I.10.4, 14–17) (*c.*40–20 BC) documents this transition from polychrome *emblemata* to black-and-white all-over mosaics (Figures 21.3 and 23.19). The mosaicist arranged diverse figural elements on a white ground in a pattern that suggests viewing from different places in the room. Although there is a limited range of colors, the mosaicist has simply made a silhouette of the black swimmer's form and filled it in with rows of black *tesserae*. He must have used some kind of one-to-one cartoon, since the same swimming figure

Figure 21.3 House of the Menander (I.10.4, 14–17), *caldarium* (48) mosaic.
Photo: Michael Larvey.

and the same heraldic dolphins appear in a contemporaneous mosaic in the House of the Cryptoporticus.[18] This "silhouette style" in figural mosaics continues through the Third Style.

THIRD-STYLE MOSAIC AND STUCCO

With the Third Style in painting, one must search for any indication of architectural members because the painter has miniaturized every element in the scheme. This reduction to utter flatness of the substantial architecture and daring, deep perspectives of the Second Style emphasizes the wall as a spatial limit rather than one that opens up through perspectival illusions. The new techniques and decorative motifs that begin to appear in mosaics and stuccoes around 20 BC parallel the changes in taste that occur in wall painting. In mosaics, both polychromy and the three-dimensional decorative motifs it served disappear in favor of flat black-and-white designs. Third-Style pavements, like the frescoed walls, avoid representation of depth. *Tesserae* are usually smaller than those employed in Second-Style mosaics. Polychromy is limited to geometrically shaped pieces of marble inserted into cement or tessellated floors. Whereas the shaded color *trompe-l'oeil* meanders and cubes in perspective begged the question of the floor's flatness in Second-Style mosaics, decorative motifs in Third-(and Fourth-) Style mosaics are emphatically two-dimensional. A phenomenon perhaps related to this emphasis on flatness is a fashion for monochrome rooms; a good example is the coordination of the black walls and *lavapesta* floors of the *atrium* and *tablinum* in the House of Lucretius Fronto (V.4.a, 11), *c.*AD 30–45.

Figure 21.4   House of Paquius Proculus (I.7.1, 20), view of *atrium* and *fauces* from room above *tablinum*. Photo: ICCD N56314.

There are few figural mosaics of the Third Style, most important being the Head of Medusa in polychromy from the House of the Centenary (IX.8.3, 6).[19] Impressive for their expanse and good state of preservation are the Third-Style *fauces* and *atrium* of the House of Paquius Proculus (I.7.1, 20); Figure 21.4. The mosaicist created a guard dog, chained to a door, to surprise the visitor and went on to decorate the *atrium* with an elaborate design inspired by lacunar ceilings. Figural motifs—unusually—appear in the fictive lacunars. The only other figural motifs in an *atrium* occur in House VII.16 [*Ins. Occ.*].15, where in each corner of the *impluvium* are images of little *amphorae* containing *garum*. The inscriptions—(A) G(ari) F(los) SCOM(bri) / SCAURI / EX OFFICI / NA SCAU / RI; (B): LIQUA(men) / FLOS; (C): G(ari)F(los) SCOM(bri) / SCAURI; (D): LIQUAMEN / OPTIMUM / EX OFFICIN / A SCAURI—announce that either the *duumvir* Umbricius Scaurus or his father was in the business of making the fish sauce.[20] Other houses rich in mosaics from this period are the

Houses of Championnet I and II (VIII.2.1 and VIII.2.3) and the House of Caecilius Iucundus (V.1.26).

Stucco decoration, just like mosaic and wall painting of the Third Style, gets smaller and avoids references to built architecture wherever decorators employ it— whether cornices at the top of walls or divisions within the wall. Whereas heavy double cornices with dentil ranges are commonplace in ensembles of the Second Style, thinner, low-relief stucco bands predominate in Third-Style walls. Made with the help of wooden molds, they complement the thinned and miniaturistic architectural forms in the wall painting (Figure 20.6).

Third-Style stuccoes at Pompeii are rare. The best evidence for figural stuccoes comes from the vault and lunettes in room (21), the *tepidarium* in the House of the Labyrinth (VI.11.9–10), *c.*AD 1–30. Prizes for athletic contests appear in the east lunette, and flying victories flank the windows in the west one; motifs similar to those of the Farnesina fill the rectilinear panels of the now-fallen vault.[21]

FOURTH-STYLE MOSAICS AND STUCCO

A gap in our knowledge of late Third- and early Fourth-Style developments arises from the lack of a securely dated pre-earthquake decorative program. The vault of the large *oecus* (A) of the Villa Imperiale may predate 62, but only the socle and median zone are in Third Style (Figure 20.6). The upper zone and stucco ceiling seem to be in the early Fourth Style of AD 45–62. The vaulted ceiling employs a highly refined scheme of concentric squares around an octagonal panel decorated with two flying figures. The stuccoist decorated the sides of the concentric square panels with figural imagery within a variety of frames (Figure 21.5). Some of the imagery is in stucco relief; some is painted. The dominant color is black, with touches of red, orange, purple and light blue.

With the Fourth Style (*c.*AD 45–79) mosaics have their heyday. Notable are the complex mosaics of the House of the Wild Boar I (VIII.3.8), the House of the Bear (VII.2.45), the House of Marcus Lucretius (IX.3.5, 24), the House of the Tragic Poet (VI.8.5), and the House of the Camillus (VII.12.23). Animal motifs often appear in *fauces*, including the boar attacked by hounds that gives its name to the House of the Wild Boar I; a wounded bear with the inscription HAVE in the House of the Bear; and the famous dog with the inscription CAVE CANEM "Beware of the dog" in the House of the Tragic Poet. Unlike the plainer mosaics of the Third Style (e.g., House of Paquius Proculus [I.7.1]; House of Caecilius Iucundus [V.1.26]), these exhibit the exuberant kind of decoration that finds a parallel in the proliferation of motifs in Fourth-Style stucco decoration.

Stucco decorations of the post-earthquake period abound at Pompeii. The strong emergence of stucco decoration, as well as its extension into walls of the Fourth Style, probably got its impetus from Rome, where statue-like figures appear, framed by the stacked *aediculae* characteristic of a theater scene-building (*scaenae frons*). Walls of Nero's palace in Rome, the *Domus Aurea* (AD 64–68), are decorated by stucco *aediculae* with integrated figures and architectural panels. In the Stabian Baths (VII.1.8), completed shortly before the eruption, the west wall of the *palaestra* conserves an elaborate stucco wall scheme modeled on the *scaenae frons*, with figures of athletes framed in niches and descending stairways (cf. Koloski-Ostrow, Ch. 15). Similarly

Figure 21.5   Villa Imperiale, *oecus* (A), vault. Photo: Michael Larvey.

Figure 21.6   House of the Menander (I.10.4, 14–17), *exedra* (24).
Photo: Michael Larvey.

enthusiastic use of stuccoes on walls appears in *tablinum* (8) of the House of Meleager (VI.9.2).

Stucco vaults become increasingly complex in this period. Stuccoists seem to have gotten inspiration for the complex decorative patterns of vaults from earlier designs in mosaic floors—themselves inspired by textiles. Another font of inspiration could have been the lacunar ceilings of built architecture, such as those of the Arch of Titus in Rome. The vault of the vestibule of the men's section of the Stabian Baths reveals the creativity of the stuccoists who based their design on an all-over pattern of circles and concave-sided octagons—each containing a figural motif and connected with figure-eight bands in red and blue. The apparently all-white design of the stucco barrel vault of room (6) of the Suburban Baths includes in the lunettes, *aediculae* with figures like those common in Fourth-Style wall designs. The stuccoist's choice to apply polychromy may have depended on the amount of lighting available to the room. The high humidity of this part of the baths may have also discouraged the use of color.

Stucco decorations appear in private houses as well. The stuccoist covered the tiny segmental barrel over the entrance to the *caldarium* of the House of the Menander, as well as the flat ceiling of the *alveus*, with free-flowing grape vines. He used the same motif in the upper part of the apses of *exedrae* (22) and (24); Figure 21.6.

The thoroughgoing rebuilding after the earthquake of AD 62 accounts in part for the large number of preserved stucco decorations, but the extension of stuccoes into wall systems is a new feature that speaks for the increased popularity of stucco work in the period.

WALL AND VAULT MOSAICS

Using the villas of the wealthy as models, and with the abundant water available after Augustus constructed the Serinus aqueduct, many Pompeians began to put fountains and *nymphaea* into their houses, often adorned with mosaic niches and vaults (cf. Jansen, Ch. 16). At the beginning of the Third Style mosaicists decorate them with thin geometric and figural designs, as in the House of the Little Bull (V.1.7, 9) and the House of the Fountain (VII.4.56). In these mosaics appear *tesserae* of colored transparent or opaque glass, with borders of shells and chips of marble and porous red and black volcanic stone. With the Fourth Style the repertory of figures expands to include Venus, fish, seaside villas, and the sea-*thiasos*, all motifs found in contemporary wall painting. Mosaicists were able to set stone and glass *tesserae* irregularly (unlike floors, walls were not levigated, or smoothed), so that the *tesserae* would catch the light and shimmer.

Despite gaps in the archaeological record between the destruction of Pompeii and the heyday of black-and-white mosaics in Rome and Ostia during the second century AD, it is clear that the most momentous change in mosaic art was the translation of polychrome *emblemata* into large-scale figural mosaics worked in uniform cubic *tesserae*. Such pavements appear in domestic and public architecture, as do both figurative and abstract stucco decoration—much of it preserved in second-century AD tombs decorated long after Pompeii had disappeared.

NOTES

1 Essential bibliography for mosaic and stucco decoration: B. Andreae, *Antike Bildmosaiken*, Mainz, 2003; M. E. Blake, "The pavements of the Roman buildings of the Republic and early empire," *MAAR*, 1930, vol. 8, pp. 7–159; J. R. Clarke, *Roman Black-and-White Figural Mosaics*, New York, 1979, now available in a revised and expanded edition, ACLS History E-book, Ann Arbor, MI, 2007, http://hdl.handle.net/2027/heb.90029; D. Corlaita Scagliarini, "Spazio e decorazione nella pittura pompeiana," *Palladio*, 1974–6, vols 23–5, pp. 3–44; M. De Vos, "Pavimenti e mosaici," in F. Zevi (ed.), *Pompei 79*, Naples, 1979, pp. 161–76; K. M. D. Dunbabin, *Mosaics of the Greek and Roman World*, Cambridge, 1999; R. Ling, *Ancient Mosaics*, London, 1998; R. Ling, "Gli stucchi," in Zevi, *Pompei 79*, pp. 145–60; R. Ling, "Stuccowork," in D. Strong and D. Brown (eds), *Roman Crafts*, New York, 1976, pp. 209–21; H. Mielsch, *Römische Stuckreliefs*, RM-EH, 21. Heidelberg, 1975; E. Pernice, *Pavimente und figürliche Mosaiken*, Die Hellenistische Kunst in Pompeji, vol. 6, Berlin, 1938; U. Riemenschneider, *Pompejanische Stuckgesimse des dritten und vierten Stils*, Frankfurt, 1986; F. B. Sear, *Roman Wall and Vault Mosaics*, RM-EH, 23, Heidelberg, 1977.

2 J. R. Clarke, "Notes on the coordination of wall, floor, and ceiling decoration in the houses of Roman Italy, 100 BCE–235 CE," in M. Aronberg Lavin (ed.), *IL 60. Essays Honoring Irving Lavin on his Sixtieth Birthday*, New York, 1990, pp. 1–29. See Pernice, *Pavimente*, for the initial articulation of a Four-Style schema for mosaics and its correlation with the painting styles.

3 For "period rooms" at the Villa at Oplontis, see J. R. Clarke, *The Houses of Roman Italy, 100 BC–AD 250. Ritual, Space, and Decoration*, Berkeley, CA, 1991, p. 140.

4 C. Scagliarini, "Spazio e decorazione."

5 K. M. D. Dunbabin, *Mosaics of the Greek and Roman World*, New York, 1999, pp. 279–303.

6 H. Joyce, "Form, function, and technique in the pavements of Delos and Pompeii," *AJA*, 1979, vol. 83, pp. 253–63; K. M. D. Dunbabin, "Technique and materials of Hellenistic mosaics," *AJA*, 1979, vol. 83, pp. 265–77. See now also R. C. Westgate, *"Pavimenta atque emblemata vermiculata*: regional styles in Hellenistic mosaic and the first mosaics at Pompeii," *AJA*, 2000, vol. 104, pp. 255–75.

7 Scholars debate whether the term *opus scutulatum* properly designates all *opus sectile* pavements: see M. L. Morricone, *Scutalata pavimenta: i pavimenti con inserti di marmo o di pietra trovati a Roma e nei dintorni*, Rome, 1980.

8 I. Lavin, "The Antioch hunting mosaics and their sources: a study of compositional principles in the development of early Medieval style," *DOP*, 1963, vol. 18, p. 186.

9 P. G. P. Meyboom, "I mosaici pompeiani con figure di pesci," *Meded*, 1977, vol. 39, pp. 49–93.

10 W. A. Daszewski, *Corpus of Mosaics from Egypt*, Mainz, 1985, cat. nos. 40, 160–3, pls. 34, 35a.

11 For the latest bibliography and a new interpretation, see B. Cohen, *The Alexander Mosaic: stories of victory and defeat*, New York, 1997. For the mosaic context of the house, see also Westgate "Pavimenta," pp. 262–74. In Autumn 2005, a full-sized replica of the mosaic, made by mosaicists from Ravenna, was installed in the original *exedra* (37) context. The original is the pride of the Naples Museum, where it was brought in 1843: MNN inv. no. 10020.

12 P. Zanker, *Pompeii: public and private life*, Cambridge, MA, 1998, p. 59, sees values of "self-Romanization" in the owner's choice of Latin as the language of greeting. But see C. Parslow's review in *BMCR*, 1999.10.25, http://ccat.sas.upenn.edu/bmcr/1999/1999-10-25.html.

13 De Vos, "Pavimenti e mosaici," p. 165 gives this address as (VII.3.?) because she was unable to locate it. It was probably mentioned in an early excavation report or in the *CIL* and is now gone.

14 J. R. Clarke, "Relationships between floor, wall, and ceiling decoration at Rome and Ostia Antica: some case studies," *BullAIEMA*, 1985, vol. 10, pp. 93–103.

15 I. Bragantini and M. De Vos, *Le decorazioni della villa romana della Farnesina, Museo Nazionale Romano 2, 1: Le Pitture*, Rome, 1982.

16 C. Ribotti, "Una sinopia musiva pavimentale a Stabia," *BdA*, 1973, vol. 58, pp. 42–4.

17 M. De Vos, "Tecnica e tipologia dei rivestimenti pavimentali e parietali," in A. Carandini and S. Settis (eds), *Settefinestre: una villa schiavistica nell'Etruria romana*, Modena, 1985, vol. 1, p. 72, with a list of *sinopie* for mosaics of the first century BC on p. 86.

18 J. R. Clarke, "Mosaic workshops at Pompeii and Ostia Antica," in P. Johnson, R. Ling and D. J. Smith (eds), *Fifth International Colloquium on Ancient Mosaics*, Ann Arbor, MI, 1994, pp. 91–6.

19 MNN inv. no. 112284.

20 R. I. Curtis, "A personalized floor-mosaic from Pompeii," *AJA*, 1984, vol. 88, pp. 557–66.

21 V. M. Strocka, *Casa del Labirinto (VI 11, 8–10)*, Häuser in Pompeji vol. 4, Munich, 1991, pp. 56–8, figs 31, 390–410.

CHAPTER TWENTY-TWO

REAL AND PAINTED
(IMITATION) MARBLE
AT POMPEII

———•◆•———

J. Clayton Fant

Imported "marble" (any fine stone capable of taking a high polish)[1] from the Hellenistic East began to come to Rome in the late second century BC, but it was not until the late first century that small quantities came to Pompeii and the cities of Vesuvius. The history of marble at Pompeii is difficult to recover because marble is scarce there, partly because of two centuries of renovation and redecoration and post-eruption salvaging parties, and partly because it always was scarce. In the case of luxury goods, scarcity is foremost a state of mind; when one variety becomes common, taste shifts to rarer options. Painted imitation marble in wall painting provides a parallel stream of evidence for house owners whose aspirations were not restricted by cost or availability.[2]

Late Hellenistic Pompeii had virtually no imported marble, but First-Style wall painting shows a keen interest, raising questions about contemporary knowledge of real marbles (cf. Strocka, Ch. 20).[3] Most of the panels of First-Style walls, especially the orthostate courses, are in solid colors easily produced from standard pigments. These do not imitate particular stones. However, the same cannot be said of the pseudo-isodomic courses, which are often elaborately painted, featuring whorls, banding or fossil-like blobs. The central pair of isodomic panels which face each other across the *fauces* of the House of the Faun (VI.12.2) feature green amoeba-like shapes on a beige ground containing target-like circles in yellow, purple and green lines. This design seems specific, but is not based on a real original. The give-away is that the ground color and the order of colors in the concentric circles are reversed from one panel to the other (Figure 22.1). This suggests painterly exploitation of a single palette of colors rather than an attempt to reproduce some geological original.

In the entry of the same house, a foreshortened colonnade with framed doors in the upper storey also employs paint to render the effect of architectural marble. The stucco colonnettes give the strong impression of white marble; their bases and the panels framing the door are in a rich dark purple. This cannot be Egyptian porphyry, since those quarries were not developed until much later (see below). The clue to its identity comes from the pavement below; one of its components is a fine limestone of the same dark purple, intersected with occasional veins of white calcite. This must be *marmor taenarium* (*rosso antico*) from the Mani peninsula of the Peloponnesus (Greece),

336

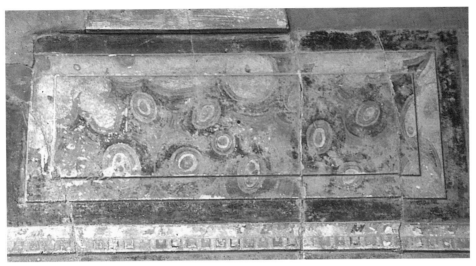

Figure 22.1 Isodomic panels in the *fauces* of the House of the Faun (VI.12). The center panels of the east wall (above) and west wall (below) use the same design and same palette but scramble the order of colors.

a marble prized since Mycenaean times.[4] It is used also to accent the mosaic greeting *have* "Hail!" set into the sidewalk before the entrance (cf. Clarke, Ch. 21).[5] Moreover, *rosso antico* molding strips line the *impluvium* tank. All are small pieces, whereas the painted imitation members are large.[6] In the quarries on the Mani peninsula, the stone is densely layered and the joints are close, so large blocks are rare. The wealthy Samnite owner of the House of the Faun saw no loss of face in using paint to "extend" prized material when the market could not supply it.

While the great majority of First-Style panels are either generic or fanciful, the coursed masonry effect carried over into the Second Style (*c.*80 BC) uses panels recognizable as *alabastro fiorito*, of unknown origin, and *alabastro cotognino*, the creamy "alabaster" (geologically an onyx) long famous in Egypt.[7] Alexandria was a center for artistic and decorative trends when Pompeii looked to the Hellenistic world in the late second century BC. Accurate knowledge of Alexandrian alabaster, whether from hand samples, actual imported objects or just the travels of itinerant artists, is therefore not surprising.[8] The workshop responsible for the walls of the Villa of Poppaea at Oplontis (Figure 1.2), (and probably the Villa of P. Fannius Synistor at Boscoreale (Figure 28.1, no. 16) and the peristyle rooms of the House of the Labyrinth [VI.11.9–10]),[9] is notable for representing the most lavish material in painted form. Alongside "tortoiseshell," "silver" and "gilded bronze" in the *atrium* are columns of *alabastro cotognino*. Real alabaster, by contrast, appears only as small pieces set into pavements; the large alabaster threshold of *triclinium* (14) at Oplontis is unique.

New painted marble types appear in Second Style, though attempts to render specific marbles remained the exception.[10] A tawny yellow-orange ground with red-outlined inclusions is an accurate rendering of Numidian marble (*giallo antico*), exploited by the late Hellenistic kings of Numidia and imported to Rome first by M. Lepidus, consul in 78 BC.[11] Numidian is a strong note in houses and villas decorated by the Oplontis-Boscoreale workshop. It also forms a border under the megalographic frieze in the Villa of the Mysteries. The appearance of painted Numidian on the most elaborate walls shows that it was highly prized as soon as it was introduced. A tan and brick-colored *breccia* resembling *breccia corallina* (usually considered a later introduction) also appears.[12] *Rosso antico* no longer comes in large panels, but reappears as column bases, moldings and cornices when its lithic counterpart begins to be employed.[13]

When did marble, in forms other than finished sculpture, begin to arrive at Pompeii? In AD 79 Campania clearly reflected the popularity of garden furniture and sculpture in the so-called neo-Attic style which had first reached the west from Athens by the second quarter of the first century BC and was the rage by mid-century.[14] The cargos of the Mahdia and Antikythera wrecks of the middle third of the first century included many neo-Attic works.[15] But if any early pieces trickled down to Pompeii, they have left little trace.[16] A scatter of objects in other marbles from the first century shows that there was interest in marble, but no steady supply.[17]

Recent studies of marble table legs and solid supports offer better evidence. The great majority at Pompeii are in Luna marble, not available in quantity before the early Augustan period.[18] About 10 percent are in Pentelic marble; they could be as early as the first Attic imports and some do appear to be early stylistically, but since Pentelic marble remained popular and was more widely available in Pompeii's last period, some may be Neronian and Flavian. Some marble, such as the *impluvium* fountain of the House of Orpheus (VI.14.20), is of poor quality, with large areas of schist and distinct bedding planes; this suggests a later date, when quarrying was moving up Mt Pentelikon to the poorer beds.

In fact, the first marble to make a real visual impression at Pompeii was Luna. The massive deposits above the colony of Luna (modern Carrara) were opened by Julius Caesar, although there was some sporadic earlier use.[19] Steep terrain slowed large-scale production.[20] Ironically, in the Augustan period painted imitation marble was disappearing as Third-Style painting, favored by the court, began to displace the ostentatious illusionism of Second Style.[21] Around Pompeii's forum, Luna marble was employed in the striking figured scroll door surround and the large solid slab of the threshold of the Eumachia Building. It was also used in the Temple of Venus.[22]

The arches at the north end of the forum, now stripped, were clad in Luna marble, to judge from the surviving bases and moldings of the north face of the Arch of Tiberius. Late republican and early imperial statue bases, such as those surviving in the middle of the west colonnade of the forum, and certainly the base of the great equestrian statue, were clad in Luna marble. In houses, Luna *impluvium* surrounds, wellheads, cistern covers and garden furniture began to displace those in tufa and travertine. Inscriptions began to be cut on plaques of Luna marble. At neighboring Capua, the displacement of herms in local stones by those in Luna has been documented.[23] Pentelic retained its prestige, however; it was used for the sacrificial reliefs on the altar of the Genius of Augustus building (cf. Dobbins, Ch. 12; Figure 12.12).[24]

Readier availability of white marble made polychrome marbles more prized, as did their adoption as key elements in the new Augustan architecture. The quarries were made imperial property for this purpose, and newly introduced Phrygian (*pavonazzetto*) and Carystian (*cipollino*) were added to the Numidian (*giallo antico*), Lucullan (*africano*), and Chian (*portasanta*).[25] These marbles were scarce outside Rome in the early Julio-Claudian period, but ambitious Pompeians found a way to display them by recycling debris from Roman workshops. In the Augustan period, black-and-white mosaic pavements were sometimes enriched with marble chunks chiefly of the new imperial marbles. The pieces range from approximately 5 to 20 cm and are set in more or less regular grids at varying densities. The finest of these pavements in the House of General Championnet (VIII.2.1) has a wide variety of polychrome marbles cut into

Figure 22.2 *Atrium* pavement with marble inserts, Augustan period, House of General Championnet (VIII.2.1).

several symmetrical shapes (Figure 22.2), but most use rather irregular pieces, suggesting that the available scraps were too small to allow further cutting.[26]

Public architecture in the post-earthquake period made greater use of marble than ever before, reflecting the general growth of imports as the imperial marble bureau (*ratio marmorum*) matured, and as private quarries strove to meet demand stimulated by court architecture. White marble from Luna was used in large sheets (*crustae*) on the walls of the municipal offices at the south end of the forum. The Temple of Venus was being reconstructed with architectural elements in Luna (some reused) as well as fresh quarry blocks, among the early imports from Proconnesus.[27] Buildings along the east side of the forum were being renovated to a unified design, and a new construction, the Imperial Cult Building, echoed contemporary Flavian design in Rome (Figures 12.10–11).[28] This exercise in curvilinear design had been fully decorated with marble sheathing on the walls, as is evident from the presence of plugs set into the brick to support bronze pins and shims for leveling on the surface of the surviving mortar beds. It has all been systematically stripped, but a pier applied to the South wall after the completion of the decoration has trapped the original cladding behind it. Two bands, each about 70 cm high, survive. The top of the upper is capped at 155 cm above present floor level by a filet of *rosso antico*. The upper *crusta* is of Scyrian marble, the lower of Lucullan, making a lively and busy juxtaposition. Traces of a plan dado in Luna are visible on the North wall.[29] A few remaining patches of Chian sheathing and dados, along with Lucullan sheathing and colonettes, show that the Macellum and Eumachia Building also made vivid use of color (Figure 22.3). At the Central Baths, decoration was just getting under way when Vesuvius interrupted work; brick walls were being fitted for marble revetment, columns of Lesbos gray marble were receiving final smoothing, and massive threshold blocks of Carystian and a gray marble were awaiting installation (Figure 22.4).[30] In the *apodyterion* at the northeast, which was being used as a marble workers' atelier, chips of Scyrian and Carystian marble suggest another lively wall scheme.

Private houses in AD 79 had more marble on display than ever, but were far behind public buildings. Marble workshops at Pompeii were modest operations devoted largely to repair and piecing, not original sculpture or architectural projects.[31] Outside three of four of the wealthiest city houses, marble wall revetment was rare.[32] Columns of genuine marble were found only in the *Praedia* of Julia Felix.[33] *Opus sectile* floors stretching from wall to wall are rare beyond the wealthy townhouse-villas on the seawall of Herculaneum (Figure 27.5) and the western city wall of Pompeii north of the Porta Marina.[34] Houses of the ordinary rich made do with small panels (averaging about one square meter) in the middle of more modest pavements.[35] Few of these descendants of the Augustan chunk pavements are as large and impressive as the *tablinum emblema* in the House of Marcus Lucretius (IX.3.5); most are small and scrappy. Unique and striking pieces of marble such as the Carystian thresholds and green porphyry blocks awaiting installation in the House of N. Popidius Priscus (VII.2.20) suggest that larger pieces of imported polychrome stones were only just beginning to be obtainable at Pompeii. White marbles from many sources were clearly available to the rich who wanted to outdo less wealthy neighbors now able to install furniture and fountains in Luna marble. In the House of the Vettii (VI.15.1; Map 3) a large number of tables, basins and fountains in the peristyle were arranged in groups by marble type and color. Large basins on the east–west cross axis are in

Figure 22.3 *Crustae* of Chian and Lucullan marbles in half-round niche, façade of the Eumachia Building (VII.9.1) facing the forum. *Crustae* with curvature are rare.

Pentelic marble, along with the prominent *cartibulum* in an intercolumniation of the east side, while the dominant group of four items extending into the garden from the middle of the north side are all of the second-quality Parian marble known as Paros 2. Shallow basins in three of the corners (that at the southeast is missing) were all apparently intended to be seen as gray, though made from heterogeneous marbles (Luna bardiglio, Lesbos gray and Proconnesian, the latter being the earliest identified import into Italy). White marble from Luna is represented only by a utilitarian cistern cover and a low pool surround.[36] The garden *triclinium* of the House of the Golden Bracelet (VI.17 [*Ins. Occ.*].42) employed three varieties of white marble.[37]

Painted imitation marble, which returns in Fourth-Style wall painted *opus sectile* panels, shows that house owners' aspirations, as usual, ran beyond the marble actually available.[38] Much about late Julio-Claudian and early Flavian taste is revealed. First, painted socles show colored marbles to the exclusion of white, now reserved for painted statues and representations of garden furniture (Figure 31.1).[39] Second, the marbles represented—Numidian, Phrygian, Lucullan, Chian, Carystian and some exotic Egyptian stones (see below)—are the marbles of the Julio-Claudian court. Alabaster has vanished, and *rosso antico* is restricted to use as fillets and moldings. Finally, socles in *opus sectile* are drawn directly from public architecture (especially the theater). It is no surprise that there is a close association of painted marble socles with theatrical scenes on stages in the central zone above them.[40]

A novelty of Fourth-Style painted marble is a dark purple punctuated with white dots, the painted imitation of purple porphyry.[41] An inscription found at the quarries

Figure 22.4 Monolithic threshold blocks in Carystian and gray marble in foreground, columns in Lesbos gray marble in the open courtyard, Central Baths (IX.4).

in Egypt shows that development of the quarry fields was under way in early Tiberian times, but the first porphyry seen at Rome under Claudius met with disapproval, and only under Nero, who loved the royal color and used the stone in his palaces, did porphyry achieve broad popularity.[42] *Graffiti* show that Nero was popular at Pompeii, and his theater claque included several Pompeians.[43] It is tempting to connect this imperial taste with the rapid diffusion of a fashion for porphyry. At the least, it is clear that Pompeian workshops watched Rome carefully, for porphyry was not the only Egyptian stone rendered in paint. A small quarry of striking black-and-white diorite (*granito bianco e nero*) at Wadi Barud was opened under Tiberius but seen in

Figure 22.5 *Triclinium* in the *nymphaeum* of the House of the Golden Bracelet
(VI.17 [*Ins. Occ.*].42); earlier painted socle left exposed above new sheathing in white
marble (Pentelic facing, Luna tank facing at left, Thasian tank front,
Parian dish rail facing with *aediculae*).

Rome only in the palaces of Nero and Domitian.[44] The fact that it was imitated in paint at Pompeii means that the wall painting workshops of the Fourth Style were still keeping up to date with trends at the imperial court (cf. Strocka, Ch. 20).

The scarcity of polychrome marbles in substantial modules was a reality that had to be faced even by wealthy municipal notables. The forecourt walls of the garden *nymphaeum* of the House of the Golden Bracelet (VI.17 [*Ins. Occ.*].42) were painted with an elaborate *opus sectile* socle and a painted revetment above. When the marble-clad masonry *triclinium* was added, the owner had no compunction about leaving the old painted wall visible behind it (Figure 22.5).[45] The unabashed juxtaposition of imitation with genuine recalls the House of the Faun (VI.12) two centuries earlier and shows that the important thing to display was not necessarily the physical object, but taste itself.

NOTES

1 I use "marble" as the Greeks and Romans did. By this convention it includes granite, porphyry, diorite, graywacke and near-metamorphic limestones as well as marble itself. Houses and objects mentioned are at Pompeii unless otherwise specified.

2 Because scholars of painting have traditionally concentrated on thematic and stylistic developments, the area of marble studies remains open. For essential bibliography, see: A. Barbet, *La Peinture murale romaine: les styles décoratifs pompéiens*, Paris, 1985; H. Dodge and B. Ward-Perkins (eds), *Marble in Antiquity. Collected Papers of J. B. Ward-Perkins*, Rome, 1992; H. Eristov, "Corpus des Faux-marbres peints a Pompéi," *MÉFR*, 1979, vol. 91, pp. 693–771; J. C. Fant, "Ideology, gift and trade: a distribution model for the Roman Imperial marbles," in W. V. Harris and S. Panciera (eds), *The Inscribed Economy: production and distribution in the Roman Empire in the light of instrumentum domesticum*, JRA Suppl. Ser. no. 6, 1993, pp. 145–70;

R. Gnoli, *Marmora romana*, 2nd edn, Rome, 1988; G. Borghini (ed.), *Marmi antichi*, Rome, 1989.

3 See A. Laidlaw, *The First Style in Pompeii: painting and architecture*, Rome, 1985; V. Bruno, "The antecedents of the Pompeian first style," *AJA*, 1969, vol. 73, pp. 305–17.

4 Gnoli, *Marmora romana*, pp. 186 ff.; Borghini, *Marmi antichi*, p. 288; S. E. Ellis, R. A. Higgins and R. Hope Simpson, "The facade of the Treasury of Atreus at Mycenae," *BSA*, 1968, vol. 63, pp. 331–6. The stone in the House of the Faun (VI.12) has not been analyzed, but the *rosso antico* of Tenaron is difficult to distinguish analytically from the red marbles of Iasos and Aphrodisias in Caria (L. Lazzarini, "Rosso antico and other red marbles used in antiquity: a characterization study," in *Marble: art historical and scientific perspectives on ancient sculpture*, Malibu, CA, 1990, pp. 237–52). But these marbles are much later, whereas *rosso antico* is strongly represented at Pompeii by the middle of the first century BC (so also Lazzarini, "Rosso antico," *pace* Gnoli, *Marmora romana*).

5 E. Pernice, *Pavimente und figürliche Mosaiken*, Die Hellenistische Kunst in Pompeji, vol. 6, Berlin, 1938, p. 90, notes that the letters were set into earlier paving but are consistent with Second-Style decoration. The use of *rosso antico*, however, is a consistent theme in the decorative scheme of the formal front of the house, not an afterthought, and it should be original. Pernice does not mention the *rosso antico* lining when he describes the *impluvium*. See J. R. Clarke, *The Houses of Roman Italy, 100 BC–AD 250. Ritual, space, and decoration*, Berkeley, CA, 1991, p. 83, not noting the presence of imported stone.

6 Similar large panels are used to frame the false door within the forward court at entrance no. 3 of the House of C. Julius Polybius (IX.13.1–3), illustrated in S. C. Nappo, *Pompeii. A guide to the ancient city*, New York, 1998, p. 53, fig. 53.

7 *Alabastro fiorito* is, to my eye, the closest visual parallel, but the stone type labeled by this traditional artisanal name does not have an agreed source or history; Gnoli, *Marmora romana*, pp. 224ff. (p. 215 for *cotognino*); Borghini, *Marmi antichi*, pp. 140ff.

8 *Alabastro fiorito* is represented in the upper molding of the Mysteries frieze (room 5) of the Villa of the Mysteries; it is known also from the late second-century House of the Griffons on the Palatine in Rome. *Alabastro cotognino*: *cubiculum* (46) of the House of the Labyrinth (VI.11.10); *cubicula* flanking *exedra* (y) of the House of the Silver Wedding (V.2.i); room (11) of the Villa of the Poppaei at Oplontis; and more modest houses such as the House of Ceres (I.9.13), *cubicula* (c, h) near the entrance, among others.

9 E. W. Leach, "Patrons, painters and patterns: the anonymity of Romano-campanian painting and the transition from the second to the third style," in B. K. Gold (ed.), *Literary and Artistic Patronage in Ancient Rome*, Austin, TX, 1982, pp. 135–73.

10 R. A. Tybout, *Aedificiorum figurae. Untersuchungen zu den Architekturdarstellungen des frühen zweiten Stils*, Amsterdam, 1989, pp. 350ff.

11 Plin., *HN* 36.44; see also below, n. 23.

12 House of Ceres (I.9.13), *cubiculum* (h), west of the *fauces*. Gnoli, *Marmora romana*, p. 208. It is difficult to sort out varieties of this marble (or marbles), whose sources are not well studied.

13 E.g., the Villa of Poppaea at Oplontis, *atrium* and *cubiculum* (11); Villa of the Mysteries, room (6).

14 H.-U. Cain and O. Dräger, "Die sogenannten neuattischen Werkstätten," in G. Hellenkemper Salies *et al.* (eds), *Das Wrack. Die antike Schiffsfund von Mahdia*, Köln, 1994, pp. 809–31; R. R. R. Smith, *Hellenistic Sculpture*, London, 1991, pp. 260f.; F. Coarelli, "Il commercio delle opere d'arte in età tardo repubblicana," *DialArch*, 1983, vol. 3.1, pp. 45–53; H. Galsterer, "Kunstraub und Kunsthandel im republikalischen Rom," in Hellenkemper Salies, *Das Wrack*, pp. 857–66. Cic., *Att.* I.8.2, I.9.2 (Shackleton Bailey, *CLA*, nos. 4–6).

15 In general, see Hellenkemper Salies, *Das Wrack*, esp. N. Himmelmann, "Mahdia und Antikythera," pp. 849–56, and supplement.

16 Ernest Pernice, in his monumental work *Hellenistische Tische, Zisternmünde, Beckenuntersätze, Altäre und Truhen*, Die hellenistische Kunst in Pompeji, vol. 5, Berlin/Leipzig, 1932, pp. 14 and 26, thought that marble came in the period of Sulla. But he admitted difficulty in distinguishing weathered travertine and limestone from marble.

17 The basin (apparently of Luna marble) in the *caldarium* of the Forum Baths; a tomb in Luna marble (visual identification) assigned a date of 90–60 BC on stylistic grounds (*PErc* N3)

and one in Chian marble (G. Kockel, *Grabbauten vor dem Herkulanische Tor*, Mainz, 1983, pp. 126–57, esp. p. 143, and p. 126, Taf. 42b, c).

18 R. Cohon, *Greek and Roman Marble Table Supports with Decorative Reliefs*, Ph.D. thesis, Institute of Fine Arts, New York University, 1984, pp. 76–93, 307–49 *et passim*. I accept his expert eye for identifying Pentelic.

19 See above, n. 16, and M. Bonamici, "Il marmo lunense in epoca preromana," in E. Dolci (ed.), *Il marmo nella civiltà Romana. La produzione e il commercio*, Carrara, 1989, pp. 83–114.

20 Suet., *Iul.* 73; Fant, "Ideology," p. 147; but I am no longer confident that the Forum Iulium could have used Luna.

21 Suet., *Aug.* 72; Paul Zanker, *The Power of Images in the Age of Augustus*, Ann Arbor, MI, 1990, ch. 4.

22 K. Wallat, "Der Marmorfries am Eingangsportal VII 9, 1 in Pompeji," *AA*, 1995, pp. 345–73.

23 M. Frederiksen, "Republican Capua," in *Campania*, ed. with additions by Nicholas Purcell, Rome, 1984, p. 293.

24 J. J. Dobbins, "The altar in the sanctuary of the Genius of Augustus in the forum at Pompeii," *RM*, 1992, vol. 99, pp. 251–63; the marble identification is mine.

25 On Phrygian: Gnoli, *Marmora romana*, pp. 169ff.; Borghini, *Marmi antichi*, p. 264; J. C. Fant, *Cavum Antrum Phrygiae: The organization and operations of the Roman imperial marble quarries at Docimium*, Oxford, 1989; M. Waelkens, *Dokimeion. Die Werkstatt der repräsentativen kleinasiatischen Sarkophage*, Berlin, 1982. Carystian: Gnoli, *Marmora romana*, pp. 180ff.; Borghini, *Marmi antichi*, p. 202; D. Vanhove, *Roman Marble Quarries in Southern Euboea and the Associated Road Networks*, Leiden, 1996. Numidian: Gnoli, *Marmora romana*, pp. 166ff.; Borghini, *Marmi antichi*, p. 214; F. Rakob (ed.), *Simmithus I. Die Steinbrüche und die antike Stadt*, Mainz, 1993. Lucullan: Gnoli, *Marmora romana*, pp. 174ff.; Borghini, *Marmi antichi*, p. 133; J. C. Fant, "Poikiloi Lithoi: the anomalous economics of the Roman imperial marble quarry at Teos," in S. Walker and A. Cameron (eds), *The Greek Renaissance in the Roman Empire*, BICS Suppl. no. 55, 1989, pp. 206–18; A. Dworakowska, "Once again on marmor Luculleum," in M. True and J. Podany (eds), *Marble: art historical and scientific perspectives on ancient sculpture*, Malibu, CA, 1990, pp. 253–62. Chian: Gnoli, *Marmora romana*, pp. 170ff.; Borghini, *Marmi antichi*, p. 285. See also J. C. Fant, "Pro imperii maiestate ornata: Augustan Rome and the new polychrome marbles," in M. Schvoerer (ed.), *Archéomatériaux. Marbres et autres roches* (ASMOSIA IV, Proceedings of the Fourth International Conference of the Association for the Study of Marble and Other Stones in Antiquity, Bordeaux, 1995), Bordeaux, 1999, pp. 277–80.

26 Other examples: the peristyle/*cryptoporticus* (29–32) paving of the House of the Stags (IV.21) at Herculaneum; *atrium* (b) of the House of M. Lucretius Fronto (V.4.a, 11); *atriolum* (46) of the bath in the House of the Menander (I.10.4); *atrium* (b) of the House of Caecilius Iucundus (V.1.26), on which see C. Dexter, *The Casa di L. Cecilio Giocondo in Pompeii*, Ph.D. thesis, Duke University, 1975, pp. 112–14. It is striking that the *impluvium* pavement (in *atrium* [27]) of the House of the Faun (VI.12) has the new marbles inserted around the base of the statue.

27 M. Bruno *et al.*, "Pompeii after the AD 62 earthquake: historical, isotopic and petrographic studies of quarry blocks in the Temple of Venus," in J. J. Herrmann, N. Herz and R. Newman (eds), *Interdisciplinary Studies on Ancient Stone* (ASMOSIA V, Proceedings of the Fifth International Conference of the Association for the Study of Marble and Other Stones in Antiquity, Boston, MA, 1998), London, 2002, pp. 282–8 (cf. also Dobbins, Ch. 12).

28 J. J. Dobbins, "Problems of chronology, decoration and urban design in the forum of Pompeii," *AJA*, 1994, vol. 98, pp. 629–94. Cf. also Dobbins, Ch. 12.

29 I owe this observation, to my knowledge not previously made (in print), to my alert undergraduate research assistant of June 2004, Kent Humrichouser. The pilaster in question is at the south end of the line tracing the north–south axis of the Imperial Cult Building in Dobbins, "Problems of chronology," p. 684, fig. 57.

30 Bruno *et al.*, "Pompeii after the AD 62 earthquake." Cf. also Koloski-Ostrow, Ch. 15.

31 C. Moss, "The Casa dello Scultore in Pompeii and the early imperial marble industry," paper at the Archaeological Institute of America 1986 annual meeting, correcting D. Mustilli, "Botteghe di scultori, marmorarii, bronzieri e caelatores in Pompei," in *Pompeiana*, Naples, 1950, pp. 206–29). I am grateful to Dr Moss for sharing a copy of the text with me.

32 Seaside room (18) of the House of the Relief of Telephus (*Ins. Or.* I.2–3) at Herculaneum, property of a senatorial family, is the richest preserved room in Campania decorated with marble. Other examples: *oecus* (62) of the House of Fabius Rufus (VII.16 [*Ins. Occ.*].17–22) (see map 3); the villa at Oplontis, with a dado in *breccia corallina* in the rooms facing the pool (64, 65); and *exedra* (46) of the House of the Dioscuri (VI.9.6), represented only by mortar beds. More modest houses include: *oecus* (34) of the House of Sallust (VI.2.4), with gray marble revetment over a white marble baseboard which was continued into the room in paint, and *opus sectile* pavement and a gray marble dado in the small rooms (22, 23) of the House of Apollo (VI.7.23) facing the garden, the walls of which were prepared for marble *crustae* also.

33 They are even more impressive because they are monolithic (see Parslow, Ch. 14). A small Carystian hexagonal base in the garden *exedra* (t) of the House of Marcus Lucretius Fronto (V.4.a, 11) must have had a marble column above it. Many such small columns may have vanished entirely.

34 Examples include rooms (5, 15–17) in the House of the Stags at Herculaneum (IV.21); room (18) of the House of the Relief of Telephus (*Ins. Or.* I.2–3) at Herculaneum; rooms (9, 12, 23 and 24) in the House of the Mosaic Atrium at Herculaneum (IV.1–2); room (M), *exedra* (D) and the ground-level *atrium* (the latter two represented by mortar beds only) in the House of Fabius Rufus (VI.17 [*Ins. Occ.*].16–19). The central *exedra* of the portico facing the *piscina* (69) of the villa at Oplontis in black marble and Numidian also stands out. Cf. Tybout, Ch. 26; Dickmann, Ch. 27.

35 Examples survive in good condition in the Houses of Cornelius Rufus (VIII.4.15, room r); the Ephebe (I.7.10–12, *triclinium* 17); Sacerdos Amandus (I.7.7). *Cubiculum* (2) of the House of the Blacksmith (I.10.7) is an example of a still more humble form with an open square of gray marble plaques and one scrap of porphyry isolated in the center.

36 J. C. Fant *et al.*, "White marble at Pompeii: sampling the House of the Vettii," in L. Lazzarini (ed.), *Interdisciplinary Studies on Ancient Stone* (ASMOSIA VI, Proceedings of the Sixth International Conference for the Association for the Study of Marble and Other Stones in Antiquity, Venice, 2000), Padova, 2003, pp. 309–16.

37 J. Clayton Fant, "White marbles in the summer triclinium of the Casa del Bracciale d'oro, Pompeii," in Y. Maniatis (ed.), (ASMOSIA VII, Proceedings of the Seventh International Conference of the Association for the Study of Marble and Other Stones in Antiquity, Thassos 2003), BCH Suppl. (in press).

38 R. Ling, *Roman Painting*, Cambridge, 1991, p. 95; A. Barbet, *La peinture murale romaine: les styles décoratifs pompéiens*, Paris, 1985, p. 198.

39 From the end walls of the poolside rooms (68 and 70) of the villa at Oplontis (Figure 31.5) one can look past painted basins and neo-Attic craters to a real neo-Attic crater by the pool (W. Jashemski, *The Gardens of Pompeii*, New Rochelle, NY, 1979, vol. I, figs 470, 473, 475, 480). Painted marble furniture appears also in *nymphaeum* (33) of the House of the Centenary (IX.8.6). Painted statues are depicted, for example, on the south peristyle wall of the House of Marine Venus (II.3.3); see Jashemksi, *Gardens*, vol. I, pp. 125–30.

40 The connections remains just as powerful even in light of E. Moorman's observation ("Rappresentazioni teatrali su scaenae frontes di quarto stile a Pompei," *Pompeii Herculaneum Stabiae*, 1983, vol. 1, pp. 73–117) that the socles were later additions.

41 E.g., the House of Pinarius Cerealis (III.4.b), room (a).

42 Inscription: W. van Rengen, "A New Paneion at Mons Porphyrites," *Chronique d'Egypte*, 1995, vol. 70, pp. 240–5. Statue: Plin., *HN* 36.75. Nero: Dio Cass. 62.6.2; Suet., *Ner.* 50.

43 J. L. Franklin, Jr, *Pompeis difficile est: studies in the political life of imperial Pompeii*, Ann Arbor, MI, 2001, pp. 101–30.

44 D. P. S. Peacock and V. Maxfield, *Mons Claudianus Survey and Excavation. Vol. I, Topography and quarries*, Cairo, 1997, pp. 275–9. The fact that the fort at Barud was called Tiberiane and the close match with Pliny's petrographic description, identify this stone as Pliny's *Tibereum* (*HN* 36.55). Imitated at Pompeii in *cubiculum* (I) of the House of the Gilded Cupids (VI.16.7) and room (h) of the House of D. Octavius Quartio (II.2.2).

45 The *triclinium* is unpublished; the glass paste mosaic of the *nymphaeum* is discussed in the exhibition catalogue *Rediscovering Pompeii*, Rome 1990, pp. 270–8.

CHAPTER TWENTY-THREE

HOUSES OF
REGIONS I AND II

——— •◆• ———

Salvatore Ciro Nappo

TOPOGRAPHY

The designation of the sector of Pompeii lying east of the strada Stabiana and south of the via dell'Abbondanza (Figure 23.1) as Regions I and II is a modern invention. Giuseppe Fiorelli devised it during his superintendency as a way of systematically cataloguing the buildings brought to light at the site (cf. Foss, Ch. 3; Laidlaw, Ch. 39). In fact, the entire sector contains two different types of urban subdivision. To the west, two rows of square *insulae* follow the line of the strada Stabiana; east of these, three rows of variably sized rectangular *insulae* are ordered along the axis of the via di Nocera. The two types of *insulae* have completely different roles and are chronologically distinct with regard to the development of the city plan (cf. Geertman, Ch. 7).

The highest altitude in the sector is right in the northwest section of Region I; from there, the ground slopes southward, dropping sharply around the middle of the row of *insulae* facing the via dell'Abbondanza. Almost all the houses there must adjust for this gradient by cutting back into the slope and building substructures. The conformation of the ground has always allowed a regular, natural, downhill flow of rainwater, which seems to have followed the north–south corridor of the streets to empty outside the walls, in some cases via actual sewers (cf. Jansen, Ch. 16).[1]

THE DEVELOPMENT OF THE URBAN PLAN

The most recent studies on the development of the city plan increasingly highlight the importance of the road that starts north of the Porta Ercolano, follows the line of the via Consolare southward, and turns east as far as the so-called "Quadrivium of Orpheus" (where Regions V, VI, VII and IX meet), where it turns south and meets the city wall again at the Porta di Stabia (Map 2). This street represents the main route into and across the earliest phase of the city, which was built on a lava plateau of some 66 ha in area and already surrounded by a boundary wall in the sixth century BC (cf. Chiaramonte, Ch. 11; Carafa, Ch. 5; Geertman, Ch. 7). The subsequent growth of the city beyond the *Altstadt* respected this route in that, we believe, its first expansion involved the stretch of the strada Stabiana where, right on the east side, two

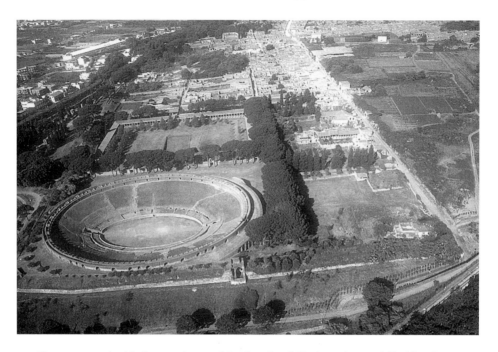

Figure 23.1 Aerial view southwest of Regions I and II, along the via dell'Abbondanza.

rows of "square" *insulae* were built (*insulae* IX.1–6, I.2–4, 6, 10). The different sizes of these *insulae*, and the inexact alignment of the two rows, suggest that growth was not planned. Rather, it took place over time according to a logic of spatial organization, through subsequent property acquisitions, that merely respected already consolidated urban forms. All the remaining territory within the walls to the east of these *insulae* was subdivided into three parts, doubtless in a later period, by two parallel streets: the via di Nola and the via dell'Abbondanza.[2]

We now turn to the *insulae* of the southern sector (Regions I and II; see Map 2). Thanks to their almost complete excavation, plus a long series of stratigraphic excavations in recent years, it is now possible to advance a hypothesis about why their lengths are slightly different. The entire sector was originally divided into three bands of equal-sized rectangular plots (roughly 87 by 33 m), bounded on the north by the via dell'Abbondanza and on the south by the circuit wall. The via di Nocera provided a perpendicular axis of orientation. Formal streets did not yet subdivide these bands; the presence of numerous wells beneath the oldest houses, but not belonging to them, suggests that the area was intended for farmland. When the via di Castricio was built, the central band ceded its northern edge to its construction (and shortened those plots to about 82 m). Meanwhile, the southern band was cut on the north end to make room for the construction of the east–west street parallel to the via di Castricio, and abbreviated on the south for a new embankment (and small retaining wall) behind the city walls, as well as a small street running just inside the wall (cf. Chiaramonte, Ch. 11). Plots of the southern band were consequently reduced to 79 m. With the dating of the construction phase of the fortification walls, we have the *terminus post quem* for true urbanization in this part of the city (300–180 BC).[3] Finally, in the area where the rectangular *insulae*, taking their orientation from the via di Nocera, meet the square ones, regulated by the via di Stabia, the city-blocks assumed an unusual trapezoidal shape (e.g., I.7), because the corner where the strada Stabiana meets the via dell'Abbondanza does not form a right-angle.

THE BUILDING TYPOLOGY

The articulation of domestic architecture in Regions I and II—at the time of the eruption in AD 79—was the result of a complex and pronounced construction history. Thanks to recent investigations, it is now possible to trace its general lines.

The first phase is characterized by the division of *insulae* into regular lots (8–10 by 32–4 m) with plans differing according to whether the street front of the short side was of particular interest—for instance, for establishing shops. In one case, lots were arranged widthwise (east–west) across the *insula* (e.g., Region II, *insulae* 8–9; Figure 23.2a). In another case, lots were arranged in two directions: on the short sides, oriented north–south; and on the long sides, arranged east–west (e.g., Region I, *insulae* 9, 11–14, 16; Figures 23.2b and 23.5). In a third instance, lots were arranged north–south on just one end; this occurred when one of the two short sides offered no particular commercial advantages (e.g., Region II, *insula* 1; Figure 23.2c).

On these lots were built modest but presentable houses. The width of the front part was practically identical to that of the *hortus* in back, although the roofed spaces of the front part took up about 60 percent of the total area, leaving the rest for uncovered garden space. The dwellings, though variable in type, were simple, modular constructions with smallish rooms. An upper story was generally lacking, and the (usually rectangular) unroofed *atrium* was set perpendicular to the entrance and parallel to the street. Sarno limestone and lava were abundantly used as building material. *Opus incertum* and *opus africanum* were the favored construction techniques, but façades

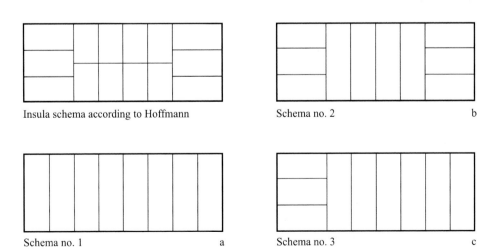

Insula schema according to Hoffmann

Schema no. 2   b

Schema no. 1   a

Schema no. 3   c

Figure 23.2 Reconstructions of the schemata for dividing *insulae* in Regions I and II into regular lots (after Nappo, "Urban transformation," fig. 4).

of *opus quadratum* in Sarno limestone are also found (cf. Adam, Ch. 8; Wallace-Hadrill, Ch. 18; Peterse, Ch. 24). The wall decoration is the imitation masonry of the First Style, while pavements are almost exclusively of *cocciopesto*. One thing seems certain: in the course of the second century BC, the whole area between the via dell'Abbondanza and the strada Stabiana was almost completely built up.[4]

This widespread urbanization, characterized by what we call "row houses," was quickly affected by phenomena of buying and selling that modified the original architectural layouts, favoring the construction of much larger, airier houses with splendid peristyles that often denote the wish of the owner to declare Greco-Hellenistic culture as his own (cf. Wallace-Hadrill, Ch. 18). In the second half of the first century BC, such large houses as the House of Marine Venus (II.3.3), the House of the Ship Europa (I.15.3), the House of the Cylindrical Columns (I.16.2), the House of the Ephebe (I.7.10–12, 19), the House of Loreius Tiburtinus (II.2.2) and houses (I.14.12) and (I.16.5), are the result of this process (Map 3).

In the turbulent years after the earthquake of AD 62, especially those following the frequent movements of the earth that occurred for some years prior to the eruption of 79, houses in this sector were substantially transformed. Many houses were gradually abandoned, to be purchased by an active and highly specialized artisan and mercantile class that transformed and adapted them to meet their specific needs. Nevertheless, despite the disturbances of nature, large homes did persist in the area, and, in their structures and decorative apparatus, attest a long building history.[5]

CASE STUDIES

Caupona of Sotericus (I.12.3); Figure 23.3

This is a small house that has kept the same ground area throughout its history.[6] Its original plan must have been the same as that of many other houses in this part of Pompeii: a vestibule at the center of the façade led into an unroofed court (2), splitting two *cubicula* (1) that opened onto the same court. On the same axis as the vestibule, beyond the court, a corridor (4) divided two more living rooms (3, 5) and led to a *viridarium* (6), onto which opened an *oecus* (7) and a small kitchen with a latrine. The house in this first phase had no upper story and the roofs were organized with a single pitch above the front range of rooms that sent rainwater onto the via dell'Abbondanza. A second roof was set over the rear range of rooms (3–5), turning perpendicular over rooms (7) and (8) and jointly draining rainwater into the *viridarium*.

Over the years, the house underwent substantial changes in the distribution of its architectural spaces while keeping their same size. Certainly in the Augustan period it received redecoration in the Third Style, as the walls of rooms (3) and (4) attest. After the earthquake of AD 62, it was probably converted from a private home into a *caupona* (cf. DeFelice, Ch. 30). At this point, the two northern rooms (1) on the street-side of the via dell'Abbondanza were radically transformed. The one to the right of the entrance was broken through and a *thermopolium* counter was installed, clad with faux tiles decorated with stylized flowers. The customary *dolia* for food storage were not set inside the counter, but were placed in court (2) against the west wall. The room to the left of the entrance (at no. 4) was sold off to others and here, after the door that had communicated with the court was walled up, was installed

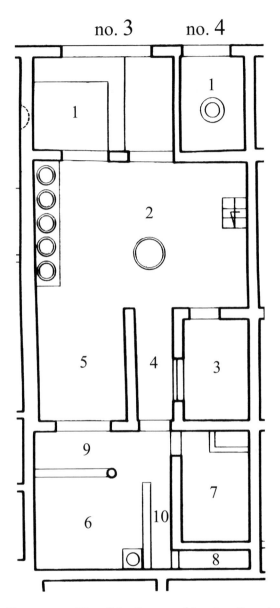

Figure 23.3 Plan of the Caupona of Sotericus (I.12.3).

a *musivarius'* (mosaicist's) atelier (or, as others believe, a felt shop).[7] The rooms opening onto the *viridarium* in the back of the building (7, 8) became an expanded kitchen, and here was found a splendid fresco with a domestic *lararium* (Figure 23.4). The house was enlarged vertically with an upper story covering practically its entire area, reached by a long wooden staircase against the east wall of the court, now entirely covered. The new roof was articulated with a large single pitch sloping toward the street and covering both the original open central area and the front range

Figure 23.4   Fresco depicting a *lararium*, Caupona of Sotericus (I.12.3).

of the house. Just above the center of the court an *opaion* was opened in the roof to provide light and air to the center of the house. Beneath this stood a large marble base on a tall foot. The back part kept free the *viridarium*, into which emptied rain-water from the roof, which had been raised to contain the upper story rooms. Thanks to its complete restoration (in 1998) and to the painstaking and faithful reconstruction of the architectural volumes and roofs, this house helps us better understand the characteristics of a *caupona* created within a building originally conceived as a residence.[8]

House (I.14.11–14); Figure 23.5

Excavated only partially in the 1950s, this *insula* was completely freed of volcanic detritus in 1992, and now the individual building nuclei can be observed.[9] The southern part, where the greatest uncertainties had been, contains three distinct residential units at nos. 12, 14 and 15. The articulation of the covered areas, the configuration of the unroofed spaces, the obliteration of earlier passageways and the presence of new openings attest a long building history that begins (as for the whole area), at the end of the third century BC. The presence of three quite regular building units appears likely in the first phase, just as, for example, on the northern end of *insula* I.16.

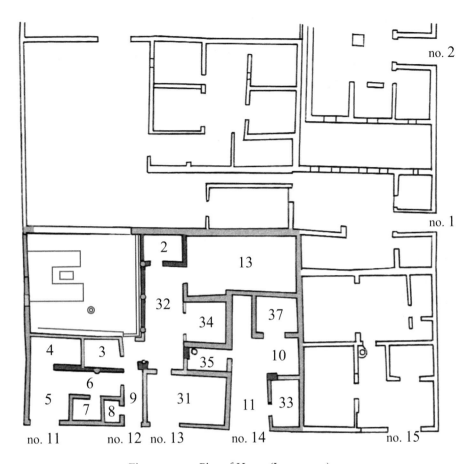

Figure 23.5   Plan of House (I.14.11–14).

This arrangement underwent a radical transformation in the Augustan period, as attested by the presence of noteworthy Third-Style decoration (Figure 23.7), when the central (at no. 14) and the western (no. 12) building units were joined. The rooms were arranged to the east around a courtyard (10) and to the west around a portico with two *ambulacra*. Passage between the eastern and western sections was made through room (35). The main entrance was at no. 14, while a *posticum* opened west onto the street parallel to the via di Nocera.

The earthquake of AD 62 caused serious damage. Some columns of the peristyle must have been replaced and remade in *opus vittatum mixtum*, while the corner column was replaced with a pillar and, what is more, *plutei* (parapet walls) were placed in the intercolumniations. An outdoor *triclinium* was built in the garden. Two new rooms (*cubicula*), decorated in the Fourth Style, were created at the extreme north (2) of the eastern portico and at the extreme west of the southern portico. This arrangement was later transformed radically: rooms (10), (11), (33), (35) and (37) came to form an independent residential unit. To increase residential capacity, a second story was built above the entire area, except room (37), which became a small internal unroofed courtyard. Here were found a great many wine *amphorae*, placed neck downward (stored as "empties"), ready to be re-filled from the imminent harvest. Despite the most recent damage suffered, the owner had to think both of the work that had to continue and of the ongoing restoration of the house itself. The western part of the house opened a new entrance at no. 12, and took over a vast area to the north behind the house at no. 1. The south portico was completely demolished, and one of the columns was incorporated in a new wall; in the space in front of the portico were built two new rooms (3) and (4), decorated in Fourth Style. A shop was opened on the street in room (5) at no. 11; room (34) was once again decorated in Fourth Style (Figure 23.6). Finally, the large *triclinium* (13), still decorated in the Third Style (Figure 23.7), was completely cleared to receive new wall decoration, as attested by

Figure 23.6   Room (34) in House (I.14.11–14), with Fourth-Style wall decoration.

Figure 23.7 *Triclinium* (13) in House (I.14.11–14), with Third-Style wall decoration depicting Perseus about to rescue Andromeda from the sea monster.

numerous containers full of lime and paints. Room (2) was also awaiting new decoration, and during the renovation of the house it served as a temporary storeroom for *instrumentum domesticum* (cf. Berry, Ch. 19). In this case too, after an initial renovation attributable to the immediate aftermath of the AD 62 earthquake, a second and more radical transformation took place.

House of the Citharist (I.4.5); Figure 23.8

The House of the Citharist has its main entrance at no. 5 on the strada Stabiana. In its first phase it was a regular *atrium* house that extended eastward up to the change in level that separated the eastern houses in the *insula* from the western, and its size and layout were comparable to the two flanking houses at no. 2 and no. 9. To this phase belongs the First-Style decoration of *cubiculum* (11) to the left of the *atrium*.

In the second phase, corresponding to the acquisition of all three properties to the east, a house was built that was splendid for its size and the daring novelty of its architectural forms. A long entrance—vestibule and *fauces* (3)—led into the *atrium* (6), where the *impluvium* pool was moved forward. On axis to the entrance opened a large rectangular *tablinum* (14), perpendicular to the *atrium*, preceded by two spacious *alae* (12) and (13). Behind and to the east were two peristyles (17) and (32) separated by a splendid wall, and a window placed directly on axis with the *tablinum* and

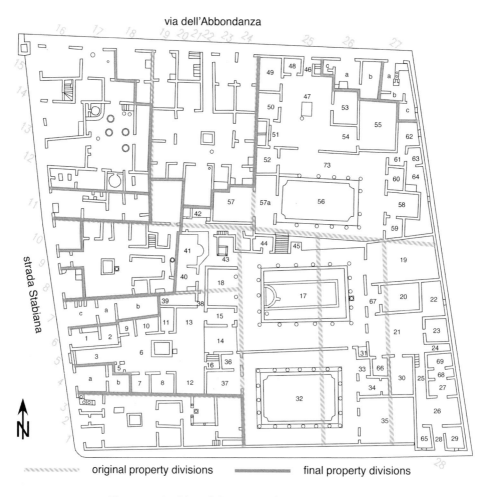

Figure 23.8   Plan of the House of the Citharist (I.4.5).

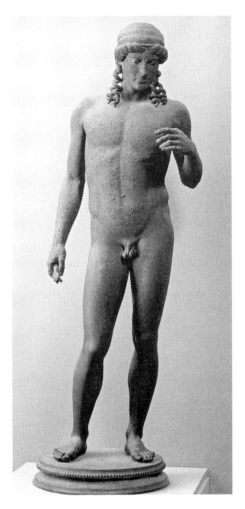

Figure 23.9 Bronze statue of Apollo Citharoedus found in the northeast corner of peristyle (32) in the House of the Citharist (I.4.5).

atrium. Further back still were three large living rooms (19–21), attesting to the importance of the owner's relationship with the outdoors. In this phase the house was embellished with elaborate Third-Style decoration, dominated by large-scale mythological paintings such as Sleeping Antiope (19); Nemesis and the Swan, Apollo and Poseidon, and Venus and Mars (20). The peristyle (17) contained many bronze statues, notably that of Apollo Citharoedus (Lyre-player); this had been moved in antiquity to the northeast corner of the peristyle (32), where it was discovered (Figure 23.9). The quality of life in the house during this period is attested equally by a gracious bath complex complete with *apodyterium, tepidarium, caldarium* (38–41) and a small tetrastyle *atrium* (43). The spectacular architectural sequences, the themes of the pictorial decoration, and the use of the peristyles clearly bespeak the Greek influence so in vogue at the end of the first century BC (Figure 23.10).

Figure 23.10   Fresco depicting seaside landscape from the architrave of peristyle (17) in the House of the Citharist (I.4.5).

The events subsequent to the earthquake of AD 62 permitted the property to grow further by incorporating the house at no. 25, which was accessed by the construction of a staircase in *opus latericium* (between 44 and 45) to overcome the sharp change in level. Continuous earth tremors made it necessary to redo a good part of the painted decoration, but its quality remained high. Room (35) received splendid Fourth-Style paintings showing Iphigenia in Tauris, and Dionysus and Ariadne, while salon (21) was decorated with a grandiose Judgment of Paris.

In the final years of its life, the house seems to have faced economic problems, and it lost the airy appearance that had characterized it. In fact, it was forced to cede some parts of the house as shops (I.4.4; I.4.26; I.4.27) or to rent out part of the upper story on the via dell'Abbondanza. The baths were no longer in working order, and the pavement with its *suspensurae* was partially dismantled; the *natatio* in the center of the middle peristyle (17) was filled with the detritus of collapse, and was replaced by a small fountain with a basin at the west end. The northern peristyle (56) was partially transformed by the construction of rooms in the intercolumniations of the west end. Finally the great *tablinum* (14) was scaled down so much (with the insertion of rooms 16 and 36) that anyone entering from the strada Stabiana no longer had that illusionistic (but also real) impression of great spaces and marvelous gardens beyond.

The House of the Citharist and its related economic activities can be ascribed to Lucius Popidius Secundus and his family, politically among the most active residents in the years after the earthquake (cf. Welch, Ch. 36 for the portrait sculptures). In terms of absolute chronology, a time frame of the second half of the third century BC can be proposed for the first phase of the house, while the second phase can reasonably be placed in the last years of the first century BC. Events that took place between the earthquake of AD 62 and the eruption of 79 determined the final modifications. It is clear that many small alterations occurred between one phase and another, but these did not involve substantial changes.[10]

Praedia of Julia Felix (II.4); Figure 23.11

This is undoubtedly one of the largest and most evocative houses in Pompeii (cf. Parslow, Ch. 14). Recent archaeological investigations have revealed that it was created by joining two *insulae* originally separated by a street, which was then eliminated and incorporated into the property probably after the earthquake of AD 62. The built-up portion of the complex lies in the north and west, along the via dell' Abbondanza, while behind it extend sweeping gardens. The structures were first excavated between March 30 and April 30, 1757, under the direction of the military engineer R. J. de Alcubierre and his assistant K. Weber. At the time, excavation focused on the recovery of only what the antiquarians defined as *objets d'art* (cf. Foss, Ch. 3). The paintings that C. Paderni, curator of the "museum" of Portici, considered worthy of enriching the personal and singularly peculiar painting collection of the Bourbon royal family were ripped from the walls. As was customary in that day, the architectural complex was reburied after it had been stripped of its treasure.[11] First, however, in May of 1757 Weber drew the plan of the building and numbered the sites where objects had been found and removed, or where paintings had been cut out, making a list of the objects which, today, is priceless for reconstructing the life and activities of the owner.[12] During that initial excavation, a crucial find clarified the characteristics of the place: at no. 6, a monumental entrance with engaged columns and small pediment of *opus latericium*, was found an inscription advertising shops, apartments and a bath complex for rent (cf. Bernstein, Ch. 34, for the inscription), and naming the owner, one Julia Felix.

The proprietor, after acquisition, constructed a multi-purpose complex that she rented out along with its commercial activities. Four distinct nuclei can be distinguished in the complex: a private house, the area around the peristyle, the baths and the garden. The private house had its own entrance (created *ex novo* after AD 62) at no. 10, the southernmost point of access on the western side of the block. The house had a compluviate *atrium* and a *tablinum* (92) on axis with the original entrance and the garden. Today the walls are still almost completely covered with frescoes, though the central figural panels are missing (having been detached and removed). *Tablinum* (92) must have been spectacular; its Fourth-Style decoration consisted of dados painted with green plants on a black background, a tripartite middle zone of red and yellow panels with villas, sanctuaries and flying figures painted in the center, and an upper part containing large still-lifes. At the time of the eighteenth-century excavations, the south wall was completely detached and carried away, while only the still-lifes were taken from the north wall, visible today in the Museo Nazionale in Naples. The peristyle quarter was accessible both from the private house (via (90); corridor (90b) branched off to service quarters; Figure 20.1) and from the via dell'Abbondanza through entrance no. 3. From the walls of entryway (24), pieces of a painted frieze depicting the Civil Forum were also detached in the 1700s (Figure 23.12).[13] The western part of the peristyle consisted of a splendid large portico with monolithic marble rectangular Corinthian pillars (Figure 23.13; cf. Fant, Ch. 22), and a back wall decorated in the Fourth Style. At its center opened a spectacular summer *triclinium* (83) with a system of waterfalls, walls frescoed with Nilotic scenes and the ceiling covered with chips of Sarno stone that gave the impression of a cave. At the center of the peristyle was a *euripus*, a long rectangular pool edged in marble, enlivened with apses, niches and little bridges (Figure 14.5). Small rectangular pillars of *opus vittatum mixtum* supported a broad pergola on the eastern and southern sides (50, 56), providing shade to a series of alternating niches and apses with cavelike walls and seats. It is not unlikely that the garden was arranged to accommodate the needs of the cult of Isis, seeing that a small shrine (55) dedicated to that goddess opened off the southern side.

The bath complex was accessible via a ramp directly off the street at entrance no. 6. From here one reached a small *quadriporticus*, with seats where clients could wait,

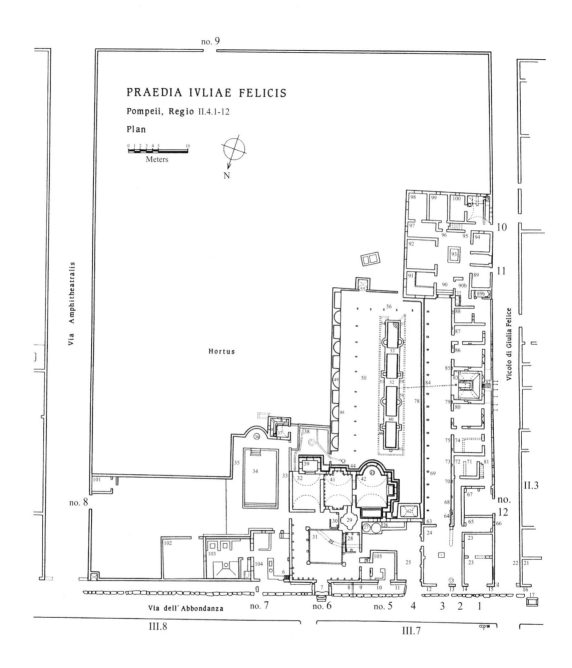

Figure 23.11 Plan of the *Praedia* of Julia Felix (II.4).
Adapted from a plan courtesy of Christopher Parslow.

Figure 23.12   Fresco showing the west side of the city forum, with candidate lists on a horizontal board in front of equestrian statues, from entryway (24) to the portico in the *Praedia* of Julia Felix (II.4).

followed by the canonical bath chambers in parallel: *frigidarium* (32), *tepidarium* (41) with the *laconicum* (29) on its north end, and *caldarium* (42). Just outside was located the *natatio* (34), used mostly in summer. The baths must have had a great deal of use, since most of the public baths in Pompeii were closed awaiting repairs of the damage suffered in the earthquake of AD 62 (cf. Koloski-Ostrow, Ch. 15). Adjacent to the bath was a *caupona* (103), accessible from the via dell'Abbondanza at no. 7. This was divided into booths with masonry seats and a *triclinium* with circular table. Annexed to the *caupona* was also a small *thermopolium* (104) that sold drinks and food directly on the street (cf. DeFelice, Ch. 30). In the spacious garden behind, fruit trees were enclosed in large squares formed by low wooden fences (Figure 15.8); access to the garden was possible also from the southern perimeter near the amphitheater at no. 9 (Map 3). The various quarters of the property intercommunicated, permitting clients to reach them easily from several directions. What once must have been a noble house became an economic center based on services to third parties.[14]

361

Figure 23.13 View northwest of the *euripus* and the portico in
the *Praedia* of Julia Felix (II.4).

House of Loreius Tiburtinus (II.2.2); Figure 23.14

The House of Loreius Tiburtinus, excavated by Vittorio Spinazzola between 1916
and 1921, occupies a large part of the *insula*, and opens to the north on the via
dell'Abbondanza, attesting the importance of this street for both commercial interests
and spacious residences. One of Pompeii's largest and most distinctive houses, it had
a long building history that wound up incorporating smaller properties, attested in
the southern and eastern perimeter walls with their succession of different building
techniques and blocked-off doors.

Its name was erroneously compiled from numerous electoral inscriptions on its
façade and those on the houses opposite, some of which solicited votes for a certain
Loreius, and others for a certain Tiburtinus. Add the representation of a priest of Isis
in the center of a panel on the south wall of *oecus* (f), with white clothing, shaved
head, *patera*, *situla* and *sistrum* (shallow bowl for libations, water-pail and metal
rattle), whose name is barely legible below: Amulius Faventinus Tiburs. The last
owner was probably one Octavius Quartio (by whose name the house is also known),
whose bronze seal was found in a *cubiculum* off the *atrium*; he seems to have renovated
the house for the domestic worship of Isis (cf. Small, Ch. 13).[15]

The lofty entrance at no. 2 was closed by two wooden doors decorated with metal
bosses, and flanked by two *cauponae* (nos. 1, 3) belonging to the house. The *atrium*,
its pavement punctuated by marble hexagons, had an *impluvium* in the center with
tall sides like a planter, and a fountain with high vertical spout. Lateral rooms were
painted in the Fourth Style (middle of the first century AD), but surmounted by
First-Style stucco cornices (second century BC), attesting to the long life of the house.

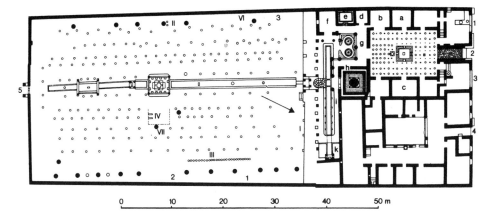

Figure 23.14 Plan of the House of Loreius Tiburtinus (II.2.2).
Archivio della Soprintendenza Archeologica di Pompei.

Noteworthy is room (b): suspended figures seem to hover in the center of red-ground panels, among them a Venus Piscatrix (fishing Venus) and soldiers in arms. High up, small hunting scenes are painted on a black background. Access from the *atrium* goes directly through a small peristyle (g) on the spot of the original *tablinum*, recognizable from traces in the *atrium*'s southern wall. Around that colonnaded *viridarium* open two of the most interesting frescoed rooms in Pompeii: *oecus* (f) and *triclinium* (h). *Oecus* (f) is embellished with extremely fine and elegant Fourth-Style decoration: a white background divided into architecturally compartmented panels with trophies. The panels are enclosed in frames with miniaturist decorations; the ceiling is articulated by circular and square partitions with fine stucco reliefs (cf. Strocka, Ch. 20; Clarke, Ch. 21); (Figure 23.15). *Triclinium* (h) displays scenes from the myth of Troy in two registers: in the upper is Hercules' expedition against Laomedon, king of Troy; in the lower, episodes of the Trojan war featuring Achilles.

Another significant element is the scenographic arrangement of two *euripi*. The upper (northern) one is covered with a pergola supported by small pillars decorated with Bacchic subjects and enriched by a considerable number of garden statues. The north wall is frescoed with a large hunting scene in an exotic setting, while the western wall shows Diana and Actaeon. Painted on the sides of an *aedicula* against the rear (eastern) wall are the myths of Narcissus and of Pyramus and Thisbe, boasting the only known signature of a painter at Pompeii: *Lucius pinxit* "Lucius painted (this)." The painter used Ovid's versions from the *Metamorphoses*, showing off his (or the owner's) literary savvy. The (Corinthian distyle) *aedicula* has an apse at the back, which held the statue of a kneeling boy pouring water from an *amphora* to fill the *euripus*, which then ran between two dining couches that formed a *biclinium* (k). The second, longer *euripus* (Figure 23.16), flanked by pergolaed avenues, extends north to south through a vast, rich garden of shady plants, acanthus and fruit trees. At the intersection of the two *euripi* is a small tetrastyle temple; at its base is a fountain with several inclined spigots arranged in a semicircle, and a vertical jet at the center. Another unusual fountain was located at the center of the lower *euripus*. It was square

Figure 23.15   Fresco of the Fourth Style in *oecus* (f) of the House of
Loreius Tiburtinus (II.2.2).

with a sort of pyramid in the center, with four sets of steps along which ran the
water, undoubtedly making a pleasant sound. The owner drew water for his fountains
directly from a *castellum plumbeum* (lead-lined reservoir) located at the northwest
corner of the *insula* (cf. Jansen, Ch. 16).[16]

House of Marine Venus (II.3.3); Figure 23.17

This house, excavated in 1952 by Amedeo Maiuri, occupies the entire northwestern
part of the *insula* and owes its name to a large fresco of the goddess on a conch shell,
located on the south wall of the garden. The *vestibulum* (1), painted reddish-purple,
had medallions with painted portrait busts, today barely recognizable. The Tuscan
atrium (2)[17] was completely frescoed with (now-faded) scenographic Fourth-Style
paintings. The center is dominated by the marble *impluvium* that gathered rainwater
from the roof through the *compluvium* and fed the cisterns beneath. On the north side
of the *atrium* open two *cubicula* (3, 7). Access to service quarters, which had their
own independent entrance on the via dell'Abbondanza at nos. 1–2 (a plaster cast of
the door is preserved), can be found at the northwest corner. In the center is a *triclinium*
(6) richly frescoed in the Fourth Style. This room has an interesting plaster cornice
that sets off the painted barrel vault from architectural frescoes of balconies supported
by a pair of *rostra* (the prows of warships), with peacocks standing above the parapets.
Also on the west side of the *atrium*, but to the south, opens a large living room (5)
with black-and-white mosaic pavement that in AD 79 was still awaiting new wall

Figure 23.16   View south at the long *euripus* in the House of
Loreius Tiburtinus (II.2.2).

decoration. The *tablinum* of the house is not in its "natural" position (on the same
axis as the *vestibulum, atrium* and peristyle), but seems to be located on the eastern
side of the peristyle, under the east *ambulacrum* at (10). Its wall decoration, unfortunately in poor condition, suggests a decorative program connected with the myth of
Apollo. The central picture on the north wall represents Apollo and Daphne, while
single figures placed in the divisions between the panels are shown in attitudes connected with the god: one plays a lyre, a woman is spinning (cf. Bernstein, Ch. 34),
and a figure making an offering seems to turn back and look toward Apollo.

It is, however, in the peristyle garden—divided into two splendid flowerbeds—
that the house's particular charm can be seen. On its southern edge, the garden
appears to merge with a wall painting in which a statue of Mars, marble fountains
and fantastic fauna dwell together (Figure 31.1).[18] In the center of the painting,
conceptually beyond the garden, a broad window opens illusionistically upon the sea.
Venus, bedecked with forehead ornament, necklace, earrings and armlets, lounges on

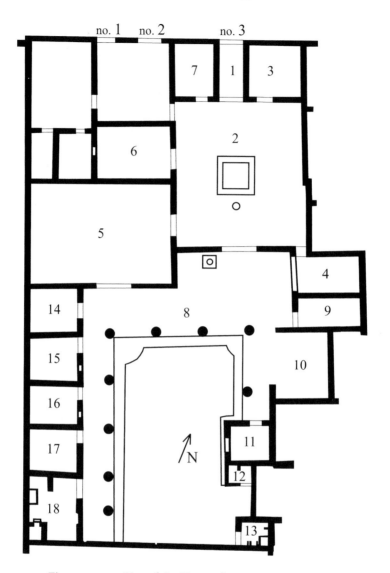

Figure 23.17 Plan of the House of Marine Venus (II.2.2).

a pink conch shell drawn by dolphins that are ridden by cupids. This painting makes sense only if viewed from the *atrium* or from the northern *ambulacrum* (8) of the peristyle. Seen from up close, it shows all the incongruities of a work by several hands. Simplistic body proportions contrast with the splendid portrait head of a woman who wears a curly hairstyle fashionable during the Neronian period.

The eastern side of the peristyle also tries to deny actual architecture. On the outer walls of room (11) is painted a garden with marble fountains, on whose edges rest doves, as can be seen for real in the reconstructed peristyle of the House of the Vettii (VI.15.1). The western and northern sides are completely porticoed (Figure 23.18):

Figure 23.18   View west in portico (8) of the House of Marine Venus (II.2.2).

the narrow *ambulacrum* of the western portico, with scenographic Fourth-Style fantastic paintings, gives access to an upper story as well as ground-floor rooms close by the garden. The wide northern portico is decorated with small impressionist paintings of sanctuaries and *villae maritimae*. Particularly interesting are rooms (11) and (14); the first lies south of the east porch, and sports blue-background panels with a central *aedicula* seen in perspective. The painting in the center is difficult to interpret, but it may be a rare image of the birth of the Hermaphrodite. The second space, located at the back of the west side of the northern *ambulacrum*, contains Fourth-Style frescoes with an elegant yellow background, depicting fantastic architecture populated by flying cupids.[19]

House of the Menander (I.10.4); Figure 23.19

This house, excavated by Amedeo Maiuri in 1930–31, is undoubtedly among the most important in Pompeii, both for the refinement of wall and pavement decoration (cf. Clarke, Ch. 21) and for the priceless furniture found within. The house probably belonged to one Quintus Poppaeus, whose family boasted kinship with Poppaea, second wife of Nero, and whose bronze seal was found in the servants' quarters. This luxurious home, which in AD 79 irregularly occupied a large part of the entire block, had been enlarged as early as the first century BC at the expense of neighboring houses. At the moment of the eruption it was being restored; there are various clues that the columns of the *atriolum* (46) in the bath quarter, which was under renovation,

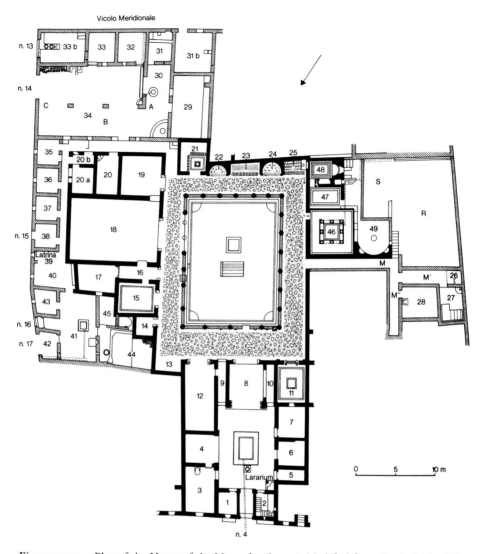

Figure 23.19   Plan of the House of the Menander (I.10.4). Modified from the Archivio della Soprintendenza Archeologica di Pompei.

were laid on the floor in the corridor (M) between the peristyle quarter and the servants' quarter, while a temporary kitchen had been set up in room (3) northeast of the *atrium*. Some *amphorae*, full of good-quality plaster ready for use, were stored in the kitchen (27) next to the bath quarter. It can be presumed that the house was only partly usable.

The house's principal nucleus has a classic plan, with *atrium*, *tablinum* (8) and peristyle on the same axis as the *vestibulum*. A passer-by looking in from the street could take it all in at a single glance—with the rectangular *exedra* (23) in the center of the south side of the peristyle as the point of departure for a marvelous architectural prospective. It seems that the architect subordinated the architectural elements of the house to this view, using two Corinthian columns as doorposts for the *tablinum*, and adjusting the space between the columns of the north and south sides of the peristyle to broaden and extend the view and direct it towards the rectangular *exedra*. It is the decorative program of that room that suggested the house's modern name: on the lateral walls are painted two Greek poets: possibly Euripides seated at the left and Menander on the right. On the south wall, visible from the street, tragic theatrical masks stand out against a yellow background.

The imposing entrance to the residence has tufa pillars with Corinthian capitals for doorjambs. It leads into a large *atrium*, where a marble *impluvium* with molded edges occupies the center, below a *compluvium* with coffered *simas* decorated with palmettes, and spouts with dolphin protomes. The *atrium* walls were decorated in the Fourth Style, with a Nilotic frieze (pygmies and crocodiles) in the upper part. The northwest corner held a domestic *lararium*; its base was decorated in faux marble, and a tempietto with two pediments supported by Tuscan columns and stucco cornices rested on top. The southern side of this tempietto, which originally took the shape of a wooden grill, has been preserved in the form of a plaster cast. Between the *lararium* and the vestibule was a room (2) containing a winding masonry staircase that led to upper-story rooms on the western side. The wing that opened on the east side of the *atrium* was decorated in the Fourth Style with paintings of the fall of Troy in the central panels. On the south was the death of Laocoon; to the east the Trojan horse; and to the north the capture of Helen and Cassandra in the presence of Priam.

Figure 23.20   View down north at the peristyle and *tablinum* (8) in the House of the Menander (I.10.4).

369

Figure 23.21 Detail of the fresco decorating the *pluteus* at the base of the peristyle in the House of the Menander (I.10.4).

Beyond the large *tablinum* (8), decorated in a showy Fourth Style, opens the peristyle (Figure 23.20). It is a *quadriporticus* with Doric columns whose lower parts are enclosed in a *pluteus* splendidly decorated with herons amid plants, hunting scenes and imaginary gardens, almost as if to deny the physical existence of the wall and suggest the continuation of the real garden (Figure 23.21; cf. Jashemski, Ch. 31). All the rooms that open onto the peristyle are luxuriously decorated: in the northwest corner is a splendid room (11) in the Fourth Style with a green background, divided into panels by vertical black bands showing flying cupids and vines growing out of a *kantharos*. At the center of the panels are framed pictures, and above the panels is a splendid frieze with Centaurs and Lapith women against a red background. The polychrome mosaic pavement of *opus vermiculatum* is also extremely recherché. The threshold is decorated with meanders alternating with rosettes in squares, the field comprises squares set off by black bands, and in the center, within a braided frame, is a small scene of life on the Nile (*emblema*). At the center of the east *ambulacrum* is an enormous living room (18) constructed over older houses that, as visible sondages reveal, have First-Style painting on both wall and pavement. In the southwest corner of the peristyle is a second *lararium* with a built-in altar and apsed niche that contained five wooden busts, probably ancestor images, preserved today thanks to their plaster casts.

The bath quarter is organized around a small octastyle *atrium* (46) with Second-Style wall paintings. Noteworthy are the mosaic pavements, especially that in the passage between the *tepidarium* (47) and the *caldarium* (48) depicting an ithyphallic servant bearing unguents and perfumes. In the *caldarium*, a polychrome mosaic depicts an acanthus bush with a small bird, around which swim fish, dolphins and marine characters (Figure 21.3).[20] The service quarter (S) for the baths was organized at a lower level, beneath the baths, and in a space underneath *atriolum* (46) was found a priceless treasure of silver utensils consisting of 118 pieces in a wooden chest.[21] The whole bath complex at the moment of the eruption of AD 79 was being restored and transformed.

Finally, in the southeast corner of the *insula* was located another servants' quarter at no. 14, where today is kept a wooden cart restored with the original pieces of metal found here. It is not unlikely, in view of the large number of agricultural implements recovered, that the owner of the house also owned farmland outside the city (cf. Moormann, Ch. 28; Jongman, Ch. 32). Perhaps the quarter of the house at no. 16, with an entrance from a narrow street to the east, was destined for the *procurator* (steward).

The wealth of the house must have been well known. A group of ancient post-eruption visitors, *fossores* (diggers), had penetrated the house through tunnels (cf. Foss, Ch. 3), but a structural collapse may have blocked them definitively in the southern room (19) of the east *ambulacrum* of the peristyle, together with the small spades and lantern that they had brought along to light their way through the congeries of volcanic detritus that filled the rooms.[22] The *domus* has been the object of a substantial and meticulous restoration (1997–98) that has brought back the original volumes and correct sequences between full spaces and empty, between light and shadows. Together with restored paintings and revived pavements, this refurbishment has once more allowed the House of the Menander to represent perhaps the clearest example of a patrician house in a provincial city of the early empire.

NOTES

1 Maureen B. Fant translated the Italian text. For an overview of the city and its surrounding territory, see *Neapolis: progetto-sistema per la valorizzazione integrale delle risorse ambientali e artistiche dell'area vesuviana*, vol. 3, Rome, 1994.

2 The following have recently addressed the problem, albeit with different results: S. De Caro, "Lo sviluppo urbanistico di Pompei," in *AttiMGrecia*, 1992, vol. 3.1, pp. 67–88; P. Sommella, "Urbanistica Pompeiana. Nuovi momenti di studio," in *Neapolis* vol. 2, Rome, 1994, pp. 163–218; H. Eschebach and L. Eschebach, *Pompeji*, Vienna, 1995; H. Geertman, "Lo sviluppo urbanistico della città e la sua storia. Il progetto olandese," in *Sotto i lapilli*, Milan, 1998, pp. 17–25. In this volume, see esp. Geertman, Ch. 7.

3 See S. C. Nappo, "Urban transformation at Pompeii in the late 3rd and early 2nd c. BC," in R. Laurence and A. Wallace-Hadrill (eds), *Domestic Space in the Roman World: Pompeii and beyond*, JRA Suppl. Ser. no. 22, 1997, pp. 96–7. On the dating of the south wall of the city, see most recently S. De Caro, "Nuove indagini sulle fortificazioni di Pompei," *AION*, 1985, vol. 7, pp. 74–114.

4 Cf. A. De Simone, "Le insulae su via di Nocera, regiones I e II," in *Restaurare Pompei*, Milan, 1990, pp. 111–20; S. C. Nappo, "Alcuni esempi di tipologie di case popolari della fine III–inizio II secolo a.C. a Pompei," *RStPomp*, 1996, vol. 6, pp. 77–104; Nappo, "Urban transformation," pp. 91–120. For Hoffman's scheme in Figure 23.2, see: A. Hoffman, "L'architettura privata," in F. Zevi (ed.), *Pompeii 79*, Naples, 1979, pp. 105–18.

5 See A. De Simone, "I terremoti precedenti l'eruzione. Nuove attestazioni da recenti scavi," in *Archäologie und Seismologie. La regione Vesuviana dal 62 al 79 d.C. Problemi archeologici e sismologici*, Munich, 1995, pp. 37–43; S. C. Nappo, "Evidenze di danni strutturali, restauri e rifacimenti nelle insulae gravitanti su 'via Nocera' a Pompei," in *Archäologie und Seismologie*, pp. 45–53.

6 On the house see G. P. Carratelli and I. Baldassarre (eds), *Pompei, pitture e mosaici*, vol. 2, Rome, 1990, pp. 701–32; I. M. Sutherland, *Colonnaded Cenacula in Pompeian Domestic Architecture*,

Ph.D. thesis, Duke University, 1991. For a generalized cross-section of this type of house in its original phase, see Nappo, "Urban transformation," p. 100, fig. 6.

7 On economic activity in this room, see W. O. Moeller, "The felt trade of Pompeii," *AJA*, 1971, vol. 75, pp. 188–9.

8 On the motivations of restorations at Pompeii in recent years, see B. Conticello, *Progetto Pompei*, Pompeii, 1988.

9 The house, like most of the *insula*, is largely unpublished; for the first reports, see Nappo, "Danni strutturali," pp. 49–51. See also S. C. Nappo, "Nuovi pavimenti in cocciopesto con decorazione geometrica da recenti scavi nella Regio I di Pompei," in A. Paribeni (ed.), *Atti VII Colloquio Alscom*, Ravenna, 2001, pp. 343–52.

10 On the house, see O. Elia, *Le pitture della Casa del Citarista*, Monumenti della pittura antica scoperta in Italia, Sez. 3.2 (Pompei), Fasc. 1, Rome, 1937; Caratelli and Baldassarre, *Pitture e mosaici*, vol. 1, 1990, pp. 117–77; F. Pesando, *"Domus," edilizia privata e società Pompeiana tra III e I secolo a.C.*, Rome, 1977, pp. 27–34; S. C. Nappo, "L'insula I-4 e la Casa del Citarista. Il progetto Italiano," in *Sotto i lapilli*, pp. 27–39. E. Dwyer, *Pompeian Domestic Sculpture*, Rome, 1982, pp. 79–108, 151–62.

11 Maiuri then brought the *Praedia* of Julia Felix back to light between 1936 and 1953. See A. Maiuri, "Due iscrizioni veneree Pompeiane," in *Saggi di varia antichità*, Venice, 1954, pp. 285–99.

12 On this plan and the excavations, see C. Parslow, *Rediscovering Antiquity. Karl Weber and the excavation of Herculaneum, Pompeii and Stabiae*, Cambridge, 1995, pp. 107–22.

13 On these paintings, see S. C. Nappo, "Fregio dipinto dal 'praedium' di Giulia Felice con rappresentazione del foro di Pompei," *RStPomp*, 1989, vol. 3, pp. 79–96.

14 On the house, see C. Parslow, "Documents illustrating the excavation of the Praedia of Iulia Felix in Pompei," *RStPomp*, 1988, vol. 2, pp. 37–48; Caratelli and Baldassarre, *Pitture e mosaici*, vol. 3, 1991, pp. 184–310.

15 On the controversy over Tiburtinus, see M. Della Corte, *Case ed abitanti di Pompei*, 3rd edn, Naples, 1965, pp. 370–81; P. Castrén, *Ordo populusque Pompeianus*, Rome, 1975, p. 32.

16 On the house, see A. Maiuri and R. Pane, *La case di Loreio Tiburtino e la Villa di Diomede in Pompei*, Rome, 1947; Caratelli and Baldassarre, *Pitture e mosaici*, vol. 3, 1991, pp. 42–108. For the painted scenes of Ovid's myths, see V. Platt, "Viewing, Desiring, Believing: confronting the divine in a Pompeian house," *Art History*, 2002, vol. 25.1, pp. 87–112.

17 The *atrium* was heavily damaged by a World War II bomb (in 1943) and the damage was not greater only because it had not yet been excavated (cf. Foss, Ch. 3).

18 See D. Michel, "Pompejanische Gartenmalereien," in *Tainia, Festschrift R. Hampe*, Mainz, 1980, pp. 399–400.

19 Caratelli and Baldassarre, *Pitture e mosaici*, vol. 3, 1991, pp. 112–71.

20 For a further discussion of these mosaics, see J. R. Clarke, "Hypersexual black men in Augustan baths: ideal somatotypes and apotropaic magic," in N. B. Kampen (ed.), *Sexuality in Ancient Art*, New York, 1996, pp. 184–98. For the *lararia*, see P. W. Foss, "Watchful *Lares*: Roman household organization and the rituals of cooking and eating," in Laurence and Wallace-Hadrill (eds), *Domestic Space in the Roman World*, pp. 214–16 and Fig. 23.

21 R. Ling, K. S. Painter and P. Arthur, *The Insula of the Menander at Pompeii, vol. 4: the silver treasure*, Oxford, 2002.

22 On the house, see A. Maiuri, *La casa del Menander e il suo tesoro*, Rome, 1932; Caratelli and Baldassarre, *Pitture e mosaici*, vol. 2, 1990, pp. 240–397; R. Ling, *The Insula of the Menander at Pompeii, vol. 1: the structures*, Oxford, 1997; R. Ling and L. Ling, *The Insula of the Menander at Pompeii, vol. 2: the decorations*, Oxford, 2005; P. M. Allison, *The Insula of the Menander at Pompeii, vol. 3: the finds, a contextual study*, Oxford, 2007. For Poppaea, cf. also Moormann, Ch. 28.

CHAPTER TWENTY-FOUR

SELECT RESIDENCES IN REGIONS V AND IX

Early anonymous domestic architecture

———— •◆• ————

Kees Peterse

Many publications refer to the House of the Surgeon (VI.1.10) as the perfect example of early domestic architecture in Pompeii.[1] This is true as far as elite architecture is concerned.[2] Most fourth- and third-century BC houses, however, were considerably smaller and had a somewhat different spatial arrangement. Good examples of these smaller houses can be found in Regions V and IX. Two of them are presented here in some detail: the "anonymous" Houses (V.4.c) and (IX.1.29).

One must bear in mind that the oldest still-standing houses of Pompeii are identified as being the oldest based on the way their walls were built. In only a few cases has the exploration of a house's structural history been accompanied by stratigraphic research (cf. Jones and Robinson, Ch. 25). None of the oldest houses were left undisturbed in the period between their construction and AD 79. In some instances, the structural interventions did not alter the initial layout thoroughly; more often, however, the oldest building phase has been preserved only fragmentarily. For obvious reasons the architectural exploration of the oldest houses must be preceded by research focused on distilling the oldest structures from the sum of walls that jointly represent a house in its final shape. Since mistakes made while identifying these oldest walls can greatly affect the outcome of the architectural analyses, a proper definition of the relevant building techniques is crucial to the success of this type of research. That is why the exploration of the houses mentioned above is preceded by a general outline on what the oldest still-standing walls look like.[3]

The architectural study of House (V.4.c) and House (IX.1.29)—as well as some houses that serve as comparative material—focuses on two main questions: what did the original layout look like, and why have certain rooms and ensembles of rooms been preserved throughout the centuries, while others were largely altered or even demolished?

OPUS QUADRATUM AND LIMESTONE FRAMEWORK

The foundations for our knowledge of the architectural history of Pompeii were laid over a century ago by G. Fiorelli, H. Nissen and A. Mau.[4] Their conclusions were not based on stratigraphic research but, rather, on a carefully constructed relative chronology that was pinned, as far as possible, to historical events or to the development of wall and floor decorations. Although the result of this effort inevitably bears some resemblance to a house of cards, no significant alternative has since been presented for the oldest building periods.[5] R. C. Carrington, M. Blake and G. Lugli[6] have followed the same general outline, although Carrington deserves credit for his detailed examination of the development of the earliest masonry.

In 1993 we presented the results of research that focused on the oldest still-visible techniques in which Pompeian houses were built: *opus quadratum* and limestone framework (i.e., *opera a telaio*); cf. Adam, Ch. 8.[7] *Opus quadratum* consists of large blocks of stone, neatly stacked, with no particular bonding (Figures 8.1 and 8.2). Generally, so-called Sarno limestone (or preferably travertine) was used; Nocera tufa was applied only incidentally. In house construction, *opus quadratum* was primarily used for façades and the sides of houses that bordered a street (e.g., House VI.10.11), whereas the remaining perimeter walls and the interior walls were executed in limestone framework. The most important exception to this is the House of the Surgeon (VI.1.10), where the walls of the *atrium* were built also in *opus quadratum* (cf. Jones and Robinson, Ch. 25).[8]

In the analysis of limestone framework, three components must be distinguished: the framework pillars, the corner posts and doorposts, and the fill of the gaps in between these massive framework structures (Figure 8.9). The framework pillars consist of a centered piling of large, (primarily) limestone blocks, alternating vertically and horizontally. The placement of pillars shows a standardized approach; they can be found particularly at the intersections of walls, where the horizontally placed blocks interlock the walls. The chief function of the framework pillars was to increase stability. Pillars can furthermore be found at regular intervals in each wall section. This, too, should be interpreted as an attempt at strengthening the wall, for stacks of large limestone blocks minimized the danger of collapse at the walls' most vulnerable spots by providing grip. Variations in spacing between pillars among the houses have been shown to fall into distinct groups. As a general tendency, pillars that stand relatively close together indicate an early date of construction.[9] The distinction between framework pillars and corner posts and doorposts is important, since the latter also generally appear in the so-called tufa period (i.e., second half of the second century BC and first quarter of the first century BC), and probably later as well, when they were combined with masonry in *opus incertum*.[10] Therefore, the presence of corner posts and doorposts is not, in itself, a criterion for identifying a building phase in limestone framework.

Limestone framework fill consists of *caementa* (i.e., hewn or broken pieces of stone) varying from the size of a fist to approximately 20 by 30 cm (cf. Dobbins, Appendix to Ch. 8). More than 90 percent of the *caementa* were of limestone; so-called *pappamonte* and red *cruma*—both provided by local quarries—as well as Nocera tufa and pieces of broken roof tiles were sporadically used.[11] Mortar was applied to assemble the *caementa*; initially mortar was restricted to the cores of walls, but it was later used in the facings as well.[12]

The fact that Nocera tufa was used to a small degree in the fill of framework walls, e.g. in House (I.6.13),[13] indicates that this material played a role in early Pompeian domestic architecture. Since the walls were covered with plaster, the amorphous pieces of Nocera tufa were not intended to be seen; therefore, they must be considered waste material. The question is why this relatively expensive material—imported from quarries located close to the neighboring town of Nocera—was applied in the first place. The most plausible explanation seems to be that the occurrence of Nocera tufa pieces is the result of on-site cutting of roughly shaped blocks into floor slabs and moulded borders for *impluvia*. It should be noticed that the vast majority of houses dating from the limestone-framework period, and which feature an *impluvium* of Nocera tufa, display a small quantity of *caementa* hewn out of the same material in the fill of their limestone-framework walls.[14] Moreover, in the House of the Scientists (VI.14.43), a Dutch team headed by the late Prof. J. A. de Waele demonstrated the presence of a fourth-century BC *impluvium*. In this house too, some pieces of Nocera tufa were applied in the fill of the limestone-framework walls. This means that at least a number of the early Pompeian *atria* were roofed from the outset (cf. Wallace-Hadrill, Ch. 18).[15]

Three interrelated processes occurred simultaneously in the development of limestone framework. First, the framework pillars were gradually placed further apart as experience taught that a more spacious disposition did not give rise to structural difficulties. Second, we can observe a development from carefully hewn *caementa* towards more irregular shapes scarcely distinguishable from the *caementa* applied in later *opus incertum*. These architectural relaxations were partially compensated for by a third development in the composition of the mortar.[16] Initially mortar was made up almost entirely of locally extracted loam. From the moment mortar was also used for wall facings, the facing *caementa* no longer had to be hewn with greatest care, because they were sufficiently held together by the loam. With the addition of volcanic material and lime, the loam-based mortar became structurally significant (Figure 24.1). Thanks to the chemical reaction between volcanic material, lime and water, the framework fill gained additional strength, allowing for a more spacious arrangement of the pillars as well as an increasingly less accurate shaping of the *caementa*. Simultaneously, the width of the joints was allowed to increase.

The continuing improvement of mortar by adding more volcanic material and lime was an important factor in the development of building techniques. This eventually caused limestone framework to lose its function while ushering in the large-scale employment of *opus incertum*. Improved mortar made it pointless to continue building walls in limestone framework (needless expense with no structural benefits). Aesthetics could not have played a role, since the walls were covered with plaster.

An extreme example of late limestone framework is the west wall of the *atrium tuscanicum* of the House of Epidius Sabinus (IX.1.22).[17] The framework pillars are positioned approximately 3 m apart and have lost any structural function. The fill of the framework, featuring amorphous *caementa* of, in particular, limestone, cannot be distinguished from later (or perhaps already contemporary) *opus incertum*. Moreover, the *caementa* are held together by a mortar that holds the highest percentage of lime among the walls executed in limestone framework.[18]

In only a few places at Pompeii can masonry be found which testifies to a transitional period from limestone framework to *opus incertum*, a topic previously explored by R. C. Carrington and E. M. Evans.[19] Earlier we made reference to the *atrium* complex in the House of Epidius Sabinus (IX.1.22), but in this context Region V is especially interesting. During Period C (see below), the expansion of the city within its pre-existing walls proceeded in an easterly direction as far as *insula* (V.4) and *insula*

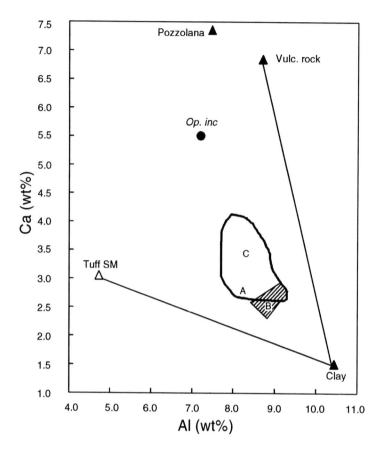

Chemical composition of mortars, clay, tuff and vulcanic rock.

Legend: ▲: Clay; ▲: Vulcanic rock (*pappamonte* and *cruma*); ▲: Pozzolana; △: Tuff SM;

A: mortar of type A; Ｂ : mortar of type B; Ｃ: mortar of type C; *Op. Inc.*: mortar of *Opus Incertum*;

Figure 24.1   This figure shows the areas in which the average values of the elements calcium and aluminum fall for the mortars of types A, B, C, and *opus incertum*. The composition of the mortars has been determined for each structurally differing wall. That is why the mortar of Type A is represented by a single dot while the mortars of Types B and C fall into areas. Mortars of Type B lie in a relatively small area, indicating the similarity between core mortars and surface mortars. The composition of the mortars of Type C covers a larger area that partially overlaps Type B. The mortar of Type C contains more volcanic material than the mortar of Types A and B. The mortar of *opus incertum* is much higher than Type C, as it contains significantly greater amounts of volcanic material (Joosten, in: Peterse, *Bouwkundige studies*). The mortar types correlate with the chronological periods on the following page.

(IX.14), located on either side of the via di Nola. In the southern half of the city, limestone framework of Period C has been documented as far east as *insula* (II.1) and *insula* (II.9) (cf. Nappo, Ch. 23).[20] Examples of a transitional stage from limestone framework to *opus incertum* may be expected especially in the area where the Period C building activity reached its borders. The western perimeter wall of Building (V.3.6)[21] shows remains of limestone framework from Period C, whereas the *atrium* walls of its easterly neighbor, House (V.3.8), seem to represent a stage immediately following Period C: its loam-based mortar contains visible lime and volcanic material and, in addition, no free-standing framework pillars have been observed.[22] In both Building (V.3.6) and House (V.3.8) predominantly limestone *caementa* were used. In House (V.3.8), parts of a First-Style wall decoration have been preserved in the *tablinum*-like room north of the *atrium*.

Dating

This leaves us with the question of chronology. It is important to bear in mind that the relative chronology mentioned above has not generally been questioned. Within all limestone-framework constructions we have distinguished three different phases: A, B and C (Figure 24.1). Period A was an experimental phase that did not last very long. Period B represents fully crystallized limestone framework, whereas Period C was characterized by a steady development toward *opus incertum*. We have dated the limestone-framework era indicatively to the period from the middle of the fifth century to the end of the first quarter of the second century BC.[23]

Chronological development of limestone-framework constructions:

Period A: *c.*450–*c.*420 BC
Period B: *c.*420–*c.*275 BC
Period C: *c.*275–*c.*175 BC

Those involved in subsoil research in the House of Amarantus (I.9.12) have expressed doubts about an early date for limestone framework (cf. Wallace-Hadrill, Ch. 18).[24] New evidence, however, substantiates the fourth-century BC date for Period B. A team of Dutch and Italian archaeologists has conducted stratigraphic research in the House of the Scientists (VI.14.43). They have demonstrated that the initial construction of the house originates in the fourth century BC.[25] This first layout of the house was executed in a combination of *opus quadratum* for the façade and limestone framework of Period B for the remaining exterior and interior walls. Furthermore, R. Ling implicitly follows this chronology when he dates the first phase of *insula* (I.10)— and more explicitly house (I.10.16)—to the late third to middle second century BC.[26] House (I.10.16) was built in the limestone framework of Period C.[27] Finally, in quite a number of cases, limestone-framework walls—as well as walls in different techniques that were verifiably built during a phase successive to the limestone-framework structures—are still partly covered with First-Style decoration. An example of the former are the north and east wall of room (2) in the House of the Scientists (VI.14.43), whereas the First-Style wall decorations in the peristyle of House (IX.1.29)— surveyed in this chapter—were applied to walls that are evidently younger than the houses' limestone-framework structures. The First-Style wall decorations provide a *terminus ante quem* or *terminus ad quem* for the construction of the relevant structures (cf. Strocka, Ch. 20). In addition, not a single *atrium tetrastylum* or *atrium corinthium*, *porticus* or peristyle can be related to a building phase in limestone framework, which means that limestone framework Period C must pre-date the second half of the second century BC.

We assert the implausibility of the equal and interchangeable use of limestone framework and *opus incertum* for any significant length of time.[28] *Opus incertum* was cheaper than limestone framework, and there were reduced costs for production and transportation, both *en route* as well as at the construction site itself. Moreover, compared to *opus incertum*, limestone framework did not offer any structural benefits.

House (V.4.c); (Figure 24.2)

In Region V the easternmost examples of limestone framework include a number of walls in House (V.4.c). The southern half of the façade in the neighboring House (V.4.b) and a fragment of the northern wall of the *andron* north of the *tablinum* in the House of M. Lucretius Fronto (V.4.a, 11) still preserve traces of an original layout in limestone framework (cf. Map 3).[29]

House (V.4.c) is one of the many examples of an average *atrium* house from the limestone-framework period (cf. Wallace-Hadrill, Ch. 18).[30] It was built in Period B. These houses generally occupied a plot of approximately 7 to 9 m wide (measured between the party walls). In most instances, the plot occupied half the depth of the *insula* (e.g., Period C House (VI.2.14)).[31] The houses of the group to which House (V.4.c) belongs had a front range featuring a centrally located entrance area that was accompanied by a room on either side. The middle zone was occupied entirely by an *atrium* which—with the exception of House (I.4.9)[32]—had no side rooms.[33] A back range of rooms accommodated a *tablinum* with an adjacent room on both sides. Generally, the latter as well as the rooms that accompanied the entrance area were accessible only from the *atrium*. At the rear of the house was a space open to the sky, probably a *hortus*. This must have been walled at least in some cases, since houses were built back-to-back from the outset.[34] The *hortus* was accessible through either a narrow corridor, i.e., the *andron* (e.g., Period B House (I.6.13)),[35] or the *tablinum* (e.g., the House of the Surgeon (VI.1.10)).

In House (V.4.c) only part of the façade dates back to the first phase.[36] Entrance area (1) still shows the original south wall and a fragment of the north wall. In both walls one observes a setback in the part closest to the street. This indicates a subdivision of the entrance area into a *vestibulum* facing the street and *fauces* that belonged to the house's interior space. Though the setbacks were not executed in limestone frame-work, they still may be a reflection of the initial plan. Close observation reveals that in both the north and south wall of the entrance area the central framework pillar stands off-center to the east. If the initial construction phase would not have had the subdivision just mentioned, one would expect the central framework pillar to stand in the center of the wall, a standardized method that is documented in so many of the limestone-framework houses—e.g., House (IX.1.29) rooms (1) and (8); Figure 24.3. Furthermore, room (3) on the south side of the *fauces* belongs to the first building phase. In the middle zone of the house, the same is true of the south wall of *atrium* (5), which did not feature doorways. In the back range of (V.4.c), the wall between *tablinum* (9) and room (10) still preserves the initial layout. The northern part of the

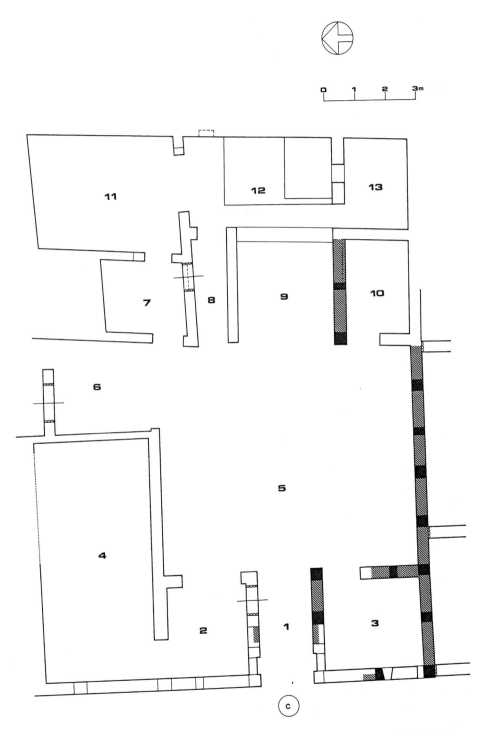

Figure 24.2 Ground plan of (V.4.c) showing the initial construction period (Period B).
Key: solid = limestone framework pillars; hatching = limestone framework fill.

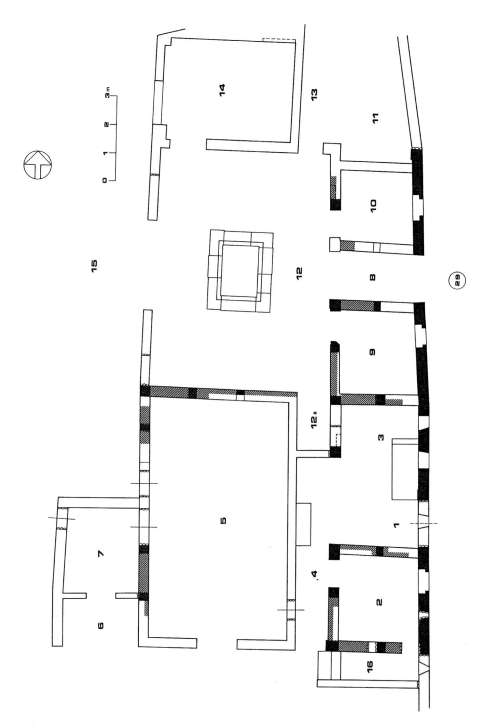

Figure 24.3 Ground plan of (IX.1.29) showing the initial construction period (Period B). Key: solid = limestone framework pillars (interior), and *opus quadratum* (eastern façade); hatching = limestone framework fill.

house underwent alteration at a later date. Nevertheless, the position of the present north wall of *atrium* (5) may coincide with the initial northern party wall, which has left no visible traces.

The presence of a *vestibulum* in (V.4.c) is quite remarkable, since during the limestone-framework period *vestibula* occurred almost exclusively in elite residences, such as the House of the Surgeon (VI.1.10).[37] This may indicate that on the street side, House (V.4.c) was architecturally upgraded to better resemble the houses of the most fortunate.[38]

The twin house of Epidius Sabinus (IX.1.29); (Figure 24.3)

Reference has already been made to the limestone framework of the *atrium* and surrounding rooms of the House of Epidius Sabinus (IX.1.22). This framework belongs to Period C and represents a very late stage. This is, however, not the only example of limestone framework in the house. In the northeast corner of the residence, which was gradually enlarged through several renovations, are traces of two smaller, identical houses from Period B that were previously explored by E. M. Evans.[39] This twin house is jointly designated by the address (IX.1.29).

The plots on which the twin house was built measure 8.55–8.65 m each (between the party walls). Evidently the party walls continued to the north–south wall, clearly visible in *insula* (IX.1), between the House of Epidius Rufus (IX.1.20) and the House of Epidius Sabinus (IX.1.22; see Map 3). In the latter house the southern section of the wall just mentioned—i.e., the west wall of the *atrium* of House (IX.1.22)—was executed in limestone framework from period C.[40]

The lower half of the façade of both residences was carried out in *opus quadratum*, whereas the upper part was continued in limestone framework. Several windows penetrate the façade; only the southernmost of these, in room (2), belongs to the first building period (Figure 24.4). This small slit window was later walled up.

The entrances to the two homes are also detectable: entrance no. 29 on the north side and an entrance, later walled up, to the southern house. *Fauces* (8) are practically intact, whereas the north wall of *fauces* (1) was later removed. In both instances, two small rooms flanked the *fauces*: (9) and (10) in the northern residence and (2) and (3) in the southern house. These rooms were entered from the *atria*. The fact that room (1) was not originally united with room (3) is apparent from the join of the separation wall, which can still be seen on the inside of the façade. The section of *opus quadratum* ashlars that met the separation wall was left rough, whereas the remaining part of the same ashlars was further worked to a smooth finish. The entrance areas (1) and (8) did not feature a *vestibulum*. The connection between room (2) and the space below staircase (16) does not belong to the original layout.

Atrium (12), stretching over the entire width of the northern plot, is still clearly visible. The east and south walls are relatively well preserved. The north wall can be reconstructed due to a clear join near room (11) on the inside of the façade. The back or west wall of the *atrium* has not been preserved in its original state. The present wall, however, is in line with the west wall of room (5), which is the back wall of the original *atrium* of the southern residence (rooms (4), (5) and (12a) jointly). Because

Figure 24.4 House (IX.1.29), *cubiculum* (2), east wall (inner side of the façade). The lower part of the façade, in which the walled up window is located (at center), was carried out in *opus quadratum*. The upper half of the facade was constructed in limestone framework and shows the original beam holes for the floor of the upper storey.

the north wall of *atrium* (12) and the south wall of former *atrium* (5) align with the original corners of the fully preserved façade, we know for sure that the two identical houses did not extend beyond the *opus quadratum* and, hence, had no side rooms.

In *atrium* (12) an athwart-lying *impluvium* of Nocera tufa has been preserved, whereas in the wall between *atrium* (12) and former *atrium* (5), a *caementum* of Nocera tufa is found in the original fill of the framework. As we explained above, the presence of the Nocera tufa *caementum* increases the plausibility that the *impluvium* originates from the Period B building phase. A definite answer, however, can only be provided by future stratigraphic research.

To the west of the *atria* no traces of the oldest masonry have been found. The original doorpost of a walled-up doorway in the west wall of room (5), however, indicates an initial extension towards the west.[41] The limestone-framework period provides ample, convincing comparative material for this arrangement.[42] At the back of the house enough space was left for a *hortus* that was probably, though not necessarily, walled.[43]

HOUSES OF DIFFERENT ORIGIN

In fourth-century BC Pompeii two different types of houses were built.[44] Best known is the type represented by the House of the Surgeon (VI.1.10), with a fully standardized layout (cf. Jones and Robinson, Ch. 25). It featured a compluviate *atrium* which— in case of the elite residences such as the House of the Surgeon—was surrounded by rooms on all four sides. For those less fortunate, a more economical version of the same type of house was built: size was reduced and side rooms were omitted. House (V.4.c) is a fine example of a minimized version of the grand-style *atrium* house of the contemporary elite.

The "traditional" *atrium tuscanicum* coexisted with a house of different typological origin. This house probably had an *atrium testudinatum* with only a small opening (the size of four roof tiles) meant for ventilation as well as for the inlet of light and, inevitably, water. The house had no side rooms and the depth of its shallow *atrium* was standardized: 4.7 m, equivalent to 17 Oscan feet of approximately 27.6 cm (e.g., Houses (VI.11.12) and (VI.11.13), built at the same time during Period C; Figure 24.5).[45] Especially from the third century BC, houses of the alternative type were generally rather small. This clearly indicates that this type was designed to accommodate non-elite citizens.

Whereas House (V.4.c) must be regarded as a minimized version of the "traditional" *atrium* house, House (IX.1.29) had its roots in the shallow type of *atrium*. In the case of House (IX.1.29), this seems to have been upgraded by replacing the testudinate *atrium* for a compluviate one. To enable the inclusion of the *impluvium*, the depth of the *atrium* had to exceed 4.7 m, otherwise, the water basin would have obstructed easy passage from one side of the *atrium* to the other. The crosswise position of the *impluvium* tells us that the enlargement of the *atrium*'s depth was restricted to a functional and budgetary minimum.

FUNCTIONAL AND FORMAL CONTINUITY

It is striking that in the houses from the limestone-framework period the rooms directly adjoining the façade as well as the party walls have been preserved best.[46] The fact that the initial construction period is still visible in several party walls makes it clear that during later periods no major changes in plot division took place. It is true that from the mid-second century BC smaller residences were often integrated into larger complexes of Hellenized Pompeii, but the original urban structure and the pattern of the party walls have remained detectable.

The continued presence of two small rooms on either side of the *fauces* was somewhat predictable, because most of the houses that were built at a later date feature the same arrangement. This, however, does not necessarily imply that there was no change in function but, rather, that there was no need for architectural intervention.

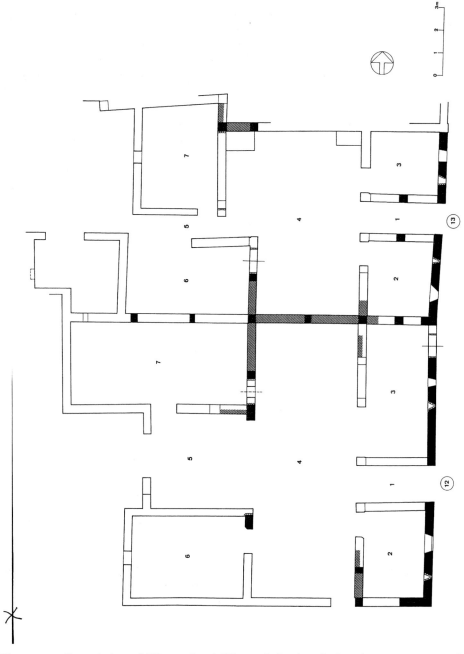

Figure 24.5 Ground plans of (VI.11.12) and (VI.11.13) showing the initial construction period (Period C). These houses represent the standardized, shallow type of home. The depth of the *atrium* in both houses is *c*.4.7 m, equivalent to 17 Oscan feet of roughly 27.6 cm each. This is the type of house that shows the most similarities with Etruscan tombs, e.g., Caere, the Banditaccia cemetery, Tomba dei Vasi Greci.

Key: solid = limestone framework pillars (interior), and *opus quadratum* (eastern façade); hatching = limestone framework fill.

The original range of rooms centered on the *tablinum* is generally less well preserved. The most important reason for this is that from the second half of the second century BC the garden area especially became the stage for fundamental changes in domestic architecture that more or less affected the entire Italo-Roman *domus* (cf. Wallace-Hadrill, Ch. 18). Within the context of this study the most decisive change was the introduction of Hellenistic living spaces featuring a portico or a peristyle in their setting. If a house that needed to incorporate new architectural forms could not be built from scratch, then the proprietor often needed to improvise. To create access to, as well as space for, the new living quarters, pre-existing rooms of the *tablinum* range were largely altered.

In the House of the Surgeon (VI.1.10), the room south of the *tablinum* was significantly enlarged. The *tablinum* in the House of the Scientists (VI.14.43) was extended in the direction of the garden, while the room on the north side of the *tablinum* was given up in favor of a large *triclinium*.[47] House (VI.10.11) was enlarged with a three-room suite that was allowed to occupy the former *hortus*.[48] One side of the suite was built back-to-back to the original *tablinum* range. A portico bordered the other side of the suite. Those present in the suite had a view onto a new garden that featured a summer *triclinium*. To enable the creation of this new garden, the former back neighbor, House (VI.10.8), was bought and subsequently demolished. Only its original façade in *opus quadratum* was spared, because it could easily serve as a garden wall.[49] House (I.6.13), too, retained the original *tablinum*, yet here large rooms were added on the west side of the *atrium*.[50] This is also true to a degree in (V.4.c), where the shallow *hortus* hardly permitted eastward expansion.

Most illuminating is the structural history of the twin house (IX.1.29). As mentioned above, residues of various limestone-framework houses were integrated in the final layout of the House of Epidius Sabinus (IX.1.22). The Period-B Houses (IX.1.29) had to give up their entire *tablinum* range in favor of a peristyle arrangement.[51] The three-sided peristyle (15) was aligned with the more or less intact northern *atrium* (12). From this *atrium* one had access to the kitchen, located to the north (rooms (11) and (13)). The *atrium* (rooms (4), (5) and (12a) jointly) of the southern of the twin residences was turned into a large room (5), whose main orientation pointed southward to a small peristyle in the center of the House of Epidius Sabinus (IX.1.22). The original *fauces* (1) and *cubiculum* (3) were joined together to accommodate a service area for the new complex.

The fact that the perimeter walls of the peristyle (15) still partly display First-Style wall decoration indicates when the alteration took place. J.-A. Dickmann dates the construction of the peristyle area to the second half of the second century BC.[52] This once more implies that the structures in limestone framework must be older. Probably in the first century BC, House (IX.1.29) in its altered form was joined to the Period-C *atrium tuscanicum* (IX.1.22), together forming the House of Epidius Sabinus.[53]

NOTES

1 Christina Williamson translated part of the Dutch text.
2 The House of the Surgeon (VI.1.10) was built according to a standardized layout that also underlies the initial construction phase of Houses (VI.10.11) and (VI.14.43): K. Peterse and J. de Waele, "The standardized design of the Casa degli Scienziati (VI.14.43) in Pompeii," in S. T. A. M. Mols and E. M. Moormann (eds), *Omni pede stare. Saggi architettonici e circumvesuviani*

in memoriam Jos de Waele, Studi della Soprintendenza archeologica di Pompeii, vol. 9, Naples, 2005, pp. 197–220. Cf. also Jones and Robinson, Ch. 25.

3 In general, differences in the outer appearance of walls simultaneously reflect structural differences. The evaluation of Pompeian masonry should be a structural, rather than aesthetic, matter.

4 G. Fiorelli, *Relazione sugli scavi di Pompei dal 1861 al 1872*, Naples, 1873, pp. 78ff.; H. Nissen, *Pompejanische Studien zur Städtekunde des Altertums*, Leipzig, 1877, passim; A. Mau, *Pompejanische Beiträge*, Berlin, 1879, passim; J. Overbeck and A. Mau, *Pompeji in seinen Gebäuden, Alterthmern und Kunstwerken*, Leipzig, 1884, pp. 30ff. and 497ff.; A. Mau, *Pompeji in Leben und Kunst*, 2nd edn, Leipzig, 1908, p. 37.

5 L. Richardson, jr, *Pompeii, an Architectural History*, London, 1988, p. 376. Reviewed by S. De Caro, "Recensione à L. Richardson, jr, Pompeii. An architectural history (1988)," *Gnomon*, 1990, vol. 62, pp. 152–61. However, cf. Wallace-Hadrill, Ch. 18.

6 R. C. Carrington, "Notes on the building materials of Pompeii," *JRS*, 1933, vol. 23, pp. 125–38; M. E. Blake, *Ancient Roman Construction in Italy*, Washington, DC, 1947, vol. 1, p. 228; G. Lugli, *La tecnica edilizia romana*, Rome, 1957, pp. 380ff.

7 The author's Ph.D. thesis, *Bouwkundige studies van huizen in Pompeii. Muurwerk, maatvoering en ontwerp*, Nijmegen, 1993, was followed by a monograph on the limestone-framework period of Pompeii, focussing on both the building techniques and a selection of architectural aspects: K. Peterse, *Steinfachwerk in Pompeji. Bautechnik und Architektur*, Amsterdam, 1999.

8 For the initial construction phase of the House of the Surgeon (VI.1.10): Peterse, *Bouwkundige studies*, pp. 273ff.; cf. Mau, *Beiträge*, pp. 37ff.; E. M. Evans, *The Atrium Complex in the Houses of Pompeii*, Birmingham, 1980, pp. 261ff.

9 K. Peterse, *Steinfachwerk*, pp. 19ff.

10 Mau, *Beiträge*, p. 3; Carrington, "Building materials," pp. 130ff.; A. R. A. Van Aken, *Nieuwe wegen in de Romeinsche woningbouw van Sulla tot Domitianus*, Utrecht, 1943, p. 15; Peterse, *Bouwkundige studies*, p. 113; Peterse, *Steinfachwerk*, pp. 9f.

11 Peterse, *Bouwkundige studies*, pp. 273ff. An exception to this is a small group of Period-C houses that show an abundance of red-*cruma caementa*: Peterse, *Bouwkundige studies*, pp. 135f.

12 I. Joosten, "Die Analyse der Mörtel im Steinfachwerk von Pompeji," in Peterse, *Steinfachwerk*, pp. 77ff.

13 Peterse, *Steinfachwerk*, pls. 8–11.

14 Among these: (I.6.13; VI.1.10; VI.14.43 and IX.1.29); from: K. Peterse, *Bouwkundige studies*, pp. 105ff.

15 For a discussion of early *atrium* houses and the issue of roofing: N. de Haan, *et al.*, "The Casa degli Scienziati (VI.14.43): elite architecture in fourth century BC Pompeii," in P. G. Guzzo and M. P. Guidobaldi (eds), *Nuove ricerche archeologiche a Pompei ed Ercolano*, Naples, 2005. Cf. S. C. Nappo, "The urban transformation at Pompeii," in R. Laurence and A. Wallace-Hadrill (eds), *Domestic Space in the Roman World: Pompeii and beyond*, JRA Suppl. Ser. no. 22, 1997, pp. 91ff.

16 Joosten, "Mörtel im Steinfachwerk," pp. 77ff. For *opus caementicium* in general, see H.-O. Lamprecht, *Opus Caementitium, Bautechnik der Römer*, Düsseldorf, 1985; J.-P. Adam, *L'arte di costruire presso i romani, materiali e tecniche*, Milan, 1988.

17 Peterse, *Bouwkundige studies*, p. 240; Peterse, *Steinfachwerk*, p. 176 and pl. 83.

18 Joosten, "Mörtel im Steinfachwerk," pp. 87, 103.

19 Also Carrington, "Building materials," p. 130; Evans, *Atrium Complex*, p. 284.

20 Peterse, *Bouwkundige studies*, pp. 150ff.

21 Peterse, *Bouwkundige studies*, p. 237; Peterse, *Steinfachwerk*, p. 173 and plate 32.

22 Also Carrington, "Building materials," p. 129; Evans, *Atrium Complex*, pp. 284f.

23 Peterse, *Bouwkundige studies*, pp. 144ff.; Peterse, *Steinfachwerk*, pp. 56ff. With thanks to Dr R. de Graaf of M.S.A. (Department of Mathematic Statistical Advice) at the Radboud University of Nijmegen.

24 The Region I, *insula* 9, project headed by A. Wallace-Hadrill of the British School at Rome. See A. L. Slayman, "The new Pompeii. Excavations beneath the AD 79 level illuminate the history of the famous Roman resort," *Archaeology*, 1997, Nov./Dec., pp. 26ff.; J. Berry (ed.), *Unpeeling Pompeii*, Catalogue of the exhibition held at the Auditorium of Pompeii October

1–December 15, 1998, Milan, 1998, pp. 63–9; cf. Peterse, *Bouwkundige studies*, p. 230; Peterse, *Steinfachwerk*, pp. 33f., pp. 71ff.

25 De Haan *et al.*, "Casa degli Scienziati."

26 R. Ling, *The Insula of the Menander at Pompeii 1: the structures*, Oxford, 1997, pp. 223ff.

27 Peterse, *Bouwkundige studies*, p. 235; Peterse, *Steinfachwerk*, pp. 170f.

28 Carrington, "Building materials," p. 130; Evans, *Atrium Complex*, p. 12; Peterse, *Bouwkundige studies*, p. 147.

29 Cf. Th. L. Heres, "L'architettura e la storia edilizia," in W. J. Th. Peters, *La casa di M. Lucretius Fronto e le sue pitture*, Scrinium no. 5, Amsterdam, 1993, pp. 41ff. See also Th. L. Heres, "L'isolata V.4 a Pompei. I risultati della ricerca olandese negli anni 1994–1995," *Meded*, 1997, vol. 56, pp. 227–47.

30 On the earliest *atrium* houses of Pompeii, see also Evans, *Atrium Complex*, pp. 260ff.

31 Peterse, *Steinfachwerk*, pl. 8.

32 Peterse, *Steinfachwerk*, pp. 125ff.; cf. Evans, *Atrium Complex*, p. 272.

33 Peterse, *Bouwkundige studies*, pp. 228ff.; cf. E. M. Evans, "A group of *atrium* houses without side rooms in Pompeii," in *Papers in Italian Archaeology I: the Lancaster Seminar*, BAR Suppl. Ser. no. 41, 1978, pp. 175–91.

34 E.g., House (IX.9.d) and House (IX.9.11), both originating from Period C.

35 Peterse, *Steinfachwerk*, pl. 2.

36 For the initial construction phase of the House (V.4.c): Peterse, *Bouwkundige studies*, p. 230; Peterse, *Steinfachwerk*, pp. 164, 121ff.

37 The side walls of the *fauces* in the House of the Surgeon (VI.1.10) display a clear distinction between the section executed in *opus quadratum* of limestone ashlars and the part built in limestone framework of Period B (Peterse, *Bouwkundige studies*, pp. 273ff; Peterse, *Steinfachwerk*, p. 109 and pl. III-3). Maiuri excavated the entrance area of the House of the Surgeon beneath the AD 79 level. There he found proof of a subdivision of the entrance area into a *vestibulum* facing the street and *fauces* facing the *atrium* (A. Maiuri, *Alla ricerca di Pompei preromana*, Naples, 1973, pp. 1ff., pls. 1–4). Cf. now Jones and Robinson, Ch. 25.

38 On the architectural and social significance of *vestibula* during the limestone-framework period: Peterse, *Steinfachwerk*, pp. 138f.

39 Cf. Nissen, *Pompejanische Studien*, pp. 450f.; Evans, "Group of *atrium* houses," p. 176 and fig. 14.3 and Evans, *Atrium Complex*, pp. 275ff., where she explores the initial construction phase. We support most of Evans' conclusions. See also J.-A. Dickmann, *Domus frequentata. Anspruchsvolles Wohnen im pompejanischen Stadthaus*, Munich, 1999, pp. 106f.

40 Peterse, *Bouwkundige studies*, p. 240; Peterse, *Steinfachwerk*, p. 176 and pl. 83.

41 See also Dickmann, *Domus frequentata*, pp. 106f.

42 Peterse, *Bouwkundige studies*, pp. 197ff.

43 Peterse, *Bouwkundige studies*, p. 152. The House of the Surgeon (VI.1.10) clearly shows how the side wall of the residence extends as far as the back wall of the northern *triclinium*. The garden wall and the architecture in the garden give no indication of limestone-framework construction.

44 Peterse, *Steinfachwerk*, pp. 107ff.; Peterse and de Waele, "Standardized design"; de Haan *et al.*, "Casa degli Scienziati."

45 Peterse, *Steinfachwerk*, pp. 127ff.

46 See Peterse, *Bouwkundige studies*, pp. 197ff., where a few of the best-preserved houses from the period of limestone framework are shown.

47 De Haan *et al.*, "Casa degli Scienziati."

48 For the initial construction phase of House (VI.10.11): Peterse, *Bouwkundige studies*, pp. 341ff.; cf. Mau, *Beiträge*, pp. 51ff.; Evans, *Atrium Complex*, pp. 266f.

49 For the initial construction phase of House (VI.10.8): Peterse, *Bouwkundige studies*, pp. 340f.

50 Peterse, *Bouwkundige studies*, p. 197; Peterse, *Steinfachwerk*, pp. 121ff., 163; cf. Evans, *Atrium Complex*, pp. 263ff.

51 Also Dickmann, *Domus frequentata*, pp. 106f.

52 Dickmann, *Domus frequentata*, p. 398.

53 Dickmann, *Domus frequentata*, p. 398.

ADDITIONAL BIBLIOGRAPHY

Bonghi Jovino, M., *Ricerche à Pompei. L'insula 5 della regio VI dalle origini al 79 d.C.*, Rome, 1984.

Carocci, F., *Le insulae 3 e 4 della regio VI di Pompei, un'analisi storico - urbanistica*, Rome, 1990.

Clarke, J. R., *The Houses of Roman Italy 100 BC–AD 250. Ritual, space and decoration*, Berkeley, CA, 1991.

Kind de, R., *Huizen in Herculaneum. Een analyse van de stedebouw en de maatvoering in de huizenblokken III en IV*, Nijmegen, 1992.

Miele, F., "La casa à schiera I.11.16, un esempio di edilizia privata a Pompei," *Rivista di Studi Pompeiani*, 1989, vol. 3, pp. 165–84.

Wallace-Hadrill, A., *Houses and Society in Pompeii and Herculaneum*, Princeton, NJ, 1994.

CHAPTER TWENTY-FIVE

INTENSIFICATION, HETEROGENEITY AND POWER IN THE DEVELOPMENT OF *INSULA* VI.1

———•◆•———

Rick Jones and Damian Robinson[1]

INTRODUCTION

Pompeii in AD 79 was a place of diverse social and economic contrasts. Wealth, poverty, power and dependency nestled together in the urban neighbourhoods of the city. *Insula* VI.1 (Figure 25.1) was a part of one such neighbourhood, situated in the northwestern corner of Pompeii on the busy Via Consolare, adjacent to the Porta Ercolano (Map 3). How does an individual city block come to take on this character and why did it occur? Was the mixture of different kinds of commercial and residential properties, of rich and of poor, the result of the concomitant social degeneration and economic development of the city (a tale present in many traditional accounts of the social and spatial development of Pompeii)?[2] Or are other factors responsible for the observable patterns in urban space? The Anglo-American Project in Pompeii[3] has investigated these fundamental questions for the past decade in *insula* VI.1. Consequently, this chapter offers an interpretation of the development of this city block, and in doing so investigates the key process of urbanisation in the area around the Porta Ercolano. The elemental themes coursing through the narrative are: intensification, heterogeneity and power. Their subtle (and at times not so subtle) interplay is instrumental in shaping this portion of the urban landscape.

THE *INSULA* BEFORE *c.*200 BC

Although the city defences seem to have been first defined as early as the sixth century BC,[4] it was some time later before recognisable traces of structures marked the space inside the Porta Ercolano (cf. Chiaramonte, Ch. 11). These were all built upon a series of "pitted earth" surfaces, which had an anthropogenic origin; it is likely that they were intended to level an uneven natural ground surface.

Several early features associated with life on the pitted earth surfaces were recovered from excavations in the northern sector of *insula* VI.1—notably beneath the level of the Inn (VI.1.4), where a section of un-mortared wall and a "toilet" feature were found (Figure 25.2), and from beneath the House of the Vestals (VI.1.7) and in the

389

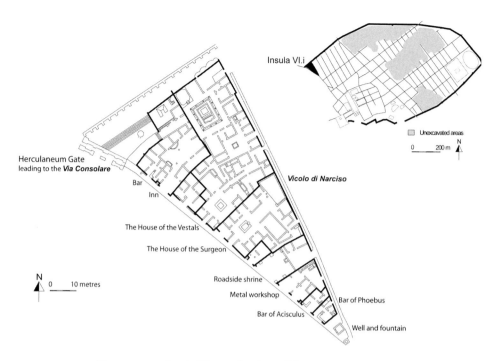

Figure 25.1 *Insula* VI.1 at the time of the eruption in AD 79.

Bar (VI.1.5), where early features were built of compacted earth or mud brick. Although finds were sparse, they included Black Gloss ware that dated to the second half of the fourth century BC.

In the central part of the *insula*, occupation commenced on top of the original ground surface at a later date than in the north. Beneath the *tablinum* of the House of the Surgeon (VI.1.10), a small length of yellow earth mortared *opus incertum* wall was discovered. A Black Gloss lamp fragment in its construction trench dated this to the third–second centuries BC. The wall was subsequently buried beneath a further levelling surface prior to the construction of the *opus quadratum* phase of the House of the Surgeon. The most coherent portion of early structure was also recovered from beneath the same house. A section of an *impluvium*-like feature, comprised of a square of *opus signinum* (Figure 25.3) surrounded by a low masonry wall with associated beaten earth floor surfaces, was encountered during excavations in a room in the "service quarter" of the property, just to the south of the later *atrium* complex.

It is interesting to note that all of the traces of early walls are aligned with the Via Consolare, which demonstrates that this road must have been a very early feature of the landscape in this area of the city, which pre-dates the orthogonal layout of the Region VI street grid to the east (cf. Geertman, Ch. 7).[5]

There were probably other similarly early structures in the southern portion of the city block, in the space now occupied by the Shrine (VI.1.13) and the commercial buildings (VI.1.14–18). However, all potential traces of these buildings have been scoured from the archaeological record by the effects of terracing, which removed much of the natural ground surface in the south of the *insula* to create a stepped

Figure 25.2   The fourth-century BC wall and toilet feature from beneath Inn (VI.1.4).

Figure 25.3   The early *impluvium* from the House of the Surgeon (VI.1.10).

sequence of building platforms. This would have involved the removal of many thousands of tonnes of earth and extended at least as far south as the House of Sallust (VI.2.4), where excavations by Laidlaw[6] revealed natural soils similar to those from the southern terrace of the *insula*.

To the north it would appear that the earliest occupation layers were also brought to a halt by the terracing activities. Beneath both the House of the Vestals (VI.1.7) and the House of the Surgeon (VI.1.10), the vestiges of former occupation were levelled for the creation of the original cores of these two properties. Both sit within a coherent building plot of approximately seventy Oscan feet wide.[7] This suggests that the landscape of *insula* (VI.1) was remade through the twin activities of terracing and plot division by the end of the third century BC or early in the second century BC. Old properties and boundaries were swept away, along with the removal of the small hill at the southern end of the *insula*. In their place came the terraces and regularly laid out plots upon which the standing archaeology that characterises the later phases of the *insula* was built.

THE BEGINNINGS OF SUBSTANTIAL STONE-BUILT ARCHITECTURE IN *INSULA* VI.1

All of the substantial stone-built architecture of the *insula* was constructed after the major period of landscaping and plot division.[8] The first two properties constructed

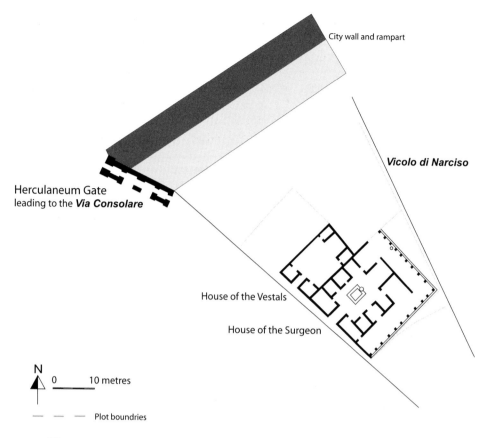

City wall and rampart

Vicolo di Narciso

Herculaneum Gate
leading to the *Via Consolare*

House of the Vestals

House of the Surgeon

N

0   10 metres

— — — — Plot boundries

Figure 25.4   The initial house layout of the House of the Surgeon (VI.1.10) and
the House of the Vestals (VI.1.7).

fronted onto the Via Consolare: the House of the Surgeon (VI.1.10) and the House
of the Vestals (VI.1.7).

Excavations beneath the *atrium* of the House of the Surgeon have revealed a layer
of building rubble comprised of mortar and plaster, into which the foundations for
the *opus quadratum* and *opus africanum* core of the property were cut. In this deposit
a coin of the late third century BC (214/212 BC) was recovered,[9] which, when taken
in combination with the third–second century BC date of the earlier wall beneath
the *tablinum* of this house, suggests that the construction of the House of the Surgeon
can now be dated to no earlier than *c*.200 BC.[10] In its initial phase this property
possessed the typical spatial layout of an *atrium* house (Figure 25.4); namely a *fauces*
and flanking rooms, a symmetrical *atrium* with two *cubicula* and an *ala* down either
side, and a *tablinum* and flanking rooms to the rear. The presence of an overflow drain
made out of a blue-grey tufa with Sarno stone capping, which led from a probable
early *impluvium*, suggests that the initial phase of the *atrium* may also have had a
compluviate roof.[11] The early drain to the south passed beneath the *cubiculum* adjacent
to the southern *ala* and through an open doorway. The house, however, also shows

some atypical architectural features. For example, the rooms adjacent to the *tablinum* were open and would have provided views through the colonnade, which flanked the south and eastern sides of the property, into a garden space. [12]

Built shortly after the construction of the initial phase of the House of the Surgeon (VI.1.10), the early House of the Vestals (VI.1.7) was a structurally simple property (Figure 25.4). It was comprised of a number of rooms around an open courtyard.[13] The house abutted the pre-existing northern wall of the House of the Surgeon, with the remaining walls being constructed from yellow earthen bricks or beaten earth, on an unbonded *opus africanum* foundation.

At the time of the construction of the House of the Vestals a large pit was dug beneath the *tablinum* and a ritual carried out, involving the burning of neonatal pigs with aromatic woods, together with the remains of a meal of bread, fruits and nuts and the deposition of a number of small incense cups.[14] This must have been a ritual act that was undertaken to celebrate the foundation of the small house.

Given the great differentiation in domestic architecture and construction style, it is apparent that even though both of these early properties occupied identically sized building plots of seventy Oscan feet wide, social, or at least architectural, differentiation was certainly a feature of *insula* VI.1 in the early years of the second century BC. The House of the Surgeon was a solidly built, substantial *atrium* property that took up its entire plot; in comparison, its neighbour, the House of the Vestals, was a smaller, less soundly built courtyard property. Indeed, it is quite unusual in Region VI to find "twin-plots" of substantial width being so diversely built up.[15]

THE INFILLING OF SPACE AND THE DEVELOPMENT OF THE URBAN ECONOMY

During the course of the second century BC, the largely open landscape to the north and south of the House of the Surgeon and the House of the Vestals becomes filled with a range of small courtyard houses and commercial properties (Figure 25.5).[16] Accompanying this period of construction would have been a major expansion in the local population. The first indications of this expansion came with the construction of a property along the line of the Vicolo di Narciso, which must have been formalised at least by the mid-second century. Although only limited traces of this property have been recovered, it was substantially built in the space to the rear of the House of the Vestals but also reached into the rear of the House of the Surgeon. This property, however, was not long lived and it was soon swept away in the drive to expand the House of the Vestals towards the end of the second century BC. At this time the House of the Vestals more than doubled its size, reaching back to the Vicolo di Narciso, where a rear entrance was constructed around 100 BC. The property now also incorporated new architectural features, including an *atrium* and a separate service area, while retaining a large garden space in the middle of the house. To the north of the House of the Vestals on the Vicolo di Narciso, two additional small courtyard houses were built, although one of these was constructed as part of the development of the rear of the House of the Vestals and so may indicate that the Vestals' owners had taken their first steps into the world of commerce and were now involved in property speculation and rental.[17]

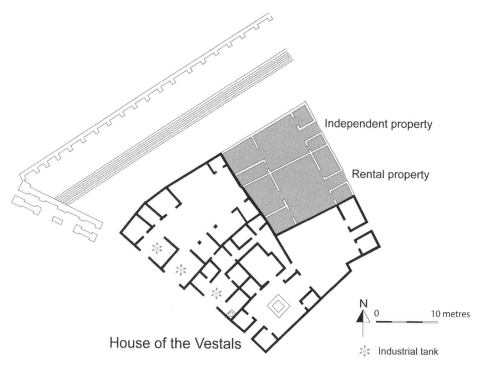

Figure 25.5 The developing *insula* during the second century BC.

In terms of its size and architectural configuration, the House of the Vestals (VI.1.7) was a much more significant property than those newer buildings surrounding it. It was also beginning to rival its neighbour, the House of the Surgeon (VI.1.10), in its size and architectural complexity, though it differed in one major aspect: its household economy possessed an obvious commercial dimension. As well as the rental property on the Vicolo di Narciso, the owners of the House of the Vestals also possessed a series of workshops along the Via Consolare that were linked to the large house. Workshops (VI.1.2, 5) comprised a series of tanks lined with waterproof plaster (Figures 25.5 and 25.6). Abundant fish remains (including a fully articulated member of the family *Sparidae*) were recovered from the bottom of one of the tanks, suggesting that they were used for fish processing activities.[18]

Towards the end of the second century BC in the south of the *insula*, a group of four small workshops was also constructed (VI.1.14–15, 17–18; Figure 25.1). Each unit had a wide "shop" doorway opening from the Via Consolare. Plaster-lined tanks, similar to those found in the north of the *insula*, were also recovered from excavations in the Soap Factory (VI.1.14) and the Bar of Acisculus (VI.1.17), as well as from the Shrine (VI.1.13). This suggests that there was a consistent phase of tank-centred industrial activity throughout the *insula* and that fish processing was a major industry in this area of Pompeii during the late second and early first centuries BC.[19]

Consequently, in the later second century BC, we witness the first substantial signs of the developing social and economic hierarchy in our neighbourhood. Although

Figure 25.6 The plaster-lined industrial tanks from workshop (VI.1.5).

the *insula* became heavily built up with a range of small houses and economic properties, we can see that as part of this development the House of the Vestals was now challenging the House of the Surgeon for the position of the largest and most important property in the *insula*. At the same time, the owners of the House of the Vestals also invested heavily in the urban economy through the construction and staffing of productive workshops located on the busy Via Consolare, and by building a separate house, probably for rental, on the quiet back street of the Vicolo di Narciso. Altogether, this period represents a crystallisation of the major changes in the social and economic history of the community that began with the phase of terracing and plot division and the construction of differently sized properties sometime around 200 BC. From this point forward, however, the densely packed landscape of this part of Pompeii possesses resolutely urban characteristics: a densely packed cityscape and a burgeoning population engaged in non-agricultural pursuits.

DEVELOPMENTS IN THE EARLY YEARS OF THE COLONY

Pompeii was one of the Campanian cities that rebelled against Rome during the Social War (cf. Descœudres, Ch. 2).[20] In 89 BC the city was laid siege by the Roman general Sulla, who appears to have targeted the strategically vulnerable Porta Ercolano with his artillery. The city wall at this point is covered in the impact craters of thousands of sling bullets and *ballistae* (Figure 25.7), and during the bombardment the northern end of *insula* VI.1 was devastated (Figure 25.8).[21]

Figure 25.7 Examples from the Social War missile assemblage.

In the aftermath of war, the owners of the House of the Vestals seized the opportunity to take over two small adjacent courtyard houses on the Vicolo di Narciso that had been badly damaged during the attack. This allowed for the enlargement of the House of the Vestals, which now covered the entire northern end of the *insula* (Figure 25.9).

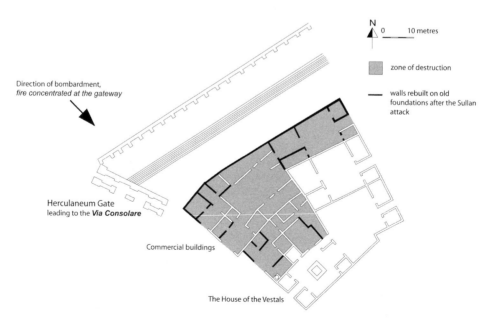

Figure 25.8 The destruction of the northern end of *insula* VI.1 caused by the Sullan bombardment.

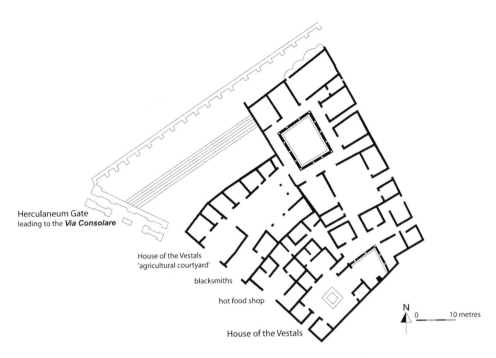

Figure 25.9 The northern sector of *insula* VI.1 during the first century BC.

These two additional properties provided the owners of the house with the space they required to build an elaborate series of reception rooms surrounding two peristyles. All of these changes were undertaken in order to create an opulent aristocratic property with a traditional axial ground plan (cf. Wallace-Hadrill, Ch. 18). Here we can see the creation of the architectural structure of the traditional Pompeian elite house. At the same time, however, it is apparent that the poorer inhabitants of the *insula* were being squeezed out in the face of the rapacious expansion of its richer inhabitants. Those who were left in the north end of the *insula* were now part of the large household (or "houseful")[22] of the House of the Vestals.

By this time the House of the Surgeon had acquired a small service area in the southeastern corner of its plot. As part of these changes, the room immediately to the south of the *tablinum* was also enlarged, creating a large *triclinium*. These changes, when compared to those taking place in the House of the Vestals, are smaller and more inconsequential; the House of the Surgeon possesses no peristyle, for example. Importantly, all of the changes in the House of the Surgeon take place inside the original 70 Oscan-foot plot, unlike the House of the Vestals, which had long-since outgrown its original property boundaries.

Were the developments in both of these houses related to differing attitudes to the urban economy on the part of the respective householders? At this time the House of the Surgeon was still without shops or workshops; it appears to play no role in the urban economy. However, in the House of the Vestals, the commercial properties that were located alongside the Via Consolare and heavily damaged during the Sullan attack were redeveloped. In the place of fish processing activities, a food and drink shop and a smithy were constructed. Also to the north of these workshops was a separate entrance to a courtyard area of the House of the Vestals (Figure 25.9). This space was structurally reminiscent of the temporally later "agricultural court" of the House of the Menander (I.10.4),[23] and may indicate that the owners of the House of the Vestals maintained agricultural interests close to the city. It is significant that all of these commercial areas were linked to the House of the Vestals. Previously its owners had embraced the opportunities offered by participation in the urban economy and presumably reaped their rewards. Did they now re-invest this capital in order to purchase all of the space in the north of the *insula*, to exploit yet more commercial opportunities along the Via Consolare, and to reconstruct the private sectors of their property along opulent lines? This must be compared and contrasted with the small-scale redevelopment of the House of the Surgeon and their apparent lack of participation in Pompeii's burgeoning urban economy.

In the aftermath of the Social War the nature of industrial and commercial activity in the south of the *insula* also changed. The fish processing tanks were abandoned and the workshops redeveloped. In the Soap Factory (VI.1.14) a group of clay and stone hearths were recovered, along with significant quantities of hammerscale, charcoal, slag and hearth bottoms. This property was now operating as a metal smithy. In contrast, a room at the rear of the Bar of Acisculus (VI.1.17) was developed into a large-scale food processing and cooking facility, the products of which were sold from the room opening onto the busy Via Consolare. Overall, the changes from an economy based solely on fish processing, potentially for an export market, to the manufacture of metal goods and feeding passersby on the streets of Pompeii, suggest a change in the nature of both the city and its urban economy. Clearly in the years after the imposition of the colony there was a growing internal market for everyday goods and foodstuffs, which was probably related both to an expanding urban population and the growing importance of the city as a regional market (cf. Jongman, Ch. 32).

POMPEII DURING THE EARLY EMPIRE

During the early empire the House of the Vestals was lavishly reappointed. An imposing columned entranceway on the Via Consolare welcomed visitors directly into the *atrium* of the property. This was painted in the latest wall painting style, floored in a black mosaic with a white double-banded border and ornamented with a decorative fountain in a new marble-lined *impluvium*. The changes were clearly intended to present a tableau of wealth and status and are illustrative of the changes that took place elsewhere in the property. For example, a second *atrium* was constructed, opening from the Vicolo di Narciso, which was even more lavishly decorated than the main *atrium* opening from the Via Consolare (Figure 25.10). Other changes also include the construction of a large private bath suite and swimming pool, as well as an enlarged service area in the centre of the property.

The decoration of the house during the early empire was built around the series of fountains (Figure 25.11).[24] The fountains were supplied with pressurised water from the city's new aqueduct-fed system. There was no attempt to store this expensive commodity, which was allowed to overflow into the streets.[25] It is significant that

Figure 25.10 The mosaic threshold from the Vicolo di Narciso *atrium* in the House of the Vestals (VI.1.7).

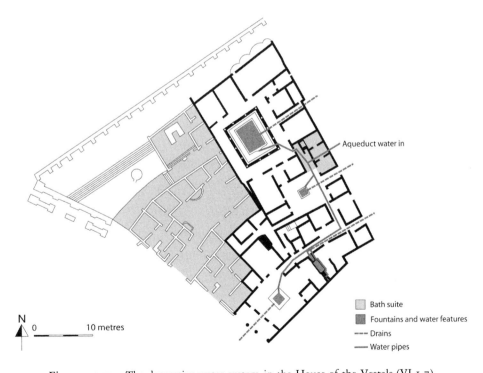

Figure 25.11 The decorative water system in the House of the Vestals (VI.1.7).

Figure 25.12   The buildings destroyed during the construction of the Shrine
to the *Lares Augusti*.

no other property in the *insula* had access to aqueduct water and this is another
signifier of inequality.

The division of space in the *insula* between residential and commercial activity
areas was well settled by the end of the second century BC. With the exceptions of
the early frontages of the House of the Surgeon and the House of the Vestals, all of
the properties fronting onto the Via Consolare were involved in the urban economy.
While the owners of the House of the Vestals rapidly embraced the opportunities
offered by the urban economy, it was only during the early years of the empire that
the inhabitants of the House of the Surgeon followed suit. Elsewhere in the insula,
a dramatic change happened to a number of economic properties in the area that
became VI.1.13 (Figure 25.12). A blacksmiths and another associated workshop were
demolished and a north–south wall was inserted, dividing the east–west building
plot in half. In the space opening onto the Via Consolare, four large brick piers were
constructed to support a roof, and the floor level was raised by over a metre. This
elevated surface was then paved with a white mosaic, with a lower step paved in
white *signinum* and decorated in a diamond pattern picked out in black *tesserae*.
Giuseppe Fiorelli first identified this space as a shrine, which can be associated with
the *Lares Augusti* through its architectural parallels with the *Lares Augusti* shrine
excavated near the Porticus Aemilia at Rome.[26] This development is significant
because throughout the remainder of the *insula* the drive to develop its commercial
base had been remorseless. Yet with the case of the shrine, presumably economically
prosperous buildings are deliberately destroyed and replaced by a religious structure.

Such an act suggests that some comparatively wealthy individual, who could afford to undertake such a deliberate and costly benefaction to the community, owned the space. It also demonstrates that at a time in Pompeii's history when tradition-ally its inhabitants are portrayed as striving to *salve lucrum*[27] and in an *insula* where an *atrium* in the house of its wealthiest inhabitant was decorated with mosaic threshold depicting twin cornucopia surrounding a staff of Mercury (Figure 25.10), the desire for profit could be tempered in order to make a political or religious statement. Clearly this was a case of putting aside economic space in order to generate social capital.

CITY LIFE AFTER THE EARTHQUAKE

The piped water system in the House of the Vestals (VI.1.7) was the greatest casualty of the earthquake of AD 62. Although the public fountain at the southern apex of the *insula* was quickly repaired and a supply reinstated, water was no longer supplied to private houses in the neighbourhood (cf. Jansen, Ch. 16). This had severe implications for the owners of the House of the Vestals, who had based the decoration of their property on the lavish provision of fountains. Consequently, another period of reconstruction and redecoration was undertaken in the house.[28] During this refurbishment, the former pressurised aqueduct water fountains were replaced by standing pools of water. Taken on its own, this abandonment of active water features could suggest that the House of the Vestals was a property in decline. Yet this could not be further from the truth. In the post-earthquake period the owners of the house redecorated all of the major public rooms in the latest wall painting style in order to bring the house decoratively up to date.[29] Architectural innovation also occurred in the form of a new upper storey that was built to provide a suite of reception rooms over the north side of the peristyle. These had large windows offering stunning views over the city walls towards Vesuvius and the sea. Such rooms with views were normally found only in the lavish properties that cascaded over the former city walls (cf. Tybout, Ch. 26). Decorative active water features, however, remained in vogue in Pompeii. In order to ensure that the House of the Vestals was still at the forefront of fashion, the roof of the new upper storey provided a large rainwater catchment area that filled an above-ground cistern in the northwest corner of the peristyle and which fed a gravity-powered fountain in the middle of the garden.

When all of the post-earthquake changes in the House of the Vestals are considered together, it can be demonstrated that the householders were clearly concerned with maintaining their property as an active status symbol after AD 62. It shows that fierce social competition, which characterised the upper classes of Pompeian society in the early years of the Imperial period, continued through the last years of the city's life.[30]

In stark contrast to the refurbishment and redevelopment of the House of the Vestals stands its neighbour, the House of the Surgeon (VI.1.10). What had initially been the most important property in the city block had fallen into a state of disrepair by the time of the eruption. This can be observed most keenly in the *atrium*, where a regularly spaced series of holes were cut through the final-phase *opus signinum* floor surface (Figure 25.13). These were clearly for beams to provide additional support

Figure 25.13   Postholes in the final phase floor surface of the House
of the Surgeon (VI.1.10).

for the roof, which must have been in a poor state of repair during the house's final
years of life.

The earthquake appears to have heralded yet another shift in the economic base
of the *insula*. The commercial properties at the northern end of the city block underwent
significant redevelopment, which resulted in the construction of a bar, a large and
well-appointed coaching inn, and an upstairs rental apartment (cf. De Felice, Ch.
30). All of these properties were now structurally separate from the House of the
Vestals and may indicate that they were also independent of its control. Parallels
from elsewhere in the city, however, suggest that this would not have been the case.[31]
Instead, it is highly likely that the bar, inn and rental apartment would still have
been owned by the House of the Vestals and were either rented out as businesses
or operated by the slaves and freedmen of the aristocratic household (cf. Pirson,
Ch. 29). Undoubtedly these properties would still have provided healthy profits for
the owners of the House of the Vestals and so helped to pay for the reconstruction
and redecoration of the house.

In the south of the *insula* the workshops also underwent another significant
redevelopment. An upper storey was created that spread right across all of the properties
in this block. The stair base, which opened directly from the Via Consolare at (VI.1.16),
provided access to a rental apartment in this new upper storey. The Soap Factory
(VI.1.14) now also encompassed its neighbouring workshop (VI.1.15), although
judging by the significant quantities of hammerscale, slag and hearth bottoms recovered
from the final occupation layer above a hard mortar floor, the workshop still appears
to have operated as a smithy. In the Bar of Acisculus (VI.1.17), the cooking platform
was demolished during the construction of the upper storey. A final surface of *opus
signinum* was laid throughout the property, over which a marble-topped bar counter
facing onto the Via Consolare was constructed (Figure 25.14).

Figure 25.14   The marble-topped counter in the Bar of Acisculus (VI.1.17).

The changes that took place in the last years of the *insula* demonstrate that Pompeii was not a decaying city still suffering from the ravages of an earthquake but a city that had returned to some form of "normality". The comparative neglect of the House of the Surgeon should not blind us into thinking about a city in ruins; it was the only property in the *insula* that had not been rebuilt along bigger and better lines. Indeed, the House of the Vestals demonstrates the commitment of its upper-class residents to play the same integral part in urban life as they had done in the years before the earthquake. The electoral *programmata* paint a vivid picture of the rise and fall of families (cf. Franklin, Ch. 33),[32] and perhaps this is also how we should also envisage the houses, waxing and waning with their owners' fortunes. We should not expect all of the properties in the city at any point in its history to be at the peak of architectural and decorative style.

The shops and workshops of the *insula* demonstrate that there was a vibrant urban economy. In this area of the city next to the Porta Ercolano, the proliferation of bars and inns on both sides of the Via Consolare, as well as the development of upper-storey rental apartments, indicates that there was an increasing amount of people entering the city—perhaps to work on rebuilding projects or do other forms of business —who required feeding and accommodating. Here we see that Pompeii was a vibrant, prosperous, flourishing city. Yet, as the changes in the economic properties at both the northern and southern extremities of the *insula* demonstrate, it was still a city in the thrall of its traditional urban elite (cf. Jongman, Ch. 32; Franklin, Ch. 33).

CONCLUSIONS

Interpreting the long and complex sequence of occupation in *insula* VI.1 has revealed that three intertwined processes are in operation during the development of this particular part of the urban landscape: intensification, heterogeneity and power.

Most obviously, the use of the space just inside of the Porta Ercolano intensifies from the fourth century BC onwards. Initially, a number of anthropogenic dumps of soil created a level surface upon which the first, ephemeral traces of activity could be observed. These low-density activities were spread throughout the area that later came to be defined as the city block, with only the "*impluvium*-like" feature, buried beneath the later House of the Surgeon (VI.1.10), representing a more substantial form of architecture. The associated processes of terracing and plot division swept away these early traces of occupation and heralded a transition from proto-urban to truly urban life. In the creation of equally sized house plots and a probable formalisation of the street network at the end of the third century BC, we see the first traces of organised city life. From this point onwards the density of occupation continually increases. Every space within the *insula* was initially colonised at ground floor level, followed in the first century BC by an encroachment onto the public land of the city's defences, and finally, in the first century AD, by an increasing use of upper storeys (for comparanda on multiple-storey buildings at Pompeii, cf. Tybout, Ch. 26). Yet space was not apportioned out equally in this intensification. The rise to prominence of the House of the Vestals (VI.1.7) during this period demonstrates that it was the poorer inhabitants of the city block who were squeezed out of their small courtyard properties as this particular house expanded, and who were eventually forced to reside in cramped upstairs rental accommodation. The rich basked in space and luxury at the expense of the lesser members of the community.

Intensification can also be traced in the economic development of the *insula*. From its early years when the occupants of VI.1 were probably involved in such basic agricultural pursuits as threshing their own cereals and slaughtering their own animals,[33] through participation in the "industrial" processing of fish, to the diversification of the economic base of the *insula*, the number of business properties increases over time. Here we also see the second theme of heterogeneity in operation. The community moves from participating in a single form of economic activity, be it subsistence agriculture or specialised fish product manufacture for a probable export market, to the complex, multifaceted economy at the time of the eruption. It also illustrates that Pompeian economic actors were not hidebound by traditional industries or longstanding relationships of production, but were clearly adaptive and perhaps even entrepreneurial in the ways by which they were prepared to change their economic strategies. The rise of the House of the Vestals clearly demonstrates the advantages that could be gained through intensifying production and participating in the urban economy, whereas the House of the Surgeon simply illustrates the dangers of being left behind.

Heterogeneity is also visible in the process through which the properties of different social class and economic orientation nestled together. Over time, the House of the Vestals was surrounded by a plethora of shops, workshops and rental apartments. In *insula* VI.1 the rich and the poor lived side by side. Such an arrangement did not arise by accident; it was specifically related to the third structural theme: power.

Indeed, this theme underlies the majority of the developments described above. The drive to expand the House of the Vestals in order to gain the necessary space on which to build status architecture, coupled with a concomitant desire to secure valuable economic space along the Via Consolare, can be interpreted as part of the development of a social and economic elite. Rich and poor lived side by side in *insula* VI.1 out of necessity; the upper classes dominated a local territory in whose economic sectors the poor toiled.[34] Such power relations played a critical role in the shaping of *insula* VI.1 and, most probably, in the development of urbanisation in Pompeii as a whole.

NOTES

1 The authors would like to record our thanks to all of our colleagues in the Anglo-American Project, especially Jane Richardson and Astrid Schoonhoven for their helpful comments on drafts of this chapter and to Jaye Pont for images 25.7 and 25.14. We would also like to extend our gratitude to Prof. Pietro Giovanni Guzzo, Dott. Antonio D'Ambrosio and all of their colleagues in the Soprintendenza Archeologica di Pompei for their enthusiastic support of our research. Damian Robinson would like to thank the British Academy for their generous award of a Postdoctoral Fellowship, during which he wrote the initial draft of this chapter.

2 See R. A. Raper, "The analysis of the urban structure of Pompeii: a sociological examination of land use (semi-micro)", in D. L. Clarke (ed.), *Spatial Archaeology*, London, 1977, pp. 189–221.

3 This chapter describes the work of the Anglo-American Project in Pompeii. The project is based in *insula* (VI.1) and is run as an international field school from the Universities of Bradford and Oxford in the UK directed by Rick Jones and Damian Robinson. See also R. Jones and D. Robinson, "The making of an élite house: the House of the Vestals at Pompeii", *JRA*, 2004, vol. 17, pp. 107–30, and "The economic development of the Commercial Triangle (VI.1.6–8, 24–6)", in P. G. Guzzo and M. P. Guidobaldi (eds), *Nuove ricerche archeologiche a pompei ed Ercolano*, Naples, 2005, pp. 270–7.

4 S. De Caro, "Nuove indagini sulle fortificazioni di Pompei", *AION*, 1985, vol. 7, pp. 75–114.

5 F. Carocci *et al.*, *Le insulae 3 e 4 della regio VI di Pompei. Un analisi storico-urbanistica*, Rome, 1990; A. V. Schoonhoven, *Metrology and Meaning in Pompeii—the urban arrangement of Regio VI*, Rome, 2006.

6 A. Laidlaw, "Excavations in the Casa del Sallustio, Pompeii: a preliminary assessment", in R. T. Scott and A. R. Scott (eds), *Eius virtutis studiosi: classical and postclassical studies in memory of Frank Edward Brown*, Washington, DC, 1993, p. 229.

7 Schoonhoven, *Metrology*; A. Schoonhoven, "Defining Space: the plot division of Insula VI.1 of Pompeii," *Oebalus*, 2006, vol. 1, pp. 113–43.

8 See Schoonhoven, *Metrology*, for an interpretation of the plot layout of the remainder of Region VI.

9 We would like to thank our project numismatist, Dr Richard Hobbs of the Department of Prehistory and Europe at the British Museum, for his work in identifying this particular coin.

10 A. Maiuri, "Saggi nella 'Casa del Chiurgo' (Reg. VI, Ins. 1, n. 10)", *NSc*, 1930, pp. 381–95, proposed a construction date for the house of the fourth–third centuries BC, which has since persevered in some accounts (cf. Adam, Ch. 8). For support of a later date, cf. also Wallace-Hadrill, Ch. 18.

11 Although see A. Wallace-Hadrill, "Rethinking the Roman atrium house", in R. Laurence and A. Wallace-Hadrill (eds), *Domestic Space in the Roman World: Pompeii and beyond*, JRA Suppl. Ser. no. 22, 1997, pp. 223–8. Cf. Wallace-Hadrill. Ch. 18.

12 We are grateful to Darren Bailey for initially suggesting this interpretation, now confirmed through excavation.

13 See S. C. Nappo, "Urban transformation at Pompeii in the late 3rd and early 2nd c. BC", in Laurence and Wallace-Hadrill, *Domestic Space*, pp. 91–120 for a study of row houses in Regions I and II from Pompeii, and Wallace-Hadrill, "Rethinking", for an introduction to the development of the *atrium* house. Cf. Wallace-Hadrill, Ch. 18; Nappo, Ch. 23.

14 M. Ciaraldi and J. Richardson, "Food, ritual and rubbish in the making of Pompeii", in G. Fincham *et al.* (eds), *TRAC 99* (Proceedings of the ninth annual Theoretical Roman Archaeology Conference, Durham 1999), Oxford, 2000, pp. 74–82; Robyn Veal, *pers. comm.*; M. Robinson "Domestic burnt offerings and sacrifices at Roman and pre-Roman Pompeii, Italy", *Vegetation History and Archaeobotany*, 2002, vol. 11, pp. 93–9.

15 See Schoonhoven, *Metrology.*

16 See above, n. 3.

17 See above, n. 3; also H. M. Parkins, "The 'consumer city' domesticated? The Roman city in élite economic strategies", in H. M. Parkins (ed.), *Roman Urbanism. Beyond the consumer city*, London, 1997, pp. 83–111; F. Pirson, "Rented accommodation at Pompeii: the *Insula Arriana Polliana*", in Laurence and Wallace-Hadrill, *Domestic Space*, pp. 165–81. See D. Robinson, "Re-thinking the social organisation of trade and industry in first century AD Pompeii", in A. MacMahon and J. Price (eds), *Roman Working Lives and Urban Living*, Oxford, 2005, pp. 88–105 for more information on property speculation and rental in Pompeii.

18 See R. I. Curtis, *Garum and Salsamenta: production and commerce in materia medica*, Leiden, 1991, for a discussion of the production of *garum* and related fish products. Dr Andrew Jones, University of Bradford, identified the fish remains. For a useful comparison also see A. I. Wilson, "Commerce and industry in Roman Sabratha", *Libyan Studies*, 1999, vol. 33, pp. 29–52.

19 Plin., *HN* 9.169–171.

20 App., *B Civ.* 1.50; Vell. Pat. 2.16.1–2; Plin., *HN* 3.70.

21 See above, n. 3; M. Burns, "Pompeii under siege: a missile assemblage from the Social War", *Journal of Roman Military Equipment Studies*, forthcoming, for more information on the Sullan attack on Pompeii.

22 See A. Wallace-Hadrill, *Houses and Society in Pompeii and Herculaneum*, Princeton, NJ, 1994, pp. 103–16, on "housefuls".

23 R. Ling, *The Insula of the Menander at Pompeii, vol. 1: the structures*, Oxford, 1997, pp. 105–32, documents the construction and function of the agricultural courtyard of the House of the Menander (I.10.4).

24 See above, n. 3.

25 For more information about the use of water in the House of the Vestals (VI.1.7), see R. Jones and D. Robinson, "Water, wealth and social status in the House of the Vestals in Pompeii", *AJA*, 2005, vol. 109.4, pp. 695–710.

26 G. Fiorelli, *Descrizione di Pompei*, Naples, 1875, p. 81; R. Laurence, *Roman Pompeii. Space and society*, London, 1994, p. 42.

27 "Say hello to profit!" (in the entryway of (VII.1.47)); see A. Maiuri, *Pompeii*, Novara, 1960, pp. 114–40.

28 See above, n. 3 and n. 25.

29 G. P. Carratelli and I. Baldassarre (eds), *Pompei, pitture e mosaici*, vol. 4, Rome, 1993, pp. 5–47.

30 H. Mouritsen, *Elections, Magistrates and Municipal Elite. Studies in Pompeian epigraphy*, Rome, 1988, uses the epigraphic record to demonstrate the continued participation of the Pompeian upper class in political life after the AD 62 earthquake. Cf. Franklin, Ch. 33; Jongman, Ch. 32.

31 See Pirson, "Rented accommodation"; Ling, *Insula of the Menander*, vol. 1, p. 250.

32 J. L. Franklin, Jr, *Pompeis difficile est: studies in the political life of imperial Pompeii*, Ann Arbor, MI, 2001; H. Mouritsen, *Elections*.

33 See Ciaraldi and Robinson, "Food, ritual and rubbish".

34 See articles by D. Robinson, "Rethinking"; "The social texture of Pompeii", in Sara E. Bon and Rick Jones (eds), *Sequence and Space in Pompeii*, Oxbow Monograph no. 77, Oxford, 1997, pp. 135–44.

CHAPTER TWENTY-SIX

ROOMS WITH A VIEW
Residences built on terraces along the edge of Pompeii (Regions VI, VII and VIII)

——— .◆. ———

Rolf A. Tybout

The layout of many a modern European city has been conditioned by the demolishing of its ramparts in the later nineteenth century. The age-old stone girdle, once untied, created virginal soil that was soon to be occupied by broad boulevards or park promenades. Often lofty residences were built to embellish their borders and supply a young bourgeoisie with elegant dwellings befitting its growing need for self-representation. Further outward extension in subsequent decades provided ample space for socio-economic zones to accommodate socially different groups of an ever more rapidly growing urban population. Changes in armament and military tactics were a prerequisite for these developments, but social shifts conditioned the patterns in which municipalities chose to organize the new public space. Thus the city, breaking out from its inveterate boundaries, marked the breakaway from the pre-industrial era in a double sense.

Though there is nothing really comparable in Greek and Roman antiquity, we may turn to late republican Pompeii to find at least some similarities. In the course of the first century BC, the southern and western sides of the city wall were allowed to be covered by buildings (Map 3): from the Porta Marina eastwards to the Triangular Forum (VIII.2) and northwards to the Porta Ercolano (VII.16 and VI.17, better known as *Insula Occidentalis* VII and VI). Pompeii was built on a prehistoric lava bed (cf. Sigurdsson, Ch. 4). The precipice along its edge provided a site for massive substructions supporting elegant multi-tiered houses, built to offer a commanding view over the Sarno valley or the Bay of Naples with Capri and the Sorrentine peninsula. These developments were conditioned by a shift in the political situation rather than in the art of war. After the Social War and the final defeat of Sulla's opponents, the seats of war moved outside Italy. The absence of foreign enemies and the foundation of a colony ensuring permanent Roman control from 80 BC (at the latest) removed the need to maintain a complete urban defense system.

However, to explain this radical alteration of the city silhouette as the result of historical developments beyond the horizon of a provincial town is only one side of the coin. Releasing the walls for private building is hardly conceivable without an official municipal decision, though nothing of the sort is preserved. The gradual disappearance of the walls from sight implies the fading out of a long-standing

407

hallmark of the original inhabitants' civic identity.[1] It is surely no coincidence that wall sections were incorporated in the foundations of two public buildings erected after the settlement of Sulla's veterans: the temple of the new city goddess Venus, built over the south-west section of the old city wall in a prominent position (cf. Small, Ch. 13), and the amphitheater occupying the opposite southeastern edge (cf. Parslow, Ch. 14). These two buildings, the conspicuous cornerstones of a re-founded Pompeii, belong to a set of impressive monuments ideologically bound up with Sulla's victory and the city's new status as a Roman colony.[2] The transformation of the city wall is yet another reflection of this major shift in the city's history: of the Pompeians' submission and subsequent peaceful integration into the Roman order,[3] and perhaps also of veterans adapting to a post-military stage of life.

The history of the exploration of the terrace houses is indicative of the paradoxical vicissitudes that befell Pompeii in its second life: of progress in scholarship, opportunities missed, and knowledge sunk into oblivion from its rediscovery up to our times (cf. Laidlaw, Ch. 39).[4] Both the western and southern city edge attracted the attention of Bourbon excavators. They generally focused on upper levels that were relatively accessible on account of their being covered only by a thin layer of ash. Single finds rather than architectural complexes attracted attention. Many of the former, including large excised fragments of wall painting, now belong to the collection of the Museum in Naples; their provenance is often unknown. On the other hand, some activities were documented in written reports stored in archives that were to lie idle for centuries. During the nineteenth century, only a few houses were known. Starting in 1883, an entire *insula* (VIII.2) and the southernmost section of the *Insula Occidentalis* were excavated. The results were published in articles scattered throughout various periodicals and were generally not noticed by mainstream architectural research. Systematic surveys of VIII.2 were undertaken in the 1910s and 1920s by F. Noack, and continued after his death in 1931 under K. Lehmann-Hartleben. Their *Baugeschichtliche Untersuchungen am Stadtrand von Pompeji*, published in 1936, was a major breakthrough. As the first publication of a complete *insula*,[5] it sheds light on the architectural history of individual buildings as parts of an interwoven complex of private and, occasionally, public buildings. Its ample attention to architectural development as an indicator of social change foreshadows modern scholarly interests, though its then-fashionable paradigm of progressive social decline in the course of the first century AD should now be considered obsolete (cf. Jongman, Ch. 32).

The *Insula Occidentalis* did not enjoy an equal fortune. The ruins were afflicted by the bombardment of Pompeii in 1943, and suffered from earth slides after World War II. Excavations were started in the late 1960s and consolidated by partial restorations in the early 1970s, but did not result in publications except for some brief preliminary reports.[6]

Among the dwellings on the west side, the House of M. Fabius Rufus (VII.16.22) takes pride of place (Figure 26.1).[7] The vast four-story complex originated from several separate houses that were unified only in the last years of Pompeii's existence. A redecoration in the Fourth Style was left unfinished in AD 79. The house's nucleus was an apsidal reception room on the second floor decorated with paintings representing Apollo, Dionysus and Venus and offering views over the sea through three large windows; a garden with a small fountain facing the central window added to the otiose ambience (cf. Dickmann, Ch. 27 for similar settings in Herculaneum). Little is left of the wall paintings belonging to the earlier habitations. The back wall of a small room in the dark inner section of the southern part of the house has an interesting painting that should be assigned to the beginning of the second phase of the Second Style (*c.*50–40 BC) (Figure 26.2; cf. Strocka, Ch. 20).[8] Its symmetrical architectural composition includes two receding walls at both sides, creating the illusion of two levels of depth separated from each other by a row of four fluted columns with Corinthian capitals. A figure of Venus wearing diadem and necklace, with a cupid seated on her shoulder and touching her chin, peeps through the partly opened wings of a monumental door with lavish bronze work, as if she just opened it to enter the colonnaded forecourt of her temple. In earlier paintings of the Second Style, Venus and other deities were represented as statues; our wall is the first to show the goddess as a living figure, still conceived of as a part of the illusionistic architecture, but foreshadowing the divine actors represented in the context of the mythological central pieces of the Third and Fourth Style. Another new motif, unknown so far from any other Roman wall painting, is the "broken door," with its left and right wings depicted at either side of the central entrance. Evidently, this is a product of pictorial imagination; as such it is typical of the advanced Second Style, in which a more or less convincing illusion of structural unity gave way to ever more fictitious architectural ensembles. The idea of cutting a door in two may have been inspired by the related motif of the "broken pediment," for which there are models in late Hellenistic architecture.

Lying in areas closed off to the general public and only partly explored, the terrace houses are generally glossed over in Pompeii guides and handbooks on Roman architecture. In spite of their particularly interesting building type they are little

Figure 26.1 House of M. Fabius Rufus (VII.16.22): view from the west; ICCD N 49327.

Figure 26.2   House of M. Fabius Rufus (VII.16.22): Second-Style painting at back of room
(71) (*c*.45–40 BC); Fourth-Style painting in front; ICCD N 45226.

known to tourists and scholars alike. Nevertheless, the development of the better-
known houses on the southern edge can be sketched in broad outlines.[9] Already in
the second century BC, during the long period of peace in Italy after the Second
Punic War, the *pomerium* inside the wall was built over to enlarge the modest dwellings
aligned to this boundary.[10] Their back parts were largely expanded with terraces that
covered the wall without hampering the latter's defensive potential. These one-level
houses generally featured a large *atrium*. Relatively little room was left for the back
premises adjacent to the terraces on the sun-side and already yielding a view over
the Sarno river, perhaps through colonnades built in perishable materials. In spite
of this prospect and the fact that they had respectable *atria*, these medium-range
dwellings could not compete with the lofty residences of the Samnitic upper echelon
such as the House of the Faun (VI.12.2) or the House of Pansa (VI.6), which offered
ample space for peristyles with gardens, for a great variety of private dining and
other reception rooms, and for storage and workforce provisions.

   This situation changes in the first century BC, when one or, more often, two lower-
level stories are built on massive substructures and eight of the original nineteen

houses[11] are united to form four (nos. 12/13, 14/16, 29/30 and 36/37), yielding a total of fifteen houses. Surface area was often doubled or tripled, causing the number of rooms to equal or even surpass that of the Samnitic mansions (e.g., thirty-five to forty rooms in no. 29/30; about fifty in no. 36/37). The pre-existing ground floor was generally rebuilt and slightly extended backwards, so as to cover the entire surface up to the outward edge of the city wall; it could now be wholly reserved for the *atrium/tablinum* and its annexes, while lower levels were assigned other functions. The first floor was generally the *bel-étage*, featuring a series of elegant private reception rooms with segmental or barrel vaults, at once a structural necessity and an aesthetic device still rare in private houses at the time. The houses in their new shape offered all sorts of refined amenities esteemed by the urban elite: bathrooms, marble lintels and moldings, wall paintings, mosaic and *opus signinum* floors, sometimes even a nursery fish-pond or a grotto-*triclinium*, features desired by owners of large villas (and hitherto unknown in town-houses). Lower stories were accessible either via vaulted corridors along the left or right sides of the houses or, where the steep hillside did not permit, by a staircase. There can be no doubt that these reconstructions, which hid large parts of the city walls, took place already in the late republican period.[12] A considerable number of wall paintings of the mature Second Style were found scattered over the south and west terrace houses. The typologically identifiable walls or fragments belong to the mature phase of this Style, and should not be dated prior to *c*.50 BC.[13] This implies that two or three decades may have elapsed after the arrival of the colonists before domestic terraces began to be built on a large scale, following the example of the temple of Venus Pompeiana erected during the second quarter of the first century BC (cf. Ling, Ch. 9; Westfall, Ch. 10; Small, Ch. 13). Indeed, the city wall was only gradually covered; lower-level extensions of some smaller houses (nos. 26 and 28) were realized as late as the Julio-Claudian period.

The picture becomes much more differentiated in the imperial period. Some houses are modernized without further extensions, while others climb farther downhill by the addition of another terrace. Upper stories, occasionally present in the first century BC, now become the rule, yielding a total of five main levels in some cases.[14] Three large (nos. 12/13, 14/16 and 29/30) and six small houses (nos. 1, 3, 5, P, 26 and 28) probably continue to exist as single-family dwellings. The remaining six houses are split up into apartments, let or sold[15] for living (on the lower stories) or commercial purposes (at the ground level). This tendency appears to have intensified after the earthquake of AD 62, as it did in other parts of the city. In the early imperial period the enormous six-storied Sarno bath complex (nos. 17–21) was built at the southwestern corner (cf. Koloski-Ostrow, Ch. 15), together with the adjacent *palaestra* (no. 23) that occupies a third of the *insula*'s surface.[16] Its top three floors contained apartments for several families.

The urban terrace house-type built on steeply sloping ground or pre-existing city walls is best attested at Pompeii, but is also known elsewhere.[17] The hills of Rome, for example, and especially the Palatine as the center of elite habitation in the late Republic, induced architects to find special solutions similar to those that enabled the walled edge of Pompeii's steep lava bed to be used as building-ground. Elements both of the *atrium* house and of the Roman villa manifest themselves in the terrace house, which consequently should be considered a typically Roman creation. The result of this reciprocal influence is a peculiarly mixed building type, which might be called a "reduced urban villa." Janus-faced, they looked like a traditional *atrium* house from the street, while providing most amenities of a suburban villa in their back premises, partly situated on lower levels.

Already the second century BC saw the development of the villa as a new architectural type befitting the lifestyle of Roman grandees.[18] The suburban villas built at the same time outside the walls of Pompeii, of which the Villa of the Mysteries may be the most famous example, probably served as an immediate model for several components of the terrace houses. Roman villas and their gardens are characteristically embedded in the landscape, with multiple vistas created where possible, preferably of sea and shoreline.[19] Often their physically and functionally heterogeneous parts are distributed over different levels, interconnected by colonnades, sloping terraces, steps and corridors. Differences in height lead to extensive use of basements, retaining walls and vaulted substructions, the latter mostly featuring cisterns and sometimes cryptoporticoes, not to mention all sorts of façade elements to cover up differences in the appearance of the building volumes. Similar experience, but on a much larger scale, was gained in the construction of terrace sanctuaries such as that of Fortuna at Praeneste (mid-second century BC).[20]

Terrace houses offered additional benefits when compared to their counterparts in the inner city. Foremost among these extras were stunning views from elegant private reception rooms, generally located on the lower levels. Another major advantage offered by their peculiar layout has so far gone unnoticed but becomes evident if we turn to recent insights on the use of social space in the Roman elite house.[21] In Roman upper-class residences, architectural space was structured according to social function. With due allowance for the flexible use of space and to uncertainties in the ancient nomenclature of specific rooms (cf. Allison, Ch. 17),[22] two major distinctions can be made. The first is between the area open to a more general public, especially the lower-status dependents of the *dominus* (especially the *vestibulum*, *fauces*, *atrium*, *tablinum* and peristyle) and the area of reception rooms (*oeci*, *triclinia*, *cubicula*, etc.) to which only invited guests (*amici*, *familiares*) had access. Roughly speaking, the division is between *negotium* and *otium*, the Roman elite house being at once the nucleus of the *dominus'* socio-political life and his refuge from it. Individual rooms occupy their place on a hierarchical scale, both by function and in the house as a whole, ranging from public to private and from elegant to plain. Transitions between the two areas may be fluid. The second distinction is between these two family-and-reception quarters on the one hand, and servile areas, transitory corridors, kitchens, storerooms etc. on the other. The latter were mostly assigned a marginal location reflecting their low status. These main groups were set off from each other by means of differences in room types; contrasts were enhanced by variation in architectural and painted decoration (or the reduction of these to a basic level in the utilitarian area; see Figure 20.1). Wall painting by its sheer variety in formal schemes also allowed for subtle distinctions within each of these areas, marking the more or less privileged status of one room relative to other rooms, yet unifying the whole domestic space by means of a common formal vocabulary.

In most town houses the three vital functional areas (public, invitation-only and service) had to be located mostly on the ground level. In the case of the terrace houses, however, the addition of new stories enabled owners to create a vertical separation of functionally different parts of the household. With few exceptions, there is a neat division between "public" space concentrated on the ground floor and directly accessible from the street, and private reception rooms located on the first floor; floors further downwards either offered additional space for representation or were, more often, assigned specific utilitarian functions. The humble rooms were situated below ground level and were always tucked away in the dark inner areas near the city wall. Leading privileged guests through winding stair-wells or long vaulted corridors to elegant rooms invisible to the average visitor—then suddenly presenting them with a landscape panorama—may have been considered by owners a major charm of their houses.

Discussion of one particular house may add concrete form to these general outlines. Clearly the residences in their re-designed shape of the first century BC represent the new architectural type in its purest form. Therefore, the focus will be on this period in the following example. The House of Joseph II (VIII.2.38–39) (Figures 26.3, 26.4 and 26.5), immediately adjacent to the Triangular Forum, was built in the third quarter of the second century BC.[23] In its original shape the main room was a large Tuscanic *atrium* (b) with tufa *impluvium* and travertine door-lintels. The *atrium*'s prominence was stressed by engaged tufa half- and quarter-columns on plinths, crowned with Corinthian capitals articulating the small wall surfaces left free by the openings or doors to the surrounding rooms and *alae* (g, h). The house was symmetrically designed, with the entrance area and *tablinum* (r) on axis at opposite ends of the *atrium*. Two corridors (q, t–u) flanking the *tablinum* gave access to the back premises, which already in this early stage must have enjoyed a panoramic view. Presumably an open colonnade gave access to a narrow terrace, which may have been connected with a somewhat larger lower terrace built over the city wall by steps on the west side.

Figure 26.3 House of Joseph II (VIII.2.38–39): view from the south; Noack and Lehmann-Hartleben, *Baugeschichtliche*, Taf. 32.1.

413

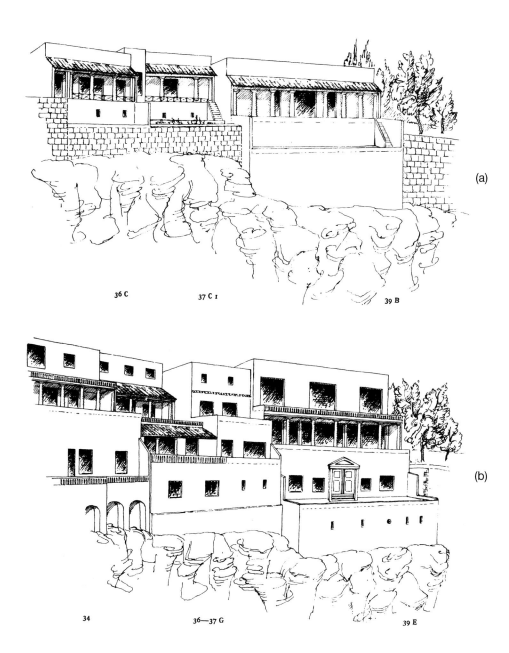

Figure 26.4 House of Joseph II (VIII.2.38–39) and adjacent houses: view from the south as reconstructed by Lehmann-Hartleben. (a) mid-first century BC; (b) mid-first century AD; Noack and Lehmann-Hartleben, *Baugeschichtliche*, Taf. 21.

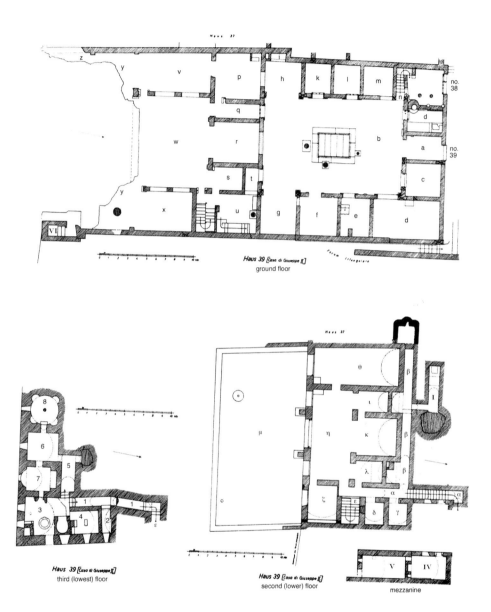

Figure 26.5 House of Joseph II (VIII.2.38–39): plan of the successive stories; after Noack and Lehmann-Hartleben, *Baugeschichtliche*, Taf. 3.

415

In the first century BC, the house was expanded by the reconstruction of the *tablinum* area and the addition of two lower stories. The *tablinum* now opened onto a spacious room (w) flanked by two oblong rooms (v, x) connected to it by doors and windows. The southern part is not preserved; it was probably built from light materials in order not to overload the vaults of the lower story. A colonnade, as reconstructed by Lehmann-Hartleben (Figure 26.4a), opened up to a view over the Sarno. This symmetrical suite of large rooms is, in all probability, a reception area accessible to the same broad category of visitors who were allowed to enter the *fauces*, *atrium* and *tablinum* located on the same axis. The central room (w) was either open (substituting for a proper peristyle) or, more probably, roofed to resemble a basilica like the *oecus Aegyptius* from the House of the Mosaic Atrium in Herculaneum (IV.1–2).[24] As in the *atrium* (c-f, k-m), small lateral rooms (p, s) may have provided more private space when necessary, e.g., to conduct business of a confidential nature or for rest.[25] Room (u) was transformed into a twofold stairwell giving access to the second (lower) storey, with one stair leading directly to the latter's reception area and the other, presumably a "servants-stair," to the back corridor and adjacent utilitarian rooms.

The symmetrically designed nucleus of the second lower story is a large central *triclinium* (κ) flanked by two smaller *cubicula* (ι, λ); (ι) directly communicates with (κ) to form a two-room suite of a type frequently found in elite habitations of the time.[26] The central hall (η) in front of these rooms also communicates with the two other elegant rooms on this floor (ζ, θ). On the outside terrace (μ), the broad central door is accentuated by two columns and was, perhaps, crowned by a pediment; together with two relatively small windows on each side it forms a rhythmically articulated symmetrical façade, stressing the distinguished place of the central *triclinium* (κ). The southern part of the second floor is certainly the house's most privileged area, used only by the *dominus* and his family and offering him a choice of five chambers in which to entertain specially invited guests. Each room enjoyed a splendid view over the Sarno Valley through its own framed opening. Limiting the size of a landscape view by an architectural frame that creates a quasi-pictorial image adapted to the "visual cone" thought to underlie human visual faculty, was considered a special effect by contemporary Romans, as noted in Cicero's deliberations with his architect Kyros, and reported to his friend Atticus.[27]

The remaining rooms of this floor serve utilitarian purposes and are situated in the darker back part, along the vaulted corridors (α) and (β). Between the ground floor and the second story are five *mezzanino* chambers (I–V; II and III are located above (ι) and (λ), which have lower vaults than the central *triclinium* (κ)) accessible only by ladders. They were storage rooms, perhaps also used as servants' sleeping rooms.[28] A bath-complex and a bakery occupied the third and lowest floor: the cupola room (8) is the *frigidarium*, originally featuring a central fountain, (6) the *apodyterium/ tepidarium* and (7) the *caldarium*, adjacent to *praefurnium*/bakery (3).

Due to several reconstructions in the course of the first century AD, this spacious house lost much of its grandeur, especially on the ground floor. The precise implication of many alterations, which defy detailed enumeration, remains unclear. The passage from *atrium* (b) to *tablinum* (r) was walled up, the *atrium* was bereft of its colonnade, the lateral *cubicula* were converted to storerooms, and in the northwest corner a shop (at no. 38) was built in with a door accessing the *atrium*. The construction of steps in (e), (n) and (u) points to the existence of an upper story now completely lost. Possibly it consisted of lodgings for the occupants of the ground floor, which was apparently used for commercial purposes. The two lower floors seem to have been left intact to a large degree and may have continued to function as a luxurious residence, with some new utilitarian facilities built in.

Might the architectural modifications of the terrace houses reflect developments in the socio-political situation? First come reconstructions in the course of the first century BC, which result in large elite residences grown out of modest habitations. The decision to build over the wall can probably be connected with the city's new colonial status, but this does not imply that the dwellings on the city edge were mainly inhabited by the veteran newcomers. Some members of the new mixed elite acquired pre-existing houses that could be expanded to meet the representative demands befitting a member of the new political aristocracy. Political peer rivalry was a feature especially typical of the late republic, even on an urban level; this was the time when municipal charters were issued obliging the *decuriones* to maintain private dwellings of a considerable minimum size.[29]

A further shift took place in the early imperial period, at least in *insula* (VIII.2), which—from a homogeneous residential district removed from the tumult of the main streets—developed into a more crowded quarter of socially and functionally mixed character. Some houses retained, and partly augmented, their former grandeur. But they now neighboured houses sheltering large apartments as well as commercial establishments surmounted by modest lodgings, as well as vast public utilitarian buildings (e.g., the Sarno Baths) that included autonomous living units of varying size and status. Recent research has shown that changes such as these cannot be considered the result of an ever-increasing decline of Pompeii's leading class, allegedly culminating in a crisis and a take-over of power by a plebeian "mercantile class" in the city's last decades. Instead, a stable elite constantly cared for its structural renewal by incorporating new families to compensate for demographic fluctuations; no rigid distinction between income from landed property and from commercial activities can be made (cf. Jongman, Ch. 32).[30] As to *insula* (VIII.2), it now featured a much broader choice of living accommodation, including a new category: large apartments with (part of the) grand rooms-cum-view once built for multi-tiered luxury houses. Far from pointing to the social decline of some "class," such housing likely met the demands of well-off families (freedmen or others belonging to the subdecurional level) who could dispense with, or simply could not afford, a complete *atrium* house. At the same time, housing at the top of the scale surpassed everything Pompeii had seen before. A telling example is the appointment of the palatial House of M. Fabius Rufus (VII.16.22) on the western edge, which testifies to the unprecedented wealth of individual *domini* even in the post-earthquake years.[31]

The broadening spectrum of housing conditions, which can also be observed in other parts of the city (cf. Jones and Robinson, Ch. 25),[32] apparently reflects the increasing social mobility (on all levels) that took place in the course of the first century AD. More individuals belonging to lower status groups were in the position to live on their own in smaller apartments, while a growing number of those higher on the scale could afford to strive for, and occasionally attain, the standards set by the nearby villas of Roman grandees.

NOTES

1 On the Greek city wall, first built in the fifth century BC, see Chiaramonte, Ch. 11; also E. La Rocca, M. De Vos and A. De Vos, *Guida archeologica di Pompei*, Verona, 1976, pp. 85–90. The symbolic meaning of Pompeii's walls is emphasized by R. Laurence (*Roman Pompeii. Space and society*, London, 1994, p. 138), who, however, does not take into account their altered function in the first centuries BC/AD. The use of *spolia* from the walls to serve as filler for the foundations of terraces seems hardly compatible, for this period, with Laurence's view of the walls as symbols of sanctified city boundaries. It should be noted, however, that some Samnian and Campanian cities at about the same time replaced their old polygonal walls with new fortifications built in typically Roman *opus quadratum*, thus "making a visible statement about their new, Romanized, cultural identity" (K. Lomas, "The idea of a city: élite ideology and the evolution of urban form in Italy, 200 BC–AD 100," in H. M. Parkins (ed.), *Roman Urbanism. Beyond the consumer city*, London, 1997, p. 34, with refs).

2 See Laurence, *Roman Pompeii*, pp. 20–7, R. Ling, *Pompeii: history, life and afterlife*, Stroud, 2005, and P. Zanker, *Pompeji. Stadtbild und Wohngeschmack*, Mainz, 1995, pp. 68–85 for convenient surveys.

3 There seems to have been some initial contention between the Pompeians and the newcomers (Cic., *Sull.* 60–61), but recent research has shown that the latter were integrated into rather than excluded from the new political organization: Laurence, *Roman Pompeii*, pp. 22–3, with refs, notably H. Mouritsen, *Elections, Magistrates and Municipal Elite. Studies in Pompeian epigraphy*, Rome, 1988, pp. 85–9.

4 For the following see: F. Noack and K. Lehmann-Hartleben, *Baugeschichtliche Untersuchungen am Stadtrand von Pompeji*, Berlin, 1936, VII–X; A. Allroggen-Bedel, "Die Malereien aus dem Haus Insula Occidentalis, 10," *CronPomp*, 1976, vol. 2, pp. 144–83; G. Cerulli Irelli, "Le case di M. Fabio Rufo e di C. Giulio Polibio," in *Pompei 1748–1980. I tempi della documentazione*, Rome, 1981, pp. 22–3; V. Kockel, "Archäologische Funde und Forschungen in den Vesuvstädten II," *AA*, 1986, pp. 507–16; V. M. Strocka, "Pompeji VI 17,41: Ein Haus mit Privatbibliothek," *RM* 1993, vol. 100, pp. 321–51, esp. pp. 321–2.

5 It is indicative of the slow pace of Pompeian studies that only recently have other publications of a Pompeian *insula* appeared: M. Bonghi Jovino *et al.*, *Ricerche a Pompei: L'insula 5 della Regio VI dalle origini al 79 d.C.*, 2 vols, Rome, 1984; R. Ling *et al.*, *The Insula of the Menander at Pompeii*, Oxford, 1997, vol. I; 2002, vol. 4; 2005, vol. 2; 2007, vol. 3; F. Coarelli and F. Pesando, *Rileggere Pompei: L'insula 10 della Regio VI*, Rome, 2006.

6 Survey in Kockel, "Funde II," pp. 507–16, with references. Some of the activities have not even been documented at all: see the disconcerting statements reported by V. M. Strocka, "Pompeji VI 17, 41," p. 322, n. 8. Cf. Foss, Ch. 3 for the bombardment.

7 Cerulli Irelli, "Le case"; A. and M. De Vos, *Pompei, Ercolano, Stabia*, Rome-Bari, 1982, p. 224; A. Barbet, *La peinture murale romaine. Les styles décoratifs pompéiens*, Paris, 1985, pp. 242–7; Kockel, "Funde II," pp. 508–13.

8 Room 71: G. P. Carratelli and I. Baldassarre (eds), *Pompei, pitture e mosaici*, Rome, 1998, vol. 8, pp. 1106–12, nos. 317–24; Cerulli Irelli, "Le case," p. 31 figs 17/18 and p. 140 fig. 3; Kockel, "Funde II," pp. 511–12; R. A. Tybout, *Aedificiorum figurae. Untersuchungen zu den Architekturdarstellungen des frühen zweiten Stils*, Amsterdam, 1989, pp. 262–3 and pl. 68. Only the upper part is visible; the lower part is now covered (or destroyed?) by a later wall erected immediately before it for unknown reasons. The latter is presumably a Fourth-Style wall imitating the architectural scheme of its predecessor.

9 Noack and Lehmann-Hartleben, *Baugeschichtliche*, pp. 161–88; cf. De Vos, *Pompei, Ercolano, Stabia*, pp. 56–9; Zanker, *Pompeji*, pp. 80–2.

10 Recent excavations have shown that Regions VII and VIII were built in the second century BC, replacing fourth-century houses which in its turn substituted pre-existing settlement presumably of the second half of the seventh century BC: P. Carafa, "What was Pompeii before 200 BC? Excavations in the House of Joseph II, in the Triangular Forum and in the House of the Wedding of Hercules," in S. E. Bon and R. Jones (eds), *Sequence and Space in Pompeii*, Oxbow Monograph no. 77, Oxford, 1997, esp. pp. 25–9; P. Carafa and M. T. D'Alessio, "Lo scavo nella Casa di Giuseppe II (VIII, 2, 38–39) e nel portico occidentale del Foro Triangolare a Pompei. Rapporto preliminare," *RStPomp*, 1995/1996 [1998], vol. 7, pp. 137–53.

11 Including the houses south of the forum not situated on the edge, and consequently without terraces or a panoramic view.

12 *Contra* L. Richardson, jr, *Pompeii. An architectural history*, Baltimore, MD, 1988, p. 231: "none of the terraces built over the city walls will have been republican," which lacks compelling arguments and neglects the presence of Second-Style wall paintings.

13 A relatively complete set of Second-Style paintings (*c.*40–35 BC) is preserved in a house at the center of the *Insula Occidentalis* (VI.17.41): Strocka, "Pompeji VI 17, 41"; Carratelli and Baldassare, *Pompei, pitture e mosaici*, 1996, vol. 6, pp. 10–43, nos. 1–73. The Second-Style wall in the House of Fabius Rufus (VII.16.22) discussed above (Figure 26.2) should probably be dated somewhat earlier (*c.*45–40 BC). For the (fragments of) Second-Style walls without vistas, i.e., the schemes with colonnades fronting a closed back wall, those reproducing masonry or marble veneer, and decorations in two zones or with simple linear patterns, see E. Heinrich, *Der zweite Stil in pompejanischen Wohnhäusern*, Munich, 2002, pp. 112–13 nos. 64–7 (House VI.17.41); pp. 113–14 nos. 68–70 (VI.17.42: House of the Golden Bracelet); pp. 123–7 nos. 88–92 and p. 145 nos. 126–7 (VII 16.12–15: House of A. Umbricius Scaurus); p. 127 no. 93 and pp. 152–3 nos. 143–4 (VII.16.16–17: House of M. Castricius); pp. 127–30 nos. 94–130 (VII.16.22: House of M. Fabius Rufus); pp. 130–2 nos. 98–9 and p. 153 no. 145 (VIII.2.1: House of Championnet); p. 132 no. 100, pp. 145–6 no. 128 and p. 154 no. 146 (VIII.2.34–35: House of the Mosaic Doves); pp. 132–3 no. 101 and p. 156 no. 149 (VIII.2.38–39: House of Joseph II); pp. 154–5 nos. 147–8 (House VIII.2.36–37). Walls including complex architectural vistas are exclusively found in private reception rooms, mostly situated on the lower floors (see below): Heinrich, *Der zweite Stil*, pp. 56 (with n. 665), 59 (with n. 690), and 65; this confirms the argument of R. A. Tybout, "Malerei und Raumfunktion im zweiten Stil," in E. M. Moormann (ed.), *Functional and Spatial Analysis of Wall Painting. Proceedings of the Fifth International Congress on Ancient Wall Painting*, BABesch Suppl. no. 3, Leiden, 1993, pp. 38–50, based on four other Second-Style complexes.

14 The presence of a *mezzanino* occasionally adds up the number of levels to six.

15 There is no compelling evidence for the suggestion of Noack and Lehmann-Hartleben, *Baugeschichtliche*, p. 184, that a considerable part of the *insula* (near the Triangular Forum) fell into the hands of one speculator who converted houses to let them out in apartments.

16 A. Koloski Ostrow, *The Sarno Bath Complex*, Rome, 1990.

17 For the following, see Noack and Lehmann-Hartleben, *Baugeschichtliche*, pp. 188–236. For building on walls, e.g., in Rome and Formia, see pp. 168, 189–90, 204. In Herculaneum, parts of the House of the Mosaic Atrium (IV.1–2) and the House of the Stags (IV.21) both large houses with seaside views, were built on the city's former ramparts: J. R. Clarke, *The Houses of Roman Italy, 100 BC–AD 250. Ritual, space, and decoration*, Berkeley, CA, 1991, pp. 21, 235–50; Dickmann, Ch. 27; Figure 27.5.

18 For surveys see J. D'Arms, *Romans on the Bay of Naples*, Cambridge, MA, 1970; H. Mielsch, *Die römische Villa. Architektur und Lebensform*, Munich, 1987.

19 Clarke, *Houses of Roman Italy*, pp. 19–23, with references; B. Bergmann, "Painted perspectives of a villa visit: landscape as status and metaphor," in E. K. Gazda (ed.), *Roman Art in the Private Sphere. New perspectives on the architecture and decor of the domus, villa, and insula*, Ann Arbor, MI, 1991, pp. 49–70.

20 H. Lauter, "Bemerkungen zur späthellenistischen Baukunst in Mittelitalien," *JdI*, 1979, vol. 94, pp. 390–459, esp. 390–415.

21 A. Wallace-Hadrill, *Houses and Society in Pompeii and Herculaneum*, Princeton, NJ, 1994, pp. 1–61; J.-A. Dickmann, *Domus frequentata. Anspruchsvolles Wohnen im pompejanischen Stadthaus*, Munich, 1999; R. A. Tybout, "Roman wall-painting and social significance," *JRA*, 2001, vol. 14, pp. 33–56, esp. 42–53 (for further literature see pp. 33–4, nn. 2, 4 and 6).

22 P. M. Allison, "How do we identify the use of space in Roman housing?" in Moormann, *Functional and Spatial Analysis*, pp. 1–8; M. George, "Repopulating the Roman House," in B. Rawson and P. Weaver (eds), *The Roman Family in Italy*, Oxford, 1997, pp. 299–319; L. Nevett, "Perceptions of domestic space in Roman Italy," in Rawson and Weaver, *Roman Family*, pp. 281–98; E. W. Leach, 1997, "Oecus on Ibycus: investigating the vocabulary of the Roman house," in Bon and Jones, *Sequence and Space*, pp. 50–72. E. W. Leach, *The Social Life of Painting in Ancient Rome and the Bay of Naples*, Cambridge, 2004. See also n. 25 below.

23 For the following, see Noack and Lehmann-Hartleben, *Baugeschichtliche*, pp. 18–30; cf. Richardson, *Pompeii*, pp. 234–40, for a description of the house's latest phase, inaccurate and incorrect in many details. For excavations in and near the house which shed light on earlier settlement, see Carafa, "What was Pompeii?" pp. 15–25.

24 Noack and Lehmann-Hartleben, *Baugeschichtliche*, p. 24, n. 2 point to Mazois' observation that the central room originally featured "eine mittlere Stützenteilung" ("a partition supported in the middle"). See F. Mazois, *Les ruines de Pompéi*, Paris, 1824, vol. 2, p. 73, Pl. XXXII, no. 11 for his plan of this room and this house. For the interpretation of the *oecus* in the House of the Mosaic Atrium in Herculaneum (IV.1–2) as a basilica see Wallace-Hadrill, *Houses and Society*, pp. 18–19, with references; cf. also Dickmann, Ch. 27.

25 In room (s) the mosaic pattern points to a bed-place on the northwestern side. On the flexible use of *cubicula* or similar rooms see A. M. Riggsby, "'Public' and 'private' in Roman culture: the case of the *cubiculum*," *JRA*, 1997, vol. 10, pp. 36–56; Wallace-Hadrill, *Houses and Society*, pp. 17, 57–8, 97 and 219; Leach, "Oecus on Ibycus," pp. 68–70; Nevett, "Perceptions," pp. 290–2.

26 Wallace-Hadrill, *Houses and Society*, pp. 57–60. Clarke, *Houses of Roman Italy*, pp. 94–6, 134–5.

27 L. Balensiefen, "Die 'Kyropädie' des Baumeisters Kyros und die antiken Sehtheorien (zu Cic. Att. II 3, 2)," *JdI*, 1994, vol. 109, pp. 301–19.

28 For the possibilities and problems of locating slave-quarters in the Roman house see M. George, "*Servus* and *domus*: the slave in the Roman house," in R. Laurence and A. Wallace-Hadrill (eds), *Domestic Space in the Roman World: Pompeii and beyond*, JRA Suppl. Ser. no. 22, 1997, pp. 15–24. See also George, Ch. 35.

29 Lomas, "The idea of a city," p. 35, with references.

30 J. D'Arms, *Commerce and Social Standing in Ancient Rome*, Cambridge, MA, 1981; H. Mouritsen, "Mobility and social change in Italian towns during the principate," in Parkins, *Roman Urbanism*, pp. 59–82. For Pompeii, see Mouritsen, *Elections*; A. Łoś, "*Quibus patet curia municipalis*. Remarque sur la structure de la classe dirigeante de Pompei," *Cahiers du Centre G. Glotz*, 1992, vol. III, Paris, pp. 259–97; Wallace-Hadrill, *Houses and Society*, pp. 118–42.

31 Unfortunately, nothing is known about the owner of the house, possibly but not necessarily the otherwise unknown M. Fabius Rufus, whose name was found inscribed on a seal-ring. On the basis of a personalized mosaic floor (AD 25–35) in one of the two secondary *atria*, the nearby split-level *domus* (VII.16.12–15), rebuilt in the early first century AD on a grand scale, can be assigned to A. Umbricius Scaurus, member of a prominent curial family which owed its wealth to the *garum* production. He is one of the very few Pompeian house-owners whose private and public activities can be reconstructed in some detail: R. I. Curtis, "A personalized mosaic floor from Pompeii," *AJA*, 1984, pp. 557–66; R. I. Curtis, "A. Umbricius Scaurus of Pompeii," in R. Curtis (ed.), *Studia pompeiana et classica in honor of W.F. Jashemsky*, New Rochelle, NY, 1988, pp. 19–50; cf. Mouritsen, "Mobility and social change," pp. 63–4. See also Clarke, Ch. 21; Cormack, Ch. 37.

32 For rented apartments see Wallace-Hadrill, *Houses and Society*, pp. 106–10; F. Pirson, *Mietwohnungen in Pompeji und Herkulaneum*, Munich, 1999; F. Pirson, "Rented accommodation at Pompeii: the evidence of the *Insula Arriana Polliana* VI.6," in Laurence and Wallace-Hadrill, *Domestic Space*, pp. 165–81; cf. H. M. Parkins, "The 'consumer city' domesticated? The Roman city in élite economic strategies," in Parkins, *Roman Urbanism*, pp. 103–7. For literary sources concerning apartments (*cenacula*), also of considerable luxury: Wallace-Hadrill, *Houses and Society*, pp. 103–6; Nevett, "Perceptions," p. 294. See also Cic., *Cael.* 17 (on high rents) and Vitr., *De arch.* 2.8.17, testifying to the fact that excellent views were considered among the advantages of apartments on higher floors. See also Pirson, Ch. 29.

CHAPTER TWENTY-SEVEN

RESIDENCES IN HERCULANEUM

———•◆•———

Jens-Arne Dickmann

According to Dionysius of Halikarnassos (*Antiq. Rom.* 1.44), Herculaneum is named after its founder, Hercules, and Strabo writes (5.4.8) that it was occupied first by Oscans, then by Tyrrhenians, Pelasgians and finally by Samnites. That is all the information we have about the prehistory of the settlement from the ancient literary sources. It is not until the first century BC that Herculaneum appears again in the sources, when its citizens rebelled against Rome side by side with other cities. Herculaneum, like Pompeii, was besieged and taken; unlike Pompeii, however, Herculaneum was given only the rights of a *municipium* and was not elevated to the rank of a Roman colony. During the course of the later first century BC and the early empire, the city attracted wealthy businessmen of Campania and the highest officials in Rome, who used it as a summer retreat or settled there permanently.

The city apparently owed its popularity to its location and a healthy climate (according to Strabo, 5.4.8), as well as the proximity of Neapolis, a city influenced by Greek culture. The ancient author Sisenna (Fragments 53–54) mentions the mountain ledge on which the city was originally located and two rivers flowing around it to the north and south. Due to a relative drop of the water level by 4 to 5 m, today's situation has changed substantially. Even if there is still an impressive view from the excavation site, the antique situation and these landmarks can be imagined only with some help of the first plans drawn in the eighteenth century.

Since Herculaneum was not covered with lava like Pompeii, but was, instead, buried under a layer of mud over 10 m deep, and because the resulting ridge has been occupied since the Middle Ages at the latest, excavations at Herculaneum have progressed with great difficulty. For this reason, we do not know the exact dimensions of the city or the location of the city wall, about which Sisenna informs us. According to the latest studies, the city extended over roughly 320 m by 350 m; that is, about one-third the size of Pompeii.[1] The section excavated to date is concentrated in the west-southwest and covers about one-fourth of the original territory of the city. Aside from the question of the main entrances to the city and its connection to the secondary road from Naples to Pompeii, we would be particularly interested to know where the city center (the forum) was located, what it looked like, and whether it was surrounded by public buildings.

A first glance at the city plan (Map 4) reveals important characteristics of the infrastructure and development of the terrain ("Map North" for directions in this chapter is at the left). With the exception of small deviations, the urban plan is based on an orthogonal grid system of streets running nearly at right angles. Selective archaeological excavations, which have studied parts of the street grid, indicate that it dates back to the fourth century BC.[2] Scholars have therefore seen influence from the Greek urban plan of Naples. Two of the original *decumani* (probably out of three) have been partially excavated, as have three of the original *cardines*, of which there were presumably five. The axis to the east of the excavated area was designated the *decumanus maximus* by Amedeo Maiuri, the most prominent excavator of Herculaneum. Maiuri called it the main street of the city because of its great width. It is adjacent to important civic buildings, such as the seat of the *augustales* (E, VI.21), the basilica (D), and the eastern complex which has most recently been identified as the *Augusteum*.[3] Thus, although we do not know the exact location of the forum, it is clear that the excavated sector lies in immediate proximity to what was the city center. Further evidence of centrality is the fact that all the streets, with the exception of two very small stretches, are lined with sidewalks. A comparison with Pompeii shows that sidewalks were used only near main streets and thoroughfares with heavy traffic. However, differences are also revealed upon closer examination. Wheel ruts, which indicate more intensive vehicular traffic, are found only along the *decumanus inferior* and on *cardo* V near the *palaestra*. This pattern corresponds to the distribution of commercial establishments, workshops, snack bars and restaurants,[4] which not only lined the streets where the wheel ruts were found, but also were concentrated along the *decumanus maximus*. The western sections of the *cardines* and *cardo* IV seem to have experienced less heavy wagon transport and delivery traffic. Such distinctions must have been nuanced, as the location of the baths and their heating system (VI.10) shows. Usually stokeholes had to be supplied by heavy traffic.

In comparison with modern cities, one aspect of Herculaneum is particularly remarkable. In spite of the many stores, workshops and public buildings, this vibrant sector of the city was primarily residential. Small, humble houses are juxtaposed with large urban villas that come close to exceeding the urban scale. While humble units afforded little more than 100 m², the great peristyle houses at the western edge of the city easily took up ten times that much space. At the time of the eruption of Vesuvius in AD 79, we can therefore rule out the existence of separate residential quarters for people from different social classes in Herculaneum, just as in Pompeii. Both the owners of large peristyle houses and the tenants of rented apartments in the upper stories were residents of the same street. A more detailed examination of individual houses shows that this situation resulted from a series of purchases and ongoing structural modifications.

The enormous differences in scale, the diversity in spatial configurations and the wide divergence in quality of the furnishings all present archaeologists and historians with not insignificant problems. The archaeological record does not reveal any hard and fast rules for residential design, much less a model house. Therefore, it is difficult to attempt the estimation of the status and social standing of a resident based on the history of the construction and use of his dwelling. A. Wallace-Hadrill, in his careful examination of Maiuri's arguments, has undermined the assumption that house forms were clearly structured and tied to social class.[5] Differentiating between a house with or without an *atrium*, for example, or one with a closed roof (*testudinatum*) as opposed to one with a central roof opening and *impluvium* (*tuscanicum*), does not provide enough information to give us detailed insights into the relative social status of various residents. For this reason, we should avoid the study of houses according to convenient typological architectural criteria, at least for social questions (cf. Allison, Ch. 17; Wallace-Hadrill, Ch. 18).

On the other hand, it is easy to read details of the urban plan and to consider particular motivations behind the divisions of *insulae* as they existed in AD 79. It appears that the blocks were usually divided in half from east to west; then they were subdivided into properties of more or less the same width. The measurements obtained by Dutch archaeologists have shown that, with the exception of the great peristyle houses, house façades generally varied between about 20 to 40 ft wide, suggesting a relatively consistent original plan for *insulae*.[6] The eastern halves of the quarters adjacent to the *decumanus maximus*, on the other hand, do not appear to have been divided in half, but rather to have been subdivided lengthwise into several parcels, so that houses there did not open onto one of the *cardines* but, rather, onto the *decumanus* itself. We can compare this situation to that of several *insulae* in the eastern section of the via dell'Abbondanza in Pompeii (I.8–9, 11–13; see Map 3).

A house such as the House of the Black Salon (VI.13), which can be attributed with certainty to the *augustalis* L. Venidius Ennychus on the basis of the discovery of an archive, demonstrates that influential men were interested in securing prominent locations near the center or on busy streets for the construction of their own houses. The plans of the House of the Black Salon and the House of the Tuscan Colonnade next door (VI.16–18) suggest, on the other hand, that *atrium* houses may have existed here previously, which were only later expanded and provided with a peristyle.[7] The original residential houses on the west side of the *decumanus* appear to have been relatively small.

We must briefly examine one difference between Herculaneum and her neighbor, Pompeii. In Herculaneum, to this date, no traces have been found of lavish façades made of tufa masonry which signal the great residences of an urban ruling class, such as contributed significantly to the economic heyday in Pompeii during the second century BC. Since even the theater, the oldest public building found in Herculaneum to date, was not constructed until the Augustan era, it becomes apparent that the city did not experience the boom observable in her southern neighbor either during the late Samnite period, or directly before the bestowal of municipal rights in 89 BC. This observation corresponds to an extremely small number of fragments of pre-Augustan wall painting, which also suggest an economic upturn only in the early imperial period.

However, there do seem to have been individual exceptions. The construction history of the recently studied Samnite House (V.1) reveals that the house must originally have been roughly twice as large, if not even larger, and possibly even extended as far as the south side of the *insula* (Map 4).[8] Accordingly, a three-sided peristyle, possibly with a *hortus*, stood at the site of the later House of the Grand Portal (V.35). This is interesting because in no other building in Herculaneum do we find preserved as many, or as qualitatively excellent, remains of wall decoration and furnishings of the First Style (Figure 27.1). The peristyle and also the faux columns with balusters in the upper story of the *atrium* both echo motifs found in

Figure 27.1   Samnite House in Herculaneum (V.1), *atrium* with colonnade on upper story; view northeast. Photo: P. W. Foss.

Hellenistic architecture that give the house the opulence of an urban palace and were also supposed to camouflage its narrowness. The decor taken in its entirety suggests a construction date in the course of the second century or at the latest the early first century BC. In spite of the oblique course of the east wall of the vestibule, one entered a regular *atrium* suite with interior walls placed at right angles and a *tablinum* whose opening was oriented to the axis of the entrance. A corridor on the west side of the *tablinum* once led to the peristyle area in the back, which consisted only of the colonnade and inner court, with no further rooms to the east. The southern limit of this garden area is not known. The great importance of this peristyle is evident in the fact that a visitor, upon entering the house—assuming that no shutters or curtains closed off the view—could have immediately glimpsed it through a window that originally opened in the rear wall of the *tablinum*.

During the course of the first century, the building was divided, and through a series of events that are not yet fully understood, a separate residential house, the House of the Grand Portal, was built on the site of the colonnaded court. The name of the new house refers to its conspicuous entryway, flanked by two brick columns and crowned by a pediment, on the west side of the *insula*.[9] A sidewalk was later laid along the entire extent of the façade; at that time, the *taberna* (V.34) still belonged to the house and was connected to the interior through a door in its north wall. The sidewalk not only marked the extent of the property, but also permitted unhindered access in front of the house and shop. It also indicates that the House of the Grand Portal never owned the southwestern section of the *insula*. The builder appears to have altered the interior of the house by shrinking the old peristyle court and constructing new residential quarters and a kitchen wing to the east. The opulence of the entryway and the high quality of the wall decorations, especially the Dionysiac imagery in the largest of the rooms, justify the assumption that the lack of an *atrium* was hardly seen as a crucial shortcoming.

The House of the Wooden Partition (III.11) is a case of the exact opposite situation. The house had a relatively large *atrium tuscanicum* with *cubicula* and *ala* on the west side and a *tablinum* on axis (Figure 27.2). The simple *cocciopesto* floor of the hall indicates a date in the late republican period, i.e., the first century BC. There is no doubt that

Figure 27.2 House of the Wooden Partition (III.11), view east into the *atrium* with marble table and sliding wooden doors.

atria of this kind were meant to express the pretensions and a certain renown of the owners, compared with smaller houses such as the House of the Brick Altar (III.17) or especially the house across the street, the House of the Painted Papyrus (IV.8). This house was probably considered one of the best in its neighborhood. Then in the early imperial period, the House of the Wooden Partition underwent major changes. The purchase of the parcel to the north and the construction of the peristyle court may have been the occasion for the lavish renovation of the wall decor in the late Third Style, a newly installed fountain in the marble-lined *impluvium*, and the furnishing of the *atrium* and *cubiculum* (2) with marble items (cf. Fant, Ch. 22). During this renovation, the depth of the *tablinum* appears to have been divided in half, as indicated by the size of room (6). Thus it was possible to erect a truncated *porticus* on the south side of the court. The broad opening of the *atrium* onto the peristyle and the possible use of the rear area as living quarters may have led to the erection of the eponymous wooden partition. Depending on the orientation of the *tablinum*, whether to the *atrium* or to the garden, the partition would have been opened or closed. We cannot pinpoint when exactly the workshops and stores on the east side and the north end of the house became integrated into the complex. Nevertheless, they demonstrate that the owners of peristyle houses did not shrink from participation in commercial activities. The owner of the House of the Wooden Partition probably charged a small fee for the use of the small public latrine behind entrance (III.7).

Let us finally turn to the House of the Skeleton (III.3) in order to clarify the extent of the purchases and structural changes in small houses during the first century AD. Its ground plan and its integration into the *insula* as a whole make it easy for us to understand its expansion in two phases. The house originally had only one small *atrium testudinatum* surrounded by rooms on three sides. As we have already observed in the House of the Wooden Partition, the *tablinum* in the House of the Skeleton also appears to have been reduced in size to allow for later installations. Ganschow's studies indicate that the owner first purchased the adjacent long and narrow "strip" house to the east.[10] Its original floor plan can no longer be reconstructed; undoubtedly it had its own entrance onto *cardo* III. Before the earthquake of AD 62, the little neighboring house to the west was also integrated, by means of a narrow corridor. The space was used for a separate residential wing in the southern section and also for a relatively large kitchen and working wing. At about the same time, the owner appears to have removed the original floor plan in the east in order to build *cenatio* (6), a *nymphaeum* with masonry *biclinia*, and a forecourt in between. Behind the *tablinum*, additional work led to the development of a similar ensemble: a dining room with an apse in its rear wall was oriented directly onto a fountain via a broad opening in its west wall. The truncation of the *tablinum* demonstrates how traditional rooms around the *atrium* had lost importance and had to give way to a third banquet room—though rooms (4) and (6) were already being so used. In spite of fundamental structural changes, in AD 79 the House of the Skeleton still had an extremely modest *atrium*, but it contained three *cenationes* independent of one another, and additional residential quarters, the rooms of which were arranged around a separate vestibule (17). The owner's efforts were obviously intended to create the largest possible residential rooms and to present lavishly appointed views. If we compare just the ensemble around *cenatio* (6) with the dimensions of earlier rooms around the *atrium*, then the raised standards of space and decor immediately become apparent.

Figure 27.3   Western side with the House of the Mosaic Atrium (IV.1–2), House of the Stags (IV.21) and House of the Gem (*Ins. Or.* I.1). The altar and tomb of M. Nonius Balbus are lower right.

The houses on the slope along the western edge of the city epitomize this evident transformation, with their great peristyles and loggias and rooms with views that reveal a spectacular panorama over the entire Gulf of Naples (Figure 27.3); cf. Tybout, Ch. 26. As already indicated, these urban villas only developed in the course of substantial purchases of older houses and fundamental structural changes. It should be noted that we know little about previous constructions because the excavations between 1927 and 1958 went down just as far as the most recent strata. Only in the House of the Stags (IV.21) were excavations undertaken (in the 1970s) below the level of the peristyle court. They revealed many-cornered walls and small-scale floor plans similar to the "strip houses" and *atrium* houses in the eastern half of the *insula*.[11] We cannot tell precisely when these additional properties were bought up or when the new construction began. Since the complexes with their substructures extended past the city wall, they can only have been built after the end of the Civil War, i.e., after 89 BC. Indications suggest that construction began not long afterwards.

The largest of these complexes is the so-called House of the Hotel (III.1–2, 18–19). It extended over the entire width of the *insula* and had extensive working quarters in the south as well as two colonnaded and pillared courts. Unfortunately, the western end of the latter is not preserved, so we cannot say anything about the arrangement of the viewing area onto the sea. Two large rooms in the substructure level underneath the courtyard appear to have opened to the west as well, so that an entire series of panoramas was available to the visitor. Connecting the two courtyards was a row of three large rooms and an enormous hall—all had mosaic floors and were oriented onto the eastern peristyle. The number of residential rooms became complete with

Figure 27.4 House of the Hotel (III.1–2), Second-Style decoration in the baths.

a group of rooms adjacent to the eastern *porticus*. The small *atrium* at no. 19 stands in stark contrast, as it retained only the function of a humble lobby. With its small size and uneven distribution of doors, the *atrium* can no longer have functioned as a prestigious foyer. However, it did provide access to the baths belonging to the house, which were usually made available to guests of the house.[12] The high quality of the Second-Style painting here suggests this (Figure 27.4). From Pompeii we know that only a few houses had their own *balnea*, and that baths were thus indicators of a high standard of living (cf. Koloski-Ostrow, Ch. 15). The findings at the House of the Hotel are particularly important because they demonstrate that the development of extensive urban villas at the western edge of Herculaneum were in full swing by the 30s of the first century BC at the latest.

The disruption this process caused is made manifest by at least two phenomena. First, in half of the new urban "palaces," a lavishly furnished *atrium* was dispensed with. This may have something to do with the small dimensions of the previous buildings. Nevertheless, a traditional element of domestic architecture up to that time thereby lost a great deal of its former significance.[13] Second, older walls were entirely, or to a large part, razed in most cases, since they were inadequate to meet the new demands for large spaces and unimpeded vistas. The remodeling was often a combination of demolition and new construction. We do not know who ordered this construction, or the origins of their economic clout. Contemporary dedications by the Balbi (cf. Small, Ch. 13), who came from Nuceria in the south but probably had their seat in Herculaneum, and who donated the city's walls, gates and basilica, among others, lead us to believe that many of the new owners of the western terrace must have recently moved there from outside Herculaneum.

Once it was determined that a famous loaf of bread with a stamp reading (C)ELERIS Q. GRANI/VERI SER[VVS] came from the House of the Stags (IV.21), it became possible to ascribe that house to Q. Granius Verus, at least for the final years before the eruption of Mt Vesuvius.[14] The Granii were probably from Puteoli and were already well known as successful merchants in the first century BC, for example, on Delos.[15] Since its exact date of construction is a matter of controversy, ranging from the earliest imperial period to the reign of Claudius,[16] it cannot be stated with certainty that a Granius originated the remodeling. Even if the house was purchased after the fact, however, the finds show that Herculaneum had lost none of its attractions in AD 79. Only in the entrance area at no. 21 were remains of the older house, with its *atrium testudinatum*, preserved. Banquet room (5) and all other areas were part of the new design. An essential feature of the new floor plan was an axis extending nearly its entire length, which clearly showed a visitor the correspondence of individual living areas to one another. A *cryptoporticus* (A–D) connected the group of rooms in the east (5–8), which had marble floors and polished walls, with the garden rooms (15–17), the *diaetae* (22, 23) and the loggia (18). In the *cryptoporticus* the visitor encountered a peculiarity of the decorative adornment of the house: small wall paintings (*pinakes*) including still-lifes and the colorful antics of little *erotes*.[17] The unusual quality of the paintings and a floor paved with mosaics and *opus sectile* indicate that use of the *cryptoporticus* as a servants' corridor is out of the question. Instead, the *pinakes*, originally 64 in number, adorned the central panels of the architecturally articulated wall panels at regular intervals and accompanied the user on his way to the garden rooms. In between, the *cryptoporticus* is repeatedly lit by windows that permit a brief, limited view of the garden outside. The garden's configuration does not appear to have disclosed its form in its entirety until viewed from room (15); Figure 27.5. In the garden foreground, statues of *Hercules mingens* ("Hercules pissing") and a satyr pouring from a wineskin—probably as a fountain—were arranged together with two stag and hunting dog *symplegmata* ("entwined groups") symmetrically flanking a three-legged marble table, or *mensa delphica*. The rigidity of this arrangement was crowned by a mosaic-clad pediment with a representation of Oceanus and mounted *erotes* that framed the opening of room (5) in the background.[18] As the grandest room in the house, *cenatio* (15) was provided with a marble floor and a dado with marble revetment. To the west, the vista wandered off through the loggia and over the sea. Since this room also had windows on its sides, the occupant had access to views in all directions. Therefore, its incorporation into a suite of three living rooms must have ceased to be perceptible. A *cenatio* of this design typically tried to separate the space from incorporation into adjacent suites of rooms, opening it rather to the landscape in several directions using wide entrances and windows. The later construction of two staircases leading to rooms in the upper story or to a kind of roof terrace via rooms (16) and (17) emphasized the importance of the view. In the other peristyle houses, living areas were also dominated by a particularly large room that must generally be considered a banqueting hall. The artificial *cryptoporticus*, which did not at all lie under the ground level, could also have served a theatrical purpose. From dark corridors that restricted the view one entered the *cenatio*, whose openness on all sides then became all the more impressive. It can hardly be doubted that the master of the house meant to place himself on the stage in this way.

Figure 27.5   House of the Stags (IV.21), view from
room (15) towards room (5) to the east.

The same is naturally also true of the neighboring houses to the north and south,
the House of the Mosaic Atrium (IV.1–2), the House of the Relief of Telephus (*Ins.
Or.* I.2–3), and the House of the Gem (*Ins. Or.* I.1). In contrast to the two urban villas
discussed so far, these retained the *atrium* and decorated it lavishly with rows of columns
and pilasters. The room located along the entrance axis of the House of the Mosaic
Atrium has achieved special fame and is generally known to archaeologists as the
only example of an *oecus aegyptius* as in—or at least similar to—Vitruvius' description
(*De arch.* 6.3.8–9; but cf. Tybout, Ch. 26). The inconspicuous door that led into the
fenestrated *porticus* without creating a prominent transition shows how isolated the

atrium remained from the rest of the house. The *porticus* was broad on three sides, but narrowed to a tight corridor that accessed a row of rooms. The central chamber (9), which extended out into the garden with a kind of terrace, was especially painted with exquisite decorations of a vibrant blue color in the Fourth Style. On the south side, instead of masonry walls pierced by windows, there was a system of frames made of wood that originally held panes of glass. These provided ample illumination to the adjacent rooms and, at the same time, opened the view to the garden area in the middle of which a fountain played in a marble-lined pool. However, the real viewing area was to the west and included the rooms as well as two small *diaetae* (23, 24) at the ends of the *porticus*. Their projecting position as corner or wing rooms and their location isolated from the banquet halls, in an arrangement similar to that found in the House of the Gem (*Ins. Or.* I.1) and the House of the Stags (IV.21), appear to have been highly prized for the purpose of creating serene cubicles embedded against the landscape.

At the House of *Opus Craticium* (III.13–15), in the immediate vicinity of these urban villas, we can observe the opposite process: the property was divided up into very small but still rentable bits which had upper stories to offer minimal living standards.[19] These units are better preserved under their layers of mud than the upper stories of Pompeii, which collapsed under the weight of the lava flows. The House of *Opus Craticium*'s location within *insula* (III) reveals that its original form probably comprised a small *atrium* house. The building has aroused a great deal of interest because its construction rests on a grid of supporting pillars. Thereupon the walls were erected in a technique similar to half-timbering, and not just in the upper story—a technique described as *opus craticium* by Vitruvius (*De arch.* 2.8.20; Figure 8.13). Other than economic reasons, the decision to use half-timbering was probably motivated by the amount of space that could be saved in the already very narrow plot by building extremely thin walls. The façade, with its three entrances, immediately signaled a multi-use character for the building (Figure 27.6).

A *taberna* with several back rooms sat to the left side of the hallway leading into the interior. On the right, a staircase led directly to the upper story and a rather dark apartment consisting of five rooms, of which only two were lit by windows onto the *atrium* of the House of the Bronze Herm (III.16) next door to the west. Remains of wooden wardrobes and two beds, including a child's bed, were preserved, together with a marble table and a marble plaque for hanging (*oscillum*). These demonstrate that efforts at a high-class decor, even in such humble circumstances, resorted to similar equipment as found in urban villas, even where the appropriate context (such as an inner courtyard or garden) was not present. The builder integrated the balcony (*maenianum*) onto the street in a clever manner, by moving the entrances to the two outer rooms onto the exterior of the house. As a result, even those occupants had access to a small *cenatio* and a *diaeta*. The apartment located in the interior of the house was even darker and more humble. It was lit almost exclusively by one airshaft at the center of the building. The two rooms were filled with furniture: three beds, wardrobes and a *lararium*. They give us an impression of the cramped quarters common to such dwellings. A narrow hallway led to a latrine. Living conditions of this kind were much more common than has generally been assumed, judging from the evidence of preserved upper stories in Herculaneum. It appears that a considerable number of homeowners in the city took advantage of the opportunity to earn additional income

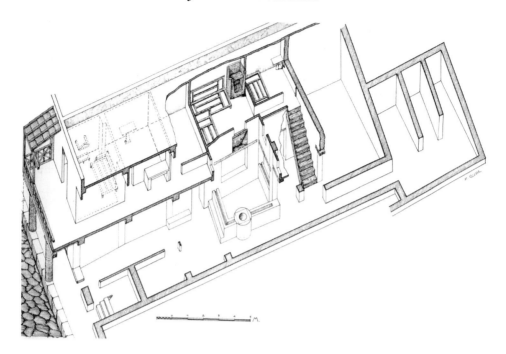

Figure 27.6 House of *Opus Craticium* (III.13–15), isometric view;
after Maiuri 1958, Taf. 36.

by remodeling and skillfully subdividing [one or more] stories (cf. Adam, Ch. 8; Figure 8.15).

Let us exit the densely populated streets of the city and move to the northern suburbs and the Villa of the Papyri (Map 4, H), which remains largely buried under the pyroclastic fill resulting from two eruptions of Mt Vesuvius in AD 79 and 1631 (cf. Moormann, Ch. 28). The complex is known principally from the floor plan reconstructed by K. Weber during tunneling excavations from 1750 to 1765, and from the sculptures and eponymous papyri removed at that time and now housed in the National Museum in Naples (Figure 28.3). The entire building extends more than 250 m along the coastline. In some areas it is similar in design and decor to other late republican villas in the neighborhood of Mt Vesuvius, especially the Villa of the Mysteries near Pompeii, the Villa at Oplontis, and the Villa San Marco at Stabiae.

The heart of the villa is a square peristyle. With its large number of tightly placed columns, its bronze herms and a sculptural fountain, the lavishly appointed inner courtyard leads towards separate wings. The most important domestic quarters were arranged around an *atrium* as their entryway, but oriented outward, with views onto the sea via a *porticus* set in front of the vestibule (these include the rooms recently and completely re-excavated; Figures 3.3 and 28.6). Apparently one could choose between several great halls and their adjoining cabinets depending on weather and light conditions. Remains of floors in *opus sectile* and Second-Style wall paintings date the construction to the later first century BC;[20] they also reveal the exceptional quality of the decor. A long, rectangular peristyle extended to the northwest. Its colonnades and garden area were filled with an overwhelming wealth of sculptures in bronze and marble. These included images of deities as well as portraits of philosophers, figures of athletes, animals, and marble furniture.[21]

Allusions to the Greek gymnasium and aspects of Greek education and upbringing were ubiquitous. It is in this context that we should consider the discovery of part of a Greek library with nearly 1,800 scrolls, primarily philosophical texts. Because numerous scrolls contain the work of Philodemos of Gadara—a contemporary philosopher—it was once believed that his patron, L. Calpurnius Piso, was the owner of the villa. Today it has clearly emerged that objects from the villa correspond more closely to a greatly standardized assemblage, and even the library cannot indicate with certainty any close personal relationship between their owner and an author, presumably his favorite.

Other changes in the interpretation and study of the villa complex have also occurred. The lack of Latin texts had always led to the suspicion that such scrolls might be discovered in unexcavated portions of the villa. In 1980, test tunnels succeeded in precisely locating the villa. In spite of the doubtful archaeological necessity to excavate the site any further—especially in view of the conspicuous amount of work remaining to be done in conserving and restoring Herculaneum—it was decided to undertake a proper excavation, involving the removal of horrendous amounts of mud from parts of the villa.[22] This has now been accomplished with the assistance of huge amounts of money, which leads one to suspect that the project has been a modern kind of treasure hunt.

In conclusion, there are several remarkable parallels between developments in the urban living conditions at Herculaneum and Pompeii, aside from those differences that are usually emphasized. First, we should note that at Herculaneum—within the inner city so far known—there is no evidence of palatial residences for a local ruling class nor any traces of public construction in the late republican era, much less in the Samnite period. Until at least the middle of the first century BC, Herculaneum appears to have been a small town that remained entirely oriented towards the metropolis of Naples. Although the absorption of Hellenistic culture into local architecture and painting at Pompeii was already under way and being actively promoted by families in residence there, in Herculaneum the construction of public buildings as well as large urban houses is probably to be ascribed to the efforts of magnates moving into the city from elsewhere. We have not demonstrated here in detail that the new standards were soon being imitated in the more modest houses, but this can easily be observed on the basis of the appropriate literature and picture books.[23] Instead we have here been more interested in highlighting the contrast between the earlier small-scale structures and the new dimensions of a villa architecture transplanted into the city. It is significant that this transformation in Herculaneum may only have begun in Augustan times, or at least not much earlier. But the construction of houses such as the House of the Stags (IV.21) or the House of the Mosaic Atrium (IV.1–2), which seem to date to the early imperial period, introduced no definitive changes. This process can be detected in Pompeii at least a generation earlier than at Herculaneum,[24] yet living conditions in the two cities appear to have increasingly converged. Herculaneum, indeed, continued to lack the family seats of the ancient local *gentes*; still, the quality and furnishings of the imperial ensembles were no longer inferior to those in Pompeii. Instead, they often surpassed them in elegance and in the use of expensive colors.

NOTES

1 Constanze Witt translated the German text. The text goes back to the original version delivered in 1998. Apart from some minor additions, the text remains unaltered. For the size of the city, see M. Pagano, "La nuova pianta della città e di alcuni edifici pubblici di Ercolano," *CronErcol*, 1996, vol. 26, p. 234. For the most recent contributions on residences, see: F. Pesando and M. P. Guidobaldi, *Gli ozi di Ercole: residenze di lusso a Pompei ed Ercolano*, Rome, 2006, pp. 179–270; R. de Kind, *Houses in Herculaneum: a new view on the town planning and the building of Insulae III and IV*, Amsterdam, 1998; V. Catalano, *Case, abitanti e culti di Ercolano*, rev. edn, Rome, 2002.

2 M. Pagano, "Ricerche sull'impianto urbano di Ercolano," in L. Franchi dell'Orto (ed.), *Ercolano 1738 - 1988. 250 anni di ricerca archeologica*. Atti del Convegno Internazionale Ravello-Ercolano-Napoli-Pompei 30 ottobre–5 novembre 1988, Rome, 1993, pp. 597ff.

3 Pagano, "La nuova pianta," pp. 240ff. See also now T. Najbjerg, "The so-called 'Basilica' in Herculaneum," in JRA Suppl. Series no. 47, 2002, pp. 157–63.

4 G. Guadagno, "Ercolano. Eredità di cultura e nuovi dati," in Franchi dell'Orto, *Ercolano 1738–1988*, p. 97, fig. 18.

5 A. Wallace-Hadrill, "Elites and trade in the Roman world," in A. Wallace-Hadrill and J. Rich (eds), *City and Country in the Ancient World*, London, 1991, pp. 250ff.

6 R. de Kind, "Houses at Herculaneum. An analysis of town planning and of measurements in *Insulae* III and IV," *CronErcol*, 1993, vol. 23, pp. 163ff.; R. de Kind and M. C. van Binnebeke, "The 'Casa dell'Atrio Corinzio' and the 'Casa del Sacello di Legno' at Herculaneum," *CronErcol*, 1996, vol. 26, pp. 198ff.

7 Contra G. Cerulli-Irelli, *La "Casa del Colonnato Tuscanico" ad Ercolano*, Naples, 1974, pp. 13ff.

8 Th. Ganschow, *Untersuchungen zur Baugeschichte in Herculaneum*, Bonn, 1989, pp. 221ff.

9 A. Wallace-Hadrill, *Houses and Society in Pompeii and Herculaneum*, Princeton, NJ, 1994, p. 119, fig. 6.1.

10 Ganschow, *Untersuchungen zur Baugeschichte*, pp. 147ff.

11 V. Tran Tam Tinh, "À la recherche d'Herculaneum préromaine," *CronPomp*, 1977, vol. 3, pp. 40ff., fig. 1f; V. Tran Tam Tinh, *La Casa dei Cervi à Herculaneum*, Rome, 1988, p. 21.

12 See J.-A. Dickmann, *Domus frequentata: Anspruchsvolles Wohnen im pompejanischen Stadthaus*, Munich, 1999, pp. 256ff.

13 M. George, "Elements of the peristyle in Campanian atria," *JRA*, 1998, vol. 11, pp. 82–100; Dickmann, *Domus frequentata*, pp. 301–12.

14 A. Allroggen-Bedel, "Der Hausherr der 'Casa dei Cervi' in Herculaneum," *CronErcol*, 1975, vol. 5, pp. 99ff.; Tran Tam Tinh, *Casa dei Cervi*, pp. 123f.

15 J. D'Arms, *Romans on the Bay of Naples*, Cambridge, MA, 1970, pp. 30f.; J. D'Arms, "Puteoli in the second century of the Roman Empire: a social and economic study," *JRS*, 1974, vol. 64, pp. 114ff.

16 A. Maiuri, *Ercolano: i nuovi scavi (1927–1958)*, Rome, 1958, pp. 302f.; Ganschow, *Untersuchungen zur Baugeschichte*, pp. 199ff., 216f.

17 Tran Tam Tinh, *Casa dei Cervi*, pl. 92ff.

18 Tran Tam Tinh, *Casa dei Cervi*, fig. 147ff.; Wallace-Hadrill, *Houses and Society*, pl. I.

19 See now F. Pirson, *Mietwohnungen in Pompeji und Herkulaneum. Untersuchungen zur Architektur, zum Wohnen und zur Sozial- und Wirtschaftsgeschichte der Vesuvstädte*, Studien zur Antiken Stadt no. 5, Munich, 1999, pp. 112–16.

20 M. Gigante, *et al.*, "Lo scavo della Villa dei Papiri," *CronErcol*, 1997, vol. 27, p. 54, fig. 16. Cf. Moorman, Ch. 28 for additional bibliography.

21 R. Neudecker, *Die Skulpturenausstattung römischer Villen in Italien*, Mainz, 1988, pp. 105ff.

22 Gigante, "Lo scavo della Villa dei Papiri," pp. 6ff., 11f., esp. 57ff.

23 E.g., A. and M. De Vos, *Pompei, Ercolano, Stabia*, Rome-Bari, 1982, *passim*; J. J. Deiss, *Herculaneum: Italy's Buried Treasure*, rev. edn, Los Angeles, 1989; on Pompeii, see P. Zanker, *Pompeji. Stadtbild und Wohngeschmack*, Mainz, 1995, pp. 141ff; R. Ling, *Pompeii: History, Life and Afterlife*, Stroud, 2005.

24 Dickmann, *Domus frequentata*, pp. 159ff.

CHAPTER TWENTY-EIGHT

VILLAS SURROUNDING POMPEII AND HERCULANEUM

——— •◆• ———

Eric M. Moormann

Ancient Campania was famous for fertility that made two vegetable crops *per annum* possible, and produced good wines. This led to intensive land use during the republican and imperial periods. After the eruption of Vesuvius, small farms disappeared, making way for large *praedia*, remains of which have been found, but never systematically investigated. Because leisure retreats became unfashionable in this region from the Vespasianic era onwards, this contribution is limited to the late republic and early empire.

In essential terms, the Roman *villa* was not the luxury house of today; rather, it owed its status to the fact that it was situated in the countryside.[1] Its main purpose was that of a farm (*villa rustica*); a residential aspect was secondary. In a few cases, luxury villas are found in rural areas (a *villa urbana*; if situated immediately near the town walls, a *villa suburbana* (cf. Tybout, Ch. 26); if along the sea shore, a *villa maritima*).[2] Ancient manuals on agriculture (Cato, Varro, Columella), encyclopedic works such as Pliny's *Naturalis historia*, and Vitruvius' *De architectura* provide us with precious data on farming and both rustic and luxury architecture; such texts are generally substantiated by the archaeological evidence.[3]

FROM TREASURE HUNTING TO RESCUE EXCAVATIONS

When Mau and Kelsey published their manual, it was possible to be an eyewitness to the excavations of ancient villas carried out by private persons on private grounds in the *suburbium* of Pompeii, as those areas were not state property like Pompeii itself (cf. Foss, Ch. 3), and therefore subject to few laws concerning monuments of antiquity. Diggers profited from their search for commercially interesting objects. Some twenty villas were partly unearthed in this way until the Italian state installed a law in 1908 that prohibited private excavations.[4] Loose finds, mosaics and paintings stripped from their architectonic setting were sold in auctions or via art dealers to museums and private collectors around the world.[5] Celebrated cases included the villa of P. Fannius Synistor in Boscoreale, the villa of Agrippa Postumus near Boscotrecase, and the "Silver Treasure Villa" in contrada Pisanella near Boscoreale, known for its

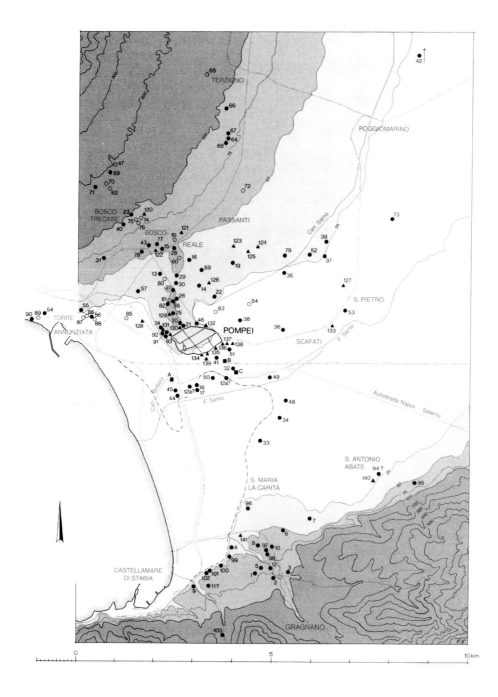

Figure 28.1 Map of the villas in the Pompeian *suburbium* as of 1985; V. Kockel, "Funde I," Figure 23, after an original by E. M. Menotti. The dot-dashed line approximates the ancient pre-eruption coastline.

436

LEGEND

[NB: At the time of the early excavations, the modern town of Pompeii did not yet exist. Therefore, find-spots lying near the ancient city were categorized under Torre Annuniziata, Boscoreale, or Scafati. Only modern place-names are used for new finds.]

VILLAS (● certain ○ probable)

1	Stabia, Casa di Miri	Ruggiero Taf. 9
2	Gragnano, Petrellune (?)	Ruggiero Taf. 10,1
3	Gragnano, Petrellune	Ruggiero Taf. 10,2
4	Stabia, Capella di S. Marco (hier Abb. 11)	Ruggiero Taf. 11
5	Stabia, Casa di Miri	Ruggiero Taf. 12
6	Gragnano, Capella degli Impisi	Ruggiero Taf. 13
7	Gragnano, Sassole	Ruggiero Taf. 14
8	Gragnano, Carmiano	Ruggiero Taf. 15
9	Stabia, Belvedere	Ruggiero Taf. 16
10	Gragnano, Medici	Ruggiero Taf. 17
11	Stabia, Varano (?)	Ruggiero Taf. 18
12	Gragnano, Ogliaro	Ruggiero Taf. 19
12a	Scafati, Contr. Murecine, Fond. Valiante, Lage umstritten	NSc 1881, 25 ff. o. Plan
13	Boscoreale, Contr. Pisanella, Fond. Pulzella und de Prisco	de Vos, Guida 1982, 242
14	Boscoreale, Contr. Giuliana, Fond. Zurlo	NSc 1897, 392
15	Boscoreale, Pzza. Mercato, Prop. Cirillo	NSc 1898, 420
16	Boscoreale, Loc. Grotta Franchina, Fond. Vona (P. Fannius Synistor)	NFP 77
17	Scafati, Contr. Murecine, Fond. Liguori	NSc 1898, 33 f. o. Plan
18	Scafati, Contr. Murecine, Fond. Malerba	NSc 1900, 204
19	Scafati, Contr. Spinelle, Fond. Acanfora	NSc 1899, 392
20	Torre Annunziata, Contr. Città, Fond. Massucci-d'Aquino	NSc 1899, 236
21	Torre Annunziata, Contr. Città, Fond. Barbatelli	NSc 1900, 599 o. Plan
22	Boscoreale, Contr. Centopiedi-al Tirone, Prop. Vitiello	NSc 1903, 65
23	Boscotrecase, Contr. Detari, Fond. Vitelli	NSc 1899, 297
24	Pompeji, Villa dei Misteri	Maiuri, La Villa d. Misteri (1931)
25	Boscoreale, Contr. Città, Fond. Prisco	NSc 1921, 416
26	Boscoreale, Contr. Città, Fond. Brancaccio	NSc 1921, 424
27	Boscoreale, Contr. Pisanella, Fond. de Martino	NSc 1921, 427

28	Boscoreale, Pzza. Staz. FFSS, Fond. d'Acunzo	NSc 1921, 436
29	Boscoreale, Contr. Pisanella, Fond. Zurlo − Pulzella (Popidius Florus)	NSc 1921, 443
30	Boscoreale, Contr. Pisanella, Fond. Agricoltura, Prop. di Palma	NSc 1921, 461; s. o. S. 521
31	Boscotrecase, Contr. Rota, Fond. Santini (Agrippa Postumus)	NSc 1922, 459
32	Scafati, Contr. S. Abbondio, Fond. Cipriano	NSc 1922, 479 f. o. Plan
33	Gragnano, Contr. Messigno, Fond. Matrone	NSc 1923, 272
34	Gragnano, Contr. Carità, Fond. Maschetti	NSc 1923, 276
35	Scafati, Contr. Spinelli, Fond. Matrone	NSc 1923, 281
36	Scafati, Contr. Crapolla, Prop. de Prisco	NSc 1923, 285
37	Scafati, Contr. Iossa, Fond. di Palma	NSc 1922, 478 f. o. Plan
38	Valle di Pompei, Contr. Crapolla, Fond. Matrone	NSc 1928, 375 o. Plan
39	Scafati, Contr. Acquavitrara, Fond. Acquino	NSc 1928, 376
40	Boscotrecase, V. Cavour 25	NSc 1929, 189 f. o. Plan
41	Valle di Pompei, Fond. de Martino	NSc 1929, 191
42	Domicella	NSc 1929, 200
43	Boscoreale, V. Vitt. Emanuele III 27	NSc 1929, 178
44	Torre Annunziata, Contr. Bottaro, Fond. Fienga	s. S. 568 Anm. 321
45	Torre Annunziata, Contr. Bottaro, Fond. Matrone	s. S. 568
46	Pompei Scavi, bei Staz. 'Scavi' der Circumves.	
47	Boscotrecase, Contr. Carotenuto, Fond. Cirillo	NSc 1886, 131 f. o. Plan
48	Scafati (?) Contr. Ponticello, Prop. Carotenuto	
49	Scafati (?) Contr. Musigno	
50	Scafati, Contr. Murecine, Fond. Cascone	s. S. 566 f.
51	Valle di Pompei, Fond. de Fusco	
52	Scafati, Contr. Iossa, Fond. di Palma	CB 150
53	Scafati, Contr. Castagno, Fond. Prete	CB 152
54	Torre Annunziata, Mass. Scognamiglio	CB 119
55	Torre Annunziata, Via Sepolcri ('Poppaea')	s. S. 549 ff.
56	Torre Annunziata, Via Murat ('L. Crassius Tertius')	s. S. 552 ff.

KEY TO ABBREVIATIONS

Ruggiero: M. Ruggiero, *Degli scavi di Stabia dal 1749 al 1782*, Naples, 1881.

NSc: *Notizie degli Scavi di Antichità*.

De Vos, Guida, 1982: A. De Vos and M. De Vos, *Guida archeologiche Laterza: Pompei, Ercolano, Stabia*, Rome, 1982.

NFP: B. Andreae and H. Kyrieleis (eds), *Neue Forschungen in Pompeji*, Recklinghausen, 1975.

Maiuri, La Villa d. Misteri (1931): A. Maiuri, *La Villa dei Misteri*, 2 vols, Rome, 1931.

RM: *Mitteilungen des Deutschen Archäologischen Instituts, Römische Abteilung*.

CB: A. Casale and A. Bianco, "Primo contributo alla topografia del suburbio pompeiano," in *Pompei 79*, Antigua, Suppl. 15, Rome, 1979, pp. 27–56.

s.S.: V. Kockel, "Fünde und Forschungen in den Vesuvstädten I," *Archäologischer Anzeiger*, 1985, pp. 519–55.

57	Boscoreale, Contr. Villa Regina	s. S. 519f.
58	Pompei, Contr. Città, Fond. Brancaccio 2 (vgl. Nr. 26)	CB 145
59	Boscoreale, Contr. Tirone, Fond. Mollica	CB 159
60	Boscoreale, Contr. Grotta Tirone, Fond. Cerulli	CB 71
61	Boscoreale, V. A. Diaz, Fond. de Gaetano	CB 50
62	Boscotrecase, Contr. Casavitelli, Fond. Bergamasco	CB 98
63	Diese Nummer des CTP entfällt. Funde nach 79 n. Chr.	CB 142
64	Terzigno (früher Ottaviano) Contr. Scocozza, Fond. Auricchio	s. S. 544 f.
65	Terzigno, Contr. Avini	CB 161
66	Terzigno, Contr. Caposecchi	CB 133
67	Terzigno, Contr. Scocozza	s. S. 545
68	Terzigno, Contr. Scocozza	s. S. 545 f.
69	Boscotrecase, V. Cantinelle	CB 27
70	Boscotrecase, V. Cinquevie	CB 42
71	Boscotrecase, V. Cinquevie	CB 28
72	Terzigno (früher Ottaviano) Contr. Scocozza	CB 53
73	Scafati, Contr. Monacelle	CB 148
74	Boscotrecase, V. Promiscua	CB 125
75	Pompei, V. Crapolla	CB 79
76	Boscotrecase, V. L. Iorio	CB 80
77	Boscoreale, V. G. della Rocca	CB 162
78	Boscoreale, V. G. della Rocca 27	CB 11
79	Scafati, Contr. Ventotto	CB 156
80	Boscoreale, Contr. Pisanella	CB 4
81	Pompei, Contr. Città, Prop. Carotenuto	CB 158
82	Pompei, Contr. Città, Prop. A. Prisco	CB 75
83	Pompei (früher Boscoreale) Contr. Fossa di Valle	CB 122
84	Pompei, Contr. Trepponti, V. Crapolla	CB 76
85	Torre Annunziata, V. Penniniello/Torrette de Siena	CB 111
86	Torre Annunziata, V. G. Murat, Prop. Fattorusso	CB 115, hier Abb. 32 Nr. 3
87	Torre Annunziata, V. G. Murat	CB 114, hier Abb. 32
88	Torre Annunziata, V. G. Murat	CB 117, hier Abb. 32
89	Torre Annunziata, Küstenstraße	CB 118, s. S. 547
90	Torre Annunziata, Terme Vesuviane	CB 120, s. S. 547
91	Pompeji, Villa delle Colonne a Mosaico	s. S. 556
92	Pompeji, Villa di Diomede	de Vos, Guida 1982, 244
93	Pompeji, Villa di Cicerone	de Vos, Guida 1982, 233
94	S. Antonio Abate, V. Buonconsiglio	s. S. 538
95	S. Antonio Abate, Loc. Casa Salese, Fond. Cuomo	s. S. 539 f.
96	S. Maria la Carità, Petraro	s. S. 541

97	Gragnano, Loc. Carmiano A	s. S. 536 f.
98	Gragnano, Loc. Carmiano B	s. S. 536
99	Castellamare di Stabia, Villa di S. Marco	s. S. 531 ff.
100	Castellamare di Stabia, Villa del Pastore	s. S. 529 ff.
101	Castellamare di Stabia, Villa di Arianna B	s. S. 529
102	Castellamare di Stabia, Villa di Arianna A	s. S. 525 ff.
103	Castellamare di Stabia, V. Pimonte, Loc. Privati	s. S. 536

NECROPOLEIS AND INDIVIDUAL GRAVES (▲)

120	Boscoreale, V. Barone Massa	CB 22
121	Boscoreale, V. A. Diaz	CB 16
122	Boscoreale, Pzza. Vargas	CB 14
123	Boscoreale, Contr. Spinelli	NSc 1929, 188 f. o. Plan
124	Boscoreale, Contr. Pizzobello	CB 55
125	Boscoreale, V. Passanti-Scati	CB 84
126	Pompeji, Friedhof in V. Nolana	NSc 1936, 352 o. Plan
127	Scafati, S. Pietro, V. Castagno	CB 153
128	Torre Annunziata, Contr. Torretta di Siena	CB 60
129	Boscoreale, Contr. Città, Fond. Prisco	s. Nr. 25
130	Pompeji, Porta del Vesuvio	NSc 1910, 400
131	Pompeji, Porta Ercolana	s. S. 555
132	Pompeji, Porta di Nola	s. S. 564 ff.
133	Scafati	s. S. 543 f.
134	Pompeji, Porta di Stabiae und Fondo Santilli	NSc 1891, 274; 1897, 275 f.
135	Pompeji, Porta di Nocera	s. S. 556 ff.
136	Pompeji, Nekropole südl. des Amphitheaters	s. S. 562 f.
137	Pompeji, Fond. Pacifico	RM 3, 1888, 122
138	Pompeji, Territorio Prelatura	s. S. 564
139	Pompeji, Fondo Azzolino	NSc 1916, 289
140	S. Antonio Abate, V. Roma	s. S. 538
141	Castellamare di Stabia, Grab des Virtius	s. S. 523

EXTRA-URBAN SANCTUARIES (■)

A	Loc. Case Bottaro, Neptun-Tempel?	s. S. 568
B	Fondo Iozzino	
C	S. Abbondio	s. S. 568 ff.

Figure 28.1   Key *(cont.)*

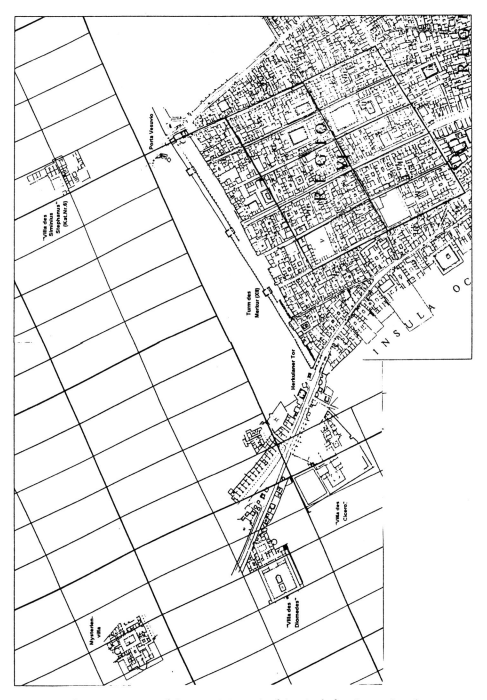

Figure 28.2   Part of the *centuriatio* north of the city before 80 BC; Oettel,
Fundkontexte, figs. 29–30.

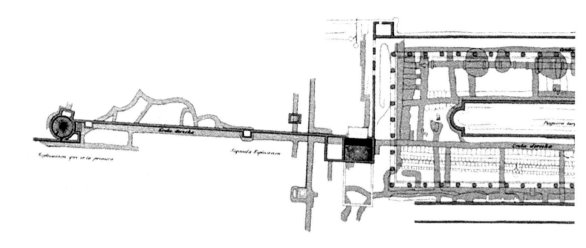

Figure 28.3 Herculaneum, Villa of the Papyri, plan, showing architecture (dark; red on original plan) and Bourbon-era tunnels (light; light brown on original); after K. Weber, 1756.

silver vessels and wall paintings (Figure 28.1, nos. 16, 31, 13). The Pisanella villa, and A. Pasqui's scientific publication (the only serious study available), provided Mau and Kelsey most of their data.[6]

Research on villas had begun in the Bourbon era with the exploration of buildings in Castellammare di Stabia (Figure 28.1, nos. 96–103), some outside Pompeii such as the Cicero and Diomedes villas (Figure 28.1, nos. 92–93; Figure 37.1), and the Villa of the Papyri, north of Herculaneum (cf. Foss, Ch. 3; Dickmann, Ch. 27; Figure 28.3).[7] In the twentieth century, state-sponsored excavations have yielded numerous remains scattered all over the region. Important examples are the Villa Item, better known as the Villa of the Mysteries after the paintings in *oecus* (5) (Figure 28.1, no. 24; Figure 28.2),[8] and the two villas in Oplontis, "Poppaea" and "L. Crassus Tertius" (Figure 28.1, nos. 55–56; Figure 31.5). The excellent excavation and publication, from 1977 to 1980 by Stefano De Caro, of a *villa rustica* near Boscoreale, contrada La Regina (Figure 28.1, no. 57; Figure 28.4), has recently produced many new insights into farming.[9] Even the villas at Stabiae were rediscovered and partly re-excavated in the 1950s and 1960s, and are now receiving new attention.[10]

Altogether, more than a hundred villas are known. V. Kockel's 1985 map (Figure 28.1) shows most of them, and each year Pompeii's archaeological superintendency reports the remains of new complexes. The label "villa," however, is sometimes given too easily to poor wall structures found outside the city. Nearly all excavations have been limited to exploring architecture, especially residential quarters embellished

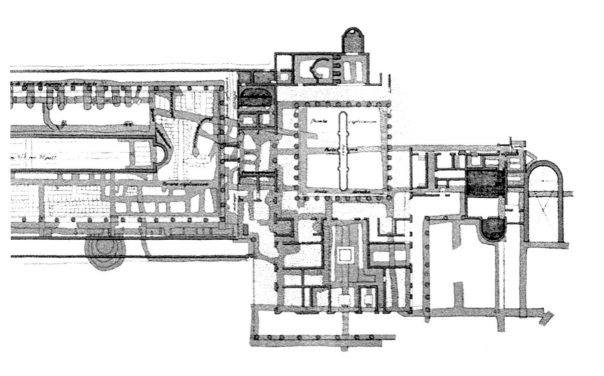

with paintings and mosaics; working quarters have tended to enjoy a lesser degree of interest.

Similarly, the organization and distribution of land (the so-called *centuriatio*) in the *ager Pompeianus* has, until recently, not received much attention from Pompeian scholars (cf. Guzzo, Ch. 1). Research has been hampered by the post-war expansion of Neapolitan suburbs, running as far as Sorrento. Few plots of land have been spared, and finds have generally been made during construction projects. Even if the land were available, the ancient land divisions could no longer be recognized under the layers of lava near Vesuvius, and under the ashes and *lapilli* around Pompeii. No grid lines can be expected like those further north in Emilia Romagna or Lombardy, where the original *centuriationes* can be reconstructed by means of air cartography, survey, excavation and even by recognition in the field, as some of the subdivisions are still in use.[11] Our understanding of ancient agriculture in the region suffers for the same reasons. However, careful botanical analysis by W. F. Jashemski in the La Regina villa has shed new light on this problem, as it did in the Villa of "Poppaea" in Oplontis (cf. Jashemski, Ch. 31; Figure 31.5).[12]

THE STATE OF RESEARCH

For a long time, relatively little attention was paid to the Pompeian countryside in the proceedings of large colloquia,[13] collections of essays,[14] or exhibition catalogs.[15]

441

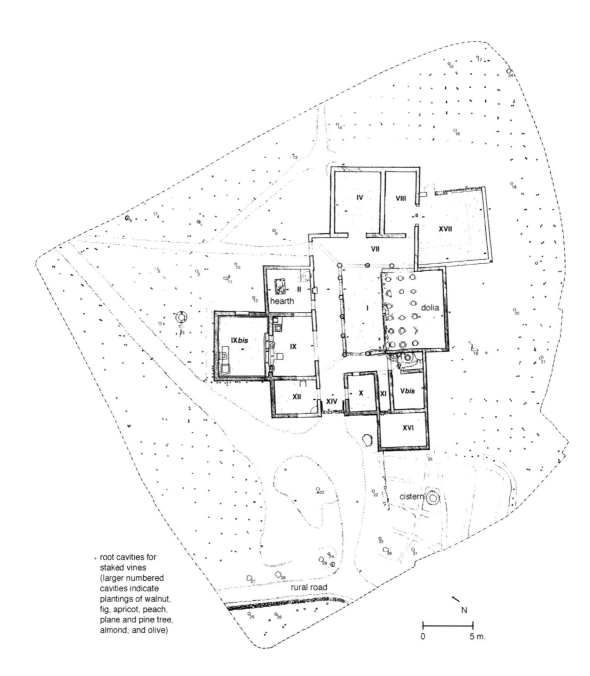

root cavities for
staked vines
(larger numbered
cavities indicate
plantings of walnut,
fig, apricot, peach,
plane and pine tree,
almond, and olive)

Figure 28.4 Boscoreale, Villa in contrada la Regina, plan;
after De Caro, *Villa rustica*, Tav. B.

Monographs on villas were rare as well,[16] but recently the excavations at Torre Annunziata (Oplontis) have received attention (cf. Jashemski, Ch. 31);[17] the villa of La Regina has been published extensively;[18] Oettel has combined old excavation data with new insights, and Jashemski has offered her latest work on the natural history of Pompeii (cf. also Guzzo, Ch. 1).[19] Finally, in 1994 an Applied Research Laboratory was established to deal with issues of restoration, preservation, conservation and the study of the ancient Vesuvian environment.[20]

OWNERS AND TENANTS

Occupation of a villa varied—from an owner and family who worked personally on their property, to a *vilicus*, "steward," who managed *praedia* with workers and slaves, while the proprietor dwelled in Rome or some other large town. Although Cato and other writers on agriculture or history always praised the agricultural roots of the Romans and their rural capacities, few of them indeed worked on the fields: the days of Cincinnatus were certainly gone by the end of the republican period.

It remains a matter of discussion whether small *villae rusticae* were rented or occupied by slaves and/or free workers paid by a proprietor. Rural slaves were unlikely to have been treated well, as shown by leg-irons found in several villas (cf. George, Ch. 35).[21]

In general, villa management was entrusted to members of the *familia* (an extended term that included household slaves) who resided on the spot. They managed daily work and production. It may be for this reason that purely luxury villas remained rare, appearing only in the age of Augustus: they tended to fall into disrepair and "die" if they were abandoned for the greater part of the year, not to mention the risks of robbery and banditry. Owners' disinterest in visiting their villas caused the disrepair of luxurious quarters, even as the caretakers concentrated upon the *pars rustica*. A good example of a *pars urbana* falling into disuse can be seen at the recently explored "villa 6" at Terzigno, 6 km north of Pompeii.[22] In any case, agricultural components were conceptually and practically central to the entire villa, helping preserve an idealized mix of *negotium*, "work" and *otium*, "leisure."

Many villas bear ancient names (Popidius Florus, Fannius Synistor, Agrippa Postumus). This suggests a sound knowledge of the proprietors, which is not the case. Some stem from a literary association, e.g., the villa of Cicero (near the Porta Ercolano, excavated from 1763–64 and then re-interred; Figure 37.1), because the famous politician and orator mentions a *Pompeianum*.[23] The "Poppaea" villa in Torre Annunziata (antique Oplontis) has been connected to this empress because of her family roots in Pompeii and the presence of a *graffito* of one of her freedmen; it does not prove that she really was the owner during the Neronian era.[24] Most of these labels are based on *graffiti*, *dipinti* on *amphorae* or *dolia*, or initials in relief on finger rings. However, these names do not prove ownership and could belong to producers (of the ceramics), visitors (the *graffiti*) or *vilici* (the finger rings). Matteo Della Corte, who worked at the excavations for decades during the twentieth century, often interpreted such "signatures" too enthusiastically in order to identify residents at Pompeii (cf. Franklin, Ch. 33).[25] We remain ignorant in most cases about the real proprietors and/or tenants of the farms; speculations on the relationships between the Roman elite and Vesuvian landowners have not yet yielded sound results.[26]

VILLA AND PROPERTY DIMENSIONS

Cato described an ideal farm as a complex of different agricultural activities (cattle, vegetables, crops, olives and wine) on a site of some 240 *iugera* (roughly four *iugera* = 1 ha), but smaller tenures of around 100 *iugera* could provide good profit as well.[27] In his calculations, a total number of thirteen personnel and slaves working constantly on the farm was high: agriculture was a labor-intensive activity, especially for grapes and vegetables. Based on excavated buildings, however, accommodation is not generally available for even ten slaves plus the *vilicus'* family (cf. George, Ch. 35).[28] Perhaps most Pompeian farms specialized in less intensive cereal crops and olives, and hired extra persons in the harvest season (cf. Jongman, Ch. 32).

Calculating the extent of productive territory for a villa is hampered by a lack of knowledge, as said before, about the distribution of land and the *centuriatio*. Normally the area is deduced from the sum of wine *dolia* found at the farms, plus extra *iugera* for supplementary production. A good example comes from the La Regina villa (Figures 1.1, 28.4 and 28.5). Here a *cella vinaria* (I) with 18 *dolia* and a capacity of 10,000 litres was found, as well as a *torcularium* (wine press; IX and IX *bis*), an oil press, and a stable (with the remains of a pig).[29] De Caro calculates a total of 3 to 8 *iugera* of vines, to which fields for crops and animal fodder must be added. This is a modest villa for five or more persons (a higher postulated population of ten to twelve seems too high).

W. Jongman has suggested a rather pessimistic image of the production capacities of Pompeian agriculture (cf. Jongman, Ch. 32).[30] Following the severe rules of Weber and Finley, he has calculated that the town was barely capable of feeding the mouths

Figure 28.5   Boscoreale, Villa in contrada la Regina, overview.

of its own inhabitants. Wine export must have been limited; besides, this product mostly caused hangovers[31] and was not prized as much as the sources suggest. However, given his calculation of a population density of 180 persons per square kilometer, grain was, indeed, sufficient in quantity. As for wine production, Jongman is incorrect in surmising that production was limited to the slopes of Vesuvius and adjacent hills. The Villa Regina excavation may change the argument to some degree; it shows that greater production, even export, was feasible.[32]

CHRONOLOGY

Pompeii has three main historical phases: the pre-colonial period, the first century BC from the foundation of the *Colonia Cornelia Veneria Pompeiana*, and the imperial period from Augustus onwards (cf. Descœudres, Ch. 2). As far as the division of the land is concerned, however, Oettel has distinguished three *centuriationes*: pre-colonial, colonial, and a third dated to 42 BC or slightly later, when veterans of the wars against Caesar's assassins received allotments in the Pompeian region.[33]

We know of only a few villas in the vicinity of Pompeii that were constructed during the pre-colonial period, and even their existence is not substantiated by deep investigation: the remains of First-Style wall paintings and some architectural remains, e.g., the terrace and *cryptoporticus* of the Villa of the Mysteries. Finds from this period remain scarce. Recent studies on early housing in Pompeii suggest that the town, with fortification walls extended in the sixth and fourth centuries BC, was not densely occupied, apart from the "*Altstadt*," until the second century BC (cf. Carafa, Ch. 5; Geertman, Ch. 7). In most districts, especially the heavily studied *regio* VI, houses were set up separately like small villas, each with their own land plots (cf. Jones and Robinson, Ch. 25).[34]

The *centuriatio* of the land immediately outside the city followed the grid of the streets of Pompeii, as can be seen from the orientation of the first villas (Figure 28.2).[35] This fact explains, for example, why the Villa of the Mysteries is set aside from the road to Herculaneum, whereas its main orientation to the northwest corresponds with that of the houseblocks in Region VI. The same is true for the so-called Villa of Diomedes, immediately outside the Porta Ercolano.[36] Those villas seem to have been oriented according to the city *insulae* and land plots (Figure 28.2). Pompeians must originally have been farmers, living in their small town, well protected against dangers and wild animals by fortifications, visiting daily the fields outside those walls. The identical orientation of plots and streets even suggests a relationship between owners of houses in town and fields *extra muros*. The apparent absence of small villas may reflect a daily migration between city and fields. The existence of "urban villas" such as the House of Pansa (VI.6.1) and the House of the Faun (VI.12), striking examples of palace-like living, contradicts an interest in living both within and out of town by the elite.[37] The same tendency can be observed for senators who lived on the Palatine and Velia hills in Rome, and had no living quarters in the country.

Agricultural activities *intra muros* as late as AD 79 have been demonstrated by W. F. Jashemski,[38] and illustrate the artificiality of a hard distinction between town and countryside. Vegetable and fruit cultivation inside and immediately outside the city guaranteed the fresh importation of these delicate products; long transport lines would have damaged them.[39] Jongman supposes the existence of many small agricultural settlements in the hinterland, and complains about a lack of intensive surveys that could prove that they existed (cf. Jongman, Ch. 32). In response, we can cite the settlement model of the Messapian town of Oria in southern Italy, recently reconstructed by intensive survey.[40] Here no small rural sites were found, and farmers must have walked out to their fields every day, unless they slept under the stars. If there were, in fact, few small farms in the vicinity of Pompeii during the early period (none have been identified by excavations), perhaps the land was not intensively worked and was underproductive.

Many villas around Pompeii were erected *ab novo* after the occupation of the town by Sulla's veterans. Some older ones, such as the Villa of the Mysteries, were entirely restructured and redecorated. Images of unfortunate local inhabitants who had dared to oppose Rome are vivid but seem exaggerated.[41] Probably they are too negative as far as the rights and possessions of native Pompeians are concerned, but certainly the town did crowd with many new, unwelcome residents who spoke another dialect than Oscan, and who brought new *mores* from Rome. They also brought new measurements: the Oscan foot of the first *centuriatio* was exchanged for the Roman foot and a new, slightly different grid. The countryside must have especially felt the impact of the new population: one consequence of an army is having to grant former soldiers a plot of land and money as a kind of pension for living. Most villas around Pompeii must have been established by veterans. A new trend in decoration, the Second Style (cf. Strocka, Ch. 20), was probably introduced from Rome by these settlers, especially those of higher social order who stimulated the development of the local economy with new impulses and demands. However, the presence of Roman elites possessing villas in Campania might have made possible an introduction of the new fashion a decade earlier.[42] A large number of Second-Style paintings in the villas remained unchanged until AD 79: this means that they were appreciated, perhaps as tokens inherited from the first veteran settlers. In that sense, the early and mature Second Style could have formed ideological means of self-representation, in that its character was highly representative. The display of architectural elements and precious objects suggested associations with the wealth of Hellenistic rulers.[43]

The villas built after 59 BC are famous for large fresco paintings in the mature Second Style (e.g., the Villa of "Poppaea" at Oplontis (cf. Jashemski, Ch. 31; Figure 1.2) and that of Fannius Synistor in Boscoreale) and the early Third Style (the Villa of Agrippa Postumus in Boscotrecase).[44] Their agricultural components are less evident; it may be at this time that the genre of the *villa urbana* came into fashion. It would be interesting to know whether large hydraulic projects such as the Augustan aqueduct, the so-called Serino aqueduct which replaced an older system that brought water from Avella (cf. Jansen, Ch. 16; Map 1), had any effects on the water level or the degree of irrigation in fields, especially for vegetable plots near the city limit.[45] In general, Augustan-era alterations cannot be detected, though the Villa Pisanella near Boscoreale did get new paintings (in a classicizing style coming from the *urbs*, i.e., Rome) during the first decades of the first century AD.[46]

At the moment Vesuvius erupted, a large number of villas were either abandoned or in a state of repair. Excavators encountered construction materials in various rooms, entire buildings empty and uninhabited, carts in former *oeci*, and rooms either closed or changed in function (e.g., many baths). It is not clear why the fashion of having a villa in the Gulf of Naples faded.[47] One reason often put forward is a decline in the Campanian economy after the earthquake of AD 62, an event that also made necessary many operations at Pompeii (cf. Dobbins, Ch.12; Koloski-Ostrow, Ch. 15; Nappo, Ch. 23). However, the latest studies contradict this old supposition, according to which the rich proprietors abandoned the town.[48] As to *villeggiatura* (vacationing), we might seek explanations related to the emperors' habits and their concentrated attention on Rome. Claudius' successors apparently seldom dwelled in the Campanian villas, and they neither enlarged them nor constructed new ones. Although Nero was often at Naples for his theatrical hobbies, he was constructing a villa within Rome, the *Domus Aurea*, a project suddenly interrupted by his death in AD 68. Vespasian was averse to the luxury displayed by Claudius and Nero, as Titus, his short-reigning son, probably was. Domitian would construct a "villa" on the Palatine, the *Domus Flavia* and/or *Augustana*, as well as villas at Castel Gandolfo and Monte Circeo— nearer to Rome—and this focus on the capital probably caused people around the throne to move to the same area.[49] If this supposition is true, villas in the Vesuvian area became less important elements in the display of wealth and power for their owners, received less attention, and changed mainly into farmsteads. Former living quarters served agricultural activities such as the traditional *pars rustica*; the tenant lived in small rooms on the first floor, as we know from the villa of La Regina at Boscoreale. The recently explored "villa 6" at Terzigno provides another example of this change (see above and n. 22).

IMAGES OF VILLAS

Depictions of villas in wall paintings and mosaics, often quoted to illustrate villa life, must be studied with care. Those in the northern and African provinces, dating from the second through sixth centuries AD, show actual farm estates and laborers on their fields; they illustrate villa life among estate buildings. The many landscapes from Pompeii do not portray realism; they belong to the idyllic world of Hellenistic and early imperial bucolic poetry (e.g., Horace). Mythological content also helps create an atmosphere that fits into the Hellenistic world of *tryphe* ("luxurious lifestyle").[50] On the other hand, a number of frescoes showing villas do seem to belong to a common repertoire (Figure 23.10). Their realistic contents include more or less standard elements for wealthy architecture: porticoes, towers, large lawns with rows of herms, and statues. None clearly depicts any known excavated villa. No agricultural activities are shown in these pictures apart from romantic impressions of shepherds with a few sheep or fishermen along a river. Therefore, I think that these (mostly small-sized) images do not constitute photo-like souvenirs for placement in town houses, but belong to the same category as entirely fantastic landscapes.[51]

STABIAE

It is generally accepted that the *ager Stabianus* did not belong to the *ager Pompeianus*; it received its own administration after the devastation of the town in 89 BC by Sullan troops. P. Miniero has demonstrated that even before that date, some (at least three) agricultural settlements were present in the region.[52] These were abandoned after the Sullan raid. Villas erected after this fatal date were collocated along the crest of the Varano hill, with a panoramic view over the Gulf of Naples; they were mainly intended as luxurious dwellings. The *villae maritimae* have elongated plans and were principally oriented to the sea. The painted images of villas mentioned just above evoke this setting, but their presence in city houses instead of villas—and their lack of details determining specific aspects—detract from their realism.

No changes to agricultural production facilities after AD 62 can be recognized. In the hinterland of Stabiae some forty-five *villae rusticae* have been identified, mainly situated near the main road to Nocera (ancient Nuceria), on the lower parts of the Sorrentine promontory (Map 1). The extent of one example measured some 1,400–1,700 m^2; most fell into the ranges of 400–800 or 800–1,200 m^2. Living spaces were few; no large numbers of slaves may be postulated. Their small dimensions and the absence of implements in most villas for wine and oil (just twelve *cellae vinariae* and five oil presses) suggest grain and vegetable farms (cf. Jongman, Ch. 32).[53]

BOSCOREALE: THE RURAL VILLA REGINA

The building that belonged to a modest property northwest of Pompeii (Figures 1.1, 28.1, no. 57; Figures 28.4 and 28.5) is similar to the "Silver Treasure Villa" studied by Mau and Kelsey. It was a good example of an ordinary private farm, built in the second century BC and used until the explosion of Vesuvius.[54] It measures approximately 450 m^2 and has a simple *pars urbana* with plain paintings of the Third Style (*triclinium* (IV), *cubicula* (V*bis*, VIII, X, XVI)). The greater part of the establishment was used for agricultural activities. Rooms (IX–IX*bis*) contained the wine press; the large room (II) formed the kitchen. Open space (XVII) was used for threshing grain. The nucleus of the building consisted of portico (VII) and the relatively enormous *cella vinaria* (I). Around the modestly constructed house, a small vegetable garden and many grapevines were situated. Fruit trees (figs, peaches and apricots) and olive trees were also present. Finds were modest, but illustrate that the farmstead was active until the final disaster.

HERCULANEUM: THE OPULENT VILLA
OF THE PAPYRI

The hinterland of Herculaneum is not well explored. No villas have been spotted on the lava-caked slopes of Vesuvius; towards the coast, only so-called villa at contrada Sora, Torre del Greco has been explored.[55] The exception is the Villa of the Papyri (Figure 28.3).[56] Since its discovery in 1750 nearly 27 m below the level of the town of Portici, this large *villa suburbana* situated along the coast northwest of Herculaneum has been admired for the existence of its large private library (cf. Foss, Ch. 3).[57] Though its ancient papyrus scrolls were first (1752) thought to be pieces of wood, nearly 1,800 scrolls have now been unrolled and revealed to contain, in large part, Greek philosophical texts (cf. Dickmann, Ch. 27). Reopening one of the Bourbon-era tunnels, at a cost of some $600,000, made a new entrance possible; the core rooms and sea front of the villa's *atrium* have now been excavated and opened to the public, revealing two additional lower levels, wall decoration and geometric mosaics (Figures 3.3, 28.6).[58] The *atrium* had Second-Style decoration, probably of the mature phase, with large still-lifes; other rooms contained Fourth-Style murals.

Figure 28.6 Herculaneum, Villa of the Papyri, new excavations, corridor (t) and reception room (f) on the west side of the atrium. Photo: P. W. Foss.

The villa had no agricultural facilities; it presented itself, from the plans made by Karl Weber shortly after the end of the excavations in 1757, as a building with an *atrium*, a small peristyle with *euripus* at the southern end, and an extensive porticoed peristyle with an elongated pool on the north (Figure 28.3). Its layout high above the shore corresponded to a Hellenistic taste for panoramically exciting terrace architecture (e.g., the Temple of Juppiter Anxur at Terracina and the coast-facing "urban villas" in Herculaneum itself); cf. Tybout, Ch. 26; Dickmann, Ch. 27.[59]

There have been various attempts to identify the owner; the prevailing opinion asserts that Lucius Calpurnius Piso, father-in-law of Julius Caesar, was the man who collected the books: he is renowned for his interest in Greek Epicurean philosophy and had Philodemos of Gadara as a personal teacher.[60] However, all arguments have foundered on the absence of epigraphic or other written evidence.[61] We may prudently conclude that the man (note that women are rarely considered as possible candidates) who had the building filled with statuary and literature belonged to the elite of the *urbs* and was, like Piso, a lover of a Greek doctrine that was a good fit to his quest for *otium*.

The original excavations brought to light numerous statues, mostly in bronze— another reason for the villa's reputation. The statuary included various genres: portraits of politicians, army heroes, writers and philosophers, "idealized" heads that quote Polykleitos (the fifth-century Greek sculptor), and images of gods, satyrs and animals (e.g., a satyr copulating with a goat); a similarly eclectic assemblage has been recovered from the Villa of "Poppaea" at Oplontis).[62] Thanks to Weber's conscientious registration of the finds (cf. Foss, Ch. 3), the original setting can largely be reconstructed. The peristyle was reminiscent of a Greek idyllic landscape, combined with a gymnasium, where sports and philosophy were practiced. The sculpted figures, however oddly eclectic they may seem, represented a sort of "Reader's Digest" of the finest elements of Hellenic culture. Greek models were not imitated blindly but were adapted to the wishes of the proprietor. A sense of *otium* was evoked by the pastoral motifs, gods and literary figures; *negotium* by portraits of politicians and military officers. These concepts were not separated out in some kind of binary opposition, but were indivisibly blended and interrelated: a *"Bildungslandschaft"* full of *"Erinnerings-kultur,"* as P. Zanker puts it.[63]

CONCLUSION

This overview by no means covers all aspects of the Roman villa in the environs of Pompeii. There is little about the architecture of farms or luxurious buildings, and interior decoration has been treated only in passing. Such topics have traditionally occupied the bulk of publications about villas. This chapter concentrates instead on the role of the villa in the context of the city, agricultural production and land use. It is clear that Pompeii's rural economy changed from the Oscan to the Roman periods: different land divisions, new farmers and perhaps even new kinds of agriculture were established in the latter phase. The villa represents only a small part of the life of a modest ancient city such as Pompeii, but the city cannot be appreciated fully if the outskirts are not included. Many Pompeians worked in their own fields or on behalf of owners who lived in Rome and periodically visited their possessions. The villa economy formed an indispensable means of income (in social currency, at least), but remained a relatively small-scale affair. At the same time, few purely luxury villas were erected; a combination of leisure and work retained primacy.

NOTES

1 In general: H. Mielsch, *Die römische Villa*, Munich, 1987, with bibliography. See also J. T. Smith, *Roman Villas. A study in social structure*, London, 1997; J. J. Rossiter, *Roman Farm Buildings in Italy*, BAR-IS 52, Oxford, 1978.

2 H. Drerup, *Die römische Villa*, Marburger Winckelmann-Programm, 1959; J. Percival, *The Roman Villa. An historical introduction*, London, 1976, pp. 54–5; X. Lafon, *Villa maritima: recherches sur les villas littorales de l'Italie romaine (IIIe siècle av. J.-C. / IIIe siècle ap. J.-C.)*, Rome, 2001.

3 M. S. Spurr, *Arable Cultivation in Italy: c. 200 BC–c. AD 100*, London, 1986; K. Greene, *The Archaeology of the Roman Economy*, Berkeley, CA, 1986, pp. 67–97; K. D. White, *Roman Farming*, Ithaca, NY, 1970; G. W. Dimbledy, "Pollen analysis of soil samples from the AD 79 level. Pompeii, Oplontis, and Boscoreale," in W. F. Jashemski and F. G. Meyer (eds), *The Natural History of Pompeii*, Cambridge, 2002, pp. 181–216; *Vitruvius: ten books on architecture* (transl. Ingrid D. Rowland; commentary and illustrations T. N. Howe), Cambridge, 1999.

4 A. Oettel, *Fundkontexte römischer Vesuvvillen im Gebiet um Pompeji*, Mainz, 1996, pp. 16–51.

5 Oettel, *Fundkontexte*, pp. 53–62.

6 A. Mau, *Pompeii: its life and art* (transl. and ed. by F. W. Kelsey), rev. edn, London, 1902, pp. 355–67; A. Pasqui, "La villa pompeiana della Pisanella presso Boscoreale," *MonAnt*, 1897, vol. 7, pp. 397–554. This is still one of the few extensive studies on Roman villas in Campania. See also R. Ling, "Villae rusticae at Boscoreale," *JRA*, 1996, vol. 9, pp. 344–50. For Boscotrecase: P. H. von Blanckenhagen and C. Alexander, *The Augustan Villa at Boscotrecase*, Mainz, 1990. Boscoreale and the meaning of its paintings, especially the *megalographia*, are hotly debated. See now the attempt at reconciling the historical and mythological interpretations by M. Torelli, "The frescoes of the Great Hall of the Villa at Boscoreale," in D. Braund and C. Gill (eds), *Myth, History and Culture in Republican Rome. Studies in honour of T. P. Wiseman*, Exeter, 2003, pp. 217–56 (with extensive bibliography).

7 See C. Parslow, *Rediscovering Antiquity. Karl Weber and the excavation of Herculaneum, Pompeii and Stabiae*, Cambridge, 1995, pp. 44–6, 177–98.

8 E. K. Gazda (ed.), *The Villa of the Mysteries in Pompeii. Ancient ritual, modern muse*, Ann Arbor, MI, 2000.

9 S. De Caro, *La villa rustica in località Villa Regina a Boscoreale*, Rome, 1994.

10 P. Miniero, "Insediamenti e trasformazioni nell'*ager Stabianus* tra VII secolo a.C. e I secolo d.C.," in L. Franchi dell'Orto (ed.), *Ercolano 1738-1988. 250 anni di ricerca archeologica*. Atti del Convegno Internazionale Ravello-Ercolano-Napoli-Pompei 30 ottobre–5 novembre 1988, Rome, 1993, pp. 581–94; L. D'Orsi, *Gli scavi di Stabiae (1950–1968)*, Rome, 1996; A. Barbet and P. Miniero (eds), *La villa di San Marco à Stabia*, Naples, 1999; G. Bonifacio and A. M. Sodo (eds), *Stabiae: storia e architettura: 250° anniversario degli scavi di Stabiae 1749-1999*, Studi della Soprintendenza archeologica di Pompei, vol. 7, Rome, 2002; *In Stabiano. Culture e archeologia da Stabiae*, Catalogo della mostra, Castellammare di Stabia, 2001.

11 *Misurare la terra*, Modena, 1983; S. L. Dyson, *The Roman Countryside*, London, 2003. For work on the territory of Pompeii, see F. Senatore, "Pompeii e l'ager Pompeianus," in F. Senatore (ed.), *Pompei, Capri e la Penisola Sorrentina*, Capri, 2004; F. Senatore, "Ager Pompeianus: viticoltura e territorio nella piana del Sarno nel I sec. d.C.," in F. Senatore (ed.), *Pompei, il Sarno e la penisola Sorrentina*, Pompei, 1998, pp. 135–66. For landuse and its documentation by means of aerial photography, see also M. Guaitoli, *Lo sguardo di Icaro: le collezioni dell'Aerofotografia Nazionale per la conoscenza del territorio*, Campisano, 2003.

12 See De Caro, *Villa rustica*, pp. 95–114; W. F. Jashemski, *The Gardens of Pompeii, Herculaneum and the Villas Destroyed by Vesuvius*, New Rochelle, NY, 1979, vol. 1, pp. 289–314; 1993, vol. 2, pp. 293–301.

13 B. Andreae and H. Kyrieleis (eds), *Neue Forschungen in Pompeji*, Recklinghausen, 1975; F. Zevi (ed.), *Pompei 79: Raccolta di studi per il decimonono centenario dell'eruzione vesuviana*, Naples, 1984; Franchi dell'Orto, *Ercolano 1738–1988*. An exception is the important overview given by J. D'Arms, "Ville rustiche e ville di 'otium'," in Zevi, *Pompei 79*, pp. 65–86.

14 "Studi su Ercolano e Pompei," *La parola del passato*, special issue, 1979, vol. 188–9, pp. 321–508; M. Kunze (ed.), *Pompeji 79–1979. Beiträge zum Vesuvausbruch und seiner Nachwirkung*, Stendal, 1982.

15 E.g., B. Andreae (ed.), *Pompeji: Leben und Kunst in den Vesuvstädten*, Essen, 1973 (also in Dutch and French editions, 1974–5); J. B. Ward-Perkins and A. Claridge, *Pompeii AD 79*, London, 1976; *Rediscovering Pompeii*, Rome, 1990; M. Borriello *et al.*, *Pompei. Abitare sotto il Vesuvio*, Ferrara, 1996. Ultimately, A. D'Ambrosio, P. Guzzo and M. Mastroroberto (eds), *Storie da un'eruzione. Pompei Ercolano Oplontis*, Milan, 2003, where several villas are presented. Another exception to the average art-historical approach is: A. Ciarallo and E. De Carolis (eds), *Homo faber. Natura, scienza e tecnica nell'antica Pompei*, Milan, 1999, with sections on farming and farming techniques.

16 Pasqui, "La villa"; A. Maiuri, *La Villa dei Misteri*, 2 vols, Rome, 1931; von Blanckenhagen and Alexander, *Augustan villa*.

17 For Oplontis, see: B. Bergmann, "Art and nature in the villa at Oplontis," in *Pompeian Brothels, Pompeii's Ancient History, Mirrors and Mysteries, Art and Nature at Oplontis, & the Herculaneum "Basilica"*, JRA Suppl. Ser. no. 47, 2002, pp. 87–120, with refs; A. Varone, "Villa of Poppea at Oplontis," in F. Coarelli (ed.), *Pompeii*, New York, 2002, pp. 360–77; P. G. Guzzo and L. Fergola, *Oplontis: la villa di Poppaea*, Milan, 2000; L. Fergola and M. Pagano, *Oplontis: le splendide ville romane di Torre Annunziata*, Naples, 1998.

18 De Caro, *Villa rustica*.

19 Oettel, *Fundkontexte*; Jashemski and Meyer, *Natural History*. Up to 1985, research on villas is summarized by V. Kockel, "Funde und Forschungen in den Vesuvstädten I," *AA*, 1985, pp. 519–55.

20 The laboratory is accessible at the Soprintendenza Archeologica di Pompei's web-site: http://www.pompeiisites.org/. Bibliographies of recent research are available.

21 Borriello, *Abitare*, p. 263, cat. 578 with fig.

22 C. Ciccirelli, "Terzigno," in D'Ambrosio, Guzzo and Mastroroberto, *Storie da un'eruzione*, pp. 200–21. I discuss the largely unknown *megalographia* in one of the luxurious republican rooms that fell into disuse during the imperial period in "Der römische Freskenzyklus mit großen Figuren in der Villa 6 in Terzigno," in Th. Ganschow (ed.), *Otium. Festschrift für Volker Michael Strocka*, Remshalden, 2005, pp. 257–66. See also V. M. Strocka, "Troja—Karthago—Rom. Ein vorvergilisches Bildprogramm in Terzigno bei Pompeji," *RM*, 2005–6, vol. 112, pp. 79–120.

23 Cic., *Fam.* 7.3.1 (to Marcus Marius), 12.20 (to Quintus Cornificius); *Q Fr.* 6.4 and 13.8 (to his brother Marcus Quintus).

24 The connection with Poppaea was surmised by the villa's excavator, Alfonso de Franciscis, "Beryllos e la villa 'di Poppea' ad Oplontis," in *Studies in Classical Art and Archaeology. A tribute to P. H. von Blanckenhagen*, Locust Valley, NY, 1979, pp. 231–3. A similar connection has been argued for the House of the Menander (I.10.4) at Pompeii; cf. Nappo. Ch. 23.

25 M. Della Corte, *Case ed abitanti di Pompei*, 3rd edn, Naples, 1965. See the criticism in P. Castrén, *Ordo populusque Pompeianus*, Rome, 1975, esp. pp. 31–3.

26 Despite the efforts of J. Day, "Agriculture in the Life of Pompeii," *YCS*, 1932, vol. 3, pp. 165–208, esp. 177. However, there were Pompeians (such as Marcus Holconius Rufus and Marcus Tullius), who clearly had political and social connections with Rome and the imperial court (cf. Ling, Ch. 9; Franklin, Ch. 33; Welch, Ch. 36). As to other means of earning money by the elite, as deduced from material found in villas, see A. Łoś, "Les affaires 'industrielles' des élites des villes campaniennes sous les Julio-Claudiens et les Flaviens," *MÉFRA*, 2000, vol. 112, pp. 243–78.

27 Cato, *Agr.* 1.7, 10.1–11.5.

28 De Caro, *Villa rustica*; cf. M. George, "*Servus* and *domus*: the slave in the Roman house," in R. Laurence and A. Wallace-Hadrill (eds), *Domestic Space in the Roman World: Pompeii and beyond*, JRA Suppl. Ser. no. 22, 1997, pp. 15–24, esp. 15.

29 De Caro, *Villa rustica*, pp. 115–30; W. F. Jashemski, "Recently excavated gardens and cultivated land of the Villas at Boscoreale and Oplontis," in E. MacDougall (ed.), *Ancient Roman Villa Gardens*, Washington, DC, 1987, pp. 33–71.

30 W. M. Jongman, *The Economy and Society of Pompeii*, Amsterdam, 1988, pp. 97–154.

31 Jongman, *Pompeii*, p. 103.

32 De Caro, *Villa rustica*; R. Etienne, "Villas du Vésuve et structure agraire," in *La regione sotterrata dal Vesuvio. Studi e prospettivi*, Atti del convegno internazionale 11–15 novembre 1979, Naples, 1982, pp. 183–91.

33 Oettel, *Fundkontexte*, pp. 147–68; F. Zevi in De Caro, *Villa rustica*, pp. 5–13; see also the criticism by Strocka and Tybout quoted below in n. 44.

34 K. Peterse, *Steinfachwerk in Pompeji: Bautechnik und Architektur*, Amsterdam, 1999, 107–48; A. Schoonhoven, *Metrology and Meaning in Pompeii: the urban arrangement of Regio VI*, Studi della Soprintendenza Archeologica di Pompeii, vol. 20, Rome, 2006.

35 Oettel, *Fundkontexte*, pp. 144–55.

36 F. Zevi, "Urbanistica di Pompei," in *Regione sotterata dal Vesuvio*, pp. 353–65.

37 J. D'Arms, *Romans on the Bay of Naples*, Cambridge, MA, 1970; J.-A. Dickmann, *Domus frequentata: Anspruchsvolles Wohnen im pompejanischen Stadthaus*, Munich, 1999.

38 Jashemski, *Gardens*, vols 1–2.

39 Jongman, *Pompeii*, p. 133.

40 D. G. Yntema, *In search of an ancient countryside: the Amsterdam Free University Field Survey at Oria Province of Brindisi, South Italy (1981–1983)*, Amsterdam, 1993, pp. 195–226, esp. 202.

41 H. Mouritsen, *Elections, Magistrates and Municipal Elite. Studies in Pompeian epigraphy*, Rome, 1988, pp. 84–9. Dickmann, *Domus frequentata*, pp. 252–5 sketches the integration of the colonists into the existing community as a peaceful process.

42 R. A. Tybout, *Aedificiorum Figurae. Untersuchungen zu den Architekturdarstellungen des frühen zweiten Stils*, Amsterdam, 1989, pp. 41–54, esp. 49. As to Oettel's proposal of dating the phases within the Second Style according to consecutive *centuriationes*, see R. A. Tybout, "Roman wall-painting and social significance," *JRA*, 2001, vol. 14, pp. 33–56, esp. 53–6.

43 See Tybout, *Aedificiorum Figurae* and "Roman wall-painting," as well as Dickmann, *Domus frequentata*, pp. 240–52.

44 Figure 28.1, nos. 55, 16, 31. The date of 59 BC is suggested by Tybout, "Roman wall-painting," p. 55 (contra Oettel's proposal in *Fundkontexte*, pp. 173–5 of 42 BC). Criticism of Oettel's chronology was also raised by V. M. Strocka in his review of Oettel in *BJb*, 1999, vol. 199, pp. 581–4. The Villa of Agrippa Postumus was probably painted by workers from a Roman studio like that which decorated the Villa della Farnesina, as proposed by I. Bragantini and M. De Vos, *Museo Nazionale Romano, II. Le pitture, 1. Le decorazioni della Villa della Farnesina*, Rome, 1982, pp. 50–61; contra A. Allroggen-Bedel, "Die Wanddekorationen der Villen am Golf von Neapel," in *Regione sotterata dal Vesuvio*, pp. 519–30, esp. 528–9.

45 C. P. J. Ohlig, *De Aquis Pompeiorum: Das Castellum Aquae in Pompeji: Herkunft, Zuleitung und Verteilung des Wassers*, Nijmegen, 2001, pp. 75–84, 270–1 (Pompeii's autonomy in using the water *decreased* with the construction of the Serino aqueduct, as the city was no longer independent and had to share resources with more distant destinations like Misenum).

46 Figure 28.1, no. 13. As to the paintings, see F. L. Bastet, "Villa rustica in contrada Pisanella," *CronPomp*, 1976, vol. 2, pp. 112–43. An update can be found in Oettel, *Fundkontexte*, no. 23, fig. 23.

47 D'Arms, *Bay of Naples*; D'Arms, "Ville rustiche."

48 See F. Pirson, *Mietwohnungen in Pompeji und Herkulaneum*, Munich, 1999, pp. 140, 144, 173 (with older literature, e.g., D'Arms, *Bay of Naples*; Allroggen-Bedel, "Die Wanddekorationen"). See also various contributions in T. Fröhlich and L. Jacobelli (eds), *Archäologie und Seismologie. La regione Vesuviana dal 62 al 79 d.C. Problemi archeologici e sismologici*, Munich, 1995.

49 The tendency to focus on Rome as the center of power is substantiated by the enormous building activities, stimulus of art and literature, and political concentration of power in the hands of the emperor. See the various contributions in A. J. Boyle and W. J. Dominik (eds), *Flavian Rome. Culture, image, text*, Leiden, 2003.

50 Jongman, *Pompeii*, pp. 105–6.

51 Bergmann, "Art and nature"; B. Bergmann, "Painted perspectives of a villa visit: landscape as status and metaphor," in E. Gazda (ed.), *Roman Art in the Private Sphere*, Ann Arbor, MI, 1991, pp. 49–70; B. Bergmann, "Exploring the grove: pastoral space on Roman walls," in J. Dixon Hunt (ed.), *The Pastoral Landscape*, Washington, DC, 1992, pp. 21–46. As to villa representations and their "realism," see W. J. Th. Peters (ed.), *La Casa di Marcus Lucretius Fronto e le sue pitture*, Assen, 1993, p. 223.

52 Miniero, "Insediamenti."

53 Miniero, "Insediamenti."

54 De Caro, *Villa rustica.*

55 M. Pagano, "Torre del Greco, Località Ponte Rivieccio, contrada Villa Sora, propr. Montella," *RStPomp*, 1989, vol. 3, pp. 287–94; M. Pagano, "La villa romana in contrada Sora a Torre del Greco," *CronErcol*, 1991, vol. 21, pp. 149–68; M. Pagano, "Torre del Greco, Villa marittima romana in contrada Sora," *RStPomp*, 1993–4, vol. 6, pp. 267–9.

56 The eighteenth-century excavations were excellently published by D. Comparetti and G. De Petra, *La villa Ercolanese dei Pisoni e la sua biblioteca*, Torino, 1883 (= facsimile, Naples, 1972). See also R. Neudecker, *Die Skulpturenausstattung römischer Villan in Italien*, Mainz, 1988, pp. 105–14; P. Stewart, *Statues in Roman society. Representation and response*, Oxford, 2003, pp. 252–9.

57 Parslow, *Rediscovering Antiquity*, pp. 77–106. See D. Snider, *The Library of the Villa dei Papiri at Herculaneum*, Los Angeles, 2005.

58 A. De Simone *et al.*, "Ercolano 1992–1997. La Villa dei Papiri e lo scavo della città," *CronErcol*, 1998, vol. 28, pp. 1–63; A. De Simone and F. Ruffo, "Ercolano 1996–1998. Lo scavo della Villa dei Papiri," *CronErcol*, 2002, vol. 32, pp. 325–44; M. Pagano, "La Villa dei Papiri," in D'Ambrosio, Guzzo and Mastroroberto, *Storie da un'eruzione*, pp. 98–101.

59 See Lafon, *Villa maritima.*

60 Following Comparetti and De Petra, *Villa Ercolanese*, pp. 1–32. So also G. Sauron, *Quis Deum? L'espression plastique des idéologies politiques et religieuses à Rome*, Rome, 1994, pp. 488–9 (cf. his index for other items discussed).

61 For instance, M. R. Wojcik, *La Villa dei Papiri ad Ercolano : contributo alla ricostruzione dell'ideologia della nobilitas tardorepubblicana*, Rome, 1986, pp. 279–84, has proposed Appius Claudius Pulcher, consul in 54 BC.

62 Wojcik, *La villa*; G. Sauron, "Templa Serena. À propos de la 'Villa des Papyri' d'Herculaneum: Contribution à l'étude des comportements aristocratiques romains à la fin de la Republique," *MÉFR*, 1980, vol. 92, pp. 277–301. For the Oplontis statues, see S. De Caro, "The sculptures of the Villa of Poppaea at Oplontis: a preliminary report," in E. Blair Macdougall (ed.), *Ancient Roman Villa Gardens*, Dumbarton Oaks Colloquium on the History of Landscape Architecture 10, Washington, DC, 1987, pp. 77–133.

63 I.e., "didactic landscape" full of "a sensibility of remembrance." P. Zanker, *Pompeji. Stadtbild und Wohngeschmack*, Mainz, 1995, p. 149; cf. pp. 23–32. Binary opposition was argued by D. Pandermalis, "Zum Programm der Statuenausstattung in der Villa dei Papyri," *AM*, 1971, vol. 86, pp. 173–209. On the sculptures, see now C. C. Mattusch, *The "Villa dei Papiri" at Herculaneum: life and afterlife of a sculpture collection*, Los Angeles, 2005.

PART IV

SOCIETY AND ECONOMY

———•·•———

CHAPTER TWENTY-NINE

SHOPS AND INDUSTRIES

———•◆•———

Felix Pirson

INTRODUCTION

As first-time visitors walk through the ruins of Pompeii and Herculaneum, they are struck by the large number of shops, workshops and taverns, distinguished from the entrances of dwellings by their wide store fronts (Figure 29.1). Particularly on the busy main roads, it is easy to get the impression that the street fronts of the buildings consist almost entirely of small business establishments, which I will designate by the Latin term *tabernae*. In antiquity, *tabernae* described not only taverns or pubs, but also artisans' workshops, stores or simple dwellings (cf. DeFelice, Ch. 30).

It is clear that *tabernae* were not exclusively business concerns, but that they were also occupied. In the cities under Vesuvius, most shops had an upper story as well as back and side rooms that could be used by the shopkeeper as dwellings. Particularly in Pompeii, many *tabernae* and even larger factories have been documented inside domestic houses or within empty lots in less densely populated parts of town. The archaeological record gives us a great deal of information, not only about diversity in commerce and the processes of production, but also about the economic strategies of the inhabitants. The incorporation of a majority of *tabernae* into private houses and public buildings demonstrates the intensive exploitation of real estate. At the same time, it provides a glimpse of the social organization of small businesses. The third section of this chapter focusses on the latter two aspects. The first section gives a brief overview of the different kinds of businesses represented in the cities under Vesuvius, and the second section explores the dynamics of living and working in *tabernae*.

A DIVERSE BUSINESS ENVIRONMENT

The excavations at Pompeii and Herculaneum have brought to light evidence of a variety of branches of industry. Inscriptions, *dipinti* and *graffiti* mention various jobs performed at Pompeii and Herculaneum. Wall paintings and shop signs illustrate scenes of manufacturing and sales.[1] The most important sources of information, however, are the shops themselves, which have been preserved in great numbers, particularly in Pompeii.[2]

457

Figure 29.1   Pompeii. *Tabernae* II.1.4–6 from the northwest.

The goods manufactured and sold there were intended primarily to meet the demands of the local market, namely Pompeii and its environs (cf. Jongman, Ch. 32; Moormann, Ch. 28).[3] Of course, it cannot be ruled out that certain products were also exported.[4] Likewise, both local and imported goods found a ready market in Pompeii and its surrounding area. The situation was probably similar in Herculaneum, where we are much less well informed about the business environment.[5] For instance, we do not yet have evidence there for large-scale manufacturing similar to the textile industry at Pompeii. This may be due to the lack of an extensive agricultural hinterland that would have provided raw materials and a market.

The manufacture of goods took place in special workshops located in *tabernae* or in converted domestic houses. We also find evidence of workshop activity in normal dwellings. This is particularly true of weaving and baking, which mainly served the needs of the occupants. There is evidence, however, that some houses produced more than what was necessary to meet immediate needs. The large kitchen (22) of the House of the Postumii (VIII.4.4, 49) contains not only a stove, latrine, fireplace and worktable, but also one small and two large basins (Figure 29.2). A fourth basin in the peristyle colonnade is connected to the kitchen via an opening. The large number of basins increases the likelihood that the kitchen was used for productive activities beyond the needs of the household itself. The kind of production is hard to establish, but it is particularly remarkable that the existence of the basins can be traced back archaeologically to the time before the earthquake of AD 62, which hitherto has been regarded as the starting point for the introduction of production-fittings into private houses (confirmed also in Region VI.1; cf. Jones and Robinson, Ch. 25).[6] Finally,

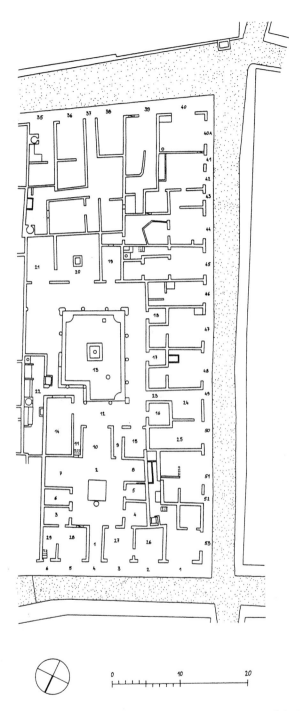

Figure 29.2 Pompeii. Western third of *insula* VIII.4 showing the House of the Postumii (VIII.4.4, 49); C. Brückener, after J.-A. Dickmann and F. Pirson, "Repräsentatives Wohnen," modified from the RICA Pompei—*insulae* 1:500 maps from H. B. Van der Poel (ed.), *Corpus Topographicum Pompeianum* Rome 1977–86, 5 vols, with the authorization of L. García y García.

observations from the House of the Postumii make clear that (commercial) production could even happen inside or close to the reception areas[7] of a luxurious private dwelling—a rather unusual solution, which points to the importance of economic factors in the layout of domestic housing.

Textile workshops and bakeries are especially prominent among the known commercial establishments in Pompeii, because of their numbers, their identifiable facilities, and their preservation.[8] Because of their evident importance in the economic life of the city, these two industries are discussed first, and in greater depth.

Bakeries

The functioning of a Pompeian bakery can be explained particularly well on the basis of *pistrinum* (VI.3.3, 27–28), which was uncovered at the beginning of the nineteenth century (Figure 29.3a).[9] The bakery is located in the rear part of the domicile. It is

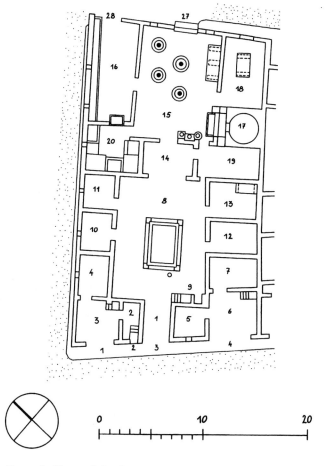

Figure 29.3a Pompeii. House of the Oven (VI.3.3, 27–28); C. Brückener, after Van der Poel, *CTP*, vol. III.1; Overbeck and Mau, *Pompeji in seinen Gebäuden*, Figure 189.

460

Figure 29.3b Shop sign from Pompeii; Overbeck and Mau, *Pompeji in seinen Gebäuden*, Figure 186.

Figure 29.3c Mill from Pompeii; Mau, *Pompeji*, Abb. 237.

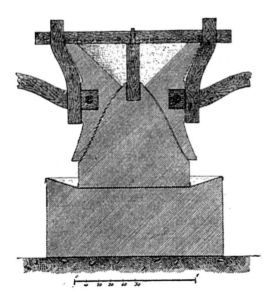

Figure 29.3d Mill from Pompeii, restored cross-section; Mau, *Pompeji*, Abb. 238.

Figure 29.3e Oven in the House of the Oven (VI.3.27–28), cross-section; Mau, *Pompeji*, Abb. 240.

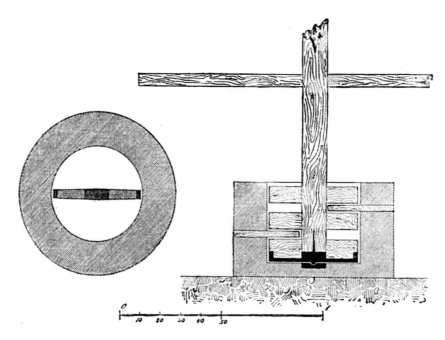

Figure 29.3f Kneading machine: plan and cross-section from bakery at the rear of the House of Laocoon (VI.14.30–32, large room south of the oven); Mau, *Pompeji*, Abb. 241.

not connected to a shop, but has its own entrance to the street, which was used for the movement of goods in and out. The center of the establishment is mill room (15), which has four millstones. This combination of bakery and mill is fairly common in the Vesuvian cities. The four millstones are arranged so as to make the best possible use of space. The floor is paved, indicating the use of mules or donkeys to turn the mills, as depicted on a shop sign from Pompeii (Figure 29.3b). The millstones are made of the usual basalt lava.[10] They consist of a conical *meta* on top of which sits the *catillus* in the shape of a double hollow cone (hourglass) (Figures 29.3c–d). Grain is poured into the upper funnel of the *catillus* and is then ground between the two stones. They are turned by means of two shafts inserted into the *catillus* and attached with bolts. The *catillus* could not sit directly on top of the *meta*, but had to move freely. For this purpose, there was a point on the tip of the *meta* for the positioning of a wooden structure which suspended the *catillus*. Milled grain then fell into a groove carved into the substructure of the mill.

The oven (17) of the bakery is located in its own baking room (Figure 29.3e). Smoke escapes through openings in the ceiling (d). The bakery is connected to adjacent rooms by two hatches: loaves of bread are shaped on a large table in room (18), while finished goods are stored in room (19). Stall (16), where animals are housed, is located on the opposite side of the mill courtyard. In several bakeries there was even found a special machine for kneading dough, which was wound around by a horizontal iron shaft at the bottom of the stone basin and then pressed through the spaces between fixed wooden slats reaching out from the sides of the basin and revolving arms on the central axis of the contraption (Figure 29.3f).

It is worth considering the distribution of *pistrina* inside Pompeii.[11] Bakeries are distributed in a more regular fashion throughout the city than other shops, in accordance with their importance as public utilities. However, concentrations of *pistrina* can be observed in several places. Those bakeries that are attached to mills are located for the most part along the main thoroughfares in the northern half of the city, along the via Consolare, via di Nola and strada Stabiana (Maps 2 and 3). The proximity of the northern part of the city to the agricultural hinterland whence the grain was delivered may explain this phenomenon. Several bakeries without mills but with shops are located in the so-called *Altstadt* (see Figure 7.1), where there was sure to be great demand because of its central location and population density.

The textile industry

The textile industry also played an important role in the economic life of Pompeii.[12] A controversial question—whether the large number of textile mills can be explained solely by the pressures of local demands, or whether Pompeii was a regional center of wool processing—cannot be discussed here. Instead, we are interested in the workshops themselves. Theoretically we can distinguish five types, although the archaeological record often does not allow a clear differentiation between the different types.[13] Raw wool was washed and combed in the *officinae lanifricariae*, and then dyed in the *officinae tinctoriae*. Spinning and weaving took place in the *textrinae*. Wool was felted in the *officinae coactiliariae*. The *fullonicae* were fullers' establishments where the finishing of woolen clothes took place, but which also took on the functions of a laundry service.[14]

Despite a great number of shops and the strong presence of textile workers in voting inscriptions, the distribution of work among different small workshops and their concentration in different areas of the city does not support the hypothesis for an organized textile industry (cf. Jongman, Ch. 32).[15] The *officinae lanifricariae* are concentrated to the east of the forum in the *Altstadt*, which was a center of small-scale industry in Pompeii.[16] On the other hand, *fullonicae* are distributed throughout the city, which may have something to do with their role as laundries, service establishments that would need to be represented throughout the city. Like most businesses, they seek the proximity of major thoroughfares, e.g. the strada Stabiana, via di Nola and via dell'Abbondanza. They are not represented in the interior *insulae* of Regions VI and VIII, which mainly consist of domestic dwellings; the powerful odors produced by fullers may be to blame. The distribution of *officinae tinctoriae* corresponds approximately to that of *fullonicae*.[17]

Fullonica (VI.8.2, 20–21) exemplifies the arrangement and furnishing of a Pompeian fullers' establishment. The house in which it is located was once a dwelling. It is the largest fullery excavated in Pompeii thus far (Figure 29.4a).[18] Well-known depictions of a textile press and *fullonica* work scenes were found on the southeast corner post of the inner courtyard. They give us important information about the production sequence (Figures 29.4b–d). The fullery was entered via corridor (8) past room (7), which may have been used to accept incoming orders. The courtyard is colonnaded on three sides; it is abutted on the south side by living quarters and the commercial wing of the complex. Room (19), containing a kitchen and home bakery, lies at the center. A flight of stairs leads from corridor (20) into an upper story.

Manufacturing equipment is located in the western and northern colonnades of the courtyard. A row of basins (26) was apparently used to rinse the fabrics (as in *fullonica* I.6.7); see Figure 35.2. The basins are connected to one another by small openings, and are constructed to allow the water to flow from one to the next. The water supply came through a pipe in the southernmost basin, at the highest level. Beside the group of basins, there is a group of six narrow cells (21), which held tubs in which the fabrics were pounded (Figure 29.4b). Urine, essential to the fuller's process, was probably gathered in the opening in the floor to the west of the two southernmost

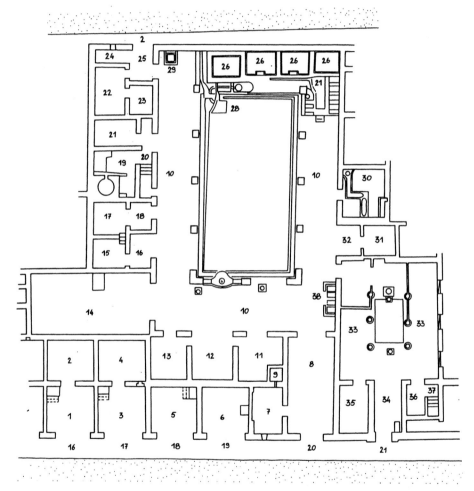

Figure 29.4a   Pompeii, *Fullonica* (VI.8.2, 20–21); C. Brückener, after Overbeck and Mau, *Pompeji in seinen Gebäuden*, Figure 193.

Figure 29.4b Wall painting from *Fullonica* (VI.8.2, 20–21): treading the fabric; Mau, *Pompeji*, Abb. 242.

Figure 29.4c Wall painting from *Fullonica* (VI.8.2, 20–21): a customer inspecting the cloth; brushing the fabric; a rack for bleaching with sulfur; Mau, *Pompeji*, Abb. 243.

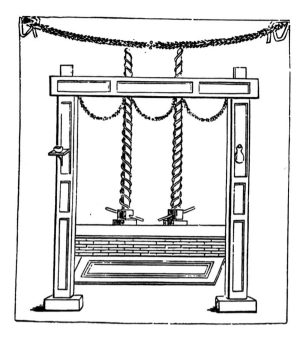

Figure 29.4d Wall painting from *Fullonica* (VI.8.2, 20–21): fuller's press;
Mau, *Pompeji*, Abb. 244.

cells. Room (30) is vaulted and contains a large stone table, a shallow basin and a
cistern. The discovery of a pot filled with fuller's earth (*creta fullonica*) shows that the
fabrics were treated with bleaching substances here. After drying the fabrics, which
presumably took place in the courtyard, they were combed or milled with a brush-
like instrument, the *aena* (Figure 29.4c). Then the cloths were treated with sulfur
on a hemispherical frame, which bleached them even more. Figure 29.4c depicts a
worker, crowned with an olive wreath, carrying such a frame. In his left hand he
holds a bucket of sulfur. The owl of Minerva, protective deity of fullers, perches on
the rack. In the foreground of the picture, a richly dressed lady is seated. She appears
to be placing an order with the girl standing in front of her. The final step in the
manufacturing process was pressing. A wooden clothes press is shown in yet another
wall painting (Figure 29.4d) from this *fullonica*, and an actual example was even
preserved at Herculaneum (shop III.10).

The *officinae lanifricariae*, *tinctoriae* and *coactiliariae* also contained specialized
equipment, which cannot be discussed in detail here. A feature of all three trades is
the presence either of basins that can be heated, or of ovens; this distinguishes them
from the *fullonicae*.

Other industries

Metalworking trades can be divided into two categories: the workers of non-ferrous
metals (*fabri aerarii*) and the ironsmiths (*fabri ferrarii*).[19] It is not always possible to
differentiate between iron and bronze smithies on the basis of furnishings and material

recovered from workshops, but we know of some forges where different kinds of metals were worked. For example, a shop was excavated outside the Porta Vesuvio at the end of the nineteenth century. This shop contained a rich assortment of finds, both in terms of raw materials (bronze, iron, lead) and tools (various anvils and hammers).[20] In addition, a plaster sculptor's model of a man's bust was found here, as well as diverse metal objects, the majority of which were probably made on-site. The most remarkable find is an under-life-size bronze statue of an *ephebe* that once functioned as a lamp stand and was apparently brought to the workshop to be repaired. There are also bronze vessels, furniture fittings, hinges and door-hinges as well as water faucets. In other workshops were found keys, surgical instruments, horse harness fittings and various other special instruments, such as a *groma*—used for land surveying. Some of the *fabri aerarii* were also metal sculptors who specialized in the manufacture of bronze statuettes (*fabri statuarii*). In contrast, ironsmiths were mainly occupied with making tools. Metalworking shops, like fulleries, avoided the proximity of residential quarters with little commercial activity. Larger forges, in particular, were probably situated outside the city walls because of fire danger. On the other hand, recent archaeological finds from the House of the Postumii (VIII.4.4, 49) located in the city center show that small-scale metalworking could even take place in half-ruined buildings or on building-sites.[21] This points to a concept of handicraft outside the well-established workshops that attract the interest of archaeologists and modern visitors. It also gives an idea of the range of productive (and perhaps commercial) activities that can no longer be traced in the excavated architectural remains of Pompeii, and hence shows how limited our insight is concerning the full range of economic life.

In the case of potteries in the urban region of Pompeii, we also cannot count on large factories,[22] which were more likely located outside the city. An inscription mentions a pottery that belonged to the imperial house somewhere in the environs of Pompeii.[23] To date, two potteries have been found inside the city walls, and a third was discovered outside the Porta di Ercolano.[24] All three workshops were small businesses rather than large factories. A lamp maker's workshop (I.20.3), furnished with two kilns, is particularly well preserved.[25] Located quite close by is another workshop (II.3.9), the façade of which was decorated with a well-known wall painting of a potter working at his wheel.[26] Evidence for the presence of two potteries in the southeastern area of Pompeii, near the amphitheater, emphasizes the productive character of this part of town, which contains not only numerous workshops but also gardens and vineyards (see below).

Inscriptions speak of many other trades and businesses in the cities under Vesuvius for which we have not yet been able to discover evidence in the archaeological record.[27] Barbers, dealers in ointments, booksellers, goldsmiths, greengrocers, onion sellers and tailors are mentioned. We have archaeological evidence for a cobbler's (VII.1.41–42), a tannery (I.5.2) and a mat weaver's (III.3.4).[28] Food was also sold in numerous *tabernae*, as shown by storage vessels sunk into the ground (*dolia*); cf. DeFelice, Ch. 30. Olive presses were found in *tabernae* (VII.4.24–25) and (VII.14.14), which suggests that oil was sold in these shops. However, it is difficult in many cases to distinguish between grocery stores and taverns or restaurants. Thus, nuts were also sold in *taberna* (IV.17–18) at Herculaneum, which has been interpreted as a snack bar (*popina*).[29]

We conclude this short overview of business concerns in Pompeii and Herculaneum with a look at food production in the city. The preparation of fish sauce (*garum*) has received much of the attention of scholars, although we know of only one *garum* shop in Pompeii to date (I.12.8; cf. also Jones and Robinson, Ch. 25).[30] Still, Pliny the Elder tells us that Pompeii was famous for its fish sauce (*HN* 31.94). It is most remarkable, concerning relations between local elites and small-scale businesses, that one of the most influential families in Pompeii, the Umbricii, participated in the production of *garum*.[31]

Extensive agricultural areas for growing fruit, vegetables and grapes are concentrated mainly in the southeastern quadrant of the city (cf. Jashemski, Ch. 31).[32] This area is considerably less densely developed, so land was open for cultivation. In addition, the topography, sloping to the southward in regions I and II, created favorable conditions for viticulture and gardening. In the largest vineyard examined to date in Pompeii, covering the entire area of *insula* (II.5), more than 2,000 vines were discovered in the excavated area alone.[33] The vineyard includes a wine pressing installation and ten *dolia* to store the wine. The wine was presumably sold in the vineyard's *taberna* that opened onto via dell'Abbondanza. The occupants of the House of the Ship Europa (I.15.2–4, 6) worked an extensive fruit and vegetable garden.[34] More than 400 roots of fruit trees, olive trees and grapevines, among others, were found here. Burnt remains of plants offer evidence for the cultivation of figs, almonds, beans and hazelnuts. Grapes, fruit and vegetables were grown, as were flowers. The latter were used in garlands and for the distillation of perfumes.[35] In all, kitchen gardens take up around 10 percent of the total area excavated so far at Pompeii.

TABERNAE AND "SHOP-HOUSES": COMBINING LIVING AND WORKING

The stores and workshops described in the previous section were mainly housed in *tabernae* that are considered to be typical commercial establishments because of their wide store fronts (Figure 29.1).[36] Accordingly, archaeological research has focussed almost exclusively on the commercial functions of the *tabernae*. Their use as living quarters has received marginal consideration at best. This situation reflects our modern conception of separate living and work-spaces which does not apply to ancient Roman life. Especially in the case of *tabernae*, which usually had access only to a limited amount of space, we should think of the boundaries between living and work areas as quite fluid. A comparison with living conditions in modern cities in southern Europe shows that shopkeepers may occupy even small shops without a back area. We can assume that *tabernae* were occupied especially in those cases where there are one or more back or side rooms adjacent to the shop itself. Most *tabernae* were also provided with mezzanines (*pergulae*) accessible by stairs or ladders (see Figure 8.14). Ventilation and light advantages connected with an upper-story location predestined the *pergulae* for use as living spaces. The significance of *tabernae* within the settlement structure of the cities of Vesuvius is underlined by their numerical strength. At Pompeii *tabernae* make up more than 40 per cent of housing units, while in Herculaneum they make up just over 30 per cent.[37]

Written sources confirm that *tabernae* were occupied as dwellings. The term *taberna*, as defined by the jurist Ulpian, is used for every building that is suitable for occupation.[38] Archaeological evidence for residential use of shops includes latrines, niches for beds and the remains of colorful wall decoration in back or side rooms off the retail space. Usually the wall painting consists of a simple decorative scheme without complicated ornamentation or figural scenes. Numerous (usually arcuated) niches in the walls point to the existence of self-sufficient households. Paintings preserved in several of these niches indicate that they were used for household cult.[39] Wells and hearths, on the other hand, may relate either to residential occupation or commercial activity.

During business hours *tabernae* were entered by the open storefront, which was closed after hours using a system of boards and a single door. The door secured the board construction and, at the same time, permitted uncomplicated access to the shop after closing time—an essential amenity if the shop was also used as a dwelling. Compared with *domus* architecture in the Vesuvian cities, *tabernae* provided a minimal standard of living, reduced progressively by greater occupation density. Colorful wall paintings in several *tabernae*, however, demonstrate that even small businessmen tried to participate in the generally accepted taste in interior decoration as they saw it in homes of the well-to-do.[40]

The size and layout of many *tabernae* are determined by their incorporation into a greater architectural complex, usually a private house. We can often observe that shops occupy several rooms of a main house as their back rooms (e.g., *tabernae* VIII.4.3, 5 in Figure 29.2). *Tabernae* may also appear in connected rows of shops, which either take up the street fronts of private houses or public buildings, or are conceived as independent structures. Especially in the latter two cases, it is appropriate to speak of *taberna* or "shop-house" complexes.[41] These complexes, usually several stories high, represent a particularly dense form of city living, since upper stories were often used as separate apartments with their own stairs and entrances. In addition to shops integrated into a larger complex, there are also freestanding *tabernae*.[42] With their expansive back wings, they often achieve the size of a small *domus*.

REAL ESTATE AND ECONOMIC STRATEGIES

In Pompeii and Herculaneum, similarly to modern cities, most stores are incorporated into larger structures: residences, public buildings or *taberna* complexes. Only about 30 percent of the Pompeiian *tabernae* cannot be connected with a larger complex and were presumably independently owned properties. Approximately 25 percent of *tabernae* are incorporated into residential houses, while almost half (45 percent) are part of a larger complex, though not connected spatially.[43] It is particularly likely in the latter cases that the *tabernae* were not run by the owners themselves, but were, rather, allocated to others. The modalities of *taberna* use legible in the archaeological record reveal various economic strategies that determined the organization of small-scale commerce.

The importance of possessing real estate as a source of income for the upper classes has repeatedly been emphasized (cf. Jongman, Ch. 32).[44] Particularly, landed elites were dependent upon capital income from rental properties or participation in business ventures. Liquid assets were needed to assure them of the leeway required for financing their political activities. Their own residences were not excepted, as numerous commercial establishments—particularly in the larger houses—attest.[45] The most minimal form of participation in a lucrative small business was the rental of *tabernae*, known to us at Pompeii from two rental notices.[46] In these cases, there was probably no relationship between the landlord and tenant above and beyond the rental contract. However, it is conceivable that rentals also took place in the context of patron–client relationships or, rather, at the beginning of such dependencies. In any case, possession of real estate was a means of binding clients more tightly to their patron and thus elevating the latter's social standing. The institution of the *institorium* played an important role in this dynamic. One *institor*, in the capacity of a business manager, ran a commercial establishment belonging to his patron, who decided the type and scope of the business.[47] In this way the property owner was in a position to skim off profits made in his *taberna* without having to be involved in the actual running of the business.

There are other possibilities for the allocation of residential and commercial spaces besides rental and *institorium*. The archaeological record cannot, unfortunately, provide us with such information in any particular case. Architecture, however, clearly reflects the interweaving of local elites with small businesses and reveals glimpses into the social organization of the commercial establishments located in *tabernae*.[48] An oft-cited example is the *Insula Arriana Polliana* (VI.6) in Pompeii, where one of the two rental notices mentioned above was found.[49] The center of the block is occupied by a manorial *atrium*-peristyle house, the so-called House of Pansa (VI.6.1, 13), which is probably where the owner of the entire property lived. Three sides of the *domus* are surrounded by smaller units that were for rent, as the advertisement indicates. Facing the street to the south, the lively via delle Terme, is a row of six *tabernae*, only one of which is connected to the interior of the house (see above). The other shops, all of which had mezzanine floors, can be equated with the *tabernae cum pergulis suis* named in the advertisement. A carefully articulated façade, consisting of ashlar masonry in tufa, helps accentuate optically the continuity between *domus* and *tabernae*. The owner of the house can have had no reason to hide his participation in small business concerns. Instead, he displays his ownership of real estate, including the shops, as a symbol of economic power. For the role of shops in urban planning and design, see Westfall, Ch. 10.

The different ways in which *tabernae* were incorporated in larger pieces of property can be examined in the House of the Postumii (VIII.4.4, 49), already mentioned above. Because of its location at the intersection of two major thoroughfares, shops surround it on the west and north (Figure 29.2).[50] The *tabernae* to the right and left of the main entrance are connected to the *atrium* via their back rooms. Presumably, the shopkeepers were residents of the central *domus* and directly under the control of the head of the house. The shops on the west side (with the exception of *taberna* (50)), however, are independent units lacking any connection with the interior. It is most probable that they, too, belonged to the same owners, as observations of the buildings' remains suggest. For example, it is striking that *tabernae* (47) and (48) dovetail in a regular manner with the floor plan of the *domus*. This and other evidence leads to the conclusion that they were planned as a unit. We could consider the isolation of the western *tabernae* an indication that they were rented out, on the analogy of the *Insula Arriana Polliana* (VI.6). However, there is also the possibility that they were managed by *institores* under contract to the master of the house. In the end, it is impossible to come to a definitive conclusion in favor of one or the other of the models. What is important to keep in mind is the potential variety of economic strategies available for a complex such as the House of the Postumii. This helps explain the attraction of urban real estate, which opened up numerous different ways for owners to participate in lucrative small business opportunities.

NOTES

1 Constanze Witt translated the German text. This article represents the state of research in 1998 when it was first submitted for publication. Since then, several important contributions have been made on the topic and are cited in the footnotes, but generally not referred to in the text. For the paintings, see T. Fröhlich, *Lararien und Fassadenbilder in den Vesuvstädten. Untersuchungen zur 'volkstümlichen' pompejanischen Malerei*, RM-EH, 32, Mainz, 1991, pp. 169–88, 236–41.

2 The text does not contain concrete numerical values, since the numbers in the literature often deviate widely from one another. The main cause for the discrepancies is the difficulty of differentiating between stores, workshops and pubs. In addition, many *tabernae* functioned as both workshops and sales areas, which has often led to their being counted twice. See V. Gassner, *Die Kaufläden in Pompeji*, Dissertationen der Universität Wien, 178, Wien, 1986, p. V: 577 shops (not counting bakeries or the textile or hospitality industries); *Pompei. L'informatica al servizio di una città antica*, Rome, 1988, p. 63: 890 "impianti commerciali", 207 "officine"; L. Eschebach, *Gebäudeverzeichnis und Stadtplan de antiken Stadt Pompeji*, Köln, 1993, pp. 453, 466: 584 stores, 301 workshops.

3 Most recently on the economic conditions in Pompeii: R. Laurence, *Roman Pompeii. Space and society*, London, 1994, pp. 51–69 with references. See also W. M. Jongman, *The Economy and Society of Pompeii*, Amsterdam, 1988.

4 Jongman, *Pompeii*, pp. 124–8, 136.

5 See E. Lepore, "Sul carattere economico-sociale di Ercolano," *PP*, 1955, vol. 10, pp. 423–39.

6 J.-A. Dickmann and F. Pirson, "Die Casa dei Postumii VIII 4, 4.49 und ihre *insula*. Bericht über die 3. Kampagne 1999," *RM*, 2000, vol. 107, pp. 454–5, figs 3–4; J.-A. Dickmann and F. Pirson, "Die Casa dei Postumii VIII 4, 4.49 und ihre Insula. Fünfter Vorbericht," *RM*, 2002, vol. 109, pp. 264, 312, fig. 17. On the importance of the AD 62 earthquake as an alleged turning-point in the social and economic history of Pompeii, see A. Wallace-Hadrill, *Houses and Society in Pompeii and Herculaneum*, Princeton, NJ, 1994, pp. 122–3; F. Pirson, *Mietwohnungen in Pompeji und Herkulaneum. Untersuchungen zur Architektur, zum Wohnen und zur Sozial- und Wirtschaftsgeschichte der Vesuvstädte*, Studien zur Antiken Stadt no. 5, Munich, 1999, pp. 137, 167.

7 J.-A. Dickmann and F. Pirson, "Repräsentatives Wohnen und kommerzielle Nutzung innerhalb eines Architekturkomplexes in Pompeji: die Casa die Postumii VIII 4,4.49 und ihre insula. Bericht über die 1. Kampagne 1997," *RM*, 1998, vol. 105, pp. 409–24.

8 La Torre, "Gli impianti commerciali," pp. 82 (nn. 67–70), 84 (n. 85) lists forty-seven businesses involved in the textile industry (the identifications are not without controversy) and thirty-four bakeries.

9 On the bakeries in Pompeii see B.-J. Mayeske, *Bakeries, Bakers and Bread at Pompeii: a study in social and economic history*, Ph.D. thesis, University of Maryland 1972; La Torre, "Gli impianti commerciali," p. 84; Laurence, *Roman Pompeii*, pp. 55–7. On *pistrinum* (VI.3.3, 27–28): Johannes Overbeck and August Mau, *Pompeji in seinen Gebäuden, Alterhümern und Kunstwerken*, 4th edn, Leipzig, 1884, pp. 385–90; August Mau, *Pompeji in Leben und Kunst*, rev. edn, Leipzig, 1908, pp. 407–10; Mayeske, *Bakeries*, pp. 95–7; G. P. Carratelli and I. Baldassarre (eds), *Pompei, pitture e mosaici*, Rome, 1993, vol. 4, pp. 271–5; Eschebach, *Gebäudeverzeichnis*, p. 162.

10 D. P. S. Peacock, "The mills of Pompeii," *Antiquity*, 1989, vol. 63, pp. 205–14.

11 See distribution maps in R. Laurence, *Roman Pompeii*, maps 4.1–2.

12 On textile-working and its respective businesses in Pompeii see W. O. Moeller, *The Wool Trade of Ancient Pompeii*, Leiden, 1976; Jongman, *Pompeii*, pp. 155–86; La Torre, "Gli impianti commerciali," pp. 82–4; Laurence, *Roman Pompeii*, pp. 57–64; M. R. Boriello *et al.* (eds),

Homo faber. Natura, scienza e tecnica nell'antica Pompei, Milan, 1999, pp. 92–4; M. Bradley, "'It all comes out in the wash': looking harder at the Roman fullonica," *JRA*, 2002, vol. 15, pp. 20–44; A. Wilson, "The archaeology of the Roman fullonica," *JRA*, 2003, vol. 16, pp. 442–6; M. Flohr, "Fullones and the Roman society," *JRA*, 2003, vol. 16, pp. 447–50.

13 This distinction and the following remarks on the distribution of the diverse workshops are largely based on Moeller, *Wool Trade*, although his method of defining and locating the workshops in the archaeological record has been criticized recently by Bradley, "It all comes out in the wash," pp. 25–7.

14 Laurence, *Roman Pompeii*, map 4.4.

15 Jongman, *Pompeii*, pp. 184–6.

16 Laurence, *Roman Pompeii*, map 4.3.

17 Laurence, *Roman Pompeii*, map 4.5.

18 Overbeck and Mau, *Pompeji in seinen Gebäuden*, pp. 390–5; Mau, *Pompeji*, pp. 412–14; Moeller, *Wool Trade*, pp. 44–6; Carratelli and Baldassare, *Pompei, pitture e mosaici*, 1993, vol. 4, pp. 604–10; Eschebach, *Gebäudeverzeichnis*, pp. 186ff.

19 On the metalworking production facilities in Pompeii see B. Gralfs, *Metallverarbeitende Produktionsstätten in Pompeji*, BAR-IS no. 433, 1988. In addition, see La Torre, "Gli impianti commerciali," pp. 84ff.; Laurence, *Roman Pompeii*, pp. 64; Boriello, *Homo faber*, pp. 104–7. Gralfs lists six *fabri aerarii*, two *fabri ferrarii* and three mixed workshops.

20 Gralfs, *Metallverarbeitende Produktionsstätten*, pp. 12–48, 149–86; Boriello, *Homo faber*, p. 191 (cat. nos. 231–9).

21 Dickman and Pirson, "Casa dei Postumii, fünfter Vorbericht," pp. 271–2, figs 25–6.

22 On pottery and the respective workshops in Pompeii see M. Annecchino, "Suppellittile fittile da cucina di Pompei," in M. Annecchino (ed.), *L'Instrumentum Domesticum di Ercolano e Pompeii nella prima età imperiale*, Rome, 1977, pp. 106–8; Boriello, *Homo faber*, pp. 100–3.

23 V. Arangio-Ruiz and G. Pugliese Carratelli, "Tabulae Herculanenses, IV," *PP*, 1954, vol. 9, p. 55 (no. LXI); see also Annecchino, *L'Instrumentum Domesticum*, p. 106 with n. 7.

24 G. Cerulli Irelli, "Una officina di lucerne fittili a Pompei," in Annecchino, *L'Instrumentum Domesticum*, pp. 53–72; Carratelli and Baldassare, *Pompei, pitture e mosaici*, 1990, vol. 2, pp. 1066–77; Eschebach, *Gebäudeverzeichnis*, pp. 80ff.

25 Carratelli and Baldassare, *Pompei, pitture e mosaici*, 1991, vol. 3, pp. 181–3; Eschebach, *Gebäudeverzeichnis*, pp. 91ff.

26 On the image of the potter, see T. Fröhlich, *Lararien und Fassadenbilder in den Vesuvustädten. Untersuchungen zur 'volkstümlichen' pompejanischen Malerei*, RM-EH, 32, Mainz, 1991, p. 313, fig. 16.1.

27 For an overview of the businesses in the cities under Vesuvius see Overbeck and Mau, *Pompeji in seinen Gebäuden*, pp. 376–96; Mau, *Pompeji*, pp. 403–18; Lepore, "Sul carattere"; Gassner, *Die Kaufläden*, pp. 17–26; La Torre, "Gli impianti commerciali."

28 On the three workshops see, respectively, Carratelli and Baldassare, *Pompei, pitture e mosaici*, 1996, vol. 6, pp. 459ff.; 1990, vol. 1, pp. 185–92; 1990, vol. 2, pp. 760–83; Eschebach, *Gebäudeverzeichnis*, pp. 250ff., 31, 103ff.

29 A. Maiuri, *Ercolano: i nuovi scavi (1927–1958)*, Rome, 1958, pp. 436–40.

30 R. I. Curtis, "The garum shop of Pompeii (1,12, 8)," *CronPomp*, 1979, vol. 5, pp. 5–23; Carratelli and Baldassare, *Pompei, pitture e mosaici*, 1990, vol. 2, pp. 760–83; Eschebach, *Gebäudeverzeichnis*, pp. 64ff. For the garden of the *garum*-shop, see Jashemski, Ch. 31.

31 R. I. Curtis, "A personalized floor mosaic from Pompeii," *AJA*, 1984, vol. 88, pp. 557–66; H. Mouritsen, "Mobility and social change in Italian towns during the principate," in H. M. Parkins (ed.), *Roman Urbanism. Beyond the consumer city*, London, 1997, pp. 63ff.; Carratelli and Baldassare, *Pompei, pitture e mosaici*, 1997, vol. 7, pp. 884ff., pls. 4–8; Pirson, *Mietwohnungen*, pp. 168–9, fig. 158. See also Clarke, Ch. 21 and Tybout, Ch. 26.

32 On kitchen gardens in Pompeii, see W. F. Jashemski, *The Gardens of Pompeii*, New Rochelle, NY, 1979, vol. 1; Laurence, *Roman Pompeii*, pp. 64–7; G. W. Dimbley, in W. F. Jashemski and F. G. Meyer (eds), *The Natural History of Pompeii*, Cambridge, 2002, pp. 181–9.

33 Jashemski, *Gardens*, vol. 1, pp. 200–18, 226ff.; W. F. Jashemski, *The Gardens of Pompeii, Herculaneum and the Villas Destroyed by Vesuvius: Appendices*, New Rochelle, NY, 1993, vol. 2,

pp. 89ff. See also P. Mastroberardino, in J. Renn and G. Castagnetti (eds), *Homo Faber: studies on nature, technology, and science at the time of Pompeii*, Rome, 2002, pp. 57–62.

34 Jashemski, *Gardens*, vol. 1, pp. 233–42; vol. 2, pp. 61–3.

35 E.g., in kitchen garden (II.8.6): Jashemski, *Gardens*, vol. 1, pp. 279–88; vol. 2, pp. 94–6.

36 On the structure, furnishing and architectural integration of *tabernae*, see Gassner, *Die Kaufläden*; F. Pirson, "Rented accommodation at Pompeii: the evidence of the *Insula Arriana Polliana* VI 6," in R. Laurence and A. Wallace-Hadrill (eds), *Domestic Space in the Roman World: Pompeii and beyond*, JRA Suppl. Ser. no. 22, 1997, pp. 165–81; Pirson, *Mietwohnungen*, pp. 85–99.

37 These numbers refer to *tabernae* in completely excavated *insulae* that have at least a back room or a mezzanine storey and are not connected to a larger private house. See Pirson, *Mietwohnungen*, pp. 161–4.

38 *tabernae appellatio declarat omne utile ad habitandum aedificium* (Dig. 50.16.183); see Pirson, *Mietwohnungen*, pp. 19, 53–5.

39 Pirson, *Mietwohnungen*, pp. 53–5, figs 42–3.

40 Pirson, *Mietwohnungen*, pp. 91–5, figs 90–3.

41 The term "shop-house" goes back to A. Boethius, "Remarks on the development of domestic architecture in Rome," *AJA*, 1934, vol. 38, pp. 158–70; see also Pirson, *Mietwohnungen*, pp. 144–52, 159–60. See, e.g., the rows of shops along the street fronts of the Forum Baths in Pompeii or the *palaestra* in Herculaneum. Freestanding complexes of *tabernae* can be found, e.g., at the southern tip of (VI.1) or along the north front of (II.1) (Figure 29.1).

42 See, e.g., the House of the Doctor (VIII.3.10–12), the upper story of which is accessed via a separate outdoor staircase (no. 10).

43 These numbers refer only to *tabernae* in completely excavated *insulae* (cf. n. 25); see Pirson, *Mietwohnungen*, p. 139.

44 P. Garnsey, "Urban property investment," in M. I. Finley (ed.), *Studies in Roman Property*, Cambridge, 1976, pp. 123–36; H. M. Parkins, "The 'consumer city' domesticated? The Roman city in élite economic strategies," in Parkins, *Roman Urbanism*, pp. 83–111.

45 Wallace-Hadrill, *Houses and Society*, pp. 118–42; Pirson, *Mietwohnungen*, p. 139.

46 CIL IV, 1136 (cf. Bernstein, Ch. 34 for the text and translation); CIL IV, 138: INSULA ARRIANA / POLLIANA [C]N AL[EI]I NIGIDI MAI / LOCANTUR EX [K(ALENDIS)] IULIS PRIMIS TABERNAE / CUM PERGULIS SUIS ET C[E]NACULA / EQUESTRIA ET DOMUS CONDUCTOR / CONVENITO PRIMUM [C]N AL[LE]I / NIGIDI MAI SER(VUM), "In the Insula Arriana Polliana of Cn. Alleius Nigidius Maius, *tabernae* with their *pergulae* and *cenacula equestria* and *domus* will be let out from July 1st onward. For letting consult Primus, slave of Cn. Alleius Nigidius Maius." See Pirson, "Rented accommodation"; Pirson, *Mietwohnungen*, pp. 15–22.

47 S. M. Treggiari, "Urban labour in Rome: *mercennarii* and *tabernarii*," in P. Garnsey (ed.), *Non-slave Labour in the Greco-Roman World*, Cambridge, 1980, pp. 48–64; J.-J. Aubert, "Workshop managers," in W. V. Harris (ed.), *The Inscribed Economy*, JRA Suppl. Ser. no. 6, 1993, pp. 171–81; H. Mouritsen, "Roman freedmen and the urban economy: Pompeii in the first century AD," in F. Senatore (ed.), *Pompei tra Sorrento e Sarno*, Rome, 2001, pp. 1–27.

48 Pirson, *Mietwohnungen*, pp. 165–73.

49 Pirson, "Rented accommodation"; Pirson, *Mietwohnungen*, pp. 23–46.

50 Pirson, *Mietwohnungen*, pp. 153–8. See a more complete treatment in Dickman and Pirson, "Casa dei Postumii, fünfter Vorbericht," pp. 243–316 and the earlier reports in *RM*, 1998–2001, vols 105–8.

CHAPTER THIRTY

INNS AND TAVERNS

————•◆•————

John DeFelice

As in many small Roman cities, Pompeii and Herculaneum had their share of hospitality businesses. However, several of the best examples remain at Pompeii. In many of Pompeii's *insulae* and around most of the city gates there were numerous taverns, inns and little restaurants to greet visitors. These probably also served Pompeii's indigenous lower-class population as well, providing food, wine, entertainment and shelter. They were an important part of Pompeii's economy and society.[1]

DEFINITIONS

It is generally agreed that there are four basic categories of hospitality businesses. These include *hospitia*, *stabula*, *tabernae* and *popinae*.[2] *Hospitia* were establishments that offered rooms for rent, and often food and drink to overnight guests. This term originally had an abstract meaning, referring to the guest/owner relationship that existed between a stranger seeking overnight accommodations and a host.[3] According to Packer, *hospitia* appear to have been expressly fabricated for business purposes, although a number of them represent secondary uses of existing private homes in Pompeii.[4]

A *caupona* was also an inn that provided meals, drink and lodging.[5] It may have catered to a lower class of customer than a *hospitium*, but some appear to have been comfortable places.[6] Often the analogy is made that a *hospitium* corresponded to a hotel while a *caupona* referred to an inn, often with a bar and snack shop. However, in most cases it is difficult to distinguish between them. A *hospitium* seems at times to have served as a lodging house for travelers as well for long-term guests. The term *caupona* gradually came to indicate a place of bad reputation and it was used less as time progressed by innkeepers themselves.[7]

Stabula were *hospitia* with facilities to shelter animals. They usually possessed wide sloping entrances on the street curb which allowed the passage of carts, and often included stalls for animals as well as rooms for guests. It was common to find these just outside the city, or just within the city gates. Businesses within the city gates had to make the most of their available room, and tended to be smaller than those in the country.[8] They tended to follow the same general plan, with the kitchen, latrine and bedrooms surrounding an open court with stables at the rear.

The term *taberna* referred to either a shop or a tavern in the first century AD. Its usage eventually came to mean a tavern in the traditional sense.[9] *Tabernae* varied in size and quality of food and drink served. This term also became linked with *caupona* (*caupona taberna*) to indicate a shop that sold food and drink and provided lodging.[10] Unfortunately, in many publications, the term *taberna* has come to refer to almost any kind of shop, so there is a good deal of confusion when compiling a list of such establishments from secondary sources (cf. also Pirson, Ch. 29).

Tabernae and *popinae* (in their first-century sense) served a variety of simple foods and drink. They usually contained a simple L-shaped marble counter, about 6 to 8 ft long, with a simmering pot of water and shelves of other food on the back wall of a tiny room, often just large enough for the proprietor and several assistants (cf. Jones and Robinson, Ch. 25; Figure 25.14). Wine and food were usually served from *dolia* embedded in the counter. Roman drinks were usually served warmed. Most bar counters were equipped for heating both food and drink.[11] For example, the Taberna of Fortunata (VI.3.18–20) was located strategically at a busy intersection next to a public fountain (Figure 30.1; Map 3). This establishment boasted four *dolia* sunk into an L-shaped marble-faced counter, a stove at the end of that counter, and two storage niches set into the base of a connecting plaster-capped counter set against the building wall. Additional cooking facilities and a latrine were located behind the counter, and a possible eating area off to the side.[12] Up the street in *insula* VI.1,

Figure 30.1   Taberna of Fortunata (VI.3.18–20), view southeast through the service counter at no. 20. Photo: P. W. Foss.

there is evidence for the development of the food service industry in the first century BC (cf. Jones and Robinson, Ch. 25). *Popinae* were suited for a quick sit-down meal, which was boorish and distasteful to upper-class Romans.[13] The Roman custom was to recline when dining, eating leisurely on a *triclinium*. Occasionally, eating and drinking establishments had indoor as well as outdoor facilities set in small gardens (e.g. I.8.8 (Figure 20.8); II.5 (Figure 31.6(e))).

It is difficult to distinguish between a *caupona* and a *hospitium*. Some *hospitia* possessed dining rooms, a garden *triclinium*, numerous bedrooms, a sophisticated kitchen, and occasionally *atria* (sometimes covered), *tablina*, *oeci*, or an *impluvium*.[14] For example, inn (I.2.24) in Pompeii boasted both an *impluvium* and an outdoor *triclinium*. It is possible that after the earthquake of AD 62 a number of private houses were converted into *hospitia*. For instance, the house at (I.9.12) was connected to the *caupona* at (I.9.11) and its *atrium* was used to store amphoras. The inn at (I.10.13) seems to have used the *posticum* of the connected house at (I.10.14) for the same purpose.[15]

LODGING AND LODGERS

The hospitality businesses at the entrances to a city such as Pompeii were placed there for the sake of travelers, such as merchants and sailors who came to trade and sell, or those who were stopping overnight along the way to other destinations. Not all travelers required their services. Those with high social standing had friends in several cities, and developed a network of *hospitae* ("hosts"), where they would stay when business needed to be transacted away from home. Rooms for rent were also available in private homes.[16]

Inns along major roads and at the city gates gained a reputation for attracting less socially significant travelers. Inns had a reputation for bedbugs, discomfort, violence and danger.[17] Apuleius and Petronius portrayed inns as dangerous places, full of low-class and poverty-stricken tenants.[18] The quality of the staff also varied. One guest wrote on the wall of Pompeian inn (VIII.6.6): "We peed in the bed. I admit we did wrong, innkeeper. If you should ask why—well, there was no chamber-pot!"[19]

Long-term guests probably stayed in Pompeian *hospitia*, perhaps at locations closer to the heart of the city. This may have contributed to the poor reputation of *hospitia*, as guests shared them with those of humble circumstance who found it difficult to lease a home.[20] In the *Satyricon*, Petronius offers a glimpse of an inn with both long-term tenants and short-term guests.[21]

The *graffiti* record provides some human insight into tavern life (cf., in general, Franklin, Ch. 33). One patron wrote on the wall of inn (I.2.24), "Curses on you, innkeeper! What you sell us is water, and you keep the wine for yourself!"[22] Another guest, in tavern (VI.10.1), made a sly request for just a single drop of water to dilute his wine, on the wall above a picture of a soldier holding out his cup to a slave.[23] However, not all innkeepers shared this reputation. At tavern (VII.2.44–45), the *copa* Hedone offered good wine for one *as*, better wine for two *asses*, and the precious *falernum* vintage for four *asses*.[24] The same establishment was also the regular meeting place of the late-night drinkers, the *seribibi universi*, who, whether in jest or seriousness, supported a political candidate with a political notice bearing their name.[25] Another visitor conflated the verses of both Ovid and Propertius on the wall of tavern

(I.11.10–11) to proclaim "A fair skinned beauty taught me to despise dusky women. I will spurn them, if I can; if not . . . I will love them reluctantly."[26] Amorous verses are common on the walls of inns and taverns.

POMPEII: REPRESENTATIVE REMAINS;
Map 3

Hospitia and *cauponae*

One famous example is the so-called House of Sallust (VI.2.3–5). This was an old Samnite house later converted into a hotel on a grand scale.[27] This *hospitium* has several interesting features. At entrance no. 5, the counter is accessible both from the street and the *atrium*, perhaps to increase business. Several bedrooms are grouped around the *atrium*. Several other large spaces could have allowed guests to dine, such as indoor spaces (22, 35) off the northeast corner of the *atrium* and the west side of the peristyle, and an outdoor masonry *triclinium* (25) covered by a pergola on two pilasters at the north end of the garden. A hearth nearby was installed to prepare food for outside dining.[28] Jashemski observed that guests could view the garden through a large picture window in *tablinum* (19). It was three steps higher than the floor of the house, and could be entered at either end of the colonnade. It was small, only 20 by 70 ft, but had a garden painting on the back wall. It showed a continuation of the real garden, with columns, garlands, three fountains and birds.[29] Jashemski noted that great care was exercised in the remodeling of this Samnite house to preserve its aesthetic characteristics, a view shared by Richardson.[30] Another old Samnite house (VI.2.18–19) was converted into a *stabulum* of a more rustic variety.[31]

At (VII.1.44–45) was a modest but better-equipped establishment. It was located across the street from the large *hospitium* at (VII.11.11, 14), and though too small even for a garden, the owner boasted of his *triclinium*.[32] In front was found a painting of an elephant entangled with a serpent—and being rescued by a pygmy.[33]

Just inside the Porta Ercolano at (VI.1.1) was a small *caupona* with a garden *triclinium* (Figure 25.1). Many small establishments made the most of limited space. This example was built adjacent to the wall, with three or so rooms to rent on the upper story.[34] It lacked a counter with *dolia*, so food was either served cold or brought in from another establishment.

Stabula

Less elegant is the *stabulum* run by Hermes at (I.1.6–9), so named because of a picture located on the entrance's left wall depicting the innkeeper Hermes emptying an *amphora* into a *dolium*.[35] This picture is no longer extant.[36] The *stabulum* entrance leads into a courtyard. A row of stalls lines the back east wall. This *stabulum* has an associated tavern, with a separate room for eating at no. 9. Rooms for lodgers included three above the stalls, reached by stairs along the north wall of the courtyard. It is interesting that despite the humble nature of this establishment, the second floor even had a latrine directly above that of the first floor. Three additional rooms for lodgers, presumably, surrounded the courtyard.

Tabernae and *popinae*

Numerous examples exist for *popinae* and *tabernae* throughout the city. Over a dozen are scattered along the strada Stabiana and via dell'Abbondanza, and almost as many along the strada Consolare and via di Nola. More are near the amphitheater, forum or baths. Around fifty are located at the corners of major intersections.

A simple single-room *taberna* with an upstairs apartment at (I.10.13) was formerly connected to the House of the Menander next door (I.10.4). Ruddell notes that although there were no *amphorae* found at this site, a number were found in the house next door. The walls were stuccoed and the floor was paved with *opus signinum*. The low masonry counter, with two *dolia*, was once painted red. The shop also contained a small hearth. This represents the most basic design, with little room for sit-down dining.[37] Somewhat larger is tavern (VI.15.15), which had an L-shaped counter with three *dolia* and a stove. Apart from the front room with its counter, was a back room, perhaps for dining or drinking. Both rooms had doors on their western walls connecting them with the House of the Matron next door (VI.15.14), so named for a mosaic portrait *emblema* from room (m).[38]

Mixed establishments

The number of establishments that incorporate two or more hospitality businesses is significant. La Torre, for example, has noted over forty establishments that appear to have rooms for overnight guests as well as facilities for food and drink.[39] One of the more remarkable can be found at (VI.1.2–4). It seems to have been at once a *hospitium, caupona, stabulum* and *taberna/popina*. See Jones and Robinson, Ch. 25, for details of its development.

At entrance no. 2 were the counter and stove usually associated with a *popina/taberna*, as well as display shelves. Three rooms were to the left of the serving room. Behind the counter was a passage to a latrine. Entrance no. 3 led to a staircase that reached the second floor, and a connecting passage under the stairs connected to the inn at entrance no. 4. This inn, labeled by various scholars a *caupona, hospitium*, or *deversorium*, possessed two rooms and a *triclinium* in the front. Food from next door was probably brought through the passage under the stairs at no. 3 for patrons. Against the north wall at the back of this business was a watering trough and three additional guest rooms. The back wall had a covered area for carts, and stalls for animals. Together with the establishment across the street, it comprised the meeting place for the wagon drivers (*statio mulionum*).[40] This is one of several hospitality businesses that made the maximum use of available space near the city gates, in this case the Porta Ercolano, to service both visitors and those transporting goods to the city.[41]

Food and camaraderie

Food in these establishments probably included simple stews, soups and other basic fare.[42] Customers probably ate sitting, not reclining, at tables. Inn (VI.10.1) in Pompeii has five preserved painted scenes that show travelers standing or sitting around wooden tables in an inn, being served by a *puer cauponis* ("serving-boy").[43] Both masonry dining tables and benches for public use are preserved at the upscale *Praedia* of Julia Felix (II.4.7; see Parslow, Ch. 14; Nappo, Ch. 23; Figure 23.11) and inn (I.8.15–16).[44]

Food quality must have varied. Horace described *popinae* as greasy (*uncta popina*).[45] Sometimes foods were displayed outside, perhaps in water-filled glass bowls, providing an illusion of size.[46] Foods such as eggs, goose liver paté, sow vulvas, fowl, game, pork, cheese, *cicer* (chick peas), vegetables either fried or in a porridge (*puls*), beans, cabbage, twice-cooked cabbage (*crambe recocta* or *repetita*), raw vegetables with vinegar, and beets may have been available in some eateries, perhaps smothered in garlic, pepper and sauces.[47]

Tiberius, Claudius, Nero and Vespasian all passed laws restricting the sale or display of certain prepared foods, especially meat and wine.[48] Casson suggests that these may have been first-century attempts to decrease traffic in inns and taverns towards promoting better "public morality." Hermansen believed that these prohibitions could have been introduced to smother potential political agitation in inns and taverns (lodging houses for travelers may have been exempted from these laws).[49] There was probably little effect on the many busy establishments of Pompeii. Evidence is fragmentary, but in the mid-fourth century AD, taverns were still the places where poorer people are said to have gathered after dark for revelry, eating and drinking. Among the problems that plagued the Rome of his day, Ammianus Marcellinus listed the poor in the city of Rome spending the entire night in wineshops (*in tabernis*).[50] Inns and taverns were probably never really outlawed as gathering places for any length of time.

Moral geography and prostitution

Roman literature assumed taverns and snack shops were places of moral turpitude.[51] Ray Laurence and Andrew Wallace-Hadrill have examined the distribution of these businesses at Pompeii towards plotting a moral geography for the city.[52] Both have assumed that a moral geography existed. Wallace-Hadrill notes, "for every area of positive charge there must be an area of negative charge set against it."[53] Laurence works along the assumption that Pompeii can be "examined to identify the areas in which deviant behavior was tolerated, and those in which it was restricted."[54] Both have chosen areas that contained a large number of these businesses as areas of "negative charge" and "deviance." Both assume that these places would only cater to customers so crude and vile that they would have to exist well out of sight of Roman matrons and children.

In Roman moralistic literature (particularly Seneca), some locations seem clearly associated with virtue and others with pleasure:

> Virtue is something lofty, elevated, regal, invincible and indefatigable; Pleasure is something lowly and servile, feeble and perishable, which has its base and residence in the brothels and the eating-houses (*popinae*). Virtue you will meet in the temple, the forum, the senate house, standing before the walls, stained with dust, with callused hands.[55]

Certainly within the mind of this moralist, there was a clear division between places characterized by pleasure and those characterized by virtue. But this passage is, at best, only a Stoic mirror that reflects the values of a few Romans. Stoic ideas, with their emphasis on social equality and the humanity of slaves, reached a limited audience even among the elite. To extend Seneca's comments to postulate zoning along moral lines is quite a leap.

Laurence includes gambling as an indicator of deviance. Certainly there was gambling and the potential for violence in some hospitality businesses. This is graphically shown in a series of wall paintings at *popina* (VI.14.35–36), which comically warned patrons that fights over gambling would not be tolerated.[56] Dice were found in tavern (VII.15.4–5), and a wall painting of men throwing dice was recovered from (VI.10.1), but such finds cannot automatically be associated with all *popinae*.[57] Furthermore, gambling was not limited to *popinae*. It is not unusual to find gaming boards cut into the pavement of the forum or sidewalks in any Roman city.[58] Even emperors were known to gamble.[59]

Altercations were also not limited to taverns. In the House of the Moralist (III.4.2–3), stern admonitions are written on the walls of *triclinium* (12) prohibiting fighting, adulterous glances and putting muddy feet on the table.[60] This does not mean that all dining rooms were places of deviance, dirt, adultery and violence. In fact, these were exactly what the owner of a tavern or inn wished to avoid.

Inn and tavern workers, as most working people in Roman society, were considered little better than slaves as far as social status was concerned, if we take Cicero seriously.[61] But using *popinae*, *cauponae* and *tabernae* as an index of deviance is problematic. Laurence's simple definition of deviance is, "In effect, the deviants in a society are those people who contravene the rules of that society."[62] But in Pompeii (as in other Roman cities), slaves, freed people and poor citizens—the large base of a steep social pyramid—represented the majority of the population.[63] His model of deviance requires revision in order to account for class and gender antagonism in the primary sources that may skew the concept of deviance as defined.

Finally, when observing the graph provided by Laurence, which marks streets as deviant if *tabernae* or *popinae* are present, one is stuck with the large number of streets considered deviant.[64] Well over 50 percent of the city would be deviant by this analysis. This theory of deviant zones or negative zones clearly needs reconsideration, although its approach to city patterns and planning may be sound. It must use criteria other than all *popinae* or *tabernae* as major indicators. Perhaps certain types of bars and snack shops would lend themselves better to a revised definition of deviance. But the positive value attached to areas that Laurence and Wallace-Hadrill consider as non-deviant must also be reconsidered. Plautus, for example, considered the forum— seen so positively by Seneca—as a place where one met perjurers, the vicious, liars, wasters, harlots and their customers.[65] Seneca, himself, knew that this was the case. He wrote, using the same metaphor of an urban landscape:

> As far as regards sensual pleasure, though it flows around us on every side and seeps through every opening, though it softens the mind with its charms and leaves no avenue untried in its attempts to seduce us in whole and in part.[66]

Seneca saw vice and pleasure as fluid entities. While he delineated certain places as centers for low living, he believed that the vice of pleasure could be found everywhere. His moral geography represented an internalized battle. He did not advocate an urban moral zoning program but, rather, a disciplined mind. Though belonging to the ranks of the Roman elite, he himself lived above the baths in a "deviant zone."[67]

Another reason why inns and taverns lend themselves to such analyses is because of the assumption that women who worked in taverns and inns were usually prostitutes. The result is that historians often labeled tavern and snack shops as *lupanars* (brothels) when initial reports followed excavation, and that label persisted through the centuries on very flimsy evidence. I will limit myself to two examples.

First, there is the notorious tavern of Asellina, located at (IX.11.2) on via dell'Abbondanza. It was first excavated at the turn of the century by Della Corte, and immediately identified as a *caupona-lupanar*. The reason for this identification would at first appear to have been because of the names of four women whose names adorn election notices painted on the front wall of the shop today.[68] The names are exotic and foreign: Smyrna, who would appear to come from the Near East; Aegle, from Greece; and Maria, who possibly was a Jew. Asellina was derived from an old Roman name, but her status can only be guessed at.

The tavern itself is unremarkable. It did have a complex phallic lamp, and on the right doorpost excavators found an odd drawing of Mercury with an ape-like head and a large phallus. It is not clear if the discovery of phalli contributed to Della Corte's identification of the location as a *lupanar*. The saying *Hic habitat felicitas* (here dwells happiness), often found below it, simply means that unhappiness has been driven away by this magic, apotropaic symbol.[69] But Della Corte seems to have identified this business on the most subjective criteria, and in euphemistic fashion: "an Asellina, perhaps the owner of the establishment, in which, according to custom, not only food and drink were served."[70]

For the second example, a *graffito* is often cited from the exterior face of the *caupona* at (I.12.3). An election notice reads: *A(ulum) Trebium aed(ilem) o(ro) v(os) f(aciatis) Soteric{us}*, "I, Sotericus, ask that you make Aulus Trebius (Valens) aedile."[71] Within the "O" is another *graffito* in tiny letters, perhaps written by a passer-by: *Futui coponam*, "I fucked the barmaid."[72]

This comment was not even located within the tavern, but as late as 1996, it was cited as proof that taverns and inns universally employed prostitutes.[73] That taverns were occasionally associated with prostitution is an assumption of later Roman law, but caution must be used when using later sources to draw conclusions about Pompeii.[74]

As evidence is handled more critically, the list of taverns and inns described as brothels grows shorter. Part of the reason is that the modern world no longer equates all sexual activity outside of marriage as prostitution. Every *graffito* that refers to sexual activity may indicate any one of a number of informal sexual relationships. Concentrations of coarse *graffiti* may sometimes indicate that a brothel was located on the premises. The *caupona* run by Hermes at (II.1.1, 13) has its share of such *graffiti*. A female worker named Palmyra is called *sitifera*, a term which can be translated as "horny animal," and another unknown worker is described as *culibona*, or "hot ass," a term Evans equates with anal sex.[75] These descriptions may indicate prostitution or sexual activity, but this location is not listed as a *caupona lupanar* in the guidebooks or in Eschebach's listing.[76] Several inns and taverns do have that label, however. For example, we find an Acria listed at the price of four *asses* and Epaphra listed for ten *asses* at tavern (V.2.b–c). Someone named "Firm" (abbreviated for Firmilla?) is also listed as available for three *asses* in this location, as well as in the tavern at (I.12.5).[77] In the tavern at (I.10.2), a woman named Prima, perhaps referred to in another *graffito* as Prima Domina, sold herself for one and one half *asses*.[78] Beyond that, there is at Pompeii only the *graffiti* record to suggest sexual activity occurring in several (but not all) inns and taverns. Indeed, many businesses probably had little space for such activities.

Furthermore, if one takes coarse *graffiti*, such as those containing the words *Hic futui*, "here I fucked" (and its grammatical derivatives) and plots them on a map, one finds them centered mainly at the well-known brothels in town.[79] These terms are not common in inns and taverns, though other romantic and sexual terms often are. A benchmark of more critical scholarship is when different types of sexual *graffiti* are distinguished from one another. Even a *graffito* with a price of a prostitute's services on a tavern's outside wall may only be the work of a passerby, or may indicate the price for services charged by a woman who walks the streets in the area. Other signs of prostitution, such as a masonry bed, a *cella meretricia* or rooms designated by pictures of different erotic acts (as is evident in the large *lupanar* found at (VII.12.18, 20) and more recently revealed in the Suburban Baths, must also be considered (Figure 35.3).[80] Even then, an element of doubt may remain. At the large *hospitium* complex at (VII.11.11, 14) a *cella meretricia* can be found at entrance 12 under a flight of stairs. However, there is no direct connection between the one-room prostitute's quarters and the large establishment. Furthermore, the *caupona* next door at (VII.11.13) has no direct entrance to the *cella* either. On the contrary, the inn possesses an outdoor sign that forbids loiterers.[81]

The complicated lives of the women who worked in these establishments cannot be discussed in full here (cf. Bernstein, Ch. 34), but there was, according to later legal sources, the potential for limited social mobility. A woman could start as a tavern servant girl, or perhaps even a slave prostitute, and eventually gain her freedom, get legally married, have a husband and legitimate children and even be a slave and tavern owner herself. It is short-sighted to see these women as prostitutes and prostitutes only.[82] The evidence of non-elite Roman lives, so richly concentrated in the inns and taverns of Pompeii and Herculaneum, at last have the chance to be seen against the background of the Roman society of their era, and not our own. I do not wish to over-criticize the idea of moral geography in Roman city planning. It is one of the many ideas that have recently been introduced by scholars expecting both criticism and dialogue when attempting to interpret Pompeii and Herculaneum on a citywide basis, and it has sparked useful responses. But as long as the very identification and number of *popinae* and *tabernae* remain uncertain, new approaches, such as the scientific analysis of food and other organic residues, are badly needed.

NOTES

1 The number of these establishments is subject to speculation. A. Wallace-Hadrill, "Public honor and private shame: the urban texture of Pompeii," in T. J. Cornell and K. Lomas (eds), *Urban Society in Roman Italy*, London, 1995, p. 46, cites G. F. La Torre, "Gli impianti commerciali ed artigianali nel tessuto urbano di Pompei," in *Pompei. L'informatica al servizio di una città antica*, Rome, 1988, p. 78 as giving a figure of 120 *cauponae* and eighty-nine *thermopolia*, twenty-nine of which functioned as *cauponae* as well. Wallace-Hadrill doubts the fantastic number of hospitality businesses for such a small town, but La Torre lists some of these establishments several times in different categories and conflates several inoperative addresses

with current ones (pp. 92–3, nn. 16–18, 20). He also uses the term *thermopolium*, which is an inaccurate term. My present count is ninety-four businesses that served food and/or drink (*popina* or *taberna*), but had no facilities for overnight guests. Another forty-two served overnight guests and possibly food and drink (*hospitium* and *caupona*) and nine businesses served overnight guests and had access to facilities for horses (*stabulum*). Another forty-seven structures have been frequently described as hospitality businesses but have questionable identifications and are not included.

2 T. Kleberg, *Hôtels, restaurants et cabarets dans l'antique romaine: études historiques et philogiques*, Uppsala, 1957, pp. 8–11, 31ff.; S. Ruddell, *The inn, restaurant and tavern business in ancient Pompeii*, M.A. thesis, University of Maryland, 1964, pp. 1–5; J. Packer, "Inns at Pompeii: a short survey," *CronPomp*, 1978, vol. 4, p. 5. Ruddell's thesis, though often cited, is difficult to obtain. See J. DeFelice, *Roman Hospitality: the professional women of Pompeii*, Warren Center, PA, 2001, pp.176–306 for a master list of hospitality businesses in Pompeii with bibliographic information on each one.

3 L. Casson, *Travel in the Ancient World*, London, 1974, p. 352; Klebeg, *Hôtels*, pp. 5–7, 14; J. H. D'Arms, *Romans on the Bay of Naples*, Cambridge, MA, 1970, p. 49.

4 Packer, "Inns at Pompeii," pp. 44–5.

5 Ruddell, *Tavern Business*, p. 2. Plin., *HN* 9.154 uses the term *cauponarum*.

6 W. F. Jashemski, "A Pompeian copa," *CJ*, 1964, vol. 59, pp. 337–49.

7 Klebeg, *Hôtels*, pp. 27–8.

8 Casson, *Travel*, pp. 205, 207; Klebeg, *Hôtels*, pp. 18, 28, 34–5; Ruddell, *Tavern Business*, pp. 7–8; Packer, "Inns at Pompeii," pp. 7–9.

9 Ruddell, *Inn, Restaurant and Tavern Business*, p. 9; Klebeg, *Hôtels*, pp. 19–23.

10 See *Dig.* 23.2.43.1 (*Taberna cauponia*).

11 Casson, *Travel*, pp. 211–12; Packer, "Inns at Pompeii," pp. 30–2; Ruddell, *Tavern Business*, pp. 9, 15.

12 L. Eschebach, *Gebäudeverzeichnis und Stadtplan de antiken Stadt Pompeji*, Köln, 1993, p. 165.

13 W. F. Jashemski, *The Gardens of Pompeii*, New Rochelle, NY, 1979, p. 167; Mart. 5.70.3.

14 Ruddell, *Tavern Business*, pp. 72–3; Packer, "Inns at Pompeii," pp. 12–14, 44.

15 DeFelice, *Roman Hospitality*, pp. 199, 201. The *amphora*-filled *atrium* of (I.9.12) can be seen in J. Berry, "Household artefacts: towards a reinterpretation of Roman domestic space," in R. Laurence and A. Wallace-Hadrill (eds), *Domestic Space in the Roman World: Pompeii and beyond*, JRA Suppl. Ser. no. 22, 1997, p. 184.

16 See *ILS* 6039 = *CIL* II, 4284, from Tarraco in Spain: *Si nitidus vivas, eccum domus exornata est. Si sordes, patior, sed pudet hospitium*, "If you're clean and neat, then here's a house ready and waiting for you. If you're dirty—well, I'm ashamed to say it, but you're welcome too." transl. Casson, *Travel*, pp. 204, 353. See also below, n. 19, for a house at Pompeii that seems to have let rooms.

17 A particularly amusing account of bugs in taverns is found in the apocryphal *Acts of John* 60.1. Pliny the Elder refers to the parasites that dwelled in *cauponae* (*HN* 9.154), and a poem attributed to Hadrian, addressed to the comic poet Florus, notes the fat, round insects plaguing inns and cook shops (SHA, *Hadr.* 16.3–9).

18 For example, see Petron., *Sat.*, 95–98 and Apul., *Met.* I. See also H. Rowell, "Satryricon 95–96," *CP*, 1957, vol. 52.4, pp. 217–27.

19 *CIL* IV, 4957, from the exterior of house (VIII.6.6), to the left of the entrance: *Miximus in lecto, fateor, peccavimus hospes. Si dices quare: nulla matella fuit* (transl. P. Foss).

20 B. Frier, "The rental market in early imperial Rome," *JRS*, 1977, vol. 67, pp. 27–37.

21 Petron., *Sat.* 95.

22 *CIL* IV, 3948. See also Petron., *Sat.* 39; Mart. 1.56.

23 *CIL* IV, 1291: "Da fridam pusillum."

24 *CIL* IV, 1679; cf. addenda on pp. 210, 463, 704.

25 *CIL* IV, 581.

26 *CIL* IV, 9847: *Candida me docuit nigras o{d}isse puellas. Odero, si potero; si non, invitus amabo.* Several instances of the same lines were found at the House of the Scientist (VI.14.43); see *CIL* IV, 1520, 1523, 1526, 1528. The lines borrow from Prop. 1.1.5 and Ov., *Am.* 3.11.35; for commentary, see: A. Keith, "Corpus eroticum: elegiac poetics and elegiac puellae in Ovid's

Amores," *CW*, 1994, vol. 88, pp. 27–40; M. Wyke, "Reading female flesh: *Amores* 3.1," in A. Cameron (ed.), *History as Text: the writing of ancient history*, London, 1989, pp. 111–43.

27 G. P. Carratelli and I. Baldassarre (eds), *Pompei, pitture e mosaici*, vol. 4, Rome, 1993, pp. 87–147; Jashemski, "A Pompeian copa," pp, 339, 349; M. Della Corte, *Case ed abitanti di Pompei*, 3rd edn, Naples, 1965, pp. 38–40.

28 Ruddell, *Tavern Business*, pp. 4–5, 88.

29 Jashemski, *Gardens*, vol. 1, p. 169. This was originally published in F. Mazois, *Les ruines de Pompéi dessinées et mesurées pendant les années 1809–1810–1811*, Paris, 1824, vol. 2, pl. 37, fig. 1.

30 L. Richardson, jr, *Pompeii. An architectural history*, Baltimore, MD, 1988, pp. 108–11.

31 Jashemski, "A Pompeian copa," p. 343.

32 *CIL* IV, 807: "*Hospitium hic locatur triclinium cum tribus lectis.*" See Jashemski, "A Pompeian copa," p. 346.

33 *CIL* IV, 806 possibly identified the innkeeper as Sittius, who boasted that he had restored the elephant. See Jashemski, "A Pompeian copa," p. 346.

34 Jashemski, "A Pompeian copa," p. 339; Ruddell, *Tavern Business*, pp. 3, 86. See also now Jones and Robinson's systematic study of *Insula* (VI.1) in Ch. 25.

35 Ruddell, *Tavern Business*, p. 70.

36 Packer, "Inns at Pompeii," p. 8, n.9.

37 Ruddell, *Tavern Business*, p. 78; Packer *Inns at Pompeii*, pp. 30–3. See now R. Ling, *The Insula of the Menander at Pompeii, vol. 1: the structures*, Oxford, 1997; P. M. Allison, *The Insula of the Menander at Pompeii 3: the finds, a contextual study*, Oxford, 2006.

38 Richardson, *Pompeii*, p. 423; Ruddell, *Tavern Business*, p. 95; Wallace-Hadrill, *Houses and Society*, pp. 214–15.

39 La Torre, "Gli impianti commerciali," pp. 92–3.

40 *CIL* IV, 97, 113.

41 Richardson, *Pompeii*, p. 424; Ruddell, *Tavern Business*, p. 86; See also H. B. Van der Poel (ed.), *Corpus Topographicum Pompeianum*, Rome, 1977–1986, vol. 2, p. 245; vol. 5, pp. 249–51.

42 Many had small kitchens and stoves. Their customers came on foot, they were considered poor, and prices were low. The price list from the *atrium* of *hospitium* (IX.7.24–25)—see *CIL* IV, 5380—may either be a daily menu or shopping list. Basic commodities are listed: cheese, bread (with a lower grade for slaves), wines of varying quality, oil, onions, wheat, porridge, leeks, dates, sausage and soft cheese. See A. E. Cooley and M. G. L. Cooley, *Pompeii. A sourcebook*, London, 2004, p. 163.

43 See Carratelli and Baldassarre, *Pitture e mosaici*, 1993, vol. 4, pp. 1005–19; T. Fröhlich, *Lararien und Fassadenbilder in den Vesuvustädten. Untersuchungen zur "volkstümlichen" pompejanischen Malerei*, RM-EH, 32, Mainz, 1991, pp. 214–22. Compare these to scenes of reclining diners from the House of the Triclinium (V.2.4); cf. Carratelli and Baldassarre, *Pitture e mosaici*, 1991, vol. 3, pp. 797–8, 811–18. See also Ruddell, *Tavern Business*, pp. 35–6; Jashemski, "A Pompeian copa," p. 338.

44 Carratelli and Baldassarre, *Pitture e mosaici*, 1991, vol. 3, pp. 184–95; 1990, vol. 1, p. 844, respectively. For (I.8.15–16), see also V. Castiglione Morelli del Franco and R. Vitale, "L'insula 8 della Regio I: un campione d'indagine socio-economica," *RStPomp*, 1989, vol. 3, pp. 205–8.

45 Hor., *Sat.* 2.4.62. The use here is unclear. However, in *Epist.* 1.14.20 he clearly uses the term pejoratively.

46 For magnifying foods, see Macrob., *Sat.* 7.14.1 (noted by E. Gowers, *The Loaded Table*, Oxford, 1993, p. 24, n. 107).

47 See *CIL* IV, 5380 at (IX.7.24–25); cf. above, n. 42. See Ruddell, *Tavern Business*, pp. 40–2; W. C. Firebaugh, *The Inns of Greece and Rome*, Chicago, IL, 1929, reprint. 1972, pp. 205–10; see also M. Della Corte, "Le inscrizioni di Ercolano," *RendNap*, 1958, vol. 33, pp. 305–7, no. 827; J. J. Deiss, *Herculaneum: Italy's buried treasure*, rev. edn, Mailbu, CA, 1989, pp. 117–24.

48 Suet., *Tib.* 34, *Claud.* 38, *Ner.* 16; Dio Cass. 60.6.7, 62.14.2. See Ruddell, *Tavern Business*, pp. 62; Klebeg, *Hôtels*, pp. 101–2.

49 Klebeg, *Hôtels*, pp. 105–7; Ruddell, *Tavern Business*, pp. 61–2; Casson, *Travel*, pp. 217, 354; G. Hermansen, "Roman inns and the law," in J. A. S. Evans (ed.), *Polis and Imperium: studies in honor of Edward Togo Salmon*, Toronto, 1974, pp. 167–73.

50 Amm. Marc. 14.6.25.

51 See P. Green (transl.), *Juvenal: the sixteen satires*, Harmondsworth, rev. edn, 1974, Satire VIII,
    p. 190 n. 17. See also Gowers, *Loaded Table*, chs 1 and 3, although she is more concerned
    with satire concerning meals held at home. See also Cic., *Pis.* 6.13.

52 Wallace-Hadrill, "Public honor," pp. 39–63; R. Laurence, *Roman Pompeii. Space and society*,
    London, 1994, pp. 70–87, to which the discussion below refers. Laurence's book has now been
    revised in a second edition (2006); *non vidi*.

53 Wallace-Hadrill, "Public honor," p. 39.

54 Laurence, *Roman Pompeii*, p. 70.

55 Sen., *De vita beata* 7.3, transl. Wallace-Hadrill, "Public honor," p. 39.

56 MNN, inv. no. 111482; CIL IV, 3494. See F. Todd, "Three Pompeian wall inscriptions and
    Petronius," *CR*, 1939, vol. 80, pp. 5–9; H. Tanzer, *The Common People of Pompeii*, Baltimore,
    MD, 1939, pp. 47–51; Packer, "Inns at Pompeii," p. 36, n. 75. In the third "cartoon" panel,
    two men gamble at a game, perhaps *XII scripta*. The first cries out: *exsi*, "I'm out" (i.e.,
    "I win"), but the other objects: *non tria; duas est*, "That's not a three, it's a two!" In the fourth
    panel, the two come to blows; the first man claims: *noxse a me tria ego fui*, "You've wronged
    me, it was a three; I was (out)." The second retorts: *orte fellator, ego fui*, "Son of a cocksucker!
    I was (out)." The proprietor shoves both of them to the door, saying: *itis foris rixiatis*, "Get
    out, do your fighting outside!" (transl. P. Foss). See G. P. Caratelli and I. Baldassarre (eds),
    Pompei, pitture e mosaici, vol. 5, Rome, 1994, pp. 366–71.

57 Ruddell, *Tavern Business*, pp. 43–4.

58 These have been found in Rome, Philippi, Timgad, Ephesus, Britain and Lepcis Magna, among
    others. See R. MacMullen, *Roman Social Relations*, New Haven, CT, 1974, pp. 64, 170 n. 22;
    U. Schädler, "XII Scripta. Alea, Tabula—new evidence for the Roman history of 'Backgammon,'"
    in A. J. de Voogt (ed.), *New Approaches to Board Games Research*, Leiden, 1995, pp. 73–98.

59 Suet., *Aug.* 71.

60 *CIL* IV, 7698: *Abluat unda pedes puer ed detergeat udos, mappa torum velet, lintea nostra cave. Lascivos
    vultus et blandos aufert ocellos coniuge ab alterius, sit tibi in ore pudor. Utere blanditiis odiosaque iurgia
    differ si potes aut gressus ad tua tecta refer*, "Let the slave wash your feet with water and wipe
    them dry; let him cover the dining-couch with a napkin; take care with our linens. Put aside
    lascivious looks and alluring eyes at the wife of another man; let decency reside in your speech.
    Speak pleasant words and avoid troublesome quarrels if you can; otherwise take steps to your
    own house." (transl. P. Foss).

61 Cic., *Off.* 1.150. Note in Pompeii for example, *CIL* IV, 9339b. See MacMullen, *Roman Social
    Relations*, pp. 119–20, 138.

62 Laurence, *Roman Pompeii*, p. 70.

63 MacMullen, *Roman Social Relations*, pp. 88–101.

64 Laurence, *Roman Pompeii*, p. 85.

65 Plaut., *Curc.* 461–85.

66 "*Nam quod ad voluptatem pertinet, licet circumfundatur undique et per omnis vias influat animumque
    blandimentis suis leniat aliaque ex aliis admoveat, quibus totos partesque nostri sollicitet*" (Sen., *De
    vita beata* 5.4), transl. C. Edwards, *The Politics of Immorality in Ancient Rome*, Cambridge, 1993,
    p. 173.

67 Sen., *Ep.* 56.1–2.

68 *CIL* IV, 7863; 7864; 7873; 7862; 7866; 7221.

69 For the use of the phallus, see Plin., *HN* 19.19.1; Varro, *Ling.* 7.97; Poll., *Onom.* 8.118. See
    also J. R. Clarke, *Roman Sex, 100 BC–AD 250*, New York, 2003, pp. 95–105, 108–11. For
    primary sources in translation concerning amulets, phallus magic and Priapus, see D. Ogden
    (ed.), *Magic, Witchcraft, and Ghosts in Greek and Roman Worlds: a sourcebook*, Oxford, 2002.

70 M. Della Corte, *Pompeii. The new excavations*, Valle di Pompeii, 1927, p. 23.

71 *CIV* IV, 7432; J. Franklin, *Pompeis difficile est*, Ann Arbor, MI, 2001, pp. 89–90, 186; Della
    Corte, *Case ed abitanti*, p. 348. Cf. Nappo, Ch. 23, for a discussion of the architecture of this
    building.

72 *CIL* IV, 8442.

73 D. E. E. Kleiner and S. B. Matherson (eds), *I Claudia. Women in ancient Rome*, New Haven,
    CT, 1996, p. 90 n. 2. I do not wish this small flaw to mar the reputation of an extraordinary

exhibit and book concerning women and Rome. See also J. Evans, *War, Women and Children in Ancient Rome*, London, 1991, p. 134.

74 *Dig.* 23.2.43, pr. 6–9.

75 Evans, *War, Women and Children*, p. 134; J. N. Adams, *The Latin Sexual Vocabulary*, Baltimore, MD, 1990, pp. 110–12.

76 H. Eschebach, *Die städbauliche Entwicklung des antiken Pompeji*, RM-EH, 17, Heidelberg, 1970, p. 122.

77 Address (V.2.b-c) is used in Carratelli and Baldassarre, *Pitture e mosaici* and Eschebach, *Die städbauliche Entwicklung*. It is listed as (V.2.C-D) in Van der Poel, *CTP*, vol. IIIa, p. 73. For the *graffiti*, see *CIL* IV, 4259, 8454.

78 *CIL* IV, 8241; 8248.

79 Wallace-Hadrill, "Public honor," pp. 51–2.

80 L. Jacobelli, *Le pitture erotiche delle Terme Suburbane Pompei*, Soprintendenza Archeologica di Pompei, Monografie 10, Rome, 1995, pp. 154–66. For critical treatments of this subject, see now T. A. J. McGinn, "Pompeian brothels and social history," JRA Suppl. Ser. no. 47, 2002, pp. 7–46; T. A. J. McGinn, *The Economy of Prostitution in the Roman World*, Ann Arbor, MI, 2004.

81 *CIL* IV, 813: *Otiosis locus hic non est. Discede morator*, "This is not a place to idle. Shove off, loiterer" (transl. P. Foss).

82 See J. DeFelice, *The Women of the Roman Inns. A study of law, occupation and status*, Ph.D. thesis, Miami University of Ohio, 1998; DeFelice, *Roman Hospitality*, ch. 3.

CHAPTER THIRTY-ONE

GARDENS

——·◆·——

Wilhelmina Jashemski

Gardens had an important place in the life of ancient Campania. Approximately 626 have been found in Pompeii, Herculaneum, and the surrounding villas, preserved by the eruption of AD 79.[1] Gardens were associated with many public buildings, and even with tombs (cf. Cormack, Ch. 37),[2] but the most were found in homes. The garden was the heart of the house, whether large or small, furnishing light, air, and ease of communication to rooms opening onto it. It was a place of work and play, a place to cook, eat and worship.[3] A large house might have three or more gardens, a small house perhaps only a tiny light well that contained plants. These gardens differed greatly not only in size, design, function and plantings, but also with respect to the role of water, sculpture and garden furniture.

The garden was a significant factor in the development of the house. The most elegant houses in Pompeii were built by the Samnites in the second century BC (cf. Wallace-Hadrill, Ch. 18). It has often been said that the house of this period was created by adding the peristyle of the contemporary luxurious Hellenistic house to the rear of the old Italic *atrium* house. But when the Italians added the peristyle to their *atrium* house they transformed the peristyle by making it a garden, instead of leaving it as a beaten clay court, or paving it with cobblestones, cement or mosaics, as was done in the Hellenistic house.

The garden might be enclosed by a portico on one, two, three or four sides. Houses with porticoed gardens, however, were not as universal as has been thought. Only about 300 such houses, some very small, have been found thus far in the entire Vesuvian area. There were also houses with interior courtyard gardens, but no portico. Sometimes wide windows gave a view into these gardens.

Some of the luxurious houses built over the city wall in the southwestern and western part of the city (after Pompeii became a Roman city and the wall was no longer needed for protection) even had roof gardens (cf. Tybout, Ch. 26).[4] Seneca scathingly deplored such unnatural practices as planting the tops of buildings with trees, with their roots where the roofs should be.[5]

Houses were by no means as uniform as is often thought. There were many smaller homes of irregular plan occupied by more humble citizens, but even the poor, if at all possible, made place in their modest homes for a tiny garden. Many homes were

Figure 31.1 Garden painting, House of Marine Venus (II.3.3), west panel of south wall.
Photo: Stanley A. Jashemski.

commercial in character (cf. Pirson, Ch. 29). We find that those who lived in rooms behind their shops, as many of the petty tradesmen did, allotted precious space for gardens. The same instinct prompted shopkeepers who lived in rooms above their shops to grow a few vines on their balconies to provide an arbor of shade. Vine-covered pergolas were not a monopoly of the rich. There were a few houses with no garden, but it is touching to discover that a neighbor who had a large garden, at times, cut a window in the wall that separated the two houses so that the poor family might enjoy the view of their neighbor's spacious garden.

Information about Vesuvian gardens is rich and varied. Garden paintings are one important source of information.[6] Painting a garden on one or more of the walls made a modest garden appear larger. Behind a painted fence, plants, trees, birds, statues, pools (sometimes shown with fish), and fountains, often too large for the actual garden, could be pictured (Figures 23.21 and 31.1). A few houses had interior rooms painted to make the room appear as a garden. These paintings furnish invaluable evidence about the ancient plant material and fauna, for the plants and birds pictured are those that would have populated ancient gardens.[7]

But only careful excavation can show how an ancient garden actually looked. The peristyle garden in the fine old Samnite House of C. Julius Polybius (IX.12.1–3), on the via dell'Abbondanza, excavated in 1973, was the first peristyle garden to be excavated using newly developed scientific techniques.[8] When the plants and trees growing at the time of the eruption died, their roots decayed, and the volcanic debris

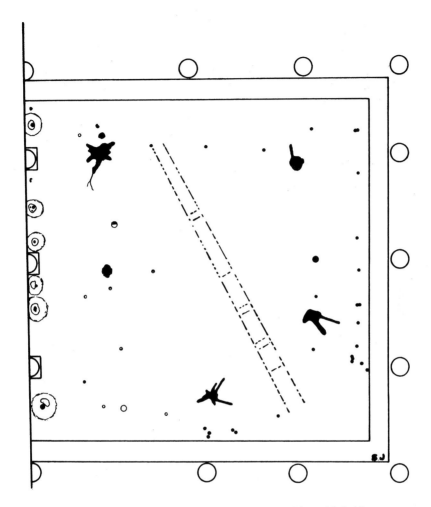

Figure 31.2 Garden of Polybius (IX.12.1–3). Plan with ladder.
Roots are indicated in black; stakes by circles; plan courtesy of the Soprintendenza
alle antichità di Pompei; garden details by Stanley A. Jashemski.

that covered the site gradually filled the cavities. During excavation, all the *lapilli* is removed until the level of the garden in AD79 is reached. At this point the *lapilli*-filled cavities are clearly visible. It is then possible with special tools to empty the cavities, reinforce them with heavy wire and fill them with cement. When the cement has hardened, the soil is removed from around the cast to reveal the shape of the ancient root. This technique, first developed by the Italian archaeologist Giuseppe Fiorelli to make casts of bodies buried in the *lapilli* (Figure 38.1), was later used by Giuseppe Spano to make root casts. Today the archaeologist carefully preserves soil contours, planting patterns, carbonized stems, ancient pollen, seed, fruit, and sometimes even insects and bacteria, all of which are studied and identified by the appropriate specialists. Garden archaeology is a complex discipline that requires the close cooperation of many specialists.[9]

The small garden in the House of Polybius, enclosed by a portico on three sides, contained five large trees, with many smaller ones, including eight trees espaliered between the engaged columns on the west wall (Figure 31.2). Fragments of terracotta pots, with four holes (three on the sides, one on the bottom) in which the trees had been started, were found in the root cavities. They suggested that the trees might have been the exotic citron, which Pliny says were transported "in pots with breathing holes for the roots,"[10] or perhaps the lemon, which the ancient Pompeians knew,[11] and which today they also start in pots. The small root cavities along the south and east edges of the garden call to mind the ornamental bushes or plants pictured so frequently at the base of Pompeian walls.

The five large trees, which would have almost completely shaded the garden, were evidently pruned high to allow planting underneath, at least along the edges. Small misshapen lumps of charcoal found around the tree cavity in the northwest corner of the garden, revealed (when sectioned) the many seeds of figs that had fallen to the ground, probably from this tree. A high concentration of olive pollen also indicates that the olive was raised in this garden. Marks left in the soil by an exceptionally long ladder (8 m long, 0.5 m wide at the bottom and 0.3 m at the top), so shaped to fit into dense branches, was recognized by the workmen as being similar to the ladders they use today to pick cherries and pears, and suggests that such fruit trees were also planted in the garden.

The discovery of this densely and informally planted garden was a great surprise, for it was very different from the formally planted gardens identified at other excavated houses. This raised questions concerning the planting of peristyle gardens and the extent to which trees may have been used. Subsoil examination of all the peristyle gardens that had been uncovered in Regions I and II during the last period of extensive excavation (1951–61)—since these had been exposed for a shorter time to the ravages of weeds and weather, making it possible to recover root cavities—revealed that in the seven peristyle gardens in which it was possible to find root cavities, all but one had been informally planted, five with trees.[12] Only one had been formally planted in low shrubs in a formal design.[13] This changed commonly accepted beliefs about plantings in peristyle gardens. Trees, which require little water in the Mediterranean area, except at first, would have been natural plantings in the period before the aqueduct, introduced during the reign of Augustus (27 BC–AD 14), made the generous use of water possible (cf. Jansen, Ch. 16). Pools, fountains, and low plantings were then installed, as in the House of the Vettii (VI.15.1).[14] During the last years of the city, showy mosaic fountains became popular, as in the House of the Great Fountain (VI.8.22).[15] Nevertheless, some owners were probably reluctant to give up the shade of trees, especially of a fig or an olive whose productivity increased with age.

A small, elegant formal garden, excavated in 1984, stretched out at the rear of the lower level of the three-story House of the Wedding of Alexander (VI.17 [*Ins. Occ.*]. 42), which was built over the western city wall (Figure 31.3).[16] A high vaulted *diaeta* (b), or garden room, its walls decorated with the most beautiful garden paintings yet found in the Vesuvian area,[17] opened out on the north end of the east side of the garden. Most of the adjacent *exedra* (c), decorated with garden paintings poorly preserved at the time of excavation, was occupied by a water *triclinium*. This was dominated by a beautiful apsidal mosaic fountain with steps over which water fell, then rose in a jet in the middle of the couches and eventually emptied into the pool in front of

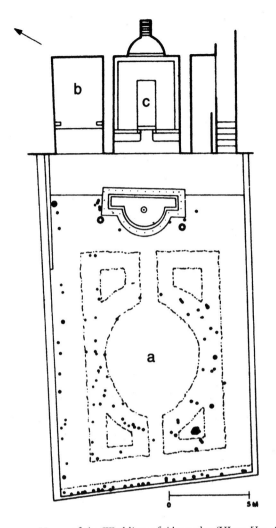

Figure 31.3 House of the Wedding of Alexander (VI.17 [*Ins. Occ.*]. 42).

the *exedra* at the east end of the garden. This pool, with a semicircular extension into the garden, was painted blue inside. Water rose in a jet from the low column in the center of the pool and from the twenty-eight jets around the rim. A column at each of the front corners of the pool apparently formed a pergola that framed the whole (cf. the *triclinium*, fountains and pergolas of the *euripi* in (II.2.2); Nappo, Ch. 23).

At the west end of the garden was a small, slightly raised bed, in which was found a row of twenty-eight small root cavities. The rest of the garden was laid out with passageways along the four walls, leaving a rectangular area with slightly raised borders. Within this rectangle, soil contours outlined an oval bed with mounded borders, which left trapezoidal-shaped beds at each corner of the garden. The many root cavities in the contoured border of the oval within the rectangular bed suggest a formal hedge, perhaps box (Figures 31.3–4). The shells, bones of fish, cow, pig,

Figure 31.4   House of the Wedding of Alexander (VI.17 [*Ins. Occ.*]. 42), view east; rendering by Victoria I.

sheep or goat, chicken and bird (rock partridge, *Alectoris graeca*) found along the north garden wall were probably debris left from meals at the nearby water *triclinium*. The bones also included the partial skeleton of a rat (*Rattus rattus* L.) and those of a dormouse (*Muscardinus avellanarius* L.). The bones of a small lizard were found in the pool.

More recently, a small formal peristyle garden was excavated in the House of the Chaste Lovers (IX.12.6–7).[18] A lattice fence made of reeds enclosed the geometrically shaped beds. Fragments of carbonized wood included the giant reed (*Arundo donax* L.), the smaller reed (*Phragmites australis* [Cav.] Trin.), Juniper (*Juniperus* sp.), and Rose (*Rosa* sp.). Pollen provided additional information.

There were also gardens in the many villas in the Vesuvian area. The luxurious villa located on the modern via Sepolcri in Torre Annunziata (ancient Oplontis) is believed to have belonged to Poppaea, wife of the emperor Nero (cf. Moormann, Ch. 28). It has thirteen remarkable gardens in the area available for excavation; these have been carefully excavated.[19] The gardens inside the villa were much like those in city homes. But the great exterior gardens, which reached out to the sea in front of the villa and toward the mountains in the rear, were unique.

The formal architectural layout of the large park-like garden at the rear of the villa reflected the plan of the villa itself (Figure 31.5). From its entrance, the perspective through the *atrium* (5) continued through the enclosed garden (20) and the grand salon (21), with its monumental entrance at the rear of the villa, to a landscaped pathway on the central axis of the villa. On either side of this pathway were contoured beds that extended to the east–west passageway (33–34) along the villa. Five marble shafts supporting white marble heads of Aphrodite, a woman of the Julio-Claudian period, a portrait of a Julio-Claudian boy, the head of the child Dionysus, and a bearded Dionysus were set among flowering shrubs. Flanking passageway (33) were four marble centaur fountains.

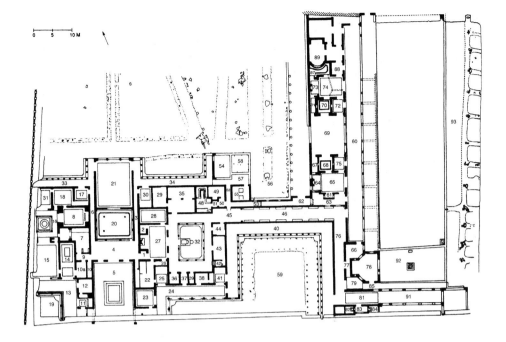

Figure 31.5 Plan of the Villa of Poppaea at Oplontis.

The large branch (1.8 m long) of a tree found in the volcanic ash at the north edge of the excavated garden, at a height of about 2.5 m, had the appearance of fresh wood. When examined, however, scientists found that the cellular structure had been almost completely destroyed. Microscopic examination of a few preserved cells finally revealed that the large tree was an olive. The cavities left by the spreading branches of this tree, along with the branches of other large trees visible in the cut of the volcanic fill, may be traces of a row of olives that grew in the yet unexcavated part of the garden. The oil press (*torcularium*) in room (83) is also proof of olive production at the villa.

The east wing of the villa, which was built later (*c.*AD 50–60), looked out on an immense swimming pool (60 by 17 m) and a magnificent sculpture garden beyond (93). Along the east side of the pool was a row of thirteen statue bases; behind each base was the root cavity of a tree. Four statue bases and their plantings, directly opposite the large open hall (69), provided a splendid picture when viewed across the pool from this room. The two outside trees were oleander and the two in the center lemon. There were also oleanders in the beds behind these trees.

The six marble statues thus far recovered, beginning from the south, were: the head of Hercules, an *ephebe* and Nike; balancing these on the left: another Nike, Diana (?) without a head, and a head of Hercules. At the south end of the swimming pool was a sculpted white marble group of a hermaphrodite and a satyr, and further to the south a small square marble pool and a large white crater fountain (92). The limits of this magnificent garden, surely worthy of an empress, are still not known.[20]

493

Pompeii had many large and important cultivated areas, usually attached to a house. The *insula* to the north of the amphitheater (II.5), since the time it was originally excavated, was believed to be the cattle market. Subsoil excavation, however, revealed a large commercial vineyard, conforming in a remarkable way to the recommendations of Roman agricultural writers, with arbored passageways and precisely spaced vines and stakes (Figure 31.6).[21] This surprising discovery led to the

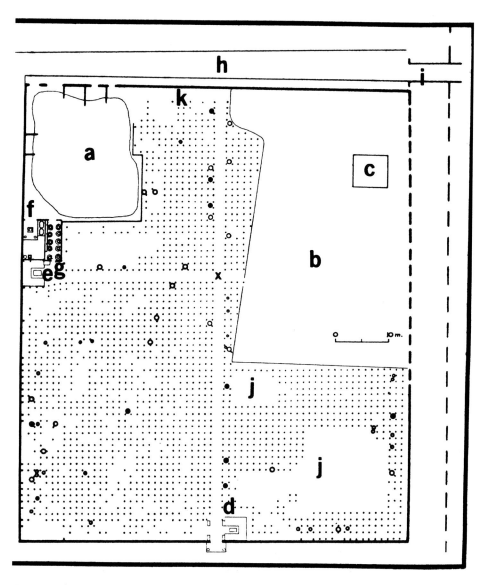

Figure 31.6 Large Vineyard (II.5). Plan. Dots indicate grapevine roots; (x) indicates the intersection of paths; circles show small tree roots; large black circles show tree roots 30 cm or more in largest dimension; plan courtesy of the Soprintendenza alle antichità di Pompei; garden details by Stanley A. Jashemski.

subsoil excavation of other large open areas hurriedly uncovered in Regions I and II during the years after World War II (cf. Foss, Ch. 3; Nappo, Ch. 23). Found were: other vineyards less formally planted,[22] a large orchard[23] and a market-garden vine-yard.[24]

The garden of Hercules (II.8.6),[25] named from the statuette found in the garden shrine, had complicated and unique soil contours, which divided the garden into many beds. In one perfectly preserved bed were small round formations; in the center of each had been a plant too small for *lapilli* to have preserved the root cavity. Around each little plant was a depression for water. Careful provisions had been made for watering these plants, even though the garden was beyond the part of Pompeii served by the aqueduct. Rainwater was collected from the roof of the house into a *dolium* on either side of the door leading into the garden. Additional water was carried to the garden and poured from the street side through an *amphora* tip inserted in the wall, so as to fill another large *dolium*. When the *dolium* overflowed, water was channeled around the edges of the garden, filling various embedded *dolia* along the wall. The young trees, perhaps lemons, started in pots along the edge of the garden, were watered in this way. Water was then led into the many irrigation channels in the garden.

Balloon photography, in a remarkable way, reveals even the badly damaged soil contours that could not be seen from the ground (Figure 31.7). The beds were not

Figure 31.7 Garden of Hercules (II.8.6), view toward the east.
Balloon photo: Julian Whittlesey Foundation.

all on the same level. Those on the north were higher than those on the south, thus conforming to the natural slope of the land. To ensure the flow of water from the higher levels to the lower levels, the water channels on the north were placed higher than the beds; those on the south, lower. Modern Pompeian gardeners shape their beds in the same way. Unfortunately, the remarkable layout of this garden with its beds of varying levels is not preserved today; the ancient evidence has been destroyed by the installation of a modern watering system, and present plantings do not match those of the ancient garden.

This garden had few tree cavities, except those of the trees started in pots along the wall and the huge cavity of an olive tree, identified by the shape of the root and plentiful olive pollen. Carbonized cherries (*Prunus cerasus* L.) probably identify another of the trees. Most of the cavities belonged to stakes or posts that supported frames covered with fiber mats or other material to furnish protection for young plants, as is done today. Vegetables or flowers were also grown in this garden (flowers for at least part of the year). A local commercial flower grower remarked to me that the ancient soil contours in this garden were the same as in his.

Ancient Pompeii was famous for its flower culture, as it still is today; commercial growers produce cut flowers and seed. In antiquity, flowers were grown for making garlands and perfume or ointment. Many glass perfume bottles were found in the house, as well as fragments of terracotta ointment containers. Olive oil was an important ingredient in making perfumed oil, probably provided by the large olive tree.

Gardens were also found in public places.[26] Pompeii and Herculaneum had their public green places, their tall and shady trees, the Great Palaestra at Pompeii its avenue of venerable plane trees (Figures 14.4 and 23.1; Map 3). The largest hotel at Pompeii (VII.11.11, 14) had a secluded garden and, along the north wall, three arbors where guests might be served (cf. DeFelice, Ch. 30).[27] Halfway across the city, the *copo* Euxinus served guests in the small vineyard attached to his *caupona* (I.12.12). There were also many gardens connected with places of business. Bakeries, fulleries and tanneries were set up in old houses, but at times the garden was retained (cf. Pirson, Ch. 29).[28] The peristyle garden in *garum* shop (I.12.8), with garden paintings placed on the north wall after the house became a workshop, had two large trees, and also smaller plants. Workers were thus sheltered from the hot Campanian sun, and their place of work enlivened by the beauty of flowers or shrubs.[29]

Formal gardens were essentially green gardens, planted with evergreens beautiful the year round: laurel, myrtle, oleander, box, ivy and rosemary. Flowers in season added accents—especially the rose, the lily, the "violet,"[30] the daisy and the colorful oleander. Many gardens, however, were less formally planted with trees (often fruit or nut) and vines, for Campanians were a practical lot. It was always possible, after all, to tuck a few flowers and herbs among the cabbages and onions growing beneath the trees or vines.

NOTES

1 For a description of these gardens see W. F. Jashemski, *The Gardens of Pompeii, Herculaneum and the Villas Destroyed by Vesuvius: Appendices*, New Rochelle, NY, 1993, vol. 2, pp. 21–312; each garden is described, together with a plan, photos, and the important evidence cited (sculpture, garden furnishings, soil contours, carbonized plant material, pollen, bones, etc.). For the subsequently excavated garden in the House of the Chaste Lovers (IX.12.6–7), see

A. Ciarallo and M. Mariotti Lippi, "Gardens of Casa dei Casti Amanti," *Garden History*, 1993, vol. 21.1, pp. 110–16.

2 W. F. Jashemski, *The Gardens of Pompeii, Herculaneum and the Villas Destroyed by Vesuvius*, New Rochelle, NY, 1979, vol. 1, pp. 141–53 ("Tomb Gardens"); Jashemski, *Gardens*, vol. 2: see specific tomb gardens. See also J. Bodel, "Tomb gardens," ch. 6 in W. F. Jashemski (ed.), *Gardens of the Roman Empire*, vol. 1, Cambridge, forthcoming.

3 Jashemski, *Gardens*, vol. 1, pp. 89–113 ("Life in the Garden"), pp. 115–35 ("Religion in the Garden"); vol. 2: see specific gardens.

4 See Plin., *HN* 15.47 for imported trees suitable for roof gardens.

5 Sen., *Ep.* 122.

6 See Jashemski, *Gardens*, vol. 1, pp. 55–87; vol. 2, pp. 313–81, a catalogue describing all the known garden paintings in the Vesuvian area, with photos and bibliography; see vol. 2, pp. 381–92 for garden paintings known elsewhere in the Roman empire. See also B. Bergmann, ch. 10 in Jashemski, *Gardens of the Roman Empire*.

7 See references in n.6 above for the identification by scientists of the flora and fauna in the garden paintings. For a more detailed description of the flora in the wall paintings, including those elsewhere in the house, see: W. F. Jashemski, F. G. Meyer and M. Ricciardi, "Plants: evidence from wall paintings, mosaics, sculpture, plant remains, graffiti, inscriptions, and ancient authors," in W. F. Jashemski and F. G. Meyer (eds), *The Natural History of Pompeii*, Cambridge, 2002, pp. 80–180. For fish: pp. 274–91; marine invertebrates, freshwater shells and land snails: pp. 292–314; insects: pp. 315–26; amphibians and reptiles: pp. 327–56; birds: pp. 357–400; mammals: pp. 401–50. For plants known to the Pompeians, see W. F. Jashemski, "Plants," ch. 13 in Jashemski, *Gardens of the Roman Empire*.

8 Jashemski, *Gardens*, vol. 1, pp. 25–30; vol. 2, pp. 249–51, no. 517.

9 See Jashemski and Meyer, *Natural History*, which contains chapters by the scientists who have cooperated with W. F. Jashemski, and identified the material found in her excavations.

10 Plin., *HN* 12.16.

11 The Romans knew both of these fruits. For lemons found in the garden paintings in the House of the Fruit Orchard (I.9.5), see Jashemski, *Gardens*, vol. 1, p. 78, fig. 126; p. 281, fig. 420. A mosaic (*c*.AD 100) in the Terme Museum, Rome (inv. no. 58596) accurately depicts both a lemon and a citron, showing their different characteristics and relative size (Jashemski, *Gardens*, vol. 1, p. 281, fig. 419).

12 See Jashemski, *Gardens*, vol. 1, pp. 30–1, figs 45–9 for the five gardens planted with trees. Only small root cavities were present in (I.11.6).

13 Jashemski, *Gardens*, vol. 1, pp. 31–2, fig. 50.

14 Jashemski, *Gardens*, vol. 1, pp. 35–8, figs 54–9; vol. 2, pp. 153–5, figs 166–78.

15 Jashemski, *Gardens*, vol. 1, pp. 41–2, figs 69–70; vol. 2, p. 135.

16 Jashemski, *Gardens*, vol. 2, pp. 166–7, no. 313.

17 Jashemski, *Gardens*, vol. 2, pp. 348–56, no. 60, figs 406–20. See also fig. 1 (frontispiece), fig. 2 on p. xvii and figs 7–12, 15–16 on pp. 12–15.

18 Ciarallo and Lippi, "Casa dei Casti Amanti."

19 Jashemski, *Gardens*, vol. 1, pp. 290–314; vol. 2, pp. 293–301, nos. 593–605; for the garden paintings: vol. 2, pp. 375–9, nos. 116–21. For the sculpture, see Stefano de Caro, "The sculptures of the Villa of Poppaea at Oplontis," in *Ancient Roman Villa Gardens*, Dumbarton Oaks Colloquium on the History of Landscape Architecture no. 10, Washington, DC, 1987, pp. 77–133.

20 See now B. Bergmann, "Art and nature in the villa at Oplontis," in *Pompeian Brothels, Pompeii's Ancient History, Mirrors and Mysteries, Art and Nature at Oplontis, & the Herculaneum "Basilica,"* JRA Suppl. Ser. no. 47, 2002, pp. 87–120, for a study of "representation, aesthetic experience, and environmental values in the 1st c. BC and the 1st AD" (p. 87).

21 See W. F. Jashemski, "Excavations in the 'Foro Boario' at Pompeii. A preliminary report," *AJA*, 1968, vol. 72, pp. 69–73; "University of Maryland excavations at Pompeii 1968," *AJA*, 1970, vol. 74, pp. 63–70; "The discovery of a large vineyard at Pompeii: University of Maryland excavations 1970," *AJA*, 1973, vol. 77, pp. 27–41; "Large vineyard discovered in ancient Pompeii," *Science*, 1973, vol. 180, pp. 821–30; Jashemski, *Gardens*, vol. 1, pp. 201–18; vol. 2, pp. 89–90, no. 146.

22 Jashemski, *Gardens*, vol. 1, pp. 221–32; vol. 2, see vineyards in: (I.11.10–11), (I.15), (I.20.1), (I.20.5), (III.7), (IX.9.6, 10).
23 Jashemski, *Gardens*, vol. 1, pp. 251–65; vol. 2, p. 73, no. 123.
24 Jashemski, *Gardens*, vol. 1, pp. 233–42; vol. 2, pp. 61–3, no. 107.
25 Jashemski, *Gardens*, vol. 1, pp. 279–88; vol. 2, pp. 94–6, no. 153.
26 Jashemski, *Gardens*, vol. 1, pp. 155–65 for gardens in *palaestras*, baths and temples. See specific gardens in vol. 2.
27 Jashemski, *Gardens*, vol. 1, pp. 167–81 for gardens in restaurants, inns and hotels. See specific gardens in vol. 2.
28 Jashemski, *Gardens*, vol. 1, pp. 183–99 for gardens connected with various places of business. See specific gardens in vol. 2.
29 Jashemski, *Gardens*, vol. 1, pp. 195–6; vol. 2, pp. 54–5, no. 84; for the garden paintings: vol. 2, p. 326, no. 20.
30 The Romans also applied the name violet (*viola*) to various flowers, including stock (*Matthiola incana* (L.) R. Br.). The violet beds (*violaria*) referred to by ancient writers would have been stock. The yellow violet of the Romans was probably the wall flower (*Erysimum cheiri* [L.] Crantz).

CHAPTER THIRTY-TWO

THE LOSS OF INNOCENCE
Pompeian economy and society
between past and present

———•◆•———

Willem M. Jongman

THE CITY AND THE ANCIENT ECONOMY

After more than two centuries of excavations, Pompeii continues to fire the imagination of scholars and tourists alike. From the beginning, the cruel fate of the city enhanced the excitement of discovering objects and remains of Roman life not normally found elsewhere. In Pompeii, visitors could walk through streets, peek into private houses, bars and brothels, and could imagine that real individuals had lived there. They could see wall paintings in vivid colours when other sites had rarely offered more than a few faded fragments. They could see household objects of luxury and refinement. Moreover, in Pompeii they could be excited by eroticism in commonplace art and crafts. Wealth, debauchery and punishment by an act of God are powerful ingredients to kindle interest (cf. Foss, Ch. 3).

Pompeii thus offered a new reading of classical antiquity, enhancing and competing with the written world of Rome. The new image became all the more vivid when, from the 1860s onwards, excavation policy began to leave and restore as much as possible *in situ*. As a conservation policy, it was the worst thing that could have happened to Pompeii. Intellectually, however, it was a clear advance, emphasizing structure and coherence over and above individual objects. It also provided a vivid sensation of time travel. A visitor not spoilt by Hollywood animation could delude himself that he was literally walking through the past.

Tourists and archaeologists were not the only ones to be impressed. In 1892 a young Russian student of ancient history, Michael Rostovtzeff, wrote his final "MA dissertation" on Pompeii and the implications of the recent excavations.[1] After he had received his degree, he travelled to Pompeii at his own expense that same year. During the next few years, he would return, to be taught by the eminent Pompeian scholar August Mau.[2] The long visits to Pompeii were formative experiences in the intellectual development of the man who would, arguably, be the most important ancient historian of the first half of the twentieth century. Already before he came to Pompeii, Rostovtzeff had been an ancient historian who believed in the value of archaeology. The visits must have deepened and enriched his sense of the texture of the Roman past such as only a personal visit can do. It is precisely his visionary style of blending archaeology into ancient history that would mark the enduring importance of Rostovtzeff for the writing of ancient history. Pompeii cannot have failed to convince him that he was right.

Pompeii also became a substantive paradigm. The sensation of time travel helped to establish the scholarly image of a Pompeian society quite similar to our own world. The step from easy recognition of material culture to the assumption that the Roman past was not so different from the modern world was easily made. The archaeologist could point to a city of fair size, with large and well-appointed houses, with "modern" facilities such as paved streets and running water, and an elite culture still highly admired.[3] It was easy to ignore what was not immediately visible, and to domesticate Pompeii to a comfortable and sanitized bourgeois world.

It was through Rostovtzeff's classic *The Social and Economic History of the Roman Empire* that this modernized Pompeii became a canonized part of ancient history. Rostovtzeff had written: "The student of economic history of the [Julio-Claudian] period might derive assistance from a careful investigation of the inscriptions and of the archaeological material, especially as furnished by Pompeii."[4] For Rostovtzeff the growth and spread of Roman urbanism represented the core of Rome's economic achievement:

[All the cities of the Empire] aimed . . . at the largest possible degree of comfort for their inhabitants; they all looked like some of our modern Western cities rather than like the cities and villages of the East at the present day. I have no doubt that some, or most, modern Italian cities differ very little from their Roman ancestors.[5]

Pompeian examples were obviously in his mind when he wrote:

The private houses were mostly of good size and equipped with modern conveniences, for example, private baths, running water, good stone stairs to the upper storeys, etc. These are all familiar facts. We may say that as regards comfort, beauty, and hygiene, the cities of the Roman Empire, worthy successors of their Hellenistic parents, were not inferior to many a modern European and American town.[6]

The corollary of such a high standard of living must have been that production was highly developed and modern. This was possible by "the formation of a city bourgeoisie, of a class of landowners, traders and industrialists, who resided in the city and who developed an energetic business activity on capitalistic lines".[7] Mau had, indeed, taught Rostovtzeff that "Pompeii was a prosperous commercial city".[8]

To an early twenty-first-century reader Rostovtzeff's modernizing anachronisms seem absurd, but that is unfair. Russia and Italy at the beginning of the twentieth century were not particularly modern societies, and only just beginning to shake off their pre-industrial past. Our personal experience of a global economy and society dominated by rapid technological innovation and economic growth has blinded us to the achievements of the Roman world. Rostovtzeff, born in what was then still pre-industrial Russia, and well-travelled in the least developed parts of the

Mediterranean, was in an excellent position to grasp the extraordinary achievements of the Roman world, often only beginning to be surpassed during the Industrial Revolution.

Rome's urbanism was indeed exceptional. The city of Rome, with its perhaps one million inhabitants in the early Empire, is unique in pre-industrial European history: the first European city to have the same number of inhabitants again was London around 1800, well after the beginning of the Industrial Revolution.[9] Rome, moreover, was not the only big city in the Empire: between them Roman Carthage, Antioch and Alexandria also had, perhaps, one million inhabitants. Around 1500, there were only four cities in all of Europe with more than 100,000 inhabitants, and between them they had only 450,000 inhabitants.[10] The prominence of big cities in the Roman Empire is truly amazing.

The Roman Empire, moreover, was not only a world of a few big cities. It was also a world of many small cities. Administratively, early imperial Italy had 431 cities, with average populations in the range of 2,000–3,000 people.[11] Again, the contrast with medieval and early-modern Europe is astounding. Even in the remotest parts of the Empire, the modern explorer still finds the remains of numerous hardly known cities.[12] Much depends on one's definition of a city, of course, but there were perhaps some 2,000 cities in all of the Roman Empire. The Romanization of the Empire entailed its urbanization. Studying the best-preserved, medium-size Roman town may be a good tactic to understand what was so special about Roman society.

The remarkably large and pervasive urbanization of the Roman Empire also matters for the debate on the history of later European economic growth and development. A pivotal place in that debate has often been given to the growth of medieval and early modern cities. Already Adam Smith wrote: "the commerce and manufactures of cities, instead of being the effect, have been the cause and occasion of the improvement and cultivation of the country."[13] Smith has not remained alone in this view. Twentieth-century economic historians, too, have given the growth of towns an important place in their accounts of the economic modernization of Europe. Their analysis rested on two arguments. The first was that the division of labour between town and country led to significant economic benefits. Farmers could do what they were best at—farming—and buy the necessary tools, garments and the like from specialized craftsmen in the cities. The growth of urban markets, moreover, encouraged agricultural specialization in market crops. Farmers, therefore, could not only specialize in farming, but also in growing what their land was best for. The second argument was that cities provided a new cultural and political environment, free from the stifling traditionalism of the feudal countryside. It was in these "non-feudal islands in the feudal seas",[14] to quote the eminent medievalist Michael Postan, that a new culture of entrepreneurship, economic rationalism and economic innovation could develop. The city, in this view, was the cradle of economic man. So, with all this ancient urbanization, did the economic modernization of Europe begin in classical antiquity, rather than in the Middle Ages?

For those who wanted to see it, however, there always was a darker side to ancient society. In Pompeii the large amphitheatre was a powerful reminder that it was dangerous to assume that Romans really were just like us (cf. Parslow, Ch. 14). When the Pompeian magistrate Cn Alleius Nigidius Maius advertised his gladiatorial games, he added: *pugnabunt . . . sine ulla dilatione*, "they will fight without intervals" (*CIL* IV, 1180). How boring, indeed, if one killing is not immediately followed by the next. The games, moreover, were not an isolated arena for cruelty. When wealthy Pompeians fled their houses during the eruption, they sometimes left the slave-doorman in place, chained so that he could not escape his duty. Indeed, slaves were everywhere. They were prostitutes in the brothels, domestic staff and sex slaves to their elite masters, they were craftsmen, and they were agricultural labour on the *villae*, chained, and locked up at night. Some Pompeians were obviously very rich, but many more were poor and miserable (cf. George, Ch. 35).

Indeed, in more recent years ancient historians have drawn a bleaker picture of the ancient world. Foremost in this effort to wipe off optimistic and anachronistic modernizing has been the late Sir Moses Finley.[15] He argued that the ancient world did not have economic growth. If ancient cities were, indeed, numerous and important, they were also critically different from those in medieval and early modern Europe. Not all urbanization, therefore, entailed modernization and development. To develop this argument he returned to some of the leading proponents of the city's importance for historical change and development in Europe: Werner Sombart and, in particular, Max Weber. Sombart and Weber had developed a typology of cities based on the nature of the relationship between the city and its countryside. They had distinguished two types in particular, the consumer city and the producer city. Consumer cities were parasites on the country; only producer cities provided the dynamics to generate economic change and development. Both types of cities depended on the countryside for their food. The difference is in how they paid for it. The consumer city did not really pay for its food: the urban elite owned much of the countryside, and received rents in kind or in money (to buy food). Urban manufacture was not for external markets, but largely for the consumer needs of the urban elite. Such urbanism did not generate growth and development. The producer city, on the other hand, paid for its food from the export of manufactures to the countryside, and to faraway markets. The relationship between town and country was that of a division of labour, beneficial to both. The economic modernization of Europe, in this view, was due to the historic emergence of producer cities.

Finley argued that whereas, indeed, medieval and early-modern cities were mostly producer cities, ancient cities were not. He could use the concept of the "consumer city" to argue that in antiquity urbanism did not lead to economic growth and development. The economy was not "an enormous conglomeration of interdependent markets", and trade and manufacturing remained at a relatively small scale.[16] Geographic division of labour was limited, and manufacture was largely for local consumption. In antiquity, and unlike the medieval and early-modern world, town and country were politically integrated: the city did not end at the city gate, but included the surrounding countryside. Therefore, "ancient cities in the great majority counted farmers, whether working or gentlemen farmers, men whose interest lay chiefly and often exclusively in the land, as the core of their citizenry".[17] The urban elite was a land-owning elite. Unlike the medieval bourgeoisie, the urban elite of the ancient world was dominated by the social values of land-ownership. It lacked the culture of economic rationality and innovation. As a result, the economy did not grow.[18]

THE POMPEIAN ECONOMY

Ancient historians and classical archaeologists only rarely indulge in explicit comparative history. The dominant modernizing view of Pompeian life, therefore, never became part of a grand scheme of historical development, or of explicit comparison with medieval or early modern history. Instead, until recently Pompeii remained stuck in the naive and uncritical anachronism such as we saw in Rostovtzeff. For years, it provided optimistic images of a world hardly different from our own, and of the comfortable and reassuring proximity of classical civilization. It beckoned the visitor to believe that the past was not at all difficult to understand. All you needed to do was experience and enjoy it.

Clearly, if urbanization matters so much for our understanding of the structure and change of both ancient and later European society, Pompeii deserves a central place in these debates. Fortunately, recent research has finally begun to introduce Pompeii into the core of the debate on ancient economy and society.[19] What can we learn from Pompeii? The simple answer is, of course, more than we can cope with: Pompeii is a large and exceptionally rich and rewarding site. Even if the standard of earlier work and its preservation is often atrocious, enough remains to baffle and confuse the curious. The multitude of "facts" is virtually infinite, and so "letting them speak for themselves" is not only conceptually problematic, but practically impossible. We must decide which questions matter more than others, and what "facts" may constitute validation.[20]

Agriculture obviously takes central stage in any reconstruction of a pre-industrial economy. For the mass of the population, food was the largest item in their spending.[21] It has been estimated that in early-modern Europe food represented close to eighty per cent of the private expenditure of most people.[22] There is no reason to assume that in the Roman Empire the standard of living for the population was significantly higher than fifteen hundred years later. Most people, therefore, were living quite close to bare subsistence, a situation aggravated by the frequent possibility of bad harvests (but cf. Lazer, Ch. 38 for health and stature evidence from skeletons). On the supply side, agriculture was similarly important. The vast majority of any pre-industrial population were working in agriculture (rarely, if ever, less than two-thirds). With agriculture so important, it is not surprising that it was also the main source of elite wealth. The rich were mostly landowners. Agricultural property was the largest investment in the economy, and relatively safe (important in a world where life was so precarious).

The urgency of food production was all the greater in Roman Italy because of its high population density—there were many hungry mouths. With an average density (excluding the city of Rome) of at least twenty to twenty-five people per square kilometre, Roman Italy was one of the most populated areas of any period of pre-industrial European history.[23] These figures, moreover, are based on the lowest possible population estimate for Roman Italy. Quite plausible recent estimates have proposed a figure two to three times larger still.[24] Densities in the core areas of Roman Italy were only surpassed during the great changes of the nineteenth century. The demands on agricultural production were consequently high. Roman agriculture was intensive agriculture. It had to (and obviously did) achieve high yields per unit area, but at the inevitable price of declining marginal returns to higher labour inputs. Labour productivity was low. Such agricultural involution, as it has been called, went with low incomes for those with nothing more to offer than their labour, but high incomes for owners of scarce land.[25] It created vast social inequality.

Inevitably, Pompeii provides some of the most graphic illustrations of Roman agriculture. Around the city, many villas were found, with often large and richly decorated residential quarters, and sometimes remarkably well-preserved (at the time of their first excavation) agricultural facilities (cf. Moormann, Ch. 28; Figure 28.1). Wine presses and storage rooms abound (e.g., Figures 1.1, 28.4). For Rostovtzeff they provided a wonderful opportunity to demonstrate his skills in writing history from archaeology.[26] Taken together, they have created the picture of a Pompeii where much of agriculture was devoted to the commercial production on slave estates of market crops such as olive oil and, in particular, wine. The owners of these estates, it was argued, were often freedmen or other members of a commercial class.

And yet, writing history from archaeology is never quite so simple. All too easily we fall into the trap of what I have called the "positivist fallacy" of believing that what remains is an unproblematic and representative image of the past ("only the facts which survived matter"). Archaeological data, however, rarely constitute a representative sample. Can we really believe that what we have—scores of excavated villas—may stand proxy for all agricultural activity there once was? The facts that did not survive may matter too, if only we can find out what they were. It was the late David Clarke, the doyen of the "new archaeology", who drew attention to what he called "filters". What is excavated or collected is only a sample of what ever survived. What survived is only a sample of what was ever deposited, and what was ever deposited only documents a sample of "the range of hominid activity patterns and social and environmental processes which once existed, over a specified time and area".[27] What happened at each of these successive samplings? For an interpretation of archaeological data what is lost may be more important than what survived. Can we think our way out of the problem?

A first tactic could be to think of the implications of the orthodox emphasis on wine production.[28] What, indeed, if (almost) the entire Pompeian territory were used to grow grapes for wine? The quantity produced would have been staggering, and enough to quench the thirst of hundreds of thousands. Without imports of food, however, Pompeians would have starved in their drunken stupor. The origin of the discrepancy between these findings is that each year 1 ha of cereal land could produce just enough grain to feed one or two people (probably two in fertile Campania), but enough wine for a year of quite serious drinking by about twenty people.[29] There is no a priori reason to reject the possibility of major exports of wine, but in that case we must accept that Pompeii needed to import part of its own staple food, and more so, the more it exported wine.[30] In fact, more recent paleobotanical research strongly suggests substantial cereal cultivation in Pompeii (cf. Moormann, Ch. 28).[31]

A second and more traditional tactic could be to look at the surviving evidence. How robust is it? The remains of Pompeian villas are not uniformly distributed across the territory, but quite strongly concentrated in the areas immediately north of the city, and to the east along what I presumed to be the ancient course of the river Sarno (Figure 28.1).[32] The question is, therefore, whether there were also many villas elsewhere in the territory, but unknown to us, or whether the absence of villa remains in some parts of the territory means that there really were only few villas in those parts. Interestingly, the pattern of surviving remains becomes even more marked when we take a closer look at the sites and eliminate those that, though classified as "villas", are no more than a few remains that could be anything. The dominant paradigm has been so strong that archaeologists in the past have tended in good faith to report any remains they found in the countryside as those of villas, even when in fact they had nothing more than a few nondescript bits of wall. With the noise of "pseudo villas" removed, what remains is a pattern of quite strong concentration in some parts, and few villas elsewhere. Was it easier to find villas north and east of the city? It does not appear, however, as if the distribution pattern can be explained by such differences in the "archaeological visibility" of remains. The villas have by and large been found precisely where it was hardest to find them, where the layers of ashes were thickest. On balance, therefore, the concentration of villa remains probably reflects an ancient distribution pattern of villas that were concentrated in some parts of the territory, and not in others (Figure 28.1, where they can be seen to follow the high ground). This is further corroborated, I think, by more recent finds of villas. Felice Senatore has insisted that the finds of quite a few more villas in the Pompeian plain have disproved my original thesis.[33] Interestingly, however, the vast majority of his examples actually come from the area north of the city, and the plain east and northeast of the city. The latter concentration I had, in fact, already noticed, even if I had connected them to river transport, rather than to the Roman road that we now know linked them.[34] For now, I think we must still conclude that our archaeological sample of surviving farm remains is heavily biased towards villas, overlooks small farms, and is, therefore, unrepresentative of the economic life of a large part of the Pompeian territory. The high visibility of villas and wine presses obscures a reality in which cereal agriculture and small farms probably played a far bigger role.

A third, and equally traditional tactic is to look at other neglected evidence. Curiously enough, the literary evidence emphasizes Campanian cereal agriculture, and is rarely kind about its wines. So far, moreover, it has been impossible to identify Pompeian (as opposed to Campanian) amphoras among those exported to Ostia.[35]

In my view, much of Pompeian agriculture was directed to meeting the pressing needs for subsistence food of Pompeii's hungry population. In the absence of major villa finds in large parts of the Pompeian territory, it seems likely that these cereals were produced by small farmers. They may have owned their land, but I think that tenant farmers are more likely on such fertile land in close proximity to large numbers of urban consumers. The prominence of cereals, however, does not exclude the possibility of considerable wine and oil production, and their export. That could be so precisely because it did not take much land. In this respect, my own earlier work was far too schematic.[36] Andreau has demonstrated conclusively that there is no evidence that significant numbers of freedmen owned such villas.[37] Instead, the owners of such villas would be among the local elite of respectable families, and members of the town council in particular (cf. Moormann, Ch. 28; Franklin, Ch. 33; Table 33.1).

The horrendous impact of high population density on labour productivity and the standard of living in cereal agriculture is graphically illustrated by comparative historical data from—mostly nineteenth-century—Campania.[38] Campania and the plain around Pompeii at that time had population densities that were as high as those in antiquity. As in antiquity, the Campanian plain (including the plain around Pompeii) was at that time largely devoted to cereals. Labour productivity was low, the standard of living, therefore, of the mass of the population was also low and mortality was high.

Oxen and plough were a rare sight, as much land was worked with the spade and the hoe. Social relations were characterized by vast social inequality and substantial "feudal" and ecclesiastical landownership. The contrast to areas practising viticulture was dramatic: labour productivity and standard of living were much higher, and mortality was correspondingly lower. Social inequality was much reduced. Clearly with vines, putting extra labour into an intensive agricultural regime paid off: labour productivity did not suffer nearly so much. In antiquity, of course, the actual outcome differed. Then, the rich could reap the benefits by using extra inputs of slave labour in viticulture. Identical economic circumstances may generate different social results.

Agriculture is important in an analysis of pre-industrial economies. The debate on the ancient economy, however, has been dominated by discussions of trade. Trade and manufacturing are, potentially, sectors where an economy can show its development rather than involution. Some would even argue that they form the engine of modernization. Modernizing and optimistic accounts of the Pompeian economy have thus emphasized the scale and sophistication of trade and manufacturing in the town. Indeed, whoever wanders through Pompeii cannot fail to be struck by the number and variety of shops and workshops along the streets: all in all eighty-five different trades have been distinguished (cf. Pirson, Ch. 29).[39] Along the main roads in particular, almost no street frontage remained unused, even if behind these shops we often find grand residences of the elite. Particularly striking is the large number of places where food was prepared and sold. Many poor Pompeians may have eaten out on a regular basis (probably because they had nowhere else to go; cf. DeFelice, Ch. 30). Pompeian shopkeepers and craftsmen catered for a complex and sophisticated urban demand (see Jones and Robinson, Ch. 25, for evidence of entrepreneurship). Pompeii was not some bleak village in Merovingian Gaul or one of those South Sea Islands beloved by anthropologists.

The examples I have given do not make Pompeii a Weberian producer city, however. The great variety of trades and the oft-luxurious character of the products indicate, if anything, an urban production to cater for local—and frequently elite—consumer demand. To be a typical producer city, it should also have produced a lot for external markets, and, like medieval exporting cities, have concentrated on particular products such as textiles. And, indeed, that claim has been made for Pompeii. It has been argued that Pompeii had so many workshops to process wool and make cloth that this was a major export industry, comparable to medieval and early-modern centres of textile industry.[40] The fullers were the entrepreneurs of this industry, controlling both the initial cleaning of raw wool and the final finishing of the woven cloth. Moreover, fullers occupied prominent places among the political elite in the town council (*ordo decurionum*). Most visibly, the large so-called "Building of Eumachia" on the forum would have been a cloth hall in medieval style, where the "guild" of the fullers met and did business.[41] If all of this were true, Pompeii would have been a major example of a producer city from classical antiquity, and a strong case could be made in favour of a more modernist reconstruction of the ancient economy.

Elsewhere I have argued at greater length that none of this is indeed true.[42] Archaeologically, the workshops identified as serving the cleaning of raw wool may well have served food instead. There is not a shred of evidence to suggest that they had anything to do with wool. That reduces the number of textile workshops significantly, and it destroys the case for the fullers as the big organizers of the industry.

What we have left are a few proper fulleries indeed, but they may have served as laundries (*ab usu*), rather than for fulling new cloth *de tela* (but cf. Pirson, Ch. 29). The vast majority of other Pompeian textile workshops and textile workers are, equally, flights of fancy. The same can be said of the social position of Pompeian fullers. It is true that they honoured their patron Eumachia in the building named after her (Figure 34.2), but that does not make the building a cloth hall, the more so since that building was also used for other memorials. There is no evidence that the Pompeian textile industry did anything more than serve local demand, or that it was a major source of income for wealthy and important people.

So where does all of this leave us? I think there is no evidence for the existence in Pompeii of the kind of large and specialized export industry that we sometimes find in later European history. Pompeii was not a Weberian "producer city". It is import-ant, however, to remember that this does not reduce crafts and trading to insignificance. Pompeians could buy a wide range of craft goods, ranging from the mundane such as bread or hot meals to the quite sophisticated. If many Pompeians dressed in second-hand clothing (or even rags), the rich exercised a strong demand—for them-selves, and for their domestics. Many Pompeians did work in trade and manufacturing. The building industry for example, though never a potential exporter, must have employed a significant proportion of the Pompeian workforce.[43] Rich Pompeians lived in grand houses indeed, a testimony to their financial resources and their craving for ostentation.[44]

The complexities and even sophistication of the urban economy are equally appar-ent in the miraculously surviving archive of the Pompeian banker and auctioneer L. Caecilius Iucundus.[45] This archive of 153 wooden writing tablets was found in July 1875 in a box in a room of house (V.1.26) in which he had lived. The box contained the receipts Iucundus had received for two kinds of payments. The first was concerned with farming some taxes or leasing public property. The second was concerned with the auctions he organized, and documented that he had, indeed, paid the sellers in these auctions. Each receipt was witnessed by a number of people, each ranked according to social status. Acting magistrates and other members of the *ordo decurionum* were at the top of the list, and freedmen at the bottom. The docu-ments give us a fascinating insight into the basis of Roman social hierarchy and the apparent need for its public display. Even small status distinctions clearly mattered in this world.

Economically, the archive is also revealing, both by what it documents, and by what it does not. It does not reveal a vast network of commercial transactions. Rather, it has local people disposing of surplus estates, slaves, and the like. That clearly mat-tered in a world where death and legacies were a fact of life, and where holdings of property and other goods had to be rearranged from time to time. The sums involved are not vast fortunes, but they are substantial enough to be well beyond the world of ordinary craftsmen. They also seem to require occasional credit from Iucundus. Both the auctions themselves and the due-dates of the credits granted by Iucundus are concentrated during the end of the year, when estate owners could expect to have sold their wine and oil.[46] Again, we see a complex, sophisticated society in which agriculture, property and death are the dominant themes.

Pompeians knew only too well of the niggardliness of nature. They had to work hard on smallish plots of land. Economically their lives were quite similar to those of their descendants, a little over a century ago. At similar population densities those distant relatives also worked exceptionally hard to make a living, doing without the benefits of oxen to plough their fields because their lands could not feed such large animals. Like their descendants, ancient Pompeians were probably mostly small cereal farmers, highly dependent on the rich and powerful for a lease of land, and for protection in bad years. Agriculture was the dominant economic activity, not because it enjoyed such high returns, but because productivity was so low that outside the elite there was little demand for anything else. The comparative success of ancient urbanism, therefore, was not because it provided an alternative to agriculture, but because more than in medieval Europe the urban elite had successfully secured for itself the revenues of the rural economy. It owed its existence to more systematic fleecing, rather than to modernization.

SOCIAL HIERARCHY

Pompeii was not a happy egalitarian society. On the contrary, rich Pompeians were very rich, and showed their riches with little restraint. We are fascinated and impressed by the splendour of Roman private homes.[47] The average ground-floor surface was some 7,000–8,000 sq ft, and they also had accommodation on the floor above. Compare that to normal modern homes, even in the US. These were magnificent houses, but again, we must think our way out of the seductions of the evidence before our eyes. Many Pompeians did live in these splendid *atrium* houses, but only as slaves or free dependants. There were never more than 500–600 of these houses in a city of maybe 10,000 inhabitants. And there were few other houses where the less well-to-do could live independent lives (though some poor Pompeians slept in their workshops). Unlike modern cities, Pompeii did not even have identifiable districts for the poor. Splendid Pompeian domestic architecture was not an expression of prosperity but of social inequality.

If inequality was large in Pompeii, was it also rigidly fixed? Many of us—and the primitivists among us in particular—have come to think of Rome as a traditional society, where little if anything of importance ever changed. Many of the details of this conventional view have never been made explicit, but I think most of us will recognize it—even if not all of us agree with it. In this view of Rome as a "primitive" and "traditional" society, the rich were rich, the poor were poor, and the poor did not even question the right of the rich to be rich and rule. There were no countervailing powers or ideologies such as bourgeois liberalism, and the dominance of the land-owning aristocracy was never challenged. The class of masters ruled from generation upon generation. It was a society that was stable not only over time, but also over space. It was a world of relatively closed communities, with limited outside contacts. People tended to stay in their ancestral communities, and few had come from elsewhere. Citizenship of the classical city-state did not normally have much room for migrants. Maybe our semi-conscious image is something like that of a modern Greek village, with many old men sitting around the village square, drinking ouzo.

The possibility of social mobility matters for the debate on the ancient economy because it is precisely the rise of the new commercial bourgeoisie that is often held responsible for medieval and early-modern modernization. Was the dominance of

Rome's landholding aristocracy ever challenged? For modernists such as Rostovtzeff that was indeed what happened, and Pompeii was their favourite case in point. This is how Tenney Frank, another modernizer from the first half of the twentieth century put it: "these leading citizens of Pompeii were, to some extent, her prosperous bakers, potters and tanners, and they did not scorn to draw their livelihood from shops and booths if only the accumulated profits summed up large enough." He concluded: "throughout the whole system industries appear in all stages of development toward capitalistic production."[48]

In my view both the primitivist emphasis on continuity and the modernist emphasis on change fail to appreciate the real nature of social succession, and the connections between continuity and change. What they both miss is that in a pre-industrial society mortality was so high and unpredictable that intergenerational succession was highly insecure. We may discuss the relative openness of elites in terms of their social norms and culture, but we must not forget that nature, and the Grim Reaper in particular, largely played the tune. As with agricultural production, our comfortable modern perspective has blinded us to the sad realities of the past, and the narrow natural constraints. That is not to say social norms and culture do not matter, but perhaps primarily as strategies and constructions to adapt to or negotiate nature.

Let us first go back to the Greek village square. The image of a society dominated by elderly mediators with tradition is, in fact, quite anachronistic: it looks ancient, because in our awareness the past and the elderly are somehow almost the same, but in reality it is a thoroughly modern experience. Antiquity was a world of many children and few old people. Life was brutish and short—death could happen at any time. For us, it is almost impossible to imagine how fragile life really was only a short time ago. In the modern western world average life expectancy at birth is in the range of seventy to eighty years, but in classical antiquity it was twenty to thirty years.[49] Much of that low life expectancy was due to high infant mortality, but unexpected death remained a real risk even for young adults. If Roman mortality patterns prevailed among modern undergraduates, almost 10 per cent would not attain their degree. Infections were the primary cause of this high mortality. Therefore, mortality was higher in the cities than in the country, and hit the rich as much as it did the poor.[50] Death was democratic. People died often without relatives, because those had already been carried away. Sometimes they died in the streets, to be eaten by vultures and dogs, or to be buried in pits, *puticuli*, together with dead animals and household refuse.[51]

At population level, a high birth rate made up for the grim reality of high mortality, but at the level of individual families, the highly varied incidence of death hindered social continuity. Intergenerational succession was not only fast, but also quite unpredictable.[52] Sometimes all children in a family died before their parents, leaving no immediate heirs to the fortune and status of the parents. Sometimes no children died before their parents, leading to much-reduced fortunes and status in the next generation.[53] The chances of having no surviving children, or too many, were far greater than the chance to have just the right number surviving until reproductive age. Behind a façade of continuity, "ancient families surviving for many generations in genetic and property continuity are not characteristic of Rome".[54] Richard Saller has recently shown that a third of all Roman landed property was in the hands of under-age orphans.[55] Land changed hands often, and from one generation to another properties were divided or reassembled.[56] Underneath a highly stable social structure, the fragility of life created vital uncertainty and countless mutations.

For the Roman Senate, Keith Hopkins has demonstrated that underneath the public image of intergenerational continuity of senatorial families, a reality was lurking where only few senators belonged to a chain of senators succeeding each other from father to son.[57] Not all of them had a surviving son to succeed them, and even of those who did, only senators at the top of the senatorial pecking order were, indeed, often succeeded by their sons. Were they succeeded because of their higher status and greater power, or were their sons simply the lucky ones in the lottery of life and death across a number of generations?

In Pompeii, too, the continuity of the local elite has been a matter of controversy. Some scholars have isolated periods of social and political discontinuity, such as the aftermath of the Sullan colonization, the end of the Republic and the beginning of the Imperial age, a possible crisis in the age of Claudius, or the years after the devastating earthquake of AD 62.[58] Those who see discontinuity at particular periods of Pompeian history do so, however, under the tacit assumption that such discontinuity is abnormal (and thus related to particular events), and that municipal elites such as those of Pompeii were a closed and largely hereditary group with a high level of intergenerational continuity. If that were true, the emergence of new faces may, indeed, be enough to indicate a period of political and social discontinuity, and imply political change. The problem is, however, that a high level of intergenerational succession was demographically very hard to achieve. Discontinuity, therefore, was part of the structure, and not a special event. What mattered politically was whether this discontinuity was translated into political change, or only involved the emergence of new players to play the same old game.

Others have pointed to the prominence of certain families over long periods of time. But what does it mean that Holconii or Popidii were important in many periods of the town's history, when we do not know how they were related (cf. Franklin, Ch. 33)?[59] First, a *gens* may have included distant relatives, who, for practical social and political purposes had nothing or almost nothing to do with each other.[60] They shared little more than a name. Second, we must appreciate that slaves and, in particular, freedmen also belonged to the *gens* of their masters. Some or all prominent Holconii or Popidii from the last days of Pompeii may well have been the descendants of freedmen of earlier Holconii or Popidii (we do not know). Roman society shows a clear desire for family continuity. In contrast to European elites before the great demographic transition, Romans could live with the thought that it was their servants who inherited their wealth, their names, and ultimately also their status.

Geographically, too, the image of physical social continuity is misleading. Urban mortality was so high that it exceeded the urban birth rate by quite a margin.[61] The best possible estimate of this urban excess mortality would put it at about five per thousand.[62] For a city with 10,000 inhabitants (such as Pompeii may have had), this implies that without immigration, its population decreased by fifty people every year. Unless Roman cities grew ever smaller, they could only exist if there was a continuous flow of immigrants to fill the vacant spaces.[63] Some of these immigrants were country dwellers moving into town, but many were slaves, brought in by their masters from far-away lands. If there is one thing that strikes any observer of the urban epigraphy of Roman towns, it is the exceptionally high proportion of freedmen among those commemorated. Some of that may be due to a desire to commemorate that they had overcome slavery (the 'epigraphic habit' argument), but even in the archive of writing tablets of L. Caecilius Iucundus, freedmen were predominant. Precision about the actual proportion of slaves and freedmen is impossible (and would have to be age-specific), but clearly there were many freedmen—and therefore slaves—in Pompeii.

As with the Senate at Rome, the analytical problem is, therefore, to reconcile the demographic reality of severe limits to social succession and continuity with the strong Roman self-image of a society with a high degree of intergenerational succession and with the obvious success of the social system to retain its structure. How could the elite renew itself without social change? How could such high social mobility exist without a challenge to the social system, or modernization?

As our starting point we may take an inscription found on the Temple of Isis (cf. Small, Ch. 13; Figure 13.3) in Pompeii (*CIL* X, 846). It reads:

N. POPIDIUS N.F. CELSINUS
AEDEM ISIDIS TERRAE MOTU CONLAPSAM
A FUNDAMENTO P.S. RESTITUIT. HUNC DECURIONES OB LIBERALITATEM
CUM ESSET ANNORUM SEXS ORDINI SUO GRATIS ADLEGERUNT.

> "Numerius Popidius Celsinus, the son of Numerius, restored from its foundations and at his own expense the temple of Isis which had collapsed in the earthquake. For his liberality the members of the town council elected him to their order for free, even though he was only six years old."

How could a boy aged six be a rich benefactor, and how could he become a member of the *ordo decurionum*, the town council, of Pompeii (Table 33.1)? In principle such councils consisted of former city magistrates, elected for life into the council after their tenure in office (these councils were a local senate, and mirrored the Senate at Rome). Children had no place in them. The answer is in the identity of the father. From other inscriptions (*CIL* X, 847; 848; 921) we know that the father was N. Popidius Ampliatus, a freedman who had served as a *minister*.[64] He was obviously sufficiently wealthy to rebuild the temple of Isis, and to entertain ambitions of social advancement. His origin as a slave precluded membership in the *ordo decurionum*, however. Since freeborn sons of freedmen were not excluded, he invested his ambitions in his freeborn son N. Popidius Celsinus (Celsinus was obviously freeborn since he has a proper filiation in his name: "son of Numerius"). Celsinus entered the *ordo* through *adlectio*, a procedure to circumvent the need for a previous tenure of office.[65] Thus, the town council was renewed with a member of slave origin, but only after one generation had passed. In the process, the social climber had to contribute as a benefactor, and show himself worthy of the new honour. In this case, the investment in the social advancement of the son was possibly in vain, since he may well have died at an early age: in *CIL* X, 848 (from a mosaic floor in the temple of Isis) both he and his father are honoured by his mother Corelia Celsa.[66]

This process of renewal from outside and socialization to the existing norms can be viewed from a wider perspective in the example of the well-documented case of the *ordo decurionum* of the city of Canusium. This city has given us a large bronze inscription (*CIL* IX, 338) with the *album*, the complete list of all 100 members of its *ordo decurionum* for the year AD 223, and of its patrons. Members of the council proper were listed in strictly hierarchical order and were ranked according to the offices they had held. The *quinquennalis* (the local *censor*) who held office longest ago came at the top. Interestingly, the list of members who had been magistrates ends after sixty-eight names. The rest are *pedani*, members of the *ordo* who had not held office but had obtained membership of the *ordo* through *adlectio* and who, presumably, had to stand during meetings (*sic*). The restricted number of former magistrates is not surprising, because with an entrance of, in principle, two former magistrates as new members each year, given prevailing high mortality levels, there could simply not be more surviving former magistrates in the *ordo*. Only at modern levels of life expectancy (i.e., with a remaining life expectancy of about fifty years in the *ordo*) could an *ordo* of 100 members retain its size with no more than two former junior magistrates each year as new entrants.[67] Under Roman mortality conditions, where remaining life expectancy for newly elected young magistrates was something like thirty years, two new entrants to the *ordo* could only have maintained an *ordo* of about sixty members (2 × 30 = 60). To retain a size of 100 an *ordo* needed additional fresh entrants who had not been—and would not be—magistrates. In Canusium, the proportion of possibly servile cognomina (the last of the three Roman names, potentially betraying servile origin) is remarkably high among *pedani*, and significantly higher than among the higher ranks of the *ordo*. We may conclude that Roman town councils probably needed a regular reinforcement from outside, and from the ranks of wealthy freedmen in particular.

In the face of the ravages wrought by high and unpredictable mortality, the continued existence of a town council could only be maintained by an influx of social climbers. The image of an urban elite that physically succeeded itself from generation upon generation is clearly false. The next question is whether this renewal led to social change. Did the newcomers challenge the social order? Did the sons of freedmen break through the prevailing aristocratic hostility towards economic innovation? Or did they simply become aristocrats themselves? Did they have a choice?

A test case for the possibilities of social change could be Pompeian elections (cf. Franklin, Ch. 33; but see also Cormack, Ch. 37, for funerary practices). Any modern visitor wandering through the town will notice the multitude of election posters, expressing support for particular candidates, and exhorting the city's population to add support to particular candidates. So was Pompeii a liberal democracy after all? The modern sceptic will appreciate that not all elections are the same (the modern world has also had its share of elections where voters had a choice of one). First, not everyone could be a candidate. Only wealthy citizens of free birth and with a good reputation could stand for office at all. Moreover, once elected, they could not be voted out of office: after their tenure they became life members of the town council, the true centre of power, unless removed by a *quinquennalis* (Table 33.1). Finally, as I have argued elsewhere, the actual elections were largely rigged. For the higher offices, there were probably never more candidates than there were slots (if only because some former aediles did not survive to stand for *duovir*), and for the lower office of *aedilis* some candidates obtained strong support from the *ordo* itself. The many election advertisements are largely those of the less successful candidates.[68] They are an indication of the difficulties faced by outsiders, rather than an indication of popular political participation. At every stage, social climbers had to conform and socialize to the norms and values of the existing elite.

That brings us back to culture. Newcomers there were, indeed, but they had to become like those in power. Precisely the social group that was most heavily involved in trade and manufacturing—slaves and freedmen—was also the focus of a multitude of subtle pressures to adopt the values and modes of behaviour of the existing powers. As slaves in the households of their masters, they had been given a prominent role in the cult of the protecting deities of the household. As slaves, they had also been guided by the carrot and the stick of the choice between manumission as a reward for good behaviour, or unrestrained violence and cruelty as punishment for even the slightest infringements on the whims of their masters. After their manumission, they had often remained in submission by their desire to see their loved ones manumitted too. By and large, freedmen had learnt their lesson well of what was best for them. In the community, moreover, they had also been given a chance to show they knew how to behave. It was precisely slaves and freedmen who were prominent in the various cults to celebrate imperial rule. They were *augustales*, *ministri Augusti*, or *magistri* and *ministri vici*.[69] Each time, they could act as surrogate magistrates, even sometimes act as benefactors, underscore their loyalty to the emperor, and demonstrate their abilities for what sociologists have so aptly termed "anticipatory socialization". Freedmen who wanted to rock the boat did not get another chance higher up the ladder of social acceptance. In fact, it does not seem that any of them ever wanted anything other than to adopt elite mentality and behaviour.

We may conclude that the primitivist image of a "traditional" society with a high degree of physical social continuity is completely wrong. Death created open spaces all the time, which needed to be filled from below, and, more remotely, from outside. The elite was constantly being renewed, and former slaves were probably the most important examples of this social mobility. As Claudius said in his famous speech in the Senate in Rome, Rome's strength had always been to incorporate outsiders, even into the very centres of power.[70] National and ethnic continuity is, after all, a nineteenth-century ideal.

CONCLUSION

Pompeii was not a happy little town, hardly different from our own world, or even from the world of the early twentieth century. For a pre-industrial city, the population in both city and countryside was large. That, however, was not a sign of good times, but a cause for a low standard of living for the mass of the population, as well as vast social inequality. When we wander through Pompeii's ruins, we are struck by the elegance of elite houses, and by the complexity and sophistication of this society. For the modern observer, that creates a problem. When we try to think what it was like to be a Roman, we imagine ourselves as senators, rather than as prostitutes or farm labourers. We also imagine ourselves as long-living senators. Consequently, we blind ourselves to the horrors of the Roman past.

In my view, the Pompeian economy does not show signs of economic development or growth. The standard of living of the mass of the population was close to subsistence, and was not improving. It was an economy dominated by the need to produce a lot of food for a large population, and constrained by the difficulties of growing enough cereals without irrigation or artificial fertilizer. Growing these cereals demanded much hard work, and sorely missed the power of machines.

The wealth of the town's elite easily disguises the structural poverty of society. At the same time that elite wealth created a substantial market for goods and services. The Pompeian urban economy showed a complexity and differentiation that clearly distinguished it from small-scale societies, including those of later European history. Historically, Roman urbanism was, and for a long time remained, unique in European history until the modern era.

The social structure of Pompeii clearly reflected the differences in income and wealth between owners of land and those who had little more to offer than their labour. It also reflected another natural constraint: the high and unpredictable incidence of mortality created new openings among the elite, and allowed substantial upward mobility, of freed slaves in particular. Interestingly that upward mobility did not change the rules of the power game. No new class took over. The first thing slaves did when they were manumitted was to try to emulate their masters. They were allowed and encouraged to do so. Thus, when uncertainty and discontinuity were endemic, the structure of power did not change. The assimilating powers of Roman elite culture and codes of behaviour were astounding. That was the real strength of Roman society.

NOTES

1 J. Andreau, in his thoughtful introduction to M. I. Rostovtseff, *Histoire économique et sociale de l'Empire Romain*, Paris, 1988, pp. viii–ix (the French translation of M. I. Rostovtzeff, *The Social and Economic History of the Roman Empire,* 2nd edn, Oxford, 1957).

2 A. Mau, *Führer durch Pompeji*, Naples, 1893 gives a good impression of how the young Rostovtzeff would be taught to look at Pompeii.

3 Mau's synthesis can be seen at its clearest in his *Pompeii: its life and art* (transl. and ed. by F. W. Kelsey), London, 1899, and in the slightly later definitive edition in German: *Pompeji in Leben und Kunst*, Leipzig, 1900. We read that, besides maritime trade, the Pompeian economy was based on the presence of rich Romans with villas in the area, the manufacture of millstones, the manufacture of fish sauces (dominated by one Umbricius Scaurus; cf. Clarke, Ch. 21), and on commercial agriculture and the growth of wine in particular. The image of commercial viticulture was quite vivid after the discovery in 1894 and 1895 of a large wine estate near modern Boscoreale, north of Pompeii (Figure 28.1, no. 13). For a picture of a similar recently excavated villa ("Regina"), see Figures 1.1 and 28.5; cf. Moormann, Ch. 28; Figure 28.1, no. 57.

4 Rostovtzeff, *Roman Empire*, p. 91.

5 Rostovtzeff, *Roman Empire*, p. 142.

6 Rostovtzeff, *Roman Empire*, p. 143.

7 Rostovtzeff, *Roman Empire*, p. 93.

8 Mau, *Führer*, p. 2: "Pompeji war eine wohlhabende Handelsstadt".

9 E. A. Wrigley, "A simple model of London's economic importance in changing English society and economy 1650–1750", in Ph. Abrams and E. A. Wrigley (eds), *Towns in Societies. Essays in economic history and historical sociology*, Cambridge, 1978, pp. 215–43; W. M. Jongman, "Slavery and the growth of Rome. The transformation of Italy in the first and second centuries BCE", in C. Edwards and G. Woolf (eds), *Rome the Cosmopolis*, Cambridge, 2003, pp. 100–22.

10 J. de Vries, *European Urbanization, 1500–1800*, London, 1984 for a survey of medieval and early-modern data.

11 The figure excludes the city of Rome. The lower figure applies to the situation in 28 BC. The most authoritative population estimates for 28 BC are in K. Hopkins, *Conquerors and Slaves*, Cambridge, 1978, p. 68 (with a summary of competing estimates). After that, population increased, but we do not really know by how much. E. Lo Cascio, "The size of the Roman population: Beloch and the meaning of the Augustan census figures", *JRS*, 1994, vol. 84,

pp. 23–40 has a higher population estimate. See W. Scheidel, "Progress and problems in Roman demography", in W. Scheidel (ed.), *Debating Roman Demography*, Leiden, 2001, pp. 1–81, and N. Morley, "The transformation of Italy, 225–28 BC", *JRS*, 2001, vol. 91, pp. 50–62 for the most recent discussions.

12 Zeugma, now flooded, is a sad case in point: D. L. Kennedy, *The Twin Towns of Zeugma on the Euphrates. Rescue work and historical studies*, JRA Suppl. Ser. no. 27, 1998.

13 A. Smith, *An Inquiry into the Nature and Causes of the Wealth of Nations*, the "Glasgow" edition, R. H. Campbell, A. S. Skinner and W. B. Todd (eds), Oxford, 1976, III, iv, 18/p. 422.

14 M. M. Postan, *The Medieval Economy and Society*, Harmondsworth, 1975, p. 239.

15 M. I. Finley, *The Ancient Economy*, 2nd edn, London, 1985. The new 1999 University of California reprint has a lucid foreword by I. Morris. For my own views, see W. M. Jongman, *The Economy and Society of Pompeii*, Amsterdam, 1988, pp. 15–55 and, more recently, W. M. Jongman, "Hunger and power. Theories, models and methods in Roman economic history", in H. Bongenaar (ed.), *Interdependency of Institutions and Private Entrepreneurs*, Midden Oosten Studies no. 2 (Proceedings of the second MOS symposium, Leiden, 1998), Istanbul 2000, pp. 259–84 and W. M. Jongman, "The Roman economy: from cities to empire", in L. de Blois and J. Rich (eds), *The Transformation of Economic Life under the Roman Empire*, Amsterdam, 2002, pp. 28–48.

16 Finley, *Ancient Economy*, p. 22.

17 Finley, *Ancient Economy*, p. 131.

18 See Jongman, "Hunger and power" and Jongman, "From cities to Empire" for conceptual scepticism.

19 J. Andreau, *Les affaires de Monsieur Jucundus*, Rome, 1974; P. Castrén, *Ordo populusque Pompeianus*, Rome, 1975; J. L. Franklin Jr, *Pompeii: the electoral programmata, campaigns and politics, AD 71–79*, Rome, 1980; Jongman, *Pompeii*; H. Mouritsen, *Elections, Magistrates and Municipal Élite: studies in Pompeian epigraphy*, Rome, 1988 (even if actually published quite a bit later than that); A. Wallace-Hadrill, *Houses and Society in Pompeii and Herculaneum*, Princeton, NJ, 1994; R. Lawrence, *Roman Pompeii: space and society*, London, 1994. See also J. Franklin, *Pompeis difficile est*, Ann Arbor, MI, 2001.

20 M. I. Finley, *Ancient History: evidence and models*, London, 1985.

21 P. Garnsey, *Food and Society in Classical Antiquity*, Cambridge, 1999.

22 C. M. Cipolla, *Before the Industrial Revolution. European society and economy, 1000–1700*, 2nd edn, London, 1981, Table 1–7, p. 30.

23 See Jongman, *Pompeii*, p. 67 for the conventional figures.

24 Lo Cascio, "The size of the Roman population"; Morley, "The transformation of Italy"; see Scheidel, "Progress and problems", pp. 49–57 for a more conservative position.

25 C. Geertz, *Agricultural Involution: the process of ecological change in Indonesia*, Berkeley, CA, 1963.

26 Rostovtzeff, *Roman Empire*, pp. 552–3.

27 D. L. Clarke, "Archaeology: the loss of innocence", *Antiquity*, 1973, vol. 47, pp. 6–18, esp. p. 16.

28 See Jongman, "Hunger and power", pp. 267–71 for a discussion of the methodological issues. J. Andreau, "Pompéi et le ravitaillement en blé et autres produits de l'agriculture (Ier siècle ap. J.-C.)", in *Le ravitaillement en blé de Rome et des centres urbains des débuts de la République jusqu'au Haut Empire*, CÉFR, no. 196, Rome, 1994, pp. 129–36.

29 Precise figures and justification may be found in Jongman, "Slavery and the growth of Rome", pp. 112–16.

30 See Jongman, *Pompeii*, pp. 136–7, for the implications of Pompeii's proximity to Puteoli, the hub of grain imports into Italy at the time.

31 A. Ciarallo, "Il frumento nell'area Vesuviana", in *Le ravitaillement en blé*, pp. 137–9 and M. Pagano, "Commercio e consumo del grano ad Ercolano", in *Le ravitaillement en blé*, pp. 141–7.

32 It now appears that this concentration to the east of the city did not so much follow the Sarno, but a Roman road: F. Senatore, "Ager Pompeianus: viticoltura e territorio nella piana del Sarno nel I sec. d.C.", in F. Senatore (ed.), *Pompei, il Sarno e la penisola Sorrentina*, Pompei, 1998, pp. 135–66, esp. 155, 163. I wish to emphasize that I greatly enjoyed meeting Dr Senatore and discussing our results.

33 Senatore, "Ager Pompeianus".

34 Jongman, *Pompeii*, pp. 116, 123, 132, 142; also p. 123 for roads, and p. 132 for the inclusion of these villas to the (north)east in my estimates of aggregate consumption.

35 Jongman, *Pompeii*, pp. 124–31. F. Zevi, in an intervention on pp. 135–6 of *Le ravitaillement en blé*, suggests that it may now be possible to distinguish Pompeian *amphorae* from those of Sorrento.

36 Jongman, *Pompeii*, pp. 131–7. I also wrongly ignored the possibilities of intercultivation, as several reviewers kindly pointed out.

37 Andreau, *Monsieur Jucundus*, pp. 224–71, for an effective criticism of earlier nonsense.

38 G. Delille, *Agricoltura e demografia nel regno di Napoli nei secoli XVIII e XIX*, Naples, 1977.

39 K. Hopkins, "Economic growth and towns in classical antiquity", in Abrams and Wrigley, *Towns in Societies*, pp. 35–77, esp. p. 72.

40 W. O. Moeller, *The Wool Trade of Ancient Pompeii*, Leiden, 1976.

41 See K. Wallat, *Die Ostseite des Forums von Pompeji*, Frankfurt am Main, 1997, for a recent account of this and nearby buildings. I admire the systematic rigour of the description, but am baffled by the unwillingness of its author to engage in a serious discussion of what actually happened in the building. Cf., however, Dobbins, Ch. 12.

42 Jongman, *Pompeii*, pp. 155–86. For my views on the place of the textile industry at large, see W. Jongman, "Wool and the textile industry of Roman Italy", in E. Lo Cascio (ed.), *Mercati permanenti e mercati periodici nel mondo romano. Atti degli incontri Caprese di storia dell'economia antica (Capri 13–15 ottobre 1997)*, Pragmateiai no. 2, Bari, 2000, pp. 187–97.

43 Though not about Pompeii, J. DeLaine, *The Baths of Caracalla: a study in the design, construction, and economics of large-scale building projects in Imperial Rome*, JRA Suppl. Ser. no. 25, 1997 is a model study of building practice and economics.

44 Wallace-Hadrill, *Houses and Society*.

45 Andreau, *Monsieur Jucundus* is the definitive study. For my own addenda, see Jongman, *Pompeii*, pp. 207–73. See also Franklin, Ch. 33.

46 Jongman, *Pompeii*, pp. 223–4.

47 See Wallace-Hadrill, *Houses and Society* for a wonderfully perceptive social and cultural analysis of Pompeian housing.

48 T. Frank, "The economic life of an ancient city", *CP*, 1918, vol. 13, pp. 225–40, esp. pp. 229 and 240.

49 See T. G. Parkin, *Demography and Roman Society*, Baltimore, MD, 1992, for a good introduction and Scheidel, "Progress and problems" for a recent survey. W. Scheidel, "Roman age structure", *JRS*, 2001, vol. 91, pp. 1–25 is critical of model life tables, and emphasizes the great variation around the mean. However, whether that matters depends critically on the argument one makes. His examples suggest that urban life expectancy was probably even worse than we thought, which only reinforces the argument I make.

50 W. Scheidel, "Emperors, aristocrats, and the grim reaper: towards a demographic profile of the Roman élite", *CQ*, 1999, vol. 49.1, pp. 254–81.

51 K. Hopkins, *Death and Renewal*, Cambridge, 1983, ch. 4 for an evocation of death in Rome; A. Scobie, "Slums, sanitation and mortality in the Roman world", *Klio*, 1986, vol. 68, pp. 399–433 for a gruesome evocation of a different antiquity.

52 See, e.g., L. E. Tacoma, *Fragile Hierarchies*, Leiden, 2004, on the urban elites of Egypt in the third century AD.

53 R. Saller, *Patriarchy, Property and Death in the Roman Family*, Cambridge, 1994 pp. 161–80.

54 J. A. Crook, *Law and Life of Rome*, London, 1967 p. 132.

55 Saller, *Patriarchy*, p. 190.

56 W. M. Jongman, "A golden age. Death, money supply and social succession in the Roman Empire", in E. Lo Cascio (ed.), *Credito e moneta nel mondo romano*, Atti degli incontri capresi di storia dell'economia antica, Capri, 12–14 ottobre 2000, Bari, 2003, pp. 181–96.

57 Hopkins, *Death and Renewal*, chs 2–3.

58 Castrén, *Ordo*, pp. 82–124 for a survey. See also Franklin, Ch. 33.

59 Castrén, *Ordo*, pp. 104, 106, 176, 207–9.

60 Saller, *Patriarchy*, ch. 4 for the best discussion of wider and smaller kinship groups.

61 See Jongman, "Slavery and the growth of Rome", pp. 103–9 for extensive discussion and bibliography.

62 Jongman, "Slavery and the growth of Rome", p. 107.

63 The picture was probably even more complex. Death occurred in waves of epidemics, leaving sudden and localized spots of labour shortage.

64 Castrén, *Ordo*, pp. 207–8.

65 He may have become a *pedanus* or a *praetextatus*; that is hard to decide. For the difference, see Jongman, *Pompeii*, pp. 317–29.

66 This implies that the N. Popidius Celsinus who died in Spain was not our man: c.f. A. Cooley, *Pompeii*, London, 2003, pp. 50–1 and n. 1. We cannot be sure, unfortunately. See Saller, *Patriarchy*, pp. 26–41 for next of kin as commemorators. In southern Italy the shift from parents to wives as commemorators occurs when men reach their mid-thirties (p. 33). Cf. Bernstein, Ch. 34.

67 The town council may best be viewed as a bathtub, with a drain (mortality) and a tap (new entrants). As long as the flow from the tap equals the flow from the tap, the level in the tub remains the same. If the drain is wider, so should be the tap to retain the same water level. If that happens, the water stays in the tub for a shorter period of time. Therefore, the annual renewal rate = size of group/length of membership. For the *Canusium* album, see: B. Salway, "Prefects, *patroni*, and decurions: a new perspective on the album of Canusium", in A. Cooley (ed.), *The Epigraphic Landscape of Roman Italy*, Bulletin of the Institute of Classical Studies, Suppl. 73, London, 2003, pp. 115–71; H. Mouritsen, "The album of Canusium and the town councils of Roman Italy", *Chiron*, 1998, vol. 28, pp. 229–54.

68 Franklin, *Electoral programmata*, pp. 94–100; Jongman, *Pompeii*, pp. 315–16.

69 Castrén, *Ordo*, pp. 72–8; Jongman, *Pompeii*, pp. 241–7; 255–64; 289–310. For criticism of my new interpretation of *vicini*: G. Amodio, "Sui vici e le circoscrizioni elettorali di Pompei", *Athenaeum*, 1996 pp. 457–78. See also George, Ch. 33.

70 Transmitted both as a literary text and in an inscription: Tac., *Ann.* 11.24 and *CIL* XIII, 1668 (spot the differences).

CHAPTER THIRTY-THREE

EPIGRAPHY
AND SOCIETY

———•◆•———

James Franklin

As August Mau drew his, now famous, survey of ancient Pompeii to a close, he turned in his final chapters to the writing that had been recovered at the site. Dividing that writing into its three major types—signs and inscriptions (both carved in stone and painted on walls), *graffiti*, and the business receipts of Caecilius Iucundus preserved on largely carbonized wax tablets[1]—he described each, noting its curiosities and the direct evidence it provided for reconstructing the daily life of this ancient city. Like so much of his volume, these descriptions remain the best short survey of the materials even today. Yet Mau's deceptively definitive presentation was also discouraging. In his very first paragraph he asserted, "It would be an exaggeration to say that they [the varieties of writing] contribute to our knowledge of antiquity much that is new."[2] And again, "Taken as a whole, the *graffiti* are less fertile for our knowledge of Pompeian life than might have been expected."[3] Mau's approach was descriptive and direct, and his straightforward treatment is admittedly the strength of these chapters, indeed of his entire volume. But for him the evidence of value was the words that the writing preserved; he did not, perhaps could not, foresee the use of those words as data that could be manipulated to address such broader issues as, for example, the level of literacy in the town. Only in the final two paragraphs of his last chapter did he proceed to observe that *signacula* (breadstamps) found in a number of houses could, in fact, be used to help identify their owners, thus suggesting the deep potential value of analysis rather than description of these written sources.

In his approach, Mau was doubtless influenced by his predecessors, who had devoted themselves to the collection, categorization and preservation of this mass of evidence in the *Corpus Inscriptionum Latinarum* (*CIL*; cf. Laidlaw, Ch. 39). There, too, it had been divided into three types, albeit types varying slightly from Mau's. Inscriptions carved into stone went into Volume X along with other carved inscriptions from throughout Campania; the parietal inscriptions—Pompeii's famous electoral *programmata*, or campaign posters, as well as painted signs, *graffiti*, and even *amphora* labels—were collected in Volume IV; and the business receipts, *apochae*, of Caecilius Iucundus were allotted separate treatment in a special supplement to Volume IV.[4] The unintended result of this categorization was the wide separation in print of texts, in fact, recovered together, so that users of the *CIL*, to which (rather than the actual excavation reports that lay only in specialized and largely inaccessible libraries) most scholars had access, were forced to shuffle these large and unwieldy volumes in seemingly endless attempts to correlate texts. Worse, the correlation was considerably hindered first by the keying of the original volume of *CIL* IV to a unique plan that was printed only with that volume (and has been omitted from re-printings), and then by the surprising lack of an index to the most recent update of *CIL* IV containing the finds through 1956. Over the years, scholars have continued to wrestle with these arrangements, and even when focussed on analysis rather than description, have tended to work within the categories of the *CIL*, centering their studies on one division of the evidence only. Progress has, therefore, been sporadic and uneven, but thanks to the accumulation of studies and approaches, we are today in a far better position to study both the individuals and the social structures of Pompeian society than Mau could ever have anticipated.

Of the varieties of evidence, the electoral *programmata* had always seemed to offer the most potential for study, and as early as 1886 Pierre Willems attempted to recover the sequence of candidacies for local municipal offices that they attested, reasoning that the most recent candidacies would be supported by the most remaining posters.[5] The approach was obviously simplistic and flawed, for any number of factors— wealth and family distinction, not to mention the incompletely recovered sample— could have affected how many *programmata* were posted on behalf of a candidate. Yet Willems' study emphasized analysis and forever raised the hope that at Pompeii, thanks to these *programmata*, we would trace factors and factions of Roman politics that could be extrapolated to other cities throughout the early Roman empire.

Nevertheless, for many years work languished on all fronts, until Emilio Magaldi produced a three-part study of references to emperors and the city of Rome that forcefully demonstrated how all sorts of written material could be assembled for far deeper insights into Pompeian life, in this case to relations between the capital and its colony, than had previously been thought possible.[6] This was followed in 1959 by a study by Veiki Väänänen on the nature of the Latin generated in the *graffiti*.[7] Väänänen not only explained thousands of errors in spelling and forms, but also demonstrated strong local variations even of pronunciation through consistent mis-spellings: Pompeians, for example, interchanged "c" and "g" as well as "c" and "q." Then, and most importantly, Matteo Della Corte offered his pioneering attempts at identifying the inhabitants of Pompeii's properties by gathering all the types of evidence for every house or shop then excavated.[8] Della Corte began with the breadstamps and correlated them with campaign posters on the façade of the property within which they were found. The posters sometimes carried the name of the person recommending the candidate for election, and he was thus able to reveal the full name abbreviated by initials on the *signacula* and to establish the general principle that names found on house façades belonged to their owners. So far so good, but in his eagerness Della Corte often proceeded beyond the evidence (there were, in fact, only 119 stamps recovered), so that his work must today be used with caution. In recent years this work has been overly criticized as an example of the so-called "Pompeian tradition," a line of less than rigorous scholarship that had, in fact, already begun to be challenged by Magaldi's studies.[9] Because of his intimate knowledge of the site and his frequent encounters with the evidence as it was found in the course of excavation, however, Della Corte's opinions must always be consulted.

In the 1970s, perhaps inspired by the impending 1900th anniversary of Pompeii's destruction, there was a flourish of new interest in the writing, as in most other aspects of this ancient city. Most significant of the work then undertaken was Paavo Castrén's compilation of references to all attested Pompeians, an indispensable companion to anyone studying Pompeian families and society.[10] The value of this volume can scarcely be overestimated; in addition to listings of every known member of the 479 families—Abonia to Vottonia—attested at Pompeii, Castrén assembled all references to the city's civic life—and his lists serve as the only, albeit awkward, index to the most recent supplement to *CIL* IV.

With the publication of first Della Corte's and then Castrén's work, students of Pompeian society at last had at hand the resources for study of a far deeper nature than had earlier been conceivable; true prosopography and social history were now possible. Individuals and families could be traced through the mass of evidence, and in several cases their houses identified to add further, non-written evidence to the discussion. It was, in fact, Castrén himself who began this deeper analysis. Thanks to a number of dated references (official inscriptions normally included the names of the consuls then holding office at Rome), he was able to determine that several families belonged to distinct eras of Pompeii's long existence and to begin to trace the rise and fall of those better-attested families. Unfortunately, a perceived lack of evidence for the Claudian years at Pompeii led him to posit a crisis that shut down local government, a theory that has now been thoroughly discredited; most of the prominent men of this and later eras were still alive when Pompeii was destroyed, so that their funerary inscriptions, which would have carried the details of their careers, were yet to be carved, while the expansive building projects that had characterized the Augustan period had ceased, with the result that dedicatory inscriptions were few as well. Castrén was also heavily influenced by the line of scholarship descending particularly through the work of Amedeo Maiuri that emphasized a change in society traceable to the famous earthquake of AD 62. Straitened circumstances, it was held, led to the rise of new, far less distinguished men and families—a commercial class—that were in the process of replacing Pompeii's land-owning grandees when the city was destroyed. Maiuri had based his analysis on supposedly different building and habitation patterns that he discerned in post-earthquake construction, when large and noble properties were partitioned into small and trade-oriented parcels. In actuality, however, Pompeii had always been a city of properties devoted to quite distinct uses jambed one against the other, and Maiuri's perceptions had been overdrawn (cf. Jongman, Ch. 32).[11] So Castrén, focussing on changes rather than continuities, also overstated the decline of Pompeii's old families and the rise of the new.

One rising class of society that proved surprisingly difficult to trace was that of the *augustales*, an order of economically successful freedmen first established under the emperor Augustus and devoted to imperial cult. Only twelve *augustales* are known from Pompeii, and of these, two, C. Calventius Quietus and M. Cerrinius Restitutus, rose to sufficient prominence to have been granted the right of a *bisellium*, the double-wide seat that was otherwise a sign of membership in the local senate, as noted with pride on their tombs (cf. Cormack, Ch. 37; Figure 37.5).[12] One of the owners of the well-known Casa dei Vettii, A. Vettius Conviva, was an *augustalis* and, to judge from the size and decoration of his house, probably also would have received the honor of a *bisellium* had Pompeii not been destroyed. Indeed, it now seems likely that many of Pompeii's *augustales* were still alive when the city was overwhelmed, so that like the men of Castrén's supposedly lost Claudian generation, their funerary inscriptions were never carved, with the result that they have escaped our record. At Herculaneum, where their local shrine was recovered (Map 4, E), study of the *augustales* has proved a significant factor in the history of the organization in general.[13] It seems unlikely, however, that the several stone-cut lists of names discovered in the course of the excavations could form *alba*, registers, of the *augustales* there, for over 450 names— far too many—have so far been recovered.[14]

At roughly the same time as Castrén's studies, several more narrowly focussed projects appeared. For the first time since their publication in the *CIL*, Jean Andreau undertook thorough analysis of the wax tablets of Caecilius Iucundus, establishing Iucundus' social milieu—decidedly that of the second rank of working businessmen and freedmen—and the importance of standing in this rank-conscious society, even in determining the order of witnesses to the transactions recorded on the tablets (cf. Welch, Ch. 36; Figures 36.11a–b for a possible portrait of Caecilius Iucundus).[15] James Franklin again attempted to date the candidacies for municipal offices, this time based on the overlaying of the posters supporting their campaigns (Table 33.1).[16] Patrizia Sabbatini Tumolesi assembled and studied the announcements of gladiatorial shows, producing reliable texts and new insights into their staging and use in local politics.[17] And in fascinating studies apart from politics, Marcello Gigante culled the *graffiti* for quotations from Greek and Latin literature,[18] while Antonio Varone collected references to Judaism and Christianity.[19]

In the 1980s Henrik Mouritsen returned again to the electoral *programmata* to produce a corrected catalogue, now indispensable for their further study, and with his catalogue he published his analysis of Pompeian society, just as Castrén had done earlier.[20] Whereas Castrén had based his studies on his lists of families, Mouritsen worked from statistical analyses of the *programmata* and inscriptions, which he assigned to one of three major time-spans. He concluded that, contrary to Castrén's theories, there were at Pompeii two types of magisterial families, one comprising a truly powerful few that remained prominent throughout the late Republic and imperial periods (the eras for which we have sufficient evidence to draw conclusions) and a second that rose to power for a generation or two in any period before falling out of sight. Indeed, we can track a few families—the Marci and Decimi Lucretii and the Marci Holconii, in particular—from Augustan through Flavian times, while most families seem to appear and then disappear rapidly. While Mouritsen identified new rising families, he could discern at most variations on traditional sources of wealth supporting them, not new sources, and he has since strongly criticized the idea of a challenging commercial class that became ascendant following the earthquake.[21]

In his roughly contemporary study of Pompeii's economy, Willem Jongman, still believing in a strong division between an old land-based elite and a rising commercial class, argued that the latter had first to acclimatize to the more aristocratic attitudes of the local senate before being allowed membership.[22] As Mouritsen showed, however, newcomers with sufficient fortune were readily accepted, for *within* the senate was the social division that mattered for these families—that between the few entrenched elite and those rising to power only for brief periods of time, into which latter category newcomers fitted. Moreover, as has been recently argued, there is, in fact, no reason

Table 33.1 The municipal government of Roman Pompeii[a]

---

ordo decurionum, decurio (-nes)

The local town senate or council and its members (decurions). Membership is for life unless removed by the quinquennials. Requirements are that members be freeborn male citizens who live in or near town, and who are honorable in character and profession. Members must meet a minimum wealth requirement (the exact amount for Pompeii is unknown), and normally be at least 25 years old. Citizens become members either automatically upon election as aedile, or through appointment (*adlectio*) by the quinquennials or the council as a whole (cf. the case of young Celsinus, Chs 32, 34). This body is responsible for public funds and municipal administration of all kinds.

comitium (-a)

The place of assembly, and (pl.) the assembly itself of the people, responsible for the annual elections of *duoviri* and *aediles*.[b]

aedilis (-es) (aedile)

duovir viis aedibus sacris publicisque procurandis, "duovir in charge of administering streets and sacred and civic buildings." This is the junior-level annual magistracy; two are elected by the *comitia* in March, to begin serving a one-year term on 1 July. They are responsible for building construction and maintenance, oversight of infrastructure (streets and water) and public services, markets and official weights and measures.

duumvir/duovir (-i) (duovir)

duovir iure dicundo, "duovir with the authority to pronounce legal decisions." This is the senior-level magistracy; two are elected by the *comitia* in March, to begin serving a one-year term on 1 July. A candidate must already have been elected as aedile. These officials act as municipal executives; they preside over meetings of the local *ordo decurionum* and implement decrees of that senatorial body.

quinquennalis (-es) (quinquennial)

duovir iure dicundo quinquennalis, "fifth-year duovir with the authority to pronounce legal decisions." This is the highest local office to which a Pompeian could aspire; two are elected every fifth year in the place of regular duovirs. A candidate must already have been elected as duovir. As with the censor in Rome, these officers take the census of citizens, revising the *ordines* and the membership of the *ordo decurionum*, which waned as members died or were expelled.

Notes

a This table is selective of the most important offices; more detail can be found in the following sources: A. E. Cooley and M. G. L. Cooley, *Pompeii. A sourcebook*, London, 2004, pp. 111–13; J. L. Franklin, Jr, *Pompeis difficile est: studies in the political life of imperial Pompeii*, Ann Arbor, MI, 2001, pp. 9–12 (with a list of known dated magistracies in the appendix); P. Castrén, *Ordo populusque Pompeianus: polity and society in Roman Pompeii*, ActaInstRomFin no. 8, Rome, 1975, pp. 55–82.

b It should be noted that while there is little doubt that *comitia* existed at Pompeii, direct evidence has yet to be found at the site. See Castrén, *Ordo*, pp. 78–9.

to assume a sharp break between Pompeii's aristocracy and its commercial ventures, mistakenly to cast the analysis in terms of early modern English patterns and attitudes, where an "aristocracy" apart from commercial interests belonged in the country, while a "bourgeoisie" inhabited the town.[23] Rather, Pompeii's elite lived both in country and city, and they exploited each.

Most recently, Franklin has again turned to studies of the political scene, this time drawing on all the varieties of the written evidence, not merely the *programmata*.[24] This has allowed him to trace the interconnections between men and families that can be demonstrated through study of the *graffiti* coupled with carved inscriptions and the *programmata*, for example, and to delineate groups of men active in six divisions of the evidence from Augustan to Flavian times. Again Mouritsen's analysis was confirmed: a few dominant families were active throughout the eras, while lesser families rose and fell. But with the addition of this evidence the picture is far more detailed. Not only can candidates be assigned more specific floruits, but throughout time, patterns of rise and fall—prominence, disappearance, advancement, returns, and newcomers—and apparent cooperation between families can be traced. In particular, the role of adoption in sustaining and combining *gentes* and wealth is clear.

Yet all this work remains to be tested or expanded by smaller, more focussed studies. There is abundant evidence, for example, for study of careers of individual men, such as the prominent Cn. Alleius Nigidius Maius, whose life has now been profitably examined by three generations of scholars.[25] Entire family lines, such as that of the distinguished Decimi Lucretii Valentes, whose family tomb has recently been recovered, must be established.[26] Lesser men, too, can be tracked through the writing; already the professional letterer Aemilius Celer has led to Crescens, *architectus* in charge of remodeling in progress just inside the Porta Marina, where surprising evidence of the workmen's level of literacy was recovered.[27] Small social units and organizations can be studied with surprising results; a traveling troupe of pantomimists visited both Pompeii and Herculaneum, even deserving mention in the *graffiti* surrounding Pompeii's most famous brothel, a neighborhood of flashy characters with their own arguments and enthusiasms (cf. DeFelice, Ch. 30).[28]

Especially begging for study are the various roles of freedmen and their descendants in society, the abundant evidence for which was first highlighted by the work of Andreau and Castrén. As discernible units within noble families or freeborn descendants striking out on their own, they form a class of society rarely studied because they are attested mainly by the relatively shallow evidence of stark funerary inscriptions in the Roman world at large. At Pompeii, in contrast, the evidence, which comes from a variety of sources, is deep, coherent and remains to be exploited. The rise of descendants of freedmen to the local senate has become a focus of the work of Andrzej Łoś,[29] but study of their roles in lower levels of society perhaps promises more insights.

Nor—perhaps because of their limited role in politics—have the women attested at Pompeii ever received the attention they deserve (cf. Bernstein, Ch. 34). Only members of Pompeii's most prominent families served as public priestesses of Ceres, Venus, and later the combined office of Ceres and Venus, an obviously distinguished and powerful position. Yet apart from listings, we currently seem able to say little about them. Women are regularly named in and wrote *graffiti*, owned slaves and directed freedmen, but as yet they have been treated only in descriptive fashion.[29]

Few are aware that masons' marks and initials carved into grain mills have been collected and remain unstudied. And while Andreau's work on the affairs of Caecilius Iucundus led him into initial exploration of the inscriptions on *amphorae* related to men named in the wax tablets, that vast store of thousands of inscriptions naming producers, contents, and shipping addresses stands largely unexplored.

Thanks to the efforts of a series of scholars working on a variety of fronts, analysis of the writing recovered at ancient Pompeii has deeply undercut Mau's original opinion that it offered little of significance to an understanding of the site. Much work, however, obviously remains to be done, especially by working with a variety of document types rather than being limited by the categories of the *CIL*. Mouritsen counted over 11,000 pieces of writing from this city, but he did not take into account the many conflated *graffiti* and election notices treated as single entries in the various publications. Over the years, focussed collections and studies of distinct types of inscriptions have made access to these materials increasingly easy, and new collectionsof the amatory and pictured *graffiti* have recently appeared.[31] The whole is an enormous mass of detail that will support study and exploration for generations to come, bringing increased knowledge of the social levels and interconnections of Pompeii's inhabitants to add to our understanding of this, the only ancient Roman society we can hope to know with any thoroughness.

NOTES

1 These tablets record both private (nos. 1–137) and public (nos. 138–52) transactions. Less well known are the wax tablets recovered at various locations in the excavations at Herculaneum: see A. Maiuri, "Tabulae Ceratae Herculanenses," *PP*, 1946, vol. 1, pp. 373–9; G. Pugliese Carratelli, "Tabulae Herculanenses I–III," *PP*, 1946, vol. 1, pp. 379–85; 1948, vol. 3, pp. 165–84; 1953, vol. 8, pp. 455–63; V. Arangio-Ruiz and G. Pugliese Carratelli, "Tabulae Herculanenses IV–VI," *PP*, 1954, vol. 9, pp. 54–74; 1955, vol. 10, pp. 448–77; 1961, vol. 16, pp. 66–73. The tablets recovered at nearby Agro Murecine in 1959 record matters relating to Puteoli across the Bay rather than Pompeii; see F. Sbordone, "Preambolo per l'edizione critica delle tavolette cerate di Pompei," *RendNap*, 1976, n.s. vol. 51, pp. 145–68.

2 A. Mau, *Pompeii: its life and art* (transl. and ed. by F.W. Kelsey), rev. edn, London, 1902, p. 485.

3 Mau, *Pompeii*, p. 491.

4 The initial issue of *CIL* IV was compiled from over 130 earlier sources by K. Zangemeister and contains many variant and often conflated readings. The first supplement to this collection, produced by Zangemeister in 1871, was the edition of the *apochae* of Caecilius Iucundus. The second supplement was again of written inscriptions in general and was prepared by Mau himself in 1909; it is the most magisterial and reliable of the volumes. The third supplement by M. Della Corte began appearing in fascicles in 1952 and records inscriptions found through 1956; following Della Corte's death, F. Weber completed it in 1970. *CIL* X was updated only by M. Ihm, "Addimenta ad corporis vol. IX et X," *EphEp*, 1899, vol. 8, pp. 1–221; pp. 86–90 pertain to Pompeii. Parietal inscriptions found after 1956 and stone-cut inscriptions found after 1899 must be traced in archaeological and learned journals.

5 P. G. H. Willems, *Les elections municipales à Pompei*, Paris, 1887, reprinted Amsterdam, 1969. It had originally appeared in *Bulletins de l'Academie royale des sciences, des lettres, et des beaux-arts de Belgique*, 1886, ser. 3, vol. 12, pp. 51–90.

6 E. Magaldi, "Echi di Roma a Pompei I–III," *RStPomp*, 1936, vol. 2, pp. 25–100, 129–209; 1939, vol. 3, pp. 21–60.

7 V. Väänänen, *Le latin vulgaire des inscriptions pompéiennes*, 2nd edn, Berlin, 1959; earlier this had appeared as *Abhandlungen der Detuschen Akademie der Wissenshaften zu Berlin*, 1958, Nr. 3.

8 M. Della Corte, *Case ed abitanti di Pompei*, 3rd edn, by P. Soprano, Naples, 1965. Earlier studies that became a part of this book had been published between 1914 and 1925 in *Neapolis* and *Rivista Indo-Greco-Italica*.

9 So P. Castrén, *Ordo populusque Pompeianus: polity and society in Roman Pompeii*, ActaInstRomFin no. 8, Rome, 1975, pp. 31–6; H. Mouritsen, *Elections, magistrates and municipal elite. Studies in Pompeian epigraphy*, AnalRom Suppl. 15, Rome, 1988, pp. 13–27. The term "la tradition pompeianiste" is owed to J. Andreau (Castrén, *Ordo*, p. 33).

10 Castrén, *Ordo*.

11 For the arguments against Maiuri's theories, see especially J. Andreau, "Histoire des séismes et histoire économique: le tremblement de terre de Pompéi (62 ap. J.-C.)," *AnnÉconSocCiv*, 1973, vol. 28, pp. 369–95. Concluding his study of Pompeii's economy, W. Jongman, *The Economy and Society of Pompeii*, Amsterdam, 1988, p. 203, categorized Pompeii as a Weberian "consumer" rather than "producer" city, as a more recent statement of Maiuri's theory might be formulated.

12 *CIL* X, 1026 and 994, 995.

13 S. E. Ostrow, "*Augustales* along the Bay of Naples: a case for their early growth," *Historia*, 1985, vol. 34, pp. 64–101. For a register of attested inhabitants of Herculaneum known by 1952, see M. Della Corte, "Onamasticon Herculanese," *RendNap*, 1952, vol. 27, pp. 211–33. See also now B. Bollmann, *Römische Vereinshäuser: Untersuchungen zu den Scholae der römische Berufs-, Kult- und Augustalen-Kollegien in Italien*, Mainz, 1998.

14 The argument is that of A. Guadagno, "Frammenti inediti di albi degli augustali," *CronErcol*, 1977, vol. 7, pp. 114–23, esp. 118–20, but see now T. Najbjerg, "The so-called 'Basilica' in Herculaneum," in *Pompeian Brothels, Pompeii's Ancient History, Mirrors and Mysteries, Art and Nature at Oplontis, & the Herculaneum "Basilica,"* JRA Suppl. Ser. no. 47, 2002, pp. 157–63, who identifies the "basilica" of Herculaneum as a *porticus* and center for the city's *augustales*, accepting the lists as those of the *ordo*'s members.

15 J. Andreau, *Les affaires de Monsieur Jucundus*, CÉFR, no. 19, Rome, 1974. The rank of witnesses can be established only generally, however, not with perfect precision, as attempted by Jongman, *Pompeii*, on which see the criticisms of H. Mouritsen, "A note on Pompeian epigraphy and social structure," *ClMed*, 1990, vol. 41, pp. 131–49, esp. 131–40.

16 J. L. Franklin, Jr, *Pompeii: the electoral programmata, campaigns and politics, ad 71–79*, PAAR, no. 28, Rome, 1980.

17 P. Sabbatini Tumolesi, *Gladiatorum paria: annunci di spettacoli gladiatorii a Pompei*, Tituli: Pubblicazioni dell'Istituto di Epigrafia e Antichità Greche e Romane dell'Università di Roma 1, Rome, 1980.

18 M. Gigante, *Civiltà delle forme letterarie nell'antica Pompei*, Naples, 1979.

19 A. Varone, *Presenze giudaiche e cristiane a Pompei*, Quaderni della Società per lo Studio e la Divulgazione dell'Archeologica Biblica 1, Naples, 1979.

20 Mouritsen, *Elections*.

21 Mouritsen, "A note," pp. 140–3, and H. Mouritsen, "Order and disorder in late Pompeian politics," in *Les élites municipales de l'Italie péninsulaire des Grecques à Néron*, CÉFR, no. 215, Naples-Rome, 1996, pp. 139–44.

22 Jongman, *Pompeii*, pp. 258–64 and 311–29.

23 Mouritsen, "A note," pp. 140–3; A. Wallace-Hadrill, "Elites and trade in the Roman town," in J. Rich and A. Wallace-Hadrill (eds), *City and Country in the Ancient World*, London, 1991, pp. 241–72, esp. 267–8.

24 J. L. Franklin, Jr, *Pompeis difficile est: studies in the political life of imperial Pompeii*, Ann Arbor, MI, 2001.

25 A. W. Van Buren, "Cnaeus Alleius Nigidius Maius of Pompeii," *AJP*, 1947, vol. 68, pp. 382–93; W. O. Moeller, "Gnaeus Alleius Nigidius Maius, princeps coloniae," *Latomus*, 1975, vol. 32, pp. 515–20; J. L. Franklin, Jr, "Cn. Alleius Nigidius Maius and the amphitheatre: munera and a distinguished career at ancient Pompeii," *Historia*, 1997, vol. 46, pp. 434–47.

26 M. De' Spagnolis Conticello, "Sul rinvenimento della villa e del monumento funerario dei Lucretii Valentes," *RStPomp*, 1993–4, vol. 6, pp. 147–66.

27 J. L. Franklin, Jr, "Literacy and the parietal inscriptions of ancient Pompeii," in J. H. Humphrey (ed.), *Literacy in the Roman World*, JRA Suppl. Ser. no. 3, 1991, pp. 77–98; J. L. Franklin, Jr, "Games and a lupanar: prosopography of a neighborhood in ancient Pompeii," *CJ*, 1985–6, vol. 81, pp. 319–28.

28 J. L. Franklin, Jr, "Pantomimists at Pompeii: Actius Anicetus and his troupe," *AJP*, 1987, vol. 108, pp. 95–107, and on the property in its context, see J. F. DeFelice, *Roman Hospitality: the professional women of Pompeii*, Warren Center, PA, 2001, esp. pp. 102–3.

29 A. Łoś, "Les affranchis dans la vie politique à Pompei," *MÉFRA*, 1987, vol. 99, pp. 847–73; "Quibus patet curia municipalis: Remarques sur la structure de la classe dirigeante de Pompei," *Cahiers de Centre Gustave Glotz*, 1992, vol. 3, pp. 259–97; "Les fils d'affranchis dans l'Ordo Pompeianus," in *Les élites municipales*, pp. 145–52.

30 See, e.g., M. D'Avino, *La donna a Pompei*, Naples, 1964; F. Bernstein, "Pompeian women and the Programmata," in R. Curtis (ed.), *Studia Pompeiana & Classica in Honor of Wilhelmina F. Jashemski*, New Rochelle, NY, 1988, pp. 1–18.

31 A. Varone, *Erotica pompeiana*, Rome, 1994; F. P. M. Vivolo, *Pompei: i graffiti figurati*, Foggia, 1993.

CHAPTER THIRTY-FOUR

POMPEIAN WOMEN

——·◆·——

Frances Bernstein

Pompeian woman of the first century AD could neither hold a magistracy, serve in the local senate, nor vote. Given these constraints, was the Pompeian matron's world limited to dutiful service to husband and household? Did her interests and achievements extend beyond domestic chores to public involvement within the community? Information gleaned from the wealth of preserved epigraphical and archaeological evidence at Pompeii clearly demonstrates that Pompeian women not only performed the traditional female duties of managing households and raising children, but also were actively involved in the economic, political and social life of their town. Capable of making astute financial decisions, they oversaw large estates, held jobs and managed households. Knowledgeable of the political process, they wielded power and were actively involved in a governmental structure that formally excluded them. Moving within the social structure, many improved their position and earned the respect of fellow citizens. The women of Pompeii played a visible and crucial public role in town life, as vital and contributing members of their community.

Who were the women of Pompeii? They were privileged women of the highest class, freedwomen working long hours in varied jobs supporting the many commercial establishments, and nameless slave women laboring in large households and businesses.[1]

As at Rome, the elite Pompeian family provided access to the instruments of power: *clientes et amici*, money, prestige and honor. Pompeian women, as respected members (daughters, wives and mothers) of elite *gentes*, gained access to and used these resources to ensure their families' status and interests. Freedwomen often working in small family-run businesses likewise served their families' interests. Since the majority of both elite and freedwomen were seen primarily within the context of the family, it is to this world that we first turn.

WOMEN AND THE FAMILY

Daughters were cherished in many Pompeian families and the birth of an infant girl was a joyous event. One proud parent announced the birth of a daughter to all passing through the Porta di Nola: *Iuvenilla nata diei Saturni hora secunda vespertina IIII nonas Augustas*, "Iuvenilla was born on Saturn's day at the second hour of vespers four days before the *nones* of August" (*CIL* IV, 294).

The death of a beloved daughter was a grievous event for parents of all classes. A mournful mother, Marcia Aucta, built a tomb for her husband and her daughter, Fabia Gratina. C(AIO) F(ABIO) SECUNDO MARCIA AUCTA UXOR FECIT ET SIBI ET FABIAE C(AI) F(ILIAE) GRATINAE FILIAE, "Marcia Aucta the wife built this for her husband Caius Fabius Secundus, also for herself and for her daughter Fabia Gratina" (*CIL* X, 1003). The freedman Marcus Petacius Dasius likewise mourned the loss of his daughters Petacia Montana and Petacia Rufilla, buried in a family plot outside the Porta di Stabia.[2] Even the deceased daughters of slaves were honored with markers, such as those outside the Porta Nocera to Helpis, four years; Psyche, three years and six months; and little Arsinoe, three years old (*PNoc* 9 ES, 9 N, 19a OS).[3]

The terms *coniunx*, *uxor* and *concubina* described relationships at Pompeii and reflected the differing and complex bonds between men and women in the Roman world. *L(ucius) Clodius/Pelagia coniunx* scrawled on a bedroom wall at (IX.3.25) clearly denoted Pelagia's status as spouse (*CIL* IV, 2321). The *duovir* Numerius Herennius Celsus dedicated a most elaborate tomb to his 22-year-old wife Aesquillia Polla, referring to her as *uxor*. Land outside the Porta di Nola was given by the town for Aesquillia's shrine: a *schola* with a slender marble column and urn (Figure 37.2).[4] The freedman banker Lucius Ceius Serapio referred to his free-born wife Helvia as *uxor* (*PNoc* 3 OS).[5] Popidia Ecdoche, also of free birth, was honored by her mate, the surveyor Nicostratus Popidius, with a tomb marker located outside the Porta Nocera (*PNoc* 17 OS) on which he openly refers to her as his concubine.

Portraits of couples and matrons painted on the walls of private houses reaffirm the central role of wives within the family. The painting of a young couple found on the wall of the house at (VII.2.6) shows a young man identified as Terentius Neo wearing a tunic and holding a sealed scroll. His wife is shown wearing a red tunic and mantle and holding a stylus and diptych; both advertise their literacy.[6]

The most important duty of a wife was to produce a legitimate heir—to become a mother. While childbirth most likely took place at home, there is evidence at (VIII.3.11–12) of a medical clinic with small rooms on the first floor for patients. Fifty-five surgical instruments were found at no. 11, and one appears to be an obstetrical forceps for use in deliveries.[7]

Portraits of women tenderly cradling babies and young children honor mothering and childcare, as shown in *cubiculum* (5) of the House of the Postumii (VIII.4.4; Figure 34.1).[8] A touching funeral monument built by Mulvia Prisca with her own money for her 22-year-old son Caius Vestorius Priscus contained a *graffito* poignantly expressing the suffering endured by the mother.[9]

Grown children lovingly remembered their mothers on tomb markers. Istacidia, member of an elite family, was honored by her daughter Tinteria, while the freedwomen and mothers Urbana and Calidia Antiochus were likewise honored by their children.[10]

For many elite Pompeian women, much of the day was spent seeing to traditional domestic chores: tending to children, supervising slaves, overseeing household expenses, providing meals, directing the spinning, worshiping at household shrines and generally keeping domestic order. A small room (51) in the House of the Dioscuri (VI.9.6) possibly served as a "day-room," where the mistress of the house could work and supervise the staff.[11]

A Pompeian matron supervised the children and their education with "home-schooling." Alphabets scrawled on walls at a child's level can be found in numerous

Figure 34.1 Maenad cradling the baby god Dionysus, from *cubiculum* (5) of the House of the Postumii (VIII.4.4). Courtesy of Wilhelmina Jashemski.

houses.[12] At the House of the Silver Wedding (V.2.i), the walls of *exedra* (y) are covered with sixteen *graffiti* referencing the teacher C. Julius Helenus (e.g., *CIL* IV, 4201, 4206, 4211).

The Pompeian matron saw to the provisioning of her family. A series of genre paintings from hall (24) in the *Praedia* of Julia Felix (II.4.3) represent scenes of daily life in the Pompeian forum and provide a unique glimpse into the daily routine for many women (Figures 23.11 and 23.12). Men and women buy and sell fruits and vegetables, shoes, fabrics, pots, pans among other objects. Spinning was also often associated with women's duties. In fact, loom weights have been found in most Pompeian homes. In the House of Marine Venus (III.3.3), a wall painting in room (10) depicts the mistress of the home spinning wool.[13]

During moments of leisure, the women of Pompeii pursued pleasures of singing, playing musical instruments, painting, reading, writing or perhaps just spending warm afternoons in the garden playing with children, visiting with friends, sharing gossip and exchanging domestic tips. They also indulged themselves at the public baths, attended theatrical events, cheered at the amphitheater and shopped at the town's many boutiques.

WOMEN AND THE ECONOMY

Pompeian women of all classes had an impact on the local economy—they possessed money either inherited from family estates or earned through hard work, and they spent it. Women were often charged with managing the domestic budget and making decisions regarding purchases for the family. Wealthy women such as Eumachia, Mamia and Corelia Celsa endowed the city with public works while lower-class women contributed to political campaigns. Women, free and freed alike, built tombs, sold property at auction, prepared their wills and, in short, had a role in money management.

Numerous and quite costly tombs that lined the streets leading into town were built by women such as Veia Barchilla of the prosperous Barca family (cf. Cormack, Ch. 37). Her sizable and prominent cylindrical tomb was located just outside the Porta Nocera, bearing the message: VEIA N(UMERI) F(ILIA) BARCHILLA SIBI ET N(UMERIO) AGRESTINO EQUITIO PULCHRO VIRO SUO, "Veia Barchilla the daughter of Numerius Veius Barchilla built this for herself and for her husband, Numerius Agrestinus Equitius Pulcher" (*PNoc* 3 ES). Likewise: ANNEDIA Q(UINTI) F(ILIA) EX TESTAMENTO SUO DE SUA PECUNIA HEREDES SUOS IUSIT FIERI MONUMENTUM SIBI ET L(UCIO) CAESIO C(AI) F(ILIO) D(UUM)V(IRO) I(URE) D(ICUNDO) VIRO SUO, "Annedia the daughter of Quintus ordered her heirs to have this monument built to her and her husband, Lucius Caesius, duovir for administering the law, according to her will from her money" (*PNoc* 29 OS). The freedwoman Muttia Salvia also set up a marker to honor her husband Caius Muttius Capito outside the Porta del Vesuvio.[14]

Accounting records of the banker Lucius Caecilius Iucundus give further testimony to the involvement of women such as Umbricia Antiochis in the financial world where they apparently saw to their own accounts and made decisions to sell or buy property.

> Umbricia Januaria declared that she had received from Lucius Caecilius Iucundus 11,039 sesterces which sum came into the hands of Lucius Caecilius Iucundus by agreement as the proceeds of an auction sale for Umbricia Ianuaria, the commission due him having been deducted. Done at Pompeii on the 12th day of December in the consulship of Lucius Duvius and Publius Clodius.[15]

Julia Felix owned and managed the large establishment that occupied the entire *insula* at (II.4), including shops, taverns, apartments and a bath (cf. Parslow, Ch. 14; Nappo, Ch. 23). An advertisement posted on the exterior wall announced that the building was for rent:

> IN PRAEDIS IULIAE SP(URII) F(ILIAE) FELICIS LOCANTUR BALNEUM VENERIUM ET NONGENTUM, TABERNAE, PERGULAE, CENACULA EX IDIBUS AUG(USTIS) PRIMIS IN IDUS AUG(USTIS) SEXTAS, ANNOS CONTINUOS QUINQUE. S(I) Q(UINQUENNIUM) D(ECURRERIT) L(OCATIO) E(RIT) N(UDO) C(ONSENSU).

> To rent for the period of five years from the thirteenth day of next August to the Thirteenth day of the sixth August, the Venus Bath fitted for the well-to-do, shops with living quarters over the shops, apartments on the second floor located in the building of Julia Felix, daughter of Spurius. At the end of five years, the agreement is terminated.[16]

Naevoleia Tyche, a freedwoman, built a costly and impressive tomb for herself and her freedman husband Caius Munatius Faustus (Figure 37.5). Located outside the Porta Ercolano, the monument stands as testimony to the wealth and position that the former slave had achieved within the community (*PErc* S 22):

NAEVOLEIA L(UCI) LIB(ERTA) TYCHE SIBI ET C(AIO) MUNATIO FAUSTO AUG(USTALIS) ET PAGANO CUI DECURIONES CONSENSU POPULI BISELLIUM OB MERITA EIUS DECREVERUNT. HOC MONI-MENTUM NAEVOLEIA TYCHE LIBERTIS SUIS LIBERTABUSQUE ET C(AI) MUNATI FAUSTI VIVA FECIT.

Naevoleia Tyche, freedwoman of Lucius, for herself and Gauis Munatius Faustus, an *augustalis* and suburban magistrate, to whom because of his merit the *decuriones* with consent of the people voted a *bisellium*. Naevoleia Tyche built this monument, while she was still living, for her freedmen and freedwomen and those of Gaius Munatius Faustus.[17]

A portrait of Naevoleia in high relief occupies the front of the tomb while a nautical scene of a ship under sail on the side of the tomb suggests her interest in trade and the shipping industry. Perhaps the large woman seen sitting in the stern of this ship under sail and giving orders to the crew is Naevoleia herself.

Numerous women served as waitresses in the many inns and taverns of Pompeii; Iris was one such barmaid: *Successus textor amat coponiaes ancilla(m), nomine Hiredem, quae quidem illum non curat. sed ille rogat, illa com(m)iseretur*, "Successus the weaver loves Iris, a waitress at the inn, but she does not care for him. He asks anyway, and she feels sorry for him".[18]

Maria, Florentina, Lalage, Doris and seven other female spinners represent the many (now nameless) women who worked long hard hours at the shops and factories of Pompeii. These workers took time off from spinning wool at the large-scale spinning and weaving establishment located at (VI.13.6) to scratch their names on the peristyle wall.[19]

WOMEN AND POLITICS

Pompeian women of all classes were actively involved in local politics, exerting influence within the confines of a system that excluded them from voting or holding elected public offices. Female members of elite families used traditional means— money and public gift-giving, political alliance, and patronage—to ensure the future of their *gentes* within the community.

In cities throughout the Roman Empire, wealthy women, in the spirit of euergetism, bestowed generous gifts upon their communities by endowing public works. At Pompeii, Eumachia, Corelia Celsa and Mamia subsidized construction of three impressive buildings: the Eumachia, the Temple of Isis, and the Temple of the Emperor respectively. The evidence, however, suggests that the gifts of Eumachia and Corelia Celsa were not purely philanthropic but were motivated by political gain.

Eumachia was born into a wealthy and respected Pompeian family, the Eumachii, whose fortune was made in the ceramic and tile industry. She married Marcus Numistrius Fronto, from an equally prestigious Pompeian family, with economic ties to sheep farming and the woolen industry. Upon the death of her father, she was heir to a sizable fortune including land holdings and mercantile ventures.

Figure 34.2 Replica of the Eumachia statue. EUMACHIAE L(UCII) F(ILIAE) SACERD(OTI) PUBL(ICAE) FULLONES, "The fullers dedicate this statue to Eumachia, daughter of Lucius, and public priestess." (*CIL* X, 813). Original in the Naples Museum. Photo: Christina Dickerson.

The large building on the southeast corner of the forum built by Eumachia in her own name and that of her son, Marcus Numistrius Fronto, was dedicated to *concordia Augusta* and *pietas* (cf. Dobbins, Ch. 12; Small, Ch. 13, Welch, Ch. 36; Figures 12.1, 12.13 and 12.14).[20] A statue of *concordia*, sculpted in the likeness of Augustus' wife Livia, stood opposite the entranceway in apse (10), while statues of her sons Tiberius and Drusus occupied flanking recesses (11). In a broad niche (13) directly behind the statue of Concordia, stood a statue dedicated to Eumachia (Figures 34.2, 36.4a–c). The implications are clear—Eumachia and her son honored Livia and her sons. Eumachia provided Pompeii with its most magnificent building and she assured the political future of her son with possible aspirations of a career at Rome.

The Temple of Isis, according to an inscription over the threshold, was rebuilt after the earthquake of AD 62–63 by the six-year-old Numerius Popidius Celsinus, who in turn was rewarded with entrance into the *ordo decurionum*. The real re-builders were, of course, the freedperson parents Numerius Popidius Ampliatus and Corelia Celsa, who paid for reconstruction of the Iseum (for the inscription, cf. Jongman, Ch. 32; see also Welch, Ch. 36). This was a generous gift and a politically astute decision to provide their family entrance into the magisterial class. Corelia Celsa also provided for the construction of room (6) at the rear of the Iseum.[21]

Wealthy families such as the Eumachii, Numistrii, Clodii, Gellii Holconii and Alleii (who intermarried to form powerful coalitions) dominated Pompeian politics (cf. Franklin, Ch. 33). While romantic interests were motivation for some marriages, politically advantageous marriages among elite families were not uncommon. Literary evidence suggests that elite women were well aware of the political ramifications of a union, and joined in marital negotiations. At Pompeii it is difficult to imagine the marriage of her son being arranged without the advice and consent of a powerful woman such as Eumachia.[22]

The patron–client relationship was a powerful Roman institution that provided Pompeian women with a means to influence elections and hence wield some political clout. Vesonia was a Pompeian woman who served as patroness to the influential and wealthy *augustalis*, Publius Vesonius Phileros (cf. Cormack, Ch. 37). As her client, he was bound by a system of duties and obligations that included political support (*PNoc* 23 OS; Figure 37.8).

Women were also active in Pompeian politics, especially elections. Of the many *programmata* painted on façades of buildings throughout Pompeii, at least forty-nine of the red and black painted election notices were sponsored and paid for by women who could themselves neither vote nor hold office. Taedia Secunda, a woman of the elite class, urged the election of her grandson as aedile: *L(ucium) Popi{dium} S{ecun}d{um} aed(ilem) o(ro) v(os) f(aciatis) / Taed{i}a Secunda cupiens avia rog(at) et fecit*, "Taedia Secunda, his grandmother, asks and demands that you make Lucius Popidius Secundus an aedile."[23] Most, however, were sponsored by lower-class women such as Iphigenia, Statia, Helpis Afra and Vatinia, e.g.: *L(ucium) Ceium Secundum aed(ilem) Vatinia (cupi)de facit*, "Vatinia desires the election of Lucius Ceius Secundus as aedile."[24]

Patterns of political endorsement show that Pompeian women, just as men, were not frivolous in selecting a candidate but, rather, based their decisions on a variety of factors inherent in Roman politics: kinship, patronage, neighborhoods, voting units and organizations, economic associations, common interest groups and the promise of lavish spectacles in the amphitheater.[25]

WOMEN AND SOCIETY

Pompeian society offered women both fluidity and visibility. Manumission and marriage were two paths to social mobility for Pompeian women who moved from the servile to the freed and on occasion into the elite class. Tironia Repentina, a former slave, married the freedman Aulus Clodius Aegialus. Their son Aulus Clodius Iustus was accordingly born free and built a tomb for himself and his parents outside the Porta Nocera (*PNoc* 50 OS). The freedwoman Naevoleia Tyche amassed a sizable fortune and earned a respected place within the community. Similarly, Muttia Salvia, a former slave, had sufficient funds to build a tomb for herself and her husband outside the Porta del Vesuvio.[26]

Vertia Philumina was able to cross social classes and rise even from slavery to become the wife of a Roman citizen. Manumitted by a female member of the Vertii family, Vertia Philumina married Marcus Octavius and together they built an impressive tomb for themselves and their son located outside the Porta Nocera. The *aedicula*-shaped shrine held the statue of Vertia Philumina standing modestly with veiled head (*PNoc* 13 OS; Figure 37.3).[27]

Roman towns honored certain elite women with statues, funereal gifts and public priesthoods, affirming their high status within the community. Viciria, the mother of an influential Herculanean named Marcus Nonius Balbus (the elder), received from the city a full-sized statue in her likeness.[28]

Pompeian women were publicly honored at their death with gifts of land and money. Aesquillia Polla, Arellia Tertulla and Mamia were buried in impressive *schola* tombs presented by the *ordo decurionum* (cf. Cormack, Ch. 37; Figure 37.2). The tomb of Mamia just outside the Porta Ercolano served the welcome needs of many a tired visitor: MAMIAE P(UBLII) F(ILIAE) SACERDOTI PUBLICAE LOCUS SEPULTUR DATUS DECURIONUM DECRETO, "The land and the tomb were given to the public priestess Mamia, daughter of Publius, by a decree of the *decuriones*" (cf. Dobbins, Ch. 12 for Mamia as a donor).[29]

But public honor was also bestowed upon a freedwoman, in the form of a small marble column located just outside the Porta Nocera: CLODIA L(IBERTA) NIGELLA PORCAR(IA) PUBLICA (LOCO DAT)O EX D(ECRETO) D(ECURIONUM), "Clodia Nigella, a freedwoman of Clodia and a public pig herder, the place having been decreed by the *decuriones*" (PN 5 OS).[30]

WOMEN AND RELIGION

Women were actively involved in the religious life at Pompeii and often officiated at both public and private rituals. The office of public priestess bestowed by the *ordo decurionum* was honorific and reserved for women of the elite class whose families dominated local politics. Duties included attending to official religious rites sanctioned by the community; accompanying honors brought special privileges at public functions. Ten extant inscriptions recall the women who served in this capacity: Eumachia, Mamia, Holconia, and Isticidia Rufilla were public priestesses of Venus; Alleia Decimilla, Clodia, Lassia and Aquvia Quarta served the goddess Ceres; Alleia Maia was public priestess of both Venus and Ceres, while Vibia Sabina was priestess to the Imperial family.[31]

Pompeian women were actively involved in domestic worship and were equally responsible for the spiritual life of the family. In wall paintings, women with veiled heads stand before altars, carrying trays of offerings, partaking in ritual and serving as priestess to many and varied cults. One Terentia Paramone was a priestess in the Greek cult of Demeter Thesmophoria. A drawing adjacent to the inscription shows an altar with a pig, the typical sacrifice for this female rite.[32]

A wall painting found on a pilaster in the House of the Dioscuri (VI.9.6) shows a young priestess holding aloft a flaming torch in one hand and a *patera* in the other.[33] In another painting, the goddess Venus sits on a throne while a priestess stands before her, apparently pouring a libation upon an altar.[34] *Cubiculum* (5) in the House of Obellius Firmus (IX.14.4) depicts a woman carrying an offering tray (Figure 34.3).

Figure 34.3 Painting from the west wall of *cubiculum* (5) in the House of Obellius Firmus (IX.14.4), showing a young woman holding an offering. Courtesy of Wilhelmina Jashemski.

Women are also present in a painting from Herculaneum, participating in a sacrifice to Isis.[35] Finally, the Great Frieze from *oecus* (5) in the Villa of the Mysteries clearly reflects the prominent role women played in religious ritual.[36]

Wall paintings from at least five *lararia* show the matron of the house (or her spiritual representation, the "Juno") sacrificing to the household deities. For example, the *lararium* painting in the House of C. Julius Polybius (IX.13.1–3), located in the kitchen court (N) next to the roofed hearth, shows two *lares* standing on either side of an altar while the matron (or Juno), wearing a blue dress and red veil, makes sacrifice.[37] The *lararium* painting in kitchen (17) of the House of Sutoria Primigenia (I.13.2) shows the matron of the house with her entire family offering sacrifice at the *Caristia*, a ritual celebrating family and held on February 22 (cf. George, Ch. 35; Figure 35.1).[38]

Thus, while Roman literary evidence ranging chiefly from male historians to poets and jurists offers valuable insights into the lives, duties and diversions of Roman women, evidence from Pompeii provides a unique glimpse into daily life in a small Roman town. At Pompeii today, we can stroll down streets and drop into the many shops and taverns; we can enter the temples honoring Venus or Isis; we can visit the homes of many Pompeian women, peeking into the kitchens and bedrooms and admiring the wall paintings; and we can read lasting tributes and epitaphs to more than two hundred individual women. Such epigraphical and archaeological evidence convincingly shows Pompeian women of all classes actively taking an active role in the economic, political and social life of their small Campanian municipality.

NOTES

1 For further reading specifically on Pompeian women, see F. S. Bernstein, *The Public Role of Pompeian Women*, Ph.D. thesis, University of Maryland, 1987, esp. Appendix I for a catalog of Pompeian women; E. L. Will, "Women in Pompeii," *Archaeology*, 1979, vol. 32, pp. 34–43; M. D'Avino, *The Women of Pompeii*, Naples, 1967.

2 For the inscription, see *NSc*, 1893, p. 334. For portraits of daughters, see MNN inv. nos. 9074, 9084, 9085; W. Helbig, *Wandegemalde der vom Vesuv Verschutteten Stadte Campaniens*, Leipzig, 1868, no. 1850. For funeral markers to daughters, see *CIL* X, 999, 1004–1007, 1061.

3 The primary reference for all tombs from the Porta Nocera necropolis is A. D'Ambrosio and S. De Caro, *Un impegno per Pompei: Fotopiano e documentazione della Necropoli di Porta Nocera*, Milan, 1983. Cf. Cormack, Ch. 37, n. 1 for an explanation of the abbreviations of the tombs used by this volume. See also George, Ch. 35, n. 26, for other child epitaphs.

4 *NSc*, 1910, p. 390; Tomb (g); see Map 3.

5 For *coniunx*, see *CIL* IV, 2321, 4933; *PNoc* 9 ES. For *uxor*, see *CIL* IV, 1567; *CIL* X, 1019, 1038; *PNoc* 3 OS, 15 ES; *NSc*, 1890, p. 422; 1910, p. 390.

6 MNN inv. no. 9058. Also see R. Ling, *Roman Painting*, Cambridge, 1992, p.160, fig. 170.

7 The House of the Graces. See L. Eschebach, *Gebäudeverzeichnis und Stadtplan de antiken Stadt Pompeji*, Köln, 1993, pp. 364–5.

8 In this case it is a mythological scene: a maenad cradling the baby Dionysus: G. P. Carratelli and I. Baldassarre (eds), *Pompei, pitture e mosaici*, vol. 8, Rome, 1998, p. 465, no. 22.

9 *AÉpigr*, 1913, no. 70 (the inscription and monument); *CIL* IV, 9160 (the *graffito*). See A. E. Cooley and M. G. L. Cooley, *Pompeii. A sourcebook*, London, 2004, p. 128, for a full translation of the former.

10 For portraits of mothers, babies and children see Bernstein, *Public Role*, pls. XXII–XXVI. For references, see *CIL* X, 926, 1071, 1273; *NSc* 1910, p. 407; 1896, p. 422; *PNoc* 5 OS, 11 OS.

11 L. Richardson, jr, *Pompeii: The Casa dei Dioscuri and its painters*, MAAR no. 23, Rome, 1955, pp. 48–9, where the room is numbered as (43). He notes other examples: the House of Meleager (VI.9.2), room (37) (cited by Richardson as room [42]); and the House of the Ephebe (I.7.10–12), room (22). Based on an analysis of the few artifacts and decoration, Allison hesitates to assign room function to the latter parallel. See P. M. Allison, *Pompeian Households: an analysis of the material culture*, Los Angeles, CA, 2004, p. 95, table 5.12b; her data are available at: P. M. Allison, "Pompeian households: an on-line companion," in R. Scaife (ed.), *The Stoa: a consortium for on-line publication in the humanities*, http://www.stoa.org/projects/ph/home/ (1 May 2005). Re: gender-designated spaces and artifacts, cf. Allison, *Pompeian Households*, pp. 156–7; E. W. Leach, *The Social Life of Painting in Ancient Rome and on the Bay of Naples*, Cambridge, 2004, p. 50; A. Wallace-Hadrill, *Houses and Society in Pompeii and Herculaneum*, Princeton, NJ, 1994, pp. 8–10; A. Wallace-Hadrill, "Engendering the Roman house," in D. E. E. Kleiner and S. B. Matheson (eds), *I Claudia. Women in ancient Rome*, New Haven, CT, 1996, pp. 104–15.

12 The House of the Tragic Poet (VI.8.5; *CIL* IV, 2515); House of the Dioscuri (VI.9.6; *CIL* IV, 2547); House of the Faun (VI.12.2; *CIL* IV, 2540); buildings (VI.9.3–5; *CIL* IV, 2549); (VI.14.38; *CIL* IV, 5475); (VI.15.21; *CIL* IV, 5482) and the Villa of the Mysteries (*CIL* IV, 9311, 9312a).

13 For the forum scenes in the *Praedia*, see Carratelli and Baldassarre, *Pitture e mosaici*, vol. 3, Rome, 1991, pp. 251–7; Ling, *Roman Painting*, pp.163–4, fig. 177; W. F. Jashemski, *The Gardens of Pompeii, Herculaneum and the Villas Destroyed by Vesuvius*, New Rochelle, NY, 1979, vol. 1, p. 12, fig. 15. On spinning, see Allison, *Pompeian Households*; W. O. Moeller, *The Wool Trade of Ancient Pompeii*, Leiden, 1976; Jashemski, *Gardens*, vol. 1, p. 102, and for the wall painting, p. 101, fig. 159.

14 *CIL* X, 1073. For other tombs built by women with their own money, see *NSc*, 1910, p. 407; 1910, p. 402; *CIL* X, 928, 1003, 1019, 1036, 1071; *PNoc* 11 OS.

15 *CIL* IV, 3340, tab. 25. Also mentioned in the 153 wax tablets (*CIL* IV, 3340) were Babia Secunda, Caesaia Optata, Cornelia Saturnini, Histria Ichmas, Lydia Tyche, Popidia, and Tullia Lampyris. See Cooley and Cooley, *Sourcebook*, pp. 181–90 for translations of several of these. Jean Andreau, *Les affaires de Monsieur Jucundus*, Rome, 1974 is the definitive socio-economic study (cf. Jongman, Ch. 32).

16 *CIL* IV, 1136 (for rental notices in general, cf. Pirson, Ch. 29).

17 *CIL* X, 1030 (for the *bisellium*, cf. Franklin, Ch. 33; for the tomb, cf. George, Ch. 35 and Cormack, Ch. 37; for sculptural comparanda, cf. Welch, Ch. 36).

18 *CIL* IV, 8259. For the rivalry of two men over Iris in a series of three *graffiti*, see: Cooley and Cooley, *Sourcebook*, pp. 77–8 (also cf. DeFelice, Ch. 30).

19 *CIL* IV, 1500 (for the wool industry, cf. Pirson, Ch. 29).

20 *CIL* X, 810. See Cooley and Cooley, *Sourcebook*, pp. 98–101. See also A. Mau, "Osservazioni sull'edifizio di Eumachia in Pompei," *RM*, 1892, vol. 7, pp. 113–43; G. Spano, "L'Edificio di Eumachia in Pompei," *RendNap*, 1961, vol. 36, pp. 5–35; L. Richardson, jr, "Concordia and concordia Augusta: Roma and Pompeii," *PP*, 1978, vol. 33, pp. 260–72; J. J. Dobbins, "Problems of chronology, decoration, and urban design in the Forum at Pompeii," *AJA*, 1994, vol. 98, pp. 647–61. See also Descœudres, Ch. 2.

21 *CIL* X, 846, 848; August Mau, *Pompeii: its life and art* (transl. and ed. by F. W. Kelsey), rev. edn, London, 1902, p. 170. See also N. Blanc, H. Eristov and M. Fincker, "*A Fundamento restituit?* Réflections dans le temple d'Isis à Pompei," *RA*, 2000, pp. 227–309. P. Castrén, *Ordo populusque Pompeianus*, Rome, 1975, pp. 157, 207–8 identifies *CIL* X, 848 as a reference to a mother, father and son. The mother Corelia Celsa's name is in the nominative; the others are in the genitive. It is possible that Corelia Celsa contributed money for the reconstruction of the room (cf. Jongman, Ch. 32).

22 Much is written concerning women and their influence in the Roman world. See, for example: J. P. V. D. Balsdon, *Roman Women, their History and Habits*, London, 1962; S. Pomeroy, *Goddesses, Whores, Wives and Slaves: women in classical antiquity*, New York, 1975; S. Dixon, "A family business: women's role in patronage and politics at Rome, 80–44 BC," *ClMed*, 1983, vol. 34, pp. 91–112; J. F. Gardner, *Women in Roman Law and Society*, Bloomington, IN, 1991; S. Treggiari, *Roman Marriage*, Oxford, 1991; Kleiner and Matheson, *I Claudia*; D. E. E. Kleiner and S. B. Matheson (eds), *I Claudia II. Women in Roman art and society*, Austin, TX, 2000.

23 *CIL* IV, 7469.

24 *CIL* IV, 7347.

25 See Bernstein, *Public Role*, pp. 77–207, esp. the table on p. 206 for a list of notices; F. S. Bernstein, "Pompeian women and the programmata," *Studia Pompeiana et Classica in Honor of Wilhelmina Jashemski*, New Rochelle, NY, 1988, pp. 1–18; L. Savunen, "Women and elections in Pompeii," in B. Levick and R. Hawley (eds), *Women in Antiquity*, London, 1995, pp. 194–206.

26 *CIL* X, 1073. See above, n. 14.

27 Cf. Cormack, Ch. 37. Female slaves manumitted by a female patroness include: Castricia Prisca (*PNoc* 25 OS); Clodia Nigella (*PNoc* 5 OS); Hegia Quinta (*NSc*, 1894, p. 385); Mescinia Veneria (*CIL* X, 1054); Stallia Haphe (*PNoc* 21 OS); Titia Optata and Titia Vesbina (*NSc*, 1887, p. 34); Tironia Repentina (*PNoc* 50 OS). Female slaves manumitted by a male patron include: Arria Utile (*CIL* X, 1044); Audia Statia (*CIL* X, 1048); Cornelia Heraes (*CIL* X, 1049); Dellia Chia (*NSc*, 1894, p. 15); Flavia Agathea (*PNoc* 7 OS); Mancia Doris (*NSc*, 1887, p. 33); Melissaea Asia (*CIL* X, 1010); Muttia Salvia (*CIL* X, 1075); Petacia Vitalis (*NSc*, 1893, p. 333); Pithia Rufilla (*PNoc* 15 ES).

28 MNN inv. no. 6168. See S. A. Muscettola, "Ritratto e società ad Ercolano," in M. Pagano (ed.), *Gli antichi Ercolanesi. Antropologia, società, economia*, Naples, 2000, p. 104; fig. 5. The statue was found in the so-called "Basilica" of Herculaneum, for which see T. Najbjerg, *Public Painted and Sculptural Programs of the Early Roman Empire: a case-study of the so-called Basilica in Herculaneum*, Ph.D. thesis, Princeton, NJ, 1997.

29 *CIL* X, 998; see Cooley and Cooley, *Sourcebook*, p. 97, pl. 5.3 for an illustration.

30 Fragmentary evidence suggests honorary statues were also dedicated to Alleia (*NSc*, 1890, p. 337) and Holconia (*CIL* X, 950).

31 Eumachia (*CIL* X, 810–13); Mamia (*CIL* X, 816, 998); Holconia (*CIL* X, 950); Istacidia Rufilla (*CIL* X, 999), Alleia Decimilla (*CIL* X, 1036); Clodia (*CIL* X, 1074a); Lassia (*CIL* X, 1074b); Aquvia Quarta (*CIL* X, 812); Alleia Maia (*NSc*, 1890, p. 333); Vabia Sabina (*CIL* X, 961).

32 *IG* XIV, 702 for the inscription and drawing.

33 The painting was located on the north face of the northeast pier in peristyle (53). See Richardson, *Casa dei Dioscuri*, p. 61. For the image, see Wm. Gell (engravings by J. P. Gandy), *Pompeiana: the topography, edifices, and ornaments of Pompeii*, London, 1832, vol. 2, p. 147, pl. 68. This figure is accessible in a digital edition of Gell: http://www.mediterranees.net/voyageurs/gell/Chapter_13.html (1 May 2005). Although Gell identifies her as the goddess Hygeia, Richardson suggests that she is a priestess.

34 MNN inv. no. 8946; J. Ward-Perkins and A. Claridge (eds), *Pompeii AD 79*, London, 1976, cat. no. 25.

35 See Ling, *Roman Painting*, p. 162, fig. 174; MNN inv. no. 8924.

36 For paintings of priestesses, see MNN inv. nos. 4946, 8949, 9454; Helbig, *Wandegemalde*, no. 1556. See also R. Herbig, *Nugae Pompeianorum. Unbekannte Wandmalereien des dritten pompejanischen Stils*, Tübingen, 1962, Taf. 32. For the Villa of the Mysteries, see A. Maiuri, *La Villa dei Misteri*, 2 vols, Rome, 1931; E. K. Gazda (ed.), *The Villa of the Mysteries in Pompeii. Ancient ritual, modern muse*, Ann Arbor, MI, 2000.

37 Carratelli and Baldassarre, *Pitture e mosaici*, 2003, vol. 10, pp. 337–40.

38 Carratelli and Baldassarre, *Pitture e mosaici*, 1990, vol. 2, pp. 876–80; Jashemski, *Gardens*, vol. 1, pp. 118–19; fig. 189.

CHAPTER THIRTY-FIVE

THE LIVES OF SLAVES

—— •❖• ——

Michele George

INTRODUCTION

Recapturing the lives of slaves in the Roman era presents a challenge to modern scholars because of the peripheral and occasional role they play in written and visual evidence. Ironically, however, the fragmentary evidence that does exist clearly demonstrates that slaves were ubiquitous in the Roman world, and that their labour in villas and in urban manufacturing establishments was both essential to the ancient economy and encompassed all facets of domestic life (cf. Jongman, Ch. 32). The written evidence for slavery from Rome provides a framework that can be combined with documentary material from Pompeii and Herculaneum to obtain an approximation of slave life. Of greater value is the quality and quantity of the archaeological evidence, which allows us to restore slaves to the Vesuvian landscape in a unique way. By looking at the tasks slaves performed, the tools they used, and the places where they worked, we can discover the scope of servile involvement in daily life and reach some understanding of the slave experience. Placing slaves in context is especially fruitful in Pompeii and Herculaneum because nowhere else are there so many well-preserved locales for slave activity.[1]

Defining the work of slaves, however, is easier than understanding the world of their thoughts and feelings, since the written evidence is so minimal. On many issues, therefore, we must be content with mere impressions of what it was like to be a Roman slave. The problem is compounded by the variegated nature of Roman slavery, which undermines any sweeping generalities we might make about the lives of slaves. Slaves might have endured great cruelty or great affection; they might have been forced to toil long hours under inhumane conditions, or have been given significant responsibilities and some degree of autonomy. The quality of slaves' lives, from the food they ate to the clothes they wore to the hardships they suffered, depended entirely on the inclination of their owners. Still, by marshalling all of the available evidence and by using inference and imagination, it is possible in some measure to reconstitute the slave's perspective.

SLAVES IN THE HOUSE

In the domestic context the slave members of the household, the *familia*, performed a wide range of jobs, both menial and administrative, and slaves are visible in the house through the items they used in their work, such as kitchen ware (food preparation and service), loom-weights (cloth production), combs, and implements of every kind (cf. Allison, Ch. 17; Berry, Ch. 19; Figures 17.3, 19.3–4). Matching slaves to their domestic jobs has been made easier by recent studies of the artefacts in Pompeian houses and their distribution, which have revealed that vessels and tools were found throughout the house, including the *atrium, triclinium* and peristyle, areas whose function has been conventionally defined as formal guest reception (cf. Allison, Ch. 17; Wallace-Hadrill, Ch. 18). Slaves were integral elements in Pompeian houses, and moved throughout as their work demanded. Obvious service areas within the house (such as kitchens and stables) were places where some slaves spent most of their lives, and the utilitarian decoration of plaster or simple wall painting that typifies them reveals the drab environment in which many slaves lived (Figure 20.1).[2] But slave activity was not confined to these areas, because the tasks they carried out in Pompeian houses varied so enormously, and were not only of a menial nature, but might include more responsible assignments such as secretarial duties, child-minding, and serving as a personal maid or manservant. Domestic slaves, moreover, were not restricted to the house, but were used as agents for the slave-owner and his family in the world beyond, giving them a visibility throughout the town—running errands in the forum for the master's wife, accompanying a child to school. In this role as instruments of their owners, slaves could even be compelled to commit acts that were socially unacceptable for slave-owners themselves: witness the gang of slaves at Herculaneum who hurled stones at the door of a neighbour because of some unknown quarrel.[3]

As in any mixed household, the emotional rhythms and daily interaction in the Pompeian house between slave and slave-owner were probably diverse, and because close contact was frequent and necessary, emotional bonds grew among slaves and family members, as abundant evidence from Rome demonstrates. An affectionate relationship sometimes developed between a slave child-minder and her charge. *Vernae*, house-born slaves who were the offspring of two domestic slaves, or sometimes of the master and a slave, were often held in high esteem and given special treatment. The domestic picture, however, should not be idealized, for slaves could never afford to forget the fundamental inequities of their circumstances or be sure of their owners' benevolence. Curtailment of freedom and even violent punishment could be inflicted on a whim, and the leg irons found in a cupboard in the House of the Venus in Bikini (I.11.6) at Pompeii attest to the dark side of the master/slave relationship in the house. Sexual coercion, moreover, of both male and female slaves at an owner's hands was common; *graffiti* which advertise *vernae* for sexual purposes stand in sharp contrast to the loving commemorations they receive in funerary inscriptions, and show that their position in the household was not always privileged.[4]

In most Campanian houses, there is little evidence of where slaves slept, and they may have been housed in missing upper storeys or underground storage rooms, or have used convenient corners near their work area, or simply the floor outside their master's door (cf. Allison, Ch. 17).[5] The lack of permanent and identifiable sleeping facilities for domestic slaves in even the largest houses betrays their marginal position in Pompeian society, despite the ties that evolved with members of their slave-owning family, and the systematic denial of a "place of their own" within the house.

Long-lasting intimate attachments did develop among household slaves themselves —abiding friendships as well as sexual relationships—and although slaves were not able to marry legally, they did form unofficial unions (*contubernia*) which produced offspring. While uncertainty about status remains, many of the *graffiti* in Pompeian houses that mention explicit sex acts must refer to slaves, belonging to the same or neighbouring households. Mutual accommodation enabled both slave and free members of the household to maintain intimate relationships in relatively cramped physical conditions, possibly because the free family regarded slaves as animate objects, omnipresent eyes and ears which could be privy to moments of anger and intimacy. The free family's ability to ignore slaves can be attributed partly to the fact that Roman slaves were "body slaves", who performed tasks of personal hygiene for their owners. Standards of modesty which operated between social peers did not apply to the same degree to slaves, who were not considered fully human, and erotic paintings from Pompeii which depict graphic sex scenes often include slaves who stand by with lamps or wash basins and towels, apparently disregarded by the participants.[6]

Domestic religion offers another glimpse into the slave *mentalité*. The shrines (*lararia*) that appear most often in Pompeian kitchens generally have depictions of the guiding spirit (*genius*) of the *paterfamilias*, or male head of the household, who sacrifices in the presence of the protective *Lares* (Figure 23.4). That these shrines were for the slave *familia* seems probable, since similar shrines are also commonly found in manufacturing and commercial establishments. Furthermore, they differ from those found in the *atrium* and peristyle, which were principally for worship by the slave-owner and his family.[7] The dichotomy in ritual suggested by these differences points to two spheres within domestic religion, which may have contributed to the formation of a collective slave identity in the house. The shared experience of cult practice thus fostered emotional bonds among slaves, creating a sense of community within the household while at the same time reinforcing the status distinctions between slave and slave-owner. More significantly, cult practice strengthened the tie between the slave's identity and his master's, for it is the *genius* of the *paterfamilias*, the spirit aspect of the master who protects and sustains the family fortunes, to whom the slave pours libations and utters prayers. Thus, the slave's subordination was renewed through the very act of household ritual.[8]

On certain feast days the entire household, free and servile, worshipped the household gods together, under the supervision of the master. A kitchen shrine in House (I.13.2) at Pompeii may depict just such an occasion (cf. Bernstein, Ch. 34; Figure 35.1).[9] The scene is unique among Pompeian *lararia* in the large number of worshippers who are shown. It has been tentatively identified as a sacrifice to the domestic *Lares* by the assembled members of the household: the *paterfamilias*, his wife and their slaves. Such an identification, though conjectural, accords with the notion that a unified, familial identity which was firmly attached to the master and his house formed a critical part of the identity of the household slave. Feast days that were celebrated in the house served a similar function. The *Saturnalia*, a holiday that fell at the end of December, was an especially significant celebration for slaves, for on this occasion a reversal of roles between slave-owner and slave occurred: slaves were served dinner by their masters, and were allowed to use more familiar forms of address. This temporary inversion of the social order can be read as a way of maintaining the status quo by providing a socially sanctioned, and therefore safe, release for frustration, thus ensuring good behaviour for the rest of the year.[10]

Figure 35.1 Kitchen shrine painting depicting a *familia*, from House (I.13.2).
Photo: P. W. Foss.

SLAVES IN BUSINESS

When the focus shifts from the house to the street, slaves remain ubiquitous if still somewhat elusive. The numerous small shops that crowded the streets of Pompeii relied on an extensive slave work force in large and small commercial and manufacturing enterprises (cf. Pirson, Ch. 29; Jongman, Ch. 32). Some establishments functioned entirely on servile labour, while others used a combination of slaves and free poor. Although freedmen probably outnumbered slaves at the supervisory level, in some cases trusted slaves also acted as business managers (*institores*) who, overseeing production and sales and answering directly to their owners, enjoyed a marked degree of freedom. Slaves could also serve as their masters' representatives in business matters, as attested by seals inscribed with slaves' names, and by the tablets of L. Caecilius Iucundus, in which slaves acted on their master's behalf in the payment of public debts.[11]

Businesses that were integrated into large houses, such as the bakery in the House of the Labyrinth (VI.11.8–10), or which used converted houses (e.g., the *fullonica* at VI.8.20–21; Figure 29.4a), had space and practical features such as kitchens and latrines to accommodate the servile work force, as did many small-scale shops (e.g., the *fullonica* of Stephanus at [I.6.7]; Figure 35.2).[12] Many shops, however, had no extra space, and it is possible in such cases that the labourers, free and servile, lived elsewhere. Paintings and sketches of life in manufacturing establishments show a coordinated workforce, suggesting that camaraderie evolved in the workplace (Figures 29.4b–d), and names scratched on the walls of shops are possible vestigial imprints of slave workers.[13] Close and complex relationships between workers are evinced by the *graffiti*, some of which are obscene, and point to group identification among workers in certain trades. A particularly skilled slave could distinguish himself in a trade despite his servile status, and business success probably eased the path to manumission. The high number of freedmen named in Pompeian inscriptions, especially among those indicating involvement in manufacturing, suggests that many followed such a path. Furthermore, the prominence of freedmen in occupational organizations (*collegia*), and the frequency with which they display themselves in work scenes on funerary monuments, demonstrates the importance of work as a vehicle for self-representation.[14] By extension, it is reasonable to assume that work was a critical element in the construction of slave identity, for it was success in business, in garnering high profits for the master and a reputation in the community for themselves, which increased the chances for manumission. The bond of identification between *liberti* and their occupations did not begin with free status, therefore, but was rooted in the servile experience, and within every prosperous freedman at Pompeii we must see the aspiring slave, while remembering the less fortunate peers with whom he once laboured.[15]

Figure 35.2 View of basins in the Fullonica of Stephanus (I.6.7).
Photo: P. W. Foss.

SLAVES IN THE COUNTRY

Slaves were even more numerous and more important in the agricultural economy of Pompeii than in the manufacturing and commercial sectors, and every Campanian villa that produced olive oil or wine used a substantial corps of slave labour (cf. Moormann, Ch. 28). Traces of rural slavery can be seen in the work areas of villas, among the mills, wine and oil presses, and stables (Figures 28.4 and 28.5); here slaves may have lived in rows of *cellae*, small, undecorated rooms with beaten earth floors, shaft windows and small niches for lamps. From the Villa of the Mosaic Columns, located just beyond the Porta Ercolano, comes a more gruesome reminder of servile existence; in the underground slave prison (*ergastulum*), a skeleton was found chained around the legs, two tibia still bound by iron circles of stocks anchored in the ground.[16]

Distinctions in living circumstances and work load existed among rural slaves as among domestics, but to a lesser degree. Overseers of villas (*vilici*), usually slaves themselves, enjoyed greater privileges than their rural counterparts, although some slaves on villas were allowed to keep livestock or a small plot to augment their rations. In general, however, agricultural slaves had a much more miserable existence than their domestic and urban counterparts. Categorized by Varro as "articulate tools", most rural slaves were given minimal clothing and rations. They spent their days at strenuous physical labour, and their nights chained in the semi-subterranean *ergastula*, several packed into a small cell. They had little chance to acquire new skills with which they might prove themselves to their owners, or to develop a relationship with him that could lead to manumission.[17]

SLAVES IN THE COMMUNITY

Other categories of slavery provided specialized services to Pompeian society and exposed slaves to danger on a daily basis. Among these were the gladiators who entertained in the amphitheatre of Pompeii, most of whom were slaves, purchased by businessmen for their natural strength and physique, and trained and rented out in groups for public performance. A school for gladiators (*ludus gladiatorius*) was built in the portico of the theatre, and excavation of its rooms has uncovered kitchen facilities, armour, and eighteen skeletons (cf. Parslow, Ch. 14). Stairs led to an *ergastulum*, where iron stocks and four more skeletons were found, though unchained. *Graffiti* which cite by name the performances of individual gladiators and even include sketches of duelling opponents, record the popularity achieved by these stars of the arena, but only the strongest and the most fortunate lived long enough to enjoy the adulation or obtain free status.[18]

Another brutal reality of Roman slavery which is well attested at Pompeii is prostitution, which involved both male and female slaves who were purchased for their youth and beauty, and forced to work in the sex trade (cf. DeFelice, Ch. 30). The most elaborate brothel (*lupanar*) at Pompeii (VII.12.18–20) is a dismal place, its narrow cells bearing crude painted sex acts over the doors, and its walls covered with *graffiti* that lists feminine names of Greek origin (Figure 35.3). While some names are probably pseudonyms used by freeborn women, it is probable that in such an establishment the majority had servile status. Advertisements for sexual services offered by individuals show that the sex trade also operated on a smaller scale, and

Figure 35.3 View into interior corridor of *lupanar* (VII.12.18–20), flanked by cubicles.
Photo: P. W. Foss.

although the status of these men and women is uncertain, some of them could have been slaves working for a procurer. Scant evidence of their lives survives, but the misery of sexual servitude, with its constant exposure to violence and disease, cannot be overestimated.[19]

There is no evidence from Pompeii for the slave social groups and burial clubs (*collegia*) which are attested at Rome, and in a small town such as Pompeii slave identity was more closely tied to his slave-owner and his family, and his servile peers. Most slaves worked for individual masters, but the town of Pompeii itself owned slaves, who were probably used for municipal construction and repair work, as well as tasks of greater responsibility.[20] Slaves of prominent families were also allowed to participate in the imperial cult as *ministri Augusti*, one of the minor priesthoods in the imperial cult. In this way preferred slaves who were marked for manumission might be introduced into the civic roles that would be open to them as freedmen, granting them a profile in the community and a degree of social status that their peers lacked. Involvement in such an institution gave the slave prestige and helped to assimilate him into the local elite, while at the same time acting as an inducement to hard work and ensuring good citizenship after manumission.[21]

Even so, slaves who received preferential treatment were still subordinate possessions, with only as much independence as their master allowed, always on the slave-owner's terms, and to his financial advantage. The close tie between slave and master that the nomenclature of slaves reflects continued after manumission, and entailed important social obligations.[22] Manumission was a critically important part of the Roman slavery system, a control mechanism that discouraged flight and bad behaviour by giving hope for a better future (cf. Jongman, Ch. 32). It was given to favoured slaves, mostly urban rather than rural, who had proven their loyalty, or whose freedom was financially beneficial to their owner. The possibility of manumission strengthened the tie between master and slave, and discouraged the development of a strong collective identity among slaves of different households. In the lives of most slaves, however, manumission's role was psychological, a powerful motivator rather than an attainable goal, a mirage pursued but never gained, and it must be remembered that, despite the high number of *liberti* among the population, the majority of Pompeian slaves died without achieving it.[23]

The obscurity in which the lives of Pompeian slaves languished extended to death and commemoration. Although slaves in wealthy Roman households were memorialized in collective tombs, most slaves lacked the resources to provide funeral markers for themselves or their loved ones, and it seems that, as in so many other things, this was contingent upon the will of the slave-owner.[24] In the *necropoleis* outside the Porta Nocera and Porta Ercolano, however, grave *stelae* were found which were possibly memorials to slaves. Dubbed "herm-*stelae*" or *columellae*, the flat, schematic silhouettes of human heads are rendered in a variety of stone, and set up at tombs, often in groups (cf. Cormack, Ch. 37; Figures 37.6a–b). Herm-*stelae* are found mostly in Campania, but their function is uncertain, for not all served as grave-markers.[25] Some are inscribed with a full Roman name (*tria nomina*), but others bear only single Greek names, which raises the possibility that they were intended for slaves. Many give the age at death, and among these young children are dominant, implying that they were favoured slaves, probably *vernae*.[26] More intriguing are those herm-*stelae* with no inscription, a group that comprises nearly two-thirds of the roughly 500 that have been found. The anonymity of such a memorial is appropriate to the low status of slaves, and their appearance in family tombs demonstrates again the subordination of the slave identity to the master's, in death as in life. Yet, if they do in fact commemorate slaves, the very existence of this crowd of nameless dead might also reflect affective ties between slave and slave-owner.

CONCLUSION

Although slaves resist our scrutiny more than any other residents of Pompeii, they were nevertheless inextricably woven into the fabric of Pompeian life, and encountered at every turn—serving at a food stand (*thermopolium*), cleaning up and stoking the furnace at the baths, shopping for the master's dinner. A more sombre scenario, however, was also played out in Pompeii's streets: slaves bought and sold at public auction, a common occurrence which might be seen in any corner of the forum or public area. The decision to sell a slave was taken at the slave-owner's convenience— to pay off debts; to obtain capital to finance a new venture; to turn a profit on a house-born slave; to be rid of an aging or feeble slave. As commodities, slaves were vulnerable to swift reversals of fortune, and servile families were routinely broken up, parents separated from children, and slave spouses cut off from one another.[27] By contrast, for the unlucky slave of a cruel master, sale to a new owner represented escape from a life of despair. The mix of dread and hope the slave auction engendered in the slave population was at once both real and profound, another symbol of the powerlessness at the centre of a slave's life. The reconstruction of its role in the consciousness of Pompeian slaves requires the same imaginative leap that accompanies every search into the past, but which is especially essential for understanding slavery. But with that leap, every glance at the Pompeian townscape conjures up the slaves who, though now evanescent, once permeated the city.

NOTES

1 General works on Roman slavery: K. Hopkins, *Conquerors and Slaves: sociological studies in Roman history*, vol. I, Cambridge, 1978; M. I. Finley, *Ancient Slavery and Modern Ideology*, London, 1980; T. Wiedemann, *Greek and Roman Slavery*, London, 1981; K. R. Bradley, *Slaves and Masters in the Roman Empire: a study in social control*, Oxford, 1987; K. R. Bradley, *Slavery and Society at Rome*, Cambridge, 1994. For the archaeology of ancient slavery, see F. H. Thompson, *The Archaeology of Greek and Roman Slavery*, London, 2003. For estimates of the servile population of Pompeii, see J. Andreau, *Les affaires de Monsieur Jucundus*, Rome, 1974, pp. 126–30. Written sources from the Vesuvian region include *graffiti*, inscriptions, the wax-tablet accounts of Pompeian banker L. Caecilius Iucundus, and legal records found in Herculaneum. For L. Caecilius Iucundus: Andreau, *Monsieur Jucundus*; for Herculaneum: V. Arangio-Ruiz, *Studi epigrafici e papirologici* (L. Bove, ed.), Naples, 1974. *Graffiti* and inscriptions are found in *CIL* IV and X; see Laidlaw, Ch. 39. See also: M. Della Corte, *Case ed abitanti di Pompei*, 3rd edn, Naples, 1965; P. Castrén, *Ordo populusque Pompeianus*, Rome, 1975; J. L. Franklin Jr, *Pompeii: the electoral programmata, campaigns and politics, AD 71–79*, Rome, 1980; H. Mouritsen, *Elections, Magistrates and Municipal Elite. Studies in Pompeian Epigraphy*, Rome, 1988; A. Varone, *Erotica pompeiana: iscrizioni d'amore sui muri di Pompei*, Naples, 1994. See also now E. Fentress, J. Bodel, F. Coarelli, P. Braconi and G. Pucci's articles in: "Selling people: five papers on Roman slave-traders and the buildings they used", *JRA*, 2005, vol. 18, pp. 180–240.

2 See A. Wallace-Hadrill, *Houses and Society in Pompeii and Herculaneum*, Princeton, NJ, 1994, p. 39–44; figs 3.2, 3.6

3 Four slaves belonging to a woman, Caria Longina, and several slaves of another owner were part of the group, which was presumably instructed to harass L. Cominius Primus (Arangio-Ruiz, *Studi epigrafici*, p. 304; Wallace-Hadrill, *Houses and Society*, pp. 178–9). For artefact distribution in Pompeian houses, see: P. M. Allison, *The Distribution of Pompeian House Contents and its Significance*, Ph.D. thesis, University of Sydney 1992, Ann Arbor, MI, 1994; J. Berry, "Household artefacts: towards a reinterpretation of Roman domestic space", in R. Laurence and A. Wallace-Hadrill (eds), *Domestic Space in the Roman World: Pompeii and beyond*, JRA Suppl. Ser. no. 22, 1997, pp. 183–95. For slave jobs in the household, see: S. Treggiari, "Domestic staff at Rome in the Julio-Claudian period, 27 BC to AD 68", *Histoire Sociale/Social History*, 1973, vol. 6, pp. 241–55; S. Treggiari, "Jobs in the household of Livia", *PBSR*, 1975, vol. 43, pp. 48–77. The famous painted scenes (Figure 23.12) showing activity in the forum, from the *Praedia* of Julia Felix (II.4), probably include, among the figures, slaves whom we cannot identify with certainty (S. C. Nappo, "Fregio dipinto dal *praedium* di Giulia Felice con rappresentazione del foro di Pompei", *RStPomp*, 1989, vol. 3, pp. 79–96).

4 Affectionate relationships: K. R. Bradley, *Discovering the Roman Family*, Oxford, 1991, pp. 13–75; the slave viewpoint: S. Joshel, "Nurturing the master's child: slavery and the Roman child-nurse", *Signs*, 1986, vol. 12, pp. 3–22; sexual abuse: Bradley, *Slaves and Masters*, pp. 118–33; leg irons: Allison, *Pompeian House Contents*, p. 151. *Vernae*: B. Rawson, "Children in the Roman *familia*", in B. Rawson (ed.), *The Family in Ancient Rome—new perspectives*, London, 1986, pp. 186–95; *vernae* in sexual *graffiti*: *CIL* IV, 4023, 4025, 4699, 5203, 5204, 5206. These women might have worked independently, gathering money for their slave savings (*peculium*), money from tips or gifts of property held by the slave (although legally the property of the slave-owner) that might be used to buy freedom, or for investment after obtaining it (Bradley, *Slaves and Masters*, pp. 108–10). But it is equally possible that they were compelled

to have sex for their masters' profit. The use of *"verna"* in advertisements indicates that some customers valued the sheltered background of the house-born slave over the unknown origins of foreign-born prostitutes. For the pre-eminence of *vernae* in the household, see Bradley, *Slavery and Society*, pp. 33–5.

5 Slave quarters are found in the House of the Menander (I.10.4), but are difficult to pinpoint in most houses. See M. George, *"Servus* and *domus*: the slave in the Roman house", in Laurence and Wallace-Hadrill, *Domestic Space*, pp. 15–24.

6 *Graffiti*: e.g., *Staphylus hic cum Quieta*, literally, "Staphylus and Quieta were here", but probably with an elliptical sexual meaning (*CIL* IV, 4087) from the house of L. Caecilius Iucundus (V.1.18); *Romula hic cum Staphylo moratur*, "Romula and Staphylos had sex here", from a column in the *atrium* of (VII.13.8), possibly the same man who could not resist an opportunity for self-advertisement. More romantic and evocative is the heartfelt plea to Venus of the slave Methe, and Chrestus, whose status is unspecified but whose Greek name makes servile status or ancestry a distinct possibility: *Methe Cominiaes Atellana amat Chrestum. Corde {si}t utreis que Venus Pompeiana propitia et sem{per} concordes veivant*, "Methe Atellana, slave of Cominia, loves Chrestus. May Venus Pompeiana favour them together (as a couple?) and may they always live in harmony", (*CIL* IV, 2457, found in a corridor of the theatre; see Varone, *Erotica pompeiana*, pp. 43–4, 154 n. 282 and *passim*). Slaves in erotic scenes: D. Michel, "Bemerkungen über Zuschauerfiguren in pompejanischen sogenannten Tafelbildern", *La regione sotterrata dal Vesuvio. Studi e prospettivi*, Atti del convegno internazionale 11–15 novembre 1979, Napoli, 1982, pp. 537–98; M. Myerowitz, "The domestication of desire: Ovid's *Parva Tabella* and the Theatre of Love", in A. Richlin (ed.), *Pornography and Representation in Greece and Rome*, Oxford, 1992, pp. 131–57; J. R. Clarke, *Looking at Lovemaking*, Berkeley, CA, 1998; A. Varone, *Eroticism in Pompeii*, Los Angeles, CA, 2001, pp. 74–9; privacy in the house: M. George, "Repopulating the Roman house", in B. Rawson and P. Weaver (eds), *The Roman Family in Italy—status, sentiment, space*, Oxford, 1997, pp. 299–319.

7 T. Fröhlich, *Lararien- und Fassadenbilder in den Vesuvstädten: Untersuchungen zur "volkstümlichen" pompejanischen Malerei*, RM-EH, 32, Mainz, 1991; P. Foss, "Watchful Lares: Roman household organization and the rituals of cooking and eating", in Laurence and Wallace-Hadrill, *Domestic Space*, pp. 196–218. Shrines in the *atrium* and peristyle usually feature the ancestral guardian deities called the *penates*, whose cult was overseen by the *paterfamilias*.

8 Note the inclusion of the servile *familia* in the prayer given by Cato for the purification of land (*Agr.* 141).

9 Fröhlich, *Lararien*, pp. 178–9, 261; pls. 28.1–2. A male and female stand beside two rows of 13 figures, uniformly attired in white, short-sleeved tunics, and making the same arm gesture.

10 For the *Saturnalia* and other festivals relevant to slaves (e.g., the *Matronalia*, March 1, when mistresses served special meals to slaves; the *Compitalia*, January 3–5, when symbols of slavery were removed from slaves): Bradley, *Slaves and Masters*, pp. 40–3. Not all masters were prepared to assume the slave's role, even for a day; see Cic., *Att.* 13.52.2; Plin., *Ep.* 2.17.22. A small sketch beside the kitchen *lararium* in the House of Obellius Firmus (IX.14.2, 4) shows a group of individuals wearing tunics, seated and drinking around a table. Fröhlich, *Lararien*, pp. 33, 299; pl. 48.1 suggests it could be a depiction of a Saturnalian celebration.

11 See Andreau, *Monsieur Jucundus*, p. 297 for *amphorae* stamped with the names of slaves who probably served as managers of *officinae*; for seals, see: Mouritsen, *Elections*, p. 14 n. 35. For slaves paying debts on L. Caecilius Iucundus' behalf, see: Andreau, *Monsieur Jucundus*, p. 44; for *institores*: J.-J. Aubert, *Business Managers in Ancient Rome*, Leiden, 1994.

12 Bakeries: B. Mayeske, *Bakeries, Bakers and Bread at Pompeii: a study in social and economic history*, Ph.D. thesis, University of Maryland 1972, pp. 177–80; fulleries: W. O. Moeller, *The Wool Trade of Ancient Pompeii*, 1976.

13 Work scenes: e.g. of fulling from (VI.8.20–22), and of a possible trial scene involving fullers from (VI.14.20): G. P. Carratelli and I. Baldassarre (eds), *Pompei, pitture e mosaici*, Rome, 1990, vol. 2, fig. 23; 1994, vol. 5, figs 34a–d, 35–9; J. R. Clarke, *Art in the Lives of Ordinary Romans*, Berkeley, CA, 2003. For workers' *graffiti*, e.g., a room in *textrina* (I.10.8) has *graffiti* with the names of five men and two women; in *textrina* (VI.13.6) *graffiti* indicates there were seven male weavers and eleven female spinners (Moeller, *Wool Trade*, pp. 39–40). A full name is often omitted in *graffiti*, and servile status cannot be ascertained from a Greek name alone,

although single Greek names have a high probability of belonging to slaves. Cf. also Pirson, Ch. 29.

14 For collegia at Pompeii, see J. Liu, *Occupation, social organization, and public service in the textile workers' associations (collegia centonariorum) in ancient Rome (first century BC-fourth century AD)*, Ph.D. thesis, Columbia University, 2004, pp. 109–14, 116–21, 247–52.

15 Freedmen and work: P. Garnsey, "Independent freedmen and the economy of Roman Italy under the principate", *Klio*, 1981, vol. 63, pp. 359–71; N. Kampen, *Image and Status: Roman working women in Ostia*, Berlin, 1981; G. Zimmer, *Römische Berufdarstellungen*, Berlin, 1982; S. Joshel, *Work, Identity and Legal Status at Rome: a study of the occupational inscriptions*, London, 1992.

16 For villas, e.g. V. Kockel and B. F. Weber, "Die Villa delle Colonne a Mosaico in Pompeji", *RM*, 1983, vol. 90, pp. 51–89; V. Kockel, "Archäologische Funde und Forschungen in den Vesuvstädten I", *AA*, 1985, p. 542. For iron stocks: M. Della Corte, "Scavi eseguiti da private nel territorio di Pompeii", *NSc*, 1922, pp. 459ff.; for stocks with two tibia extant: G. Spano, *NSc*, 1910, pp. 259ff., fig. 3; for stocks with a capacity for fourteen slaves at a time: M. Della Corte, *NSc*, 1923, p. 277.

17 Varro, *Rust.* 1.17.1; for a summary of the ancient sources on rural slavery, see K. D. White, *Roman Farming*, Ithaca, NY, 1970, pp. 332–83.

18 Among the skeletons was a female with costly jewellery, probably not a slave, but a citizen trying to escape the disaster of the eruption. For gladiators at Pompeii: P. Sabbatini Tumolesi, *Gladiatorum paria—annunci di spettacoli gladiatorii à Pompei*, Rome, 1980; F. Maulucci Vivolo, *Pompei: i graffiti figurati*, Foggia, 1993; L. Jacobelli, *Gladiators at Pompeii*, Los Angeles, CA, 2003. For the *ludus gladiatorius* in the theatre portico: J. Overbeck and A. Mau, *Pompeji in seinen Gebäuden, Alterhümern und Kunstwerken*, 4th edn, Leipzig, 1884, pp. 193–6; A. and M. De Vos, *Pompei, Ercolano, Stabia*, Rome-Bari, 1982, pp. 67–9; Jacobelli, *Gladiators*, pp. 66–7. A private *ludus gladiatorius* has been identified in a house at (V.5.3), because of numerous gladiatorial *graffiti* on the columns of the peristyle: A. Mau, "Iscrizioni gladiatorie di Pompei", *RM*, 1890, vol. 5, pp. 25–39; A. Sogliano, *NSc*, 1899, pp. 228ff., 347; Jacobelli, *Gladiators*, pp. 65–6.

19 A. Wallace-Hadrill, "Public honor and private shame: the urban texture of Pompeii", in T. J. Cornell and K. Lomas (eds) *Urban Society in Roman Italy*, London, 1995, pp. 33–62. For wall paintings in the *lupanar* at Pompeii, see Clarke, *Ordinary Romans*, pls. 79–85. See also now T. A. J. McGinn, *The Economy of Prostitution in the Roman World*, Ann Arbor, MI, 2004. A cleaned and restored *lupanar* was re-opened to the public in 2006.

20 One *servus coloniae*, Secundus, appears in the accounts of L. Caecilius Iucundus first as a witness to debt payments in AD 53, and then in AD 58 as a freedman and witness to another transaction (Andreau, *Monsieur Jucundus*, p. 53; cf. Welch, Ch. 36, re: Vesonius Primus). For public slaves, see W. Eder, *Servitus Publica: Untersuchungen zur Entstehung, Entwicklung und Funktion der öffentlichen Sklaverei in Rom*, Wiesbaden, 1980.

21 *Ministri Augusti*: e.g., Nymphodotus, one of several slaves who appear in the records of L. Caecilius Iucundus first as servile *ministri*, and then as *liberti* in later tablets. See Andreau, *Monsieur Jucundus*, pp. 205–8; Castrén, *Ordo*, pp. 76f.; Mouritsen, *Elections*, p. 92.

22 Freed slaves usually retained their servile personal name as a *cognomen* and assumed their master's *praenomen* and *nomen*.

23 Manumission: W. M. Jongman, *The Economy and Society of Pompeii*, Amsterdam, 1988, p. 241; Bradley, *Slavery and Society*, pp. 154–65.

24 Slaves in the *columbarium* of Livia at Rome: Treggiari, "Jobs in the household".

25 A. D'Ambrosio and S. De Caro, *Un impegno per Pompei: Fotopiano e documentazione della Necropoli di Porta Nocera*, Milan, 1983; A. D'Ambrosio and S. De Caro, "La necropoli di Porta Nocera. Campagna di scavo 1983", in H. von Hesberg and P. Zanker (eds), *Römische Gräberstrassen—Selbstdarstellung—Status—Standard*, Munich, 1987, pp. 199–228. V. Kockel, *Die Grabbauten vor dem Herkulaner Tor in Pompeji*, Mainz, 1983, pp. 16–18; V. Kockel, "Im Tode gleich? Die sullanischen Kolonisten und ihr kulturelles Gewicht in Pompeji am Beispiel der Nekropolen", in Von Hesberg and Zanker, *Römische Gräberstrassen*, pp. 183–98, suggests that rather than grave markers, herm-*stelae* were meant to represent the guiding spirit (the *genius* for men, the

Juno for women) of the deceased (cf. Small, Ch. 13). See also V. Hope, "A roof over the dead: communal tombs and family structure", in Laurence and Wallace-Hadrill, *Domestic Space*, pp. 84–6.

26 E.g., from the necropolis outside the Porta Ercolano: FORTUNATUS VIXIT ANNIS II, "Fortunatus lived two years" (*CIL* X, 1012; Kockel, *Herkulaner Tor*, p. 69); Porta Nocera necropolis: HELLE PUELLA VIXIT ANNIS IV, "the girl Helle lived four years" (D'Ambrosio and De Caro, *Un impegno*, *PNoc* 19a OS). The tomb of C. Munatius Faustus and Naevoleia Tyche (*PErc* S22; Figure 37.5) contains eight herm-*stelae*, of which five are inscribed with typical slave names, raising the possibility that they represent loyal members of the domestic *familia*. Of the remaining three herm-*stelae*, one has C. Munatius Faustus' own name, and two others are probably for two of his *liberti* (*PNoc* 9 ES). Naevoleia Tyche had her own substantial tomb in the Porta Nocera necropolis: Kockel, *Herkulaner Tor*, p. 100 (cf. Bernstein, Ch. 34; Cormack, Ch. 37, n.1 for an explanation of the numbering and abbreviation system for cemeteries at Pompeii).

27 Slaves sold at auction: Andreau, *Monsieur Jucundus*, pp. 107–9; 118–19; Bradley, *Slaves and Masters*, pp. 55–6, Bradley, *Slavery and Society*, pp. 51–6; Fentress *et al.*, "Selling People".

CHAPTER THIRTY-SIX

POMPEIAN MEN
AND WOMEN IN PORTRAIT
SCULPTURE

———— •◆• ————

Katherine E. Welch

INTRODUCTION[1]

In preserving Pompeii, the eruption of Vesuvius in AD 79 has provided the opportunity to examine the sculpted portraits of men and women of the early imperial period in a uniquely complete archaeological context—a context that enables one to describe vividly the social identities of the portrayed individuals. While most portrait statues that have come down from antiquity lack any precise indication of provenance or date, with the portraits from Pompeii, not only is there evidence of provenance and date, but also we often know where the portraits were displayed, and sometimes the occupations, public offices, religious affiliations, and even the taste in domestic decoration of the individuals portrayed. This unusually detailed information permits Pompeii to function as an important test case in the investigation of a key aspect of Roman portraiture: the relationship between portrait style (a somewhat subjective term, basically meaning "mode of representation"), social identity, and portrait setting. It also provides an opportunity to test the reliability of our traditional chronological model of stylistic development in portraiture—a model constructed in order to classify images in museums that lack such documentation.

There are some fifty private portraits from Pompeii about which a fair amount is known, more than from any other Roman site in the West. We are, therefore, better equipped here than anywhere else to reconstruct the intent and effect of these images within the social and aesthetic parameters of the community that produced them. We may interpret these images in relation to their viewers, and we may also investigate how portrait style and statue types were modified in relation to social identity and their intended architectural settings. As a group, the portraits from Pompeii offer an unparalleled opportunity to understand the conventions of self-representation of ancient Roman men and women from a range of different social levels and backgrounds within a single Italian municipality during the first century AD.

A portrait's find-spot indicates the relative prominence of an individual's image within the space of the community and thus suggests the individual's social status. If the portrait of a person was set up in a public context (forum, basilica, temple, etc.), it is likely that he or she was a person of influence. Portraits of less prominent members of the community, on the other hand, were confined to private (domestic or funerary) contexts. Besides the find-spot, the quality and format of the sculpture—equestrian (on horseback), cuirassed (with military breastplate), nude, hip mantle (nude with cloak wrapped around hips), togate, bust, herm (bust placed on vertical shaft)—are important indications of the social position of the represented person and how he or she may have wished to be viewed by society. Furthermore, dedicatory inscriptions, when they accompany the portrait, often provide information concerning social position and status. Other epigraphic sources that mention the person—building inscriptions, election posters, etc.—may provide additional relevant information.[2]

The best way to illustrate the remarkable strengths of the Pompeian material is to offer a survey of some of the portraits with a known find-spot and context, illustrating the portrait options selected by the different types of people in Pompeii. This can be done most effectively by proceeding from the public to the private and funerary spheres, beginning with portraits of elite individuals in the city, and then moving to the middle, or sub-elite, levels of the community.

PORTRAITS FROM PUBLIC CONTEXTS

The forum was the most prominent venue for public statuary display at Pompeii.[3] This space was dominated by a great pedestal, probably for a statue of Augustus in a *quadriga* (four-horse chariot) at the center of the south side of the forum. Originally used for the Roman state god, Jupiter Optimus Maximus, this was the most elevated of Roman statue formats, reserved only for the imperial family. On either side of this were two other bases for colossal statues of members of the imperial family. On the north side of the forum, on either side of the Temple of Jupiter, stood arches. On analogy with the Forum of Augustus in Rome (Tac., *Ann.* 2.64), it is possible that these two arches were dedicated to Germanicus and Drusus Minor, nephew and son of Tiberius, respectively; the former was designated heir to the principate (see Figure 36.1 for the Julio-Claudian family tree). The northeastern arch (so-called "of Tiberius") has niches for statuary, and it has been hypothesized that one of these niches might have held a standing statue of Nero Caesar, son of Germanicus.[4] The arch west of the temple is smaller and, unlike the "Arch of Tiberius," has no niches. Two equestrian statues that stood on either side of the Temple of Jupiter (they are attested by extant bases) presumably also represented members of the Julio-Claudian imperial family.[5]

So that local aristocracies could share in the emperor's glory, it was important that the space of a forum not be entirely monopolized by the emperor and his family. For this reason, statues of local citizens were also present in the forum at Pompeii, although less prominently positioned, and smaller in scale. Equestrian statues of private citizens were placed on smaller bases, and only at the margins of the forum in front of the colonnades, as shown by a painted frieze from the *atrium* of the *Praedia* ("properties") of Julia Felix (II.4; Figure 23.12).[6] In addition, several standing statues of local benefactors were located in front of the forum's porticoes, as we know from surviving statue bases.[7] What separated the statues of the emperor and his family from the statues of private citizens was not, therefore, the type of statues (except in the case of the *quadriga*), but their scale and position.

While many of the statue bases from the forum at Pompeii have survived, the statues themselves are not preserved, except in fragments, probably because of looting after the eruption of Vesuvius in AD 79, as well as damage to the forum inflicted by the earthquake of AD 62. One statue has survived from quite close to the forum, however.

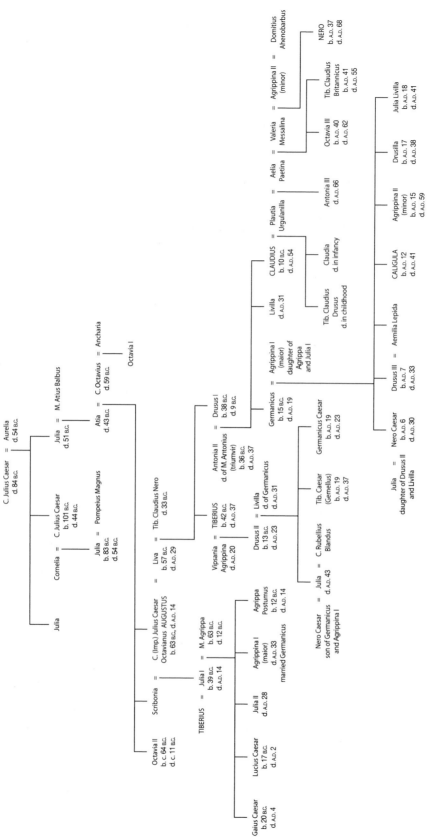

Figure 36.1 Genealogical chart of the Julio-Claudians. From B. Rose, *Dynastic Commemoration and Imperial Portraiture in the Julio-Claudian Period*, Cambridge, 1997, p. 204, table 4.

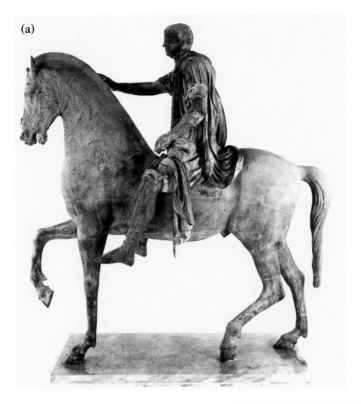

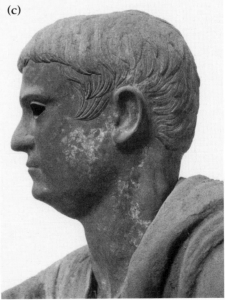

Figure 36.2a–c Bronze equestrian statue from atop the so-called Arch of Caligula, north of the forum at Pompeii (a: MNN inv. no. 5635, neg. no. 2047; b: MNN inv. no. 5635, neg. no. 1399; c: MNN inv. no. 5635, neg. no. 1401).

It is a bronze equestrian statue that stood atop an arch north of the forum, the so-called Arch of Caligula (Figures 36.2a–c).[8] The statue was found beneath the arch, broken into pieces. This arch is smaller and less conspicuous than the previously mentioned arches flanking the Temple of Jupiter, which exhibited statues of members of the imperial family. This was fitting, since the "Arch of Caligula" was a monument evidently set up in honor of a non-imperial person. The figure wears a toga and has his arm extended in a gesture of *adlocutio* (public address). The employment of togas for equestrian statues is less common than the more usual formats of tunic and *paludamentum* (short military cloak) or cuirass.[9] The toga is a more civic, less "charged" type of garment, and its employment may have been intended to express the subject's humbler status with respect to the nearby statues (equestrian and in chariot) of members of the imperial family. The subject wears *calcei patricii* ("senatorial shoes"), a type of shoe laced around the ankles with four straps and tied into two knots, which was originally reserved only for men who had senatorial status in Rome but which was eventually appropriated by high ranking officials in Rome's municipalities.[10] The equestrian statue format and the gesture were appropriate for a statue positioned on top of an arch.

The portrait head may now be examined. The flesh surfaces of the face are rendered stiffly and the brow line rather sharply. The thick hair is arranged in locks straight across the forehead and is cut into corners at the temples. These traits reflect the influence of the portraiture of the Julio-Claudian house, particularly the pre-accession portraits of Tiberius.[11] Yet the Pompeian portrait is a frank representation of an individual who is nearly middle-aged. There has been no attempt to regularize his sagging underchin or the odd square shape of his head. The tightly compressed lips and thrusting facial expression, which had been common elements of republican portraits, were signs of aggressive manliness, personal power, and seriousness (*virtus, auctoritas* and *gravitas*). The dynamic quality of the image is appropriate to the statue format (equestrian) and to the prestigious architectural context (arch), both of which had military associations. The equestrian statue type functioned to elevate the portrait image through its symbolic associations of personal prowess.

Judging from the prominent location of his equestrian statue, this individual must have been one of the most important magistrates at Pompeii. The arch on which the statue was placed is located immediately to the west of the Temple of Fortuna Augusta, dedicated in the reign of Augustus.[12] An inscription on the entablature of the Temple of Fortuna Augusta (*CIL* X, 820)[13] reveals that the building was paid for by a certain Marcus Tullius, who was a member of a powerful land-owning family at Pompeii during the Augustan period and who was *tribunus militum a populo* (this office, which did not necessarily imply any military involvement, is to be distinguished from the *tribuni militum* who were the senior officers of the Roman legions).[14] The holder of this title was granted equestrian rank, which meant that he could sit on juries in Rome, and could hold the offices of procurator and prefect in the capital. The fact that the arch and the temple are adjacent presents the possibility that this equestrian statue portrait represents the donor of the temple, Marcus Tullius himself. If the portrait represents M. Tullius, it may be suggested that the allusions to Tiberius' portraiture expressed his allegiance to the heir apparent in the later Augustan period, and that the statue format advertised his equestrian rank. The location of this equestrian statue, atop an arch, distinguished this figure from the many other equestrian portrait statues crowded in front of the colonnades of the forum, each competing for the viewer's attention.

By contrast, at Rome in the early imperial period the possibilities for statuary self-representation were considerably more restricted. Epigraphical evidence indicates that at Rome, it was possible for a non-imperial personage to have been granted the privilege of having an equestrian statue of himself set up, but this type of honor was rare in the early imperial period. The only known example of a non-imperial equestrian statue at Rome during this period is that of L. Volusius Saturninus (*consul suffectus*, AD 3). The dedications to him at Rome included: three standing statues in triumphal toga (one in bronze in the Forum of Augustus and two of marble on the Palatine inside a triple gate and in front of the Temple of Apollo); one augural statue in the Regia (i.e., with *toga* drawn over the head and carrying a *lituus*, or augural staff); one equestrian statue near the Rostra; and one seated on the *sella curulis* (curule chair) in the *porticus* of the Theatre of Pompey.[15] The extensive variety of statue types shows how closely controlled statue format and location were in the capital.

On the one hand, it was important that portrait statues of non-imperial dignitaries at Rome be set up in prominent public spaces, lest the imperial family appear to monopolize all available display space. On the other hand, statue type, scale and position had to be carefully worked out so that no non-imperial statue should seem more important than an imperial one. Thus, while Saturninus' most imposing statue, the bronze in Augustus' Forum, was equipped with a triumphal toga (purple), the dominant focus would have been the colossal statue of Augustus in a *quadriga* in the center of the Forum square. Statues of Saturninus were set up in all the most important parts of the city (Forum, Palatine, Campus Martius), yet dedications were not allowed to congregate in any one area; this would have had the effect of elevating him beyond what was considered appropriate. A non-imperial person in Rome would not have been awarded a commemorative arch such as the one at Pompeii; at Rome this was an honor reserved for members of the imperial family. The evidence provided by the equestrian statue from the "Arch of Caligula" at Pompeii, in conjunction with the painting from the *Praedia* of Julia Felix (Figure 23.12) showing equestrian statues in front of the forum colonnades, shows that the possibilities of public self-display for members of the elite were much greater in provincial cities than in the capital.[16]

Another magistrate awarded a statue in a prominent position at Pompeii was M. Holconius Rufus (cf. Ling, Ch. 9; Small, Ch. 13; Parslow, Ch. 14; Figures 36.3a–c).[17] His statue was conspicuously located at the intersection of the *cardo maximus* (the strada Stabiana) and the lower *decumanus* (the via dell'Abbondanza), two of the city's main arteries. The Holconii, a family attested only in Pompeii, were part of the land-owning elite and made their money through wine production (the *vitus Holconia* was one of the most famous wines of Campania: Plin., *HN* 2.6.35; Col., *Rust.* 3.2.27).[18] The inscription on Holconius' statue base (*CIL* X, 830) gives a list of his titles and allows the statue to be dated.[19] The fact that Augustus is not called *divus* in the inscription gives a latest possible date for the dedication of AD 14. The earliest possible date is determined by another inscription (*CIL* X, 890), recording that Holconius' fourth duumvirate occurred in 2/1 BC. At the time of the dedication, Holconius was *duovir* for the fifth time and *quinquennalis* for the second time. Holconius was also *patronus coloniae*, which indicates that he had connections at the imperial court (this was a title awarded by the emperor). He was *Augusti Caesaris sacerdos*, the most distinguished priesthood at Pompeii (Holconius is the earliest documented imperial priest in Italy).[20] Finally, he was *tribunus militum a populo*. This title is attested

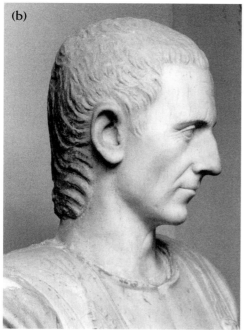

Figure 36.3a–c Statue of M. Holconius Rufus from the intersection of the strada Stabiana and the via dell'Abbondanza at Pompeii (a: photo DAI Rom 74.1288; b: photo DAI Rom 83.1820; c: photo DAI Rom 83.1818).

only in the Augustan period and only in Italian municipalities; it is not found at Rome or outside of Italy.[21] It is significant that *tribunus militum a populo* appears as the first title in the inscription. This novel, pseudo-military appellation probably had a more flamboyant air to Pompeians than the titles pertaining to Holconius' political career in the town itself.

This statue would have had an arresting effect on the Pompeian observer in the Augustan period. First, the statue body is of very high quality. Like the equestrian statue discussed above, it wears *calcei patricii*. Second, the cuirass, with its decoration consisting of a *gorgoneion*, facing griffins, and masks on the shoulder straps, is in fact a close version of the statue of Mars Ultor of the Forum of Augustus in Rome, consecrated in 2 BC.[22] Cuirassed statues had been relatively rare in the Republic, and decorated ones such as this were employed mainly for statues of members of the imperial family (the cuirasses used for the statues of one M. Nonius Balbus of Herculaneum in the early Augustan period, for example, were plain and belted— the type of breastplate that local people could actually have seen military officials wearing).[23] It may have been because of his priesthood of Augustus that such an elevated type of cuirass was deemed appropriate for M. Holconius Rufus.

The portrait head is not as high in quality as is the statue body (the folds and wrinkles of the face—particularly in the contracted brow—are not rendered in organic harmony with the surface of the flesh). The head is also somewhat too small for the body. P. Zanker's explanation for this fact is that the head was reworked from an imperial portrait, the original head having been knocked off the body during the earthquake of AD 62. Following Zanker, J. D'Arms suggested that the statue's original location was in the forum and that it was moved to this lesser location when the forum was under construction after the earthquake of AD 62.[24]

The head is, indeed, reworked (possibly from a portrait of the disgraced emperor Caligula, as the configuration of residual locks at the nape of the neck suggests). Since the statue was set on a high pedestal, however, the discrepancy between head and body in terms of size and quality would have been less apparent when the statue was viewed from below. In any case, the aesthetic harmony of the monument was evidently less important than the fact that the statue's head and body successfully conveyed their respective messages: the body suggested Holconius' connections in Rome; the head advertised Holconius as a dignified, resolute Pompeian magistrate.

The reworked head follows the lost, original portrait very closely. Indeed, Holconius' features are highly individualized, the face thin, bony and wrinkled, and the ears protruding, in the manner of portraits of the republican period (a style often referred to as "verism"). The triangular shape of the head and the relatively thick hair is formed into a forked motif at the forehead and cut into corners at the temples. These traits reflect the influence of portraits of Augustus.[25] These borrowings from the portraits of Augustus were presumably a means of suggesting Holconius' loyalty to that emperor.

Holconius' loyalty to Augustus may also help to explain the location of the statue: during the early imperial period, crossroads were often the sites of shrines to the *genius* of Augustus where the emperor was worshipped together with the *Lares*.[26] Holconius was priest of Augustus, and the symbolic nature of the crossroads may have made the display context of his portrait statue a poignant one. The context was also close to the theater at Pompeii which Holconius himself had rebuilt on the model of the Theater of Marcellus in Rome (*CIL* X, 833–5; cf. Parslow, Ch. 14).

There is, therefore, no particular need to assume, as did D'Arms, that the statue was moved to its current location at the junction of the strada Stabiana and the via dell'Abbondanza from an original location in the forum.

The Holconii were one in a group of families that were quite influential in the Pompeian *ordo* (town council) during the Augustan period. Another family in this group was the *gens Eumachia*. One portrait of a member of the Eumachii has survived (Figures 36.4a–c).[27] The portrait of Eumachia was found *in situ* in the so-called Edifice of Eumachia on the east side of the forum. An inscription on the entablature of the portico of the building indicates that Eumachia and her son M. Numistrius Fronto paid for the building and dedicated it to Concordia Augusta (*CIL* X, 810), a statue of whom stood in the largest apse at the rear.[28]

The statue of Eumachia stood in a niche in a separated corridor at the rear of the building. It was a secondary dedication, which explains its less prominent location; an inscription on the statue pedestal reveals that the fullers of Pompeii erected her portrait: EUMACHIAE L(UCII) F(ILIAE) SACERD(OTI) / PUBL(ICAE) FULLONES, "To Eumachia, daughter of Lucius, public priestess [dedicated by] the fullers" (*CIL* X, 813) (Figure 34.2). The wool workers of Pompeii had good reason to be grateful to their benefactress, as her family were holders of extensive farmland and were involved in wool (as well as wine) production.[29] Because of this dedicatory inscription it is sometimes said that the building was a social club, guild-house, or even a commercial center for the buying and selling of wool or slaves. However, these activities are more likely to have taken place in the forum itself. Eumachia's building, with its large open court and surrounding porticoes without the small rooms or booths suited to commercial transactions, was a public promenade (*porticus*), outfitted with statues like the Porticus of Livia in Rome, which was also dedicated to Concordia Augusta and which the Edifice of Eumachia in certain architectural respects resembles.[30]

Like many portrait statues of women from Pompeii, Eumachia is shown draped in Hellenistic style with a *tunica* (an undergarment that reached down to the ankles and that was made of two pieces of cloth pinned at the shoulders or buttoned at the upper arms) and *palla* (an overgarment worn as a mantle and draped around the body). But unlike most statues of women from Pompeii and other municipalities of the Roman West, there is no trace of individuality in Eumachia's facial features or hairstyle. Both are rendered in the purely idealized style of the late classical period. The face and hair on their own could be taken for an Aphrodite or Hellenistic queen. In Eumachia's case, it was evidently considered appropriate to exploit the symbolic value of a purist classical style for her portrait statue. This could have been because her family seems ultimately to have been of Greek origin.[31] The Eumachii had one of the few Greek *nomina* among the Pompeian elite, and the portrait style may have been intended to call attention to those (perhaps genuinely ancient) origins.[32] More important may have been Eumachia's office of city priestess. In Pompeii there were two kinds of priestess: those serving Venus, and those of Ceres.[33] As Pompeii was better known for its cult of Venus, the priesthood of Venus was the more important office of the two. Eumachia was probably a priestess of Venus, which is another possible reason that it was considered appropriate to portray her as young, beautiful and Aphrodite-like. (The Edifice is dedicated both in Eumachia's name and in that of her son M. Numistrius Fronto. It is usually assumed that in dedicating the building in her son's name, Eumachia was attempting to advance his career—he may have been

Figure 36.4a–c Portrait of Eumachia from the Edifice of Eumachia
(a: MNN inv. no. 6232, neg. no. 2363; b: MNN inv. no. 6232, neg. no. 2658;
c: MNN inv. no. 6232, neg. no. 2659).

Figure 36.5a–c   Female portrait statue from the Macellum
(a: photo DAI Rom 76.1157; b: photo DAI Rom 76.1161;
c: photo DAI Rom 76.1159).

running for public office. In any case, for Eumachia to have a son old enough to enter public life, she would have been well over forty at the time her portrait statue was set up in the Edifice.)

The portrait statue of Eumachia is not wholly idealized, however. Eumachia's *palla* is draped over her head (a visual reminder of her office as *sacerdos publica*), and she delicately holds up the edge of her *palla* so that it hangs down loosely, and, piquantly, between her breasts (her left nipple is articulated under the *tunica*). This drapery format, replicated in a number of other portrait statues, follows the Hellenistic tradition of portrait statues of women; that is, it is realistically rendered and is apparently not based on a particular classical statue of a divinity.[34] The choice of this "realistic"-looking statue body in Eumachia's case would have tempered the elevated and rather aloof effect of the idealized portrait head and would have allowed the Pompeian viewer immediately to engage with the figure as a portrait, before he or she noticed the dedicatory inscription on the statue base.

Other women of the Pompeian elite chose to have themselves portrayed with an ideal Greek portrait style similar to that of Eumachia's image, but with fashionable, contemporary Roman hairstyle and dress. An example is a portrait statue from the Macellum, the fish and meat market in the northeast corner of the forum (Figures 36.5a–c).[35] The statue, which was paired with a male portrait statue, was located at the back of the building in a small, enclosed shrine reached by a flight of steps. The large niche at the rear of this room probably featured a statue of an emperor in the seated Jupiter type, as an arm holding a globe was found on the floor there.[36] The smaller niche on the north side of this room contained the male and female portrait statues. The statues that occupied the other niches are gone, but it is probable that they depicted members of the imperial family.

The woman is represented in the act of sacrifice, holding an incense box in her left hand and a *patera* (libation bowl) in her right (the latter is a modern replacement). She wears a sleeved *tunica*; a *palla*, which is draped over her left shoulder and head, emerges from under her right arm, and is pulled across her waist. This same drapery configuration—known as the "Artemisia type," named after the well-known female portrait statue from the Mausoleum at Halicarnassus dating to the mid-fourth century BC—is used for several other Roman female portrait statues.[37] Here, however, there is inserted between the *tunica* and *palla* a third garment: a *stola* (a sleeveless, long garment worn by Roman matrons of the upper classes), held by straps over the shoulders, which falls in a characteristic V-shape below the neck, revealing the *tunica* beneath it. In addition, the figure wears a wreath of leaves and myrtle berries and an *infula*, a beaded fillet seen on representations of sacrificial animals which became an elevating attribute for portraits of imperial princesses, such as Drusilla, the sister of Caligula (cf. Figure 36.1 for the genealogy),[38] and—as this Pompeian example suggests—a stylish accouterment in the portraiture of municipal priestesses.

The face resembles a Hellenistic Aphrodite, although it is also subtly individualized, by means of the break in profile at the root of the nose and the slightly smiling mouth. The hair is arranged in a contemporary fashionable style reminiscent of the portraits of the empress Agrippina Minor, wife of Claudius. It has recently been suggested by A. Small that the portrait, in fact, depicts Agrippina. Others have seen this portrait as Octavia Minor, sister of Augustus, or Claudia Octavia, daughter of Claudius.[39] Against these interpretations are the facts that: (1) Agrippina Minor and Octavia Minor both have securely identified portrait types to which the hairstyle and facial formulation of this image do not conform, and (2) we possess no securely identified portrait of Octavia the daughter of Claudius with which to compare this image.[40] Moreover, the face is almost wholly idealized, and while portraits of women from the Roman East often feature such "ideal" physiognomies, those from Rome and Italy are usually more individualized. The Macellum portrait, therefore, likely represents a non-imperial person. We may say with confidence, however, that in its hairstyle the portrait draws on the image of Agrippina Minor (especially the so-called Milan and Stuttgart portrait types) and probably dates to around the reign of Nero.

The corresponding male portrait in the Macellum depicts an individual with a light beard and mustache indicating that he was still an adolescent (Figures 36.6a–c).[41] He is represented with a cloak draped across his lower body (in the "hip mantle" statue format). His crimped locks of hair at the forehead follow a dandified hairstyle that was popular among the elite youth of Rome from the late Claudian period to the early second century.[42] The hooked nose and mild facial expression are reminiscent of the portraits of some Julio-Claudian princes, particularly Drusus Minor, the son of Tiberius.[43] The most recent proposal for the identification of this statue (A. Small) holds that it represents Britannicus, for whom there are no securely identified portraits in the round and only highly generalized coin portraits with which to compare it.[44] The strongly individualized physiognomy and bumpiness of the nose, however, argue against an imperial identification for this portrait.

S. Adamo Muscettola has hypothesized that the male portrait represents the Pompeian magistrate Gn. Alleius Nigidius Maius, *duovir quinquennalis* in AD 55–56, *flamen {Ti. Claudii} Caesaris Augusti* and *princeps coloniae*. She also argues that the female portrait statue could show his daughter Alleia Nigidia Maia, a priestess of Venus and Ceres.[45] (The Nigidii Maii were prominent in the Neronian period at Pompeii and were involved in the bronze industries of Capua.) Against this interpretation is the fact that both the male and female figures are represented as being the same age (very young), which lessens the likelihood that they depict a father and daughter. M. Torelli has argued that the male statue may represent one Sp. Turranius Proculus Gellianus, a Pompeian who was a Roman citizen (he belonged to the *tribus Fabia* or "Fabian tribe"), was *praefectus cohortis Gaetulorum, tribunus militum legionis* X ("praefect of the cohort of the Gaetulii, military tribune of the tenth legion"), and is perhaps to be identified with the Gellianus who was friend to Nero's praetorian prefect, Ninfidius Sabinus (Plut., *Galba* 9).[46] In addition, Torelli suggests that the female statue represents HOLCONIA M. F. SACERDOS PUBLICA (*CIL* X, 950), public priestess and relative of M. Holconius Rufus (probably his niece). The identification of the male statue as Sp. Turrianus Proculus Gellianus is based largely on the fact that the figure has a sword in his left hand which, according to Torelli, signifies that he was a military tribune. But the sword need not be interpreted literally. It is more easily seen as an attribute that carried a general evocation of manly prowess. While there is no proof either for Torelli's or Adamo Muscettola's proposed identifications for the Macellum statues, they do plausibly indicate the kind of individuals whom these statues could have represented. The man and woman were probably members of the family that had paid for the erection of the newly refurbished Macellum in the Julio-Claudian period.

The statues of these two young members of Pompeii's elite, set up in the Macellum, use a type of portraiture that draws on the style of Julio-Claudian portraits and on

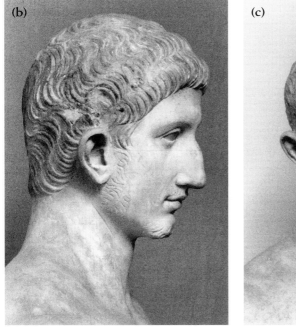

Figure 36.6a–c   Male portrait statue from the Macellum
(a: photo DAI Rom 76.1152; b: photo DAI Rom 76.1155;
c: photo DAI Rom 76.1154).

Greek ideal portraits, but which also incorporates enough individual specificity in physiognomy and/or coiffure to render the images recognizably individual.[47] The woman's idealized face and the man's semi-nude statue type were intended to distance the images from reality, to an extent.[48] Such elevating devices may have been considered appropriate both to the ostensible youth of the individuals represented and to the elevated architectural context of the portrait statues (a shrine of the imperial cult).

An example of a portrait set up in a temple is shown in Figure 36.7. It was discovered *in situ* in the southwest corner of the *porticus* surrounding the Temple of Isis.[49] The Temple of Isis was one of the few public buildings at Pompeii that was entirely rebuilt after the earthquake. The donor for the restoration was N. Popidius Ampliatus (see below for the Popidii). The herm portrait is inscribed as follows: C. NORBANI SORICIS SECUNDARUM / MAG. PAGI AVG. FELICIS SVBVRBANI EX D. D. LOC. D. (*CIL* X, 1814: "To Gaius Norbanus Sorex, player of second parts. The *magistri* of the *Pagus Augustus Felix Suburbanus*, by decree of the decurions, set

Figure 36.7   Herm portrait of C. Norbanus Sorex from the Temple of Isis; photo DAI Rom 89.1216.

it up here"). The herm represents C. Norbanus Sorex, an actor described as a player of second parts. The portrait was dedicated by the *magistri* of a wealthy suburban district of Pompeii.[50] Sorex was probably one of these magistrates himself. Men of lowly birth, mostly freedmen who could not become ordinary magistrates, occupied this office, which was connected with the cult of the *Lares*.[51] Sorex, however, seems to have had considerable influence despite his being a freedman and an actor.[52] His portrait was set up with the formal approval of the town council (*ex decurionum decreto*), and another herm portrait of him stood in the Edifice of Eumachia.[53]

Sorex's portrait is rendered in a matter-of-fact, realistic-looking style. His face is irregularly shaped, his jaw is quite prominent and his underchin sags in the manner of many Roman republican period portraits. Yet the upward tilt to his head is an element one sees often in Hellenistic Greek portraits. It may be that this refinement was deemed appropriate to the representation of an actor. As the Temple of Isis was also associated with Dionysus (that deity's statue was displayed in a niche in the rear wall of the *cella*) and was adjacent to the theater, it was perhaps a resonant display context for the portrait of an actor.

There has been considerable controversy, however, concerning the date and identification of this portrait. An older interpretation, espoused again by M. Torelli, is that the herm represents the famous *archimimus* (chief mimic actor) Norbanus Sorex, who accompanied the dictator Sulla to Puteoli after he retired.[54] Against this interpretation is the fact that Sulla's companion Norbanus Sorex was an *archimimus*, while the Norbanus Sorex whose portraits were set up in Pompeii was only a player of second parts. Also, the inclusion of the name Augustus in the designation *Pagus Augustus Felix Suburbanus* suggests a *terminus post quem* of 27 BC for the portrait (Torelli and others have tried to get around this point by arguing that the portrait from the Temple of Isis is a later copy of the original portrait from the time of Sulla). Other scholars have rejected the idea that the portrait represents the *archimimus* Norbanus Sorex and have, instead, identified the figure as a local Pompeian of the late republican or early Augustan period, based on stylistic considerations.[55] This dating raises a question: why would a Pompeian actor who lived in the late first century BC, who only had played second parts, still be important enough to have two portraits of himself set up in architectural contexts that post-date the earthquake of AD 62?

Some external evidence suggests that the portrait of Norbanus Sorex may have been later in date than the Augustan period. A third copy of Sorex's herm portrait (missing the portrait head, like the copy in the Edifice of Eumachia) was discovered in the sanctuary of Diana Nemorensis at Nemi, along with several other herm portraits representing actors, tradesmen and their women. It refers again to Sorex as a "player of second parts" and as *parisitus Apollonis* (Apollo's actor). At least three portraits of actors were included in this group: Norbanus Sorex, Fundilius Doctus and L. Faenius Faustus, player of fourth parts. Based on the male and female hairstyles and the physiognomic renderings, all of these herm portraits are dated to the Julio-Claudian period, between the reigns of Tiberius and Claudius (*c*.AD 14–56).[56] It is likely, then, that Sorex's portrait, of which at least three replicas were made (two from Pompeii, one from Nemi) was commissioned sometime during the Julio-Claudian period.

The presence of Sorex's portrait in the Temple of Isis raises the possibility that Sorex may have helped pay for the restoration of the building after AD 62. If his portrait was initially commissioned when he was about thirty (in AD 40, for example), he could easily have lived into the 60s AD. A Julio-Claudian date for Sorex might also explain the presence of a (headless) portrait of him in the Edifice of Eumachia (*CIL* X, 814), which—like the Temple of Isis—was substantially rebuilt after the earthquake of AD 62 (cf. Dobbins, Ch. 12) and which Sorex may also have helped to fund. Finally, we may speculate that Norbanus Sorex was descended from the *familia* of Norbanus Sorex the *archimimus*, who had settled with Sulla nearby Pompeii at Puteoli.

PORTRAIT SCULPTURE FROM THE DOMESTIC SPHERE

A portrait of a prominent Pompeian individual (Figures 36.8a–b) comes from the House of the Gilded Cupids (VI.16.7).[57] The portrait was found in the peristyle and was not a bust but was originally inserted into a togate statue, as indicated by the irregular configuration of the worked surface at the bottom of the neck. The middle-aged physiognomy is highly individualized, though influenced to an extent by the early imperial, posthumous portrait type of Julius Caesar (Divus Julius) in terms of its formal structure, its artfully arranged locks of hair, its pronounced naso-labial lines and diagonal wrinkles on the neck.[58] A head found at Herculaneum depicts the very same person.[59] It was evidently sculpted from the same model, although executed in a more plastic style. The different styles of execution suggest that one of these portraits did not serve as the model for the other, but that the prototype was another portrait, perhaps an "official" portrait displayed in a public context either at Pompeii

Figure 36.8a–b   Male bust of togate statue from the House of the Gilded Cupids (VI.16.7) (a: MNN inv. no. 4989, neg. no. 1369; b: MNN inv. no. 4989, neg. no. 1370).

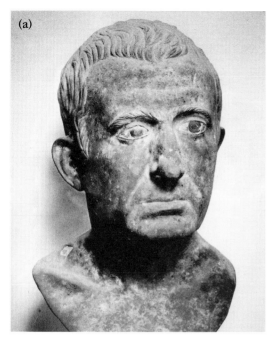

Figure 36.9a–b Bronze bust of a man from the south *anta* of *tablinum* (14) in the House of the Citharist (I.4.25) (a: photo DAI Rom 38.1287; b: photo DAI Rom 38.1286).

or Herculaneum. The person depicted must have had substantial social standing to have had portraits of himself set up in two different cities.

One of the better-documented (though prosopographically complicated) families from Pompeii was that of the Popidii. They may have lived in the House of the Citharist (I.4.5), which occupies nearly an entire *insula* of the city (Figure 23.8). Abundant *graffiti* in and around the house suggest that two men, L. Popidius Ampliatus and L. Popidius Secundus, occupied the house in the later period of Pompeii's history. The former is a first-generation freedman and has retained his slave name "Ampliatus" (which means "he who has been augmented," a cognomen that could be read in different ways, but that basically signifies that he has made a lot of money). A relation, N. Popidius Ampliatus, paid for the restoration of the Temple of Isis after the earthquake of AD 62 (see above), in exchange for which his six-year-old son was elected to the town *ordo* (*CIL* X, 846; cf. Jongman, Ch. 32). Second-generation freedmen were eligible for public office, but first-generation ones like N. Pop. Ampliatus were not. Secundus (or his son) was perhaps a second-generation freedman, because we know he was running for the office of aedile in the last phase of the town's history.[60] Two bronze busts exhibited in the *atrium* of this house allow us to examine the types of images that members of the municipal sub-elite (in this case, wealthy individuals of servile origin) commissioned for use in a domestic context, the setting to which their portraits were largely confined.

The first bronze bust (Figures 36.9a–b) was discovered *in situ* against the south *anta* of *tablinum* (14).[61] It was found nailed to the wall 1.5 m above the floor, indicating

(a)

(b)

Figure 36.10a–b Bronze bust of a woman from the north *anta*
of *tablinum* (14) in the House of the Citharist (I.4.25) (a: photo DAI Rom 39.605;
b: photo DAI Rom 39.604).

that it originally stood on a wooden herm. The portrait was rendered in a highly
realistic manner, with no attempt to regularize the weak chin and large, pointed
nose. Close to this bust—in the north *ala* of the *atrium*—the bronze bust of a woman
was discovered (Figures 36.10a–b).[62] The workmanship and size of the bust are
comparable to that of the man, and it is likely that the two were a pair, placed on
herms on either side of the entrance to the *tablinum*. The woman's image is somewhat
blander in appearance than the male's. It does, however, include individualized
elements such as thick lips and a weak chin. Her hair is arranged in a fashionable
style similar to that of portraits of Agrippina Maior, wife of Germanicus and mother
of Caligula. In profile her nose also resembles Agrippina's.[63] We see, then, that these
members of Pompeii's wealthy middle class chose to portray themselves in a style
influenced by the realism of late republican portraiture, updated in the woman's case
with Julio-Claudian portrait "quotations."

If the male portrait stood in a museum and did not have a known archaeological
context, we might date it to the late republican period because of its realistic-looking
portrait style. The fact that it was paired with the female portrait, which uses a
hairstyle fashionable in Rome during the Julio-Claudian period, indicates that the
portraits represent the owner of the house and his wife during Julio-Claudian times.[64]

A particularly well-documented herm portrait (Figures 36.11a–b) was displayed
at the entrance to the *tablinum* of the House of L. Caecilius Iucundus (V.1.26).[65]
The inscription on the herm states: GENIO L. NOSTRI / FELIX L. ("to the *genius*

[guardian spirit] of our Lucius; his freedman Felix [dedicated it]") (*CIL* X, 860). This is an exceedingly prosaic representation of an individual, fully within the heightened realism of Roman republican portraiture. The realism is almost "cruelly" observed; all of the subject's unattractive features are carefully rendered, including a prominent wart on his left cheek.

On stylistic grounds alone, this portrait might be (and usually is) dated to the late first century BC. But a series of inscribed wax tablets found in this house reveal that its owner, L. Caecilius Iucundus, was a second-generation freedman and *argentarius coactor* (broker) active during the Neronian period.[66] It is logical to think that the

(a)

(b)

Figure 36.11a–b Herm portrait of L. Caecilius Iucundus from the entrance to *tablinum* (i) of his house (V.1.26). (a: author's photo; b: MNN inv. no. 110663, neg. no. 2568).

portrait represents this individual (as the *praenomen* in the inscription hints). Some commentators, including R. Bonifacio and now L. H. Petersen, have thought that the portrait does not represent Iucundus, but a forebear of his, partly because they find it difficult to accept that such a republican-looking portrait could have been made as late as the 50s AD. Citing K. Zangemeister (*CIL* IV suppl., p. 277), Bonifacio argues that, because the dedicator of the herm portrait was a freedman called Felix, the subject must be L. Caecilius Felix, the father of Iucundus, a first-generation freedman who is mentioned once in a wax tablet of AD 15.[67] But there is no epigraphical reason to think that the dedicator Felix, simply because of his name, was a freedman of the obscure L. Caecilius Felix rather than of his son L. Caecilius Iucundus.[68] The portrait no doubt represents L. Caecilius Iucundus the broker (whose cognomen, meaning "pleasant," may have been his slave name).

Like the portrait of Norbanus Sorex, this image indicates that the style of objective-looking realism, which we associate primarily with the Roman Republic, was evidently still in use well into the first century AD.[69] The portrait of L. Caecilius Iucundus possesses all the emphases on age and plasticity of flesh surfaces that a republican-period portrait would have. As such, it stands at one end of the spectrum of choices used for Pompeian men in their portraits. Some reasons for the use of this portrait style in Iucundus' case may be suggested. The emphatic realism and the stress on real features of age may have been intended to make the portrait of Iucundus look as Roman as possible—perhaps to compensate for his servile ancestry.[70] But the aggressive characteristics (tight lips, brow knitted in concentration) seen in so many republican portraits, as well as in the equestrian statue that stood on the "Arch of Caligula" (Figures 36.2a–c)—are missing here. The pointed absence of aggressive qualities seems to convey something not seen in elite portraiture—excessive modesty or compliance. This is the representation of a man who has demonstrated that he knows how to serve. It might be suggested, then, that Iucundus' portrait was intended to convey the quality of *fides*—loyalty and trustworthiness, a virtue traditionally associated with freedmen (in part because it constituted the underpinning of the legal obligation that existed between freedman and patron[71]) and one that any well-heeled Pompeian would certainly value in his broker. In reconstructing the personality of this rich freedman, one cannot help thinking of Petronius' Trimalchio, whose patron deity was Mercury, protector of traders (Petron., *Sat.* 29, 67), and whose household gods were Gain, Luck and Profit (60).[72]

Evidence from the wax tablets of L. Caecilius Iucundus suggests that he had business dealings with a man of comparable wealth and mercantile status, Vesonius Primus, who lived right across the street in the House of Orpheus (VI.14.20), a dwelling that was combined with a fullery (VI.14.22; cf. Map 3).[73] In the peristyle of this house is a painting of Orpheus charming the beasts, crude in design but colossal in scale (size evidently being considered more important than quality here).[74] From *tablinum* (i) of this house comes the herm portrait of Vesonius Primus (Figures 36.12a–b).[75] This individual was presumably the owner of the house and operator of the fullery during the last period of Pompeii's history. Bonifacio (*Ritratti*, p. 92) dates the portrait to the early Augustan period, on the basis of its republican-looking face and its similarity to the portrait of Caecilius Iucundus. There is no good evidence for this dating. The fact that Vesonius Primus appears as a witness on a wax tablet dating to AD 57, and the existence of a painted *graffito* on the façade of the fullery,

Figure 36.12a–b   Herm portrait of Vesonius Primus from *tablinum* (i) of the House of Orpheus (VI.14.20) (a: photo DAI Rom 39.970; b: photo DAI Rom 39.969).

in Vesonius Primus' name, endorsing candidates for election, suggest that the represented individual lived during the Neronian period at least.[76] The herm is inscribed: PRIMO / ANTEROS ARCAR ("to Primus. His cashier Anteros [dedicated it]") (*CIL* X, 865). A Greek slave made the dedication, and there is evidence that Primus himself was a freedman. Primus was in a position to endorse candidates for public office, but there is no record of his having held any such office himself (first-generation freedmen were not permitted to hold public office); his cognomen is not attested for any earlier member of the *gens Vesonia* at Pompeii, and "The First" was a likely name to have been chosen by a first-generation freedman.[77] Primus' portrait is placed on a *cippolino* (imported Greek marble) herm nearly identical to Iucundus', suggesting that the two portraits were contemporary, as does the comparability of the category of dedicator in each case: with Iucundus it was "his freedman Felix"; with Primus it was "his cashier."

The portrait of Vesonius Primus is executed in a style of heightened realism. It depicts a balding individual whose face is deeply engraved with wrinkles. The irises and pupils of his eyes were painted, as was usual in ancient sculpture. Primus seems to have been aiming for the same type of self-presentation in his portrait as was Iucundus, but the portrait is of lesser quality (it is less plastic and more linear in execution).

It is striking that the same mundane, realistic-looking style was used for the portraits of Vesonius Primus, L. Caecilius Iucundus, the male portrait from the House of the Citharist (I.4.25), and Norbanus Sorex. These individuals, all of whom lived *c.* the middle of the first century AD, evidently preferred not to have themselves represented using contemporary metropolitan (Julio-Claudian) fashions, but rather with the style of heightened realism associated primarily with the Roman Republic. Taken together, these portraits indicate that this particular mode of representation was still used for portraiture well into the mid-first century AD at Pompeii.[78] This, in turn, suggests that such a portrait option was also available in Rome, where closely dated private portraits for this period are lacking.[79]

That this phenomenon is not well recognized in the most recent study of portraits from Pompeii (Bonifacio, *Ritratti*) has to do, on the one hand, with the imposition of the prevailing stylistic developmental model onto the material, and, on the other hand, with a lingering but groundless tendency (not exclusive to Bonifacio) to label portraits found in Pompeian *atria* as forebears of the man that owned the house. It has been seen, however, in the portraits of Vesonius Primus, Caecilius Iucundus and the House of the Citharist bronzes, that this assumption privileges a traditional chronology of stylistic development over the archaeological evidence. The *atrium* of a Roman house was, indeed, the usual display place for ancestor portraits, at least in Rome during the Republican period (Plin., *HN* 35.5–8; Polyb. 6.53). However, the herm portraits from houses at Pompeii, positioned on either side of the *tablinum*, do not appear to be ancestor portraits—at least not remote ancestors—but rather the *paterfamilias* and his wife.[80] It is difficult to determine from the surviving evidence how common it was for the current owner of a house to have a portrait of himself displayed in his *atrium*.[81] We may speculate that in the case of wealthy individuals of servile origin (such as the Pompeians discussed above), there was a special imperative to place portraits of the current *paterfamilias* in the *atrium*, as a kind of substitute for traditional ancestor portraits, precisely because such individuals did not have a pedigree comparable to their elite colleagues. Interestingly, the (more private) peristyle, rather than the *atrium*, is attested as a display context for portraits in one case at Pompeii, and it is probably not a coincidence that the portrait is a full-length statue —not a bust—and that it represented a member of the Pompeian elite.[82] Members of the elite had less to prove, and thus may have been less concerned with placing portrait busts of themselves in the quasi-public *atrium*.[83]

It is also worth considering why herms were used for all of the surviving portraits found in the *atria* of middle-class houses at Pompeii—the herm format is more generally associated with portraits of thinkers, writers and famous Greeks of the past, for example those from the Villa of the Papyri.[84] At a general level, the herm format may have been favored because it evoked the cultured ambiance of the Greek gymnasium or the elite Roman villa. More specifically, the herm format seems not to have been used for the portraits of freeborn members of the Roman political elite, as far the evidence suggests—there are no surviving documented examples.[85] It is worth noting that at Pompeii all of the surviving portrait-herms with accompanying inscriptions or other identificatory information represent freedmen.[86] In general, herm portraits, when they represent contemporary Romans, often depict individuals who were freedmen, tradesmen and their relatives.[87] The herm was associated with the Greek Hermes, god of merchants, which may have made it a popular choice for freedmen, who were often of Greek descent and made their money through mercantile activities (Trimalchio, for example, came to Italy as a slave from Asia and made his fortune from trade in wine, bacon, beans, perfumes and slaves (Petron., *Sat.* 76)).[88] It is also possible that the herm, originally the exclusive statue format for representations of Hermes (and in the Roman period, of Greek cultural heroes—philosophers and Hellenistic kings), may have been particularly favored by freedmen who were often of Greek origin themselves. One might suggest, in addition, that the herm was used by newly "arrived" members of the middle and freedmen class for the same reason that they often chose a republican-looking portrait style: because it lent their portraits the appearance of a venerable, time-honored authority in the *atrium* setting.

FUNERARY PORTRAITS

Thus far we have examined portraits dating between the Augustan period and AD 79. Funerary portrait sculpture from Pompeii is plentiful (though not well published), and some of it dates to the late republican period, affording a glimpse of the modes of self-presentation of Pompeian men and women during the colonial period of the town's history (*c.* 80–30 BC).[89] The streets leading out of Pompeii began to be lined with impressive tombs by the Sullan colonists (80 BC) and their descendants in imitation of funerary practices in Rome. We may look at two examples that decorated the façade of an aediculated tomb from the cemetery outside the Porta Ercolano.[90]

The first is a male portrait (Figure 36.13), cut down from a full statue, that is powerfully expressive, although lower in quality than the portraits from public and domestic contexts examined thus far.[91] The carving is somewhat linear and abbreviated, and the head and body are block-like. The figure wears a tunic and over it a late republican type of toga, without the voluminous swathe of drapery at the midsection (*umbo*) that characterizes togas in the Augustan period and later. The garment is simple in its drapery scheme, hanging from the right shoulder to below breast level and thrown over the left shoulder, creating a sling-like fold in which the right forearm rests. The figure's hair is closely cropped, and his ears protrude in a quasi-military fashion. The brow is furrowed, the eyes creased, the nose wide, and the lips individualized— they are full with downturned corners. The expression is severe and direct, creating the impression of an immediate, individual presence, successfully catching the viewer's attention.

In a world where an afterlife was by no means guaranteed, a funerary monument was one of the best ways of being remembered, since a steady stream of travelers passing in and out of the city would view it for the foreseeable future. In this case, the portrayed individual was probably from a family that had arrived at Pompeii with the Sullan colonists. The portrait projects the Roman qualities of *auctoritas* (personal power), *gravitas* (gravity) and *virtus* (aggressive manliness) with which a Pompeian descended from the citizen colonists from Rome would have forcefully impressed the indigenous Osco-Samnite population of the city.[92]

A female portrait statue comes from the same tomb and represents a woman of approximately the same period, who was perhaps the man's wife (Figures 36.14a–b).[93] The statue is of the same level of quality as the male portrait but it is considerably less weathered. The portrait has a stolid, matronly aspect with feet planted solidly apart. The statue body is in the very latest fashion: the *pudicitia* format, in which the *palla* is tightly wrapped around the body in a modest fashion, with one arm bent at a 90° angle across the body and the other reaching upwards towards the chin. The *palla* envelops the body and head and hangs to just below the knees where the *tunica* becomes visible, and the right hand holds an end of the *palla* that hangs down beneath. The *pudicitia* statue format was adopted from Hellenistic female portrait

Figure 36.13 Male portrait statue from the façade of *aedicula* tomb (*PErc* 38N).
Photo DAI Rom 77.1840.

statues, and was used quite commonly in Italy during the late republican period. The pose, with right hand at the chin, is somewhat pensive (it is also a bridal gesture) and was thus considered suitable for a wife's funerary statue.

The facial expression is serious, although less severe than that of the male portrait. The only concessions to fashion in the hair are the tendrils that appear at each temple, escaping from the centrally parted hair, which is pulled back tightly over the ears. The statue lacks the contrived elegance of the portrait of Eumachia or that of the woman from the Macellum. The pose is tight, and the body is substantial. The point was not to represent this woman as youthful and attractive, but as a virtuous, wise and practical (if not intractable) wife—supporter of her family through good works done in the home and occasional public appearances in which she is careful to comport herself modestly. In its expression of the traditional female virtues of *modestia*, *decor* and *castitas* (modesty, grace or propriety, and moral fidelity), the statue inspires confidence.

Since many of the funerary portraits from Pompeii date from the period of the Sullan colony (80–30 BC), they are important because they give an idea of the range

(a)

(b)

Figure 36.14a–b Female portrait statue from the façade of *aedicula* tomb (*PErc* 38N) (a: photo DAI Rom 77.2278; b: photo DAI Rom 77.2276).

of options used in contemporary funerary portraiture for middle-class individuals at Rome. Indeed, for Rome at this time we have no securely dated and identified portrait sculpture in the round, except for images of some of the major figures of the elite class (Pompey, Caesar, Cato the Younger, M. Antonius, and possibly Cicero and Crassus), and these are later copies that lack statue bodies and are not *in situ*. For women, we have only Octavia, sister of Augustus, who appears on M. Antony's coin reverses. For the middle class, there are funerary reliefs with portrait busts, but these only began to be produced at the end of the first century BC.[94] The instances of early funerary sculpture at Pompeii are thus comparable in importance to (if fewer in number and lower in quality than) the main body of portrait sculpture at Delos, which also has a fairly narrow chronological span (late second century BC to *c.*70 BC). In fact, the Pompeian portraits often represent a comparable category of individuals— middle-class merchants and their wives, and they suggest how such individuals presented themselves in statuary in a funerary context.

A preliminary suggestion may be made concerning the significance of the Pompeian funerary statues depicting men. We have an idea, from surviving examples, of the repertoire of choices for portrait statue format used for men during the late Republic: togate, cuirassed, nude with cloak over the shoulder or wrapped around the hips. We remain unsure, however, of the relative numbers of such statues. From the evidence available, it seems that in the late republican/early imperial periods togate statues were the most common and the elevated, nude or hip mantle statue format was less so, being used mostly by members of the elite for display in public contexts (e.g., at Pompeii a nude youth of the Julio-Claudian period;[95] C. Ofellius Ferus in the Agora of the Italians on Delos; the statues from the Forum at Formiae; L. Cartilius Poplicola from the Temple of Hercules at Ostia; the "Tivoli general" from the Sanctuary of Hercules Victor at Tivoli).[96] The Pompeian evidence raises the possibility that during the late Republic the sub-elites of a community may have preferred to be represented in their funerary statues wearing costumes they actually wore in life (i.e., togate). Part of the explanation for this might be that relatives visiting the tombs and banqueting there could more effectively engage with an image of the deceased with a "realistic-looking" body type, as he had appeared in life. Most importantly, however, members of the middle levels of society in Roman cities did not have public, honorific statues. Funerary statues comprised an available substitute, which may explain their choice of standard public honorific dress: the toga.

CONCLUSIONS

In the past, Roman portraiture has been (and often still is) discussed in terms of a linear scheme of stylistic evolution, with private portraits understood as "period-faces" following a fashion fixed by the reigning emperor and his wife.[97] At Pompeii, however, there seems to have been a wide range of stylistic options in use during the first century AD, upon which the inhabitants could draw when commissioning their portraits. At one end of the portrait spectrum is the style that we know as "republican;" it is characterized by short-cropped hair with an emphasis on an individual's less youthful and attractive facial features. At the other end is a blander, less realistic-looking portraiture, "sub-Julio-Claudian" in appearance.[98] Between these extremes is a style that may be termed "diluted" or "sub-republican," distinguished by the depiction of the real features of age, yet combined with a stiff treatment of the flesh and a reduction in the richness of detail evident in securely dated republican portraits.[99] Such a style was used for the portraits of both Pompeian men and women, and was sometimes combined with an overlay of portrait elements drawn from the imperial family.

In each of the examples of Pompeian portraiture considered here, it can be argued that there is a clear connection between an individual's social position and the portrait style with which he chose to represent himself to the community. Younger individuals of the city's elite often used a bland, more or less idealized style, usually influenced by (the often Classicizing) imperial portraiture of the Julio-Claudian period (itself a contrived combination of Classicizing elements with ostensibly realistic physiognomies). We suggest that this style was considered appropriate to those whose youth might, in theory, allow them to possess such physical features. Portraits of individuals from the middle levels of Pompeian society are usually rendered in a sub-republican style, sometimes also showing the influence of imperial portraits. A style of heightened realism seems to have been favored by some members of the middle class, particularly freedmen, because it looked venerable and conveyed Romanness. The Pompeian corpus of private portraits thus allows us to begin to reconstruct how metropolitan fashions were received in Italy outside of Rome—which categories of individuals adopted them and which did not.

The evidence from Pompeii also suggests that the choice of portrait style, as well as statue format (equestrian, cuirassed, togate, hip-mantle, bust, or herm), may have been determined to some extent by the intended architectural setting of the portrait. The portraits most elevated in appearance come from the most elevated settings, such as shrines of the imperial cult (the Macellum portraits) or a *porticus* dedicated to *Concordia Augusta* (Eumachia's portrait). An authoritative, rather grave portrait style was used for the equestrian statue that stood on the so-called Arch of Caligula. A style connected with that of Augustus and Tiberius was used by individuals who held the office of *tribunus militum a populo*—a title conferred by the emperor—and/or were imperial priests, such as M. Holconius Rufus. Portraits commissioned for a domestic context tend to be less elevated in statue-body format and facial formulation, and more immediate and accessible in appearance. The preferred location for portraits of the owners of a house, at least in the case of individuals from the middle levels of Pompeian society, was in the *atrium* at the entrance to the *tablinum*. The herm format seems to have been widely used for the display of portraits in middle-class houses, particularly for the portraits of freedmen. Members of the elite had less to prove, and this might account for the fact that their portraits in domestic contexts are rare, where they survive, and are full statues found in the (more private) peristyle.

Portrait sculpture from Pompeii affords an excellent opportunity to investigate a fundamental aspect of Roman visual culture. As this summary has revealed, by exploring connections between portrait style, display context, as well as issues of social hierarchy, personal background, and gender, the evidence from Pompeii allows us to make significant strides towards reconstructing the nuanced visual codes of portrait style, statue format, and architectural setting used for self-representation by ancient Romans in Italy during the first century AD.

NOTES

1 Many of the ideas in this chapter were delivered as a lecture at Lincoln College, Oxford. I would like to thank S. Dillon, C. H. Hallett, R. R. R. Smith and J. Van Voorhis for their helpful comments. Fundamental works on Pompeian portraiture are: R. Bonifacio, *Ritratti romani da Pompei*, Rome, 1997; A. De Franciscis, *Il ritratto romano a Pompei*, MemNap, Naples, 1951; P. Zanker, *Pompeii: public and private life*, Cambridge, MA, 1998; H. Döhl and P. Zanker, "La Scultura," in F. Zevi (ed.), *Pompei 79*, Naples, 1979, pp. 177–210. On the social history of Pompeii and its families, see P. Castrén, *Ordo populusque Pompeianus*, Rome, 1975 and H. Mouritsen, *Elections, Magistrates and Municipal Élite. Studies in Pompeian epigraphy*, Rome, 1988.

Important works on private (non-imperial) portraiture: L. Giuliani, *Bildnis und Botschaft: Hermeneutische Untersuchungen zur Bildniskunst der römischen Republik*, Frankfurt am Main, 1986; K. Fittschen, "Pathossteigerung und Pathosdämpfung: Bemerkungen zu griechischen und römischen Porträts des 2. und 1. Jahrhunderts v. Chr.," *AA*, 1991, pp. 253–70; N. Bonacasa and G. Rizza (eds), *Ritratto ufficiale e ritratto privato*, Rome, 1988; P. Zanker, "Individuum und Typus: zur Bedeutung des realistischen Individualporträts der späten Republik," *AA*,

1995, pp. 473–81; P. Zanker, "Zur Rezeption des hellenistischen Individual-porträts in Rom und in den italienischen Städten," in P. Zanker (ed.), *Hellenismus in Mittelitalien*, Göttingen, 1976, vol. 2, pp. 581–609; P. Zanker, "Zur Bildnisrepräsentation führender Männer in mittelitalischen und campanischen Städten zur Zeit der späten Republik und der Julisch-Claudischen Kaiser," in *Les "Bourgeoisies" municipales italiennes aux IIe et Ier siècle av. J.-C.*, Naples, 1983, pp. 251–66; E. Gazda and A. E. Haeckl, "Roman portraiture: reflections on the question of context," *JRA*, 1993, vol. 6, pp. 289–302.

For the Greek East: P. Zanker, "Brüche im Bürgerbild? Zur bürgerlichen Selbstdarstellung in den hellenistischen Städten," in M. Wörrle and P. Zanker (eds), *Stadtbild und Bürgerbild im Hellenismus*, Munich, 1995, pp. 251–73; J. Inan and E. Alföldi-Rosenbaum, *Roman and Early Byzantine Portrait Sculpture in Asia Minor*, London, 1970; id., *Römische und frühbyzantinische Porträtplastik aus der Türkei: neue Funde*, Mainz, 1979; and now R. R. R. Smith (with contributions by Sheila Dillon, Christopher H. Hallett, Julia Lenaghan and Julie Van Voorhis), *Roman Portrait Statuary from Aphrodisias*, Mainz, 2006. On the garments discussed here, see J. Sebesta and L. Bonfante (eds), *The World of Roman Costume*, Madison, WI, 1994.

2 The recent book on Pompeian portraits by Bonifacio, *Ritratti*, while comprehensive in stylistic and iconographical analysis, bibliographical treatment, and enumeration of find-spots, strangely neglects to consider what the Pompeian material is capable of offering, namely a reconstruction of the relationship between statue type, portrait head, content of inscribed statue base and display context. Cf. Table 33.1 for political offices at Pompeii.

3 Cf. Dobbins, Ch. 12.

4 S. De Maria, *Gli archi onorari di Roma e dell'Italia romana*, Rome, 1988, p. 254 no. 38; F. Kleiner, *The Arch of Nero in Rome*, Rome, 1985, p. 56.

5 See the relief from the *lararium* in the House of Caecilius Iucundus (V.1.26), which shows the Temple of Jupiter, with its equestrian statues on either side, during the earthquake of AD 62: Zanker, *Pompeii*, p. 106, fig. 54a. The *lararium* reliefs were stolen in the 1990s and have not been recovered. Cf. also Small, Ch. 13.

6 G. P. Carratelli and I. Baldassarre (eds), *Pompei, pitture e mosaici*, Rome, 1991, vol. 3, pp. 251–7, esp. fig. 122; R. Brilliant, *Gesture and Rank in Roman Art*, New Haven, CT, 1963, fig. 2.15.

7 *CIL* X, 789, 790, 791, 792.

8 MNN inv. no. 5635; Bonifacio, *Ritratti*, pp. 31–4; Döhl and Zanker, "La Scultura," pp. 187, 191; De Franciscis, *Il Ritratto*, pp. 60–1; J. Bergemann, *Römische Reiterstatuen*, Mainz, 1990, pp. 91–4, P35 with excellent photographs (taf. 69–72).

9 See Bergemann, *Römische Reiterstatuen*, pp. 5–6 and 6–8. On the gesture of *adlocutio* see Brilliant, *Gesture and Rank*, pp. 57–8. The gilded bronze equestrian statue (of a private person) from Cartoceto features the portrait of a man who is similarly clad in a toga: *Bronzi dorati da Cartoceto*, Florence, 1987, pl. 32.

10 See H. R. Goette, "Mulleus—Embas—Calceus. Ikonographische Studien zu römischen Schuhwerke," *JdI*, 1988, vol. 103 pp. 401–64, esp. 456f., 464, with Abb. 35a; and Bergemann, *Römische Reiterstatuen*, p. 23.

11 Tiberius: K. Fittschen and P. Zanker, *Katalog der römischen Porträts in den Capitolinischen Museen und den anderen kommunalen Sammlungen der Stadt Rom*, Mainz, 1985, vol. I, pp. 12–15, nos. 11–12, Taf. 13–14.

12 Cf. Small, Ch.13.

13 *CIL* X, 820: M. TULLIUS M. F. D. V. I. D. TER. QUINC. / AUGUR TR. MIL. A POP. AEDEM FORTUNAE / AUGUST. SOLO ET PEQ, "Marcus Tullius, son of Marcus, *duovir* for the fifth time, by official decree *quinquennalis* for the third time, *augur*, *tribunus militum a populo*, [dedicated] the Temple of Fortuna Augusta with his own money."

14 Castrén, *Ordo*, pp. 97–9, 231–2.

15 For an inscription from the Villa at Lucus Feroniae, see W. Eck, "Die Familie der Volusii Saturnini in den neuen Inschriften aus Lucus Feroniae," *Hermes*, 1972, vol. 100, pp. 461–84; W. Eck, "Senatorial self-representation: developments in the Augustan period," in F. Millar and E. Segal (eds), *Caesar Augustus: seven aspects*, Oxford, 1984, pp. 129–68, esp. 143. On the Volusii, see M. T. Boatwright, *I Volusii Saturnini: una famiglia romana della prima età imperiale*, Bari, 1982; R. Syme, *The Augustan Aristocracy*, Oxford, 1986, pp. 319–20.

16 This was also the case at Herculaneum, where many statues of the proconsul M. Nonius Balbus stood in one small area of town, near the so-called Basilica, in the early imperial period. See Zanker, "Zur Bildnisrepräsentation."

17 MNN inv. no. 6233; Bonifacio, *Ritratti*, pp. 34–8; Döhl and Zanker, "La Scultura," pp. 187, 191–2; Zanker, *Pompeii*, p. 109; De Franciscis, *Il Ritratto*, pp. 37–9; P. Zanker, "Das Bildnis des M. Holconius Rufus," *AA*, 1981, pp. 349ff.; K. Stemmer, *Untersuchungen zur Typologie, Chronologie und Ikonographie der Panzerstatuen*, Berlin, 1978, p. 578, n. 65; Goette, "Mulleus—Embas—Calceus," p. 456.

18 Castrén, *Ordo*, p. 176.

19 *CIL* X, 830: M. HOLCONIO M. F. RUFO / TRIB. MIL. A POPUL. II VIR I. D. V / QUINC. ITER AUGUST. CAESARIS SACERD. / PATRONO COLONIAE, "To Marcus Holconius Rufus, son of Marcus, *tribunus militum a populo, duovir* for the fifth time and by official decree *quinquennalis* for the second time, priest of Augustus Caesar, patron of the colony." See the statue base at the center right of Figure 10.4.

20 M. Torelli, "Il culto imperiale a Pompei," *I culti della Campania antica*, Rome, 1998, pp. 245–70, esp. 249–50.

21 Castrén, *Ordo*, pp. 62–7, 98–9.

22 Paul Zanker, *The Power of Images in the Age of Augustus*, Ann Arbor, MI, 1990, fig. 155 (statue of Mars Ultor in the Musei Capitolini).

23 See Stemmer, *Panzerstatuen*, pp. 142ff. On the statues of M. Nonius Balbus, see Zanker, "Zur Bildnisrepräsentation," pp. 251ff., and S. Adamo Muscettola, "I Nonii Balbi e il foro di Ercolano," *Prospettiva*, 1982, vol. 28, pp. 2ff.

24 Zanker, "M. Holconius Rufus," p. 352; J. D'Arms, "Pompeii and Rome in the Augustan age and beyond: the eminence of the gens Holconia," in R. I. Curtis (ed.), *Studia pompeiana et classica*, New Rochelle, 1988, vol. I, pp. 55ff.

25 On Augustus' portraits, see Fittschen and Zanker, *Capitolinischen Museen*, vol. I, pp. 3–6, taf. 4–6; K. Vierneisel and P. Zanker, *Die Bildnisse des Augustus*, Munich, 1979; S. Walker and A. Burnet, *The Image of Augustus*, London, 1981; D. Boschung, *Die Bildnisse des Augustus*, Berlin, 1993; R. R. R. Smith, "Typology and diversity in the portraits of Augustus," *JRA*, 1996, vol. 9, pp. 30–47.

26 See Zanker, *Power of Images*, pp. 126–35; *Kaiser Augustus und die verlorene Republik*, Mainz, 1988, nos. 217–24; T. Hölscher, *Staatsdenkmal und Publikum: vom Untergang der Republik bis zur Festigung des Kaiserturms in Rom*, Konstanz, 1984, pp. 27–9. For worship of the *genius* of Augustus at Pompeii, see Ling, Ch. 9, Dobbins, Ch. 12 and esp. Small, Ch. 13.

27 MNN inv. no. 6232; Bonifacio, *Ritratti*, pp. 51–3; Döhl and Zanker, "La Scultura," pp. 180, 192–3; Zanker, *Pompeii*, pp. 97–101; De Franciscis, *Il Ritratto*, pp. 53–5.

28 For Eumachia, cf. Descœudres, Ch. 2; Dobbins, Ch. 12; Small, Ch. 13; Bernstein, Ch. 34; Cormack, Ch. 37.

29 Castrén, *Ordo*, pp. 165–6. Cf. Pirson, Ch. 29.

30 See Torelli, "Il culto imperiale," pp. 251ff.; L. Richardson, jr, *Pompeii. An architectural history*, Baltimore, MD, 1988, pp. 194–8; C. Panella, "Porticus Liviae," *LTUR*, vol. IV, pp. 127–9. See now T. Najbjerg, "A reconstruction and reconsideration of the so-called Basilica in Herculaneum," in *Pompeian Brothels, Pompeii's Ancient History, Mirrors and Mysteries, Art and Nature at Oplontis, & the Herculaneum "basilica,"* JRA Suppl. Ser. no. 47, 2002, pp. 123–65.

31 Castrén, *Ordo*, p. 165. The Eumachii may have been related to a historian from Neapolis called Eumachus (Ath. 13.577a).

32 This idea is also supported by Eumachia's tomb, in the Porta Nocera cemetery, which is unusual in taking the (Hellenistic Greek) form of a monumental *exedra*, such as we find in the city gate at Perge, or the Philopappos monument in Athens. See H. von Hesberg, *Römische Grabbauten*, Darmstadt, 1992, p. 193; Richardson, *Pompeii*, p. 257; A. D'Ambrosio and S. De Caro, "La necropoli di Porta Nocera. Campagna di scavo 1983," in H. von Hesberg and P. Zanker (eds), *Römische Gräberstrassen—Selbstdarstellung—Status—Standard*, Munich, 1987, pp. 199–228. Cf. Cormack, Ch. 37.

33 Castrén, *Ordo*, pp. 70–3. Cf Bernstein, Ch. 34.

34 There are four other surviving portrait statues with statue bodies in the "Eumachia" format, all dating to the Augustan and Tiberian periods, from Aquileia, Valle di Pompei, the via

Tiburtina outside Rome, and Nemi (Fundilia C. F. Rufa); these are discussed in detail by J. Lenaghan, *Portrait Statues of Women in the Roman World*, Ph.D. thesis, New York University, Institute of Fine Arts, 1999. On draped portrait statues of women in the Hellenistic period, see R. R. R. Smith, *Hellenistic Sculpture*, London, 1991, pp. 83–6.

35 MNN inv. no. 6041; Bonifacio, *Ritratti*, pp. 53–6; Döhl and Zanker, "La Scultura," p. 185–94, fig. 40; De Franciscis, *Il Ritratto*, pp. 63–5. Two other examples of female portraits with "ideal" Greek facial formulation and contemporary Roman hairstyles come from the Temple of Isis: MNN inv. nos. 6285, 6289; Bonifacio, *Ritratti*, nos. 9, 10, pp. 46–51. For the Macellum, see Dobbins, Ch. 12.

36 A. Mau, *Pompeii: its life and art* (transl. and ed. by F. W. Kelsey), rev. edn, London, 1902, pp. 98–100.

37 A statue of Livia in Holkham Hall, two statues from Cyrene, and a statue of a Vestal Virgin from the *Atrium Vestae* in Rome; these statues are discussed and interpreted by Lenaghan, *Portrait Statues*. On the "Artemisia type" see A. Heckler, "Römische weibliche Gewandstatuen," *Münchener Archäologische Studien dem Andeken Adolf Furtwänglers gewidmet*, Munich, 1909, pp. 134–5.

38 C. B. Rose, *Dynastic Commemoration and Imperial Portraiture in the Julio-Claudian Period*, Cambridge, 1997, p. 36; D. Boschung, "Die Bildnistypen der iulish-claudischen Kaiserfamilie," *JRA*, 1993, vol. 6, pp. 39–79, esp. 68–9 (Drusilla).

39 A. Small, "The shrine of the imperial family in the Macellum at Pompeii," in A. Small (ed.), *Subject and Ruler: the cult of the ruling power in classical antiquity*, JRA Suppl. Ser. no. 17, 1996, pp. 115–36; Small, Ch. 13; De Franciscis, *Il Ritratto*, p. 63–5 for the various identifications.

40 Drusus Minor: Boschung, "Die Bildnistypen," pp. 73–5 (Agrippina Minor), 43–5 (Octavia Minor) and 75–6 (Claudia Octavia); Fittschen and Zanker, *Capitolinischen Museen*, Mainz, 1983, vol. III, pp. 6–7, no. 5, taf. 6, Beilage 3–6 (Agrippina Minor).

41 MNN inv. no. 6044; Bonifacio, *Ritratti*, pp. 44–6; Döhl and Zanker, "La Scultura," pp. 194, 197; Zanker, *Pompeji*, p. 85; De Franciscis, *Il Ritratto*, pp. 63–4.

42 See P. Cain, *Männerbildnisse Neronisch-Flavischer Zeit*, Munich, 1993, esp. pp. 33 ff., 175–7; Fittschen and Zanker, *Capitolinischen Museen*, vol. I, no. 31, p. 35; M. Bergmann and P. Zanker, "Damnatio Memoriae. Umgearbeitete Nero- und Domitiansporträts. Zur Ikonographie der flavischen Kaiser und des Nerva," *JdI*, 1981, vol. 96, pp. 317–412, esp. 326–32; U. W. Hiesinger, "The portraits of Nero," *AJA*, 1975, vol. 79, pp. 120ff.

43 Britannicus: Boschung, "Die Bildnistypen," pp. 62–3; Rose, *Dynastic Commemoration*, pl. 172.

44 Small, "The shrine"; Boschung, "Die Bildnistypen," pp. 74–5; Rose, *Dynastic Commemoration*, p. 252 n. 190 for references to numismatic representations of Brittanicus.

45 S. Adamo Muscettola, "I Nigidi Mai di Pompei: fra politica tra l'età neroniana e l'età flavia," *RivIstArch*, 1991–92, vols 14–15, pp. 193–218; Castrén, *Ordo*, pp. 72, 133.

46 Torelli, "Il culto imperiale," pp. 265–6.

47 There are other portraits at Pompeii that use individualized physiognomies combined with an overlay of the portraits of members of the imperial family. Two bronze male busts from the area of the Basilica (MNN inv. nos. 5584, 19; Bonifacio, *Ritratti*, nos. 4–5, pp. 39–41), a draped male head from the area of the Temple of Venus (Pompei, Deposito del Foro inv. no. 6317; Bonifacio, *Ritratti*, no. 6, pp. 41–2), a bust from the House of the Citharist (I.4.25) (MNN inv. no. 111386; Bonifacio, *Ritratti*, no. 40, pp. 100–2), and a male head (MNN inv. no. 109516; Bonifacio, *Ritratti*, no. 47, pp. 116–18) all resemble imperial princes. A female bust from the House of the Citharist (MNN inv. no. 6192; Bonifacio, *Ritratti*, no. 43, pp. 107–9) resembles an imperial princess. A male bust from House (I.2.17) (MNN inv. no. 109611; Bonifacio, *Ritratti*, no. 34, pp. 89–90) and a male bust from the House of the Citharist (MNN inv. no. 6028; Bonifacio, *Ritratti*, no. 38, pp. 97–8) both resemble Agrippa. A bronze bust (MNN inv. no. 5617; Bonifacio, *Ritratti*, no. 50, pp. 122–3) resembles Tiberius. A nude statue with cloak over the shoulder (MNN inv. no. 6055; Bonifacio, *Ritratti*, no. 51, pp. 124–5) and a male bust (MNN inv. no. 109516; Bonifacio, *Ritratti*, no. 47, pp. 116–18) resemble Drusus Maior, brother of Tiberius (cf. Fittschen and Zanker, *Capitolinischen Museen*, vol. I, no. 19, taf. 21). A draped female statue from the *atrium* of the Villa of the Mysteries (MNN inv. no. 4400; Bonifacio, *Ritratti*, no. 42, pp. 104–7) resembles Livia and is doubtfully identified as such by Bonifacio and others, most recently E. Bartman, *Portraits of Livia. Imaging the imperial woman in Augustan Rome*, Cambridge, 1999, pp. 157–8.

48 The "hip mantle" statue format had first been used for the representations of divinities with bare chests and draped lower body, such as the Poseidon from Melos in the Athens National Museum. The hip mantle was then adopted in the late republican period for statues of Roman magistrates (for example, the "Tivoli General" in the Museo Nazionale Romano delle Terme) and in the early imperial period began to be used for portraits of imperial princes, as well as for private portraits. The hip mantle was not worn in reality by Romans—hence its "distancing" effect. Notwithstanding the use of this statue format for representations of Divus Julius (for example, on the so-called Ravenna relief), there is no evidence that the use of the hip mantle indicated that the represented person was deceased at the time that the statue was made, as is sometimes said (for example, by Bonifacio, *Ritratti*, p. 26). The use of nudity or partial nudity in portrait sculpture had a more general elevating effect. For these points, see C. H. Hallett, *The Roman Nude: heroic portrait statuary 200 BC–AD 300*, Oxford, 2005. The actual cult statue of Divus Julius, as shown on coins depicting this temple, was togate and carried an augural staff.

49 MNN inv. no. 4991; Bonifacio, *Ritratti*, pp. 28–31; De Franciscis, *Il Ritratto*, pp. 27–31.

50 The inscription is written in the genitive rather than usual dative case. The dedication seems to have been made to the *genius*, or "guardian spirit" (understood) of Norbanus Sorex, in a way analogous to the dedication to the *genius* of L. Caecilius Iucundus on his portrait herm (*CIL* X, 860; discussed below). On the Sorex inscription, see Torelli, "Il culto imperiale," p. 257. Also, cf. Cormack, Ch. 37.

51 Castrén, *Ordo*, p. 72.

52 A. M. Duff, *Freedmen in the Early Roman Empire*, Oxford, 1928, p. 104.

53 *CIL* X, 814; only the herm survives.

54 Plut., *Sull.* 36; *CIL* X, 814. Torelli, "Il culto imperiale," pp. 257ff., argues that the herm portrait of Norbanus Sorex that stood in the Edifice of Eumachia was part of a gallery of *viri illustri*, or famous Pompeians, on analogy with such galleries in the Forum of Augustus in Rome.

55 Late republican: Bonifacio, *Ritratti*, pp. 30–1. Augustan: Döhl and Zanker, "La Scultura," p. 197; S. Adamo Muscettola, "La decorazione architettonica e l'arredo," in S. De Caro *et al.*, *Alla ricerca di Iside*, Rome, 1992, p. 67; De Franciscis, *Il Ritratto*, pp. 27–35. See L. H. Petersen, *Freedmen in Roman Art and History*, Cambridge, 2006, p. 54.

56 M. G. Granino Cecere, "Nemi: l'erma di C. Norbanus Sorex," *RendPontAcc*, 1988–89, vol. 61 pp. 131–51, figs 1–3; F. Johansen, *Catalogue of Roman Portraits I. Ny Carlsberg Glyptotek*, Copenhagen, 1994, pp. 182–3, 192–7 (nos. 84–6). The herm shaft of Sorex is in Nemi; the other herm portraits, which are now in Copenhagen and Nottingham, include: (1) an actor, Fundilius Doctus, (2) his patron Fundilia, (3) a woman called Licinia Chrisarion, (4) L. Faenius Faustus, an actor and player of fourth parts; (5) L. Aninius Rufus, *quaestor* of Aricia, whose herm portrait was erected by his wife Prima (probably a freedwoman), (6) Q. Hostius Capito, teacher of rhetoric, (7) Staia Quinta, freedwoman of Lucius.

57 Pompeii, Deposito del Foro, inv. no. 3015; Bonifacio, *Ritratti*, pp. 99–100; Döhl and Zanker, "La Scultura," p. 196; De Franciscis, *Il Ritratto*, p. 23.

58 For Julius Caesar's portraiture, see F. S. Johansen, "Antichi ritratti di Caio Giulio Cesare nella scultura," *AnalRom*, 1967, vol. 4, pp. 7–68.

59 Döhl and Zanker, "La Scultura," p. 196, fig. 108.

60 Castrén, *Ordo*, pp. 207–9. Petersen, *Freedmen*, pp. 50–1, 248 n.132.

61 MNN inv. no. 4989; Bonifacio, *Ritratti*, pp. 87–9; De Franciscis, *Il Ritratto*, p. 25.

62 MNN inv. no. 4990; Bonifacio, *Ritratti*, pp. 109–11; Döhl and Zanker, "La Scultura," p. 195; De Franciscis, *Il Ritratto*, pp. 49–50.

63 Fittschen and Zanker, *Capitolinischen Museen*, vol. III, pp. 5f., no. 4, Taf. 4–5; Boschung, "Die Bildnistypen," pp. 61–2 (Agrippina Maior).

64 Despite the fact that the two bronze busts are obviously a pair (they are both the same size, 38 cm high, and are of comparable workmanship and quality), Bonifacio (*Ritratti*, pp. 88, 110–11) dates the male bust to the later republican or Augustan period and the female bust to the Claudian period.

65 MNN inv. no. 110663; Bonifacio, *Ritratti*, pp. 92–4; Döhl and Zanker, "La Scultura," p. 194; De Franciscis, *Il Ritratto*, p. 31.

66 Jean Andreau, *Les affaires de Monsieur Jucundus*, Rome, 1974; Castrén, *Ordo*, p. 144. Cf. Jongman, Ch. 32; Franklin, Ch. 33.

67 An Augustan date for the portrait and identification with L. Caecilius Felix is also proposed in Döhl and Zanker, "La Scultura," p. 197. See Petersen, *Freedmen*, pp. 75, 163–83, esp. 166.

68 I am grateful to John Bodel for this information.

69 Other portraits from Pompeii that use a style of heightened realism: the herm portrait of Vesonius Primus (see below); a male bust (MNN inv. no. 6169; Bonifacio, *Ritratti*, no. 46, pp. 115–16); a bronze male bust that resembles Cato the Younger (MNN inv. no. 4992; Bonifacio, *Ritratti*, no. 49, pp. 120–2).

70 This style of heightened realism, or "verism," is used particularly for freedmen during the early imperial period in their grave reliefs: see P. Zanker, "Grabreliefs römischer Freigelassener," *JdI*, 1975, vol. 90, pp. 267–315; also V. Kockel, *Porträtreliefs stadtrömischer Grabbauten*, Mainz, 1993. Many of these portraits have a bland, generic quality, interpreted by Zanker as a function of the level of production. We may also suggest that signs of assertiveness were thought to be out of keeping with the social status and professions of freedmen. Such an assertive "veristic" style had been characteristic of the portraits of Roman elite during the first century BC, as is known from dated coins (e.g., J. M. C. Toynbee, *Roman Historical Portraits*, Ithaca, NY, 1978, pp. 17ff., figs 1, 7, 8), and was probably used earlier during the second century BC when we hear of realistic-looking portrait masks (*imagines*) of deceased family members kept in cupboards in *atria* and worn by family members during funeral processions (Polyb. 6.53; Plin. *HN* 35.5–8); see G. Lahusen, "Zur Funktion und Rezeption des römischen Ahnenbildes," *RM*, 1985, vol. 92, 1985, pp. 261–84; H. Flower, *Ancestor Masks and Aristocratic Power in Roman Culture*, Oxford, 1996.

71 See S. Treggiari, *Roman Freedmen during the Late Republic*, Oxford, 1969, p. 8, and S. van Houte, *The Freedmen at Pompeii*, Ph.D. thesis, University of Maryland, 1971, pp. 13ff.

72 J. D'Arms, "The typicality of Trimalchio," in *Commerce and Social Standing in Ancient Rome*, Cambridge, MA, 1981, pp. 97–120; A. Maiuri, *La cena di Trimalchione di Petronio Arbitro*, Naples, 1945, p. 157.

73 The name *Vesonius Pri{mus}* appears on wax tablet no. 31 from the House of L. Caecilius Iucundus (*c*.AD 57). Primus evidently served as a witness for at least one of Iucundus' business transactions. There is some possible evidence that Iucundus may have rented Primus' fullery, but this is debated: see Andreau, *Monsieur Jucundus*, pp. 281–4.

74 Likewise the Pentelic marble of the *impluvium* fountain is "exotic" but low in quality; cf. Fant, Ch. 22. For the frescoes, see Caratelli and Baldassarre, *Pitture e mosaici*, vol. V, pp. 284–7. Paintings such as these are interpreted by P. Zanker as the least expensive form of villa imitation; elite Romans frequently had game preserves in their villas, in which at least on one occasion a slave dressed up as Orpheus in order to entertain his master's guests (Varro, *Rust.* 3.13). See Zanker, *Pompeii*, pp. 184ff.

75 Deposito del Foro, inv. no. 407/4; Bonifacio, *Ritratti*, pp. 90–2; De Franciscis, *Il Ritratto*, pp. 30–1.

76 For the *graffito*, see M. Della Corte, *Case ed abitanti di Pompei*, 3rd edn, Naples, 1965, p. 275; A. and M. De Vos, *Pompei, Ercolano, Stabia*, 2nd edn, Rome-Bari, 1982, p. 209.

77 L. R. Taylor, "Freedmen and freeborn in the epitaphs of imperial Rome," *AJP*, 1961, vol. 82, pp. 113–32, esp. 125; van Houte, *Freedmen at Pompeii*, pp. 54–5; Castrén, *Ordo*, p. 238. The large theater at Pompeii was architecturally designed by a freedman, who took Primus as his cognomen, as is attested by an inscription found there: "*M. Artorius M. l. Primus architectus*" ("Marcus Artorius Primus, freedman of Marcus, [was] architect") (*CIL* X, 841).

78 Portraits from Pompeii that use a similar style (but lack a known find-spot): a male bust (MNN inv. no. 6169; Bonifacio, *Ritratti*, no. 46, pp. 115–16); a bronze male bust that resembles Cato the Younger (MNN inv. no. 4992; Bonifacio, *Ritratti*, no. 49, pp. 120–2). That such a style was regularly used for members of the municipal elite in the mid-first century AD is also indicated by the image of Vespasian, who hailed from the Sabine town of Reate. See P. Zanker, "Principat und Herrscherbild," *Gymnasium*, 1979, vol. 86, pp. 353–68, esp. 362–4; Bergmann and Zanker, "Damnatio Memoriae," pp. 332ff.

79 That a republican-looking portrait style was still being used in first-century Rome for members of the elite is also, of course, indicated by the coin portraits of Galba (AD 68) and Vitellius

(AD 69); and for members of the middle class by grave reliefs of the first century AD that feature portraits in different period styles on the same panel. An example is a Flavian relief formerly in the *Palazzo dei Conservatori* (Mus. Nuovo inv. no. 9828 and now in an exhibition at *La Centrale Montemartini* on the via Ostiense). It shows three men—two brothers (Apemantus and Thalerus), and Uliades, dedicator of the monument. Thalerus has a Flavian-looking portrait similar to that of the emperor Titus, and Uliades has a portrait that appears wholly late republican, in the manner of Julius Caesar's lifetime portraits: see Kockel, *Porträtreliefs*, pp. 204–5, taf. 120a.

80 Contrary to what is said in the literature, there is no evidence that any of the busts from the House of the Citharist (I.4.25) were part of a gallery of ancestor portraits, as alleged by Flower, *Ancestor Masks*, pp. 40, 79 n. 78; and E. Dwyer, *Pompeian Domestic Sculpture: a study of five Pompeian houses and their contents*, Rome, 1982, pp. 127–8. A female bust (MNN inv. no. 6192; Bonifacio, *Ritratti*, no. 43, pp. 107–9), found in the *tablinum*, is probably Claudian in date; two male busts of early Augustan date (MNN inv. nos. 6025, 6028; Bonifacio, *Ritratti*, nos. 37–38, pp. 94–8) were not on display in the *atrium* but were found on an upper floor and were probably being kept in storage—they had been cut down to bust form from statues.

81 Cf. Allison, Ch. 17. In the case of villas, the garden or *cubiculum* seems to have been the preferred display context for portraits of the current owner or members of his family; evidence collected by R. Neudecker, *Die Skulpturen-Ausstattung römischer Villen in Italien*, Mainz, 1988, pp. 75–91.

82 This is the so-called statue of Livia found *in situ* in the peristyle of the Villa of the Mysteries (MNN inv. no. 4400; Bonifacio, *Ritratti*, no. 42, pp. 104–7), which probably instead represents one of the members of the family that owned the villa.

83 In the Villa of the Papyri, the *atrium* contained only ideal sculpture and portraits of Hellenistic kings; the portraits of contemporary Romans from this villa were not found in the *atrium* but in a private room between the small and large peristyles; see M. George, "Elements of the peristyle in Campanian *atria*," *JRA*, 1998, vol. 11, pp. 82–100; Neudecker, *Skulpturen-Ausstattung*, pp. 105–14.

84 Neudecker, *Skulpturen-Ausstattung*, pp. 105–14.

85 As noted by K. Fittschen, "Die Statuen des Poseidippos und des Pseudo-Menander," *AM*, 1992, vol. 107, pp. 229–71, esp. 247. There exist several unidentified herm-portraits of men of the imperial period that are of high quality and are therefore likely to represent prominent people. For a detailed discussion of one of these, identified as a man of letters, see R. Wünsche, "Eine Bildnisherme in der Münchner Glyptothek," *MüJb*, 1980, vol. 31, pp. 13–34.

86 Vesonius Primus, L. Caecilius Iucundus, the bronze busts from the House of the Citharist (I.4.25), Norbanus Sorex. The herm portrait from the House of Cornelius Rufus (VIII.4.15) (Bonifacio, *Ritratti*, no. 32) is inscribed simply: C. CORNELIO RUFO, "To Gaius Cornelius Rufus" (*CIL* X, 864), but the identity of the individual is not specifically known: Castrén, *Ordo*, p. 157. Two other herm portraits from Pompeii (Bonifacio, *Ritratti*, nos. 4, 49) are uninscribed.

87 See Johansen, *Catalogue of Roman Portraits* and Granino Cecere, "Nemi." A series of portrait herms of charioteers comes from a shrine of Hercules in Trastevere in Rome; see L. Nista, *Sacellum Herculis. Le sculture del tempio di Ercole a Trastevere*, Rome, 1991.

88 See H. Wrede, *Die Antike Herme*, p. 77. A painted portrait of Trimalchio (Petron., *Sat.* 28) holding a caduceus appeared on a wall of his house; similarly, portraits of freedmen were often represented with the attributes of Hermes: evidence collected by H. Wrede, *Consecratio in Formam Deorum*, Mainz, 1981, pp. 273–83.

89 Cf. Cormack, Ch. 37.

90 The statues were found together in (*PErc* 38 N). Cf. Cormack, Ch. 37, n. 1, for an explanation of the numbering and abbreviation system for cemeteries at Pompeii. Middle-class tombs of the republican era often featured full-length statues on the façade, whereas middle-class tombs of the Julio-Claudian period and later were often more enclosed and tended to use relief sculpture, rather than portrait sculpture, on their façades; see von Hesberg, *Römische Grabbauten*, p. 71.

91 Bonifacio, *Ritratti*, no. 13, pp. 61–2; V. Kockel, *Die Grabbauten vor dem Herkulaner Tor in Pompeji*, Mainz, 1983, p. 171.

92 Döhl and Zanker, "La Scultura," pp. 189–91; Zanker, *Pompeii*, pp. 76–7.

93 Pompei Antiquarium inv. no. 14205; Bonifacio, *Ritratti*, no. 14, pp. 62–4; Kockel, *Porträtreliefs*, p. 172.

94 P. Zanker, "Grabreliefs"; Giuliani, *Bildnis und Botschaft*, pp. 200–38, figs 57–64; J. M. C. Toynbee, *Roman Historical Portraits*, pp. 24–46; Kockel, *Porträtreliefs*.

95 MNN inv. no. 6055; Bonifacio, *Ritratti*, no. 51, pp. 124–5.

96 See N. Himmelmann, *Herrscher und Athlet. Die Bronzen vom Quirinal*, Milan, 1989, pp. 100–25, with figs 46–50; Smith, *Hellenistic Sculpture*, pp. 255–61.

97 On this phenomenon, see P. Zanker, "Herrscherbild und Zeitgesicht," in *Römisches Porträt: Wege zur Erforschung eines gesellschaftlichen Phänomenons. Wissenschaftliche Konferenz, Berlin 1981*, Berlin, 1982, pp. 307–12; for a critique, see M. Bergmann, "Zeittypen im Kaiserporträt?" in *Römisches Porträt*, pp.143–7.

98 For selected examples, see above, n. 47, less the "pseudo-Livia." Also, a male portrait head from the House of the Gilded Cupids (VI.16.7) (MNN inv. no. 3015; Bonifacio, *Ritratti*, no. 39, pp. 99–100) draws on portraits of Divus Julius (discussed above).

99 Selected examples of middle-aged men: male bust from (*PNoc* 4 EN) (Pompei, Deposito del Foro inv. no. 10942; Bonifacio, *Ritratti*, no. 23, pp. 73–4); herm portrait of Cornelius Rufus (Pompei, Deposito del Foro; Bonifacio, *Ritratti*, no. 32, pp. 86–7); male bust from House (IX.6.3) (MNN inv. no. 111385; Bonifacio, *Ritratti*, no. 41, pp. 102–3).

CHAPTER THIRTY-SEVEN

THE TOMBS AT POMPEII

———— · ◆ · ————

Sarah Cormack

The narrative presented by the tombs at Pompeii is in many ways unique. Unlike other necropoleis that may represent decades or centuries of use, transformation, and accumulation of debris before gradual abandonment, the tombs at Pompeii present a snapshot of how the necropolis looked at a particular moment in time. As Vesuvius erupted, some of the inhabitants of Pompeii fled out of the city along the streets lined with tombs. Some of them sought shelter in the entrances or inner chambers of the monumental tombs, finding, inadvertently, their own final resting places. These victims were obviously not the occupants for whom the tombs were intended; due, however, to the unique archaeological circumstances at Pompeii, archaeologists and epigraphists can reconstruct a great deal concerning the identity of the original tomb occupants, and the way in which the tomb environment conveyed various messages concerning, for example, social status, family or political connections. The purpose here is to present the sorts of evidence that the tombs preserve, and to interpret that evidence in the framework of the broader social environment at Pompeii. After a brief discussion of the locations and typology of the Pompeian tombs, we shall turn to the evidence for their functions and usage, their decorative schemes and the implications of this decoration, and the contribution of the epitaph towards the creation of an individual or group identity. Finally, observations will be offered regarding whether the tombs can be viewed as a mirror of society (as attested in the urban evidence), or whether they constitute an idealised, utopian space.[1]

LOCATIONS, TYPOLOGY AND CHRONOLOGY

As is common with most cities of the Roman West, the major cemeteries (necropoleis) at Pompeii are grouped outside the city gates or strung out along the major approaches to the city, intramural burial being traditionally forbidden except under special circumstances. The most important cemeteries of the Roman colonial period, the extensive Porta Nocera necropolis and the necropolis outside the Porta Ercolano, have been well published.[2] Furthermore, smaller groups of tombs exist outside the Porta del Vesuvio, the Porta di Nola, the Porta Marina, and the Porta di Stabia, although these tombs have not been as extensively—or as recently—studied (Map 3; Figure 28.1).[3] Far less accessible for the modern scholar is the funerary material at Herculaneum, where eighteenth-century archaeologists occasionally stumbled upon structures that they interpreted as tombs, but where systematic research into the funerary picture has not yet been carried out (Map 4, B).[4] From the extremely scant evidence available for Herculaneum, it seems likely that there, too, tombs of prominent citizens were clustered at areas of highest visibility, namely, outside the city gates and along the important approach roads.[5] Thus, at both Pompeii and Herculaneum, the visitor to the city was welcomed by images of the dead, images which transmitted important messages about familial connections, social status, and who wielded power in the city.

At Pompeii, the preserved monumental tombs date without exception to the post-colony period. A Samnite cemetery has come to light, however, revealing that the pre-colonial inhabitants practised inhumation burial as opposed to the cremation burials of the late republican and imperial periods.[6] In this cemetery, outside the Porta di Stabia, inhumation burials, in which the corpse was commonly placed in a simple *fossa* or covered with tiles, have been excavated. In addition, a total of 119 cremation burials of the Roman period were also unearthed. In spite of the presence of these two distinct burial practices, the majority of the tombs of both phases belonged to an indigenous family, the Epidii. Thus, a single family rapidly adopted cremation after the arrival of the colonists. This example of the willingness of one social group to adopt and adapt its burial practices to that of the "other" will be encountered again.

This enclosed cemetery with its modest burials, however, is not the dominant picture for funerary architecture at Pompeii. After the transformation of the city to a colony under Sulla in 80 BC, the picture changes drastically: the monumental built tomb appears, unequivocally constituting a new architectural type.[7] The two major arterial roads along which tombs were built—outside the Porta Ercolano and the Porta Nocera—differ from each other in subtle ways. The Porta Nocera necropolis contains an unbroken row of tombs, while those of the Porta Ercolano necropolis are interspersed with shops and extramural residences (Figure 37.1). Furthermore, the Porta Nocera tombs are predominantly the resting places of socially ambitious freedmen and their families, although the tomb of Eumachia provides an exception (cf. George, Ch. 35). Although tombs of *liberti* are indeed found in the Porta Ercolano necropolis, there is a higher concentration here of tombs belonging to members of the magisterial order. Support for this observation is also provided by the complete absence in the Porta Nocera necropolis of the *schola* tomb, a tomb type associated without exception with the magisterial order (cf. Bernstein, Ch. 34).

The *schola* tomb serves as a good introduction to the variety of tomb types at Pompeii. This tomb type generally consists of a semicircular bench with high back, sides terminating in sculpted lion's or griffin-lion's feet, and often supporting a graceful column (which in turn may be capped with an elegant stone urn) (Figure 37.2). Furthermore, the type is only found directly outside four of the city gates, the Porta di Nola, the Porta di Stabia, the Porta del Vesuvio and the Porta Ercolano.[8] In form, the *schola* tombs seem to have some connection to honorific benches erected in the Hellenistic East, but they differ from these via their funerary function. Funerary urns have only been found in a few of the enclosures which *scholae* mark, and in many cases the actual burial method remains obscure. Inscriptions associated with these *schola*

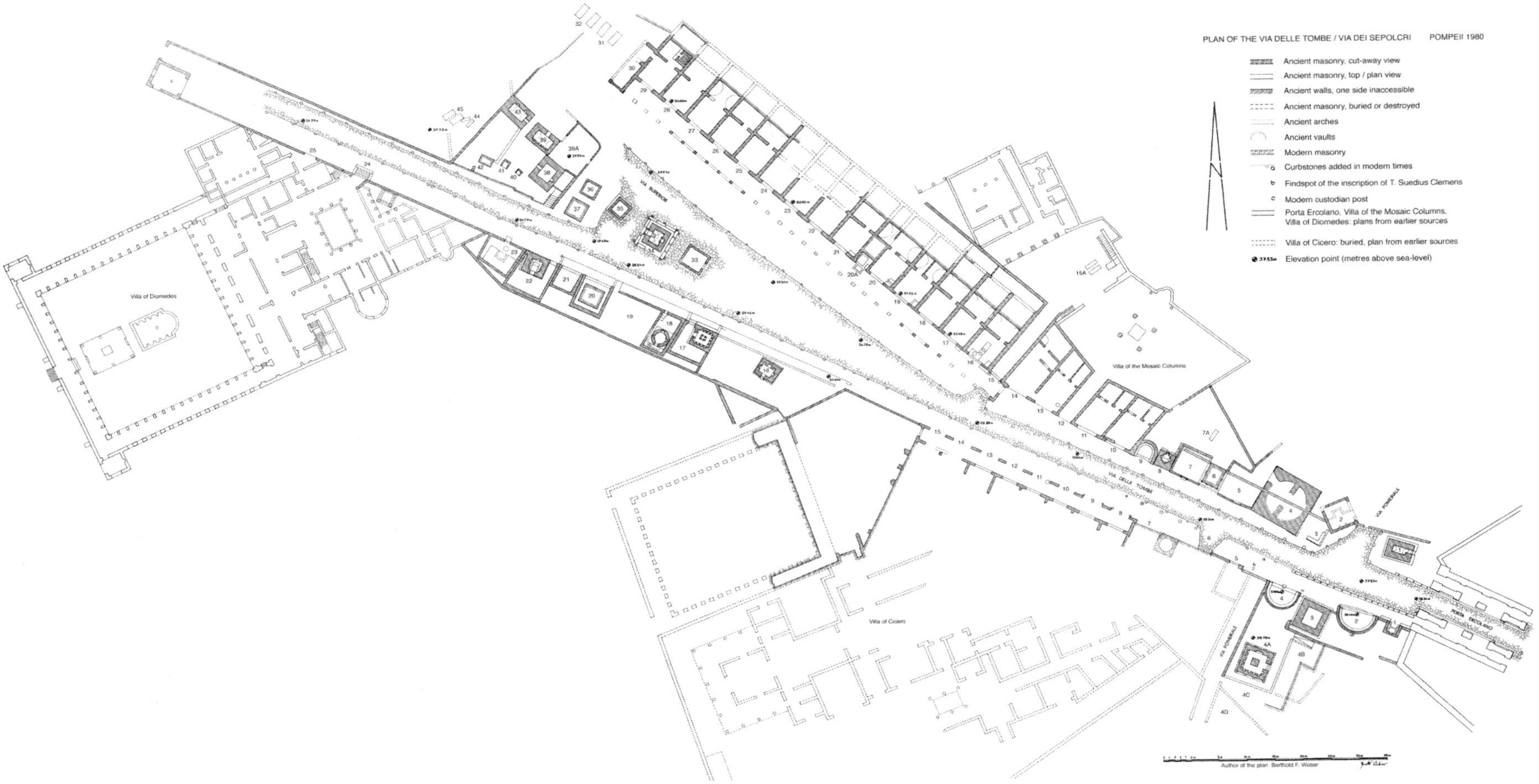

Figure 37.1 Plan of Porta Eccolano necropolis, Pompeii; after Kockel 1983, drawn by B. F. Weber and reproduced with permission.

Figure 37.2 View of *schola* tomb of Aesquillia Polla, Porta di Nola necropolis.
Photo: DAI Rom 63.1279.

tombs indicate that they were the preserve of the highest echelon of Pompeian society: *duoviri*, *quinquennales*, priests, or their wives (Table 33.1). Furthermore, it has recently been demonstrated that these tombs were all situated within, roughly, a thirty-metre zone outside the city wall. Not only did this prominent location assure the families of a continuous presence in the urban fabric, but the zone in which they were built can be interpreted as corresponding to the *pomerium* of Pompeii.[9] Since burial within the pomerial zone was forbidden for religious—and occasionally military—reasons, these *schola* tombs constituted marks of singular honour, possibly signalling connections between those who were buried there and the imperial household.[10]

Beyond these bench tombs, which constitute a uniquely Pompeian type, the remaining tombs at Pompeii resist easy classification. What is evident is the tremendous variation possible in the form of the tomb, a circumstance paralleled at numerous other Roman sites. There are examples of:

1   Multi-storey *aedicula* tombs, often elevated on a tall podium; e.g., the tomb of Marcus Octavius and Vertia Philumina (Figure 37.3).[11]
2   Podium tombs supporting a circular superstructure; e.g., the tomb of Veia Barchilla and Numerius Pulcher.[12]

3   Altar tombs, also often elevated on a high base; e.g., the tomb of Umbricius Scaurus (Figure 37.5).[13]

4   Tombs with large arcuated niches built into their façades; e.g., the tomb of L. Barbidius.[14]

5   Tombs with numerous niches, either interior or exterior, for the location of cinerary urns; e.g., the tomb of the Flavii (Figure 37.4).[15]

There does seem to be some evidence for the concentration of certain types of tombs in certain areas. For example, the tomb type with a prominent niche in the façade and associated burial *stelae* does not occur in the Porta Ercolano necropolis,

Figure 37.3   View of *PNoc* 13 OS—tomb of Octavii, Porta Nocera necropolis;
DAI Rom 58.1942.

Figure 37.4   View of *PNoc* 7 OS—tomb of the Flavii, Porta Nocera necropolis;
DAI Rom 70.883.

while it is only in this necropolis that the small funerary altar on elevated socle is to be found.[16] The *columella* or funerary *stelae* often associated with many of these freestanding tombs constitutes another burial monument unique to Pompeii (Figures 37.6a–b). Its sociological implications are further discussed below.

In addition to these broad typological observations, a chronological development for the various tomb types can be proposed. The monumental, "multi-storey" tomb with tall podium and *cella* or *aedicula*, often containing statues of the deceased, utterly inaccessible and somewhat macabre in their isolation and frontal pose, is found predominantly during the republican period (cf. Welch, Ch. 36).[17] In the Porta Nocera necropolis, such tombs tend to be found in the western region of the necropolis street, towards the direction of the Porta di Stabia where the earlier Samnite burials have come to light. In general, these republican tombs utilise tufa and *opus incertum* as facing material, and when columns are employed they are frequently of stuccoed masonry.

During the late republican and early Augustan periods new types appear, including the tomb with circular superstructure, perhaps representing a modification of the circular tomb of the late republic attested at the city of Rome; and the *schola* tomb, only attested in the Augustan and early Tiberian periods.[18] The chamber tomb with a façade containing multiple niches for the insertion of portrait busts or *stelae* is another type appropriated by the inhabitants of Pompeii from the funerary repertoire of the capital city. The new Pompeian type, however, did not simply mimic the

Roman examples but took on a unique local form through the presence of *stelae* (*columellae*) which are otherwise absent from the Roman record.[19] The outward appearance of such tombs, exemplified by the tomb of the Flavii (*PNoc* 7 OS), constitutes an amalgamation of freedmen's tombs from the city of Rome (with their portrait reliefs confronting passers-by), and the *columbarium* tomb, whose walls were covered with niches containing plaques or busts of the dead (Figure 37.4). In the early imperial period even altar tombs undergo a transformation that seemingly reflects a shift in emphasis, from the commemoration of a wealthy and prominent individual, to the assertion of the individual's place within a larger group. In the republican period, altar tombs were free-standing, relatively large monuments, for example the tomb of M. Porcius, dated to *c.*50 BC, from the Porta Ercolano necropolis.[20] Over time, the altar tomb decreased in size, became more elaborately decorated (sometimes with marble reliefs depicting events from the life of the deceased), and was placed on top of an elevated socle which now housed a funerary chamber for multiple burials (Figure 37.5).[21]

Figure 37.5 Altar tombs *PErc* S 20 (showing a *bisellium*), of C. Calventius Quietus, and S 22, tomb of Munatius Faustus and Naevoleia Tyche, Porta Ercolano necropolis, Pompeii; DAI Rom 77.2128.

The increasing exploitation of marble for decorative effects is another feature of Augustan tomb architecture (cf. Fant, Ch. 22). The monumental tomb of Eumachia, priestess probably of the cult of Venus and benefactrix of the forum building which bears her name, supported an elaborate scenographic display of alternating niches, decorated with marble reliefs (an Amazonomachy) and free-standing marble sculpture. Altars carved with *erotes*, garlands and masks stood on a flat terrace in front of the *exedra* tomb (cf. Dobbins, Ch. 12; Welch, Ch. 36).[22]

In the Julio-Claudian period, tombs often resemble public, honorific architecture: the tomb with large arcuated entrance seems directly to reflect such commemorative civic structures as the triumphal arch. In the post-earthquake period, however, scholars have detected a substantial impoverishment in the funerary record, with many tombs containing simple vaulted niches and decorated with painted scenes as opposed to more elaborate marble or stucco reliefs. Furthermore, the latest tombs often appear to have been squeezed into spaces between earlier, more elaborate tombs, suggesting a struggle for real estate.[23]

Not all of the tombs of the last twenty-five years of the colony's life are modest. Such tombs as that of Lucius Barbidius Communis, freedman and *magister* of the *Pagus Augustus Felix Suburbanus* (cf. Guzzo, Ch. 1), had an elaborate façade punctuated with niches framed by half-columns on high podia. This elaborate scheme indicates the eagerness with which the freedman class now displayed its wealth and status via the medium of the tomb monument.[24] In spite of the wide variety of the funerary repertoire at Pompeii, a basic transformation can be detected from a monumental, imposing, and physically isolated type (e.g., the multi-storey *aedicula* tomb) to a tomb that could accommodate multiple burials and whose façade adopts elements of domestic architecture (doorways, brickwork niches, etc.). These communal tombs, in turn, develop from a type with emphasis on the façade, where exterior niches signal the minimum number of people buried within, to a type with interior tomb chamber, the façade now reserved for more or less elaborate architectonic display. Such architectural changes reflect social changes as well: the powerful *gentes* who dominated the magisterial order were gradually joined, and perhaps even displaced, by families, often of servile origin, anxious to announce their newly acquired wealth and position. In this regard the funerary evidence mirrors wider social changes in the city: epigraphic analysis has documented that, after the Julio-Claudian period, the magisterial *ordo* contained names previously unattested, and possibly of freedman origin (cf. Jongman, Ch. 32; cf. Franklin, Ch. 33).[25]

THE FUNCTION AND USAGE OF TOMBS

Pompeian tombs also preserve evidence for burial practice and ritual. After the Samnite period, the burial practice preferred was, almost without exception, cremation.[26] The dead were either cremated in common areas designated for this purpose in the necropolis (an *ustrinum*); or, in some cases, the cremation took place within the private tomb enclosure itself (a *bustum*).[27] Remains of the deceased were gathered and placed in a cinerary urn (usually of terracotta or glass; rarely of marble) which was then either buried in the ground in the funerary enclosure, placed in a niche inside the tomb chamber, or inserted in a niche in the tomb façade. No specific chronological or social patterns have emerged to explain these various placements.

Figure 37.6a   View of basalt stelae (*columellae*), Porta Nocera necropolis, Tomb 16.
Photo: P. W. Foss.

Figure 37.6b
View of inscribed limestone stele
(*columella*), Porta Ercolano necropolis,
at Tomb 42, naming a freedman of
Marcus Arrius Diomedes: *CIL* X,
1044. Photo: P. W. Foss.

Another common feature of many burials at Pompeii is the *columella* or burial stele. These *stelae*, of which approximately 500 have so far come to light, are a distinctive Pompeian type: they are lava, tufa, basalt, limestone, or, after the Augustan period, marble slabs whose upper element resembles an abstracted human head (Figures 37.6a–b); cf. George, Ch. 35. Of this group, about 180 were inscribed with basic information regarding the deceased.[28] In many cases gender is distinguished, female *columellae* being differentiated by the addition of a knob at the back representing a stylized coiffure.[29] The *columellae* not only served as aboveground markers for cinerary urns, but also marked the mouths of tubes via which libations could be poured, symbolic sustenance for the deceased. Remarkably, even when the *stelae* were placed in the façade of a tomb, tubes frequently led to the cinerary urn housed in the tomb chamber.[30] *Columellae* were not restricted to a particular social class: children, slaves, *liberti* and magistrates all had *stelae*. Furthermore, the *columella* was an element of the pre-colonial funerary repertoire that was rapidly adopted by the colonists, and integrated into the monumental tomb structures that appeared after the arrival of the new social group.[31] These observations indicate the crucial role of the *columella* in the cult of the dead at Pompeii.

In addition to the abundant evidence from Pompeii that the dead were symbolically provided with sustenance, there is also evidence, albeit less widespread, that visitors to the tomb also banqueted there on prescribed days dedicated to the memory of the dead. The tomb of Gnaeus Vibrius Saturninus outside the Porta Ercolano contains benches in a *triclinium* arrangement.[32] The presence of areas identified as gardens adjacent to the tombs also suggests that the entire area was intended to represent a *locus amoenus*, "pleasant spot", in which the living were invited to spend time (cf. Jashemski, Ch. 31). If the tomb garden yielded produce, the income from this harvest contributed to the *tutela* (money dedicated for the maintenance of the tomb). In this sense the tomb had an economic function, albeit one whose implications did not reach beyond its own boundaries.[33]

Tombs at Pompeii functioned not only as burial spaces for the dead and locations of ritual activity on the part of the living. Their architectural design, if it incorporated benches or an *exedra*, might invite passers-by to relax and, ideally, contemplate the life and beneficence of the deceased (Figure 37.2). The walls of the tombs also served as public "bulletin boards": in addition to the primary epitaph, community announcements such as electoral notices, advertisements for gladiatorial or theatrical events, or more personal messages such as salutations to friends or sexual insults were scratched (*graffiti*) or painted (*dipinti*) on the tomb.[34] Such notices reveal that the cemetery was heavily frequented, due to its location along highways, and that tombs were treated as public space. Since these messages also reveal a stark contrast between the social rank of the tomb's patron and that of those who congregated there, we are invited to reconsider who actually had access to the tomb and how, or if, the space was controlled. Thus, although these secondary inscriptions cannot properly be considered part of the tomb's original framework, the interaction which they reveal between the living and the dead suggests an absence of barriers or borders in the ancient cemetery, a situation that contrasts with the way in which modern graveyards are often maintained.

THE DECORATION OF THE TOMB:
IMAGE AND TEXT

It is evident that the architectonic scheme of the tombs, combined with their location along the roads outside Pompeii, played an important role in transmitting the intended message of power to those passing by. Although the patron may have had some input into the choice of tomb type, additional decorative elements such as statues, portraits, reliefs, paintings, and the tomb epitaph itself, seem more revealing of the personal wishes of the patron. Furthermore, if anything can be determined regarding the owner's beliefs concerning death and the afterlife, it is likely to be gleaned from these more personal expressions. Perhaps in contrast to our expectations, full-length statues are preserved in surprisingly few tombs. Furthermore, to judge by the extant evidence, the funerary statue was a phenomenon restricted to the late republican and Augustan periods (cf. Welch, Ch. 36). The most common type was a standing figure— usually togate if male, or, if female, draped modestly in *pudicitia* pose (a pose denoting female chastity, based on images of the personification of this virtue, Pudicitia)— and often of tufa coated with stucco to imitate marble (Figures 36.13–14; 37.3).[35] In nearly all examples, husbands and wives are shown together, emphasising the marital bond. However, that bond is not underscored via such emotive gestures as the *dextrarum iunctio*, the clasping of the right hands adopted elsewhere as a convenient visual symbol for conjugal union.[36]

Such full-length statues were almost always placed in an *aedicula*, as if in emulation of a cult statue in a shrine. Unique for Pompeii is the pair of seated statues depicting an elderly couple from (*PNoc* 9 OS) (Figure 37.7). The tufa figures, the male togate with a *rotulus* (scroll) and the female in high-girt tunic with mantle covering her head, are placed against the rear wall of the *naiskos* (small shrine) that forms the crowning element of their tower-like late republican tomb. They manage to convey a combination of aloofness and accessibility: isolated yet seemingly welcoming the visitor to the tomb in much the same manner as the seated limestone ancestors with outstretched hands known from Etruscan tombs.[37] At Pompeii, the location of both the standing and seated statues, rising phoenix-like above their own ashes buried below, suggests apotheosis, a transformation that is reinforced by the adoption of certain architectural elements from the religious realm.

Funerary portraits in the form of busts do not appear to have been widespread at Pompeii, if we discount the abstract and stylised rendition of the human form represented by the *columella*.[38] Busts of the deceased were incorporated into the façade of the tomb of the Flavii in the Porta Nocera necropolis, their cumulative effect likened to individuals looking out of the windows of an apartment building (Figure 37.4).[39] In contrast to ancient Greek funerary portraiture, with its idealising concerns, these Pompeian images—both portrait busts and life-size statues—rely on attributes and the variability of physiognomic form to express the notion of the individual; in this dynamic presence the Pompeian material is, again, reminiscent of Etruscan funerary art.

The career and important events in the life of the deceased were frequent subjects for tomb decoration in the form of carved or stucco reliefs. A public career might be alluded to by an image of the *bisellium*, for example on the tombs of C. Calventius Quietus and C. Munatius Faustus near the Porta Ercolano (Figure 37.5), or by a

Figure 37.7   View of *PNoc* 9 OS, *aedicula* tomb with seated statues,
Porta Nocera necropolis; DAI Rom 63.1296.

representation of the *fasces* on the tomb of the *duovir* L. Caesius in the Porta Nocera necropolis.[40] A painted and stuccoed military panoply, including a sword, dagger, javelin and shield with tondo of a barbarian, provides a further example of the biographical content of much Pompeian funerary art, doubtless reflecting a military career in this case.[41] Although there is evidence that some stuccowork was repaired after the earthquake of AD 62, indicating continued concern for the upkeep of the tomb, much of this decoration, placed on the exterior of the tomb for greatest visibility, has no doubt been damaged and destroyed in the intervening centuries.

Of particular interest are instances where painted decoration is preserved. Like stucco and relief plaques, tomb painting at Pompeii often commemorated the career and social position of the dead. Images of gardens or scenes to which symbolic content can be ascribed indicate that tomb painting also encompassed a broader repertoire. An outstanding example of such a scheme comes from the tomb (j) of C. Vestorius Priscus outside the Porta del Vesuvio. Both the inner face of the enclosure wall and the podium of the tomb altar itself were painted with a rich assortment of scenes, including Priscus' public life and successful career (a seated judge on a *sella curulis*, gladiatorial games, and a table heaped with coins), interspersed with scenes of more symbolic nature (a half-open door, funerary banquet, pomegranates and garden scenes, *erotes*, hunting scenes, and a marine-scape with pygmies).[42] Although the tomb of Vestorius Priscus is a complex example of biography and symbolism, this combination is not unique at Pompeii: the scenes of public beneficence and naval trade from the tomb erected for C. Munatius Faustus convey a similar message (Figure 37.5). Munatius Faustus attains safe harbour after navigating the stormy waters of life, just as Vestorius Priscus enjoys the fruits of the afterlife after a distinguished—albeit brief—public career.

Scenes with mythological content are notably absent from the decorative repertoire of Pompeian tombs. This is hardly surprising, given the fact that the tombs were buried in AD 79. There are some hints, however, of the self-deification and mythological imagery that would come to dominate Roman funerary art in the late first and second centuries AD. Examples include the reliefs of Oedipus and the sphinx, along with a seated Hercules, from the tomb of C. Calventius Quietus; also: the herm-form representation of M. Cerrinius Restitutus in the guise of Mercury, this latter example constituting a rare instance of private apotheosis at Pompeii. The female statue of Vesonia, holding a torch in one hand and a small animal in the other, and thus associated with Ceres, may now be added to this group (Figure 37.8); cf. Bernstein, Ch. 34.[43]

In sum, the visual decoration of tombs had as its primary aim the advertisement of the social position of the deceased: the dead is shown in his official capacity, wearing a toga, while accessories and attributes (the *sella curulis*, *fasces*, dispensing of largesse, etc.) underscore his public, civic career. Given the exterior location of much of this decoration, the intended audience was passers-by rather than the immediate family, who had access to the inner chamber. Interior decoration is not completely unknown, although it tended to avoid narrative, emulating instead the painted schemes common in Pompeian houses, in particular that of the Third Style (cf. Strocka, Ch. 20).[44] Even in the instances where the deceased is heroised, e.g., M. Cerrinius Restitutus as Mercury or Vesonia P. f. as Ceres, the heroisation may, perhaps, be viewed as an embellishment of daily roles: for example, Cerrinius Restitutus might have been a successful trader, or Vesonia may have served as *sacerdos* of the cult of Ceres.

Figure 37.8   View of *PNoc* 23 OS, tomb of the Vesonii, Porta Nocera necropolis;
DAI Rom 58.1937.

The epitaph also constituted an important element of the tomb's overall message. Epitaphs were prominently located, usually on the podium or in the gable, and therefore were intended to attract the attention of passers-by. Most of the epitaphs conform to the *titulus* type, providing name, filiation and, occasionally, tribal association, rather than to the lengthier epigram with its poetic pretensions.[45] In many cases the *cursus honorum* of the deceased might be listed, but in only five cases is occupation (as opposed to magisterial career) mentioned.[46] A unique exception to the generally terse epitaph may, however, be cited. It is the declamation by P. Vesonius Phileros, freedman and *augustalis*, on the tomb erected for himself, his former patroness Vesonia, and M. Orfellius Faustus, *amicus*. The original *titulus* of the tomb records these circumstances, and indeed three full-length statues are preserved in the *aedicula* (Figure 37.8). However, the friends fell out, and Vesonius issued his own *damnatio memoriae* of Faustus in the form of a vocative epigram in the middle of the podium.[47]

Of the approximately 380 names known from funerary inscriptions at Pompeii, almost half are known from *columellae*, attesting to the importance of the *stela* as part of the tomb furnishing. What this number also reveals is the inability of the patron to control, via the titular epitaph, who the subsequent tomb occupants would be.[48] An analysis of epitaphs from the Porta Nocera necropolis, comparing the number of persons named in each with the minimum number of persons actually buried (as deduced from the number of *columellae* and/or ash urns) confirms this view: in nearly every case the number of burials far exceeds the number mentioned in the epitaph.[49] In the cases where epitaphs are preserved and *columellae* are inscribed, it is possible to reach conclusions regarding the familial or servile relationships between those buried. Where original epitaphs are absent and/or *columellae* are not inscribed, relationships can only be surmised. What emerges in both cases is the fluid and constantly shifting nature of the burial environment, in contrast to the rigid picture expressed by the titular epitaph. Thus, compared to the freedman reliefs from the city of Rome, where the *titulus* and image combine to represent the "family as a group",[50] the evidence of epitaphs and *columellae* from Pompeii suggests that the "family group" was a flexible one indeed.[51]

CONCLUSIONS

It has been demonstrated that the necropoleis at Pompeii in the post-colony period were sites of individual expression, with each patron attempting to create a monument in which his or her memory might live on for posterity and in which his or her deeds might be fore-grounded. However, the overall picture that emerges is, paradoxically, one of conformity. From the earliest days of the colony, individuals do not appear to have exploited the tomb as a form of challenge to social or cultural norms: the colonists rapidly adopted the indigenous funerary marker, the *columella*, adding it to the monumental tomb form which appeared contemporaneously, thereby creating a new hybrid sepulchral environment. By the same token, indigenes at Pompeii did not reject the monumental tomb type, but willingly appropriated it, perhaps realising its potential for the very public announcement of a new social status that they were keen to attain. It is tempting to conclude from these actions that a social divide between colonist and indigene did not exist (and if it did, at least not for long), a conclusion that is in part supported by analysis of other aspects of civic life at Pompeii.[52] Perhaps it is safer, however, only to conclude that if social distinctions did exist between colonist and non-colonist, they were not expressed in the medium of funerary architecture (cf. Lazer, Ch. 38).

Tombs at Pompeii also conform to models of civic architecture in their use of materials and technique. The changes in material witnessed in the urban environment —broadly characterised as a gradual abandonment of tufa and *opus incertum* facing in favour of brick facings and stucco (and, in the Augustan period, the increased use of marble)—are also documented in the sepulchral realm (cf. Adam, Ch. 8; Wallace-Hadrill, Ch. 18; Fant, Ch. 22; Peterse, Ch. 24).[53] Paradigmatic for the early period is the tomb of the Stronnii, a freestanding, monumental altar tomb on a podium faced with tufa (carved to imitate isodomic masonry), symbolically guarded by tufa lions.[54] During the Augustan period, the "Romanization" apparent in other areas of art and society at Pompeii, and the prominence of the landowning aristocracy, are perhaps best mirrored in the funerary record by the appearance of the *schola* tomb, which must be viewed as a signal of adherence to conservative social values (Figure 37.2).[55] The tomb of Eumachia, although post-Augustan in date, exemplifies the manner in which members of the Pompeian aristocracy gestured allegiance to imperial ideals. The rise to social and political power of new families in the Neronian and Flavian periods is well documented in the sepulchral realm, in particular in the Porta Nocera necropolis, where the majority of the tombs datable to the period AD 50–75 belonged to freedmen who held such positions as *augustalis* or *magister pagus*. These later tombs of freedmen are, in many cases, more elaborate than tombs erected earlier for *duoviri* or other magistrates.

Although the actual circumstances controlling the physical development of the necropoleis can, perhaps, never be reconstructed, a dynamic of compliance with social expectations appears to have been in play, a dynamic to which each class conformed. A certain kind of conformity also characterises many of the decorative elements of the tombs (cf. Welch, Ch. 36). From the mute statues of couples, conservatively decked in toga and mantle, to such reliefs as that of C. Calventius Quietus with its proud display of the *corona civica*, an Imperial icon filtered down the social scale, the overall message is of adherence to social norms and values. Completely absent from the tombs are any expressions of sentiment or affection, of personal emotion as opposed to public expectation.[56] From these observations it can only be concluded that what was displayed was that which was socially acceptable.

If Pompeian society can be classified as highly stratified with regard to class, these distinctions did not disappear after death. However, evidence such as that provided by the *graffiti* and *dipinti* reveals that, although a patron might attempt to create a tomb environment in which social status was displayed, ultimately this setting became the site of interaction between various social classes. In this regard the funerary record at Pompeii mirrors the domestic one, where an elite house actually served as a point of intersection between "public" and "private". Thus, in the necropoleis of Pompeii, a mirror was held up to society, a mirror in which was reflected the aims and ideals of the social formation itself.

NOTES

1 Following A. D'Ambrosio and S. De Caro, *Un impegno per Pompei: Fotopiano e documentazione della Necropoli di Porta Nocera*, Milan, 1983, tombs from the Porta Nocera (or via Nocera) necropolis are identified as *PNoc*. This is followed by their number and cardinal location (in Italian) relative to the street intersection just outside that gate, e.g., (*PNoc* 23 OS) = Porta Nocera tomb 23 Ovest "west" (of the intersection), Sud "south" (side of road). (N = Nord = "north"; E = Est = "east".) Tombs from the Porta Ercolano necropolis are designated as *PErc* followed by their cardinal position and tomb number, e.g., (*PErc* S 4) = Porta Ercolano necropolis, south side of street, tomb 4.

General discussions of the tombs appear in F. Coarelli, E. La Rocca and M. and A. De Vos, *Pompeji: archäologischer Führer*, Bergisch Gladbach, 1990, pp. 335–56, 428–30; W. F. Jashemski, *The Gardens of Pompeii, Herculaneum and the Villas Destroyed by Vesuvius*, vol. 1, New Rochelle, NY, 1979, pp. 141–53; L. Richardson, jr, *Pompeii. An architectural history*, Baltimore, MD, 1988, pp. 185–8, 246–58, 361–8. For a plan showing the location of tombs in relation to the city: V. Kockel, "Funde und Forschungen in den Vesuvstädten I", *AA*, 1985, fig. 23 opposite p. 534 (Figure 28.1, this volume). All of the tombs are also numbered on Map 3 of this volume. See also the "Read Me" file on the enclosed CD for additional references.

2 Porta Nocera necropolis: *c.*275 m of tombs in the extensive necropolis outside the Porta di Nocera, with about forty-four tombs: D'Ambrosio and De Caro, *Un impegno*, reviewed by V. Kockel in *Gnomon*, 1985, vol. 57, pp. 545–51. Twelve additional tombs southeast of the amphitheatre, along the Via Nocera: A. D'Ambrosio and S. De Caro, "La necropoli di Porta Nocera. Campagna di scavo 1983", in H. von Hesberg and P. Zanker (eds), *Römische Gräberstrassen—Selbstdarstellung—Status—Standard*, Munich, 1987, pp. 199–228; A. D'Ambrosio and S. De Caro, in Kockel, "Funde I", pp. 562–3. Six tombs several hundred metres to the north-east (Fondo Pacifico): A. Mau, "Sepolcri della Via Nucerina", *RM*, 1888, vol. 3, pp. 120–49; August Mau, *Pompeji in Leben und Kunst*, rev. edn, Leipzig, 1908, pp. 450–4, figs 265–7. Five more tombs *c.*60 m further to the east of the Fondo Pacifico (Fondo Prelatura): P. Cipriotti, *NSc*, 1961, pp. 189ff.; Kockel, "Funde I", p. 564.

Porta Ercolano necropolis: V. Kockel, *Die Grabbauten vor dem Herkulaner Tor in Pompeji*, Mainz, 1983; Kockel, "Funde I", p. 555.

3 Porta del Vesuvio tombs: J.-M. Dentzer, "La tombe de C. Vestorius Priscus dans la tradition de la peinture italique", *MÉFRA*, 1962, vol. 74, pp. 533–94; Mau, *Pompeji*, pp. 424–54; G. Spano, *NSc*, 1910, pp. 399–416; G. Spano, "La tomba dell'edile C. Vestorio Prisco in Pompei", *MemLinc*, 1943, pp. 237–315 (*non vidi*).

Porta di Nola tombs: Coarelli *et al.*, *Pompeji*, pp. 428–30; S. de Caro, "Scavi nell'area fuori Porta Nola à Pompei", *CronPomp*, 1979, vol. 5, pp. 61–101; E. Pozzi, "Exedra funeraria Pompeiana fuori Porta di Nola", *RendNap*, 1960, vol. 35, pp. 175–86; Kockel, "Funde I", pp. 564–6; Mau, *Pompeji*, p. 448; Spano, *NSc*, 1910, pp. 385–99.

Porta di Stabia tombs (incl. Fondo Azzolino and Fondo Santilli; Figure 28.1, nos. 139 and 134): M. Della Corte, "Necropoli sannitico-romana, scoperti fuori la Porta di Stabia", *NSc*, 1916, pp. 287–309; Mau, *Pompeji*, pp. 448–9; A. Sogliano, *NSc*, 1890, pp. 329–30; A. Sogliano, *NSc*, 1891, p. 274; A. Sogliano, *NSc*, 1916, p. 289.

Porta Marina: Single tomb with apse of *opus incertum* masonry outside the gate, perhaps one of several. I thank L. Richardson, jr for this information.

4 The early excavation reports at Herculaneum are discussed in C. Parslow, *Rediscovering Antiquity. Karl Weber and the excavation of Herculaneum, Pompeii and Stabiae*, Cambridge, 1995, with references to tombs on pp. 49, 129, 144, 335, 338, 350, 352. Also: L. Franchi dell'Orto (ed.), *Ercolano 1738–1988. 250 anni di ricerca archeologica*, Rome, 1993 (*non vidi*).

5 E.g., the tomb of M. Nonius Balbus, in the plaza of the Suburban Baths at Herculaneum; cf. Small, Ch. 13; Figures 15.13 and 27.3.

6 Forty-four inhumation graves of the Samnite period were discovered in an enclosed cemetery area outside the Porta di Stabia (Fondo Azzolino; Figure 28.1, no. 139). Excavation reported by Della Corte, "Necropoli sannitico-romana", pp. 287–309; summarised by P. Castrén, *Ordo populusque Pompeianus*, 2nd edn, Rome, 1983, p. 41. V. Kockel, "Im Tode gleich? Die sullanischen Kolonisten und ihr kulturelles Gewicht in Pompeji am Beispiel der Nekropolen", in von

Hesberg and Zanker, *Römische Gräberstrassen*, p. 187, questions whether the absence of monumental tombs from the Samnite period provides a true picture of pre-colonial burial: "would an individual such as the owner of the Casa del Fauno have allowed himself to be buried in such a manner, or have we not yet found his 'hellenistic mausoleum' on his own property?" For additional Samnite inhumation burials along the via Sepolcri (outside the Porta Ercolano), see Kockel, *Herkulaner Tor*, p. 11.

7 For the complex architectural picture at Pompeii immediately following colonisation, and the contribution of the colonists to indigenous styles (particularly in the funerary realm), see Kockel, "Im Tode gleich?" pp. 183–7. Kockel makes the valid point that although monumental tomb architecture first followed the founding of the colony, the tombs "are not unconditionally a result of the colonial foundation" (p. 187). As monumental tombs are a phenomenon attested elsewhere throughout Italy at this time, monumental tombs might well have appeared at Pompeii even without the arrival of the colonists.

8 For the *schola* tomb in general: L. Borelli, *Le tombe di Pompei à schola semicircolare*, Naples, 1937; Kockel, *Herkulaner Tor*, pp. 18ff. Sketch plans of *schola* tombs and their locations can be found in Jashemski, *Gardens*, vol. 1, figs 220, 226, 227, 235.

Porta di Nola *schola* tombs: Tomb (g): Tomb of Aesquillia Polla, dedicated by her husband Numerius Herennius Celsus, twice *duovir iure dicundo* (one of two magistrates elected with the power to pronounce judgment; Table 33.1) and *praefectus fabrum* (superintendent of public works); tomb location given by decurional decree. See Spano, *NSc*, 1910, p. 387; the tomb illustrated in H. von Hesberg, *Römische Grabbauten*, Darmstadt, 1992, p. 65, fig. 22 (misidentified as a tomb outside the "Porta di Vesuvio"). For Herennius: Castrén, *Ordo*, p. 174 no. 191.9. Tomb (h): tomb of uncertain patronage, supporting an altar on its rear wall: Spano, *NSc*, 1910, pp. 393–6.

Porta di Stabia *schola* tombs: Tomb of M. Tullius (d, h): tomb in an enclosed area (a garden, or the space of the *bustum?*), belonging to M. Tullius M. f., possibly the same M. Tullius responsible for the Temple of Fortuna Augusta at Pompeii (cf. Small, Ch. 13; Welch, Ch. 36). Here again the space was given by decurional decree. See Sogliano, *NSc*, 1890, pp. 329–30; Mau, *Pompeji*, pp. 448. For M. Tullius: Castrén, *Ordo*, p. 231, no. 420.4. Tomb of M. Alleius Minius (f, g): a tomb similarly enclosed by a wall and given by decurional decree. See Sogliano, *NSc*, 1890; Castrén, *Ordo*, p. 133, no. 23.15. Beyond these two *schola* tombs, the excavators report a further two benches, unexplored.

Porta del Vesuvio *schola* tomb: Tomb (k): possibly belonging to (Ar?)ellia N. f. Tertulla, wife of M. Stlaborius Veius Fronto, *augur, duovir quinquennalis* in AD 25/26; not only was the burial location given *ex decreto decurionum*, but also the funeral was held at public expense. See Spano, *NSc*, 1910, pp. 404–6. For Stlaborius Veius and his wife: Castrén, *Ordo*, pp. 137, no. 41.3; 225, no. 393.1.

Porta Ercolano *schola* tombs: Tomb (S 2): tomb of A. Veius M. f., twice *duovir iure dicundo, quinquennalis, tribunus militum a populo* (one of two magistrates elected with the power to pronounce judgment; a magistrate holding office every fifth year; a military tribune elected by the people); burial location given *ex decreto decurionum*. See Kockel, *Herkulaner Tor*, pp. 51–3. For Veius: Castrén, *Ordo*, p. 235, no. 434.3. Tomb (S 4): tomb of Mam(m)ia P. f., *sacerdos publica*, "public priestess" (probably of the cult of Venus), burial given *ex d.d.* See Kockel, *Herkulaner Tor*, pp. 57–9. For Mamia: Castrén, *Ordo*, p. 188, no. 237.1 (cf. Bernstein, Ch. 34).

9 Kockel, *Herkulaner Tor*, pp. 11–14 marshals the evidence, developing the point made earlier by Jashemski, *Gardens*, vol. 1, p. 146. For injunctions against intramural and pomerial burial, see Kockel, *Herkulaner Tor*, p. 13, n. 108.

10 Two of those persons awarded *schola* tombs (Tullius and Mamia) had funded the erection of temples for the imperial cult (cf. Ling, Ch. 9; Dobbins, Ch. 12; Small, Ch. 13). The other families associated with *schola* burials belonged to a social group consolidated under Augustus: Kockel, *Herkulaner Tor*, p. 19, discussed further by Castrén, *Ordo*, p. 96.

11 D'Ambrosio and De Caro, *Un impegno*, PNoc 13 OS; republican period.

12 D'Ambrosio and De Caro, *Un impegno*, PNoc 3 ES; see Bernstein, Ch. 34, for its inscription. Kockel, "Im Tode gleich?" p. 191 fig. 55; late republican or early imperial period. The tomb with circular superstructure is relatively infrequent at Pompeii.

13 Kockel, *Herkulaner Tor*, pp. 70–5. This altar tomb, *PErc* S 16, has been re-attributed to Umbricius Scaurus even though his epitaph was rebuilt into the adjacent tomb (S 17), that said to be of Festus Ampliatus.

14 D'Ambrosio and De Caro, *Un impegno*, *PNoc* 15 ES.

15 D'Ambrosio and De Caro, *Un impegno*, *PNoc* 7 OS.

16 Kockel, *Herkulaner Tor*, p. 193.

17 For example, the earliest monumental tomb at Pompeii, the Garland Tomb in the Porta Ercolano necropolis, belongs to this type, although it seems to have had no statues: Kockel, *Herkulaner Tor*, pp. 126–51.

18 On the circular tomb in Rome, see M. Eisner, *Zur Typologie der Grabbauten im Suburbium Roms*, RM-EH, 26, Mainz, 1986. Kockel, however, notes important differences between the monumental, isolated circular tombs of the late republic outside Rome, and the smaller circular tomb type at Pompeii: Kockel, *Herkulaner Tor*, pp. 34–6. On the *schola* tomb, see above, n. 8.

19 On the form and function of these *columellae*, see further below.

20 *PErc* S 3: Kockel, *Herkulaner Tor*, pp. 53–7, pls. 6–7.

21 E.g., the tomb attributed to Festus Ampliatus, *PErc* S 17: Kockel, *Herkulaner Tor*, pp. 75–85, pls. 18–21; or the tomb of Naevoleia Tyche and Munatius Faustus, *PErc* S 22: Kockel, *Herkulaner Tor*, pp. 100–9, pls. 27–9.

22 Tomb of Eumachia = *PNoc* 11 OS in D'Ambrosio and De Caro, *Un impegno*. Kockel, *Herkulaner Tor*, p. 20 omits this tomb from his list of *schola* tombs, characterising it instead as "a monumentalization of the *schola*-concept" and pointing out its differences from the type. For a reconstruction of the tomb, see Kockel, "Funde I", p. 559, fig. 41, where it is posited that the Amazonomachy frieze may date to the post-earthquake period.

23 D'Ambrosio and De Caro, *Un impegno*.

24 D'Ambrosio and De Caro, *Un impegno*, *PNoc* 15 ES, late Neronian or early Flavian. For the family: Castrén, *Ordo*, p. 143 no. 70; for the position of *magister pagi*: Castrén, *Ordo*, pp. 72–3 (and cf. Welch, Ch. 36).

25 For a discussion of the social and political make-up of the colony during this period, see Castrén, *Ordo*, pp. 118–22.

26 Only one post-Samnite inhumation burial, dating to the Claudian period, has thus far been identified, the burial of a child in the Fondo Azzolino cemetery: Della Corte, "Necropoli sannitico-romana", p. 302.

27 Carbon, ashes and fragments of bone discovered within the enclosure of the tomb of M. Obellius Firmus outside the Porta di Nola indicate the location of the pyre: De Caro, "Fuori Porta Nola", pp. 65–79. A common cremating area, or *ustrinum*, has not been identified with certainty in the necropoleis at Pompeii.

28 See the observations by S. De Caro in D'Ambrosio and De Caro, *Un impegno*. The discussion here includes the 100 *columellae*, of which twenty-one were inscribed, excavated outside the Porta Nocera: see D'Ambrosio and De Caro, "La necropoli di Porta Nocera". For a more detailed discussion of the *columellae*, including their relationship to funerary ritual, and their possible identification as the "Genius" or "Juno" of the deceased, see Kockel, "Im Tode gleich?" (cf. Bernstein, Ch. 34; George, Ch. 35).

29 E.g. D'Ambrosio and De Caro, "La necropoli di Porta Nocera", pl. 33.h: rear view of the *columella* of Verania Clara Q. l., re-carved from a cornice block.

30 For example, the tomb of Veia Barchilla (*PNoc* 3 ES), where built-in pipes led from the *stelae* on the exterior of the tomb to corresponding ash urns inside. Kockel, "Im Tode gleich?" p. 188 argues that these symbols of the human body facilitated participation in the funerary cult on the part of the living when the tomb chamber itself, with its urns, was not easily accessible—as was the case with the tomb of Veia Barchilla (cf. Bernstein, Ch. 34).

31 Kockel, "Im Tode gleich?" pp. 189ff. The stele-urn-niche combination charted by Kockel appears only in the Porta Nocera necropolis—there are no examples from the Porta Ercolano necropolis. It is difficult, however, to draw conclusions based on social status from this fact.

32 *PErc* S 23: Kockel, *Herkulaner Tor*, pp. 109–11, pl. 31b; Jashemski, *Gardens*, vol. 1, p. 153 fig. 241; von Hesberg, *Römische Grabbauten*, p. 68 fig. 24. For banquets in honour of deceased

ancestors, in particular the religious festival of the *Parentalia* (on the Ides of February), cf. J. M. C. Toynbee, *Death and Burial in the Roman World*, Baltimore, MD, 1996, pp. 43–64.

33 For the identification of tomb gardens as well as their economic role, see Jashemski, *Gardens*, vol. 1, pp. 141–53; Spano, *NSc*, 1910, pp. 385–93; von Hesberg, *Römische Grabbauten*, pp. 229–30. Others have seen the tomb enclosure as the area of the *bustum*, e.g., Mau, *Pompeji*, p. 448, although such views do not need to be mutually exclusive.

34 A total of 189 messages were scratched or painted onto the tombs of the Porta Nocera necropolis, and of the forty-four tombs immediately outside the Porta Nocera, twenty had some sort of *graffiti* or *dipinti* preserved. In most cases it is impossible to determine how much time elapsed between the completion of the tomb, and the addition of the *graffiti/dipinti*. One inscription, "Ataude wrote this with Dio doing the whitewashing", *Scr(ipsit) Ataude(?) dealbante Dione* (*CIL* IV, 9968b) suggests that tombs were constantly re-plastered, just as the houses inside Pompeii were. I thank Gil Renberg for sharing his insights on the *graffiti* and *dipinti* from Pompeii. For a brief discussion of this material, cf. A. D'Ambrosio, in D'Ambrosio and De Caro, *Un impegno*. Five additional *graffiti* and *dipinti* appear in D'Ambrosio and De Caro, "La necropoli di Porta Nocera", pp. 204–6. Cf. Franklin, Ch, 33, for epigraphy in general.

35 A. D'Ambrosio, in D'Ambrosio and De Caro, *Un impegno*, notes that the effect of these "modest products of a local workshop" was enhanced by their elevated location and distance from the spectator. The following tombs contained standing statues: (*PNoc* 34a EN), Augustan period: male *togatus* holding a scroll, female in tunic and mantle, headless male *togatus*. D'Ambrosio and De Caro, *Un impegno*; Kockel, "Funde I", p. 562, fig. 45. (*PNoc* 13 OS), Tomb of M. Octavius and Vertia Philumina, Republican period (probably shortly after colonisation): elderly male *togatus*, soldier with short tunic and cuirass, female in tunic and mantle. The soldier is not named in the inscription; D'Ambrosio and De Caro, *Un impegno*. (*PNoc* 23 OS), Tomb of Publius Vesonius Phileros, Vesonia, and M. Orfellius Faustus, 1st quarter of first century AD (?): two male *togati* and a female in tunic and mantle, all now headless. M. Orfellius Faustus was damned by Vesonius (see below) in an epitaph added later, although his statue was not removed; D'Ambrosio and De Caro, *Un impegno*. (*PNoc* Tomb H N, Fondo Pacifico), Tomb of Marcus Blaesius *et al.*: female head from *pudicitia*-pose statue. D'Ambrosio and De Caro, "La necropoli di Porta Nocera", p. 213. (Fondo Pacifico Tomb 4), Tomb of L. Caesius and Titia: three male and one female statue. Mau, "Sepolcri", pp. 120–49. (Fondo Pacifico Tomb 5), Tomb of P. Mancius Diogenes: two female statues preserved. Mau, "Sepolcri", pp. 120–49. (Fondo Pacifico Tomb 6): male *togatus* with scroll, male *togatus*, draped female. Mau, "Sepolcri", pp. 120–49. (Fondo Prelatura Tomb 7 or 8), see Figure 28.1, no. 138; late republican to mid-Augustan period: male *togatus* and two draped females in *pudicitia* pose. Cipriotti, *NSc*, 1961, pp. 194f., figs 7–11. (*PErc* S 2), male *togatus* (possibly deriving from S 3 or S 4a): Kockel, *Herkulaner Tor*, p. 51. (*PErc* S 4A), Tomb of the Istacidii, probably early first century AD: three draped female statues, five male draped figures or fragments thereof. Kockel, *Herkulaner Tor*, pp. 61–2, pl. 12b. (*PErc* N 4): male *togatus* (association with this tomb is uncertain); Kockel, *Herkulaner Tor*, p. 121. (*PErc* N 38–43): four male *togati*, three females in *pudicitia* pose. Kockel, *Herkulaner Tor*, pp. 171–3, pls. 62–3 (cf. Welch, Ch. 36).

36 For examples of the *dextrarum iunctio* in funerary reliefs of freedmen from Rome, see D. E. E. Kleiner, *Roman Group Portraiture*, New York, 1977, figs 28, 34, 68, 80, 85, 92. On the gesture, see G. Davies, "The significance of the handshake motif in classical funerary art", *AJA*, 1985, vol. 89, pp. 627–40.

37 For example, the seated figures identified as ancestors from the seventh century BC Tomb of the Five Chairs at Cerveteri: F. Prayon, "Zum ursprünglichen Aussehen und zur Deutung des Kultraums in der Tomba della Cinque Sedie bei Cerveteri", *MarbWPr*, 1974, pp. 1–15. For a discussion of the development of Etruscan funerary sculpture and its relationship to the cult of ancestors, see H. D. Anderson, "The Etruscan ancestor cult—its origin and development and the importance of anthropomorphization", *AnalRom*, 1993, vol. 21, pp. 7–66.

38 Only three examples of these *columellae* have been identified with any certainty as intentional "portraits" of the deceased: a basalt stele behind the Tomb of the Vesonii (*PNoc* 23 OS): Kockel, "Im Tode gleich?" pl. 29b; and two *columellae* from Roman graves found in the Fondo Azzolino cemetery near the Porta di Stabia: Della Corte, "Necropoli sannitico-romana", pp. 299, fig. 12; 301, fig. 14.

39 Tomb of the Flavii = (Tomb 7 OS) in D'Ambrosio and De Caro, *Un impegno*. Tomb and sculpture also included in P. Zanker, "Grabreliefs römischer Freigelassener", *JdI*, 1975, vol. 90, p. 264, fig. 6. For the analogy, see Zanker, "Grabreliefs", p. 274; M. Koortbojian, "*In commemorationem mortuorum*: text and image along the 'streets of tombs'", in J. Elsner (ed.), *Art and Text in Roman Culture*, Cambridge, 1996, p. 221.

40 C. Calventius Quietus = (*PErc* S 20): Kockel, *Herkulaner Tor*, pp. 90–7, pls. 23–5. Tomb of Munatius Faustus = (*PErc* S 22): Kockel, *Herkulaner Tor*, pp. 100–9. His wife Naevoleia Tyche dedicated the tomb, although Faustus was actually buried in (*PNoc* 9 ES). Both Quietus and Faustus were *augustales* (Castrén, *Ordo*, p. 74, n. 11). Tomb of L. Caesius = (*PNoc* 29 OS) in D"Ambrosio and De Caro, *Un impegno*. L. Caesius, whose tomb was built by his wife Annedia, was a *duovir iure dicundo*, an important municipal magistracy; he had powers of legal administration: cf. Castrén, *Ordo*, pp. 88, 146, no. 85. The tomb imagery also gives insights into the women who built the tombs; see Bernstein, Ch. 34.

41 (*PNoc* 13 ES) in D'Ambrosio and De Caro, *Un impegno*. The tomb is dated to the second quarter of the first century AD, and Kockel, noting the peculiar hairstyle of the barbarian, suggests that the tomb's occupants might have participated in a particular campaign, perhaps against German tribes: Kockel, "Funde I", p. 562.

42 For the tomb, see Spano, *NSc*, 1910, pp. 401–3; Spano, "La tomba dell'edile", pp. 237–315. For a thorough discussion of the iconography, see Dentzer, "C. Vestorius Priscus". For Priscus and his career, see Castrén, *Ordo*, p. 120. He was aedile in AD 75/76, and died in office, making this one of the latest magisterial tombs at Pompeii. Since he was only twenty-two when he died, many of the images may perhaps be read as prospective rather than retrospective.

43 Tomb of C. Calventius Quietus (*PErc* S 20): Kockel, *Herkulaner Tor*, pp. 25ff., 92ff. Tomb of M. Cerrinius Restitutus = (*PErc* S 1): Kockel, *Herkulaner Tor*, p. 37. Female statue from the tomb of the Vesonii = (*PNoc* 23 OS) in D'Ambrosio and De Caro, *Un impegno*. For the association with Ceres, see Kockel, *Gnomon*, 1985, pp. 545–51. For private apotheosis in funerary art, see H. Wrede, *Consecratio in formam deorum: Vergöttlichte Privatpersonen in der römischen Kaiserzeit*, Mainz, 1981.

44 Painted inner tomb chambers: (*PErc* S 4A): Kockel, *Herkulaner Tor*, pl. 12a; (*PErc* S 18): Kockel, *Herkulaner Tor*, pl. 22. The inner enclosure wall of the tomb of Cn. Vibrius Saturninus added peacocks, associated with Juno and possibly symbols of apotheosis, to the basic architectonic scheme: (*PErc* S 23): Kockel, *Herkulaner Tor*, pl. 31b.

45 For a discussion of the often-problematic relationship between image and text in Roman sepulchral art, see Koortbojian, "*Commemorationem*", pp. 210–33, esp. n. 21 for the distinction between *titulus* and epigram.

46 Kockel, *Herkulaner Tor*, p. 36 n. 305 for the list. The occupations mentioned are *miles*, "soldier" (twice), *argentarius*, "money-changer" or "silver-smith", *porcaria publica*, "public pig herder" (cf. Bernstein, Ch. 34), and *calcaria*, "lime-burner". At the other end of the social scale, Kockel, "Im Tode gleich?" Anhang II provides a useful list correlating civic magistrates and their tombs.

47 (*PNoc* 23 OS) in D'Ambrosio and De Caro, *Un impegno*, with the inscription: "Wanderer, rest awhile, if it is no trouble, and learn what you should avoid. He whom I believed to be my friend, accused me without cause. In court I was freed from trouble, thanks to the gods and my innocence; may he who has accused me wrongly be received neither by the Penates nor by the gods of the underworld". HOSPES PAUILLISPER MORARE / SI NON EST MOLESTUM ET QUID EVITES / COGNOSCE. AMICUM HUNC QUEM / SPERAVERAM MI ESSE AB EO MIHI ACCUSATO / RES SUBIECTI. ET IUDICIA INSTAURATA DEIS / GRATIAS AGO ET MEAE INNOCENTIAE OMNI / MOLESTIA LIBERATUS SUM; QUI NOSTRUM MENTITUR / EUM NEC DI PENATES NEC INFERI RECIPIANT. M. Orfellius suffered the equivalent of a *damnatio* through this public vilification; interestingly, however, his statue remained in place. See Figures 36.12a–b for the herm-portrait of Vesonius.

48 Kockel, "Im Tode gleich?" p. 189 cites 340 names known from funerary inscriptions, 160 deriving from *stelae*. To this number can now be added about forty names: D'Ambrosio and De Caro, "La necropoli di Porta Nocera", pp. 227–8. A recent study analysing epitaphs from Ostia and Pompeii concludes that these inscriptions were often intentionally vague with regard to future tomb usage: V. Hope, "A roof over the dead: communal tombs and family structure",

in R. Laurence and A. Wallace-Hadrill (eds), *Domestic Space in the Roman World: Pompeii and beyond*, JRA Suppl. Ser. no. 22, 1997, pp. 69–88, esp. 82–4. As Hope notes, frequently the epitaph presents the tomb patron as a solitary figure, while the archaeological evidence reveals him/her as a member of a much larger group.

49 In only one case are more people mentioned in the epitaph than appear to have been buried: (*PNoc* 17 OS), where the epitaph lists five members of the Tillii family, while only two anepigraphic male *columellae* were found. Obviously accidents of preservation might explain this. In only one of the epitaphs I was able to survey is provision made for posterity: (PNoc 13 OS), the tomb of M. Octavius M. f. and Vertia Philumina, for themselves and their descendants. Inscriptions published in D'Ambrosio and De Caro, *Un impegno*.

50 Koortbojian, "*Commemorationem*", p. 220.

51 Hope, "Roof over the dead", extrapolates from the funerary evidence back to the domestic environment at Pompeii, reinforcing observations regarding the flexible nature of the Pompeian household. See A. Wallace-Hadrill, *Houses and Society in Pompeii and Herculaneum*, Princeton, NJ, 1994, esp. pp. 3–61.

52 For the architectural contributions of the colonists in the public realm, and their conformity to pre-existing models, see Kockel, "Im Tode gleich?" pp. 183–7.

53 For a discussion of the tombs from the perspective of their materials and techniques, see Richardson, *Pompeii*.

54 Tomb of the Stronnii = (*PNoc* 31 OS) in D'Ambrosio and De Caro, *Un impegno*; see also Kockel, "Im Tode gleich?" p. 190 fig. 54 for a reconstruction. Early (post-colonial) tombs from the Porta Ercolano necropolis include the Garland Tomb (*PErc* N 3) and the tomb of M. Porcius (*PErc* S 3): Kockel, *Herkulaner Tor*.

55 For the *schola* tomb, see above. On "Romanization" in the Augustan period at Pompeii, see P. Zanker, *Pompeji. Stadtbilder als Spiegel von Gesellschaft und Herrschaftsform*, TrWPr no. 9, 1988.

56 Koortbojian, "*Commemorationem*", p. 225 eloquently makes this point, noting that the "formula" of image plus text more readily displays biography and commemoration than emotional content. Even in the funerary markers of children, where one might expect grief to be indulged, rarely is anything expressed other than the age at death.

CHAPTER THIRTY-EIGHT

VICTIMS OF
THE CATACLYSM

——•◆•——

Estelle Lazer

INTRODUCTION

S keletal evidence was regularly found in Pompeii from the first excavations in 1748
(cf. Foss, Ch. 3). Skeletons were initially only considered to be of interest as grim
reminders of the tragedy. They were retained to create macabre tableaux for the
edification of visiting dignitaries.[1] In the first hundred years of excavation skeletons
were not well documented. Further, they were not carefully stored and, over time,
the skeletal remains became disarticulated.

Herculaneum, on the other hand, yielded so little skeletal material before 1982
that it was assumed that most of its inhabitants had escaped, either by sea or by
travelling north to Naples.[2] In 1982, a number of well-preserved skeletons were
uncovered on the ancient beachfront and in nearby chambers. A total of 296 skeletons
have now been excavated. The majority of these skeletons were found in the barrel-
vaulted chambers. Only fifty-nine victims were found on the beachfront.[3]

As a result of the differential preservation of the skeletons, the remains from
Pompeii and Herculaneum have not lent themselves to the same types of investigation.
The Herculaneum material can undergo traditional skeletal analyses based on complete
skeletons. The largely disarticulated Pompeian material (1,150 victims at last count)
is best studied by statistical analysis of samples of specific bones.[4]

CASTS

As a result of differences in post-eruption groundwater levels, the shapes of some
individuals were preserved in Pompeii and its immediate vicinity, but not in Herculaneum. The only bodies preserved in this way were victims encased in the fine ash
above the layer of *lapilli* belonging to the Plinian phase of the eruption (cf. Sigurdsson,
Ch. 4).[5] The fine ash that covered Pompeii in the surge that killed the majority of
victims hardened and sealed organic material. Over time, the organic remains
decomposed and were drained through the porous layers of ash and pumice on which
they lay. This left what were essentially moulds of organic remains, shaped as they
were at the time of destruction.[6] These forms were first recognized in the ash in the

607

Figure 38.1   Injected cement casts of bodies found at Pompeii in 1989 (*insula* I.22).

eighteenth century. A technique of making casts of the forms by pouring plaster of Paris into the voids left by decomposed organic material was first applied by Giuseppe Fiorelli to human victims in 1863 (Figure 38.1; cf. Foss, Ch. 3; Berry, Ch. 19).[7]

The poses of the casts reveal details about the manner of death and the time it took. Baxter examined photographs of forty-one complete casts and observed that about half of them were frozen in positions consistent with exposure to extremely high temperatures at or about the time of death.[8] The most typical position is described as "pugilistic", because the limbs are flexed and the spine extended. This posture is typical of perimortem exposure to at least 200–250 degrees Celsius.[9]

The non-pugilistic poses in the Pompeian cast collection require a different explanation. It appears that some of these victims were preserved in the positions they had assumed at the time of death. This phenomenon is known as "cadaveric spasm", and is generally explained in terms of total muscle contraction in the body at the time of death, specifically in cases of sudden and violent death.[10]

These observations are consistent with the interpretation of the main cause of death being hot gas avalanches or *nuées ardentes* associated with the second phase of the eruption (cf. Sigurdsson, Ch. 4).[11] From comparison with autopsies of victims of the Mt St Helens eruption in North America in 1980, it was initially thought that the majority of the victims from both Pompeii and Herculaneum died within a few minutes from asphyxiation. Arguments were also made for thermal shock to have been a major cause of death. It has recently been suggested that exposure to the intense heat of the first surge resulted in almost instantaneous death for a number of the victims found at the beachfront in Herculaneum.[12]

THE SAMPLE OF VICTIMS

It has traditionally been asserted that the sample of victims in Pompeii is skewed towards the old, the infirm, the very young, and women, all of whom were assumed to have been less likely to escape.[13] There was no such assumption of bias at Herculaneum, since most inhabitants were presumed to have survived, until the discovery of skeletal evidence in 1982.

It is important to establish whether skeletal samples are biased in any way, such as by sex, age-at-death or infirmity, as this would imply that the samples cannot provide reliable indicators of the AD 79 populations of Pompeii and Herculaneum. Normally distributed samples would suggest that these samples are random and could well reflect these populations during the last occupation phase of the towns.

Sex attribution and age-at-death

The skeletal evidence from the Pompeian and Herculanean adult samples suggested that there was no significant sex or age bias among the victims.[14] Very young juveniles were underrepresented in both collections, but this is not uncommon in archaeological contexts. The bones of neonates and young juveniles are often poorly preserved or not recognized as human by untrained excavators and, hence, not even collected.[15]

General health

Stature

Bone inheritance is multifactorial, i.e., it is determined by a combination of genetic and environmental factors. This means that the ultimate height an individual attains is a compromise between their genetic potential and environmental factors, especially health and nutrition during the years of bone growth. Information about the stature of earlier populations can provide insight into the health status of individuals in a sample.[16]

Bisel calculated the mean heights for the Herculanean sample at 155.2 cm for females and 169.1 cm for males. Capasso obtained slightly lower values from what was essentially the same sample. He calculated a mean of about 151.7 cm for females and 163.8 cm for males. He found it difficult to account for the difference between his results and Bisel's as she did not provide details of her methodology for calculations.[17] The Pompeian results were comparable with those obtained from the Herculaneum sample, as they fell within this range. The mean height calculated for Pompeian females was 154.75 ± 3.72 cm and for males was 167.6 ± 3.94 cm.[18] One would expect the stature reconstructions for the Herculanean sample to be more reliable because the sexing of individuals was based on entire skeletons, rather than the individual long bones used to estimate height in Pompeii.[19]

The Pompeian and Herculanean stature estimates are comparable to, or exceed, recent Neapolitan female and male mean heights, which are respectively 152.6 cm and 164 cm.[20] These results indicate regional continuity and suggest that the diet of the ancient Campanians was adequate, and that they enjoyed relatively good health during the period of bone growth.

Pathology

There does not appear to be any bias in the Pompeian sample towards bones with pathological change.[21] The post-excavation disarticulation of the sample has proved a constraint to interpretation of pathology, however, as many diagnoses require examination of the entire skeleton. As a result, only gross pathologies able to be diagnosed from individual bones were examined to determine whether pathological changes exerted an impact on the potential for escape from the eruption.

Because of the completeness of the Herculanean skeletons, it is possible to interpret, with more reliability, a greater range of pathology. A number of scholars have published detailed accounts of the evidence for disease and trauma that can be observed on the bones from Herculaneum.[22] For the purpose of this work, however, only a few types of pathology are considered.

Healed fractures were observed in the Pompeian sample with a frequency of about 0.6 per cent, which is comparable to or slightly lower than that reported for other archaeological sites (Figures 38.2 and 38.3).[23] While it appears that the sample was not skewed towards people with healed injuries, it is possible that specific individuals were not able to escape as a result of their pathology.

Bisel documented the cases of trauma she observed in the Herculaneum sample but did not separate healed fractures from other traumas, such as dislocations and inflammatory responses. This impedes comparison with the Pompeian data. She reported that 32 per cent of the male sample, compared to 11.4 per cent of the female sample, displayed signs of trauma, with a population average of 22.7 per cent. She did not consider that these figures indicated any bias towards pathology in the sample.[24]

Capasso separated cases of fractured bones from those with inflammatory responses. He observed thirty-one fractures in seventeen of the 162 subjects in his sample. Like Bisel, he found the majority of cases involved males. The ratio of males to females with fractures in his sample is 4.7 : 1. He attributed this to gender-related division of labour in Herculaneum.[25]

One age-related pathology, *hyperostosis frontalis interna* (HFI), proved to be a valuable population descriptor. HFI is a syndrome usually associated with postmenopausal women. This syndrome has a suite of signs and symptoms, including obesity, increased hairiness, or hirsutism, non-insulin dependent diabetes and headaches.[26] It presents on the skull as bilaterally symmetrical deposits of bone overgrowth on the inner table of the frontal bone. Forty-three of 360-odd skulls that were examined displayed bone thickening, or hyperostotic changes consistent with a diagnosis of HFI (Figure 38.4).[27] This frequency of 11.9 per cent is comparable with the upper end of the normal range for a modern western population. As this syndrome is often sub-clinical, it is likely that it is underreported in modern populations. It can, therefore, be argued that the incidence of HFI observed in the Pompeian sample of victims is a reflection of its population occurrence and not a skewing of the sample. This suggests that the total Pompeian sample is representative of a normally distributed population with no apparent bias towards this pathology.

Figure 38.2 A healed depressed fracture of the left parietal bone of the skull, outer table of the skull, consistent with a wound made by a blunt instrument. Brain damage would certainly have resulted from an injury of this magnitude. The site of the injury corresponds with Broca's area of the brain, which is concerned with sentence construction. Though the individual might have had difficulty with sentence production, they would not have had a problem with comprehension. It is unlikely that this injury would have played a part in their decision to remain in Pompeii in the early stages of the eruption.

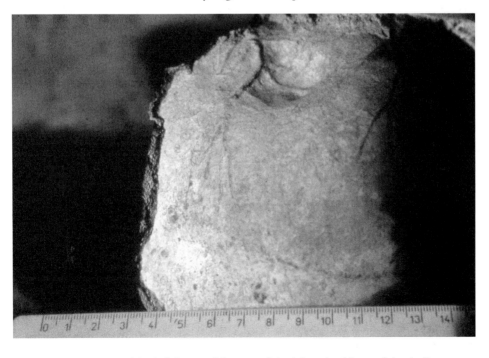

Figure 38.3 A healed depressed fracture of the left parietal bone of the skull, inner table of the skull.

Figure 38.4 Inner table of the frontal bone of a skull, showing *Hyperostosis frontalis interna*. The upper portion of the eye sockets is at the top of the image.

Medical intervention

There is little unequivocal evidence of medical or dental intervention that can be observed on either Pompeian or Herculanean skeletons. The only clear example of surgery observed in the Pompeian sample was a case of trepanation. Trepanation involves the cutting and removal of a portion of the skull. This procedure was performed for a number of reasons, such as to reduce intracranial swelling from head trauma. The observed case had been successful, as there was considerable evidence of healing.[28]

Other indicators of health and nutrition

Because of her involvement in the excavation of the Herculaneum material, Bisel was able to collect samples for laboratory studies to establish diet and to determine lead content in the bones. She analysed bones for the presence of calcium, magnesium, strontium and zinc.[29] She argued that strontium would provide more dietary information than other trace elements because the strontium/calcium ratio in bones indicates the relative proportion of animal to vegetable protein consumed during life. She concluded that most people in the Herculanean sample had not relied on mammals or birds for their main protein source. Instead, they probably relied on vegetables, seafood or a combination of the two.[30] Subsequent trace element analysis of the large number of skeletons that have been excavated since Bisel's pioneering work essentially confirms her results.[31] Bisel also examined the Herculanean bones for the presence of lead. It has been claimed that lead poisoning was a primary cause of the demise of Roman civilization. Gilfillan, for example, argued that the use of lead, especially in vessels used for the cooking and manufacture of wine, was responsible for the decline in the birthrate of the Roman aristocracy from the second century BC.[32] Though the arguments for this contention are problematic and largely unproven, it continues to influence popular thought to the extent that scholars embarking on skeletal analysis of Roman remains are compelled to, at least, test the hypothesis that Roman populations suffered from significant lead exposure.[33]

Population affinities

It has been presumed that the AD 79 inhabitants of Pompeii, a port town with a mixed history, constituted a heterogeneous population.[34] Strabo (5.4.8), for example, wrote that Pompeii and Herculaneum were occupied over time by peoples that included Oscans, Etruscans, Pelasgians, Samnites and Romans (cf. Descœudres, Ch. 2). This assumption was based on ancient literary and epigraphic sources. Oscan and Greek inscriptions on walls and the identification of Greek names in a list of accounts and on *amphorae* have been interpreted as evidence of Oscan and Greek presence in the population. The existence of a Jewish element in the Pompeian population is argued on the basis of Semitic inscriptions on *amphorae* and the presence of names such as Martha and Mary on wall inscriptions (cf. DeFelice, Ch. 30).[35] This evidence, however, could also be interpreted as contact between cultures rather than actual presence; names inscribed on *amphorae* could equally reflect the dealers of the commodities, or the owners of the estates where they were found.[36] Archaeological evidence, such as wall painting subject matter and stereotypical features associated with certain ethnic groups observed on sculptures, has also been invoked to demonstrate the heterogeneous nature of the Pompeian population.[37]

Bisel reported that the Herculanean sample she studied was heterogeneous on the basis of metrical analysis of the skulls of the adults in the sample.[38] Her interpretation of the data, however, is problematic and open to question.[39] Accordingly, several of her measurements were compared with those obtained from the Pompeian sample.[40] These results, in turn, were compared with Pompeian metric data collected by Nicolucci in the nineteenth century,[41] and with data from a variety of European and African populations.[42]

Skull measurements provided insufficient evidence to establish whether the Pompeian and Herculanean samples reflect heterogeneous or homogeneous populations. Not surprisingly, the data from the Pompeian samples were closest to those of the Herculanean sample, though there were exceptions for some measurements. A large portion of the observed differences was intra-populational rather than inter-populational and probably reflected male and female variation.

Non-metric cranial and post-cranial data from Pompeii were also analysed to establish whether the population was heterogeneous.[43] Non-metric traits are anomalous skeletal variations, which generally are not pathological. They are also known as epigenetic traits and occur with varying frequencies in all populations. Since skeletal inheritance is multifactorial, the environmental and genetic components of epigenetic traits cannot easily be separated. It should be noted that it is not necessary for a non-metric trait to have a genetic basis for it to function as a useful population indicator.[44]

Twenty-eight cranial non-metric traits were scored on 126 skulls in the Pompeian collection.[45] The standard definitions of Hauser and De Stefano were used to score the skulls.[46] Because of the comparatively low retention of maxillae (upper jaws) and mandibles, and the high rate of post-mortem tooth loss as a result of poor storage techniques, only one dental non-metric trait was scored. This was the presence or absence of double-rooted canines. Ten post-cranial non-metric traits were scored.[47]

Interpretation was limited by a lack of appropriate comparative material. This is primarily due to cremation being the main method for disposing of the dead in the Roman world of the first century AD. Comparison was made with data collected from the Herculaneum material,[48] as well as other available data that were both temporally and geographically removed from Pompeii. When using such comparative data, it should be noted that there is no reason to assume regional immutability over time, in particular for traits with a strong environmental component.

The Pompeian cranial non-metric data were compared to the data collected from the cemetery populations excavated at San Vincenzo at Volturno in central southern Italy. Two groups of skeletons were unearthed at this site—one from the late Roman era and one from the early Medieval period.[49] Other comparative material involved data from European populations dating from the prehistoric to the modern period. Ancient Egyptian samples, prehistoric African samples from Mali, and a modern Nubian sample were compared with the Pompeian material as an acknowledgement of the possibility of Pompeian contact with Africa.[50]

The results for the majority of these thirty-nine traits were inconclusive. This can largely be attributed to the lack of appropriate comparative material for a number of the traits. It is unfortunate that the same traits were not always scored for the Pompeian and Herculanean material.[51] The non-metric traits that yielded the most interesting results in relation to the issue of heterogeneity in the Pompeian sample were palatine torus, double-rooted canines and lateral squatting facets in the tibia.

Palatine torus is a trait associated with excessive ossification of structures that are usually made up of cartilage or dura.[52] A palatine torus, if present, can be observed on the palate as a median, or more frequently, paramedian bony mound, varying in height, width and length. Some degree of expression for this trait was found on all but two cases of the fifty-two Pompeian skulls where the palate was well enough preserved to score this trait. This means that there was a cranial index of 96.2 per cent for palatine torus. The presence of this trait did not appear to be linked with either age or gender. No other population presented in the available literature has a comparable incidence to the Pompeian sample for this trait. It is notable that only three cases of palatine torus were observed in the Herculaneum sample studied by Capasso.[53]

Canine teeth usually have a single root. Double-rooted canines are occasionally observed in the mandible or lower jaw. Double-rooted canines were observed in a number of mandibles from Pompeii. This trait was also detected in mandibles where the teeth had been lost post-mortem, as there were two distinct socket holes. Six of the twenty-one mandibles from which it was possible to make observations had teeth with roots that were divided. This is probably too small a sample to describe in terms of percentages. But bearing in mind the sample size, Pompeians appear to have exhibited a higher frequency of this trait than any other recorded population.[54] This trait was not recorded for the Herculaneum sample.

Lateral squatting facets, when present, are located on the lower articular surface of the tibia. These are extensions of the articular surface, which are generally thought to result from the habitual use of a squatting posture. This trait was found more frequently on the right leg, with a prevalence of 87 per cent as compared to 78.7 per cent on the left leg. These frequencies are very high when compared to other recorded populations, such as American white males and females. Capasso only documented five cases of squatting facets in the Herculaneum tibiae that he studied.[55]

The relatively high frequencies of these non-metric traits compared to other populations suggest homogeneity within the ancient Pompeian skeletal sample. Further research, involving both non-metric trait analysis of the Pompeian and Herculanean collections and comparative studies of contemporary regional material for these traits, is required for corroboration.

The results of this study are unexpected and require some explanation to account for the apparent homogeneity of the Pompeian skeletal collection. The evidence presented above for sex, age-at-death and frequency of pathology, such as HFI, indicates that the sample is representative of a normally distributed population. It should also be remembered that the Pompeian skeletal sample is a reflection of the victims of the eruption. While it might constitute a statistically representative sample, it may exclude portions of the original population. It is possible that the Pompeian population was never as heterogeneous as suggested by the literary evidence. However, consideration should also be given to the notion that there may have been some alteration to the composition of the population by some sections of the population leaving Pompeii, either as a direct result of the AD 62 earthquake or because of continuing seismic activity. Seneca certainly railed against those who abandoned the region after the AD 62 earthquake.[56] The population could also have changed for other reasons, as would be expected in a dynamic community with a long occupation history.[57]

It would be extremely valuable to score these three traits on other Italian skeletal material, especially in the Campanian region. Calculation of the frequency of these traits over time and space should aid in the determination of whether they are regional features or if they are specific to Pompeii. It would not be reasonable to draw conclusions from the relative frequencies of just one trait, but the difference between the Pompeian and Herculanean samples for palatine torus underlines the need for further research.

Molecular biology has the potential to provide valuable insights into the population affinities of the victims of the AD 79 eruption. DNA analysis has been attempted on samples from both Pompeii and Herculaneum, but the results to date have been somewhat disappointing.[58] The high temperatures to which the bodies were exposed at the time of death have been used to explain the poor preservation of nucleic acids in samples from the Herculaneum skeletons. Human skeletal remains from Pompeii have also yielded limited information due to poor preservation of DNA. Nonetheless, these preliminary studies indicate that, at least in some cases, there is sufficient endogenous DNA in the human remains to enable amplification and analysis.

CONCLUSION

The evidence provided by the Pompeian and Herculanean skeletal samples is consistent with the current volcanological explanation of the eruption sequence. The human skeletal remains from the sites destroyed by the eruption of Mt Vesuvius appear to reflect a random sample of a normally distributed population. This means that the sample of victims is not skewed towards any particular sector of the population. Furthermore, the Pompeian material suggests that the sample may reflect a homogeneous population, a discovery that challenges traditional views about the composition of the population.

NOTES

1 A. and M. De Vos, *Pompei, Ercolano, Stabia*, Rome-Bari, 1982, p. 59.

2 H. Sigurdsson *et al.*, "The eruption of Vesuvius in AD 79", *NatGeogRes*, 1985, vol. 1.3, p. 364; S. C. Bisel, "The human skeletons of Herculaneum", *International Journal of Anthropology*, 1991, vol. 6.1, p. 1.

3 E. De Carolis and G. Patricelli, "Le vittime dell'eruzione", in A. d'Ambrosio, P. G. Guzzo and M. Mastroroberto (eds), *Storie da un'eruzione: Pompei, Ercolano, Oplontis*, Milan, 2003, pp. 56–72; E. De Carolis and G. Patricelli, *Vesuvius, AD 79: The destruction of Pompeii and Herculaneum*, Rome, 2003; Bisel, "Human skeletons", p. 1.

4 Studies of the skeletons of the victims of the AD 79 eruption in Herculaneum have been undertaken by Bisel: S. C. Bisel, "The Herculaneum Project; preliminary report", *Palaeopathology Newsletter*, 1983, vol. 41, pp. 6–7; S. C. Bisel, "The people of Herculaneum", *Helmartica*, 1986, vol. 37, pp. 11–23; S. C. Bisel, "Human bones at Herculaneum", *RStPomp*, 1987, vol. 1, pp. 123–31; S. C. Bisel, "Nutrition in first century Herculaneum", *Anthropologie*, 1988, vol. 27, pp. 61–6; S. C. Bisel, "The skeletons of Herculaneum, Italy", in B. A. Purdy (ed.), *Wet Site Archaeology*, Caldwell, NJ, 1988, pp. 207–18; Bisel, "Human skeletons"; S. C. Bisel and Jane Bisel, "Health and nutrition at Herculaneum: an examination of human skeletal remains", in W. F. Jashemski and F. G. Meyer (eds), *The Natural History of Pompeii*, Cambridge, 2002, pp. 451–75. See also now L. Capasso, *I fuggiaschi di Ercolano. Paleobiologia delle vittime dell'eruzione vesuviana del 79 d.C.*, Rome, 2001; M. Pagano, "Gli scheletri dei fuggiaschi di ercolano: l'indagine archeologica", in M. Pagano (ed.), *Gli antichi Ercolanesi. Antropologia, società, economia*, Naples, 2000, pp. 39–41, and pp. 42–44, 51–63 in the same volume. See also L. Capasso, "Herculaneum victims of the volcanic eruptions of Vesuvius in 79 AD", *The Lancet*, 2000, vol. 356, pp. 1344–6; L. Capasso, "Indoor pollution and respiratory diseases in ancient Rome", *The Lancet*, 2000, vol. 356, p. 1774; L. Capasso, "Brucellosis at Herculaneum (79 AD)", *International Journal of Osteoarchaeology*, 1999, vol. 9, pp. 277–88; L. and L. Capasso, "Mortality in Herculaneum before the volcanic eruption in 79 AD", *The Lancet*, 1999, vol. 354 (no. 9192), p. 1826; L. Capasso and G. di Tota, "Lice buried under the ashes of Herculaneum", *The Lancet*, 1998, vol. 351 (no. 9107), p. 992; L. Capasso and L. di Domenicantonio, "Work-related syndesmoses on the bones of children who died at Herculaneum", *The Lancet*, 1998, vol. 352 (no. 9140), p. 1634; P. P. Petrone, A. Coppa and L. Fattore, "La populazione di Ercolano", in P. P. Petrone and F. Fedele (eds), *Vesuvio 79 ad: Vita e morte ad Ercolano*, Naples, 2002, pp. 67–73; P. P. Petrone, A. Coppa, and L. Fattore, "Alimentazione e malattie ad Ercolano", in Petrone and Fedele, *Vita e morte*, pp. 75–83.

For studies at Pompeii: G. Niccolucci, "Crania pompeiana. Descrizione de'crani umani rinvenuti fra le ruine dell'anitica pompei", *Atti della R. Accademia delle Scienze Fisiche e Matematiche*, 1882, vol. 9, no. 10; C. D'Amore, F. Mallegni and M. Schiano Di Zenise, "Antropologia pompeiana del 79 d.C.; sesso ed età di morte", *Archivio per l'Antropologia e la Etnologia*, 1979, vol. 109, pp. 297–308; C. D'Amore, F. Mallegni and M. Schiano Di Zenise, "Primi risultalti degli studi sull'antropologia pompeiana del 79 d.C.", in *La regione sotterrata dal Vesuvio. Studi e prospettivi*, Atti del convegno internazionale 11–15 novembre 1979, Naples, 1982, pp. 927–43; E. Lazer, "The people of Pompeii", in J. P. Descœudres (ed.), *Pompeii Revisited: the life and death of a Roman town*, Sydney, 1994, pp. 144–9; E. Lazer, *Human Skeletal Remains in Pompeii*, Ph.D. thesis, University of Sydney, 1995; E. Lazer, "Revealing secrets of a lost city", *Medical Journal of Australia*, 1996, vol. 165, pp. 620–3; E. Lazer, "Pompeii AD 79: a Population in Flux?" in Sara E. Bon and Rick Jones (eds), *Sequence and Space in Pompeii*, Oxbow Monograph no. 77, Oxford, 1997, pp. 102–20; M. Henneberg and R. Henneberg, "Skeletal material from the House of C. Iulius Polybius in Pompeii, 79 AD", in A. Ciarallo and E. de Carolis (eds), *La Casa di Giulio Polibio: studi interdisciplinari*, Tokyo–Pompeii, 2001, pp. 79–92; E. Lazer, *Resurrecting Pompeii*, London, 2007. On counting the victims, see: G. Patricelli and A. Ciarallo, "Rinvenimenti di corpi umani nell'area urbana di Pompeii", *RStPomp*, 1998, vol. 9, pp. 75–123; G. Luongo *et al.*, "Impact of the AD 79 explosive eruption on Pompeii, II. Causes of death of the inhabitants inferred by stratigraphic analysis and areal distribution of the human casualties", *Journal of Volcanology and Geothermal Research*, 2003, vol. 126, pp. 169–200, who estimate (p. 179) that a total of *c*.1,600 persons lost their lives within Pompeii during the eruption.

5 H. Sigurdsson, S. Cashdollar and S. R. J. Sparks, "The eruption of Vesuvius in AD 79: reconstruction from historical and volcanological evidence", *AJA*, 1982, vol. 86, pp. 49–50; P. J. Baxter, "Medical effects of volcanic eruptions", *Bulletin of Volcanology*, 1990, vol. 52, p. 539; P. Francis, *Volcanoes: a planetary perspective*, Oxford, 1993, pp. 70–1.

6 Sigurdsson *et al.*, "The eruption", pp. 365–6.

7 Carolis and Patricelli, "Le vittime", p. 66; Carolis and Patricelli, *Vesuvius, AD 79*, p. 111.

8 Baxter, "Medical effects", p. 539.

9 Baxter, "Medical effects", pp. 535–7, 539, 541; V. D. Plueckhahn, *Ethics, Legal Medicine and Forensic Pathology*, Melbourne, 1983, p. 168.

10 Baxter, "Medical effects", p. 542.

11 Sigurdsson *et al.*, "The eruption", pp. 364–6. See now Luongo *et al.*, "Impact of the AD 79 explosive eruption".

12 J. W. Eisele *et al.*, "Deaths during the May 18, 1980, eruption of Mt St Helens", *The New England Journal of Medicine*, 1981, vol. 305.16, p. 933; Baxter, "Medical effects", pp. 533–4; Sigurdsson *et al.*, "The eruption", p. 365; Francis, *Volcanoes*, p. 98; Carolis and Patricelli, *Vesuvius, AD 79*, p. 102; G. Mastrolorenzo *et al.*, "Archaeology: Herculaneum victims of Vesuvius in AD 79", *Nature*, 2001, vol. 410 (no. 6830), pp. 769–70.

13 E.g., by Niccolucci, "Crania pompeiana", p. 1.

14 Bisel, "Nutrition", p. 61; Bisel, "Human skeletons", p. 2; Lazer, *Human Skeletal Remains*, pp.110–19; Petrone *et al.*, "Populazione di Ercolano", pp. 67–73.

15 H. V. Vallois, "Vital statistics in prehistoric population as determined from archaeological data", in R. F. Heizer and S. F. Cook (eds), *The Application of Quantitative Methods in Archaeology*, Chicago, IL, 1960, pp. 205–22; S. Mays, *The Archaeology of Human Bones*, London, 1998, p. 15.

16 D. H. Ubelaker, *Human Skeletal Remains: excavation, analysis, interpretation*, 2nd edn, Taraxacum, WA, 1989, pp. 60–3; V. Higgins, *Rural Agricultural Communities of the Late Roman and Early Medieval Periods Including a Study of two Skeletal Groups from San Vincenzo al Volturno*, Ph.D. thesis, University of Sheffield, UK, 1990, pp. 355–6.

17 Bisel and Bisel, "Health and nutrition", p. 455; Capasso, *I fuggiaschi*, p. 927.

18 Lazer, *Human Skeletal Remains*, p. 203.

19 Lazer, *Human Skeletal Remains*, pp. 202–5.

20 S. D'Amore, M. Carfagna and G. Matarese, "Definizione antropologica della popolazione adulta di un comune della provincia di Napoli", *Rendiconto dell'Accademia delle Scienze, Fisiche e Matematiche della Societa Nazionale di Scienze. Lettere ed Arti in Napoli*, 1964, ser. 4, vol. 31, p. 409.

21 Lazer, *Human Skeletal Remains*, pp. 200–67.

22 For example: Bisel and Bisel, "Health and nutrition", pp. 451–5; Bisel, "Human skeletons"; Bisel, "Herculaneum Project"; Bisel, "People of Herculaneum"; Bisel, "Human bones"; Bisel, "Nutrition"; Bisel, "The skeletons"; Capasso, *I fuggiaschi*; Capasso, "Herculaneum victims"; Capasso, "Indoor pollution"; Capasso, "Brucellosis"; Capasso and di Domenicantonio, "Work-related syndesmoses"; Petrone *et al.*, "Alimentazione e malattie".

23 C. Roberts and K. Manchester, *The Archaeology of Disease*, 2nd edn, Ithaca, NY, 1995, pp. 74–9.

24 Bisel, "Human bones", pp. 124–5.

25 Capasso, *I fuggiaschi*, pp. 998–1002.

26 D. J. Ortner and W. G. J. Putschar, "Identification of pathological conditions in human skeletal remains", *Smithsonian Contributions to Anthropology*, no. 28, Washington, DC, 1981, p. 294; J. J. Cocheton, L. Finaltain and J. Poulet, "Le syndrome de Morgagni-Stewart-Morel: mythe ou realite?" *Semaine des Hopitaux*, 1974, vol. 50, p. 2946; F. J. Fernandez-Nogueras and V. Fernandez-Nogueras, "The Stewart-Morel Syndrome in the differential diagnosis of patients with frontal headache", *Anales Ortorrinolaringologicos Ibero-Americanos*, 1993, vol. 20.4, pp. 383–91.

27 Lazer, *Human Skeletal Remains*, pp. 244–66.

28 Lazer, "Revealing secrets", p. 623; Bisel, "Human bones"; Bisel, "Nutrition"; Bisel, "Human skeletons"; Bisel and Bisel, "Health and nutrition", p. 473; Roberts and Manchester, *Archaeology of Disease*, pp. 91–4. The first-century AD author Celsus, *Med.*, 8.3–4, describes trepanation.

29 Bisel, "Nutrition"; Bisel, "The skeletons"; Bisel and Bisel, "Health and nutrition", pp. 456–60.

30 Bisel, "Nutrition", p. 65; Bisel, "The skeletons", pp. 214–15; Bisel, "Human skeletons", p. 11; Bisel and Bisel, "Health and nutrition", pp. 456–9.

31 E.g., Capasso, *I fuggiaschi*, pp. 1065–7; Petrone *et al.*, "Alimentazione e malattie", pp. 78–80.

32 S. C. Gilfillan, "Lead poisoning and the fall of Rome", *Journal of Occupational Medicine*, 1965, vol. 7, pp. 53–60, esp. 54.

33 For more detail on the effects of lead on bones and its likely impact on ancient Romans see Lazer, *Human Skeletal Remains*, pp. 30–3; Lazer, *Resurrecting Pompeii*; Bisel and Bisel, "Health and nutrition", pp. 459–60. Bisel's results were inconclusive but she did note that her results reflected significant lead ingestion during the course of people's lives.

34 Niccolucci, "Crania pompeiana", pp. 3–5, 21–3; August Mau, *Pompeii: its life and art* (transl. and ed. by F. W. Kelsey), rev. edn, London, 1902, p. 16; A. Maiuri, *Pompei: the new excavations, the "Villa dei Misteri"—the Antiquarium*, Rome, 1962, p. 17.

35 Mau, *Pompeii*, pp. 16–18; J. B. Ward-Perkins and A. Claridge, *Pompeii AD 79*, 2nd edn, Sydney, 1980, pp. 15, 33; E. C. C. Corti, *The Destruction and Resurrection of Pompeii and Herculaneum* (transl. by R. G. Smith), London, 1951, p. 208; C. Giordano and I. Kahn, *The Jews in Pompeii, Herculaneum, Stabiae and in the Cities of Campania Felix*, Naples, 1979, p. 44.

36 Mau, *Pompeii*, p. 18. A century of study of *amphora* epigraphy has begun to yield a clearer understanding of the written elements and to what they refer. E.g., E. Rodríguez-Almeida, "Graffiti e produzione anforaria della Betica", in W. V. Harris (ed.), *The Inscribed Economy*, JRA Suppl. Ser. no. 6, 1993, pp. 95–106. What is needed is a re-study of the Pompeian evidence using these new techniques developed elsewhere in the Roman world (cf. Franklin, Ch. 33).

37 Lazer, "Pompeii AD 79", p. 102. For example, wall paintings with subject matter interpreted as depicting scenes from the Old Testament, such as the Judgment of Solomon (MNN inv. no. 73879, from House VIII.6.6), have been used as evidence for the presence of a Jewish community in Pompeii. Similarly, some sculptures have been identified as representations of Semitic types on the questionable basis of stereotypical facial features. See Giordano and Kahn, *Jews in Pompeii*, pp. 56–8, 60–70, Lazer, *Human Skeletal Remains*, p. 37.

38 Bisel, "Human skeletons", p. 4; Bisel and Bisel, "Health and nutrition", pp. 454–5.

39 Lazer, *Human Skeletal Remains*, p. 276.

40 Lazer, *Human Skeletal Remains*, pp. 269–77; Lazer, "Pompeii AD 79", p. 111.

41 Niccolucci, "Crania pompeiana".

42 W. W. Howells, *Cranial Variation in Man: a study by multivariate analysis of patterns of difference among recent populations*, Papers of the Peabody Museum of Archaeology and Ethnology, Harvard University, vol. 67, Cambridge, MA, 1973; W. W. Howells, *Skull Shapes and the Map: craniometric analyses in the dispersion of modern homo*, Papers of the Peabody Museum of Archaeology and Ethnology, Harvard University, vol. 79, Cambridge MA, 1989, pp. 89–93, 112.

43 Bisel unfortunately did not concentrate on non-metric data at Herculaneum, and did not publish that which she had collected prior to her death.

44 S. R. Saunders, "Nonmetric skeletal variation", in M. Y. Iscan and K. A. R. Kennedy (eds), *Reconstruction of Life from the Skeleton*, New York, 1989, p. 106; D. R. Brothwell, Institute of Archaeology, University College, London, pers. comm., 1988.

45 Lazer, *Human Skeletal Remains*, pp. 277–313; Lazer, "Pompeii AD 79", p. 112.

46 G. Hauser and G. F. De Stefano, *Epigenetic Variants of the Human Skull*, Stuttgart, 1989.

47 I.e., from parts of the skeleton other than the skull. See Lazer, *Human Skeletal Remains*, pp. 316–20; Lazer, "Pompeii AD 79", p. 112.

48 Capasso, *I fuggiaschi*, pp. 981–97, 1031–5.

49 V. Higgins, "A model for assessing health patterns from skeletal remains", in C. A. Roberts, F. Lee and J. Bintliff (eds), *Burial Archaeology: current research, methods and developments*, BAR no. 211, Oxford, 1989, pp. 175–6.

50 The data for these samples was presented in D. R. Brothwell, *Digging up Bones: the excavation, treatment and study of human skeletal remains*, 3rd edn, London, 1981, p. 92; Hauser and De Stefano, *Epigenetic*, p. 17.

51 See Lazer, *Resurrecting Pompeii*, ch. 7.

52 N. S. Ossenberg, "The influence of artificial cranial deformation on discontinuous morphological traits", *American Journal of Physical Anthropology*, 1970, vol. 33, pp. 362–3.

53 Lazer, "Pompeii AD 79", p. 114; Capasso, *I fuggiaschi*, p. 982.

54 C. G. Turner II, Department of Anthropology, Arizona State University, pers. comm., 1993.

55 Lazer, *Human Skeletal Remains*, p. 321; D. Donlon, *The value of postcranial nonmetric variation in studies of global populations in modern* Homo Sapiens, Ph.D. thesis, University of New England, Armidale, 1990, pp. 87, 90; Mays, *Archaeology of Human Bones*, pp. 118–19; Capasso, *I fuggiaschi*, p. 996.

56 Sen., *Q Nat.* 6.1.10.

57 Lazer, "Pompeii AD 79", pp. 103–6.

58 M. Cipollaro *et al.*, "Histological analysis and ancient DNA amplification of human bone remains found in Caius Iulius Polybius House in Pompeii", *Croatian Medical Journal Online*, 1999, vol. 40.3, pp. 392–7; R. M. Costantini and L. Capasso, "Sulla presenza di DNA endogeno nei resti schletri dei *fuggiaschi* di Ercolano", in Capasso, *I fuggiaschi*, Appendix 3, pp. 1069–74; G. Geraci, R. del Gaudio and R. di Giaimo, "Le analisi paleogenetiche", in Petrone and Fedele, *Vita e morte*, pp. 85–8.

CHAPTER THIRTY-NINE

MINING THE EARLY
PUBLISHED SOURCES
Problems and pitfalls

——•◆•——

Anne Laidlaw

The literature on Pompeii is not only vast, but complicated by the fact that Pompeii and its sister cities are the earliest continuously excavated Roman sites that exist. Thus, the most important adjunct to any study of Pompeii is access to a good Classical library, and for the eighteenth- and nineteenth-century publications, especially the periodicals and illustrated folios, these are difficult if not impossible to find in the United States.[1] In deciphering the early published accounts, a knowledge of the modern social and political history of southern Italy is also necessary, since the vicissitudes of the newly re-established Bourbon Kingdom of the Two Sicilies and its familial interrelationships with the Austro-Hungarian Empire, with France and England during the Napoleonic Wars, and later, when the Italians were struggling to throw off the Bourbon rule to establish the Kingdom of Italy, often were decisive elements in what was published where, by whom, and with what purpose.[2]

Above and beyond this background information, I cannot stress too strongly the necessity of an intimate knowledge of the site itself, since in almost all the early published accounts and far too often even today, scholars have relied on the information in earlier publications without checking for themselves. Thus every error is compounded by repetition: as the Bellman says in Lewis Carroll's *Hunting of the Snark*, "I have said it thrice: what I tell you three times is true," and unfortunately this is doubly apposite for Pompeii.[3] It should also be borne in mind that Pompeii was initially regarded mainly as a source of finds, listed in the official reports, which throughout the eighteenth and much of the nineteenth centuries were stripped out of the excavations and turned over to the Museo Reale and its narrow circle of scholars who had the king's ear.

Consequently, from its very beginning in 1748 under Charles of Bourbon (later Charles III of Spain) as king of the newly re-established Kingdom of the Two Sicilies, the excavation of Pompeii rapidly became rife with political intrigues among the officials and Neapolitan scholars, who jealously guarded the right to study and publish the finds. By royal decree it was strictly forbidden to make sketches or plans, or even to take notes, except for the few who had the King's—or more often, the Queen's—favor. Depending on political circumstances this situation basically obtained until the establishment of the Kingdom of Italy in 1860, when Giuseppe Fiorelli was appointed as the Inspector of the Excavations, a career that led eventually to his being made the Director General of Antiquities for all Italy in 1875. For Pompeii, he should be considered as the father of a systematic and logical approach to the excavations, which also opened up the site not only to foreign scholars but also to ordinary tourists (cf. Foss, Ch. 3 for an overview of the history of excavations).

The following comments are meant as observations on the contents and use of some of the early publications from 1748 to 1900, along with a few modern sources that I have found invaluable. They are not meant to be exhaustive.[4]

BIBLIOGRAPHIES AND INDICES

A useful source for the early publications is F. Furchheim's annotated *Bibliografia di Pompei, Ercolano e Stabia* (2nd edn, Naples, 1891), with a commentary on the various sources arranged chronologically in the Introduction, pp. xiii–xxx, followed by the publications listed alphabetically by author or title. K. Zangemeister's first publication of Pompeian inscriptions in *CIL* IV (1871) also has a numbered list of his sources with a commentary on his opinion of their reliability in his Introduction.[5] This is still in print, but the modern reprint (1958) omits the original topographical index and plan at the back, which are essential for locating the inscriptions he records;[6] and many libraries only have August Mau's edition (*CIL* IV, Suppl. 2, 1909), on the incorrect assumption that Zangemeister's edition has been totally replaced. It has not.

For the Naples museum collections, A. Reusch (ed.), *Guida Illustrata del Museo Nazionale di Napoli*, Naples, 1908, referred to as the *Guida Reusch*, is still indispensable, since it contains "precise physical descriptions, formal and iconographic commentary, general provenance, and references to earlier inventories and bibliographies."[7] Karl Schefold, *Die Wände Pompejis: Topographisches Verzeichnis der Bildmotive*, Berlin, 1957, is also very useful for locating subject paintings and general wall decorations, although his dates are not universally accepted and the locations in the Museo Nazionale have sometimes been changed. The book is arranged topographically, with excellent indices that list a concordance to W. Helbig (below) with the museum inventory numbers, and a reverse concordance that includes the *Guida Reusch*; topographical indices arranged both by numerical addresses and by names of buildings; and an index of the motifs. H. Eschebach, who published the standard plan now in use (*RM* Suppl. 17, Heidelberg, 1970; rev. edn, L. Eschebach/Müller-Trollius, Cologne, 1993), has an even better topographical listing of buildings, also arranged both ways (addresses and common names), in which he attempts to identify the type of building (private house, shop, owner, etc.). On p. 115 (1970 edn) he lists the changes between the modern identifications by region, *insula*, and entrance and those of Mau's plan in *CIL* IV, Suppl. 2 (1909),[8] which was the only standard plan available until then.

The most voluminous modern bibliography is that of H. B. Van der Poel, *Corpus Topographicum Pompeianum* (*CTP*) IV, 1977, but it is arranged so idiosyncratically that it is almost impossible to use, compounded by the fact that any individual author may be listed under multiple categories (Books, Art and Culture, Articles, Inscriptions, etc.), in each case with the authors arranged alphabetically, so that you have to know when and where a given writer was working in order to locate what he wrote about any specific monument. The other volumes in this series are: *CTP* II,

1983 ("Toponomy"), containing an encyclopedic topographical set of indices; *CTP* III, 1984 ("The RICA Maps of Pompeii"), plans at a scale of 1 : 1000; *CTP* III A, 1986 ("The Insulae of Regions I–V"), the same plans at a scale of 1 : 500, but only for Regions I to V; and *CTP* V, 1981 ("Cartography"), a mine of information on the extant plans of the city, which includes redrawn plans of Latapie (1776) between pp. 111 and 112, and of F. La Vega (end of 1808) between pp. 116 and 117; *CTP* I, which was to have contained a numerical index "of all structural entities within or without the city walls," was never published.[9]

Van der Poel based his work on that of Tatiana Warscher, a White Russian who had devoted her life from the 1920s until her death in 1960 to assembling in typescript the multivolume *Codex Topographicus Pompeianus*, in which she attempted to copy all the references to every building in each *insula*, which she further documented with her own commentary and snapshots; for the *insulae* that she covered, the arrangement proceeds logically according to the numeration of Fiorelli, and often contains information now lost. The Warscher Codices can be disconcerting to use, since the language changes from page to page according to the author being excerpted and every version is slightly different; but often her comments and photos are the only evidence remaining of details for the buildings that she recorded.[10]

EXCAVATION REPORTS

In the beginning, weekly or monthly reports on the course of the excavations, written by the Director and based on the observations of his Capomaestro, who was in charge of the actual work crew, were sent to the Prime Minister and the King.[11] There are also daybooks, called the "Notizie degli Scavi," and a variety of records, stored in various archives, which contain a morass of contemporary information. The major published sources for the early official reports are *Pompeianarum Antiquitatum Historia* (*PAH*) compiled by Giuseppe Fiorelli, which he published between 1860 and 1864, and *I diari di scavo di Pompei, Ercolano e Stabiae di Francesco e Pietro La Vega (1764–1810)*, published in 1997 by Mario Pagano. *PAH* consists of three volumes, but these are divided into various parts and occasional Addenda, and the pagination is not always consecutive. The following list may be of use in sorting this out:[12]

- *Vol. I, Part 1, 1748 to 1780, pp. 1–316*, written in Spanish up to July 14, 1764 (p. 167),[13] and continued in Italian, with a brief introduction in Latin in which Fiorelli lists his sources;

- *Vol. I, Part 2, 1781 to 1807, pp. 1–91*, with Addenda, pp. 92–187, divided into four parts: Parts I and II, a letter from Paderni describing statues found in the *Praedia* of Julia Felix, and a numbered list corresponding to that on Weber's plan of rooms and finds (which is put as pl. I at the end of vol. I, Part 3, after the Addenda for 1818); Part III, the Giornale degli Scavi of Francesco La Vega from 1763 to 1790, which is divided into section A: Villa of Cicero (pl. II); B: Porta Ercolano and adjacent tombs (pl. III); and C: Villa of Diomedes (pls. IV–VI); and Part IV, an epitome of the daily reports from 1748 to 1806, which ends with the proposed plan of further excavations in Pompeii from the officials of the excavation and the Museo Reale to the King (at this time, Joseph Bonaparte);

- *Vol. I, Part 3, 1808 to 1818, pp. 1–280*, with a Supplement for 1812–13, and Addenda from the notes of Pietro La Vega and Michele Arditi, which include detailed records of the costs of the excavations and two proposals for systematizing them, along with the six plans described in the Addenda to vol. I, part 2;
- *Vol. II, pp. 1–688*, divided into three parts: 4, 1819 to 1830; 5, 1831 to 1850; 6, 1851 to 1860;
- *Vol. III, pp. 1–200*, Addenda for 1814 to 1844.

Fiorelli devised the system of identification by region, *insula* and entrance at the end of the 1860s, over 100 years after the excavations had begun in 1748. His arrangement has been revised from time to time (especially for many *insulae* in Regions I and II in 1957)[14] in order to correlate the regions with the actual street grid as it has emerged in the course of excavation. During the middle of the nineteenth century (*c*.1852 to 1870) the identification of locations being excavated followed a "shoelace" pattern, with the numbers alternating on either side of the street, a system introduced by Sangiorgio Spinelli, the General Superintendent of the Excavations of the Kingdom.[15] Therefore, it is usually possible to locate fairly precisely where the excavators were working from the 1850s to the present.

Before then we are dependent on *PAH* and the *Diari*. To decipher these early reports it is necessary to know where the workmen were digging at specific dates, and also whatever still extant or recorded features—a painting, mosaic, identifiable find, etc.—had caught the attention of the excavators, since basically the digging was done from the farmland above the ruins, and if nothing turned up the hole was back-filled or left to disintegrate and another spot was chosen. Consequently, especially in the first sixty years or more, the reports consist mostly of long lists of finds and not much else, unless a particular object or architectural feature was of interest.

Between 1858 and 1860, Fiorelli also published his *Tabula*, a large-scale plan (approximately 1 : 350) which is a useful record for parts of buildings no longer extant, especially for details such as the locations of windows. In our modern plans, the directions are usually based on "Pompeian North," a convention which considers Vesuvius as north although it is actually northwest of the town. In the early reports in *PAH*, when compass points are given, the excavators considered that the tombs along the via dei Sepolcri were located on the north and south of the road, a designation which was maintained when they reached the via Consolare, so that there "Bourbon north" actually equals modern east, a quarter turn clockwise for each compass point.

BOURBON PERIOD (1748 TO 1860), INCLUDING THE FRENCH HEGEMONY FROM 1806 TO 1815

1 PIRANESI. The two volumes of *Antiquités de Pompeïa* are part of Francesco Piranesi's publication, *Antiquités de la Grand-Grèce*, printed in 1804. They contain some of the earliest plans and views of the via dei Sepolcri, the via Consolare, and the "Quartiere dei Soldati" (Reg. VIII, ins. 7, which includes the theaters and the Temple of Isis), mostly drawn by Francesco, Giovanni Battista's son, but based on the father's work.[16]

2   MAZOIS. François Mazois (1783–1826) was a deaf French architect who began a series of large folios based on his personal tracings and measurements made on the site from 1809 to 1811 (Figure 15.4)[17] under the patronage of Queen Caroline Murat. The first two volumes of *Les ruines de Pompéi* appeared in 1824; two more were published after his death by F. C. Gau and L. Barré. Mazois' drawings and descriptions of the Basilica and House of Actaeon (= H. of Sallust, VI.2.4) are valuable as the first comprehensive publications of these buildings. The work is arranged as follows: vol. 1 (1824): streets, tombs, gates and walls; vol. 2 (1824): public fountains and a selection of houses; vol. 3 (1829): municipal monuments (the forum and the public buildings around it); vol. 4 (1838): temples, theaters, baths, and a general plan of the town.

3   GELL. In 1817 Sir William Gell (1777–1836) began publishing popularizing books on Pompeii (most notably *Pompeiana*), based on personal observations and pro-fusely illustrated with his own drawings (Figures 3.2 and 15.5). These were the first relatively accurate accounts to appear in English; they were repeatedly reprinted in a variety of editions, revised and kept up to date with the collaboration of the architect John Gandy. From 1830 to 1835, as resident minister plenipotentiary in Naples to the Society of the Dilettanti, Gell also corresponded regularly with William Hamilton, secretary of the Society, to report on the most recent discoveries in Pompeii and elsewhere. Since these observations were made on the spot while excavations were still in progress, they can be extremely valuable. Contents, first and second editions (1817–19, 1821): drawings and commentaries on tombs along the via dei Sepolcri, Porta Ercolano and Porta di Nola, Villa of Diomedes, various houses along the via Consolare (Vestals, Surgeon, Sallust, Pansa), House of Championnet, buildings around the forum, theater quarter and temple of Isis, amphitheater. Contents, two-volume edition (1832): Chalcidicum (= Eumachia Building), Forum, "Pantheon" (= Macellum), Temple of Fortune, Thermae (= Forum Baths), Women's Baths (the plans on pp. 131 and 141 of vol. 1 are not those of the women's section of the Forum Baths whose plan appears on p. 80 of vol. 2. Editor); houses in Reg. VI, ins. 8 (Tragic Poet, Fullonica, Large and Small Fountains), House of the Dioscuri.

4   ZAHN. Wilhelm Zahn (1800–71) published *Die schönsten Ornamente und merkwürdigsten Gemälde aus Pompeji, Herkulanum und Stabiae* in three elephant folios in six parts between 1828 and 1859. These were intended for the archaeological community, but were also used as pattern-books: he freely transposes subject paintings or decorative motifs from one wall to another, and only occasionally identifies the precise location in Pompeii or Herculaneum. Most useful is his plan of Pompeii (vol. 2.2, pl. 100) on which he has listed the dates of excavation for major buildings up to 1844.

5   NICCOLINI. Antonio Niccolini (1772–1850) and his sons, Fausto and Felice, and grandson, Antonio, were all involved in the excavations during the nineteenth century. The elder Antonio initiated the publication of the Museo Borbonico series and was later responsible for the removal of the Alexander mosaic to the Museo Nazionale. *Le case ed i monumenti di Pompei* consists of four elephant folios containing individually paged fascicles on a variety of Pompeian subjects, published by the sons and grandson between 1854 and 1896. Like Zahn, the Niccolinis freely transposed

motifs and colors from one painting to another, so that the book must be used with caution. Vol. 1 (1854) contains fascicles on public monuments and private houses, including the House of the Faun, with plans and descriptions that often contain quotations from the original excavation reports recorded in *PAH*; vol. 2 (1862) has a long topographical description of the town ("Descrizione Generale") which is augmented in vol. 3 (1890) by eleven plates of city plans; vol. 4 contains fascicles on *graffiti*, plaster casts, imaginative restorations of a number of buildings, and two descriptions of new excavations: the "Appendice—nuovi scavi dal 1874 a tutto il 1882" and the "Nuovi scavi" which includes later finds up to 1896.[18]

6   BECHI. Guglielmo Bechi (1791–1852) became the first secretary of the Istituto Reale di Belle Arti (now the Accademia di Belle Arti) in Naples, at the invitation of Antonio Niccolini. In this position he collaborated with Niccolini in the systematic publication of the collections of the Museo Borbonico from 1824 to 1848. His youthful work on the *chalcidicum* and *crypta* of Eumachia (Naples, *c.*1821) is the first publication of that building, and he was later responsible for a number of the excavation reports that appear at the back of each volume of the *Museo Borbonico*.

7   AVELLINO. Francesco Maria Avellino (1788–1850) was one of the foremost internationally recognized Italian scholars of his time. He was originally educated as a lawyer, and held university chairs in Political Economy and Jurisprudence in Naples. In the 1820s he began an inventory of the medallions in the Naples Museum, and was made a member of a committee concerned with restorations in Pompeii. In 1832 he became the permanent secretary of the Reale Accademia Ercolanese; in 1837 he was put in charge of publishing the *Museo Borbonico* series, and in 1839 became Director of the Museum and Superintendent of the Excavations of the Kingdom of the Two Sicilies. In 1842 he began the *Bullettino Archeologico Napolitano* which was later continued by Minervini. His published descriptions in *Memorie della Regale Accademia Ercolanese di Archeologia* of the large houses on the north side of Region VII (VII.4.56, 57 and 59) are verbose, but useful for the descriptions and drawings of details that are now lost.

8   MINERVINI. Giulio Minervini (1819–91) was the nephew of Avellino, and followed closely in his footsteps. Thus, in the mid-nineteenth century he became the central figure in the group of archaeological scholars who had been trained by his uncle. He, too, was a corresponding member of a number of foreign and Italian archaeological societies; he was also permanent secretary of the Accademia Pontaniana, an honorary professor of the university, and Inspector of the Naples Museum. He wrote many of the articles in the first series of the *Bulletino Archeologico Napolitano*, and then published a continuation of it until 1859.

FIORELLI AND COLLEAGUES (1860–1910)

1   FIORELLI. Giuseppe Fiorelli (1823–96) began his career as a numismatist, but he is far better known as the scholar who reorganized the excavations of Pompeii on a rigorously scientific basis in the 1860s. Other important contributions to Pompeian studies were his publications of excavation reports (*PAH*, *Relazione*), a guidebook

(*Descrizione*),[19] a detailed large-scale plan (*Tabula*), and the series of periodicals that he initiated (*GdSc, NSc*). He also reorganized the collections of the Museo Nazionale in Naples, and founded the Scuola di Archeologia in Pompeii, which was eventually transferred to Rome when he became the first Inspector General of Antiquities for the Kingdom of Italy in 1875.

2   OVERBECK. Johannes Overbeck (1826–95) first published *Pompeji in seinen Gebäuden, Alterthümern und Kunstwerken*, a general survey of Pompeii arranged typologically, in 1856. He entrusted the fourth edition (1884) to August Mau, who rewrote the first half of the book completely, leaving only the chapters on small finds and inscriptions and the final section on works of art relatively untouched. Although outdated in some respects, this is still the best general book on Pompeii of its kind.

3   HELBIG. Wolfgang Helbig (1839–1915) studied ancient painting in Campania from 1863 to 1867. His book, *Wandgemälde der vom Vesuv verschütteten Städte Campaniens*, Leipzig, 1868, consists of a numbered catalogue, arranged by subject, of all the subject paintings from Pompeii, Herculaneum and Stabiae excavated up to 1867, with dimensions and bibliographies. It also contains an essay by Otto Donner on the techniques of ancient painting, and, unlike most books of this period, detailed indices (which use the Spinelli numbers to indicate locations). Since so many of these paintings are no longer extant, Helbig is still the standard source for descriptions of paintings excavated up to 1867.

4   ZANGEMEISTER. Karl Zangemeister (1837–1902) was chosen by Henzen and Mommsen to edit volume IV of the *CIL* on the *dipinti* and *graffiti* of Pompeii, Herculaneum and Stabiae. He spent the spring of 1865 at these sites, while he located and checked the transcription of inscriptions already published and added many new ones. Included at the back of the first printing of his edition (Berlin, 1871) is a plan of Pompeii with indices in which the buildings are identified by the Spinelli shoelace numbers in use before Fiorelli established the present system. Thus, Zangemeister's plan and commentaries are often helpful for determining the locations of houses excavated between 1852 and 1870, especially those described in *BAN* and *GdSc*.

5   NISSEN. Heinrich Nissen (1839–1912) was Professor of History at the University of Bonn. His *Pompejanische Studien*, Leipzig, 1877, is essentially a study of Pompeian architecture and building techniques. It was planned as a joint work in collaboration with Richard Schoene, but after working on his part from 1866 to 1868 Schoene gave up the project and handed over all his material to Nissen. Nissen did his preliminary research in 1865–66; after incorporating much of Schoene's work, he checked the rough draft and the measurements in Pompeii in 1872–73. Although some of the material is outdated, Nissen's careful observations are still useful, especially his descriptions and measurements of limestone *atria*.

6   *Relazione: Gli scavi di Pompei da 1861 al 1872* (Naples, 1873). This is Fiorelli's official report to the Ministry of Public Instruction on the excavations of Pompeii from 1861 to 1872. It contains chapters on the topography, structure and monuments

(inscriptions, paintings, mosaics, sculpture, small finds), including accurate plans, at a scale of 1 : 400, for the following areas: Reg. I, ins. 3 and 4; Reg. VII, ins. 1–3, 7, 10–12, 15; Reg. VIII, ins. 4; Reg. IX, ins. 1–3. Pl.13 gives the levels above sea level for the street plan of the western half of the town. The room-by-room descriptions are identical with those in *Descrizione di Pompei*, the guidebook that he published two years later.

7   RUGGIERO (ed.), *Pompei e la regione sotterrata dal Vesuvio nell'anno LXXIX*, Naples, 1879. Michele Ruggiero compiled a collection of articles to mark the eighteen-hundredth anniversary of the eruption of Vesuvius. In Part 2, there is a brief description by Giacomo Tascone of how he designed the cork model that is now in the National Museum in Naples (pp. 3–6);[20] Luigi Viola's report, "Gli scavi di Pompei dal 1873 al 1878," (pp. 7–85), which is essentially a continuation of Fiorelli's *Relazione*, with descriptions and plans covering the following: Reg. I, ins. 1, 2 and 5; Reg. V, ins.1; Reg. VI, ins. 13 and 14; Reg. VIII, ins. 8; a plan of the *insulae* excavated up to 1878, divided into the periods from 1748–1859, 1860–72, and 1873–78; and Antonio Sogliano's catalogue of the wall paintings excavated between 1867 and 1879, which is a continuation of Helbig's catalogue.

8   MAU. August Mau (1840–1909) first came to Pompeii in 1873 and, in effect, devoted the rest of his life to the study of the town. One of his earliest publications, "Osservazioni intorno alle decorazioni murali di Pompei," *GdSc*, 1873, N.S. vol. 2, pp. 439–56, foreshadowed his larger work, *Geschichte der decorativen Wandmalerei in Pompeji*, Berlin, 1882, in which he categorized the four styles of Pompeian wall decoration and meticulously catalogued the extant examples of each type. In 1879 he published his *Pompejanische Beiträge*, a commentary with corrections of Nissen's *Pompejanische Studien*, and in 1884 the almost totally rewritten fourth edition of Overbeck. English speakers know him best for Francis W. Kelsey's translation of *Pompeji in Leben und Kunst* (*Pompeii: its life and art*, New York, 1899, rev. Eng. edn, 1902, 1907; rev. German edn, 1908), still the most comprehensive scholarly survey of Pompeii in English. In 1913 F. Drexel published a supplementary bibliography, *Pompeji in Leben und Kunst, Anhang zur zweiten Auflage*. Throughout the last third of the nineteenth century Mau wrote annual reports on the progress of the excavations, first in *BdI* and then in *RM*, as the representative of the German Archaeological Institute in Rome. He also wrote a number of articles on specific buildings for the same periodicals, many of which are still useful (e.g., the bibliography in Dobbins Ch. 12). His final work was Supplement 2 of *CIL* IV (1909) with an updated plan of the western half of the town numbered according to Fiorelli's system;[21] this was the standard plan of Pompeii until 1970, when it was supplanted by the one of Eschebach.

9   PRESUHN. In 1878 and 1881 Emil Presuhn published two accounts of the most recent excavations, which were intended for the general public. Both volumes are divided into a number of parts with separate pagination; each part includes an *insula* plan (frequently repeated, but colored to indicate the house being discussed in that particular part), a bibliography, brief descriptions, and a number of colored plates

copied from originals made by an artist named Discanno, who was connected with the excavations. Although Presuhn tried to be accurate, he notes in his preface that the plans were drawn freehand and that the printing of the plates did not do justice to the originals. Contents, vol. 1 (1874–78): Part 1: V.1.26, 20–32, 1–9; Part 2: V.1.18, 13–19; Part 3: VI.14.20, 18, 19; Part 4: VI.14.21–32; Part 5: VI.14.1–17, 33–44; Part 6: VI.13.21; Part 7: IX.4.1–14, IX.5.1–13. Vol. 2 (1878–81): Part 7 [*sic*]: IX.5.1–10, 17–22; Part 8: IX.5.11–16; Part 9: IX.8 (House of the Centenary); Part 10: IX.4 (Central Baths), IX.6 and 7.

10 SOGLIANO. Antonio Sogliano (1854–1942) was Director of the Excavations from 1905 to 1910, after a long apprenticeship under Ruggiero (1875–93) and De Petra (1893–1901). His early study, *Le pitture murali campane scoperte negli anni 1867–1879*, Naples, was a continuation of Helbig's catalogue. It was written in the same format, regrettably without indices, and was printed both as a chapter in Ruggiero's collection, *Pompei e la regione sotterrata dal Vesuvio nell'anno LXXIX* (Part 2, pp. 87–243), and as a separate book with its own pagination. As Director, Sogliano concentrated on restoration and preservation of existing buildings; his later years were devoted to writing *Pompei nel suo sviluppo storico*, Rome, 1937, in which he discusses the development of Pompeii from its origins down to 80 BC.

PERIODICALS AND SERIES

1 *Le antichità di Ercolano esposte con qualche spiegazione* (Naples, 1757–92): This was the first official publication by the Accademici Ercolanesi of the finds from Herculaneum and Pompeii, commanded and paid for by King Charles of Bourbon, printed in the Regia Stamperia, and then distributed to the royal court; it was never put on public sale. The nine volumes were printed in elephant folios from etchings on copper plates, and are extremely rare. The contents are divided into a series of catalogues:

- *Catalogo degli antichi monumenti dissotterrati dalla discoperta Città di Ercolano*, vol. I (1754), by Monsignor Ottavio Antonio Bayardi;
- *Pitture*, 5 vols: I (1757) with 50 plates, II (1760) with 60 plates, III (1762) with 60 plates, IV (1765) with 70 plates, V [= No. VII in the series] (1779) with 84 plates;
- *Bronzi*, 2 vols: I [= No.V] (1767) *Buste*, with 79 plates, II [= No. VI] (1771) *Statue*, with 101 plates;
- *Lucerne e Candelabri*, vol. VIII (1792), with 93 plates.

2 *Museo Borbonico* (*MusBorb*): From 1823 to 1857 a brief "Relazione degli Scavi di Pompei" was published at the end of each of the sixteen volumes of the *Real Museo di Napoli*, mostly written by Guglielmo Bechi within a year of the actual excavations. These reports sometimes contain the same lists as in *PAH*, but usually add information since they summarize the results of work on an entire building at one time (e.g., the House of the Faun). They are especially valuable for the detailed plans, sections, and occasional reconstructions, which are often the earliest and sometimes the only records left.

3   AdI, BdI, JdI, RM: From 1829 to 1885 two periodicals, the *Annali dell'Instituto di Corrispondenza Archeologica* (*AdI*), subsequently replaced by the *Jahrbuch des Deutschen Archaeologischen Instituts* (*JdI*, 1886–date), and the *Bullettino dell'Instituto di Corrispondenza Archeologica* (*BdI*), subsequently replaced by the *Römische Mitteilungen* (*RM*, 1886–date), were published at regular intervals. Between 1829 and the 1860s these contain occasional accounts of recent excavations. From 1874 up to 1904 August Mau wrote reports in *BdI* and *RM* which parallel the official Italian ones in *NSc* but appear approximately a year later and often in much more detail.

4   BAN: The *Bullettino Archeologico Napolitano* appeared from 1842 to 1848 edited by Francesco Avellino, and in a new series from 1852 to 1859 edited by Giulio Minervini. This contains monthly reports on current excavations, with special attention to lists of finds recorded day by day. In 1861–62 it was briefly succeeded by the *Bollettino Archeologico Italiano* (*BAIt*) edited by Minervini.

5   GdSc: The *Giornale degli Scavi* first appeared in 1850–51 in three fascicles, published by Fiorelli in two parts. He then began it again in 1861 as a series under the same name and published nos. 1–4 and 8–10 in 1861, nos. 13–15 in 1862, and no. 31 in 1865. These journals contain sporadic general reports under the heading of "Descrizioni dei nuovi scavi," and the daily report of the excavations for 1861 under the separate heading of "Giornale dei Soprastanti," which is a continuation of the reports formerly published in *BAN*. A new series of *GdSc* was published by Fiorelli between 1868 and 1879, in which the reports written under his supervision by the Soprastanti are headed "Relazione officiale dei lavori eseguiti" with inclusive dates of excavation.

6   NSc: From 1876 to the present, excavation reports have been published in the *Notizie degli Scavi di Antichità*.[22] These reports are fairly detailed until 1910, when Spinazzola began the "Nuovi Scavi" along the via dell'Abbondanza (ultimately published in book form in 1953). When Maiuri became Superintendent of Antiquities in 1924, he published some summaries of his own excavations in the *NSc*, but in a very selective fashion, reserving the houses with spectacular finds (e.g., House of the Menander, Villa of the Mysteries) for separate studies, and omitting the ongoing excavations of the houses in Regions I and II altogether. The specialized reports on his stratigraphical excavations were collected and reprinted by the Amici di Pompei in 1973, under the title of *Alla ricerca di Pompei preromana*.

7   MonAnt: The series of *Monumenti Antichi* was begun in 1889 by the Accademia dei Lincei. It was intended as a supplement to the brief notices in *NSc* in order to provide a format for more extensive and complete publication of important monuments. Thus, while the earliest mention of many finds is in the *NSc*, more detailed studies of the same material may appear at a later date in the *Monumenti*.

8   *Revista di Studi Pompeiani*:[23] This periodical appeared sporadically between 1935 and 1946, edited by Professor Emilio Magaldi of the University of Naples. The five issues contain articles on various subjects connected with Pompeii and Campania; notices of recent publications; and occasional brief book reviews. For the revival of the title, see below.

9 *CronPomp*, 1975–79, vols. I–IV: *Cronache Pompeiane* was an annual periodical begun in 1975 by the Amici di Pompei. It contains articles on recent research in Campania; book reviews; and short reports on excavations and restoration in a special section under the heading "Attività archeologica." This was replaced by *Pompeii Herculaneum Stabiae* I (1983), replaced in turn by the *Rivista di Studi Pompeiani* (1987–date), which took only its name from the earlier periodical by Magaldi. It has a larger format, but basically is a continuation of the previous publications sponsored by the Amici di Pompei, with the recent notices of excavations listed under "Notiziario" for Pompeii and Pompei-Suburbio.

10 *Pompeian Gleanings*, Oct. 1979–Aug. 1981, vols. 1–9, was a xeroxed newsletter, distributed jointly by Professor Eugene Dwyer of Kenyon College and Doctor Hartmut Döhl of the Archaeological Institute in Göttingen. It contains invaluable bibliographical materials, with miscellaneous information on Pompeian documents of all sorts; notices of work in progress; and vitae of active Pompeianists.

In this chapter I have attempted to outline the contents and reliability of some of the basic eighteenth- and nineteenth-century sources, along with a few more recent publications that I have found useful for the excavations in Pompeii, and also to provide a guide for the more complicated reports such as Fiorelli's *PAH*. I owe a profound debt of gratitude to Professor Lawrence Richardson, jr, not only for my initial introduction to these studies at Yale in the 1950s, but also for his continued interest in my work and frequent counsel over the years. Nothing can replace a firsthand knowledge of both the site and the publications, but I believe strongly that the knowledge and experience acquired over many years of repeated wrestling with both should be shared as broadly as possible. If in this chapter I have saved anyone from some of the pitfalls I have encountered (and often fallen into, both literally on the site and figuratively in studying the literature), it will have served its purpose.

NOTES

1 Few libraries in the United States have essential early materials on Pompeii, especially periodicals, before the twentieth century, and those that do are difficult to use, since for want of space or because of their valuable illustrations these books are kept either in depositories or Rare Book Rooms separate from the main collections. Now that H. Van der Poel's collection, which includes the papers of Tatiana Warscher and of Matteo Della Corte, has been donated to the Getty Research Institute Library (searchable contents now available at http://www.getty.edu /research/conducting_research/special_collections/ [click Selected Special Collections Finding Aids and proceed to the letter "V"]), it may be easier to work on the west coast than the east, but I have found that the libraries of the foreign schools and academies in Rome have the largest and most accessible collections, particularly those of the German Archaeological Institute and the American Academy in Rome. Individual Roman library catalogues may be accessed on the Internet at http://www-urbs.vatlib.it/ under "General Online Catalogues," or the entire index may be searched under "Library and Local Opac." (Anne Laidlaw has been a mentor and a friend since I was a graduate student. Her scholarly experience and her teacher's desire to share knowledge are evident in this chapter, and will be appreciated by future students of Pompeii. I am most grateful for her contribution to this book.—John Dobbins, *ed.*)

2 An excellent and readable source for this period is Harold Acton, *The Bourbons of Naples*, London, 1957, and *The Last Bourbons of Naples*, London, 1961. For the intrigues and internal politics of the early excavations, see Christopher Parslow, *Rediscovering Antiquity: Karl Weber*

and the Excavations of Herculaneum, Pompeii, and Stabiae, Cambridge, 1995. The most recent book geared specifically to the history of the excavations is Alison Cooley, *Pompeii,* London, 2003, chs 4–5, published in the Duckworth Archaeological Histories.

3   For example, one of the standard articles on *cubicula* by the then Directress of Pompeii, Olga Elia, "I cubicoli nelle case di Pompei: Contributo alla storia della domus," *Historia* 6, 1932, 394–421, locates some of her examples in the wrong *insulae* (e.g., cub.d, VI.14.38, which she puts in *Insula* 13), errors which are consistently repeated in later discussions of Pompeian *cubicula.* Conversely, in August Mau's *Geschichte der decorativen Wandmalerei in Pompeji,* Berlin, 1882, when I checked on the site every extant trace of First-Style wall paintings catalogued by him, I found only two minor errors in 105 pages, a remarkable degree of accuracy when one considers that so much of the material was very fragmentary and I was examining it 100 years later.

4   A substantial number of these comments, edited and updated, are reprinted from my "Commentary on Bibliography" in A. Laidlaw, *The First Style in Pompeii, Painting and Architecture,* Rome, 1985 pp. 2–13.

5   This includes a lucid analysis of Fiorelli's sources for *PAH,* cited as "Acta" in the bibliography for each inscription.

6   Since he did his work in Pompeii before Fiorelli established the present system of locations by region, *insula* and entrances, Zangemeister uses Spinelli's numbering (see note 15).

7   Eugene Dwyer, *Pompeian Gleanings* 3, January 1980, p. 4. Reusch numbers are often used rather than the museum inventory numbers in later publications to identify objects in the museum, even today. In *Pompeian Gleanings* 2, January 1980, pp. 1–11, Hartmut Döhl has transcribed a concordance of the Reusch numbers with the museum inventory numbers, slightly edited by Eugene Dwyer.

8   Mau disagreed with Fiorelli's final division of Pompeii into nine regions, so on this plan he has used his own regionary numbers, followed in parentheses by those of Fiorelli.

9   Van der Poel's *Corpus Topographicum Pompeianum* was privately printed in runs of 1,000 numbered copies, with a courtesy logo from the University of Texas. The volumes were then distributed free to a number of classical libraries and also to individual Pompeian scholars, but, to the best of my knowledge, were never put up for sale to the public. They contain a morass of information on Pompeii, but are arranged so haphazardly that they are extremely difficult to use.

10 In Laidlaw, *The First Style in Pompeii,* pp. 10–11, I attempted to list the locations and contents of all extant Warscher Codices (see Marginalia on the World of Pompeii website). Subsequently, I have come across some in the John Miller Burnam Classical Library of the University of Cincinnati, and there are probably others here and there. The major collection in the United States, from which the microfilms now in some university libraries were made, was formerly at Yale and is presently on permanent loan to Duke University. In Rome the libraries of the American Academy in Rome, the German Archaeological Institute, the British School, and the Swedish Institute also have slightly variant copies of most of her Codices.

11 Zangemeister, Preface p. vi. His chart of the officials and their positions from 1748 to 1860 is reprinted here in Appendix 1.

12 Eugene Dwyer, *Pompeian Gleanings* 1, October 1979, pp. 2–3, gives a more detailed index, in Italian.

13 Typescript copies of a modern Italian translation of the Spanish part of Fiorelli's text, *Giornale degli scavi di Pompei,* Rome, 1997, done by Paola Poli-Capri under the direction of H.B.Van der Poel, are in the library collections of the American Academy, the German Archaeological Institute, the British School, and the Swedish Institute in Rome.

14 Della Corte kept the earlier numeration (before 1957) for his publications of inscriptions in the *NSc* and the second edition of *Case ed Abitanti di Pompei,* Pompeii, 1954, which also has a sketch plan of Pompeii with these numbers. In the reprint (Naples 1965), Maiuri's revision of the numeration of Regions I and II has been substituted, with a new plan and two topographical indices, although the text remains the same. The tombs outside the Porta Nocera were also numbered separately by Della Corte and Maiuri. There is a concordance of these on the back of the page with the modern plan in A. D'Ambrosio and S. De Caro, *Un Impegno per Pompei: Fotopiano e documentazione della necropoli di Porta Nocera,* Milan, 1983. Van der Poel,

CTP V, 1981, pp. 36–7, also lists a concordance of Maiuri's and Della Corte's numbers for these tombs.

15 Spinelli's system is mentioned casually in *BAN* N.S. 4, August, 1852, p. 25, in reference to a shop described as the "seventh and eighth after . . . the andron [= *fauces*] of the House of Marcus Lucretius [IX.3.5] . . . [which] has been distinguished by numbers 55 and 56, through a praiseworthy usage introduced recently to indicate by consecutive numbers all the entrances of the buildings on the different streets of Pompeii: this arrangement is owed to the Principe di Sangiorgio Spinelli, actually the General Superintendent of the excavations of the Kingdom." Spinelli's numbers are used in *PAH* II, Part 6, beginning on p. 521 (March 24, 1852). They are also indicated on Zangemeister's plan in *CIL* IV, and used to identify locations of buildings excavated after this date in many of the reports and catalogues (e.g., Helbig). There is a concordance of these numbers with the modern equivalents of Fiorelli's system in Van der Poel, *CTP* V, 1981, pp. 505–10. He also lists them in his Numerical Index in *CTP* II, 1983, pp. 225–326 at the beginning of each *insula* where they had been in use.

16 Van der Poel (*CTP* IV, 1977, p. 131) notes that Giovanni Battista visited Pompeii five times in the 1770s. The end of the via Consolare by the Porta Ercolano was being excavated at this time; the Quartiere dei Soldati (VIII.7) had been uncovered slightly earlier. For further information on both father and son in relation to Pompeii, see *CTP* V, pp. 181–8, and 491–6 (Appendix 4) which lists the drawings of Pompeii by Piranesi and his School, with a bibliography by John Ely.

17 All four volumes have been made available on the internet by Professor Masanori Aoyagi of the University of Tokyo at http://www.picure.l.u-tokyo.ac.jp/arc/mazois/index.html. The full text is given in both Japanese and French, with thumbnails which can be enlarged on the computer of all 202 plates. Mazois also made a series of watercolors, which correspond almost completely to the published drawings. These are conserved in the Département des Estampes et Photographie in the Bibliothèque Nationale in Paris. Although Mazois made his drawings in Pompeii while he was in Naples when the French were in control, he did the commentaries and captions in Rome and Paris, which led to a certain number of errors, although, for the most part, he was a meticulous draftsman. For a discussion of his work, see Van der Poel, *CTP* V, pp. 188–91.

18 A detailed table of contents for all four volumes is given in *Le Case e i monumenti di Pompei nell'opera di Fausto e Felice Niccolini*, Novara, 1997, p. 24 n. 41, ed. by Stefano De Caro.

19 There is a modern reprint, Umberto Pappalardo (ed.), *La descrizione di Pompei per Giuseppe Fiorelli*, Naples, 2001, printed in a larger format but with the original pagination indicated in square brackets. In the first section there is also a chronology of Fiorelli's life, and a listing of his publications.

20 For a discussion of the cork model see Van der Poel, *CTP* V, 1981, pp. XXIX and 107–8 (s.v. Domenico Padiglione).

21 See note 8.

22 From 1876 to 1904 these appeared both as reports in the *Atti della Reale Accademia Nazionale dei Lincei* and as separate volumes. Citations are usually made to the separate volumes.

23 The tables of contents are reprinted in *Pompeian Gleanings* 6, July 1980, pp. 6–8.

APPENDIX 1

Zangemeister's lists of Pompeian officials, 1748–1860

CIL IV (1871), Praefatio VI, Note 2

For the early excavations beginning in 1748, there were three kinds of reports ("*acta*"): (1) The ones made by the foremen of the actual workers ("*Maestri fabbricatori*" (sometimes referred to in *PAH* as "*Capo maestri*")) to the Pompeian officials ("*Soprastanti*" or "*Architetti*"); (2) the ones made by these to the directors of the excavation ("*Architetti direttori*" or "*Soprintendenti degli scavi*"; and (3) the ones made by the directors to the royal officials in Naples (generally the prime minister and the king) or to the directors of the Museo Reale. Zangemeister obtained this list from Fiorelli personally. The names and dates in square brackets were added by Zangemeister.

(Translated from the Latin, slightly edited by author.)

I *Soprintendenti degli Scavi*
   Felice Nicolas 1806
   Michele Arditi 1807–1839
   Francesco M. Avellino 1839–1850
   San Giorgio Spinelli 11 May 1850–10 April 1863
   Giuseppe Fiorelli 29 November 1863

II *Ispettori*
   Raffaele Minervini 1811–1815
   Giuseppe Fiorelli 1847–1849
   Giuseppe Fiorelli 1860–1863

III *Architetti direttori dello scavo*
   Rocco Gioacchin. Alcubiere 1748–1780
   Francesco La Vega 1780–1804
   Pietro La Vega 1804–1815
   Antonio Bonucci 1815–1825
   Nicola d'Apuzzo 1825–1828
   Pietro Bianchi 1832–1848
   Giuseppe Settembre 1849–1851
   Gugliemo Bechi 1851–1852
   Gaetano Genovese 1852–1862
   Michele Ruggiero 15 September 1862

IV *Architetti locali o subalterni*
   Carlo Weber 1750–1764
   Francesco La Vega 1765
   Mariano Manzilli 1811–1815
   Carlo Bonucci 1828–1848
   Raffaele Campanelli 1852

V *Soprastanti*

Gioacchino Perez Conde 1766–1799
Giuseppi Civitelli 1811–1824
Antonio Imparato 1811–1824
Raffaele Amicone 1813 [–10 April 1829; 15 May 1837–1846]
Francesco Sconamiglio 1813
Mauro Imparato 1820
Francesco Imparato 1820
Gabriele Cirillo 1847–1849
Andrea Galella 1850
Gabriele Cirillo 1851–1860
Antonio Imparato 1859 [–1867]
Nicola Pagano 1860–1862
Domenico Scognamiglio 1860
Andrea Freja 1860

VI *Uffici minori e diversi*

Antonio Scognamiglio *capo maestro* 1757–1781
Pasquale Scognamiglio *capo maestro* 1781
Antonio *Imparato capo d'opere* 1781
[Nicola Gargano *incaricato degli scavi* 1807, v. Fiorelli Pomp. ant. hist. I 2 pp. 177 et 185]
Mariano Manzilli *sorvegliante* 1815
Pasquale Scognamiglio *sorvegliante* 1815

APPENDIX 2

Glossary of terms associated with the early sources

"Bourbon North": Approximately modern east inside the city walls for the early excavation reports in *PAH* and *Diari*, especially along the via Consolare.

Cadastral Plan: See **Plan, Cadastral Map**.

Camino Reale: The "Royal Road" (Strada Reale) built by Charles of Bourbon, the first king of the re-established Kingdom of the Two Sicilies, in order to link Naples with Calabria. It is shown on the early maps, and ran just to the south of the ancient city.

Casa Pseudourbano: Villa of Diomedes at the end of the via dei Sepolcri (Figure 37.1).

Casino dell'Aquilla: Seventeenth-century building located on the farmland above the via dell'Abbondanza, now used for small exhibits on a variety of subjects.

Comparative tables of weights and measures: (1) Neapolitan and metric: Pagano, *Diari*, p. 185; 2) R. E. Zapko, *Italian Weights and Measures from the Middle Ages to the Nineteenth Century*, Philadelphia, 1981; 3) General table of measures from the sixteenth to the twentieth centuries: Van der Poel, *CTP*, 1981, vol. 5, Appendix IX, pp. 504–5. These vary slightly from author to author, but as a rule of thumb the following measurements are useful:

Oscan foot: *c*.27.5 cm.

Roman foot: *c*.29.6 cm.

Neapolitan palm: 26.4 cm subdivided into 12 *oncia*;

Once = 2.2 cm, subdivided into 5 *minuti* (Pagano).

French pied: 32.5 cm.

French toise = 6 pieds = 1.95 m.

Compass Points: See "Bourbon North," "Pompeian North."

Direzione Nuova: Current site director's office, VII.4.10.

Direzione Vecchia: Former site director's office, VI. *Ins. Occ.* 27.

Excavation dates by buildings: Zahn 2.2, pl. 100, up to 1844; for First-Style decorations, Laidlaw, 1985, at the beginning of each entry in the catalogue.

Excavation dates by *insulae*: Fiorelli, *Descrizione di Pompei*, 1875, at the beginning of the description of each *insula*; Van der Poel, *CTP*, 1981, vol. 5, pp. 498–500.

Fondo Pacifico: Property southwest of the amphitheater, where six tombs were found in 1886–87. These are a continuation of the tombs outside the Porta Nocera, but the buildings of the modern town have surrounded them.

Isola di Minervini: VI.5.

Masseria: Farms owned by various proprietors, located above the ruins of Pompeii, which, in the early reports, identified, roughly speaking, where the excavators were working. These were gradually bought or expropriated by the State. La Vega's plan (1808) lists a number of them on the Indice in the lower right corner (detailed photo, DAI, Rome, Inst. Neg. 76.1260), but the boundaries are always vague in relation to the unexcavated buildings underneath them, so they can only give an approximate location. See also **Podere, Cadastral Plan**.

Masseria di Balzano: Part of the via dei Sepolcri.

Masseria di Cuomo: VI, *Ins. Occ.* (on the "south" [= west] side of the via Consolare, Helbig 481; entrance No. 31, Eschebach).

Masseria di Irace: VIII.2/VII.6, next to the Masseria di Cuomo.

"Pantheon": The Macellum, VII.9.7.

Plan, Allied Bombing, September 1943: (1) Sketch plan, with note that there were 160 bombs that hit the town: Photo from the Ufficio Disegnatori, Scavi di Pompei, Disegno N. 14. Presumably unpublished; (2) Sketch plan labeled: "Pompeii: Bomb—Damage 1943." Source unknown; (3) Sketch plan of Regions I and II: V. Spinazzola, *Pompei alla luce degli scavi nuovi di via dell'Abbondanza (anni 1910–1923)*, Rome, 1953, vol. 1, p. XX. Van der Poel, *CTP*, 1986, vol. III A, p. XVI, gives a brief description and bibliography dealing with the bombing.

Plan, Cadastral Map: Plan of southern half of Pompeii, showing ownership of farms, 1807: C. Parslow, *Rediscovering Antiquity*, Cambridge and New York, 1995, p. 108 Figure 28 (unfortunately printed in too small a size for the names of the owners to be legible).

Plan, Della Corte's numbering: Regions I and II: (1) Sketch plan of whole town: M. Della Corte, *Case ed abitanti di Pompei*, 2nd edn, Naples, 1954, between pp. xxiii and xxiv; (2) Sketch plan of Regions I and II, from the Ufficio degli Scavi, labeled "Pianta di Pompei, Reg. I e Reg. II, Scala 1 : 2000," with notation "Numeri in cerchio usati dal Prof. Della Corte." Unpublished.

Plan, Della Corte's numbering, tombs outside the Porta Nocera: From the Ufficio di Disegno in Pompeii. Unpublished. For concordances for these numbers, see my Note 14.

Plan, Latapie, 1776: redrawn for Van der Poel, *CTP*, 1981, vol. 5, between pp. 110 and 111.

Plan, La Vega brothers, excavations from 1748 up to December, 1808: redrawn for Van der Poel, *CTP*, 1981, vol. 5 between pp. 116 and 117. Photographs of the original: DAI, Rome, Inst. Neg. Nos. 76.1259–62.

Podere: Farm.

Podere di Montemurro: Temple of Isis (June 1765).

Podere di Vicenzo Grasso: the large theater (July 1764) and the *Praedia* of Julia Felix.

"Pompeian North": modern simplification of compass points based on the location of Vesuvius in relation to Pompeii.

Quartiere dei Soldati: Designation in early reports for the Caserma dei Gladiatori, VIII.7.

Sarno Canal: This was engineered by Domenico Fontana between 1594 and 1600, to carry water from the Sarno river to the munitions factories ("Polviera") at Torre Annunziata. Since Pompeii was built on a hill created by a prehistoric lava flow from Vesuvius, Fontana tunneled through the southern half of ancient Pompeii, which was then known simply as "Città." In the dry season it is possible to walk through large sections of this canal, which can be traced from above by the occasional metal gratings used for ventilation and cleaning. Cf. Foss, Ch. 3, n. 13 for a description; Figure 3.1 for a map of the canal's course.

Spinelli numbers: System of numbering the entrances between 1852 and about 1870, when Fiorelli's system supplanted it. This consisted along the strada Stabiana of alternating numbered doorways on each side of the street—hence the term "shoelace" numbers. In some parts of Region VII these numbers run consecutively the length of a street and then double back on the other side. For further explanation, see my note 15.

Strada delle Suonatrici: Strada di Stabia, between Reg. VII.2 and IX.3.

Taverna del Rapillo/Lapillo: Hosteria just outside the southwest corner of Pompeii, later the Hotel Diomedes. Its precise location is shown on Zangemeister's plan at the end of the original edition of *CIL* IV (1867), on the small inset, as No. 148.

Tempio di Venere: term used to identify the Tempio d'Apollo in the early reports, including the entry in Fiorelli's *Descrizione* (1875).

GLOSSARY

———•◆•———

Note. Because not all scholars agree about the exact physical correlates of ancient terms, particularly concerning spaces within Roman houses, the definitions below describe how such terms have traditionally been used. When appropriate, Latin, Greek and Italian terms appear with the plural form after the singular.

adlocutio (-ones)   A formal speech or public address, artistically indicated by the gesture of an outstretched, uplifted right hand (Figures 36.2a, 36.6a).

aedicula (-ae)   A decorative architectural opening, real or painted, featuring two columns or pilasters supporting an entablature and pediment (Figures 13.5, 20.4).

aedilis (-es) (aedile)   A civic magistrate responsible for public buildings, urban maintenance, ritual and entertainment (Table 33.1).

ager (agri)   A plot or area of land with definite boundaries, private or public; specified when applied to territory under the jurisdiction of a city or town, e.g., *ager Pompeianus* (Figure 28.2).

ala (-ae)   An open space, or "wing" off the side of an *atrium* in a Roman house (Figure 17.1).

album (-a)   A tablet containing a notice or edict; a register listing public officials.

Altstadt (the old city)   A modern German term denoting the southwestern part of Pompeii where many scholars believe that the earliest, pre-Samnite settlement was located (Figure 7.1).

alveus (-i)   A tub or basin for a hot bath, or the recess for such a tub, constructed on or into the floor of the *caldarium* (cf. Ch. 15).

ambulacrum (-a)   A walk planted with trees, commonly near a house (Figure 23.13).

amicus (-i)   A personal friend; a supporter.

amphora (-ae)   A large earthenware jar with a narrow neck and two handles at the top, often with the base narrowed to a point, used for the storage or transport of liquid or granular goods.

analemma (analemmata)   The wall(s) supporting the end(s) of the *cavea* of a theater (Figure 14.1).

andron (-ones)   A Vitruvian term designating a narrow passageway within a house, especially the hallway that often connects an *atrium* court to an open garden or peristyle court at the back (Figure 17.1, unlabelled).

anta (-ae) A square pillar, often decorated, that is installed at the end of the flanking wall of a room or structure, usually marking the edge of a doorway, and appearing in sets of two to frame the opening (Figure 37.8).

apodyterium (-a) A room for changing and storing clothes in a bath (cf. Ch. 15).

apotropaic The perceived quality of an object, image or symbol to ward off evil.

architrave The lowest part of the entablature resting immediately atop the abacus of a column or pilaster capital; the principal horizontal element in trabeated architecture (Figures 12.3, 12.4, 23.16).

as (asses) A unit of value in Roman copper currency; during the Augustan period, four *asses* equaled one *sestertius*; the daily wage of an unskilled laborer was about three sesterces.

ashlar construction A technique of wall construction in which large, regularly cut stone blocks are laid in courses; also called *opus quadratum* (cf. Ch. 8 and Figures 8.1, 8.2).

atriolum (-i) A small *atrium* or hall.

atrium (-a) The entrance hall of a Roman house; its most recognizable form was characterized by an opening in the roof (*compluvium*), a pool for collecting rain water (*impluvium*), and surrounding household rooms (cf. Chs 17 and 18; Figures 17.1, 18.1, 27.1). In an *atrium tetrastylum*, the roof opening was supported by four columns.

auctoritas Authority stemming from prestigious reputation; unofficial power; influence; clout.

augur (-es) A religious official who observes and interprets patterns of bird behavior.

augustalis (-es) A priest of the imperial cult, usually a freedman, who could use the honor to increase personal prestige through benefactions; a kind of semi-official magistracy.

Augusteum (-a) A temple dedicated to the imperial cult, maintained by *augustales*.

balneum (-a) A small private bathhouse, or a bath-suite that belongs to a private home. Generally understood to be smaller than *thermae*.

biclinium (-a) A dining area named for the two *klinai*, or couches, on which the diners reclined (Figure 23.14 (k)).

bisellium (-a) A double-wide seat, like those set up for *decuriones* in the theater, or as an honor for municipal service (Figure 37.5, tomb at left).

bouleuterion (-a) The assembly hall for the *boulé*, or city council, of a Greek or Hellenistic city.

bucchero Italian term for a kind of pottery characteristic of the Etruscans, produced in the Archaic period. Its fabric is gray to black in color (from a reducing atmosphere during firing), often with a smooth, shiny surface that imitates metal wares.

bustum (-i) An open spot adjoining a burial ground upon which a funeral pyre is raised; a locus for cremation. Cf. *ustrinum*.

caementum (-a) Irregular pieces of stone, terracotta or brick used to help bind the mortar of Roman concrete (Figure 8.10; Appendix to Ch. 8).

calcei patricii A four-strap shoe laced around the ankles, reserved for Roman senators or high-ranking muncipal officials (Figure 36.2a).

caldarium (-a) An artificially heated room in a bath, containing hot plunge basins (cf. Ch. 15).

campus (-i) An open area of ground upon which meetings or festivals could be held, recreation arranged, or military drills performed (Figure 14.4). Identified with the Great or Large Palaestra.

cardo (-ines) A north–south street in a Roman settlement, aligned with the principal axis of the main road, the *cardo maximus*, and perpendicular to the *decumanus*.

cartibulum A stone table (often of marble) set in the *atrium* or sometimes the peristyle of a Roman house (Figures 27.2 and 27.5).

castellum aquae The municipal water distribution center; a building located just inside the Porta Vesuvio (Map 3).

catillus The hourglass-shaped upper millstone of a grain mill which rested over the *meta* (Figure 29.3d).

caupona (-ae) An inn, hostel or tavern serving the accommodation of travelers (cf. Ch. 30).

cavea (-ae) The auditorium, or seating area in a theater, divided into wedges of seating called *cunei* (cf. *cuneus*). The *cavea* is frequently divided vertically into three zones of seating, from bottom to top: the *ima cavea*, *media cavea*, and *summa cavea* (Figures 14.1, 14.3).

cella (-ae) In a domestic context, a niche, closet or store-room; in a sacred context, the main interior room of a temple.

cenaculum (-a) A term which early on often designated a dining-room on the upper floor of a Roman house and later came to mean the whole upper story.

cenatio (-ones) A dining room; effectively synonymous with *triclinium*.

censor (-ores) A Roman magistrate elected every four or five years to conduct a census determining the economic classification of citizens and therefore their political rights, with additional authority to demote individuals on moral grounds.

centuriatio (centuriation) A system of dividing agricultural land (as at the foundation of a Roman colony) into a regular grid pattern. Each square, whose sides were 2,400 Roman feet, was called a *centuria* (Figure 28.2).

CIL (*Corpus Inscriptionum Latinarum*) A multi-volume compilation of Latin inscriptions from the Roman world. Inscriptions from Pompeii are published in *CIL* volumes IV and X (cf. Ch. 39).

clientela (-ae) A person or group in a position of social, economic and/or political dependency to a *patronus*.

cocciopesto Crushed red pottery or roof tiles set in mortar (cf. *opus signinum*).

collegium (-a) A formally structured social club, with officers, whose members paid periodical dues and which existed on the basis of common religious, professional, ethnic, geographic or other interests.

columbarium (-a) Literally, "dovecote"; a collection of niches for holding cinerary urns in a sepulchral tomb (Figure 37.4).

columella (-ae) A pillar or slab erected for a tombstone, sometimes containing a cavity for the placement of an urn (Figures 37.6a–b).

compital shrine A small altar or shrine located at an intersection and dedicated to the *Lares Compitales*, the deities protecting crossroads (Figure 10.2; the shrine is located to the left of the water tower and behind a modern cement trash container).

compluvium (-a) The rectangular opening in the roof of an *atrium* that admitted light into the hall and directed rain water into the *impluvium* below (Figure 8.19).

concordia Harmony; peace; agreement in common.

console   A projecting ornament in wood, stone or plaster, used to help demarcate the transition between wall and ceiling (Figure 21.2).

consul (-es)   The twin office of the chief Roman magistrate who presided at Rome over the senate, assembly and foreign affairs. A *consul suffectus* was originally a replacement for a consul who had died or resigned while in office; during the Empire, regular mid-year replacement by *suffecti* was instituted.

contrada   Italian term for a traditional, unofficial territorial division, commonly used to locate a site or special find. Usually larger than a *fondo.*

corona civica   A crown or garland made of oak leaves presented to a Roman soldier who saved the life of a citizen in battle.

cruma   A tough but porous igneous rock.

crypta (-ae)   A covered corridor, such as that surrounding the portico of the Eumachia Building or the vaulted passage (now largely broken) above the *media cavea* of the theater (Figure 14.3; the doors at the top of the steps lead into the *crypta*).

cryptoporticus   A covered portico or arcade, usually vaulted and located underground.

cubiculum (-a)   A domestic bedroom, by its most common definition (Figure 17.1).

cuneus (-i)   A term used to describe a wedge-shaped section of seating in a theater or amphitheater (Figures 14.1–3).

cursus honorum   The sequential order of advancement through public office.

dado   The lower (bottom) horizontal zone of any schema of wall decoration (cf. Chs 20, 22). Cf. socle.

damnatio memoriae   A form of public accusation and dishonor; in its most serious form, any mention of the accused enemy, in written or pictorial form, is destroyed.

decumanus (-i)   An east–west street in a Roman settlement, aligned with the principal axis of the main road, the *decumanus maximus*, and perpendicular to the *cardo.*

decurio (-ones) (decurion)   A member of the city council, or *ordo decurionum* (Table 33.1).

destrictarium (-a)   A room in the baths where dirt and oil are removed from the body after outdoor exercise (cf. Ch. 15).

diaeta (-ae)   A room or set of rooms with an orchestrated view onto a garden, courtyard, landscape or seascape (Figures 27.3 and 31.3–4).

dipinto (-i)   An inscription painted on the surface of a wall or object (cf. *graffito*).

dolium (-a)   A large coarse earthenware vessel with a wide mouth and spherical form, used for storage and processing (Figure 1.1).

domina (-ae)   The lady or mistress of the household, who might also be the owner.

dominus (-i)   The male owner, lord, or master of a household.

domus (-us)   A private residence; a home.

duumvir/duovir (-i)   The senior-level municipal magistracy, held by two men each year (Table 33.1).

emblema (emblemata)   A panel of mosaic or marble set centrally into a pavement, reserved for special, more detailed representations, usually figural in nature (cf. Ch. 21).

ephebe   Greek term for a youth at the stage between adolescence and adulthood.

epigram   A short, witty poem or verse inscription.

ergastulum (-a)   A prison in which slaves were kept in chains.

eros (erotes)   A youthful winged god of love; cupid.

euripus (-i) An artificial canal or watercourse in the garden of a Roman house, often edged in marble or decorated with arbors, bridges, sculptures or fountains (Figures 14.5, 23.13, 23.14, 23.16).

exedra (-ae) A term often applied in domestic or public architecture to a largish room with one side open to a courtyard and/or portico; also designates a semi-circular or Π-shaped seating area at the site of a tomb (Figure 37.2).

familia (-ae) Collectively, the members of a household, including family, relatives, freedmen and slaves, not all necessarily living under the same roof.

fascis (-es) A tied bundle of rods, with an axe in the middle, carried before certain Roman magistrates as a symbol of their authority and power to compel.

fauces (pl.) A narrow passage, usually used in reference to the entrance corridor of a house (Figures 17.1, 21.4). See *vestibulum*.

ferculum (-a) A tray used for carrying dishes for meals or objects for sacrifice (Figure 13.2).

fides Trust, loyalty, honesty, good faith.

fillet Architecturally, a thin strip distinguished by color, decoration or surface level, set between larger decorative zones (Figure 22.3); in figural representations, a thin band, often decorated, tied around the head of an animal about to be sacrificed, or around the head of a person or god (Figure 23.9).

flamen (-ines) A priest devoted to the service of any one god or divinized emperor.

fondo The Italian term for "property," combined with the last name of a long-time owner, often locates an ancient site or the find-spot of notable artifacts. Usually smaller than a *contrada*.

fossa (-ae) A long, narrow, shallow depression in the ground; a ditch; a trench used for burial.

frigidarium (-a) The cold (unheated) room in a bath (cf. Ch. 15).

fuller A launderer who cleaned linen and woolen clothes (Figures 29.4b–c).

fullonica (-ae) A fuller's establishment (Figure 29.4a).

garum A pungent Roman fish sauce essential to Roman cooking.

genius (-i) The guardian spirit of a *gens*, embodied in the male head of household (Figure 13.5, center).

gens (-tes) A clan; a set of families sharing the same *nomen* and original ancestor.

gorgoneion (-eia) The head and face of the gorgon Medusa, used in apotropaic fashion to ward off evil (Figure 36.3a, on the breastplate).

graffito (-i) An inscription scratched into the surface of a wall or object (cf. *dipinto*).

gravitas Dignity, gravity, seriousness.

groma A Roman surveying instrument used to establish straight lines and right angles, used for *centuriatio* and for laying out streets (cf. *cardo*).

hectare (abbrev. ha) A unit of area covering 10,000 m^2 (e.g., a square 100 m by 100 m); *c.*2.47 acres.

herm A squared stone pillar originally featuring an erect phallus and topped by a bust of the god Hermes, later adapted for portraits (Figures 36.11a–b).

hortus (-i) A Roman garden (cf. Ch. 31).

hospitium (-a) An establishment that offers room and board (cf. *caupona*).

hypocaust system A system of heating the baths in which the floor (*suspensura*) is supported on pillars of tiles (*pilae*) so that hot air from the furnace can circulate under the floor and then rise within the walls in flue tiles or behind *tegulae mammatae*, "nipple tiles," whose projections allowed the face of the tile to stand in front of the structural wall, thereby creating a space for the hot air to rise (cf. Ch. 15).

impluvium   A basin in the floor of the *atrium* into which rain water fell from the roof via the *compluvium*, in order to be stored in a subfloor cistern (Figures 16.1, 18.1, 18.2, 21.4, 25.3).

in situ (in place)   In its natural or original position. An archaeological term denoting an intact context.

institor (-es), institorium (-a)   A shopkeeper; a shopkeeper's place of business.

instrumentum domesticum   Personal belongings; the artifacts of daily domestic life.

insula (-ae)   A large tenement-style house or apartment block (ancient sense); a city block in a Roman settlement (modern sense). The ancient term *insulae*, particularly as it is used in the Regionaries of Rome, is much debated, and recent scholarly work argues that it might, in fact, refer more generally to individual residences of varying size and configuration within apartment blocks.

isodomic   A method of building in which large stone (ashlar) blocks are regular in size and stacked in parallel layers (cf. *opus quadratum*); in pseudo-isodomic masonry, the layers appear to be largely parallel and uniform, but are in fact unequal or irregular in detail.

iugerum (-a)   A unit of area covering 240 by 120 Roman feet; approximately five-eighths of an acre; roughly, 4 *iugera* = 1 ha.

kantharos (-oi)   A large two-handled drinking vessel for drinking wine, sacred to Dionysus/Bacchus.

kline (-ai)   A Greek-style couch with a headboard and sometimes a footboard, used for reclining during dinner and/or drinking parties. Essential furniture for a *biclinium* or *triclinium*.

koiné   The Greek word for "common" that originally meant the most popular dialect of Greek in the classical world. More generally, it now denotes a shared commonality amongst otherwise distinct groups, often in reference to language, culture or custom.

kymation   A double-curved molding.

labrum   A shallow tub or basin, usually built up off the floor and set in the end niche of a *caldarium* in a Roman bath, around which bathers stood to splash its fountain-fed cool water for relief from the heat.

laconicum (-a)   The sweat room in a bath (cf. Ch. 15).

lacunar   A recessed ceiling panel (cf. Ch. 21).

lapilli   The Italian word for "pebbles" is frequently employed to identify volcanic ejecta consisting of fingertip to thumb-sized pumice stones; see volcano terms.

lararium (-a)   A small shrine for the *Lares* of a household (Figures 13.5, 23.4).

Lar (-es)   A guardian deity of a household.

lavapesta   A term used to designate cement floors that are dark in color due to the inclusion of black volcanic rock.

lex (leges)   A law; statute.

libertus (-i)   A male slave who has been set free (feminine: *liberta*). A freedman.

limestone framework As defined by K. Peterse in Chapter 24, limestone framework consists of three components: framework pillars, corner posts and doorposts, and fill. The framework pillars consist of a concentrated piling of large blocks of stone, alternating vertically and horizontally. The technique is also called *opus africanum*, *opera a telaio*, and masonry chains (cf. Ch. 8 and Figure 8.9).

limitatio The Roman ritual of land surveying by which a city is divided into quarters by the *cardo* and *decumanus*, or the countryside is divided into arable plots by *centuriatio* (Figures 7.3, 28.2).

lituus A staff with incurved top, borrowed by Rome from Etruscan ritual practice, and used by an *augur* during ceremonies of augury.

lucus A sacred grove; a wooded place of ritual.

lupanar A brothel or house of prostitution (cf. Chs 30, 35; Figure 35.3).

macellum (-a) A marketplace for perishable foods consisting of shops around a central court (cf. Ch. 12 for the Macellum at Pompeii; Figure 12.9).

maenianum (-a) A balcony projecting from the wall of a house (Figure 27.6).

magister, minister vici An honorific title for an official, most often a slave or freedman, in a *vicus* or city district.

megalographia/megalography Large single figures or figural scenes in wall painting (Figure 20.11).

meta Any object with a circular base and of conical shape; the lower part of a grinding mill (Figure 29.3d).

mezzanino A small upper story lying between two others of larger size; mezzanine; loft.

munus (munera) A service or duty; gift or tribute. A term also used for gladiatorial games organized and donated by local elites.

natatio (-ones) A swimming pool in a bath or *palaestra* (cf. Ch. 15; Figure 14.4).

negotium Work; business, politics. The opposite of *otium*.

nomen (nomina) Name; *gens* name.

nuée ardente Literally, burning cloud; the cloud of hot particles and gases that travels down the slopes of a volcano. See pyroclastic flow and pyroclastic surge.

nymphaeum (nymphaea) An elaborately decorated public or private fountain (Figure 22.5).

obol A Greek silver coin; six obols equal one *drachma*.

oecus (-i) A Vitruvian term designating a reception room in a private residence (cf. Ch. 17; Figure 17.1).

officina (-ae) A workshop (cf. Ch. 29).

omphalos A stone-carved "navel" which served as a cultic icon in sanctuaries of Apollo; the original example was located at Delphi in Greece, where it marked the "center of the world." A stone *omphalos* is preserved in the *cella* of the Temple of Apollo at Pompeii. (Figure. 6.3).

opaion A skylight; an opening in the roof of a building permitting the entry of light, air and rain, either at the top of an *atrium*, a dome, or a single-pitched roof (cf. *compluvium*; Figure 8.19).

opera a telaio Cf. limestone framework (cf. Chs 8 and 24).

opus africanum Cf. limestone framework (cf. Chs 8 and 24).

opus caementicium Roman concrete. A wall consisting of a mortared rubble core between faces of brick or stone (cf. Ch. 8, Appendix to Ch. 8, and associated figures).

opus craticium A mixed construction of rubble and wood, mainly used for internal partitions and, because of its lightness, for the external walls of upper floors projected or cantilevered over a street (Figure 8.13, upper story).

opus incertum The facing of an *opus caementicium* wall in which roughly cut stones of various sizes form an irregular pattern (Figures 8.9, A8.1).

opus latericium Cf. *opus testaceum*.

opus quadratum A construction technique using squared blocks; ashlar masonry (Figures 8.1, 8.2).

opus quasi-reticulatum The facing of an *opus caementicium* wall in which the pattern of stones is more regular than in *opus incertum*, and verges towards *opus reticulatum* (cf. Ch. 8 and Appendix to Ch. 8).

opus reticulatum The facing of an *opus caementicium* wall in which the square ends of pyramidally shaped stones form a regular netlike pattern (Figures 8.12, A8.1).

opus sectile Technique using thin, variously colored marble pieces in designs on floors or walls (cf. Chs 21, 22).

opus signinum Construction technique of crushed brick set in mortar to seal walls and floors, especially in baths; also called *cocciopesto*.

opus testaceum Brick-faced Roman concrete (cf. Appendix to Ch. 8). Also called *opus latericium*.

opus vermiculatum Mosaic technique in which a figural mosaic is made up of small, closely set, and sometimes tapered *tesserae* (cf. Ch. 21).

opus vittatum mixtum The combination of brick and small stone blocks used as the facing of an *opus caementicium* wall, in which one course of block alternates with two courses of brick (Figure 8.12, outer edges; cf. Appendix to Ch. 8).

orchestra The area of a theater located between the *cavea* and the stage (Figures 14.1, 14.3).

ordo decurionum The members of a town council (Table 33.1).

orthostate In First-Style wall painting, the zone of tall panels above the socle (lowest zone) and the narrow string course and below the course of ashlar panels (cf. Ch. 20 and Figure 20.2).

oscillum (-a) An ornament of marble suspended from the architrave of a peristyle in a house.

otium Leisure. The opposite of *negotium*.

paideia The system of education for an (aristocratic) young man in the Greco-Roman world, often in the setting of a gymnasium or *palaestra*. By extension, it can also connote the learning process for initiation into cults such as that of Isis.

pagus (-i) The smallest unit of land in the territorial system of Roman Italy; a country area; a village. *Pagus Augustus Felix Suburbanus*: a district outside Pompeii known from inscriptions, but not yet located.

palaestra (-ae) An open-air courtyard surrounded by a colonnade; public *palaestrae*, such as the Samnite Palaestra, the Large or Great Palaestra (Figure 14.4; cf. *campus*), and the *palaestrae* in baths (cf. Ch. 15) were used for exercise.

palla (-ae) A rectangular mantle worn as an outer garment by women (Figures 36.4a–c).

pappamonte A local tufa used in early construction (cf. Chs 5, 11, 24).

parados (paradoi) The passageway or passageways, vaulted at Pompeii, between the *cavea* and the scene building that lead into and out of the orchestra of a theater (Figures 14.1, 14.3).

pars rustica, pars urbana   Terms commonly used to designate the predominantly agricultural and residential portions of a Roman villa, respectively (cf. *villa urbana*, etc.).

patera (-ae)   A rounded bowl, sometimes with a long handle, used for libation pouring or in sacrifices (Figure 36.5a).

paterfamilias   The male head of the household.

patronus (-i)   A patron. The former owner of a freed slave (feminine: *patrona*).

penaria (-ae)   A room for storing food or provisions.

Penates   Household gods representing familial ancestors, believed to bestow good fortune and blessings upon a *familia.*

peristyle   The screen of columns surrounding a temple forming a colonnade along its side (Figure 13.1); peristyles of the *domus* contained the private living quarters of the family and might be planted as a garden (Figure 23.20).

pietas   The Roman virtue of responsibility or duty to family, nation and gods.

pinax (pinakes)   A painting on a wooden panel.

pistrinum (-a)   A mill for grinding grain.

plebs   The Roman lower class.

Plinian eruption   Named for Pliny the Younger who described the AD 79 eruption of Vesuvius, this type of explosive eruption is characterized by columns of tephra and gas that reach into the stratosphere (>11 km). Cf. volcano terms.

pluteus (-i)   A low partition wall separating columns; a balustrade (Figure 23.21).

pomerium   A line marking the sacred enclosure of a town by means of stone pillars, inside of which burials were forbidden (cf. Ch. 2).

pontifex (-ices)   Member of the council of high priests, the *collegium pontificum*, at Rome. The *pontifex maximus* was the chief priest of that council, an office held for life and attached to the emperor starting with Augustus. He held ritual authority over calendars, consecrations, expiations, marriages, burials and successions.

popina (-ae)   A tavern or snack bar where food and drink were sold (cf. Ch. 30).

porticus (-us)   A portico or colonnade, such as the *porticus* of Popidius around the forum (Figure 12.7); a building type, such as the Eumachia Building (Figure 12.13), or the Porticus of Livia at Rome that served as a large, public promenade.

posticum (-a)   A back door to a home.

pozzolana   Italian word for sandy volcanic ash from the Bay of Naples which, when mixed with lime, forms strong mortar or cement that can set underwater.

praedia   Properties, such as the *Praedia* of Julia Felix (Figure 23.11).

praefurnium   The furnace room in a bath (cf. Ch. 15).

praenomen (-ina)   The given name or forename of a Roman as opposed to the *nomen*, or *gens* name, and *cognomen*, family name.

predella   A painted zone above or beneath a painting's main panel that contains small figures (Figure 20.6).

programmata   Campaign posters.

protome   Decorative motif in the form of a human or animal head.

pudicitia Modesty, chastity; this female virtue is represented sculpturally by the wrapping of the *palla* tightly around the body, the placement of the left arm across the body, and the extension of the right hand and arm to the chin (cf. Ch. 36 and Figure 36.14a–b).

puteal A cylindrical cover for a cistern mouth or well-head. About a half-meter tall and made of stone or terracotta, it aids both in the drawing of water and in the prevention of accidental falls (Figure 18.2).

pyroclastic flow The lower part of a volcanic cloud, or *nuée ardente*, that travels down the slopes of a volcano, containing a high-concentration mixture of gas and particles. Cf. volcano terms.

pyroclastic surge The upper part of a volcanic cloud, or *nuée ardente*, that travels down the slopes of a volcano, containing a low-concentration, highly turbulent mixture of gas and particles. Cf. volcano terms.

quadriga (-ae) A chariot with four horses yoked abreast.

quadriporticus (-us) A four-sided colonnade.

quaestor (-es) A political official who tried criminal cases, was in charge of public money, and paid the army.

quinquennalis (-es) The local censor; these magistrates were responsible for performing the census at Pompeii every five years (Table 33.1).

quoin Quoining is a technique for bonding sturdy, straight-edged masonry (such as brick or block) at the corners or doorways of buildings with less sturdy masonry of the main body of a wall. The bonding is achieved by allowing toothlike masonry units (the quoins) to project at regular intervals into the less regular body of the wall. Squared quoins are seen in Figures 8.12 and 8.13 (lower right); serrated quoins appear in Figure 8.11.

rotulus (-i) A scroll.

sacerdos (-otes) A priest or priestess.

scaena and *scaenae frons* The *scaena* is the scene building that includes the stage, the backdrop behind the stage (called the *scaenae frons*), and the rooms behind the *scaenae frons*.

schola (-ae) A tomb in the form of a semicircular bench with a high back (cf. Ch. 37 and Figure 37.2).

sella curulis (**curule chair**) A folding stool decorated in ivory, granted to magistrates at least of aedile rank, to use while conducting official business, as a symbol of office.

signaculum (-a) A seal or stamp used for marking bread.

sima The roof gutter.

sinopia (sinopie) A preparatory drawing made in red pigment on the second to last coat of plaster in fresco painting. Fresh plaster is then applied over the *sinopia* and the artist executes the final painting. Also applies to a sketch scratched into, or painted onto, the initial layer of cement before the *tesserae* of a mosaic are laid down.

socle A plain block forming a low pedestal to a column or around the bottom of a wall; the lowest zone in First-Style painting (Figure 20.2); cf. *dado*.

spectacula The amphitheater (Figure 14.2); this is the term used to identify the building in the dedicatory inscription for the amphitheater at Pompeii.

spolia Booty taken in war; captured arms or implements of war.

stabulum (-a) A place to house transport animals, such as horses; a term used for a dwelling of the poor.

stela (-ae) An upright, freestanding stone monument often inscribed or carved in relief (Figures 37.6a–b).

still-life A depiction in painting or mosaic of a carefully arranged set of vessels, fruit, flowers, birds, animals, seafood or other objects.

stola (-ae) A long, sleeveless, dresslike garment worn by Roman matrons below the *palla* (cf. Ch. 36 and Figure 36.5).

sudatorium (-a) A sweat room in a bath (cf. Ch. 15).

suspensura (-ae) Generally, anything that is supported, used often to describe the floor of a heated room in a bath (cf. Ch. 15).

symplegma (symplegmata) In art, an entwined group of figures.

taberna (-ae) A retail shop; a wine shop or tavern (cf. Chs 29, 30).

tablinum (-a) A multifunctional room in a Roman house associated with the *paterfamilias*, used as bedroom, reception, storage and office space. It is identified as an open-fronted room set at or near the back of the *atrium*, usually on axis with the *fauces* (Figures 17.1, 18.1 and 18.2).

telamon (-ones) The figure of a man that replaces a column to support an entablature (Figure 15.5).

tephra Fragments of rock and lava hurled into the air by volcanic explosions (see **volcano terms**).

tepidarium (-a) The warm room in a bath where bathers rested and socialized (Figure 15.5).

terminus ante sive post quem Archaeological terms referring to a date before (*ante*) or after (*post*) which a particular deposit or construction must have been made.

terra sigillata A fine, mass-produced Roman pottery usually red glazed or glossed, and mold-made.

tessera (-ae) Stone, colored glass or tile pieces used to make mosaics.

testudinatum A closed roof as opposed to an open one with *compluvium* and *impluvium* (cf. Figure 24.5).

tetrapylon Literally, a quadruple gate or entrance. A four-sided urban structure comprised of four piers that define a square. When they occur, such structures typically are sited within a major intersection, but at Pompeii the tetrapylon near the important via dell'Abbondanza–strada Stabiana intersection is actually located within the largo Stabiana (Figures 10.4 and 15.3).

thermae Literally a "thermal establishment," the term refers to a bathing establishment, or to several baths collectively. Generally understood to be larger than *balnea*.

thermopolium (-a) A Greek term found especially in the Roman playwright Plautus for a refreshment shop in which warm drinks were sold. Now commonly used for *popina* or *taberna* (cf. Ch. 30).

thiasos A procession of Dionysus/Bacchus and his retinue.

titulus (-i) An epitaph or inscription on a monument (Figure. 37.8).

toga (-ae) The formal attire of a Roman (male) citizen, comprised of a long cloth wrapped around the body and worn over a tunic. The *toga praetexta* was edged with a broad purple stripe and identified certain magistrates and priests as well as young freeborn boys who had not yet donned the *toga virilis* as a mark of manhood and citizenship (Figures 36.2a, 36.13, 37.8).

togatus (-i) A statue that is wearing the *toga*.

tondo Painted, carved or mosaic design within a circular border (Figure 21.3).

tribunalia Special box seats above the *paradoi* (entrances) of a theater for sponsors of the events and their guests (Figure 14.3).

tribunus militum a populo   "Military tribune (chosen) by the people"; an honorific title conferred by Augustus on distinguished individuals, such as M. Tullius, who had been nominated by their local assembly.

tribus (-i)   Tribe. A division of Roman free society, used for voting, taxation and conscription purposes.

triclinium (-a)   A dining area named for the three *klinai*, or couches, on which the diners reclined (Figures 17.1, 20.8, 22.5, 31.3(c)).

trompe l'oeil   Literally, "fools the eye"; a painting or mosaic that creates a highly realistic three-dimensional effect.

tufa   A compact and easily quarried volcanic stone (brown, grey, yellow) that was used in numerous buildings (Figure 8.2).

tunica (-ae)   Tunic. The principal garment worn by men and women; a woolen shirt tight around the neck and waist and coming down to the knee with short sleeves to the elbow. Worn under a *toga* for men and under a *palla* for women (Figures 29.4b, 35.1).

tuscanicum   A "tuscan" *atrium* in which the roof was supported by four beams which formed the *compluvium* (Figure 8.19 for a reconstructed *compluvium*).

ustrinum (-a)   A public place for burning the bodies of the dead within the necropolis. Cf. *bustum*.

velum (-a)   The awnings that provided shade for spectators at the theater or the amphitheater (as seen in the famous painting of the AD 59 brawl in the amphitheater in House (I.3.23), west wall of courtyard (n)).

venatio (venationes)   Animal hunt in the amphitheater involving animals against each other, or men against animals.

verna (-ae)   House-born slaves, born either of two slaves, or the master and a slave (cf. Ch. 35).

vestibulum (-a)   A small entrance space separate from the *fauces* that is sometimes present immediately inside the door of a house (Figures 17.1, 24.2).

victimarius   An attendant who kills a sacrificial animal with an axe.

vicus (-i)   A quarter or district of a town.

vilicus (-i)/vilica (-ae)   The overseer of a villa. A steward. Usually a slave, but could also be a freedperson or even free-born.

villa urbana, suburbana, rustica, maritima (villae urbanae, suburbanae, rusticae, maritimae)   Terms commonly used to designate various aspects of utility (*rustica* = farming operations), luxury (*urbana* = fine living quarters for the owners) and location (*suburbana* = just outside a town's walls; *maritima* = along the seaside) in villas (cf. Ch. 28).

viridarium (-a)   An ornamental garden.

virtus   The Roman quality of manly virtue.

volcano terms   Consult the United States Geological Survey for a "Photo glossary of volcano terms": http://volcanoes.usgs.gov/Products/Pglossary.

INDEX

———•◆•———